Caravan &
Camping Guide
Britain & Ireland
2012

AA Lifestyle Guides

This 44th edition published 2012
© AA Media Limited 2011
AA Media Limited retains the copyright in the current edition
©2011 and in all subsequent editions, reprints and amendments to editions.

To contact us:
Advertisement Sales: advertisingsales@theAA.com
Editorial: lifestyleguides@theAA.com

Co-ordinator, AA Caravan & Camping Scheme: David Hancock
Editors: David Hancock and Lin Hutton

Front cover: (t) AA/M Kipling; (bl) AA/C Hill; (br) Woodclose Caravan Park;
Back cover: (l) AA/J A Tims; (c) Outwell; (b) ilovedust.

Typeset and colour organisation by Wellcom, London
Printed and bound by Printers Trento srl, Italy

Published by AA Publishing, a trading name of AA Media Limited,
whose registered office is Fanum House, Basing View, Basingstoke,
Hampshire, RG21 4EA. Registered number 06112600

A CIP catalogue record for this book is available from the British Library
ISBN: 978-0-7495-7201-3
A04681

Maps prepared by the
Mapping Services Department of
AA Publishing.

Maps © AA Media Limited 2011.

Contains Ordnance Survey data
© Crown copyright and database right 2011

 Land &
Property
Services.
This is based upon Crown Copyright and is reproduced with the permission of Land & Property Services under delegated authority from the Controller of Her Majesty's Stationery Office.
© Crown copyright and database rights 2011
Licence number 100,363.
Permit number 110026

 Ordnance Survey Ireland
Ireland's National Mapping Agency
Republic of Ireland mapping based on © Ordnance Survey Ireland/Government of Ireland Copyright Permit number MP000611

Information on National Parks in England provided by the Countryside Agency (Natural England).

Information on National Parks in Scotland provided by Scottish Natural Heritage.

Information on National Parks in Wales provided by The Countryside Council for Wales.

Contents

How to Use the Guide

1 LOCATION

Place names are listed alphabetically within each county.

2 MAP REFERENCE

Each site is given a map reference for use in conjunction with the atlas section at the back of the guide. The map reference comprises the guide map page number, the National Grid location square and a two-figure map location reference.

For example: **Map 15 SJ52**.

15 refers to the page number of the map section at the back of the guide.

SJ is the National Grid lettered square (representing 100,000sq metres) in which the location will be found.

5 is the figure reading across the top or bottom of the map page.

2 is the figure reading down each side of the map page.

3 PLACES TO VISIT

Suggestions of nearby places to visit for adults and children.

4 AA CAMPING CARD SCHEME

See explanation on page 7.

5 RATING & SITE NAME

Campsites are listed in descending order of their Pennant Quality rating (see pages 10 & 11). Sites are rated from one to five pennants and are also awarded a score ranging from 50%-100% according to how they compare with other parks within the same pennant rating. Some sites are given a Holiday Centre grading. For a fuller explanation see page 10. A category for parks catering only for recreational vehicles (**RV**) has been created, (no toilet facilities are provided at these sites).

NEW indicates that the site is new in the guide this year. Where the name appears in *italic* type the information that follows has not been confirmed by the campsite for 2012.

6 6-FIGURE MAP REFERENCE

Each entry also includes a 6-figure National Grid reference as many sites are in remote locations. To help you find the precise location of a site the 6-figure map reference, based on the National Grid, can be used with the relevant Ordnance Survey maps in conjunction with the atlas at the back of the guide.

7 CONTACT DETAILS

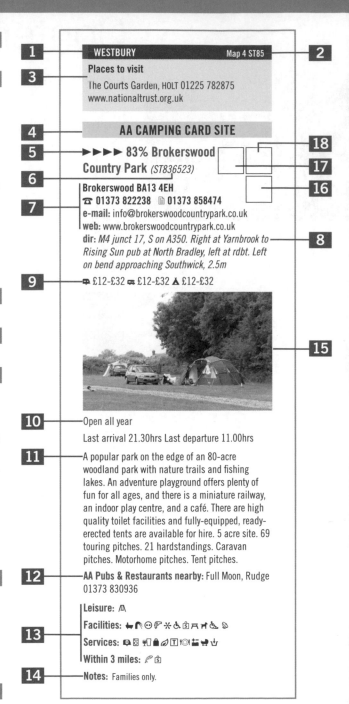

1 WESTBURY   Map 4 ST85   **2**

3 Places to visit
The Courts Garden, HOLT 01225 782875
www.nationaltrust.org.uk

4 **AA CAMPING CARD SITE**

5 ►►►► 83% Brokerswood
Country Park *(ST836523)*   **6**   **18** **17** **16**

7 Brokerswood BA13 4EH
☎ 01373 822238   🖺 01373 858474
e-mail: info@brokerswoodcountrypark.co.uk
web: www.brokerswoodcountrypark.co.uk
dir: *M4 junct 17, S on A350. Right at Yarnbrook to Rising Sun pub at North Bradley, left at rdbt. Left on bend approaching Southwick, 2.5m*   **8**

9 ⊕ £12-£32 ⇔ £12-£32 ▲ £12-£32

15

10 Open all year
Last arrival 21.30hrs Last departure 11.00hrs

11 A popular park on the edge of an 80-acre woodland park with nature trails and fishing lakes. An adventure playground offers plenty of fun for all ages, and there is a miniature railway, an indoor play centre, and a café. There are high quality toilet facilities and fully-equipped, ready-erected tents are available for hire. 5 acre site. 69 touring pitches. 21 hardstandings. Caravan pitches. Motorhome pitches. Tent pitches.

12 AA Pubs & Restaurants nearby: Full Moon, Rudge 01373 830936

Leisure: ⋀
Facilities: ⇃⋔⊙⌿⋇⅙🖺⋤⋔⅋🐾
Services: ⊕🖺🍴🛢⌀◻🍽🎠⊶⛽
Within 3 miles: ⋒🏛   **13**

14 Notes: Families only.

8 DIRECTIONS

Brief directions from a recognisable point, such as a main road, are included in each entry. Please contact the individual site for more detailed directions or try the online AA Route Planner, **theAA.com**, and enter the postcode.

9 CHARGES

Rates are given after each appropriate symbol (⚬ Caravan, ⚬ Campervan, ⚬ Tent) and are the overnight cost for one caravan or tent, one car and two adults, or one motorhome and two adults. The prices vary according to the number of people in the party, but some parks have a fixed fee per pitch regardless of the number of people. Please note that some sites charge separately for certain facilities, including showers; and some sites charge a different rate for pitches with or without electricity. Prices are supplied to us in good faith by the site operators and are as accurate as possible. They are, however, only a guide and are subject to change during the currency of this publication.
* If this symbol appears before the prices, it indicates that the site has not advised us of the prices for 2012; they relate to 2011.

10 OPENING, ARRIVAL & DEPARTURE TIMES

Parks are not necessarily open all year and while most sites permit arrivals at any time, checking beforehand is advised (see page 12).

11 DESCRIPTION

These are based on information supplied by the AA inspector at the time of the last visit.

Please note: The AA pennant classification is based on the touring pitches and the facilities only. AA inspectors do not visit or report on statics or chalets for hire under the AA Caravan & Camping quality standards scheme. The AA takes no responsibility for the condition of rented accommodation and can take no action in the event of complaints relating to these. We only include the number of static caravan pitches in order to give an indication of the nature and size of the site.

12 AA PUBS & RESTAURANTS

An entry may include suggestions for nearby pubs and/or restaurants recognised by the AA. Some of these establishments will have been awarded Rosettes for food excellence.

13 SYMBOLS & ABBREVIATIONS

These are divided into Leisure, Facilities, Services and Within 3 miles sections. Explanations can be found on page 9 and at the bottom of the pages throughout the guide.

14 NOTES

This includes information about any restrictions the site would like their visitors to be aware of and any additional facilities.
⊜ As most sites now accept credit and debit cards, we have only indicated those that don't accept cards.

15 PHOTOGRAPH

Optional photograph supplied by the campsite.

16 COUNTRYSIDE DISCOVERY

 A group of over 30 family-run parks with fewer than 150 pitches, each sharing a common theme of tranquillity. **www.countryside-discovery.co.uk**

17 BEST OF BRITISH

 A group of over 40 parks, both large and small, which focus on high quality facilities and amenities. **www.bob.org.uk**

18 DAVID BELLAMY AWARDS

 Many AA recognised sites are also recipients of a David Bellamy Award for Conservation. The awards are graded Gold, Silver and Bronze. The symbols we show indicate the 2010/11 winners as this was the most up-to-date information at the time of going to press. For the 2011/12 winners please contact:
British Holiday & Homes Parks Association Tel: 01452 526911

Facilities for disabled guests

The Equality Act 2010 provides legal rights for disabled people including access to goods, services and facilities, and means that service providers may have to consider making adjustments to their premises.

For more information about the Act see:
www.equalities.gov.uk
or **www.direct.gov.uk/en/DisabledPeople/RightsAndObligations/ DisabilityRights/DG_4001068**

♿ If a site has told us that they provide facilities for disabled visitors their entry in the guide will include this symbol. The sites in this guide should be aware of their responsibilities under the Act. However, we recommend that you always telephone in advance to ensure the site you have chosen has facilities to suit your needs.

AA Camping Card Scheme

The AA Camping Card

In this edition of the AA Caravan & Camping Guide Britain & Ireland you will find some sites highlighted with the **AA CAMPING CARD SITE** banner. This indicates that the site has signed up to the AA Camping Card Scheme, and means they have agreed to offer reduced rates to campers who book in advance, citing the AA Camping Card, and show the card on arrival at the site. The offers are provided by and are available entirely at the discretion of participating campsites. Offers may include, for example, reduced pitch prices at certain times of the week or year. These discounts will only be available to those booking in advance, stating at the time of booking that an AA Camping Card is being used, and showing the card on arrival. Scheme terms and campsite terms of booking will apply.

You'll need to contact the site to find out what they are offering. We hope this will encourage you to visit sites and explore parts of the country you may not have considered before.

Terms and conditions

This card may be used at any campsite specified as accepting the AA Camping Card within the AA Caravan & Camping Guide Britain & Ireland 2012 and is valid for and may be applied to stays that expire before 31.1.2013.

To make use of the benefits of the AA Camping Card Scheme you must notify any participating campsite that you are a cardholder at your time of advance booking and provide details. Scheme Cards are issued and enclosed with your copy of AA Caravan & Camping Guide Britain & Ireland 2012 at the point of initial purchase.

The card entitles the bearer to any discount or other benefits being offered by the campsite under the scheme at the time of making an advance booking. Participating campsites may formulate, provide, vary or withdraw offers at their discretion. Offers may vary from campsite to campsite. Acceptance by you of any offer made by a campsite is an agreement between you and the campsite. Offers are subject to availability at time of booking and presentation of the booker person's AA Camping Card on arrival. Photocopies will not be accepted. Campsite terms and conditions will apply.

Only one card per person or party accepted. No change given. This card is valid during the period(s) specified by the campsites concerned, and will not be valid after 31 Jan 2013. This card cannot be used in conjunction with any other discount voucher or special offer. No cash alternative available.

This scheme will be governed by English law.

AA Camping Card on back cover flap; for a list of sites that accept this card please see page 511

Symbols & Abbreviations

Facilities
 Bath
 Shower
 Electric Shaver
 Hairdryer
 Ice Pack Facility
 Disabled Facilities
 Public Telephone
 Shop on Site or within 200yds
 Mobile Shop (calling at least 5 days per week)
 BBQ Area
 Picnic Area
 Wi-fi Access
 Internet Access
 Recycling Facilities
 Tourist Information
 Dog Exercise Area

Leisure
 Indoor Swimming Pool
 Outdoor Swimming Pool
 Tennis Court
 Games Room

 Children's Playground
 Kid's Club
 Stables & Horse Riding
 9/18 hole Golf Course
 Boats for Hire
 Cinema
 Entertainment
 Fishing
 Mini Golf
 Watersports
 Gym
 Sports Field
Spa Spa
 Separate TV room

Services
 Toilet Fluid
 Café or Restaurant
 Fast Food/Takeaway
 Baby Care
 Electric Hook Up
 Motorvan Service Point
 Launderette
 Licensed Bar

 Calor Gas
 Camping Gaz
 Battery Charging

Abbreviations
BH   bank holiday/s
Etr   Easter
Whit   Whitsun
dep   departure
fr   from
hrs   hours
m   mile
mdnt   midnight
rdbt   roundabout
rs   restricted service
RV   Recreational Vehicles
U   rating not confirmed
wk   week
wknd   weekend

 no dogs
 no credit or debit cards

AA Pennant Classification

AA Pennant Rating and Holiday Centres

AA parks are classified on a 5-point scale according to their style and the range of facilities they offer. As the number of pennants increases, so the quality and variety of facilities is generally greater. There is also a separate category for Holiday Centres which provide full day and night holiday entertainment as well as offering complete touring facilities for campers and for caravanners.

What can you expect at an AA-rated park?

All AA parks must meet a minimum standard: they should be clean, well maintained and welcoming. In addition they must have a local authority site licence (unless specially exempted), and satisfy local authority fire regulations.

The AA inspection

Each campsite that applies for AA recognition receives an unannounced visit each year by one of the AA's highly qualified team of inspectors. They make a thorough check of the site's touring pitches, facilities and hospitality. The sites pay an annual fee for the inspection, the recognition and rating, and receive a text entry in the AA Caravan & Camping Guide Britain & Ireland. AA inspectors pay when they stay overnight on a site. The criteria used by the inspectors in awarding the AA Pennant rating is shown on the opposite page. **Please note:** the AA does not, under the AA Caravan and Camping quality standards scheme, inspect any statics or chalets that are for hire. The AA takes no responsibility for the condition of rented accommodation and can take no action in the event of complaints relating to these.

AA Quality % Score

AA Rated Campsites, Caravan Parks and Holiday Centres are awarded a percentage score alongside their pennant rating or holiday centre status. This is a qualitative assessment of various factors including customer care and hospitality, toilet facilities and park landscaping. The % score runs from 50% to 100% and indicates the relative quality of parks with the same number of pennants. For example, one 3-pennant park may score 60%, while another 3-pennant park may achieve 70%. Holiday Centres also receive a % score between 50% and 100% to differentiate between quality levels within this grading. Like the pennant rating, the percentage is reassessed annually.

Holiday Centres

In this category we distinguish parks which cater for all holiday needs including cooked meals and entertainment.

They provide:

- A wide range of on-site sports, leisure and recreational facilities
- Supervision and security at a very high level
- A choice of eating outlets
- Facilities for touring caravans that equal those available to rented holiday acommodation
- A maximum density of 25 pitches per acre
- Clubhouse with entertainment provided
- Laundry with automatic washing machines

AA Pennant Rating Guidelines

 One Pennant Parks

These parks offer a fairly simple standard of facilities including:

- No more than 30 pitches per acre
- At least 5% of the total pitches allocated to touring caravans
- An adequate drinking water supply and reasonable drainage
- Washroom with flush toilets and toilet paper provided, unless no sanitary facilities are provided in which case this should be clearly stated
- Chemical disposal arrangements, ideally with running water, unless tents only
- Adequate refuse disposal arrangements that are clearly signed
- Well-drained ground, and some level pitches
- Entrance and access roads of adequate width and surface
- Location of emergency telephone clearly signed
- Emergency telephone numbers fully displayed

 Two Pennant Parks

Parks in this category should meet all of the above requirements, but offer an increased level of facilities, services, customer care, security and ground maintenance. They should include the following:

- Separate washrooms, including at least 2 male and 2 female WCs and washbasins per 30 pitches
- Hot and cold water direct to each basin
- Externally-lit toilet blocks
- Warden available during day, times to be indicated
- Whereabouts of shop/chemist clearly signed
- Dish-washing facilities, covered and lit
- Reception area

 Three Pennant Parks

Many parks come within this rating and the range of facilities is wide. All parks will be of a very good standard and will meet the following minimum criteria:

- Facilities, services and park grounds are clean and well maintained, with buildings in good repair and attention paid to customer care and park security
- Evenly-surfaced roads and paths
- Clean modern toilet blocks with all-night lighting and containing toilet seats in good condition, soap and hand dryers or paper towels, mirrors, shelves and hooks, shaver & hairdryer points, and lidded waste bins in female toilets
- Modern shower cubicles with sufficient hot water and attached, private changing space
- Electric hook-ups
- Some hardstanding/wheel runs/firm, level ground
- Laundry with automatic washing and drying facilities, separate from toilets

- Children's playground with safe equipment
- 24 hours public telephone on site or nearby where mobile reception is poor
- Warden availability and 24-hour contact number clearly signed

 Four Pennant Parks

These parks have achieved an excellent standard in all areas, including landscaping of grounds, natural screening and attractive park buildings, and customer care and park security.

Toilets are smart, modern and immaculately maintained, and generally offer the following facilities:

- Spacious vanitory-style washbasins, at least 2 male and 2 female per 25 pitches
- Fully-tiled shower cubicles with doors, dry areas, shelves and hooks, at least 1 male and 1 female per 30 pitches
- Availability of washbasins in lockable cubicles, or combined toilet/washing cubicles, or a private/family room with shower/toilet/washbasin

Other requirements are:

- Baby changing facilities
- A shop on site, or within reasonable distance
- Warden available 24 hours
- Reception area open during the day, with tourist information available
- Internal roads, paths and toilet blocks lit at night
- Maximum 25 pitches per campable acre
- Toilet blocks heated October to Easter
- Minimum 50% electric hook-ups
- Minimum 10% hardstandings where necessary
- Late arrivals enclosure

 Five Pennant Premier Parks

Premier parks are of an extremely high standard, set in attractive surroundings with superb mature landscaping. Facilities, security and customer care are of an exceptional quality. As well as the above they will also offer:

- First-class toilet facilities including several designated self-contained cubicles, ideally with WC, washbasin and shower.
- Electricity to most pitches
- Minimum 20% hardstandings (where necessary)
- Some fully-serviced 'super' pitches: of larger size and with water and electricity supplies connected
- A motorhome service point

Many Premier Parks will also provide:

- Heated swimming pool
- Well-equipped shop
- Café or restaurant and bar
- A designated walking area for dogs (if accepted)

Useful Information

Booking Information

It is advisable to book in advance during peak holiday seasons and in school or public holidays. It is also wise to check whether or not a reservation entitles you to a particular pitch. It does not necessarily follow that an early booking will secure the best pitch; you may simply have the choice of what is available at the time you check in.

Some parks may require a deposit on booking which may be non-returnable if you have to cancel your holiday. If you do have to cancel, notify the proprietor at once because you may be held legally responsible for partial or full payment unless the pitch can be re-let. Consider taking out insurance such as AA Travel Insurance, tel: 0800 085 7240 or visit the AA website: **theAA.com** for details to cover a lost deposit or compensation. Some parks will not accept overnight bookings unless payment for the full minimum period (e.g. two or three days) is made.

Last Arrival – Unless otherwise stated, parks will usually accept arrivals at any time of the day or night, but some have a special 'late arrivals' enclosure where you have to make temporary camp to avoid disturbing other people on the park. Please note that on some parks access to the toilet block is by key or pass card only, so if you know you will be late, do check what arrangements can be made.

Last Departure – Most parks will specify their overnight period – e.g. noon to noon. If you overstay the departure time you can be charged for an extra day.

Chemical Closet Disposal Point (cdp)

You will usually find one on every park, except those catering only for tents. It must be a specially constructed unit, or a WC permanently set aside for the purpose of chemical disposal and with adjacent rinsing and soak-away facilities. However, some local authorities are concerned about the effect of chemicals on bacteria in cesspools etc, and may prohibit or restrict provision of CDPs in their areas.

Complaints

Speak to the park proprietor or supervisor immediately if you have any complaints, so that the matter can be sorted out on the spot. If this personal approach fails, you may decide, if the matter is serious, to approach the local authority or tourist board.

AA guide users may also write to:

The Co-ordinator, AA Caravan & Camping Scheme,
AA Lifestyle Guides, 13th floor, Fanum House, Basingstoke,
RG21 4EA

The AA may at its sole discretion investigate any complaints received from guide users for the purpose of making any necessary amendments to the guide. The AA will not in any circumstances act as representative or negotiator or undertake to obtain compensation or enter into further correspondence or deal with the matter in any other way whatsoever. The AA will not guarantee to take any specific action.

Dogs

Dogs may or may not be accepted at parks, and this is entirely at the owner's or warden's discretion (assistance dogs should be accepted). Even when the park states that they accept dogs, it is still discretionary, and certain breeds may not be considered as suitable, so we strongly advise that you check when you book.*
Dogs should always be kept on a lead and under control, and letting them sleep in cars is not encouraged.

*Some sites have told us they do not accept dangerous breeds.
The following breeds are covered under the Dangerous Dogs Act 1991 –
Pit Bull Terrier, Japanese Tosa, Dogo Argentino and Fila Brazilerio.

Electric Hook-Up

This is becoming more generally available at parks with three or more pennants, but if it is important to you, you should check before booking. The voltage is generally 240v AC, 50 cycles, although variations between 200v and 250v may still be found. All parks in the AA scheme which provide electric hook-ups do so in accordance with International Electrotechnical Commission regulations. Outlets are coloured blue and take the form of a lidded plug with recessed contacts, making it impossible to touch a live point by accident. They are also waterproof. A similar plug, but with protruding contacts which hook into the recessed plug, is on the end of the cable which connects the caravan to the source of supply, and is dead. This equipment can usually be hired on site, or a plug connector supplied to fit your own cable. You should ask for the male plug; the female plug is the one already fixed to the power supply. This supply is rated for either 5, 10 or 16 amps and this is usually displayed on a triangular yellow plate attached to source of supply. If it is not, be sure to check at the site reception. This is important because if you overload the circuit, the trip switch will operate to cut off the power supply. The trip switch can only be reset by a park official, who will first have to go round all the hook-ups on park to find the cause of the trip. This can take a long time and will make the culprit distinctly unpopular with all the other caravanners deprived of power, to say nothing of the park official. Tents and trailer tents are recommended to have a Residual Circuit Device (RCD) for safety reasons and to avoid overloading the circuit. It is a relatively simple matter to calculate whether your appliances will overload the circuit. The amperage used by an appliance depends on its wattage and the total amperage used is the total of all the appliances in use at any one time. If you are not sure whether your camping or caravanning equipment can be used at a park, check beforehand.

Average amperage

Portable black & white TV 50 watts approx.	0.2 amp
Small colour TV 90 watts approx.	0.4 amp
Small fan heater 1000 watts (1kW) approx.	4.2 amp
One-bar electric fire NB each extra bar rates 1000 watts (1kW)	4.2 amp
60 watt table lamp approx.	0.25 amp
100 watt light bulb approx.	0.4 amp
Battery charger 100 watts approx.	0.4 amp
Small fridge 125 watts approx.	0.4 amp
Domestic microwave 600 watts approx.	2.5 amp

Motor Caravans

At some parks motor caravans are only accepted if they remain static throughout the stay. Also check that there are suitable level pitches at the parks where you plan to stay.

Overflow Pitches

Campsites are legally entitled to use an overflow field which is not a normal part of their camping area for up to 28 days in any one year as an emergency method of coping with additional numbers at busy periods. When this 28 day rule is being invoked site owners should increase the numbers of sanitary facilities accordingly. In these circumstances the extra facilities are sometimes no more than temporary portacabins.

Parking

Some park operators insist that cars be put in a parking area separate from the pitches; others will not allow more than one car for each caravan or tent.

Park Restrictions

Many parks in our guide are selective about the categories of people they will accept on their parks. In the caravan and camping world there are many restrictions and some categories of visitor are banned altogether. Where a park has told us of a restriction/s this is included in notes in their entry.

On many parks in this guide, unaccompanied young people, single-sex groups, single adults, and motorcycle groups will not be accepted. The AA takes no stance in this matter, basing its pennant classification on facilities, quality and maintenance. On the other hand, some parks cater well for teenagers and offer magnificent sporting and leisure facilities as well as discos; others have only very simple amenities. A small number of parks in our guide exclude all children in order to create an environment aiming at holiday makers in search of total peace and quiet. (See p.47)

Pets Travel Scheme

The importation of animals into the UK is subject to strict controls. Penalties for trying to avoid these controls are severe. However, the Pet Travel Scheme (PETS) allows cats, dogs, ferrets and certain other pets coming from the EU and certain other countries to enter the UK without quarantine provided the appropriate conditions are met. For details:
www.defra.gov.uk/wildlife-pets/pets/travel/pets/index.htm
PETS HELPLINE on 0870 241 1710
E-mail: quarantine@animalhealth.gsi.gov.uk
Pets resident in the British Isles (UK, Republic of Ireland, Isle of Man and Channel Islands) are not subject to any quarantine or PETS rules when travelling within the British Isles.

Seasonal Touring Pitches

Some park operators allocate a number of their hardstanding pitches for long-term seasonal caravans. These pitches can be reserved for the whole period the campsite is open, generally between Easter and September, and a fixed fee is charged for keeping the caravan on the park for the season. These pitches are in great demand, especially in popular tourist areas, so enquire well in advance if you wish to book one.

Shops

The range of food and equipment in shops is usually in proportion to the size of the park. As far as our pennant requirements are concerned, a mobile shop calling several times a week, or a general store within easy walking distance of the park is acceptable.

Unisex Toilet Facilities

An ever-increasing number of parks now offer unisex toilet facilities instead of (or sometimes as well as) separate units for men and women. If the type of toilet facility is important to you, please check what the park has to offer at the time of booking.

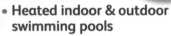

Island Camping

Channel Islands

Tight controls are operated because of the narrow width of the mainly rural roads. On all of the islands tents can be hired on recognised campsites.

Alderney

Neither caravans nor motor caravans are allowed, and campers must have a confirmed booking on the one official camp site before they arrive.

Guernsey

Only islanders may own and use towed caravans, but a limited number of motor caravans are now permitted on the island. The motor caravan, used for overnight accommodation, must be not more than 6.9mtrs long, must be booked into an authorised site (Fauxquets Valley Campsite or Le Vaugrat Camp Site) and must obtain a permit from the site operator before embarking on a ferry for Guernsey - Condor Ferries will not accept motor caravans without this permit. A window sticker must be displayed, motor caravans must return to the site each night, and the visits are limited to a maximum of one month. Permission is not required to bring a trailer tent to the island. For further details see **www.visitguernsey.com/faqs.aspx**

Herm and Sark

These two small islands are traffic free. Herm has a small campsite for tents, and these can also be hired. Sark has three campsites. New arrivals are met off the boat by a tractor which carries people and luggage up the steep hill from the harbour. All travel is by foot, on bicycle, or by horse and cart.

Jersey

Visiting caravans are now allowed into Jersey, provided they are to be used as holiday accommodation only. Caravans will require a permit for travelling to and from the port and campsite on their arrival and departure days only. Motorvans may travel around the island on a daily basis, but must return to the campsite each night. Bookings should be made through the chosen campsite, who will also arrange for a permit. Early booking is strongly recommended during July and August.

Isle of Man

Motor caravans may enter with prior permission. Trailer caravans are generally only allowed in connection with trade shows and exhibitions, or for demonstration purposes, not for living accommodation. Written application for permission should be made to the Secretary, Planning Committee, Isle of Man Local Government Board, Murray House, Mount Havelock, Douglas. The shipping line cannot accept caravans without this written permission.

Isles of Scilly

Caravans and motor caravans are not allowed, and campers must stay at official sites. Booking is advisable on all sites, especially during school holidays.

Scottish Islands

Inner Isles (including Inner Hebrides)

Skye is accessible to caravans and motor caravans, and has official camping sites, but its sister isles of Rhum and Eigg have no car ferries, and take only backpackers. Official camping only is allowed at Rothsay on the Isle of Bute. The islands of Mull, Islay, Coll and Arran have official campsites, and welcome caravans, motor caravans and tenters. Offsite camping is also allowed with the usual permission. Iona is car free, and a backpacker's paradise, while Tiree does not accept caravans or motor caravans, and has no official sites. Colonsay and Cumbrae allow no caravanning or camping, although organized groups such as the Guides or Scouts may stay with official permission. Jura and Gigha allow neither camping nor caravanning, and Lismore bans caravans but permits camping, although there are no official sites and few suitable places.

Orkney

There are no camping and caravanning restrictions, and plenty of beauty spots in which to pitch camp.

Shetland

There are four official campsites on the Shetlands, but visitors can camp anywhere with prior permission. Caravans and motor caravans must stick to the main roads. Camping 'böds' offer budget accommodation in unisex dormitories for campers with their own bed rolls and sleeping bags. There is no camping or caravanning on Noss and Fair Isle, and the Tresta Links in Fetlar.

Western Isles (Outer Hebrides)

There are official campsites on these islands, but 'wild' camping is allowed within reason, and with the landowner's prior permission.

AA Campsites of the Year

ENGLAND & OVERALL WINNER OF THE AA BEST CAMPSITE OF THE YEAR

►►►►► **96%** ROSS PARK

NEWTON ABBOT, DEVON Page 171

From the moment you arrive at this exceptional touring park, owners Mark and Helen Lowe's all-consuming passion since taking over in 1999, you know you are in for a real camping treat. 32-acres of parkland are devoted to camping and caravanning, with at least two thirds being devoted to green open space, creating a mini nature reserve for guest to explore and enjoy. What sets this park above all other contenders is Mark and Helen's dedication and attention to detail, which is evident at every turn, from the breathtaking colourful flower displays (savour the wonderful floral walk to the loos and the glorious themed flower beds) and the large, secluded, fully serviced hardstanding pitches surrounded by lush flowerbeds, to the impressive dog shower and grooming cabin, and the provision of hand sanitizers at the dustbin/recycling points. Spotless, high quality toilet facilities include eight first-class family rooms and there's a bar and restaurant in a converted barn, replete with flower-festooned conservatory, plus an adventure play area, space for ball games, a well-stocked shop selling local and home-grown produce, a 4-acre dog exercising field, and a conservation walk through glorious wild flower meadows, where guests can relax on benches and savour rolling country views towards Dartmoor. A top-class park in every way.

SCOTLAND

►►►► **83%** SKYE CAMPING & CARAVANNING CLUB SITE
EDINBANE, ISLE OF SKYE, HIGHLAND Page 389

David Weller and Nicky Sellier were so taken with the Isle of Skye that they bought a 200-acre croft and campsite on the shores of Loch Greshornish in 2007. They later became franchisees to the Camping and Caravanning Club and have continued investing and improving the facilities to create a great campsite. The views from the pitches over Loch Greshornish are amazing and the surrounding countryside is truly impressive. There are camping pods with loch views, cars for hire and guided bus tours leave from the site, so you don't even need your own transport or accommodation to enjoy a stay on this site. The amenity block, built to exacting standards, provides high quality and immaculately maintained modern amenities for all campers, and there is even a dog wash! The old croft buildings have been converted to camper's shelters, information rooms, and produce from David & Nicky's own working croft is also available from their well-stocked shop. Their desire is to provide a top quality holiday experience for everyone staying with them and their aim, when they bought the croft, to be the best campsite in Scotland has now been fulfilled.

WALES

►►►►► **88%** ISLAWRFFORDD CARAVAN PARK
TAL-Y-BONT, GWYNEDD Page 416

Situated on the coast between Barmouth and Harlech, and within the Snowdonia National Park, with clear views of Cardigan Bay, the Lleyn Peninsula and the Snowdonia and Cader Idris mountain ranges, this excellent, family-friendly park has been owned and run with enthusiasm and dedication by the Evans family since 1957. The whole park, which comprises 200 holiday homes and over 100 touring pitches, has seen considerable investment in recent years and the first-class facilities include a leisure complex with heated indoor swimming pool, a sauna and jacuzzi, and a tanning suite. In 2011, the reception, Henry's Bar & Bistro, and the games room were smartly refurbished to complement the excellent leisure facilities. The well-stocked shop has an in-store bakery. Now fully matured, the touring area boasts 75 fully serviced hardstanding pitches (including TV with freeview), new roadways and fresh tree planting, a superb toilet block with under-floor heating, top-quality fittings and two fully serviced family rooms, and 30 excellent tent pitches (all with electric) in the New Beach Paddock. The park also has private access to miles of sandy beach.

Why not spend less and relax more on UK breaks?

cottages4you
property ref GRL

Make AA Travel your first destination and you're on the way to a more relaxing short break or holiday.

AA Members and customers can get great deals on accommodation, from B&Bs to farmhouses, inns and hotels.

You can also save up to 10% at cottages4you, enjoy a 5% discount with Hoseasons, and up to 60% off the very best West End shows.

Thinking of going further afield?

Check out our attractive discounts on car hire, airport parking, ferry bookings, travel insurance and much more.

Then simply relax.

These are just some of our well-known partners:

Visit theAA.com/travel

For the road ahead

AA Campsites of the Year – Regional Award Winners

SOUTH WEST ENGLAND

▶▶▶▶▶ **91%** SOUTH LYTCHETT MANOR CARAVAN & CAMPING PARK

LYTCHETT MINSTER, DORSET Page196

This quality family park is set in the tranquil grounds of the former Lytchett Manor estate and is a perfect location for visiting the many attractions in this area of Dorset, including Poole, Swanage and Purbeck. There is even a bus stop right outside the gate where you can get the famous 'Jurassic Coast' bus, the X53, which runs from Poole to Exeter. The owners, Joanne and David Bridgen, took over the park in 2006 and have since embarked on a programme of continuous improvement, transforming the park into one of the best in the country. The modern facilities are maintained to the highest standards and provide excellent family rooms and disabled units. Pitches are both spacious and well appointed and some are fully serviced. Tents are also well catered for which makes the park even more popular with families. The park is also very dog friendly. Customer care is high on Joanne and David's list of priorities so visitors can expect a warm welcome to this top park in Dorset.

SOUTH EAST ENGLAND

▶▶▶▶▶ **88%** TANNER FARM TOURING CARAVAN & CAMPING PARK

MARDEN, KENT Page 227

At the heart of a 150-acre Wealden farm, replete with oast house, this extensive, long-established touring park is tucked away down a quiet farm drive deep in unspoilt Kentish countryside, yet close to Sissinghurst Castle and within easy reach of London (Marden station 3 miles). Campers enjoy the total peace and quiet at this well organised and beautifully laid-out park on former farmland, the two big meadows have a parkland feel with plenty of mature trees and pitch density is excellent, with neatly mown and spacious grassy pitches, plus there's plenty of room for ball games. Generous hardstanding pitches have neat wood edging and twelve are fully serviced. The huge restored barn by the entrance houses a very efficient reception/well-stocked shop, where you can buy fresh-baked bread and local produce, and an excellent information room. Tanner Farm is perfect for families, with its two excellent play areas, recreation room (computer/TV), woodland and farm walks, and a menagerie of birds and farm animals – kids can help feed the lambs in April. Refurbished toilets are spotlessly clean and there are good privacy cubicles, a unisex bathroom and a baby bathroom. Expect high levels of security and customer care.

After Bite

Fast relief from bites and stings.

Don't let bites and stings stop the family fun
– take After Bite away with you.

Easy-to-apply, fast-acting After Bite provides
instant relief from the effects of mosquitoes,
bees, wasps, nettles and jellyfish.

From Boots, Superdrug, Tesco, Lloydspharmacy
and good chemists everywhere.
Online at **www.afterbite.co.uk**
Contains ammonia 3.5% w/v. Always read the label.

AA Campsites of the Year – Regional Award Winners *continued*

HEART OF ENGLAND

▶▶▶▶▶ 85% TWO MILLS TOURING PARK

NORTH WALSHAM, NORFOLK Page 252

Two Mills is an intimate, beautifully presented adults-only park set in gently rolling countryside and provides a convenient base for exploring the Broads, the north Norfolk coast, and for visiting Norwich. Throughout the park there is a profusion of flowers and hanging baskets and the mature, wooded perimeter provides the park with an atmosphere of peaceful, rural seclusion and a wonderful wildlife habitat. There are immaculate fully serviced pitches, separated by neatly mown grass, and first-class modern toilet blocks, and a small shop. Accessed via a steep tarmac road, the newly developed 'Top Acre' section of the park is starting to mature and features a fine terrace of 26 fully serviced pitches, all with panoramic views over the site, a smart toilet block and good planting, plus the layout of pitches and facilities is excellent. The good information centre has a TV lounge, where campers can relax with tea and coffee, and a lending library. The rustic dog walk around the perimeter of the former sand quarry is an especially attractive feature, plus the park is only a short stroll from the Weavers Way Walk. Ray and Barbara Barnes are the very friendly, helpful and hands-on owners and they maintain the park in pristine condition.

NORTH WEST ENGLAND

▶▶▶▶▶ 80% RIVERSIDE CARAVAN PARK

HIGH BENTHAM, NORTH YORKSHIRE Page 337

In a tranquil setting on the banks of the River Wenning, within walking distance of High Bentham, this well-managed riverside park is located in a stunning area close to the Yorkshire/ Lancashire border and makes the perfect base for exploring the Yorkshire Dales, the Forest of Bowland, Morecambe Bay and is within easy reach of the Lake District (1 hour). It has been developed from a green field to a top quality park by the hands-on and dedicated Marshall family, who have owned the park since the late 1960s. The 12-acre site includes 200 static holiday caravans, while the touring area offers level grass pitches and 27 hardstandings, all for caravans and motorhomes and all with electric and TV connection, set in avenues separated by trees. There are excellent facilities for children, including a superb games room and adventure play area, and they are made to feel as important as the adults. It has an excellent, modern toilet block, including a new family bathroom, and a good shop, laundry and information room. The river is ideal for paddling, small dinghies and fishing (permits from reception) and Bentham Golf Club (1 mile away) is also under same ownership with facilities available for Riverside guests.

NORTH EAST ENGLAND

▶▶▶▶▶ 83% ST HELENS CARAVAN PARK

WYKEHAM, NORTH YORKSHIRE Page 350

Set on the edge of the North York Moors National Park, just six miles from Scarborough and the glorious Yorkshire coastline, this delightfully landscaped and immaculately maintained park is set in the heart of the Wykeham Estate. Arrival at this popular holiday destination creates a warm feeling of anticipation, with stunning floral displays at the entrance and around reception, and this is matched by excellent customer care from Chris and Jane Tedman, the enthusiastic wardens, who have been gradually upgrading the park in recent years. The site is thoughtfully laid out and divided into terraces with tree-screening creating smaller areas, including an adults-only zone with twelve new fully serviced super pitches for those wanting some peace and quiet, and the beautiful, eye-catching floral displays around the park are impressive. Two camping pods were added for the 2011 season and these are already proving very popular. The touring areas are well maintained and high standards of cleanliness are a real strength at this first-class park. A cycle route leads through the surrounding Wykeham Estate, and there is a short pathway to the adjoining Downe Arms country pub.

ROGER ALMOND AWARD – MOST IMPROVED CAMPSITE

▶▶▶▶▶ 89% TRETHEM MILL TOURING PARK

ST JUST-IN-ROSELAND. CORNWALL Page 113

Owned and run by three generations of the Ackroyd family, Trethem Mill stands tucked away in a sheltered valley in the heart of the beautiful Roseland Peninsula, close to St Mawes and Portscatho, and just a mile from the sea and glorious coast path walks. Roger Almond spent many years inspecting this tranquil park for the AA, offering advice and guidance on how to improve and upgrade the facilities. Ian and Jane Ackroyd, who continually look for ways to enhance the facilities, have embraced some of Roger's ideas, transforming Trethem Mill into one of Cornwall's top 5-pennant parks. Recent improvements include impressive landscaping at the park entrance, excellent planting throughout resulting in glorious flower displays, widening of tarmac roads to give better access to the spacious, fully serviced hardstanding pitches, and upgrading of the reception/shop, and to the now ultra-modern and spotlessly clean toilets. The latter has seen the addition of combined WC/WHB cubicles and, for 2012, the conversion of the former games room into three fully serviced cubicles with under-floor heating. In addition, expect great attention to detail around the park, from beautifully manicured grassy pitches and weed-free hardstandings to expertly trimmed trees and shrubbery, and a very high level of customer care. A worthy winner indeed.

A WEEK

The Life

MKH 401E

END IN
of Brian

In his quest to experience everything 'cool' about 21st-century camping, DAVID HANCOCK spends a weekend with Brian, a beautifully restored classic VW camper, in the New Forest.

Two new words in our vocabulary have changed the look of camping and caravanning in Britain in recent years. 'Staycation' describes the trend for holidaying closer to home rather than abroad due to the dire economy and the weak pound, while 'glamping', or glamorous camping, the perfect term for those too posh to pitch a tent, represents the growing number of boutique alternative campsites that offer luxury and style in spades. Combine the two and it's no wonder that camping has suddenly become very chic and 'cool', appealing to a wider cross-section of society. It's true to say that camping has been 'cool' for several years, with many traditional campsites offering wooden camping pods, domes, tipis, wigwams, bell tents and yurts for those campers who crave a little style and comfort while experiencing the great outdoors. However, 'glamping' has taken camping to a luxurious level. A new breed of quirky, eco-friendly, boutique campsites, often located deep in woodland on isolated farms, are leading the glamping trend, with stylish and unusual accommodation in treehouses, beautifully converted shepherd's huts, heated micro-lodges (Hobbit Houses) with electricity and a TV, the odd 1950s airstream trailer, or perhaps a replica Iron Age roundhouse. Yurts now come filled with antiques, hand-made wooden beds, duck-down duvets, en suite bathrooms with roll-top baths, and even an outside hot-tub. ▷

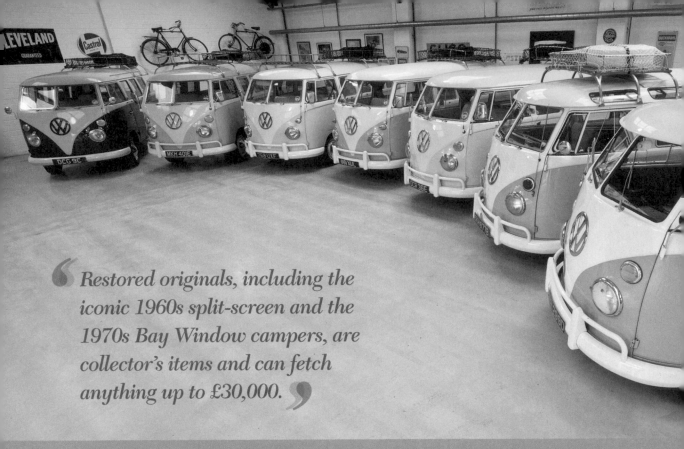

> *Restored originals, including the iconic 1960s split-screen and the 1970s Bay Window campers, are collector's items and can fetch anything up to £30,000.*

Above: The split-screen range at Vanilla Splits

If you love the idea of glamping it up in style and being mobile at the same time the answer is to hire a re-conditioned classic VW Camper van. Long a favourite of the surfing fraternity and festival-goers, and a regular at classic car shows, the legendary 'Combi' or 'Hippy Bus' is once again fulfilling many people's dreams as a holiday camper. Restored originals, including the iconic 1960s split-screen and the 1970s Bay Window campers, are collector's items and can fetch anything up to £30,000. So, if you can't afford to buy one, why not borrow a revamped classic from one of the hire companies that are springing up across the country.

Vanilla Splits – Cool Campers

Located just off the A27 east of Chichester in West Sussex, Vaniila Splits was my choice for hiring a spruced-up 'Splittie', not just for their cool website and their gorgeous fleet of buses but for their proximity to the perfect weekend destinations of the Isle of Wight, the New Forest and the magnificent Dorset coast.

Having found some of the finest 1960s split-screen and 1970s bay window campers from as far afield as California, Vanilla Splits have skilfully and lovingly restored each bus, maintaining their original integrity and adding some funky interiors with 21st-century features and comforts to enhance the whole VW experience. Every bus is unique

family get-away - kids can be accommodated in pop-up roofs in three of the campers.

The ten classy classic campers share a pristine showroom with a collection of equally stunning classic cars (also for hire), an old AA roadside emergency box, and boiler-suited Ian, who looks after the elegant collection of campers, all named after characters in the 1960s children's television series *Magic Roundabout* (Bongo, Bart, Boris, Florence, Dougal, Dylan, Mr McHenry, Mclovin, Zebedee, Brian), with passion and enthusiasm.

With 1940s/50s music drifting through the open windows of Dougal Ian proudly showed us Brian, a gorgeous 1967 split-screen painted in a cool two-tone light green and white, who was already prepped up and ready to go. Ian showed us how the electric hook-up, water pump, stove and iPod connector worked, where everything is neatly stored, including the all-important DVD player and bottle opener, and joked that it's best to pull-over in heavy rain as the tiny wipers on the split-screens are not that effective.

Top: Brian prepped and ready to go

Above: The cool interior of Florence

and personally styled, with colourful fabrics and cushions, radio with iPod connector, and a drop-down DVD player, plus a fridge, gas-powered two-ring cooker, sink, soft spotlighting, essential cooking equipment, and a proper set of crockery, cutlery and glasses. For those wanting to enjoy the great outdoors, the use of roof racks (ideal for the surf board), bike racks and drive-away awnings are also available free of charge.

Everything, including full insurance cover and AA Roadside Recovery, is provided for the coolest adventure on four wheels, be it a festival weekend away with mates, couples looking for a dream trip to Cornwall, a wedding day surprise with a difference, or the ultimate

On the road with Brian

We were eager to head west but before I could be let loose at the wheel on the M27 in the Friday rush hour, Ian had to run through Brian's (very limited) controls in the cockpit, which are totally original, explaining that the 21st-century luxuries are well and truly confined to the living quarters. A startling test drive around the parking area quickly revealed that driving a ▷

Above: Brian's original 1967 controls

> *by going back to the basics of driving and divorcing myself from the way I drive a modern-day car, I found the whole experience exciting and great fun.*

1967 vintage camper was going to be a unique and somewhat stressful experience, especially for the first few hours on the motorway.

Don't expect synchromesh gears! Finding neutral, let alone any of the four gears in Brian, is pretty much a lottery, and to engage reverse you must push the long gear stick down, then sideways and back. Mastering the gears early on is vital as the original braking system is not that effective, so they are essential in slowing down and eventually stopping the van. Take note and quiz Ian more when he quips 'You'll get used to the brakes' during your test drive. God help you if you normally drive an automatic!

And don't expect power steering – turning any corner involves wrestling with a bus driver's wheel, which is mounted across your lap, so negotiating a tight corner at speed (over 20mph) can be nerve-wracking as I found out on the A27

near Romsey. General handling can be awkward at times as Brian appeared to float, especially on nearing the top speed of 50mph, requiring constant manoeuvering of the wheel to keep it stable and in lane.

Having conquered the idiosyncrasies of how to drive Brian, by going back to the basics of driving and divorcing myself from the way I drive a modern-day car, I found the whole experience exciting and great fun. You may be slower than most on the road but the sight of an iconic camper, especially a rare, poshed-up vintage split-screen, always brings a smile to people's faces and gains huge respect on the road. Rarely are you tooted in annoyance, only in conjunction with an enthusiastic wave and a big smile.

Saturday saw me into the groove at the wheel of Brian, loving the experience and raring to trundle further west to Devon and Cornwall. If we had booked Brian for the full week, rather then the 3-night weekend break, Brian would have joined his many friends beside the surfing beaches of north Cornwall.

The Camping Experience

The distinctive sound and gorgeous retro-look of Brian certainly turned a few heads as we pulled into Hill Farm Caravan Park, a well-run 5 Pennant park on the edge of the New Forest near Romsey. As a life-long camper, setting up on the pitch was a breeze compared to erecting even the smallest of tents and I can see why campers make the transition to a motorhome or invest in a VW campervan at a certain age after years in a tent.

In just a couple of minutes, having plugged the socket into the electric hook-up and dropped the water pump into the water canister under the sink, we had the kettle on and were relaxing and reliving the exciting first journey in Brian along the M27.

Time spent finding the fridge switch, the fold-away table base and the corkscrew are essential in daylight as you soon realise how small the living space is in a vintage VW camper. Intimacy with whoever you are travelling with is guaranteed. It may be compact but the interior has been brilliantly designed, which is a credit to German efficiency and the excellent modernisation by Vanilla Splits, who have added effective spotlights and a decent gas stove. Organisation and getting into a good routine is key to easy living in Brian, especially when it comes to sleeping.

Working out how the bed slots together takes time, then you have to retrieve the duvet and pillows from the deep compartment beside the sink before pulling all the doll's house curtains (all with pretty double-sided designs) for privacy. With bags stowed away at the back or front, the result is a very cosy, small double bed, with Brian's original louvred windows, a genius design with mosquito mesh, allowing a gentle flow of fresh air into the bus during the night.

A good night's sleep was followed by a relaxed start and a decent fry-up breakfast before setting off to Salisbury in heavy rain, with Brian's tiny motorised window wipers just about coping with the downpour. Sunday saw Brian pootling through sun-drenched New Forest lanes, including the glorious Bolderwood and Rhinefield Ornamental Drives, before the M27 beckoned in the late afternoon and the journey to Ellscott Park near the Witterings south of Chichester, as Brian had to be back home at 10am on the Monday morning.

That evening, following a slap-up pasta meal, we made the bed up early and settled down cosy and warm to watch a DVD with a glass of wine while wild wind and rain from Hurricane Katia raged outside. It was the perfect way to end our all too brief love affair with Brian and we look forward to being reunited with him for a longer, more adventurous trip in the future.

VW – A LITTLE HISTORY

The first generation of VW buses were built from 1950 to 1967. Very distinctive, with their split windshield, these first T1 vans were powered by the 1100cc (24hp) Beetle engine. Initially two versions were offered, the Commercial (or Panel) Van, and the Kombi with two rows of removable seats and three windows down each side. Larger engines followed, together with other versions of the van, including the Deluxe Microbus (or Samba) with its distinctive roof lights, cloth sunroof and chrome plated ornamental band separating the two-tone colour scheme.

The Westfalia camper version started in 1950 and luxuries were added to the basic vans, including various foldout seat arrangements for sleeping; birch plywood interior panels; laminated plywood cabinets for storage; an ice box or cold-box; a sink; a water storage and pump; electric hook ups; louvred windows; and a laminated folding table.

All the vans at Vanilla Splits are restored with these original concepts in mind.

In late 1967, the 'Splittie' was given a thorough make over, and the T2 was introduced. This second generation Type 2 lost its distinctive split front windshield, and was slightly larger and considerably heavier than its predecessor. Nicknamed The Bay, after the panoramic front window, it introduced many new features to the iconic van, and even to this day is still in production in Brazil. Being slightly larger than the 'Splitties', they're ideal for families with kids or a couple looking for a little more room to stretch.

Vanilla Splits
Barnham Road, Barnham, Chichester, West Sussex PO22 0HD
Tel: 01243 545725; info@vanillasplits.com; www.vanillasplitscom

Brave new

world

Outdoor Journalist
CLIVE GARRETT
considers camping technology

We live in an age where everything appears to be judged on technical merit. Multi-function mobile phones that tap into the wonders of the web, mp4 players and e-books are just the tip of a technological iceberg that appears to spread far and wide. These gadgets are designed to improve the day-to-day quality of our lives and to entertain. Ultra-small packages instantly bring the total knowledge of man's endeavours to our fingertips, and we now border on full integration with this virtual world.

You would expect such technology to impact heavily on the world of camping. And it has - but possibly not in the way that you might imagine...

Camping is enjoying a resurgence. It is impossible to claim that this is down to a single cause, but talk to campers, and certain topics keep cropping up. Of course, many are attracted to camping as a cheap holiday option, however many more are realising the benefits of spending quality time with friends and family, away from the pressures and sophistication of modern life; perhaps to escape and experience an adventure – no matter how ▷

> *with camping's green credentials rubber-stamping concerns about the environment, the pastime is finding a far wider audience.*

small. And, with camping's green credentials rubber-stamping concerns about the environment, the pastime is finding a far wider audience than previously enjoyed.

However, while tents undoubtedly bring you closer to nature, it could be argued that many of the new generation of campers are not prepared to forsake all their modern luxuries, and consequently look to technology to improve the experience.

Mains effect

The demands placed on campsites to provide caravan and motorhome campers with electric hook-ups has had a knock-on effect. Realising that they have to pay for the service whether they use it or not, tent campers are investing in a suitable mains hook-up board to make use of electric equipment designed for camping.

There are benefits to having a BS-approved mains unit in the tent. Cooking under cover has long been a problem for campers unless using a tarp or cook tent; the twin dangers of fire and carbon monoxide poisoning should always be in the back of a camper's mind when using traditional camping stoves. Electricity (ie flameless cooking) minimises the risks by using induction hobs and cookers such as the popular Remoska. And I, for one, happily enjoy the ready supply of fresh food and chilled drinks provided by running my three-way fridge on electric in my tent. Campers have long enjoyed using gas to power these units, but the threat from carbon monoxide has always meant that they had to be situated in an open awning.

An electricity supply provides a suitable power source for travel kit. For instance, parents with young families are able to use travel sterilisers and bottle warmers. It also encourages the development of powered camping equipment such as the electric lights and heaters that are needed in the spring or autumn months.

Redundant skills

Safety is one area that technology can have a direct influence - advanced braking and stability systems for caravans is an obvious example. Likewise, anyone participating in outdoor pursuits will probably have had some experience with using the latest GPS navigation systems. But, technology is no substitute for learning and improving upon the relevant skills needed to enjoy life outdoors. After all, human error can cause accidents when towing, and you can still get lost if those GPS batteries fail!

Much reliance is placed upon technology in modern camping gear and, unfortunately, it appears that when something goes wrong the blame is placed squarely on the equipment rather than the user's lack of camping skills. Last year, leading family camping brand Outwell applied a Wind Stabilizer System to a number of its tent categories. Under test, it was shown that these could withstand Force

9 and 10 winds – dependent upon category. Of course, they can only do this if pitched correctly, so the fact remains that if a camper lacks the skill to pitch a tent appropriately then no matter how good the technology the product will fail.

Emerging materials and production techniques allow designers to experiment, and sometimes the results are stunning. But, the very best new designs are often based on old tried and tested ideas that fulfill the consumer's basic requirements.

Most tent designs had already been tried out by midway through the last century. Dome tents had been created using wooden poles that had been shaped under steam; hooped tents were used on wagon trains and camping punts. Ridge and pyramid tents were the norm, with variations being developed for expedition use. Since the beginning of the last century lightweight campers were using their walking staffs as the tent's centre pole to

keep weight down. Many of these ideas are still applied to modern tents. In fact, some lightweight tents are again using walking poles as the tent frame. Pneumatic tents had been around for half a century before Vango applied the latest materials to create an inflatable tent in a design more suitable to the needs of a modern family rather than the igloos of old.

Zips and aluminium opened up tent design after World War II, closely followed by the use of synthetic materials. The 1950s saw a hike in costs when mounting major mountaineering expeditions. This was recognised by Robert Saunders, a man who was to become one of the UK's leading tent designers. He started experimenting with synthetic materials, used for spinnakers, to create lighter tents needed for faster, smaller and thus cheaper expeditions. This eventually developed into his famous double-sided silicon elastomer-coated Ripstop nylon outer fabric ▷

> *Generations of campers have been brought up with the convenience of synthetic materials. Unfortunately, this has meant many of the old skills have never been learnt*

that, decades on, is just being adapted and improved upon by many leading European tent manufacturers.

Recent years has seen fabric technology improve to the extent that it is easier to stitch and bond lighter fabrics, and seams in silicon elastomer-coated materials can to be taped against leakage. German tent manufacturer Vaude has made great strides using such technology on its lightweight tents, but it is UK manufacturer, Terra Nova that is now in the Guinness Book of Records for manufacturing the world's lightest tent - the 581g Laser Ultra 1. Like the early Saunder's tents, the company looked to sail materials for increased strength and reduced weight when creating the latest innovative products.

Generations of campers have been brought up with the convenience of synthetic materials. Unfortunately, this has meant many of the old skills have never been learnt, especially as now maintenance is minimal and gear is often treated as a consumable. Such a mentality cannot be employed when using conventional, natural fibres that demand more intensive maintenance and a different approach to camping. For instance, the popularity for polycotton and cotton tents has risen in recent years as campers look to quality natural fabrics that are perceived to have green credentials. But there has been a rise in complaints concerning leaking fabrics and seams, apparently down to lack of knowledge. Many campers believe

cotton, like a coated synthetic, is totally waterproof, and do not realise that in order to work effectively natural fabrics have to be weathered before use.

Green light

Having green credentials when camping is important these days and many campers explore power sources such as solar panels and wind-up products. Large panels using the latest technology are important sources of power for caravans and motorhomes that are pitched beyond the reach on an electric hook-up for any length of time. Unfortunately, panels on a smaller scale have yet prove themselves reliable for tent campers.

While a wind-up torch is ideal for children who regularly waste batteries by leaving a torch on overnight, the noise and inconvenience created by winding a radio up for one minute in every 20 is just not worth the hassle. But, improvements in rechargeable battery performance and LED technology is certainly a major step forward, creating lighter, brighter and more energy efficient lights. Torches, although pricey, that store and control electricity in capacitors and can be fully recharged in 90 seconds, point to the latest exciting energy-efficient developments that could change the way we light up our tents.

One would expect the greatest use of technology in the most glamorous camping circles but, in fact, such seekers of the outdoor life have returned to traditional equipment as used during the early part of last century. The book, *First in the field; A Century of The Camping and Caravanning Club* reports that in 1917 a Club member wrote a feature on family camping that describes his 22ft long and 12 ft high tent (designed for fixed camping) as including a solid floor, beds, chest of drawers, washstand, book shelves, meat safe, provisions cupboard, table and chairs! This book also shows examples of adverts for the latest camping stoves that resemble a small kitchen range.

Yet while it appears that glamping is hardly a new idea there has been improvements in camping furniture. Tables, kitchens and storage units are becoming lighter, easier to pack and more ergonomically designed. This is mirrored in seating that also boasts greater support and cushioning – a far cry from traditional, finger-trapping, deckchairs.

If you decide to stay on a basic site you can equip a toilet tent with an electric-flush chemical toilet that uses the latest environmentally friendly and nice-smelling chemicals. And you can now buy portable gas-fired water systems that provide hot water for your shower or kitchen.

Sleeping bags and beds also benefit. The latest synthetic fills like Primaloft, closely mimic the properties of down without the maintenance problems. Memory foam marks out more expensive models and guarantees a great night's sleep no matter how cold the weather outside or how

Some think it far better to have an instant pop-up palace for their outdoor adventure.

lumpy the ground. Self-inflating mattresses take the hassle out of preparing your bed – just open the valve and the internal foam sucks in air.

Outside factors

While developments will continue to build on old ideas, arguably the greatest changes will be through the campers' own expectations and through social change. For instance, many now expect ready-made equipment to provide home-from-home comforts – after all, the skills needed to manufacturer your own using natural materials on

site are now, sadly, virtually non-existent. Some think it far better to have an instant pop-up palace for their outdoor adventure.

So, as you decide whether or not to buy new camping gear this year, just pause to consider if that latest gadget really will improve your camping experience. Chances are that if you keep things simple, the money will be better spent improving your camping skills, and maybe extending your stay at your favourite AA-rated site by a night or two.

A day in the life of a Campsite Inspector

The AA Caravan & Camping Guide features over 900 campsites offering a diverse choice for the camper. Our inspectors visit campsites of every type and size that provide a wide range of good facilities, from the large family-orientated Holiday Centres to the more humble, more basic sites where peace, quiet and wonderful views are all that is required.

But, how do we grade a campsite, what do we look for, and what exactly do we do during an inspection visit? Senior Inspector Colin Church unravels the mystery and takes you through a typical inspection day.

So what does an AA Campsite Inspector do?

Well, we visit campsites and holiday parks, unannounced, to carry out a detailed inspection using the AA Pennant Scheme's prescribed set of criteria (very similar to that used for hotel inspections) which covers the general facilities and overall quality at each campsite. The inspectors have either their own caravan, motorhome or tent - yes, one inspector does use a tent - as we travel around the country, plus we all have many years experience of camping and caravanning.

Each inspector has his or her allocated area, and mine for this year covers Somerset, Dorset, Gloucestershire, Wiltshire, Hampshire, Oxfordshire, Berkshire, Isle of Wight and the Channel Islands. This equates to about 160 campsites that are required to be inspected between Easter and August, so planning my route and identifying how many sites I can inspect in a single day is a key element of the job - if a site is missed it will mean a long drive back!

The day begins

Today I'm in sunny Dorset, having based my caravan at Wareham Forest Touring Park, a lovely park set in the heart of the Wareham Forest. From here I am well positioned to visit sites in the Poole and Purbeck area. My caravan will become my home and office for the next few days while I carry out my ▷

> *Today I'm in sunny Dorset, having based my caravan at Wareham Forest Touring Park, a lovely park set in the heart of the Wareham Forest.*

> *If the site, or the guidebook, tell you not to rely on Sat Nav please take the advice – ignore warnings at your peril.*

Above: South Lytchett Manor Caravan & Camping Park

'work'. Yes, it really is work, or at least that's what I tell everyone!

Today's schedule is to visit Ridge Farm Camping & Caravan Park and Lookout Holiday Park, both near Wareham, but first it's off to South Lytchett Manor Caravan and Camping Park near Poole.

The inspection starts well before arriving at the actual site, as I need to verify the directions and signs, and also to see if the Sat Nav will get me there in one piece – especially important if you happen to be towing a large twin-axle caravan. If the site, or the guidebook, tell you NOT to

rely on Sat Nav please take the advice – I have been to sites using Sat Nav and, if I had been towing the caravan, I would have become well and truly stuck in a narrow and twisty lane! Ignore warnings at your peril.

On arrival at South Lytchett Manor, through its very impressive gated entrance, I first head for the reception to meet the owners Joanne and David, who run the park with their son Matthew and an experienced team. Joanne and David accompany me around the park pointing out the changes that have been made since my visit last year, as well as outlining any future plans. The inspection is very detailed and all facilities and areas of the site are thoroughly checked. In particular the toilet and shower blocks are inspected for the quality of fittings, how well they are appointed (ie hairdryers, mirrors, hooks, soap dispensers etc), how spacious the showers are, and most importantly how clean they are. I note my findings on the report sheet which will be discussed with the owners at the end of tour.

Finding the unexpected

Inspectors find themselves in some quite unusual and unexpected situations, and today is no exception. A visiting RSPB group, from nearby Arne Nature Reserve, have set up a stand on the site to talk to the children about their work and show them the animals that can be found on the reserve. I'm impressed at this excellent educational children's activity

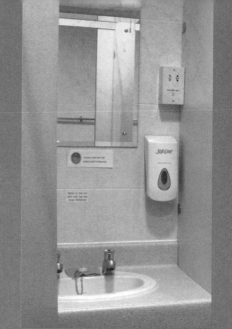

and the kids love it too. I have to admit that I did decline the offer to hold a grass snake, much to the amusement of the children who had no such fear.

My tour then took me to the far end of the site, where last year several old static caravans were parked, and quite frankly, let the site down. Well, what a transformation, all the statics have gone and the whole area has been landscaped with new pitches and roadways. The result is excellent and it's now one of the most popular areas of the park.

The details of the inspection

As part of the inspection process, pitch size, quality of hardstanding, electric, non-electric or fully serviced pitches are taken into consideration. 1- and 2-pennant sites are not required to have hardstandings, but sites with 3 pennants and above are required to have some, and those with 5-pennants, our top rating, must have fully-serviced pitches as well. These top rated sites must also provide good disabled rooms and family rooms; South Lytchett Manor scores well, both are spacious and of excellent quality.

Another key part of the inspection process is to spot the attention to detail owners lavish on their parks. I look for neat and tidy edges to hardstandings, weed-free flower beds, well mown and strimmed grass (especially just after a pitch has been vacated), perhaps fresh flowers in toilet blocks, and maybe screening panels around the

chemical disposal points, because no one wants to see people using this facility! It's these little details that make a park look just that much sharper and stand out from others. I'm happy to say South Lytchett Manor sets a fine example.

Customer service plays an important part of my inspection, for example, the way customers are received when they arrive, especially after perhaps a long and tiring journey. A friendly welcome, an easy booking-in process and making sure that customers are

Top and above: South Lytchett Manor Caravan & Camping Park

escorted to their allotted pitch without any fuss, goes a long way to making the holiday or short break a relaxing and enjoyable experience. As an inspector, I only need to stand in the reception office to see and hear how well the staff ▷

greet their guests. South Lytchett Manor places great importance on customer care and service. While I'm in reception I also take into consideration the provision of good local tourist information, such as nearby attractions, local walks, good pubs and restaurants, and what birds or animals can be seen on the park. At South Lytchett Manor they have an excellent information cabin which also has a free Wi-fi area.

Other facilities we inspect are the laundry rooms; the dish-wash areas especially to see if they are undercover and well lit; the chemical disposal points, which need to have a water supply, a means of flushing and must be clean; and if the site has them, the children's play areas and games rooms.

Safe and secure

Access and security is next on the check list. Manoeuvering around the site and ease of access onto the pitch is checked carefully; at some long-established sites access can be quite tight for a large twin-axle caravan or very large motorhome. The inspector will point this out to the owners and can nearly always make suggestions and recommendations to improve the situation.

A 1-pennant site may only have a simple, lockable gate, whilst at 5-pennants we expect a barrier system and maybe also CCTV. The protection of both customers and their expensive units (car and caravan) is vital, and we find that virtually all campsites take these matters very seriously.

Security is also important not only for customers but also the owners. I recently visited a site to be told by a proud owner that he had at last installed a new and expensive, commercial washing machine and tumble drier. Following my inspection I asked him where he had put the machines, as I'd seen no sign of them. He rushed over to the laundry to find both gone! It turned out that the previous evening, just after he had closed reception and had gone home, two men had turned up and loaded the new machines into their van. A customer told the owner that these uninvited visitors had spun the story that the machines had to be replaced as they were the wrong type. The customer even helped the men put the machines in the van! A timely warning to all campsite owners perhaps.

The rating scores

Next is to assess the 'AA Quality Percentage Score' for each campsite. This quality score is assessed for each pennant rating and we consider customer service, toilets and showers (quality of fittings, cleanliness etc); other site facilities (swimming pools, bar, children's activities and so on); pitches, landscaping and ground maintenance. The percentage score appears alongside the pennant rating in this guide. So, for example, there could be a 1-pennant site at 90%, which indicates that although a fairly small and basic site it has very good facilities and good pitches.

On the other hand, a 4-pennant site at 78%, meets all the criteria for that number of pennants but the percentage score reflects a lower quality - this may be due to small pitch sizes or a slightly lower number of private washing cubicles. However we always require clean and decent toilet facilities at all levels.

Back to my now completed inspection tour of South Lytchett Manor which finishes with a short debrief with the owners on any findings or further suggestions. Happily I can tell them that there are no problems and my report will reflect the improvements made since last year. A copy of my detailed report will be sent to the owners within two weeks of this visit.

THE GOOD, THE BAD, AND THE GOOD HUMOURED

What's good about the job?
You get to visit a great variety of campsites in some wonderful parts of the country, meet plenty of interesting owners, managers and wardens, and you have the satisfaction of knowing that most sites take on board your suggestions and recommendations which will result in an improved experience for everyone.

What's bad about the job?
Very little really. Sometimes you encounter a bad tempered owner, especially if you have to point out that something is not quite right, and, in British's unpredictable climate it's not very nice when it is cold and wet...!

Who can do the job?
Anyone who is an experienced camper or caravanner, who likes meeting people and has a good sense of humour. Next time you see an advert for an AA Campsite Inspector, you might think of applying.

 I go through the same detailed inspection procedure and quality assessment at each site

The day's not over yet
Next, it's off to Ridge Farm near Wareham, which is a 3-pennant site offering a smaller and more peaceful camping or caravanning environment. I go through the same detailed inspection procedure and quality assessment. Again I find the facilities are fresh and very clean, however this site does not have cubicled washing facilities or family rooms and is restricted on hardstandings, hence it achieves a lower grading, but of course it will suit what many of our readers are looking for.

The final site visit of the day is to Lookout Holiday Park at Stoborough, near Wareham, which presents different choices, and is well suited to families who appreciate the provision of a good games room, plus an excellent play and football area.

I can now head back home to my caravan in Wareham Forest to write up the reports and plan the next day or, if I'm lucky, settle down and read the paper with a glass of wine – perhaps you can guess which one I prefer!

Above: Lookout Holiday Park

Best for...

The AA thinks these are the best sites for...

...waterside pitches

ENGLAND

PENTEWAN SANDS HOLIDAY PARK,
Pentewan, Cornwall
SOUTH END CARAVAN PARK,
Barrow-in-Furness, Cumbria
SLENINGFORD WATERMILL CC PARK,
North Stainley, North Yorkshire
SWALE VIEW CARAVAN PARK,
Richmond, North Yorkshire

SCOTLAND

INVER MILL FARM CARAVAN PARK,
Dunkeld, Perth & Kinross
SKYE C&C CLUB SITE,
Edinbane, Isle of Skye

WALES

RIVERSIDE CAMPING,
Caernarfon, Gwynedd

NORTHERN IRELAND

**DRUMAHEGLIS MARINA & CARAVAN
PARK**, Ballymoney, Co Antrim

...stunning views

ENGLAND

TRISTRAM C&C PARK,
Polzeath, Cornwall
TROUTBECK C&C CLUB SITE,
Troutbeck, Cumbria
GALMPTON TOURING PARK,
Brixham, Devon
HIGHLANDS END HOLIDAY PARK,
Bridport, Dorset
WIMBLEBALL LAKE,
Dulverton, Somerset
WOLDS WAY CARAVAN PARK,
West Knapton, North Yorkshire

CHANNEL ISLANDS

ROZEL CAMPING PARK,
St Martin, Jersey

SCOTLAND

OBAN C&C PARK, Oban, Argyll & Bute
LINNHE LOCHSIDE HOLIDAYS,
Corpach, Highland
INVERCOE C&C PARK,
Glencoe, Highland
JOHN O'GROATS CARAVAN SITE,
John O'Groats, Highland

WALES

BRON-Y-WENDON CARAVAN PARK,
Llanddulas, Conwy
BEACH VIEW CARAVAN PARK,
Abersoch, Gwynedd
TRAWSDIR TOURING C&C PARK,
Barmouth, Gwynedd
EISTEDDFA, Criccieth, Gwynedd
BARCDY TOURING C&C PARK,
Talsarnau, Gwynedd
CARREGLWYD C&C PARK,
Port Einon, Swansea

...good on-site restaurants

ENGLAND

STROUD HILL PARK,
St Ives, Cambridgeshire
TRISTRAM C&C PARK,
Polzeath, Cornwall
BINGHAM GRANGE T&C PARK,
Bridport, Dorset
HIGHLANDS END HOLIDAY PARK,
Bridport, Dorset
BAY VIEW HOLIDAY PARK,
Bolton-Le-Sands, Lancashire
THE OLD BRICK KILNS,
Barney, Norfolk
**BEACONSFIELD FARM CARAVAN
PARK,** Shrewsbury, Shropshire

CHANNEL ISLANDS

BEUVELANDE CAMP SITE,
St Martin, Jersey

SCOTLAND

GLEN NEVIS C&C PARK,
Fort William, Highland

...top toilets

ENGLAND

CARNON DOWNS C&C PARK,
Truro, Cornwall
BEECH CROFT FARM,
Buxton, Derbyshire
RIVERSIDE C&C PARK,
South Molton, Devon
SHAMBA HOLIDAYS,
St Leonards, Dorset
DELL TOURING PARK,
Bury St Edmunds, Suffolk
MOON & SIXPENCE,
Woodbridge, Suffolk
RIVERSIDE CARAVAN PARK,
High Bentham, North Yorkshire
WAYSIDE HOLIDAY PARK,
Pickering, North Yorkshire
MOOR LODGE PARK,
Bardsey, West Yorkshire

SCOTLAND

SKYE C&C CLUB SITE,
Edinbane, Isle of Skye
BEECRAIGS C&C SITE,
Linlithgow, West Lothian

...on-site fishing

ENGLAND

FIELDS END WATER CP,
Doddington, Cambridgeshire
BACK OF BEYOND TOURING PARK,
St Leonards, Dorset
BLACKMORE VALE C&C PARK,
Shaftesbury, Dorset
WOODLAND WATERS, Ancaster,
Lincolnshire
SALTFLEETBY FISHERIES,
Saltfleetby by Peter, Lincolnshire
**LAKESIDE CARAVAN PARK &
FISHERIES,** Downham Market, Norfolk
THORNEY LAKES CARAVAN PARK,
Langport, Somerset
**MARSH FARM CARAVAN SITE, &
CARLTON MERES COUNTRY PARK**
Saxmundham, Suffolk
**SUMNERS PONDS FISHERY &
CAMPSITE,** Barns Green, West Sussex

SCOTLAND

HODDOM CASTLE CARAVAN PARK,
Ecclefechan, Dumfries & Galloway
MILTON OF FONAB CARAVAN SITE,
Pitlochry, Perth & Kinross
GART CARAVAN PARK,
Callander, Stirling

WALES

AFON TEIFI C&C PARK,
Newcastle Emlyn, Carmarthenshire
YNYSYMAENGWYN CARAVAN PARK,
Tywyn, Gwynedd

...the kids

ENGLAND

TREVORNICK HOLIDAY PARK,
Holywell Bay, Cornwall
EDEN VALLEY HOLIDAY PARK,
Lostwithiel, Cornwall
GOLDEN VALLEY C&C PARK,
Ripley, Derbyshire
FRESHWATER BEACH HOLIDAY PARK,
Bridport, Dorset
SANDY BALLS HOLIDAY CENTRE,
Fordingbridge, Hampshire
HEATHLAND BEACH CARAVAN PARK,
Kessingland, Suffolk
GOLDEN SQUARE TOURING PARK,
Helmsley, North Yorkshire
RIVERSIDE CARAVAN PARK,
High Bentham, North Yorkshire
GOOSEWOOD CARAVAN PARK,
Sutton-on-the-Forest, North Yorkshire

SCOTLAND

BLAIR CASTLE CARAVAN PARK,
Blair Atholl, Perth & Kinross

WALES

HOME FARM CARAVAN PARK,
Marian-Glas, Isle of Anglesey
**HENDRE MYNACH TOURING C&C
PARK**, Barmouth, Gwynedd
TRAWSDIR TOURING C&C PARK,
Barmouth, Gwynedd

...being eco-friendly

ENGLAND

SOUTH PENQUITE FARM,
Blisland, Cornwall
RIVER DART COUNTRY PARK,
Ashburton, Devon
BROOK LODGE FARM C&C PARK,
Cowslip Green, Somerset

SCOTLAND

SHIELING HOLIDAYS,
Craignure, Isle of Mull

WALES

**CAERFAI BAY CARAVAN & TENT
PARK**, St David's, Pembrokeshire

...glamping it up

and staying in a pod or wigwam

ENGLAND

TREGOAD PARK, Looe, Cornwall
RUTHERN VALLEY HOLIDAYS,
Ruthernbridge, Cornwall
**LOW WRAY NATIONAL TRUST
CAMPSITE**, Ambleside Cumbria
WILD ROSE PARK,
Appleby-in-Westmorland,
Cumbria (wigwams)
ESKDALE C&C CLUB SITE,
Boot, Cumbria
**GREAT LANGDALE NATIONAL TRUST
CAMPSITE**, Great Langdale, Cumbria
WOODCLOSE CARAVAN PARK,
Kirkby Lonsdale, Cumbria (wigwams)
**WASDALE HEAD NATIONAL TRUST
CAMPSITE**, Wasdale Head, Cumbria
THE QUIET SITE,
Watermillock, Cumbria
LEE VALLEY CAMPSITE,
London E4
BELLINGHAM C&C CLUB SITE,
Bellingham, Northumberland
COTSWOLD VIEW TOURING PARK,
Charlbury, Oxfordshire

SCOTLAND

LINWATER CARAVAN PARK,
East Calder, West Lothian

...or staying in a yurt

ENGLAND

SOUTH PENQUITE FARM,
Blisland, Cornwall
**GREAT LANGDALE NATIONAL TRUST
CAMPSITE**, Great Langdale, Cumbria
ACTON FIELD CAMPING SITE,
Swanage, Dorset
HERSTON C&C PARK, Swanage, Dorset

...or staying in a tipi

ENGLAND

**LOW WRAY NATIONAL TRUST
CAMPSITE**, Ambleside, Cumbria
SYKESIDE CAMPING PARK,
Patterdale, Cumbria
SANDY BALLS HOLIDAY CENTRE,
Fordingbridge, Hampshire
**ROEBECK CAMPING & CARAVAN
PARK**, Ryde, Isle of Wight

WALES

EISTEDDFA, Criccieth, Gwynedd

...or staying in a safari tent

ENGLAND

**BURNHAM-ON-SEA HOLIDAY
VILLAGE**, Burnham-on-Sea, Somerset

Premier Parks ►►►►►

ENGLAND

BERKSHIRE
HURLEY
Hurley Riverside Park

CAMBRIDGESHIRE
ST IVES
Stroud Hill Park

CHESHIRE
CODDINGTON
Manor Wood Country Caravan Park
WHITEGATE
Lamb Cottage Caravan Park

CORNWALL
BUDE
Wooda Farm Holiday Park
CARLYON BAY
Carlyon Bay Caravan & Camping Park
CRANTOCK
Trevella Tourist Park
GOONHAVERN
Silverbow Park
MEVAGISSEY
Seaview International Holiday Park
PADSTOW
Padstow Touring Park
PENTEWAN
Sun Valley Holiday Park
ST AUSTELL
River Valley Holiday Park
ST IVES
Ayr Holiday Park
Polmanter Touring Park
ST JUST-IN-ROSELAND
Trethem Mill Touring Park
TRURO
Carnon Downs Caravan & Camping Park
Truro Caravan & Camping Park

CUMBRIA
AMBLESIDE
Skelwith Fold Caravan Park
APPLEBY-IN-WESTMORLAND
Wild Rose Park
BOOT
Eskdale C & C Club Site
KESWICK
Castlerigg Hall Caravan & Camping Park

KIRKBY LONSDALE
Woodclose Caravan Park
TROUTBECK [NEAR KESWICK]
Troutbeck C & C Club Site
WINDERMERE
Park Cliffe Camping & Caravan Estate

DEVON
BRAUNTON
Hidden Valley Park
DARTMOUTH
Woodlands Grove C & C Park
NEWTON ABBOT
Dornafield
Ross Park
SIDMOUTH
Oakdown Country Holiday Park
TAVISTOCK
Woodovis Park

DORSET
ALDERHOLT
Hill Cottage Farm C & C Park
BRIDPORT
Bingham Grange T & C Park
Highlands End Holiday Park
CHARMOUTH
Wood Farm Caravan & Camping Park
CHRISTCHURCH
Meadowbank Holidays
LYTCHETT MINSTER
South Lytchett Manor C & C Park
ST LEONARDS
Shamba Holidays
WAREHAM
Wareham Forest Tourist Park
WEYMOUTH
East Fleet Farm Touring Park
WIMBORNE MINSTER
Merley Court
Wilksworth Farm Caravan Park

HAMPSHIRE
ROMSEY
Hill Farm Caravan Park

HEREFORDSHIRE
PEMBRIDGE
Townsend Touring Park

KENT
ASHFORD
Broadhembury Caravan & Camping Park
MARDEN
Tanner Farm Touring Caravan & Camping Park

LANCASHIRE
SILVERDALE
Silverdale Caravan Park

LINCOLNSHIRE
WOODHALL SPA
Woodhall Country Park

NORFOLK
BARNEY
Old Brick Kilns
CLIPPESBY
Clippesby Hall
NORTH WALSHAM
Two Mills Touring Park

NORTHUMBERLAND
BELLINGHAM
Bellingham C & C Club Site
BERWICK-UPON-TWEED
Ord House Country Park

NOTTINGHAMSHIRE
TEVERSAL
Teversal Camping & Caravanning Club Site

OXFORDSHIRE
HENLEY-ON-THAMES
Swiss Farm Touring & Camping
STANDLAKE
Lincoln Farm Park Oxfordshire

SHROPSHIRE
BRIDGNORTH
Stanmore Hall Touring Park
SHREWSBURY
Beaconsfield Farm Caravan Park
Oxon Hall Touring Park
TELFORD
Severn Gorge Park
SOMERSET
GLASTONBURY
Old Oaks Touring Park
PORLOCK
Porlock Caravan Park

WIVELISCOMBE
Waterrow Touring Park

SUFFOLK
WOODBRIDGE
Moon & Sixpence

SUSSEX, EAST
BEXHILL
Kloofs Caravan Park

WIGHT, ISLE OF
NEWBRIDGE
The Orchards Holiday Caravan Park
RYDE
Whitefield Forest Touring Park

WORCESTERSHIRE
HONEYBOURNE
Ranch Caravan Park

YORKSHIRE, NORTH
ALLERSTON
Vale of Pickering Caravan Park
HARROGATE
Ripley Caravan Park
Rudding Holiday Park
HELMSLEY
Golden Square Touring Caravan Park
HIGH BENTHAM
Riverside Caravan Park
OSMOTHERLEY
Cote Ghyll Caravan & Camping Park
SCARBOROUGH
Jacobs Mount Caravan Park
SUTTON-ON-THE-FOREST
Goosewood Caravan Park
WYKEHAM
St Helens Caravan Park

CHANNEL ISLANDS

JERSEY
ST MARTIN
Beuvelande Camp Site

SCOTLAND

ABERDEENSHIRE
HUNTLY
Huntly Castle Caravan Park

DUMFRIES & GALLOWAY
BRIGHOUSE BAY
Brighouse Bay Holiday Park
CREETOWN
Castle Cary Holiday Park
ECCLEFECHAN
Hoddom Castle Caravan Park

EAST LOTHIAN
DUNBAR
Thurston Manor Leisure Park

FIFE
ST ANDREWS
Cairnsmill Holiday Park
Craigtoun Meadows Holiday Park

HIGHLAND
CORPACH
Linnhe Lochside Holidays

PERTH & KINROSS
BLAIR ATHOLL
Blair Castle Caravan Park
River Tilt Caravan Park

WALES

ANGLESEY, ISLE OF
DULAS
Tyddyn Isaf Caravan Park
MARIAN-GLAS
Home Farm Caravan Park

CARMARTHENSHIRE
NEWCASTLE EMLYN
Cenarth Falls Holiday Park

CONWY
LLANDDULAS
Bron-Y-Wendon Caravan Park
LLANRWST
Bron Derw Touring Caravan Park

GWYNEDD
BARMOUTH
Hendre Mynach Touring C & C Park
Trawsdir Touring Caravans
& Camping Park

TAL-Y-BONT
Islawrffordd Caravan Park

MONMOUTHSHIRE
USK
Pont Kemys Caravan & Camping Park

PEMBROKESHIRE
ST DAVID'S
Caerfai Bay Caravan & Tent Park

POWYS
BRECON
Pencelli Castle Caravan & Camping Park

WREXHAM
EYTON
Plassey Leisure Park

NORTHERN IRELAND

CO ANTRIM
BALLYMONEY
Drumaheglis Marina & Caravan Park
BUSHMILLS
Ballyness Caravan Park

CO FERMANAGH
BELCOO
Rushin House Caravan Park

Pack up your troubles and... leave them in the UK

You can now go farther afield without worrying you'll end up camping in some random field.

We've enlisted the help of European camping experts ANWB, to offer a list of inspected and trusted campsites you can choose from.

Check availability and prices in almost 900 campsites in Europe, then book your campsite pitch or rental accommodation directly with us. You can be confident that they've been inspected by ANWB, with many also offering independent scores and visitor reviews.

We guarantee that you'll pay the same price with the AA as with the campsite directly and, if you visit **theAA.com/european-camping** before you visit the continent, you could also benefit from discounts of up to 15% on ferry fares.

So, now you can camp in Europe without losing sleep over where to stay.

These are just some of our well-known partners:

Visit theAA.com/european-camping

Adults – No Children Parks

Over 40 of the parks in the AA pennant rating scheme have opted to provide facilities for adults only, and do not accept children. The minimum age for individual parks may be 18, or 21, while one or two pitch the limit even higher. For more information please contact the individual parks.

ENGLAND

CAMBRIDGESHIRE
Stanford Park, Burwell
Fields End Water CP, Doddington,
Stroud Hill Park, St Ives

CHESHIRE
Lamb Cottage Caravan Park, Whitegate

CORNWALL
St Day Holiday Park, St Day
Wayfarers C&C Park, St Hilary

CUMBRIA
Green Acres Caravan Park, Carlisle
Larches Caravan Park, Mealsgate

DERBYSHIRE
Clover Fields Touring CP, Buxton

DEVON
Woodland Springs Adult TP, Drewsteignton
Zeacombe House CP, East Anstey
Widdicombe Farm Touring Park, Torquay

DORSET
Bingham Grange T&CP, Bridport
Fillybrook Farm TP, Hurn
Back of Beyond TP, St Leonards

GREATER MANCHESTER
Gelderwood Country Park, Rochdale

HEREFORDSHIRE
Arrow Bank HP, Eardisland
Cuckoo's Corner Campsite,
Moreton on Lugg

LINCOLNSHIRE
Long Acre CP, Boston
Orchard Park, Boston
Saltfleetby Fisheries, Saltfleetby St Peter

NORFOLK
Two Mills Touring Park, North Walsham
The Rickels C&C Park, Stanhoe
Breckland Meadows TP, Swaffham
Lode Hall HP, Three Holes

NOTTINGHAMSHIRE
New Hall Farm Touring Park, Southwell

SHROPSHIRE
Beaconsfield Farm CP, Shrewsbury
Severn Gorge Park, Telford

SOMERSET
Exe Valley Caravan Site, Bridgetown
Cheddar Bridge Touring Park, Cheddar
The Old Oaks Touring Park, Glastonbury
Long Hazel Park, Sparkford
Greenacres Touring Park, Wellington
Homestead Park, Wells
Waterrow Touring Park, Wiveliscombe

SUFFOLK
Moat Barn Touring CP, Woodbridge

WEST MIDLANDS
Somers Wood Caravan Park, Meriden

WIGHT, ISLE OF
Riverside Paddock Camp Site, Newport

YORKSHIRE, EAST RIDING OF
Blue Rose Caravan Country Park,
Brandesburton

YORKSHIRE, NORTH
Shaws Trailer Park, Harrogate
Foxholme C&C Park, Helmsley
Maustin CP, Netherby

YORKSHIRE, WEST
Moor Lodge Park, Bardsey
St Helena's Caravan Park, Horsforth

SCOTLAND

FIFE
Woodland Gardens C&C Site,
Lundin Links

WALES

PEMBROKESHIRE
Rosebush Caravan Park, Rosebush

POWYS
Riverside C&C Park, Crickhowell
Dalmore C&C Park, Llandrindod Wells

Discover
Haven Touring and Camping

Choice of 23 UK coastal locations

23 fun-filled UK coastal touring and camping Holiday Parks

- Dedicated touring and camping areas with shower blocks, 24/7 security and Touring Wardens on many Parks
- 5 pitch types - ranging from Basic to Premier pitches with electric hook-up, water and drainage facility
- We welcome tourers, motorhomes, tents and trailer tents
- Save even more with Freedom Trail, our touring and camping loyalty club!
- Enjoy **FREE** use of the indoor pools, sports facilities, kids' clubs, children's play areas, family entertainment and much more!
- £100 million invested over the past few years on touring shower blocks, pitches and holiday facilities on many Parks
- Monthly and seasonal pitches available
- Pets welcome
- Open mid March - end of October

SAVE UP TO
50%*
ON 2012 HOLIDAYS
Please call or go online for details

Haven touring +camping

Awarded in 2010 for the 2nd year running and nominated for 2011 awards

---

AA Holiday Centres

ENGLAND

CORNWALL
BUDE
Sandymouth Holiday Park
HAYLE
St Ives Bay Holiday Park
HOLWELL BAY
Holywell Bay Holiday Park
Trevornick Holiday Park
LOOE
Tencreek Holiday Park
MULLION
Mullion Holiday Park
NEWQUAY
Hendra Holiday Park
Newquay Holiday Park
PENTEWAN
Pentewan Sands Holiday Park
PERRANPORTH
Perran Sands Holiday Park
REJERRAH
Monkey Tree Holiday Park
ST MERRYN
Harlyn Sands Holiday Park
WIDEMOUTH BAY
Widemouth Bay Caravan Park

CUMBRIA
FLOOKBURGH
Lakeland Leisure Park
POOLEY BRIDGE
Park Foot Caravan & Camping Park

SILLOTH
Stanwix Park Holiday Centre

DEVON
CROYDE BAY
Ruda Holiday Park
DAWLISH
Lady's Mile Holiday Park
Peppermint Park
EXMOUTH
Devon Cliffs Holiday Park
MORTEHOE
Twitchen House Holiday Parc
PAIGNTON
Beverley Parks C&C Park
WOOLACOMBE
Golden Coast Holiday Park
Woolacombe Bay Holiday Village
Woolacombe Sands Holiday Park

DORSET
BRIDPORT
Freshwater Beach Holiday Park
West Bay Holiday Park
HOLTON HEATH
Sandford Holiday Park
POOLE
Rockley Park
WEYMOUTH
Littlesea Holiday Park
Seaview Holiday Park

CO DURHAM
BLACKHALL COLLIERY
Crimdon Dene

ESSEX
CLACTON-ON-SEA
Highfield Grange
Martello Beach Holiday Park
MERSEA ISLAND
Waldegraves Holiday Park
ST LAWRENCE
Waterside St Lawrence Bay
ST OSYTH
Orchards Holiday Park
WALTON ON THE NAZE
Naze Marine

HAMPSHIRE
FORDINGBRIDGE
Sandy Balls Holiday Centre

KENT
EASTCHURCH
Warden Springs Caravan Park
WHITSTABLE
Seaview Holiday Park

LANCASHIRE
BLACKPOOL
Marton Mere Holiday Village

▷

CASTLE CARY HOLIDAY PARK

Creetown, Nr Newton Stewart, Wigtownshire DG8 7DQ
Telephone: 01671 820264
Fax: 01671 820670
www.castlecary-caravans.com
enquiries@castlecarypark.f9.co.uk

For that quiet relaxing holiday in the heart of romantic Galloway Castle Cary has much to offer, and constantly adds to and improves its facilities year after year, views over fields, woodlands and the estuary of the river cree.

Your very own luxurious holiday home on Castle Cary Holiday Park is no longer a dream but has became a reality for more and more customers who have became aware of the virtues that your own holiday home has to offer, we have a comprehensive selection of new and used Caravans, and a wide range of luxury lodges for sale.

FACILITIES
- Shower and toilets Family room
- Outdoor heated swimming pool Games room/ Shop
- Indoor heated swimming pool Donkey park
- Snooker room Restaurant/Inn
- Giant Draughts Crazy Golf
- Course Fishing New for 2011 Glamping
- Childrens Play Park C.W Points
- Tourers, tents, motor homes all welcome
- Special 10% discount for weekly bookings

AA Holiday Centres *continued*

LINCOLNSHIRE
CLEETHORPES
Thorpe Park Holiday Centre
MABLETHORPE
Golden Sands Holiday Park
SALTFLEET
Sunnydale
SKEGNESS
Southview Leisure Park

MERSEYSIDE
SOUTHPORT
Riverside Holiday Park

NORFOLK
BELTON
Wild Duck Holiday Park
BURGH CASTLE
Breydon Water
CAISTER-ON-SEA
Caister Holiday Park
GREAT YARMOUTH
Vauxhall Holiday Park
HUNSTANTON
Manor Park HP
Searles Leisure Resort

NORTHUMBERLAND
BERWICK-UPON-TWEED
Haggerston Castle
NORTH SEATON
Sandy Bay

SOMERSET
BREAN
Holiday Resort Unity
Warren Farm Holiday Centre
BRIDGWATER
Mill Farm C&C Park
BURNHAM-ON-SEA
Burnham-on-Sea Holiday Village
CHEDDAR
Broadway House Holiday Park

SUFFOLK
KESSINGLAND
Kessingland Beach Holiday Park

SUSSEX, EAST
CAMBER
Camber Sands

SUSSEX, WEST
SELSEY
Warner Farm Touring Park

WIGHT, ISLE OF
COWES
Thorness Bay Holiday Park
ST HELENS
Nodes Point Holiday Park
SHANKLIN
Lower Hyde Holiday Park
WHITECLIFF BAY
Whitecliff Bay Holiday Park

YORKSHIRE, EAST RIDING OF
SKIPSEA
Searles Leisure Resort
Skipsea Sands
WITHERNSEA
Withernsea Sands

YORKSHIRE, NORTH
FILEY
Blue Dolphin Holiday Park
Flower of May Holiday Park
Primrose Valley Holiday Park
Reighton Sands Holiday Park

SCOTLAND

DUMFRIES & GALLOWAY
GATEHOUSE-OF-FLEET
Auchenlarie Holiday Park
SOUTHERNESS
Southerness Holiday Village

EAST LOTHIAN
LONGNIDDRY
Seton Sands Holiday Village

HIGHLAND
DORNOCH
Grannie's Heilan Hame HP

NAIRN
Nairn Lochroy Holiday Park

NORTH AYRSHIRE
SALTCOATS
Sandylands

PERTH & KINROSS
TUMMEL BRIDGE
Tummel Valley Holiday Park

SCOTTISH BORDERS
EYEMOUTH
Eyemouth

SOUTH AYRSHIRE
AYR
Craig Tara Holiday Park
COLYTON
Sundrum Castle Holiday Park

WALES

CEREDIGION
BORTH
Brynowen Holiday Park

CONWY
TOWYN
Ty Mawr Holiday Park

DENBIGHSHIRE
PRESTATYN
Presthaven Sands

GWYNEDD
PORTHMADOG
Greenacres
PWLLHELI
Hafan Y Mor Holiday Park

PEMBROKESHIRE
TENBY
Kiln Park Holiday Centre

SWANSEA
SWANSEA
Riverside Caravan Park

England

Bibury, Gloucestershire

FANTASTIC
UK CAMPING & TOURING HOLIDAYS

FROM ONLY

£5*
PER PITCH, PER NIGHT

PLUS ALL OF THIS FREE

- Modern touring amenities
- Super swimming pools
- Local attraction discount booklet
- Great entertainment

- Cool kids' clubs
- Massive investment on our Parks for 2012

Across 24 Award-Winning Holiday Parks

BOOK YOUR FAMILY HOLIDAY TODAY!

WWW.PARK-RESORTS.COM/AA12
or Call 0843 320 2368 & QUOTE AA12

*Price based on a non-electric pitch Sun-Thurs in low season. Subject to availability. Facilities vary by Park

Park Resorts
Creating Amazing Memories

ISLE OF - Places incorporating the words 'Isle of' of 'Isle' will be found under the actual name, eg Isle of Wight is listed under Wight, Isle of. Channel Islands and Isle of Man, however, are between England and Scotland, and there is also a section in the guide for Scottish Islands.

BERKSHIRE

FINCHAMPSTEAD   MAP 5 SU76

Places to visit

West Green House Gardens, HARTLEY WINTNEY 01252 844611 www.westgreenhouse.co.uk

Museum of English Rural Life, READING 0118 378 8660 www.merl.org.uk

Great for kids: The Look Out Discovery Centre, BRACKNELL 01344 354400 www.bracknell-forest.gov.uk/be

AA CAMPING CARD SITE

►►► **74% California Chalet & Touring Park** *(SU788651)*

Nine Mile Ride RG40 4HU
☎ 0118 973 3928   📠 0118 932 8720
e-mail: enquiries@californiapark.co.uk
dir: *From A321 (S of Wokingham), right onto B3016 to Finchampstead. Follow Country Park signs on Nine Mile Ride*

* 🚐 £23-£25 🚥 £23-£25 ▲ £19-£30

Open all year

Last arrival flexible Last departure noon

A simple, peaceful woodland site with secluded pitches among the trees, adjacent to the country park. Several pitches have a prime position beside the lake with their own fishing area. Plans for the future include better hardstanding pitches, refurbished toilets and more lodges. 5.5 acre site. 44 touring pitches. 44 hardstandings. Caravan pitches. Motorhome pitches. Tent pitches.

California Chalet & Touring Park

AA Pubs & Restaurants nearby: The Broad Street Tavern, Wokingham 0118 977 3706

L'ortolan, Shinfield 0118 988 8500

Facilities: 📶 ⊙ 🅿 ⚏ ♻ ❼
Services: 🔌 🗑 🛒 ⚒
Within 3 miles: 🚶 🚴 ⊚ 🏠 🗑 ∪
Notes: No ground fires, no ball games, no washing of caravans. Dogs must be kept on leads.

HURLEY

Places to visit

Cliveden, CLIVEDEN 01628 605069 www.nationaltrust.org.uk

The Hell-Fire Caves, WEST WYCOMBE 01494 524411 (office) www.hellfirecaves.co.uk

Great for kids: Bekonscot Model Village and Railway, BEACONSFIELD 01494 672919 www.bekonscot.co.uk

HURLEY   Map 5 SU88

PREMIER PARK

►►►►► **81% Hurley Riverside Park** *(SU826839)*

Park Office SL6 5NE
☎ 01628 824493   & 823501   📠 01628 825533
e-mail: info@hurleyriversidepark.co.uk
dir: *Signed off A4130 (Henley to Maidenhead road), just W of Hurley*

🚐 £15-£30 🚥 £15-£30 ▲ £13-£28

Open Mar-Oct

Last arrival 20.00hrs Last departure noon

A large Thames-side site with a good touring area close to river. Now a quality park following major investment, there are three beautifully appointed toilet blocks, one of which houses quality, fully-serviced unisex facilities. Level grassy pitches are sited in small, sectioned areas, and this is a generally peaceful setting. There are furnished tents for hire. 15 acre site. 200 touring pitches. 18 hardstandings. Caravan pitches. Motorhome pitches. Tent pitches. 290 statics.

continued

SERVICES: 🔌 Electric hook up   🗑 Launderette   🍺 Licensed bar   🛢 Calor Gas   🔥 Camping Gaz   🚽 Toilet fluid   🍴 Café/Restaurant   🍟 Fast Food/Takeaway   🔋 Battery charging
🍼 Baby care   ⚒ Motorvan service point
ABBREVIATIONS: BH/bank hols-bank holidays   Etr-Easter   Whit-Whitsun   dep-departure   fr-from   hrs-hours   m-mile   mdnt-midnight   rdbt-roundabout   rs-restricted service   wk-week
wknd-weekend   ⊛ No credit cards   ⊗ No dogs   See page 7 for details of the AA Camping Card Scheme

HURLEY continued

AA Pubs & Restaurants nearby: Black Boys Inn, Hurley 01628 824212

Hotel du Vin, Henley-on-Thames 01491 848400

Facilities: ⌂ ⊙ ☔ ✳ ⅄ ☺ 🍴 🚿 🗑 🌐 ♻ ❶

Services: 🚐 🗑 🖍 ⊘ 🕭 ⅄

Within 3 miles: ⅃ 👣 🎬 ✎ 🍴 🛒

Notes: No unsupervised children, no young groups, no commercial vehicles, quiet park policy. Dogs must be kept on leads. Fishing in season, slipway, nature trail.

see advert on page 55

NEWBURY   Map 5 SU46

Places to visit

Highclere Castle & Gardens, HIGHCLERE 01635 253210 www.highclerecastle.co.uk

West Berkshire Museum, NEWBURY 01635 519231 www.westberkshiremuseum.org.uk

Great for kids: The Living Rainforest, HAMPSTEAD NORREYS 01635 202444 www.livingrainforest.org

▶▶▶ 79% Bishops Green Farm Camp Site (SU502630)

Bishops Green RG20 4JP
☎ 01635 268365
dir: Exit A339 (opp New Greenham Park) towards Bishops Green & Ecchinswell. Site on left, approx 0.5m by barn

🚐 🚌 ▲

Open Apr-Oct

Last arrival 21.30hrs

A sheltered and secluded meadowland park close to the Hampshire/Berkshire border, offering very clean and well-maintained facilities, including a toilet block with a disabled/family room. There are woodland and riverside walks to be enjoyed around the farm, and coarse fishing is also available. 1.5 acre site. 30 touring pitches. 6 hardstandings. Caravan pitches. Motorhome pitches. Tent pitches.

AA Pubs & Restaurants nearby: The Yew Tree Inn, near Highclere 01635 253360

Facilities: ⌂ ⊙ ✳ 🚿 **Services:** 🚐 🗑 ⅄

Within 3 miles: ⅃ ✎ 🛒

Notes: 🐕 Dogs must be kept on leads.

RISELEY   Map 5 SU76

Places to visit

Basildon Park, LOWER BASILDON 0118 984 3040 www.nationaltrust.org.uk/basildonpark

Mapledurham House, MAPLEDURHAM 0118 972 3350 www.mapledurham.co.uk

Great for kids: Beale Park, LOWER BASILDON 0870 777 7160 www.bealepark.co.uk

---

AA CAMPING CARD SITE

▶▶▶ 84% Wellington Country Park

(SU728628)

Odiham Rd RG7 1SP
☎ 0118 932 6444   📄 0118 932 6445
e-mail: info@wellington-country-park.co.uk
web: www.wellington-country-park.co.uk
dir: M4 junct 11, A33 south towards Basingstoke. M3 junct 5, B3349 north towards Reading

🚐 🚌 ▲

Open Mar-Nov

Last arrival 17.30hrs Last departure noon

A peaceful woodland site set within an extensive country park, which comes complete with lakes and nature trails, and these are accessible to campers after the country park closes. There's also a herd of Red and Fallow deer that roam the meadow area. This site is ideal for those travelling on the M4. 80 acre site. 72 touring pitches. 10 hardstandings. Caravan pitches. Motorhome pitches. Tent pitches.

AA Pubs & Restaurants nearby: The George & Dragon, Swallowfield 0118 988 4432

Leisure: 🎠 🎵

Facilities: ⌂ ⊙ ☔ ✳ ⅄ ☺ 🗑 🚿 ♻ ❶

Services: 🚐 🗑 🖍 🍴

Within 3 miles: ⅃ ⊙ 👣 🛒 🏒 U

Notes: No open fires, latest arrival time 16.30hrs low season. Dogs must be kept on leads. Miniature railway, crazy golf, maze, animal corner, access to Country Park.

BRISTOL

See Cowslip Green, Somerset

CAMBRIDGESHIRE

BURWELL   Map 12 TL56

Places to visit

Anglesey Abbey, Gardens & Lode Mill, LODE 01223 810080 www.nationaltrust.org.uk/angleseyabbey

National Horseracing Museum and Tours, NEWMARKET 01638 667333 www.nhrm.co.uk

▶▶▶ 69% *Stanford Park* (TL578675)

Weirs Drove CB25 0BP
☎ 01638 741547   & 07802 439997
e-mail: enquiries@stanfordcaravanpark.co.uk
dir: Signed from B1102

🚐 🚌 ▲

Open all year

Last arrival 20.00hrs Last departure 11.00hrs

A secluded site on the outskirts of Burwell set in four large fields with several attractive trees. The amenities are modern and well kept, and there are eight hardstandings hedged with privet. 20 acre site. 100 touring pitches. 20 hardstandings. Caravan pitches. Motorhome pitches. Tent pitches.

AA Pubs & Restaurants nearby: Dyke's End, Reach 01638 743816

Hole in the Wall, Little Wilbraham 01223 812282

Facilities: ⌂ ⊙ ☔ 🕭 🚿

Services: 🚐 🗑 🖍 ⊘ 🕭 ⅄

Within 3 miles: ⅃ 👣 🏊 ✎ 🛒 🛒 U

Notes: Adults only. 🐕 No group bookings.

see advert on opposite page

LEISURE: 🏊 Indoor swimming pool 🏊 Outdoor swimming pool 🎠 Children's playground 🪁 Kid's club 🎾 Tennis court 🎱 Games room 📺 Separate TV room ⅃ 9/18 hole golf course ⛵ Boats for hire 🎬 Cinema 🎵 Entertainment ✎ Fishing ⊙ Mini golf 🏄 Watersports 🏋 Gym 🏒 Sports field Spa U Stables
FACILITIES: 🛁 Bath ⌂ Shower ⊙ Electric shaver ☔ Hairdryer ✳ Ice Pack Facility ⅄ Disabled facilities 🕭 Public telephone 🛒 Shop on site or within 200yds 🛒 Mobile shop (calls at least 5 days a week) 🍴 BBQ area 🗑 Picnic area 🌐 Wi-fi 🖥 Internet access ♻ Recycling ❶ Tourist info 🚿 Dog exercise area

COMBERTON Map 12 TL35

Places to visit

Imperial War Museum Duxford, DUXFORD 01223 835000 www.iwm.org.uk/duxford

Audley End House & Gardens, AUDLEY END 01799 522842 www.english-heritage.org.uk

Great for kids: Linton Zoological Gardens, LINTON 01223 891308 www.lintonzoo.co.uk

►►►► 91% *Highfield Farm Touring Park* *(TL389572)*

Best of British

Long Rd CB23 7DG
☎ 01223 262308 📠 01223 262308
e-mail: enquiries@highfieldfarmtouringpark.co.uk
dir: *From M11 junct 12, take A603 (Sandy) for 0.5m, then right onto B1046 to Comberton*

🚐 🚌 ⛺

Open Apr-Oct

Last arrival 22.00hrs Last departure 14.00hrs

Run by a very efficient and friendly family, the park is on a well-sheltered hilltop, with spacious pitches including a cosy backpackers/cyclists' area, and separate sections for couples and families. There is a one and a half mile marked walk around the family farm, with stunning views. 8 acre site. 120 touring pitches. 52 hardstandings. Caravan pitches. Motorhome pitches. Tent pitches.

AA Pubs & Restaurants nearby: The Three Horseshoes, Madingley 01954 210221

Restaurant 22, Cambridge 01223 351880

Leisure: /🛝

Facilities: 🚿 ⊙ ❄ ☎ [S] 🐕 [Wi-fi]

Services: ⚡ 🧺 🛢 🍃 [T] 🔋 ⛛

Within 3 miles: ⛳ 🎣 [S] 🧺 U

Notes: 💳 Postbox.

DODDINGTON

Places to visit

WWT Welney Wetland Centre, WELNEY 01353 860711 www.wwt.org.uk

Flag Fen Archaeology Park, PETERBOROUGH 01733 313414 www.flagfen.org

DODDINGTON Map 12 TL49

►►►► 85% Fields End Water Caravan Park & Fishery *(TL378908)*

Benwick Rd PE15 0TY
☎ 01354 740199
e-mail: info@fieldsendfishing.co.uk
dir: *Exit A141, follow signs to Doddington. At clock tower in Doddington turn right into Benwick Rd. Site 1.5m on right after sharp bends*

* 🚐 £15-£17 🚌 £15-£20 ⛺ £12-£14

Open all year

Last arrival 20.30hrs Last departure noon

Now in its third year, this meticulously planned and executed park makes excellent use of its slightly elevated position in The Fens. The 33 fully serviced pitches, all with very generous hardstandings, are on smart terraces with sweeping views of the countryside. The two toilet blocks contain several combined cubicle spaces and there are shady walks through mature deciduous woodland adjacent to two large and appealingly landscaped fishing lakes. 20 acre site. 52 touring pitches. 16 hardstandings. Caravan pitches. Motorhome pitches. Tent pitches.

AA Pubs & Restaurants nearby: The Crown, Broughton 01487 824428

The Old Bridge Hotel, Huntingdon 01480 424300

Facilities: 🚿 ⊙ ❄ ♿ [S] 🐕 [Wi-fi] ♻ ⓘ

Services: ⚡ 🧺 🛢 [T]

Within 3 miles: 🎣 ◎ [S] 🧺

Notes: Adults only. 2 fishing lakes.

SERVICES: ⚡ Electric hook up 🧺 Launderette 🍺 Licensed bar 🛢 Calor Gas 🍃 Camping Gaz [T] Toilet fluid 🍴 Café/Restaurant 🍔 Fast Food/Takeaway 🔋 Battery charging 👶 Baby care ⛛ Motorvan service point
ABBREVIATIONS: BH/bank hols-bank holidays Etr-Easter Whit-Whitsun dep-departure fr-from hrs-hours m-mile mdnt-midnight rdbt-roundabout rs-restricted service wk-week wknd-weekend 💳 No credit cards 🚫🐕 No dogs

See page 7 for details of the AA Camping Card Scheme

HEMINGFORD ABBOTS   Map 12 TL27

►►► 77% Quiet Waters Caravan Park *(TL283712)*

PE28 9AJ
☎ 01480 463405 📠 01480 463405
e-mail: quietwaters.park@btopenworld.com
web: www.quietwaterscaravanpark.co.uk
dir: *Follow village signs off A14 junct 25, E of Huntingdon, site in village centre*

* 🚐 £15.50-£19.50 🚐 £15.50-£19.50
🛖 £15.50-£19.50

Open Apr-Oct

Last arrival 20.00hrs Last departure noon

This attractive little riverside site is found in a most charming village just one mile from the A14, making an ideal centre to tour the Cambridgeshire area. There are nine holiday statics for hire. 1 acre site. 20 touring pitches. 18 hardstandings. Caravan pitches. Motorhome pitches. Tent pitches. 40 statics.

AA Pubs & Restaurants nearby: The Cock Pub & Restaurant, Hemingford Grey 01480 463609

The Old Bridge Hotel, Huntingdon 01480 424300

Facilities: 🐾⊙🅟❄🔥🕒📶 ❓
Services: 🔌🛢️🔋⚡
Within 3 miles: 🎣🛝🎍🖊️🏧🛒∪

Notes: Dogs must be kept on leads. Fishing & boating.

HUNTINGDON

Places to visit

Ramsey Abbey Gatehouse, RAMSEY 01480 301494 www.nationaltrust.org.uk

Fitzwilliam Museum, CAMBRIDGE 01223 332900 www.fitzmuseum.cam.ac.uk

Great for kids: The Raptor Foundation, WOODHURST 01487 741140 www.raptorfoundation.org.uk

HUNTINGDON   Map 12 TL27

►►► 79% Huntingdon Boathaven & Caravan Park *(TL249706)*

The Avenue, Godmanchester PE29 2AF
☎ 01480 411977 📠 01480 411977
e-mail: boathaven.hunts@virgin.net
dir: *S of town. Exit A14 at Godmanchester junct, through Godmanchester on B1043 to site (on left by River Ouse)*

🚐 🚐 🛖

Open all year (rs Open in winter when weather permits)

Last arrival 21.00hrs

A small, well laid out site overlooking a boat marina and the River Ouse, set close to the A14 and within walking distance of Huntingdon town centre. The toilets are clean and well kept. A pretty area has been created for tents beside the marina, with wide views across the Ouse Valley. Weekend family activities are organised throughout the season. 2 acre site. 24 touring pitches. 18 hardstandings. Caravan pitches. Motorhome pitches. Tent pitches.

AA Pubs & Restaurants nearby: The Old Bridge Hotel, Huntingdon 01480 424300

King William IV, Fenstanton 01480 462467

Facilities: 🐾⊙🅟❄🔥🔥📶 ❓
Services: 🔌🔋⚡📺📦
Within 3 miles: 🎣🛝🎍🖊️🚣🏧

Notes: No cars by tents. Dogs must be kept on leads.

►►► 79% The Willows Caravan Park *(TL224708)*

Bromholme Ln, Brampton PE28 4NE
☎ 01480 437566
e-mail: willows@willows33.freeserve.co.uk
dir: *Exit A14/A1 signed Brampton, follow Huntingdon signs. Site on right close to Brampton Mill pub*

* 🚐 £18 🚐 £18 🛖 £15

Open all year

Last arrival 20.00hrs Last departure noon

A small, friendly site in a pleasant setting beside the River Ouse, on the Ouse Valley Walk. Bay areas have been provided for caravans and motorhomes, and planting for screening is gradually maturing. There are launching facilities and free river fishing. 4 acre site. 50 touring pitches. 10 hardstandings. Caravan pitches. Motorhome pitches. Tent pitches.

AA Pubs & Restaurants nearby: The Old Bridge Hotel, Huntingdon 01480 424300

Leisure: 🅰️☉❄
Facilities: 🐾⊙❄🔥📶 ❓
Services: 🔌🛢️🔒
Within 3 miles: 🎣🛝🎍🖊️🏧

Notes: 🚫 No cars by tents. Ball games on field provided, no generators, no groundsheets, 5mph one-way system. Dogs must be kept on leads. Free book lending/exchange.

ST IVES   Map 12 TL37

Places to visit

The Farmland Museum and Denny Abbey, WATERBEACH 01223 860988 www.dennyfarmlandmuseum.org.uk

Oliver Cromwell's House, ELY 01353 662062 www.visitely.org.uk

AA CAMPING CARD SITE

PREMIER PARK

►►►►► 95% Stroud Hill Park   Best of British *(TL335787)*

Fen Rd PE28 3DE
☎ 01487 741333 📠 01487 741365
e-mail: stroudhillpark@btconnect.com
dir: *Off B1040 in Pidley follow signs for Lakeside Lodge Complex, down Fen Rd, site on right*

* 🚐 £23.50-£25.50 🚐 £23.50-£25.50 🛖 £17

Open all year

Last arrival 20.00hrs Last departure noon

A superb adults-only caravan park designed to a very high specification in a secluded and sheltered spot not far from St Ives. A modern timber-framed barn houses the exceptional facilities. These include the beautifully tiled toilets with spacious cubicles, each containing a shower, washbasin and toilet. A bar and café, restaurant, small licensed shop, tennis court and course fishing are among the attractions. There are three pay-as-

LEISURE: 🏊 Indoor swimming pool   ⊜ Outdoor swimming pool   🅰️ Children's playground   🛝 Kid's club   🎾 Tennis court   🎱 Games room   📺 Separate TV room   ⛳ 9/18 hole golf course   🚣 Boats for hire   🎬 Cinema   🎵 Entertainment   🎣 Fishing   ◉ Mini golf   🏄 Watersports   🏋️ Gym   ⚽ Sports field   Spa   ∪ Stables
FACILITIES: 🛁 Bath   🚿 Shower   ⊙ Electric shaver   🅿 Hairdryer   ❄ Ice Pack Facility   ♿ Disabled facilities   ☎ Public telephone   🏪 Shop on site or within 200yds   🚐 Mobile shop (calls at least 5 days a week)   🍖 BBQ area   🌲 Picnic area   📶 Wi-fi   💻 Internet access   ♻ Recycling   ❓ Tourist info   🐕 Dog exercise area

you-go golf courses plus ten-pin bowling nearby. 6 acre site. 60 touring pitches. 44 hardstandings. Caravan pitches. Motorhome pitches. Tent pitches.

Stroud Hill Park

AA Pubs & Restaurants nearby: The Old Ferryboat Inn, Holywell 01480 463227

The Lazy Otter, Stretham 01353 649780

Leisure: ⚑

Facilities: ⬖⊙🅿❄⬓🅒🅢🛏🚻 ♻ 🄸

Services: 🔌🅖🍴🔒🛢🅣🍽

Within 3 miles: ↧🎠🦮◎⛵🅢🅖🅤

Notes: Adults only. No large motorhomes.

WISBECH   Map 12 TF40

Places to visit

Peckover House & Garden, WISBECH 01945 583463 www.nationaltrust.org.uk/peckover

Sandringham House, Gardens & Museum, SANDRINGHAM 01485 545408 www.sandringhamestate.co.uk

Great for kids: Butterfly & Wildlife Park, SPALDING 01406 363833 www.butterflyandwildlifepark.co.uk

▶▶▶ **80% Little Ranch Leisure**

(TF456062)

Begdale, Elm PE14 0AZ
☎ 01945 860066   📠 01945 860114
dir: *From rdbt on A47 (SW of Wisbech) take Redmoor Lane to Begdale*

🚐 £12-£17 🚍 £12-£17 ⛺ £12-£17

Open all year

A friendly family site set in an apple orchard, with 25 fully-serviced pitches and a beautifully designed, spacious toilet block. The site overlooks a large fishing lake, and the famous horticultural auctions at Wisbech are nearby. 10 acre site. 25 touring pitches. 25 hardstandings. Caravan pitches. Motorhome pitches. Tent pitches.

Little Ranch Leisure

AA Pubs & Restaurants nearby: The Crown Lodge Hotel, Wisbech 01945 773391

The Hare Arms, Stow Bardolph 01366 382229

Facilities: ⬖⊙🅿❄⬓🛏🚻 ♻ 🄸

Services: 🔌🅖🛠

Within 3 miles: 🎣🅢

Notes: 🚫

CHESHIRE
See Walk 1 in Walks & Cycle Rides section at the end of the guide

---

CODDINGTON   Map 15 SJ45

Places to visit

Cholmondeley Castle Gardens, CHOLMONDELEY 01829 720383 www.cholmondeleycastle.com

Hack Green Secret Nuclear Bunker, NANTWICH 01270 629219 www.hackgreen.co.uk

Great for kids: Dewa Roman Experience, CHESTER 01244 343407 www.dewaromanexperience.co.uk

---

AA CAMPING CARD SITE

PREMIER PARK

▶▶▶▶▶ **82% Manor Wood Country Caravan Park** *(SJ453553)*

Manor Wood CH3 9EN
☎ 01829 782990 & 782442   📠 01829 782990
e-mail: info@manorwoodcaravans.co.uk
dir: *From A534 at Barton, turn opposite Cock O'Barton pub signed Coddington. Left in 100yds. Site 0.5m on left*

* 🚐 £13.50-£24 🚍 £13.50-£24 ⛺ £13.50-£24

Open all year (rs Oct-May swimming pool closed)

Last arrival 19.00hrs Last departure 11.00hrs

A secluded landscaped park in a tranquil country setting with extensive views towards the Welsh

Hills across the Cheshire Plain. This park offers fully serviced pitches, modern facilities, a heated outdoor pool and tennis courts. Wildlife is encouraged, and lake fishing with country walks and pubs are added attractions. Generous pitch density provides optimum privacy and the park is immaculately maintained, with a diligent approach to cleanliness throughout. 8 acre site. 45 touring pitches. 38 hardstandings. Caravan pitches. Motorhome pitches. Tent pitches. 12 statics.

AA Pubs & Restaurants nearby: The Calveley Arms, Handley 01829 770619

1851 Restaurant at Peckforton Castle, Peckforton 01829 260930

Leisure: ⚓♨🎾◎🎣

Facilities: ⬖⊙🅿❄⬓🅒🅢🚽🛏🚻 📺 ♻ 🄸

Services: 🔌🅖🛠

Within 3 miles: ↧🎣🅢🅖

Notes: No cars by caravans. No cycles, no noise after 23.00hrs. Dogs must be kept on leads.

DELAMERE   Map 15 SJ56

Places to visit

Jodrell Bank Discovery Centre, JODRELL BANK 01477 571766 www.jodrellbank.net

Little Moreton Hall, CONGLETON 01260 272018 www.nationaltrust.org.uk

Great for kids: Chester Zoo, CHESTER 01244 380280 www.chesterzoo.org

---

AA CAMPING CARD SITE

▶▶▶▶ **82% Fishpool Farm Caravan Park** *(SJ567672)*

Fishpool Rd CW8 2HP
☎ 01606 883970 & 07501 506583
📠 01606 301022
e-mail: enquiries@fishpoolfarmcaravanpark.co.uk
dir: *From Tarporley take A49 towards Cuddington. Left onto B5152. Continue on B5152 (now Fishpool Rd). Site on right*

* 🚐 £20-£22 🚍 £22-£25 ⛺ £20-£22

Open 15 Feb-15 Jan

Last arrival 19.00hrs Last departure mdnt
Developed on a former hay field on the owner's farm, this excellent park has a shop/reception, a superb purpose-built toilet block with laundry facilities, a picnic area, and 50 spacious pitches,

continued

SERVICES: 🔌 Electric hook up 🅖 Launderette 🍴 Licensed bar 🔒 Calor Gas 🛢 Camping Gaz 🅣 Toilet fluid 🍽 Café/Restaurant 🍟 Fast Food/Takeaway 🔋 Battery charging 🛏 Baby care 🛠 Motorvan service point

ABBREVIATIONS: BH/bank hols-bank holidays Etr-Easter Whit-Whitsun dep-departure fr-from hrs-hours m-mile mdnt-midnight rdbt-roundabout rs-restricted service wk-week wknd-weekend 🚫 No credit cards 🚫 No dogs

See page 7 for details of the AA Camping Card Scheme

DELAMERE *continued*

all with electric hook-up. Plans include additional toilet facilities (under construction at our last inspection), a lakeside lodge, coarse fishing and a nature walk. 5.5 acre site. 50 touring pitches. Caravan pitches. Motorhome pitches. Tent pitches.

AA Pubs & Restaurants nearby: The Dysart Arms, Bunbury 01829 260183

Alvanley Arms Inn, Tarporley 01829 760200

Leisure: ⚙

Facilities: ♠ ⊙ ☞ ✻ ⚤ 🖄 ♠ 🛒 ♻

Services: 🔌 🗄 📸 ⬇

Within 3 miles: ⚓ ☞ ◎ ≋ 🖄 🗄 ∪

Notes: Dogs must be kept on leads. Dog walks available.

KNUTSFORD   Map 15 SJ77

►►► **75% Woodlands Park** (SJ743710)

Wash Ln, Allostock WA16 9LG
☎ 01565 723429 & 01332 810818
dir: *M6 junct 18 take A50 N to Holmes Chapel for 3m, turn into Wash Ln by Boundary Water Park. Site 0.25m on left*

* 🚐 £14 �90 £14 🛆 £12

Open Mar-6 Jan

Last arrival 21.00hrs Last departure 11.00hrs

A very tranquil and attractive park in the heart of rural Cheshire, and set in 16 acres of mature woodland. Tourers are located in three separate wooded areas that teem with wildlife and you will wake up to the sound of birdsong, plus the rhododendrons look stunning in the spring. This park is just three miles from Jodrell Bank. 16 acre site. 40 touring pitches. Caravan pitches. Motorhome pitches. Tent pitches. 140 statics.

AA Pubs & Restaurants nearby: The Dog Inn, Knutsford 01625 861421

The Duke of Portland, Lach Dennis 01606 46264

Facilities: ♠ ⊙ &

Services: 🔌 🗄

Within 3 miles: ⚓ ☞ 🗄

Notes: ⊘ No skateboards. Dogs must be kept on leads.

WETTENHALL   Map 15 SJ66

AA CAMPING CARD SITE

►►► **82% New Farm Caravan Park**
(SJ613608)

Long Ln CW7 4DW
☎ 01270 528213 & 07970 221112
e-mail: info@newfarmcheshire.com
dir: *M6 junct 16, A500 towards Nantwich, right onto Nantwich bypass (A51). At lights turn right, follow A51 Caster & Tarporely signs. After Calveley right into Long Ln (follow site sign). Site in 2m*

* 🚐 fr £18 �90 fr £18 fr £18

Open all year

Last arrival 20.00hrs Last departure 14.00hrs

Diversification at New Farm has seen the development of four fishing lakes, quality AA-listed B&B accommodation in a converted milking parlour, and the creation of a peaceful small touring park. The proprietors are to be commended for their investment to provide a very welcome touring destination within this peaceful part of Cheshire. Expect good landscaping, generous hardstanding pitches, a spotless toilet block, and good attention to detail throughout. Please note there is no laundry. 40 acre site. 24 touring pitches. 17 hardstandings. Caravan pitches. Motorhome pitches.

AA Pubs & Restaurants nearby: The Nags Head, Haughton Moss 01829 260265

The Brasserie at Crewe Hall, Crewe 01270 253333

Facilities: ♠ ☞ 🛒 🛒

Services: 🔌 ⊘ 📸 ⬇

Within 3 miles: ⚓ ≋ ☞ 🗄 ∪

WHITEGATE   Map 15 SJ66

Places to visit

The Cheshire Military Museum,
CHESTER 01244 327617
www.cheshiremilitarymuseum.co.uk

Chester Cathedral, CHESTER 01244 500961
www.chestercathedral.com

PREMIER PARK

►►►►► **91% Lamb Cottage**
Caravan Park (SJ613692)

Dalefords Ln CW8 2BN
☎ 01606 882302 📄 01606 888491
e-mail: info@lambcottage.co.uk
dir: *From A556 turn at Sandiway lights into Dalefords Ln, signed Winsford. Site 1m on right*

* 🚐 £20-£26 �90 £19-£25

Open Mar-Oct

Last arrival 20.00hrs Last departure noon

A secluded and attractively landscaped adults-only park in a glorious location where the emphasis is on peace and relaxation. The serviced pitches are spacious with wide grass borders for sitting out and the high quality toilet block is spotlessly clean and immaculately maintained. A good central base for exploring this area, with access to nearby woodland walks and cycle trails. 6 acre site. 45 touring pitches. 45 hardstandings. 14 seasonal pitches. Caravan pitches. Motorhome pitches. 26 statics.

AA Pubs & Restaurants nearby: The Bear's Paw, Warmingham 01270 526317

Facilities: ♠ ⊙ ☞ & ⊙ 🛒 📶 ♻ ❶

Services: 🔌 🗄 🔒

Within 3 miles: ⚓ ☞ 🗄 ∪

Notes: Adults only. No tents (except trailer tents), no commercial vehicles. Dogs must be kept on leads.

LEISURE: 🏊 Indoor swimming pool   🏊 Outdoor swimming pool   🎠 Children's playground   🧒 Kid's club   🎾 Tennis court   🎱 Games room   📺 Separate TV room   ⛳ 9/18 hole golf course   ⛵ Boats for hire   🎬 Cinema   🎵 Entertainment   🎣 Fishing   ⛳ Mini golf   🏄 Watersports   🏋 Gym   🏟 Sports field   **Spa**   ∪ Stables

FACILITIES: 🛁 Bath   🚿 Shower   ⊙ Electric shaver   ☞ Hairdryer   ✻ Ice Pack Facility   & Disabled facilities   ⊙ Public telephone   🖄 Shop on site or within 200yds   🏪 Mobile shop (calls at least 5 days a week)   🍴 BBQ area   🛒 Picnic area   📶 Wi-fi   💻 Internet access   ♻ Recycling   ❶ Tourist info   🛒 Dog exercise area

SERVICES: ⚡ Electric hook up ⬛ Launderette 🍷 Licensed bar 🛢 Calor Gas ⊘ Camping Gaz Ⓣ Toilet fluid 🍴 Café/Restaurant 🍟 Fast Food/Takeaway 🔋 Battery charging
🍼 Baby care ♨ Motorvan service point
ABBREVIATIONS: BH/bank hols-bank holidays Etr-Easter Whit-Whitsun dep-departure fr-from hrs-hours m-mile mdnt-midnight rdbt-roundabout rs-restricted service wk-week
wknd-weekend Ⓒ No credit cards ⊗ No dogs See page 7 for details of the AA Camping Card Scheme

Cornwall

Known for its wild moorland landscapes, glorious river valleys, quaint towns and outstanding coastline, Cornwall is one of the country's most popular holiday destinations. Boasting the mildest and sunniest climate in the United Kingdom, as a result of its southerly latitude and the influence of the Gulf Stream, the county benefits from more than 1,500 hours of sunshine each year.

Bordered to the north and west by the Atlantic and to the south by the English Channel, the county boasts prehistoric sites, colourful mythology, a wealth of ancient traditions, a legacy of tin mining and impressive cultural diversity. Cornwall is acknowledged as one of the Celtic nations by many locals and use of the revived Cornish language has increased.

St Piran's flag is regarded by many as the national flag of Cornwall and an emblem of the Cornish people. It is said that St Piran, who is alleged to have discovered tin, adopted the flag's two colours – a white cross on a black background – after spotting the white tin amongst the black coals and ashes.

The coast

The Cornish coastline offers miles of breath-takingly beautiful scenery. The northern coast is open and exposed; the 735-ft High Cliff, between Boscastle and St Gennys, represents the highest sheer drop cliff in the county. In contrast are long stretches of golden sandy beaches, including those at St Ives, and Newquay, now an internationally renowned surfing destination.

The Lizard, at Cornwall's most southerly point, is a geological masterpiece of towering cliffs, stacks and arches as is Land's End, on the county's south-west corner. The legendary 603-mile (970km) walk from this point to John O'Groats at the northern tip of Scotland ▶

creates a daunting challenge that numerous people, including sportsmen and TV personalities, have tackled with varying degrees of success over the years.

Truro is Cornwall's great cathedral city, with a wealth of Georgian buildings, quaint alleyways and historic streets adding to its charm. Compared to many cathedrals throughout the country, Truro's is relatively young; the foundation stones were laid in 1880 and the western towers were finally dedicated some thirty years later.

Inspirational Cornwall

Mysterious Bodmin Moor lies at the heart of Cornwall. In 1930 the writer Daphne du Maurier spent a night at Jamaica Inn in Bolventor, which inspired the famous novel of the same name; *Menabilly*, her home near Fowey, on Cornwall's south coast, was the inspiration for *'Manderley'*, the house in *Rebecca*, almost certainly her best-known and best-loved book. It is said that one day while out walking she spotted a flock of seagulls diving and wheeling above a newly ploughed field, which gave her the idea for the short story *The Birds*, which Alfred Hitchcock memorably turned into a horror film.

Walking and Cycling

Naturally, walking and cycling are very popular pursuits in Cornwall. The South West Coast Path offers many miles of rugged coastal grandeur and stunning views, while inland there is the chance to combine this most simple of outdoor pursuits with suitably green and environmentally friendly train travel. Tourist information centres provide leaflets showing a variety of linear or circular walks incorporating branch line stations; easy-to-

● Biodomes, Eden Project

follow maps are included. One popular route involves taking the train along the scenic Atlantic Coast line to Luxulyan, then cutting across country on foot for 2.5 miles (4km) to reach the Eden Project.

Festivals and Events

- The Newlyn Fish Festival takes place on August Bank Holiday Monday.
- Penzance hosts the Golowan Festival and Mazey Day for two weeks in mid-June.
- St Ives has its Feast Day in early February and the St Ives Festival of Music and the Arts for two weeks in early September.
- Victorian Day on Cotehele Quay near Calstock in mid-August is family fun and involves dressing up.
- Tamar Growers' Harvest at Cotehele Quay in mid-September. Here you will find local growers on the quay at an outdoor market.

● Coverack harbour, Lizard Peninsula

CORNWALL & ISLES OF SCILLY

See Walk 2 in the Walks & Cycle Rides section at the end of the guide

ASHTON   Map 2 SW62

Places to visit

Godolphin House, GODOLPHIN CROSS 01736 763194 www.nationaltrust.org.uk/godolphin

Poldark Mine and Heritage Complex, WENDRON 01326 573173 www.poldark-mine.com

Great for kids: The Flambards Theme Park, HELSTON 01326 573404 www.flambards.co.uk

►►► 76% Boscrege Caravan & Camping Park (SW595305)

TR13 9TG
☎ 01736 762231   📠 01736 762152
e-mail: enquiries@caravanparkcornwall.com
dir: From Helston on A394 turn right in Ashton by Post Office into lane. Site in 1.5m, signed

🚐 ⛺ ⛺

Open Mar-Nov

Last arrival 22.00hrs Last departure 11.00hrs

A quiet and bright little touring park divided into small paddocks with hedges, and offering plenty of open spaces for children to play in. The family-owned park offers clean, well-painted toilets facilities and neatly trimmed grass. In an Area of Outstanding Natural Beauty at the foot of Tregonning Hill. 14 acre site. 50 touring pitches. Caravan pitches. Motorhome pitches. Tent pitches. 26 statics.

AA Pubs & Restaurants nearby: The Victoria Inn, Perranuthnoe 01736 710309

New Yard Restaurant, Helston 01326 221595

Leisure: 🏊 ⚽ 🎱 🖵

Facilities: 🔌 ⊙ 🕮 ✳ ❄ 🚿 🛏 🚻 Wi-Fi ♻ 🛈

Services: 🚽 🗑 🔋 🧹 🛒 🖸 🏧

Within 3 miles: ↓ 🚴 ⛵ ◎ 🛶 ⛳ 🛒 ♨ U

Notes: Dogs must be kept on leads. Microwave available. Nature trail.

see advert below

BLACKWATER

Places to visit

Royal Cornwall Museum, TRURO 01872 272205 www.royalcornwallmuseum.org.uk

East Pool Mine, POOL 01209 315027 www.nationaltrust.org.uk

Great for kids: National Maritime Museum Cornwall, FALMOUTH 01326 313388 www.nmmc.co.uk

BLACKWATER   Map 2 SW74

►►►► 83% Chiverton Park

(SW743468)

East Hill TR4 8HS
☎ 01872 560667 & 07789 377169
e-mail: chivertonpark@btopenworld.com
dir: Exit A30 at Chiverton rdbt (Starbucks) onto unclass road signed Blackwater (3rd exit). 1st right, site 300mtrs on right

🚐 ⛺ ⛺

Open 3 Mar-3 Nov

Last arrival 21.00hrs Last departure noon

A small, well-maintained site with some mature hedges dividing pitches, sited midway between Truro and St Agnes. Facilities include a good toilet block and a steam room, sauna and gym. A games room with pool table, and children's outside play equipment prove popular with families. 4 acre site. 12 touring pitches. 10 hardstandings. Caravan pitches. Motorhome pitches. Tent pitches. 50 statics.

AA Pubs & Restaurants nearby: Driftwood Spars, St Agnes 01872 552428

Leisure: ⛳ ⚲ ⚲ Spa

Facilities: ⚲ ⊙ ⚲ ✳ ⚲ ⚲ ⚲ ⚲ ⚲ ⚲ ⚲ ⚲ *ℹ*

Services: ⚲ ⚲ ⚲

Within 3 miles: ⚲ ⚲ ⚲ ⚲ ⚲ ⚲ ⚲

Notes: No ball games. Dogs must be kept on leads. Drying lines.

►►►► 80% Trevarth Holiday Park

(SW744468)

TR4 8HR
☎ **01872 560266** 🖷 **01872 560379**
e-mail: trevarth@btconnect.com
web: www.trevarth.co.uk
dir: *Exit A30 at Chiverton rdbt onto B3277 signed St Agnes. At next rdbt take road signed Blackwater. Site on right in 200mtrs*

* ⚲ £10.50-£17.50 ⚲ £10.50-£17.50 ⚲ £10.50-£17.50

Open Apr-Oct

Last arrival 22.00hrs Last departure 11.30hrs

A neat and compact park with touring pitches laid out on attractive, well-screened high ground adjacent to A30/A39 junction. This pleasant little park is centrally located for touring, and is maintained to a very good standard. 4 acre site. 30 touring pitches. 10 hardstandings. 2 seasonal pitches. Caravan pitches. Motorhome pitches. Tent pitches. 20 statics.

AA Pubs & Restaurants nearby: Driftwood Spars, St Agnes 01872 552428

Leisure: ⚲ ⚲

Facilities: ⚲ ⊙ ⚲ ✳ ⚲ ⚲ ⚲ *ℹ*

Services: ⚲ ⚲ ⚲ ⚲ ⚲

Within 3 miles: ⚲ ⚲ ⚲ ⚲

Notes: Dogs must be kept on leads.

BLISLAND   Map 2 SX17

Places to visit
Tintagel Old Post Office, TINTAGEL 01840 770024 www.nationaltrust.org.uk/ main/w-tintageloldpostoffice

►►► 81% South Penquite Farm

(SX108751)

South Penquite PL30 4LH
☎ **01208 850491**
e-mail: thefarm@bodminmoor.co.uk
dir: *From Exeter on A30 exit at 1st sign to St Breward on right, (from Bodmin 2nd sign on left). Follow narrow road across Bodmin Moor. Ignore left & right turns until South Penquite Farm Lane on right in 2m*

⚲ £14 ⚲ £14

Open May-Oct

Last departure 14.00hrs

This 'cool camping' site is situated high on Bodmin Moor and on a farm committed to organic farming. As well as camping there are facilities to learn about conservation, organic farming and the local environment, including a fascinating and informative farm trail (pick up a leaflet). Toilet facilities have been considerably enhanced by the construction of an additional timber building with quality showers and a good disabled facility. There are organic home-reared lamb burgers and sausages for sale and one field contains four Mongolian yurts, available for holiday let. 4 acre site. 40 touring pitches. Motorhome pitches. Tent pitches. 4 bell tents/yurts.

AA Pubs & Restaurants nearby: The Blisland Inn, Blisland 01208 850739

The Old Inn & Restaurant, St Breward 01208 850711

Leisure: ⚲ ⚲

Facilities: ⚲ ⊙ ⚲ ✳ ⚲ ⚲ ⚲ *ℹ*

Services: ⚲

Within 3 miles: ⚲ ⚲ ⚲ ⚲ ⚲

Notes: ⚲ ⚲ No caravans. Organic produce available.

BODMIN

See also Lanivet

BODMIN   Map 2 SX06

AA CAMPING CARD SITE

►►► 81% Mena Caravan & Camping Park *(SW041626)*

PL30 5HW
☎ **01208 831845** 🖷 **01208 831845**
e-mail: mena@campsitesincornwall.co.uk
dir: *Exit A30 onto A389 N signed Lanivet & Wadebridge. In 0.5m 1st right & pass under A30. 1st left signed Lostwithiel & Fowey. In 0.25m right at top of hill. 0.5m then 1st right. Entrance 100yds on right*

* ⚲ £10-£15 ⚲ £10-£15 ⚲ £10-£15

Open all year

Last arrival 22.00hrs Last departure noon

Set in a secluded, elevated location with high hedges for shelter, and plenty of peace. This grassy site is about four miles from the Eden Project and midway between the north and south Cornish coasts. There is a small coarse fishing lake on site, 21 hardstanding pitches, a shop selling take-away snacks, and two static caravans for holiday hire. 15 acre site. 25 touring pitches. 4 hardstandings. Caravan pitches. Motorhome pitches. Tent pitches. 2 statics.

AA Pubs & Restaurants nearby: The Borough Arms, Dunmere 01208 73118

Trehellas House Hotel & Restaurant, Bodmin 01208 72700

Leisure: ⚲ ⚲

Facilities: ⚲ ⊙ ⚲ ✳ ⚲ ⚲ ⚲ ⚲ ⚲ *ℹ*

Services: ⚲ ⚲ ⚲ ⚲ ⚲ ⚲ ⚲

Within 3 miles: ⚲ ⚲ ⚲ ⚲ ⚲

BOLVENTOR

Places to visit
Tintagel Castle, TINTAGEL 01840 770328 www.english-heritage.org.uk

Great for kids: Tamar Otter & Wildlife Centre, LAUNCESTON 01566 785646 www.tamarotters.co.uk

---

SERVICES: ⚲ Electric hook up ⚲ Launderette ⚲ Licensed bar ⚲ Calor Gas ⚲ Camping Gaz ⚲ Toilet fluid ⚲ Café/Restaurant ⚲ Fast Food/Takeaway ⚲ Battery charging ⚲ Baby care ⚲ Motorvan service point
ABBREVIATIONS: BH/bank hols-bank holidays Etr-Easter Whit-Whitsun dep-departure fr-from hrs-hours m-mile mdnt-midnight rdbt-roundabout rs-restricted service wk-week wknd-weekend ⚲ No credit cards ⚲ No dogs
See page 7 for details of the AA Camping Card Scheme

BOLVENTOR
Map 2 SX17

AA CAMPING CARD SITE

►►► 74% Colliford Tavern Campsite
(SX171740)

Colliford Lake, St Neot PL14 6PZ
☎ 01208 821335 ▤ 01208 821661
e-mail: info@colliford.com
web: www.colliford.com
dir: *Exit A30 1.25m W of Bolventor onto unclass road signed Colliford Lake. Site 0.25m on left*

Open all year

Last arrival 22.00hrs Last departure 11.00hrs

An oasis on Bodmin Moor, a small site with spacious grassy pitches, and the advantage of a comfortable lounge bar and restaurant in the tavern. Attractions for children are greatly enhanced by the merger of the site with the neighbouring children's play park. 3.5 acre site. 40 touring pitches. 8 hardstandings. Caravan pitches. Motorhome pitches. Tent pitches.

AA Pubs & Restaurants nearby: Jamaica Inn, Bolventor 01566 86250

Leisure: /A\
Facilities: ↖⊙℗✳& ⚙ ↾ ♯
Services: ⮑ ⌦ ⏳ ❦
Within 3 miles: ℓ
Notes: Dogs must be kept on leads.

BOSCASTLE
Map 2 SX09

Places to visit

Tintagel Castle, TINTAGEL 01840 770328
www.english-heritage.org.uk

Tintagel Old Post Office,
TINTAGEL 01840 770024
www.nationaltrust.org.uk/
main/w-tintageloldpostoffice

Great for kids: The Milky Way Adventure Park,
CLOVELLY 01237 431255
www.themilkyway.co.uk

►► 80% Lower Pennycrocker Farm
(SX125927)

PL35 0BY
☎ 01840 250257 ▤ 01840 250613
e-mail: karynheard@btinternet.com
dir: *Exit A39 at Marshgate onto B3263 towards Boscastle, site signed in 2m*

* ⮑ fr £10 ⮑ fr £10 ▲ fr £10

Open Etr-Oct

Last arrival anytime Last departure anytime

Mature Cornish hedges provide shelter for this small, family-run site on a dairy farm. Spectacular scenery and the nearby coastal footpath are among the many attractions, along with fresh eggs, milk and home-made clotted cream for sale. The excellent, upgraded toilets and showers enhance this site's facilities, and there are plans for further modernisation. Two traditional Cornish cottages are available to let. 6 acre site. 40 touring pitches. Caravan pitches. Motorhome pitches. Tent pitches.

AA Pubs & Restaurants nearby: The Port William, Tintagel 01840 770230

The Wellington Hotel, Boscastle 01840 250202

Facilities: ↖⊙℗✳& ⚙ ↾
Services: ⮑ ⌦ ⏳
Within 3 miles: ⏚ ℓ ⛷ U
Notes: ⊘ Dogs must be kept on leads.

BRYHER (ISLES OF SCILLY)
Map 2 SV81

On the Isles of Scilly caravans and motor caravans are not allowed, and campers must stay at official sites. Booking is advisable on all sites, especially during school holidays.

AA CAMPING CARD SITE

►►► 79% Bryher Camp Site
(SV880155)

TR23 0PR
☎ 01720 422559 ▤ 01720 423092
e-mail: relax@bryhercampsite.co.uk
web: www.bryhercampsite.co.uk
dir: *Accessed by boat from main island of St Marys*

* ▲ £9.50

Open Apr-Oct

Set on the smallest inhabited Scilly Isle with spectacular scenery and white beaches, this tent-only site is in a sheltered valley surrounded by hedges. Pitches are located in paddocks at the northern end of the island, and easily reached from the quay. There is a good modern toilet block, and plenty of peace and quiet. 2.25 acre site. 38 touring pitches. Tent pitches.

AA Pubs & Restaurants nearby: Hell Bay Hotel, Bryher 01720 422947

Leisure: ✪ **Facilities:** ↖⊙℗✳♻ ❶
Services: ⓢ 🠗⌀⏳
Within 3 miles: ⏚⛷ ℓ ◎ ⛷ 🐚 U
Notes: No cars by tents. No pets.

BUDE
Map 2 SS20

See also Kilkhampton & Bridgerule (Devon)

AA CAMPING CARD SITE

 89% Sandymouth Holiday Park *(SS214104)*

Sandymouth Bay EX23 9HW
☎ 08442 729530
e-mail: enquiries@sandymouthbay.co.uk
web: www.sandymouthbay.co.uk
dir: *Signed from A39 approx 0.5m S of Kilkhampton, 4m N of Bude*

* ⮑ £16-£28 ⮑ £16-£28 ▲ £16-£28

Open Mar-26 Nov (rs 16 May-9 Jul (excl half term week) closed for private booking)

Last arrival 21.00hrs Last departure 10.00hrs

A bright and friendly holiday park with glorious and extensive sea views from all areas. Darwin Leisure bought the park in 2010 and have completely refurbished it. The park offers modern and well maintained touring facilities, alongside excellent leisure and entertainment facilities, notably the eye-catching pirate galleon in the fabulous children's play area. 24 acre site. 22 touring pitches. 22 hardstandings. Caravan pitches. Motorhome pitches. Tent pitches.

AA Pubs & Restaurants nearby: The Bush Inn, Morwenstow 01288 331242

The Castle Restaurant, Bude 01288 350543

Leisure: ≈/A\↓☺✦♫
Facilities: ↖⊙℗✳☺🖩🛒♻ ❶
Services: ⮑ⓢ🠗Ⓣ⏳🛒🐕
Within 3 miles: ⏚⛷ℓ◎🐚🖥U
Notes: Dogs must be kept on leads. Sauna, pirate ship.

see advert on opposite page

LEISURE: ≈ Indoor swimming pool ⚊ Outdoor swimming pool /A\ Children's playground ↓ Kid's club ≗ Tennis court ✦ Games room ⬚ Separate TV room ⏚ 9/18 hole golf course ⛷ Boats for hire ⊞ Cinema ♫ Entertainment ℓ Fishing ◎ Mini golf 🐚 Watersports ✦ Gym ☺ Sports field **Spa** U Stables
FACILITIES: ↓ Bath ↖ Shower ⊙ Electric shaver ℗ Hairdryer ✳ Ice Pack Facility & Disabled facilities ☺ Public telephone 🖩 Shop on site or within 200yds ⬚ Mobile shop (calls at least 5 days a week) ⚙ BBQ area ↾ Picnic area ▦ Wi-fi ▤ Internet access ♻ Recycling ❶ Tourist info ♯ Dog exercise area

AA CAMPING CARD SITE

PREMIER PARK

►►►►► 90% Wooda Farm Holiday Park

Best of British GOLD

(SS229080)

Poughill EX23 9HJ
☎ 01288 352069 📠 01288 355258
e-mail: enquiries@wooda.co.uk
web: www.wooda.co.uk
dir: 2m E. From A39 at outskirts of Stratton follow unclassified road signed Poughill

* 🚐 £15-£29 🚙 £15-£29 ▲ £12-£25

Open Apr-Oct (rs Apr-May & mid Sep-Oct shop hours limited, bar & takeaway)

Last arrival 20.00hrs Last departure 10.30hrs

An attractive park set on raised ground overlooking Bude Bay, with lovely sea views. The park is divided into paddocks by hedges and mature trees, and offers high quality facilities in extensive colourful gardens. A variety of activities are provided by the large sports hall and hard tennis court, and there's a super children's playground. There are holiday static caravans for hire. 50 acre site. 200 touring pitches. 80 hardstandings. Caravan pitches. Motorhome pitches. Tent pitches. 55 statics.

Wooda Farm Holiday Park

AA Pubs & Restaurants nearby: The Bush Inn, Morwenstow 01288 331242

The Castle Restaurant, Bude 01288 350543

Leisure: 🎱 ⛰ 🎾 🏊 🎣 🖵

Facilities: 🚿 📶 ⊙ 🅿 ✳ ⚒ 🔥 🛒 📶 ♻ 🛈

Services: 🔌 🧺 🍴 💧 🚰 🚻 🍵 🍽 🧹 🛒 ⬇

Within 3 miles: ♨ 🚴 🏌 ◎ 🛥 🏪 🛢 🎯 ∪

Notes: Restrictions on certain dog breeds, skateboards, rollerblades & scooters. Dogs must be kept on leads. Coarse fishing, clay pigeon shooting, pets corner, woodland walks.

AA CAMPING CARD SITE

►►►► 84% Widemouth Fields Caravan & Camping Park (SS215010)

Park Farm, Poundstock EX23 0NA
☎ 01288 361351 📠 01288 361115
e-mail: enquiries@widemouthbaytouring.co.uk
dir: M5 junct 27, A361, A39 signed Bideford & Bude. (NB do not exit A39 at Stratton). 3m, follow sign just past x-rds to Widemouth Bay. Into lay-by, site on the left

🚐 £12-£26 🚙 £12-£26 ▲ £12-£19

Open Apr-Sep

Last arrival dusk Last departure noon

In a quiet location with far reaching views over rolling countryside; only one mile from the golden beach at Widemouth Bay and three miles from Bude. The park has a shop and small café/takeaway, and offers many hardstanding pitches. The toilets are of outstanding quality with a wealth of combined fully-serviced cubicles. The owner, having acquired Widemouth Bay Holiday Village, runs courtesy shuttle buses into Bude and to the Holiday Village, where the facilities can be used by the touring campers. Caravan, motorhome and tent pitches.

AA Pubs & Restaurants nearby: Bay View Inn, Widemouth Bay 01288 361273

Leisure: ⛰ 🎣 🖵

Facilities: 🚿 📶 ⊙ 🅿 ✳ ⚒ 🔥 🛒 📶

Services: 🔌 🧺 💧 🚰 🍽 🧹 🛒 ⬇

Within 3 miles: ♨ 🚴 🏌 ◎ 🛥 🏪 🛢 🎯 ∪

Notes: Entry to site by swipecard only, deposit taken when booking in.

SERVICES: 🔌 Electric hook up 🧺 Launderette 🍴 Licensed bar 🛢 Calor Gas ⊘ Camping Gaz 💧 Toilet fluid 🍽 Café/Restaurant 🧹 Fast Food/Takeaway 🔋 Battery charging 🚼 Baby care ⬇ Motorvan service point

ABBREVIATIONS: BH/bank hols-bank holidays Etr-Easter Whit-Whitsun dep-departure fr-from hrs-hours m-mile mdnt-midnight rdbt-roundabout rs-restricted service wk-week wknd-weekend 🚫 No credit cards 🚫 No dogs   See page 7 for details of the AA Camping Card Scheme

BUDE *continued*

►►►► 83% Budemeadows Touring Park *(SS215012)*

Widemouth Bay EX23 0NA
☎ 01288 361646 📄 0870 7064825
e-mail: holiday@budemeadows.com
dir: *3m S of Bude on A39. Follow signs after turn to Widemouth Bay. Site accessed via layby*

* 🚐 £10.50-£26.50 ⛺ £10.50-£26.50
▲ £10.50-£26.50

Open all year (rs mid Sep-late May shop, bar & pool closed)

Last arrival 21.00hrs Last departure 11.00hrs

A very well kept site of distinction, with good quality facilities, hardstandings and eight fully-serviced pitches. Budemeadows is set on a gentle sheltered slope in nine acres of naturally landscaped parkland, surrounded by mature hedges. Just one mile from Widemouth Bay, and three miles from the unspoilt resort of Bude. 9 acre site. 145 touring pitches. 24 hardstandings. Caravan pitches. Motorhome pitches. Tent pitches.

AA Pubs & Restaurants nearby: Bay View Inn, Widemouth Bay 01288 361273

The Castle Restaurant, Bude 01288 350543

Leisure: ⛵ 🅰 🔍 📺
Facilities: 🛁 📳 ⊙ 🦅 ✳ ⛑ 🕙 🔊 🛗 ⚊ wifi 🖥 ♻ ❶
Services: 🔌 🔋 🔧 ⛽ 🚽 ⚱ 🛒 ⛟
Within 3 miles: ♨ ❄ 🏕 ℰ ⊚ 🛥 🔊 🔋 ∪

Notes: No noise after 23.00hrs. Dogs must be kept on leads. Table tennis, giant chess. baby changing facility.

►►►► 78% Willow Valley Holiday Park *(SS236078)*

Bush EX23 9LB
☎ 01288 353104
e-mail: willowvalley@talk21.com
dir: *On A39, 0.5m N of junct with A3072 at Stratton*

* 🚐 £12-£17 ⛺ £12-£17 ▲ £12-£17

Open Mar-end Oct

Last arrival 21.00hrs Last departure 11.00hrs

A small sheltered park in the Strat Valley with level grassy pitches and a stream running through it. The friendly family owners have improved all areas of this attractive park, including a smart toilet block and an excellent reception/shop. The park has direct access off the A39, and is only two miles from the sandy beaches at Bude. There are four pine lodges for holiday hire. 4 acre site. 41 touring pitches. Caravan pitches. Motorhome pitches. Tent pitches. 4 statics.

AA Pubs & Restaurants nearby: The Bickford Arms, Holsworthy 01409 221318

The Castle Restaurant, Bude 01288 350543

Leisure: 🅰
Facilities: 📳 ⊙ 🦅 ✳ ⛑ 🕙 🔊 🛗 🖗 ♻ ❶
Services: 🔌 🔋 🔧 ⛽ 🚽 ⛟
Within 3 miles: ♨ ❄ ℰ ⊚ 🔊 🔋 ∪

Notes: ⊜ Dogs must be kept on leads.

►►► 80% Upper Lynstone Caravan Park *(SS205053)*

Lynstone EX23 0LP
☎ 01288 352017 📄 01288 359034
e-mail: reception@upperlynstone.co.uk
dir: *0.75m S of Bude on coastal road to Widemouth Bay*

* 🚐 £13.50-£21.50 ⛺ £13.50-£21.50
▲ £13.50-£21.50

Open Apr-Oct

Last arrival 22.00hrs Last departure 10.00hrs

There are extensive views over Bude to be enjoyed from this quiet family-run park set on sheltered ground. There is a reception/shop selling basic food supplies and camping spares, a children's playground, and static caravans for holiday hire. A path leads directly to the coastal footpath with its stunning sea views, and the old Bude Canal is a stroll away. 6 acre site. 65 touring pitches. Caravan pitches. Motorhome pitches. Tent pitches. 41 statics.

AA Pubs & Restaurants nearby: The Castle Restaurant, Bude 01288 350543

Leisure: 🅰
Facilities: 📳 ⊙ 🦅 ✳ ⛑ 🕙 🔊 🛗 ❶
Services: 🔌 🔋 🔧 ⛽ 🚽 ⛟
Within 3 miles: ♨ ❄ 🏕 ℰ ⊚ 🛥 🔊 🔋 ∪

Notes: No groups. Baby changing room.

CAMELFORD   Map 2 SX18

►►►► 85% Juliot's Well Holiday Park *(SX095829)*

PL32 9RF
☎ 01840 213302 📄 01840 212700
e-mail: holidays@juliotswell.com
web: www.juliotswell.com
dir: *Through Camelford, A39 at Valley Truckle turn right onto B3266, then 1st left signed Lanteglos, site 300yds on right*

🚐 ⛺ ▲

Open all year

Last arrival 20.00hrs Last departure 11.00hrs

Set in the wooded grounds of an old manor house, this quiet site enjoys lovely and extensive views across the countryside. A rustic inn on site offers occasional entertainment, and there is plenty to do, both on the park and in the vicinity. The superb, fully-serviced toilet facilities are very impressive. There are also self-catering pine lodges, static caravans and five cottages. 33 acre site. 39 touring pitches. Caravan pitches. Motorhome pitches. Tent pitches. 82 statics.

AA Pubs & Restaurants nearby: The Mill House Inn, Trebarwith 01840 770200

Leisure: ⛵ 🅰 🔍
Facilities: 🛁 📳 🦅 ⛑ 🕙 🔊 🛗 🐕 wifi
Services: 🔌 🔋 🔧 🍽 ⛟
Within 3 miles: ♨ ℰ 🔊 🔋 ∪

Notes: Complimentary use of cots & high chairs.

LEISURE: ⛵ Indoor swimming pool ⛵ Outdoor swimming pool 🅰 Children's playground 🪁 Kid's club ⚲ Tennis court 🔍 Games room 📺 Separate TV room
♨ 9/18 hole golf course ⚓ Boats for hire 🎬 Cinema 🎵 Entertainment ℰ Fishing ⊚ Mini golf 🛥 Watersports 🏌 Gym ⊕ Sports field **Spa** ∪ Stables
FACILITIES: 🛁 Bath 📳 Shower ⊙ Electric shaver 🦅 Hairdryer ✳ Ice Pack Facility ⛑ Disabled facilities 🕙 Public telephone 🔊 Shop on site or within 200yds
🖗 Mobile shop (calls at least 5 days a week) 🛒 BBQ area 🖼 Picnic area wifi Wi-fi 🖥 Internet access ♻ Recycling ❶ Tourist info 🐕 Dog exercise area

►►► 76% Lakefield Caravan Park
(SX095853)

Lower Pendavey Farm PL32 9TX
☎ 01840 213279
e-mail: lakefieldcaravanpark@btconnect.com
dir: *From A39 in Camelford onto B3266, then right at T-junct, site 1.5m on left*

* 🚐 £11-£13.50 🚃 £11-£13.50 ▲ £11-£13.50

Open Etr or Apr-Sep

Last arrival 22.00hrs Last departure 11.00hrs

Set in a rural location, this friendly park is part of a specialist equestrian centre, and offers good quality services. Riding lessons and hacks always available, with a BHS qualified instructor. 5 acre site. 40 touring pitches. Caravan pitches. Motorhome pitches. Tent pitches.

AA Pubs & Restaurants nearby: The Old House Inn & Restaurant, St Breward 01208 850711

Facilities: 🚿☉🅿☀🛬 🐕

Services: 🚐🖭🛒⊘Ⓣ🍴🔋

Within 3 miles: ⚓🏌️♨️🛍️🗄️↻

Notes: Dogs must be kept on leads. On-site lake.

CARLYON BAY　　　　　Map 2 SX05

Places to visit

Charlestown Shipwreck & Heritage Centre, ST AUSTELL 01726 69897 www.shipwreckcharlestown.com

Eden Project, ST AUSTELL 01726 811911 www.edenproject.com

Great for kids: Wheal Martyn Museum & Country Park, ST AUSTELL 01726 850362 www.wheal-martyn.com

---

PREMIER PARK

►►►►► 87% Carlyon Bay Caravan & Camping Park *(SX052526)*

Bethesda, Cypress Av PL25 3RE
☎ 01726 812735　📠 01726 815496
e-mail: holidays@carlyonbay.net
dir: *Exit A390 W of St Blazey, left onto A3092 for Par, right in 0.5m. On private road to Carlyon Bay*

🚐🚃▲

Open Etr-3 Oct (rs Etr-mid May & mid Sep-3 Oct swimming pool, takeaway & shop closed; Jul-Aug only - children's entertainment)

Last arrival 21.00hrs Last departure 11.00hrs

An attractive, secluded site set amongst a belt of trees with background woodland. The spacious grassy park is beautifully landscaped and offers quality toilet and shower facilities and plenty of on-site attractions, including a well-equipped games room, TV room, café, an inviting swimming pool, and occasional family entertainment. It is less than half a mile from a sandy beach and the Eden Project is only two miles away. 35 acre site. 180 touring pitches. 12 hardstandings. Caravan pitches. Motorhome pitches. Tent pitches.

AA Pubs & Restaurants nearby: Austell's, St Austell 01726 813888

Leisure: 🏊♨️🎣🎱♨️🖥

Facilities: 🚿☉🅿☀♿Ⓢ🔋🐕📶 ♻ ❸

Services: 🚐🖭🛒⊘Ⓣ🍴🔋⛽↻

Within 3 miles: 🏌️♨️🍴♨️◎♨️🗄️🛍️↻

Notes: No noise after 23.00hrs. Dogs must be kept on leads. Crazy golf.

►►► 80% East Crinnis Camping & Caravan Park *(SX062528)*

Lantyan, East Crinnis PL24 2SQ
☎ 01726 813023　& 07950 614780
📠 01726 813023
e-mail: eastcrinnis@btconnect.com
dir: *From A390 (Lostwithiel to St Austell) take A3082 signed Fowey at rdbt by Britannia Inn, site on left*

* 🚐 £11-£19 🚃 £11-£19 ▲ £10-£19

Open Etr-Oct

Last arrival 21.00hrs Last departure 11.00hrs

A small rural park with spacious pitches set in individual bays about one mile from the beaches at Carlyon Bay, and just two miles from the Eden Project. The friendly owners keep the site very clean and well maintained and also offer three self-catering holiday lodges. 2 acre site. 25 touring pitches. 6 hardstandings. Caravan pitches. Motorhome pitches. Tent pitches. 2 bell tents/yurts.

AA Pubs & Restaurants nearby: The Rashleigh Inn, Polkerris 01726 813991

Austell's, St Austell 01726 813888

Leisure: 🏊

Facilities: 🚿☉☀♿Ⓢ🔋🐕📶 🖥 ♻ ❸

Services: 🚐🖭

Within 3 miles: 🏌️♨️🍴♨️◎♨️🗄️🛍️↻

Notes: Dogs must be kept on leads. Coarse fishing, wildlife & pond area with dog walk.

see advert on page 93

COVERACK　　　　　Map 2 SW71

Places to visit

Trevarno Estate Garden & Museum of Gardening, HELSTON 01326 574274 www.trevarno.co.uk

Goonhilly Satellite Earth Station Experience, HELSTON 0800 679593 www.goonhilly.bt.com

Great for kids: National Seal Sanctuary, GWEEK 0871 423 2110 www.sealsanctuary.co.uk

---

AA CAMPING CARD SITE

►►► 79% Little Trevothan Caravan & Camping Park *(SW772179)*

Trevothan TR12 6SD
☎ 01326 280260
e-mail: sales@littletrevothan.co.uk
web: www.littletrevothan.co.uk
dir: *A3083 onto B3293 signed Coverack, approx 2m after Goonhilly ESS, right at Zoar Garage onto unclass road. Approx 1m, 3rd left. Site 0.5m on left*

* 🚐 £12-£15 🚃 £12-£15 ▲ £12-£15

Open Mar-Oct

Last arrival 21.00hrs Last departure noon

A secluded site near the unspoilt fishing village of Coverack, with a large recreation area. The nearby sandy beach has lots of rock pools for children to play in, and the many walks both from the park and the village offer stunning scenery. 10.5 acre site. 70 touring pitches. 10 hardstandings. Caravan pitches. Motorhome pitches. Tent pitches. 40 statics.

AA Pubs & Restaurants nearby: The New Inn, Manaccan 01326 231323

Leisure: 🏊❀🎱🖥

Facilities: 🚿☉🅿☀♨️🔋🐕♻ ❸

Services: 🚐🖭🛒⊘Ⓣ🔋

Within 3 miles: 🍴♨️🗄️🛍️

Notes: ❸ Dogs must be kept on leads.

CRACKINGTON HAVEN   Map 2 SX19

►►► 77% Hentervene Holiday Park

(SX155944)

EX23 0LF
☎ **01840 230365**
e-mail: contact@hentervene.co.uk
dir: *Exit A39 approx 10m SW of Bude (1.5m beyond Wainhouse Corner) onto B3263 signed Boscastle & Crackington Haven. 0.75m to Tresparret Posts junct, right signed Hentervene. Site 0.75m on right*

Open Mar-Oct

Last arrival 21.00hrs Last departure 11.00hrs

This much improved park is set in a rural location a short drive from a golden sandy beach. It is in an Area of Outstanding Natural Beauty, and pitches are in paddocks which are bordered by mature hedges, with a small stream running past. Some pitches are on level terraces, and there are also hardstandings. Static caravans and three pine lodges are available for self-catering holiday hire and a new woodland walk was created for the 2011 season. 11 acre site. 8 touring pitches. 8 hardstandings. Caravan pitches. Motorhome pitches. 24 statics.

Leisure: 🅰 🔍 ⊡
Facilities: ⋔ ☉ ℘ ✳ ⊙ ⟁ wifi ♻ 𝒊
Services: 🔌 🔋 🛢 ⌀ Ⓣ
Within 3 miles: ℘ ≛ 🅱 🅶 U
Notes: Microwave & freezer for campers.

CRANCOCK (NEAR NEWQUAY)   Map 2 SW76

PREMIER PARK

►►►►► 88% *Trevella Tourist Park* *(SW801599)*

TR8 5EW
☎ **01637 830308**   🖷 **01637 830155**
e-mail: holidays@trevella.co.uk
dir: *Between Crantock & A3075*

Open Etr-Oct

A well established and very well run family site, with outstanding floral displays. Set in a rural area close to Newquay, this attractive park boasts three teeming fishing lakes for both the experienced and novice angler, and a superb outdoor swimming pool and paddling area. The toilet facilities include excellent en suite wet

rooms. All areas are neat and clean and the whole park again looked stunning at our last inspection. 15 acre site. 313 touring pitches. 53 hardstandings. Caravan pitches. Motorhome pitches. Tent pitches.

AA Pubs & Restaurants nearby: The Smugglers' Den Inn, Cubert 01637 830209

The Lewinnick Lodge Bar & Restaurant, Newquay 01637 878117

Leisure: ⊜ 🅰 🔍 ⊡
Facilities: ⋔ ☉ ℘ ✳ ⅖ ⊙ 🅱 ⋔
Services: 🔌 🔋 🛢 ⌀ Ⓣ ⊙ 🛒 ⅊
Within 3 miles: ⅃ ≛ 🅱 ℘ ◎ ≛ 🅱 🅶 U
Notes: Crazy golf, badminton.

see advert on page 93

►►► 87% *Treago Farm Caravan Site*

(SW782601)

TR8 5QS
☎ **01637 830277**   🖷 **01637 830277**
e-mail: treagofarm@aol.com
dir: *From A3075 (W of Newquay) turn right for Crantock. Site signed beyond village*

Open mid May-mid Sep

Last arrival 22.00hrs Last departure 18.00hrs

A grass site in open farmland in a south-facing sheltered valley. This friendly family park has direct access to Crantock and Polly Joke beaches, National Trust land and many natural beauty spots. 5 acre site. 90 touring pitches. Caravan pitches. Motorhome pitches. Tent pitches. 10 statics.

AA Pubs & Restaurants nearby: The Smugglers' Den Inn, Cubert 01637 830209

The Lewinnick Lodge Bar & Restaurant, Newquay 01637 878117

Leisure: 🔍 ⊡
Facilities: ⋔ ☉ ℘ ✳ ⊙ 🅱 ⋒ ⋔
Services: 🔌 🔋 ⅊ 🛢 ⌀ Ⓣ ⅊
Within 3 miles: ⅃ ≛ ℘ ◎ ≛ 🅱 🅶 U

►►► 80% Crantock Plains Touring Park *(SW805589)*

TR8 5PH
☎ **01637 830955**   & **07967 956897**
e-mail: matthew-milburn@btconnect.com
dir: *Exit Newquay on A3075, 2nd right signed to park & Crantock. Site on left in 0.75m on narrow road*

Open mid Apr-end Sep

Last arrival 22.00hrs Last departure noon

A small rural park with pitches on either side of a narrow lane, surrounded by mature trees for shelter. This spacious, family-run park has good modern toilet facilities and is ideal for campers who appreciate peace and quiet and is situated approximately 1.2 miles from pretty Crantock, and Newquay is within easy reach. 6 acre site. 60 touring pitches. 20 seasonal pitches. Caravan pitches. Motorhome pitches. Tent pitches.

AA Pubs & Restaurants nearby: The Smugglers' Den Inn, Cubert 01637 830209

The Lewinnick Lodge Bar & Restaurant, Newquay 01637 878117

Leisure: 🅰 ⚽ 🔍
Facilities: ⋔ ☉ ℘ ✳ ⅖ ⊙ 🅱 ⋔ 𝒊
Services: 🔌 🔋 ⅊
Within 3 miles: ⅃ ℘ ≛ 🅱 🅶 U
Notes: No skateboards. Dogs must be kept on leads.

AA CAMPING CARD SITE

►►► 80% Quarryfield Holiday Park

(SW793608)

TR8 5RJ
☎ **01637 872792**   & **830338**   🖷 **01637 872792**
e-mail: quarryfield@crantockcaravans.orangehome.co.uk
dir: *From A3075 (Newquay-Redruth road) follow Crantock signs. Site signed*

* 🔌 £20-£23.50 ⇆ £20-£23.50 🅰 £20-£23.50

Open Etr to end Oct (rs May/Sep pool closed)

Last arrival 23.00hrs Last departure 10.00hrs

This park has a private path down to the dunes and golden sands of Crantock Beach, about ten minutes away, and it is within easy reach of all that Newquay has to offer, particularly for families. The park has very modern facilities, and provides plenty of amenities. 10 acre site. 145

LEISURE: 🏊 Indoor swimming pool   🏊 Outdoor swimming pool   🅰 Children's playground   🪁 Kid's club   🎾 Tennis court   🔍 Games room   ⊡ Separate TV room
⅃ 9/18 hole golf course   ⅊ Boats for hire   🎬 Cinema   ♫ Entertainment   ℘ Fishing   ◎ Mini golf   ≛ Watersports   ⅄ Gym   ⊙ Sports field   Spa   U Stables
FACILITIES: ⊔ Bath   🚿 Shower   ⊙ Electric shaver   ℘ Hairdryer   ✳ Ice Pack Facility   ⅖ Disabled facilities   ⊙ Public telephone   🅱 Shop on site or within 200yds
🏪 Mobile shop (calls at least 5 days a week)   🍖 BBQ area   ⋔ Picnic area   wifi Wi-fi   🖳 Internet access   ♻ Recycling   𝒊 Tourist info   ⋔ Dog exercise area

touring pitches. Caravan pitches. Motorhome pitches. Tent pitches. 43 statics.

AA Pubs & Restaurants nearby: The Smugglers' Den Inn, Cubert 01637 830209

The Lewinnick Lodge Bar & Restaurant, Newquay 01637 878117

Leisure: ⛵🅰🔍

Facilities: 📶⊙🅿✳🔥🕐🖪🎏🖈

Services: 🔌🖪🍴🔋⊘🍽🛒🏧🍼⛽

Within 3 miles: 🎣⛳🗓🔎◎🖪🔵🔄

Notes: No campfires, quiet after 22.30hrs. Dogs must be kept on leads.

CUBERT   Map 2 SW75

Places to visit

Blue Reef Aquarium, TYNEMOUTH 0191 258 1031 www.bluereefaquarium.co.uk

Trerice, TRERICE 01637 875404 www.nationaltrust.org.uk

Great for kids: Dairy Land Farm World, NEWQUAY 01872 510246 www.dairylandfarmworld.com

►►► 80% Cottage Farm Touring Park *(SW786589)*

Treworgans TR8 5HH
☎ 01637 831083
web: www.cottagefarmpark.co.uk
dir: From A392 towards Newquay, left onto A3075 towards Redruth. In 2m right signed Cubert, right again in 1.5m signed Crantock, left in 0.5m

* 🚐 £12-£16 🚐 £12-£16 ⛺ £12-£16

Open Apr-end Sep

Last arrival 22.30hrs Last departure noon

A small grassy touring park nestling in the tiny hamlet of Treworgans, in sheltered open countryside close to a lovely beach at Holywell Bay. This quiet family-run park boasts very good quality facilities. 2 acre site. 45 touring pitches. 2 hardstandings. Caravan pitches. Motorhome pitches. Tent pitches. 1 static.

AA Pubs & Restaurants nearby: The Smugglers' Den Inn, Cubert 01637 830209

The Plume of Feathers, Mitchell 01872 510387

Facilities: 📶⊙🅿✳♻🖈

Services: 🔌🖪🏧

Within 3 miles: 🎣⛳🗓🔎◎🛒🔵🔄

Notes: No noise after 23.00hrs. Dogs must be kept on leads.

EDGCUMBE   Map 2 SW73

Places to visit

Poldark Mine and Heritage Complex, WENDRON 01326 573173 www.poldark-mine.com

Trevarno Estate Garden & Museum of Gardening, HELSTON 01326 574274 www.trevarno.co.uk

Great for kids: National Seal Sanctuary, GWEEK 0871 423 2110 www.sealsanctuary.co.uk

►►► 78% Retanna Holiday Park
(SW711327)

TR13 0EJ
☎ 01326 340643 🖹 01326 340643
e-mail: retannaholpark@btconnect.com
web: www.retanna.co.uk
dir: On A394 towards Helston, site signed on right. Site in 100mtrs

* 🚐 £16.50-£22.50 ⛺ £16.50-£22.50

Open Apr-Oct

Last arrival 21.00hrs Last departure noon

A small family-owned and run park in a rural location midway between Falmouth and Helston. Its well-sheltered grassy pitches make this an ideal location for visiting the lovely beaches and towns nearby. 8 acre site. 24 touring pitches. Caravan pitches. Tent pitches. 23 statics.

AA Pubs & Restaurants nearby: Trengilly Wartha Inn, Constantine 01326 340332

Leisure: 🅰⊙🍴🔲

Facilities: 📶⊙✳🔥🕐🖪🎏♻❔

Services: 🔌🖪🔋⊘🔲🏧🔵🔄

Within 3 miles: 🎣🔎◎🔵🖪🔵🔄

Notes: No pets, no disposable BBQs, no open fires. Free use of fridge/freezer in laundry room, free air bed inflation, free mobile phone charging.

FALMOUTH   Map 2 SW83

Places to visit

Pendennis Castle, FALMOUTH 01326 316594 www.english-heritage.org.uk

Trebah Garden, MAWNAN SMITH 01326 252200 www.trebah-garden.co.uk

Great for kids: National Maritime Museum Cornwall, FALMOUTH 01326 313388 www.nmmc.co.uk

►►► 78% *Pennance Mill Farm Touring Park* *(SW792307)*

Maenporth TR11 5HJ
☎ 01326 317431 🖹 01326 317431
dir: From A39 (Truro to Falmouth road) follow brown camping signs towards Maenporth Beach. At Hill Head rdbt take 2nd exit for Maenporth Beach

🚐🚐⛺

Open Etr-Xmas

Last arrival 22.00hrs Last departure 10.00hrs Set approximately half a mile from the safe, sandy bay at Maenporth, accessed by a private woodland walk direct from the park, this is a mainly level, grassy park in a rural location sheltered by mature trees and shrubs and divided into three meadows. It has a modern toilet block. 6 acre site. 75 touring pitches. 8 hardstandings. Caravan pitches. Motorhome pitches. Tent pitches. 4 statics.

AA Pubs & Restaurants nearby: Trengilly Wartha Inn, Constantine 01326 340332

Budock Vean - Hotel on the River, Mawnan Smith 01326 252100

Leisure: 🅰⛱🔍

Facilities: 📶⊙✳🕐🖪🖈

Services: 🔌🖪🔋⊘🏧🍼⛽

Within 3 miles: 🎣⛳🗓🔎◎🔵🖪🔵🔄

Notes: ◎ 0.5m private path to walk or cycle to beach.

FALMOUTH *continued*

►► 78% Tregedna Farm Touring Caravan & Tent Park *(SW785305)*

Maenporth TR11 5HL
☎ 01326 250529
e-mail: enquiries@tregednafarmholidays.co.uk
dir: *Take A39 from Truro to Falmouth. Turn right at Hill Head rdbt. Site 2.5m on right*

🚐 🚃 Å

Open Apr-Sep

Last arrival 22.00hrs Last departure 13.00hrs

Set in the picturesque Maen Valley, this gently-sloping, south-facing park is part of a 100-acre farm. It is surrounded by beautiful wooded countryside just minutes from the beach, with spacious pitches and well-kept facilities. 12 acre site. 40 touring pitches. Caravan pitches. Motorhome pitches. Tent pitches.

AA Pubs & Restaurants nearby: Trengilly Wartha Inn, Constantine 01326 340332

Budock Vean - Hotel on the River, Mawnan Smith 01326 252100

Leisure: ⚠
Facilities: ⋔ ☉ ✳ ◷ 🛇 ⇥ ♻ ❶
Services: ⬛ 🛢 ⌀
Within 3 miles: ♨ ⊟ ∕ ◎ ⇲ 🛍 🛍
Notes: ☻ One dog only per pitch.

FOWEY

Places to visit

St Catherine's Castle, FOWEY
www.english-heritage.org.uk

Restormel Castle, RESTORMEL 01208 872687
www.english-heritage.org.uk

Great for kids: Wheal Martyn Museum & Country Park, ST AUSTELL 01726 850362
www.wheal-martyn.com

FOWEY Map 2 SX15

►►► 81% Penmarlam Caravan & Camping Park *(SX134526)*

Bodinnick PL23 1LZ
☎ 01726 870088 📄 01726 870082
e-mail: info@penmarlampark.co.uk
dir: *From A390 at East Taphouse take B3359 signed Looe & Polperro. Follow signs for Bodinnick & Fowey, via ferry. Site on right at entrance to Bodinnick*

* 🚐 £14.50-£25 🚃 £14.50-£25 Å £14.50-£25

Open Apr-Oct

Last departure noon

This tranquil park set above the Fowey Estuary in an Area of Outstanding Natural Beauty, with access to the water, continues to improve with the addition of six more fully-serviced pitches. Pitches are level, and sheltered by trees and bushes in two paddocks, while the toilets are spotlessly clean and well maintained. The shop is licensed and sells local and other Cornish produce. 4 acre site. 63 touring pitches. 20 seasonal pitches. Caravan pitches. Motorhome pitches. Tent pitches. 1 static.

AA Pubs & Restaurants nearby: Old Ferry Inn, Bodinnick 01726 870237

The Ship Inn, Fowey 01726 832230

Facilities: ⋔ ☉ ∕ ✳ ⅋ 🛇 ⇥ ♯ ⧠ ⧉ ♻ ❶
Services: ⬛ 🛢 ⬛ ⌀ 🅣 🛁
Within 3 miles: ♨ ⊀ ⊟ ∕ ⇲ 🛍 🛍 ♺
Notes: Dogs must be kept on leads. Private slipway, small boat storage.

LEISURE: 🏊 Indoor swimming pool 🏊 Outdoor swimming pool ⚠ Children's playground ⛳ Kid's club ♨ Tennis court ⚲ Games room ⧠ Separate TV room ♨ 9/18 hole golf course ⛵ Boats for hire ⊟ Cinema ♫ Entertainment ∕ Fishing ◎ Mini golf ⇲ Watersports ⚡ Gym ⚘ Sports field Spa ♺ Stables
FACILITIES: ⌖ Bath ⋔ Shower ☉ Electric shaver ⚐ Hairdryer ✳ Ice Pack Facility ⅋ Disabled facilities ◷ Public telephone 🛍 Shop on site or within 200yds 🏪 Mobile shop (calls at least 5 days a week) ♯ BBQ area ⇥ Picnic area ⧉ Wi-fi ⧠ Internet access ♻ Recycling ❶ Tourist info ⇥ Dog exercise area

GOONHAVERN   Map 2 SW75

See also Rejerrah

Places to visit

Trerice, TRERICE 01637 875404
www.nationaltrust.org.uk

Blue Reef Aquarium, NEWQUAY 01637 878134
www.bluereefaquarium.co.uk

Great for kids: Dairy Land Farm World,
NEWQUAY 01872 510246 www.
dairylandfarmworld.com

PREMIER PARK

▶▶▶▶▶ 84% Silverbow Park

(SW782531)

GOLD

Perranwell TR4 9NX
☎ 01872 572347
e-mail: silverbowhols@btconnect.com
dir: *Adjacent to A3075, 0.5m S of village*

* ➡ £20-£33 ➡ £20-£33 ▲ £14-£27

Open May-end Sep

Last arrival 22.00hrs Last departure 10.30hrs

This park has a quiet garden atmosphere, and
appeals to families with young children. The
superb landscaped grounds and good quality
toilet facilities, housed in an attractive chalet-
style building, including four family rooms, are
maintained to a very high standard with attention
paid to detail. Leisure facilities include two
inviting swimming pools (outdoor and indoor), a
bowling green and a nature reserve. 14 acre site.
100 touring pitches. 2 hardstandings. Caravan
pitches. Motorhome pitches. Tent pitches. 15
statics.

AA Pubs & Restaurants nearby: The Smugglers'
Den Inn, Cubert 01637 830209

The Plume of Feathers, Mitchell 01872 510387

Leisure: ⏊ ⚓ ⚲
Facilities: ⬅ ♣ ☉ 🅿 ✳ ⚐ 🖿 ⍽ ♒

Services: ⚡ 🗵 ⚬ 🅃 ⛢

Within 3 miles: ⚓ ✛ 🅿 ☉ ⚓ 🖿 ⚬ ↺

Notes: ⊗ No cycling, no skateboards. Short mat
bowls rink, conservation/information area, indoor/
outdoor table tennis.
see advert on opposite page

AA CAMPING CARD SITE

▶▶▶▶ 84% Penrose Holiday Park

(SW795534)

TR4 9QF
☎ 01872 573185   🖷 01872 571972
e-mail: info@penroseholidaypark.com
web: www.penroseholidaypark.com
dir: *From Exeter take A30, past Bodmin & Indian
Queens. Just after Wind Farm take B3285 towards
Perranporth, site on left on entering Goonhavern*

* ➡ £14-£32 ➡ £14-£32 ▲ £14-£32

Open Apr-Oct

Last arrival 21.30hrs Last departure 10.00hrs

A quiet sheltered park set in five paddocks divided
by hedges and shrubs, only a short walk from the
village. Lovely floral displays enhance the park's
appearance, and the grass and hedges are neatly
trimmed. Four cubicled family rooms are very
popular, and there is a good laundry, and a smart
reception building. 9 acre site. 110 touring
pitches. 48 hardstandings. Caravan pitches.
Motorhome pitches. Tent pitches. 24 statics.

AA Pubs & Restaurants nearby: The Smugglers'
Den Inn, Cubert 01637 830209

The Plume of Feathers, Mitchell 01872 510387

Leisure: ⚲
Facilities: ♣ ☉ 🅿 ✳ ⚐ ⚲ 🖿 ⍽ 🖳 ♒ ⓘ
Services: ⚡ 🗵 ⚬ ⚬ 🅃 ⍾ ⛢ 🖢 ⛢
Within 3 miles: ⚓ ✛ 🅿 ☉ ⚓ 🖿 ⚬ ↺

Notes: Families & couples only. Dogs must be
kept on leads. Camper's kitchen.

▶▶▶ 77% Sunny Meadows Tourist
Park *(SW782542)*

Rosehill TR4 9JT
☎ 01872 571333   🖷 01872 571491
dir: *From A30 onto B3285 signed Perranporth. At
Goonhavern turn left at T-junct, then right at rdbt
to Perranporth. Site on left*

➡ ➡ ▲

Open Etr-Oct

Last arrival 22.30hrs Last departure 10.30hrs

A gently-sloping park in a peaceful, rural location,
with mostly level pitches set into three small
hedge-lined paddocks. Run by a friendly family,
the park is just two miles from the long sandy
beach at Perranporth. 14.5 acre site. 100 touring
pitches. 1 hardstanding. Caravan pitches.
Motorhome pitches. Tent pitches. 4 statics.

Sunny Meadows Tourist Park

AA Pubs & Restaurants nearby: The Smugglers'
Den Inn, Cubert 01637 830209

The Plume of Feathers, Mitchell 01872 510387

Leisure: ⚲
Facilities: ♣ ☉ ✳ ⚐ ♒ 🖿 ♻
Services: ⚡ ⚬ ⚬ 🅃 ⛢
Within 3 miles: ⚓ 🅿 🖿 ⚬ ↺

Notes: ⊗ One car per pitch. Dogs must be kept
on leads. Pool table & family TV room; washing
machine & tumble dryer.
see advert on page 76

▶▶▶ 75% *Roseville Holiday Park*

(SW787540)
TR4 9LA
☎ 01872 572448   🖷 01872 572448
dir: *From mini-rdbt in Goonhavern follow B3285
towards Perranporth, site 0.5m on right*

➡ ➡ ▲

Open Whit-Oct (rs Apr-Jul, Sep-Oct shop closed)

Last arrival 21.30hrs Last departure 11.00hrs

A family park set in a rural location with sheltered
grassy pitches, some gently sloping. The toilet
facilities are modern, and there is an attractive
outdoor swimming pool complex. This park is
approximately two miles from the long sandy
beach at Perranporth. 8 acre site. 95 touring
pitches. Caravan pitches. Motorhome pitches.
Tent pitches. 5 statics.

AA Pubs & Restaurants nearby: The Smugglers'
Den Inn, Cubert 01637 830209

The Plume of Feathers, Mitchell 01872 510387

Leisure: ⏊ ⚲ ⚲
Facilities: ♣ ☉ 🅿 ✳ ⚐ ♒
Services: ⚡ 🗵 ⚬ ⚬ 🅃 ⛢
Within 3 miles: ⚓ 🅿 ☉ ⚓ 🖿 ⚬ ↺

Notes: ⊗ Families only. Off-licence in shop.

GOONHAVERN *continued*

►► 81% *Little Treamble Farm Touring Park* (SW785560)

Rose TR4 9PR
☎ 01872 573823 & 07971 070760
e-mail: info@treamble.co.uk
dir: *A30 onto B3285 signed Perranporth. Approx 0.5m right into Scotland Rd signed Newquay. Approx 2m to T-junct, right onto A3075 signed Newquay. 0.25m left at Rejerrah sign. Site signed 0.75m on right*

🚐 🚐 Å

Open all year

Last departure noon

This site is set in a quiet rural location with extensive countryside views across an undulating valley. There is a small toilet block and a well-stocked shop. This working farm is next to a Caravan Club site. 1.5 acre site. 20 touring pitches. Caravan pitches. Motorhome pitches. Tent pitches.

AA Pubs & Restaurants nearby: The Smugglers' Den Inn, Cubert 01637 830209

The Plume of Feathers, Mitchell 01872 510387

Facilities: �🏠 ✳ 🅂
Services: 🔌 🅃 🔧
Within 3 miles: ⬇ 🎣 ◎ 🅂 ∪

GORRAN   Map 2 SW94

Places to visit

Caerhays Castle Gardens, GORRAN 01872 501144 www.caerhays.co.uk

The Lost Gardens of Heligan, PENTEWAN 01726 845100 www.heligan.com

Great for kids: Wheal Martyn Museum & Country Park, ST AUSTELL 01726 850362 www.wheal-martyn.com

---

AA CAMPING CARD SITE

►►► 80% Treveague Farm Caravan & Camping Site (SX002410)

PL26 6NY
☎ 01726 842295   🖷 01726 842295
e-mail: treveague@btconnect.com
web: www.treveaguefarm.co.uk
dir: *From St Austell take B3273 towards Mevagissey, past Pentewan at top of hill, turn right signed Gorran. Past Heligan Gardens towards Gorran Churchtown. Follow brown tourist signs from fork in road*

🚐 £9-£22 🚐 £9-£22 Å £7-£20

Open Apr-Sep

Last arrival 21.00hrs Last departure noon

Spectacular panoramic coastal views can be enjoyed from this rural park, which is set on an organic farm and well equipped with modern facilities. A stone-faced toilet block with a Cornish slate roof is an attractive and welcome feature, as is the building that houses the smart reception, café and shop, which sells meat produced on the farm. A footpath leads to the fishing village of Gorran Haven in one direction, and the secluded sandy Vault Beach in the other. 4 acre site. 40 touring pitches. Caravan pitches. Motorhome pitches. Tent pitches.

AA Pubs & Restaurants nearby: The Ship Inn, Mevagissey 01726 843324

The Crown Inn, St Ewe 01726 843322

Leisure: ⚠ ⊙
Facilities: �🏠 ⊙ 🔧 ✳ 🅃 🍴 🖽 📶 ♻ 🛈
Services: 🔌 🅃 🍴 🖼 🛒 🚜
Within 3 miles: ⬇ 🎣 ⬇ 🅂 🅂
Notes: Bird hide with observation cameras.

►►► 77% Treveor Farm Caravan & Camping Site (SW988418)

PL26 6LW
☎ 01726 842387   🖷 01726 842387
e-mail: info@treveorfarm.co.uk
web: www.treveorfarm.co.uk
dir: *From St Austell bypass left onto B3273 for Mevagissey. On hilltop before descent to village turn right on unclass road for Gorran. Right in 3.5m, site on right*

* 🚐 £4.50-£16.50 🚐 £4.50-£16.50
Å £4.50-£16.50

Open Apr-Oct

Last arrival 20.00hrs Last departure 11.00hrs

A small family-run camping park set on a working farm, with grassy pitches backing onto mature

LEISURE: 🏊 Indoor swimming pool 🏊 Outdoor swimming pool ⚠ Children's playground ⚓ Kid's club 🎾 Tennis court 🎯 Games room 📺 Separate TV room ⛳ 9/18 hole golf course ⛵ Boats for hire 🎬 Cinema 🎵 Entertainment 🎣 Fishing ◎ Mini golf 🏄 Watersports 🏋 Gym ⚽ Sports field Spa ∪ Stables
FACILITIES: 🛁 Bath 🚿 Shower ⊙ Electric shaver ✳ Hairdryer ✳ Ice Pack Facility ♿ Disabled facilities ☎ Public telephone 🅂 Shop on site or within 200yds 🛒 Mobile shop (calls at least 5 days a week) 🍴 BBQ area 🗖 Picnic area 📶 Wi-fi 💻 Internet access ♻ Recycling 🛈 Tourist info 🐕 Dog exercise area

hedging. This quiet site, with good facilities, is close to beaches and offers a large coarse fishing lake. 4 acre site. 50 touring pitches. Caravan pitches. Motorhome pitches. Tent pitches.

AA Pubs & Restaurants nearby: The Ship Inn, Mevagissey 01726 843324

The Crown Inn, St Ewe 01726 843322

Leisure: ⚁

Facilities: ↿⊙🅿✳♻ ❼

Services: ⚫🔲🔋

Within 3 miles: ⚡⚓🖫

Notes: No hard balls, kites or frizbees. Dogs must be kept on leads.

GORRAN HAVEN — Map 2 SX04

Places to visit

Caerhays Castle Gardens, GORRAN 01872 501144 www.caerhays.co.uk

The Lost Gardens of Heligan, PENTEWAN 01726 845100 www.heligan.com

Great for kids: Wheal Martyn Museum & Country Park, ST AUSTELL 01726 850362 www.wheal-martyn.com

▶▶ 74% Trelispen Caravan & Camping Park *(SX008421)*

PL26 6NT
☎ 01726 843501 📠 01726 843501
e-mail: trelispen@care4free.net
dir: *B3273 from St Austell towards Mevagissey, on hilltop at x-roads before descent into Mevagissey turn right on unclass road to Gorran. Through village, 2nd right towards Gorran Haven, site signed on left in 250mtrs*

* 🚐 £14-£18 🚃 £12-£16 ▲ £12-£16

Open Etr & Apr-Oct

Last arrival 22.00hrs Last departure noon

A quiet rural site set in three paddocks, and sheltered by mature trees and hedges. The simple toilets have plenty of hot water, and there is a small laundry. Sandy beaches, pubs and shops are nearby, and Mevagissey is two miles away. 2 acre site. 40 touring pitches. Caravan pitches. Motorhome pitches. Tent pitches.

AA Pubs & Restaurants nearby: The Ship Inn, Mevagissey 01726 843324

The Crown Inn, St Ewe 01726 843322

Leisure: ⚁ **Facilities:** ↿⊙✳
Services: ⚫🔲 **Within 3 miles:** ⚡⚓🖫
Notes: ⊛ 30-acre nature reserve.

GWITHIAN — Map 2 SW54

Places to visit

East Pool Mine, POOL 01209 315027
www.nationaltrust.org.uk

▶▶▶▶ 87% Gwithian Farm Campsite

(SW586412)

Gwithian Farm TR27 5BX
☎ 01736 753127
e-mail: camping@gwithianfarm.co.uk
dir: *Exit A30 at Hayle rdbt, take 4th exit signed Hayle, 100mtrs. At 1st mini-rdbt turn right onto B3301 signed Portreath. Site 2m on left on entering village*

🚐 🚃 ▲

Open 31 Mar-1 Oct

Last arrival 22.00hrs Last departure 17.00hrs

An unspoilt site located behind the sand dunes of Gwithian's golden beach, which can be reached directly by footpath from the site. The site boasts stunning floral displays, a superb toilet block with excellent facilities, including a bathroom and baby-changing unit, and first-class hardstanding pitches. There is a good pub opposite. 7.5 acre site. 87 touring pitches. 26 hardstandings. Caravan pitches. Motorhome pitches. Tent pitches.

AA Pubs & Restaurants nearby: The Basset Arms, Portreath 01209 842077

Porthminster Beach, St Ives
01736 795352

Facilities: ↿⊙🅿✳♿🖫🗟🛁🏐🚻♻ ❼
Services: ⚫🔲🛒🚿⚧🛒⚦
Within 3 miles: ⚡🖉◎⚓🖫🔲∪
Notes: Surf board & wet suit hire, table tennis.

HAYLE — Map 2 SW53

Places to visit

Tate St Ives, ST IVES 01736 796226
www.tate.org.uk/stives

Barbara Hepworth Museum & Sculpture Garden, ST IVES 01736 796226
www.tate.org.uk/stives

86% St Ives Bay Holiday Park

(SW577398)

73 Loggans Rd, Upton Towans TR27 5BH
☎ 01736 752274 📠 01736 754523
e-mail: stivesbay@btconnect.com
web: www.stivesbay.co.uk
dir: *Exit A30 at Hayle then immediate right onto B3301 at mini-rdbts. Site entrance 0.5m on left*

* 🚐 £10-£32 🚃 £10-£32 ▲ £10-£32

Open Etr-1 Oct

Last arrival 21.00hrs Last departure 09.00hrs

An extremely well maintained holiday park with a relaxed atmosphere, built on sand dunes adjacent to a three mile beach. The touring section forms a number of separate locations around this extensive park. The park is specially geared for families and couples, and as well as the large indoor swimming pool there are two pubs with seasonal entertainment. 90 acre site. 240 touring pitches. Caravan pitches. Motorhome pitches. Tent pitches. 250 statics.

AA Pubs & Restaurants nearby: White Hart, Ludgvan 01736 740574

Porthminster Beach Restaurant, St Ives 01736 795352

Leisure: ⚑⚁⚌🏐⊡🎵
Facilities: ↿⊙🅿✳♿⏱🖫🌐🖥♻ ❼
Services: ⚫🔲🛒🛁🚿⚧🍽⚧🚻⚦
Within 3 miles: ⚡🖉◎🖫🔲∪
Notes: No pets. Crazy golf, video room.

HAYLE *continued*

►►► 83% Higher Trevaskis Caravan & Camping Park *(SW611381)*

Gwinear Rd, Connor Downs TR27 5JQ
☎ **01209 831736**
dir: At Hayle rdbt on A30 take exit signed Connor Downs, in 1m turn right signed Carnhell Green. Site 0.75m just past level crossing

* 🚐 £11-£19 🚃 £11-£19 ▲ £11-£19

Open mid Apr-Sep

Last arrival 20.00hrs Last departure 10.30hrs

An attractive paddocked park in a sheltered rural position with views towards St Ives. This secluded park is personally run by owners who keep it quiet and welcoming. Three unisex showers are a great hit with visitors. Fluent German is spoken. 6.5 acre site. 82 touring pitches. 3 hardstandings. Caravan pitches. Motorhome pitches. Tent pitches.

AA Pubs & Restaurants nearby: White Hart, Ludgvan 01736 740574

Porthminster Beach Restaurant, St Ives 01736 795352

Leisure: 🅰 ⊕
Facilities: 🏕 ⊙ ☂ ✳ ⊕ 🅢 ♻ ❶
Services: 🖭 🗟 🛆 🕗 🖵 🛒
Within 3 miles: ⌂ 🖉 ◎ 🛥 🛗 🗟

Notes: ⊕ Max speed 5mph, max 2 dogs, no dangerous dogs, balls on field only. Dogs must be kept on leads.

►►► 81% Atlantic Coast Caravan Park *(NW580400)*

GOLD

53 Upton Towans, Gwithian TR27 5BL
☎ **01736 752071** 🖨 **01736 758100**
e-mail: enquiries@atlanticcoastpark.co.uk
dir: From A30 into Hayle, turn right at double rdbt. Site 1.5m on left

* 🚐 £17-£20 🚃 £17-£20 ▲ £17-£20

Open Mar-early Jan

Last arrival 20.00hrs Last departure 11.00hrs

Fringed by the sand-dunes of St Ives Bay and close to the golden sands of Gwithian Beach, the small, friendly touring area offers fully serviced pitches. There's freshly baked bread, a takeaway and a bar next door. This park is ideally situated for visitors to enjoy the natural coastal beauty and attractions of south-west Cornwall. Static caravans for holiday hire. 4.5 acre site. 15 touring pitches. 5 seasonal pitches. Caravan pitches. Motorhome pitches. Tent pitches. 50 statics.

AA Pubs & Restaurants nearby: White Hart, Ludgvan 01736 740574

Porthminster Beach Restaurant, St Ives 01736 795352

Facilities: 🏕 ⊙ ☂ ✳ ⊕ 🕗 🅢 🖭 ♻ ❶
Services: 🖭 🗟 🖵 🍽 🛒
Within 3 miles: ⌂ 🖉 ◎ 🛥 🗟 🛗 ∪

Notes: No commercial vehicles, gazebos or day tents. Dogs must be kept on leads.

►►► 79% Parbola Holiday Park *(SW612366)*

Wall, Gwinear TR27 5LE
☎ **01209 831503**
e-mail: bookings@parbola.co.uk
dir: At Hayle rdbt on A30 take Connor Downs exit. In 1m turn right signed Carnhell Green. In village right to Wall. Site in village on left

🚐 🚃 ▲

Open all year (rs Etr-end of Jun & Sep shop closed, pool unheated)

Last arrival 21.00hrs Last departure 10.00hrs

Pitches are provided in both woodland and open areas in this spacious park in Cornish downland. The park is centrally located for touring the seaside resorts and towns in the area, especially nearby Hayle with its three miles of golden sands. 16.5 acre site. 110 touring pitches. 4 hardstandings. Caravan pitches. Motorhome pitches. Tent pitches. 28 statics.

AA Pubs & Restaurants nearby: White Hart, Ludgvan 01736 740574

Porthminster Beach Restaurant, St Ives 01736 795352

Leisure: ⊜ 🅰 ⊕ 🔍
Facilities: 🏕 ⊙ ☂ ✳ ⊕ 🅢 🖭 🖳 ♻ ❶
Services: 🖭 🗟 🛆 🕗 🛒 🛒
Within 3 miles: ⌂ 🖉 ◎ 🗟 🗟 ∪

Notes: Dogs not allowed Jul-Aug. Dogs must be kept on leads. Crazy golf & table tennis, giant chess & draughts, hairdresser, make-up room, herb garden.

►►► 79% Treglisson Touring Park *(SW581367)*

Wheal Alfred Rd TR27 5JT
☎ **01736 753141**
e-mail: enquiries@treglisson.co.uk
dir: 4th exit off rdbt on A30 at Hayle. 100mtrs, left at 1st mini-rdbt. Approx 1.5m past golf course, site sign on left

🚐 £10-£17.50 🚃 £10-£17.50 ▲ £10-£17.50

Open Etr-Sep

Last arrival 20.00hrs Last departure 11.00hrs

A small secluded site in a peaceful wooded meadow, a former apple and pear orchard. This quiet rural site has level grass pitches and a well-planned modern toilet block, and is just two miles from the glorious beach at Hayle with its vast stretch of golden sand. 3 acre site. 26 touring pitches. 3 hardstandings. Caravan pitches. Motorhome pitches. Tent pitches.

AA Pubs & Restaurants nearby: White Hart, Ludgvan 01736 740574

Porthminster Beach Restaurant, St Ives 01736 795352

Leisure: ⊜ 🅰
Facilities: 🏕 ⊙ ☂ ✳ ⊕ 🕗 🖈 🖭 ♻ ❶
Services: 🖭 🗟 🛒
Within 3 miles: ⌂ 🖉 🛥 🗟 🗟

Notes: Max 6 people to one pitch. Dogs must be kept on leads. Milk deliveries.

HELSTON

See also Ashton

Places to visit

Trevarno Estate Garden & Museum of Gardening, HELSTON 01326 574274 www.trevarno.co.uk

Goonhilly Satellite Earth Station Experience, HELSTON 0800 679593 www.goonhilly.bt.com

Great for kids: The Flambards Theme Park, HELSTON 01326 573404 www.flambards.co.uk

---

LEISURE: 🏊 Indoor swimming pool 🏊 Outdoor swimming pool 🅰 Children's playground 🛝 Kid's club 🎾 Tennis court 🎱 Games room 🖵 Separate TV room 🏌 9/18 hole golf course ⛵ Boats for hire 🎬 Cinema 🎵 Entertainment 🎣 Fishing ◎ Mini golf 🏄 Watersports 🏋 Gym ⊕ Sports field **Spa** ∪ Stables
FACILITIES: 🛁 Bath 🚿 Shower ⊕ Electric shaver ☂ Hairdryer ✳ Ice Pack Facility ⊕ Disabled facilities 🕗 Public telephone 🅢 Shop on site or within 200yds 🚐 Mobile shop (calls at least 5 days a week) 🍽 BBQ area 🌲 Picnic area 🖭 Wi-fi 🖳 Internet access ♻ Recycling ❶ Tourist info 🖈 Dog exercise area

HELSTON
Map 2 SW62

►►► 85% *Lower Polladras Touring Park* (SW617308)

Carleen, Breage TR13 9NX
☎ 01736 762220 ▤ 01736 762220
e-mail: lowerpolladras@btinternet.com
web: www.lower-polladras.co.uk
dir: *From Helston take A394 then B3302 (Hayle road) at Ward Garage, 2nd left to Carleen, site 2m on right*

Open Apr-Jan

Last arrival 22.00hrs Last departure noon

An attractive rural park with extensive views of surrounding fields, appealing to families who enjoy the countryside. The planted trees and shrubs are maturing, and help to divide the area into paddocks with spacious grassy pitches. The site has a dishwashing area, a games room, a dog and nature walk, with plans for campers' kitchen and two fully-serviced family rooms. 4 acre site. 39 touring pitches. 23 hardstandings. Caravan pitches. Motorhome pitches. Tent pitches. 3 statics.

AA Pubs & Restaurants nearby: The Ship Inn, Porthleven 01326 564204

The Kota Restaurant with Rooms, Porthleven 01326 562407

The New Yard Restaurant, Helston 01326 221595

Leisure: ⚓ 🔍
Facilities: 🐾 ⊙ 🅿 ⚒ ⅄ 🖐 ⑤ 🛒 🛏 📶
Services: 🔌 ⑤ 🔥 ⊘ T 🛠 ⬇
Within 3 miles: ⅃ ⛽ ⚂ 🎣 ◎ ⛵ 🗿 🎠 ∪
Notes: ⊗ Caravan storage area.

AA CAMPING CARD SITE

►►► 77% Poldown Caravan Park
(SW629298)

Poldown, Carleen TR13 9NN
☎ 01326 574560
e-mail: stay@poldown.co.uk
dir: *From Helston follow Penzance signs for 1m, right onto B3302 to Hayle, 2nd left to Carleen, 0.5m to site*

* 🚐 £10.50-£16.25 🚗 £10.50-£16.25
Å £10.50-£16.25

Open Apr-Sep

Last arrival 21.00hrs Last departure noon

A small, quiet site set in attractive countryside with bright toilet facilities. All of the level grass pitches have electricity. This sunny park is sheltered by mature trees and shrubs. 2 acre site. 13 touring pitches. 2 hardstandings. Caravan pitches. Motorhome pitches. Tent pitches. 7 statics. 2 bell tents/yurts.

AA Pubs & Restaurants nearby: The Ship Inn, Porthleven 01326 564204

The Kota Restaurant with Rooms, Porthleven 01326 562407

The New Yard Restaurant, Helston 01326 221595

Leisure: ⚓
Facilities: 🐾 ⊙ 🅿 ⚒ ⅄ ⑤ ◎ 🛏 📶 🖥 ♻ ℹ
Services: 🔌 ⑤ 🔋
Within 3 miles: ⅃ ⛽ ⚂ 🎣 ⛵ 🗿 🎠 ∪
Notes: ⊗ Dogs must be kept on leads. Table tennis.

AA CAMPING CARD SITE

►►► 76% Skyburriowe Farm
(SW698227)

Garras TR12 6LR
☎ 01326 221646
e-mail: bkbenney@hotmail.co.uk
web: www.skyburriowefarm.co.uk
dir: *From Helston A3083 to The Lizard. After Culdrose Naval Airbase continue straight at rdbt, in 1m left at Skyburriowe Ln sign. In 0.5m right at Skyburriowe B&B/Campsite sign. Pass bungalow to farmhouse. Site on left*

🚐 £12-£18 🚗 £12-£18 Å £10-£16

Open Apr-Oct

Last arrival 22.00hrs Last departure 11.00hrs

A leafy no-through road leads to this picturesque farm park in a rural location on the Lizard Peninsula. The toilet block offers excellent quality facilities, and most pitches have electric hook-ups. There are some beautiful coves and beaches nearby. 4 acre site. 30 touring pitches. 2 hardstandings. Caravan pitches. Motorhome pitches. Tent pitches.

Skyburriowe Farm

AA Pubs & Restaurants nearby: The Ship Inn, Porthleven 01326 564204

The Kota Restaurant with Rooms, Porthleven 01326 562407

The New Yard Restaurant, Helston 01326 221595

Facilities: 🐾 ⊙ ⚒ ⅄ ⑤ 🎠 ♻ ℹ
Services: 🔌 🔋
Within 3 miles: ⅃ ⚂ 🎣 ⛵ 🗿 🎠 ∪
Notes: ⊗ Quiet after 23.00hrs. Dogs must be kept on leads.

HOLYWELL BAY

Places to visit

Trerice, TRERICE 01637 875404
www.nationaltrust.org.uk

Blue Reef Aquarium, NEWQUAY 01637 878134
www.bluereefaquarium.co.uk

Great for kids: Newquay Zoo, NEWQUAY 0844 474 2244
www.newquayzoo.org.uk

SERVICES: 🔌 Electric hook up ⑤ Launderette 🍺 Licensed bar 🔥 Calor Gas ⊘ Camping Gaz T Toilet fluid 🍽 Café/Restaurant 🍔 Fast Food/Takeaway 🔋 Battery charging 🍼 Baby care ⬇ Motorvan service point
ABBREVIATIONS: BH/bank hols-bank holidays Etr-Easter Whit-Whitsun dep-departure fr-from hrs-hours m-mile mdnt-midnight rdbt-roundabout rs-restricted service wk-week wknd-weekend ⊗ No credit cards ⊗ No dogs
See page 7 for details of the AA Camping Card Scheme

HOLYWELL BAY — Map 2 SW75

94% Trevornick Holiday Park
(SW776586)

TR8 5PW
☎ 01637 830531 📠 01637 831000
e-mail: info@trevornick.co.uk
web: www.trevornick.co.uk
dir: 3m from Newquay off A3075 towards Redruth. Follow Cubert & Holywell Bay signs

Open Etr & mid May-mid Sep

Last arrival 21.00hrs Last departure 10.00hrs

A large seaside holiday complex with excellent facilities and amenities. There is plenty of entertainment including a children's club and an evening cabaret, adding up to a full holiday experience for all the family. A sandy beach is just a 15-minute footpath walk away. The park has 68 ready-erected tents for hire. 20 acre site. 593 touring pitches. 50 hardstandings. Caravan pitches. Motorhome pitches. Tent pitches.

AA Pubs & Restaurants nearby: The Smugglers' Den Inn, Cubert 01637 830209

Leisure: 🏄 🎠 🏊 🎣 🎱 🎵 Spa
Facilities: 🚿 🔫 ☉ 🅿 ❄ ⚓ 🔥 🛎 🐕 📶 ♻ ℹ
Services: 🔌 🔋 🚽 🔒 ⚡ 🔓 🚰 🍽 🚮
Within 3 miles: ↓ 🎿 🎣 🅿 ◎ 🔔 🛒 🛎 ∪

Notes: Families & couples only. Fishing, golf course, entertainment.

see advert on page 94

77% Holywell Bay Holiday Park (SW773582)

TR8 5PR
☎ 0844 335 3756 📠 01637 831166
e-mail: touringandcamping@parkdeanholidays.com
web: www.parkdeantouring.com
dir: Exit A30 onto A392, take A3075 signed Redruth, right in 2m signed Holywell/Cubert. Through Cubert past Trevornick to site on left

* 🚐 £13-£41 🚗 £13-£41 ⛺ £10-£36

Open Mar-Oct (rs May-19 Sep pool open)

Last arrival 23.00hrs Last departure 10.00hrs

Close to lovely beaches in a rural location, this level grassy park borders on National Trust land, and is only a short distance from the Cornish Coastal Path. The park provides a popular entertainment programme for the whole family (including evening entertainment), and there is an outdoor pool with a water slide and children's clubs. Newquay is just a few miles away. 16 acre site. 40 touring pitches. Caravan pitches. Motorhome pitches. Tent pitches. 156 statics.

Holywell Bay Holiday Park

AA Pubs & Restaurants nearby: The Smugglers' Den Inn, Cubert 01637 830209

Leisure: 🏄 🎠 🏊 🎣 🎵
Facilities: 🔫 ☉ ⚓ 🕐 🛎 🔥
Services: 🔌 🔋 🚽 ⏳ 🍽 🚮 ♻
Within 3 miles: ↓ 🅿 ◎ 🔔 🛒 🛎 ∪

Notes: No pets. Surf school & hire shop, adventure playground.

see advert in preliminary section

INDIAN QUEENS — Map 2 SW95

Places to visit

Lanhydrock, LANHYDROCK 01208 265950
www.nationaltrust.org.uk

Charlestown Shipwreck & Heritage Centre, ST AUSTELL 01726 69897
www.shipwreckcharlestown.com

Great for kids: Eden Project, ST AUSTELL 01726 811911
www.edenproject.com

▶▶▶ 74% Gnome World Caravan & Camping Site (SW890599)

Moorland Rd TR9 6HN
☎ 01726 860812 & 860101 📠 01726 861749
e-mail: gnomesworld@btconnect.com
dir: Signed from slip road at A30 & A39 rdbt in village of Indian Queens - site on old A30, now unclassified road

Open Mar-Dec

Last arrival 22.00hrs Last departure noon

Set in open countryside, this spacious park is set on level grassy land only half a mile from the A30 (Cornwall's main arterial route) and in a central holiday location for touring the county. Please note that there are no narrow lanes to negotiate. 4.5 acre site. 50 touring pitches. 25 hardstandings. Caravan pitches. Motorhome pitches. Tent pitches. 60 statics.

AA Pubs & Restaurants nearby: Ship Inn, Mitchell 01726 843324

Leisure: 🎠
Facilities: 🔫 ☉ ❄ ⚓ 🔥 🔨
Services: 🔌 🔋 🔒
Within 3 miles: ↓ 🛒 🛎 ∪

Notes: Dogs must be kept on leads. Nature trail.

see advert on opposite page

JACOBSTOW — Map 2 SX19

Places to visit

Launceston Castle, LAUNCESTON 01566 772365
www.english-heritage.org.uk

Tamar Otter & Wildlife Centre, LAUNCESTON 01566 785646 www.tamarotters.co.uk

Great for kids: Launceston Steam Railway, LAUNCESTON 01566 775665
www.launcestonsr.co.uk

▶▶▶ 76% Edmore Tourist Park
(SX184955)

Edgar Rd, Wainhouse Corner EX23 0BJ
☎ 01840 230467 📠 01840 230467
e-mail: enquiries@cornwallvisited.co.uk
dir: Exit A39 at Wainhouse Corner onto Edgar Rd, site signed on right in 200yds

* 🚐 £14-£16 🚗 £14-£16 ⛺ £8-£16

Open 1 wk before Etr-Oct

Last arrival 21.00hrs Last departure noon

A quiet family-owned site in a rural location with extensive views, set close to the sandy surfing beaches of Bude, and the unspoilt sandy beach and rock pools at Crackington Haven. The friendly owners keep all facilities in a very good condition and the site has hardstanding pitches and gravel access roads. 3 acre site. 28 touring pitches. Caravan pitches. Motorhome pitches. Tent pitches.

AA Pubs & Restaurants nearby: Bay View Inn, Widemouth Bay 01288 361273

Leisure: 🎠 **Facilities:** 🔫 ☉ 🅿 ❄ 🕐
Services: 🔌 🔋 🚮 **Within 3 miles:** 🛎
Notes: ⚘ Dogs must be kept on leads.

LEISURE: 🏊 Indoor swimming pool 🏊 Outdoor swimming pool 🎠 Children's playground 🎣 Kid's club 🎾 Tennis court 🎱 Games room 📺 Separate TV room
⛳ 9/18 hole golf course ⛵ Boats for hire 🎬 Cinema 🎵 Entertainment 🎣 Fishing ◎ Mini golf 🏄 Watersports 🏋 Gym ⚽ Sports field Spa ∪ Stables
FACILITIES: 🚿 Bath 🔫 Shower ☉ Electric shaver 🅿 Hairdryer ❄ Ice Pack Facility ⚓ Disabled facilities 🕐 Public telephone 🛎 Shop on site or within 200yds
🚐 Mobile shop (calls at least 5 days a week) 🍖 BBQ area 🔥 Picnic area 📶 Wi-fi 📡 Internet access ♻ Recycling ℹ Tourist info 🔨 Dog exercise area

KENNACK SANDS
Map 2 SW71

Places to visit

National Seal Sanctuary, GWEEK 0871 423 2110
www.sealsanctuary.co.uk

Trevarno Estate Garden & Museum of
Gardening, HELSTON 01326 574274
www.trevarno.co.uk

Great for kids: Goonhilly Satellite Earth Station
Experience, HELSTON 0800 679593
www.goonhilly.bt.com

►►► 86% *Chy Carne Holiday Park*
(SW725164)

Kuggar, Ruan Minor TR12 7LX
☎ **01326 290200** & **291161**
e-mail: enquiries@camping-cornwall.com
web: www.chycarne.co.uk
dir: *From A3083 turn left on B3293 after Culdrose
Naval Air Station. At Goonhilly ESS right onto
unclass road signed Kennack Sands. Left in 3m
at junct*

Open Etr-Oct

Last arrival dusk

A small but spacious park in a quiet, sheltered
spot with extensive sea and coastal views from
the grassy touring area. A village pub with
restaurant is a short walk by footpath from the
touring area, and a sandy beach is less than half
a mile away. 12 acre site. 30 touring pitches. 4
hardstandings. Caravan pitches. Motorhome
pitches. Tent pitches. 18 statics.

AA Pubs & Restaurants nearby: Cadgwith Cove
Inn, Cadgwith 01326 290513

Leisure:
Facilities:
Services:
Within 3 miles:

AA CAMPING CARD SITE

►►► 82% Silver Sands
Holiday Park *(SW727166)*

Gwendreath TR12 7LZ
☎ **01326 290631** 📠 **01326 290631**
e-mail: info@silversandsholidaypark.co.uk
dir: *From Helston follow signs to Future World
Goonhilly. After 300yds turn right at x-roads
signed Kennack Sands, 1m, left at Gwendreath
sign, site 1m*

* 🚐 £14.50-£20.50 🚗 £14.50-£20.50
Å £12.50-£20.50

Open all year

Last arrival 21.00hrs Last departure 11.00hrs

A small park in a remote location, with
individually screened pitches providing sheltered
suntraps. The owners continue to upgrade the
park, improving the landscaping, access roads
and toilets; there are lovely floral displays that
greet you on arrival. A footpath through the woods
from the family-owned park leads to the beach
and the local pub. 9 acre site. 16 touring pitches.
Caravan pitches. Motorhome pitches. Tent
pitches. 17 statics.

AA Pubs & Restaurants nearby: Cadgwith Cove
Inn, Cadgwith 01326 290513

Leisure:
Facilities:
Services:
Within 3 miles:

Notes: No noise after mdnt. Dogs must be kept on
leads.

►►► 72% Gwendreath Farm Holiday
Park *(SW738168)*

TR12 7LZ
☎ **01326 290666**
e-mail: tom.gibson@virgin.net
dir: *From A3083 turn left past Culdrose Naval Air
Station onto B3293. Right past Goonhilly Earth
Station signed Kennack Sands, left in 1m. At end
of lane turn right over cattle grid. Right, through
Seaview to 2nd reception*

🚐 £14 Å £14

Open May-Sep

Last arrival 21.00hrs Last departure 10.00hrs

A grassy park in an elevated position with
extensive sea and coastal views, and the beach
just a short walk through the woods. Campers can
use the bar and takeaway at an adjoining site. It
is advisable to phone ahead and book before
arrival. 5 acre site. 10 touring pitches. Caravan
pitches. Tent pitches. 17 statics.

AA Pubs & Restaurants nearby: Cadgwith Cove
Inn, Cadgwith 01326 290513

Leisure: **Facilities:**
Services:
Within 3 miles:

Notes: Dogs must be kept on leads.

SERVICES: 🔌 Electric hook up 🧺 Launderette 🍺 Licensed bar 🫙 Calor Gas 🔥 Camping Gaz 🚽 Toilet fluid 🍽 Café/Restaurant 🍟 Fast Food/Takeaway 🔋 Battery charging
🍼 Baby care ⛟ Motorvan service point
ABBREVIATIONS: BH/bank hols-bank holidays Etr-Easter Whit-Whitsun dep-departure fr-from hrs-hours m-mile mdnt-midnight rdbt-roundabout rs-restricted service wk-week
wknd-weekend 🚫 No credit cards 🐕 No dogs   See page 7 for details of the AA Camping Card Scheme

KILKHAMPTON — Map 2 SS21

Places to visit

Dartington Crystal, GREAT TORRINGTON 01805 626242 www.dartington.co.uk

RHS Garden Rosemoor, GREAT TORRINGTON 01805 624067 www.rhs.org.uk/rosemoor

Great for kids: The Milky Way Adventure Park, CLOVELLY 01237 431255 www.themilkyway.co.uk

►► 72% Upper Tamar Lake (SS288118)

Upper Tamar Lake EX23 9SB
☎ 01288 321712
e-mail: info@swlakestrust.org.uk
dir: From A39 at Kilkhampton onto B3254, left in 0.5m onto unclass road, follow signs approx 4m to site

* Å £13-£15

Open Apr-Oct

A well-trimmed, slightly sloping site overlooking the lake and surrounding countryside, with several signed walks. The site benefits from the excellent facilities provided for the watersports centre and coarse anglers, with a rescue launch on the lake when the flags are flying. A good family site, with Bude's beaches and surfing waves only eight miles away. 2 acre site. 28 touring pitches. Tent pitches.

AA Pubs & Restaurants nearby: The Bush Inn, Morwenstow 01288 331242

Leisure: Å
Facilities: ♠ ℙ & ♉ ♻ ❼
Services: ⦿ ⛟
Within 3 miles: ⥮ ⥥ ℘ ⛵ ⓢ ⓤ U

Notes: No swimming in lake. Dogs must be kept on leads. Watersports centre, canoeing, sailing, windsurfing.

LANDRAKE

Places to visit

Cotehele, CALSTOCK 01579 351346 www.nationaltrust.org.uk

Mount Edgcumbe House & Country Park, TORPOINT 01752 822236 www.mountedgcumbe.gov.uk

Great for kids: The Monkey Sanctuary, LOOE 01503 262532 www.monkeysanctuary.org

---

LANDRAKE — Map 3 SX36

►►►► 87% Dolbeare Park Caravan and Camping (SX363616)

Best of British SILVER

St Ive Rd PL12 5AF
☎ 01752 851332 📠 01752 547871
e-mail: reception@dolbeare.co.uk
web: www.dolbeare.co.uk
dir: A38 to Landrake, 4m W of Saltash. At footbridge over A38 turn right, follow signs to site (0.75m from A38)

⦿ £16.50-£23 ⛟ £16.50-£23 Å £6-£23

Open all year

Last arrival 18.00hrs Last departure noon

Set in meadowland close to the A38 and the Devon/Cornwall border, this attractive touring park is run by innovative, forward-thinking owners, who have adopted a very 'green' approach to running the park. The smart, newly refubished toilet block is very eco-friendly, electronic sensor showers, a new on-demand boiler system, flow control valves on the taps, and the low-energy lighting, as well as impressive family room. The park is extremely well presented, with excellent hardstanding pitches, a good tenting field, offering spacious pitches, and good provision for children with a separate ball games paddock. Expect high levels of customer care and cleanliness. 9 acre site. 60 touring pitches. 54 hardstandings. Caravan pitches. Motorhome pitches. Tent pitches. 1 tipi.

AA Pubs & Restaurants nearby: The Crooked Inn, Saltash 01752 848177

The Farmhouse, Saltash 01752 854661

Leisure: Å ☉
Facilities: ♠ ⦿ ℙ ✳ & ① ⓢ ♉ ✈ 🅆
🖥 ♻ ❼
Services: ⦿ ⓢ ♨ ♟ ⌀ Ⓣ ⛟ ⛟ ⥧
Within 3 miles: ⥮ ⥥ ℘ ⓢ ⓤ U

Notes: No cycling, no kite flying, fee applies for arrivals after 18.00hrs. Dogs must be kept on leads. Off licence, free fridge & freezer.

see advert on page 89

LEEDSTOWN (NEAR HAYLE)

Places to visit

East Pool Mine, POOL 01209 315027 www.nationaltrust.org.uk

Godolphin House, GODOLPHIN CROSS 01736 763194 www.nationaltrust.org.uk/godolphin

---

LEEDSTOWN (NEAR HAYLE) — Map 2 SW63

►►►► 82% Calloose Caravan & Camping Park (SW597352)

TR27 5ET
☎ 01736 850431 & 0800 328 7589
📠 01736 850431
e-mail: calloose@hotmail.com
dir: From Hayle take B3302 to Leedstown, turn left opposite village hall, before entering village. Site 0.5m on left at bottom of hill

⦿ ⛟ Å

Open all year

Last arrival 22.00hrs Last departure 11.00hrs

A comprehensively equipped leisure park in a remote rural setting in a small river valley. This very good park is busy and bustling, and offers bright, clean and newly upgraded toilet facilities, an excellent games room, an inviting pool, a good children's play area, and log cabins and static caravans for holiday hire. 12.5 acre site. 109 touring pitches. 29 hardstandings. Caravan pitches. Motorhome pitches. Tent pitches. 25 statics.

AA Pubs & Restaurants nearby: Mount Haven Hotel & Restaurant, Marazion 01736 710249

Leisure: ⛱ Å ⥌ ♠ ▢
Facilities: ♠ ⦿ ℙ ✳ & ① ⓢ ♉ ✈
Services: ⦿ ⓢ ♨ ♟ ⌀ Ⓣ ⛟ ⥧ ⥧ ⛟
Within 3 miles: ℘ ⓢ ⓢ

Notes: No noise after mdnt, no pets in statics or lodges. Crazy golf, skittle alley.

LOOE

Places to visit

Antony House, TORPOINT 01752 812191 www.nationaltrust.org.uk/antony

Mount Edgcumbe House & Country Park, TORPOINT 01752 822236 www.mountedgcumbe.gov.uk

Great for kids: The Monkey Sanctuary, LOOE 01503 262532 www.monkeysanctuary.org

---

LEISURE: ⛱ Indoor swimming pool ⥌ Outdoor swimming pool Å Children's playground ⥮ Kid's club ⥥ Tennis court ♠ Games room ▢ Separate TV room ⥮ 9/18 hole golf course ⥥ Boats for hire ⊞ Cinema ♫ Entertainment ℘ Fishing ◉ Mini golf ⓢ Watersports ✣ Gym ☉ Sports field Spa U Stables
FACILITIES: ⛟ Bath ♠ Shower ⊙ Electric shaver ℙ Hairdryer ✳ Ice Pack Facility & Disabled facilities ① Public telephone ⓢ Shop on site or within 200yds ⛟ Mobile shop (calls at least 5 days a week) ♨ BBQ area ♉ Picnic area 🅆 Wi-fi ⌀ Internet access ♻ Recycling ❼ Tourist info ✈ Dog exercise area

LOOE   Map 2 SX25

AA CAMPING CARD SITE

 81% Tencreek Holiday Park *(SX233525)*

Polperro Rd PL13 2JR
☎ 01503 262447 🖷 01503 262760
e-mail: reception@tencreek.co.uk
web: www.dolphinholidays.co.uk
dir: *Take A387 1.25m from Looe. Site on left*

* ➡ £11-£20.50 ⇔ £11-£20.50 ▲ £11-£20.50

Open all year

Last arrival 23.00hrs Last departure 10.00hrs

Occupying a lovely position with extensive countryside and sea views, this holiday centre is in a rural spot but close to Looe and Polperro. There is a full family entertainment programme, with indoor and outdoor swimming pools, an adventure playground and an exciting children's club. The superb new amenities blocks opened for the 2011 season and include several private family shower rooms with WC and washbasin. 24 acre site. 254 touring pitches. 12 hardstandings. 120 seasonal pitches. Caravan pitches. Motorhome pitches. Tent pitches. 101 statics.

AA Pubs & Restaurants nearby: Barclay House, Looe 01503 262929

Trelaske Hotel & Restaurant, Looe 01503 262159

Leisure: 🏊🏖🅰🚶🎣🎵
Facilities: 🅽☉🅿✳🕎🕙🖺🛱🅆🕼🖥♻🛈
Services: 🔌🗄🍽🛢🚿🚾🛁♨🛒🚽
Within 3 miles: ⬇🏌🎣🅿◎🛶🛍🗄🛍⛳

Notes: Families & couples only. Dogs must be kept on leads. Nightly entertainment, 45-metre pool flume.

▶▶▶▶ **81% Camping Caradon Touring Park** *(SX218539)*

Trelawne PL13 2NA
☎ 01503 272388
e-mail: enquiries@campingcaradon.co.uk
dir: *Site signed from B3359 near junct with A387, between Looe & Polperro. Also signed on junct A387/B3359*

➡⇔▲

Open all year (rs Nov-Mar by booking only)

Last arrival 22.00hrs Last departure noon

Set in a quiet rural location between the popular coastal resorts of Looe and Polperro, this family-run and developing eco-friendly park is just one and half miles from the beach at Talland Bay. The site, run by hands-on owners, has a bar and restaurant (food can also be delivered to your pitch), and two fully-serviced family/disabled wet rooms. 3.5 acre site. 85 touring pitches. 23 hardstandings. Caravan pitches. Motorhome pitches. Tent pitches.

AA Pubs & Restaurants nearby: Old Mill House Inn, Polperro 01503 272362

Barclay House, Looe 01503 262929

Leisure: 🅰🎣🖵
Facilities: 🅽☉🅿✳🕙🖺🛱🅆♻🛈
Services: 🔌🗄🍽🛢🛢🚾🍽♨🚽
Within 3 miles: 🏌🅿◎🛶🗄🛍

Notes: No noise 23.00hrs-07.00hrs & barrier not operational. Dogs must be kept on leads.

▶▶▶▶ **77% Tregoad Park** *(SX272560)*

St Martin PL13 1PB
☎ 01503 262718 🖷 01503 264777
e-mail: info@tregoadpark.co.uk
web: www.tregoadpark.co.uk
dir: *Signed with direct access from B3253, or from E on A387 follow B3253 for 1.75m towards Looe. Site on left*

➡⇔▲

Open all year (rs mid & high season bistro open)

Last arrival 20.00hrs Last departure 11.00hrs

Investment continues at this smart, terraced park with extensive sea and rural views, about a mile and a half from Looe. All pitches are level. The facilities are well maintained and spotlessly clean, and there is a swimming pool with adjacent jacuzzi and sun patio, and a licensed bar where bar meals are served in the conservatory. American trailers, static caravans, holiday cottages and two camping pods are available for holiday hire. 55 acre site. 200 touring pitches. 60 hardstandings. Caravan pitches. Motorhome pitches. Tent pitches. 7 statics.

AA Pubs & Restaurants nearby: Barclay House, Looe 01503 262929

Trelaske Hotel & Restaurant, Looe 01503 262159

Leisure: 🏊🅰🎣🖵
Facilities: 🛒🅽☉🅿✳🕙🖺🛱🅆
Services: 🔌🗄🍽🛢🛢🚾🍽♨🚽
Within 3 miles: 🏌🅿◎🛶🗄🛍⛳

Notes: Pets on leads at all times. Fishing lake, crazy golf, ball sports area.

▶▶▶ **82% Polborder House Caravan & Camping Park** *(SX283557)*

Bucklawren Rd, St Martin PL13 1NZ
☎ 01503 240265
e-mail: reception@polborderhouse.co.uk
dir: *Approach Looe from E on A387, follow B3253 for 1m, left at Polborder & Monkey Sanctuary sign. Site 0.5m on right*

➡⇔▲

Open all year

Last arrival 22.00hrs Last departure 11.00hrs

A very neat and well-kept small grassy site on high ground above Looe in a peaceful rural setting. Friendly and enthusiastic owners continue to invest in the park. The toilet facilities have upmarket fittings (note the infra-red operated taps and under floor heating). The whole park again looked immaculate at our last inspection, with a new laundry and shop for 2011. 3.3 acre site. 31 touring pitches. 19 hardstandings. Caravan pitches. Motorhome pitches. Tent pitches. 5 statics.

AA Pubs & Restaurants nearby: Barclay House, Looe 01503 262929

Trelaske Hotel & Restaurant, Looe 01503 262159

Leisure: 🅰
Facilities: 🅽☉🅿✳🕙🖺🛱🅆♻🛈
Services: 🔌🗄🛢🛢🚾🍽
Within 3 miles: ⬇🏌🅿🛶🗄🛍⛳

Notes: Dogs must be kept on leads.

▶▶▶ **80% Trelay Farmpark** *(SX210544)*

Pelynt PL13 2JX
☎ 01503 220900 🖷 01503 220902
e-mail: stay@trelay.co.uk
dir: *From A390 at East Taphouse, take B3359 S towards Looe. After Pelynt, site 0.5m on left*

➡⇔▲

Open Dec-Oct

Last arrival 21.00hrs Last departure 11.00hrs

A small site with a friendly atmosphere set in a pretty rural area with extensive views. The good-size grass pitches are on slightly-sloping ground, and the toilets are immaculately kept, as is the excellent washing-up room. Looe and Polperro are just three miles away. 4.5 acre site. 66 touring pitches. 3 hardstandings. 7 seasonal pitches. Caravan pitches. Motorhome pitches. Tent pitches. 45 statics.

continued

SERVICES: 🔌 Electric hook up 🗄 Launderette 🍽 Licensed bar 🛢 Calor Gas 🚾 Camping Gaz 🅣 Toilet fluid 🍽 Café/Restaurant 🍔 Fast Food/Takeaway 🔋 Battery charging 🍼 Baby care 🚽 Motorvan service point
ABBREVIATIONS: BH/bank hols-bank holidays Etr-Easter Whit-Whitsun dep-departure fr-from hrs-hours m-mile mdnt-midnight rdbt-roundabout rs-restricted service wk-week wknd-weekend 🚫 No credit cards 🚫 No dogs
See page 7 for details of the AA Camping Card Scheme

LOOE *continued*

AA Pubs & Restaurants nearby: Old Mill House Inn, Polperro 01503 272362

Barclay House, Looe 01503 262929

Leisure: 𝖠

Facilities: ⬤○𝒫✻&⬤☂ᗄ📶

Services: 🔌🛢️🔋⬤🇹⛽

Within 3 miles: 🎣🛶🦮⬤♨️⛵

Notes: No skateboards, ball games or kites. Fridge & freezer.

LOSTWITHIEL	Map 2 SX15

Places to visit

Restormel Castle, RESTORMEL 01208 872687
www.english-heritage.org.uk

Eden Project, ST AUSTELL 01726 811911
www.edenproject.com

AA CAMPING CARD SITE

▶▶▶▶ **81% Eden Valley Holiday Park** *(SX083593)*

SILVER

PL30 5BU
☎ **01208 872277** 📠 **01208 871236**
e-mail: enquiries@edenvalleyholidaypark.co.uk
dir: *1.5m SW of Lostwithiel on A390 turn right at brown/white sign in 400mtrs*

🚐 £13-£17 🚛 £13-£17 ⛺ £13-£17

Open Etr or Apr-Oct

Last arrival 22.00hrs Last departure 11.30hrs

A grassy park set in attractive paddocks with mature trees. A gradual upgrading of facilities continues, and both buildings and grounds are carefully maintained and contain an impressive children's play area. This park is ideally located for visiting the Eden Project, the nearby golden beaches and sailing at Fowey. There are also two self-catering lodges. 12 acre site. 56 touring pitches. 12 hardstandings. 20 seasonal pitches. Caravan pitches. Motorhome pitches. Tent pitches. 38 statics.

AA Pubs & Restaurants nearby: The Crown Inn, Lanlivery 01208 872707

Leisure: 𝖠⊛⬤▢

Facilities: ⬤○𝒫✻&⬤ᗄ♻️𝒊

Services: 🔌🛢️🔋⬤🇹⛽

Within 3 miles: 🎣🛶𝒫◎♨️⛵

Notes: Dogs must be kept on leads. Table football, pool, table tennis, putting green, football.

LUXULYAN	Map 2 SX05

Places to visit

Restormel Castle, RESTORMEL 01208 872687
www.english-heritage.org.uk

Eden Project, ST AUSTELL 01726 811911
www.edenproject.com

▶▶▶ **77% Croft Farm Holiday Park** *(SX044568)*

DAVID BELLAMY CONSERVATION AWARD GOLD

PL30 5EQ
☎ **01726 850228** 📠 **01726 850498**
e-mail: enquiries@croftfarm.co.uk
dir: *Exit A30 at Bodmin onto A391 towards St Austell. In 7m left at double rdbt onto unclass road towards Luxulyan/Eden Project, continue to rdbt at Eden, left signed Luxulyan. Site 1m on left. (NB Do not approach any other way as roads are very narrow)*

* 🚐 £12.50-£17.50 🚛 £12.50-£17.50 ⛺ £11.50-£16.50

Open 21 Mar-21 Jan

Last arrival 18.00hrs Last departure 11.00hrs

A peaceful, picturesque setting at the edge of a wooded valley, and only one mile from The Eden Project. Facilities include a well-maintained toilet block, a well-equipped dishwashing area, replete with freezer and microwave, and a children's play area reached via an attractive woodland trail. 10.5 acre site. 52 touring pitches. 42 hardstandings. 32 seasonal pitches. Caravan pitches. Motorhome pitches. Tent pitches. 45 statics.

AA Pubs & Restaurants nearby: The Crown Inn, Lanlivery 01208 872707

Leisure: 𝖠🔍

Facilities: ⬤⬤○𝒫✻◎🛢️ᗄ♿📶♻️𝒊

Services: 🔌🛢️🔋⬤🇹⛽🐕

Within 3 miles: 🎣🛶🍴🦮♨️◎♨️

Notes: No skateboarding, ball games only in playing field, quiet between 23.00hrs-07.00hrs. Woodland walk.

MARAZION	Map 2 SW53

See also St Hilary

Places to visit

St Michael's Mount, MARAZION 01736 710507
www.stmichaelsmount.co.uk

Trengwainton Garden, PENZANCE 01736 363148
www.nationaltrust.org.uk

AA CAMPING CARD SITE

▶▶▶ **78% Wheal Rodney Holiday Park** *(SW525315)*

Gwallon Ln TR17 0HL
☎ **01736 710605**
e-mail: reception@whealrodney.co.uk
dir: *Exit A30 at Crowlas, signed Rospeath. Site 1.5m on right. From Marazion centre turn opposite Fire Engine Inn, site 500mtrs on left*

* 🚐 £16-£42 🚛 £16-£42 ⛺ £13-£42

Open Etr-Oct

Last arrival 20.00hrs Last departure 11.00hrs

Set in a quiet rural location surrounded by farmland, with level grass pitches and well-kept facilities. Within half a mile are the beach at Marazion and the causeway or ferry to St Michael's Mount. A cycle route is just 400 yards away. 2.5 acre site. 30 touring pitches. Caravan pitches. Motorhome pitches. Tent pitches.

AA Pubs & Restaurants nearby: Godolphin Arms, Marazion 01736 710202

Mount Haven Hotel & Restaurant, Marazion 01736 710249

Leisure: 🏊

Facilities: ⬤○𝒫✻◎🛢️📶♻️𝒊

Services: 🔌🛢️⛽

Within 3 miles: 🎣𝒫◎♨️🦮◎⛵

Notes: Quiet after 22.00hrs. Dogs must be kept on leads.

LEISURE: 🏊 Indoor swimming pool ⊛ Outdoor swimming pool 𝖠 Children's playground 🦮 Kid's club ⬤ Tennis court 🔍 Games room ▢ Separate TV room 🎣 9/18 hole golf course 🛶 Boats for hire 🎬 Cinema 🎵 Entertainment 𝒫 Fishing ◎ Mini golf 🌊 Watersports 🏋 Gym ⬤ Sports field **Spa** ⛵ Stables
FACILITIES: ⬤ Bath ⬤ Shower ⊙ Electric shaver 𝒫 Hairdryer ✻ Ice Pack Facility & Disabled facilities ◎ Public telephone 🛢️ Shop on site or within 200yds ⬤ Mobile shop (calls at least 5 days a week) 🍖 BBQ area ᗄ Picnic area 📶 Wi-fi ⬛ Internet access ♻️ Recycling 𝒊 Tourist info 🐕 Dog exercise area

MAWGAN PORTH — Map 2 SW86

▶▶▶▶ 81% Sun Haven Valley Holiday Park

(SW861669)

TR8 4BQ
☎ 01637 860373 📠 01637 860373
e-mail: sunhaven@sunhavenvalley.com
dir: Exit A30 at Highgate Hill junct for Newquay; follow signs for airport. At T-junct turn right. At beach level in Mawgan Porth take only road inland, then 0.25m. Site 0.5m beyond S bend

* 🚐 £15-£26 🚐 £15-£26 ▲ £15-£26

Open Apr-Oct

Last arrival 22.00hrs Last departure 10.30hrs

An attractive site with level pitches on the side of a river valley. The very high quality facilities include a TV lounge and a games room in a Swedish-style chalet, and a well-kept adventure playground. Trees and hedges fringe the park, and the ground is well drained. 5 acre site. 109 touring pitches. Caravan pitches. Motorhome pitches. Tent pitches. 38 statics.

AA Pubs & Restaurants nearby: The Falcon Inn, St Mawgan 01637 860225

The Scarlet Hotel, Mawgan Porth 01637 861800

Leisure: 🄰 🔍 🖵
Facilities: ⇞ ⚕ ⊙ ☞ ✳ ⛟ ⊙ 🟦 WiFi ♲ 🄕
Services: ⊟ 🗄 🍴 ⊘ Ⓣ 🛒
Within 3 miles: ↓ ✗ ◎ ⛳ 🟦 🄱 U

Notes: Families and couples only. Dogs must be kept on leads.

▶▶▶ 79% Trevarrian Holiday Park

(SW853661)

TR8 4AQ
☎ 01637 860381 & 0845 2255910
e-mail: holiday@trevarrian.co.uk
dir: From A39 at St Columb rdbt turn right onto A3059 towards Newquay. Fork right in approx 2m for St Mawgan onto B3276. Turn right, site on left

* 🚐 £15-£25 🚐 £15-£25 ▲ £15-£25

Open all year

Last arrival 22.00hrs Last departure 11.00hrs

A well-established and well-run holiday park overlooking Mawgan Porth beach. This park has a wide range of attractions including a free entertainment programme in peak season and a 10-pin bowling alley with licensed bar. 7 acre site. 185 touring pitches. 10 hardstandings. Caravan pitches. Motorhome pitches. Tent pitches.

AA Pubs & Restaurants nearby: The Falcon Inn, St Mawgan 01637 860225

Leisure: 🔍 🄰 ⊙ 🔍 🖵 🎵
Facilities: ⇞ ⚕ ⊙ ☞ ✳ ⛟ ⊙ 🟦 🐾 WiFi ♲ 🄕
Services: ⊟ 🗄 🍴 ⊘ Ⓣ 🍴 🛒 ⇞ ↯
Within 3 miles: ↓ ✗ 🟦 ⛳ ◎ 🄱 🄱 U

Notes: No noise after mdnt. Dogs must be kept on leads. Crazy golf.

MEVAGISSEY — Map 2 SX04

See also Gorran & Pentewan

AA CAMPING CARD SITE

PREMIER PARK

▶▶▶▶▶ 91% Seaview International Holiday Park

(SW990412)

Boswinger PL26 6LL
☎ 01726 843425 📠 01726 843358
e-mail: holidays@seaviewinternational.com
web: www.seaviewinternational.com
dir: From St Austell take B3273 signed Mevagissey. Turn right before entering village. Follow brown tourist signs to site

* 🚐 £6-£58 🚐 £6-£58 ▲ £6-£58

Open Mar-Oct (rs Late May-Early Sep swimming pool opens late)

Last arrival 21.00hrs Last departure 10.00hrs

An attractive holiday park set in a beautiful environment overlooking Veryan Bay, with colourful landscaping, including attractive flowers and shrubs. It continues to offer an outstanding

continued

MEVAGISSEY ***continued***

holiday experience, with its luxury family pitches, super toilet facilities, takeaway, shop and static caravans for holiday hire. The beach and sea are just half a mile away. 28 acre site. 201 touring pitches. 28 hardstandings. 8 seasonal pitches. Caravan pitches. Motorhome pitches. Tent pitches. 35 statics.

Seaview International Holiday Park

AA Pubs & Restaurants nearby: The Ship Inn, Mevagissey 01726 843324

Leisure: 🏊 🛝 🎾 ⚽ 🎱

Facilities: 🛁 🚿 🪒 💨 ❄ ♿ 🏪 🧺 🐕 📶 ♻ ℹ

Services: 🔌 🧺 🔒 🥬 [T] 🍴 🛒 🚐 🍦

Within 3 miles: ⛵ 🎣 ◎ 🏄 🏪 🧺

Notes: Restrictions on certain dog breeds. Crazy golf, volleyball, badminton, scuba diving.

see advert on page 85

MULLION

Places to visit

Trevarno Estate Garden & Museum of Gardening, HELSTON 01326 574274 www.trevarno.co.uk

Goonhilly Satellite Earth Station Experience, HELSTON 0800 679593 www.goonhilly.bt.com

Great for kids: National Seal Sanctuary, GWEEK 0871 423 2110 www.sealsanctuary.co.uk

MULLION Map 2 SW61

76% Mullion Holiday Park *(SW699182)*

SILVER

Ruan Minor TR12 7LJ

☎ 0844 335 3756 & 01326 240428

📠 01326 241141

e-mail: touringandcamping@parkdeanholidays.com

web: www.parkdeantouring.com

dir: *A30 onto A39 through Truro towards Falmouth. A394 to Helston, A3083 for The Lizard. Site 7m on left*

🚐 🚗 ⛺

Open Apr-Oct (rs 17 May-20 Sep outdoor pool open)

Last arrival 22.00hrs Last departure 10.00hrs

A comprehensively-equipped leisure park geared mainly for self-catering holidays, and set close to the sandy beaches, coves and fishing villages on The Lizard peninsula. There is plenty of on-site entertainment for all ages, with indoor and outdoor swimming pools and a bar and grill. 49 acre site. 69 touring pitches. 9 hardstandings. Caravan pitches. Motorhome pitches. Tent pitches. 305 statics.

AA Pubs & Restaurants nearby: The Halzephron Inn, Gunwalloe 01326 240406

Leisure: 🏊 🏊 🛝 👋 ⚽ 🎱 📺 🎭

Facilities: 🚿 🪒 💨 ❄ ♿ ☎ 🏪 🧺 🐕 📶 💻 ♻ ℹ

Services: 🔌 🧺 🍺 🔒 🥬 🍴 🛒 🚐

Within 3 miles: ⛳ 🎣 ◎ 🏄 🏪 🧺 🐎

Notes: Dogs must be kept on leads. Scuba diving, football pitch, surf & cycle hire, multi-sports court.

see advert in preliminary section

►►► 75% 'Franchis' Holiday Park *(SW698203)*

BRONZE

Cury Cross Lanes TR12 7AZ

☎ 01326 240301

e-mail: enquiries@franchis.co.uk

web: www.franchis.co.uk

dir: *Exit A3083 on left 0.5m past Wheel Inn PH, between Helston & The Lizard*

* 🚐 £15-£18 🚗 £15-£18 ⛺ £13-£18

Open Apr-Oct

Last arrival 20.00hrs Last departure 10.30hrs

A grassy site surrounded by hedges and coppices, and divided into two paddocks for tourers, in an ideal position for exploring the Lizard Peninsula. The pitches are a mixture of level and slightly sloping. 16 acre site. 70 touring pitches. Caravan pitches. Motorhome pitches. Tent pitches. 12 statics.

AA Pubs & Restaurants nearby: The Halzephron Inn, Gunwalloe 01326 240406

Facilities: 🚿 🪒 ❄ 🏪 🐕 📶 ♻ ℹ

Services: 🔌 🧺 🔒 🥬 [T] 🛏

Within 3 miles: ⛳ ⛵ 🎣 🏪 🧺 🐎

Notes: Dogs must be kept on leads. Woodland walks.

NEWQUAY

See also Rejerrah

Places to visit

Blue Reef Aquarium, NEWQUAY 01637 878134 www.bluereefaquarium.co.uk

Newquay Zoo, NEWQUAY 0844 474 2244 www.newquayzoo.org.uk

Great for kids: Dairy Land Farm World, NEWQUAY 01872 510246 www.dairylandfarmworld.com

LEISURE: 🏊 Indoor swimming pool 🏊 Outdoor swimming pool 🛝 Children's playground 👋 Kid's club 🎾 Tennis court 🎱 Games room 📺 Separate TV room ⛳ 9/18 hole golf course ⛵ Boats for hire 🎬 Cinema 🎭 Entertainment 🎣 Fishing ◎ Mini golf 🏄 Watersports 🏋 Gym ⚽ Sports field **Spa** 🐎 Stables
FACILITIES: 🛁 Bath 🚿 Shower 🪒 Electric shaver 💨 Hairdryer ❄ Ice Pack Facility ♿ Disabled facilities ☎ Public telephone 🏪 Shop on site or within 200yds 🚚 Mobile shop (calls at least 5 days a week) 🍖 BBQ area 🧺 Picnic area 📶 Wi-fi 💻 Internet access ♻ Recycling ℹ Tourist info 🐕 Dog exercise area

NEWQUAY
Map 2 SW86

AA CAMPING CARD SITE

87% Hendra Holiday Park

(SW833601)

TR8 4NY
☎ 01637 875778 📄 01637 879017
e-mail: enquiries@hendra-holidays.com
dir: *A30 onto A392 signed Newquay. At Quintrell Downs over rdbt, signed Lane, site 0.5m on left*

* 🚐 £11.55-£20.35 ⛺ £11.55-£20.35
🛖 £11.55-£20.35

Open Apr-Oct (rs Apr-Spring BH, Sep-Oct outdoor pool closed)

Last arrival dusk Last departure 10.00hrs

A large complex with holiday statics and superb facilities including an indoor fun pool and an outdoor pool. There is a children's club for the over 6s, and evening entertainment during high season. The touring pitches are set amongst mature trees and shrubs, and some have fully-serviced facilities. All amenities are open to the public. 80 acre site. 548 touring pitches. 28 hardstandings. Caravan pitches. Motorhome pitches. Tent pitches. 283 statics. 1 wooden pod.

AA Pubs & Restaurants nearby: Lewinnick Lodge Bar & Restaurant, Pentire Headland, Newquay 01637 878117

Leisure: 🏊🏄⛰️🎣🎠🎱🎵

Facilities: 🅿️☉🍴✳️♿🕙🏧🔥🎯 WiFi 🖥️ ♻️ ⓘ

Services: 🔌🗑️🍷🛢🚿🚽🍴🎪👶♿

Within 3 miles: 🚶🎣♨️🅿️◎⛳🎣🏪🛒⛵

Notes: Families and couples only. Solarium, fish bar, train rides.

see advert on page 92

 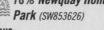 **78%** *Newquay Holiday Park* (SW853626)

TR8 4HS
☎ 0844 335 3756 📄 01637 850818
e-mail: touringandcamping@parkdeanholidays.com
web: www.parkdeantouring.com
dir: *From Bodmin on A30, under low bridge, right towards RAF St Mawgan. Take A3059 towards Newquay, site past Treloy Golf Club*

* 🚐 £10-£42 ⛺ £10-£42 🛖 £10-£41

Open Mar-Oct (rs May-19 Sep outdoor pool complex open)

Last arrival 21.00hrs Last departure 10.00hrs

A well-maintained park with a wide range of indoor and outdoor activities. A children's playground and bar and grill enhance the facilities, and the club and bars offer quality entertainment. Three heated outdoor pools and a giant waterslide are very popular. 60 acre site. 53 touring pitches. 10 hardstandings. Caravan pitches. Motorhome pitches. Tent pitches. 312 statics.

AA Pubs & Restaurants nearby: Lewinnick Lodge Bar & Restaurant, Pentire Headland, Newquay 01637 878117

Leisure: 🏄⛰️🎣🎱🎵

Facilities: 🅿️☉🍴✳️♿🕙🏧🔥 WiFi

Services: 🔌🗑️🍷🛢🚿🚽🍴♿🎪🚿

Within 3 miles: 🚶🎣🅿️◎🏪🛒⛵

Notes: Pool room, family entertainment, children's clubs.

see advert in preliminary section

▶▶▶▶ **82% Trencreek Holiday Park**
(SW828609)

Hillcrest, Higher Trencreek TR8 4NS
☎ 01637 874210 📄 01637 879526
e-mail: trencreek@btconnect.com
dir: *A392 to Quintrell Downs, right towards Newquay, left at 2 mini-rdbts into Trevenson Rd to site*

* 🚐 £11.30-£17.90 ⛺ £11.30-£17.90
🛖 £11.30-£17.90

Open Whit-mid Sep

Last arrival 22.00hrs Last departure noon

An attractively landscaped park in the village of Trencreek, with modern toilet facilities of a very high standard. Two well-stocked fishing lakes, and evening entertainment in the licensed clubhouse, are extra draws. Located about two miles from Newquay with its beaches and surfing. 10 acre site. 194 touring pitches. 8 hardstandings. Caravan pitches. Motorhome pitches. Tent pitches. 6 statics.

AA Pubs & Restaurants nearby: Lewinnick Lodge Bar & Restaurant, Pentire Headland, Newquay 01637 878117

Leisure: 🏄⛰️🎣🎱

Facilities: 🅿️☉🍴✳️♿🕙🏧🔥ⓘ

Services: 🔌🗑️🍷🛢🚿🚽🍴🎪👶🚿

Within 3 miles: 🚶🎣♨️🅿️◎⛳🎣🏪🛒⛵

Notes: 🏠🐕 Families and couples only. Free coarse fishing.

SERVICES: 🔌 Electric hook up 🗑️ Launderette 🍷 Licensed bar 🛢 Calor Gas ⊘ Camping Gaz 🅃 Toilet fluid 🍴 Café/Restaurant 🍔 Fast Food/Takeaway 🔋 Battery charging 👶 Baby care 🚿 Motorvan service point
ABBREVIATIONS: BH/bank hols-bank holidays Etr-Easter Whit-Whitsun dep-departure fr-from hrs-hours m-mile mdnt-midnight rdbt-roundabout rs-restricted service wk-week wknd-weekend 🚫 No credit cards 🚫 No dogs
See page 7 for details of the AA Camping Card Scheme

NEWQUAY *continued*

AA CAMPING CARD SITE

▶▶▶▶ 79% Treloy Touring Park *(SW858625)*

SILVER

TR8 4JN
☎ 01637 872063 & 876279 🖹 01637 872063
e-mail: treloy.tp@btconnect.com
web: www.treloy.co.uk
dir: *Off A3059 (St Columb Major-Newquay road)*

🚐 🚙 ⚠

Open May-15 Sep (rs Sep pool, takeaway, shop & bar)

Last arrival 21.00hrs Last departure 10.00hrs

An attractive site with fine countryside views, that is within easy reach of resorts and beaches. The pitches are set in four paddocks with mainly level but some slightly sloping grassy areas. Maintenance and cleanliness are very high. 18 acre site. 223 touring pitches. 24 hardstandings. Caravan pitches. Motorhome pitches. Tent pitches.

AA Pubs & Restaurants nearby: Lewinnick Lodge Bar & Restaurant, Pentire Headland, Newquay 01637 878117

Leisure: 🏊 ⚲ ⬇ ⚽ 🎱 🏓 🎪

Facilities: 🚿 ⊙ ⌷ ✳ ⚡ 🕐 🛁 🎣 WiFi ♻ ❶

Services: 🔌 ⭕ 🍺 🛢 🚿 🔧 🇹 🍴 🔋 ♿ ⚓

Within 3 miles: ⬇ 🎿 🎏 🎯 ⊙ 🛥 🐟 🎣 ♾ ⛵

Notes: Concessionary green fees for golf, entertainment.
see advert on page 90

▶▶▶▶ 78% *Porth Beach Tourist Park (SW834629)*

Porth TR7 3NH
☎ 01637 876531 🖹 01637 871227
e-mail: info@porthbeach.co.uk
dir: *1m NE off B3276 towards Padstow*

🚐 🚙 ⚠

Open Mar-Nov

Last arrival 18.00hrs Last departure 10.00hrs

This attractive, popular park offers level, grassy pitches in neat and tidy surroundings. A well-run site set in meadowland and adjacent to sea and a fine sandy beach. 6 acre site. 200 touring pitches. 19 hardstandings. Caravan pitches. Motorhome pitches. Tent pitches. 18 statics.

AA Pubs & Restaurants nearby: Lewinnick Lodge Bar & Restaurant, Pentire Headland, Newquay 01637 878117

Leisure: 🏔

Facilities: 🚿 ⊙ ⌷ ⚡ 🕐 🛁

Services: 🔌 ⭕ 🛢 🚿 🔧 🇹 🍴 🔋 ⚓

Within 3 miles: ⬇ 🎿 ⛵ 🎯 ⊙ 🛥 🐟 🎣 ♾ ⛵

Notes: Families and couples only.
see advert on page 90

▶▶▶▶ 75% Trenance Holiday Park *(SW818612)*

Edgcumbe Av TR7 2JY
☎ 01637 873447 🖹 01637 852677
e-mail: enquiries@trenanceholidaypark.co.uk
dir: *Exit A3075 near viaduct. Site by boating lake rdbt*

* 🚐 £17-£20 🚙 £17-£20 ⚠ £16-£19

Open 26 May-Oct

Last arrival 22.00hrs Last departure 10.00hrs

A mainly static park popular with tenters, close to Newquay's vibrant nightlife, and serving excellent breakfasts and takeaways. Set on high ground in an urban area of town, with cheerful owners and clean facilities. 12 acre site. 50 touring pitches. Caravan pitches. Motorhome pitches. Tent pitches. 190 statics.

AA Pubs & Restaurants nearby: Lewinnick Lodge Bar & Restaurant, Pentire Headland, Newquay 01637 878117

Leisure: ⚲

Facilities: 🚿 ⊙ ✳ ⚡ 🕐 🛁 ♻ ❶

Services: 🔌 ⭕ 🛢 🚿 🇹 🍴 🔋 ♿

Within 3 miles: ⬇ 🎿 🎏 🎯 ⊙ 🛥 🐟 🎣 ♾ ⛵

Notes: No pets.

▶▶▶ 80% Trebellan Park *(SW790571)*

Cubert TR8 5PY
☎ 01637 830522 🖹 01637 830522
e-mail: enquiries@trebellan.co.uk
dir: *4m S of Newquay, turn W off A3075 at Cubert sign. Left in 0.75m onto unclass road*

* 🚐 £17.50-£25 🚙 £17.50-£25 ⚠ £13-£20

Open May-Oct

Last arrival 21.00hrs Last departure 10.00hrs

A terraced grassy rural park within a picturesque valley with views of Cubert Common, and adjacent to the Smuggler's Den, a 16th-century thatched inn. This park has three well-stocked coarse

fishing lakes on site. 8 acre site. 150 touring pitches. Caravan pitches. Motorhome pitches. Tent pitches. 7 statics.

AA Pubs & Restaurants nearby: Lewinnick Lodge Bar & Restaurant, Pentire Headland, Newquay 01637 878117

Leisure: 🏊 🏔 🖵

Facilities: 🚿 ⊙ ⌷ ✳ ⚡ 🕐 🛁 🎣

Services: 🔌 ⭕ ⚓

Within 3 miles: ⬇ 🎏 ⊙ 🛥 🐟 🎣 ♾ ⛵

Notes: Families and couples only.

▶▶▶ 79% Trethiggey Touring Park *(SW846596)*

GOLD

Quintrell Downs TR8 4QR
☎ 01637 877672 🖹 01637 879706
e-mail: enquiries@trethiggey.co.uk
dir: *A30 onto A392 signed Newquay at Quintrell Downs rdbt, left onto A3058, pass Newquay Pearl centre. Site 0.5m on left*

* 🚐 £11.10-£17.90 🚙 £11.10-£17.90 ⚠ £11.10-£17.90

Open Mar-Dec

Last arrival 22.00hrs Last departure 10.30hrs

A family-owned park in a rural setting that is ideal for touring this part of Cornwall. It is pleasantly divided into paddocks with maturing trees and shrubs, and offers coarse fishing and tackle hire. 15 acre site. 145 touring pitches. 35 hardstandings. Caravan pitches. Motorhome pitches. Tent pitches. 12 statics.

AA Pubs & Restaurants nearby: Lewinnick Lodge Bar & Restaurant, Pentire Headland, Newquay 01637 878117

Leisure: 🏔 ⚲ 🖵

Facilities: 🛒 🚿 ⊙ ⌷ ✳ ⚡ 🕐 🛁 🎣 🔧 WiFi 🖥 ♻ ❶

Services: 🔌 ⭕ 🍺 🛢 🚿 🇹 🍴 🔋 ♿ ⚓

Within 3 miles: ⬇ 🎿 🎏 🎯 ⊙ 🛥 🐟 🎣 ♾ ⛵

Notes: No noise after mdnt. Off licence, recreation field.
see advert on page 91

SERVICES: 🔌 Electric hook up 🅱 Launderette 🍺 Licensed bar 🛢 Calor Gas ⚗ Camping Gaz 🇹 Toilet fluid 🍴 Café/Restaurant 🍟 Fast Food/Takeaway 🔋 Battery charging 🚼 Baby care ♿ Motorvan service point
ABBREVIATIONS: BH/bank hols-bank holidays Etr-Easter Whit-Whitsun dep-departure fr-from hrs-hours m-mile mdnt-midnight rdbt-roundabout rs-restricted service wk-week wknd-weekend ⊛ No credit cards ⊗ No dogs
See page 7 for details of the AA Camping Card Scheme

NEWQUAY *continued*

▶▶▶ 77% Riverside Holiday Park

(SW829592)

Gwills Ln TR8 4PE
☎ 01637 873617 📄 01637 877051
e-mail: info@riversideholidaypark.co.uk
web: www.riversideholidaypark.co.uk
dir: *A30 onto A392 signed Newquay. At Quintrell Downs cross rdbt signed Lane. 2nd left in 0.5m onto unclass road signed Gwills. Site in 400yds*

🚐 🚉 ⊼

Riverside Holdiay Park

Open Mar-Oct

Last arrival 22.00hrs Last departure 10.00hrs

A sheltered valley beside a river in a quiet location is the idyllic setting for this lightly wooded park. The fairly simple facilities continue to be upgraded, and the park caters for families and couples only. The site is close to the wide variety of attractions offered by this major resort and the park has self-catering lodges, cabins and static vans for hire. 11 acre site. 65 touring pitches. Caravan pitches. Motorhome pitches. Tent pitches. 65 statics.

AA Pubs & Restaurants nearby: Lewinnick Lodge Bar & Restaurant, Pentire Headland, Newquay 01637 878117

Leisure: 🏊 🎠 🎱 🖵
Facilities: 🖍 ☺ ⚡ ✳ 🖒 ⓒ 🗟 🛈
Services: 🚐 🗟 🍴 🛢 🗑 Ⓣ 🛆 🛒
Within 3 miles: 🎣 🚣 🎬 ♪ 🐟 ◎ 🖄 🖹 🗟 ∪

Notes: Families and couples only. Dogs must be kept on leads.

OTTERHAM	Map 2 SX19

Places to visit
Launceston Castle, LAUNCESTON 01566 772365
www.english-heritage.org.uk

Launceston Steam Railway, LAUNCESTON
01566 775665 www.launcestonsr.co.uk

Great for kids: Tamar Otter & Wildlife Centre, LAUNCESTON 01566 785646
www.tamarotters.co.uk

▶▶▶ 79% *St Tinney Farm Holidays* *(SX169906)*

PL32 9TA
☎ 01840 261274
e-mail: info@st-tinney.co.uk
dir: *Signed 1m off A39 via unclass road signed Otterham*

🚐 🚉 ⊼

Open Etr-Oct

Last arrival 21.00hrs Last departure 10.00hrs

A family-run farm site in a rural area with nature trails, lakes, valleys and offering complete seclusion. Visitors are free to walk around the farmland lakes and lose themselves in the countryside. 34 acre site. 20 touring pitches. Caravan pitches. Motorhome pitches. Tent pitches. 15 statics.

AA Pubs & Restaurants nearby: The Wellington Hotel, Boscastle 01840 250202

Leisure: 🚣 🎠 🎣
Facilities: 🖍 ☺ ⚡ ✳ 🗟 🛱 Wi-fi
Services: 🚐 🗟 🍴 🛢 🗑 Ⓣ 🍴 🍺
Within 3 miles: 🖉 🗟

Notes: Coarse fishing.

PADSTOW	Map 2 SW97

See also Rumford

Places to visit
Prideaux Place, PADSTOW 01841 532411
www.prideauxplace.co.uk

PREMIER PARK

▶▶▶▶▶ 87% Padstow Touring Park *(SW913738)*

PL28 8LE
☎ 01841 532061
e-mail: mail@padstowtouringpark.co.uk
dir: *1m S of Padstow, on E side of A389 (Padstow to Wadebridge road)*

✱ 🚐 £14-£22 🚉 £14-£22 ⊼ £10-£18

Open all year

Last arrival 21.00hrs Last departure 11.00hrs

Improvements continue at this popular park set in open countryside above the quaint fishing town of Padstow, which can be approached by footpath directly from the park. It is divided into paddocks by maturing bushes and hedges to create a peaceful and relaxing holiday atmosphere. Improvements in 2011 included more hardstanding pitches, an improved entrance, refurbished toilets, better landscaping, and a new dishwashing area. 13.5 acre site. 150 touring pitches. 27 hardstandings. Caravan pitches. Motorhome pitches. Tent pitches.

AA Pubs & Restaurants nearby: The Cornish Arms, St Merryn 01841 532700

Paul Ainsworth at No 6, Padstow 01841 532093
Rosel & Co, Padstow 01841 521289

Leisure: 🎠
Facilities: 🖍 ☺ ⚡ ✳ 🖒 🗟 🛱 Wi-fi 💻 ♻ 🛈
Services: 🚐 🗟 🛢 🗑 Ⓣ 🍴 🍺 🍴
Within 3 miles: 🎣 🚣 🖉 ◎ 🖄 🗟 🗟 ∪

Notes: No groups, no noise after 22.00hrs. Dogs must be kept on leads.

▶▶▶ 76% Dennis Cove Camping

(SW919743)

Dennis Ln PL28 8DR
☎ 01841 532349
e-mail: denniscove@freeuk.com
dir: *Approach Padstow on A389, right at Tesco into Sarah's Ln, 2nd right to Dennis Ln, follow to site at end*

✱ 🚐 £15-£23 🚉 £15-£23 ⊼ £15-£23

Open Apr-end Sep

Last arrival 21.00hrs Last departure 11.00hrs

Set in meadowland with mature trees, this site overlooks Padstow Bay, with access to the Camel Estuary and the nearby beach. The centre of town is just a 10-minute walk away, and bike hire is

---

LEISURE: 🏊 Indoor swimming pool 🏊 Outdoor swimming pool 🎠 Children's playground 🎣 Kid's club 🎾 Tennis court 🎱 Games room 🖵 Separate TV room
🏌 9/18 hole golf course 🚣 Boats for hire 🎬 Cinema ♪ Entertainment 🎣 Fishing ◎ Mini golf 🏄 Watersports 🏋 Gym ⚽ Sports field Spa ∪ Stables
FACILITIES: 🛁 Bath 🚿 Shower ☺ Electric shaver ✳ Hairdryer ✱ Ice Pack Facility ♿ Disabled facilities ☎ Public telephone 🗟 Shop on site or within 200yds
🛒 Mobile shop (calls at least 5 days a week) 🍴 BBQ area 🛱 Picnic area Wi-fi Wi-fi 💻 Internet access ♻ Recycling 🛈 Tourist info 🐕 Dog exercise area

available on site, with the famous Camel Trail beginning right outside. 3 acre site. 42 touring pitches. Caravan pitches. Motorhome pitches. Tent pitches.

AA Pubs & Restaurants nearby: Margot's, Padstow 01841 533441

The Seafood Restaurant, Padstow 01841 532700

Facilities: ⬤ ⬤ ⬤ ⬤ ⬤ ⬤

Services: ⬤ ⬤ ⬤ ⬤ ⬤

Within 3 miles: ⬤ ⬤ ⬤ ⬤ ⬤ ⬤ ⬤ ⬤ ⬤

Notes: ⬤ Arrivals from 14.00hrs. Dogs must be kept on leads.

►►► 74% Padstow Holiday Park

(SW009073)

Cliffdowne PL28 8LB
☎ **01841 532289** 📠 **01841 532289**
e-mail: mail@padstowholidaypark.co.uk
dir: *Exit A39 onto either A389 or B3274 to Padstow. Site signed 1.5m before Padstow*

* ⬤ £10-£18 ⬤ £10-£18 ⬤ £10-£18

Open Mar-Dec

Last arrival 17.00hrs Last departure noon

A mainly static park with some touring pitches in a small paddock and others in an open field. This quiet holiday site is only a mile from Padstow and can be reached by a footpath. Three holiday letting caravans are available. 5.5 acre site. 27 touring pitches. Caravan pitches. Motorhome pitches. Tent pitches. 74 statics.

AA Pubs & Restaurants nearby: The Cornish Arms, St Merryn 01841 532700

Leisure: ⬤

Facilities: ⬤ ⬤ ⬤ ⬤ ⬤ ⬤ ⬤ ⬤ ⬤ ⬤

Services: ⬤ ⬤ ⬤ ⬤ ⬤

Within 3 miles: ⬤ ⬤ ⬤ ⬤ ⬤ ⬤ ⬤ ⬤ ⬤

Notes: ⬤

PENTEWAN   Map 2 SX04

Places to visit

The Lost Gardens of Heligan, PENTEWAN 01726 845100 www.heligan.com

Charlestown Shipwreck & Heritage Centre, ST AUSTELL 01726 69897 www.shipwreckcharlestown.com

Great for kids: Eden Project, ST AUSTELL 01726 811911 www.edenproject.com

---

 90% Pentewan Sands Holiday Park *(SX018468)*

PL26 6BT
☎ **01726 843485** 📠 **01726 844142**
e-mail: info@pentewan.co.uk
dir: *On B3273 4m S of St Austell*

⬤ ⬤ ⬤

Open Apr-Oct

Last arrival 22.00hrs Last departure 10.30hrs

A large holiday park with a wide range of amenities, set on grassy pitches beside a private beach where plenty of aquatic activities are available. A short stroll leads to the pretty village of Pentewan, and other attractions are a short drive away. The very impressive 'Seahorse Complex' comprises swimming pools, a well-stocked bar and restaurant, with a choice of dining options, a kids' zone, a fully-equipped gym, and outside terraces with stunning sea views. 32 acre site. 500 touring pitches. Caravan pitches. Motorhome pitches. Tent pitches. 120 statics.

AA Pubs & Restaurants nearby: The Ship Inn, Mevagissey 01726 843324

Leisure: ⬤ ⬤ ⬤ ⬤ ⬤ ⬤ ⬤

Facilities: ⬤ ⬤ ⬤ ⬤ ⬤ ⬤ ⬤ ⬤ ⬤ ⬤ ⬤ ⬤ ⬤

Services: ⬤ ⬤ ⬤ ⬤ ⬤ ⬤ ⬤ ⬤ ⬤ ⬤ ⬤

Within 3 miles: ⬤ ⬤ ⬤ ⬤ ⬤ ⬤ ⬤ ⬤

Notes: ⬤ No jet skis. Cycles, boat launch, water sports, caravan store.

PREMIER PARK

►►►►► 84% Sun Valley Holiday Park

(SX005486)

Pentewan Rd PL26 6DJ
☎ **01726 843266** & **844393** 📠 **01726 843266**
e-mail: reception@sunvalley-holidays.co.uk
dir: *From St Austell take B3273 towards Mevagissey. Site 2m on right*

* ⬤ £15-£32.50 ⬤ £15-£32.50 ⬤ £15-£32.50

Open all year (rs Winter pool, restaurant & touring field)

Last arrival 22.00hrs Last departure 10.30hrs

In a picturesque valley amongst woodland, this neat park is kept to a high standard. The extensive amenities include tennis courts, indoor swimming pool, licensed clubhouse and

---

restaurant. The sea is just a mile away, and can be accessed via a footpath and cycle path along the river bank. 20 acre site. 29 touring pitches. 13 hardstandings. Caravan pitches. Motorhome pitches. Tent pitches. 75 statics.

AA Pubs & Restaurants nearby: The Crown Inn, St Ewe 01726 843322

Leisure: ⬤ ⬤ ⬤ ⬤ ⬤ ⬤

Facilities: ⬤ ⬤ ⬤ ⬤ ⬤ ⬤ ⬤ ⬤ ⬤ ⬤ ⬤ ⬤

Services: ⬤ ⬤ ⬤ ⬤ ⬤ ⬤ ⬤ ⬤ ⬤ ⬤

Within 3 miles: ⬤ ⬤ ⬤ ⬤ ⬤ ⬤ ⬤ ⬤

Notes: Certain pet restrictions apply, please contact the site for details. No motorised scooters, skateboards or bikes at night. Dogs must be kept on leads. Pets' corner, bike hire, outdoor & indoor play areas.

►►► 82% *Heligan Woods* *(SW998470)*

PL26 6BT
☎ **01726 842714** & **844414** 📠 **01726 844142**
e-mail: info@pentewan.co.uk
dir: *From A390 take B3273 for Mevagissey at x-roads signed 'No caravans beyond this point'. Right onto unclass road towards Gorran, site 0.75m on left*

⬤ ⬤ ⬤

Open 16 Jan-26 Nov

Last arrival 22.30hrs Last departure 10.30hrs

A pleasant peaceful park adjacent to the Lost Gardens of Heligan, with views over St Austell Bay, and well-maintained facilities. Guests can also use the extensive amenities at the sister park, Pentewan Sands, and there's a footpath with direct access to Heligan Gardens. 12 acre site. 89 touring pitches. 24 hardstandings. 3 seasonal pitches. Caravan pitches. Motorhome pitches. Tent pitches. 17 statics.

AA Pubs & Restaurants nearby: Austell's, St Austell 01726 813888

Leisure: ⬤

Facilities: ⬤ ⬤ ⬤ ⬤ ⬤ ⬤ ⬤

Services: ⬤ ⬤ ⬤ ⬤ ⬤ ⬤

Within 3 miles: ⬤ ⬤ ⬤ ⬤ ⬤ ⬤ ⬤ ⬤

PENZANCE

See also Rosudgeon

Places to visit

Trengwainton Garden, PENZANCE 01736 363148 www.nationaltrust.org.uk

St Michael's Mount, MARAZION 01736 710507 www.stmichaelsmount.co.uk

---

►►►► 77% Higher Chellew Holiday Park (SW496353)

PENZANCE   Map 2 SW43

Higher Trenowin, Nancledra TR20 8BD
☎ 01736 364532 & 07818 025884
e-mail: higherchellew@btinternet.com
web: www.higherchellewcamping.co.uk
dir: From A30 turn towards St Ives, left at mini-rdbt towards Nancledra. Left at B3311 junct, through Nancledra. Site 0.5m on left

🚐 £10-£16 🚙 £10-£16 ▲ £10-£16

Open Fri before Etr-Oct

Last departure 10.30hrs

A small rural park quietly located just four miles from the golden beaches at St Ives, and a similar distance from Penzance. This well sheltered park occupies an elevated location, and all pitches are level. 1.25 acre site. 25 touring pitches. Caravan pitches. Motorhome pitches. Tent pitches.

AA Pubs & Restaurants nearby: Turk's Head Inn, Penzance 01736 363093

The Navy Inn, Penzance 01736 333232

Facilities: 🇫 ⊙ 🏳 ✳ 🔥 🇸 ♻ ❶

Services: 🚿 🔧

Within 3 miles: 🏪 🔧 ∪

Notes: ⊗ No pets. Microwave & freezer available. Farm shop opposite.

►►► 76% Bone Valley Caravan & Camping Park (SW472316)

Heamoor TR20 8UJ
☎ 01736 360313 📠 01736 360313
e-mail: wardmandie@yahoo.co.uk
dir: Exit A30 at Heamoor/Madron rdbt. 4th on right into Josephs Lane. 800yds left into Bone Valley. Entrance 200yds on left

🚐 🚙 ▲

Open all year

Last arrival 22.00hrs Last departure 10.00hrs

A compact grassy park on the outskirts of Penzance, with well maintained facilities. It is divided into paddocks by mature hedges, and a small stream runs alongside. 1 acre site. 17 touring pitches. 6 hardstandings. Caravan pitches. Motorhome pitches. Tent pitches. 3 statics.

AA Pubs & Restaurants nearby: Dolphin Tavern, Penzance 01736 364106

Harris's Restaurant, Penzance 01736 364408

Leisure: ▭

Facilities: ⊷ 🇫 ⊙ 🏳 ✳ 🔥 🇸 🛒 �🏦 wifi

Services: 🚿 🔧 🔩 T

Within 3 miles: ⌀ ⊞ 🏪 🔧 ∪

Notes: Dogs must be kept on leads. Campers' lounge, kitchen & laundry room.

PERRANPORTH   Map 2 SW75

See also Rejerrah

Places to visit

Royal Cornwall Museum, TRURO 01872 272205
www.royalcornwallmuseum.org.uk

Trerice, TRERICE 01637 875404 www.nationaltrust.org.uk

Great for kids: Blue Reef Aquarium, NEWQUAY 01637 878134 www.bluereefaquarium.co.uk

76% Perran Sands Holiday Park (SW767554)

TR6 0AQ
☎ 0871 231 0871 📠 01872 571158
e-mail: perransands@haven.com
dir: A30 onto B3285 towards Perranporth. Site on right before descent on hill into Perranporth

🚐 🚙 ▲

Open mid Mar-Oct (rs mid Mar-May & Sep-Oct some facilities may be reduced)

Last arrival 22.00hrs Last departure 10.00hrs

LEISURE: 🏊 Indoor swimming pool 🏊 Outdoor swimming pool 🄰 Children's playground 🎣 Kid's club 🎾 Tennis court Games room ▭ Separate TV room 🏌 9/18 hole golf course ⛵ Boats for hire 🎬 Cinema 🎵 Entertainment 🎣 Fishing ◉ Mini golf 🏄 Watersports 🏋 Gym ⊙ Sports field Spa ∪ Stables
FACILITIES: ⊷ Bath 🚿 Shower ⊙ Electric shaver 🏳 Hairdryer ✳ Ice Pack Facility 🔥 Disabled facilities 🕐 Public telephone 🏦 Shop on site or within 200yds 🛒 Mobile shop (calls at least 5 days a week) 🍖 BBQ area 🪑 Picnic area wifi Wi-fi 🖥 Internet access ♻ Recycling ❶ Tourist info 🐕 Dog exercise area

Situated amid 500 acres of protected dune grassland, and with a footpath through to the surf and three miles of golden sandy beach, this lively park is set in a large village-style complex. It offers a complete range of on-site facilities and entertainment for all the family, which makes it an extremely popular park. 550 acre site. 360 touring pitches. 20 hardstandings. Caravan pitches. Motorhome pitches. Tent pitches. 600 statics.

AA Pubs & Restaurants nearby: Driftwood Spars, St Agnes 01872 552428

Leisure: 🏊 🏊 ⛺ ✋ ⚽ ♫

Facilities: 🛁 🚿 🔌 ✳ ♿ ☎ $ Wi-fi ♻ ℹ

Services: 🔌 🧺 🍺 🔥 ⛽ 🍴 🍟 👶

Within 3 miles: ⚓ ⛳ ◎ 🚤 $ 🧺 U

Notes: Max 2 dogs per booking, certain dog breeds banned, no commercial vehicles, no bookings by persons under 21yrs unless a family booking.

see advert on opposite page

AA CAMPING CARD SITE

►►►► 80% Tollgate Farm Caravan & Camping Park *(SW768547)*

Budnick Hill TR6 0AD

☎ 01872 572130 & 0845 166 2126

e-mail: enquiries@tollgatefarm.co.uk

dir: *Exit A30 onto B3285 to Perranporth. Site on right 1.5m after Goonhavern*

🚐 🚗 ⛺

Open Etr-Sep

Last arrival 21.00hrs Last departure 11.00hrs

A quiet site in a rural location with spectacular coastal views. Pitches are divided into four paddocks sheltered and screened by mature hedges. Children will enjoy the play equipment and pets' corner. The three miles of sand at Perran Bay are just a walk away through the sand dunes, or by car it will be a three-quarter mile drive. 10 acre site. 102 touring pitches. 10 hardstandings. 12 seasonal pitches. Caravan pitches. Motorhome pitches. Tent pitches.

Tollgate Farm Caravan & Camping Park

AA Pubs & Restaurants nearby: Driftwood Spars, St Agnes 01872 552428

Leisure: ⛺ ⚽

Facilities: 🚿 ⊙ 🔌 ✳ ♿ ☎ $ ⛩ 🐕 Wi-fi ♻ ℹ

Services: 🔌 🧺 🔥 ⛽ [T] 🔋 🍟 ⛽

Within 3 miles: ⚓ 🚤 ⛩ ⛳ ◎ 🚤 $ 🧺 U

Notes: No large groups. Dogs must be kept on leads.

see advert below

AA CAMPING CARD SITE

►►► 80% Higher Golla Touring & Caravan Park *(SW756514)*

Penhallow TR4 9LZ

☎ 01872 573963 & 07800 558407

📠 01872 328635

e-mail: cornish.hair@btconnect.com

web: www.highergollatouringpark.co.uk

dir: *A30 onto B3284 towards Perranporth. (Straight on at junct with A3075). Approx 2m. Site signed on right*

🚐 £13-£20 🚗 £13-£20 ⛺ £9-£14

Last arrival 20.00hrs Last departure 10.30hrs

Extensive country views can be enjoyed from all pitches on this quietly located site, which now has high quality and immaculate toilet facilities. Every pitch has electricity and a water tap and this peaceful park is just two miles from Perranporth and its stunning beach. 1.5 acre site. 18 touring pitches. Caravan pitches. Motorhome pitches. Tent pitches. 2 statics.

Open Etr-mid Oct

continued

PERRANPORTH *continued*

AA Pubs & Restaurants nearby: Driftwood Spars, St Agnes 01872 552428

Facilities: ⚫⊙℮✳️🔥🎯🐕♻️ ❶

Services: ⚡🔌 T ↯

Within 3 miles: ↕️℘◎≋🔥🎯U

Notes: No kite flying, quiet between 21.00hrs-08.00hrs. Dogs must be kept on leads.

▶▶▶ 67% Perranporth Camping & Touring Park *(SW768542)*

Budnick Rd TR6 0DB

☎ 01872 572174   📠 01872 572174
dir: 0.5m E off B3285

* ⚐ £16-£22 ⚎ £16-£22 ▲ £16-£22

Open Whit-Sep (rs Etr & end Sep shop, swimming pool & club facilities closed)
Last arrival 23.00hrs Last departure noon

A mainly tenting site with few level pitches, located high above a fine sandy beach, which is much-frequented by surfers. The park is attractive to young people, and is set in a lively town on a spectacular part of the coast. 9 static caravans for holiday hire. 6 acre site. 120 touring pitches. 4 hardstandings. Caravan pitches. Motorhome pitches. Tent pitches. 9 statics.

Perranporth Camping & Touring Park

AA Pubs & Restaurants nearby: Driftwood Spars, St Agnes 01872 552428

Leisure: ≋ 𝘼 🔍 ⬜

Facilities: 🛁⚫⊙℮✳️♿🔥🎯❶

Services: ⚡🔌🍽️🛒🧼 T 🔌

Within 3 miles: ↕️≋℘◎≋🔥🎯U

Notes: No noise after 23.00hrs. Dogs must be kept on leads.

see advert below

POLPERRO Map 2 SX25

▶▶ 77% Great Kellow Farm Caravan & Camping Site *(SX201522)*

Lansallos PL13 2QL

☎ 01503 272387   📠 01503 272387
e-mail: kellow.farm@virgin.net
dir: From Looe to Pelynt. In Pelynt left at church follow Lansallos sign. Left at x-rds, 0.75m. At staggered x-rds left, follow site signs

⚐ ⚎ ▲

Open Mar-3 Jan

Last arrival 22.00hrs Last departure noon

Set on a high level grassy paddock with extensive views of Polperro Bay, this attractive site is on a working dairy and beef farm, and close to National Trust properties and gardens. It is situated in a very peaceful location close to the fishing village of Polperro. 3 acre site. 30 touring pitches. Caravan pitches. Motorhome pitches. Tent pitches. 10 statics.

AA Pubs & Restaurants nearby: Old Mill House Inn, Polperro 01503 272362

Barclay House, Looe 01503 262929

Facilities: ⚫⊙✳️🎯 **Services:** ⚡
Within 3 miles: ≋℘🔥 **Notes:** 🚫

POLRUAN
Map 2 SX15

AA CAMPING CARD SITE

►►► 84% Polruan Holidays-Camping & Caravanning *(SX133509)*

Polruan-by-Fowey PL23 1QH
☎ **01726 870263**
e-mail: polholiday@aol.com
web: www.polruanholidays.co.uk
dir: *A38 to Dobwalls, left onto A390 to East Taphouse. Left onto B3359. Right in 4.5m signed Polruan*

🚐 🚕 Å

Open Etr-Oct

Last arrival 21.00hrs Last departure noon

A very rural and quiet site in a lovely elevated position above the village, with good views of the sea. The River Fowey passenger ferry is close by, and the site has a good shop, and barbecues to borrow. 3 acre site. 47 touring pitches. 7 hardstandings. Caravan pitches. Motorhome pitches. Tent pitches. 10 statics.

AA Pubs & Restaurants nearby: Old Ferry Inn, Bodinnick 01726 870237

Leisure: ⚐

Facilities: 🏕☉🅿☀🕙🖎📶🛒♻ 𝓲

Services: 🔌🅶🔋⌀🅣🍴🔋

Within 3 miles: ≯𝓟⤓🔥🔵∪

Notes: No skateboards, rollerskates, bikes, water pistols or water bombs. Dogs must be on leads.

POLZEATH
Map 2 SW97

►►► 82% South Winds Caravan & Camping Park *(SW948790)*

Polzeath Rd PL27 6QU
☎ **01208 863267** 🖷 **01208 862080**
e-mail: info@southwindscamping.co.uk
web: www.polzeathcamping.co.uk
dir: *Exit B3314 onto unclass road signed Polzeath, site on right just past turn to New Polzeath*

* 🚐 £16-£38 🚕 £16-£38 Å £10-£36

Open May-mid Sep (rs mid Jul-end Aug Stepper Field open)

Last arrival 21.00hrs Last departure 10.30hrs

A peaceful site with beautiful sea and panoramic rural views, within walking distance of a golf complex, and just three quarters of a mile from beach and village. There's an impressive reception building, replete with tourist information, TV, settees and a range of camping spares. 16 acre site. 165 touring pitches. Caravan pitches. Motorhome pitches. Tent pitches.

South Winds Caravan & Camping Park

AA Pubs & Restaurants nearby: Restaurant Nathan Outlaw, Rock 01208 863394

Facilities: 🏕☉🅿☀🕙🖎📶🛒♻ 𝓲

Services: 🔌🅶🔋⌀🅣🔋⌄

Within 3 miles: ≯🔥𝓟◎🔵∪

Notes: Families & couples only. No disposable BBQs, no noise 23.00hrs-07.00hrs. Dogs must be kept on leads. Restaurant & farm shop adjacent.
see advert on page 102

►►► 82% Tristram Caravan & Camping Park *(SW936790)*

PL27 6TP
☎ **01208 862215** 🖷 **01208 862080**
e-mail: info@tristramcampsite.co.uk
web: www.polzeathcamping.co.uk
dir: *From B3314 onto unclassified road signed Polzeath. Through village, up hill, site 2nd right*

* 🚐 £24-£40 🚕 £24-£40 Å £12-£40

Open Mar-Nov (rs mid Sep reseeding the site)

Last arrival 21.00hrs Last departure 10.00hrs

An ideal family site, positioned on a gently sloping cliff with grassy pitches and glorious sea views, which are best enjoyed from the terraced premier pitches, or over lunch at the Salt Water Café adjacent to the reception/shop. There is direct, gated access to the beach, where surfing is very popular, and the park has a holiday bungalow for rent. The local amenities of the village are only a few hundred yards away. 10 acre site. 100 touring pitches. Caravan pitches. Motorhome pitches. Tent pitches.

AA Pubs & Restaurants nearby: Restaurant Nathan Outlaw, Rock 01208 863394

Facilities: 🏕☉🅿☀🕙🖎📶♻ 𝓲

Services: 🔌🅶🔋⌀🅣🍴🔋

Within 3 miles: ≯🔥🍴𝓟◎🔵∪

Notes: No ball games, no disposable BBQs, no noise between 23.00hrs-07.00hrs. Dogs must be kept on leads. Surf equipment hire.
see advert on page 102

PORTHTOWAN
Map 2 SW64

►►►► 90% Porthtowan Tourist Park *(SW693473)*

Mile Hill TR4 8TY
☎ **01209 890256**
e-mail: admin@porthtowantouristpark.co.uk
web: www.porthtowantouristpark.co.uk
dir: *Exit A30 at junct signed Redruth/Porthtowan. Take 3rd exit at rdbt. 2m, right at T-junct. Site on left at top of hill*

* 🚐 £9.25-£17 🚕 £9.25-£17 Å £9.25-£17

Open Apr-Sep

Last arrival 21.30hrs Last departure 11.00hrs

A neat, level grassy site on high ground above Porthtowan, with plenty of shelter from mature trees and shrubs. The superb toilet facilities considerably enhance the appeal of this peaceful rural park, which is almost midway between the small seaside resorts of Portreath and Porthtowan, with their beaches and surfing. 5 acre site. 80 touring pitches. 2 hardstandings. 8 seasonal pitches. Caravan pitches. Motorhome pitches. Tent pitches.

AA Pubs & Restaurants nearby: Driftwood Spars, St Agnes 01872 552428

Leisure: ⚐☺🎣

Facilities: 🏕☉🅿☀🕙🖎📶🛒♻ 𝓲

Services: 🔌🅶🔋⌀🅣🔋

Within 3 miles: ≯🔥𝓟🔵∪

Notes: No bikes or skateboards during Jul & Aug. Dogs must be kept on leads.

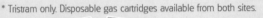

PORTHTOWAN *continued*

AA CAMPING CARD SITE

►►►► 71% Wheal Rose Caravan & Camping Park *(SW717449)*

Wheal Rose TR16 5DD
☎ 01209 891496
e-mail: whealrose@aol.com
dir: *Exit A30 at Scorrier sign, follow signs to Wheal Rose. Site 0.5m on left (Wheal Rose to Porthtowan road)*

* 🚐 £12-£17 🚎 £12-£17 ⛺ £12-£17

Open Mar-Dec

Last arrival 21.00hrs Last departure 11.00hrs

A quiet, peaceful park in a secluded valley setting, central for beaches and countryside, and two miles from the surfing beaches of Porthtowan. The friendly owners work hard to keep this park immaculate, with a bright toilet block and well-trimmed pitches. 6 acre site. 50 touring pitches. 6 hardstandings. Caravan pitches. Motorhome pitches. Tent pitches. 3 statics.

Leisure: ⚓ ⋒ ⊙ ⚄

Facilities: ⟋ ⊙ ℙ ☀ ⅙ ⓢ 🏠 ⧟ 🖥 ♻ ❶

Services: 🚐 ⓢ 🛢 ⌀ ⊤ 🔋

Within 3 miles: ⌿ ⊟ ℐ 🏄 🛇 🛒 ↺

Notes: 5mph speed limit, minimum noise after 23.00hrs, gates locked 23.00hrs. Dogs must be kept on leads.

PORTREATH   Map 2 SW64

Places to visit

East Pool Mine, POOL 01209 315027
www.nationaltrust.org.uk

►►► 87% Tehidy Holiday Park *(SW682432)*

GOLD

Harris Mill, Illogan TR16 4JQ
☎ 01209 216489   📄 01209 216489
e-mail: holiday@tehidy.co.uk
web: www.tehidy.co.uk
dir: *Exit A30 at Redruth/Portreath junct onto A3047 to 1st rdbt. Left onto B3300. At junct straight over signed Tehidy Holiday Park. Past Cornish Arms pub, site 800yds at bottom of hill on left*

* 🚐 £12-£19 🚎 £12-£19 ⛺ £12-£19

Open all year (rs Nov-Mar part of shower block & shop closed)

Last arrival 20.00hrs Last departure 10.00hrs

An attractive wooded location in a quiet rural area only two and half miles from popular beaches. Mostly level pitches on tiered ground, and the toilet facilities are bright and modern. Holiday static caravans for hire. 4.5 acre site. 18 touring pitches. 11 hardstandings. Caravan pitches. Motorhome pitches. Tent pitches. 32 statics.

AA Pubs & Restaurants nearby: The Basset Arms, Portreath 01209 842077

Leisure: ⋒ ⊙ ⚄ ▭

Facilities: ⟋ ⊙ ℙ ☀ ⅙ ⓢ 🏠 ⧟ ♻ ❶

Services: 🚐 ⓢ ⌀ ⊤ 🔋 🍼

Within 3 miles: ⌿ ⊹ ⊟ ℐ 🏄 🛇 🛒 ↺

Notes: No pets, no noise after 23.00hrs. Trampoline, off-licence.

see advert on page 94

PORTSCATHO   Map 2 SW83

Places to visit

St Mawes Castle, ST MAWES 01326 270526
www.english-heritage.org.uk

Trelissick Garden, TRELISSICK GARDEN 01872 862090 www.nationaltrust.org.uk

►►► 78% Trewince Farm Touring Park *(SW868339)*

TR2 5ET
☎ 01872 580430   📄 01872 580430
e-mail: info@trewincefarm.co.uk
dir: *From St Austell take A390 towards Truro. Left on B3287 to Tregony, following signs to St Mawes. At Trewithian, turn left to St Anthony. Site 0.75m past church*

* 🚐 fr £11.50 🚎 fr £11.50 ⛺ fr £11.50

Open May-Sep

Last arrival 23.00hrs Last departure 11.00hrs

A site on a working farm with spectacular sea views from its elevated position. There are many quiet golden sandy beaches close by, and boat launching facilities and mooring can be arranged at the nearby Percuil River Boatyard. The village of Portscatho with shops and pubs and attractive harbour is approximately one mile away. 3 acre site. 25 touring pitches. Caravan pitches. Motorhome pitches. Tent pitches.

AA Pubs & Restaurants nearby: The New Inn, Veryan 01872 501362

The Quarterdeck at The Nare, Veryan 01872 500000

Facilities: ⟋ ⊙ ℙ ☀ 🏠 ⧟ ♻ ❶

Services: 🚐 ⓢ 🔋

Within 3 miles: ⊹ ℐ 🏄 🛇 ↺

Notes: ⊘ Dogs must be kept on leads.

REDRUTH

Places to visit

East Pool Mine, POOL 01209 315027
www.nationaltrust.org.uk

Pendennis Castle, FALMOUTH 01326 316594
www.english-heritage.org.uk

Great for kids: National Maritime Museum Cornwall, FALMOUTH 01326 313388
www.nmmc.co.uk

SERVICES: 🚐 Electric hook up   ⓢ Launderette   🍷 Licensed bar   🛢 Calor Gas   ⌀ Camping Gaz   ⊤ Toilet fluid   🍽 Café/Restaurant   🍟 Fast Food/Takeaway   🔋 Battery charging   🍼 Baby care   ⚡ Motorvan service point
ABBREVIATIONS: BH/bank hols-bank holidays   Etr-Easter   Whit-Whitsun   dep-departure   fr-from   hrs-hours   m-mile   mdnt-midnight   rdbt-roundabout   rs-restricted service   wk-week
wknd-weekend   ⊘ No credit cards   ⊗ No dogs   See page 7 for details of the AA Camping Card Scheme

REDRUTH

Map 2 SW64

►►►► 85% Globe Vale Holiday Park

(SW708447)

Radnor TR16 4BH
☎ 01209 891183 📄 01209 890590
e-mail: info@globevale.co.uk
dir: *A30 take Redruth/Porthtowan exit then Portreath/North Country exit from rdbt, right at x-rds into Radnor Rd, left after 0.5m, site on left after 0.5m*

Open all year

Last arrival 20.00hrs Last departure 10.00hrs

A family owned and run park set in a quiet rural location yet close to some stunning beaches and coastline. The park's touring area has a number of full facility hardstanding pitches, a high quality toilet block, a comfortable lounge bar serving bar meals, and holiday static caravans. 13 acre site. 138 touring pitches. 19 hardstandings. Caravan pitches. Motorhome pitches. Tent pitches. 10 statics.

AA Pubs & Restaurants nearby: The Basset Arms, Portreath 01209 842077

Leisure: 🄰 🔍

Facilities: 🕭 ✳ ⚹ ♻ 𝒊

Services: 🚰 🔧 🐕 🍴 ✂ 🚽 🍴 🛒 ⬇

Within 3 miles: ↓ 🎠 ≋ 🏧 🛒

Notes: Dogs must be kept on leads.

see advert on page 91

see advert on page 91

AA CAMPING CARD SITE

►►► 80% Lanyon Holiday Park

(SW684387)

Loscombe Ln, Four Lanes TR16 6LP
☎ 01209 313474
e-mail: info@lanyonholidaypark.co.uk
web: www.lanyonholidaypark.co.uk
dir: *Signed 0.5m off B2397 on Helston side of Four Lanes village*

Open Mar-Oct

Last arrival 21.00hrs Last departure noon

Small, friendly rural park in an elevated position with fine views to distant St Ives Bay. This family owned and run park continues to be upgraded in all areas, and is close to a cycling trail. Stithian's Reservoir for fishing, sailing and windsurfing is

two miles away. Two holiday cottages are available. 14 acre site. 25 touring pitches. Caravan pitches. Motorhome pitches. Tent pitches. 49 statics.

Lanyon Holiday Park

AA Pubs & Restaurants nearby: The Basset Arms, Portreath 01209 842077

Leisure: 🏊 🄰 🔍 🖵

Facilities: ♿ 🕭 ⊙ 🄿 ✳ 🚻 🏧 📶

Services: 🚰 🔧 🐕 🍴 🛒 ⬇

Within 3 miles: ↓ ➕ 🎠 ♪ ◎ ≋ 🛒 � U

Notes: Family park. Take-away service, all-day games room.

►►► 79% Cambrose Touring Park

(SW684453)

Portreath Rd TR16 4HT
☎ 01209 890747
e-mail: cambrosetouringpark@supanet.com
dir: *A30 onto B3300 towards Portreath. Approx 0.75m at 1st rdbt right onto B3300. Take unclassified road on right signed Porthtowan. Site 200yds on left*

Open Apr-Oct

Last arrival 22.00hrs Last departure 11.30hrs

Situated in a rural setting surrounded by trees and shrubs, this park is divided into grassy paddocks. It is situated about two miles from the harbour village of Portreath. 6 acre site. 60 touring pitches. Caravan pitches. Motorhome pitches. Tent pitches.

AA Pubs & Restaurants nearby: The Basset Arms, Portreath 01209 842077

Leisure: 🏊 🄰 🔍 🔍

Facilities: 🕭 🕭 ⊙ 🄿 ✳ ⚹ 🕭 🐕 🕭 📶 ♻ 𝒊

Services: 🚰 🔧 🐕 ✂ 🚽 🍴 🛒

Within 3 miles: ↓ 🎠 🔔 ♪ ◎ 🛒 🔔 U

Notes: Mini football pitch.

AA CAMPING CARD SITE

NEW ►►► 71% Stithians Lake Country Park *(SW705369)*

Stithians Lake, Menherion TR16 6NW
☎ 01209 860301 📄 01209 861503
e-mail: stithianswatersports@swlakestrust.org.uk
dir: *From Redruth take the B3297 towards Helston. Follow the brown tourist signs to Stithians Lake, entrance by the Golden Lion Inn*

* 🚐 £11-£13 🚛 £11-£13 ⛺ £11-£13

Open all year

Last arrival 17.30hrs Last departure noon

Opened in 2011, this simple campsite is a 2-acre field situated adjacent to the Watersports Centre, which forms part of a large activity complex beside Stithians Lake. Campers have to use the functional toilet/shower facilities at the centre, and there is an excellent waterside café that also serves breakfasts. This is the perfect campsite for water sport enthusiasts. 2.1 acre site. 40 touring pitches. Caravan pitches. Motorhome pitches. Tent pitches.

AA Pubs & Restaurants nearby: Bassett Arms, Portreath 01209 842077

Leisure: 🄰

Facilities: 🕭 🕭 🐕 🏧 ♻ 𝒊

Services: 🚰 🔧 🍴

Within 3 miles: ➕ ♪ ≋ 🛒 🔔

Notes: Dogs must be kept on leads.

REJERRAH

Places to visit

Trerice, TRERICE 01637 875404
www.nationaltrust.org.uk

Blue Reef Aquarium, NEWQUAY 01637 878134
www.bluereefaquarium.co.uk

Great for kids: Newquay Zoo, NEWQUAY
0844 474 2244 www.newquayzoo.org.uk

LEISURE: 🏊 Indoor swimming pool 🏊 Outdoor swimming pool 🄰 Children's playground 🪁 Kid's club 🎾 Tennis court 🔍 Games room 🖵 Separate TV room
↓ 9/18 hole golf course ⛵ Boats for hire 🎬 Cinema ♪ Entertainment 🎣 Fishing ◎ Mini golf ≋ Watersports 🏋 Gym 🔔 Sports field **Spa** U Stables
FACILITIES: ♿ Bath 🕭 Shower ⊙ Electric shaver 🄿 Hairdryer ✳ Ice Pack Facility 🕭 Disabled facilities 🕙 Public telephone 🏪 Shop on site or within 200yds
🏪 Mobile shop (calls at least 5 days a week) 🍴 BBQ area 🏧 Picnic area 📶 Wi-fi 📶 Internet access ♻ Recycling 𝒊 Tourist info 🐕 Dog exercise area

REJERRAH — Map 2 SW75

82% Monkey Tree Holiday Park (SW803545)

GOLD

Scotland Rd TR8 5QR
☎ 01872 572032 📠 01872 573577
e-mail: enquiries@monkeytreeholidaypark.co.uk
web: www.monkeytreeholidaypark.co.uk
dir: *Exit A30 onto B3285 to Perranporth, 0.25m right into Scotland Rd, site on left in 1.5m*

🚐 🚕 Å

Open all year

Last arrival 22.00hrs Last departure 10.00hrs

A busy holiday park with plenty of activities and a jolly holiday atmosphere. Set close to lovely beaches between Newquay and Perranporth, it offers an outdoor swimming pool, children's playground, two bars with entertainment, and a good choice of eating outlets including a restaurant and a takeaway. 56 acre site. 750 touring pitches. 17 hardstandings. Caravan pitches. Motorhome pitches. Tent pitches. 48 statics.

AA Pubs & Restaurants nearby: The Smugglers' Den Inn, Cubert 01637 830209

Leisure: ⌖ ⋀ 🐎 👁 🐾 🎵
Facilities: ♨ ♠ ⊙ ✳ ⅙ ⏰ 👁 ☕ ⛱ ♲ 🟰 ❼
Services: 🔌 🗑 🍽 🧺 🛢 ⊘ 🔲 🍴 🔋 🛒 ♻ ♿
Within 3 miles: ↨ ☞ ◎ ⛳ 🚲 🗿 🐴 ↻

Notes: Family & couples park. Dogs must be kept on leads. Mini diggers, amusement arcade, aqua-blaster, remote control cars/boats, indoor soft play area, animal encounters, mini golf, fishing.

►►►► 87% Newperran Holiday Park (SW801555)

TR8 5QJ
☎ 01872 572407 📠 01872 571254
e-mail: holidays@newperran.co.uk
dir: *4m SE of Newquay & 1m S of Rejerrah on A3075. Or A30 Redruth, exit B3275 Perranporth, at 1st T-junct right onto A3075 towards Newquay, site 300mtrs on left*

🚐 🚕 Å

Open Etr-Oct

Last arrival mdnt Last departure 10.00hrs

A family site in a lovely rural position near several beaches and bays. This airy park offers screening to some pitches, which are set in paddocks on level ground. High season entertainment is available in the park's country inn, and the café has an extensive menu. 25 acre site. 357 touring pitches. 14 hardstandings. Caravan pitches. Motorhome pitches. Tent pitches. 16 statics.

AA Pubs & Restaurants nearby: The Smugglers' Den Inn, Cubert 01637 830209

Leisure: ⌖ ⋀ 🔍
Facilities: ♠ ⊙ ⅙ ✳ ⅙ ⏰ 👁 ⛱ 🟰
Services: 🔌 🗑 🍽 🛢 ⊘ 🔲 🍴 ⛱ 🔋 ♻
Within 3 miles: ↨ ☞ 🎣 ☞ ⛳ ◎ 🚲 🗿 🐴 ↻

Notes: Families & couples only. No skateboards. Dogs must be kept on leads. Adventure playground.

see advert on page 91

ROSUDGEON — Map 2 SW52

Places to visit

Trengwainton Garden, PENZANCE 01736 363148 www.nationaltrust.org.uk

Goonhilly Satellite Earth Station Experience, HELSTON 0800 679593 www.goonhilly.bt.com

Great for kids: The Flambards Theme Park, HELSTON 01326 573404 www.flambards.co.uk

---

►►►► 84% Kenneggy Cove Holiday Park (SW562287)

Higher Kenneggy TR20 9AU
☎ 01736 763453
e-mail: enquiries@kenneggycove.co.uk
web: www.kenneggycove.co.uk
dir: *On A394 between Penzance & Helston, turn S into signed lane to site & Higher Kenneggy*

🚐 🚕 Å

Open 12 May-Sep

Last arrival 21.00hrs Last departure 11.00hrs

Set in an Area of Outstanding Natural Beauty with spectacular sea views, this family-owned park is quiet and well kept, with a well-equipped children's play area, superb, newly refurbished toilets, and a new takeaway food facility offering home-cooked meals. A short walk along a country footpath leads to the Cornish Coastal Path, and on to the golden sandy beach at Kenneggy Cove. 4 acre site. 45 touring pitches. Caravan pitches. Motorhome pitches. Tent pitches. 7 statics.

AA Pubs & Restaurants nearby: The Victoria Inn, Perranuthnoe 01736 710309

The Ship Inn, Porthleven 01326 564204

Leisure: ⋀
Facilities: 🚿 ♠ ⊙ ⅙ ✳ ⏰ 👁 ⛱ ♲ ❼
Services: 🔌 🗑 🛢 ⊘ 🔲 ⛱
Within 3 miles: ↨ 🎣 ☞ 🚲 🗿 🐴 ↻

Notes: ⊜ No large groups. Dogs must be kept on leads. Fresh bakery items.

RUMFORD — Map 2 SW87

Places to visit

Prideaux Place, PADSTOW 01841 532411 www.prideauxplace.co.uk

AA CAMPING CARD SITE

►►► 80% Music Water Touring Park (SW906685)

PL27 7SJ
☎ 01841 540257
dir: *A39 at Winnards Perch rdbt onto B3274 signed Padstow. Left in 2m onto unclass road signed Rumford & St Eval. Site 500mtrs on right*

🚐 🚕 Å

Open Apr-Oct

Last arrival 23.00hrs Last departure 11.00hrs

Set in a peaceful location yet only a short drive to the pretty fishing town of Padstow, and many sandy beaches and coves. This family owned and run park has grassy paddocks, and there is a quiet lounge bar and a separate children's games room. 8 acre site. 55 touring pitches. 2 hardstandings. Caravan pitches. Motorhome pitches. Tent pitches. 2 statics.

AA Pubs & Restaurants nearby: The Cornish Arms, St Merryn 01841 532700

Leisure: ⌖ ⋀ 🔍
Facilities: ♠ ⊙ ⅙ ✳ 🟰 🟰
Services: 🔌 🗑 🍽 ⊘ 🛢 ⛱
Within 3 miles: 🎣 ☞ 🚲 🗿 🐴 ↻

Notes: ⊜ Maximum 2 dogs per pitch, one tent per pitch. Pets' corner (donkeys).

RUTHERNBRIDGE Map 2 SX06

Places to visit

Prideaux Place, PADSTOW 01841 532411 www.prideauxplace.co.uk

Cornwall's Regimental Museum, BODMIN 01208 72810

Great for kids: Pencarrow, BODMIN 01208 841369 www.pencarrow.co.uk

AA CAMPING CARD SITE

►►► 78% Ruthern Valley Holidays *(SX014665)*

DAVID BELLAMY CONSERVATION AWARD GOLD

PL30 5LU

☎ 01208 831395

e-mail: camping@ruthernvalley.com

web: www.ruthernvalley.com

dir: *A389 through Bodmin, follow St Austell signs, then Lanivet signs. At top of hill turn right on unclass road signed Ruthernbridge. Follow signs*

* 🚐 £16-£20 🚌 £16-£20 ⛺ £12.50-£17

Open all year

Last arrival 20.30hrs Last departure noon

An attractive woodland site peacefully located in a small river valley west of Bodmin Moor. This away-from-it-all park is ideal for those wanting a quiet holiday, and the informal pitches are spread in four natural areas, with plenty of sheltered space. There are also 12 lodges, heated wooden wigwams, camping pods, and static holiday vans for hire. 7.5 acre site. 26 touring pitches. 2 hardstandings. Caravan pitches. Motorhome pitches. Tent pitches. 3 statics. 3 tipis. 3 wooden pods.

AA Pubs & Restaurants nearby: The Swan, Wadebridge 01208 812526

Trehellas House Hotel & Restaurant, Bodmin 01208 72700

Leisure: 🛝

Facilities: 🚿 ⊙ ✱ ☏ 🏪 🧺 📶 ℹ

Services: ⚡ 🗄 🔥 🍃 [T] 🥡 🚼

Within 3 miles: ⛳ 🎣 🏪 🗄 Ս

Notes: No dogs in camping pods or wigwams. No fires, no noise 22.30hrs-07.00hrs. Woodland area, farm animals.

ST AGNES Map 2 SW75

Places to visit

Royal Cornwall Museum, TRURO 01872 272205 www.royalcornwallmuseum.org.uk

Trerice, TRERICE 01637 875404 www.nationaltrust.org.uk

AA CAMPING CARD SITE

►►►► 76% Beacon Cottage Farm Touring Park *(SW705502)*

Beacon Dr TR5 0NU

☎ 01872 552347 & 07879 413862

e-mail: beaconcottagefarm@lineone.net

web: www.beaconcottagefarmholidays.co.uk

dir: *From A30 at Threeburrows rdbt take B3277 to St Agnes, left into Goonvrea Rd, right into Beacon Drive, follow brown sign to site*

* 🚐 £16-£22 🚌 £16-£22 ⛺ £16-£22

Open Apr-Oct (rs Etr-Whit shop closed)

Last arrival 20.00hrs Last departure noon

A neat and compact site on a working farm, utilizing a cottage and outhouses, an old orchard and adjoining walled paddock. The unique location on a headland looking north-east along the coast comes with stunning views towards St Ives, and the keen friendly family owners keep all areas very well maintained. 5 acre site. 70 touring pitches. 2 seasonal pitches. Caravan pitches. Motorhome pitches. Tent pitches.

AA Pubs & Restaurants nearby: Driftwood Spars, St Agnes 01872 552428

Leisure: 🛝

Facilities: 🚿 ⊙ 💇 ✱ 🏪 🧺 🐕 ♻ ℹ

Services: ⚡ 🗄 🔥 🍃 🥡 ⚓

Within 3 miles: ⛳ ⛵ 🎣 ◎ 🏄 🏪 🗄 Ս

Notes: No large groups. Dogs must be kept on leads. Secure year-round caravan storage.

►►► 82% Presingoll Farm Caravan & Camping Park *(SW721494)*

TR5 0PB

☎ 01872 552333 📠 01872 552333

e-mail: pam@presingollfarm.co.uk

dir: *From A30 Chiverton rdbt take B3277 towards St Agnes. Site 3m on right*

* 🚐 fr £13.50 🚌 fr £13.50 ⛺ fr £13.50

Open Etr/Apr-Oct

Last departure 10.00hrs

An attractive rural park adjoining farmland, with extensive views of the coast beyond. Family owned and run, with level grass pitches, and modernised toilet block in smart converted farm buildings. There is also a campers' room with microwave, freezer, kettle and free coffee and tea, and a children's play area. 5 acre site. 90 touring pitches. 6 hardstandings. Caravan pitches. Motorhome pitches. Tent pitches.

Presingoll Farm Caravan & Camping Park

AA Pubs & Restaurants nearby: Driftwood Spars, St Agnes 01872 552428

Leisure: 🛝

Facilities: 🚿 ⊙ 💇 ✱ ♿ 🏪 🚚 🧺 🐕 ♻ ℹ

Services: ⚡ 🗄 🥡

Within 3 miles: 🎣 🏪 Ս

Notes: 🚫 No large groups. Dogs must be kept on leads.

ST ALLEN Map 2 SW85

Places to visit

Royal Cornwall Museum, TRURO 01872 272205 www.royalcornwallmuseum.org.uk

Trerice, TRERICE 01637 875404 www.nationaltrust.org.uk

Great for kids: Dairy Land Farm World, NEWQUAY 01872 510246 www.dairylandfarmworld.com

NEW ►► 82% Tolcarne Campsite *(SW826513)*

Tolcarne Bungalow TR4 9QX

☎ 01872 540652 & 07881 965477

e-mail: dianemcd@talktalk.net

dir: *A30 towards Redruth. Approx 1m W of Carland Cross rdbt 2nd left to St Allen. 1m, 3rd left to site*

🚐 £8 🚌 £8 ⛺ £8

Open all year

Last arrival 22.00hrs Last departure noon

A new rural site with fantastic countyside views

from the terraced pitches. Expect level, beautifully mown pitches and a spotlessly clean and purpose-built facilities block. The owners have great vision for the site and extra facilities should be in place for the 2012 season. 1 acre site. 10 touring pitches. 5 seasonal pitches. Caravan pitches. Motorhome pitches. Tent pitches.

AA Pubs & Restaurants nearby: Plume of Feathers, Mitchell 01872 510387

Facilities: ⬤⊙✲⛆🖧🛒🚿❔

Services: ⬤🡕🔋

Within 3 miles: ↓🖉🛒

Notes: 🚫 No noise after 22.30hrs. Dogs must be kept on leads.

ST AUSTELL
Map 2 SX05

See also Carlyon Bay

Places to visit

Charlestown Shipwreck & Heritage Centre, ST AUSTELL 01726 69897
www.shipwreckcharlestown.com

Eden Project, ST AUSTELL 01726 811911
www.edenproject.com

Great for kids: Wheal Martyn Museum & Country Park, ST AUSTELL 01726 850362
www.wheal-martyn.com

PREMIER PARK

▶▶▶▶▶ **81% River Valley Holiday Park** *(SX010503)*

London Apprentice PL26 7AP
☎ **01726 73533**
e-mail: mail@cornwall-holidays.co.uk
web: www.rivervalleyholidaypark.co.uk
dir: *Direct access to site signed on B3273 from St Austell at London Apprentice*

* ⬤ £12-£28 ⬤ £12-£28 ⛺ £12-£28

Open Apr-end of Sep

Last arrival 21.00hrs Last departure 11.00hrs

A neat, well-maintained family-run park set in a pleasant river valley. The quality toilet block and attractively landscaped grounds make this a delightful base for a holiday. All pitches are hardstanding, mostly divided by low fencing and neatly trimmed hedges, and the park offers a good range of leisure facilities, including an inviting swimming pool, a games room, an internet room, and an excellent children's play area. There is direct access to river walks and the cycle trail to the beach at Pentewan. 2 acre site. 45 touring

---

pitches. 45 hardstandings. Caravan pitches. Motorhome pitches. Tent pitches. 40 statics.

AA Pubs & Restaurants nearby: Austell's, St Austell 01726 813888

Leisure: ⬤🏊🔍

Facilities: ⬤⊙📷✲🖧🕒🖧🛒🚿⛽🖥♻❔

Services: ⬤🖧🛒

Within 3 miles: ↓⛳🎇🖉⚓🖧🛒

Notes: Off-road cycle trail to beach.
see advert below

▶▶▶ **86% Meadow Lakes** *(SW966485)*

Hewas Water PL26 7JG
☎ **01726 882540** 📠 **01726 883254**
e-mail: info@meadow-lakes.co.uk
web: www.meadow-lakes.co.uk
dir: *From A390 4m SW of St Austell onto B3287, Tregony. 1m, site on left*

* ⬤ £7-£20 ⬤ £7-£20 ⛺ £7-£20

Open mid Mar-end Oct

Last arrival 21.00hrs

Set in a quiet rural area, this extensive park is divided into paddocks with mature hedges and trees, and with its own coarse fishing lakes. This friendly, family park has enthusiastic and hands-in owners, who have made significant changes in the past year, adding new roads, improving the landscaping and building a new reception and toilet block - all facilities are immaculate and spotlessly clean. The park offers organised activities for children indoors (a new, well-equipped games room) and out in the summer holidays, and at other times caters for
continued

SERVICES: ⬤ Electric hook up 🖧 Launderette 🍺 Licensed bar 🛢 Calor Gas 🛢 Camping Gaz 🚽 Toilet fluid 🍽 Café/Restaurant 🍔 Fast Food/Takeaway 🔋 Battery charging 🚼 Baby care ⛟ Motorvan service point

ABBREVIATIONS: BH/bank hols-bank holidays Etr-Easter Whit-Whitsun dep-departure fr-from hrs-hours m-mile mdnt-midnight rdbt-roundabout rs-restricted service wk-week wknd-weekend 🚫 No credit cards ⊗ No dogs

See page 7 for details of the AA Camping Card Scheme

ST AUSTELL *continued*

adult breaks. There are animals in pens, which children can enter. Self-catering lodges, static caravans and nine bungalows are also found at this site. 56 acre site. 108 touring pitches. 9 hardstandings. 30 seasonal pitches. Caravan pitches. Motorhome pitches. Tent pitches. 32 statics. 3 wooden pods.

AA Pubs & Restaurants nearby: Austell's, St Austell 01726 813888

Leisure: ⚅🅰🏊⚽☺🔍🖵

Facilities: 🏴🅱🚿🛡🅰🛠WiFi 🛒♻ℹ

Within 3 miles: 🎣🌊🏅🏪🛒

Notes: Dogs must be kept on leads.

►►► 78% Court Farm Holidays

(SW953524)

St Stephen PL26 7LE
☎ 01726 823684 📃 01726 823684
e-mail: truscott@ctfarm.freeserve.co.uk
dir: *From St Austell take A3058 towards Newquay. Through St Stephen (pass Peugeot garage). Right at St Stephen/Coombe Hay/Langreth/Industrial site sign. 400yds, site on right*

🚐 🚗 🅰

Open Apr-Sep

Last arrival by dark Last departure 11.00hrs

Set in a peaceful rural location, this large camping field offers plenty of space, and is handy for the Eden Project and the Lost Gardens of Heligan. Coarse fishing and star-gazing facilities at the Roseland Observatory are among the on-site attractions. 4 acre site. 20 touring pitches. 5 hardstandings. Caravan pitches. Motorhome pitches. Tent pitches.

AA Pubs & Restaurants nearby: Austell's, St Austell 01726 813888

Leisure: 🅰

Facilities: 🏴☉🚿🅰🛠WiFi

Services: 🔌🛒

Within 3 miles: 🎣🎗🌊🏪🛒🔄

Notes: No noise after dark. Astronomy lectures, observatory, solar observatory.

Places to visit

Eden Project, ST AUSTELL 01726 811911
www.edenproject.com

St Catherine's Castle, FOWEY
www.english-heritage.org.uk

Great for kids: Wheal Martyn Museum & Country Park, ST AUSTELL 01726 850362
www.wheal-martyn.com

►►► 84% Doubletrees Farm

(SX060540)

Luxulyan Rd PL24 2EH
☎ 01726 812266
e-mail: doubletrees@eids.co.uk
dir: *On A390 at Blazey Gate. Turn by Leek Seed Chapel, almost opposite BP filling station. After approx 300yds turn right by public bench into site*

✱ 🚐 fr £15 🚗 fr £15 🅰 fr £15

Open all year

Last arrival 22.30hrs Last departure 11.30hrs

A popular park with terraced pitches offering superb sea and coastal views. Close to beaches, and the nearest park to the Eden Project, it is very well maintained by friendly owners. 1.57 acre site. 32 touring pitches. 6 hardstandings. Caravan pitches. Motorhome pitches. Tent pitches.

AA Pubs & Restaurants nearby: Austell's, St Austell 01726 813888

Facilities: 🏴☉🚿🛡🅰🛠

Services: 🔌🛒🛒

Within 3 miles: 🎣🌊◎🏪🛒🔄

Notes: 🚭 No noise after mdnt. Dogs must be kept on leads.

| ST BURYAN | Map 2 SW42 |

►►► 85% *Treverven Touring Caravan & Camping Park* (SW410237)

Treverven Farm TR19 6DL
☎ 01736 810200 & 810318 📃 01736 810200
e-mail: trevervenpark@btconnect.com
dir: *A30 onto B3283 1.5m after St Buryan, left onto B3315. Site on right in 1m*

🚐 🚗 🅰

Open Etr-Oct

Last departure noon

Situated in a quiet Area of Outstanding Natural Beauty, with panoramic sea and country

---

views,this family-owned site is located off a traffic-free lane leading directly to the coastal path. The toilet facilities are very good, and Treverven is ideally placed for exploring west Cornwall. 6 acre site. 115 touring pitches. Caravan pitches. Motorhome pitches. Tent pitches.

Leisure: 🅰

Facilities: 🏴☉🚿🛡🅰🛠🛡🅰🛠WiFi

Services: 🔌🛒🛡🛒🛒🛒

Within 3 miles: 🎣🌊🏅🏪🛒

Notes: Toaster & kettle available.

| ST COLUMB MAJOR | Map 2 SW96 |

Places to visit

Prideaux Place, PADSTOW 01841 532411
www.prideauxplace.co.uk

Cornwall's Regimental Museum, BODMIN 01208 72810

Great for kids: Pencarrow, BODMIN 01208 841369 www.pencarrow.co.uk

►►► 87% *Southleigh Manor Naturist Park* (SW918623)

TR9 6HY
☎ 01637 880938 📃 01637 881108
e-mail: enquiries@southleigh-manor.com
dir: *Exit A30 at junct with A39 signed Wadebridge. At Highgate Hill rdbt take A39. At Halloon rdbt take A39. At Trekenning rdbt take 4th exit. Site 500mtrs on right*

🚐 🚗 🅰

Open Etr-Oct (rs Peak times shop open)

Last arrival 20.00hrs Last departure 10.30hrs

A very well maintained, naturist park in the heart of the Cornish countryside, catering for families and couples only. Seclusion and security are very well planned, and the lovely gardens provide a calm setting. There are two lodges and static caravans for holiday hire. 4 acre site. 50 touring pitches. Caravan pitches. Motorhome pitches. Tent pitches.

Leisure: ⚅🅰

Facilities: 🏴☉🚿🛡🅰

Services: 🔌🛒🛡🛡🔌🛒🛒🛒

Within 3 miles: 🎣🌊🏪🛒🔄

Notes: 🚭 Sauna, spa bath, pool table, putting green.

ST DAY
Map 2 SW74

Places to visit

Royal Cornwall Museum, TRURO 01872 272205
www.royalcornwallmuseum.org.uk

East Pool Mine, POOL 01209 315027
www.nationaltrust.org.uk

▶▶▶ 82% St Day Touring Park
(SW733422)

Church Hill TR16 5LE
☎ 01209 821086 & 07989 996175
e-mail: jo@stdaytouringpark.co.uk
dir: *From A30 at Scorrier onto B3298 towards Falmouth. Site signed on right in 2m*

🚐 £10-£12 🚐 £10-£12 ▲ £8-£12

Open Etr & Apr-Oct

Last departure noon

A very good touring area with modern toilet facilities. This rurally located park run by keen friendly owners is situated in a quiet area between Falmouth and Newquay and within close walking distance of the attractive village of St Day. 4 acre site. 30 touring pitches. 9 hardstandings. 9 seasonal pitches. Caravan pitches. Motorhome pitches. Tent pitches.

Facilities: 🕭⊙🅿⚹🕭🕙🖺🚾♻🚻
Services: 🔌🖥🔋
Within 3 miles: ⚓🏄🎣🌊🛶♨🖺🔋U

Notes: Adults only. ⊛ No ball games. Dogs must be kept on leads.

ST GILES-ON-THE-HEATH

See Chapmans Well (Devon)

ST HILARY

Places to visit

Godolphin House,
GODOLPHIN CROSS 01736 763194
www.nationaltrust.org.uk/godolphin

Great for kids: The Flambards Theme Park,
HELSTON 01326 573404 www.flambards.co.uk

ST HILARY
Map 2 SW53

▶▶▶▶ 81% Wayfarers Caravan & Camping Park *(SW558314)*

Relubbus Ln TR20 9EF
☎ 01736 763326
e-mail: elaine@wayfarerspark.co.uk
dir: *Exit A30 onto A394 towards Helston. Left at rdbt onto B3280 after 2m. Site 1.5m on left*

* 🚐 £16-£22 🚐 £16-£22 ▲ £14-£19

Open May-Sep

Last arrival 19.00hrs Last departure 11.00hrs

A quiet sheltered park in a peaceful rural setting within two and half miles of St Michael's Mount. It offers spacious, well-drained pitches and very well cared for facilities. 4.8 acre site. 39 touring pitches. 25 hardstandings. Caravan pitches. Motorhome pitches. Tent pitches. 3 statics.

AA Pubs & Restaurants nearby: Trevelyan Arms, Goldsithney 01736 710453

Godolphin Arms, Marazion 01736 710202

Facilities: 🕭⊙🅿⚹🕭🕙🖺🚰♻🚻
Services: 🔌🖥🔋⊘🅣🔋🔋
Within 3 miles: ⚓🏄🎣⊙🌊🖺🔋U
Notes: Adults only. ⊛ No pets.

▶▶▶ 77% Trevair Touring Park
(SW548326)

South Treveneague TR20 9BY
☎ 01736 740647
e-mail: info@trevairtouringpark.co.uk
dir: *A30 onto A394 signed Helston. 2m to rdbt, left onto B3280. Through Goldsithney. Left at brown site sign. Through 20mph zone to site, 1m on right*

🚐 🚐 ▲

Open Etr-Nov

Last arrival 22.00hrs Last departure 11.00hrs

Set in a rural location adjacent to woodland, this park is level and secluded, with grassy pitches. Marazion's beaches and the famous St Michael's Mount are just three miles away. The friendly owners live at the farmhouse on the park. 3.5 acre site. 40 touring pitches. Caravan pitches. Motorhome pitches. Tent pitches. 2 statics.

AA Pubs & Restaurants nearby: Trevelyan Arms, Goldsithney 01736 710453

Godolphin Arms, Marazion 01736 710202

Facilities: 🕭⊙⚹♻🚻
Services: 🔌🖥🔋
Within 3 miles: ⚓🎣🌊🖺U
Notes: ⊛ Dogs must be kept on leads.

ST IVES
Map 2 SW54

Places to visit

Barbara Hepworth Museum & Sculpture Garden, ST IVES 01736 796226
www.tate.org.uk/stives

Tate St Ives, ST IVES 01736 796226
www.tate.org.uk/stives

PREMIER PARK

▶▶▶▶▶ 94% Polmanter
Touring Park *(SW510388)*

Best of British

Halsetown TR26 3LX
☎ 01736 795640
e-mail: reception@polmanter.com
dir: *Signed from B3311 at Halsetown*

🚐 🚐 ▲

Open Whit-10 Sep (rs Whit shop, pool, bar & takeaway food closed)

Last arrival 21.00hrs Last departure 10.00hrs

A well-developed touring park on high ground, Polmanter offers high quality in all areas, from the immaculate modern toilet blocks to the outdoor swimming pool and hard tennis courts. Pitches are individually marked and sited in meadows, and the park has been tastefully landscaped, which includes a field with full-facility hardstanding pitches to accommodate larger caravans and motorhomes. The fishing port and beaches of St Ives are just a mile and a half away, and there is a bus service in high season. 20 acre site. 270 touring pitches. 60 hardstandings. Caravan pitches. Motorhome pitches. Tent pitches.

AA Pubs & Restaurants nearby: The Tinners Arms, Zennor 01736 796927

The Gurnard's Head, Zennor 01736 796928

Leisure: 🏊🏘🎮🎱🎯
Facilities: 🕭⊙🅿⚹🕭🕙🖺🚾🚾🖥♻🚻
Services: 🔌🖥🔋🔋⊘🅣🍽🔋🍟🔋🔋
Within 3 miles: ⚓🏄🏖🎣⊙🌊🖺🔋U

Notes: No skateboards, roller blades or heelys, family camping only. Dogs must be kept on leads. Putting.

SERVICES: 🔌 Electric hook up 🖥 Launderette 🍺 Licensed bar 🛢 Calor Gas ⊘ Camping Gaz 🅣 Toilet fluid 🍽 Café/Restaurant 🍟 Fast Food/Takeaway 🔋 Battery charging 🍼 Baby care ⚕ Motorvan service point

ABBREVIATIONS: BH/bank hols-bank holidays Etr-Easter Whit-Whitsun dep-departure fr-from hrs-hours m-mile mdnt-midnight rdbt-roundabout rs-restricted service wk-week wknd-weekend ⊛ No credit cards ⊗ No dogs

See page 7 for details of the AA Camping Card Scheme

ST IVES continued

PREMIER PARK

▶▶▶▶▶ 86% Ayr Holiday Park *(SW509408)*

TR26 1EJ

☎ 01736 795855 📄 01736 798797

e-mail: recept@ayrholidaypark.co.uk

dir: *From A30 follow St Ives 'large vehicles' route via B3311 through Halsetown onto B3306. Site signed towards St Ives town centre*

* 🚐 £15.75-£31.50 🚃 £15.75-£31.50
Å £15.75-£31.50

Open all year

Last arrival 22.00hrs Last departure 10.00hrs

A well-established park on a cliff side overlooking St Ives Bay, with a heated toilet block that makes winter holidaying more attractive. There are stunning views from most pitches, and the town centre, harbour and beach are only half a mile away, with direct access to the coastal footpath. 4 acre site. 40 touring pitches. 20 hardstandings. Caravan pitches. Motorhome pitches. Tent pitches.

AA Pubs & Restaurants nearby: The Watermill, Hayle, near St Ives 01736 757912

Leisure: 🅰 🔍

Facilities: ⊷ 🇷 ⊙ 🄿 ✳ ↻ 💷 🇷 🇾 🅿 🕴

WIFI ♻ 🛈 **Services:** 🚇 🗑 🔋 ⌀ 🎃 ⛟ ♨

Within 3 miles: ⚓ ♨ 🎱 🗜 🍴 🎱 🚲 ⚓

Notes: No disposable BBQs. Dogs must be kept on leads.

see advert below

▶▶▶▶ 86% Little Trevarrack Holiday Park *(SW525379)*

Laity Ln, Carbis Bay TR26 3HW

☎ 01736 797580

e-mail: info@littletrevarrack.co.uk

dir: *A30 onto A3074 signed 'Carbis Bay & St Ives'. Left opposite turn to beach. 150yds, over x-rds, site 2nd on right*

* 🚐 £14-£25.25 🚃 £14-£25.25 Å £14-£25.25Open Apr-Sep (rs Etr-Whit, mid-end Sep games room & pool closed)

Last arrival 21.00hrs Last departure 10.00hrs

A pleasant grass park set in countryside but close to beaches and local amenities. Plenty of tree planting has resulted in more shelter and privacy in this landscaped park, and there are superb sea views. There are impressive floral displays, well maintained toilets, a good children's play area, and a spacious games field. A private bus service runs to St Ives in high season. 20 acre site. 200 touring pitches. Caravan pitches. Motorhome pitches. Tent pitches.

Little Trevarrack Holiday Park

AA Pubs & Restaurants nearby: The Watermill, Hayle, near St Ives 01736 757912

Leisure: 🏊 🅰 🎱 🔍

Facilities: 🇷 ⊙ 🄿 ✳ ↻ 🕴 WIFI 🖥 ♻ 🛈

Services: 🚇 🗑 🔋 ⌀ 🎃

Within 3 miles: ⚓ ♨ 🎱 🗜 🍴 ◎ 🚲 ⚓

Notes: No groups, no noise after 23.30hrs. Dogs must be kept on leads. Night warden.

LEISURE: 🏊 Indoor swimming pool 🏊 Outdoor swimming pool 🅰 Children's playground 🛝 Kid's club 🎾 Tennis court 🔍 Games room 📺 Separate TV room 🏌 9/18 hole golf course 🚣 Boats for hire 🎬 Cinema 🎵 Entertainment 🎣 Fishing ◎ Mini golf 🏄 Watersports 🏋 Gym 🏟 Sports field **Spa** ⚓ Stables

FACILITIES: ⊷ Bath 🇷 Shower ⊙ Electric shaver 🄿 Hairdryer ✳ Ice Pack Facility ↻ Disabled facilities ↻ Public telephone 🏪 Shop on site or within 200yds 🛒 Mobile shop (calls at least 5 days a week) 🍖 BBQ area 🇾 Picnic area WIFI Wi-fi 🖥 Internet access ♻ Recycling 🛈 Tourist info 🕴 Dog exercise area

►►►► 78% Penderleath Caravan & Camping Park (SW496375)

Towednack TR26 3AF
☎ 01736 798403 & 07840 208542
e-mail: holidays@penderleath.co.uk
dir: From A30 take A3074 towards St Ives. Left at 2nd mini-rdbt, approx 3m to T-junct. Left then immediately right. Next left

* ⊑ £13.50-£24.50 ⊑ £13.50-£24.50
▲ £13.50-£24.50

Open Etr-Oct

Last arrival 21.30hrs Last departure 10.30hrs

Set in a rugged rural location, this tranquil park has extensive views towards St Ives Bay and the north coast. Facilities are all housed in modernised granite barns, and include spotless toilets with fully-serviced shower rooms, and there's a quiet licensed bar with beer garden, a food takeaway, breakfast room and bar meals. The owners are welcoming and helpful. 10 acre site. 75 touring pitches. Caravan pitches. Motorhome pitches. Tent pitches.

AA Pubs & Restaurants nearby: The Watermill, Hayle, Nr Ives 01736 757912

Leisure: 🅐 🔍

Facilities: 🏕 ⊙ 🅿 ⚒ 🔥 🕙 🖎 ➕ ♻ ⓘ

Services: 🔌 🖥 🍴 🏧 🖉 🛢 🍴 🔋 ⊞ 🍼

Within 3 miles: 🚴 ♨ 🎣 🅿 ◎ ⛴ 🛢 🛢 ∪

Notes: No campfires, no noise after 23.00hrs, dogs must be well behaved and kept on leads. Bus to St Ives in high season.

►►►► 78% Trevalgan Touring Park (SW490402)

Trevalgan TR26 3BJ
☎ 01736 792048
e-mail: recept@trevalgantouringpark.co.uk
dir: From A30 follow holiday route to St Ives. B3311 through Halsetown to B3306. Left towards Land's End. Site signed 0.5m on right

* ⊑ £14-£24 ⊑ £14-£24 ▲ £14-£24

Open Etr-Sep

Last arrival 22.00hrs Last departure 10.00hrs

An open park next to a working farm in a rural area on the coastal road from St Ives to Zennor. The park is surrounded by mature hedges, but there are extensive views over the sea. There are very good toilet facilities including family rooms, and a large TV lounge and recreation room with drinks machine. 4.9 acre site. 120 touring pitches. Caravan pitches. Motorhome pitches. Tent pitches.

AA Pubs & Restaurants nearby: The Tinners Arms, Zennor 01736 796927

The Gurnard's Head, Zennor 01736 796928

Leisure: 🅐 ⊛ 🔍 ▢

Facilities: 🏕 ⊙ 🅿 ⚒ 🔥 🕙 🖎 🛢 🔥 ♻ ⓘ

Services: 🔌 🖥 🛢 🖉 ⊞ 🔋 🍼 ↻

Within 3 miles: 🚴 ♨ 🎣 🅿 ◎ ⛴ 🛢 🛢 ∪

Notes: Dogs must be kept on leads. Farm trail.

►► 85% Balnoon Camping Site (SW509382)

Halsetown TR26 3JA
☎ 01736 795431
e-mail: nat@balnoon.fsnet.co.uk
dir: From A30 take A3074, at 2nd mini-rdbt 1st left signed Tate/St Ives. In 3m turn right after Balnoon Inn

⊑ ⊑ ▲

Open Etr-Oct

Last arrival 20.00hrs Last departure 11.00hrs

Small, quiet and friendly, this sheltered site offers superb views of the adjacent rolling hills. The two paddocks are surrounded by mature hedges, and the toilet facilities are kept spotlessly clean. The beaches of Carbis Bay and St Ives are about two miles away. 1 acre site. 23 touring pitches. Caravan pitches. Motorhome pitches. Tent pitches.

AA Pubs & Restaurants nearby: The Tinners Arms, Zennor 01736 796927

The Gurnard's Head, Zennor 01736 796928

Facilities: 🏕 ⊙ 🅿 ⚒ 🛢

Services: 🔌 🖉 ⊞ 🔋

Within 3 miles: 🚴 ♨ 🎣 🅿 ◎ 🛢 🛢 ∪

Notes: ⊛ No noise between 23.00hrs-07.30hrs.

ST JUST (NEAR LAND'S END)   Map 2 SW33

Places to visit

Geevor Tin Mine, PENDEEN 01736 788662
www.geevor.com

Carn Euny Ancient Village, SANCREED
www.english-heritage.org.uk

►►► 83% Roselands Caravan and Camping Park (SW387305)

Dowran TR19 7RS
☎ 01736 788571
e-mail: info@roselands.co.uk
dir: From A30 Penzance bypass turn right for St Just on A3071. 5m, turn left at sign after tin mine chimney, follow signs to site

⊑ ⊑ ▲

Open all year

Last arrival 21.00hrs Last departure 11.00hrs

A small, friendly park in a sheltered rural setting, an ideal location for a quiet family holiday. The owners continue to upgrade the park, and in

continued

ST JUST (NEAR LAND'S END) *continued*

addition to the attractive little bar there is an indoor games room, children's playground, and good toilet facilities. 3 acre site. 15 touring pitches. Caravan pitches. Motorhome pitches. Tent pitches. 15 statics.

AA Pubs & Restaurants nearby: The Wellington, St Just 01736 787319

Harris's Restaurant, Penzance 01736 364408

The Navy Inn, Penzance 01736 333232

Leisure: Ⓐ🔍▢

Facilities: 🝙⊙🅟✳🕒🔆🚿Ⓦⓘ🝙

Services: 🔌🔋🔫🧺Ⓣ🛒

Within 3 miles: ⌀🎣🛥🍴Ⓤ

Notes: No cars by caravans.

►►► 78% *Kelynack Caravan & Camping Park* (SW374301)

Kelynack TR19 7RE
☎ 01736 787633 📠 01736 787633
e-mail: kelynackholidays@tiscali.co.uk
dir: *1m S of St Just, 5m N of Land's End on B3306*

🚐🚌🅰

Open Apr-Oct

Last arrival 22.00hrs Last departure 10.00hrs

A small secluded park nestling alongside a stream in an unspoilt rural location. The level grass pitches are in two areas, and the park is close to many coves, beaches and ancient villages. 3 acre site. 20 touring pitches. 3 hardstandings. Caravan pitches. Motorhome pitches. Tent pitches. 13 statics.

AA Pubs & Restaurants nearby: The Wellington, St Just 01736 787319

Harris's Restaurant, Penzance 01736 364408

The Navy Inn, Penzance 01736 333232

Kelynack Caravan & Camping Park

Leisure: Ⓐ🔍

Facilities: 🝙⊙🅟✳🔆🚿Ⓦⓘ🝙

Services: 🔌🔋🔫🧺Ⓣ🛒🔽

Within 3 miles: ⌀🛥🍴Ⓤ

Notes: Dining & cooking shelter.

►►► 78% Trevaylor Caravan & Camping Park (SW368222)

Botallack TR19 7PU
☎ 01736 787016
e-mail: trevaylor@cornishcamping.co.uk
dir: *On B3306 (St Just-St Ives road), site on right 0.75m from St Just*

🞰 🚐 £13.50-£17.50 🚌 £13.50-£17.50 🅰 fr £11

Open Fri before Etr-Oct

Last departure 11.00hrs

A sheltered grassy site located off the beaten track in a peaceful location at the western tip of Cornwall. The dramatic coastline and the pretty villages nearby are truly unspoilt. Clean, well-maintained facilities and a good shop are offered along with a bar serving meals. 6 acre site. 50 touring pitches. Caravan pitches. Motorhome pitches. Tent pitches. 5 statics.

AA Pubs & Restaurants nearby: The Wellington, St Just 01736 787319

Harris's Restaurant, Penzance 01736 364408

The Navy Inn, Penzance 01736 333232

Leisure: Ⓐ🔍

Facilities: 🝙⊙🅟✳🚿🔆🚿🅰Ⓦⓘ♻🅘

Services: 🔌🔋🔫🍴🧺Ⓣ🍽🛒🔽

Within 3 miles: ⌀🎣🅿🛥🍴🅿

Notes: Quiet between 22.30hrs-07.30hrs. Dogs must be kept on leads.

AA CAMPING CARD SITE

►►► 75% Secret Garden Caravan & Camping Park (SW370305)

Bosavern House TR19 7RD
☎ 01736 788301
e-mail: mail@bosavern.com
web: www.secretbosavern.com
dir: *Exit A3071 near St Just onto B3306 Land's End road. Site 0.5m on left*

🞰 🚐 fr £15 🚌 fr £15 🅰 fr £15

Open Mar-Oct

Last arrival 22.00hrs Last departure noon

A neat little site in a walled garden behind a guest house, where visitors can enjoy breakfast and snacks in the bar in the evening. This site is in a fairly sheltered location with all grassy pitches. Please note that there is no children's playground. 1.5 acre site. 12 touring pitches. Caravan pitches. Motorhome pitches. Tent pitches.

AA Pubs & Restaurants nearby: The Wellington, St Just 01736 787319

Harris's Restaurant, Penzance 01736 364408

The Navy Inn, Penzance 01736 333232

Leisure: ▢

Facilities: 🝙⊙✳🔆Ⓦⓘ🖥♻🅘

Services: 🔌🔋🔫🧺🛒🔽

Within 3 miles: ⌀🅿🛥🍴Ⓤ

Notes: No pets.

LEISURE: 🏊 Indoor swimming pool 🏊 Outdoor swimming pool Ⓐ Children's playground 🏃 Kid's club 🎾 Tennis court 🔍 Games room ▢ Separate TV room ⌀ 9/18 hole golf course 🛥 Boats for hire 🎬 Cinema 🎵 Entertainment 🎣 Fishing ⊙ Mini golf 🏄 Watersports 💪 Gym 🏟 Sports field **Spa** Ⓤ Stables

FACILITIES: 🛁 Bath 🝙 Shower ⊙ Electric shaver 🅟 Hairdryer ✳ Ice Pack Facility 🔆 Disabled facilities 🕒 Public telephone 🅘 Shop on site or within 200yds 🚚 Mobile shop (calls at least 5 days a week) 🍖 BBQ area 🟥 Picnic area Ⓦⓘ Wi-fi 🖥 Internet access ♻ Recycling 🅘 Tourist info 🐕 Dog exercise area

ST JUST-IN-ROSELAND   Map 2 SW83

Places to visit

St Mawes Castle, ST MAWES 01326 270526
www.english-heritage.org.uk

Trelissick Garden, TRELISSICK GARDEN
01872 862090 www.nationaltrust.org.uk

Roger Almond Award for the Most Improved Campsite

PREMIER PARK

▶▶▶▶▶ 89%
Trethem Mill Touring Park
(SW860365)

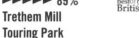

TR2 5JF
☎ 01872 580504   ▤ 01872 580968
e-mail: reception@trethem.com
dir: From Tregony on A3078 to St Mawes. 2m after Trewithian, follow signs to site

* ⊞ £17-£25 ⊞ £17-£25 ▲ £17-£25

Open Apr-mid Oct

Last arrival 20.00hrs Last departure 11.00hrs

A quality park in all areas, with upgraded amenities including a reception, shop, laundry, and disabled/family room. This carefully-tended and sheltered park is in a lovely rural setting, with spacious pitches separated by young trees and shrubs. The very keen family who own the site are continually looking for ways to enhance its facilities. 11 acre site. 84 touring pitches. 61 hardstandings. Caravan pitches. Motorhome pitches. Tent pitches.

AA Pubs & Restaurants nearby: The Victory Inn, St Mawes 01326 270324

Hotel Tresanton, St Mawes 01326 270055

Driftwood, Porthscatho 01872 580644

Leisure: ⋒ ⊛
Facilities: ⋔ ⊙ ⨍ ⚹ ⅋ ⊙ ⓢ ⊞ ⌂ ♻ ❶
Services: ⊞ ⓢ ⬛ ⊘ ⊤ ⛟ ⬇
Within 3 miles: ⚲ ⫽ ⛵ ⓢ ⓢ ↺
Notes: No skateboards or rollerblades. Information centre.

ST MARY'S (ISLES OF SCILLY)   Map 2 SV91

On the Isles of Scilly caravans and motor caravans are not allowed, and campers must stay at official sites. Booking is advisable on all sites, especially during school holidays.

Places to visit

Isles of Scilly Museum, ST MARY'S
01720 422337 www.iosmuseum.org

▶▶▶ 80% **Garrison Campsite**
(SV897104)

Tower Cottage, The Garrison TR21 0LS
☎ 01720 422670   ▤ 01720 422670
e-mail: tedmoulson@aol.com
dir: 10 mins' walk from quay to site

▲

Open Etr-Oct

Last arrival 20.00hrs Last departure 19.00hrs

Set on the top of an old fort with superb views, this park offers tent-only pitches in a choice of well-sheltered paddocks. There are modern toilet facilities (with powerful showers), a superb children's play area, and a good shop at this attractive site, which is only ten minutes from the town, the quay and the nearest beaches. 9.5 acre site. 120 touring pitches. Tent pitches.

Facilities: ⋔ ⊙ ⨍ ⚹ ⊙ ⓢ ⊞ ❶
Services: ⊞ ⓢ ⬛ ⊘ ⬇
Within 3 miles: ⚲ ⫽ ⛵ ⓢ ⓢ ↺
Notes: ⊗ No cars on site, no open fires.

ST MERRYN (NEAR PADSTOW)

Places to visit

Prideaux Place, PADSTOW 01841 532411
www.prideauxplace.co.uk

ST MERRYN (NEAR PADSTOW)   Map 2 SW87

78% **Harlyn Sands Holiday Park** (SW873752)

Lighthouse Rd, Trevose Head PL28 8SQ
☎ 01841 520720 & 01752 841485
▤ 01841 521251
e-mail: enquiries@harlynsands.co.uk
web: www.harlynsands.co.uk
dir: Exit B3276 in St Merryn centre onto unclassified road towards Harlyn Sands & Trevose Head. Follow brown site signs for approx 1m. (NB Do not turn right to Harlyn Sands)

⊞ £8-£35 ⊞ £8-£35 ▲ £8-£35

Open Etr-Nov

Last arrival 22.00hrs Last departure 10.00hrs

A family park for 'bucket and spade' holidays, surrounded by seven bays each with its own sandy beach. On site entertainment for children and adults is extensive, and there is an indoor swimming pool complex, excellent restaurant and takeaway, and a quiet over-30s lounge bar. 21 acre site. 160 touring pitches. 6 hardstandings. 60 seasonal pitches. Caravan pitches. Motorhome pitches. Tent pitches. 350 statics.

AA Pubs & Restaurants nearby: The Cornish Arms, St Merryn 01841 532700

Leisure: ⧈ ⋒ ♞ ♫
Facilities: ⋔ ⊙ ⨍ ⚹ ⅋ ⊙ ⓢ ⌂ ⊞ ♻ ❶
Services: ⊞ ⓢ ⬛ ⬛ ⊤ ⍟ ⛟ ⬇
Within 3 miles: ⚲ ⊞ ⫽ ⛵ ⓢ ↺
Notes: Families only. Dogs must be kept on leads. Arcade, clubhouse, chip shop.

▶▶▶▶ 80% **Carnevas Holiday Park & Farm Cottages** (SW862728)

Carnevas Farm PL28 8PN
☎ 01841 520230 & 521209 ▤ 01841 520230
e-mail: carnevascampsite@aol.com
dir: From St Merryn on B3276 towards Porthcothan Bay. Approx 2m turn right at site sign onto unclass road opposite Tredrea Inn. Site 0.25m on right

* ⊞ £10-£17 ⊞ £10-£17 ▲ £10-£17

Open Apr-Oct (rs Apr-Whit & mid Sep-Oct shop, bar & restaurant closed)

A family-run park on a working farm, divided into four paddocks on slightly sloping grass.

continued

ST MERRYN (NEAR PADSTOW) *continued*

The toilets are central to all areas, and there is a small licensed bar serving bar meals. 8 acre site. 195 touring pitches. Caravan pitches. Motorhome pitches. Tent pitches. 14 statics.

Carnevas Holiday Park & Farm Cottages

AA Pubs & Restaurants nearby: The Cornish Arms, St Merryn 01841 532700

Leisure: 🄰 🔍

Facilities: 🏕⊙🖤✳🛠🕙🖫 WIFI ♻ ℹ

Services: 🖵🖥🍴🛒🗑🛎🛒

Within 3 miles: ♨🏊⛵🛝🎿🏌️🎣⛳

Notes: No skateboards. Dogs must be kept on leads.

see advert on page 89

AA CAMPING CARD SITE

▶▶▶▶ **78% Atlantic Bays Holiday Park** *(SW890717)*

St Merryn PL28 8PY
☎ 01841 520855   📠 01841 520419
e-mail: info@atlanticbaysholidaypark.co.uk
dir: *Take B3274 towards Padstow, in 3m left onto unclassified road to St Merryn, follow brown signs to park*

* 🚐 £18-£32 🚍 £18-£32 ▲ £10-£28

Open Mar- 2 Jan

Last arrival 19.00hrs Last departure 10.00hrs

Atlantic Bays has a mix of hardstanding and grass pitches, a high quality toilet/shower block and a comfortable bar/restaurant. The park is set in a rural area yet only two miles from the coast

and beautiful sandy beaches, and within easy reach of the quaint fishing village of Padstow. 27 acre site. 70 touring pitches. 50 hardstandings. Caravan pitches. Motorhome pitches. Tent pitches. 171 statics.

AA Pubs & Restaurants nearby: The Cornish Arms, St Merryn 01841 532700

Leisure: 🄰 🔍

Facilities: 🏕⊙🖤✳🛠🕙🖫🛒🛎 WIFI ♻ ℹ

Services: 🖵🖥🛒🛎🛒

Within 3 miles: ♨🏊🛝🎣⛳🎿🏌️⛳

Notes: Dogs must be kept on leads.

▶▶▶ **78% Trevean Caravan & Camping Park** *(SW875724)*

Trevean Ln PL28 8PR
☎ 01841 520772   📄 01841 520772
e-mail: trevean.info@virgin.net
dir: *From St Merryn take B3276 to Newquay for 1m. Turn left for Rumford. Site 0.25m on right*

🚐 £8-£12 🚍 £8-£12 ▲ £8-£12

Open Apr-Oct (rs Whit-Sep shop open)

Last arrival 22.00hrs Last departure 11.00hrs

A small working farm site with level grassy pitches in open countryside. The toilet facilities are clean and well kept, and there is a laundry and good children's playground. 1.5 acre site. 68 touring pitches. 35 seasonal pitches. Caravan pitches. Motorhome pitches. Tent pitches. 3 statics.

AA Pubs & Restaurants nearby: The Cornish Arms, St Merryn 01841 532700

Leisure: 🄰

Facilities: 🏕⊙🖤✳🛠🕙🖫🛒♻ ℹ

Services: 🖵🖥🛎🛒

Within 3 miles: ♨🏊🏌️⛳🎣🛝⛳

▶▶ **80% Tregavone Touring Park** *(SW898732)*

Tregavone Farm PL28 8JZ
☎ 01841 520148
e-mail: info@tregavone.co.uk
dir: *From A389 towards Padstow, right after Little Petherick. In 1m just beyond Padstow Holiday Park turn left into unclass road signed Tregavone. Site on left, approx 1m*

🚐 £10-£12 🚍 £10-£12 ▲ £10-£12

Open Mar-Oct

Situated on a working farm with unspoilt country views, this spacious grassy park, run by friendly family owners, makes an ideal base for exploring the north Cornish coast and the seven local golden beaches with surfing areas, or for enjoying quiet country walks from the park. 3 acre site. 40 touring pitches. Caravan pitches. Motorhome pitches. Tent pitches.

AA Pubs & Restaurants nearby: The Cornish Arms, St Merryn 01841 532700

Facilities: 🏕⊙✳🛒

Services: 🖵🖥🛒

Within 3 miles: ♨🏊🏌️⛳🎣🛝⛳

Notes: 😐

ST MINVER
Map 2 SW97

▶▶▶▶ **82% Gunvenna Caravan Park** *(SW969782)*

PL27 6QN
☎ 01208 862405   📄 01208 869107
dir: *From A39 N of Wadebridge take B3314 (Port Isaac road), site 4m on right*

🚐 🚍 ▲

Open Etr-Oct

Last arrival 21.00hrs Last departure 11.00hrs

An attractive park with extensive rural views in a quiet country location, yet within three miles of Polzeath. This popular park is family owned and run, and provides good facilities in an ideal position for touring north Cornwall. The park has excellent hardstanding pitches, improved and maturing landscaping, and static caravans and a cottage for holiday hire. 10 acre site. 75 touring pitches. 23 hardstandings. Caravan pitches. Motorhome pitches. Tent pitches. 44 statics. 2 wooden pods.

AA Pubs & Restaurants nearby: The Swan, Wadebridge 01208 812526

Restaurant Nathan Outlaw, Rock 01208 863394

Leisure: 🏊 ⚲ 🎣

Facilities: ⛟ 📷 ⊙ 🖗 ⚙ 🛎 🔥 🚻 🚮 WiFi ♻ 🅰

Services: 🔌 🗑 🛢 🚰 🚽 ⚒

Within 3 miles: ⚲ ⚲ 🚣 🛒 🐴

Notes: Owners must clear up after their dogs. Dogs must be kept on leads.

SENNEN
Map 2 SW32

Places to visit

Geevor Tin Mine, PENDEEN 01736 788662 www.geevor.com

Carn Euny Ancient Village, SANCREED www.english-heritage.org.uk

►►► 81% Trevedra Farm Caravan & Camping Site *(SW368276)*

TR19 7BE
☎ **01736 871818 & 871835**
e-mail: trevedra@btconnect.com
dir: *Take A30 towards Land's End. After junct with B3306 turn right into farm lane. (NB Sat Nav directs past site entrance to next lane which is unsuitable for caravans)*

🚐 🚛 🅰

Open Etr or Apr–Oct

Last arrival 19.00hrs Last departure 10.30hrs

A working farm with dramatic sea views over to the Scilly Isles, just a mile from Land's End. The popular campsite offers well-appointed toilets, a well-stocked shop, and a cooked breakfast or evening meal from the food bar. There is direct access to the coastal footpath, and two beautiful beaches are a short walk away. 8 acre site. 100 touring pitches. Caravan pitches. Motorhome pitches. Tent pitches.

AA Pubs & Restaurants nearby: The Old Success Inn, Sennen 01736 871232

Facilities: 📷 ⊙ 🖗 ⚙ 🛎 🔥 🗑 WiFi ♻ 🅰

Services: 🔌 🗑 🛢 🚰 🚽 🍴 ⚒ 🔋 ⚒

Within 3 miles: ⚲ ⚲ 🛒 🐴 🗑

Notes: No open fires. Dogs must be kept on leads.

SUMMERCOURT
Map 2 SW85

Places to visit

Trerice, TRERICE 01637 875404 www.nationaltrust.org.uk

Blue Reef Aquarium, NEWQUAY 01637 878134 www.bluereefaquarium.co.uk

Great for kids: Dairy Land Farm World, NEWQUAY 01872 510246 www.dairylandfarmworld.com

---

AA CAMPING CARD SITE

RV ►►►► 95% Carvynick Country Club *(SW878564)*

TR8 5AF
☎ **01872 510716** 📠 **01872 510172**
e-mail: info@carvynick.co.uk
web: www.carvynick.co.uk
dir: *Off A3058*

🚐

Open all year (rs Jan–early Feb restricted leisure facilities)

Set within the gardens of an attractive country estate this spacious dedicated American RV Park (also home to the 'Itchy Feet' retail company) provides all full facility pitches on hardstandings. The extensive on-site amenities, shared by the high quality time share village, include an excellent restaurant with lounge bar, indoor leisure area with swimming pool, fitness suite and badminton court. 47 touring pitches. Motorhome pitches.

AA Pubs & Restaurants nearby: The Plume of Feathers, Mitchell 01872 510387

Leisure: 🏊 🎾 ⚲ 🎣

Facilities: 📷 ⊙ 🖗 ♻ 🅰

Services: 🔌 🗑 🍴 🍴 ⚒

Within 3 miles: ⚲ 🗑 🗑

Notes: Dogs must be exercised off site.

see advert on page 116

TINTAGEL
Map 2 SX08

See also Camelford

Places to visit

Tintagel Castle, TINTAGEL 01840 770328 www.english-heritage.org.uk

Tintagel Old Post Office, TINTAGEL 01840 770024 www.nationaltrust.org.uk/main/w-tintageloldpostoffice

Great for kids: Tamar Otter & Wildlife Centre, LAUNCESTON 01566 785646 www.tamarotters.co.uk

►►► 75% Headland Caravan & Camping Park *(SX056887)*

Atlantic Rd PL34 0DE
☎ **01840 770239** 📠 **01840 770925**
e-mail: headland.caravan@talktalkbusiness.net
dir: *From B3263 follow brown tourist signs through village to Headland*

* 🚐 £12.50–£16 🚛 £11–£14.50 🅰 £12.50–£16

Open Etr–Oct

Last arrival 21.00hrs

A peaceful family-run site in the mystical village of Tintagel, close to the ruins of King Arthur's Castle. There are two well terraced camping areas with sea and countryside views, immaculately clean and updated toilet facilities, and good, colourful planting across the park. The Cornish coastal path and the spectacular scenery are just two of the attractions here, and there are safe bathing beaches nearby. There are holiday statics for hire. 5 acre site. 62 touring pitches. Caravan pitches. Motorhome pitches. Tent pitches. 28 statics.

AA Pubs & Restaurants nearby: The Port William, Tintagel 01840 770230

Leisure: ⚲

Facilities: 📷 ⊙ 🖗 ⚙ 🗑 🚮 WiFi ♻ 🅰

Services: 🔌 🗑 🚰 🍴 🔋 ⚒

Within 3 miles: 🚣 ⚲ 🛒 🗑 🗑 🐴

Notes: Dogs must be kept on leads and exercised off site, quiet after 23.00hrs.

TORPOINT
Map 3 SX45

Places to visit

Antony House, TORPOINT 01752 812191
www.nationaltrust.org.uk/antony

Mount Edgcumbe House & Country Park,
TORPOINT 01752 822236
www.mountedgcumbe.gov.uk

Great for kids: The Monkey Sanctuary, LOOE
01503 262532 www.monkeysanctuary.org

▶▶▶▶ **80% Whitsand Bay Lodge &
Touring Park** *(SX410515)*

Millbrook PL10 1JZ
☎ 01752 822597 📠 01752 823444
e-mail: enquiries@whitsandbayholidays.co.uk
dir: *From Torpoint take A374, turn left at Anthony
onto B3247 for 1.25m to T-junct. Turn left, 0.25m
then right onto Cliff Rd. Site 2m on left*

* 🚐 £15–£30 🚏 £15–£30 ⛺ £10–£30

Open all year (rs Sep-Mar opening hours at shop/
pool/bar restricted)

Last arrival 19.00hrs Last departure 10.00hrs

A very well equipped park with panoramic coastal,
sea and countryside views from its terraced

pitches. A very high quality park with upmarket
toilet facilities and other amenities. 27 acre site.
49 touring pitches. 30 hardstandings. 15 seasonal
pitches. Caravan pitches. Motorhome pitches. Tent
pitches. 5 statics.

AA Pubs & Restaurants nearby: The Halfway
House Inn, Kingsand 01752 822279

Leisure: 🌊 ⛳ 🎱 ♨ 🎾 ♫

Facilities: 🛉 🚿 🔌 ⚡ ✂ 🧊 🛗 ⛑ 🐕 📶 🛒 ♻ ℹ

Services: 🚐 🛢 🚽 💧 🍴 🔥 ⬆ 🛒 ♿

Within 3 miles: ⚓ ⛵ 🎣 ◎ ⛳ 🛢 ♫ ⛲

Notes: Families & couples only. Sauna, putting,
chapel, library, amusement arcade.

TRURO

See also Portscatho

Places to visit

Royal Cornwall Museum, TRURO 01872 272205
www.royalcornwallmuseum.org.uk

Trewithen Gardens, PROBUS 01726 883647
www.trewithengardens.co.uk

Great for kids: Pencarrow, BODMIN
01208 841369 www.pencarrow.co.uk

TRURO
Map 2 SW84

AA CAMPING CARD SITE

PREMIER PARK

▶▶▶▶▶ **92% Carnon Downs
Caravan & Camping Park**
(SW805406)

Carnon Downs TR3 6JJ
☎ 01872 862283 📠 01872 870820
e-mail: info@carnon-downs-caravanpark.co.uk
dir: *Take A39 from Truro towards Falmouth. Site
just off main Carnon Downs rdbt, on left*

* 🚐 £19.50–£27.50 🚏 £19.50–£27.50
⛺ £19.50–£27.50

Open all year

Last arrival 22.00hrs Last departure 11.00hrs

A beautifully mature park set in meadowland and
woodland close to the village amenities of Carnon
Downs. The four toilet blocks provide exceptional
facilities in bright modern surroundings. An
extensive landscaping programme has been
carried out to give more spacious pitch sizes, and
there is an exciting children's playground with

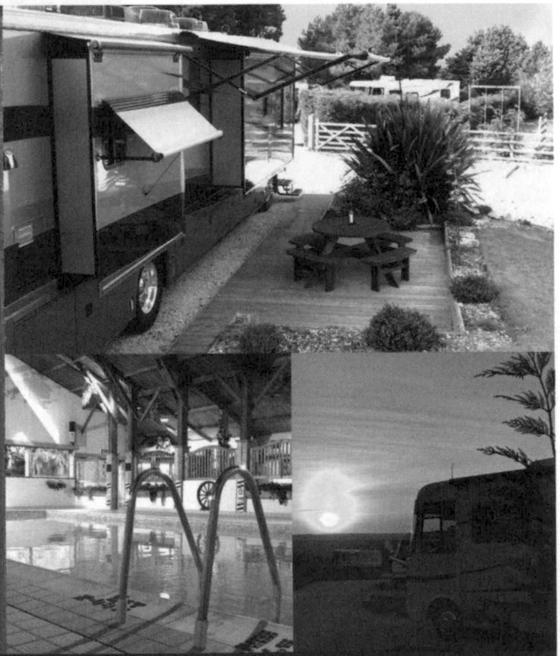

LEISURE: 🌊 Indoor swimming pool 🌊 Outdoor swimming pool 🎠 Children's playground 🎣 Kid's club 🎾 Tennis court 🎱 Games room ▭ Separate TV room
⛳ 9/18 hole golf course ⛵ Boats for hire 🎬 Cinema ♫ Entertainment 🎣 Fishing ◎ Mini golf 🏄 Watersports 🏌 Gym 🏟 Sports field **Spa** ⛲ Stables

FACILITIES: 🛁 Bath 🚿 Shower ⚡ Electric shaver 🔥 Hairdryer ✳ Ice Pack Facility ♿ Disabled facilities 📞 Public telephone 🛒 Shop on site or within 200yds
🚚 Mobile shop (calls at least 5 days a week) 🍖 BBQ area 🌲 Picnic area 📶 Wi-fi 🖥 Internet access ♻ Recycling ℹ Tourist info 🐕 Dog exercise area

modern equipment, and a football pitch. 33 acre site. 150 touring pitches. 80 hardstandings. Caravan pitches. Motorhome pitches. Tent pitches. 1 static.

AA Pubs & Restaurants nearby: The Pandora Inn, Mylor Bridge 01326 372678

Tabb's, Truro 01872 262110

Leisure: ⚲ ▢

Facilities: ⬤ ⬤ ⊙ ℗ ✳ ⬤ ☺ ☌ ♻ ❶

Services: ⬤ ⬛ ⬛ ⬛ ⊤ ⬛ ⬛

Within 3 miles: ↓ ⬤ ⽇ ℘ ⬤ ⬤ ⬤ ∪

Notes: No children's bikes in Jul & Aug. Baby & child bathroom.

PREMIER PARK

▶▶▶▶▶ **82% Truro Caravan and Camping Park** *(SW772452)*

TR4 8QN
☎ **01872 560274** 🖷 **01872 561413**
e-mail: info@trurocaravanandcampingpark. co.uk
dir: *Exit A390 at Threemilestone rdbt onto unclass road towards Chacewater. Site signed on right in 0.5m*

⬤ £18.50-£25.50 ⬤ £18.50-£25.50
⬤ £18.50-£25.50

Open all year

Last arrival 19.00hrs Last departure 10.30hrs

An attractive south-facing and well laid out park with spacious pitches, including good hardstandings, and quality modern toilets that are kept spotlessly clean. It is situated on the edge of the city of Truro yet close to many beaches, with St Agnes being just ten minutes away by car. It is equidistant from both the rugged north coast and the calmer south coastal areas. There is a good bus service from the gate of the park to Truro. 8.5 acre site. 51 touring pitches. 26 hardstandings. Caravan pitches. Motorhome pitches. Tent pitches. 49 statics.

Truro Caravan & Camping Park

AA Pubs & Restaurants nearby: The Wig & Pen Inn, Truro 01872 273028

Probus Lamplighter Restaurant, Probus, Nr Truro 01726 882453

Facilities: ⬤ ⬤ ⊙ ℗ ✳ ⬤ ☺ ☌ wifi ⬛ ♻ ❶

Services: ⬤ ⬛ ⬛ ⬛ ⊤ ⬛ ⬛

Within 3 miles: ↓ ⽇ ℘ ⬤ ⬤ ⬤ ∪

Notes: Dogs must be kept on leads.

see advert below

TRURO *continued*

▶▶▶ 80% *Summer Valley* (SW800479)

Shortlanesend TR4 9DW
☎ 01872 277878
e-mail: res@summervalley.co.uk
dir: *3m NW off B3284*

Open Apr-Oct

Last arrival 20.00hrs Last departure noon

A very attractive and secluded site in a rural setting midway between the A30 and the cathedral city of Truro. The keen owners maintain the facilities to a good standard. 3 acre site. 60 touring pitches. Caravan pitches. Motorhome pitches. Tent pitches.

AA Pubs & Restaurants nearby: Old Ale House, Truro 01872 271122

Bustophers Bar Bistro, Truro 01872 279029

Leisure: 🅰 **Facilities:** 🏾⊙🅿✳⊕🖾🚻
Services: 🔌🖾🔒🖊🆃🖾
Within 3 miles: 🎣🕀🖊◎🖾🖾U

Notes: Campers' lounge.

WADEBRIDGE

Places to visit

Prideaux Place, PADSTOW 01841 532411
www.prideauxplace.co.uk

Cornwall's Regimental Museum, BODMIN 01208 72810

Great for kids: Pencarrow, BODMIN 01208 841369 www.pencarrow.co.uk

---

WADEBRIDGE   Map 2 SW97

AA CAMPING CARD SITE

▶▶▶ 89% The Laurels Holiday Park (SW957715)

Padstow Rd, Whitecross PL27 7JQ
☎ 01209 313474
e-mail: info@thelaurelsholidaypark.co.uk
web: www.thelaurelsholidaypark.co.uk
dir: *Off A389 (Padstow road) near junct with A39, W of Wadebridge*

Open Apr or Etr-Oct

Last arrival 20.00hrs Last departure 11.00hrs

A very smart and well-equipped park with individual pitches screened by hedges and young shrubs. The enclosed dog walk is of great benefit to pet owners, and the Camel cycle trail and Padstow are not far away. 2.2 acre site. 30 touring pitches. 2 hardstandings. Caravan pitches. Motorhome pitches. Tent pitches.

AA Pubs & Restaurants nearby: The Swan, Wadebridge 01208 812526

Leisure: 🅰
Facilities: 🏾⊙🅿✳🖾🚻
Services: 🔌🖾🖾
Within 3 miles: 🎣🏂🕀🖊⮑🖾🖾U

Notes: No group bookings, family park. Dogs must be kept on leads. Wet suit dunking bath & drying area.

AA CAMPING CARD SITE

▶▶▶ 87% St Mabyn Holiday Park (SX055733)

Longstone Rd, St Mabyn PL30 3BY
☎ 01208 841677 📠 01208 841514
e-mail: info@stmabyn.co.uk
web: www.stmabynholidaypark.co.uk
dir: *S of Camelford on A39, left after BP garage onto B3266 to Bodmin, 6m to Longstone, right at x-rds to St Mabyn, site approx 400mtrs on right*

Open 15 Mar-Oct (rs 15 Mar-Spring BH & mid Sep-Oct swimming pool may be closed)

Last arrival 22.00hrs Last departure noon

A family run site ideally situated close to the picturesque market town of Wadebridge, and within easy reach of Bodmin. The park offers peace and tranquillity in a country setting and at the same time provides plenty of on-site activities including a swimming pool and children's play areas. Holiday chalets and fully-equipped holiday homes are available to rent, along with a choice of pitches. 12 acre site. 120 touring pitches. 49 hardstandings. Caravan pitches. Motorhome pitches. Tent pitches. 20 statics. 1 wooden pod.

AA Pubs & Restaurants nearby: The Swan, Wadebridge 01208 812526

The Borough Arms, Dunmere 01208 73118

LEISURE: 🏊 Indoor swimming pool 🏊 Outdoor swimming pool 🅰 Children's playground 🚸 Kid's club 🎾 Tennis court 🎱 Games room 📺 Separate TV room 🏌 9/18 hole golf course ⛵ Boats for hire 🎬 Cinema 🎵 Entertainment 🎣 Fishing ◎ Mini golf 🏄 Watersports 🏋 Gym ⚽ Sports field **Spa** U Stables
FACILITIES: 🛁 Bath 🚿 Shower ⊙ Electric shaver 🅿 Hairdryer ✳ Ice Pack Facility ♿ Disabled facilities ☎ Public telephone 🏪 Shop on site or within 200yds 🛒 Mobile shop (calls at least 5 days a week) 🍖 BBQ area 🪑 Picnic area 📶 Wi-fi 💻 Internet access ♻ Recycling ⓘ Tourist info 🐕 Dog exercise area

Leisure: ☺ ⚠ ⚲ ▢

Facilities: 🟊 ⊙ ℗ ✳ ⚹ ⊘ 🛁 🚽 🛒 WI-FI ▤ ♻ ❶

Services: 🔌 🗑 🛢 ⊘ T 🛒

Within 3 miles: ↓ ℘ ⊙ 🛒 U

Notes: Quiet from 23.00hrs-07.00hrs. Information book given on arrival. Small animal area with goats.

AA CAMPING CARD SITE

►►► 79% Little Bodieve Holiday Park (SW995734)

Bodieve Rd PL27 6EG

☎ 01208 812323

e-mail: info@littlebodieve.co.uk

dir: From A39 rdbt on Wadebridge by-pass take B3314 signed Rock/Port Isaac, site 0.25m on right

🚐 🚗 ⚠

Open Apr-Oct (rs Early & late season pool, shop & clubhouse closed)

Last arrival 21.00hrs Last departure 11.00hrs

Rurally located with pitches in three large grassy paddocks, this family park is close to the Camel Estuary. The licensed clubhouse provides bar meals, with an entertainment programme in high season, and there is a swimming pool with sun terrace plus a separate waterslide and splash pool, and 7 static holiday caravans. 22 acre site. 195 touring pitches. Caravan pitches. Motorhome pitches. Tent pitches. 75 statics.

AA Pubs & Restaurants nearby: The Swan, Wadebridge 01208 812526

Leisure: ☺ ⚠ ⚲ ♫

Facilities: 🚼 🟊 ⊙ ℗ ✳ ⚹ ⊘ 🛁 🚽 🐾 ♻ ❶

Services: 🔌 🗑 🛒 🛢 ⊘ T 🍽 🛒 🛒

Within 3 miles: ↓ ⊟ ℘ ⊙ 🛒 🛒 U

Notes: Families & couples only. Dogs must be kept on leads. Crazy golf, water shute/splash pool, pets' corner.

WATERGATE BAY   Map 2 SW86

AA CAMPING CARD SITE

►►►► 87% Watergate Bay Touring Park (SW850653)

SILVER

TR8 4AD

☎ 01637 860387   🖨 0871 661 7549

e-mail: email@watergatebaytouringpark.co.uk

web: www.watergatebaytouringpark.co.uk

dir: 4m N of Newquay on B3276 (coast road)

* 🚐 £11-£20 🚗 £11-£20 ⚠ £11-£20

Open Mar-Nov (rs Mar-Spring BH & Sep-Oct restricted bar, café, shop & pool)

Last arrival 22.00hrs Last departure noon

A well-established park above Watergate Bay, where acres of golden sand, rock pools and surf are seen as a holidaymakers' paradise. The toilet facilities are appointed to a high standard, and there is a well-stocked shop and café, an inviting swimming pool, and a wide range of activities including tennis courts and outdoor facilities for all ages, and a regular entertainment programme in the clubhouse. 30 acre site. 171 touring pitches. 14 hardstandings. Caravan pitches. Motorhome pitches. Tent pitches. 2 statics.

AA Pubs & Restaurants nearby: Fifteen Cornwall, Watergate Bay 01637 861000

Leisure: ☺ ☺ ⚠ ⚲ 🏊 ☺ ⚲ ▢ ♫

Facilities: 🚼 🟊 ⊙ ℗ ✳ ⚹ ⊘ 🛁 🐾 WI-FI ▤ ♻ ❶

Services: 🔌 🗑 🛒 🛢 ⊘ T 🍽 🛒 🛒 ⚗

Within 3 miles: ↓ ℘ ⊙ 🛒 🛒

Notes: Dogs must be kept on leads. Free minibus to beach during main school hols.

see advert on opposite page

WIDEMOUTH BAY   Map 2 SS20

72% Widemouth Bay Caravan Park (SS199008)

EX23 0DF

☎ 01271 866766   🖨 01271 866791

e-mail: bookings@jfhols.co.uk

dir: Take Widemouth Bay coastal road off A39, turn left. Site on left

🚐 🚗 ⚠

Open Etr-Oct

Last arrival dusk Last departure 10.00hrs

A partly sloping rural site set in countryside overlooking the sea and one of Cornwall's finest beaches. Nightly entertainment in high season with emphasis on children's and family club programmes. This park is located less than half a mile from the sandy beaches of Widemouth Bay. 58 acre site. 220 touring pitches. 90 hardstandings. Caravan pitches. Motorhome pitches. Tent pitches. 200 statics.

AA Pubs & Restaurants nearby: The Bay View Inn, Widemouth Bay 01288 361273

Castle Restaurant, Bude 01288 350543

Leisure: ☺ ☺ ⚠ ⚲ ⚲ ♫

Facilities: 🟊 ⊙ ℗ ✳ ⚹ ⊘ 🛁 🚽 🐾 WI-FI

Services: 🔌 🗑 🛒 🍽 🛒

Within 3 miles: ↓ ⚲ ⊟ ℘ ⊙ 🛒 🛒 🛒 U

Notes: Crazy golf.

WIDEMOUTH BAY *continued*

▶▶▶ 75% *Cornish Coasts Caravan & Camping Park* (SS202981)

Middle Penlean, Poundstock, Bude EX23 0EE
☎ 01288 361380
e-mail: enquiries5@cornishcoasts.co.uk
dir: *5m S of Bude on A39, 0.5m S of Rebel Cinema on right*

🚐 🚍 Å

Open Apr-Oct

Last arrival 22.00hrs Last departure 10.30hrs

A quiet park with lovely terraced pitches that make the most of the stunning views over the countryside to the sea at Widemouth Bay. The reception is in a 13th-century cottage, and the park is well equipped and tidy, with the well maintained and quirky toilet facilities (note the mosaic vanity units) housed in a freshly painted older-style building. Planned ongoing improvements for this small and friendly park sounded very positive. 3.5 acre site. 46 touring pitches. 8 hardstandings. Caravan pitches. Motorhome pitches. Tent pitches. 4 statics.

AA Pubs & Restaurants nearby: The Bay View Inn, Widemouth Bay 01288 361273

Castle Restaurant, Bude 01288 350543

Leisure: ⚠

Facilities: 🐾 ⊙ ℱ ✳ ♿ 🏪

Services: 🚐 🔋 🛢 📶 T 🍴

Within 3 miles: 🎣 ✎ ◎ ⛵ 🏪 ∪

Notes: Quiet after 22.00hrs. Post office.

▶▶▶ 74% **Penhalt Farm Holiday Park** (SS194003)

EX23 0DG
☎ 01288 361210 📄 01288 361210
e-mail: denandjennie@penhaltfarm.fsnet.co.uk
web: www.penhaltfarm.co.uk
dir: *From Bude take 2nd right to Widemouth Bay road off A39, left at end by Widemouth Manor signed Millook onto coastal road. Site 0.75m on left*

🚐 🚍 Å

Open Etr-Oct

Splendid views of the sea and coast can be enjoyed from all pitches on this sloping but partly level site, set in a lovely rural area on a working farm. About one mile away is one of Cornwall's finest beaches which prove popular with all the family as well as surfers. 8 acre site. 100 touring pitches. Caravan pitches. Motorhome pitches. Tent pitches.

AA Pubs & Restaurants nearby: The Bay View Inn, Widemouth Bay 01288 361273

Castle Restaurant, Bude 01288 350543

Leisure: ⚠ 🔍

Facilities: 🐾 ⊙ ℱ ✳ ♿ 🕐 🏪 🐕

Services: 🚐 🔋 📶 🍴

Within 3 miles: 🎣 ✎ 日 ⛵ 🏪 ∪

Notes: Pool table, netball & football posts, air hockey & table tennis.

● Wasdale Head and Wast Water from Great Gable

Cumbria

Think of Cumbria and you immediately picture a rumpled landscape of magical lakes and mountains and high green fells. For sheer natural beauty and grandeur, the English Lake District is hard to beat, and despite traffic congestion and high visitor numbers, this enchanting corner of the country manages to retain its unique individuality and sense of otherness.

Even on a glorious summer's day, you can still escape the 'madding crowd' and discover Lakeland's true heart and face. It is a fascinating place, characterised by ever changing moods and a timeless air of mystery. By applying a little effort and leaving the tourist hotspots and the busy roads far behind, you can reach and appreciate the Lake District that inspired William Wordsworth, Samuel Taylor Coleridge, Arthur Ransome and Robert Southey.

Derwentwater – the 'Queen of the English Lakes' is one of the most popular lakes in the region and certainly the widest. Shelley described it as 'smooth and dark as a plain of polished jet.' Windermere, to the south, is the largest lake and the town of the same name is a popular tourist base; this is one of the few places in the Lake District that has a railway. Away from the lakes and the various watersports are miles of country for the adventurous to explore. The towering summits of Helvellyn, Scafell, Scafell Pike and Great Gable are the highest peaks in England.

Along the eastern edge of the 866-square mile National Park and handy for the West Coast main line and the M6 are several well-known towns – Kendal and Penrith. To the north is the ancient and historic city of Carlisle; once a Roman camp – its wall still runs north of the city – it was captured during the Jacobean rising of 1745. The cathedral dates back to the early 12th century.

The southern half of Cumbria is often bypassed and overlooked in favour of the more obvious attractions of the Lake District. Visitors who do journey beyond the park boundaries are usually impressed and inspired in equal measure by its wealth of delights. The Lune Valley, for example, remains as lovely as it was when Turner came here to paint, and the 19th-century writer John Ruskin described the view from 'The Brow,' a walk running behind Kirkby Lonsdale's parish church, as 'one of the loveliest scenes in England.'

Walking and Cycling

Walkers are spoilt for choice in Cumbria and the Lake District. Numerous paths and trails crisscross this rugged mountain landscape. That is part of its appeal – the chance to get up close and personal with Mother Nature. For something even more ambitious and adventurous, there are several long-distance trails. ▶

● Lake Buttermere

The 70-mile (112km) Cumbria Way follows the valley floors rather than the mountain summits, while the 190-mile (305km) Coast to Coast has just about every kind of landscape and terrain imaginable. The route, pioneered by the well-known walker and writer, Alfred Wainwright, cuts across the Lake District, the Yorkshire Dales and the North York Moors, spanning the width of England between St Bees on the Cumbrian west coast, and Robin Hood's Bay on the North Yorkshire and Cleveland Heritage Coast.

The region also offers a walk with a difference and one which brings a true sense of drama and adventure. At the extreme southern end of Cumbria, in the reassuring company of official guide Cedric Robinson, MBE, you can cross the treacherous, deceptively beautiful sands of Morecambe Bay on foot. The bay, which is Britain's largest continuous intertidal area, is renowned for its quick sand and shifting channels. Many lives have been lost here over the years but in Cedric's expert hands, it is safe to cross.

● Herdwick sheep at Eskdale Show

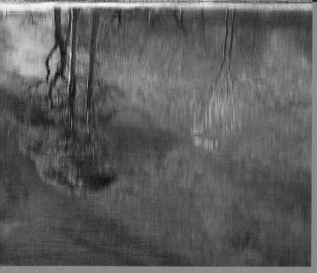

Festivals and Events

Cumbria offers something in the region of 500 festivals and events throughout the year.
The choice includes:

- Ambleside Daffodil and Spring Flower Festival in late March.
- Ulverston Walking Festival at the end of April and beginning of May.
- In July there is the Coniston Water Festival, famous for its Duck Race at Church Bridge; the Carlisle Festival of Nations; the Carlisle Summer Classical Music Festival at the cathedral.
- The Westmorland County Show takes place at Crooklands, near Kendal, in early September while the Dickensian Festival is staged in Ulverston in late November.
- Model Railway and Transport Exhibition at Barrow-in-Furness, in October.
- There are winter lighting events along Hadrian's Wall in November and December; and Christmas at the Castle at Muncaster Castle, Ravenglass.

The region is also popular with cyclists with lots of cycle hire outlets and plenty of routes to choose from. The 12-mile Wast Water to Santon Bridge cycle route passes England's deepest lake and is reputed to offer the finest view of the Lake District. It's quite a tough challenge and not suitable for under-11s. There are also waymarked bike trails in Grizedale Forest and Whinlatter Forest.

CUMBRIA

See Walks 3 & 4 in the Walks & Cycle Rides section at the end of the guide.

AMBLESIDE   Map 18 NY30

Places to visit

The Armitt Collection, AMBLESIDE 015394 31212 www.armitt.com

Beatrix Potter Gallery, HAWKSHEAD 015394 36269 www.nationaltrust.org.uk

Great for kids: Lakes Aquarium, LAKESIDE 015395 30153 www.lakesaquarium.co.uk

PREMIER PARK

►►►►► 86% *Skelwith Fold Caravan Park* (NY355029)

GOLD

LA22 0HX
☎ 015394 32277   📄 015394 34344
e-mail: info@skelwith.com
dir: *From Ambleside on A593 towards Coniston, left at Clappersgate onto B5286 (Hawkshead road). Site 1m on right*

🚐 🚐

Open Mar-15 Nov

Last arrival dusk Last departure noon

In the grounds of a former mansion, this park is in a beautiful setting close to Lake Windermere. Touring areas are dotted in paddocks around the extensively wooded grounds, and the all-weather pitches are set close to the many facility buildings. The premium pitches are quite superb.

There is a five-acre family recreation area, which has spectacular views of Loughrigg Fell. 130 acre site. 150 touring pitches. 150 hardstandings. Caravan pitches. Motorhome pitches. 300 statics.

AA Pubs & Restaurants nearby: Wateredge Inn, Ambleside 015394 32332

Drunken Duck Inn, Ambleside 015394 36347

Leisure: 🎬 🎣
Facilities: 🏪⊙🍴✳🔥🕙🚽🚻🏕 📶
Services: 🚐🔌🛢🎱🚽🛒🔧
Within 3 miles: ⬇🚣🎏🏇◎🛶🏌🎣🐴🐴🎣🚫
Notes: Family recreation area.

►►► 78% Low Wray National Trust Campsite *(NY372013)*

Low Wray LA22 0JA
☎ 015394 63862 & 32733   📄 015394 32684
e-mail: campsite.bookings@nationaltrust.org.uk
dir: *3m SW of Ambleside on A593 to Clappersgate, then B5286. Approx 1m turn left at Wray sign. Site less than 1m on left*

* 🚐 fr £13 ⛺ fr £13

Open wk before Etr-Oct

Last arrival variable Last departure 11.00hrs

Picturesquely set on the wooded shores of Lake Windermere, this site is a favourite with tenters and watersports enthusiasts. The toilets facilities are housed in wooden cabins and these were smartly refurbished in 2011, and tents can be pitched in wooded glades with lake views or open grassland, here there are wooden camping pods, and a mini-reservation of tipis and solar-heated bell tents. There's a new shop and reception and a

superb decked walkway through wetland teeming with wildlife. Off-road biking, walks and pubs serving food are all nearby. 10 acre site. 140 touring pitches. Motorhome pitches. Tent pitches. 4 wooden pods.

AA Pubs & Restaurants nearby: Wateredge Inn, Ambleside 015394 32332

Drunken Duck Inn, Ambleside 015394 36347

Kings Arms, Hawkshead 015394 36372

Leisure: 🎬
Facilities: 🏪⊙✳🕙🚽🔁 ⓘ
Services: 🛢
Within 3 miles: 🚣🎏🎣◎🛶🏌
Notes: No cars by tents. No groups of more than 4 unless a family group with children, takeaway catering van/outdoor activities bookable during school hols. Dogs must be kept on leads. Launching for sailing craft, orienteering course.

see advert below

NEW ►►► 77% The Croft Caravan & Campsite *(SD352981)*

North Lonsdale Rd, Hawkshead LA22 0NX
☎ 015394 36374
e-mail: enquiries@hawkshead-croft.com
dir: *From B5285 in Hawkshead turn into site opposite main public car & coach park*

* 🚐 £18.75-£24 ⛺ £15.75-£24 ⛺ £15.75-£18.75

Open Mar-Nov

Last arrival 21.30hrs Last departure noon

In the historic village of Hawkshead, which is now a popular destination for Beatrix Potter fans, this

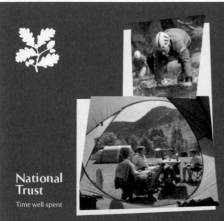
LEISURE: 🏊 Indoor swimming pool 🏊 Outdoor swimming pool 🎠 Children's playground 🧒 Kid's club 🎾 Tennis court 🎯 Games room 📺 Separate TV room ⛳ 9/18 hole golf course 🚤 Boats for hire 🎬 Cinema 🎵 Entertainment 🎣 Fishing ◎ Mini golf 🏄 Watersports 🏋 Gym 🏈 Sports field **Spa** 🐴 Stables
FACILITIES: 🛁 Bath 🚿 Shower ⊙ Electric shaver 🎀 Hairdryer ✳ Ice Pack Facility ♿ Disabled facilities 🕙 Public telephone 🏪 Shop on site or within 200yds 🚐 Mobile shop (calls at least 5 days a week) 🍖 BBQ area 🪑 Picnic area 📶 Wi-fi 💻 Internet access ♻ Recycling ⓘ Tourist info 🐕 Dog exercise area

former working farm has a large tent field that borders a beck, and the sound of running water and birdsong are welcome distractions. A well maintained amenities block and games room are additional benefits. 5 acre site. 75 touring pitches. 15 hardstandings. Caravan pitches. Motorhome pitches. Tent pitches. 20 statics.

AA Pubs & Restaurants nearby: The Queen's Head, Hawkshead 015394 36271

Kings Arms, Hawkshead 015394 36372

Leisure: 🔍

Facilities: ⬛☉🍴❄️🔥🛝🏕🐕♻️ⓘ

Services: 🔌🔲

Within 3 miles: ✐🛍🔲

Notes: No noise 23.00hrs-07.00hrs. Dogs must be kept on leads.

NEW ►►► 75% Hawkshead Hall Farm (SD349988)

Hawkshead LA22 0NN
☎ **015394 36221**
e-mail: enquiries@hawksheadhall-campsite.com
dir: From Ambleside take A593 signed Coniston, then B5286 signed Hawkshead. Site signed on left just before Hawkshead. Or from Coniston take B5285 to T-junct. Left, then 1st right into site

🚐 � Å

Open Mar-Oct

Last arrival 21.00hrs Last departure noon

A mainly camping site a few minutes' walk from village centre in a landscape of gentle rolling hills. The pitch sizes are generous, and there's a very well-equipped, purpose-built amenities block. There is no laundry on this site, but there is direct access to the adjacent Croft site, under same ownership, where this facility can be used. 55 touring pitches. Caravan pitches. Motorhome pitches. Tent pitches.

AA Pubs & Restaurants nearby: The Queen's Head, Hawkshead 015394 36271

Kings Arms, Hawkshead 015394 36372

APPLEBY-IN-WESTMORLAND   Map 18 NY62

Places to visit

Brougham Castle, BROUGHAM 01768 862488
www.english-heritage.org.uk

Acorn Bank Garden and Watermill, TEMPLE SOWERBY 017683 61893
www.nationaltrust.org.uk

Great for kids: Wetheriggs Animal Rescue & Conservation Centre, PENRITH 01768 866657
www.wetheriggsanimalrescue.co.uk

AA CAMPING CARD SITE

PREMIER PARK

►►►►► 86% Wild Rose Park (NY698165)

Best of British

Ormside CA16 6EJ
☎ **017683 51077**   📠 **017683 52551**
e-mail: reception@wildrose.co.uk
web: www.wildrose.co.uk
dir: Signed on unclass road to Great Ormside, off B6260

* 🚐 £16-£33.50 � £17-£33.50 Å £16-£26.50

Open all year (rs Nov-Mar shop closed, restaurant rs, pool closed 6 Sep-27 May)

Last arrival 22.00hrs Last departure noon

Situated in the Eden Valley, this large family-run park has been carefully landscaped and offers superb facilities maintained to an extremely high standard, including four wooden wigwams for hire. There are several individual pitches, and extensive views from most areas of the park. Traditional stone walls and the planting of lots of indigenous trees help it to blend into the environment, and wildlife is actively encouraged. 85 acre site. 226 touring pitches. 140 hardstandings. Caravan pitches. Motorhome pitches. Tent pitches. 273 statics. 4 tipis.

AA Pubs & Restaurants nearby: The Royal Oak Appleby, Appleby-in-Westmorland 017683 51463

Tufton Arms Hotel, Appleby-in-Westmorland 017683 51593

Wild Rose Park

Leisure: 🏊⛰🔍🖥

Facilities: ⬛☉🍴❄️🔥🛝🏕🐕♻️ⓘ

Services: 🔌🔲🔋⌀Ⓣ🍴🛒🚚🔧

Within 3 miles: ⚓✐◎🛍🔲🪑

Notes: No unaccompanied teenagers, no group bookings, no dangerous dogs, no noise after 22.30hrs. Dogs must be kept on leads. Pitch & putt.

AYSIDE   Map 18 SD38

Places to visit

Hill Top, NEAR SAWREY 015394 36269
www.nationaltrust.org.uk

Levens Hall, LEVENS 015395 60321
www.levenshall.co.uk

Great for kids: Lakes Aquarium, LAKESIDE 015395 30153 www.lakesaquarium.co.uk

►►► 74% Oak Head Caravan Park (SD389839)

LA11 6JA
☎ **015395 31475**
web: www.oakheadcaravanpark.co.uk
dir: M6 junct 36, A590 towards Newby Bridge, 14m. From A590 bypass follow signs for Ayside

🚐 � Å

Open Mar-Oct

Last arrival 22.00hrs Last departure noon

A pleasant terraced site with two separate areas - grass for tents and all gravel pitches for caravans and motorhomes. The site is enclosed within mature woodland and surrounded by hills. This site is located in a less busy area but convenient for all the Lake District attractions. 3 acre site. 60 touring pitches. 30 hardstandings. Caravan pitches. Motorhome pitches. Tent pitches. 71 statics.

continued

SERVICES: 🔌 Electric hook up 🔲 Launderette 🍷 Licensed bar 🔥 Calor Gas ⌀ Camping Gaz Ⓣ Toilet fluid 🍴 Café/Restaurant 🚚 Fast Food/Takeaway 🔋 Battery charging 🚼 Baby care 🔧 Motorvan service point
ABBREVIATIONS: BH/bank hols-bank holidays Etr-Easter Whit-Whitsun dep-departure fr-from hrs-hours m-mile mdnt-midnight rdbt-roundabout rs-restricted service wk-week wknd-weekend 🚫 No credit cards 🚫 No dogs
See page 7 for details of the AA Camping Card Scheme

AYSIDE *continued*

AA Pubs & Restaurants nearby: White Hart Inn, Bouth 01229 861229

Rogan & Company Bar & Restaurant, Cartmel 015395 35917

Facilities: 🏠⊙🅿✕🕭🕙

Services: 🔌🛢🧴🚮

Within 3 miles: 🐟🏌🏊🛒🕙

Notes: 🐕 No open fires.

BARROW-IN-FURNESS   Map 18 SD26

Places to visit

The Dock Museum, BARROW-IN-FURNESS 01229 876400 www.dockmuseum.org.uk

Furness Abbey, BARROW-IN-FURNESS 01229 823420 www.english-heritage.org.uk

Great for kids: South Lakes Wild Animal Park, DALTON-IN-FURNESS 01229 466086 www.wildanimalpark.co.uk

---

▶▶▶ 82% South End Caravan Park

(SD208628)

Walney Island LA14 3YQ
☎ 01229 472823 & 471556   📠 01229 472822
e-mail: enquiries@secp.co.uk
web: www.walneyislandcaravanpark.co.uk
dir: *M6 junct 36, A590 to Barrow, follow signs for Walney Island. Cross bridge, turn left. Site 6m south*

🔌🚐

Open Mar-Oct (rs Mar-Etr & Oct pool closed)

Last arrival 22.00hrs Last departure noon

A friendly family-owned and run park next to the sea and close to a nature reserve, on the southern end of Walney Island. It offers an extensive range of quality amenities including an adult lounge, and high standards of cleanliness and maintenance. 7 acre site. 50 touring pitches. 20 hardstandings. 29 seasonal pitches. Caravan pitches. Motorhome pitches. 250 statics.

South End Caravan Park

Leisure: 🏄⛰🚣🔍🖵

Facilities: 🏠⊙✕🕭🕙⊙🏕♻

Services: 🔌🛢🍽🧴🚮🛒🍺

Within 3 miles: 🏌🏊🛒🕙

Notes: Dogs must be kept on leads. Bowling green, snooker table.

BASSENTHWAITE LAKE

See map for locations of sites in the vicinity

BOOT   Map 18 NY10

Places to visit

Steam Yacht Gondola, CONISTON 015394 41288 www.nationaltrust.org.uk/gondola

The Ruskin Museum, CONISTON 015394 41164 www.ruskinmuseum.com

Great for kids: Ravenglass & Eskdale Railway, RAVENGLASS 01229 717171 www.ravenglass-railway.co.uk

---

PREMIER PARK

▶▶▶▶▶ 83% Eskdale Camping & Caravanning Club Site *(NY178011)*

CA19 1TH
☎ 019467 23253 & 0845 130 7633
e-mail: eskdale.site@thefriendlyclub.co.uk
dir: *Exit A595 at Gosforth or Holmrook to Eskdale Green & then to Boot. Site on left towards Hardknott Pass after railway & 150mtrs after Brook House Inn*

🚐Å

Open Mar-14 Jan

Last arrival 20.00hrs Last departure noon

Stunningly located in Eskdale, a feeling of peace and tranquillity prevails at this top quality Club site, with the sounds of running water and birdsong the only welcome distractions. Although mainly geared to campers, the facilities here are

---

very impressive, with a smart amenities block, equipped with efficient modern facilities including an excellent fully-serviced wet room-style, family room with power shower, and the surroundings of mountains, mature trees and shrubs create a wonderful 'back to nature' feeling. There's a nest of camping pods under the trees, with gravel access paths and barbeques, and a super new lush backpackers' field (opened in 2011). Expect great attention to detail and a high level of customer care. The park is only a quarter of a mile from Boot station on the Ravenglass/Eskdale railway (La'al Ratty). 8 acre site. 80 touring pitches. Motorhome pitches. Tent pitches. 10 wooden pods.

AA Pubs & Restaurants nearby: Boot Inn, Boot 019467 23224

Brook House Inn, Boot 019467 23288

Leisure: ⛰♿

Facilities: 🏠⊙🅿✕🕭🕙🖼🏕➤𝒊

Services: 🔌🛢🧴🚮🅣🚮🛒⛏

Within 3 miles: 🏌🏊🛒🕙

Notes: Site gates closed & no noise 23.00hrs-07.00hrs, no open fires. Dogs must be kept on leads. 1 camping barn.

BOWNESS-ON-WINDERMERE

Sites are listed under Windermere

CARLISLE   Map 18 NY35

Places to visit

Carlisle Castle, CARLISLE 01228 591992 www.english-heritage.org.uk

Tullie House Museum & Art Gallery, CARLISLE 01228 618718 www.tulliehouse.co.uk

Great for kids: Trotters World of Animals, BASSENTHWAITE 017687 76239 www.trottersworld.com

---

▶▶▶ 86% Dandy Dinmont Caravan & Camping Park *(NY399620)*

Blackford CA6 4EA
☎ 01228 674611   📠 01228 674611
e-mail: dandydinmont@btopenworld.com
dir: *M6 junct 44, A7 N. Site 1.5m on right, after Blackford sign*

🔌 £14 🚐 £14 Å £12-£13

Open Mar-Oct

Last arrival 21.00hrs Last departure 14.00hrs

A sheltered, rural site, screened on two sides by hedgerows and only one mile from the M6 and Carlisle. The grass pitches are immaculately kept, and there are some larger hardstandings for motor homes. This park attracts mainly adults; please note that cycling and ball games are not allowed. Touring customers are invited to view the private award-winning garden. 4.5 acre site. 47 touring pitches. 14 hardstandings. Caravan pitches. Motorhome pitches. Tent pitches. 15 statics.

Facilities: 🚿 ⊙ ✱ 🪑 ♻ ℹ

Services: 🔌 🧺 ⛽

Within 3 miles: ⛳ 🎣 ◎ [$] 🧺 🐎

Notes: 💳 Dogs must be kept on leads and exercised off site. Children's activities are restricted. Covered dishwashing area.

►►► 84% Green Acres Caravan Park

(NY416614)

High Knells, Houghton CA6 4JW
☎ 01228 675418
e-mail: info@caravanpark-cumbria.com
dir: *Exit M6 junct 44, A689 towards Brampton for 1m. Left at Scaleby sign. Site 1m on left*

* 🔌 £14-£18 🚐 £14-£18 ⛺ £10-£13

Open Apr-Oct

Last arrival 21.00hrs Last departure noon

A small touring park in rural surroundings close to the M6 with distant views of the fells. A convenient stopover, this pretty park is run by keen, friendly owners who maintain high standards throughout. The site has a caravan and motorhome pressure-washer area. 3 acre site. 30 touring pitches. 30 hardstandings. 12 seasonal pitches. Caravan pitches. Motorhome pitches. Tent pitches.

Leisure: ⚽

Facilities: 🚿 ⊙ ✱ 🐕 ♻ ℹ

Services: 🔌 🧺

Within 3 miles: ⛳ [$]

Notes: Adults only. 💳 Dogs must be kept on leads.

CARTMEL — Map 18 SD37

Places to visit

Holker Hall & Gardens, HOLKER 015395 58328 www.holker.co.uk

Hill Top, NEAR SAWREY 015394 36269 www.nationaltrust.org.uk

Great for kids: Lakes Aquarium, LAKESIDE 015395 30153 www.lakesaquarium.co.uk

►►► 75% Greaves Farm Caravan Park *(SD391823)*

Field Broughton LA11 6HU
☎ 015395 36329 & 36587
dir: *M6 junct 36 onto A590 signed Barrow. Approx 1m before Newby Bridge, turn left at x-roads signed Cartmel/Staveley. Site 2m on left just before church*

* 🔌 £16-£18 🚐 £16-£18 ⛺ £16-£18

Open Mar-Oct

Last arrival 21.00hrs Last departure noon

A small family-owned park close to a working farm in a peaceful rural area. Motorhomes are parked in a paddock, and there is a large field for tents and caravans. This simple park is carefully maintained, offers electric pitches (6amp), and there is always a sparkle to the toilet facilities. Static holiday caravans for hire. 3 acre site. 12 touring pitches. Caravan pitches. Motorhome pitches. Tent pitches. 20 statics.

AA Pubs & Restaurants nearby: Cavendish Arms, Cartmel 015395 36240

Rogan & Company Bar & Restaurant, Cartmel 015395 35917

Facilities: 🚿 ⊙ 💨 ✱ ☎ 🍼 ♻ ℹ

Services: 🔌 ⛽

Within 3 miles: ⛳ ⛵ 🎣 🚤 [$] 🐎

Notes: 💳 Dogs must be kept on leads. Separate chalet for dishwashing. Small freezer & fridge available.

CROOKLANDS — Map 18 SD58

Places to visit

Levens Hall, LEVENS 015395 60321 www.levenshall.co.uk

RSPB Leighton Moss Nature Reserve, SILVERDALE 01524 701601 www.rspb.org.uk/leightonmoss

Great for kids: South Lakes Wild Animal Park, DALTON-IN-FURNESS 01229 466086 www.wildanimalpark.co.uk

►►► 83% Waters Edge Caravan Park

(SD533838)

LA7 7NN
☎ 015395 67708
e-mail: info@watersedgecaravanpark.co.uk
dir: *M6 junct 36 take A65 towards Kirkby Lonsdale, at 2nd rdbt follow signs for Crooklands/Endmoor. Site 1m on right at Crooklands garage, just beyond 40mph limit*

* 🔌 £15.80-£22.90 🚐 £15.80-£22.90 ⛺ £12-£26.50

Open Mar-14 Nov (rs Low season bar not always open on week days)

Last arrival 22.00hrs Last departure noon

A peaceful, well-run park close to the M6, pleasantly bordered by streams and woodland. A Lakeland-style building houses a shop and bar, and the attractive toilet block is clean and modern. This is ideal either as a stopover or for longer stays. 3 acre site. 26 touring pitches. 26 hardstandings. Caravan pitches. Motorhome pitches. Tent pitches. 20 statics.

Leisure: 🏓 📺

Facilities: 🚿 ⊙ 💨 ✱ ♿ [$] 🪑 ℹ

Services: 🔌 🧺 🍷 ⛽ 🔥 [T]

Within 3 miles: 🎣 [$] 🐎

Notes: No cars by tents. Dogs must be kept on leads.

SERVICES: 🔌 Electric hook up 🧺 Launderette 🍷 Licensed bar ⛽ Calor Gas 🔥 Camping Gaz [T] Toilet fluid 🍴 Café/Restaurant 🍔 Fast Food/Takeaway 🔋 Battery charging 🍼 Baby care 🚰 Motorvan service point
ABBREVIATIONS: BH/bank hols-bank holidays Etr-Easter Whit-Whitsun dep-departure fr-from hrs-hours m-mile mdnt-midnight rdbt-roundabout rs-restricted service wk-week wknd-weekend 💳 No credit cards 🚫 No dogs
See page 7 for details of the AA Camping Card Scheme

CUMWHITTON   Map 18 NY55

Places to visit

Nenthead Mines, ALSTON 01434 382294
www.npht.com/nentheadmines

Lanercost Priory, BRAMPTON 01697 73030
www.english-heritage.org.uk

►►► 69% Cairndale Caravan Park

(NY518523)

CA8 9BZ
☎ 01768 896280
dir: *Exit A69 at Warwick Bridge on unclassified road through Great Corby to Cumwhitton, left at village sign, site 1m*

🚐 £10-£11 🚐 £10-£11

Open Mar-Oct

Last arrival 22.00hrs

Lovely grass site set in the tranquil Eden Valley with good views to distant hills. The all-weather touring pitches have electricity, and are located close to the immaculately maintained toilet facilities. Static holiday caravans for hire. 2 acre site. 5 touring pitches. 5 hardstandings. Caravan pitches. Motorhome pitches. 15 statics.

AA Pubs & Restaurants nearby: String of Horses Inn, Faugh 01228 670297

Facilities: 🅿⊙✳♻

Services: 🕿🛏🛒

Within 3 miles: ⌊⇞🎣🛶

Notes: 🐾

FLOOKBURGH   Map 18 SD37

Places to visit

Holker Hall & Gardens, HOLKER 015395 58328
www.holker.co.uk

Hill Top, NEAR SAWREY 015394 36269
www.nationaltrust.org.uk

Great for kids: Lakes Aquarium, LAKESIDE 015395 30153 www.lakesaquarium.co.uk

78% Lakeland Leisure Park *(SD372743)*

Moor Ln LA11 7LT
☎ 0871 231 0883 🖷 01539 558559
e-mail: lakeland@haven.com
dir: *On B5277 through Grange-over-Sands to Flookburgh. Left at village square, site 1m*

🚐🚐Å

Open mid Mar-end Oct (rs Mar-May & Sep-Oct reduced activities, outdoor pool closed)

Last arrival anytime Last departure 10.00hrs

A complete leisure park with full range of activities and entertainments, making this flat, grassy site ideal for families. The touring area is quietly situated away from the main amenities, but the swimming pools, all-weather bowling green and evening entertainment are just a short stroll away. 105 acre site. 190 touring pitches. 10 seasonal pitches. Caravan pitches. Motorhome pitches. Tent pitches. 800 statics.

AA Pubs & Restaurants nearby: Cavendish Arms, Cartmel 015395 36240

Rogan & Company Bar & Restaurant, Cartmel 015395 35917

Leisure: 🏊🏊‍♂️🎠♨🎱🎮🎵

Facilities: 🅿⊙♿🛁📷🛒📺🖥🚿♻🅿

Services: 🕿🛒🍴📺🍽🛒🛏

Within 3 miles: ⌊🏌◎🛶🎿🎣🛒U

Notes: No cars by caravans or tents. Family park, max 2 dogs per booking, certain dog breeds banned, no commercial vehicles, no bookings by persons under 21yrs unless a family booking.

see advert below

GRANGE-OVER-SANDS

See Cartmel

LEISURE: 🏊 Indoor swimming pool   🏊‍♂️ Outdoor swimming pool   🅰 Children's playground   🏌 Kid's club   🎾 Tennis court   🎱 Games room   📺 Separate TV room
⌊ 9/18 hole golf course   🛶 Boats for hire   🎬 Cinema   🎵 Entertainment   🎣 Fishing   ◎ Mini golf   🎿 Watersports   🏋 Gym   ⚽ Sports field   **Spa**   U Stables
FACILITIES: 🛁 Bath   🚿 Shower   ⊙ Electric shaver   🅿 Hairdryer   ✳ Ice Pack Facility   ♿ Disabled facilities   🕿 Public telephone   🛒 Shop on site or within 200yds
🛒 Mobile shop (calls at least 5 days a week)   🍴 BBQ area   🍽 Picnic area   🕸 Wi-fi   🖥 Internet access   ♻ Recycling   🅰 Tourist info   🐾 Dog exercise area

GREAT LANGDALE — Map 18 NY20

Places to visit

Dove Cottage and The Wordsworth Museum, GRASMERE 015394 35544
www.wordsworth.org.uk

Honister Slate Mine, BORROWDALE
01768 777230 www.honister.com

►►► 76% Great Langdale National Trust Campsite (NY286059)

LA22 9JU
☎ 015394 63862 & 32733
e-mail: campsite.bookings@nationaltrust.org.uk
web: www.ntlakescampsites.org.uk
dir: From Ambleside, A593 to Skelwith Bridge, right onto B5343, approx 5m to New Dungeon Ghyll Hotel. Site on left just before hotel

* ⇌ fr £13 ▲ fr £13

Open all year

Last departure 11.00hrs

Nestling in a green valley, sheltered by mature trees and surrounded by stunning fell views, this site is an ideal base for campers, climbers and fell walkers. The large grass tent area has some gravel parking for cars, and there is a separate area for groups, and one for families with a children's play area. Attractive wooden cabins house the toilets, a refurbished reception and shop (selling fresh baked bread and pastries), and drying rooms, and there are wooden camping pods and two yurts for hire. 9 acre site. 220 touring pitches. Motorhome pitches. Tent pitches. 3 wooden pods.

AA Pubs & Restaurants nearby: New Dungeon Ghyll Hotel, Great Langdale 015394 37213

Britannia Inn, Elterwater 015394 37210

Purdey's (Langdale Hotel & Country Club), Elterwater 015394 37302

Leisure: ⚙

Facilities: ⬤☉❄&☉⑤♻☘

Services: ⑤ 🔋⌀

Within 3 miles: ✎⑤

Notes: No cars by tents. No noise between 23.00hrs-07.00hrs, no groups of 4 or more unless a family with children. Dogs must be kept on leads.

see advert on page 126

HOLMROOK — Map 18 SD09

Places to visit

The Beacon, WHITEHAVEN 01946 592302
www.thebeacon-whitehaven.co.uk

The Rum Story, WHITEHAVEN 01946 592933
www.rumstory.co.uk

Great for kids: Ravenglass & Eskdale Railway, RAVENGLASS 01229 717171
www.ravenglass-railway.co.uk

►►► 75% Seven Acres Caravan Park (NY078014)

CA19 1YD
☎ 01946 822777 ⑤ 01946 824442
e-mail: reception@seacote.com
dir: Off A595 between Holmrook & Gosforth

* ⇌ £18-£21 ⇌ £18-£21 ▲ £10-£18

Open Mar-15 Jan

Last arrival 21.00hrs Last departure 10.30hrs

This sheltered park is close to the quiet West Cumbrian coastal villages and beaches, and handy for Eskdale and Wasdale. There is a good choice of pitches, some with hedged bays for privacy, and some with coastal views. The park has a heated toilet block, and a children's play area, and there is plenty to do and see in the area. 7 acre site. 37 touring pitches. 20 hardstandings. Caravan pitches. Motorhome pitches. Tent pitches. 16 statics.

AA Pubs & Restaurants nearby: Bower House Inn, Eskdale Green 019467 23244

Cumbrian Lodge, Seascale 019467 27309

Facilities: ⬤☉❄❄🛏🐕♻ ❶

Services: ⑤⑤⌀

Within 3 miles: ⚓✎◎⑤∪

KESWICK

Places to visit

Cumberland Pencil Museum, KESWICK
017687 73626 www.pencilmuseum.co.uk

Honister Slate Mine, BORROWDALE
01768 777230 www.honister.com

Great for kids: Mirehouse, KESWICK
017687 72287 www.mirehouse.com

KESWICK — Map 18 NY22

PREMIER PARK

►►►►► 86% *Castlerigg Hall Caravan & Camping Park* (NY282227)

Castlerigg Hall CA12 4TE
☎ 017687 74499 ⑤ 017687 74499
e-mail: info@castlerigg.co.uk
dir: 1.5m SE of Keswick on A591, turn right at sign. Site 200mtrs on right past Heights Hotel

⇌ ⇌ ▲

Open mid Mar-7 Nov

Last arrival 21.00hrs Last departure 11.30hrs

Spectacular views over Derwentwater to the mountains beyond are among the many attractions at this lovely Lakeland park. Old farm buildings have been tastefully converted into excellent toilets with private washing and family bathroom, reception and a well-equipped shop, and there is a kitchen/dining area for campers, and a restaurant/takeaway. There is a superb toilet block and wooden camping pods in the tent field, and a further ten all-weather pitches have been created. 8 acre site. 48 touring pitches. 48 hardstandings. Caravan pitches. Motorhome pitches. Tent pitches. 30 statics.

AA Pubs & Restaurants nearby: Kings Head, Keswick 017687 72393

Leisure: ⊡

Facilities: 🛏⬤☉❄❄&☉⑤🛏 ᴡ-ꜰ

Services: ⑤⑤🔋⌀🅣🍽🛒⬤⌀

Within 3 miles: ⚓❄🗓✎◎❄⑤⑤∪

Notes: Dogs must be kept on leads and not left unattended. Campers' kitchen, sitting room.

SERVICES: 🔌 Electric hook up ⑤ Launderette 🍷 Licensed bar 🔥 Calor Gas ⌀ Camping Gaz 🅣 Toilet fluid 🍽 Café/Restaurant 🍔 Fast Food/Takeaway 🔋 Battery charging
🛏 Baby care ⌀ Motorvan service point
ABBREVIATIONS: BH/bank hols-bank holidays Etr-Easter Whit-Whitsun dep-departure fr-from hrs-hours m-mile mdnt-midnight rdbt-roundabout rs-restricted service wk-week
wknd-weekend ⊛ No credit cards ⊗ No dogs
See page 7 for details of the AA Camping Card Scheme

KESWICK continued

▶▶▶▶ 78% Gill Head Farm Caravan & Camping Park (NY380269)

Troutbeck CA11 0ST
☎ 017687 79652 📄 017687 79130
e-mail: enquiries@gillheadfarm.co.uk
web: www.gillheadfarm.co.uk
dir: M6 junct 40 take A66, then A5091 towards Troutbeck. Right after 100yds, then right again

🚐 🚍 ▲

Open Apr-Oct

Last arrival 22.00hrs Last departure noon

A family-run park on a working hill farm with lovely fell views. It has level touring pitches, and a log cabin dining room that is popular with families. Tent pitches are gently sloping in a separate field with glorious views towards Keswick. 5.5 acre site. 42 touring pitches. 21 hardstandings. Caravan pitches. Motorhome pitches. Tent pitches. 17 statics.

AA Pubs & Restaurants nearby: The George, Keswick 017687 72076

Leisure: 🄰 ▢
Facilities: 🔦 ☉ 🅿 ✳ ☉ 🖰 🛱 ⊁
Services: 🔌 🖥 🛢 ⌀
Within 3 miles: ↨ ⚘ ✔ 🖉 🍴 🖥 ↻
Notes: ⊘ No fires.

▶▶▶ 82% Castlerigg Farm Camping & Caravan Site (NY283225)

Castlerigg Farm CA12 4TE
☎ 017687 72479
e-mail: info@castleriggfarm.com
dir: From Keswick on A591 towards Windermere, turn right at top of hill at camping sign. Farm 2nd site on left

* 🚐 £17-£20 🚍 £17-£20 ▲ £14-£16.20

Open Mar-Nov (rs at quiet times café & shop restricted hours)

Last arrival 21.30hrs Last departure 11.30hrs

Nestling at the foot of Walla Crag, this tranquil fell-side park enjoys lake views, and is popular with families and couples seeking a quiet base for fell walking. The modern facilities include a shop, laundry and spotless toilet facilities, and a café in a converted barn. Castlerigg Stone Circle and the attractions of Keswick are nearby. 3 acre site. 48 touring pitches. Caravan pitches. Motorhome pitches. Tent pitches.

AA Pubs & Restaurants nearby: Horse & Farrier Inn, Keswick 017687 79688

The Swinside Inn, Keswick 017687 78253

Facilities: 🔦 ☉ 🅿 ✳ ☉ 🖥 🛱 🕾
Services: 🔌 🖥 🛢 🅿 ⊕ 🅣 🍴 🎪 🖩 ⌄
Within 3 miles: ↨ ⚘ 🎗 🖉 ◎ ⚓ 🖥 🖥
Notes: No noise after 22.30hrs, no fires on the ground. Dogs must be kept on leads. Cycle storage.

▶▶▶ 77% Burns Farm Caravan Park (NY307244)

St Johns in the Vale CA12 4RR
☎ 017687 79225 & 79112
e-mail: linda@burns-farm.co.uk
dir: Exit A66 signed Castlerigg Stone Circle/Youth Centre/Burns Farm. Site on right in 0.5m

🚐 🚍 ▲

Open Mar-4 Nov

Last departure noon

Lovely views of Blencathra and Skiddaw can be enjoyed from this secluded park, set on a working farm which extends a warm welcome to families. This is a good choice for exploring the beautiful and interesting countryside. Food can be found in the pub at Threlkeld. 2.5 acre site. 32 touring pitches. Caravan pitches. Motorhome pitches. Tent pitches.

AA Pubs & Restaurants nearby: Farmers Arms, Keswick 017687 72322

Facilities: 🔦 ☉ ✳ ⚒ ☉ 🕾
Services: 🔌 🖥 🛢 🎪
Within 3 miles: ↨ ⚘ 🎗 ⒣ 🖉 ◎ ⚓ 🖥 🖥 ↻
Notes: ⊘ No noise after mdnt.

Places to visit

Sizergh Castle & Garden, SIZERGH
015395 60951 www.nationaltrust.org.uk

Kendal Museum, KENDAL 01539 815597
www.kendalmuseum.org.uk

Great for kids: Dales Countryside Museum & National Park Centre, HAWES 01969 666210
www.yorkshiredales.org.uk/dcm

▶▶▶▶▶ 80% Woodclose Caravan Park (SD618786)

GOLD

High Casterton LA6 2SE
☎ 01524 271597 📄 01524 272301
e-mail: info@woodclosepark.com
web: www.woodclosepark.com
dir: On A65, 0.25m after Kirkby Lonsdale towards Skipton, on left

* 🚐 £12-£22 🚍 £12-£22 ▲ £13-£17

Open Mar-Oct

Last arrival 21.00hrs Last departure noon

A peaceful park with excellent toilet facilities set in idyllic countryside in the beautiful Lune Valley. Ideal for those seeking quiet relaxation, and for visiting the Lakes and Dales, with the riverside walks at Devil's Bridge, and historic Kirkby Lonsdale both an easy walk from the park. There are four wigwam cabins for hire, and Freeview TV is available via a booster cable from reception. There are now 8 fully-serviced all-weather pitches and more are planned. 9 acre site. 29 touring pitches. 8 hardstandings. Caravan pitches. Motorhome pitches. Tent pitches. 54 statics.

AA Pubs & Restaurants nearby: Sun Inn, Kirkby Lonsdale 015242 71965

The Whoop Hall, Kirkby Lonsdale 015242 71284

Pheasant Inn, Kirkby Lonsdale 01524 271230

Leisure: 🄰
Facilities: 🔦 ☉ 🅿 ✳ ⚒ ☉ 🖥 🛱 🕾
Services: 🔌 🖥 🛢 ⌀
Within 3 miles: ↨ 🖉 🖥 🖥 ↻
Notes: No arrivals before 13.00hrs. Dogs must be kept on leads. Cycle hire, internet access, wigwams & crock boxes for hire.

LEISURE: 🏊 Indoor swimming pool 🏊 Outdoor swimming pool 🄰 Children's playground 🛝 Kid's club 🎾 Tennis court 🎱 Games room 📺 Separate TV room ↨ 9/18 hole golf course 🚣 Boats for hire 🎬 Cinema 🎵 Entertainment 🎣 Fishing ◎ Mini golf 🏄 Watersports ⚽ Gym ⚓ Sports field **Spa** ↻ Stables
FACILITIES: 🛁 Bath 🔦 Shower ☉ Electric shaver 🅿 Hairdryer ✳ Ice Pack Facility ⚒ Disabled facilities ☉ Public telephone 🖥 Shop on site or within 200yds 🛒 Mobile shop (calls at least 5 days a week) 🛱 BBQ area 🛱 Picnic area 🕾 Wi-fi 🖥 Internet access ♻ Recycling ⓘ Tourist info ⊁ Dog exercise area

►►►► 79% New House Caravan Park (SD628774)

LA6 2HR
☎ 015242 71590
e-mail: colinpreece9@aol.com
dir: *1m SE of Kirkby Lonsdale on A65, turn right into site entrance 300yds past Whoop Hall Inn*

* ⚐ £17 ⚐ £17

Open Mar-Oct Last arrival 20.00hrs

A very pleasant base in which to relax or tour the surrounding area, developed around a former farm. The excellent toilet facilities are purpose built, and there are good roads and hardstandings, all in a lovely rural setting. 3 acre site. 50 touring pitches. 50 hardstandings. Caravan pitches. Motorhome pitches.

AA Pubs & Restaurants nearby: Sun Inn, Kirkby Lonsdale 015242 71965

The Whoop Hall, Kirkby Lonsdale 015242 71284

Pheasant Inn, Kirkby Lonsdale 01524 271230

Facilities: ⟨icons⟩
Services: ⟨icons⟩
Within 3 miles: ⟨icons⟩
Notes: ⊗ No cycling.

LONGTOWN Map 21 NY36
Places to visit
Carlisle Castle, CARLISLE 01228 591992 www.english-heritage.org.uk
Tullie House Museum & Art Gallery, CARLISLE 01228 618718 www.tulliehouse.co.uk

►► 75% Camelot Caravan Park
(NY391666)

CA6 5SZ
☎ 01228 791248
dir: *M6 junct 44, site in 5m*

⚐ ⚐ Å

Open Mar-Oct

Last arrival 22.00hrs Last departure noon

A very pleasant level grassy site in a wooded setting near the M6, with direct access from the A7, and simple, clean toilet facilities. The park is an ideal stopover site. 1.5 acre site. 20 touring pitches. Caravan pitches. Motorhome pitches. Tent pitches. 2 statics.

Facilities: ⟨icons⟩ **Services:** ⚐
Within 3 miles: ⟨icons⟩ **Notes:** ⊗

MEALSGATE Map 18 NY24
Places to visit
Jennings Brewery Tour and Shop, COCKERMOUTH 0845 129 7190 www.jenningsbrewery.co.uk
Wordsworth House and Garden, COCKERMOUTH 01900 820882 www.nationaltrust.org.uk

►►►► 78% Larches Caravan Park
(NY205415)

CA7 1LQ
☎ 016973 71379 & 71803 ▤ 016973 71782
dir: *On A595 (Carlisle to Cockermouth road)*

* ⚐ £15-£20.90 ⚐ £15-£20.90 Å £15-£20.90

Open Mar-Oct (rs Early & late season)

Last arrival 21.30hrs Last departure noon

This over 18s-only park is set in wooded rural surroundings on the fringe of the Lake District National Park. Touring units are spread out over two sections. The friendly family-run park offers well cared for facilities, and a small indoor swimming pool. 20 acre site. 73 touring pitches. 30 hardstandings. Caravan pitches. Motorhome pitches. Tent pitches.

AA Pubs & Restaurants nearby: Oddfellows Arms, Caldbeck 016974 78227

Leisure: ⟨icon⟩
Facilities: ⟨icons⟩
Services: ⟨icons⟩
Within 3 miles: ⟨icons⟩
Notes: Adults only. ⊗

MILNTHORPE
Places to visit
Levens Hall, LEVENS 015395 60321 www.levenshall.co.uk
RSPB Leighton Moss Nature Reserve, SILVERDALE 01524 701601 www.rspb.org.uk/leightonmoss
Great for kids: Lakes Aquarium, LAKESIDE 015395 30153 www.lakesaquarium.co.uk

MILNTHORPE Map 18 SD48

►►► 76% Hall More Caravan Park (SD502771)

GOLD

Hale LA7 7BP
☎ 01524 781453 ▤ 01524 782243
e-mail: enquiries@pureleisure-holidays.co.uk
dir: *M6 junct 35, A6 towards Milnthorpe for 4m. Left at Lakeland Wildlife Oasis, follow brown signs*

* ⚐ £15-£17 ⚐ £15-£17 Å £13-£14

Open Mar-Jan

Last arrival 22.00hrs Last departure 10.00hrs

A pleasant meadowland site with hardstanding and grass pitches in two neat and tidy hedged areas, simple, well maintained toilet facilities, a new dish-washing facility in the tenting field for 2011, and seven wooden cabins for hire. It is close to a farm and stables offering pony trekking, and there is trout fishing nearby. 4 acre site. 44 touring pitches. 7 hardstandings. Caravan pitches. Motorhome pitches. Tent pitches. 60 statics.

AA Pubs & Restaurants nearby: The Wheatsheaf, Beetham 015395 62123

Facilities: ⟨icons⟩
Services: ⟨icons⟩
Within 3 miles: ⟨icons⟩

PATTERDALE Map 18 NY31

►►► 78% Sykeside Camping Park
(NY403119)

Brotherswater CA11 0NZ
☎ 017684 82239 ▤ 017684 82239
e-mail: info@sykeside.co.uk
dir: *Direct access off A592 (Windermere to Ullswater road) at foot of Kirkstone Pass*

* ⚐ £17.50-£25 ⚐ £17.50-£25 Å £13.50-£23.50

Open all year

Last arrival 22.30hrs Last departure 14.00hrs

A camper's delight, this family-run park is sited at the foot of Kirkstone Pass, under the 2,000ft Hartsop Dodd in a spectacular area with breathtaking views. The park has mainly grass pitches with a few hardstandings, an area with tipis for hire, and for those campers without a tent there is bunkhouse accommodation. There's a small campers' kitchen and the bar serves breakfast and bar meals. There is abundant

continued on page 135

SERVICES: ⚐ Electric hook up ▤ Launderette ⚐ Licensed bar ⚐ Calor Gas ⚐ Camping Gaz ⊤ Toilet fluid ⚐ Café/Restaurant ⚐ Fast Food/Takeaway ⚐ Battery charging ⚐ Baby care ⚐ Motorvan service point
ABBREVIATIONS: BH/bank hols-bank holidays Etr-Easter Whit-Whitsun dep-departure fr-from hrs-hours m-mile mdnt-midnight rdbt-roundabout rs-restricted service wk-week wknd-weekend ⊗ No credit cards ⊗ No dogs
See page 7 for details of the AA Camping Card Scheme

PATTERDALE *continued*

wildlife. 10 acre site. 86 touring pitches. 5 hardstandings. Caravan pitches. Motorhome pitches. Tent pitches.

AA Pubs & Restaurants nearby: Inn on the Lake, Glenridding 017684 82444

The Brackenrigg, Watermillock 017684 86206

Leisure:

Facilities:

Services:

Within 3 miles:

Notes: Laundry & drying room.

PENRITH — Map 18 NY53

Places to visit

Dalemain Mansion & Historic Gardens, DALEMAIN 017684 86450 www.dalemain.com

Shap Abbey, SHAP www.english-heritage.org.uk

Great for kids: The Rheged Centre, PENRITH 01768 868000 www.rheged.com

►►►► 84% *Lowther Holiday Park* *(NY527265)*

GOLD

Eamont Bridge CA10 2JB
☎ 01768 863631 01768 868126
e-mail: sales@lowther-holidaypark.co.uk
dir: *3m S of Penrith on A6*

Open mid Mar-mid Nov

Last arrival 22.00hrs Last departure 22.00hrs

A secluded natural woodland site with lovely riverside walks and glorious countryside surroundings. The park is home to a rare colony of red squirrels, and trout fishing is available on the two-mile stretch of the River Lowther which runs through it. A birdwatch scheme with a coloured brochure has been introduced inviting guests to spot some of 30 different species that can be seen on the park. 50 acre site. 180 touring pitches. 50 hardstandings. Caravan pitches. Motorhome pitches. Tent pitches. 403 statics.

AA Pubs & Restaurants nearby: Yanwath Gate Inn, Yanwath 01768 862386

Queen's Head Inn, Tirril 01768 863219

Martindale Restaurant, Penrith 01768 868111

Leisure:

Facilities:

Services:

Within 3 miles:

Notes: Families only, no cats, rollerblades, skateboards or commercial vehicles.

see advert on opposite page

►►►► 81% Flusco Wood

(NY345529)

GOLD

Flusco CA11 0JB
☎ 017684 80020 017684 80794
e-mail: info@fluscowood.co.uk
dir: *From Penrith to Keswick on A66 turn right signed Flusco. Approx 800mtrs, up short incline to right. Site on left*

Open all year (rs Etr-Nov tourers & motorhomes)

Last arrival 20.00hrs Last departure noon

Flusco Wood is set in mixed woodland with outstanding views towards Blencathra and the fells around Keswick. It combines two distinct areas, one of which has been designed specifically for touring caravans in neat glades with hardstandings, all within close proximity of the excellent log cabin-style toilet facilities. 24 acre site. 53 touring pitches. 53 hardstandings. Caravan pitches. Motorhome pitches.

AA Pubs & Restaurants nearby: Yanwath Gate Inn, Yanwath 01768 862386

Queen's Head Inn, Tirril 01768 863219

Martindale Restaurant, Penrith 01768 868111

Leisure:

Facilities:

Services:

Within 3 miles:

Notes: Quiet site, not suitable for large groups. Dogs must be kept on leads.

PENRUDDOCK — Map 18 NY42

►►► 78% Beckses Caravan Park

(NY419278)

CA11 0RX
☎ 01768 483224 01768 483006
dir: *M6 junct 40 onto A66 towards Keswick. Approx 6m at caravan park sign turn right onto B5288. Site on right in 0.25m*

Open Etr-Oct

Last arrival 20.00hrs Last departure 11.00hrs

A small, pleasant site on sloping ground with level pitches and views of distant fells, on the edge of the National Park. This sheltered park is in a good location for touring the North Lakes. 4 acre site. 23 touring pitches. Caravan pitches. Motorhome pitches. Tent pitches. 18 statics.

AA Pubs & Restaurants nearby: Queen's Head, Troutbeck 015394 32174

Facilities:

Services: **Within 3 miles:**

PENTON — Map 21 NY47

AA CAMPING CARD SITE

►►► 76% Twin Willows *(NY449771)*

The Beeches CA6 5QD
☎ 01228 577313 & 07850 713958
e-mail: davidson_b@btconnect.com
dir: *M6 junct 44/A7 Longtown, right onto Netherby St, 6m to Bridge Inn pub. Right then 1st left, site 300yds on right*

Open all year

Last arrival 22.00hrs Last departure 10.00hrs

Twin Willows is a spacious park in a rural location on a ridge overlooking the Scottish border. All facilities, including all-weather pitches, are of a high quality. The park is suited to those who enjoy being away-from-it-all yet at the same time being able to explore the rich history of this area.

continued

PENTON *continued*

The attractive city of Carlisle is 20 miles from the park. 3 acre site. 10 touring pitches. 10 hardstandings. 10 seasonal pitches. Caravan pitches. Motorhome pitches. Tent pitches.

Leisure: 🌳 ⛳ ☺

Facilities: 🝆 ☉ ℙ ✶ 🕭 ⓒ 🖺 🏄 🚾
🖥 ♻ 🅘

Services: 🔌 🛢 🔒 ⌀ 🚰 🍽 🛒 🏧 ♿

Within 3 miles: 🎣 🛍 U

Notes: 🐕 Dogs must be kept on leads.

| **POOLEY BRIDGE** | **Map 18 NY42** |

AA CAMPING CARD SITE

 83% Park Foot Caravan & Camping Park *(NY469235)*

Howtown Rd CA10 2NA
☎ 017684 86309 📠 017684 86041
e-mail: holidays@parkfootullswater.co.uk
web: www.parkfootullswater.co.uk
dir: *M6 junct 40, A66 towards Keswick, then A592 to Ullswater. Turn left for Pooley Bridge, right at church, right at x-roads signed Howtown*

* 🚐 £20-£36 🚛 £14-£28 ⛺ £14-£28

Open Mar-Oct (rs Mar-Apr, mid Sep-Oct clubhouse open wknds only)

Last arrival 22.00hrs Last departure noon

A lively park with good outdoor sports facilities, and boats can be launched directly onto Lake Ullswater. The attractive mainly tenting park has many mature trees, lovely views across the lake, and a superb new amenities block has been built in the family-only field. The Country Club bar and restaurant provides good meals, as well as discos, live music and entertainment

---

in a glorious location. There are lodges and static caravans for holiday hire. 18 acre site. 323 touring pitches. 32 hardstandings. Caravan pitches. Motorhome pitches. Tent pitches. 131 statics.

AA Pubs & Restaurants nearby: The Brackenrigg, Watermillock 017684 86206

Leisure: 🎢 🏊 🎣 ◻ 🎵

Facilities: 🝆 ☉ ℙ ✶ 🕭 ⓒ 🖺 🏄 🚾 ♻ 🅘

Services: 🔌 🛢 🍴 🔒 ⌀ 🚰 🍽 🛒 🏧 🚮 ♿

Within 3 miles: ⛳ 🎣 🛶 🛍 U

Notes: Families & couples only. Dogs must be kept on leads. Boat launch, pony trekking, pool table, table tennis, bike hire.

▶▶▶ **80% Waterfoot Caravan Park** *(NY462246)*

GOLD

CA11 0JF
☎ 017684 86302 📠 017684 86728
e-mail: enquiries@waterfootpark.co.uk
web: www.waterfootpark.co.uk
dir: *M6 junct 40, A66 for 1m, then A592 for 4m, site on right before lake. (NB do not leave A592 until site entrance; Sat Nav not compatible)*

* 🚐 £18.50-£30 🚛 £18.50-£30

Open Mar-14 Nov

Last arrival dusk Last departure noon

A quality touring park with neat, hardstanding pitches in a grassy glade within the wooded grounds of an elegant Georgian mansion. Toilets facilities are clean and well maintained, and the lounge bar with a separate family room enjoys lake views, and there is a path to Ullswater. Aira Force waterfall, Dalemain House and Gardens and Pooley Bridge are all close by. Please note that there is no access via Dacre. 22 acre site. 34 touring pitches. 30 hardstandings. Caravan pitches. Motorhome pitches. 146 statics.

AA Pubs & Restaurants nearby: The Brackenrigg, Watermillock 017684 86206

Leisure: 🎢 🎣

Facilities: 🝆 ☉ ℙ ✶ 🕭 ⓒ 🖺 🏄 ♻ 🅘

Services: 🔌 🛢 🍴 🔒 🅣 🛒 ♿

Within 3 miles: ⛳ 🎣 🛶 🛍 U

Notes: Families only, no tents, no large RVS. Dogs must be kept on leads.

| **SANTON BRIDGE** |

Places to visit

Brantwood, CONISTON 015394 41396
www.brantwood.org.uk

| **SANTON BRIDGE** | **Map 18 NY10** |

▶▶▶ **75% The Old Post Office Campsite** *(NY110016)*

CA19 1UY
☎ 01946 726286 & 01785 822866
e-mail: enquiries@theoldpostofficecampsite.co.uk
dir: *A595 to Holmrook and Santon Bridge, 2.5m*

🚐 🚛 ⛺

Open Mar-15 Nov

Last departure noon

A family-run campsite in a delightful riverside setting next to an attractive stone bridge, with very pretty pitches. The enthusiastic owner is steadily upgrading the park. Permits for salmon, sea and brown trout fishing are available, and there is an adjacent pub serving excellent meals. 2.2 acre site. 40 touring pitches. 5 hardstandings. Caravan pitches. Motorhome pitches. Tent pitches.

AA Pubs & Restaurants nearby: Bower House Inn, Eskdale Green 019467 23244

Wasdale Head Inn, Wasdale Head 019467 26229

Leisure: 🎢

Facilities: 🝆 ☉ ℙ ✶ 🕭 🖺 🏄

Services: 🔌 🛢 ♿

Within 3 miles: 🎣 🛍 U

Notes: 🐕

| **SILLOTH** | **Map 18 NY15** |

 90% Stanwix Park Holiday Centre *(NY108527)*

Greenrow CA7 4HH
☎ 016973 32666 📠 016973 32555
e-mail: enquiries@stanwix.com
dir: *1m SW on B5300. From A596 (Wigton bypass), follow signs to Silloth on B5302. In Silloth follow signs to site, approx 1m on B5300*

* 🚐 £20-£25.10 🚛 £20-£25.10 ⛺ £20-£25.10

Open all year (rs Nov-Feb (ex New Year) no entertainment/shop closed)

Last arrival 21.00hrs Last departure 11.00hrs

A large well-run family park within easy reach of the Lake District. Attractively laid out, with lots of amenities to ensure a lively holiday, including a 4-lane automatic, 10-pin bowling alley. Excellent touring areas with hardstandings, one in a peaceful glade well away from the main leisure complex, and there's a campers' kitchen and clean, well

---

maintained toilet facilities. 4 acre site. 121 touring pitches. 100 hardstandings. Caravan pitches. Motorhome pitches. Tent pitches. 212 statics.

Stanwix Park Holiday Park

AA Pubs & Restaurants nearby: New Inn, Blencogo 016973 61091

Leisure: 🏊⛵🎾⚲🛶⛳🎣⛱🎱🎵
Facilities: 🚿🔌☺☔✳♿☎🛁♻ ⓘ
Services: 🔌🖥🍺∅🗑Ⓣ🍽🍔🛒⛽
Within 3 miles: 🚴⛳◎🛒🏇

Notes: Families only. Amusement arcade.
see advert below

▶▶▶▶ 86% **Hylton Caravan Park**

(NY113533)
Eden St CA7 4AY
☎ **016973 31707 & 32666** 📠 016973 32555
e-mail: enquiries@stanwix.com
dir: *On entering Silloth on B5302 follow signs Hylton Caravan Park, approx 0.5m on left, (end of Eden St)*

* 🚐 £18-£22.10 🚌 £18-£22.10 ⛺ £18-£22.10

Open Mar-15 Nov

Last arrival 21.00hrs Last departure 11.00hrs

A smart, modern touring park with excellent toilet facilities including several bathrooms. This high quality park is a sister site to Stanwix Park, which is just a mile away and offers all the amenities of a holiday centre, which are available to Hylton tourers. 18 acre site. 90 touring pitches. Caravan pitches. Motorhome pitches. Tent pitches. 213 statics.

AA Pubs & Restaurants nearby: New Inn, Blencogo 016973 61091

Leisure: ⛱
Facilities: 🚿🔌☺☔♿☎
Services: 🔌🖥∅⛽
Within 3 miles: 🚴⛳◎🛒🏇

Notes: Families only. Use of facilities at Stanwix Park Holiday Centre.

SERVICES: 🔌 Electric hook up 🖥 Launderette 🍺 Licensed bar 🛢 Calor Gas ∅ Camping Gaz Ⓣ Toilet fluid 🍽 Café/Restaurant 🍔 Fast Food/Takeaway 🔋 Battery charging 🛒 Baby care ⛽ Motorvan service point

ABBREVIATIONS: BH/bank hols-bank holidays Etr-Easter Whit-Whitsun dep-departure fr-from hrs-hours m-mile mdnt-midnight rdbt-roundabout rs-restricted service wk-week wknd-weekend 🚫 No credit cards ⊗ No dogs   See page 7 for details of the AA Camping Card Scheme

TEBAY	Map 18 NY60

►►► 75% Westmorland Caravan Park *(NY609060)*

Orton CA10 3SB
☎ 01539 711322 📠 015396 24944
e-mail: caravans@westmorland.com
web: www.westmorland.com/caravan
dir: *Exit M6 at Westmorland Services, 1m from junct 38. Site accessed through service area from either N'bound or S'bound carriageways. Follow park signs*

Open Mar-Nov

Last arrival anytime Last departure noon

An ideal stopover site adjacent to the Tebay service station on the M6, and handy for touring the Lake District. The park is screened by high grass banks, bushes and trees, and is within walking distance of an excellent farm shop and restaurant. 4 acre site. 70 touring pitches. 70 hardstandings. 43 seasonal pitches. Caravan pitches. Motorhome pitches. 7 statics.

AA Pubs & Restaurants nearby: Fat Lamb Country Inn, Ravenstonedale 015396 23242

Black Swan, Ravenstonedale 015396 23204

Facilities: 📶 ⊙ 🅿 ✳ 🔥 💺 🛏 🚿 ♻ ❶
Services: 🚽 🔄 🗑 📶 🛁 T 🍽 🚿
Within 3 miles: 🚲 🏪 🛒

TROUTBECK (NEAR KESWICK)	Map 18 NY32

PREMIER PARK

►►►►► 81% Troutbeck Camping and Caravanning Club Site *(NY365271)*

Hutton Moor End CA11 0SX
☎ 017687 79149
dir: *M6 junct 40, A66 towards Keswick. In 9.5m sharp left for Wallthwaite. Site 0.5m on left*

Open 9 Mar-11 Nov

Last arrival 20.00hrs Last departure noon

Beautifully situated between Penrith and Keswick, this quiet, well managed Lakeland park offers two immaculate touring areas, one a sheltered paddock for caravans and motorhomes, with serviced hardstanding pitches, and a maturing lower field, which has spacious hardstanding pitches and a superb and very popular small tenting area that enjoys stunning and extensive views of the surrounding fells. The toilet block is appointed to a very high standard and includes two family cubicles, and the log cabin reception/shop stocks local and organic produce. The enthusiastic franchisees offer high levels of customer care and are constantly improving the park, which is well-placed for visited Keswick, Ullswater and the north lakes. 5 acre site. 54 touring pitches. 36 hardstandings. Caravan pitches. Motorhome pitches. Tent pitches. 20 statics.

Leisure: 🛝
Facilities: 📶 ⊙ 🅿 ✳ 🔥 💺 🛏 🚿 wm ♻ ❶
Services: 🚽 🔄 🗑 📶 🛁 T 🚿
Within 3 miles: 🚲 🛒 🐴

Notes: Site gates closed 23.00hrs-07.00hrs. Dogs must be kept on leads. Dog walk.

ULVERSTON	Map 18 SD27

Places to visit

The Dock Museum, BARROW-IN-FURNESS 01229 876400 www.dockmuseum.org.uk

Furness Abbey, BARROW-IN-FURNESS 01229 823420 www.english-heritage.org.uk

Great for kids: South Lakes Wild Animal Park, DALTON-IN-FURNESS 01229 466086 www.wildanimalpark.co.uk

►►►► 85% *Bardsea Leisure Park* *(SD292765)*

Priory Rd LA12 9QE
☎ 01229 584712 📠 01229 580413
e-mail: reception@bardsealeisure.co.uk
dir: *Off A5087*

Open all year

Last arrival 21.00hrs Last departure 18.00hrs

An attractively landscaped former quarry, making a quiet and very sheltered site. Many of the generously-sized pitches offer all-weather full facilities, and a luxury toilet block provides plenty of fully-serviced cubicles. Set on the southern edge of the town, it is convenient for both the coast and the Lake District and there's an excellent caravan accessories shop on site. Please note that this site does not accept tents. 5 acre site. 83 touring pitches. 83 hardstandings. Caravan pitches. Motorhome pitches. 83 statics.

AA Pubs & Restaurants nearby: Farmers Arms, Ulverston 01229 584469

Leisure: 🛝
Facilities: 📶 ⊙ 🅿 ✳ 🔥 💺 🛏 🚿 🏪 🛏
Services: 🚽 🔄 🗑 📶 🛁 T 🚿 🛒 🚿
Within 3 miles: 🚲 🏨 🚲 🏪 🛒 🐴

WASDALE HEAD	Map 18 NY10

►►► 76% Wasdale Head National Trust Campsite *(NY183076)*

CA20 1EX
☎ 015394 63862 & 32733
e-mail: campsite.bookings@nationaltrust.org.uk
web: www.ntlakescampsites.org.uk
dir: *From A595(N) left at Gosforth; from A595(S) right at Holmrook for Santon Bridge, follow signs to Wasdale Head*

* 🚐 fr £13 ⛺ fr £13

Open all year (rs Wknds Nov-Feb shop open)

Last departure 11.00hrs

Set in a remote and beautiful spot at Wasdale Head, under the stunning Scafell peaks at the head of the deepest lake in England. Clean, well-kept facilities are set centrally amongst open grass pitches and trees, where camping pods are also located. There are eight hardstanding pitches for motorhomes. The renowned Wasdale Head Inn is close by. 5 acre site. 120 touring pitches. 6 hardstandings. Motorhome pitches. Tent pitches. 3 wooden pods.

AA Pubs & Restaurants nearby: Wasdale Head Inn, Wasdale Head 019467 26229

Facilities: 📶 ⊙ 🅿 ✳ 🔥 💺 🛏 ♻
Services: 🚽 🔄 🗑

Notes: No cars by tents. No groups of more than 4 unless a family with children. Dogs must be kept on leads.

see advert on page 126

LEISURE: 🏊 Indoor swimming pool 🏊 Outdoor swimming pool 🛝 Children's playground 🧒 Kid's club 🎾 Tennis court 🎱 Games room 📺 Separate TV room 🏌 9/18 hole golf course ⛵ Boats for hire 🎬 Cinema 🎵 Entertainment 🎣 Fishing 🏌 Mini golf 🏄 Watersports 💪 Gym 🏟 Sports field Spa ∪ Stables
FACILITIES: 🛁 Bath 🚿 Shower ⊙ Electric shaver 🧖 Hairdryer ✳ Ice Pack Facility 💺 Disabled facilities 🕿 Public telephone 🏪 Shop on site or within 200yds 🚐 Mobile shop (calls at least 5 days a week) 🔥 BBQ area 🚿 Picnic area wm Wi-fi 🖥 Internet access ♻ Recycling ❶ Tourist info 🚶 Dog exercise area

WATERMILLOCK
Map 18 NY42

▶▶▶▶ 87% The Quiet Site

(NY431236)

GOLD

Ullswater CA11 0LS
☎ 07768 727016
e-mail: info@thequietsite.co.uk
dir: *M6 junct 40, A592 towards Ullswater. Right at lake junct, then right at Brackenrigg Hotel. Site 1.5m on right*

* 🚐 £12-£30 🚐 £12-£30 ▲ £12-£30

Open all year (rs Low season park open wknds only)

Last arrival 22.00hrs Last departure noon

A well-maintained site in a lovely, peaceful location, with good terraced pitches offering great fells views, very good toilet facilities including family bathrooms, and a charming 'olde-worlde' bar. There are wooden camping pods for hire and a self-catering stone cottage. Ongoing improvements for 2011 included new terraced tent pitches, more camping pod, and extra planting for privacy. 10 acre site. 100 touring pitches. 60 hardstandings. Caravan pitches. Motorhome pitches. Tent pitches. 23 statics.

AA Pubs & Restaurants nearby: The Brackenrigg, Watermillock 017684 86206

Leisure: 🄰 ☺ 🔍 ▢
Facilities: ➡ 📵 ☉ 🅟 ❄ ⚓ ☺ 📵 🄰 ➰ WiFi 🛒 🟤 ❸ 🅸
Services: 🔌 🖾 🍴 🛢 🔥 🚰 🛒 ➰ ⚒
Within 3 miles: ⚓ 🖉 💧 🛢 🛒 ∪

Notes: Quiet from 22.00hrs onwards. Pool table, soft play area for toddlers, caravan storage.

▶▶▶ 84% Ullswater Caravan, Camping & Marine Park *(NY438232)*

High Longthwaite CA11 0LR
☎ 017684 86666 📠 017684 86095
e-mail: info@uccmp.co.uk
web: www.ullswatercaravanpark.co.uk
dir: *M6 junct 40 take A592, W for Ullswater for 5m. Right alongside Ullswater for 2m, then right at phone box. Site 0.5m on right*

* 🚐 £14-£26 🚐 £14-£26 ▲ £14-£26

Open Mar-Nov (rs Low season bar open wknds only)

Last arrival 21.00hrs Last departure noon

A pleasant rural site with its own nearby boat launching and marine storage facility, making it ideal for sailors. The family-owned and run park enjoys fell and lake views, and there is a bar, café and shop on site. Many of the pitches are fully serviced and there are two wooden cabins with barbecues. Please note that the Marine Park is one mile from the camping area. 12 acre site. 160 touring pitches. 58 hardstandings. Caravan pitches. Motorhome pitches. Tent pitches. 55 statics.

AA Pubs & Restaurants nearby: The Brackenrigg, Watermillock 017684 86206

Leisure: 🄰 🔍 ▢
Facilities: 🏕 ☉ 🅟 ❄ ⚓ 🅸 ➰ WiFi ❸
Services: 🔌 🖾 🍴 🛢 🔥 ➰ 🅣 🛒
Within 3 miles: ⚓ 🖉 💧 🛢 🛒 ∪

Notes: No open fires, no noise after 23.30hrs. Dogs must be kept on leads. Boat launching & moorings 1m.

▶▶▶ 79% Cove Caravan & Camping Park *(NY431236)*

Ullswater CA11 0LS
☎ 017684 86549 📠 017684 86549
e-mail: info@cove-park.co.uk
dir: *M6 junct 40 take A592 for Ullswater. Right at lake junct, then right at Brackenrigg Inn. Site 1.5m on left*

* 🚐 £18-£30 🚐 £18-£30 ▲ £14-£25

Open Mar-Oct

Last arrival 21.00hrs Last departure noon

A peaceful family site in an attractive and elevated position with extensive fell views and glimpses of Ullswater Lake. The ground is gently sloping grass, but there are also eight fully serviced hardstandings for motorhomes and caravans. The simple toilet facilities are fresh, clean and well maintained by the enthusiastic and welcoming wardens. 3 acre site. 50 touring

continued

SERVICES: 🔌 Electric hook up 🖾 Launderette 🍴 Licensed bar 🛢 Calor Gas ⚖ Camping Gaz 🅣 Toilet fluid 🍽 Café/Restaurant 🍟 Fast Food/Takeaway 🔋 Battery charging 🚼 Baby care ⚒ Motorvan service point
ABBREVIATIONS: BH/bank hols-bank holidays Etr-Easter Whit-Whitsun dep-departure fr-from hrs-hours m-mile mdnt-midnight rdbt-roundabout rs-restricted service wk-week wknd-weekend ⊛ No credit cards ⊗ No dogs
See page 7 for details of the AA Camping Card Scheme

WATERMILLOCK *continued*

pitches. 17 hardstandings. 5 seasonal pitches. Caravan pitches. Motorhome pitches. Tent pitches. 39 statics.

AA Pubs & Restaurants nearby: The Brackenrigg, Watermillock 017684 86206

Leisure: ⚠

Facilities: ♠⊙⛱☀⚠☉⛱⚲♻❶

Services: ⚥⚊🔋🌿

Within 3 miles: ⚘⚖⚓💈🛥∪

Notes: No open fires, no noise after 22.30hrs.

see advert on page 139

WINDERMERE Map 18 SD49

Places to visit

Holehird Gardens, WINDERMERE 015394 46008
www.holehirdgardens.org.uk

Blackwell The Arts & Crafts House, BOWNESS-ON-WINDERMERE 015394 46139
www.blackwell.org.uk

Great for kids: Lake District Visitor Centre at Brockhole, WINDERMERE 015394 46601
www.lake-district.gov.uk

PREMIER PARK

▶▶▶▶▶ **84% Park Cliffe Camping & Caravan Estate**

(SD391912)

Birks Rd, Tower Wood LA23 3PG
☎ 01539 531344 📠 01539 531971
e-mail: info@parkcliffe.co.uk
dir: *M6 junct 36, A590. Right at Newby Bridge onto A592. 3.6m right into site. (NB due to difficult access from main road this is only advised direction for approaching site)*

* 🚐 £25-£29 🚏 £25-£29 ⛺ £20-£34

Open Mar-11 Nov (rs Wknds/school hols facilities open fully)

Last arrival 22.00hrs Last departure noon

A lovely hillside park set in 25 secluded acres of fell land. The camping area is sloping and uneven in places, but well drained and sheltered; some pitches have spectacular views of Lake Windermere and the Langdales. The park offers a high level of customer care and is very well

equipped for families (family bathrooms), and there is an attractive bar and brasserie restaurant serving quality food, and three static holiday caravans for hire. 25 acre site. 60 touring pitches. 60 hardstandings. 25 seasonal pitches. Caravan pitches. Motorhome pitches. Tent pitches. 55 statics. 4 wooden pods.

Park Cliffe Camping & Caravan Estate

AA Pubs & Restaurants nearby: Eagle & Child Inn, Staveley 01539 821320

Jerichos, Windermere 015394 42522

Leisure: ⚠ ♠

Facilities: ♠⊙⛱☀⚠☉⛱⚲♻❶

Services: ⚥⚊🔋🌿⊞🍽♻⚊⚓

Within 3 miles: ⚘⚖⚓💈🛥∪

Notes: No noise 23.00hrs-07.30hrs. Dogs must be kept on leads. Off-licence, playground.

▶▶▶▶ **87% Fallbarrow Park**

(SD401973)

Rayrigg Rd LA23 3DL
☎ 015394 44422 📠 015394 88736
e-mail: enquiries@southlakelandparks.co.uk
dir: *0.5m N of Windermere on A591. At mini-rdbt take road to Bowness Bay & the Lake. Site 1.3m on right*

* 🚐 £24-£32 🚏 £24-£32

Open Mar-mid Nov

Last arrival 22.00hrs Last departure 12.00hrs

A park set in impressive surroundings just a few minutes' walk from Bowness on the shore of Lake Windermere. There is direct access to the lake through the park. The site has good, hedged, fully serviced pitches, quality toilet facilities, a deli and café serving meals using locally sourced produce, and 30 holiday hire statics. 32 acre site. 32 touring pitches. Caravan pitches. Motorhome pitches. 269 statics.

AA Pubs & Restaurants nearby: Eagle & Child Inn, Staveley 01539 821320

Jerichos, Windermere 015394 42522

Leisure: ⚠ ♠ ⬜

Facilities: ♠⊙⛱☀⚠☉⛱⚲♻❶

Services: ⚥⚊🔋🌿🍽♻⚊⚓

Within 3 miles: ⚘⚖⚓💈🛥∪

Notes: ⊗ No tents, no cycling, no scooters. Boat launching.

▶▶▶▶ **80% Hill of Oaks & Blakeholme** *(SD386899)*

LA12 8NR
☎ 015395 31578 📠 015395 30431
e-mail: enquiries@hillofoaks.co.uk
web: www.hillofoaks.co.uk
dir: *M6 junct 36 onto A590 towards Barrow. At rdbt signed Bowness turn right onto A592. Site approx 3m on left*

* 🚐 £27-£35 🚏 £27-£35

Open Mar-14 Nov

Last departure noon

A secluded, heavily wooded park on the shores of Lake Windermere. Pretty lakeside picnic areas, woodland walks and a play area make this a delightful park for families, with excellent serviced pitches, a licensed shop and a heated toilet block. Watersports include sailing and canoeing, with private jetties for boat launching. Combined toilet/wash-hand basin cubicles were added in 2011. 31 acre site. 43 touring pitches. Caravan pitches. Motorhome pitches. 215 statics.

AA Pubs & Restaurants nearby: Eagle & Child Inn, Staveley 01539 821320

Jerichos, Windermere 015394 42522

Leisure: ⚠

Facilities: ♠⊙⛱☀⚠☉⛱⚲❶

Services: ⚥⚊🔋⊞⚓

Within 3 miles: ⚘⚖⚓💈🛥∪

Notes: Dogs must be kept on leads.

LEISURE: 🏊 Indoor swimming pool 🏊 Outdoor swimming pool ⚠ Children's playground 🪁 Kid's club 🎾 Tennis court ♠ Games room ⬜ Separate TV room ⚘ 9/18 hole golf course ⚓ Boats for hire 🎬 Cinema 🎵 Entertainment 🎣 Fishing ⊙ Mini golf 🏄 Watersports 🏋 Gym ⚙ Sports field Spa ∪ Stables
FACILITIES: 🛁 Bath ♠ Shower ⊙ Electric shaver 💈 Hairdryer ☀ Ice Pack Facility ⚠ Disabled facilities ☎ Public telephone 🏪 Shop on site or within 200yds 🚐 Mobile shop (calls at least 5 days a week) 🍖 BBQ area ⛱ Picnic area 📶 Wi-fi 💻 Internet access ♻ Recycling ❶ Tourist info 🐾 Dog exercise area

SERVICES: ⊡ Electric hook up ⑤ Launderette ⏻ Licensed bar 🛢 Calor Gas ∅ Camping Gaz ⊤ Toilet fluid ⦿ Café/Restaurant 🍴 Fast Food/Takeaway ⊟ Battery charging
🍼 Baby care ⌁ Motorvan service point
ABBREVIATIONS: BH/bank hols-bank holidays Etr-Easter Whit-Whitsun dep-departure fr-from hrs-hours m-mile mdnt-midnight rdbt-roundabout rs-restricted service wk-week
wknd-weekend ⊗ No credit cards ⊗ No dogs   See page 7 for details of the AA Camping Card Scheme

Derbyshire

Think of Derbyshire and you instantly think of the Peak District, the first of Britain's glorious and much-loved National Parks and still the most popular. This is where the rugged, sometimes inhospitable landscape of north England meets the gentler beauty of the Midland counties.

● Walking in the Derwent Valley

Within the National Park lies the upland country of the Dark Peak, shaped over the centuries by silt from the region's great rivers, and where gritstone outcrops act as monuments to the splendour and magic of geology. History was made in this corner of Derbyshire in 1932 when 500 ramblers spilled on to Kinder Scout to argue for the right of public access to the countryside.

Southern landscape

To the south is the White Peak, different in both character and appearance. This is a land of limestone, of deep wooded gorges, underground caves and high pastures crisscrossed by traditional drystone walls. There are dales, too – the most famous among them being Dovedale, the haunt of countless writers and artists over the years. Not surprisingly, Wordsworth and Tennyson sought inspiration here and much of it retains a rare, magical quality.

Fine buildings

Look in and around the Peak District National Park and you'll find an impressive range of fine buildings. Calke Abbey (NT) is not an abbey at all but a magnificent baroque mansion dating back to the beginning of the 18th century.

World-famous Chatsworth, the palatial home of the Duke of Devonshire, is one of Derbyshire's ▶

Curbar Edge

The Pudding Shop in Bakewell

more demanding and adventurous routes, including the High Peak Trail, which runs from Hurdlow to Cromford, and the Monsal Trail, which extends from Haddon Park to Topley Pike. There is also the 26-mile (42km) Limestone Way from Matlock to Castleton and the 35-mile (56km) Gritstone Trail from Disley to Kidsgrove. Derbyshire's most famous walk is undoubtedly the Pennine Way, which starts at Edale in the Peak District and runs north for 251 miles (404km) to Kirk Yetholm in Scotland.

In common with other parts of the country, the Peak District includes a number of disused railway tracks that have been adapted to user-friendly cycle trails. Among many popular cycle trails are several family routes around Derwent reservoir, where 617 Squadron, 'The Dambusters', famously practised low-level flying during the Second World War.

most cherished visitor attractions. Work began on the original building in 1549 and the house has been substantially altered and enlarged over the years. The 1,000-acre park is the jewel in Chatsworth's crown; designed by 'Capability' Brown, it includes rare trees, a maze and the highest gravity-fed fountain in the world.

Towns and villages

As well as the county's palatial houses, there is an impressive array of quaint villages and historic towns. Chesterfield is known for the crooked spire of its church, while Buxton is acknowledged as one of the country's loveliest spa towns. Bakewell introduced the tradition of the Bakewell Pudding and the villagers of Tissington still maintain the old custom of well dressing on Ascension Day.

Walking and Cycling

Derbyshire is just the place for exhilarating walking where almost every person you pass is pleasant and friendly. The Peak District offers

Festivals and Events

Among many fixtures are the following:
- The Ashbourne Shrovetide Football on Shrove Tuesday and Ash Wednesday.
- The Bamford Sheep Dog Trials, the Chatsworth Horse Trials and the Castleton Garland Ceremony in May.
- In July there is the Bakewell Carnival, the Padley Pilgrimage and the Buxton Festival.
- September sees the Matlock Bath Illuminations and Firework Display and December the Castleton Christmas Lights and the Boxing Day Raft Race at Matlock Bath.

DERBYSHIRE

See Cycle Ride 1 in the Walks & Cycle Rides section at the end of the guide

ASHBOURNE Map 10 SK14

Places to visit

Kedleston Hall, KEDLESTON HALL 01332 842191 www.nationaltrust.org.uk

Wirksworth Heritage Centre, WIRKSWORTH 01629 825225 www.storyofwirksworth.co.uk

Great for kids: Crich Tramway Village, CRICH 01773 854321 www.tramway.co.uk

►► 83% Carsington Fields Caravan Park *(SK251493)*

Millfields Ln, Nr Carsington Water DE6 3JS
☎ 01335 372872
dir: *From Belper towards Ashbourne on A517, right approx 0.25m past Hulland Ward into Dog Ln. 0.75m right at x-roads signed Carsington. Site on right approx 0.75m*

* ☞ £20-£23 ☞ £20-£23 ▲ £19-£23

Open end Mar-Sep

Last arrival 21.00hrs Last departure 18.00hrs

A very well presented and spacious park with a good toilet block, open views and a large fenced pond that attracts plenty of wildlife. The popular tourist attraction of Carsington Water is a short stroll away, with its variety of leisure facilities including fishing, sailing, windsurfing and children's play area. The park is also a good base for walkers. 6 acre site. 20 touring pitches. 12 hardstandings. Caravan pitches. Motorhome pitches. Tent pitches.

AA Pubs & Restaurants nearby: Barley Mow Inn, Ashbourne 01335 370306

The Dining Room, Ashbourne 01335 300666

Facilities: ►⊙✻⚷♥ ⬚ ♻ ❶
Services: ☒
Within 3 miles: ≿ ⌒ ⚓ ⬚ ∪
Notes: No large groups or group bookings, no noise after 23.00hrs.

BAKEWELL Map 16 SK26

Places to visit

Chatsworth, CHATSWORTH 01246 565300 www.chatsworth.org

Chesterfield Museum and Art Gallery, CHESTERFIELD 01246 345727 www.visitchesterfield.info

AA CAMPING CARD SITE

►►► 78% Greenhills Holiday Park
(SK202693)

Crowhill Ln DE45 1PX
☎ 01629 813052 & 813467 ≣ 01629 815760
e-mail: info@greenhillsholidaypark.co.uk
web: www.greenhillsholidaypark.co.uk
dir: *1m NW of Bakewell on A6. Signed before Ashford-in-the-Water, 50yds along unclass road on right*

* ☞ £15-£30 ☞ £15-£30 ▲ £15-£30

Open Feb-Nov (rs Mar, Apr & Oct bar & shop closed)

Last arrival 22.00hrs Last departure noon

A well-established park set in lovely countryside within the Peak District National Park. Many pitches enjoy uninterrupted views, and there is easy accessibility to all facilities. A clubhouse, shop and children's playground are popular features. 8 acre site. 172 touring pitches. 30 hardstandings. Caravan pitches. Motorhome pitches. Tent pitches. 63 statics.

AA Pubs & Restaurants nearby: Bull's Head, Bakewell 01629 812931

Piedaniel's, Bakewell 01629 812687

Leisure: ⚠ ☺ ♫
Facilities: ►⊙☞✻⚷♥⬚♻❶
Services: ☒☒♨♻⬚⟟⬚⬚
Within 3 miles: ≿⌒⬚⬚∪

BIRCHOVER Map 16 SK26

Places to visit

Haddon Hall, HADDON HALL 01629 812855 www.haddonhall.co.uk

The Heights of Abraham Cable Cars, Caverns & Hilltop Park, MATLOCK BATH 01629 582365 www.heightsofabraham.com

AA CAMPING CARD SITE

NEW ►►►► 81% Barn Farm Campsite *(SK238621)*

Barn Farm DE4 2BL
☎ 01629 650245 ≣ 01629 650151
e-mail: gilberthh@msn.com
dir: *From A6 take B5056 towards Ashbourne. Follow brown signs to site*

* ☞ £15-£17 ☞ £15-£17 ▲ £10-£15

Open Apr-Oct

Last arrival 21.00hrs Last departure noon

An interesting park on a former dairy farm with the many and varied facilities housed in high quality conversions of old farm buildings. Three large and well maintained touring fields offer sweeping views across the Peak National Park. There is an excellent choice in the provision of privacy cubicles, including shower and wash basin cubicles and even a shower and sauna. There are five stylish camping barns for hire. 15 acre site. 25 touring pitches. Caravan pitches. Motorhome pitches. Tent pitches.

AA Pubs & Restaurants nearby: The Peacock at Rowsley, Rowsley 01629 733518

Leisure: ⚠☺♣
Facilities: ►⊙☞✻⚷♥⬚♻❶
Services: ☒☒♨♻⟟⬚
Within 3 miles: ≿⌒⬚⬚∪
Notes: No music after 22.30hrs, minimum noise 22.30hrs-07.00hrs. Dogs must be kept on leads.

LEISURE: ☀ Indoor swimming pool ☀ Outdoor swimming pool ⚠ Children's playground ♣ Kid's club ☺ Tennis court ♣ Games room ☐ Separate TV room ♪ 9/18 hole golf course ☀ Boats for hire ☐ Cinema ♫ Entertainment ⌒ Fishing ☺ Mini golf ☀ Watersports ♀ Gym ☺ Sports field **Spa** ∪ Stables
FACILITIES: ♥ Bath ► Shower ⊙ Electric shaver ☞ Hairdryer ✻ Ice Pack Facility ⚷ Disabled facilities ♨ Public telephone ⬚ Shop on site or within 200yds ☺ Mobile shop (calls at least 5 days a week) ♨ BBQ area ⬚ Picnic area ⬚ Wi-fi ■ Internet access ♻ Recycling ❶ Tourist info ⬚ Dog exercise area

BUXTON
Map 16 SK07

Places to visit

Eyam Hall, EYAM 01433 631976
www.eyamhall.com

Poole's Cavern (Buxton Country Park), BUXTON
01298 26978 www.poolescavern.co.uk

AA CAMPING CARD SITE

▶▶▶▶ 83% Lime Tree Park (SK070725)

Dukes Dr SK17 9RP
☎ 01298 22988 📠 01298 22988
e-mail: info@limetreeparkbuxton.co.uk
dir: 1m S of Buxton, between A515 & A6

* 🚐 £18-£22 🚏 £18-£22 ▲ £10-£20

Open Mar-Oct

Last arrival 21.00hrs Last departure noon

A most attractive and well-designed site, set on the side of a narrow valley in an elevated location, with separate, neatly landscaped areas for statics, tents, touring caravans and motorhomes. There's good attention to detail throughout including the clean toilets and showers. Its backdrop of magnificent old railway viaduct and views over Buxton and the surrounding hills, make this a sought-after destination. There are eight static caravans, a pine lodge and two apartments available for holiday lets. 10.5 acre site. 106 touring pitches. 22 hardstandings. Caravan pitches. Motorhome pitches. Tent pitches. 43 statics.

AA Pubs & Restaurants nearby: Queen Anne Inn, Buxton 01298 871246

Leisure: 🅰 🎣 ▢
Facilities: 🅝 ⊙ 🅟 🌣 ♿ ⊙ 🅖 🖈
Services: 🚐 🅢 ⊘ 🅣 🔋
Within 3 miles: ⬇ ◎ ⛴ 🅖 🅢 ♻

▶▶▶ 87% Clover Fields Touring Caravan Park (SK075704)

1 Heath View, Harpur Hill SK17 9PU
☎ 01298 78731
e-mail: cloverfields@tiscali.co.uk
dir: A515, B5053, then immediately right. Site 0.5m on left

* 🚐 £18 🚏 £18 ▲ £16

Open all year

Last departure 18.00hrs

A developing and spacious adults-only park with very good facilities, including an upmarket, timber

chalet-style toilet block, just over a mile from the attractions of Buxton. All pitches are fully serviced including individual barbecues, and are set out on terraces, each with extensive views over the countryside. Swathes of natural meadow grasses and flowers cloak the terraces and surrounding fields. 12 acre site. 25 touring pitches. 25 hardstandings. Caravan pitches. Motorhome pitches. Tent pitches.

AA Pubs & Restaurants nearby: Queen Anne Inn, Buxton 01298 871246

Facilities: 🅝 ⊙ 🌣 ♿ ⊙ 🅖 🖈 ♻ 🚗
Services: 🚐 🅢 🔋 🅣 🔋
Within 3 miles: ⬇ ♻ 🅖 🅢 ♻

Notes: Adults only. No commercial vehicles. Dogs must be kept on leads. Small fishing pond, boules area.

▶▶▶ 84% Beech Croft Farm
(SK122720)

Beech Croft, Blackwell in the Peak SK17 9TQ
☎ 01298 85330
e-mail: mail@beechcroftfarm.net
dir: Off A6 midway between Buxton & Bakewell. Site signed

* 🚐 £16-£20 🚏 £16-£20 ▲ £12.50-£14.60

Open all year

Last arrival 21.30hrs

Winter 2010/11 saw huge changes at this small terraced farm site with lovely Peak District views. With planning issues resolved, there's now a fine stone-built toilet block with ultra-modern fittings, underfloor heating and extra unisex facilities, 31 enlarged, fully-serviced hardstanding pitches (11 in the camping field), new gravel roads, new electric points, and a super tarmac pathway leading from the camping field to the toilet block. An ideal, much improved site for those touring or walking in the Peak District. 3 acre site. 30 touring pitches. 30 hardstandings. Caravan pitches. Motorhome pitches. Tent pitches.

AA Pubs & Restaurants nearby: Queen Anne Inn, Buxton 01298 871246

Facilities: 🅝 ⊙ 🌣 ♿ 🅖 🖈 🚗 WiFi ♻ 🄯
Services: 🚐 🅢 🔋 ⊘ 🅣
Notes: No noise after 23.00hrs.

EDALE
Map 16 SK18

Places to visit

Blue-John Cavern & Mine, CASTLETON
01433 620638 www.bluejohn.gemsoft.co.uk

▶▶ 69% *Coopers Camp & Caravan Park* (SK121859)

Newfold Farm, Edale Village S33 7ZD
☎ 01433 670372
dir: From A6187 in Hope take minor road signed Edale for 4m. In Edale right onto unclassified road, site on left in 800yds opposite school

🚐 🚏 ▲

Open all year

Last arrival 23.30hrs Last departure 15.00hrs

Rising grassland behind a working farm, divided by a wall into two fields, culminating in the 2,062ft Edale Moor. Facilities have been converted from original farm buildings, and include a café for backpackers, and a well-stocked shop. 6 acre site. 135 touring pitches. Caravan pitches. Motorhome pitches. Tent pitches. 11 statics.

AA Pubs & Restaurants nearby: Cheshire Cheese Inn, Hope 01433 620381

Ye Olde Nag's Head, Castleton 01433 620248

The Peaks Inn, Castleton 01433 620247

Facilities: 🅝 ⊙ 🅟 🌣 ⊙ 🅖
Services: 🚐 🔋 ⊘ 🍽 🔋
Within 3 miles: 🅖 ♻
Notes: 🚫

HOPE Map 16 SK18

Places to visit

Speedwell Cavern, CASTLETON 01433 620512 www.speedwellcavern.co.uk

Peveril Castle, CASTLETON 01433 620613 www.english-heritage.org.uk

►► 76% Pindale Farm Outdoor Centre *(SK163825)*

Pindale Rd S33 6RN
☎ 01433 620111 📠 01433 620729
e-mail: pindalefarm@btconnect.com
dir: *From A6187 in Hope take turn signed Pindale between church & Woodrough pub. Centre 1m on left*

* ⛺ fr £12

Open Mar-Oct

Set around a 13th-century farmhouse and a former lead mine pump house (now converted to a self-contained bunkhouse for up to 60 people), this simple, off-the-beaten track site is an ideal base for walking, climbing, caving and various outdoor pursuits. Around the farm are several deeply wooded closes available for tents, and old stone buildings that have been well converted to house modern toilet facilities. 4 acre site. 60 touring pitches. Tent pitches.

AA Pubs & Restaurants nearby: Cheshire Cheese Inn, Hope 01433 620381

Ye Olde Nag's Head, Castleton 01433 620248

The Peaks Inn, Castleton 01433 620247

Facilities: 🚿 🪒 ❄

Services: 🧺 ⛽

Within 3 miles: 🏪 🐎

Notes: 🚫 No anti-social behaviour, noise must be kept to minimum after 21.00hrs, no fires. Dogs must be kept on leads.

MATLOCK

Places to visit

Peak District Mining Museum, MATLOCK BATH 01629 583834 www.peakmines.co.uk

Haddon Hall, HADDON HALL 01629 812855 www.haddonhall.co.uk

Great for kids: The Heights of Abraham Cable Cars, Caverns & Hilltop Park, MATLOCK BATH 01629 582365 www.heightsofabraham.com

MATLOCK Map 16 SK35

►►►► 80% Lickpenny Caravan Site *(SK339597)*

Lickpenny Ln, Tansley DE4 5GF
☎ 01629 583040 📠 01629 583040
e-mail: lickpenny@btinternet.com
dir: *From Matlock take A615 towards Alfreton for 3m. Site signed to left, into Lickpenny Ln, right into site near end of road*

* 🚐 £15-£25 🚌 £15-£25

Open all year

Last arrival 20.00hrs Last departure noon

A picturesque site in the grounds of an old plant nursery with areas broken up and screened by a variety of shrubs, and spectacular views, which are best enjoyed from the upper terraced areas. Pitches, several fully serviced, are spacious, well screened and well marked, and facilities are to a very good standard. The bistro/coffee shop is popular with visitors. 16 acre site. 80 touring pitches. 80 hardstandings. 20 seasonal pitches. Caravan pitches. Motorhome pitches.

AA Pubs & Restaurants nearby: Red Lion, Matlock 01629 584888

Stones Restaurant, Matlock 01629 56061

Leisure: 🛝

Facilities: 🚿 🪒 💨 ♿ 📞 🏪 🪑 🐕 ♻ ℹ

Services: 🧺 ⛽ 🔋 [T] 🛏 🚰

Within 3 miles: ⛳ 🚣 🎣 🎯 🏪 ⛽ 🐎

Notes: Dogs must be kept on leads. Child bath available.

NEWHAVEN

Places to visit

Middleton Top Engine House, MIDDLETON 01629 823204 www.derbyshire.gov.uk/countryside

Peak District Mining Museum, MATLOCK BATH 01629 583834 www.peakmines.co.uk

NEWHAVEN Map 16 SK16

►►► 77% Newhaven Caravan & Camping Park *(SK167602)*

SK17 0DT
☎ 01298 84300 📠 01332 726027
e-mail: newhavencaravanpark@btconnect.com
web: www.newhavencaravanpark.co.uk
dir: *Between Ashbourne & Buxton at A515 & A5012 junct*

* 🚐 £14-£17.75 🚌 £14-£17.75 ⛺ £14-£17.75

Open Mar-Oct

Last arrival 21.00hrs

Pleasantly situated within the Peak District National Park, this park has mature trees screening the three touring areas. Very good toilet facilities cater for touring vans and a large tent field, and there's a restaurant adjacent to the site. 30 acre site. 125 touring pitches. 18 hardstandings. 40 seasonal pitches. Caravan pitches. Motorhome pitches. Tent pitches. 73 statics.

AA Pubs & Restaurants nearby: Red Lion Inn, Birchover 01629 650363

Druid Inn, Birchover 01629 650302

Leisure: 🛝 🎱

Facilities: 🚿 🪒 💨 ❄ 📞 🏪 🪑 🐕 ℹ

Services: 🧺 ⛽ [T] 🛏

Within 3 miles: 🎣 🏄 🏪 ⛽ 🐎

Notes: Dogs must be kept on leads.

RIPLEY Map 16 SK35

Places to visit

Midland Railway Butterley, RIPLEY 01773 747674 www.midlandrailwaycentre.co.uk

Denby Pottery Visitor Centre, DENBY 01773 740799 www.denbyvisitorcentre.co.uk

►►►► 80% Golden Valley Caravan & Camping Park *(SK408513)*

Coach Rd DE55 4ES
☎ 01773 513881 & 746786 📠 01773 746786
e-mail: enquiries@goldenvalleycaravanpark.co.uk
web: www.goldenvalleycaravanpark.co.uk
dir: *M1 junct 26, A610 to Codnor. Right at lights, then right into Alfreton Rd. In 1m left into Coach Rd, park on left. (NB it is advised that Sat Nav is ignored for last few miles & guide directions are followed)*

LEISURE: 🏊 Indoor swimming pool 🌊 Outdoor swimming pool 🛝 Children's playground 🧒 Kid's club 🎾 Tennis court 🎱 Games room 📺 Separate TV room ⛳ 9/18 hole golf course 🚣 Boats for hire 🎬 Cinema 🎭 Entertainment 🎣 Fishing 🎯 Mini golf 🏄 Watersports 🏋 Gym ⚽ Sports field **Spa** 🐎 Stables
FACILITIES: 🛁 Bath 🚿 Shower 🪒 Electric shaver 💨 Hairdryer ❄ Ice Pack Facility ♿ Disabled facilities 📞 Public telephone 🏪 Shop on site or within 200yds 🚚 Mobile shop (calls at least 5 days a week) 🍖 BBQ area 🪑 Picnic area 📶 Wi-fi 💻 Internet access ♻ Recycling ℹ Tourist info 🐕 Dog exercise area

🚐 £22-£30 🚎 £22-£27.50 ▲ £15-£27.50

Open all year (rs Wknds only in low season bar/café open)

Last arrival 21.00hrs Last departure noon

This superbly landscaped park is set within 30 acres of woodland in the Amber Valley. The fully-serviced pitches are set out in informal groups in clearings amongst the trees. The park has a cosy bar and bistro with outside patio, a fully stocked fishing lake, an innovative and well-equipped play area, an on-site jacuzzi and fully equipped fitness suite. There is also a wildlife pond and a nature trail. 30 acre site. 45 touring pitches. 45 hardstandings. Caravan pitches. Motorhome pitches. Tent pitches. 1 static.

AA Pubs & Restaurants nearby: Santo's Higham Farm Hotel, Higham 01773 833812

Leisure: 🏌 🇦 🎣 ☐

Facilities: ⬅ 🐕 ⊙ 🇵 ☀ ⛴ 🔥 🍴 🚿 Wi-Fi ♻ ❓

Services: 🔌 🔥 🍴 🛢 🗑 ⊘ ⊤ 🍴 🔋 🍔 ⚓

Within 3 miles: ↕ 🏇 🚶 🏌 🐕 ⛳ ♻

Notes: No open fires or disposable BBQs, no noise after 22.30hrs, no vehicles on grass. Gym, jacuzzi, zip slide, donkey rides, tractor train.

ROSLISTON   Map 10 SK21

Places to visit

Sudbury Hall and Museum of Childhood, SUDBURY 01283 585305 www.nationaltrust.org.uk

Ashby-de-la-Zouch Castle, ASHBY-DE-LA-ZOUCH 01530 413343 www.english-heritage.org.uk

Great for kids: Conkers, MOIRA 01283 216633 www.visitconkers.com

---

▶▶▶ **81% Beehive Woodland Lakes** (SK249161)

DE12 8HZ
☎ 01283 763981 📧 01283 763981
e-mail: info@beehivefarm-woodlandlakes.co.uk
dir: From A444 in Castle Gresley into Mount Pleasant Rd, follow Rosliston signs for 3.5m through Linton to T-junct. Left signed Beehive Farms

🚐 🚎 ▲

Open Mar-Nov

Last arrival 20.00hrs Last departure 10.30hrs

A small, informal and rapidly developing caravan area secluded from an extensive woodland park in the heart of the National Forest National Park. Toilet facilities were extended for 2011 and include four family rooms and improved washing-up facilities. Young children will enjoy the on-site animal farm and playground, whilst anglers will appreciate fishing the three lakes within the park; bikes can be hired. The Honey Pot tearoom provides snacks and is open most days. 2.5 acre site. 25 touring pitches. 12 hardstandings. Caravan pitches. Motorhome pitches. Tent pitches.

AA Pubs & Restaurants nearby: The Waterfront, Barton-under-Needwood 01283 711500

Leisure: 🇦

Facilities: 🐕 ⊙ 🇵 ☀ ⛴ 🔥 🍴

Services: 🔌 🛢 📱 ⊤ 🔋

Within 3 miles: ↕ 🏇 🚶 🐕 ⊙ 🍴

Notes: Last arrival time 18.00hrs low season. 3 coarse fishing lakes, takeaway food delivered to site.

ROWSLEY   Map 16 SK26

Places to visit

Hardwick Hall, HARDWICK HALL 01246 850430 www.nationaltrust.org.uk/main/w-hardwickhall

Temple Mine, MATLOCK BATH 01629 583834 www.peakmines.co.uk

Great for kids: The Heights of Abraham Cable Cars, Caverns & Hilltop Park, MATLOCK BATH 01629 582365 www.heightsofabraham.com

---

▶▶▶ **73% Grouse & Claret** (SK258660)

Station Rd DE4 2EB
☎ 01629 733233 📧 01629 735194
e-mail: grouseandclaret.matlock@marstons.co.uk
dir: M1 junct 29. Site on A6, 5m from Matlock & 3m from Bakewell

* 🚐 fr £25 🚎 fr £25 ▲ fr £12

Open all year

Last arrival 20.00hrs Last departure noon

A well-designed, purpose-built park at the rear of an eating house on the A6 between Bakewell and Chatsworth, and adjacent to the New Peak Shopping Village. The park comprises a level grassy area running down to the river, and all pitches have hardstandings and electric hook-ups. 2.5 acre site. 26 touring pitches. 26 hardstandings. Caravan pitches. Motorhome pitches. Tent pitches.

AA Pubs & Restaurants nearby: Grouse & Claret (on site); Peacock at Rowsley 01629 733518

Leisure: 🇦

Facilities: 🐕 ⊙ 🍴 Wi-Fi

Services: 🔌 🍴 🍴 🍔 ⚓

Within 3 miles: ↕ 🐕 🍴 ♻

Notes: No cars by tents. Dogs must be kept on leads & under strict control.

SHARDLOW   Map 11 SK43

Places to visit

Melbourne Hall & Gardens, MELBOURNE 01332 862502 www.melbournehall.com

---

AA CAMPING CARD SITE

▶▶▶ **69% Shardlow Marina Caravan Park** (SK444303)

London Rd DE72 2GL
☎ 01332 792832 📧 01332 792832
e-mail: admin@shardlowmarina.co.uk
dir: M1 junct 24a, A50 signed Derby. Exit junct 1 at rdbt signed Shardlow. Site 1m on right

* 🚐 £13-£20 🚎 £13-£20 ▲ £13-£20

Open Mar-Jan (rs office closed between 13.00-14.00hrs)

Last arrival 17.00hrs Last departure noon

A large marina site with restaurant facilities, situated on the Trent/Merseyside Canal. Pitches are on grass surrounded by mature trees, and for the keen angler the site offers fishing within the marina. The attractive grass touring area overlooks the marina. 25 acre site. 35 touring pitches. 10 hardstandings. 10 seasonal pitches. Caravan pitches. Motorhome pitches. Tent pitches. 73 statics.

AA Pubs & Restaurants nearby: Old Crown Inn, Shardlow 01332 792392

Priest House on the River, Castle Donington 0845 072 7502

Facilities: 🐕 ⊙ ☀ ⛴ 🔥 ❓

Services: 🔌 🛢 📱 ⊘ ⊤ 🍴 🔋

Within 3 miles: ↕ 🏊 🏇 🐕 🍴 ♻

Notes: Max 2 dogs & 1 child per unit. Dogs must be kept on leads.

Devon

With two magnificent coastlines, two historic cities and a world-famous national park, Devon sums up all that is best about the British landscape. For centuries it has been a fashionable and much-loved holiday destination – especially south Devon's glorious English Riviera.

The largest and most famous seaside resort on the southern coast is Torquay, created in the 19th century and still retaining a tangible air of Victorian charm mixed with a pleasing hint of the Mediterranean. Palm trees grace the bustling harbour where colourful yachts and cabin cruisers vie for space and the weather is pleasantly warm and sunny for long hours in the summer.

In and around Torquay

In recent years television and literature have helped to boost Torquay's holiday image. The

The beach at Woolacombe

hotel that was the inspiration for *Fawlty Towers*, starring the incomparable John Cleese, is located in the town, while Agatha Christie, the Queen of Crime, was born and raised in Torquay. A bust of her, unveiled in 1990 to mark the centenary of her birth, stands near the harbour and tourist information centre.

Greenway, Christie's splendid holiday home, now managed by the National Trust and open to the public, lies outside the town, overlooking a glorious sweep of the River Dart. By taking a nostalgic ride on the Paignton and Dartmouth Steam Railway you can wallow in the world of Poirot and Miss Marple, Christie's famous sleuths, passing close to the house and its glorious grounds.

Dartmoor

One of Agatha Christie's favourite Devon landscapes was Dartmoor. The National Park which contains it covers 365 square miles and includes vast moorland stretches, isolated granite tors and two summits exceeding 2,000 feet. This bleak and brooding landscape is the largest tract of open wilderness left in southern England. More than 100 years ago Sir Arthur Conan Doyle gave ▶

Dartmoor something of a boost when he set his classic and most famous Sherlock Holmes' story, *The Hound of the Baskervilles*, in this romantic and adventurous area.

South Devon

Plymouth lies in Devon's south-west corner and is a fine city and naval port with a wide range of visitor attractions, including the Plymouth Mayflower, overlooking Sutton Harbour, an interactive exhibition explaining the city's history. There is particular emphasis on the Spanish Armada and the voyage of the Pilgrim Fathers to America. The ancient city of Exeter can also occupy many hours of sightseeing. As well as the famous cathedral with its Norman twin towers, there is the Guildhall, which includes a Mayor's Parlour with five original Tudor windows, and the Quay House Visitor Centre where the history of the city is illustrated.

Walking and Cycling

The beauty of Devon, of course, is also appreciated on foot. The Dart Valley Trail offers views of the river at its best, while at Dartmouth you can join the South West Coast Path, renowned for its stunning views and breezy cliff-top walking. The trail heads along the coast to South Hams, a rural farming district where gently rolling hills sweep down to the majestic coastline. One of the area's great landmarks is Salcombe, a bustling fishing port with a magnificent natural harbour.

Another popular trail is the 103-mile (164km) Two Moors Way which begins at Ivybridge and crosses Dartmoor before passing through the delightful hidden landscape of R.D.Blackmoor's classic novel *Lorna Doone* to reach Exmoor, which straddles the Devon/Somerset border. On reaching picturesque Lynton and Lynmouth you can link up with the South Coast Path again to explore north Devon's stunning coastline. Don't miss the Valley of Rocks, an extraordinary collection of peaks and outcrops which add a wonderful sense of drama to this stretch of coast.

There are various leaflets and booklets on cycling available from tourist information centres throughout the county. The Dartmoor Way is a great introduction to the National Park with a choice of off-road cycle routes; there is also a range of cycle trails in the Exmoor National Park.

Festivals and Events

- The Ashburton Carnival takes place at Ashburton in early July and there is a Winter Carnival in early November.
- Chagford has an Agricultural and Flower show in August.
- During July, Honiton hosts a Fair with the Hot Pennies ceremony; in August there is an Agricultural Show and in October a carnival.
- Ilfracombe is the setting for the North Devon Festival and there is evening entertainment on the seafront throughout the summer.
- Plymouth Navy Days takes place on the August Bank Holiday weekend.

Haytor Rocks, Dartmoor

Clovelly

Watersmeet, near Lynmouth

DEVON

See Walk 5 & Cycle Ride 2 in the Walks & Cycle Rides section at the end of the guide

ASHBURTON — Map 3 SX77

Places to visit

Compton Castle, COMPTON 01803 842382
www.nationaltrust.org.uk/devoncornwall

Tuckers Maltings, NEWTON ABBOT 01626 334734
www.tuckersmaltings.com

Great for kids: Prickly Ball Farm and Hedgehog Hospital, NEWTON ABBOT 01626 362319
www.pricklyballfarm.com

▶▶▶▶ 85% River Dart Country Park (SX734700)

Holne Park TQ13 7NP
☎ 01364 652511 🖷 01364 652020
e-mail: info@riverdart.co.uk
web: www.riverdart.co.uk
dir: *M5 junct 31, A38 towards Plymouth. In Ashburton at Peartree junct follow brown site signs. Site 1m on left. (NB Peartree junct is 2nd exit at Ashburton - do not exit at Linhay junct as narrow roads are unsuitable for caravans)*

* ⬛ £17-£28.50 ⬛ £17-£28.50 ▲ £17-£28.50

Open Apr-Sep (rs Low season café bar restricted opening hours)

Last arrival 21.00hrs Last departure 11.00hrs

Set in 90 acres of magnificent parkland that was once part of a Victorian estate, with many specimen and exotic trees, this peaceful, hidden away touring park occupies several camping areas, all served with good quality toilet facilities. In spring the park is a blaze of colour from the many azaleas and rhododendrons. There are numerous outdoor activities for all ages including abseiling, caving and canoeing, plus high quality, well-maintained facilities. The open moorland of Dartmoor is only a few minutes away. 90 acre site. 170 touring pitches. 23 hardstandings. Caravan pitches. Motorhome pitches. Tent pitches.

AA Pubs & Restaurants nearby: Dartbridge Inn, Buckfastleigh 01364 642214

Agaric, Ashburton 01364 654478

Leisure: 🅰 ♨ ✎

Facilities: ⬛ ⬛ ⬛ ⬛ ⬛ ⬛ ⬛ ⬛ ⬛ ⬛ ⬛ ⬛ ⬛

Services: ⬛ ⬛ ⬛ ⬛ ⬛ ⬛ ⬛ ⬛ ⬛

Within 3 miles: ⬛ ⬛ ⬛ ⬛ ♨

Notes: Dogs must be kept on leads. Adventure playground, climbing, canoeing.

▶▶▶▶ 84% Parkers Farm Holiday Park (SX779713)

Higher Mead Farm TQ13 7LJ
☎ 01364 654869 🖷 01364 654004
e-mail: parkersfarm@btconnect.com
dir: *From Exeter on A38, 2nd left after Plymouth/26m sign, signed Woodland & Denbury. From Plymouth on A38 take A383 Newton Abbot exit, turn right across bridge, rejoin A38, then as above*

⬛ ⬛ ▲

Open Etr-end Oct (rs Wknds only bar/restaurant open out of season)

Last arrival 22.00hrs Last departure 10.00hrs

A well-developed site terraced into rising ground with stunning views across rolling countryside to the Dartmoor tors. Part of a working farm, this park offers excellent fully serviced hardstanding pitchs, which make the most of the fine views, beautifully maintained and good quality toilets facilities, and a popular games room and a bar/restaurant that serves excellent meals. Large family rooms with two shower cubicles, a large sink and a toilet are especially appreciated by families with small children. There are regular farm walks when all the family can meet and feed the various animals. 25 acre site. 100 touring pitches. 20 hardstandings. Caravan pitches. Motorhome pitches. Tent pitches. 18 statics.

AA Pubs & Restaurants nearby: Dartbridge Inn, Buckfastleigh 01364 642214

Agaric, Ashburton 01364 654478

Leisure: 🅰 ✎ ▭

Facilities: ⬛ ⬛ ⬛ ⬛ ⬛ ⬛ ⬛ ⬛ ⬛

Services: ⬛ ⬛ ⬛ ⬛ ⬛ ⬛ ⬛ ⬛ ⬛

Within 3 miles: ⬛ ⬛ ⬛

Notes: Large field for dog walking.

AXMINSTER — Map 4 SY29

Places to visit

Branscombe - The Old Bakery, Manor Mill and Forge, BRANSCOMBE 01752 346585
www.nationaltrust.org.uk

Allhallows Museum, HONITON 01404 44966
www.honitonmuseum.co.uk

Great for kids: Pecorama Pleasure Gardens, BEER 01297 21542 www.pecorama.info

▶▶▶▶ 83% Andrewshayes Caravan Park (ST248088)

Dalwood EX13 7DY
☎ 01404 831225 🖷 01404 831893
e-mail: info@andrewshayes.co.uk
web: www.andrewshayes.co.uk
dir: *3m from Axminster (towards Honiton) on A35, right at Taunton Cross signed Dalwood & Stockland. Site 150mtrs on right*

* ⬛ £12-£27 ⬛ £12-£27 ▲ £12-£24

Open Mar-Nov (rs Sep-Nov shop, bar hours limited, pool closed Sep-mid May)

Last arrival 22.00hrs Last departure 11.00hrs

An attractive family park within easy reach of Lyme Regis, Seaton, Branscombe and Sidmouth in an ideal touring location. This popular park offers modern toilet facilities, an outdoor swimming pool and a quiet, cosy bar with a wide-screen TV. 12 acre site. 150 touring pitches. 105 hardstandings. Caravan pitches. Motorhome pitches. Tent pitches. 80 statics.

AA Pubs & Restaurants nearby: Tuckers Arms, Dalwood 01404 881342

Leisure: ♨ 🅰 ♨ ✎ ▭

Facilities: ⬛ ⬛ ⬛ ⬛ ⬛ ⬛ ⬛ ⬛ ⬛ ⬛ ⬛

Services: ⬛ ⬛ ⬛ ⬛ ⬛ ⬛ ⬛ ⬛

Within 3 miles: ⬛ ⬛ ⬛

Notes: Dogs must be kept on leads.

LEISURE: 🏊 Indoor swimming pool 🏊 Outdoor swimming pool 🅰 Children's playground 👶 Kid's club 🎾 Tennis court 🎱 Games room 📺 Separate TV room
🏌 9/18 hole golf course ⛵ Boats for hire 🎬 Cinema 🎵 Entertainment 🎣 Fishing 🏌 Mini golf 🏄 Watersports 🏋 Gym 🎯 Sports field **Spa** ♨ Stables
FACILITIES: 🛁 Bath 🚿 Shower ⚡ Electric shaver 💈 Hairdryer ❄ Ice Pack Facility ♿ Disabled facilities ☎ Public telephone 🏪 Shop on site or within 200yds
🚐 Mobile shop (calls at least 5 days a week) 🍖 BBQ area 🎋 Picnic area 📶 Wi-fi 💻 Internet access ♻ Recycling ℹ Tourist info 🐕 Dog exercise area

AA CAMPING CARD SITE

▶▶▶ 81% *Hawkchurch Country Park*

(SY344985)

Hawkchurch EX13 5UL
☎ 08442 729502
e-mail: enquiries@hawkchurchpark.co.uk
dir: *From Axminster towards Charmouth on A35 left onto B3165. Left into Wareham Rd, site on left, follow signs. (NB the lanes near Hawkchurch are narrow)*

* ⊕ £13-£20 ⊕ £13-£20 ▲ £13-£20

Open 15 Feb-4 Jan

Last arrival 21.00hrs Last departure 10.00hrs

This peaceful park is set in mature woodlands right on the Devon and Dorset border, with easy access to the Jurassic Coast Heritage Site, Lyme Regis, Charmouth and West Bay. The site has huge potential, with hardstandings plus tent and rally fields. 30 acre site. 369 touring pitches. 225 hardstandings. Caravan pitches. Motorhome pitches. Tent pitches.

AA Pubs & Restaurants nearby: The Mariners, Lyme Regis 01297 442753

Pilot Boat Inn, Lyme Regis 01297 442753

Leisure: 🎿 🎱 🎵
Facilities: 🚿⊙🅿☀♿🕐🖥🎣ℹ
Services: 🔌🗑🍺💧⌀🚽🍽
Within 3 miles: 🚴🎡🏌◎🛥🍴🗑

Notes: Quiet period 22.00hrs-08.00hrs. Dogs must be kept on leads.

see advert below

BERRYNARBOR   Map 3 SS54

Places to visit

Arlington Court, ARLINGTON 01271 850296 www.nationaltrust.org.uk/main/w-arlingtoncourt

Exmoor Zoological Park, BLACKMOOR GATE 01598 763352 www.exmoorzoo.co.uk

Great for kids: Combe Martin Wildlife Park & Dinosaur Park, COMBE MARTIN 01271 882486 www.dinosaur-park.com

▶▶▶ 84% Mill Park (SS559471)

Mill Ln EX34 9SH
☎ 01271 882647
e-mail: millparkdevon@btconnect.com
dir: *M5 junct 27, A361 towards Barnstaple. Right onto A399 towards Combe Martin. At Sawmills Inn take turn opposite signed Berrynarbor*

⊕ ⊕ ▲

Open Mar-30 Oct (rs Low season on-site facilities closed)

Last arrival 22.00hrs Last departure 10.00hrs

This family owned and run park is set in an attractive wooded valley with a stream running into a lake where coarse fishing is available. There is a quiet bar/restaurant with a family room, and the park now has two lakeside cocoons and a four bedroom apartment for hire. The park is two miles from Combe Martin and Ilfracombe and just a stroll across the road from the small harbour at Watermouth. 23 acre site. 178 touring pitches. 20 hardstandings. Caravan pitches. Motorhome pitches. Tent pitches. 1 static. 2 wooden pods.

AA Pubs & Restaurants nearby: George & Dragon, Ilfracombe 01271 863851

The Quay, Ilfracombe 01271 868090

Leisure: 🎿 🎱
Facilities: 🚿⊙🅿☀♿🕐🖥🎣🎾 Wi-fi
Services: 🔌🗑🍺⌀🚽🍽🔋
Within 3 miles: 🚴🎡🏌🗑U

Notes: No large groups.

BICKINGTON (NEAR ASHBURTON)

Places to visit

Bradley Manor, NEWTON ABBOT 01803 843235 www.nationaltrust.org.uk/devoncornwall

Great for kids: Living Coasts, TORQUAY 01803 202470 www.livingcoasts.org.uk

BICKINGTON (NEAR ASHBURTON)   Map 3 SX87

▶▶▶▶ **81% Lemonford Caravan Park** (SX793723)

TQ12 6JR
☎ **01626 821242**
e-mail: info@lemonford.co.uk
web: www.lemonford.co.uk
dir: From Exeter on A38 take A382, then 3rd exit at rdbt, follow Bickington signs

* 🚐 £10-£18.50 🚏 £10-£18.50 ▲ £10-£18.50

Open all year

Last arrival 22.00hrs Last departure 11.00hrs

Small, secluded and well-maintained park with a good mixture of attractively laid out pitches. The friendly owners pay a great deal of attention to detail, and the toilets in particular are kept spotlessly clean. This good touring base is only one mile from Dartmoor and ten miles from the seaside at Torbay. 7 acre site. 82 touring pitches. 55 hardstandings. Caravan pitches. Motorhome pitches. Tent pitches. 44 statics.

AA Pubs & Restaurants nearby: Wild Goose Inn, Combeinteignhead 01626 872241

Agaric, Ashburton 01364 654478

Leisure: ⚠
Facilities: 🚾🅿️⊙🎣✳️♿🛈🗑️🛈
Services: 🚐🅿️🛢️⊘🚽🍴⚡
Within 3 miles: ⚓️🎇🛒🛈U
Notes: Dogs must be kept on leads. Clothes drying area.

see advert below

BRAUNTON   Map 3 SS43

Places to visit

Marwood Hill Gardens, BARNSTAPLE 01271 342528
www.marwoodhillgarden.co.uk

Great for kids: Combe Martin Wildlife Park & Dinosaur Park, COMBE MARTIN 01271 882486
www.dinosaur-park.com

PREMIER PARK

▶▶▶▶▶ **85% *Hidden Valley Park*** (SS499408)
Best of British

West Down EX34 8NU
☎ **01271 813837**
dir: Direct access off A361, 8m from Barnstaple & 2m from Mullacott Cross

🚐 🚏 ▲

Open all year

A delightful, well-appointed family site set in a wooded valley, with superb facilities and a café. The park is set in a very rural, natural location not far from the beautiful coastline around Ilfracombe. The woodland is now home to nesting buzzards, and otters have taken up residence by the lake. 25 acre site. 115 touring pitches. Caravan pitches. Motorhome pitches. Tent pitches.

AA Pubs & Restaurants nearby: The Williams Arms, Braunton 01271 812360

▶▶▶ **79% Lobb Fields Caravan & Camping Park** (SS475378)

Saunton Rd EX33 1HG
☎ **01271 812090** 📠 01271 812090
e-mail: info@lobbfields.com
dir: At x-rds in Braunton take B3231 to Croyde. Site signed on right leaving Braunton

* 🚐 £9-£27 🚏 £9-£27 ▲ £8-£27

Open 23 Mar-28 Oct

Last arrival 22.00hrs Last departure 10.30hrs

A bright, tree-lined park with the gently-sloping grass pitches divided into two open areas and a camping field in August. Braunton is an easy walk away, and the golden beaches of Saunton Sands and Croyde are within easy reach. 14 acre site. 180 touring pitches. 6 hardstandings. Caravan pitches. Motorhome pitches. Tent pitches.

LEISURE: 🏊 Indoor swimming pool 🏊 Outdoor swimming pool ⚠ Children's playground 🧒 Kid's club 🎾 Tennis court 🎱 Games room 📺 Separate TV room ⛳ 9/18 hole golf course ⛵ Boats for hire 🎬 Cinema 🎵 Entertainment 🎣 Fishing ⛳ Mini golf 🏄 Watersports 🏋️ Gym ⚽ Sports field **Spa** U Stables
FACILITIES: 🚿 Bath 🚿 Shower ⊙ Electric shaver 🎣 Hairdryer ✳️ Ice Pack Facility ♿ Disabled facilities ☎ Public telephone 🛒 Shop on site or within 200yds 🏪 Mobile shop (calls at least 5 days a week) 🍖 BBQ area 🪑 Picnic area 📶 Wi-fi 💻 Internet access ♻ Recycling 🛈 Tourist info 🐕 Dog exercise area

AA Pubs & Restaurants nearby: The Williams Arms, Braunton 01271 812360

Leisure: ⚠ **Facilities:** 🏪⊙🍴✳⚒☎🐕♻ 𝒊

Services: 🔌🗑 🏠⚿💧👶♨🛠⚡

Within 3 miles: ↨🔎⚓🛥🎣🛒∪

Notes: No under 18s unless accompanied by an adult. Dogs must be kept on leads. Surfing, boards & wet suits for hire, wet suit washing areas.

BRIDESTOWE   Map 3 SX58

Places to visit

Lydford Castle and Saxon Town, LYDFORD www.english-heritage.org.uk

Museum of Dartmoor Life, OKEHAMPTON 01837 52295 www.museumofdartmoorlife.eclipse.co.uk

Great for kids: Tamar Otter & Wildlife Centre, LAUNCESTON 01566 785646 www.tamarotters.co.uk

---

AA CAMPING CARD SITE

▶▶▶ 75% **Bridestowe Caravan Park**

(SX519893)

EX20 4ER
☎ 01837 861261
e-mail: ali.young53@btinternet.com
dir: Exit A30 at A386/Sourton Cross junct, follow B3278 signed Bridestowe, turn left in 3m. In village centre, left onto unclassified road for 0.5m

* 🚐 £13-£18 �" £13-£18 ▲ £10-£15

Open Mar-Dec

Last arrival 22.30hrs Last departure noon

A small, well-established park in a rural setting close to Dartmoor National Park. This mainly static park has a small, peaceful touring space, and there are many activities to enjoy in the area including fishing and riding. Part of the National Cycle Route 27 - the Devon coast to coast - passes close to this park. 1 acre site. 13 touring pitches. 3 hardstandings. Caravan pitches. Motorhome pitches. Tent pitches. 40 statics.

AA Pubs & Restaurants nearby: Highwayman Inn, Sourton 01837 861243

Lewtrenchard Manor, Lewdown 01566 783222

Leisure: ⚠ 🎣 **Facilities:** 🏪⊙✳🛒♻ 𝒊
Services: 🔌🗑 🏠⊘⛽🛠
Within 3 miles: 🔎🛒🛒∪ **Notes:** ⊗

BRIDGERULE   Map 2 SS20

▶▶▶ 82% **Hedleywood Caravan & Camping Park** (SS262013)

EX22 7ED
☎ 01288 381404 📠 01288 382011
e-mail: alan@hedleywood.co.uk
dir: M5 south to Exeter, A30 to Launceston, B3254 towards Bude. Left into Tackbear Rd signed Marhamchurch & Widemouth (at Devon/Cornwall border). Site on right

* 🚐 £12.50-£19 �" £12.50-£19 ▲ £12.50-£19

Open all year (rs Main hols bar/restaurant open)

Last arrival anytime Last departure anytime

Set in a very rural location about four miles from Bude, this relaxed family-owned site has a peaceful, easy-going atmosphere. Pitches are in separate paddocks, some with extensive views, and this wooded park is quite sheltered in the lower areas. 16.5 acre site. 120 touring pitches. 30 hardstandings. Caravan pitches. Motorhome pitches. Tent pitches. 16 statics.

AA Pubs & Restaurants nearby: The Bickford Arms, Holsworthy 01409 221318

Bay View Inn, Widemouth Bay 01288 361273

Leisure: ⚠ 🎣 ⊡
Facilities: 🏪⊙🍴✳⚒☎🗑🐕✈🌐 📺 ♻ 𝒊
Services: 🔌🗑 🍴🏠⊘🚽🍽♨🚐♨⚡
Within 3 miles: 🔎🛒🛒∪
Notes: ⊗ Dog kennels, nature trail/dog walk, caravan storage.

▶▶ 89% **Highfield House Camping & Caravanning** (SS279035)

Holsworthy EX22 7EE
☎ 01288 381480
e-mail: njt@btinternet.com
dir: Exit A3072 at Red Post x-rds onto B3254 towards Launceston. Direct access just over Devon border on right

🚐 �" ▲

Open all year

Set in a quiet and peaceful rural location, this park has extensive views over the valley to the sea at Bude, five miles away. The friendly owners, with children of their own, offer a relaxing holiday for families, with the simple facilities carefully looked after. 4 acre site. 20 touring pitches. Caravan pitches. Motorhome pitches. Tent pitches. 4 statics.

AA Pubs & Restaurants nearby: The Bickford Arms, Holsworthy 01409 221318

Bay View Inn, Widemouth Bay 01288 361273

Facilities: 🏪⊙✳⚒✈
Services: 🔌🗑
Within 3 miles: 🔎🛒◎🎣🛒∪
Notes: ⊗ Dogs must be kept on leads.

SERVICES: 🔌 Electric hook up 🗑 Launderette 🍴 Licensed bar 🏠 Calor Gas ⊘ Camping Gaz 🚽 Toilet fluid 🍽 Café/Restaurant ♨ Fast Food/Takeaway 🚐 Battery charging 👶 Baby care 🛠 Motorvan service point
ABBREVIATIONS: BH/bank hols-bank holidays Etr-Easter Whit-Whitsun dep-departure fr-from hrs-hours m-mile mdnt-midnight rdbt-roundabout rs-restricted service wk-week wknd-weekend ⊗ No credit cards ⊗ No dogs

See page 7 for details of the AA Camping Card Scheme

BRIXHAM — Map 3 SX95

Places to visit

Greenway, CHURSTON FERRERS 01803 842382
www.nationaltrust.org.uk/devoncornwall

Great for kids: Paignton Zoo Environmental
Park, PAIGNTON 0844 474 2222 www.
paigntonzoo.org.uk

▶▶▶ 80% *Galmpton Touring Park* (SX885558)

Greenway Rd TQ5 0EP
☎ 01803 842066
e-mail: galmptontouringpark@hotmail.com
dir: *Signed from A3022 (Torbay to Brixham road) at Churston*

🏕🚐⛺

Open Etr-Sep

Last arrival 21.00hrs Last departure 11.00hrs

New experienced owners have taken over this stunningly located site, set on high ground overlooking the River Dart and with outstanding views of the creek and anchorage. The park is looking smarter and improved pitches are set on level terraces, plus the older-style toilets facilities have been spruced up and the reception/shop has been extended and improved. Plans include upgrading the toilet block with privacy cubicles. 10 acre site. 120 touring pitches. 15 hardstandings. Caravan pitches. Motorhome pitches. Tent pitches.

AA Pubs & Restaurants nearby: Quayside Hotel, Brixham 01803 855751

Leisure: 🅰

Facilities: 🍴⊙🅿✶♿🕐🛒📶

Services: 🔌🔟🔒🗑🚰🅣

Within 3 miles: 🎣🏌🎠📡🛶🏖🛒🗑

Notes: Families & couples only, no dogs during peak season. Bathroom for under 5s (charges apply).

BROADWOODWIDGER — Map 3 SX48

Places to visit

Museum of Dartmoor Life,
OKEHAMPTON 01837 52295
www.museumofdartmoorlife.eclipse.co.uk

Finch Foundry, STICKLEPATH 01837 840046
www.nationaltrust.org.uk

▶▶▶ 75% Roadford Lake (SX421900)

Lower Goodacre PL16 0JL
☎ 01409 211507 📠 01566 778503
e-mail: info@swlakestrust.org.uk
dir: *Exit A30 between Okehampton & Launceston at Roadford Lake signs, across dam wall, site 0.25m on right*

✻ 🚐 £13-£15 🚐 £13-£15 ⛺ £13-£15

Open Apr-Oct

Located right at the edge of Devon's largest inland water, this popular rural park is well screened by mature trees and shrubs. It boasts a brand new toilet block and an excellent watersports school (sailing, windsurfing, rowing and kayaking) with hire and day launch facilities, and is an ideal location for fly fishing for brown trout. 1.5 acre site. 30 touring pitches. 4 hardstandings. Caravan pitches. Motorhome pitches. Tent pitches.

AA Pubs & Restaurants nearby: Arundell Arms, Lifton 01566 784666

Facilities: 🍴⊙🅿✶♿🏕♻🛈

Services: 🔌🗑🍴

Within 3 miles: 🎣🏌🛶🗑

Notes: Dogs must be kept on leads.

BUCKFASTLEIGH — Map 3 SX76

Places to visit

Buckfast Abbey, BUCKFASTLEIGH 01364 645500
www.buckfast.org.uk

Great for kids: Buckfast Butterfly Farm &
Dartmoor Otter Sanctuary, BUCKFASTLEIGH
01364 642916 www.ottersandbutterflies.co.uk

▶ 88% Churchill Farm Campsite (SX743664)

TQ11 0EZ
☎ 01364 642844 & 07964 730578
e-mail: apedrick@btinternet.com
dir: *From A38 Dart Bridge exit for Buckfastleigh/ Totnes towards Buckfast Abbey. Pass Abbey entrance, up hill, left at x-roads to site opposite Holy Trinity Church*

✻ 🚐 £12 🚐 £12 ⛺ £12

Open Etr-Sep

Last arrival 22.00hrs

A working family farm in a relaxed and peaceful setting, with keen, friendly owners. Set on the hills above Buckfast Abbey, this attractive park is maintained to a good standard. The spacious pitches in the neatly trimmed paddock enjoy extensive country views towards Dartmoor, and the clean, simple toilet facilities now include smartly refurbished showers. This is a hidden gem for those who love traditional camping. 3 acre site. 25 touring pitches. Caravan pitches. Motorhome pitches. Tent pitches.

AA Pubs & Restaurants nearby: Dartbridge Inn, Buckfastleigh 01364 642214

Facilities: 🍴⊙✶♿♻🛈

Services: 🔌🚰

Within 3 miles: 🗑

Notes: 🐕 Working farm, no ball games. Dogs must be kept on leads. Within a Site of Special Scientific Interest.

▶ 84% Beara Farm Caravan & Camping Site (SX751645)

Colston Rd TQ11 0LW
☎ 01364 642234
dir: *From Exeter take Buckfastleigh exit at Dart Bridge, follow South Devon Steam Railway/ Butterfly Farm signs. In 200mtrs 1st left to Old Totnes Rd, 0.5m right at brick cottages signed Beara Farm*

🏕🚐⛺

Open all year

A very good farm park with clean unisex facilities and very keen and friendly owners. A well-trimmed camping field offers peace and quiet. Close to the River Dart and the Dart Valley steam railway line, within easy reach of the sea and moors. Please note that the approach to the site is narrow, with passing places, and care needs to be taken. 3.63 acre site. 30 touring pitches. 1 hardstanding. Caravan pitches. Motorhome pitches. Tent pitches.

AA Pubs & Restaurants nearby: Dartbridge Inn, Buckfastleigh 01364 642214

Facilities: 🍴⊙✶🏕🐕♻

Services: 🚰

Within 3 miles: 🏌🗑

Notes: 🐕 Dogs must be kept on leads.

LEISURE: 🏊 Indoor swimming pool 🏊 Outdoor swimming pool 🅰 Children's playground 🧒 Kid's club 🎾 Tennis court 🎱 Games room ▭ Separate TV room 🏌 9/18 hole golf course 🚣 Boats for hire 🎬 Cinema 🎵 Entertainment 🎣 Fishing 🏌 Mini golf 🛶 Watersports 🏋 Gym 🏟 Sports field **Spa** ⛲ Stables
FACILITIES: 🛁 Bath 🍴 Shower ⊙ Electric shaver 🅿 Hairdryer ✶ Ice Pack Facility ♿ Disabled facilities 🕐 Public telephone 🛒 Shop on site or within 200yds 🛒 Mobile shop (calls at least 5 days a week) 🍴 BBQ area 🏕 Picnic area 📶 Wi-fi 📧 Internet access ♻ Recycling 🛈 Tourist info 🐕 Dog exercise area

BUDLEIGH SALTERTON — Map 3 SY08

Places to visit

Otterton Mill, OTTERTON 01395 568521
www.ottertonmill.com

Great for kids: Bicton Park Botanical Gardens,
BICTON 01395 568465
www.bictongardens.co.uk

AA CAMPING CARD SITE

▶▶▶ 79% Pooh Cottage Holiday Park
(SY053831)

Bear Ln EX9 7AQ
☎ 01395 442354 & 07928 486938
e-mail: info@poohcottage.co.uk
web: www.poohcottage.co.uk
dir: *M5 junct 30, A376 towards Exmouth. Left onto
B3179 towards Woodbury & Budleigh Salterton.
Left into Knowle onto B3178. Through village, at
brow of hill take sharp left into Bear Lane. Site
200yds*

* ⊕ £14-£20 ⊕ £14-£20 ▲ £14-£20

Open 15 Mar-Oct

Last arrival 20.00hrs Last departure 11.00hrs

A rural park with widespread views of the sea and
surrounding peaceful countryside. Expect a
friendly welcome to this attractive site, with its
lovely play area, and easy access to plenty of
walks, as well as the Buzzard Cycle Way. 8 acre
site. 52 touring pitches. 40 seasonal pitches.
Caravan pitches. Motorhome pitches. Tent
pitches. 3 statics.

AA Pubs & Restaurants nearby: The Blue Ball,
Sidford 01395 514062

Salty Monk, Sidford 01395 513174

Leisure: ⚐
Facilities: ⚐⊙⚒⚓⚑⚑ ⚏ ♻ ❼
Services: ⚐⚏🔌⚗️⚏️🆃
Within 3 miles: ⚓⚑🚲🔵◎⚓🔵🔵U

Notes: Dogs must be kept on leads. Cycle track,
bike hire.

CHAPMANS WELL — Map 3 SX39

Places to visit

Launceston Steam Railway, LAUNCESTON
01566 775665 www.launcestonsr.co.uk

Launceston Castle, LAUNCESTON 01566 772365
www.english-heritage.org.uk

Great for kids: Tamar Otter & Wildlife Centre,
LAUNCESTON 01566 785646
www.tamarotters.co.uk

AA CAMPING CARD SITE

▶▶▶ 84% Chapmanswell Caravan
Park *(SX354931)*

St Giles-on-the-Heath PL15 9SG
☎ 01409 211382 ▤ 01409 211154
e-mail: george@chapmanswellcaravanpark.co.uk
web: www.chapmanswellcaravanpark.co.uk
dir: *Take A338 from Launceston towards
Holsworthy, 6m. Site on left at Chapmans Well*

* ⊕ £13.50-£18 ⊕ £13.50-£18 ▲ £10.50-£25.50

Open all year

Last arrival anytime by prior agreement Last
departure anytime by prior agreement

Set on the borders of Devon and Cornwall in
peaceful countryside, this park is just waiting to
be discovered. It enjoys extensive views towards
Dartmoor from level pitches, and is within easy
driving distance of Launceston (7 miles) and the
golden beaches at Bude (14 miles). 10 acre site.
50 touring pitches. 35 hardstandings. 32
seasonal pitches. Caravan pitches. Motorhome
pitches. Tent pitches. 50 statics.

AA Pubs & Restaurants nearby: The Bickford
Arms, Holsworthy 01409 221318

Blagdon Manor, Ashwater 01409 211224

Leisure: ⚐ ♪
Facilities: ⚐⊙⚒⚓⚏⚏ ♻ ❼
Services: ⚐⚏⚑🔌⚗️🆃🍽🔋🥤⚓
Within 3 miles: ⚓⚑🚲⚓🔵🔵U

Notes: Dogs must be kept on leads.

CHUDLEIGH — Map 3 SX87

Places to visit

Canonteign Falls, CHUDLEIGH 01647 252434
www.canonteignfalls.co.uk

Exeter's Underground Passages, EXETER
01392 665887 www.exeter.gov.uk/passages

Great for kids: Prickly Ball Farm and Hedgehog
Hospital, NEWTON ABBOT 01626 362319
www.pricklyballfarm.com

▶▶▶ 83% Holmans Wood
Holiday Park *(SX881812)*

Harcombe Cross TQ13 0DZ
☎ 01626 853785 ▤ 01626 853792
e-mail: enquiries@holmanswood.co.uk
dir: *M5 junct 31, A38. After racecourse at top
of Haldon Hill left at BP petrol station signed
Chudleigh, site entrance on left of slip road*

* ⊕ £18-£23 ⊕ £18-£23 ▲ £12-£16

Open mid Mar-end Oct

Last arrival 22.00hrs Last departure 11.00hrs

A delightful small park set back from the A38 in a
secluded wooded area, handy for touring Dartmoor
National Park, and the lanes and beaches of
South Devon. The facilities are bright and clean,
and the grounds are attractively landscaped. 12
acre site. 73 touring pitches. 71 hardstandings.
Caravan pitches. Motorhome pitches. Tent
pitches. 34 statics.

AA Pubs & Restaurants nearby: The Cridford Inn,
Trusham 01626 853694

Leisure: ⚐
Facilities: ⚐⊙⚒⚒⚓⚏🔵❼
Services: ⚐⚏🔌⚗️
Within 3 miles: 🔵🔵U
Notes: No pets.

COMBE MARTIN

See also Berrynarbor

Places to visit

Arlington Court, ARLINGTON 01271 850296
www.nationaltrust.org.uk/
main/w-arlingtoncourt

Great for kids: Combe Martin Wildlife Park &
Dinosaur Park, COMBE MARTIN 01271 882486
www.dinosaur-park.com

SERVICES: ⚐ Electric hook up ⚏ Launderette ⚑ Licensed bar ⚗ Calor Gas ⚖ Camping Gaz 🆃 Toilet fluid 🍽 Café/Restaurant 🔋 Fast Food/Takeaway 🔌 Battery charging
🥤 Baby care ⚓ Motorvan service point
ABBREVIATIONS: BH/bank hols-bank holidays Etr-Easter Whit-Whitsun dep-departure fr-from hrs-hours m-mile mdnt-midnight rdbt-roundabout rs-restricted service wk-week
wknd-weekend ⊛ No credit cards ⊗ No dogs   See page 7 for details of the AA Camping Card Scheme

COMBE MARTIN — Map 3 SS54

►►►► 88% Stowford Farm Meadows (SS560427)

GOLD

Berry Down EX34 0PW
☎ 01271 882476 📠 01271 883053
e-mail: enquiries@stowford.co.uk
dir: M5 junct 27, A361 to Barnstaple. Take A39 from town centre towards Lynton, in 1m left onto B3230. Right at garage at Lynton Cross onto A3123, site 1.5m on right

* ⚲ £8.40-£23 ⛺ £9.40-£23 ⛺ £8.40-£22

Open all year (rs Winter bars & catering closed)

Last arrival 20.00hrs Last departure 10.00hrs

Very gently sloping, grassy, sheltered and south-facing site approached down a wide, well-kept driveway. This large farm park is set in 500 acres, and offers many quality amenities, including a large swimming pool, horse riding and crazy golf. A 60-acre wooded nature trail is an added attraction, as is the mini zoo with its stock of friendly animals. 100 acre site. 700 touring pitches. 115 hardstandings. Caravan pitches. Motorhome pitches. Tent pitches.

AA Pubs & Restaurants nearby: George & Dragon, Ilfracombe 01271 863851

Fox & Goose, Parracombe 01598 763239

The Quay, Ilfracombe 01271 868090

Leisure: 🏊🏻‍♀️ 🎠 ⚽ 🎣 🎵
Facilities: 🚾 🚿 ⊙ 💇 ✳ ♿ 🕐 🏧 ☎ wifi ♻ ❶
Services: 🚐 🔋 🍴 🛢 🚽 🍽 🛒 🎪 🚮
Within 3 miles: ↓ ✐ ◎ 🏧 🐴 ∪

Notes: Dogs must be kept on leads. Caravan accessory shop/storage/workshop/sales.

AA CAMPING CARD SITE

►►►► 83% Newberry Valley Park (SS576473)

GOLD

Woodlands EX34 0AT
☎ 01271 882334
e-mail: relax@newberryvalleypark.co.uk
dir: M5 junct 27, A361 to North Aller rdbt. Right onto A399, through Combe Martin to sea. Left into site

⚲ £15-£38 ⛺ £15-£38 ⛺ £15-£38

Open Apr-Oct

Last arrival 20.45hrs Last departure 10.00hrs

A family owned and run touring park on the edge of Combe Martin, with all its amenities just a five-minute walk away. The park is set in a wooded valley with its own coarse fishing lake and has a stunning new toilet block with underfloor heating and excellent unisex privacy cubicles. The safe beaches of Newberry and Combe Martin are reached by a short footpath opposite the park entrance, where the South West Coast Path is located. 20 acre site. 120 touring pitches. 18 hardstandings. 20 seasonal pitches. Caravan pitches. Motorhome pitches. Tent pitches.

AA Pubs & Restaurants nearby: George & Dragon, Ilfracombe 01271 863851

Fox & Goose, Parracombe 01598 763239

The Quay, Ilfracombe 01271 868090

Leisure: 🎣
Facilities: 🚾 🚿 ⊙ 💇 ✳ ♿ 🕐 🏧 🐕
Services: 🚐 🔋 🚽 🛒
Within 3 miles: ↓ ✐ 🏧 🏧

Notes: No camp fires, latest arrival time dusk in winter. Dogs must be kept on leads.

CROYDE — Map 3 SS43

Places to visit

Marwood Hill Gardens, BARNSTAPLE 01271 342528 www.marwoodhillgarden.co.uk

Great for kids: Watermouth Castle & Family Theme Park, ILFRACOMBE 01271 863879 www.watermouthcastle.com

►►► 80% Bay View Farm Caravan & Camping Park (SS443388)

EX33 1PN
☎ 01271 890501
dir: M5 junct 27, A361, through Barnstaple to Braunton, left onto B3231. Site at entry to Croyde village

⚲ ⛺ ⛺

Open Mar-Oct

Last arrival 21.30hrs Last departure 11.00hrs

A very busy and popular park close to surfing beaches and rock pools, with a public footpath leading directly to the sea. Set in a stunning location with views out over the Atlantic to Lundy Island, it is just a short stroll from Croyde. Facilities are clean and well maintained, with the addition of a new family bathroom in 2011, and there is a fish and chip shop on site. Please note that no dogs are allowed. 10 acre site. 70 touring pitches. 38 hardstandings. 10 seasonal pitches. Caravan pitches. Motorhome pitches. Tent pitches. 3 statics.

AA Pubs & Restaurants nearby: The Williams Arms, Braunton 01271 812360

George & Dragon, Ilfracombe 01271 863851

The Quay, Ilfracombe 01271 868090

Leisure: 🎣
Facilities: 🚾 ⊙ 💇 ✳ ♿ 🕐 ♻ ❶
Services: 🚐 🔋 🛢 🚽 🍽 🎪 🚮
Within 3 miles: ↓ 🎣 ✐ ◎ 🏧 🏧 ∪
Notes: ⊗

CROYDE BAY — Map 3 SS43

84% Ruda Holiday Park (SS438397)

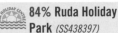

GOLD

EX33 1NY
☎ 0844 335 3756 📠 01271 890656
e-mail: touringandcamping@parkdeanholidays.com
web: www.parkdeantouring.com
dir: M5 junct 27, A361 to Braunton. Left at main lights, follow Croyde signs

⚲ ⛺ ⛺

Open mid Mar-Oct

Last arrival 21.00hrs Last departure 10.00hrs

A spacious, well-managed park with its own glorious award-winning sandy beach, a surfer's paradise. Set in well-landscaped grounds, and with a full leisure programme plus daytime and evening entertainment for all the family. Cascades tropical adventure pool and an entertainment lounge are very popular features. 220 acre site. 312 touring pitches. Caravan pitches. Motorhome pitches. Tent pitches. 278 statics.

AA Pubs & Restaurants nearby: The Williams Arms, Braunton 01271 812360

George & Dragon, Ilfracombe 01271 863851

The Quay, Ilfracombe 01271 868090

LEISURE: 🏊 Indoor swimming pool 🏊 Outdoor swimming pool 🎠 Children's playground 🧒 Kid's club 🎾 Tennis court 🎱 Games room 📺 Separate TV room ⛳ 9/18 hole golf course ⛵ Boats for hire 🎬 Cinema 🎵 Entertainment 🎣 Fishing ◎ Mini golf 🏄 Watersports 🏋 Gym ⚽ Sports field **Spa** ∪ Stables
FACILITIES: 🛁 Bath 🚿 Shower ⊙ Electric shaver 💇 Hairdryer ✳ Ice Pack Facility ♿ Disabled facilities 🕐 Public telephone 🏪 Shop on site or within 200yds 🚚 Mobile shop (calls at least 5 days a week) 🍖 BBQ area 🌲 Picnic area wifi Wi-fi 🖥 Internet access ♻ Recycling ❶ Tourist info 🐕 Dog exercise area

Leisure: 🏊🚶⬇🎯⚽🔍🎱🎵
Facilities: ➡🐾☉🅿✳♿🕙🚿🎯🚻
Services: 🔌🔅🍽🛡🧺🚽🍴🛒🚰
Within 3 miles: 🎣🏇🔅U

Notes: No pets. Family entertainment, children's clubs, Coast Bar & Kitchen.

see advert in preliminary section

CULLOMPTON

See Kentisbeare

DARTMOUTH — Map 3 SX85

Places to visit

Dartmouth Castle, DARTMOUTH 01803 833588 www.english-heritage.org.uk

Coleton Fishacre House & Garden, KINGSWEAR 01803 752466 www.nationaltrust.org.uk

Great for kids: Woodlands Family Theme Park, DARTMOUTH 01803 712598 www.woodlandspark.com

AA CAMPING CARD SITE

PREMIER PARK

►►►►► 88% Woodlands Grove Caravan & Camping Park (SX813522)

Best of British

Blackawton TQ9 7DQ
☎ 01803 712598 📠 01803 712680
e-mail: holiday@woodlandsgrove.com
web: www.woodlands-caravanpark.com
dir: *4m from Dartmouth on A3122. From A38 take turn for Totnes & follow brown tourist signs*

* 🚐 £13.50-£23 🚐 £13.50-£23 ⛺ £13.50-£23

Open 8 Apr-30 Oct

Last departure 11.00hrs

A quality caravan or tent park with smart, newly refurbished toilet facilities (including excellent family rooms), spacious pitches, including decent hardstandings, and good attention to detail throughout, all set in an extensive woodland environment with a terraced grass camping area. Free entry to the adjoining Woodlands Theme Park makes an excellent package holiday for families, but also good for adults travelling without children who are perhaps seeking a low season break. 16 acre site. 350 touring pitches. 113 hardstandings. Caravan pitches. Motorhome pitches. Tent pitches.

Woodlands Grove Caravan & Camping Park

AA Pubs & Restaurants nearby: The Seahorse, Dartmouth 01803 835147

Jan and Freddies Brasserie, Dartmouth 01803 832491

Leisure: 🏕🔍🎱🎵
Facilities: ➡🐾☉🅿✳♿🕙🚿🎯🚻🚻💻🖥ℹ
Services: 🔌🔅🛡🧺🚽🍴🛒🚰
Within 3 miles: 🏇🔅🔅

Notes: Dogs must be kept on leads. Falconry centre, woodland walk, mini golf. Discount available at local golf course & spa.

see advert on page 162

►►►► 84% Little Cotton Caravan Park (SX858508)

Little Cotton TQ6 0LB
☎ 01803 832558 📠 01803 834887
e-mail: enquiries@littlecotton.co.uk
dir: *Exit A38 at Buckfastleigh, A384 to Totnes, A381 to Halwell, take A3122 (Dartmouth Rd), site on right at entrance to town*

🚐 🚐 ⛺

Open 15 Mar-Oct

Last arrival 22.00hrs Last departure 11.00hrs

A very good grassy touring park set on high ground above Dartmouth, with quality facilities, and park-and-ride to the town from the gate. The immaculate toilet blocks are heated and superbly maintained and more spacious hardstandings were added in 2011. The friendly owners offer high levels of customer care and are happy to offer advice on touring in this pretty area. Excellent base for visiting Totnes, Slapton Sands and Kingsbridge. 7.5 acre site. 95 touring pitches. 42 hardstandings. Caravan pitches. Motorhome pitches. Tent pitches.

AA Pubs & Restaurants nearby: The Seahorse, Dartmouth 01803 835147

Jan and Freddies Brasserie, Dartmouth 01803 832491

Facilities: 🐾☉🅿✳♿🕙🚿🎯🚻🚻♻ℹ
Services: 🔌🔅🛡🧺🚽🍴🛒
Within 3 miles: 🏇🔅🔅🔅

Notes: Dogs must be kept on leads.

DAWLISH — Map 3 SX97

Places to visit

Kents Cavern, TORQUAY 01803 215136 www.kents-cavern.co.uk

Powderham Castle, POWDERHAM 01626 890243 www.powderham.co.uk

Great for kids: Babbacombe Model Village, TORQUAY 01803 315315 www.model-village.co.uk

 83% *Lady's Mile Holiday Park* (SX968784)

GOLD

EX7 0LX
☎ 0845 026 7252 📠 01626 888689
e-mail: info@ladysmile.co.uk
dir: *1m N of Dawlish on A379*

🚐 🚐 ⛺

Open 17 Mar-27 Oct

Last arrival 20.00hrs Last departure 11.00hrs

A holiday site with a wide variety of touring pitches, including some fully serviced pitches. There are plenty of activities for everyone, including two swimming pools with waterslides, a large adventure playground, 9-hole golf course, and a bar with entertainment in high season all add to the enjoyment of a stay here. Facilities are kept very clean, and the surrounding beaches are easily accessed. Holiday homes are also available. 16 acre site. 243 touring pitches. 30 hardstandings. Caravan pitches. Motorhome pitches. Tent pitches. 43 statics.

AA Pubs & Restaurants nearby: The Elizabethan Inn, Luton 01626 775425

Anchor Inn, Cockwood 01626 890203

Leisure: 🏊🏊🏕🔍
Facilities: ➡🐾☉♿🕙🎯🚻🚻
Services: 🔌🔅🍽🛡🧺🚽🍴🛒🚰
Within 3 miles: 🏇🔅🔅🔅U

SERVICES: 🔌 Electric hook up 🔅 Launderette 🍽 Licensed bar 🛡 Calor Gas 🧺 Camping Gaz 🚽 Toilet fluid 🍴 Café/Restaurant 🛒 Fast Food/Takeaway 🚰 Battery charging ➡ Baby care ⚙ Motorvan service point
ABBREVIATIONS: BH/bank hols-bank holidays Etr-Easter Whit-Whitsun dep-departure fr-from hrs-hours m-mile mdnt-midnight rdbt-roundabout rs-restricted service wk-week wknd-weekend 🚫 No credit cards 🚫 No dogs
See page 7 for details of the AA Camping Card Scheme

Families Free Entry To Theme Park! - With a 2 night stay

ADDING FUN TO YOU HOLIDAY

Woodlands Grove CARAVAN & CAMPING DARTMOUTH

Adult Midweek Special Discounts! Adults only low season

5 STAR CAMPING IN GLORIOUS SOUTH DEVON

Baths & Shower Rooms - Award Winning Facilities
Superb setting and Views - Beautiful beaches close by
Licensed Shop - Spacious Pitches - Under 5's Facilities
Baby and family rooms - Wi-fi

Blackawton, Totnes, South Devon TQ6 7DQ
www.woodlands-caravanpark.com 01803 712598

DAWLISH *continued*

78% *Peppermint Park*
(SX978788)

SILVER

Warren Rd EX7 0PQ
☎ **01626 863436** 📠 **01626 866482**
e-mail: peppermint@parkholidaysuk.com
web: www.parkholidaysuk.com
dir: *From A379 at Dawlish follow signs for Dawlish Warren. Site 1m on left at bottom of hill*

🏕🚐⛺

Open Mar-end Oct

Last arrival 18.00hrs Last departure 10.00hrs

A well managed, attractive park close to the coast, with excellent facilities including a club and bar, which are well away from pitches. Nestling close to sandy beaches, the park offers individually marked pitches on level terraces in pleasant, sheltered grassland. The many amenities include a heated swimming pool and water chute, coarse fishing and a launderette. 26 acre site. 25 touring pitches. Caravan pitches. Motorhome pitches. Tent pitches. 82 statics.

AA Pubs & Restaurants nearby: The Elizabethan Inn, Luton 01626 775425

Anchor Inn, Cockwood 01626 890203

Leisure: ⚠

Facilities: 🏠🐕🕐🛏📶 ❶

Services: 🔌🔲

Within 3 miles: ↓🐎🎣◎🔩🛒🔲

Notes: No cars by tents. Families & couples only. Dogs must be kept on leads.

AA CAMPING CARD SITE

►►►► 84% Cofton Country
Holidays *(SX967801)*

GOLD

Starcross EX6 8RP
☎ **01626 890111** & **0800 085 8649**
📠 **01626 890160**
e-mail: info@coftonholidays.co.uk
dir: *On A379 (Exeter/Dawlish road) 3m from Dawlish*

* 🚐 £14.50-£29 ⛺ £14.50-£29 ⛺ £14.50-£29

Open all year (rs Spring BH-mid Sep; Etr-end Oct pool, bar & shop open)

Last arrival 20.00hrs Last departure 11.00hrs

This park is set in a rural location surrounded by spacious open grassland, with plenty of well-kept

---

flowerbeds throughout. Most pitches overlook either the swimming pool complex or the fishing lakes and woodlands. A new purpose-built toilet block offers smart modern facilities and the on-site pub serves drinks, meals and snacks for all the family, and a mini-market caters for most shopping needs. 45 acre site. 450 touring pitches. 30 hardstandings. 110 seasonal pitches. Caravan pitches. Motorhome pitches. Tent pitches. 76 statics.

Cofton Country Holidays

AA Pubs & Restaurants nearby: The Elizabethan Inn, Luton 01626 775425

Anchor Inn, Cockwood 01626 890203

Leisure: 🏊⚠❀🔍

Facilities: 🛁🏠◎🎣☀🐕🕐🔩🏠🛏📶❹❶

Services: 🔌🔲🍴🔥📶🚿🔲🍴🛒🚚

Within 3 miles: ↓🐎🎣◎🔩🔲🔲

Notes: Dogs must be kept on leads. Coarse fishing, pub with family room, camping orchard, games room.

see advert on page 164

AA CAMPING CARD SITE

►►► 76% Leadstone Camping
(SX974782)

Warren Rd EX7 0NG
☎ **01626 864411** 📠 **01626 873833**
e-mail: info@leadstonecamping.co.uk
web: www.leadstonecamping.co.uk
dir: *M5 junct 30, A379 to Dawlish. Before village turn left on brow of hill, signed Dawlish Warren. Site 0.5m on right*

* 🚐 £17.50-£22 ⛺ £13.50-£18 ⛺ £13.50-£18

Open 8 Jun-2 Sep

Last arrival 22.00hrs Last departure noon

A traditional, mainly level, grassy camping park approximately a half-mile' walk from the sands and dunes at Dawlish Warren, an Area of Outstanding Natural Beauty. This mainly tented park has been run by the same friendly family for many years, and is an ideal base for touring south

---

Devon. A regular bus service from outside the gate takes in a wide area. A new wood-clad cabin will replace the old portaloos facilities for the 2012 season. 8 acre site. 137 touring pitches. 14 seasonal pitches. Caravan pitches. Motorhome pitches. Tent pitches.

Leadstone Camping

AA Pubs & Restaurants nearby: The Elizabethan Inn, Luton 01626 775425

Anchor Inn, Cockwood 01626 890203

Leisure: ⚠

Facilities: 🏠◎🎣☀🕐🔩📶♻❶

Services: 🔌🔲🍴🚿🚚

Within 3 miles: ↓🐎◎🔲🔲

Notes: No noise after 23.00hrs. Dogs must be kept on leads. Portable/disposable BBQs allowed.

DREWSTEIGNTON   Map 3 SX79

Places to visit

Castle Drogo, DREWSTEIGNTON 01647 433306
www.nationaltrust.org.uk/main

Finch Foundry, STICKLEPATH 01837 840046
www.nationaltrust.org.uk

NEW ►►►► 84% Woodland Springs
Adult Touring Park *(SX695912)*

Venton EX6 6PG
☎ **01647 231695**
e-mail: enquiries@woodlandsprings.co.uk
web: www.woodlandsprings.co.uk
dir: *Exit A30 at Whiddon Down junct onto A382 towards Moretonhampstead. Site 1.5m on left*

🚐 £18-£21 ⛺ £18-£21 ⛺ £15-£21

Open all year

Last arrival 20.00hrs Last departure 11.00hrs

An attractive park in a rural area within Dartmoor National Park. This site is surrounded by woodland and neighbouring farmland, and is very peaceful. The toilet block offers superb facilities for the disabled. Please note that children are not

continued

SERVICES: 🔌 Electric hook up 🔲 Launderette 🍴 Licensed bar 🔥 Calor Gas ⛽ Camping Gaz 🔲 Toilet fluid 🍴 Café/Restaurant 🛒 Fast Food/Takeaway 🔋 Battery charging 🍼 Baby care ⚡ Motorvan service point
ABBREVIATIONS: BH/bank hols-bank holidays Etr-Easter Whit-Whitsun dep-departure fr-from hrs-hours m-mile mdnt-midnight rdbt-roundabout rs-restricted service wk-week wknd-weekend 🚫 No credit cards 🚫 No dogs
See page 7 for details of the AA Camping Card Scheme

DREWSTEIGNTON *continued*

accepted. 4 acre site. 81 touring pitches. 45 hardstandings. 17 seasonal pitches. Caravan pitches. Motorhome pitches. Tent pitches.

Facilities: ↑ ⊙ ℙ ✳ ♿ 🖁 🛒 ⋈ Wi-Fi ♻ ℹ

Services: ⊕🖥 🛢 ⌿ 🔲 🛒 ↧

Within 3 miles: ↓ ✐ 🏪 🖆 ∪

Notes: Adults only. No fires, no noise 23.00hrs-08.00hrs. Dogs must be kept on leads. Day kennels, freezer, coffee vending machine.

EAST ALLINGTON

Places to visit

Coleton Fishacre House & Garden, KINGSWEAR 01803 752466 www.nationaltrust.org.uk

Kingsbridge Cookworthy Museum, KINGSBRIDGE 01548 853235 www.kingsbridgemuseum.org.uk

---

EAST ALLINGTON Map 3 SX74

AA CAMPING CARD SITE

▶▶▶ **74% Mounts Farm Touring Park**

(SX757488)

The Mounts TQ9 7QJ
☎ 01548 521591
e-mail: mounts.farm@lineone.net
web: www.mountsfarm.co.uk
dir: *A381 from Totnes towards Kingsbridge (NB ignore signs for East Allington). At 'Mounts', site 0.5m on left*

* 🚐 £15-£23 ⛺ £15-£23 ▲ £10-£20

Open 15 Mar-Oct

Last arrival anytime Last departure anytime

A neat grassy park divided into four paddocks by mature natural hedges. Three of the paddocks house the tourers and campers, and the fourth is the children's play area. The laundry and well-stocked little shop are in converted farm buildings. 7 acre site. 50 touring pitches. 10 seasonal pitches. Caravan pitches. Motorhome pitches. Tent pitches.

AA Pubs & Restaurants nearby: Fortescue Arms, East Allington 01548 521215

Tower Inn, Slapton 01548 580216

Leisure: 𝔸 ☼

Facilities: ↑ ⊙ ℙ ✳ 🖁 ♻ ℹ

Services: ⊕🖥 🛢 ⌿ 🔲 🛒

Within 3 miles: ≽ 日 ✐ ⇶ 🖁 🏪 ∪

Notes: Dogs must be kept on leads. Camping accessories shop on site.

EAST ANSTEY

Places to visit

Quince Honey Farm, SOUTH MOLTON 01769 572401 www.quincehoney.com

Tiverton Museum of Mid Devon Life, TIVERTON 01884 256295 www.tivertonmuseum.org.uk

LEISURE: 🏊 Indoor swimming pool 🏊 Outdoor swimming pool 𝔸 Children's playground 🏄 Kid's club ♨ Tennis court ⚲ Games room ☐ Separate TV room ↓ 9/18 hole golf course ⛵ Boats for hire 🎬 Cinema ♫ Entertainment ✐ Fishing ⊙ Mini golf ⇶ Watersports 🏌 Gym ☼ Sports field **Spa** ∪ Stables
FACILITIES: 🛁 Bath ↑ Shower ⊙ Electric shaver ℙ Hairdryer ✳ Ice Pack Facility ♿ Disabled facilities ☏ Public telephone 🏪 Shop on site or within 200yds 🏬 Mobile shop (calls at least 5 days a week) 🍖 BBQ area 🛒 Picnic area Wi-Fi Wi-fi 🖥 Internet access ♻ Recycling ℹ Tourist info ⋈ Dog exercise area

EAST ANSTEY | Map 3 SS82

AA CAMPING CARD SITE

►►►► 86% Zeacombe House Caravan Park *(SS860240)*

Blackerton Cross EX16 9JU
☎ **01398 341279**
e-mail: enquiries@zeacombeadultretreat.co.uk
dir: *M5 junct 27, A361 signed Barnstaple, right at next rdbt onto A396 signed Dulverton & Minehead. In 5m at Exeter Inn left, 1.5m, at Black Cat junct left onto B3227 towards South Molton, site 7m on left*

🚐 £10-£20 🚐 £10-£20 ▲ £10-£20

Open 7 Mar-Oct

Last arrival 21.00hrs Last departure noon

Set on the southern fringes of Exmoor National Park, this 'garden' park is nicely landscaped in a tranquil location, and enjoys panoramic views towards Exmoor. This adult-only park offers a choice of grass or hardstanding pitches, and a unique restaurant-style delivery service allows you to eat an evening meal in the comfort of your own unit. 5 acre site. 50 touring pitches. 12 hardstandings. Caravan pitches. Motorhome pitches. Tent pitches.

AA Pubs & Restaurants nearby: Masons Arms, Knowstone 01398 341231

Woods Bar & Dining Room, Dulverton 01398 324007

Facilities: ♠⊙♟✳♿🛁🔌⚿ℹ️
Services: 🔌🗄🔋🖊️🔧丁🛒⬆️♿
Within 3 miles: 🎣♟🎿🛍🗄♿⛳

Notes: Adults only. Dogs must be kept on leads. Store & stay system.

EAST WORLINGTON | Map 3 SS71

►►►► 80% Yeatheridge Farm Caravan Park *(SS768110)*

EX17 4TN
☎ **01884 860330**
e-mail: yeatheridge@talk21.com
dir: *M5 junct 27, A361, at 1st rdbt at Tiverton take B3137 for 9m towards Witheridge. Fork left 1m past Nomansland onto B3042. Site on left in 3.5m. (NB do not enter East Worlington)*

* 🚐 £9-£17.50 🚐 £9-£17.50 ▲ £9-£17.50

Open Etr-Sep

Last arrival 22.00hrs Last departure 10.00hrs

Gently sloping grass site with mature trees, set in meadowland in rural Devon. There are good views of distant Dartmoor, and the site is of great appeal to families with its two new play areas, farm animals, horse riding, and two indoor swimming pools, one with flume. There are many attractive villages in this area. 9 acre site. 85 touring pitches. Caravan pitches. Motorhome pitches. Tent pitches. 12 statics.

Yeatheridge Farm Caravan Park

Leisure: 🏊⛰🎠🎣
Facilities: ♠♟⊙♟✳♿🕐🛁🔌WiFi♻️ℹ️
Services: 🔌🗄🔋🖊️🗑丁🍽️🛒⬆️♿
Within 3 miles: ♟🗄♿⛳

Notes: Dogs must be kept on leads. Fishing, pool table.

EXETER

See Kennford

EXMOUTH

See also Woodbury Salterton

Places to visit

A la Ronde, EXMOUTH 01395 265514
www.nationaltrust.org.uk

Bicton Park Botanical Gardens, BICTON 01395 568465 www.bictongardens.co.uk

Great for kids: The World of Country Life, EXMOUTH 01395 274533
www.worldofcountrylife.co.uk

EXMOUTH | Map 3 SY08

90% Devon Cliffs Holiday Park *(SY036807)*

Sandy Bay EX8 5BT
☎ **0871 231 0870** 📠 **01395 226267**
e-mail: devoncliffs@haven.com
dir: *M5 junct 30/A376 towards Exmouth, follow brown signs to Sandy Bay*

🚐 🚐

Open mid Mar-end Oct (rs mid Mar-May & Sep-Oct some facilities may be reduced)

Last arrival anytime Last departure 10.00hrs

A large and exciting holiday park on a hillside setting close to Exmouth, with spectacular views across Sandy Bay. The all-action park offers a superb entertainment programme for all ages throughout the day, with the very modern sports and leisure facilities available for everyone. An internet café is just one of the quality amenities, and though some visitors may enjoy relaxing and watching others play, the temptation to join in is overpowering. Please note that this park does not accept tents. 163 acre site. 43 touring pitches. 43 hardstandings. Caravan pitches. Motorhome pitches. 1800 statics.

AA Pubs & Restaurants nearby: Globe Inn, Lympstone 01395 263166

Les Saveurs at The Seafood Restaurant, Exmouth 01395 269459

Leisure: 🏊⛰🎾⛰🎿🎵 Spa
Facilities: ♠♟⊙♟♿🕐🛁🔌♻️WiFi♻️
Services: 🔌🗄🔋🍽️🛒♿
Within 3 miles: ⛳🏇♟◎🎿🗄♿⛳

Notes: Max 2 dogs per booking, certain dog breeds banned, no dogs on beach May-Sep. No commercial vehicles, no bookings by under 21s unless a family booking. Dogs must be kept on leads. Crazy golf, fencing, archery, bungee trampoline, aqua jets.

EXMOUTH *continued*

▶▶ 81% Prattshayes Farm National Trust Campsite *(SY030810)*

Maer Ln EX8 5DB
☎ 01395 276626 📄 01395 276626
dir: A376 Exmouth, follow signs towards Sandy Bay. Right at narrow bridge by Clinton Arms pub, site 0.5m on right

🚐 £12-£14 🚙 £12-£14 ⛺ £12-£14

Open Apr-Oct

Last arrival 21.00hrs Last departure 10.30hrs

Set in a quiet rural location, with grassy pitches surrounded by mature hedging. Converted farm buildings house the good toilet/shower facilities. There is also a National Trust 'Base Camp' with dormitories, kitchen and wet rooms available for groups or families. Takeaway breakfasts are also available at certain times. An ideal spot for exploring the Jurassic Coast. 30 touring pitches. Caravan pitches. Motorhome pitches. Tent pitches.

AA Pubs & Restaurants nearby: Globe Inn, Lympstone 01395 263166

Les Saveurs at The Seafood Restaurant, Exmouth 01395 269459

Facilities: 🚿⊙🦶✳🛁🕓📶🛒♻ *ℹ*

Services: 🖃

Within 3 miles: ⚓🛶🎇🎣◎🏊🏪🛍🎢U

Notes: 🐕 Dogs to be kept on leads, and exercised off site, no generators, no open fires or ground level BBQs. Baby changing unit.

HOLSWORTHY

Places to visit

Dartington Crystal, GREAT TORRINGTON 01805 626242 www.dartington.co.uk

RHS Garden Rosemoor, GREAT TORRINGTON 01805 624067 www.rhs.org.uk/rosemoor

Great for kids: The Milky Way Adventure Park, CLOVELLY 01237 431255 www.themilkyway.co.uk

---

HOLSWORTHY   Map 3 SS30

AA CAMPING CARD SITE

▶▶▶ 77% Headon Farm Caravan Site *(SS367023)*

Headon Farm, Hollacombe EX22 6NN
☎ 01409 254477 📄 0870 705 9052
e-mail: reader@headonfarm.co.uk
dir: From Holsworthy A388 signed Launceston. 0.5m, at hill brow left into Staddon Rd. 1m, (follow site signs) right signed Ashwater. 0.5m, left at hill brow. Site 25yds

* 🚐 £13.50-£15.50 🚙 £13.50-£15.50

Open all year

Last arrival 19.00hrs Last departure noon

Set on a working farm in a quiet rural location. All pitches have extensive views of the Devon countryside, yet the park is only two and a half miles from the market town of Holsworthy, and within easy reach of roads to the coast and beaches of north Cornwall. 2 acre site. 19 touring pitches. 5 hardstandings. Caravan pitches. Motorhome pitches.

AA Pubs & Restaurants nearby: The Bickford Arms, Holsworthy 01409 221318

Leisure: ⛹ ⊙

Facilities: 🚿⊙✳🛁🐕♻ *ℹ*

Services: 🖃🍴

Within 3 miles: ⚓🎣🏪🛍U

Notes: 🐕 Breathable groundsheets only. Dogs must be kept on leads. Secure caravan & motorhome storage.

AA CAMPING CARD SITE

▶▶ 77% Tamarstone Farm *(SS286056)*

Bude Rd, Pancrasweek EX22 7JT
☎ 01288 381734
e-mail: camping@tamarstone.co.uk
dir: A30 to Launceston, then B3254 towards Bude, approx 14m. Right onto A3072 towards Holsworthy, approx 1.5m, site on left

* 🚐 £10-£13 🚙 £10-£13 ⛺ £10-£13

Open Etr-end Oct

Last arrival 22.00hrs Last departure noon

Four acres of river-bordered meadow and woodland providing a wildlife haven for those who enjoy peace and seclusion. The wide, sandy beaches of Bude are just five miles away, and

---

coarse fishing is provided free on site for visitors. 1 acre site. 16 touring pitches. Caravan pitches. Motorhome pitches. Tent pitches. 1 static.

AA Pubs & Restaurants nearby: The Bickford Arms, Holsworthy 01409 221318

Leisure: 🎣

Facilities: 🚿⊙✳🛁🐕♻ *ℹ*

Services: 🖃

Within 3 miles: ⚓🎣🛍

Notes: 🐕 Dogs must be kept on leads.

▶ 75% Noteworthy Caravan and Campsite *(SS303052)*

Noteworthy, Bude Rd EX22 7JB
☎ 01409 253731
e-mail: enquiries@noteworthy-devon.co.uk
dir: On A3072 between Holsworthy & Bude. 3m from Holsworthy on right

🚐 🚙 ⛺

Open all year

This campsite is owned by a friendly young couple with their own small children. There are good views from the quiet rural location, and simple toilet facilities. 5 acre site. 5 touring pitches. Caravan pitches. Motorhome pitches. Tent pitches. 1 static.

AA Pubs & Restaurants nearby: The Bickford Arms, Holsworthy 01409 221318

Leisure: ⛹

Facilities: 🚿⊙✳🕓🐕♻

Services: 🖃🛒

Within 3 miles: ⚓🎣🏊🏪🛍U

Notes: 🐕 No open fires. Dogs must be kept on leads. Dog grooming.

ILFRACOMBE

See also Berrynarbor

Places to visit

Arlington Court, ARLINGTON 01271 850296 www.nationaltrust.org.uk/main/w-arlingtoncourt

Exmoor Zoological Park, BLACKMOOR GATE 01598 763352 www.exmoorzoo.co.uk

Great for kids: Watermouth Castle & Family Theme Park, ILFRACOMBE 01271 863879 www.watermouthcastle.com

---

LEISURE: 🏊 Indoor swimming pool 🏊 Outdoor swimming pool ⛹ Children's playground 🛶 Kid's club ⛹ Tennis court 🎱 Games room ⧉ Separate TV room ⛳ 9/18 hole golf course 🚣 Boats for hire 🎦 Cinema 🎵 Entertainment 🎣 Fishing ◎ Mini golf 🏄 Watersports 🏋 Gym 🏉 Sports field **Spa** U Stables
FACILITIES: 🛁 Bath 🚿 Shower ⊙ Electric shaver 🦶 Hairdryer ✳ Ice Pack Facility ♿ Disabled facilities 🕓 Public telephone 🏪 Shop on site or within 200yds 🛍 Mobile shop (calls at least 5 days a week) 🍴 BBQ area 🎡 Picnic area 📶 Wi-fi 💻 Internet access ♻ Recycling *ℹ* Tourist info 🐕 Dog exercise area

ILFRACOMBE — Map 3 SS54

AA CAMPING CARD SITE

▶▶▶▶ 83% Hele Valley Holiday Park (SS533472)

Hele Bay EX34 9RD
☎ 01271 862460 📄 01271 867926
e-mail: holidays@helevalley.co.uk
dir: M5 junct 27 onto A361. Through Barnstaple & Braunton to Ilfracombe. Then A399 towards Combe Martin. Follow brown Hele Valley signs. In 400mtrs sharp right, to T-junct. Park on left

* ⚏ £14-£31 ⚏ £14-£31 Å £14-£33

Open Etr-Oct

Last arrival 18.00hrs Last departure 11.00hrs

A deceptively spacious park set in a picturesque valley with glorious tree-lined hilly views from most pitches. High quality toilet facilities are provided, and the park is close to a lovely beach, with the harbour and other attractions of Ilfracombe just a mile away. 17 acre site. 50 touring pitches. 18 hardstandings. Caravan pitches. Motorhome pitches. Tent pitches. 80 statics.

AA Pubs & Restaurants nearby: George & Dragon, Ilfracombe 01271 863851

The Quay, Ilfracombe 01271 868090

Leisure: ⌂ Spa
Facilities: ⬆️⊙🅿️✳️&⊙🖾&🚿🛒🎮♻️❶
Services: ⚏🖥️🍴⊘🎫⛽🚼♨️
Within 3 miles: ⅃⅄☰🅿️◎⌕🅰️🚲🎮↻

Notes: Groups by arrangement only. Dogs must be kept on leads. Post collection, nature trail.

KENNFORD

Places to visit
St Nicholas Priory, EXETER 01392 665858 www.exeter.gov.uk/priory

Quay House Visitor Centre, EXETER 01392 271611 www.exeter.gov.uk/quayhouse

Great for kids: Crealy Adventure Park, CLYST ST MARY 01395 233200 www.crealy.co.uk

KENNFORD — Map 3 SX98

▶▶▶▶ 79% Kennford International Caravan Park (SX912857)

EX6 7YN
☎ 01392 833046 📄 01392 833046
e-mail: ian@kennfordinternational.com
web: www.kennfordinternational.co.uk
dir: At end of M5, take A38, site signed at Kennford slip road

⚏ ⚏ Å

Open all year (rs Winter arrival times change)

Last arrival 21.00hrs Last departure 11.00hrs

Screened from the A38 by trees and shrubs, this park offers many pitches divided by hedging for privacy. A high quality toilet block complements the park's facilities. A good, centrally-located base for touring the coast and countryside of Devon, and Exeter is easily accessible via buses that stop nearby. 15 acre site. 96 touring pitches. Caravan pitches. Motorhome pitches. Tent pitches. 53 statics.

AA Pubs & Restaurants nearby: The Bridge Inn, Topsham 01392 873862

Leisure: ⌂ ⚲
Facilities: 🚿⬆️⊙&⊙🚿🐕❶
Services: ⚏🖥️🍴❶🎫⛽♨️
Within 3 miles: ⅃⅄☰🅿️🎮↻

KENTISBEARE

Places to visit
Killerton House & Garden, KILLERTON HOUSE & GARDEN 01392 881345 www.nationaltrust.org.uk

Allhallows Museum, HONITON 01404 44966 www.honitonmuseum.co.uk

Great for kids: Diggerland, CULLOMPTON 0871 227 7007 www.diggerland.com

KENTISBEARE — Map 3 ST00

▶▶▶▶ 79% Forest Glade Holiday Park (ST101073)

GOLD

EX15 2DT
☎ 01404 841381 📄 01404 841593
e-mail: enquiries@forest-glade.co.uk
dir: Tent traffic: from A373 turn left past Keepers Cottage Inn (2.5m E of M5 junct 28). Touring caravans: via Honiton/Dunkeswell road. Please phone for access details

* ⚏ £14.50-£20.50 ⚏ £14.50-£20.50 Å £12.50-£19.50

Open mid Mar-end Oct (rs Low season limited shop hours)

Last arrival 21.00hrs Last departure noon

A quiet, attractive park in a forest clearing with well-kept gardens and beech hedge screening. One of the main attractions is the immediate proximity of the forest, which offers magnificent hillside walks with surprising views over the valleys. Please telephone for route details. 15 acre site. 80 touring pitches. 40 hardstandings. 28 seasonal pitches. Caravan pitches. Motorhome pitches. Tent pitches. 57 statics.

AA Pubs & Restaurants nearby: Five Bells Inn, Clyst Hydon 01884 277288

Leisure: 🏊⌂♨️⊙⚲
Facilities: ⬆️⊙🅿️✳️&⊙🖾🅰️🐕🖾♻️❶
Services: ⚏🖥️🍴⊘🎫⛽♨️
Within 3 miles: 🅿️🎮↻

Notes: Families & couples only. Dogs must be kept on leads. Adventure/soft play area, wildlife information room, paddling pool.
see advert on page 168

SERVICES: ⚏ Electric hook up 🖥️ Launderette 🍴 Licensed bar ❶ Calor Gas ⊘ Camping Gaz 🎫 Toilet fluid 🍽️ Café/Restaurant 🍟 Fast Food/Takeaway ⛽ Battery charging 🚼 Baby care ♨️ Motorvan service point
ABBREVIATIONS: BH/bank hols-bank holidays Etr-Easter Whit-Whitsun dep-departure fr-from hrs-hours m-mile mdnt-midnight rdbt-roundabout rs-restricted service wk-week wknd-weekend ⊛ No credit cards ⊗ No dogs
See page 7 for details of the AA Camping Card Scheme

LYNTON
Map 3 SS74

See also Oare (Somerset)

Places to visit

Arlington Court, ARLINGTON 01271 850296
www.nationaltrust.org.uk/
main/w-arlingtoncourt

Great for kids: Exmoor Zoological Park,
BLACKMOOR GATE 01598 763352
www.exmoorzoo.co.uk

AA CAMPING CARD SITE

►►►► 71% Channel View
Caravan and Camping Park
(SS724482)

Manor Farm EX35 6LD
☎ 01598 753349 📠 01598 752777
e-mail: relax@channel-view.co.uk
web: www.channel-view.co.uk
dir: *A39 E for 0.5m on left past Barbrook*

* 🚐 £11-£19 ⛺ £11-£19 ⛺ £11-£19

Open 15 Mar-15 Nov

Last arrival 22.00hrs Last departure noon

On the top of the cliffs overlooking the Bristol
Channel, a well-maintained park on the edge of
Exmoor, and close to both Lynton and Lynmouth.
Pitches can be selected from either those in a
hidden hedged area or those with panoramic
views over the coast. 6 acre site. 76 touring
pitches. 15 hardstandings. Caravan pitches.
Motorhome pitches. Tent pitches. 31 statics.

AA Pubs & Restaurants nearby: The Rising Sun
Hotel, Lynmouth 01598 753223

Rockford Inn, Brendon 01598 741214

Leisure: 🅰

Facilities: 🚿🔥☉🗲✳❄🕐🖩🚻 ᠊᠊᠊᠊ ♻ 🛈

Services: 🖃🔘🚽🗑🍽📶⛟

Within 3 miles: 🥘🗲◎⛵🏇🐴🎣⛳

Notes: Groups by prior arrangement only. Dogs
must be kept on leads. Parent & baby room.

►►► 76% Sunny Lyn Holiday Park
(SS719486)

Lynbridge EX35 6NS
☎ 01598 753384 📠 01598 753273
e-mail: info@caravandevon.co.uk
web: www.caravandevon.co.uk
dir: *M5 junct 27, A361 to South Molton. Right onto
A399 to Blackmoor Gate, right onto A39, left onto
B3234 towards Lynmouth. Site 1m on right*

* 🚐 £14.75-£15.50 ⛺ £14.75-£15.50
⛺ £11.50-£13.50

Open Mar-Oct

Last arrival 20.00hrs Last departure 11.00hrs

Set in a sheltered riverside location in a wooded
combe within a mile of the sea, in Exmoor National
Park. This family-run park offers good facilities
including an excellent café. 4.5 acre site. 9
touring pitches. 5 hardstandings. Caravan
pitches. Motorhome pitches. Tent pitches. 7
statics.

Sunny Lyn Holiday Park

AA Pubs & Restaurants nearby: The Rising Sun
Hotel, Lynmouth 01598 753223

Rockford Inn, Brendon 01598 741214

Facilities: 🔥☉🗲✳❄🕐🖩🚻 ᠊᠊᠊᠊ ♻ 🛈

Services: 🖃🔘🚽🗑🍽⛟

Within 3 miles: 🏇🥘🗲◎🔘⛳

Notes: No cars by tents. No wood fires, quiet after
22.30hrs.

MODBURY

Places to visit

Kingsbridge Cookworthy Museum,
KINGSBRIDGE 01548 853235
www.kingsbridgemuseum.org.uk

Overbeck's, SALCOMBE 01548 842893
www.nationaltrust.org.uk

Great for kids: National Marine Aquarium,
PLYMOUTH 01752 600301
www.national-aquarium.co.uk

LEISURE: 🅰 Indoor swimming pool 🅰 Outdoor swimming pool 🅰 Children's playground 🅰 Kid's club 🅰 Tennis court 🅰 Games room 🅰 Separate TV room
🅰 9/18 hole golf course 🅰 Boats for hire 🅰 Cinema 🅰 Entertainment 🅰 Fishing ◎ Mini golf 🅰 Watersports 🅰 Gym 🅰 Sports field **Spa** ᑌ Stables
FACILITIES: 🅰 Bath 🅰 Shower ☉ Electric shaver 🗲 Hairdryer ✳ Ice Pack Facility ❄ Disabled facilities 🕐 Public telephone 🖩 Shop on site or within 200yds
🅰 Mobile shop (calls at least 5 days a week) 🅰 BBQ area 🅰 Picnic area 🚾 Wi-fi 🅰 Internet access ♻ Recycling 🛈 Tourist info 🅰 Dog exercise area

MODBURY
Map 3 SX65

►►► 81% Pennymoor Camping & Caravan Park (SX685516)

PL21 0SB
☎ 01548 830542 & 830020 ▤ 01548 830542
e-mail: enquiries@pennymoor-camping.co.uk
dir: *Exit A38 at Wrangaton Cross. Left & straight over x-roads. 4m, pass petrol station, 2nd left. Site 1.5m on right*

Open 15 Mar-15 Nov (rs 15 Mar-mid May one toilet & shower block only open)

Last arrival 20.00hrs Last departure 10.00hrs

A well-established rural park on part level, part gently sloping grass with good views over distant Dartmoor and the countryside in between. The park has been owned and run by the same family since 1935, and is very carefully tended, with a relaxing atmosphere. 12.5 acre site. 119 touring pitches. Caravan pitches. Motorhome pitches. Tent pitches. 76 statics.

AA Pubs & Restaurants nearby: California Country Inn, Modbury 01548 821449

Rose & Crown, Yealmpton 01752 880223

Leisure: ⚙

Facilities: ⚓☉⚑✳️♿☉📶🐾♻️

Services: 🔌🆘🔒⌀🚰🔋

Within 3 miles: 🚴🅿️

Notes: ⊗ No skateboards. Dogs must be kept on leads.

see advert below

MOLLAND
Map 3 SS82

Places to visit

Quince Honey Farm, SOUTH MOLTON
01769 572401 www.quincehoney.com

Cobbaton Combat Collection, CHITTLEHAMPTON
01769 540740 www.cobbatoncombat.co.uk

►►► 75% Yeo Valley Holiday Park (SS788265)

The Blackcock Inn EX36 3NW
☎ 01769 550297
e-mail: info@yeovalleyholidays.co.uk
dir: *From A361 onto B3227 towards Bampton. Follow brown signs for Blackcock Inn. Site opposite*

* 🚐 £15.50-£21.50 🚌 £15.50-£21.50
🛖 £14.50-£18

Open Mar-Nov

Last arrival 20.30hrs Last departure 10.30hrs

Set in a beautiful secluded valley on the edge of Exmoor National Park, this family-run park has easy access to both the moors and the north Devon coastline. The park is adjacent to the Blackcock Inn (under the same ownership), and has a very good heated indoor pool. 8 acre site. 36 touring pitches. 16 hardstandings. Caravan pitches. Motorhome pitches. Tent pitches. 5 statics.

AA Pubs & Restaurants nearby: Woods Bar & Dining Room, Dulverton 01398 324007

Leisure: 🏊♿🎣💻⬚

Facilities: ⚓☉⚑✳️♿☉📶🐾

Services: 🔌🆘🛠🔒⌀🚰🍽🔋

Within 3 miles: 🚴🅿️🆘↻

Notes: Dogs must be kept on leads.

MORTEHOE

See also Woolacombe

Places to visit

Marwood Hill Gardens, BARNSTAPLE
01271 342528 www.marwoodhillgarden.co.uk

Great for kids: Watermouth Castle & Family Theme Park, ILFRACOMBE 01271 863879
www.watermouthcastle.com

MORTEHOE · Map 3 SS44

85% Twitchen House Holiday Village (SS465447)

Station Rd EX34 7ES
☎ 01271 870343 📄 01271 870089
e-mail: goodtimes@woolacombe.com
dir: From Mullacott Cross rdbt take B3343 (Woolacombe road) to Turnpike Cross junct. Take right fork, site 1.5m on left

* 🚐 £16.14-£58.60 🚙 £16.14-£58.60
🛖 £10.76-£38

Open Mar-Oct (rs mid May & mid Sep outdoor pool closed)

Last arrival mdnt Last departure 10.00hrs

A very attractive park with good leisure facilities. Visitors can use the amenities at all three of Woolacombe Bay holiday parks, and a bus service connects them all with the beach. The touring area features pitches (many fully serviced, including 80 for tents) with either sea views or a woodland countryside outlook. 45 acre site. 334 touring pitches. 110 hardstandings. Caravan pitches. Motorhome pitches. Tent pitches. 278 statics.

AA Pubs & Restaurants nearby: George & Dragon, Ilfracombe 01271 863851

The Quay, Ilfracombe 01271 868090

Leisure: 🏊🏖️🎠🎣🎱⬜🎵
Facilities: 🚿☀️💈✂️♿🕐📞🏪🍴📶🖥️♻️
Services: 🔌🚾🔧💧🚽🍴🛒🚮💧
Within 3 miles: 🏌️🚣📅🎣🎯◎♨️🏪🎳⛵

Notes: Table tennis, sauna, swimming & surfing lessons.

AA CAMPING CARD SITE

▶▶▶▶ 83% Warcombe Farm Caravan & Camping Park

(SS478445)

Station Rd EX34 7EJ
☎ 01271 870690 & 07774 428770
📄 01271 871070
e-mail: info@warcombefarm.co.uk
web: www.warcombefarm.co.uk
dir: On B3343 towards Woolacombe turn right towards Mortehoe. Site less than 2m on right

* 🚐 £12.50-£36 🚙 🛖

Open 15 Mar-Oct (rs Low season no takeaway food)

Last arrival 21.00hrs Last departure 11.00hrs

Extensive views over the Bristol Channel can be enjoyed from the open areas of this attractive park, while other pitches are sheltered in paddocks with maturing trees. 14 excellent super pitches with hardstandings were added in 2011. The superb sandy beach with a Blue Flag award at Woolacombe Bay is only a mile and a half away, and there is a fishing lake with direct access from some pitches. 19 acre site. 250 touring pitches. 10 hardstandings. Caravan pitches. Motorhome pitches. Tent pitches.

AA Pubs & Restaurants nearby: George & Dragon, Ilfracombe 01271 863851

The Quay, Ilfracombe 01271 868090

Leisure: 🎣
Facilities: 🚿☀️💈✂️♿🕐🏪🍴📶🖥️♻️
Services: 🔌🚾💧🚽🍴🛒🚮💧
Within 3 miles: 🏌️🚣🎣◎♨️🏪🎳⛵

Notes: No groups unless booked in advance. Dogs must be kept on leads. Private fishing.

▶▶▶▶ 82% North Morte Farm Caravan & Camping Park (SS462455)

North Morte Rd EX34 7EG
☎ 01271 870381 📄 01271 870115
e-mail: info@northmortefarm.co.uk
dir: From B3343 into Mortehoe, right at post office. Site 500yds on left

* 🚐 £15.75-£20.50 🚙 £12-£20.50 🛖 £12-£18.50

Open Apr-Oct

Last arrival 22.30hrs Last departure noon

Set in spectacular coastal countryside close to National Trust land and 500 yards from Rockham Beach. This attractive park is very well run and maintained by friendly family owners, and the quaint village of Mortehoe with its cafés, shops and pubs, is just a five-minute walk away. 22 acre site. 180 touring pitches. 25 hardstandings. Caravan pitches. Motorhome pitches. Tent pitches. 73 statics.

AA Pubs & Restaurants nearby: George & Dragon, Ilfracombe 01271 863851

The Quay, Ilfracombe 01271 868090

Leisure: 🎣
Facilities: 🚿☀️💈✂️♿🕐🏪🍴📶🖥️♻️🌳
Services: 🔌🚾💧🚽🍴🛒🚮💧
Within 3 miles: 🏌️🎣◎♨️🏪🎳⛵

Notes: No large groups. Dogs must be kept on leads.

▶▶▶ 78% Easewell Farm Holiday Park & Golf Club (SS465455)

EX34 7EH
☎ 01271 870343 📄 01271 870089
e-mail: goodtimes@woolacombe.com
dir: B3343 to Mortehoe. Turn right at fork, site 2m on right

* 🚐 £9-£35 🚙 £9-£35 🛖 £9-£26.60

Open Mar-Oct (rs Etr)

Last arrival 22.00hrs Last departure 10.00hrs

A peaceful cliff-top park with full facility pitches for caravans and motorhomes, and superb views. The park offers a range of activities including indoor bowling and a 9-hole golf course, and all the facilities at the three other nearby holiday centres within this group are open to everyone. 17 acre site. 302 touring pitches. 50 hardstandings. Caravan pitches. Motorhome pitches. Tent pitches. 1 static.

AA Pubs & Restaurants nearby: George & Dragon, Ilfracombe 01271 863851

The Quay, Ilfracombe 01271 868090

Leisure: 🏊🎠🎱🎣🎵
Facilities: 🚿☀️💈✂️♿🕐🏪🍴📶🖥️♻️
Services: 🔌🚾🔧💧🚽🍴🛒🚮
Within 3 miles: 🏌️🚣📅🎣◎♨️🏪🎳⛵

Notes: Indoor bowls, snooker.

NEWTON ABBOT

See also Bickington

Places to visit

Tuckers Maltings, NEWTON ABBOT 01626 334734
www.tuckersmaltings.com

Bradley Manor, NEWTON ABBOT 01803 843235
www.nationaltrust.org.uk/devoncornwall

Great for kids: Prickly Ball Farm and Hedgehog Hospital, NEWTON ABBOT 01626 362319
www.pricklyballfarm.com

LEISURE: 🏊 Indoor swimming pool 🏖️ Outdoor swimming pool 🎠 Children's playground 🎣 Kid's club 🎾 Tennis court 🎱 Games room ⬜ Separate TV room 🏌️ 9/18 hole golf course 🚣 Boats for hire 🎬 Cinema 🎵 Entertainment 🎣 Fishing ◎ Mini golf 🏄 Watersports 🏋️ Gym 🏐 Sports field Spa ⛵ Stables
FACILITIES: 🛁 Bath 🚿 Shower ☀️ Electric shaver 💈 Hairdryer ✂️ Ice Pack Facility ♿ Disabled facilities 📞 Public telephone 🏪 Shop on site or within 200yds 🚐 Mobile shop (calls at least 5 days a week) 🍴 BBQ area 🏕️ Picnic area 📶 Wi-fi 🖥️ Internet access ♻️ Recycling 🌐 Tourist info 🌳 Dog exercise area

NEWTON ABBOT — Map 3 SX87

AA Campsite of the Year for England and overall winner of the AA Best Campsite of the Year 2012

AA CAMPING CARD SITE

PREMIER PARK

►►►►► 96%

Ross Park (SX845671)

Best of British GOLD

Park Hill Farm, Ipplepen TQ12 5TT
☎ 01803 812983 📇 01803 812983
e-mail: enquiries@rossparkcaravanpark.co.uk
web: www.rossparkcaravanpark.co.uk
dir: Exit A381 3m from Newton Abbot towards Totnes, signed opposite Texaco garage towards 'Woodland'

* 🚐 £14-£27.20 🚎 £14-£27.50 ▲ £14-£27.50

Open Mar-2 Jan (rs Nov-Jan & 1st 3 wks in Mar restaurant/bar closed (ex Xmas/New Year))

Last arrival 21.00hrs Last departure 10.00hrs

A top-class park in every way, with large secluded pitches, high quality toilet facilities, which include excellent family rooms, and colourful flower displays throughout - note the wonderful floral walk to the toilets. The beautiful tropical conservatory also offers a breathtaking show of colour. There's a conservation walk through a glorious wild flower meadows, replete with nature trail, a dog shower/grooming area, and six new fully-serviced pitches. This very rural park enjoys superb views of Dartmoor, and good quality meals to suit all tastes and pockets are served in the restaurant. Expect high levels of customer care - this park gets better each year. 32 acre site. 110 touring pitches. 94 hardstandings. Caravan pitches. Motorhome pitches. Tent pitches.

AA Pubs & Restaurants nearby: The Church House Inn, Marldon 01803 558279

Union Inn, Denbury 01803 812595

Leisure: 🅰️🌀🎱▢

Facilities: 🍄☉🅿️⚘🔆🔕🛁🚻 Wi-Fi

Services: 🔌🅖🔌🧺🅣🍽️🚰🚮🔧

Within 3 miles: ↨🏇🎣🏌️🅟🛢️🅢∪

Notes: Bikes, skateboards/scooters allowed only on leisure field. Snooker, table tennis, badminton, croquet.

AA CAMPING CARD SITE

PREMIER PARK

►►►►►► 94%

Dornafield (SX838683)

Best of British GOLD

Dornafield Farm, Two Mile Oak TQ12 6DD
☎ 01803 812732 📇 01803 812032
e-mail: enquiries@dornafield.com
web: www.dornafield.com
dir: From Newton Abbot take A381 signed Totnes for 2m. At Two Mile Oak Inn right, left at x-roads in 0.5m. Site on right

* 🚐 £16-£33 🚎 £16-£33 ▲ £16-£33

Open 16 Mar-3 Jan

Last arrival 22.00hrs Last departure 11.00hrs

An immaculately kept park in a tranquil wooded valley between Dartmoor and Torbay, offering either deluxe or fully-serviced pitches. A lovely 15th-century farmhouse sits at the entrance, and the park is divided into three separate areas, served by two superb, ultra-modern toilet blocks. The friendly family owners are always available. Well positioned for visiting nearby Totnes or the resorts of Torbay. 30 acre site. 135 touring pitches. 119 hardstandings. 13 seasonal pitches. Caravan pitches. Motorhome pitches. Tent pitches.

AA Pubs & Restaurants nearby: The Church House Inn, Marldon 01803 558279

Union Inn, Denbury 01803 812595

Leisure: 🅰️🎱🎣

Facilities: 🍄☉🅿️⚘🔆🔕🛁🚻 Wi-Fi ♻️ ❓

Services: 🔌🅖🔌🧺🅣🚼🚮🔧

Within 3 miles: ↨🏇🎣🅢🛢️

Notes: Caravan storage (all year).

►►► 78% **Twelve Oaks Farm Caravan Park** (SX852737)

Teigngrace TQ12 6QT
☎ 01626 335015
e-mail: info@twelveoaksfarm.co.uk
dir: A38 from Exeter left signed Teigngrace (only), 0.25m before Drumbridges rdbt. 1.5m, through village, site on left. Or from Plymouth pass Drumbridges rdbt, take slip road for Chudleigh Knighton. Right over bridge, rejoin A38 towards Plymouth. Left for Teigngrace (only), then as above

* 🚐 £8.50-£15.50 🚎 £8.50-£15.50
▲ £8.50-£15.50

Open all year

Last arrival 21.00hrs Last departure 10.30hrs

An attractive small park on a working farm close to Dartmoor National Park, and bordered by the River Teign. The tidy pitches are located amongst trees and shrubs, and the modern facilities are very well maintained. Children will enjoy all the farm animals, and nearby is the Templar Way walking route. 2 acre site. 50 touring pitches. 25 hardstandings. Caravan pitches. Motorhome pitches. Tent pitches.

AA Pubs & Restaurants nearby: Elizabethan Inn, Luton (near Chudleigh) 01626 775425

Union Inn, Denbury 01803 812595

Leisure: 🚣

Facilities: 🍄☉🅿️⚘🔆🔕🛁🚻♻️❓

Services: 🔌🅖🔌🧺🅣🔧

Within 3 miles: ↨🏇🎣🅟☉🛢️∪

Notes: No noise after 23.00hrs. Dogs must be kept on leads.

PAIGNTON

Places to visit

Dartmouth Steam Railway & River Boat Company, PAIGNTON 01803 555872
www.dartmouthrailriver.co.uk

Kents Cavern, TORQUAY 01803 215136
www.kents-cavern.co.uk

Great for kids: Paignton Zoo Environmental Park, PAIGNTON 0844 474 2222
www.paigntonzoo.org.uk

SERVICES: 🔌 Electric hook up 🅖 Launderette 🔌 Licensed bar 🅒 Calor Gas 🅖 Camping Gaz 🅣 Toilet fluid 🍽️ Café/Restaurant 🚮 Fast Food/Takeaway 🔋 Battery charging 🚼 Baby care 🔧 Motorvan service point

ABBREVIATIONS: BH/bank hols-bank holidays Etr-Easter Whit-Whitsun dep-departure fr-from hrs-hours m-mile mdnt-midnight rdbt-roundabout rs-restricted service wk-week wknd-weekend 🚫 No credit cards ⊗ No dogs

See page 7 for details of the AA Camping Card Scheme

PAIGNTON
Map 3 SX86

AA CAMPING CARD SITE

89% Beverley Parks Caravan & Camping Park *(SX886582)*

Goodrington Rd TQ14 7JE
☎ 01803 661979 📄 01803 845427
e-mail: info@beverley-holidays.co.uk
dir: *On A380, A3022, 2m S of Paignton left into Goodrington Rd. Beverley Park on right*

* 🚐 £15.20-£38.50 🚍 £15.20-£38.50
▲ £13-£32.50

Open all year

Last arrival 21.00hrs Last departure 10.00hrs

A high quality family-run park with extensive views of the bay and plenty of on-site amenities. The park boasts indoor and outdoor heated swimming pools, plus tasteful bars and restaurants. The toilet facilities are modern and very clean and include excellent new fully serviced family rooms. The park complex is attractively laid out with the touring areas divided into nicely screened areas. 12 acre site. 172 touring pitches. 49 hardstandings. Caravan pitches. Motorhome pitches. Tent pitches.

AA Pubs & Restaurants nearby: Church House Inn, Marldon 01803 558279

Elephant Restaurant & Brasserie, Torquay 01803 200044

No 7 Fish Bistro, Torquay 01803 295055

Beverley Parks Caravan & Camping Park

Leisure: 🏊 🏊 ⛱ 🎠 🛝 🎱 🎵 Spa
Facilities: 🛁 📷 ⊙ 🏮 ✳ 🔌 🚿 🕐 🅿 🛒 WiFi 💻 ♻ ℹ️
Services: 🔌 🔄 🍽 🔒 🛢 📷 T 🍴 🛒 🐕 🛒
Within 3 miles: 🛶 🎣 ⛳ ◎ 🚣 🏪 U

Notes: No pets. Table tennis, sauna, crazy golf, letter box trail.

▶▶▶▶ **79% *Widend Touring Park*** *(SX852619)*

Berry Pomeroy Rd, Marldon TQ3 1RT
☎ 01803 550116 📄 01803 550116
dir: *Signed from Torbay ring road*

🚐 🚍 ▲

Open Apr-end Sep (rs Apr-mid May & mid Sep swimming pool & club house closed)

Last arrival 20.00hrs Last departure 10.00hrs

A terraced grass park divided into paddocks and screened on high ground overlooking Torbay with views of Dartmoor. This attractive park is well laid out, divided up by mature trees and bushes but with plenty of open grassy areas. Facilities are of a high standard and offer a heated outdoor swimming pool with sunbathing area, a small lounge bar and a well-stocked shop. 22 acre site. 207 touring pitches. 6 hardstandings. Caravan pitches. Motorhome pitches. Tent pitches. 16 statics.

AA Pubs & Restaurants nearby: Church House Inn, Marldon 01803 558279

Elephant Restaurant & Brasserie, Torquay 01803 200044

No 7 Fish Bistro, Torquay 01803 295055

Leisure: 🏊 ⛱ 🎱
Facilities: 📷 ⊙ ✳ 🔌 🕐 🅿 🛒
Services: 🔌 🔄 🍽 🔒 📷 T 🏓 🛒
Within 3 miles: 🛶 🎣 ⛳ ◎ 🚣 🏪 U

Notes: No dogs mid Jul-Aug.

AA CAMPING CARD SITE

▶▶▶ **84% Whitehill Country Park** *(SX857588)*

Stoke Rd TQ4 7PF
☎ 01803 782338 📄 01803 782722
e-mail: info@whitehill-park.co.uk
dir: *A385 through Totnes towards Paignton. Turn right by Parkers Arms into Stoke Rd towards Stoke Gabriel. Site on left after approx 1.5m*

🚐 🚍 ▲

Open Etr-Sep

Last arrival 21.00hrs Last departure 10.00hrs

A family-owned and run park set in rolling countryside, with many scenic beaches just a short drive away. This extensive country park covers 40 acres with woodland walks, and plenty of flora and fauna, and features an excellent outdoor swimming pool, a café, plus a bar/restaurant with summer entertainment. It offers ideal facilities, including luxury lodges and new camping pods, for an excellent holiday. 40 acre site. 260 touring pitches. Caravan pitches. Motorhome pitches. Tent pitches. 60 statics.

AA Pubs & Restaurants nearby: Church House Inn, Marldon 01803 558279

Elephant Restaurant & Brasserie, Torquay 01803 200044

No 7 Fish Bistro, Torquay 01803 295055

LEISURE: 🏊 Indoor swimming pool 🏊 Outdoor swimming pool 🎠 Children's playground 🛶 Kid's club 🎾 Tennis court 🎱 Games room 📺 Separate TV room 🛶 9/18 hole golf course 🚣 Boats for hire 🎬 Cinema 🎵 Entertainment 🎣 Fishing ◎ Mini golf 🚣 Watersports 🏋 Gym 🏟 Sports field **Spa** U Stables
FACILITIES: 🛁 Bath 📷 Shower ⊙ Electric shaver 🏮 Hairdryer ✳ Ice Pack Facility 🔌 Disabled facilities 🕐 Public telephone 🏪 Shop on site or within 200yds 🏪 Mobile shop (calls at least 5 days a week) 🍖 BBQ area 🏓 Picnic area WiFi Wi-fi 💻 Internet access ♻ Recycling ℹ️ Tourist info 🐕 Dog exercise area

Leisure: ⛱ ⛰ 🎣 ▢
Facilities: 🖍 🏴 🍴 ✳ ♿ 🕐 💲 🚿 🧺 🔲 ♻ ❶
Services: 🔌🔋 🍴🚰 📶 🍴 🛒 🍴
Within 3 miles: ↓ ☂ 🛎 ℓ ◎ 🛥 🏧 🔽 ∪

Notes: Dogs only allowed 5 Apr-1 Jun, 12 Jun-20 Jul & 4-28 Sep. Dogs must be kept on leads. Walking & cycling trails, letter box trail, craft room, table tennis.

PLYMOUTH   Map 3 SX45

Places to visit
Plymouth City Museum & Art Gallery, PLYMOUTH 01752 304774 www.plymouthmuseum.gov.uk

The Elizabethan House, PLYMOUTH 01752 304774 www.plymouth.gov.uk/museums

Great for kids: National Marine Aquarium, PLYMOUTH 01752 600301 www.national-aquarium.co.uk

▶▶▶▶ **81% Riverside Caravan Park** (SX515575)

Leigham Manor Dr PL6 8LL
☎ 01752 344122   📄 01752 344122
e-mail: office@riversidecaravanpark.com
dir: A38 follow signs at Marsh Mills rdbt, take 3rd exit, then left. 400yds turn right (keep River Plym on right) to site

* 🚐 £12-£24 🚐 £14-£24 ▲ £10.50-£20

Open all year (rs Oct-Etr bar, restaurant, takeaway & pool closed)

Last arrival 22.00hrs Last departure 10.00hrs

A well-groomed site on the outskirts of Plymouth on the banks of the River Plym, in a surprisingly peaceful location surrounded by woodland. The toilet facilities are to a very good standard, and include private cubicles, plus there's a good games room and bar/restaurant serving food. This park is an ideal stopover for the ferries to France and Spain, and makes an excellent base for touring Dartmoor and the coast. 11 acre site. 259 touring pitches. Caravan pitches. Motorhome pitches. Tent pitches. 22 statics.

AA Pubs & Restaurants nearby: Fishermans Arms, Plymouth 01752 661457

Tanners Restaurant, Plymouth 01752 252001

Artillery Tower Restaurant, Plymouth 01752 257610

Leisure: ⛱ ⛰ 🎣 ▢
Facilities: 🖍 ⊙ 🍴 ✳ ♿ 🕐 💲 🍴 ♻ ❶
Services: 🔌🔋 🍴🚰 📶 🍴 🔳 🍴 🛒 🍴
Within 3 miles: ↓ ☂ 🛎 ℓ ◎ 🛥 🏧 🔽 ∪

Notes: Dogs must be kept on leads.

SALCOMBE   Map 3 SX73

Places to visit
Overbeck's, SALCOMBE 01548 842893 www.nationaltrust.org.uk

Kingsbridge Cookworthy Museum, KINGSBRIDGE 01548 853235 www.kingsbridgemuseum.org.uk

▶▶▶ **79% *Higher Rew Caravan & Camping Park*** (SX714383)

Higher Rew, Malborough TQ7 3BW
☎ 01548 842681   📄 01548 843681
e-mail: enquiries@higherrew.co.uk
dir: A381 to Malborough. Right at Townsend Cross, follow signs to Soar for 1m. Left at Rew Cross

🚐 🚐 ▲

Open Etr-Oct

Last arrival 22.00hrs Last departure noon

A long-established park in a remote location within sight of the sea. The spacious, open touring field has some tiered pitches in the sloping grass, and there are lovely countryside or sea views from every pitch. Friendly family owners are continually improving the facilities. 5 acre site. 85 touring pitches. Caravan pitches. Motorhome pitches. Tent pitches.

AA Pubs & Restaurants nearby: Victoria Inn, Salcombe 01548 842604

Soar Mill Cove Hotel, Salcombe 01548 561566

Leisure: ⛱ 🎣
Facilities: 🖍 ⊙ 🍴 ✳ 🕐 💲 🔲
Services: 🔌🔋 🍴 📶 🔳 🛒
Within 3 miles: ☂ ℓ 🛥 🏧 🔽
Notes: 🐾 Play barn.

▶▶▶ **79% Karrageen Caravan & Camping Park** (SX686395)

Bolberry, Malborough TQ7 3EN
☎ 01548 561230   📄 01548 560192
e-mail: phil@karrageen.co.uk
dir: At Malborough on A381, sharp right through village, in 0.6m right, 0.9m, site on right

* 🚐 £13-£22 🚐 £13-£22 ▲ £12-£27

Open Etr-Sep

Last arrival 21.00hrs Last departure 11.30hrs

A small friendly, family-run park with secluded hidden dells for tents and terraced grass pitches giving extensive sea and country views. There is a varied takeaway menu available every evening, and a well-stocked shop. This park is just one mile from the beach and pretty hamlet of Hope Cove and is a really peaceful park from which to explore the South Hams coast. 7.5 acre site. 70 touring pitches. Caravan pitches. Motorhome pitches. Tent pitches. 25 statics.

AA Pubs & Restaurants nearby: Victoria Inn, Salcombe 01548 842604

Soar Mill Cove Hotel, Salcombe 01548 561566

Facilities: 🖍 ⊙ 🍴 ✳ ♿ 🕐 💲 ♻ ❶
Services: 🔌🔋 📶 🍴 🔳 🛒 🍴
Within 3 miles: ↓ ☂ ℓ 🛥 💲
Notes: 🐾 Dogs must be kept on leads.

▶▶▶ **76% *Bolberry House Farm Caravan & Camping Park*** (SX687395)

Bolberry TQ7 3DY
☎ 01548 561251
e-mail: enquiries@bolberryparks.co.uk
dir: At Malborough on A381 turn right signed Hope Cove/Bolberry. Take left fork after village signed Soar/Bolberry. Right in 0.6m. Site signed in 0.5m

🚐 🚐 ▲

Open Etr-Oct

Last arrival 20.00hrs Last departure 11.30hrs

A very popular park in a peaceful setting on a coastal farm with sea views, fine cliff walks and nearby beaches. Customers are assured of a warm welcome and the nicely tucked away portaloo facilities are smart and beautifully maintained. There's a super dog-walking area. 6 acre site. 70 touring pitches. Caravan pitches. Motorhome pitches. Tent pitches. 10 statics.

continued

SERVICES: 🔌 Electric hook up 🔋 Launderette 🍴 Licensed bar 🔥 Calor Gas ∅ Camping Gaz 🔳 Toilet fluid 🍴 Café/Restaurant 🛒 Fast Food/Takeaway 🔋 Battery charging 🍼 Baby care ♨ Motorvan service point
ABBREVIATIONS: BH/bank hols-bank holidays Etr-Easter Whit-Whitsun dep-departure fr-from hrs-hours m-mile mdnt-midnight rdbt-roundabout rs-restricted service wk-week wknd-weekend 🚫 No credit cards 🚫 No dogs
See page 7 for details of the AA Camping Card Scheme

SALCOMBE *continued*

AA Pubs & Restaurants nearby: Victoria Inn, Salcombe 01548 842604

Soar Mill Cove Hotel, Salcombe 01548 561566

Leisure: 🅰

Facilities: 🐴 ⊙ 🅿 ❄ ⊙ 🔯 ⚡

Services: 🔌 🔵 🗑

Within 3 miles: ⬇ 🕁 🎠 🎣 ◎ ⛵ 🎯 🗑 ♻ ∪

Notes: 🐕

AA CAMPING CARD SITE

►► **69% Alston Camping and Caravan Site** *(SX716406)*

Malborough, Kingsbridge TQ7 3BJ
☎ 01548 561260 & 0780 803 0921
e-mail: info@alstoncampsite.co.uk
dir: *1.5m W of town off A381 towards Malborough*

* 🚐 £11.50-£20 🚕 £11.50-£20 ▲ £10.50-£20

Open 15 Mar-Oct

An established farm site in a rural location adjacent to the Kingsbridge/Salcombe estuary. The site is well sheltered and screened, and approached down a long, well-surfaced narrow farm lane with passing places. The toilet facilities are basic. 16 acre site. 90 touring pitches. Caravan pitches. Motorhome pitches. Tent pitches. 58 statics.

AA Pubs & Restaurants nearby: Victoria Inn, Salcombe 01548 842604

Soar Mill Cove Hotel, Salcombe 01548 561566

Leisure: 🅰

Facilities: 🔌 ⊙ 🅿 ❄ 🐕 ⊙ 🔯 ⚡ wifi ♻ 🛈

Services: 🔌 🔵 🔋 🖊 🔲 🗑

Within 3 miles: ⬇ 🕁 🎠 🎣 ⛵ 🎯 🗑

Notes: 🐕 Dogs must be kept on leads.

SAMPFORD PEVERELL

Places to visit

Tiverton Castle, TIVERTON 01884 253200
www.tivertoncastle.com

Tiverton Museum of Mid Devon Life, TIVERTON 01884 256295 www.tivertonmuseum.org.uk

Great for kids: Diggerland, CULLOMPTON 0871 227 7007 www.diggerland.com

---

SAMPFORD PEVERELL   Map 3 ST01

►►►► **87% Minnows Touring Park**
(SS042148)

Holbrook Ln EX16 7EN
☎ 01884 821770 📄 01884 829199
dir: *M5 junct 27, A361 signed Tiverton & Barnstaple. In 600yds take 1st slip road, then right over bridge, site ahead*

* 🚐 £13.50-£25.40 🚕 £13.50-£25.40 ▲

Open 5 Mar-28 Oct

Last arrival 20.00hrs Last departure 11.30hrs

A small, well-sheltered park, peacefully located amidst fields and mature trees. The toilet facilities are of a high quality in keeping with the rest of the park, and there is a good laundry. The park has direct gated access to the canal towpath - a brisk 20-minute walk will take you to a choice of pubs plus a farm shop. All pitches have hardstandings. 5.5 acre site. 59 touring pitches. 59 hardstandings. Caravan pitches. Motorhome pitches. Tent pitches. 1 static.

Leisure: 🅰

Facilities: 🐴 ⊙ 🅿 ❄ 🐕 ⊙ 🔯 🎋 🖥 ♻ 🛈

Services: 🔌 🔵 🔋 🖊 🔲 🗑 ⬇

Within 3 miles: ⬇ 🎣 ⛵ 🗑

Notes: No cycling, no groundsheets on grass. Dogs must be kept on leads.

SIDMOUTH

Places to visit

Branscombe - The Old Bakery, Manor Mill and Forge, BRANSCOMBE 01752 346585 www.nationaltrust.org.uk

Otterton Mill, OTTERTON 01395 568521 www.ottertonmill.com

Great for kids: Pecorama Pleasure Gardens, BEER 01297 21542 www.pecorama.info

---

SIDMOUTH   Map 3 SY18

AA CAMPING CARD SITE

PREMIER PARK

►►►►► **91% Oakdown Country Holiday Park**
(SY167902)

Gatedown Ln, Weston EX10 0PT
☎ 01297 680387 📄 01297 680541
e-mail: enquiries@oakdown.co.uk
web: www.oakdown.co.uk
dir: *Exit A3052, 2.5m E of junct with A375*

* 🚐 £17.50-£27.50 🚕 £17.50-£27.50
▲ £11.30-£17.50

Open Apr-Oct

Last arrival 22.00hrs Last departure 10.30hrs

A quality, friendly, well-maintained park with good landscaping and plenty of maturing trees that makes it well screened from the A3502. Pitches are grouped in paddocks surrounded by shrubs, with a 50-pitch development replete with an upmarket toilet block. Stunning new facilities were created for 2011, plus the park has an excellent 9 hole par 3 golf course and a good shop and café. The park's conservation areas, with their natural flora and fauna, offer attractive walks, and there is a hide by the Victorian reed bed for both casual and dedicated bird watchers. A delightful park in every respect. 16 acre site. 150 touring pitches. 90 hardstandings. Caravan pitches. Motorhome pitches. Tent pitches. 62 statics.

AA Pubs & Restaurants nearby: The Blue Ball, Sidford 01395 514062

The Salty Monk, Sidford 01395 513174; Dukes, Sidmouth 01395 513320

LEISURE: 🏊 Indoor swimming pool 🏊 Outdoor swimming pool 🅰 Children's playground 🛝 Kid's club 🎾 Tennis court 🎱 Games room 📺 Separate TV room ⛳ 9/18 hole golf course ⛵ Boats for hire 🎬 Cinema 🎵 Entertainment 🎣 Fishing ◎ Mini golf 🏄 Watersports 💪 Gym ⚽ Sports field Spa ∪ Stables
FACILITIES: 🛁 Bath 🚿 Shower ⊙ Electric shaver 🅿 Hairdryer ❄ Ice Pack Facility 🐕 Disabled facilities ⊙ Public telephone 🔯 Shop on site or within 200yds 🛒 Mobile shop (calls at least 5 days a week) 🍖 BBQ area 🎋 Picnic area wifi Wi-fi 🖥 Internet access ♻ Recycling 🛈 Tourist info ⚡ Dog exercise area

Leisure: ⚲ ⚄ 🖵

Facilities: ⛽ ⌂ ☉ ⚘ ⚒ ⚖ ⚠ ⚘ 🔥 WI-FI 🖥 ♺ ❶

Services: 🔌 🗑 🍺 ⌀ Ⓣ ⦿ 🛒 ⚡

Within 3 miles: ↕ ⚲ 日 ✎ ◎ 🦆 🎣 🎱 ⟲

Notes: No bikes, skateboards or kite flying. Dogs must be kept on leads. Use of microwave. Field trail to donkey sanctuary.

see advert below

AA CAMPING CARD SITE

▶▶▶ **83% Salcombe Regis Caravan & Camping Park** *(SY153892)*

Salcombe Regis EX10 0JH
☎ 01395 514303 📠 01395 514314
e-mail: contact@salcombe-regis.co.uk
web: www.salcombe-regis.co.uk
dir: *Exit A3052 1m E of junct with A375. From opposite direction turn left past Donkey Sanctuary*

* 🚐 £12-£22 🚐 £22 ▲ £22

Open Etr-end Oct

Last arrival 20.15hrs Last departure 10.30hrs

Set in quiet countryside with glorious views, this spacious park has well-maintained facilities, and a good mix of grass and hardstanding pitches. A footpath runs from the park to the coastal path and the beach. There is a self-catering holiday cottage and static caravans for hire. 16 acre site. 100 touring pitches. 40 hardstandings. Caravan pitches. Motorhome pitches. Tent pitches. 10 statics.

Salcombe Regis Caravan & Camping Park

AA Pubs & Restaurants nearby: The Blue Ball, Sidford 01395 514062

The Salty Monk, Sidford 01395 513174; Dukes, Sidmouth 01395 513320

Salcombe Regis Caravan & Camping Park

Leisure: ⚲

Facilities: ⛽ ⌂ ☉ ⚘ ⚒ ⚖ ⚠ 🔥 WI-FI ♺ ❶

Services: 🔌 🗑 🍺 ⌀ Ⓣ 🛒 ⚡

Within 3 miles: ↕ ⚲ 日 ✎ ◎ 🦆 🎣 🎱 ⟲

Notes: Dogs must be kept on leads. Putting.

SIDMOUTH *continued*

▶▶▶ 76% Kings Down Tail Caravan & Camping Park *(SY173907)*

Salcombe Regis EX10 0PD
☎ 01297 680313 📄 01297 680313
e-mail: info@kingsdowntail.co.uk
dir: *Exit A3052 3m E of junct with A375*

🚐 🚏 ⛺

Open 15 Mar-15 Nov

Last arrival 22.00hrs Last departure noon

A well-kept site on level ground in a tree-sheltered spot on the side of the Sid Valley. This neat family-run park makes a good base for exploring the east Devon coast. 5 acre site. 102 touring pitches. 61 hardstandings. Caravan pitches. Motorhome pitches. Tent pitches.

AA Pubs & Restaurants nearby: The Blue Ball, Sidford 01395 514062

The Salty Monk, Sidford 01395 513174; Dukes, Sidmouth 01395 513320

Leisure: Ⅶ 🔍
Facilities: ⌐ ⊙ 𝒫 ✳ ఈ 🛁 🛒 ♻
Services: 🔌 🔄 🏧 ⌀ T 🚽
Within 3 miles: ↓ ⛄ ⽬ 🔦 🛒 🔄 ∪

Notes: Dogs must be kept on leads.

see advert below

AA CAMPING CARD SITE

▶▶▶ 78% Bundu Camping & Caravan Park *(SX546916)*

EX20 4HT
☎ 01837 861611
e-mail: frances@bundu.plus.com
dir: *W on A30, past Okehampton. Take A386 to Tavistock. Take 1st left & left again*

🚐 🚏 ⛺

Open all year

Last arrival 23.30hrs Last departure 14.00hrs

Welcoming, friendly owners set the tone for this well-maintained site, ideally positioned on the border of the Dartmoor National Park. Along with fine views, well maintained toilet facilities and level grassy pitches, the Granite Way cycle track from Lydford to Okehampton along the old railway line (part of the Devon Coast to Coast cycle trail)

passes the edge of the park. 4.5 acre site. 38 touring pitches. 11 hardstandings. Caravan pitches. Motorhome pitches. Tent pitches.

AA Pubs & Restaurants nearby: Highwayman Inn, Sourton 01837 861243

Facilities: ⌐ ⊙ 𝒫 ✳ ఈ 🏧 🛒
Services: 🔌 🔄 ⌀ T 🚽
Within 3 miles: ⽬ 🔦 🛒 🔄
Notes: Dogs must be kept on leads.

LEISURE: 🏊 Indoor swimming pool   🏊 Outdoor swimming pool   Ⅶ Children's playground   🏊 Kid's club   🎾 Tennis court   🎯 Games room   📺 Separate TV room   ⛳ 9/18 hole golf course   🚣 Boats for hire   🎬 Cinema   🎵 Entertainment   🎣 Fishing   ⛳ Mini golf   🏄 Watersports   🏋 Gym   ⚽ Sports field   Spa   ∪ Stables
FACILITIES: 🛁 Bath   🚿 Shower   ⊙ Electric shaver   🔦 Hairdryer   ✳ Ice Pack Facility   ఈ Disabled facilities   📞 Public telephone   🏧 Shop on site or within 200yds   🛒 Mobile shop (calls at least 5 days a week)   🍖 BBQ area   🌲 Picnic area   Wi-fi   Internet access   ♻ Recycling   Tourist info   🐕 Dog exercise area

SOUTH MOLTON
Map 3 SS72

AA CAMPING CARD SITE

▶▶▶▶ 88% Riverside Caravan & Camping Park (SS723274)

Marsh Ln, North Molton Rd EX36 3HQ
☎ 01769 579269 📄 01769 574853
e-mail: relax@exmoorriverside.co.uk
web: www.exmoorriverside.co.uk
dir: *M5 junct 27 onto A361 towards Barnstaple. Site signed 1m before South Molton on right*

🚐 £15-£22 🚎 £15-£22 ▲ £10-£20

Open all year

Last arrival 22.00hrs Last departure 11.00hrs

A family-run park, set alongside the River Mole, where supervised children can play, and fishing is available. This is an ideal base for exploring Exmoor, as well as north Devon's golden beaches. The site has an award for the excellence of the toilets. 40 acre site. 42 touring pitches. 42 hardstandings. Caravan pitches. Motorhome pitches. Tent pitches.

AA Pubs & Restaurants nearby: The Rising Sun Inn, Umberleigh 01769 560447

Leisure: ⋒ ◉ ♫

Facilities: 🖗 ☉ 🅿 ⚒ ⚓ & ⊙ 🗓 🗛 ⌁ ♻ **θ**

Services: 🔌 🗓 🍺 🛢 🥛 🚽 🍽 🛍 🏧 ⌁

Within 3 miles: ↨ 🖽 🖋 ◎ ≿ 🖷🖷 ∪

Notes: Dogs must be kept on leads. Fishing.

STARCROSS

See Dawlish

STOKE GABRIEL

Places to visit

Berry Pomeroy Castle, TOTNES 01803 866618
www.english-heritage.org.uk

Totnes Museum, TOTNES 01803 863821
www.devonmuseums.net/totnes

Great for kids: Paignton Zoo Environmental Park, PAIGNTON 0844 474 2222
www.paigntonzoo.org.uk

STOKE GABRIEL
Map 3 SX85

▶▶▶ 84% Higher Well Farm Holiday Park (SX857577)

Waddeton Rd TQ9 6RN
☎ 01803 782289
e-mail: higherwell@talk21.com
dir: *From Exeter A380 to Torbay, turn right onto A385 for Totnes, in 0.5m left for Stoke Gabriel, follow signs*

🚐 £11-£18 🚎 £11-£18 ▲ £11-£18

Open 31 Mar-4 Nov

Last arrival 22.00hrs Last departure 10.00hrs

Set on a quiet farm yet only four miles from Paignton, this rural holiday park is on the outskirts of the picturesque village of Stoke Gabriel. A toilet block, with some en suite facilities, is an excellent amenity, and tourers are housed in an open field with some very good views. 10 acre site. 80 touring pitches. 3 hardstandings. Caravan pitches. Motorhome pitches. Tent pitches. 19 statics.

AA Pubs & Restaurants nearby: Durant Arms, Ashprington 01803 732240

Steam Packet Inn, Totnes 01803 863880

White Hart, Totnes 01803 847111

Facilities: 🖗 ☉ 🅿 ⚒ ⚓ & ⊙ 🗓 🗛 ♻ **θ**

Services: 🔌 🗓 🛢 ⌁ 🏧 ⌁

Within 3 miles: ↨ 🖋 🖷🖷

Notes: No commercial vehicles. Dogs must be kept on leads.

AA CAMPING CARD SITE

▶▶▶ 80% Broadleigh Farm Park (SX851587)

Coombe House Ln, Aish TQ9 6PU
☎ 01803 782422
e-mail: enquiries@broadleighfarm.co.uk
web: www.broadleighfarm.co.uk
dir: *From Exeter on A38 then A380 towards Torbay. Right onto A385 for Totnes. In 0.5m right at Whitehill Country Park. Site approx 0.75m on left*

🚐 🚎 ▲

Open Mar-Oct

Last arrival 21.00hrs Last departure 11.30hrs

Set in a very rural location on a working farm bordering Paignton and Stoke Gabriel. The large sloping field with a timber-clad toilet block in the centre is sheltered and peaceful, surrounded by rolling countryside but handy for the beaches. There is also an excellent rally field with good toilets and showers. 7 acre site. 80 touring pitches. Caravan pitches. Motorhome pitches. Tent pitches.

AA Pubs & Restaurants nearby: Rumour, Totnes 01803 864682

Facilities: 🖗 ☉ 🅿 ⚒ ⚓ & 🗛 ♻ **θ**

Services: 🔌 🗓 🏧

Within 3 miles: ↨ 🖽 🖋 ◎ ≿ 🖷🖷

Notes: ⊗ Dogs must be kept on leads.

STOKENHAM
Map 3 SX84

Places to visit

Kingsbridge Cookworthy Museum, KINGSBRIDGE 01548 853235
www.kingsbridgemuseum.org.uk

AA CAMPING CARD SITE

▶▶▶ 80% Old Cotmore Farm (SX804417)

TQ7 2LR
☎ 01548 580240
e-mail: info@holiday-in-devon.com
dir: *From Kingsbridge take A379 towards Dartmouth, through Frogmore & Chillington to mini rdbt at Stokenham. Right towards Beesands, site 1m on right*

* 🚐 £12-£17 🚎 £12-£17 ▲ £12-£17

Open 15 Mar-Oct

Last arrival 20.00hrs Last departure 11.00hrs

A small and peaceful, family run touring caravan and campsite well located in the South Hams region of Devon, close to Slapton and within easy reach of Salcombe and Dartmouth. Facilities are very clean and well maintained and there is a basic shop and small play area. Sought-after tent pitches overlook fields and rolling fields. Pebble and sandy beaches with cliff walks through woods and fields are within walking distance. Self-catering cottages are available. 22 acre site. 30 touring pitches. 25 hardstandings. Caravan pitches. Motorhome pitches. Tent pitches.

AA Pubs & Restaurants nearby: The Cricket Inn, Beesands 01548 580215

Leisure: ⋒ 🔍

Facilities: 🖗 ⚒ & ⊙ 🗓 🗛 📶 💻 ♻ **θ**

Services: 🔌 🗓 🛢 ⌁ 🏧

Within 3 miles: ≿ 🖋 ≿ 🖷🖷

Notes: Dogs must be kept on leads.

SERVICES: 🔌 Electric hook up 🗓 Launderette 🍺 Licensed bar 🛢 Calor Gas ⌀ Camping Gaz 🗓 Toilet fluid 🍽 Café/Restaurant 🏧 Fast Food/Takeaway 🔋 Battery charging 🍼 Baby care ⌁ Motorvan service point
ABBREVIATIONS: BH/bank hols-bank holidays Etr-Easter Whit-Whitsun dep-departure fr-from hrs-hours m-mile mdnt-midnight rdbt-roundabout rs-restricted service wk-week wknd-weekend ⊛ No credit cards ⊗ No dogs
See page 7 for details of the AA Camping Card Scheme

TAVISTOCK Map 3 SX47

Places to visit

Morwellham Quay, MORWELLHAM 01822 832766 www.morwellham-quay.co.uk

Yelverton Paperweight Centre, YELVERTON 01822 854250 www.paperweightcentre.co.uk

Great for kids: National Marine Aquarium, PLYMOUTH 01752 600301 www.national-aquarium.co.uk

AA CAMPING CARD SITE

PREMIER PARK

►►►►► 85% Woodovis Park *(SX431745)*

Gulworthy PL19 8NY
☎ 01822 832968 📠 01822 832948
e-mail: info@woodovis.com
dir: *A390 from Tavistock signed Callington & Gunnislake. At hill top right at rdbt signed Lamerton & Chipshop. Site 1m on left*

🚃 £17-£38 🚐 £17-£38 ⛺ £17-£38

Open 23 Mar-2 Nov

Last arrival 20.00hrs Last departure 11.00hrs

A well-kept park in a remote woodland setting on the edge of the Tamar Valley. Peacefully located park at the end of a private, half-mile, tree-lined drive, it offers superb on-site facilities and high levels of customer care from hands-on owners. The toilets are immaculate and well maintained, plus there is an indoor swimming pool, sauna and a good information/games room, all in a friendly, purposeful atmosphere. 14.5 acre site. 50 touring pitches. 20 hardstandings. 8 seasonal pitches. Caravan pitches. Motorhome pitches. Tent pitches. 35 statics. 1 wooden pod.

AA Pubs & Restaurants nearby: Dartmoor Inn, Lydford 01822 820221

Leisure: 🏊 🛝 ⚽ 🎱

Facilities: 🛁 🚿 ⊙ 💨 ❄ ♿ 📞 🛍 🧺 🐕 [Wi-fi] 💻 ♻ ℹ

Services: 🔧 🌀 🛢 ⛽ [T] 🛏 👶 🔌

Within 3 miles: ⛳ 🎣 ◎ 🏄 🛍 🌀 🐴

Notes: Dogs must be kept on leads. Archery, water-walking, physiotherm infra-red therapy cabin, petanque court.

AA CAMPING CARD SITE

►►►► 80% Langstone Manor Camping & Caravan Park *(SX524738)*

Moortown PL19 9JZ
☎ 01822 613371 📠 01822 613371
e-mail: jane@langstone-manor.co.uk
web: www.langstone-manor.co.uk
dir: *B3357 from Tavistock to Princetown. Approx 1.5m right at x-rds, follow signs. Over bridge, cattle grid, up hill, left at sign, left to park*

🚃 £13-£17.50 🚐 £13-£17.50 ⛺ £13-£17.50

Open 15 Mar-Oct

Last arrival 22.00hrs Last departure 11.00hrs

A secluded and very peaceful site set in the well-maintained grounds of a manor house in Dartmoor National Park. Many attractive mature trees provide a screen within the park, yet the west-facing terraced pitches on the main park enjoy the superb summer sumsets. Toilet facilities are being refurbished and extended for the 2012 season and there is a popular lounge bar with an excellent menu of reasonably priced evening meals, and camping pods to hire. Plenty of activities and places of interest can be found within the surrounding moorland. 6.5 acre site. 40 touring pitches. 10 hardstandings. 5 seasonal pitches. Caravan pitches. Motorhome pitches. Tent pitches. 25 statics. 3 wooden pods.

AA Pubs & Restaurants nearby: Royal Inn, Horsebridge 01822 870214

Leisure: 🛝 🎱

Facilities: 🛁 🚿 ⊙ 💨 ❄ ♿ 📞 🧺 ♻ ℹ

Services: 🔧 🌀 🍷 ⛽ [T] 🍴 🛏 👶 🔌

Within 3 miles: ⛳ 🎬 🎣 ◎ 🏄 🛍 🌀 🐴

Notes: No skateboards, scooters, cycles, ball games. Dogs must be kept on leads. Baguettes, croissants etc available.

AA CAMPING CARD SITE

►►► 82% Harford Bridge Holiday Park *(SX504767)*

Peter Tavy PL19 9LS
☎ 01822 810349 & 07773 251457
📠 01822 810028
e-mail: stay@harfordbridge.co.uk
web: www.harfordbridge.co.uk
dir: *2m N of Tavistock, off A386 Okehampton Rd, take Peter Tavy turn, entrance 200yds on right*

* 🚃 £12.75-£21.70 🚐 £12.75-£21.70 ⛺ £12.75-£19.95

Open all year (rs Nov-Mar statics only & 5 hardstandings)

Last arrival 21.00hrs Last departure noon

This beautiful spacious park is set beside the River Tavy in the Dartmoor National Park. Pitches are located beside the river and around the copses, and the park is very well equipped for the holidaymaker. An adventure playground and games room entertain children, and there is fly-fishing and a free tennis court. 16 acre site. 120 touring pitches. 5 hardstandings. Caravan pitches. Motorhome pitches. Tent pitches. 80 statics.

AA Pubs & Restaurants nearby: The Peter Tavy Inn, Peter Tavy 01822 810348

Leisure: 🛝 🎾 ⚽ 🎱 📺

Facilities: 🚿 ⊙ 💨 ❄ ♿ 📞 🧺 🐕 [Wi-fi] ♻ ℹ

Services: 🔧 🌀 🛢 ⛽ [T] 🛏 🔌

Within 3 miles: ⛳ 🎬 🎣 🏄 🛍 🌀 🐴

Notes: No large groups. Dogs must be kept on leads. Fly fishing. Baguettes, croissants, snacks, sweets available.

TEDBURN ST MARY — Map 3 SX89

Places to visit

Finch Foundry, STICKLEPATH 01837 840046
www.nationaltrust.org.uk

Castle Drogo, DREWSTEIGNTON 01647 433306
www.nationaltrust.org.uk/main

Great for kids: Prickly Ball Farm and Hedgehog
Hospital, NEWTON ABBOT 01626 362319
www.pricklyballfarm.com

AA CAMPING CARD SITE

▶▶▶▶ 80% Springfield Holiday Park

(SX788935)

EX6 6EW
☎ 01647 24242
e-mail: enquiries@springfieldholidaypark.co.uk
dir: M5 junct 31, A30 towards Okehampton, exit
at junct, signed to Cheriton Bishop. Follow brown
tourist signs to site. (For Sat Nav use postcode
EX6 6JN)

⊟ £12-£20 ⊟ £12-£20 Å £10-£20

Open 15 Mar-15 Nov

Last arrival 22.00hrs Last departure noon

Set in a quiet rural location with countryside
views, this park continues to be upgraded to a
smart standard. It has the advantage of being
located close to Dartmoor National Park, with
village pubs and stores just two miles away. 9
acre site. 48 touring pitches. 38 hardstandings.
Caravan pitches. Motorhome pitches. Tent
pitches. 49 statics.

AA Pubs & Restaurants nearby: Old Thatch Inn,
Cheriton Bishop 01647 24204

Leisure: ⚓ ⛰ ☍

Facilities: ⚮ ☉ ☼ 🌂 ⬚ ☴ 🛒 Wi-fi

Services: ⊡ ⬚ 🛢 ⬚ ⚊ ↯

Within 3 miles: ↧ ⌁ ⬚ ⬚

Notes: Dogs must be kept on leads.

TIVERTON

See East Worlington

TORQUAY — Map 3 SX96

See also Newton Abbot

Places to visit

Torre Abbey, TORQUAY 01803 293593
www.torre-abbey.org.uk

'Bygones', TORQUAY 01803 326108
www.bygones.co.uk

Great for kids: Living Coasts, TORQUAY
01803 202470 www.livingcoasts.org.uk

▶▶▶▶ 82% Widdicombe Farm Touring Park (SX876643)

Marldon TQ3 1ST
☎ 01803 558325 🖷 01803 559526
e-mail: info@widdicombefarm.co.uk
dir: On A380, midway between Torquay & Paignton
ring road

⊟ ⊟ Å

Open mid Mar-end Oct

Last arrival 20.00hrs Last departure 11.00hrs

A friendly family-run park on a working farm with
good quality facilities and extensive views. The
level pitches are terraced to take advantage of the
views towards the coast and Dartmoor. This is the
only adult touring park within Torquay, and is also
handy for Paignton and Brixham. There's a bus
service from the park to the local shopping centre
and Torquay's harbour. There is a small shop, a
restaurant and a lounge bar with entertainment
from Easter to the end of September. 8 acre site.
180 touring pitches. 180 hardstandings. 20
seasonal pitches. Caravan pitches. Motorhome
pitches. Tent pitches. 3 statics.

AA Pubs & Restaurants nearby: Church House
Inn, Marldon 01803 558279

Elephant Restaurant & Brasserie, Torquay
01803 200044

No 7 Fish Bistro, Torquay 01803 295055

Leisure: ♫

Facilities: ⚮ ☉ ⌁ ☼ ⬚ ⬚ 🛒 Wi-fi ♻ ⬚ ❶

Services: ⊡ ⬚ 🍴 🛢 ⬚ ⊤ ⍾ ⬚ ⬚ ↯

Within 3 miles: ↧ ⌕ ☰ ⌁ ◎ ⬚ ⬚ ⬚

Notes: Adults only. Most dog breeds accepted.
Dogs must be kept on leads.

WOODBURY SALTERTON — Map 3 SY08

Places to visit

The World of Country Life, EXMOUTH
01395 274533 www.worldofcountrylife.co.uk

A la Ronde, EXMOUTH 01395 265514
www.nationaltrust.org.uk

Great for kids: Crealy Adventure Park,
CLYST ST MARY 01395 233200 www.crealy.co.uk

▶▶▶ 87% Browns Farm Caravan Park (SY016885)

Browns Farm EX5 1PS
☎ 01395 232895
dir: M5 junct 30, A3052 for 3.7m. Right at White
Horse Inn, follow sign to Woodbury. At junct with
village road turn right, site on left

* ⊟ £11-£14 ⊟ £11-£15 Å £11-£14

Open all year

Last departure 11.00hrs

A small farm park adjoining a 14th-century
thatched farmhouse, and located in a quiet
village. Pitches back onto hedgerows, and friendly
owners keep the excellent facilities very clean. The
tourist information and games room, with table
tennis, chess etc, is housed in a purpose-built
building. The park is just a mile from the historic
heathland of Woodbury Common with its superb
views. 2.5 acre site. 29 touring pitches. 24
hardstandings. Caravan pitches. Motorhome
pitches. Tent pitches.

AA Pubs & Restaurants nearby: Golden Lion Inn,
Tipton St John 01404 812881

Moore's Restaurant & Rooms, Newton Poppleford
01395 568100

Leisure: ☍ ☐

Facilities: ⚮ ☉ ⌁ ☼ ⬚ ☉ ❶

Services: ⊡ ⬚ ⚊ ⬚

Within 3 miles: ↧ ⌁ ⬚ ∪

Notes: ⊗ No ground sheets in awnings, no
music. Dogs must be kept on leads.
Hardstandings for winter period, caravan storage.

WOOLACOMBE

Map 3 SS44

See also Mortehoe

Places to visit

Arlington Court, ARLINGTON 01271 850296
www.nationaltrust.org.uk/
main/w-arlingtoncourt

Great for kids: Watermouth Castle & Family
Theme Park, ILFRACOMBE 01271 863879
www.watermouthcastle.com

 80% Woolacombe Bay Holiday Village *(SS465442)*

Sandy Ln EX34 7AH
☎ 01271 870343 📄 01271 870089
e-mail: goodtimes@woolacombe.com
dir: *From Mullacott Cross rdbt take B3343 (Woolacombe road) to Turnpike Cross junct. Right towards Mortehoe, site approx 1m on left*

* 🚐 £17.80-£60.60 🚌 £17.80-£60.60 ▲ £12.50-£39.90

Open Mar-Oct (rs Mar-mid May, mid Sep-Oct no touring, camping only available)

Last arrival mdnt Last departure 10.00hrs

A well-developed touring section in a holiday complex with a full entertainment and leisure programme. This park offers excellent facilities including a steam room and sauna. For a small charge a bus takes holidaymakers to the other Woolacombe Bay holiday centres where they can take part in any of the activities offered, and there is also a bus to the beach. 8.5 acre site. 180 touring pitches. Caravan pitches. Motorhome pitches. Tent pitches. 237 statics.

AA Pubs & Restaurants nearby: George & Dragon, Ilfracombe 01271 863851

The Quay, Ilfracombe 01271 868090

The Williams Arms, Braunton 01271 812360

Leisure: 🏊 🏖 ♨ 🎣 🎠 ⚽ 🔍 🎱 🎵 Spa
Facilities: 🔦 ⊙ 🍳 ✳ ♿ 🏪 🍴 🐕 ♻
Services: 🔌 🗑 🍺 ⊘ 🍴 🧺 🛒 ♨
Within 3 miles: ↓ ✚ 🎯 ♬ ◎ 🎿 🏌 🎮 ♄

Notes: Health suite, surfing & swimming lessons.
see advert on opposite page & inside front cover

 78% Golden Coast Holiday Village *(SS482436)*

Station Rd EX34 7HW
☎ 01271 870343 📄 01271 870089
e-mail: goodtimes@woolacombe.com
dir: *From Mullacott Cross towards Woolacombe Bay, site 1.5m on left*

* 🚐 £9-£61.80 🚌 £9-£61.80 ▲ £9-£40.70

Open Feb-Dec (rs mid Sep-May outdoor pools closed)

Last arrival mdnt Last departure 10.00hrs

A holiday village offering excellent leisure facilities together with the amenities available at the other Woolacombe Bay holiday parks. There is a neat touring area with a unisex toilet block, maintained to a high standard. Bowling alleys, a new 'Waves' pool (the only one in Europe), a number of bars and plenty of activities add to the holiday experience. 10 acre site. 91 touring pitches. 53 hardstandings. Caravan pitches. Motorhome pitches. Tent pitches. 444 statics.

AA Pubs & Restaurants nearby: George & Dragon, Ilfracombe 01271 863851

The Quay, Ilfracombe 01271 868090

The Williams Arms, Braunton 01271 812360

Leisure: 🏊 🏖 ♨ 🎣 🎠 ⚽ 🔍 🎱 🎵
Facilities: 🔦 ⊙ 🍳 ✳ ♿ 🏪 🍴 🐕 📶 🖥 ♻
Services: 🔌 🗑 🍺 ⊘ 🍴 🧺 🛒 ♨
Within 3 miles: ↓ ✚ 🎯 ♬ ◎ 🎿 🏌 🎮 ♄

Notes: No pets on touring pitches. Sauna, solarium, golf, fishing, snooker, cinema, swimming & surfing lessons.

AA CAMPING CARD SITE

 77% Woolacombe Sands Holiday Park *(SS471434)*

Beach Rd EX34 7AF
☎ 01271 870569 📄 01271 870606
e-mail: lifesabeach@woolacombe-sands.co.uk
dir: *M5 junct 27, A361 to Barnstaple. Follow Ilfracombe signs to Mullacott Cross. Left onto B3343 to Woolacombe. Site on left*

* 🚐 £10.50-£31 🚌 £10.50-£31 ▲ £10.50-£31

Open Apr-Oct

Last arrival 22.00hrs Last departure 10.00hrs

Set in rolling countryside with grassy terraced pitches, most with spectacular views overlooking the sea at Woolacombe. The lovely Blue Flag beach can be accessed directly by footpath in 10-15 minutes, and there is a full entertainment programme for all the family in high season. 20 acre site. 200 touring pitches. 75 hardstandings. 40 seasonal pitches. Caravan pitches. Motorhome pitches. Tent pitches. 80 statics.

AA Pubs & Restaurants nearby: George & Dragon, Ilfracombe 01271 863851

The Quay, Ilfracombe 01271 868090

The Williams Arms, Braunton 01271 812360

Leisure: 🏊 🏖 ♨ 🎣 ⚽ 🔍 🎱 🎵
Facilities: 🔦 ⊙ 🍳 ✳ ♿ 🏪 🍴 🐕 📶 ♻ ℹ
Services: 🔌 🗑 🍺 🛢 ⊘ 🍴 🧺 🛒 ♨
Within 3 miles: ↓ 🎯 ◎ 🎿 🏌 🎮 ♄

Notes: Crazy golf.

see advert on page 183

LEISURE: 🏊 Indoor swimming pool 🏊 Outdoor swimming pool 🛝 Children's playground 🧒 Kid's club 🎾 Tennis court 🎱 Games room 📺 Separate TV room
⛳ 9/18 hole golf course ⛵ Boats for hire 🎬 Cinema 🎵 Entertainment 🎣 Fishing ⛳ Mini golf 🏄 Watersports 🏋 Gym ⚽ Sports field **Spa** ♘ Stables
FACILITIES: 🛁 Bath 🚿 Shower 😊 Electric shaver 💇 Hairdryer ❄ Ice Pack Facility ♿ Disabled facilities 📞 Public telephone 🏪 Shop on site or within 200yds
🏪 Mobile shop (calls at least 5 days a week) 🍖 BBQ area 🍴 Picnic area 📶 Wi-fi 💻 Internet access ♻ Recycling ❶ Tourist info 🐕 Dog exercise area

WOOLACOMBE *continued*

►►► 77% Europa Park *(SS475435)*

Beach Rd EX34 7AN

☎ 01271 871425   📠 01271 871425

e-mail: europaparkwoolacombe@yahoo.co.uk

dir: *M5 junct 27, A361 through Barnstaple to Mullacott Cross. Left onto B3343 signed Woolacombe. Site on right at Spa shop/garage*

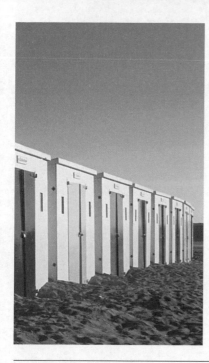

Open all year

Last arrival 23.00hrs Last departure 10.00hrs

A very lively family-run site handy for the beach at Woolacombe, and catering well for surfers but maybe not suitable for a quieter type of stay (please make sure the site is suitable for you before making your booking). Set in a stunning location high above the bay, it provides a wide range of accommodation including surf cabins, 10 camping pods and generous touring pitches. Visitors can enjoy the indoor pool and sauna, games room, restaurant/café/bar and clubhouse. 16 acre site. 200 touring pitches. 20 hardstandings. Caravan pitches. Motorhome pitches. Tent pitches. 22 statics.

Europa Park

AA Pubs & Restaurants nearby: George & Dragon, Ilfracombe 01271 863851

The Quay, Ilfracombe 01271 868090

The Williams Arms, Braunton 01271 812360

Leisure: 🎣 ⚖ 🎱 ☐

Facilities: 🔌 ☉ ✳ ☉ 💰

Services: 🔌 🛢 🍽 ⊘ Ⓣ 🍴 🛒 🛍 ⚒

Within 3 miles: ⬆ 🎡 ⚲ ◎ 🛥 🎣 🛢 U

Notes: Beer deck, off licence, pub, big screen TV.

Dorset

Dorset means rugged varied coastline and high chalk downland, with more than a hint of Thomas Hardy, its most famous son. The coastal grandeur is breathtaking with two famous local landmarks, Lulworth Cove and Durdle Door, shaped and sculpted to perfection by the elements. Squeezed in among the cliffs and set amid some of Britain's most beautiful scenery is a chain of picturesque villages and occasionally seaside towns.

Most prominent among these seaside towns is Lyme Regis, with its sturdy breakwater, known as the Cobb, made famous by Jane Austen in *Persuasion*, and John Fowles in *The French Lieutenant's Woman*. It's the sort of place where Georgian houses and quaint cottages jostle with historic pubs and independently run shops. With its blend of architectural styles and old world charm, Lyme looks very much like a film set, and fans of Austen and Fowles and the big-screen adaptations of their work flock to point their cameras and enjoy its beauty. Before the era of sea-bathing and Victorian respectability, the town was a haunt of smugglers.

● Durdle Door

Chesil Beach

In sharp contrast to Lyme's steep streets and dramatic inclines is Chesil Beach, a long shingle reef extending for 10 miles (16.1km) between Abbotsbury and Portland. The beach is covered by a vast wall of shingle resulting from centuries of violent weather-influenced activity along the Devon and Dorset coastline. The novelist Ian McEwan chose the setting for his recent novel *On Chesil Beach*.

Thomas Hardy

Rural Dorset is where you can be 'far from the madding crowd'- to quote Thomas Hardy. For fans of this popular and much-admired writer there is the chance to visit two National Trust properties - the cob-and-thatch cottage in Higher Bockhampton where he was born and lived until the age of 34, and Max Gate in Dorchester, his home for 40 years and where he wrote some of his best-known works.

Walking and Cycling

For the true walker, however, there is nowhere to beat the magnificent Dorset coastline, particularly in the vicinity of Charmouth and Bridport where the domed Golden Cap stands tall and proud amid the cliffs. At 619ft it is the highest cliff on the south coast. Getting there, however, involves about 0.75 mile (1.2km) of steep walking. The Golden Cap is part of Dorset's spectacular Jurassic Coast, a World Heritage Site. This designated coastline stretches to East Devon.

The South West Coast Path, one of Britain's great walks, extends the length of the Dorset ▶

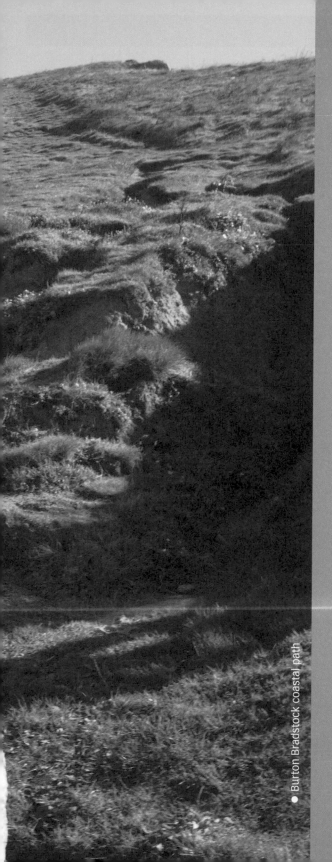

● Burton Bradstock coastal path

coast, from Lyme Regis to Studland Bay and Poole Harbour, and offers constant uninterrupted views of the coast and the Channel. Away from the sea there are miles of rolling downland walks which are no less impressive than the coastal stretches. The Purbeck Hills, between Weymouth and Poole Harbour, are great for exploring on foot. Cranborne Chase, to the north of Blandford Forum and once a royal forest, is a remote, rural backwater where the walker can feel totally at home.

The National Cycle Network offers the chance to ride from Dorchester through the heart of Dorset to Lyme Regis or north to Sherborne, taking in some of the county's most picturesque villages. There is also the chance to tour the ancient hill forts of Pilsdon Pen, Coneys Castle and Lamberts Castle around Charmouth and the Marshwood Vale – among a wide choice of Dorset cycle routes.

Festivals and Events

- Among numerous live shows, exhibitions, flower festivals and craft fairs, is the Great Dorset Steam Fair in September. This famous event draws many visitors who come to look at vintage and classic vehicles. There are also heavy horse shows and rural crafts.
- Also in September is the two-day Dorset County Show which includes over 450 trade stands, exciting main ring attractions and thousands of animals.
- For something a bit more light-hearted – but perhaps a little uncomfortable - there is the annual Nettle Eating Contest in June, which attracts fans from all over Europe.

DORSET

See Walk 6 in the Walks & Cycle Rides section at the end of the guide

ALDERHOLT   Map 5 SU11

Places to visit

Furzey Gardens, MINSTEAD 023 8081 2464
www.furzey-gardens.org

Breamore House & Countryside Museum, BREAMORE 01725 512468
www.breamorehouse.com

Great for kids: Rockbourne Roman Villa, ROCKBOURNE 0845 603 5635
www.hants.gov.uk/rockbourne-roman-villa

AA CAMPING CARD SITE

PREMIER PARK

►►►►► 81% **Hill Cottage Farm Camping and Caravan Park** (SU119133)

Sandleheath Rd SP6 3EG
☎ 01425 650513 & 07714 648690
📠 01425 652339
e-mail:
hillcottagefarmcaravansite@supanet.com
dir: Take B3078 W of Fordingbridge. Exit at Alderholt, site 0.25m on left after railway bridge

* 🚐 £17-£25 🚏 £17-£25 ▲ £14-£26

Open Mar-Nov

Last arrival 19.00hrs Last departure 11.00hrs

Set within extensive grounds this rural, beautifully landscaped park offers all fully-serviced pitches set in individual hardstanding bays with mature hedges between giving adequate pitch privacy. The modern toilet block is kept immaculately clean, and there's a good range of leisure facilities. In high season there is an area available for tenting plus a rally field. 40 acre site. 35 touring pitches. 35 hardstandings. Caravan pitches. Motorhome pitches. Tent pitches.

AA Pubs & Restaurants nearby: The Augustus John, Fordingbridge 01425 652098

Leisure: ⚠ 🔍
Facilities: 📶☉🅿☀♿🕙🖎🚮 wifi ♻ ❶
Services: 🔌🖻🛢🥄🔌
Within 3 miles: ↧🚶🛒🚶∪
Notes: No noise after 22.30hrs. Dogs must be kept on leads.

BERE REGIS   Map 4 SY89

Places to visit

Kingston Lacy, WIMBORNE 01202 883402 (Mon-Fri) www.nationaltrust.org.uk

Priest's House Museum and Garden, WIMBORNE 01202 882533 www.priest-house.co.uk

Great for kids: Monkey World-Ape Rescue Centre, WOOL 01929 462537
www.monkeyworld.org

►►► 81% **Rowlands Wait Touring Park** (SY842933)

Rye Hill BH20 7LP
☎ 01929 472727 📠 01929 472275
e-mail: enquiries@rowlandswait.co.uk
web: www.rowlandswait.co.uk
dir: On approach to Bere Regis follow signs to Bovington Tank Museum. At top of Rye Hill, 0.75m from village turn right. 200yds to site

🚐🚏▲

Open mid Mar-Oct (winter by arrangement)

Last arrival 21.00hrs Last departure noon

This park lies in a really attractive setting overlooking Bere Regis and the Dorset countryside, set amongst undulating areas of trees and shrubs. The toilet facilities include two family rooms. Located within a few miles of the Tank Museum with its mock battles. 8 acre site. 71 touring pitches. 2 hardstandings. 23 seasonal pitches. Caravan pitches. Motorhome pitches. Tent pitches.

AA Pubs & Restaurants nearby: Botany Bay Inne, Winterborne Zelston 01929 459227

Leisure: ⚠ 🔍
Facilities: 📶☉🅿☀♿🛢🚮🚻♻ ❶
Services: 🔌🖻🛢🥄🔌🛒🥄
Within 3 miles: ↧🚶◎🛒🛒∪
Notes: No open fires. Dogs must be kept on leads.

BLANDFORD FORUM   Map 4 ST80

Places to visit

Kingston Lacy, WIMBORNE 01202 883402 (Mon-Fri) www.nationaltrust.org.uk

Old Wardour Castle, TISBURY 01747 870487
www.english-heritage.org.uk

Great for kids: Monkey World-Ape Rescue Centre, WOOL 01929 462537
www.monkeyworld.org

►►►► 81% **The Inside Park** (ST869046)

Down House Estate DT11 9AD
☎ 01258 453719 📠 01258 459921
e-mail: inspark@aol.com
dir: From town, over River Stour, follow Winterborne Stickland signs. Site in 1.5m

* 🚐 £14.90-£22.20 🚏 £14.90-£22.20
▲ £14.90-£22.20

Open Etr-Oct

Last arrival 22.00hrs Last departure noon

An attractive, well-sheltered and quiet park, half a mile off a country lane in a wooded valley. Spacious pitches are divided by mature trees and shrubs, and amenities are housed in an 18th-century coach house and stables. There are some lovely woodland walks within the park and an excellent fenced play area for children. 12 acre site. 125 touring pitches. Caravan pitches. Motorhome pitches. Tent pitches.

AA Pubs & Restaurants nearby: Crown Hotel, Blandford Forum 01258 456626

Anvil Inn, Blandford Forum 01258 453431

Leisure: ⚠ 🔍
Facilities: 📶☉🅿☀♿🕙🖎🚮 wifi ♻ ❶
Services: 🔌🖻🛢🥄🛒🥄
Within 3 miles: ↧🚶🛒🛒∪
Notes: Dogs must be kept on leads. Kennels for hire.

BRIDPORT

Places to visit

Forde Abbey, CHARD 01460 221290
www.fordeabbey.co.uk

Dorset County Museum, DORCHESTER 01305 262735 www.dorsetcountymuseum.org

Great for kids: Abbotsbury Swannery, ABBOTSBURY 01305 871858
www.abbotsbury-tourism.co.uk

TOURING   HOLIDAY HOMES   CAMPING

Freshwater Beach
HOLIDAY PARK

Private Beach

- Family Pools
- Children's Activities
- Great Entertainment*
- Family Friendly Bars
- Restaurant and Take-Away
- On Site Supermarket
- Launderette
- Excellent Camping Facilities
- Luxurious Holiday Homes

All on Dorset's World Heritage Coast.

* Spring Bank Holiday to mid Sept.

PLUS...
OUR NEW INDOOR
LEISURE COMPLEX

JURASSiC fun centre

INCLUDING 10-PIN BOWLING,
INDOOR SWIMMING POOLS
& WATER SLIDES, HOT TUB,
SAUNA, STEAM ROOM, GYM
& RESTAURANTS.

Call 01308 897 317

freshwaterbeach.co.uk   Burton Bradstock Dorset DT6 4PT

BRIDPORT
Map 4 SY49

90% Freshwater Beach Holiday Park (SY493892)

Burton Bradstock DT6 4PT
☎ 01308 897317 📠 01308 897336
e-mail: office@freshwaterbeach.co.uk
web: www.freshwaterbeach.co.uk
dir: *Take B3157 from Bridport towards Burton Bradstock. Site 1.5m from Crown rdbt on right*

* 🚐 £14-£42 🚎 £14-£42 ▲ £14-£42

Open mid Mar-mid Nov

Last arrival 22.00hrs Last departure 10.00hrs

A family holiday centre sheltered by a sand bank and enjoying its own private beach. The park offers a wide variety of leisure and entertainment programmes for all the family; there's a new indoor pool, bowling alley and restaurant/take-away, plus a gym and sauna. It is well placed at one end of the Weymouth/Bridport coast with spectacular views of Chesil Beach. There are three immaculate toilet blocks, with excellent private rooms. 40 acre site. 500 touring pitches. 25 hardstandings. Caravan pitches. Motorhome pitches. Tent pitches. 250 statics.

AA Pubs & Restaurants nearby: Shave Cross Inn, Bridport 01308 868358

Riverside Restaurant, Bridport 01308 422011

Anchor Inn, Chideock 01297 489215

Leisure: 🏊‍♂️ 🏊 ⛳ 🎾 🎱 🎵 Spa
Facilities: 🚿 📶 ☀️ 🔌 ⚗️ 🛒 🏪 💈 Wi-fi 🖥️ ℹ️
Services: 🚰 🔋 🍴 🛢️ 🚿 🅃 🍽️ 🛒 🛍️ 🛁
Within 3 miles: 🏇 🎣 ⛳ ◎ 💰 🛍️ 🛒 ♻️

Notes: Families & couples only. Dogs must be kept on leads. Large TV, entertainment in high season & BHs.

see advert on page 189

83% West Bay Holiday Park (SY461906)

West Bay DT6 4HB
☎ 0844 335 3756 📠 01308 421371
e-mail: touringandcamping@parkdeanholidays.com
web: www.parkdeantouring.com
dir: *From A35 (Dorchester road), W towards Bridport, take 1st exit at 1st rdbt, 2nd exit at 2nd rdbt into West Bay, site on right*

* 🚐 £15-£45 🚎 £15-£45 ▲ £15-£42

Open Mar-Oct

Last arrival 23.00hrs Last departure 10.00hrs

Overlooking the pretty little harbour at West Bay, and close to the shingle beach, this park offers a full entertainment programme for all ages. There are children's clubs and an indoor pool with flume for all the family, and plenty of evening fun with shows and cabaret etc. The grassy touring area is terraced to enjoy the sea views and has plenty of hardstandings. The large adventure playground is very popular. 6 acre site. 116 touring pitches. Caravan pitches. Motorhome pitches. Tent pitches. 298 statics.

AA Pubs & Restaurants nearby: George Hotel, Bridport 01308 423187

West Bay, Bridport 01308 422157

Riverside Restaurant, Bridport 01308 422011

Leisure: 🏊 🎢 🎱 🎵
Facilities: 🛁 🚿 ☀️ 🔌 ☀️ 🔌 ⚗️ 🏪 💈 🚻 Wi-fi
Services: 🚰 🔋 🍴 🛢️ 🚿 🅃 🍽️ 🛒 🛍️ 🛁
Within 3 miles: 🏇 🎣 ⛳ ◎ 💰 🛍️ ♨️

Notes: No skateboards.

see advert in preliminary section

AA CAMPING CARD SITE

PREMIER PARK

▶▶▶▶▶ 88%

Highlands End Holiday Park

(SY454913)

Eype DT6 6AR
☎ 01308 422139 & 426947 📠 01308 425672
e-mail: holidays@wdlh.co.uk
dir: *1m W of Bridport on A35, turn south for Eype. Site signed*

🚐 £15.10-£25 🚎 £15.10-£25 ▲ £13-£22

Open 16 Mar-4 Nov

Last arrival 22.00hrs Last departure 11.00hrs

A well-screened site with magnificent cliff-top views over the Channel and Dorset coast, adjacent to National Trust land and overlooking Lyme Bay. The pitches are mostly sheltered by hedging and well spaced on hardstandings. The facilities are excellent. There is a mixture of statics and tourers, but the tourers enjoy the best cliff-top positions. 9 acre site. 195 touring pitches. 45 hardstandings. Caravan pitches. Motorhome pitches. Tent pitches. 160 statics.

AA Pubs & Restaurants nearby: Shave Cross Inn, Bridport 01308 868358

Riverside Restaurant, Bridport 01308 422011

Anchor Inn, Chideock 01297 489215

Leisure: 🏊 ⛳ 🎢 🎱 🎵
Facilities: 🚿 ☀️ 🔌 ⚗️ 🏪 💈 🚻 Wi-fi ♻️ ℹ️
Services: 🚰 🔋 🍴 🛢️ 🚿 🅃 🍽️ 🛒 🛍️ 🛁 🚽
Within 3 miles: 🏇 ⛳ 💰 🛍️

Notes: Dogs must be kept on leads. Steam room, sauna, pitch & putt.

see advert on opposite page

PREMIER PARK

►►►►► **85% Bingham Grange Touring & Camping Park** *(SY478963)*

Melplash DT6 3TT
☎ 01308 488234 📄 01308 488426
e-mail: enquiries@binghamsfarm.co.uk
dir: *From A35 at Bridport take A3066 N towards Beaminster. Site on left after 3m*

🐕 🚐 👍

Open 16 Mar-Oct (rs Wed (high season), Tue & Wed (low season) restaurant & bar closed)

Last departure 11.00hrs

Set in a quiet rural location but only five miles from the Jurassic Coast, this adults-only park enjoys views over the west Dorset countryside. The mostly level pitches are attractively set amongst shrub beds and ornamental trees. There is an excellent restaurant with lounge bar and takeaway, and all facilities are of a high quality. A very dog-friendly site. 20 acre site. 150 touring pitches. 83 hardstandings. Caravan pitches. Motorhome pitches. Tent pitches.

AA Pubs & Restaurants nearby: George Hotel, Bridport 01308 423187

West Bay, Bridport 01308 422157

Riverside Restaurant, Bridport 01308 422011

Facilities: 🏪 ⊙ 🅿 ⚒ 🕭 🕒 🖄 🚿 📶 ♻ 🛈
Services: 🔌 🗑 🍴 🛢 🖉 🚰 🍽 ⛟
Within 3 miles: 🎣 ⛳ 🛒 U

Notes: Adults only, (no under 18s to stay or visit), no noise after 23.00hrs. Dogs must be kept on leads. Woodland walks & dog exercise trail leading to riverbanks.

CERNE ABBAS   Map 4 ST60

Places to visit

Athelhampton House & Gardens, ATHELHAMPTON 01305 848363 www.athelhampton.co.uk

Hardy's Cottage, DORCHESTER 01305 262366 www.nationaltrust.org.uk

Great for kids: Maiden Castle, DORCHESTER www.english-heritage.org.uk

►►► **86% Lyons Gate Caravan and Camping Park** *(ST660062)*

Lyons Gate DT2 7AZ
☎ 01300 345260
e-mail: info@lyons-gate.co.uk
dir: *Signed with direct access from A352, 3m N of Cerne Abbas*

* 🚐 fr £13 🚐 fr £13 👍 fr £13

Open all year

Last arrival 20.00hrs Last departure 11.30hrs

A peaceful park with pitches set out around the four attractive coarse fishing lakes. It is surrounded by mature woodland, with many footpaths and bridleways. Other easily accessible attractions include the Cerne Giant carved into the hills, the old market town of Dorchester, and the superb sandy beach at Weymouth. Holiday homes are now available for sale. 10 acre site. 90 touring pitches. 24 hardstandings. Caravan pitches. Motorhome pitches. Tent pitches. 14 statics.

AA Pubs & Restaurants nearby: The Piddle Inn, Piddletrenthide 01300 348468

Poachers Inn, Piddletrenthide 01300 348358

Leisure: ♨ 🎣 💻
Facilities: 🏪 ⊙ 🅿 ⚒ 🕭 🖄 🚿 🚽 📶 🛈
Services: 🔌 🗑 🛢 🖉
Within 3 miles: 🎣 ⛳ 🛒 U

Notes: Dogs must be kept on leads.

AA CAMPING CARD SITE

►► **69% Giants Head Caravan & Camping Park** *(ST675029)*

Giants Head Farm, Old Sherborne Rd DT2 7TR
☎ 01300 341242
e-mail: holidays@giantshead.co.uk
dir: *From Dorchester into town avoiding by-pass, at Top O'Town rdbt take A352 (Sherborne road), in 500yds right fork at BP (Loder's) garage, site signed*

* 🚐 £8-£16 🚐 £8-£16 👍 £8-£16

Open Etr-Oct (rs Etr shop & bar closed)

Last arrival anytime Last departure 13.00hrs

A pleasant, though rather basic, park set in Dorset downland near the Cerne Giant (the famous landmark figure cut into the chalk) with stunning views. This is a good stopover site, ideal for tenters and backpackers on the Ridgeway route. Holiday chalets to let. 4 acre site. 50 touring pitches. Caravan pitches. Motorhome pitches. Tent pitches.

continued

SERVICES: 🔌 Electric hook up 🗑 Launderette 🍴 Licensed bar 🛢 Calor Gas 🖉 Camping Gaz 🚽 Toilet fluid 🍽 Café/Restaurant ⛟ Fast Food/Takeaway 🔋 Battery charging 🚼 Baby care ⛟ Motorvan service point

ABBREVIATIONS: BH/bank hols-bank holidays Etr-Easter Whit-Whitsun dep-departure fr-from hrs-hours m-mile mdnt-midnight rdbt-roundabout rs-restricted service wk-week wknd-weekend 🚫 No credit cards 🚫 No dogs

See page 7 for details of the AA Camping Card Scheme

CERNE ABBAS continued

AA Pubs & Restaurants nearby: Greyhound Inn, Sydling St Nicholas 01300 341303

European Inn, Piddletrenthide 01300 348308

Facilities: �⊙☞⁂⊞🐕♻

Services: 🅿🗄🔋🥄🍽

Within 3 miles: 🎣🗄🖼

Notes: ⊛ Dogs must be kept on leads.

CHARMOUTH   Map 4 SY39

Places to visit

Forde Abbey, CHARD 01460 221290
www.fordeabbey.co.uk

Dorset County Museum, DORCHESTER
01305 262735 www.dorsetcountymuseum.org

Great for kids: Abbotsbury Swannery, ABBOTSBURY 01305 871858
www.abbotsbury-tourism.co.uk

PREMIER PARK

►►►►► 89% Wood Farm Caravan & Camping Park

Best of British

(SY356940)

Axminster Rd DT6 6BT
☎ 01297 560697 📠 01297 561243
e-mail: holidays@woodfarm.co.uk
web: www.woodfarm.co.uk
dir: *Site entered directly off A35 rdbt, on Axminster side of Charmouth*

* 🚐 £14-£28 🚌 £14-£28 ▲ £14-£28

Open Etr-Oct

Last arrival 19.00hrs Last departure noon

This top quality park is set amongst mature native trees with the various levels of the site falling away into a beautiful valley below. The park offers excellent facilities including family rooms and fully serviced pitches. The facilities throughout the park are spotless. At the bottom end of the park there is an excellent indoor swimming pool and leisure complex, plus the licensed, conservatory-style Offshore Café. There's a good children's play room plus tennis courts and a well-stocked, coarse-fishing lake. The park is well positioned on the Heritage Coast near Lyme Regis. Static holiday homes are also available for hire. 13 acre site. 216 touring pitches. 175 hardstandings. 20 seasonal pitches. Caravan pitches. Motorhome pitches. Tent pitches. 92 statics.

AA Pubs & Restaurants nearby: Pilot Boat Inn, Lyme Regis 01297 443157

Leisure: 🏊🏖🎠🔍🖥

Facilities: ↑⊙☞⁂🐕♿🕿🛡🌳🐕📶

Services: 🅿🗄🔋🛡🚿🔩🍽🛒🚮🚽

Within 3 miles: 🏌🚣🎣🖼◎🎿🗄🐴🎣⛵

Notes: No skateboards, scooters, roller skates or bikes. Dogs must be kept on leads.

►►►► 86% Newlands Caravan & Camping Park (SY374935)

GOLD SILVER

DT6 6RB
☎ 01297 560259 📠 01297 560787
e-mail: enq@newlandsholidays.co.uk
web: www.newlandsholidays.co.uk
dir: *4m W of Bridport on A35*

* 🚐 £14-£38 🚌 £14-£38 ▲ £14-£38

Open 10 Mar-4 Nov

Last arrival 22.30hrs Last departure 10.00hrs

A very smart site with excellent touring facilities. The park offers a full cabaret and entertainment programme for all ages, and boasts an indoor swimming pool with spa and an outdoor pool with water slide. Set on gently sloping ground in hilly countryside near the sea. Holiday homes and lodges are available for hire or sale. 23 acre site. 240 touring pitches. 52 hardstandings. Caravan pitches. Motorhome pitches. Tent pitches. 86 statics.

AA Pubs & Restaurants nearby: Pilot Boat Inn, Lyme Regis 01297 443157

Leisure: 🏊🏖🎠🖐🔍🖥🎶

Facilities: ↑⊙☞⁂♿🕿🛡🌳🐕📶 🖥♻🛈

Services: 🅿🗄🔩🛡🚿🔩🍽🔩🚮🚽

Within 3 miles: 🏌🚣🎣🖼◎🎿🗄🐴🎣⛵

Notes: Kid's club only during school hols.

►►► 84% Manor Farm Holiday Centre (SY368937)

DT6 6QL
☎ 01297 560226
e-mail: enquiries@manorfarmholidaycentre.co.uk
dir: *W on A35 to Charmouth, site 0.75m on right*

* 🚐 £14-£24 🚌 £14-£24 ▲ £14-£24

Open all year (rs End Oct-mid Mar statics only)

Last arrival 20.00hrs Last departure 10.00hrs

Set just a short walk from the safe sand and shingle beach at Charmouth, this popular family park offers a good range of facilities. Children enjoy the activity area and outdoor swimming pool (so do their parents!), and the park also offers a lively programme in the extensive bar and entertainment complex. Excellent new outdoor/indoor swimming pool, plus café, sun terrace and gym complex. 1- to 5-bedroom cottages are available for hire. 30 acre site. 400 touring pitches. 80 hardstandings. Caravan pitches. Motorhome pitches. Tent pitches. 29 statics.

AA Pubs & Restaurants nearby: Pilot Boat Inn, Lyme Regis 01297 443157

Leisure: 🏊🏖🎠🔍🎶

Facilities: ↑⊙☞⁂♿🕿🛡🌳🐕📶 ♻🛈

Services: 🅿🗄🔩🛡🚿🔩🍽🚮🚽🚽

Within 3 miles: 🏌🚣🎣🖼◎🎿🗄🐴🎣⛵

Notes: No skateboards. Dogs must be kept on leads.

CHIDEOCK

Places to visit

Branscombe - The Old Bakery, Manor Mill and Forge, BRANSCOMBE 01752 346585
www.nationaltrust.org.uk

Mapperton, BEAMINSTER 01308 862645
www.mapperton.com

Great for kids: Pecorama Pleasure Gardens, BEER 01297 21542 www.pecorama.info

---

LEISURE: 🏊 Indoor swimming pool 🏖 Outdoor swimming pool 🎠 Children's playground 🖐 Kid's club 🎾 Tennis court 🎱 Games room 📺 Separate TV room 🏌 9/18 hole golf course 🚣 Boats for hire 🎬 Cinema 🎶 Entertainment 🎣 Fishing ◎ Mini golf 🎿 Watersports 🏋 Gym ⚽ Sports field **Spa** ⛵ Stables
FACILITIES: 🛁 Bath 🚿 Shower ⊙ Electric shaver ☞ Hairdryer ⁂ Ice Pack Facility ♿ Disabled facilities 🕿 Public telephone 🏪 Shop on site or within 200yds 🚐 Mobile shop (calls at least 5 days a week) 🍴 BBQ area 🌳 Picnic area 📶 Wi-fi 🖥 Internet access ♻ Recycling 🛈 Tourist info 🐕 Dog exercise area

CHIDEOCK
Map 4 SY49

AA CAMPING CARD SITE

►►►► 83% Golden Cap Holiday Park (SY422919)

GOLD

Seatown DT6 6JX
☎ 01308 422139 & 426947 📠 01308 425672
e-mail: holidays@wdlh.co.uk
dir: On A35, in Chideock follow Seatown signs, site signed

🚐 £15.10-£25 🚎 £15.10-£25 ▲ £13-£22

Open 16 Mar-4 Nov

Last arrival 22.00hrs Last departure 11.00hrs

A grassy site, overlooking sea and beach and surrounded by National Trust parkland. This uniquely placed park slopes down to the sea, although pitches are generally level. A slight dip hides the view of the beach from the back of the park, but this area benefits from having trees, scrub and meadows, unlike the barer areas closer to the sea which do have a spectacular outlook. This makes an ideal base for touring Dorset and Devon. 11 acre site. 108 touring pitches. 24 hardstandings. Caravan pitches. Motorhome pitches. Tent pitches. 234 statics.

AA Pubs & Restaurants nearby: George Hotel, Bridport 01308 423187

West Bay, Bridport 01308 422157

Riverside Restaurant, Bridport 01308 422011

Leisure: ⚽

Facilities: 🏪⊙🅿✳🔧⚙☺🖥🚿🚽 WiFi ♻ 🅾

Services: 🚐🔌💧🧴✏🚻🍴🔋

Within 3 miles: ⬇🎣📷🔌

Notes: Dogs must be kept on leads. Fishing lake.

CHRISTCHURCH

Places to visit

Red House Museum & Gardens, CHRISTCHURCH 01202 482860 www.hants.gov.uk/museum/redhouse

Hurst Castle, HURST CASTLE 01590 642344 www.english-heritage.org.uk

Great for kids: Oceanarium, BOURNEMOUTH 01202 311993 www.oceanarium.co.uk

CHRISTCHURCH
Map 5 SZ19

PREMIER PARK

►►►►► 85% Meadowbank Holidays (SZ136946)

SILVER

Stour Way BH23 2PQ
☎ 01202 483597 📠 01202 483878
e-mail: enquiries@meadowbank-holidays.co.uk
web: www.meadowbank-holidays.co.uk
dir: A31 onto A338 towards Bournemouth. Take 1st exit after 5m then left towards Christchurch on B3073. Right at 1st rdbt into St Catherine's Way/River Way. Stour Way 3rd right, site at end of road

* 🚐 £10-£30 🚎 £10-£30

Open Mar-Oct

Last arrival 21.00hrs Last departure noon

A very smart park on the banks of the River Stour, with a colourful display of hanging baskets and flower-filled tubs placed around the superb reception area. An excellent new facility block was completed for 2011. Visitors can choose between the different pitch sizes, including luxury fully-serviced ones. There is also an excellent play area and a good shop on site. Statics are available for hire. 2 acre site. 41 touring pitches. 22 hardstandings. Caravan pitches. Motorhome pitches. 180 statics.

AA Pubs & Restaurants nearby: Ship in Distress, Christchurch 01202 485123

Splinters, Christchurch 01202 483454

Leisure: ⚽ 🎣

Facilities: 🚿🏪⊙🅿☺🖥🚿 WiFi ♻ 🅾

Services: 🚐🔌💧🧴🚻🔋

Within 3 miles: ⬇🎿🅷🔌📷🚶🔌🚲🔌∪

Notes: No pets. Fishing on site.

CORFE CASTLE
Map 4 SY98

Places to visit

Corfe Castle, CORFE CASTLE 01929 481294 www.nationaltrust.org.uk

Brownsea Island, BROWNSEA ISLAND 01202 707744 www.nationaltrust.org.uk

Great for kids: Swanage Railway, SWANAGE 01929 425800 www.swanagerailway.co.uk

►►►► 85% Corfe Castle Camping & Caravanning Club Site (SY953818)

GOLD

Bucknowle BH20 5PQ
☎ 01929 480280 & 0845 130 7633
dir: From Wareham A351 towards Swanage. In 4m turn right at foot of Corfe Castle signed Church Knowle. 0.75m right to site on left at top of lane

🚐 £19.25-£31.60 🚎 £19.25-£31.60
▲ £20.90-£31.60

Open Mar-Oct

Last arrival 20.00hrs Last departure noon

This lovely park is set in woodland near to the famous Corfe Castle. It has a smart new stone reception building and modern toilet and shower facilities, which are spotless. Although the site is sloping, pitches are level and include 33 spacious hardstandings. The site is perfect for visiting the many attractions of the Purbeck area including Swanage and Studland, as well has having the nearby station at Corfe for the Swanage Steam Railway. 5 acre site. 80 touring pitches. 33 hardstandings. 80 seasonal pitches. Caravan pitches. Motorhome pitches. Tent pitches.

AA Pubs & Restaurants nearby: Greyhound Inn, Corfe Castle 01929 480205

New Inn, Church Knowle 01929 480357

Leisure: ⚽

Facilities: 🏪⊙🅿✳🔧☺🖥♻ 🅾

Services: 🚐🔌💧🧴🔋🔌

Within 3 miles: ⬇🎿🅷🔌📷🚶🔌🚲🔌∪

Notes: Site gates closed between 23.00hrs-07.00hrs, any arrival time after 20.00hrs by prior arrangement. Dogs must be kept on leads.

SERVICES: 🚐 Electric hook up 🔌 Launderette 🍺 Licensed bar 🔥 Calor Gas 🧴 Camping Gaz 🚻 Toilet fluid 🍴 Café/Restaurant 🍟 Fast Food/Takeaway 🔋 Battery charging 🚼 Baby care ♨ Motorvan service point
ABBREVIATIONS: BH/bank hols-bank holidays Etr-Easter Whit-Whitsun dep-departure fr-from hrs-hours m-mile mdnt-midnight rdbt-roundabout rs-restricted service wk-week wknd-weekend ⊗ No credit cards ⊗ No dogs
See page 7 for details of the AA Camping Card Scheme

CORFE CASTLE *continued*

►► 82% Woody Hyde Camp Site

(SY974804)

Valley Rd BH20 5HT

☎ 01929 480274

e-mail: camp@woodyhyde.fsnet.co.uk

dir: *From Corfe Castle towards Swanage on A351, site approx 1m on right*

* £14 £14

Open Apr-Oct

A large grassy campsite in a sheltered location for tents and motorhomes only, set into three paddocks - one is dog free. There is a well-stocked shop on site, and a regular bus service located near the site entrance. This site offers traditional camping in a great location on Purbeck. Electric hook-ups and some hardstandings are now available. The new toilet/shower block should be open for the 2012 season. 13 acre site. 150 touring pitches. Motorhome pitches. Tent pitches.

AA Pubs & Restaurants nearby: Greyhound Inn, Corfe Castle 01929 480205

New Inn, Church Knowle 01929 480357

Facilities:

Services:

Within 3 miles:

Notes: No noise after 23.00hrs, no open fires. Dogs must be kept on leads.

DORCHESTER

See Cerne Abbas

DRIMPTON Map 4 ST40

Places to visit

Forde Abbey, CHARD 01460 221290 www.fordeabbey.co.uk

Mapperton, BEAMINSTER 01308 862645 www.mapperton.com

►►►► 80% Oathill Farm Touring and Camping Site *(ST404055)*

Oathill TA18 8PZ

☎ 01460 30234 01460 30234

e-mail: oathillfarm@btconnect.com

dir: *From Crewkerne take B3165. Site on left just after Clapton*

£17.50-£22.50 £17.50-£22.50 £13-£14.50

Open all year

Last arrival 20.00hrs Last departure noon

This small peaceful park is located on the borders of Somerset and Devon, with the Jurassic coast of Lyme Regis, Charmouth and Bridport only a short drive away. The modern facilities are spotless and there are hardstandings and fully-serviced pitches available. Lucy's Tea Room serves breakfast and meals. Three luxury lodges are available for hire. 9 acre site. 13 touring pitches. 13 hardstandings. 3 seasonal pitches. Caravan pitches. Motorhome pitches. Tent pitches. 3 statics.

AA Pubs & Restaurants nearby: The Wild Garlic, Beaminster 01308 861446

Leisure:

Facilities:

Services:

Within 3 miles:

Notes: No washing lines, no quad bikes, no noise after 23.00hrs. Separate recreational areas, landscaped fish ponds.

FERNDOWN Map 5 SU00

Places to visit

Poole Museum, POOLE 01202 262600 www.boroughofpoole.com/museums

Kingston Lacy, WIMBORNE 01202 883402 (Mon-Fri) www.nationaltrust.org.uk

Great for kids: Oceanarium, BOURNEMOUTH 01202 311993 www.oceanarium.co.uk

►►► 76% St Leonards Farm Caravan & Camping Park *(SU093014)*

Ringwood Rd, West Moors BH22 0AQ

☎ 01202 872637

e-mail: enquiries_stleonards@yahoo.co.uk

web: www.stleonardsfarm.biz

dir: *From E (Ringwood): entrance directly off A31, after crossing rdbt, opposite Texaco garage. From W: U-turn at rdbt after Texaco garage, turn left into site*

* £11-£16 £11-£16 £11-£16

Open Apr-Sep

Last departure 14.00hrs

A private road off the A31 leads to this well-screened park divided into paddocks, with spacious pitches. This is one of the nearest parks to Bournemouth with its many holiday amenities. 12 acre site. 151 touring pitches. Caravan pitches. Motorhome pitches. Tent pitches.

AA Pubs & Restaurants nearby: Les Bouviers, Wimborne Minster 01202 889555

Leisure:

Facilities:

Services:

Within 3 miles:

Notes: No large groups, no noise after 23.00hrs, no disposable BBQs, no gazebos. Dogs must be kept on leads.

HOLTON HEATH — Map 4 SY99

Places to visit

Royal Signals Museum, BLANDFORD FORUM
01258 482248 www.royalsignalsmuseum.com

Larmer Tree Gardens, TOLLARD ROYAL
01725 516228 www.larmertreegardens.co.uk

Great for kids: Moors Valley Country Park,
RINGWOOD 01425 470721
www.moors-valley.co.uk

84% Sandford Holiday Park (SY939916)

SILVER

Organford Rd BH16 6JZ
☎ 0844 335 3756 & 01202 631600
📠 01202 625678
e-mail:
touringandcamping@parkdeanholidays.com
web: www.parkdeantouring.com
dir: *A35 from Poole towards Dorchester, at
lights onto A351 towards Wareham. Right at
Holton Heath. Site 100yds on left*

* ⚡ £15.50-£44 ⛺ £15.50-£44 ▲ £12.50-£41

Open Mar-Oct (rs May-Sep outdoor pool open)

Last arrival 20.00hrs Last departure 10.00hrs

With touring pitches set individually in 20 acres
surrounded by woodland, this park offers a full
range of leisure activities and entertainment
for the whole family. The touring area, situated
at the far end of the park, is neat and well
maintained, and there are children's clubs
in the daytime and nightly entertainment.
A reception area with lounge, bar, café and
restaurant creates an excellent and attractive
entrance, with a covered area outside with
tables and chairs and well-landscaped
gardens. 64 acre site. 354 touring pitches. 20
hardstandings. 79 seasonal pitches. Caravan
pitches. Motorhome pitches. Tent pitches. 344
statics.

AA Pubs & Restaurants nearby: Kemps Country
House, Wareham 0845 862 0315

Greyhound Inn, Corfe Castle 01929 480205

New Inn, Church Knowle 01929 480357

Leisure: 🏊🏊♨♨🎱🎣🎵

Facilities: 🛁📶☺🍴🔥👶♿⚽🍴WiFi
🖥♻ℹ

Services: ⚡🖲🍴🔒⚗🚽🍴🔋⛽

Within 3 miles: 🚴🏇☂🐾◎🏊🎱🎱⛵

Notes: No noise after 23.00hrs, no motorised
scooters or carts, max 2 dogs per pitch. Dogs
must be kept on leads. Bowling, crazy golf, bike
hire, adventure playground.

see advert in preliminary section

HURN — Map 5 SZ19

Places to visit

Red House Museum & Gardens,
CHRISTCHURCH 01202 482860
www.hants.gov.uk/museum/redhouse

Oceanarium, BOURNEMOUTH 01202 311993
www.oceanarium.co.uk

NEW ▶▶ 83% Fillybrook Farm Touring Park (SZ128997)

Matchams Ln BH23 6AW
☎ 01202 478266
e-mail: enquiries@fillybrookfarm.co.uk
dir: *M27 junct 1, A31 to Ringwood. Continue
towards Poole, left immediately after Texaco
Garage signed Verwood & B3081, left into Hurn Ln
signed Matchams. Site on right in 4m*

* ⚡ £15-£18 ⛺ £15-£18 ▲ £15-£18

Open Etr-Oct

Last arrival 20.00hrs Last departure 11.00hrs

A small adults-only park well located on the edge
of Hurn Forest, with Bournemouth, Christchurch,
Poole and the New Forest within easy reach. The
facilities are both modern and very clean. A dry-
ski slope, with an adjoining restaurant and small
bar, is a short walk from the site. There is also a
separate rally field. 1 acre site. 18 touring pitches.
Caravan pitches. Motorhome pitches. Tent
pitches.

Facilities: 📶☺🍴🔥🍴♻ℹ

Services: ⚡🍴🔋 **Within 3 miles:** 🚴🐾◎⛵

Notes: Adults only. 🚫 No large groups, no
commercial vehicles. Dogs must be kept on leads.

LYME REGIS — Map 4 SY39

See also Charmouth

Places to visit

Marwood Hill Gardens, BARNSTAPLE
01271 342528 www.marwoodhillgarden.co.uk

Pecorama Pleasure Gardens, BEER
01297 21542 www.pecorama.info

Great for kids: The World of Country Life,
EXMOUTH 01395 274533
www.worldofcountrylife.co.uk

▶▶▶▶ 85% Shrubbery Touring Park (SY300914)

Rousdon DT7 3XW
☎ 01297 442227   📠 01297 446086
e-mail: enq@shrubberypark.co.uk
web: www.shrubberypark.co.uk
dir: *3m W of Lyme Regis on A3052 (coast road)*

⚡⛺▲

Open Apr-Oct

Last arrival 22.00hrs Last departure 11.00hrs

Mature trees enclose this peaceful park, which
has distant views of the lovely countryside. The
modern facilities are well kept, the hardstanding
pitches are spacious, and there is plenty of space
for children to play in the grounds. This park is
right on the Jurassic Coast bus route, which is
popular with visitors to this area. 10 acre site.
120 touring pitches. 10 hardstandings. Caravan
pitches. Motorhome pitches. Tent pitches.

AA Pubs & Restaurants nearby: Pilot Boat Inn,
Lyme Regis 01297 443157

Leisure: 🎱

Facilities: 📶☺🍴🔥👶♿🍴

Services: ⚡🖲🍴⚗

Within 3 miles: 🚴🏇☂🐾◎🏊🎱🎱

Notes: No motor scooters, roller skates or
skateboards, no groups (except rallies). Crazy golf.

LYME REGIS *continued*

AA CAMPING CARD SITE

►►► 83% *Hook Farm Caravan & Camping Park* (SY323930)

Gore Ln, Uplyme DT7 3UU
☎ 01297 442801 📱 01297 442801
e-mail: information@hookfarm-uplyme.co.uk
dir: *A35 onto B3165 towards Lyme Regis & Uplyme at Hunters Lodge pub. In 2m right into Gore Ln, site 400yds on right*

🚐 £12-£29 🚙 £12-£29 ⛺ £10-£29

Open 15 Mar-Oct (rs Low season shop closed)

Last arrival 21.00hrs Last departure 11.00hrs

Set in a peaceful and very rural location, the popular farm site enjoys lovely views of Lym Valley and is just a mile from the seaside at Lyme Regis. There are modern toilet facilities and good on-site amenities. Most pitches are level due to excellent terracing - a great site for tents. 5.5 acre site. 100 touring pitches. 4 hardstandings. Caravan pitches. Motorhome pitches. Tent pitches. 17 statics.

AA Pubs & Restaurants nearby: Pilot Boat Inn, Lyme Regis 01297 443157

Leisure: ⚐

Facilities: 📶☉🖍✳♿◷🖾🐾

Services: 🚐🖥🧺🚿

Within 3 miles: ⛳🎣🎿🏇▣◎♨🏕🏤🏦U

Notes: ⊗ No groups of 6 adults or more, no dangerous dog breeds.

LYTCHETT MATRAVERS

Places to visit

Brownsea Island, BROWNSEA ISLAND 01202 707744 www.nationaltrust.org.uk

Poole Museum, POOLE 01202 262600 www.boroughofpoole.com/museums

Great for kids: Swanage Railway, SWANAGE 01929 425800 www.swanagerailway.co.uk

---

LYTCHETT MATRAVERS   Map 4 SY99

AA CAMPING CARD SITE

►►► 78% Huntick Farm Caravan Park (SY955947)

Huntick Rd BH16 6BB
☎ 01202 622222
e-mail: huntickcaravans@btconnect.com
dir: *Between Lytchett Minster & Lytchett Matravers. From A31 take A350 towards Poole. Follow Lytchett Minster signs, then Lytchett Matravers signs. Huntick Rd by Red Cow pub*

* 🚐 £15.50-£21.50 🚙 £15.50-£21.50
⛺ £13.50-£28

Open Apr-Oct

Last arrival 21.00hrs Last departure noon

A really attractive little park nestling in rural surroundings edged by woodland, a mile from the village amenities of Lytchett Matravers. This neat grassy park is divided into three paddocks offering a peaceful location, yet it is close to the attractions of Poole and Bournemouth. 4 acre site. 30 touring pitches. Caravan pitches. Motorhome pitches. Tent pitches.

AA Pubs & Restaurants nearby: Coventry Arms, Corfe Mullen 01258 857284

Botany Bay Inne, Winterborne Zelston 01929 459227

Leisure: ⚐⚽

Facilities: 📶☉✳🐾

Services: 🚐

Within 3 miles: 🏤🏦

Notes: No ball games on site.

LYTCHETT MINSTER

Places to visit

Clouds Hill, BOVINGTON CAMP 01929 405616 www.nationaltrust.org.uk

Poole Museum, POOLE 01202 262600 www.boroughofpoole.com/museums

Great for kids: Monkey World-Ape Rescue Centre, WOOL 01929 462537 www.monkeyworld.org

---

LYTCHETT MINSTER   Map 4 SY99

> Regional Winner –
> AA South West of England
> Campsite of the Year 2012

AA CAMPING CARD SITE

PREMIER PARK

►►►►► 91% South Lytchett Manor Caravan & Camping Park (SY954926)

Best of British

Dorchester Rd BH16 6JB
☎ 01202 622577
e-mail: info@southlytchettmanor.co.uk
dir: *Exit A35 onto B3067, 1m E of Lytchett Minster, 600yds on right after village*

* 🚐 £15-£30 🚙 £15-£30 ⛺ £13-£28

Open Mar-2 Jan

Last arrival 21.00hrs Last departure 11.00hrs

Situated in the grounds of a historic manor house the park has modern facilities, which are spotless and well maintained. A warm and friendly welcome awaits at this lovely park which is well located for visiting Poole and Bournemouth; the Jurassic X53 bus route (Exeter to Poole) has a stop just outside the park. This park continues to improve each year. 20 acre site. 150 touring pitches. 80 hardstandings. Caravan pitches. Motorhome pitches. Tent pitches.

AA Pubs & Restaurants nearby: The Rising Sun, Poole 01202 771246

Guildhall Tavern, Poole 01202 671717

Leisure: ⚐⚽🎱▭

Facilities: 📶☉🖍✳♿◷🖾🐾📶
🖥♻ℹ

Services: 🚐🖥🔋🧺🆃🚿↧

Within 3 miles: ⛳🏇♨🏕🏤🏦U

Notes: No camp fires or Chinese lanterns. Dogs must be kept on leads.

LEISURE: 🏊 Indoor swimming pool 🏊 Outdoor swimming pool ⚐ Children's playground 🏐 Kid's club ⚲ Tennis court 🎱 Games room ▭ Separate TV room
⛳ 9/18 hole golf course ⛵ Boats for hire 🎬 Cinema ♫ Entertainment 🎣 Fishing ◎ Mini golf 🎿 Watersports 🏋 Gym ⚽ Sports field Spa U Stables
FACILITIES: 🛁 Bath 🚿 Shower ☉ Electric shaver 🖍 Hairdryer ✳ Ice Pack Facility ♿ Disabled facilities ◷ Public telephone 🖾 Shop on site or within 200yds
🚐 Mobile shop (calls at least 5 days a week) 🍴 BBQ area 🌲 Picnic area 📶 Wi-fi 🌐 Internet access ♻ Recycling ℹ Tourist info 🐾 Dog exercise area

ORGANFORD — Map 4 SY99

Places to visit

Tolpuddle Martyrs Museum, TOLPUDDLE 01305 848237 www.tolpuddlemartyrs.org.uk

Kingston Lacy, WIMBORNE 01202 883402 (Mon-Fri) www.nationaltrust.org.uk

Great for kids: Farmer Palmer's Farm Park, ORGANFORD 01202 622022 www.farmerpalmers.co.uk

AA CAMPING CARD SITE

▶▶▶▶ 84% Pear Tree Holiday Park

(SY938915)

Organford Rd, Holton Heath BH16 6LA
☎ 0844 272 9504
e-mail: enquiries@peartreepark.co.uk
web: www.peartreepark.co.uk
dir: *From Poole take A35 towards Dorchester, onto A351 towards Wareham, at 1st lights turn right, site 300yds on left*

* 🚐 £20-£28 🚗 £20-£28 ▲ £18-£25

Open Mar-Oct

Last arrival 19.00hrs Last departure 11.00hrs

A quiet, sheltered country park with many colourful flowerbeds, and toilet facilities that offer quality and comfort. The touring area is divided into terraces with mature hedges for screening, with a separate level tenting area on the edge of woodland. The friendly atmosphere at this attractive park help to ensure a relaxing holiday.

A bridle path leads into Wareham Forest. 9 acre site. 154 touring pitches. 82 hardstandings. Caravan pitches. Motorhome pitches. Tent pitches. 40 statics.

Pear Tree Holiday Park

AA Pubs & Restaurants nearby: Coventry Arms, Corfe Mullen 01258 857284

Botany Bay Inne, Winterborne Zelston 01929 459227

Leisure: 🏊

Facilities: 🏪⊙🅿✳🕙👷♻🅱

Services: 🔌🛁🔒♿🚽🔋

Within 3 miles: ◎

Notes: No noise after 22.30hrs. Dogs must be kept on leads.

see advert below

OWERMOIGNE — Map 4 SY78

Places to visit

RSPB Nature Reserve Radipole Lake, WEYMOUTH 01305 778313 www.rspb.org.uk

Clouds Hill, BOVINGTON CAMP 01929 405616 www.nationaltrust.org.uk

Great for kids: Weymouth Sea Life Adventure Park & Marine Sanctuary, WEYMOUTH 0871 423 2110 www.sealifeeurope.com

AA CAMPING CARD SITE

▶▶▶ 77% Sandyholme Holiday

Park (SY768863)

Moreton Rd DT2 8HZ
☎ 01308 422139 & 426947
e-mail: sandyholme@wdlh.co.uk
web: www.wdlh.co.uk
dir: *From A352 (Wareham to Dorchester road) turn right to Owermoigne for 1m. Site on left*

* 🚐 £14.60-£21.90 🚗 £14.60-£21.90 ▲ £12-£17.50

Open 16 Mar-4 Nov (rs Etr)

Last arrival 22.00hrs Last departure 11.00hrs

A pleasant site in a tree-lined rural setting within easy reach of the coast at Lulworth Cove, and handy for several seaside resorts. The facilities are very good, including a superb toilet block, and good food is available in the lounge/bar. 6 acre site. 46 touring pitches. Caravan pitches. Motorhome pitches. Tent pitches. 52 statics.

continued

SERVICES: 🔌 Electric hook up 🛁 Launderette 🍺 Licensed bar 🪣 Calor Gas ⊘ Camping Gaz 🚽 Toilet fluid 🍽 Café/Restaurant 🍟 Fast Food/Takeaway 🔋 Battery charging 🚼 Baby care ♿ Motorvan service point
ABBREVIATIONS: BH/bank hols-bank holidays Etr-Easter Whit-Whitsun dep-departure fr-from hrs-hours m-mile mdnt-midnight rdbt-roundabout rs-restricted service wk-week wknd-weekend ◎ No credit cards ⊗ No dogs   See page 7 for details of the AA Camping Card Scheme

OWERMOIGNE *continued*

AA Pubs & Restaurants nearby: Smugglers Inn, Osmington Mills 01305 833125

Lulworth Cove Inn, West Lulworth 01929 400333

Castle Inn, West Lulworth 01929 400311

Leisure: ⚑ ⊕ ✎

Facilities: ⬈ ☞ ✻ ☖ ⊕ 🗟 ⌁ ⚐ 📶 ♺ ❶

Services: 🖳 🗟 🛢 ✐ 🔲 🛒 🜄

Within 3 miles: ✐ 🗟 🗟

Notes: Dogs must be kept on leads. Table tennis, wildlife lake.

POOLE

See also Lytchett Minster, Organford & Wimborne Minster

Places to visit

Compton Acres Gardens, CANFORD CLIFFS
01202 700778 www.comptonacres.co.uk

Brownsea Island, BROWNSEA ISLAND
01202 707744 www.nationaltrust.org.uk

Great for kids: Oceanarium, BOURNEMOUTH
01202 311993 www.oceanarium.co.uk

POOLE

Map 4 SZ09

86% Rockley Park
(SY982909)

Hamworthy BH15 4LZ
☎ 0871 231 0880   📠 01202 683159
e-mail: rockleypark@haven.com
dir: M27 junct 1, A31 to Poole centre, then follow signs to site

🚐 � 🛖

Open mid Mar-end Oct (rs mid Mar-May & Sep-Oct some facilities may be reduced)

Last departure 10.00hrs

A complete holiday experience, including a wide range of day and night entertainment, and plenty of sports and leisure activities, notably watersports. There is also mooring and launching from the park. The touring area has 60 fully serviced pitches and an excellent toilet and shower block. A great base for all the family set in a good location to explore Poole or Bournemouth. 90 acre site. 60 touring pitches. 60 hardstandings. Caravan pitches. Motorhome pitches. Tent pitches. 1077 statics.

AA Pubs & Restaurants nearby: The Rising Sun, Poole 01202 771246

Guildhall Tavern, Poole 01202 671717

Leisure: ⚑ ⊕ ⚑ 🡣 ⚒ ✎ 🎵 Spa

Facilities: ⬈ ⊙ ☞ ✻ ☖ 🗟 ⌁ 📶 ♺ ❶

Services: 🖳 🗟 ⚑ 🔲 🍴 🛒

Within 3 miles: ⚓ 🎏 ✐ ◎ 🡣 🗟 🗟

Notes: Max 2 dogs per booking, certain dog breeds banned, no commercial vehicles, no bookings by persons under 21yrs unless a family booking. Dogs must be kept on leads. Sailing school.

see advert below

▶▶▶ **76%** *Beacon Hill Touring Park* *(SY977945)*

Blandford Road North BH16 6AB
☎ 01202 631631   📠 01202 624388
e-mail: bookings@beaconhilltouringpark.co.uk
dir: On A350, 0.25m N of junct with A35, 3m NW of Poole

🚐 🚐 🛖

Open Etr-end Oct (rs Low & mid season some services closed/restricted opening)

Last arrival 23.00hrs Last departure 11.00hrs

Set in an attractive, wooded area with conservation very much in mind. There are two large ponds for coarse fishing within the grounds, and the terraced pitches, with fine views, are informally sited so that visitors can choose their favourite spot. The outdoor swimming pool and tennis court are popular during the summer

---

LEISURE: ⚑ Indoor swimming pool ⚑ Outdoor swimming pool ⚑ Children's playground 🡣 Kid's club ⚒ Tennis court ✎ Games room 🖵 Separate TV room
🡣 9/18 hole golf course 🚣 Boats for hire 🎞 Cinema 🎵 Entertainment ✐ Fishing ◎ Mini golf 🡣 Watersports 🡣 Gym ⊕ Sports field **Spa** ♨ Stables
FACILITIES: 🛁 Bath 🚿 Shower ⊙ Electric shaver ☞ Hairdryer ✻ Ice Pack Facility ☖ Disabled facilities ⌁ Public telephone 🗟 Shop on site or within 200yds
📇 Mobile shop (calls at least 5 days a week) ⌁ BBQ area ⌁ Picnic area 📶 Wi-fi ▪ Internet access ♺ Recycling ❶ Tourist info ⌁ Dog exercise area

period. 30 acre site. 170 touring pitches. 10 hardstandings. Caravan pitches. Motorhome pitches. Tent pitches.

AA Pubs & Restaurants nearby: The Rising Sun, Poole 01202 771246

Guildhall Tavern, Poole 01202 671717

Leisure: ⟶⚘♨♣⌼

Facilities: ♙☉ℱ☀♿⌂🍴🛒 Wi-Fi

Services: ☎🗑🍺🅣🍴🎪🛗

Within 3 miles: ⤋♞🅟ℰ◎⛴🖼🗑☉

Notes: Groups of young people not accepted during high season.

PORTESHAM   Map 4 SY68

Places to visit

Tutankhamun Exhibition, DORCHESTER 01305 269571 www.tutankhamun-exhibition.co.uk

Maiden Castle, DORCHESTER www.english-heritage.org.uk

Great for kids: Teddy Bear Museum, DORCHESTER 01305 266040 www.teddybearmuseum.co.uk

▶▶▶▶ 80% Portesham Dairy Farm Campsite (SY602854)

Weymouth DT3 4HG
☎ **01305 871297**
e-mail: info@porteshamdairyfarm.co.uk
dir: From Dorchester on A35 towards Bridport. In 5m left at Winterbourne Abbas, follow Portesham signs. Through village, left at Kings Arms pub, site 350yds on right

* ⊞ £11.50-£28.50 ⚏ £11.50-£28.50 Ⓐ £11.50-£28.50

Open mid Mar-Oct

Last arrival 21.00hrs Last departure 16.00hrs

Located at the edge of the picturesque village of Portesham, this family run, level park is part of a small working farm in a quiet rural location. Near the site entrance is a pub where meals are served, and that has a garden for children. Fully serviced and seasonal pitches available. 8 acre site. 90 touring pitches. 61 hardstandings. Caravan pitches. Motorhome pitches. Tent pitches.

AA Pubs & Restaurants nearby: Manor Hotel, West Bexington 01308 897660

Leisure: ⟑

Facilities: ♙☉ℱ☀♿⌂🍴🛒🐾🛈

Services: ☎🗑🍺⌀

Within 3 miles: 🅟🖼🗑

Notes: No commercial vehicles, minimal noise after 22.00hrs. Dogs must be kept on leads. Caravan storage.

PUNCKNOWLE   Map 4 SY58

Places to visit

Dinosaur Museum, DORCHESTER 01305 269880 www.thedinosaurmuseum.com

Hardy's Cottage, DORCHESTER 01305 262366 www.nationaltrust.org.uk

Great for kids: Abbotsbury Swannery, ABBOTSBURY 01305 871858 www.abbotsbury-tourism.co.uk

AA CAMPING CARD SITE

▶▶ 84% Home Farm Caravan and Campsite (SY535887)

Home Farm, Rectory Ln DT2 9BW
☎ **01308 897258**
dir: Dorchester towards Bridport on A35, left at start of dual carriageway, at hill bottom right to Litton Cheney. Through village, 2nd left to Puncknowle (Hazel Ln). Left at T-junct, left at phone box. Site 150mtrs on right. Caravan route: approach via A35 Bridport, then Swyre on B3157, continue to Swyre Lane & Rectory Lane

⊞ ⚏ Ⓐ

Open Etr or Apr-Oct

Last arrival 21.00hrs Last departure noon

A quiet site hidden away on the edge of this little hamlet. It offers sweeping views of the Dorset countryside from most pitches, and is just five miles from Abbotsbury, and one and a half miles from the South West Coastal Footpath. A really good base from which to tour this attractive area. 6.5 acre site. 47 touring pitches. Caravan pitches. Motorhome pitches. Tent pitches.

AA Pubs & Restaurants nearby: Crown Inn, Puncknowle 01308 897711

Anchor Inn, Burton Bradstock 01308 897228

Manor Hotel, West Bexington 01308 897660

Facilities: ♙☉ℱ☀♲⌂♻ 🛈

Services: ☎🗑🍺⌀🛗⌁

Within 3 miles: 🅟

Notes: ⊛ No cats. No wood burning fires, skateboards, rollerblades, loud music or motorised toys. Dogs must be kept on leads. Calor gas exchange only.

ST LEONARDS   Map 5 SU10

Places to visit

Rockbourne Roman Villa, ROCKBOURNE 0845 603 5635 www.hants.gov.uk/rockbourne-roman-villa

Red House Museum & Gardens, CHRISTCHURCH 01202 482860 www.hants.gov.uk/museum/redhouse

Great for kids: Moors Valley Country Park, RINGWOOD 01425 470721 www.moors-valley.co.uk

PREMIER PARK

▶▶▶▶▶ 84% Shamba Holidays (SU105029)

230 Ringwood Rd BH24 2SB
☎ **01202 873302** 🖷 **01202 873392**
e-mail: enquiries@shambaholidays.co.uk
web: www.shambaholidays.co.uk
dir: From Poole on A31, pass Texaco garage on left, straight on at next 2 rdbts, 100yds, left into Eastmoors Lane. Site 0.25m on right (just past Woodman Inn)

⊞ ⚏ Ⓐ

Open Mar-Oct (rs Low season some facilities only open at wknds)

Last arrival 22.00hrs Last departure 11.00hrs

This top quality park has excellent modern facilities particularly suited to families. You can be certain of a warm welcome by the friendly staff. There is a really good indoor/outdoor heated pool, plus a tasteful bar supplying a good range of meals. The park is well located for visiting the

continued

SERVICES: ☎ Electric hook up 🗑 Launderette 🍺 Licensed bar 🅰 Calor Gas ⌀ Camping Gaz 🅣 Toilet fluid 🍴 Café/Restaurant 🛗 Fast Food/Takeaway 🔋 Battery charging 🍼 Baby care ⌁ Motorvan service point
ABBREVIATIONS: BH/bank hols-bank holidays Etr-Easter Whit-Whitsun dep-departure fr-from hrs-hours m-mile mdnt-midnight rdbt-roundabout rs-restricted service wk-week wknd-weekend ⊛ No credit cards ⊗ No dogs   See page 7 for details of the AA Camping Card Scheme

ST LEONARDS *continued*

south coast, which is just a short drive away, and also for the New Forest National Park. 7 acre site. 150 touring pitches. Caravan pitches. Motorhome pitches. Tent pitches.

Shamba Holidays

AA Pubs & Restaurants nearby: Old Beams Inn, Ibsley 01425 473387

Leisure: 🏊🏊♨Ⓜ☺🔍

Facilities: 🛁🚿☺🖊✳🚿🕙🛒🚻

Services: 🔌🗑️🔃🚰⚙️Ⓣ🍴🛒🚮

Within 3 miles: 🎣🏌️🛒🛍️🎰♺

Notes: No large groups, no commercial vehicles. Phone card top-up facility.

see advert below

▶▶▶▶ 83% **Back of Beyond Touring Park** *(SU103034)*

234 Ringwood Rd BH24 2SB
☎ 01202 876968 📠 01202 876968
e-mail: melandsuepike@aol.com
web: www.backofbeyondtouringpark.co.uk
dir: *From E: on A31 over Little Chef rdbt, pass St Leonard's Hotel, at next rdbt U-turn into lane immediately left to site at end of lane. From W: on A31 pass Texaco garage & Woodman Inn, immediately left to site*

* 🚐 £17.50-£25 🚍 £17.50-£25 ▲ £17.50-£20.50

Open Mar-Oct

Last arrival 19.00hrs Last departure noon

Set well off the beaten track in natural woodland surroundings, with its own river and lake, yet close to many attractions. This tranquil park is run by keen, friendly owners, and the quality facilities are for adults only. 28 acre site. 80 touring pitches. 20 seasonal pitches. Caravan pitches. Motorhome pitches. Tent pitches.

AA Pubs & Restaurants nearby: Old Beams Inn, Ibsley 01425 473387

Facilities: 🖊☺🖊✳🕙🛒🚻🚮🐕♺ ℹ️

Services: 🔌🗑️🔃🚰⚙️Ⓣ🛒🚮

Within 3 miles: 🎣🏌️🎰🛒🛍️♺

Notes: Adults only. No commercial vehicles. Lake & river fishing, 9-hole pitch & putt course, boules.

▶▶▶ 78% **Forest Edge Touring Park** *(SU104024)*

229 Ringwood Rd BH24 2SD
☎ 01590 648331 📠 01590 645610
e-mail: holidays@shorefield.co.uk
dir: *From E: on A31 over 1st rdbt (Little Chef), pass St Leonards Hotel, left at next rdbt into Boundary Ln, site 100yds on left. From W: on A31 pass Texaco garage & Woodman Inn, right at rdbt into Boundary Ln*

🚐 £12-£36 🚍 £12-£36 ▲ £10-£36

Open Feb-3 Jan (rs School & summer hols pool open)

Last arrival 21.00hrs Last departure 10.00hrs

A tree-lined park set in grassland with plenty of excellent amenities for all the family, including an outdoor heated swimming pool and toddlers' pool, an adventure playground, and two launderettes. Visitors are invited to use the superb leisure club plus all amenities and entertainment at the sister site of Oakdene Forest Park, which is less than a mile away. Some pitches may experience some traffic noise from the nearby A31. 9 acre site. 72 touring pitches. 29 seasonal pitches. Caravan, motorhome & tent pitches. 30 statics.

AA Pubs & Restaurants nearby: Old Beams Inn, Ibsley 01425 473387

Leisure: ♨Ⓜ🔍

Facilities: 🖊☺🖊✳🕙🛒♺ ℹ️

Services: 🔌🗑️🔃🚰⚙️Ⓣ

Within 3 miles: 🎣🏌️🎰🛒🛍️♺

Notes: Families & couples only. 1 dog & 1 car per pitch, no gazebos. Rallies welcome. Dogs must be kept on leads.

LEISURE: 🏊 Indoor swimming pool ♨ Outdoor swimming pool Ⓜ Children's playground 🎣 Kid's club 🎾 Tennis court 🔍 Games room 📺 Separate TV room 🎣 9/18 hole golf course ⛵ Boats for hire 🎬 Cinema 🎵 Entertainment 🎣 Fishing ◎ Mini golf 🏄 Watersports 🏋️ Gym ☀ Sports field **Spa** ♺ Stables

FACILITIES: 🛁 Bath 🚿 Shower ☺ Electric shaver 🖊 Hairdryer ✳ Ice Pack Facility ♿ Disabled facilities 🕙 Public telephone 🛒 Shop on site or within 200yds 🛍️ Mobile shop (calls at least 5 days a week) 🍴 BBQ area 🪑 Picnic area 📶 Wi-fi 💻 Internet access ♺ Recycling ℹ️ Tourist info 🐕 Dog exercise area

SHAFTESBURY — Map 4 ST82

Places to visit

Shaftesbury Abbey Museum & Garden, SHAFTESBURY 01747 852910 www.shaftesburyheritage.org.uk

Royal Signals Museum, BLANDFORD FORUM 01258 482248 www.royalsignalsmuseum.com

Great for kids: Sherborne Castle, SHERBORNE 01935 813182 (office) www.sherbornecastle.com

▶▶▶ 74% Blackmore Vale Caravan & Camping Park (ST835233)

Sherborne Causeway SP7 9PX
☎ 01747 851523 & 851497 📠 01747 851671
e-mail: info@dche.co.uk
dir: *From Shaftesbury's Ivy Cross rdbt take A30 signed Sherborne. Site 2m on right*

* 🚐 £14-£16 🚎 £12-£14 ▲ £10

Open all year

Last arrival 21.00hrs

Improvements continue at this pleasant touring park with spacious pitches and well-maintained facilities. There is a fully-equipped gym which is open to visitors, and there are plans for a new toilet block. Blackmore Vale, about two miles from Shaftesbury, is set behind a caravan sales showground and dealership. 5 acre site. 26 touring pitches. 6 hardstandings. Caravan pitches. Motorhome pitches. Tent pitches. 20 statics.

AA Pubs & Restaurants nearby: Kings Arms Inn, Gillingham 01747 838325

Coppleridge Inn, Motcombe 01747 851980

Le Chanterelle, Shaftesbury 01747 852821

Leisure: 🎯
Facilities: 🌳☀❄🐕🚿🛒♻ℹ
Services: 🚐🔋🎫🚽🍴🔌🛒
Within 3 miles: 🎣💰🛒♻U

Notes: Dogs must be kept on leads. Caravan sales & accessories.

SIXPENNY HANDLEY — Map 4 ST91

Places to visit

Larmer Tree Gardens, TOLLARD ROYAL 01725 516228 www.larmertreegardens.co.uk

Shaftesbury Abbey Museum & Garden, SHAFTESBURY 01747 852910 www.shaftesburyheritage.org.uk

Great for kids: Moors Valley Country Park, RINGWOOD 01425 470721 www.moors-valley.co.uk

▶▶▶▶ 84% Church Farm Caravan & Camping Park (ST994173)

The Bungalow, Church Farm, High St SP5 5ND
☎ 01725 552563 & 07766 677525
e-mail: churchfarmcandcpark@yahoo.co.uk
dir: *1m S of Handley Hill rdbt. Exit for Sixpenny Handley, right by school, site 300yds by church*

🚐 £15-£17 🚎 £15-£17 ▲ £15-£17

Open all year (rs Nov-Mar 10 vans max)

Last arrival 21.00hrs Last departure 11.00hrs

A spacious, open park located within the Cranborne Chase in an Area of Outstanding Natural Beauty. There is a first-class facility block with good private facilities and an excellent café/restaurant. The pretty village of Sixpenny Handley with all its amenities is just 200 yards away. 10 acre site. 35 touring pitches. 4 hardstandings. 5 seasonal pitches. Caravan pitches. Motorhome pitches. Tent pitches. 2 statics.

AA Pubs & Restaurants nearby: Museum Inn, Farnham 01725 516261

Drovers Inn, Gussage All Saints 01258 840084

Leisure: 🎱
Facilities: 🌳☀❄♿🚿🐕📶♻ℹ
Services: 🚐🔋🎫🛢🚽🍴🔌🛒🚻
Within 3 miles: ♿💰

Notes: Quiet after 23.00hrs. Dogs must be kept on leads. Caravan storage, use of fridge/freezer & microwave.

SWANAGE — Map 5 SZ07

Places to visit

Corfe Castle, CORFE CASTLE 01929 481294 www.nationaltrust.org.uk

Brownsea Island, BROWNSEA ISLAND 01202 707744 www.nationaltrust.org.uk

Great for kids: Swanage Railway, SWANAGE 01929 425800 www.swanagerailway.co.uk

▶▶▶▶ 83% Ulwell Cottage Caravan Park (SZ019809)

SILVER

Ulwell Cottage, Ulwell BH19 3DG
☎ 01929 422823 📠 01929 421500
e-mail: enq@ulwellcottagepark.co.uk
web: www.ulwellcottagepark.co.uk
dir: *From Swanage N for 2m on unclass road towards Studland*

🚐🚎▲

Open Mar-7 Jan (rs Mar-Spring BH & mid Sep-early Jan takeaway closed, shop open variable hrs)

Last arrival 22.00hrs Last departure 11.00hrs

Nestling under the Purbeck Hills and surrounded by scenic walks, this park is only two miles from the beach. A family-run park that caters well for families and couples, and offers a toilet and shower block complete with good family rooms, all appointed to a high standard. There is a good indoor swimming pool and village inn offering a good range of meals. 13 acre site. 77 touring pitches. 19 hardstandings. Caravan pitches. Motorhome pitches. Tent pitches. 140 statics.

AA Pubs & Restaurants nearby: Bankes Arms Hotel, Studland 01929 450225

Square and Compass, Worth Matravers 01929 439229

Leisure: 🏊♿
Facilities: 🌳☀❄♿🚿🐕📶♻ℹ
Services: 🚐🔋🎫🛢🚽🍴🛒
Within 3 miles: ♿⚓🎣🎯◎💰🛒♻U

see advert on page 202

SERVICES: 🔌 Electric hook up 🧺 Launderette 🍺 Licensed bar 🔥 Calor Gas ⛽ Camping Gaz 🚽 Toilet fluid 🍴 Café/Restaurant 🍟 Fast Food/Takeaway 🔋 Battery charging 🍼 Baby care ⛽ Motorvan service point
ABBREVIATIONS: BH/bank hols-bank holidays Etr-Easter Whit-Whitsun dep-departure fr-from hrs-hours m-mile mdnt-midnight rdbt-roundabout rs-restricted service wk-week wknd-weekend 💳 No credit cards 🚫 No dogs
See page 7 for details of the AA Camping Card Scheme

SWANAGE *continued*

AA CAMPING CARD SITE

▶▶▶ 77% Herston Caravan & Camping Park *(SZ018785)*

Washpond Ln BH19 3DJ
☎ 01929 422932　📠 01929 423888
e-mail: office@herstonleisure.co.uk
dir: *From Wareham on A351 towards Swanage. Washpond Ln on left just after 'Welcome to Swanage' sign*

* 🚐 £20-£40　🚎 £20-£40　⛺ £15-£50

Open all year

Set in a rural area, with extensive views of the Purbecks, this tree-lined park has many full facility pitches and quality toilet facilities. Herston Halt is within walking distance, a stop for the famous Swanage steam railway between the town centre and Corfe Castle. There are also yurts available for hire. 10 acre site. 100 touring pitches. 71 hardstandings. Caravan pitches. Motorhome pitches. Tent pitches. 5 statics. 6 bell tents/yurts.

AA Pubs & Restaurants nearby: Bankes Arms Hotel, Studland 01929 450225

Square and Compass, Worth Matravers 01929 439229

Leisure: ⋀

Facilities: 🆘⊙🅿✳🔥🛐🍴🚽 WiFi ♻ ❶

Services: 🔌🖥🔧🧺🚰🍴🛒🚮♻

Within 3 miles: ↕🚴🎯🏇🅿◎⛴📍⛳🎳⛵

Notes: No noise after 23.00hrs. Dogs must be kept on leads.

▶▶ 73% Acton Field Camping Site *(SY991785)*

Acton Field, Langton Matravers BH19 3HS
☎ 01929 424184 & 439424　📠 01929 424184
e-mail: enquiries@actonfieldcampsite.co.uk
dir: *From A351 right after Corfe Castle onto B3069 to Langton Matravers, 2nd right after village sign (bridleway)*

🚐 🚎 ⛺

Open mid Jul-early Sep (rs Apr-Oct open for organised groups)

Last arrival 22.00hrs Last departure noon

The informal campsite, bordered by farmland on the outskirts of Langton Matravers, now has upgraded toilet facilities. There are superb views of the Purbeck Hills and towards the Isle of Wight, and a footpath leads to the coastal path. The site occupies what was once a stone quarry, and rock pegs may be required. 7 acre site. 80 touring pitches. Caravan pitches. Motorhome pitches. Tent pitches.

AA Pubs & Restaurants nearby: Bankes Arms Hotel, Studland 01929 450225

Square and Compass, Worth Matravers 01929 439229

Facilities: 🆘⊙✳🔥♻

Services: 🚰 **Within 3 miles:** ↕🚴🏇🅿◎⛴⛳🎳⛵

Notes: 🚫 No open fires, no noise after mdnt. Dogs must be kept on leads.

LEISURE: 🏊 Indoor swimming pool　🏊 Outdoor swimming pool　⋀ Children's playground　🪀 Kid's club　🎾 Tennis court　🎱 Games room　📺 Separate TV room
↕ 9/18 hole golf course　⛵ Boats for hire　🎬 Cinema　🎵 Entertainment　🎣 Fishing　⛳ Mini golf　🏄 Watersports　🏋 Gym　🏟 Sports field　**Spa**　⛎ Stables
FACILITIES: 🛁 Bath　🚿 Shower　🔌 Electric shaver　🗲 Hairdryer　✳ Ice Pack Facility　♿ Disabled facilities　📞 Public telephone　🛒 Shop on site or within 200yds
🏪 Mobile shop (calls at least 5 days a week)　🍴 BBQ area　🪵 Picnic area　WiFi Wi-fi　🖥 Internet access　♻ Recycling　❶ Tourist info　🐕 Dog exercise area

THREE LEGGED CROSS — Map 5 SU00

Places to visit

Portland Castle, PORTLAND 01305 820539
www.english-heritage.org.uk

Moors Valley Country Park, RINGWOOD
01425 470721 www.moors-valley.co.uk

Great for kids: Monkey World-Ape Rescue
Centre, WOOL 01929 462537
www.monkeyworld.org

►►►► 79% Woolsbridge Manor Farm Caravan Park

(SU099052)

BH21 6RA
☎ 01202 826369 📠 01202 820603
e-mail: woolsbridge@btconnect.com
web: www.woolsbridgemanorcaravanpark.co.uk
dir: *From Ringwood take A31 towards Bournemouth. Approx 1m follow signs for Three Legged Cross & Horton. Site 2m on right*

🚐 🚐 ▲

Open Mar-Oct

Last arrival 20.00hrs Last departure 10.30hrs

A small farm site with spacious pitches on a level field. This quiet site is an excellent central base for touring the New Forest, Salisbury and the south coast, and is close to Moors Valley Country Park for outdoor family activities. Facilities are good and very clean and there are excellent family rooms available. 6.75 acre site. 60 touring pitches. Caravan pitches. Motorhome pitches. Tent pitches.

AA Pubs & Restaurants nearby: Old Beams Inn, Ibsley 01425 473387

Leisure: ⚙

Facilities: 🏕⊙🅿✳🕏⚘🔥✕

Services: 🔌🔴🛢🚿🧴🚽🔋

Within 3 miles: 🚶🎣🏇🛒🎯↺

Notes: Dogs must be kept on leads.

WAREHAM — Map 4 SY98

Places to visit

Compton Acres Gardens, CANFORD CLIFFS
01202 700778 www.comptonacres.co.uk

Brownsea Island, BROWNSEA ISLAND
01202 707744 www.nationaltrust.org.uk

Great for kids: Oceanarium, BOURNEMOUTH
01202 311993 www.oceanarium.co.uk

AA CAMPING CARD SITE

PREMIER PARK

►►►►► 91% Wareham Forest Tourist Park

(SY894912)

North Trigon BH20 7NZ
☎ 01929 551393 📠 01929 558321
e-mail: holiday@warehamforest.co.uk
dir: *Telephone for directions*

🚐 🚐 ▲

Open all year (rs Off-peak season limited services)

Last arrival 21.00hrs Last departure 11.00hrs

A woodland park within the tranquil Wareham Forest, with its many walks and proximity to Poole, Dorchester and the Purbeck coast. Two luxury blocks, with combined washbasin and toilets for total privacy, maintain a high standard of cleanliness. A heated outdoor swimming pool, off licence, shop and games room add to the pleasure of a stay on this top quality park. 55 acre site. 200 touring pitches. 70 hardstandings. 70 seasonal pitches. Caravan pitches. Motorhome pitches. Tent pitches.

AA Pubs & Restaurants nearby: Kemps Country House, Wareham 0845 862 0315

Greyhound Inn, Corfe Castle 01929 480205

New Inn, Church Knowle 01929 480357

Leisure: ⛱ ⚙ 🔍

Facilities: 🏕⊙🅿✳🕏⚘🔥✕ 🛜 ♻ ❓

Services: 🔌🔴🛢🚿🚽🔋

Within 3 miles: 🚶🎯🎣🛒🛒↺

Notes: Families & couples only, no group bookings.

►►►► 78% Birchwood Tourist Park

(SY896905)

Bere Rd, Coldharbour BH20 7PA
☎ 01929 554763 📠 01929 556635
dir: *From Poole (A351) or Dorchester (A352) on N side of railway line at Wareham, follow Bere Regis signs (unclassified). 2nd park after 2.25m*

* 🚐 fr £16.25 🚐 fr £16.25 ▲ fr £12.75

Open 13 Dec-23 Nov (rs 31 Oct-1 Mar shop/ reception open for 2-3 hrs daily in winter)

Last arrival 21.00hrs Last departure 11.30hrs

Set in 50 acres of parkland located within Wareham Forest, this site offers direct access into ideal areas for walking, mountain biking, and horse and pony riding. The modern facilities are in two central locations and are very clean. There is a good security barrier system. 25 acre site. 175 touring pitches. 25 hardstandings. Caravan pitches. Motorhome pitches. Tent pitches.

AA Pubs & Restaurants nearby: Kemps Country House, Wareham 0845 862 0315

Greyhound Inn, Corfe Castle 01929 480205

New Inn, Church Knowle 01929 480357

Leisure: ⚙ ⚽ 🔍

Facilities: 🏕⊙🅿✳🕏⚘🔥✕ 🛜 ♻ ❓

Services: 🔌🔴🛢🚿🚽🔋

Within 3 miles: 🚶🎣🛒

Notes: No generators, no groups on BHs, no camp fires. Dogs must be kept on leads. Bike hire, pitch & putt, paddling pool.

see advert on page 204

SERVICES: 🔌 Electric hook up 🔴 Launderette 🍺 Licensed bar 🛢 Calor Gas ⊘ Camping Gaz 🚽 Toilet fluid 🍴 Café/Restaurant 🍟 Fast Food/Takeaway 🔋 Battery charging 🚿 Baby care ↯ Motorvan service point
ABBREVIATIONS: BH/bank hols-bank holidays Etr-Easter Whit-Whitsun dep-departure fr-from hrs-hours m-mile mdnt-midnight rdbt-roundabout rs-restricted service wk-week wknd-weekend ❷ No credit cards ❌ No dogs
See page 7 for details of the AA Camping Card Scheme

WAREHAM *continued*

►►► 81% East Creech Farm Campsite *(SY928827)*

East Creech Farm, East Creech BH20 5AP
☎ 01929 480519 & 481312 📄 01929 480519
e-mail: east.creech@virgin.net
dir: From Wareham on A351 S towards Swanage. On bypass at 3rd rdbt take Furzebrook/Blue Pool Rd exit, approx 2m site on right

🚐 £11-£19 🚕 £11-£19 ▲ £11-£19

Open Apr-Oct

Last arrival 20.00hrs Last departure noon

A grassy park set in a peaceful location beneath the Purbeck Hills, with extensive views towards Poole and Brownsea Island. The park boasts a woodland play area, bright, clean toilet facilities, and a farm shop selling milk, eggs and bread. There are also three coarse fishing lakes teeming with fish. The park is close to the Norden Station on the Swanage to Norden steam railway, and is well located for visiting Corfe Castle, Swanage and the Purbeck coast. 4 acre site. 80 touring pitches. Caravan pitches. Motorhome pitches. Tent pitches.

AA Pubs & Restaurants nearby: Kemps Country House, Wareham 0845 862 0315

Greyhound Inn, Corfe Castle 01929 480205

New Inn, Church Knowle 01929 480357

Leisure: ⚙ **Facilities:** 🔥⊙℗✳🍴♻
Services: 🔌🚽
Within 3 miles: ⊟✏🏪🛒
Notes: ⊘ No camp fires. Dogs must be kept on leads.

►►► 81% Lookout Holiday Park
(SY927858)

Stoborough BH20 5AZ
☎ 01929 552546 📄 01929 556662
e-mail: enquiries@caravan-sites.co.uk
web: www.caravan-sites.co.uk
dir: Take A351 through Wareham, after crossing River Frome & through Stoborough, site signed on left

🚐 £17-£30 🚕 £17-£30 ▲ £12-£25

Open all year

Last arrival 22.00hrs Last departure noon

Divided into two paddocks and set well back from the Swanage road, this touring park is separated from the static part of the operation. A superb children's playground and plenty of other attractions make this an ideal centre for families; it is also close to the popular attractions of the area. 15 acre site. 150 touring pitches. 94 hardstandings. Caravan pitches. Motorhome pitches. Tent pitches. 89 statics.

AA Pubs & Restaurants nearby: Kemps Country House, Wareham 0845 862 0315

Greyhound Inn, Corfe Castle 01929 480205

New Inn, Church Knowle 01929 480357

Leisure: ⚙ 🎱
Facilities: 🔥⊙℗✳🔥⚙🛒🚿 ♻ 🛈
Services: 🔌🚽🛒🧴T🛁🚚
Within 3 miles: ⚓✚⊟✏🏪🛒U
Notes: No pets.

see advert on opposite page

►►► 78% Ridge Farm Camping & Caravan Park *(SY939868)*

Barnhill Rd, Ridge BH20 5BG
☎ 01929 556444
e-mail: info@ridgefarm.co.uk
web: www.ridgefarm.co.uk
dir: From Wareham take B3075 towards Corfe Castle, cross river to Stoborough, then left to Ridge. Follow site signs for 1.5m

🚐🚕▲

Open Etr-Sep

Last arrival 21.00hrs Last departure noon

A quiet rural park, adjacent to a working farm and surrounded by trees and bushes. This away-from-it-all park is ideally located for touring this part of Dorset, and especially for birdwatchers, or those who enjoy walking and cycling. This site is perfect for visiting the Arne Nature Reserve. 3.47 acre site. 60 touring pitches. 2 hardstandings. Caravan pitches. Motorhome pitches. Tent pitches.

LEISURE: 🏊 Indoor swimming pool 🏊 Outdoor swimming pool ⚙ Children's playground 🧒 Kid's club 🎾 Tennis court 🎱 Games room 📺 Separate TV room ⛳ 9/18 hole golf course ⛵ Boats for hire 🎬 Cinema 🎵 Entertainment 🎣 Fishing ⛳ Mini golf 🏄 Watersports 🏋 Gym 🏟 Sports field **Spa** U Stables
FACILITIES: 🛁 Bath 🚿 Shower ⊙ Electric shaver ℗ Hairdryer ✳ Ice Pack Facility ♿ Disabled facilities ☎ Public telephone 🏪 Shop on site or within 200yds 🛒 Mobile shop (calls at least 5 days a week) 🍖 BBQ area 🌳 Picnic area 📶 Wi-fi 💻 Internet access ♻ Recycling 🛈 Tourist info 🐕 Dog exercise area

AA Pubs & Restaurants nearby: Greyhound Inn, Corfe Castle 01929 480205

New Inn, Church Knowle 01929 480357

Facilities: 🅿☉🎣✻🕐🛁♻ ❶

Services: ⚡🛢🍴🧺🚽🔋

Within 3 miles: 🚶🎣🎯🐾🛒🎡⛵

Notes: No dogs Jul-Aug. Dogs must be on leads.

WEYMOUTH — Map 4 SY67

Places to visit

RSPB Nature Reserve Radipole Lake, WEYMOUTH 01305 778313 www.rspb.org.uk

Portland Castle, PORTLAND 01305 820539 www.english-heritage.org.uk

Great for kids: Weymouth Sea Life Adventure Park & Marine Sanctuary, WEYMOUTH 0871 423 2110 www.sealifeeurope.com

 85% Littlesea Holiday Park *(SY654783)*

Lynch Ln DT4 9DT

☎ 0871 231 0879 📠 01305 759186

e-mail: littlesea@haven.com

dir: *A35 onto A354 signed Weymouth. Right at 1st rdbt, 3rd exit at 2nd rdbt towards Chickerell. Left into Lynch Lane after lights. Site at far end of road*

🚐🚙⛺

Open end Mar-end Oct (rs End Mar-May & Sep-Oct facilities may be reduced)

Last arrival mdnt Last departure 10.00hrs

Just three miles from Weymouth with its lovely beaches and many attractions, Littlesea has a cheerful family atmosphere and fantastic facilities. Indoor and outdoor entertainment and activities are on offer for all the family, and the toilet facilities on the touring park are of a good quality. The touring section of this holiday complex is at the far end of the site adjacent to the South West Coast path. 100 acre site. 124 touring pitches. Caravan pitches. Motorhome pitches. Tent pitches. 720 statics.

AA Pubs & Restaurants nearby: Old Ship Inn, Weymouth 01305 812522

Perry's Restaurant, Weymouth 01305 785799

Leisure: 🏊🏊🎱🎣⚽☺🏹🎵

Facilities: 🛁🅿☉🎣✻🛁🕐🛢🎄🐾 📶♻ ❶

Services: ⚡🛢🍴🍴🧺🚽🍽🛒🔋

Within 3 miles: 🚶🎣🎯🐾◎🚣🎡⛵

Notes: Max 2 dogs per booking, certain dog breeds banned, no commercial vehicles, no bookings by persons under 21yrs unless a family booking, no boats.

SERVICES: ⚡ Electric hook up 🛢 Launderette 🍴 Licensed bar 🍴 Calor Gas 🅖 Camping Gaz 🚽 Toilet fluid 🍽 Café/Restaurant 🍟 Fast Food/Takeaway 🔋 Battery charging 🍼 Baby care ♿ Motorvan service point

ABBREVIATIONS: BH/bank hols-bank holidays Etr-Easter Whit-Whitsun dep-departure fr-from hrs-hours m-mile mdnt-midnight rdbt-roundabout rs-restricted service wk-week wknd-weekend ⊗ No credit cards ⊗ No dogs

See page 7 for details of the AA Camping Card Scheme

WEYMOUTH *continued*

82% *Seaview Holiday Park*
(SY707830)

Preston DT3 6DZ
☎ 0871 231 0877 📠 01305 833169
e-mail: seaview@haven.com
dir: *A354 to Weymouth, signs for Preston/ Wareham onto A353. Site 3m on right just after Weymouth Bay Holiday Park*

🚐 �55 Å

Open mid Mar-Oct (rs mid Mar-May & Sep-Oct facilities may be reduced)

Last arrival mdnt Last departure 10.00hrs

A fun-packed holiday centre for all the family, with plenty of activities and entertainment during the day and evening. Terraced pitches are provided for caravans, and there is a separate field for tents. The park is close to Weymouth and other coastal attractions. There's a smart toilet and shower block, plus fully-serviced hardstanding pitches. 20 acre site. 87 touring pitches. 24 hardstandings. Caravan pitches. Motorhome pitches. Tent pitches. 259 statics.

AA Pubs & Restaurants nearby: Old Ship Inn, Weymouth 01305 812522

Smugglers Inn, Osmington Mills 01305 833125

Perry's Restaurant, Weymouth 01305 785799

Leisure: 🏊 ⛱ 🛝 🪁 🎾 🎵
Facilities: 🛁 🚿 ☉ 🪒 ✂ ♿ 🕓 🏪 🐕 ♻ 🎧 WiFi
♻ 🎧
Services: 🔌 🗑 🍴 🛒 🍴 🛒 🚛
Within 3 miles: ♨ 🚤 🎣 ◎ ⛵ 🏪 🛒 🎣 Ս

Notes: Max 2 dogs per booking, certain dog breeds banned, no commercial vehicles, no bookings by persons under 21yrs unless a family booking.

►►►►► 84% East Fleet Farm Touring Park (SY640797)

GOLD

Chickerell DT3 4DW
☎ 01305 785768
e-mail: enquiries@eastfleet.co.uk
dir: *On B3157 (Weymouth-Bridport road), 3m from Weymouth*

* 🚐 £15-£23.50 �55 £15-£23.50 Å £15-£23.50

Open 16 Mar-Oct

Last arrival 22.00hrs Last departure 10.30hrs

Set on a working organic farm overlooking Fleet Lagoon and Chesil Beach, with a wide range of amenities and quality toilet facilities with family rooms in a Scandinavian log cabin. The friendly owners are welcoming and helpful, and their family bar serving meals and takeaway food is open from Easter, with glorious views from the patio area. There is also a good accessory shop. 21 acre site. 400 touring pitches. 50 hardstandings. Caravan pitches. Motorhome pitches. Tent pitches.

AA Pubs & Restaurants nearby: Old Ship Inn, Weymouth 01305 812522

Perry's Restaurant, Weymouth 01305 785799

Leisure: 🛝 😊 🔍
Facilities: 🛁 🚿 ☉ 🪒 ✂ ♿ 🕓 🏪 🐕 ♻ WiFi
🖥 ♻ 🎧
Services: 🔌 🗑 🍴 🛒 🍴 🛒 🚛
Within 3 miles: ♨ 🚤 🎣 ◎ ⛵ 🏪 🛒 Ս

Notes: Dogs must be kept on leads.

►►►► 81% *Bagwell Farm Touring Park* (SY627816)

Knights in the Bottom, Chickerell DT3 4EA
☎ 01305 782575 📠 01305 780554
e-mail: aa@bagwellfarm.co.uk
web: www.bagwellfarm.co.uk
dir: *4m W of Weymouth on B3157 (Weymouth-Bridport), past Chickerell, left into site 500yds after Victoria Inn*

🚐 �55 Å

Open all year (rs Winter bar closed)

Last arrival 21.00hrs Last departure 11.00hrs

An idyllically placed, terraced site on a hillside of a valley overlooking Chesil Beach. The park is well equipped with 25 fully-serviced pitches, a mini-supermarket, children's play area, pets' corner and a bar and grill serving food in high season.

---

14 acre site. 320 touring pitches. 10 hardstandings. Caravan pitches. Motorhome pitches. Tent pitches.

AA Pubs & Restaurants nearby: Old Ship Inn, Weymouth 01305 812522

Perry's Restaurant, Weymouth 01305 785799

Leisure: 🛝
Facilities: 🛁 🚿 ☉ 🪒 ✂ ♿ 🕓 🏪 🐕 ♻
Services: 🔌 🗑 🍴 🛒 🍴 🛒 🚛
Within 3 miles: 🏪 🛒 Ս

Notes: Families only. Dogs must be kept on leads. Wet suit shower, campers' shelter.

►►► 83% West Fleet Holiday Farm
(SY625811)

Fleet DT3 4EF
☎ 01305 782218 📠 01305 775396
e-mail: aa@westfleetholidays.co.uk
web: www.westfleetholidays.co.uk
dir: *From Weymouth take B3157 towards Abbotsbury for 3m. Past Chickerell turn left at mini-rdbt to Fleet, site 1m on right*

* 🚐 £16-£25 �55 £13-£22 Å £13-£22

Open Etr-Sep (rs May-Sep clubhouse & pool available)

Last arrival 21.00hrs Last departure 11.00hrs

A spacious farm site with both level and sloping pitches divided into paddocks, and screened with hedging. Good views of the Dorset countryside, and a relaxing site for a family holiday with its new heated outdoor pool (in 2011) and interesting clubhouse. 12 acre site. 250 touring pitches. Caravan pitches. Motorhome pitches. Tent pitches.

AA Pubs & Restaurants nearby: Old Ship Inn, Weymouth 01305 812522

Perry's Restaurant, Weymouth 01305 785799

Leisure: ⛱ 🛝 😊 🎵
Facilities: 🛁 🚿 ☉ 🪒 ✂ ♿ 🏪 ♻ 🎧
Services: 🔌 🗑 🍴 🛒 🍴 🛒 🚛
Within 3 miles: ♨ 🏪 Ս

Notes: Non-family groups by arrangement only, dogs restricted to certain areas. Dogs must be kept on leads.

►►► 82% Pebble Bank Caravan Park

(SY659775)

Camp Rd, Wyke Regis DT4 9HF
☎ **01305 774844**
dir: *From Weymouth take Portland road. At last rdbt turn right, then 1st left to Army Tent Camp. Site opposite*

* ⇌ £15.50-£27.50 ⇌ £15.50-£27.50 ▲ £10-£25

Open Etr-mid Oct (rs High season & wknds only bar open)

Last arrival 21.00hrs Last departure 11.00hrs

This site, although only one and a half miles from Weymouth, is in a peaceful location overlooking Chesil Beach and the Fleet. There is a friendly little bar, which offers even better views. The toilet and shower block is spotlessly maintained. 4 acre site. 40 touring pitches. Caravan pitches. Motorhome pitches. Tent pitches. 80 statics.

AA Pubs & Restaurants nearby: Old Ship Inn, Weymouth 01305 812522

Perry's Restaurant, Weymouth 01305 785799

Leisure: /Ⴥ
Facilities: �ͣ⊙℘⁂å WiFi ❶
Services: ⬅⯑ 🔌⬀🔋
Within 3 miles: ↥⇟⊟℘◎⇟🔋⬀U

►►► 80% Rosewall Camping

(SY736820)

East Farm Dairy, Osmington Mills DT3 6HA
☎ **01305 832248**
e-mail: holidays@weymouthcamping.com
dir: *Take A353 towards Weymouth. At Osmington Mills sign (opposite garage) turn left, 0.25m, site on first right*

⇌ ▲

Open Etr-Oct (rs Apr, May & Oct shop opening times)

Last arrival 22.00hrs Last departure 10.00hrs

A large, slightly sloping field with hedging and natural screening providing bays, in a peaceful setting close to the Dorset coastline and footpaths. The facilities are of a very good quality. This park offers an excellent spacious environment for tents and families. 13 acre site. 225 touring pitches. Motorhome pitches. Tent pitches.

AA Pubs & Restaurants nearby: Old Ship Inn, Weymouth 01305 812522

Smugglers Inn, Osmington Mills 01305 833125

Perry's Restaurant, Weymouth 01305 785799

Leisure: /Ⴥ
Facilities: ⍅⊙⁂å🔋♻❶
Services: ⬅🔋⬀🔋
Within 3 miles: ⊟℘⇟🔋⬀U

Notes: Families & couples only. Dogs must be kept on leads. Riding stables & coarse fishing.

<hr>

AA CAMPING CARD SITE

►►► 78% Sea Barn Farm *(SY625807)*

Fleet DT3 4ED
☎ **01305 782218** 📠 **01305 775396**
e-mail: aa@seabarnfarm.co.uk
web: www.seabarnfarm.co.uk
dir: *From Weymouth take B3157 towards Abbotsbury for 3m. Past Chickerell turn left at mini-rdbt towards Fleet. Site 1m on left*

* ⇌ £12-£21 ▲ £12-£21

Open 15 Mar-Oct (rs Mar-Jun & Sep use of facilities at West Fleet)

Last arrival 21.00hrs Last departure 11.00hrs

This site is set high on the Dorset coast and has spectacular views over Chesil Beach, The Fleet and Lyme Bay, and it is also on the South West coast path. Optional use of the clubhouse and swimming pool at West Fleet Holiday Farm is available. Pitches are sheltered by hedging, and there is an excellent toilet facility block, and plenty of space for games. 12 acre site. 250 touring pitches. Motorhome pitches. Tent pitches. 1 static.

AA Pubs & Restaurants nearby: Old Ship Inn, Weymouth 01305 812522

Perry's Restaurant, Weymouth 01305 785799

Leisure: /Ⴥ
Facilities: ⍅⍄⊙℘⁂å🔋⬀♻❶
Services: ⬅🔋⬀🔋
Within 3 miles: ↥🔋U

Notes: Non-family groups by arrangement. Dogs must be kept on leads.

WIMBORNE MINSTER   Map 5 SZ09

Places to visit

Kingston Lacy, WIMBORNE 01202 883402 (Mon-Fri) www.nationaltrust.org.uk

Priest's House Museum and Garden, WIMBORNE 01202 882533 www.priest-house.co.uk

Great for kids: Moors Valley Country Park, RINGWOOD 01425 470721 www.moors-valley.co.uk

PREMIER PARK

►►►►► 84% Wilksworth Farm Caravan Park *(SU004018)*

GOLD

Cranborne Rd BH21 4HW
☎ **01202 885467** 📠 **01202 885467**
e-mail: rayandwendy@wilksworthfarmcaravanpark.co.uk
web: www.wilksworthfarmcaravanpark.co.uk
dir: *1m N of Wimborne on B3078*

⇌ ⇌ ▲

Open Apr-Oct (rs Oct no shop)

Last arrival 20.00hrs Last departure 11.00hrs

A popular and attractive park peacefully set in the grounds of a listed house in the heart of rural Dorset. The spacious site has much to offer visitors, including an excellent heated swimming pool, takeaway and café, plus a games room. The modern toilet facilities contain en suite rooms and good family rooms. 11 acre site. 85 touring pitches. 20 hardstandings. Caravan pitches. Motorhome pitches. Tent pitches. 77 statics.

AA Pubs & Restaurants nearby: Les Bouviers, Wimborne Minster 01202 889555

Coventry Arms, Corfe Mullen 01258 857284

Botany Bay Inne, Winterborne Zelston 01929 459227

Leisure: ⬗/Ⴥ♨🔍
Facilities: ⍅⍄⊙℘⁂å🕓🔋🏇🀫
Services: ⬅🔋⬀T🍽⬀⬓↯
Within 3 miles: ↥⊟℘🔋🔋

Notes: Max 2 dogs per pitch. Dogs must be kept on leads. Paddling pool, volley ball, mini football pitch.

WIMBORNE MINSTER *continued*

PREMIER PARK

▶▶▶▶▶ 80% Merley Court

Best of British

(SZ008984)

Merley BH21 3AA
☎ 01590 648331 📠 01590 645610
e-mail: holidays@shorefield.co.uk
dir: *Site signed on A31, Wimborne by-pass & Poole junct rdbt*

🚐 £16-£42.50 🚐 £16-£42.50 ▲ £14.50-£37

Open 6 Feb-2 Jan (rs Low season pool closed & bar, shop open limited hrs)

Last arrival 21.00hrs Last departure 10.00hrs

A superb site in a quiet rural position on the edge of Wimborne, with woodland on two sides and good access roads. The park is well landscaped and offers generous individual pitches in sheltered grassland. There are plenty of amenities for all the family, including a heated outdoor pool, tennis court and adventure playground. This park tends to get busy in summer and therefore advance booking is advised. 20 acre site. 160 touring pitches. 50 hardstandings. Caravan pitches. Motorhome pitches. Tent pitches. 2 statics.

AA Pubs & Restaurants nearby: Les Bouviers, Wimborne Minster 01202 889555

Coventry Arms, Corfe Mullen 01258 857284

Botany Bay Inne, Winterborne Zelston 01929 459227

Leisure: 🏊 🅰 🎱 🎠 🔍
Facilities: 🛁 🛖 ☉ 🅿 ☼ ♿ 🕐 🅱 🍴 🚮 ♻ 🔓
Services: 🔌 🗑 🍺 🔥 ⌀ 🅃 🍴 🔋 ♨ ⌁
Within 3 miles: 🚶 ⚘ 🎅 🎣 🅿 ◉ 🅱 🅶 ⛳

Notes: Families & couples only, rallies welcome. Dogs must be kept on leads. Use of facilities at Oakdene Forest Park (7m). 2 Euro tents for hire.

see advert on opposite page

▶▶▶ 81% Springfield Touring Park

(SY987989)

Candys Ln, Corfe Mullen BH21 3EF
☎ 01202 881719
e-mail: john.clark18@btconnect.com
dir: *From Wimborne on Wimborne by-pass (A31) W end turn left after Caravan Sales, follow brown sign*

🚐 £15-£20 🚐 £15-£20 ▲ £10-£20

Open Apr-Oct

Last arrival 21.00hrs Last departure 11.00hrs

A small touring park with extensive views over the Stour Valley and a quiet and friendly atmosphere. The park is maintained immaculately, and has a well-stocked shop. 3.5 acre site. 45 touring pitches. 18 hardstandings. Caravan pitches. Motorhome pitches. Tent pitches.

AA Pubs & Restaurants nearby: Les Bouviers, Wimborne Minster 01202 889555

Coventry Arms, Corfe Mullen 01258 857284

Botany Bay Inne, Winterborne Zelston 01929 459227

Leisure: 🅰
Facilities: 🛖 ☉ 🅿 ☼ ♿ 🅱 ♻ 🔓
Services: 🔌 🗑 🍺 ⌁
Within 3 miles: 🚶 🎅 🎣 🅿 🅱 🅶 ⛳

Notes: No skateboards. Dogs must be kept on leads.

AA CAMPING CARD SITE

▶▶▶ 79% Charris Camping & Caravan Park *(SY992988)*

Candy's Ln, Corfe Mullen BH21 3EF
☎ 01202 885970
e-mail: bookings@charris.co.uk
web: www.charris.co.uk
dir: *From E, exit Wimborne bypass (A31) W end. 300yds after Caravan Sales, follow brown sign. From W on A31, over A350 rdbt, take next turn after B3074, follow brown signs*

🚐 £12.50-£17.25 🚐 £12.50-£17.25
▲ £11.50-£13.50

Open all year

Last arrival 21.00hrs Last departure 11.00hrs

A sheltered park of grassland lined with trees on the edge of the Stour Valley. The owners are friendly and welcoming, and they maintain the park facilities to a good standard. Barbecues are

a popular, occasional event. 3.5 acre site. 45 touring pitches. 12 hardstandings. Caravan pitches. Motorhome pitches. Tent pitches.

AA Pubs & Restaurants nearby: Les Bouviers, Wimborne Minster 01202 889555

Coventry Arms, Corfe Mullen 01258 857284

Botany Bay Inne, Winterborne Zelston 01929 459227

Facilities: 🛖 ☉ 🅿 ☼ 🕐 🅱 📶 ♻ 🔓
Services: 🔌 🗑 🍺 ⌀ 🅃 ⌁
Within 3 miles: 🚶 🅿 🅱 🅶 ⛳

Notes: Earliest arrival time 11.00hrs.

WOOL
Map 4 SY88

Places to visit

The Tank Museum, BOVINGTON CAMP 01929 405096 www.tankmuseum.org

Clouds Hill, BOVINGTON CAMP 01929 405616 www.nationaltrust.org.uk

Great for kids: Monkey World-Ape Rescue Centre, WOOL 01929 462537 www.monkeyworld.org

---

▶▶▶▶ 81% Whitemead Caravan Park *(SY841869)*

East Burton Rd BH20 6HG
☎ 01929 462241 📠 01929 462241
e-mail: whitemeadcp@aol.com
dir: *Signed from A352 at level crossing on Wareham side of Wool*

* 🚐 £13.50-£21 🚐 £13.50-£21 ▲ £11-£18.50

Open mid Mar-Oct

Last arrival 22.00hrs Last departure noon

A well laid-out site in the valley of the River Frome, close to the village of Wool, and surrounded by woodland. A shop and games room enhance the facilities here, and the spotless, modern toilets are heated, providing an excellent amenity. Only a short walk away are the shops

continued

SERVICES: 🔌 Electric hook up 🗑 Launderette 🍺 Licensed bar 🛢 Calor Gas ⌀ Camping Gaz 🅃 Toilet fluid 🍴 Café/Restaurant 🍟 Fast Food/Takeaway 🔋 Battery charging 🍼 Baby care ⌁ Motorvan service point

ABBREVIATIONS: BH/bank hols-bank holidays Etr-Easter Whit-Whitsun dep-departure fr-from hrs-hours m-mile mdnt-midnight rdbt-roundabout rs-restricted service wk-week wknd-weekend 🚫 No credit cards 🚫 No dogs

See page 7 for details of the AA Camping Card Scheme

WOOL continued

and pubs, plus the main bus route and mainline station to Poole, Bournemouth and Weymouth. 5 acre site. 95 touring pitches. 20 seasonal pitches. Caravan pitches. Motorhome pitches. Tent pitches.

AA Pubs & Restaurants nearby: New Inn, Church Knowle 01929 480357

Leisure: ⋔ ⚲

Facilities: ⋔ ⊙ ℱ ✳ ⅋ Ⓢ ⟊ ⅏ ♲ ❶

Services: ⊞ ⓢ ⬤ ⬢ ⊤ ≊

Within 3 miles: ↨ ⟋ ⓢ ⓢ ∪

CO DURHAM

BARNARD CASTLE   Map 19 NZ01

Places to visit

Barnard Castle, BARNARD CASTLE 01833 638212 www.english-heritage.org.uk

The Bowes Museum, BARNARD CASTLE 01833 690606 www.thebowesmuseum.org.uk

Great for kids: Raby Castle, STAINDROP 01833 660202 www.rabycastle.com

►►► 77% Pecknell Farm Caravan Park (NZ028178)

Lartington DL12 9DF
☎ **01833 638357**
dir: 1.5m from Barnard Castle. From A66 take B6277. Site on right 1.5m from junct with A67

* ⊞ £12-£14 ⛺ £12-£14

Open Apr-Oct

Last arrival 20.00hrs Last departure noon

A small well laid out site on a working farm in beautiful rural meadowland, with spacious marked pitches on level ground. There are many walking opportunities directly from this friendly site. 1.5 acre site. 20 touring pitches. 5 hardstandings. Caravan pitches. Motorhome pitches.

AA Pubs & Restaurants nearby: Fox and Hounds, Cotherstone 01833 650241

Morritt Arms Hotel, Barnard Castle 01833 627232

Rose & Crown, Romaldkirk 01833 650213

Facilities: ⋔ ⊙ ℱ ⓒ ♲

Services: ⊞ ≊

Within 3 miles: ↨ ⟋ ⓒ ⓢ ⓢ ∪

Notes: ⊛ Maximum 2 dogs, no noise after 22.30hrs. Dogs must be kept on leads.

BEAMISH   Map 19 NZ25

Places to visit

Tanfield Railway, TANFIELD 0191 388 7545 www.tanfieldrailway.co.uk

Beamish Museum, BEAMISH 0191 370 4000 www.beamish.org.uk

Great for kids: Diggerland, LANGLEY PARK 0871 227 7007 www.diggerland.com

►►► 78% Bobby Shafto Caravan Park (NZ232545)

Cranberry Plantation DH9 0RY
☎ **0191 370 1776** 🖹 **0191 370 1783**
dir: From A693 signed Beamish to sign for Beamish Museum. Take approach road, turn right immediately before museum, left at pub to site 1m on right

⊞ ⛺ ⋏

Open Mar-Oct

Last arrival 23.00hrs Last departure 11.00hrs

A tranquil rural park surrounded by trees, with very clean and well organised facilities. The suntrap touring area has plenty of attractive hanging baskets, and there is a clubhouse with bar, TV and pool. The hardstandings and the 28 fully serviced pitches enhance the amenities. 9 acre site. 83 touring pitches. 47 hardstandings. Caravan pitches. Motorhome pitches. Tent pitches. 54 statics.

AA Pubs & Restaurants nearby: Beamish Park Hotel, Beamish 01207 230666

Leisure: ⋔ ⚲ ▭

Facilities: ⋔ ⊙ ℱ ✳ ⅋ ⓒ ⓢ

Services: ⊞ ⓢ ⬤ ⬤ ⬢ ⊤ ≊

Within 3 miles: ↨ ⅏ ⟋ ⓢ ∪

BLACKHALL COLLIERY

Places to visit

Hartlepool's Maritime Experience, HARTLEPOOL 01429 860077 www.hartlepoolsmaritimeexperience.com

Auckland Castle, BISHOP AUCKLAND 01388 602576 www.auckland-castle.co.uk

Great for kids: Captain Cook Birthplace Museum, MIDDLESBROUGH 01642 311211 www.captcook-ne.co.uk

BLACKHALL COLLIERY   Map 19 NZ43

79% Crimdon Dene (NZ477378)

Coast Rd TS27 4BN
☎ **0871 664 9737**
e-mail: crimdon.dene@park-resorts.com
dir: From A19 just S of Peterlee, take B1281 signed Blackhall. Through Castle Eden, left in 0.5m signed Blackhall. Approx 3m right at T-junct onto A1086 towards Crimdon. Site in 1m signed on left, by Seagull pub

⊞ ⛺

Open Apr-Oct

Last arrival 23.00hrs Last departure 10.00hrs

A large, popular coastal holiday park, handily placed for access to Teeside, Durham and Newcastle. The park contains a full range of holiday centre facilities for both children and their parents. Touring facilities are appointed to a very good standard. 44 touring pitches. 44 hardstandings. 12 seasonal pitches. Caravan pitches. Motorhome pitches. 586 statics.

Leisure: ⌘ ⋔ ⚲ ⚲ ♫

Facilities: ⋔ ⊙ ℱ ⓒ ⓢ ⅏ ♲ ❶

Services: ⊞ ⓢ ⬤ ⅃⊙⅃ ⬤ ⬢

Within 3 miles: ↨ ⅏ ⟋ ⓢ ⓢ ∪

Notes: No cars by caravans. No quad bikes. Dogs must be kept on leads.

CONSETT

Places to visit

Beamish Museum, BEAMISH 0191 370 4000 www.beamish.org.uk

Tanfield Railway, TANFIELD 0191 388 7545 www.tanfieldrailway.co.uk

Great for kids: Gibside, ROWLANDS GILL 01207 541820 www.nationaltrust.org.uk/gibside

---

LEISURE: ⛱ Indoor swimming pool ⚘ Outdoor swimming pool ⋔ Children's playground ⚑ Kid's club ⚲ Tennis court ⚲ Games room ▭ Separate TV room ↨ 9/18 hole golf course ⚓ Boats for hire ⊟ Cinema ♫ Entertainment ⟋ Fishing ⊙ Mini golf ⚲ Watersports ⚲ Gym ⚲ Sports field **Spa** ∪ Stables
FACILITIES: ⚲ Bath ⋔ Shower ⊙ Electric shaver ℱ Hairdryer ✳ Ice Pack Facility ⅋ Disabled facilities ⓒ Public telephone ⓢ Shop on site or within 200yds ⅌ Mobile shop (calls at least 5 days a week) ⟊ BBQ area ⌒ Picnic area ⅏ Wi-fi ▤ Internet access ♲ Recycling ❶ Tourist info ⟊ Dog exercise area

CONSETT
Map 19 NZ15

▶▶▶ 75% Byreside Caravan Site

(NZ122560)

Hamsterley NE17 7RT
☎ 01207 560280 📠 01207 560280
dir: *From A694 onto B6310 & follow signs*
🚐 £12-£14 🚍 £12-£14 ▲ £8-£12

Open all year

Last arrival 22.00hrs Last departure noon

A small, secluded family-run site on a working farm, with well-maintained facilities. It is immediately adjacent to the coast-to-coast cycle track so makes an ideal location for walkers and cyclists. Handy for Newcastle and Durham; the Roman Wall and Northumberland National Park are within an hour's drive. Please note that there is no laundry on the park. 1.5 acre site. 31 touring pitches. 29 hardstandings. Caravan pitches. Motorhome pitches. Tent pitches.

AA Pubs & Restaurants nearby: Manor House Inn, Carterway Heads 01207 255268

Facilities: 🅟 ⊙ ✳ ⅙ 🗟 🛒 ♻ 🛈

Services: 🖬 🔒 🆃 🚿

Within 3 miles: ⅃ 🎠 🗟 🖥

Notes: No ball games on site. Dogs must be kept on leads. Caravan storage.

ESSEX

CANEWDON
Map 7 TQ99

Places to visit
RHS Garden Hyde Hall, CHELMSFORD
01245 402006 www.rhs.org.uk

Southend's Pier Museum,
SOUTHEND-ON-SEA 01702 611214
www.southendpiermuseum.co.uk

Great for kids: Southend Museum and Planetarium, SOUTHEND-ON-SEA 01702 434449
www.southendmuseums.co.uk

AA CAMPING CARD SITE

▶▶▶ 79% Riverside Village Holiday Park *(TQ929951)*

Creeksea Ferry Rd, Wallasea Island SS4 2EY
☎ 01702 258297 📠 01702 258555
e-mail: riversidevillage@tiscali.co.uk
dir: *M25 junct 29, A127, towards Southend-on-Sea. Take B1013 towards Rochford. Follow signs for Wallasea Island & Baltic Wharf*

* 🚐 £16-£25 🚍 £16-£25 ▲ £16-£25

Open Mar-Oct

Next to a nature reserve beside the River Crouch, this holiday park is surrounded by wetlands but only eight miles from Southend. A modern toilet block with disabled facilities is provided for tourers and there's a handsome reception area. Several restaurants and pubs are within a short distance. 25 acre site. 60 touring pitches. Caravan pitches. Motorhome pitches. Tent pitches. 159 statics.

Leisure: 🅰

Facilities: 🅟 ⊙ 🅵 ✳ ⅙ 🕒 🗟 🛒 ♻ 🛈

Services: 🖬 🗟 🔒 ⌀ 🆃

Within 3 miles: ⅃ ⌀ 🗟 🖥 ∪

Notes: No dogs in tents. Dogs must be kept on leads. Freshwater fishing, mobile newspaper vendor Sun & BH.

CLACTON-ON-SEA
Map 7 TM11

Places to visit
Harwich Redoubt Fort, HARWICH 01255 503429
www.harwich-society.com

The Beth Chatto Gardens, COLCHESTER
01206 822007 www.bethchatto.co.uk

Great for kids: Colchester Zoo, COLCHESTER
01206 331292 www.colchester-zoo.com

78% Highfield Grange

(TM173175)

London Rd CO16 9QY
☎ 0871 664 9746 📠 01255 689805
e-mail: highfield.grange@park-resorts.com
dir: *A12 to Colchester, A120 (Harwich), A133 to Clacton-on-Sea. Site on B1441 clearly signed on left*

🚐 🚍

Open Apr-Oct

Last arrival mdnt Last departure 10.00hrs

The modern leisure facilities at this attractively planned park make it an ideal base for a lively family holiday. The swimming complex with both indoor and outdoor pools and a huge water shoot is especially popular. There are fully serviced touring pitches, each with its own hardstanding, located at the heart of the park. The nearby resorts of Walton on the Naze, Frinton and Clacton all offer excellent beaches and a wide range of popular seaside attractions. 30 acre site. 43 touring pitches. 43 hardstandings. Caravan pitches. Motorhome pitches. 509 statics.

AA Pubs & Restaurants nearby: Rose & Crown, Colchester 01206 866677

Whalebone, Fingringhoe 01206 729307

Leisure: ⦵ ⦵ 🅰 🛝 🕒 🎯 🎵

Facilities: 🅟 ⊙ 🅵 ⅙ 🕒 🗟 🛒 📶 🖥

Services: 🖬 🗟 🕎 🍽 🍴

Within 3 miles: ⅃ 🎣 🎠 ⌀ 🎯 ⅏ 🗟 🖥 ∪

Notes: No fold-in campers or trailer tents.

SERVICES: 🖬 Electric hook up 🗟 Launderette 🕎 Licensed bar 🔒 Calor Gas ⌀ Camping Gaz 🆃 Toilet fluid 🍽 Café/Restaurant 🍴 Fast Food/Takeaway ⅏ Battery charging 🛒 Baby care ⅄ Motorvan service point

ABBREVIATIONS: BH/bank hols-bank holidays Etr-Easter Whit-Whitsun dep-departure fr-from hrs-hours m-mile mdnt-midnight rdbt-roundabout rs-restricted service wk-week wknd-weekend ⊛ No credit cards ⊗ No dogs
See page 7 for details of the AA Camping Card Scheme

CLACTON-ON-SEA *continued*

75% *Martello Beach Holiday Park* (TM136128)

BRONZE

Belsize Av, Jaywick CO15 2LF
☎ 0871 664 9782 & 01442 830100
e-mail: martello.beach@park-resorts.com
dir: *Telephone for directions*

Open Apr-Oct

Last arrival 21.30hrs Last departure 10.00hrs

Direct access to a seven-mile long Blue Flag beach is an undoubted attraction at this holiday park. The much improved touring area (refurbished toilet block, road resurfacing, new planting) is next to the leisure complex, where an indoor and outdoor swimming pool, shops, cafés and bars and evening entertainment are all provided. 40 acre site. 100 touring pitches. Caravan pitches. Motorhome pitches. Tent pitches. 294 statics.

AA Pubs & Restaurants nearby: Rose & Crown, Colchester 01206 866677

Whalebone, Fingringhoe 01206 729307

Leisure: 🏊🏊🛝🪁🎮🎱🎵
Facilities: 🚿☉🅿✂♿🕙🛒 Wi-Fi 🖥
Services: 🚐🔌🍴🧺🍽🛒
Within 3 miles: 🎣🏌⛴🎿🛒🎱⛵
Notes: ⊗ Water sports.

COLCHESTER — Map 13 TL92

Places to visit
Colchester Castle Museum, COLCHESTER
01206 282939 www.colchestermuseums.org.uk

Layer Marney Tower, LAYER MARNEY
01206 330784 www.layermarneytower.co.uk

Great for kids: Colchester Zoo, COLCHESTER
01206 331292 www.colchester-zoo.com

▶▶▶▶ 85% *Colchester Holiday Park* (TL971252)

Cymbeline Way, Lexden CO3 4AG
☎ 01206 545551 📄 01206 710443
e-mail: enquiries@colchestercamping.co.uk
dir: *Follow tourist signs from A12, then A133 Colchester Central slip road*

Open all year

Last arrival 20.30hrs Last departure noon

A well-designed campsite on level grassland, on the west side of Colchester near the town centre. Close to main routes to London (A12) and east coast. There is good provision for hardstandings, and the owner's attention to detail is reflected in the neatly trimmed grass and well-cut hedges. Toilet facilities are housed in three buildings, two of which are modern and well equipped. 12 acre site. 168 touring pitches. 44 hardstandings. Caravan pitches. Motorhome pitches. Tent pitches.

AA Pubs & Restaurants nearby: Rose & Crown, Colchester 01206 866677

Whalebone, Fingringhoe 01206 729307

Swan Inn, Chappel 01787 222353

Leisure: 🛝
Facilities: 🚿☉🅿✂♿🕙🛒🎪🐕
Services: 🚐🔌🧺🍴T🛒🛠
Within 3 miles: 🎣🎬🏌⛴🎿🛒⛵
Notes: No commercial vehicles. Badminton court.

MERSEA ISLAND — Map 7 TM01

Places to visit
Layer Marney Tower, LAYER MARNEY
01206 330784 www.layermarneytower.co.uk

80% *Waldegraves Holiday Park* (TM033133)

GOLD

CO5 8SE
☎ 01206 382898 📄 01206 385359
e-mail: holidays@waldegraves.co.uk
web: www.waldegraves.co.uk
dir: *A12 junct 26, B1025 to Mersea Island across The Strood. Left to East Mersea, 2nd right, follow tourist signs to site*

* 🚐 £16-£26 🚐 £16-£26 ⛺ £16-£26

Open Mar-Nov (rs Mar-Jun & Sep-Nov (excl BH & school half terms) pool, shop & clubhouse reduced opening hrs low season, pool open May-Sep (weather permitting))

Last arrival 22.00hrs Last departure 15.00hrs

A spacious and pleasant site, located between farmland and its own private beach on the Blackwater Estuary. Facilities include two freshwater fishing lakes, heated swimming pool, club, amusements, café and golf, and there is generally good provision for families. 25 acre site. 60 touring pitches. 30 seasonal pitches. Caravan pitches. Motorhome pitches. Tent pitches. 250 statics.

AA Pubs & Restaurants nearby: Peldon Rose, Peldon 01206 735248

Leisure: 🏊🛝🪁🎮🎱🎵
Facilities: 🚿☉🅿✂♿🕙🛒🎪🐕 Wi-Fi ♻ ⓘ
Services: 🚐🔌🍴🧺🧺T🍽🛒🛒🛠
Within 3 miles: 🎣🏌◎🎿🛒🎱
Notes: No large groups or groups of under 21s. Boating/slipway, pitch & putt/driving range.

see advert on opposite page

SERVICES: Electric hook up Launderette Licensed bar Calor Gas Camping Gaz Toilet fluid Café/Restaurant Fast Food/Takeaway Battery charging Baby care Motorvan service point

ABBREVIATIONS: BH/bank hols-bank holidays Etr-Easter Whit-Whitsun dep-departure fr-from hrs-hours m-mile mdnt-midnight rdbt-roundabout rs-restricted service wk-week wknd-weekend No credit cards No dogs

See page 7 for details of the AA Camping Card Scheme

ST LAWRENCE — Map 7 TL90

Places to visit

RHS Garden Hyde Hall, CHELMSFORD 01245 402006 www.rhs.org.uk

Kelvedon Hatch Secret Nuclear Bunker, BRENTWOOD 01277 364883 www.secretnuclearbunker.co.uk

Great for kids: Hadleigh Castle, HADLEIGH 01760 755161 www.english-heritage.org.uk

79% Waterside St Lawrence Bay

(TL953056)

Main Rd CMO 7LY
☎ 0871 664 9794
e-mail: waterside@park-resorts.com
dir: *A12 towards Chelmsford, A414 signed Maldon. Follow B1010 & signs to Latchingdon, then signs for Mayland/Steeple/St Lawrence. Left towards St Lawrence. Site on right*

Open Apr-Oct (rs Wknds)

Last arrival 22.00hrs Last departure 10.00hrs

Waterside occupies a scenic location overlooking the Blackwater estuary. In addition to the range of on-site leisure facilities there are opportunities for beautiful coastal walks and visits to the attractions of Southend. Tents are welcome on this expansive site, which has some touring pitches with electricity and good toilet facilities. The park has its own boat storage and slipway onto the Blackwater. 72 touring pitches. Caravan pitches. Motorhome pitches. Tent pitches. 271 statics.

Waterside St Lawrence Bay

AA Pubs & Restaurants nearby: Ye Olde White Harte Hotel, Burnham-on-Crouch 01621 782106

Ferryboat Inn, North Fambridge 01621 740208

Leisure:
Facilities:
Services:
Within 3 miles:
Notes: Sauna, spa pool.

see advert on page 213

ST OSYTH

Places to visit

Harwich Redoubt Fort, HARWICH 01255 503429 www.harwich-society.com

Colchester Castle Museum, COLCHESTER 01206 282939 www.colchestermuseums.org.uk

Great for kids: Colchester Zoo, COLCHESTER 01206 331292 www.colchester-zoo.com

ST OSYTH — Map 7 TM11

79% The Orchards Holiday Park *(TM125155)*

CO16 8LJ
☎ 0871 231 0861 📠 01255 820184
e-mail: theorchards@haven.com
dir: *From Clacton-on-Sea take B1027 towards Colchester. Left after petrol station, then straight on at x-rds in St Osyth. Follow signs to Point Clear. Park in 3m*

Open end Mar-end Oct (rs mid Mar-May & Sep-Oct some facilities may be reduced)

Last arrival anytime Last departure 10.00hrs

The Orchards offers much improved touring facilities with a quality toilet block which includes two very spacious family rooms. The touring pitches are generously sized and the touring area has its own laundry and play area. There's also direct access to all the leisure, entertainment and dining outlets available

LEISURE: 🏊 Indoor swimming pool 🏊 Outdoor swimming pool 🎠 Children's playground 👦 Kid's club 🎾 Tennis court 🎱 Games room 📺 Separate TV room ⛳ 9/18 hole golf course ⛵ Boats for hire 🎬 Cinema 🎵 Entertainment 🎣 Fishing ⊙ Mini golf 🏄 Watersports 🏋 Gym ⚽ Sports field **Spa** ♨ Stables
FACILITIES: 🛁 Bath 🚿 Shower 🔌 Electric shaver 💨 Hairdryer ❄ Ice Pack Facility ♿ Disabled facilities 📞 Public telephone 🏪 Shop on site or within 200yds 🏪 Mobile shop (calls at least 5 days a week) 🍖 BBQ area 🎪 Picnic area 📶 Wi-fi 💻 Internet access ♻ Recycling ⊙ Tourist info 🐕 Dog exercise area

on this large popular holiday park on the Essex coast. 140 acre site. 54 touring pitches. Caravan pitches. Tent pitches. 1000 statics.

AA Pubs & Restaurants nearby: Rose & Crown, Colchester 01206 866677

Whalebone, Fingringhoe 01206 729307

Leisure: ⛱ ⚲ Ⓜ **Facilities:** ⍾ ⚲ ⚹ ⚙ Ⓢ WI-FI

Services: ⊞ Ⓢ ⚑ 🛢 ⓘⓄ ⚒

Within 3 miles: ⌖ ⚲ ⊚ ⚌ Ⓢ Ⓢ ∪

Notes: No cars by tents. Max 2 dogs per booking, certain dog breeds banned, no commercial vehicles, no bookings by persons under 21yrs unless a family booking.

see advert on opposite page

WALTON ON THE NAZE   Map 7 TM22

Places to visit

Ipswich Museum, IPSWICH 01473 433550
www.ipswich.gov.uk

Harwich Redoubt Fort, HARWICH 01255 503429
www.harwich-society.com

 73% Naze Marine
(TM255226)

Hall Ln CO14 8HL
☎ 0871 664 9755
e-mail: naze.marine@park-resorts.com
dir: *A12 to Colchester. Then A120 (Harwich road) then A133 to Weeley. Take B1033 to Walton seafront. Site on left*

⊞ ⊟

Open Apr-Oct

Last arrival anytime Last departure 10.00hrs

With its modern indoor swimming pool, show bar, bar/restaurant and amusements, this park offers a variety of on-site attractions The park is within easy access of the beaches and attractions of Walton on the Naze, Frinton and Clacton, and the more historic places of interest inland. Please note that this site does not cater for tents. 46 acre site. 41 touring pitches. Caravan pitches. Motorhome pitches. 540 statics.

Leisure: ⛱ Ⓜ ⚽ ⚞ **Facilities:** ⍾ ☺ ⚙ ⚙ Ⓢ ⚟ WI-FI 💻

Services: ⊞ Ⓢ ⚑ ⓘⓄ ⚒

Within 3 miles: ⌖ ⚲ ⚌ Ⓢ Ⓢ

Notes: Nature walk, natural meadow.

WEST MERSEA   Map 7 TM01

Places to visit

Layer Marney Tower, LAYER MARNEY
01206 330784 www.layermarneytower.co.uk

Great for kids: Colchester Zoo, COLCHESTER
01206 331292 www.colchester-zoo.com

NEW ►►► 79% Seaview Holiday Park *(TM025125)*

Seaview Av CO5 8DA
☎ 01206 382534
e-mail: seaviewholidaypark@googlemail.com
dir: *From A12 (Colchester), onto B1025 (Mersea Island), cross causeway, left towards East Mersea, 1st right, follow signs*

* ⊞ £15-£21 ⊟ £17-£23

Open Apr-Oct

Last arrival 18.00hrs Last departure noon

With sweeping views across the Blackwater estuary, this interesting, well established park has its own private beach, complete with boat slipway and photogenic beach cabins, a modern shop, café and a stylish clubhouse which offers evening meals and drinks in a quiet family atmosphere. The touring area is well maintained and has 40 fully serviced pitches. 30 acre site. 106 touring pitches. 40 hardstandings. 30 seasonal pitches. Caravan pitches. Motorhome pitches. 240 statics.

Facilities: ⍾ ☺ ⚙ ⚹ ❶

Services: ⊞ Ⓢ ⚑ ⓘⓄ ⚒

Within 3 miles: ⌖ ⚲ Ⓢ Ⓢ ∪

Notes: No noise after mdnt. Phone site if late arrival expected. Dogs must be kept on leads. Private beach.

GLOUCESTERSHIRE

BERKELEY   Map 4 ST69

Places to visit

Edward Jenner Museum, BERKELEY
01453 810631 www.jennermuseum.com

WWT Slimbridge, SLIMBRIDGE 01453 891900
www.wwt.org.uk

Great for kids: Berkeley Castle & Butterfly House, BERKELEY 01453 810332
www.berkeley-castle.com

AA CAMPING CARD SITE

►►► 74% Hogsdown Farm Caravan & Camping Park *(ST710974)*

Hogsdown Farm, Lower Wick GL11 6DD
☎ 01453 810224
dir: *M5 junct 14 (Falfield), take A38 towards Gloucester. Through Stone & Woodford. After Newport turn right signed Lower Wick*

⊞ ⊟ Å

Open all year

Last arrival 21.00hrs Last departure 16.00hrs

A pleasant site with good toilet facilities, located between Bristol and Gloucester. It is well positioned for visiting Berkeley Castle and the Cotswolds, and makes an excellent overnight stop when travelling to or from the West Country. 5 acre site. 45 touring pitches. 12 hardstandings. Caravan pitches. Motorhome pitches. Tent pitches.

AA Pubs & Restaurants nearby: Malt House, Berkeley 01453 511177

Anchor Inn, Oldbury-on-Severn 01454 413331

Leisure: Ⓜ **Facilities:** ⍾ ☺ ❈ ♻ ❶

Services: ⊞ Ⓢ ≣

Within 3 miles: ⌖ ⚲ Ⓢ Ⓢ ∪

Notes: ⊛ No skateboards or bicycles. Dogs must be kept on leads.

CHELTENHAM — Map 10 SO92

Places to visit

Holst Birthplace Museum, CHELTENHAM
01242 524846 www.holstmuseum.org.uk

Sudeley Castle, Gardens & Exhibitions,
WINCHCOMBE 01242 602308
www.sudeleycastle.co.uk

Great for kids: Gloucester City Museum & Art
Gallery, GLOUCESTER 01452 396131
www.gloucester.gov.uk/citymuseum

AA CAMPING CARD SITE

▶▶▶▶ **80% Briarfields Motel &
Touring Park** (SO909218)

Gloucester Rd GL51 0SX
☎ **01242 235324**
e-mail: briarfields@hotmail.co.uk
dir: M5 junct 11, A40 towards Cheltenham. At rdbt
left onto B4063, site 150mtrs on left

⇔ £15-£18 ⇔ £15-£18 ▲ £11-£15

Open all year

A well-designed level park, with a motel, where
the facilities are modern and very clean. The park
is well-positioned between Cheltenham and
Gloucester, with easy access to the Cotswolds.
And, being close to the M5, it makes a perfect
overnight stopping point. 5 acre site. 72 touring
pitches. 72 hardstandings. Caravan pitches.
Motorhome pitches. Tent pitches.

Facilities: ⊓⊙ℱ✳⊙ WiFi ♻ ❶
Services: ⊟⑤
Within 3 miles: ↓☐ℱ◎⑤⑤∪
Notes: No noise after 23.00hrs. Dogs must be
kept on leads.

CIRENCESTER

Places to visit

Corinium Museum, CIRENCESTER 01285 655611
www.coriniummuseum.cotswold.gov.uk

Chedworth Roman Villa,
CHEDWORTH 01242 890256
www.nationaltrust.org.uk/chedworth

Great for kids: Prinknash Abbey, CRANHAM
01452 812066 www.prinknashabbey.org.uk

CIRENCESTER — Map 5 SP00

AA CAMPING CARD SITE

▶▶▶▶ **80% Mayfield Touring Park**
(SP020055)

Cheltenham Rd GL7 7BH
☎ **01285 831301**
e-mail:
mayfield-park@cirencester.fsbusiness.co.uk
dir: From Cirencester bypass take Burford road/
A429 junct exit towards Cirencester, then follow
brown signs to site (approx 3.5m)

* ⇔ £14-£22 ⇔ £14-£22 ▲ £14-£22

Open all year

Last arrival 20.00hrs Last departure noon

A gently sloping park on the edge of the
Cotswolds, with level pitches and a warm
welcome. Popular with couples and families, it
offers a good licensed shop selling a wide
selection of home-cooked takeaway food. Although
some traffic noise can be heard at times, this
lovely park makes an ideal base for visiting the
Cotswolds and the many attractions of the area.
12 acre site. 72 touring pitches. 31
hardstandings. Caravan pitches. Motorhome
pitches. Tent pitches.

AA Pubs & Restaurants nearby: The Crown of
Crucis, Cirencester 01285 851806

Hare & Hounds, Chedworth 01285 720288

Facilities: ⊓⊙ℱ✳⊙⑤♣ WiFi ♻ ❶
Services: ⊟⑤⬛∅T⬛
Within 3 miles: ↓⑤⑤
Notes: Dogs only by by prior arrangement, and
must be kept on leads. No cycles or skateboards.
Off licence.

GLOUCESTER

Places to visit

Gloucester Folk Museum,
GLOUCESTER 01452 396868
www.gloucester.gov.uk/folkmuseum

Nature in Art, GLOUCESTER 01452 731422
www.nature-in-art.org.uk

Great for kids: The National Waterways
Museum, GLOUCESTER 01452 318200
www.nwm.org.uk

GLOUCESTER — Map 10 SO81

▶▶▶ **73% Red Lion Caravan &
Camping Park** (SO849258)

Wainlode Hill, Norton GL2 9LW
☎ 01452 730251 & 731810 ⬛ 01452 730251
dir: Exit A38 at Norton, follow road to river

⇔ ⇔ ▲

Open all year

Last arrival 22.00hrs Last departure 11.00hrs

An attractive meadowland park, adjacent to a
traditional pub, with the River Severn just across
a country lane. This is an ideal touring and fishing
base. 24 acre site. 60 touring pitches. 10
hardstandings. Caravan pitches. Motorhome
pitches. Tent pitches. 85 statics.

AA Pubs & Restaurants nearby: Queens Head,
Gloucester 01452 301882

Queens Arms, Ashleworth 01452 700395

Boat Inn, Ashleworth 01452 700272

Leisure: ⋀
Facilities: ⊓⊙ℱ✳⊙⑤♣
Services: ⊟⑤⬛∅T⬛
Within 3 miles: ↓ℱ⑤∪
Notes: ⊛ Freshwater fishing & private lake.

NEWENT — Map 10 SO72

Places to visit

Odda's Chapel, DEERHURST
www.english-heritage.org.uk

Westbury Court Garden, WESTBURY-ON-SEVERN
01452 760461 www.nationaltrust.org.uk

Great for kids: The National Birds of Prey
Centre, NEWENT 0870 9901992 www.nbpc.co.uk

▶▶▶ **82% Pelerine Caravan and
Camping** (SO645183)

Ford House Rd GL18 1LQ
☎ **01531 822761**
e-mail: pelerine@hotmail.com
dir: 1m from Newent

* ⇔ £18-£22 ⇔ £18-£22 ▲ £18-£22

Open Mar-Nov

Last arrival 22.00hrs Last departure 16.00hrs

A pleasant site divided into two areas, one of
which is for adults only, with some hardstandings
and electric hook-ups in each area. Facilities are

LEISURE: ⊛ Indoor swimming pool ⊛ Outdoor swimming pool ⋀ Children's playground ↓ Kid's club ⊙ Tennis court ⚡ Games room ☐ Separate TV room
↓ 9/18 hole golf course ⚓ Boats for hire ☐ Cinema ⬛ Entertainment ℱ Fishing ◎ Mini golf ⬛ Watersports ⬛ Gym ⊕ Sports field Spa ∪ Stables
FACILITIES: ⬛ Bath ⊓ Shower ⊙ Electric shaver ℱ Hairdryer ✳ Ice Pack Facility ⑤ Disabled facilities ⊙ Public telephone ⑤ Shop on site or within 200yds
⬛ Mobile shop (calls at least 5 days a week) ⬛ BBQ area ⬛ Picnic area WiFi Wi-fi ⬛ Internet access ♻ Recycling ❶ Tourist info ♣ Dog exercise area

very good, especially for families. It is close to several vineyards, and well positioned in the north of the Forest of Dean with Tewkesbury, Cheltenham and Ross-on-Wye within easy reach. 5 acre site. 35 touring pitches. 2 hardstandings. Caravan pitches. Motorhome pitches. Tent pitches.

AA Pubs & Restaurants nearby: Yew Tree Inn, Cliffords Mesne 01531 820719

Penny Farthing Inn, Aston Crews 01989 750366

Facilities: ⬤⬤⬤⬤⬤⬤⬤⬤⬤⬤

Services: ⬤⬤⬤

Within 3 miles: ⬤⬤⬤⬤⬤⬤⬤

Notes: ⬤ Dogs must be kept on leads. Woodburners, chimneas, burning pits.

SLIMBRIDGE   Map 4 SO70

Places to visit

Dean Forest Railway, LYDNEY 01594 843423 (info) www.deanforestrailway.co.uk

Berkeley Castle & Butterfly House, BERKELEY 01453 810332 www.berkeley-castle.com

Great for kids: WWT Slimbridge, SLIMBRIDGE 01453 891900 www.wwt.org.uk

▶▶▶▶ 84% Tudor Caravan & Camping (SO728040)

GOLD

Shepherds Patch GL2 7BP
☎ 01453 890483
e-mail: aa@tudorcaravanpark.co.uk
web: www.tudorcaravanpark.com
dir: *M5 juncts 13 & 14 follow WWT Wetlands Wildlife Centre-Slimbridge signs. Site at rear of Tudor Arms pub*

* ⬤ £11.50-£20 ⬤ £11.50-£20 ▲ £7.50-£20

Open all year

Last arrival 20.00hrs Last departure noon

An orchard-style park sheltered by mature trees and shrubs, set in an attractive meadow beside the Sharpness to Gloucester canal. A facility block has been added in the more open area of the site

and the site now benefits from a new reception and tourist information office. This tidy site offers both level grass and gravel pitches complete with electric hook-ups, and there is a separate adults-only area. The Wildfowl and Wetlands Trust at Slimbridge is close by, and there is much scope locally for birdwatching. 8 acre site. 75 touring pitches. 48 hardstandings. Caravan pitches. Motorhome pitches. Tent pitches.

AA Pubs & Restaurants nearby: Old Passage Inn, Arlingham 01452 740547

Facilities: ⬤⬤⬤⬤⬤⬤⬤⬤⬤⬤⬤

Services: ⬤⬤⬤⬤⬤⬤⬤⬤⬤

Within 3 miles: ⬤⬤⬤⬤⬤

Notes: Debit cards only accepted. Dogs must be kept on leads.

STONEHOUSE   Map 4 SO80

Places to visit

Painswick Rococo Garden, PAINSWICK 01452 813204 www.rococogarden.org.uk

WWT Slimbridge, SLIMBRIDGE 01453 891900 www.wwt.org.uk

NEW ▶▶▶ 86% Apple Tree Park Caravan and Camping Site (SO766063)

A38, Claypits GL10 3AL
☎ 01452 742362 & 07708 221457
📠 01452 742362
e-mail: appletreepark@hotmail.co.uk
dir: *M5 junct 13 onto A38. 1st exit on rdbt. Site 0.7m on left (400mtrs past filling station)*

* ⬤ £14-£15.50 ⬤ £14-£15.50 ▲ £14-£15.50

Open Mar-Oct

Last arrival 21.00hrs Last departure noon

Apple Tree park is a new family owned park conveniently located on the A38, not far from the M5. A peaceful site with glorious views of the Cotswolds, it offers modern and spotlessly clean toilet facilities with under-floor heating. The park is well located for visiting Slimbridge Wildfowl & Wetlands Trust, and makes an excellent stopover for M5 travellers. Very much a hidden gem. 6.5 acre site. 65 touring pitches. 14 hardstandings. 10 seasonal pitches. Caravan pitches. Motorhome pitches. Tent pitches.

Leisure: ⬤

Facilities: ⬤⬤⬤⬤⬤⬤⬤⬤⬤⬤⬤

Services: ⬤⬤⬤⬤⬤

Within 3 miles: ⬤⬤⬤⬤⬤

Notes: Minimum noise after 22.30hrs. Dogs must be kept on leads.

GREATER MANCHESTER

LITTLEBOROUGH   Map 16 SD91

Places to visit

Imperial War Museum North, MANCHESTER 0161 836 4000 www.iwm.org.uk

Manchester Art Gallery, MANCHESTER 0161 235 8888 www.manchestergalleries.org

Great for kids: Heaton Park, PRESTWICH 0161 773 1085 www.heatonpark.org.uk

▶▶▶ 70% Hollingworth Lake Caravan Park (SD943146)

Round House Farm, Rakewood Rd, Rakewood OL15 0AT
☎ 01706 378661 & 373919
dir: *From Littleborough or Milnrow (M62 junct 21), follow 'Hollingworth Lake Country Park' signs to Fishermans Inn/The Wine Press. Take 'No Through Road' to Rakewood, then 2nd on right*

* ⬤ £12-£16 ⬤ £12-£16 ▲ £8-£16

Open all year

Last arrival 20.00hrs Last departure noon

A popular park adjacent to Hollingworth Lake, at the foot of the Pennines, within easy reach of many local attractions. Backpackers walking the Pennine Way are welcome at this family-run park, and there are also large rally fields. 5 acre site. 50 touring pitches. 25 hardstandings. Caravan pitches. Motorhome pitches. Tent pitches. 53 statics.

AA Pubs & Restaurants nearby: The White House, Littleborough 01706 378456

Facilities: ⬤⬤⬤⬤⬤⬤⬤

Services: ⬤⬤⬤⬤⬤⬤⬤

Within 3 miles: ⬤⬤⬤⬤⬤⬤⬤

Notes: ⬤⬤ Family groups only. Pony trekking.

SERVICES: ⬤ Electric hook up ⬤ Launderette ⬤ Licensed bar ⬤ Calor Gas ⬤ Camping Gaz ⬤ Toilet fluid ⬤ Café/Restaurant ⬤ Fast Food/Takeaway ⬤ Battery charging ⬤ Baby care ⬤ Motorvan service point
ABBREVIATIONS: BH/bank hols-bank holidays Etr-Easter Whit-Whitsun dep-departure fr-from hrs-hours m-mile mdnt-midnight rdbt-roundabout rs-restricted service wk-week wknd-weekend ⬤ No credit cards ⬤ No dogs
See page 7 for details of the AA Camping Card Scheme

ROCHDALE Map 16 SD81

Places to visit

People's History Museum, MANCHESTER
0161 838 9190 www.phm.org.uk

Gallery of Costume, MANCHESTER 0161 245 7245
www.manchestergalleries.org.uk .

▶▶▶ **76%** *Gelderwood Country Park* (SD852127)

GOLD

Ashworth Rd OL11 5UP
☎ 01706 364858 & 620300 📄 01706 364858
e-mail: gelderwood@aol.com
dir: *Signed midway from B6222 (Bury/Rochdale road). Turn into Ashworth Rd, continue past mill. Uphill for 800yds, site on right*

🚐 🚙

Open all year Last departure noon

A very rural site in a peaceful private country park with excellent facilities. All pitches have extensive views of the moor, and this is a popular base for walkers and birdwatchers. The park is for adults only. 10 acre site. 34 touring pitches. 26 hardstandings. Caravan pitches. Motorhome pitches.

AA Pubs & Restaurants nearby: The White House, Littleborough 01706 378456

Nutters, Rochdale 01706 650167

The Peacock Room, Rochdale 01706 368591

Facilities: 🏕 ⊙ 🅿 ⅃ 🛒 **Services:** 🔌 🔒
Within 3 miles: ✒ 🏷 🛍 ∪
Notes: Adults only. 🐕

HAMPSHIRE

BRANSGORE Map 5 SZ19

Places to visit

Sammy Miller Motorcycle Museum, NEW MILTON
01425 620777 www.sammymiller.co.uk

Red House Museum & Gardens,
CHRISTCHURCH 01202 482860
www.hants.gov.uk/museum/redhouse

Great for kids: Moors Valley Country Park,
RINGWOOD 01425 470721
www.moors-valley.co.uk

▶▶▶ **84% Harrow Wood Farm Caravan Park** (SZ194978)

Harrow Wood Farm, Poplar Ln BH23 8JE
☎ 01425 672487 📄 01425 672487
e-mail: harrowwood@caravan-sites.co.uk
dir: *From Ringwood take B3347 towards Christchurch. At Sopley, left for Bransgore, to T-junct. Turn right. Straight on at x-rds. Left in 400yds (just after garage) into Poplar Lane*

🚐 £16.50-£31.50 🚙 £16.50-£31.50
⛺ £16.50-£23.50

Open Mar-6 Jan

Last arrival 22.00hrs Last departure noon

A well laid-out and spacious site in a pleasant rural position adjoining woodland and fields. Free on-site coarse fishing is available at this peaceful park. Well located for visiting Christchurch, the New Forest National Park and the south coast. 6 acre site. 60 touring pitches. 60 hardstandings. Caravan pitches. Motorhome pitches. Tent pitches.

Harrow Wood Farm Caravan Park

AA Pubs & Restaurants nearby: Three Tuns, Bransgore 01425 672232

Facilities: 🏕 ⊙ 🅿 ✳ ⅃ 🕓 📶
Services: 🔌 🔲 🔒 🛒
Within 3 miles: ✒ 🏷
Notes: ⊗ No open fires.

see advert below

FORDINGBRIDGE

Places to visit

Rockbourne Roman Villa,
ROCKBOURNE 0845 603 5635
www.hants.gov.uk/rockbourne-roman-villa

Breamore House & Countryside Museum,
BREAMORE 01725 512468
www.breamorehouse.com

Great for kids: Moors Valley Country Park,
RINGWOOD 01425 470721
www.moors-valley.co.uk

Situated in a pleasant village right on the edge of the New Forest, our six acre site offers the perfect centre from which to explore the surrounding area. Christchurch, Highcliffe and the market town of Ringwood are but a short drive away. In the village at Bransgore, there are a variety of shops to suit your everyday needs, all within walking distance. Sorry no dogs.

HARROW WOOD FARM
Caravan Park
AA ▶▶▶ ETB ★★★ **BH&HPA** Member
Open 1 March – 6 January
Bransgore, nr. Christchurch, Dorset BH23 8JE
Telephone: 01425 672487
Email: harrowwood@caravan-sites.co.uk
http://www.caravan-sites.co.uk

LEISURE: 🏊 Indoor swimming pool 🏊 Outdoor swimming pool 🛝 Children's playground 🧒 Kid's club 🎾 Tennis court 🎱 Games room 📺 Separate TV room ⛳ 9/18 hole golf course ⛵ Boats for hire 🎬 Cinema 🎵 Entertainment 🎣 Fishing ⛳ Mini golf 🏄 Watersports 🏋 Gym ⚽ Sports field Spa ∪ Stables
FACILITIES: 🛁 Bath 🚿 Shower ⊙ Electric shaver ✂ Hairdryer ✳ Ice Pack Facility ♿ Disabled facilities ☎ Public telephone 🏪 Shop on site or within 200yds 🏪 Mobile shop (calls at least 5 days a week) 🔥 BBQ area 🏕 Picnic area 📶 Wi-fi 💻 Internet access ♻ Recycling ❶ Tourist info 🐕 Dog exercise area

FORDINGBRIDGE — Map 5 SU11

92% Sandy Balls Holiday Centre

Best of British GOLD

(SU167148)

Sandy Balls Estate Ltd, Godshill SP6 2JZ
☎ 0845 270 2248 📠 01425 653067
e-mail: post@sandyballs.co.uk
web: www.sandyballs.co.uk
dir: M27 junct 1 onto B3078, B3079, 8m to Godshill. Site 0.25m after cattle grid

* ⊞ £10-£50 ⊟ £10-£50 ▲ £25

Open all year (rs Nov-Feb pitches reduced, no activities)

Last arrival 21.00hrs Last departure 11.00hrs

A large, mostly wooded New Forest holiday complex with good provision of touring facilities on terraced, well laid-out fields. Pitches are fully serviced with shingle bases, and groups can be sited beside the river and away from the main site. There are excellent sporting, leisure and entertainment facilities for the whole family, a bistro and information centre, and now also four tipis and eight ready-erected tents for hire. 120 acre site. 233 touring pitches. 233 hardstandings. Caravan pitches. Motorhome pitches. Tent pitches. 233 statics. 4 bell tents/yurts.

AA Pubs & Restaurants nearby: The Augustus John, Fordingbridge 01425 652098

Leisure: 🏊⛵🎯🎠🎣♫ Spa
Facilities: 🛁🚿⊙⚡🎣✳❤🕐🛒🧺🎯 WiFi ♻ ℹ
Services: 🔌🛢🧺🚿♨🚽🍴🛒🛒🚮
Within 3 miles: 🎣🏊🛒🛍⛳U

Notes: Groups only by arrangement, no gazebos, no noise after 23.00hrs. Dogs must be kept on leads. Jacuzzi, sauna, beauty therapy, gym, horse riding, bistro.

see advert on page 219

HAMBLE-LE-RICE — Map 5 SU40

Places to visit

Royal Armouries Fort Nelson, FAREHAM
01329 233734 www.royalarmouries.org

Southampton City Art Gallery, SOUTHAMPTON
023 8083 2277 www.southampton.gov.uk/art

Great for kids: Southampton Maritime Museum, SOUTHAMPTON 023 8022 3941
www.southampton.gov.uk/leisure

►►►► 80% Riverside Holidays (SU481081)

COUNTRYSIDE DISCOVERY

21 Compass Point, Ensign Way
SO31 4RA
☎ 023 8045 3220 📠 023 8045 3611
e-mail: enquiries@riversideholidays.co.uk
web: www.riversideholidays.co.uk
dir: M27 junct 8, follow signs to Hamble on B3397. Left into Satchell Lane, site in 1m

⊞ ⊟ ▲

Open Mar-Oct

Last arrival 22.00hrs Last departure 11.00hrs

A small, peaceful park next to the marina, and close to the pretty village of Hamble. The park is neatly kept, and there are two toilet and shower blocks complete with good family rooms. A pub and restaurant are very close by. Lodges and static caravans are available for hire. 6 acre site. 77 touring pitches. Caravan pitches. Motorhome pitches. Tent pitches. 45 statics.

AA Pubs & Restaurants nearby: The Bugle, Hamble-le-Rice 023 8045 3000

Facilities: 🛁🚿⊙⚡🎣✳❤🛒ℹ
Services: 🔌🛢🛒🚮
Within 3 miles: 🎿🛶🎣🏊🛒🛍⛳U

Notes: Dogs must be kept on leads. Bike hire, baby changing facilities.

see advert on opposite page

LINWOOD — Map 5 SU10

Places to visit

The New Forest Centre, LYNDHURST
023 8028 3444 www.newforestmuseum.org.uk

Furzey Gardens, MINSTEAD 023 8081 2464
www.furzey-gardens.org

Great for kids: Paultons Park, OWER
023 8081 4442 www.paultonspark.co.uk

►►► 84% Red Shoot Camping Park

(SU187094)

BH24 3QT
☎ 01425 473789 📠 01425 471558
e-mail: enquiries@redshoot-campingpark.com
dir: A31 onto A338 towards Fordingbridge & Salisbury. Right at brown signs for caravan park towards Linwood on unclassified roads, site signed

⊞ ⊟ ▲

Open Mar-Oct

Last arrival 20.30hrs Last departure 13.00hrs

Located behind the Red Shoot Inn in one of the most attractive parts of the New Forest, this park is in an ideal spot for nature lovers and walkers. It is personally supervised by friendly owners, and offers many amenities including a children's play area. There are modern and spotless facilities plus a smart reception and shop. 3.5 acre site. 130 touring pitches. Caravan pitches. Motorhome pitches. Tent pitches.

AA Pubs & Restaurants nearby: High Corner Inn, Linwood 01425 473973

Leisure: 🎠
Facilities: 🚿⊙⚡🎣✳❤🕐🛒
Services: 🔌🛢🧺🛒♨♻T🍴🚮
Within 3 miles: 🎣🏊🛒🛍U

Notes: Quiet after 22.30hrs. Dogs must be kept on leads. Family shower room.

MILFORD ON SEA

Places to visit

Buckler's Hard, BUCKLERS HARD 01590 616203
www.bucklershard.co.uk

Exbury Gardens & Railway,
EXBURY 023 8089 1203 www.exbury.co.uk

Great for kids: Beaulieu, BEAULIEU
01590 612345 www.beaulieu.co.uk

LEISURE: 🏊 Indoor swimming pool 🏊 Outdoor swimming pool 🎠 Children's playground 🧒 Kid's club 🎾 Tennis court 🎱 Games room 📺 Separate TV room ⛳ 9/18 hole golf course 🚣 Boats for hire 🎬 Cinema 🎭 Entertainment 🎣 Fishing ⛳ Mini golf 🏄 Watersports 🏋 Gym 🏟 Sports field Spa U Stables
FACILITIES: 🛁 Bath 🚿 Shower ⊙ Electric shaver 🎣 Hairdryer ✳ Ice Pack Facility ♿ Disabled facilities 🕐 Public telephone 🛒 Shop on site or within 200yds 🚚 Mobile shop (calls at least 5 days a week) 🍖 BBQ area 🧺 Picnic area WiFi Wi-fi 💻 Internet access ♻ Recycling ℹ Tourist info 🐕 Dog exercise area

MILFORD ON SEA
Map 5 SZ29

►►►► 84% Lytton Lawn Touring Park (SZ293937)

Lymore Ln SO41 0TX
☎ 01590 648331 📄 01590 645610
e-mail: holidays@shorefield.co.uk
dir: *From Lymington A337 to Christchurch for 2.5m to Everton. Left onto B3058 to Milford on Sea. 0.25m, left onto Lymore Lane*

🚐 £12-£39.50 🚗 £12-£39.50 ▲ £12-£36

Open 6 Feb-2 Jan (rs Low season shop/reception limited hrs. No grass pitches)

Last arrival 22.00hrs Last departure 10.00hrs

A pleasant well-run park with good facilities, located near the coast. The park is peaceful and quiet, but the facilities of a sister park 2.5 miles away are available to campers, including swimming pool, tennis courts, bistro and bar/carvery, and large club with family entertainment. Fully-serviced pitches provide good screening, and standard pitches are on gently-sloping grass. 8 acre site. 136 touring pitches. 53 hardstandings. Caravan pitches. Motorhome pitches. Tent pitches.

AA Pubs & Restaurants nearby: Royal Oak, Downton 01590 642297

Leisure: 🅰 🌣 🔍
Facilities: ♠ ☉ 🗝 ✳ ⚹ ⏰ 🍴 ♨ ➡ 🎱 ♻ ❔
Services: 🔌 🗑 🛢 🖉 ⊤ ⚡
Within 3 miles: 🚲 ♬ ◎ ⛵ 🎱 🗑 ∪

Notes: Families & couples only. Rallies welcome. Dogs must be kept on leads. Free use of Shorefield Leisure Club (2.5m), bar.

OWER
Map 5 SU31

Places to visit
The New Forest Centre, LYNDHURST 023 8028 3444 www.newforestmuseum.org.uk

Furzey Gardens, MINSTEAD 023 8081 2464 www.furzey-gardens.org

Great for kids: Paultons Park, OWER 023 8081 4442 www.paultonspark.co.uk

►►► 80% Green Pastures Farm (SU321158)

SO51 6AJ
☎ 023 8081 4444

e-mail: enquiries@greenpasturesfarm.com
dir: *M27 junct 2. Follow Salisbury signs for 0.5m. Then follow brown tourist signs for Green Pastures. Also signed from A36 & A3090 at Ower*

* 🚐 fr £17 🚗 fr £17 ▲ fr £17

Open 15 Mar-Oct

Last departure 11.00hrs

A pleasant site on a working farm, with good screening of trees and shrubs around the perimeter. The touring area is divided by a border of shrubs and, at times, colourful foxgloves. This peaceful location is close to the M27 and the New Forest, and is also very convenient for visiting Paultons Family Theme Park. 5 acre site. 45 touring pitches. 2 hardstandings. Caravan pitches. Motorhome pitches. Tent pitches.

AA Pubs & Restaurants nearby: Sir John Barleycorn, Cadnam 023 8081 2236

Facilities: ♠ ☉ ✳ ⚹ 🗑 ➡ ♻ ❔
Services: 🔌 🗑 🛢 🖉 ⊤
Within 3 miles: 🚲 ♬ 🗑

Notes: Dogs must be kept on leads. Day kennels.

RINGWOOD

See St Leonards (Dorset)

ROMSEY

Places to visit
The Sir Harold Hillier Gardens, AMPFIELD 01794 369318 www.hilliergardens.org.uk

Avington Park, AVINGTON 01962 779260 www.avingtonpark.co.uk

Great for kids: Longdown Activity Farm, ASHURST 023 8029 2837 www.longdownfarm.co.uk

SERVICES: 🔌 Electric hook up 🗑 Launderette 🍴 Licensed bar 🛢 Calor Gas 🖉 Camping Gaz ⊤ Toilet fluid 🍴 Café/Restaurant ➡ Fast Food/Takeaway ⚡ Battery charging 🚼 Baby care ⚡ Motorvan service point
ABBREVIATIONS: BH/bank hols-bank holidays Etr-Easter Whit-Whitsun dep-departure fr-from hrs-hours m-mile mdnt-midnight rdbt-roundabout rs-restricted service wk-week wknd-weekend ⊗ No credit cards ⊗ No dogs
See page 7 for details of the AA Camping Card Scheme

ROMSEY
Map 5 SU32

PREMIER PARK

▶▶▶▶▶ **86% Hill Farm Caravan Park** (SU287238)

Branches Ln, Sherfield English SO51 6FH
☎ 01794 340402 📠 01794 342358
e-mail: gjb@hillfarmpark.com
dir: *Signed from A27 (Salisbury to Romsey road) in Sherfield English, 4m NW of Romsey & M27 junct 2*

* 🚐 £16-£30 🚐 £16-£30 ▲ £16-£30

Open Mar-Oct

Last arrival 20.00hrs Last departure noon

A small, well-sheltered park peacefully located amidst mature trees and meadows. The two toilet blocks offer smart unisex showers as well as a fully en suite family/disabled room and plenty of privacy in the washrooms. Bramleys, a good restaurant, with an outside patio, serves a wide range of snacks and meals. This attractive park is well placed for visiting Salisbury and the New Forest National Park, and the south coast is only a short drive away, making it an appealing holiday location. 10.5 acre site. 70 touring pitches. 60 hardstandings. Caravan pitches. Motorhome pitches. Tent pitches. 6 statics.

AA Pubs & Restaurants nearby: Dukes Head, Romsey 01794 514450

Three Tuns, Romsey 01794 512639

Leisure: ⚒ ⊛
Facilities: 🅁 ⊙ 🅿 ✶ ৬ 🖻 🛇 🗚 🚿 💷 ♻
Services: 🖧 🖃 🛢 🖉 🅣 🍴 🛒 🖫
Within 3 miles: ♨ ⊞ 🎣 ⊚ 🖻 🖫 ∪

Notes: ⊜ Minimum noise at all times & no noise after 23.00hrs. One unit per pitch. Unsuitable for teenagers. 9-hole pitch & putt.

see advert below

WARSASH
Map 5 SU40

▶▶▶▶ **80% Dibles Park** (SU505060)

Dibles Rd SO31 9SA
☎ 01489 575232
e-mail: dibles.park@btconnect.com
dir: *M27 junct 9, at rdbt 5th exit (Parkgate A27), 3rd rdbt 1st exit, 4th rdbt 2nd exit. Site 500yds on left. Or M27 junct 8, at rdbt 1st exit (Parkgate), next rdbt 3rd exit (Brook Ln), 4th rdbt 2nd exit. Site 500yds on left*

🚐 🚐 ▲

Open all year

Last arrival 20.30hrs Last departure 11.00hrs

A small peaceful touring park adjacent to a private residential park. The facilities are excellent and spotlessly clean. A warm welcome awaits visitors to this well-managed park, which is very convenient for the Hamble, the Solent and the cross-channel ferries. Excellent information on local walks from the site is available. 0.75 acre site. 14 touring pitches. 14 hardstandings. Caravan pitches. Motorhome pitches. Tent pitches. 46 statics.

AA Pubs & Restaurants nearby: The Jolly Farmer Country Inn, Warsash 01489 572500

Facilities: 🅁 ⊙ 🅿 ✶ ◔ ♻ 𝒊
Services: 🖧 🖃 🛢
Within 3 miles: ⚡ 🎣 ⚓ 🖻 🖫 ∪
Notes: Dogs must be kept on leads.

LEISURE: ⊜ Indoor swimming pool ⊛ Outdoor swimming pool ⚒ Children's playground ⛳ Kid's club ⚏ Tennis court ⚙ Games room ▭ Separate TV room ♨ 9/18 hole golf course ⚓ Boats for hire ⊞ Cinema ♫ Entertainment 🎣 Fishing ⊚ Mini golf ⚴ Watersports ⚡ Gym ⊛ Sports field Spa ∪ Stables
FACILITIES: 🛁 Bath 🅁 Shower ⊙ Electric shaver 🗚 Hairdryer ✶ Ice Pack Facility ৬ Disabled facilities ◔ Public telephone 🖻 Shop on site or within 200yds 🖫 Mobile shop (calls at least 5 days a week) 🍴 BBQ area 🚿 Picnic area 💷 Wi-fi 🖥 Internet access ♻ Recycling 𝒊 Tourist info 🗚 Dog exercise area

HEREFORDSHIRE

EARDISLAND
Map 9 SO45

Places to visit

Berrington Hall, ASHTON 01568 615721 www.nationaltrust.org.uk/main/w-berringtonhall

Hergest Croft Gardens, KINGTON 01544 230160 www.hergest.co.uk

▶▶▶ 87% Arrow Bank Holiday Park (SO419588)

Nun House Farm HR6 9BG
☎ 01544 388312   📠 01544 388312
e-mail: enquiries@arrowbankholidaypark.co.uk
dir: *From Leominster A44 towards Rhayader. Right to Eardisland, follow signs*

* 🚐 £18-£20 �90 £18-£20 ▲ £15-£20

Open Mar-7 Jan

This peaceful, adults-only park is set in the beautiful 'Black and White' village of Eardisland with its free exhibitions, tea rooms and heritage centre. The park is well positioned for visiting the many local attractions, as well as those further afield such as Ludlow Castle, Ross-on-Wye, Shrewsbury and Wales. The modern toilet facilities are spotlessly clean. 45 touring pitches. 36 hardstandings. 16 seasonal pitches. Caravan pitches. Motorhome pitches. Tent pitches. 62 statics.

AA Pubs & Restaurants nearby: New Inn, Pembridge 01544 388427

The Bateman Arms, Shobdon 01568 708374

Stagg Inn & Restaurant, Titley 01544 230221

Facilities: 🏕️⊙🕐&🕐🐕📶 🛈
Services: 🔌🗑️🎫
Within 3 miles: ✎🛒🗑️

Notes: Adults only. No ball games, no skateboards/cycles in park. Dogs must be kept on leads.

HEREFORD
Map 10 SO53

Places to visit

Cider Museum & King Offa Distillery, HEREFORD 01432 354207 www.cidermuseum.co.uk

Great for kids: Goodrich Castle, GOODRICH 01600 890538 www.english-heritage.org.uk

▶ 68% Ridge Hill Caravan and Campsite (SO509355)

HR2 8AG
☎ 01432 351293
e-mail: ridgehill@fsmail.net
dir: *From Hereford on A49, then B4399 signed Rotherwas. At 1st rdbt follow Dinedor/Little Dewchurch signs, in 1m signed Ridge Hill/Twyford turn right, then right at phone box, 200yds, site on right*

🚐 £7 �90 £7 ▲ £6

Open Mar-Oct

Last departure noon

A simple, basic site set high on Ridge Hill a few miles south of Hereford. This peaceful site offers outstanding views over the countryside. It does not have toilets or showers, and therefore own facilities are essential, although toilet tents can be supplied on request at certain times of the year. Please do not rely on Sat Nav directions to this site - guidebook directions should be used for caravans and motorhomes. 1.3 acre site. 5 touring pitches. Caravan pitches. Motorhome pitches. Tent pitches.

Facilities: ♻️ 🛈
Within 3 miles: ⚓🎏✎🗑️
Notes: ⊗ Dogs must be kept on leads.

MORETON ON LUGG
Map 10 SO54

Places to visit

The Weir Gardens, SWAINSHILL 01981 590509 www.nationaltrust.org.uk

Brockhampton Estate, BROCKHAMPTON 01885 482077 www.nationaltrust.org.uk/brockhampton

▶▶ 80% Cuckoo's Corner Campsite (SO501456)

Cuckoo's Corner HR4 8AH
☎ 01432 760234
e-mail: cuckooscorner@gmail.com
dir: *Direct access from A49. From Hereford 2nd left after Moreton on Lugg sign. From Leominster 1st right (non gated road) after brown sign. Right just before island*

* 🚐 £10-£12 �90 £10-£12 ▲ £10-£12

Open all year

Last arrival 21.00hrs Last departure 13.00hrs

This small, adults-only site is well positioned just north of Hereford, with easy access to the city. The site is in two areas, and offers hardstandings and some electric pitches. It is an ideal spot for an overnight stop or longer stay to visit the attractions of the area. There's a bus stop just outside the site and a full timetable is available from the reception office. 3 acre site. 19 touring pitches. 15 hardstandings. Caravan pitches. Motorhome pitches. Tent pitches.

AA Pubs & Restaurants nearby: England's Gate Inn, Bodenham 01568 797286

The Wellington, Wellington 01432 830367

Facilities: 🏕️⊙✳️🐕📶 ♻️ 🛈
Services: 🔌🗑️🍺
Within 3 miles: ⚓✎🗑️

Notes: Adults only. ⊗ No large groups, no noise after 22.30hrs. Dogs must be kept on leads. DVD library, books & magazines.

PEMBRIDGE
Map 9 SO35

Places to visit

The Weir Gardens, SWAINSHILL 01981 590509 www.nationaltrust.org.uk

Brockhampton Estate, BROCKHAMPTON 01885 482077 www.nationaltrust.org.uk/brockhampton

SERVICES: 🔌 Electric hook up 🗑️ Launderette 🍺 Licensed bar ⛽ Calor Gas ⊘ Camping Gaz 🎫 Toilet fluid 🍽️ Café/Restaurant 🍟 Fast Food/Takeaway 🔋 Battery charging 🍼 Baby care ♨️ Motorvan service point
ABBREVIATIONS: BH/bank hols-bank holidays Etr-Easter Whit-Whitsun dep-departure fr-from hrs-hours m-mile mdnt-midnight rdbt-roundabout rs-restricted service wk-week wknd-weekend ⊗ No credit cards ⊗ No dogs
See page 7 for details of the AA Camping Card Scheme

PEMBRIDGE *continued*

PREMIER PARK

▶▶▶▶▶ **87% Townsend Touring Park** *(SO395583)*

Best of British

Townsend Farm HR6 9HB
☎ 01544 388527
e-mail: info@townsend-farm.co.uk
dir: *A44 through Pembridge. Site 40mtrs from 30mph on E side of village*

🚐 🚍 ⛺

Open Mar-mid Jan

Last arrival 22.00hrs Last departure noon

This outstanding park is spaciously located on the edge of one of Herefordshire's most beautiful Black and White villages. The park offers excellent facilities, and all hardstanding pitches are fully serviced, and it has its own award-winning farm shop and butchery. It also makes an excellent base from which to explore the local area, including Ludlow Castle and Ironbridge. There are four camping pods available for hire. 12 acre site. 60 touring pitches. 23 hardstandings. Caravan pitches. Motorhome pitches. Tent pitches.

AA Pubs & Restaurants nearby: New Inn, Pembridge 01544 388427

The Bateman Arms, Shobdon 01568 708374

Stagg Inn & Restaurant, Titley 01544 230221

Leisure: ⚙
Facilities: 🛁 🚿 ⊙ ℗ 🔥 🕐 🛒 🎁 🚻 ✈
Services: 🔌 🔋 🛢 ⛽
Within 3 miles: 🏊 🛒 🎁 ♨

STANFORD BISHOP   Map 10 SO65

▶▶▶ **80% Boyce Caravan Park**
(SO692528)

WR6 5UB
☎ 01886 884248 📠 01886 884187
e-mail: enquiries@boyceholidaypark.co.uk
web: www.boyceholidaypark.co.uk
dir: *From A44 take B4220. In Stanford Bishop take 1st left signed Linley Green, then 1st right down private driveway*

* 🚐 fr £20 🚍 fr £20 ⛺ fr £20

Open Feb-Dec (static) (rs Mar-Oct (touring))

Last arrival 18.00hrs Last departure noon

A friendly and peaceful park with access allowed onto the 100 acres of farmland. Coarse fishing is also available in the grounds, and there are

extensive views over the Malvern and Suckley Hills. There are many walks to be enjoyed. 10 acre site. 14 touring pitches. 3 hardstandings. 18 seasonal pitches. Caravan pitches. Motorhome pitches. Tent pitches. 200 statics.

AA Pubs & Restaurants nearby: Three Horseshoes Inn, Little Cowarne 01885 400276

Leisure: ⚙
Facilities: 🛁 ⊙ ℗ 🔥 🕐 🛒 🚻 ✈ ℹ
Services: 🔌 🔋 🛢 ⛽
Within 3 miles: 🏊 🎁 ♨

Notes: Certain dog breeds are not accepted (call for details). Farm walks.

SYMONDS YAT (WEST)   Map 10 SO51

Places to visit
The Nelson Museum & Local History Centre, MONMOUTH 01600 710630
Great for kids: Goodrich Castle, GOODRICH 01600 890538 www.english-heritage.org.uk

▶▶▶ **85% Doward Park Camp Site**
(SO539167)

Great Doward HR9 6BP
☎ 01600 890438
e-mail: enquiries@dowardpark.co.uk
dir: *A40 from Monmouth towards Ross-on-Wye. In 2m exit left signed Crockers Ash, Ganarew & The Doward. Cross over A40, 1st left at T-junct, in 0.5m 1st right signed The Doward. Follow park signs up hill (NB do not follow Sat Nav for end of journey)*

🚍 ⛺

Open Mar-Oct

Last arrival 20.00hrs Last departure 11.30hrs

This delightful little park is set in peaceful woodlands on the hillside above the Wye Valley. It is ideal for campers and motorhomes but not caravans due to the narrow twisting approach roads. A warm welcome awaits and the facilities are kept spotless. 1.5 acre site. 28 touring pitches. 6 seasonal pitches. Motorhome pitches. Tent pitches.

AA Pubs & Restaurants nearby: Mill Race, Walford 01989 562891

Leisure: ⚙ **Facilities:** 🚿 ⊙ ℗ 🔥 🕐 🎁 ℹ
Services: 🔌 🔋 🛢 🏍 ⛽
Within 3 miles: 🚶 🎿 🎬 🏊 ◎ ♨ 🎁 ♨

Notes: No fires, quiet after 22.00hrs. Dogs must be kept on leads.

KENT

See Walk 7 in the Walks & Cycle Rides section at the end of the guide

ASHFORD   Map 7 TR04

Places to visit
Leeds Castle, MAIDSTONE 01622 765400 www.leeds-castle.com

Great for kids: Thorpe Park, CHERTSEY 0870 444 4466 www.thorpepark.com

PREMIER PARK

▶▶▶▶▶ **85% Broadhembury Caravan & Camping Park**
(TR009387)

Best of British

Steeds Ln, Kingsnorth TN26 1NQ
☎ 01233 620859 📠 01233 620918
e-mail: holidaypark@broadhembury.co.uk
web: www.broadhembury.co.uk
dir: *M20 junct 10, A2070. Left at 2nd rdbt signed Kingsnorth, left at 2nd x-roads in village*

* 🚐 £16-£25 🚍 £16-£25 ⛺

Open all year

Last arrival 22.00hrs Last departure noon

A well-run and well-maintained small family park surrounded by open pasture; it is neatly landscaped with pitches sheltered by mature hedges. There is a well-equipped campers' kitchen adjacent to the spotless toilet facilities and children will love the play areas, games room and football pitch. The adults-only area, close to the excellent reception building, has some popular fully serviced hardstanding pitches; this area has its own first-class, solar heated toilet block. 10 acre site. 110 touring pitches. 20 hardstandings. Caravan pitches. Motorhome pitches. Tent pitches. 25 statics.

AA Pubs & Restaurants nearby: Wife of Bath, Wye 01233 812232

Leisure: ⚙ ⚽ 🎱 📺
Facilities: 🚿 ⊙ ℗ 🔥 🕐 🛒 🎁 ✈ 📶 💻 ♻ ℹ
Services: 🔌 🔋 🛢 🏍 📞 🛒 ⛽
Within 3 miles: 🚶 🎬 🏊 ◎ 🎁 🛒 ♨

Notes: No noise after 23.00hrs. Dogs must be kept on leads.

LEISURE: 🏊 Indoor swimming pool 🏊 Outdoor swimming pool ⚙ Children's playground 🎈 Kid's club 🎾 Tennis court 🎱 Games room 📺 Separate TV room
🏌 9/18 hole golf course 🚣 Boats for hire 🎬 Cinema 🎭 Entertainment 🎣 Fishing ◎ Mini golf 🏄 Watersports 🏋 Gym ⚽ Sports field Spa ♨ Stables
FACILITIES: 🛁 Bath 🚿 Shower ⊙ Electric shaver ℗ Hairdryer ❋ Ice Pack Facility ♿ Disabled facilities 🕐 Public telephone 🛒 Shop on site or within 200yds
🚐 Mobile shop (calls at least 5 days a week) 🍖 BBQ area 🪑 Picnic area 📶 Wi-fi 💻 Internet access ♻ Recycling ℹ Tourist info ✈ Dog exercise area

BELTRING
Map 6 TQ64

►► 73% The Hop Farm Touring & Camping Park *(TQ674469)*

Maidstone Rd TN12 6PY
☎ **01622 870838**
e-mail: touring@thehopfarm.co.uk
dir: *M20 junct 4, M25 junct 5 onto A21 S, follow brown tourist signs*

Open Mar-Oct (rs Major Hop Farm events - camping occasionally closed)

Last arrival 19.00hrs Last departure 14.00hrs

Occupying a large field (for tents) and neat paddocks close to a collection of Victorian oast houses and its surrounding family attractions, which include indoor and outdoor play areas, animal farm, shire horses and restaurant, this popular touring park makes a great base for families. One paddock has good hardstanding pitches and the older-style toilet facilities are kept clean and tidy. 16 acre site. 106 touring pitches. 25 hardstandings. Caravan pitches. Motorhome pitches. Tent pitches. 12 statics.

Facilities: ⛆⊙☍☕&⑤☂⼌
Services: 🔌🔥⌀
Within 3 miles: ⌿☇⑤🔲

Notes: No open fires, no large or 'same age' groups, no mini motors or quad bikes. Dogs must be kept on leads. Site campers entitled to half price entry to Hop Farm Family Park.

BIRCHINGTON

Places to visit
Reculver Towers & Roman Fort, RECULVER 01227 740676 www.english-heritage.org.uk

Great for kids: Richborough Roman Fort & Amphitheatre, RICHBOROUGH 01304 612013 www.english-heritage.org.uk

BIRCHINGTON
Map 7 TR36

►►► 83% Two Chimneys Caravan Park *(TR320684)*

Shottendane Rd CT7 0HD
☎ **01843 841068** & **843157** 🖴 **01843 848099**
e-mail: info@twochimneys.co.uk
dir: *A28 to Birchington Sq, right into Park Ln (B2048). Left at Manston Rd (B2050), 1st left*

* ⛺ £15-£24 ⛟ £15-£24 ⛺ £15-£24

Open Mar-Oct (rs Mar-May & Sep-Oct shop, bar, pool & takeaway restricted)

Last arrival 22.00hrs Last departure noon

An impressive entrance leads into this well-managed site, which boasts two swimming pools and a fully-licensed clubhouse. Other attractions include a tennis court and children's play area, and the immaculately clean toilet facilities fully meet the needs of this busy family park. 40 acre site. 200 touring pitches. 5 hardstandings. 20 seasonal pitches. Caravan pitches. Motorhome pitches. Tent pitches. 200 statics.

Leisure: ⛱⛰♒
Facilities: ⛆⊙☍☀✳&⑤☕☂⼍♻ ❼
Services: 🔌⑤🔥⌀⛽T🍴🔌♨⻌
Within 3 miles: ⌿☇目⼿◎♨⑤🔲U

Notes: ⊗ No gazebos, no noise between 23.00hrs & 07.00hrs, no bikes after dusk. Amusement arcade, bus service.

►►► 81% Quex Caravan Park *(TR321685)*

Best of British · SILVER

Park Rd CT7 0BL
☎ **01843 841273**
e-mail: h@keatfarm.co.uk
dir: *From Birchington (A28) turn SE into Park Rd to site in 1m*

* ⛺ £13.50-£26 ⛟ £13.50-£26

Open Mar-Nov

Last arrival 18.00hrs Last departure noon

A small parkland site in a quiet and secluded woodland glade, with a very clean toilet block housed in a log cabin. This picturesque site is just one mile from the village of Birchington, while Ramsgate, Margate and Broadstairs are all within easy reach. 11 acre site. 48 touring pitches. Caravan pitches. Motorhome pitches. 145 statics.

Leisure: ⛰⊗
Facilities: ⛆⊙☍✳©⑤☕☂⼍♻ ❼
Services: 🔌⑤🔥⌀T🍴⻌♨
Within 3 miles: ⌿☇目⼿◎♨⑤🔲U

Notes: Dogs must be kept on leads.

DOVER
Map 7 TR34

Places to visit
The White Cliffs of Dover, DOVER 01304 202756 www.nationaltrust.org.uk

Walmer Castle & Gardens, DEAL 01304 364288 www.english-heritage.org.uk

Great for kids: Dover Castle & Secret Wartime Tunnels, DOVER 01304 211067 www.english-heritage.org.uk

►►►► 79% Hawthorn Farm Caravan Park *(TR342464)*

GOLD

Station Rd, Martin Mill CT15 5LA
☎ **01304 852658** & **852914** 🖴 **01304 853417**
e-mail: hawthorn@keatfarm.co.uk
dir: *Signed from A258*

* ⛺ £13.50-£26 ⛟ £13.50-£26 ⛺ £13.50-£29

Open Mar-Nov

Last arrival 22.00hrs Last departure noon

This pleasant rural park set in 28 acres of beautifully-landscaped gardens is screened by young trees and hedgerows, in grounds which include woods and a rose garden. A popular night-halt to and from the cross-channel ferry port, it has decent facilities including a shop/café and good hardstanding pitches. 28 acre site. 147 touring pitches. 15 hardstandings. Caravan pitches. Motorhome pitches. Tent pitches. 163 statics.

AA Pubs & Restaurants nearby: Bay Restaurant (White Cliffs Hotel), St Margaret's at Cliffe 01304 852229

Facilities: ⛆⊙☍&©⑤☕☂⼍♻ ❼
Services: 🔌⑤🔥⌀T🍴♨
Within 3 miles: ⌿☇目⼿◎♨⑤🔲U

Notes: No noise after 22.00hrs. Dogs must be kept on leads.

SERVICES: 🔌 Electric hook up ⑤ Launderette 🔥 Licensed bar 🛢 Calor Gas ⌀ Camping Gaz T Toilet fluid 🍴 Café/Restaurant ⻌ Fast Food/Takeaway ♨ Battery charging 🔲 Baby care ♨ Motorvan service point
ABBREVIATIONS: BH/bank hols-bank holidays Etr-Easter Whit-Whitsun dep-departure fr-from hrs-hours m-mile mdnt-midnight rdbt-roundabout rs-restricted service wk-week wknd-weekend ⊗ No credit cards ⊗ No dogs
See page 7 for details of the AA Camping Card Scheme

EASTCHURCH
Map 7 TQ97

Places to visit

Upnor Castle, UPNOR 01634 718742
www.english-heritage.org.uk

The Historic Dockyard Chatham, CHATHAM
01634 823807 www.thedockyard.co.uk

►► 74% Warden Springs Caravan Park (TR019722)

Warden Point ME12 4HF
☎ 01795 880216 📠 01795 880218
*dir: M2 junct 5 (Sheerness/Sittingbourne), A249
for 8m, right onto B2231 to Eastchurch. In
Eastchurch left after church, follow park signs*

🚐 🚉 ▲

Open Apr-Oct (rs BH & peak wks)

Last arrival 22.00hrs Last departure noon

Panoramic views from the scenic cliff-top
setting can be enjoyed at their best from the
touring area of this holiday park. All of the
many and varied leisure activities provided
by the park are included in the pitch tariff, ie
the heated outdoor swimming pool, adventure
playground, family entertainment and a good
choice of food outlets. 66 touring pitches.
Caravan pitches. Motorhome pitches. Tent
pitches. 198 statics.

Leisure: 🏊 🎠 🚣 🎵
Facilities: 🎿 ⊙ 🅿 ⚿ 🕐 🔆 🍴 📶 🖥
Services: 🗄 🍴 🍽 🛒
Within 3 miles: 🎣 🛒 📮 ∪
Notes: No cars by caravans or tents.

FOLKESTONE
Map 7 TR23

Places to visit

Dymchurch Martello Tower, DYMCHURCH
01304 211067 www.english-heritage.org.uk

Great for kids: Port Lympne Wild Animal Park,
LYMPNE 0844 8424 647 www.totallywild.net

►►► 83% Little Satmar Holiday Park (TR260390)

Winehouse Ln, Capel Le Ferne CT18 7JF
☎ 01303 251188 📠 01303 251188
e-mail: satmar@keatfarm.co.uk
dir: Signed off B2011

* 🚐 £13.50-£26 🚉 £13.50-£26 ▲ £13.50-£29

Open Mar-Nov

Last arrival 21.00hrs Last departure 12.00hrs

A quiet, well-screened site well away from the
road and statics, with clean and tidy facilities. A
useful base for visiting Dover and Folkestone, or
as an overnight stop for the Channel Tunnel and
ferry ports, and it's just a short walk from cliff
paths with their views of the Channel, and sandy
beaches below. 5 acre site. 47 touring pitches.
Caravan pitches. Motorhome pitches. Tent pitches.
75 statics.

Leisure: 🎠
Facilities: 🎿 ⊙ 🅿 ⚿ 🕐 🍴 📶 🖥 ♻ ⊙
Services: 🗄 🗄 🔒 📮 🕎 T
Within 3 miles: 🎣 🚽 📮 🛒 ∪
Notes: No noise after 22.00hrs. Dogs must be
kept on leads.

►► 74% Little Switzerland Camping & Caravan Site (TR248380)

Wear Bay Rd CT19 6PS
☎ 01303 252168
e-mail: btony328@aol.com
*dir: Signed from A20 E of Folkestone. Approaching
from A259 or B2011 on E outskirts of Folkestone
follow signs for Wear Bay/Martello Tower, then
tourist sign to site, follow signs to country park*

🚐 🚉 ▲

Open Mar-Oct

Last arrival mdnt Last departure noon

Set on a narrow plateau below the white cliffs,
this unusual site has sheltered camping in
secluded dells and enjoys fine views across Wear
Bay and the Strait of Dover. The licensed café with
an alfresco area is popular; please note that the
basic toilet facilities (showers refurbished in
2011) are unsuitable for disabled visitors. 3 acre
site. 32 touring pitches. Caravan pitches.
Motorhome pitches. Tent pitches. 13 statics.

Facilities: 🎿 ⊙ 🔆 🕐 🍴 📶
Services: 🗄 🗄 🍴 📮 🍽 🛒 ⬇
Within 3 miles: 🚽 🚣 🚽 📮 ⊚ 🚴 🛒 🗄 ∪
Notes: 🐕 No open fires.

LEYSDOWN-ON-SEA
Map 7 TR07

►►► 71% Priory Hill (TR038704)

Wing Rd ME12 4QT
☎ 01795 510267
e-mail: touringpark@prioryhill.co.uk
*dir: M2 junct 5, A249 signed Sheerness, then
B2231 to Leysdown, follow brown tourist signs*

🚐 🚉 ▲

Open Mar-Oct (rs Low season shorter opening
times for pool & club)

Last arrival 20.00hrs Last departure noon

A small well-maintained touring area on an
established family-run holiday park close to the
sea, with views of the north Kent coast. Amenities
include a clubhouse and a swimming pool. The
pitch price includes membership of the clubhouse
with live entertainment, and use of indoor
swimming pool. 1.5 acre site. 37 touring pitches.
Caravan pitches. Motorhome pitches. Tent pitches.

Leisure: 🏊 ⊙ 🔍 🗔
Facilities: 🎿 ⊙ 🅿 🔆 🕐 🍴 📮 📶 ⊙
Services: 🗄 🗄 🍴 📮 🍽 🛒
Within 3 miles: 📮 ⊚ 🛒 🗄
Notes: Dogs must be kept on leads.

LEISURE: 🏊 Indoor swimming pool 🏊 Outdoor swimming pool 🎠 Children's playground 🚣 Kid's club 🎾 Tennis court 🎱 Games room 🗔 Separate TV room 🏌 9/18 hole golf course 🚣 Boats for hire 🎬 Cinema 🎵 Entertainment 🎣 Fishing ⊚ Mini golf 🚴 Watersports 🏋 Gym ⚽ Sports field Spa ∪ Stables
FACILITIES: 🛁 Bath 🚿 Shower ⊙ Electric shaver 🅿 Hairdryer 🔆 Ice Pack Facility ⚿ Disabled facilities 🕐 Public telephone 🗄 Shop on site or within 200yds 🚚 Mobile shop (calls at least 5 days a week) 🍴 BBQ area 🍴 Picnic area 📶 Wi-fi 🖥 Internet access ♻ Recycling ⊙ Tourist info 🎯 Dog exercise area

MARDEN — Map 6 TQ74

**Regional Winner –
AA South East of England
Campsite of the Year 2012**

PREMIER PARK

▶▶▶▶▶ **88% Tanner
Farm Touring Caravan
& Camping Park**

Best of British

(TQ732415)

Tanner Farm, Goudhurst Rd TN12 9ND
☎ 01622 832399 & 831214
📠 01622 832472
e-mail: enquiries@tannerfarmpark.co.uk
dir: *From A21 or A229 onto B2079. Midway
between Marden & Goudhurst*

* 🚐 £14-£24.50 🚐 £14-£24.50
▲ £14-£24.50

Open all year

Last arrival 20.00hrs Last departure noon

At the heart of a 150-acre Wealden farm,
replete with oast house, this extensive, long-
established touring park is peacefully tucked
away down a quiet farm drive deep in unspoilt
Kentish countryside, yet close to Sissinghurst
Castle and within easy reach of London
(Marden station 3 miles). Perfect for families,
with its farm animals, two excellent play
areas and recreation room (computer/TV), it
offers quality toilet blocks with privacy
cubicles, a good shop, spacious
hardstandings (12 fully serviced), and high
levels of security and customer care. 15 acre
site. 100 touring pitches. 36 hardstandings.
Caravan pitches. Motorhome pitches. Tent
pitches.

Leisure: 🏊⊙🔍▢

Facilities: ⬅🏠⊙🟢✳🔥🛒 etc.

Services: 🚐🔋🍴📶🛒♻

Within 3 miles: 🏪🏧

Notes: No groups, 1 car per pitch, no
commercial vehicles. Dogs must be kept on
leads.

ST NICHOLAS AT WADE — Map 7 TR26

Places to visit

Reculver Towers & Roman Fort, RECULVER
01227 740676 www.english-heritage.org.uk

Great for kids: Richborough Roman Fort &
Amphitheatre, RICHBOROUGH 01304 612013
www.english-heritage.org.uk

▶▶ **76% St Nicholas Camping Site**
(TR254672)

Court Rd CT7 0NH
☎ 01843 847245
dir: *Signed from A299 & A28, site at W end of
village near church*

* 🚐 £18.50-£20 🚐 £18.50-£20 ▲ £15-£17

Open Etr-Oct

Last arrival 22.00hrs Last departure 14.00hrs

A gently-sloping field with mature hedging, on the
edge of the village close to the shop. This pretty
site offers upgraded facilities, including a family/
disabled room, and is conveniently located close
to primary routes and the north Kent coast. 3 acre
site. 75 touring pitches. Caravan pitches.
Motorhome pitches. Tent pitches.

Leisure: 🏊 Facilities: 🏠⊙🟢✳🔥 etc.

Services: 🚐🔋📶

Within 3 miles: 🏪🏧

Notes: No music after 22.30hrs. Dogs must be
kept on leads. Baby changing area.

WHITSTABLE

Places to visit

Royal Engineers Museum, Library & Archive,
GILLINGHAM 01634 822839
www.re-museum.co.uk

Canterbury West Gate Towers, CANTERBURY
01227 789576 www.canterbury-museum.co.uk

Great for kids: Howletts Wild Animal Park,
BEKESBOURNE 0844 8424 647
www.totallywild.net

WHITSTABLE — Map 7 TR16

 **73% Seaview Holiday
Park** *(TR145675)*

St John's Rd CT5 2RY
☎ 01227 792246 📠 01227 792247
e-mail: info@parkholidaysuk.com
dir: *A299 onto A2990 then B2205 to Swalecliffe,
site between Herne Bay & Whitstable*

🚐 £9-£25 🚐 £9-£25 ▲ £7-£25

Open Mar-Oct

Last arrival 21.30hrs Last departure noon

A pleasant open site on the edge of Whitstable,
set well away from the static area, with a
smart, modern toilet block and both super and
hardstanding pitches. This popular holiday
centre has an excellent bar, restaurant,
clubhouse (with entertainment) and games
room complex, and an outdoor swimming
pool area. 12 acre site. 16 hardstandings. 25
seasonal pitches. Caravan pitches. Motorhome
pitches. Tent pitches. 523 statics.

AA Pubs & Restaurants nearby: The
Sportsman, Whitstable 01227 273370

Crab & Winkle Seafood Restaurant, Whitstable
01227 779377

Leisure: ⚽🏊⚘⊙🔍▢🎵
Facilities: 🏠⊙🟢✳🔥🛒 etc.
Services: 🚐🔋📶🍴🛒♻
Within 3 miles: 🏪🏧🏧

Notes: Dogs must be kept on leads.
Amusements in games room.

▶▶▶▶ **84% Homing Park**
(TR095645)

Church Ln, Seasalter CT5 4BU
☎ 01227 771777 📠 01227 273512
e-mail: info@homingpark.co.uk
dir: *Exit A299 for Whitstable & Canterbury, left at
brown camping-caravan sign into Church Ln. Site
entrance has 2 large flag poles*

* 🚐 £19.50-£27 🚐 £19.50-£27 ▲ £19.50-£27

Open Etr-Oct

Last arrival 20.00hrs Last departure 11.00hrs

A small touring park close to Seasalter Beach and
Whitstable, which is famous for its oysters. All
pitches are generously sized and fully serviced,
and most are separated by hedging and shrubs.

continued

SERVICES: 🔌 Electric hook up 🔋 Launderette 🍴 Licensed bar 🔋 Calor Gas 🔋 Camping Gaz 🔋 Toilet fluid 🍴 Café/Restaurant 🛒 Fast Food/Takeaway 🔋 Battery charging 🔋 Baby care ♻ Motorvan service point
ABBREVIATIONS: BH/bank hols-bank holidays Etr-Easter Whit-Whitsun dep-departure fr-from hrs-hours m-mile mdnt-midnight rdbt-roundabout rs-restricted service wk-week wknd-weekend 🚫 No credit cards 🚫 No dogs
See page 7 for details of the AA Camping Card Scheme

WHITSTABLE *continued*

A clubhouse and swimming pool are available on site with a small cost for the use of the swimming pool. Please note there is some traffic noise from the nearby A229. 12.6 acre site. 43 touring pitches. Caravan pitches. Motorhome pitches. Tent pitches. 195 statics.

AA Pubs & Restaurants nearby: The Sportsman, Whitstable 01227 273370

Crab & Winkle Seafood Restaurant, Whitstable 01227 779377

Leisure: ⚓ ⅍ ♨

Facilities: ♠ ☉ ⚲ ✳ ⅙ ☎ wi-fi ♻ ❶

Services: ⊡ ⊠ ⬛ ⬛ ⚱ 🍺

Within 3 miles: ⌛ ⊞ ⚲ ⚖ 🛍 ∪

Notes: No commercial vehicles, no tents greater than 8 berth or 5mtrs, no unaccompanied minors, no cycles/scooters. Dogs must be kept on leads.

WROTHAM HEATH   Map 6 TQ65

► ► ► **78% *Gate House Wood Touring Park*** (TQ635585)

Ford Ln TN15 7SD
☎ 01732 843062
e-mail: gatehousewood@btinternet.com
dir: *M26 junct 2a, A20 S towards Maidstone, through lights at Wrotham Heath. 1st left signed Trottiscliffe, left at next junct into Ford Ln. Site 100yds on left*

🚐 🚐 Å

Open Mar-Oct

Last arrival 22.00hrs Last departure noon

A well-sheltered and mature site in a former quarry surrounded by tall deciduous trees and gorse banks. The well-designed facilities include reception, shop and smart toilets, and there is good entrance security. Colourful flowers beds and hanging baskets are impressive and give a positive first impression. Conveniently placed for the M20 and M25. 3.5 acre site. 55 touring pitches. Caravan pitches. Motorhome pitches. Tent pitches.

Leisure: ⅍

Facilities: ♠ ☉ ⚲ ✳ ⅙ ☎ 🛍

Services: ⊡ ⊠ ⚱ ⚲ Ⓣ ⅃

Within 3 miles: ⌛ 🛍 ∪

Notes: ⊛ ⊗ No commercial vehicles.

LANCASHIRE

See Cycle Ride 3 in Walks & Cycle Rides section at the end of the guide

BLACKPOOL   Map 18 SD33

See also Lytham St Annes & Thornton

Places to visit

Blackpool Zoo, BLACKPOOL 01253 830830
www.blackpoolzoo.org.uk

83% Marton Mere Holiday Village

(SD347349)   GOLD

Mythop Rd FY4 4XN
☎ 0871 231 0881   📠 01253 791252
e-mail: martinmere@haven.com
dir: *M55 junct 4, A583 towards Blackpool. Right at Clifton Arms lights, onto Mythop Rd. Site 150yds on left*

🚐 🚐

Open mid Mar-Oct (rs Mar-end May & Sep-Oct reduced facilities, splash zone closed)

Last arrival 22.00hrs Last departure 10.00hrs

A very attractive holiday centre in an unusual setting on the edge of the mere, with plenty of birdlife to be spotted. The on-site entertainment is directed at all ages, and includes a superb show bar. There's a regular bus service into Blackpool for those who want to explore further afield. The separate touring area is well equipped with hardstandings and electric pitches, and there are good quality facilities, including a superb new amenities block in 2011. 30 acre site. 85 touring pitches. 85 hardstandings. Caravan pitches. Motorhome pitches. 700 statics.

AA Pubs & Restaurants nearby: Jali Fine Indian Dining, Blackpool 01253 622223

Leisure: ⚓ ⅍ ↯ ♫

Facilities: ♣ ♠ ☉ ⚲ ✳ ⅙ ☎ 🛍 🍺 🚐 ♻ ❶

Services: ⊡ ⊠ ⬛ ⚱ ⚲ 🍴 ⬛ 🍺

Within 3 miles: ⌛ ≽ ⊞ ⚲ ◎ ⚖ 🛍 🛍 ∪

Notes: Max 2 dogs per booking, certain dog breeds banned, no commercial vehicles, no bookings by persons under 21yrs unless a family booking.

see advert on opposite page

BOLTON-LE-SANDS   Map 18 SD46

Places to visit

Lancaster Maritime Museum, LANCASTER 01524 382264 www.lancashire.gov.uk/museums

Lancaster City Museum, LANCASTER 01524 64637 www.lancashire.gov.uk/museums

Great for kids: Lancaster Castle, LANCASTER 01524 64998 www.lancastercastle.com

---

AA CAMPING CARD SITE

► ► ► **86% Bay View Holiday Park** (SD478683)

BRONZE

LA5 9TN
☎ 01524 732854 & 701508   📠 01524 730612
e-mail: info@holgatesleisureparks.co.uk
dir: *W of A6, 1m N of Bolton-le-Sands*

✳ 🚐 £20-£23 🚐 £20-£23 Å £13-£31

Open Mar-Oct (rs Mar-May shop & café hours restricted)

Last arrival 20.00hrs Last departure noon

Developments at this family orientated seaside destination are ongoing and include for 2011 an outstanding new camping field, with 92 fully serviced pitches, including 15 tent pitches. All have glorious views across Morecambe Bay to the Cumbrian Hills. The four amenity blocks are currently of differing standard but all are well maintained and offer a high standard of cleanliness. All will be of an exceptional standard as work progresses and match the overall quality of the rest of this newly developed park, which includes a tastefully designed bar/restaurant. It makes a great place for a family holiday by the seaside as there is a wide range of activities and attractions within a few miles. 10 acre site.

LEISURE: ⚓ Indoor swimming pool ⚓ Outdoor swimming pool ⅍ Children's playground ↯ Kid's club ♨ Tennis court ♞ Games room ▢ Separate TV room ⌛ 9/18 hole golf course ⚓ Boats for hire ⊞ Cinema ♫ Entertainment ⚲ Fishing ◎ Mini golf ⚖ Watersports ♟ Gym ⚘ Sports field **Spa** ∪ Stables
FACILITIES: ♣ Bath ♠ Shower ☉ Electric shaver ⚲ Hairdryer ✳ Ice Pack Facility ⅙ Disabled facilities ☎ Public telephone 🛍 Shop on site or within 200yds 🚐 Mobile shop (calls at least 5 days a week) ⬛ BBQ area 🏮 Picnic area wi-fi Wi-fi ⬛ Internet access ♻ Recycling ❶ Tourist info 🐕 Dog exercise area

100 touring pitches. 50 hardstandings. 127 seasonal pitches. Caravan pitches. Motorhome pitches. Tent pitches. 100 statics. 2 wooden pods.

AA Pubs & Restaurants nearby: Longland Inn & Restaurant, Carnforth 01524 781256

Hest Bank Hotel, Hest Bank 01524 824339

Leisure: ⚙ ⊙ ⚲ ▢

Facilities: ℕ ⊙ ✳ ⊙ 🖾 🚻 🎬 🚾 ♻ ❶

Services: 🔌 🗄 🍴 🛢 ⊘ T 🍽 🚰 ⚓

Within 3 miles: ↧ ⚞ 目 ℐ 🏦 🖼

Notes: Dogs must be kept on leads.

▶▶▶ **84% Sandside Caravan & Camping Park** (SD472681)

The Shore LA5 8JS
☎ 01524 822311 🖨 01524 822311
e-mail: sandside@btconnect.com
dir: M6 junct 35, A6 through Carnforth. Right after Far Pavillion in Bolton-le-Sands, over level crossing to site

* 🚐 £18-£21 🚐 £18-£21 ▲ £17

Open Mar-Oct

Last arrival 20.00hrs Last departure 13.00hrs

A well-kept family park located in a pleasant spot overlooking Morecambe Bay, with distant views of the Lake District. The site is next to a West Coast railway line with a level crossing. The shop and reception are assets to this welcoming park. Booking is advisable at peak periods. 9 acre site. 70 touring pitches. 70 hardstandings. Caravan pitches. Motorhome pitches. Tent pitches. 33 statics.

AA Pubs & Restaurants nearby: Longland Inn & Restaurant, Carnforth 01524 781256

Hest Bank Hotel, Hest Bank 01524 824339

Facilities: ℕ ⊙ 🏠 🚻

Services: 🔌 🗄

Within 3 miles: ↧ 目 ℐ ◎ 🏦 🖼 U

Notes: 🚭

▶▶▶ **78% Red Bank Farm** (SD472681)

LA5 8JR
☎ 01524 823196 🖨 01524 824981
e-mail: mark.archer@hotmail.co.uk
dir: Take A5105 (Morecambe road), after 200mtrs right on Shore Lane. At rail bridge turn right to site

🚐 ▲

Open Mar-Oct

A gently sloping grassy field with mature hedges, close to the sea shore and a RSPB reserve. This farm site has smart toilet facilities, a superb view across Morecambe Bay to the distant Lake District hills, and is popular with tenters. Archers Café serves a good range of cooked food, including home reared marsh lamb. 3 acre site. 60 touring pitches. Motorhome pitches. Tent pitches.

AA Pubs & Restaurants nearby: Longland Inn & Restaurant, Carnforth 01524 781256

Hest Bank Hotel, Hest Bank 01524 824339

Facilities: ℕ ⊙ 🏠 ✳ ♻

Services: 🔌 🗄

Within 3 miles: ↧ ⚞ 目 ℐ ◎ ⚓ 🏦 🖼

Notes: Dogs must be kept on leads. Pets' corner.

SERVICES: 🔌 Electric hook up 🗄 Launderette 🍴 Licensed bar 🛢 Calor Gas ⊘ Camping Gaz T Toilet fluid 🍽 Café/Restaurant 🚰 Fast Food/Takeaway ⚓ Battery charging 🚼 Baby care ⚲ Motorvan service point

ABBREVIATIONS: BH/bank hols-bank holidays Etr-Easter Whit-Whitsun dep-departure fr-from hrs-hours m-mile mdnt-midnight rdbt-roundabout rs-restricted service wk-week wknd-weekend 🚭 No credit cards ⊗ No dogs

See page 7 for details of the AA Camping Card Scheme

CAPERNWRAY   Map 18 SD57

Places to visit

Sizergh Castle & Garden, SIZERGH
015395 60951 www.nationaltrust.org.uk

Levens Hall, LEVENS 015395 60321
www.levenshall.co.uk

►►►► 86% Old Hall Caravan Park *(SD533716)*

LA6 1AD
☎ 01524 733276   📄 01524 734488
e-mail: info@oldhallcaravanpark.co.uk
web: www.oldhallcaravanpark.co.uk
dir: *M6 junct 35 follow signs to Over Kellet, left onto B6254, left at village green signed Capernwray. Site 1.5m on right*

🚐 🚎

Open Mar-Oct

Last departure noon

A lovely secluded park set in a clearing amongst trees at the end of a half-mile long drive. This peaceful park is home to a wide variety of wildlife, and there are marked walks in the woods. The facilities are well maintained by friendly owners, and booking is advisable. 3 acre site. 38 touring pitches. 38 hardstandings. Caravan pitches. Motorhome pitches. 220 statics.

AA Pubs & Restaurants nearby: The Highwayman, Burrow 01524 273338

Lunesdale Arms, Tunstall 015242 74203

Leisure: 🛝

Facilities: 🚿 ⊙ 📁 ৬ 🕒 🚽 📶 🖥 ♻ ❼

Services: 🔌 🔲 💧 🧼 🚮

Within 3 miles: ⭢ 🎣 ⤳ 🛥 🏪 🐎 ∪

Notes: No skateboards, rollerblades or roller boots. Dogs must be kept on leads.

COCKERHAM

Places to visit

Lancaster Maritime Museum,
LANCASTER 01524 382264
www.lancashire.gov.uk/museums

Lancaster City Museum,
LANCASTER 01524 64637
www.lancashire.gov.uk/museums

Great for kids: Blackpool Zoo, BLACKPOOL
01253 830830 www.blackpoolzoo.org.uk

COCKERHAM   Map 18 SD45

►►►► 82% *Moss Wood Caravan Park (SD456497)*

Crimbles Ln LA2 0ES
☎ 01524 791041   📄 01524 792444
e-mail: info@mosswood.co.uk
dir: *M6 junct 33, A6, approx 4m to site. From Cockerham take W A588. Left into Crimbles Lane to site*

🚐 🚎 🏕

Open Mar-Oct

Last arrival 20.00hrs Last departure 16.00hrs

A tree-lined grassy park with sheltered, level pitches, located on peaceful Cockerham Moss. The modern toilet block is attractively clad in stained wood, and the facilities include cubicled washing facilities and a launderette. 25 acre site. 25 touring pitches. 25 hardstandings. Caravan pitches. Motorhome pitches. Tent pitches. 143 statics.

AA Pubs & Restaurants nearby: Bay Horse Inn, Forton 01524 791204

Facilities: 🚿 ⊙ 📁 ৬ 🕒 🛒 🏪 🚽

Services: 🔌 🔲 💧 🧼 🔲

Within 3 miles: ⭢ 🎣 🏪 ∪

Notes: Woodland walks.

CROSTON   Map 15 SD41

Places to visit

Harris Museum & Art Gallery, PRESTON
01772 905427 www.harrismuseum.org.uk

AA CAMPING CARD SITE

►►► 83% Royal Umpire Caravan Park *(SD504190)*

Southport Rd PR26 9JB
☎ 01772 600257   📄 01704 505886
e-mail: info@royalumpire.co.uk
dir: *From Chorley take A581, 3.5m towards Croston, site on right*

✱ 🚐 £16-£25 🚎 £16-£25 🏕 £10-£18

Open all year

Last arrival 20.00hrs Last departure 16.00hrs

A pleasant level site set in open countryside, with an attractive sunken garden and seating area. Plenty of leisure opportunities include an interesting children's playground, and a large playing field. The toilets, laundry and dishwashing

area are of a very good quality. At our last inspection the ongoing upgrade programme was well underway. A restaurant and a pub are within walking distance. 60 acre site. 195 touring pitches. 180 hardstandings. Caravan pitches. Motorhome pitches. Tent pitches.

AA Pubs & Restaurants nearby: Farmers Arms, Heskin Green 01257 451276

Leisure: 🛝 ⊙ 🎵

Facilities: 🚿 ⊙ 📁 ✳ ৬ 🕒 🛒 🏪 ❼

Services: 🔌 🔲 💧 🧼 🚮 ⛟

Within 3 miles: ⭢ 🎣 ⤳ 🛥 🏪 🐎 ∪

Notes: Dogs must be kept on leads.

FAR ARNSIDE   Map 18 SD47

AA CAMPING CARD SITE

►►►► 81% Hollins Farm Camping & Caravanning *(SD450764)*

LA5 0SL
☎ 01524 701508
e-mail: reception@holgates.co.uk
dir: *M6 junct 35, A601/Carnforth. Left in 1m at rdbt to Carnforth. Right in 1m at lights signed Silverdale. Left in 1m into Sands Ln, signed Silverdale. 2.4m over auto-crossing, 0.3m to T-junct. Right, follow signs to site, approx 3m & take 2nd left after passing Holgates*

✱ 🚐 fr £26 🚎 fr £26 🏕 fr £26

Open 14 Mar-Oct

Last arrival 20.00hrs Last departure noon

Hollins Farm is a long established park that is currently being upgraded by the new owners. There are now 50 fully serviced hardstanding pitches for tourers and 25 fully serviced tent pitches; a new quality amenities block will open for the 2012 season. It has a traditional family camping feel and offers high standard facilities; most pitches offer views towards Morecambe Bay. The leisure and recreation facilities of the nearby, much larger, sister park (Silverdale Holiday Park) can be accessed by guests here. 30 acre site. 12 touring pitches. 12 hardstandings. 38 seasonal pitches. Caravan pitches. Motorhome pitches. Tent pitches.

Facilities: 🚿 ⊙ ✳ ❼

Services: 🔌 💧 🧼

Within 3 miles: ⭢ 🎣 ◎ 🏪 📖

Notes: No unaccompanied children. Dogs must be kept on leads.

LEISURE: 🏊 Indoor swimming pool 🏊 Outdoor swimming pool 🛝 Children's playground 🧒 Kid's club ⚲ Tennis court 🎱 Games room 📺 Separate TV room 🏌 9/18 hole golf course 🚣 Boats for hire 🎬 Cinema 🎵 Entertainment 🎣 Fishing ◎ Mini golf 🏄 Watersports 🏋 Gym ⚽ Sports field Spa ∪ Stables
FACILITIES: 🛁 Bath 🚿 Shower ⊙ Electric shaver 📁 Hairdryer ✳ Ice Pack Facility ৬ Disabled facilities 🕒 Public telephone 🛒 Shop on site or within 200yds 🚐 Mobile shop (calls at least 5 days a week) 🍖 BBQ area 🏪 Picnic area 📶 Wi-fi 🖥 Internet access ♻ Recycling ❼ Tourist info 🐕 Dog exercise area

GARSTANG — Map 18 SD44

Places to visit

Lancaster Maritime Museum, LANCASTER 01524 382264 www.lancashire.gov.uk/museums

Lancaster City Museum, LANCASTER 01524 64637 www.lancashire.gov.uk/museums

Great for kids: Lancaster Castle, LANCASTER 01524 64998 www.lancastercastle.com

AA CAMPING CARD SITE

►►►► 83% Claylands Caravan Park

(SD496485)

Cabus PR3 1AJ
☎ 01524 791242 🖹 01524 792406
e-mail: alan@claylands.com
dir: *From M6 junct 33 S to Garstang, approx 6m pass Quattros Restaurant, signed from A6 into Weavers Lane, follow lane to end, over cattle grid*

* 🚐 £20-£25 🚐 £20-£25 ⛺ £17-£22

Open Mar-Jan

Last arrival 23.00hrs Last departure noon

A well-maintained site with lovely river and woodland walks and good views over the River Wyre towards the village of Scorton. This friendly park is set in delightful countryside where guests can enjoy fishing, and the atmosphere is very relaxed. The quality facilities and amenities are of a high standard, and everything is immaculately maintained. Colourful seasonal floral displays create an excellent first impression. 14 acre site. 30 touring pitches. 30 hardstandings. Caravan pitches. Motorhome pitches. Tent pitches. 68 statics.

AA Pubs & Restaurants nearby: Owd Nell's Tavern, Bilsborrow 01995 640010

Leisure: ⚂

Facilities: 🛁⊙☀️⚡👶🕐🚽🎈♻️❓

Services: 🔌🚿🗑️🚮🚽🍽️🔋⛽

Within 3 miles: 🎣🚴🏌️🛒🍴🎣↻

Notes: No roller blades or skateboards. Dogs must be kept on leads.

►►► 76% Bridge House Marina & Caravan Park *(SD483457)*

Nateby Crossing Ln, Nateby PR3 0JJ
☎ 01995 603207 🖹 01995 601612
e-mail: edwin@bridgehousemarina.co.uk
dir: *Exit A6 at pub & Knott End sign, immediately right into Nateby Crossing Ln, over canal bridge to site on left*

🚐 🚐

Open Feb-1 Jan

Last arrival 22.00hrs Last departure 13.00hrs

A well-maintained site in attractive countryside by the Lancaster Canal, with good views towards the Trough of Bowland. The boatyard atmosphere is interesting, and there is a good children's playground. 4 acre site. 30 touring pitches. 25 hardstandings. Caravan pitches. Motorhome pitches. 40 statics.

AA Pubs & Restaurants nearby: Owd Nell's Tavern, Bilsborrow 01995 640010

Leisure: ⚂

Facilities: 🛁⊙☀️⚡👶🕐🚽❓

Services: 🔌🗑️👶🚮🚽🔋

Within 3 miles: 🎣🚴🏌️🛒🍴

Notes: Dogs must be kept on leads.

KIRKHAM

Places to visit

Castle Howard, MALTON 01653 648333 www.castlehoward.co.uk

Duncombe Park, HELMSLEY 01439 778625 www.duncombepark.com

Great for kids: Eden Camp Modern History Theme Museum, MALTON 01653 697777 www.edencamp.co.uk

KIRKHAM — Map 18 SD43

►►► 80% Little Orchard Caravan Park *(SD399355)*

Shorrocks Barn, Back Ln PR4 3HN
☎ 01253 836658
e-mail: info@littleorchardcaravanpark.com
web: www.littleorchardcaravanpark.com
dir: *M55 junct 3, A585 signed Fleetwood. Left in 0.5m opposite Ashiana Tandoori restaurant into Greenhalgh Ln in 0.75m, right at T-junct, site entrance 1st left*

🚐 £17.50-£18.50 🚐 £17.50-£18.50 ⛺ £14.50-£16.50

Open 14 Feb-1 Jan

Last arrival 20.00hrs Last departure noon

Set in a quiet rural location in an orchard, this attractive park welcomes the mature visitor. The toilet facilities are to a very high standard but there is no laundry. Two excellent fisheries are within easy walking distance. The site advises that bookings should be made by phone only, not on-line. 7 acre site. 45 touring pitches. 45 hardstandings. Caravan pitches. Motorhome pitches. Tent pitches.

Facilities: 🛁⊙☀️⚡♿🚽🎈📶♻️❓

Services: 🔌🔋

Within 3 miles: 🏌️◎🏊🛒🍴↻

Notes: ⊗ No cars by tents. No ball games or skateboards, no dangerous dog breeds, children must be supervised in toilet blocks. Dogs must be kept on leads.

LANCASTER

Places to visit

Lancaster Maritime Museum, LANCASTER 01524 382264 www.lancashire.gov.uk/museums

Lancaster City Museum, LANCASTER 01524 64637 www.lancashire.gov.uk/museums

Great for kids: Lancaster Castle, LANCASTER 01524 64998 www.lancastercastle.com

SERVICES: 🔌 Electric hook up 🗑 Launderette 🍺 Licensed bar 🛢 Calor Gas 🛢 Camping Gaz 🚽 Toilet fluid 🍽 Café/Restaurant 🍟 Fast Food/Takeaway 🔋 Battery charging 👶 Baby care ⛽ Motorvan service point
ABBREVIATIONS: BH/bank hols-bank holidays Etr-Easter Whit-Whitsun dep-departure fr-from hrs-hours m-mile mdnt-midnight rdbt-roundabout rs-restricted service wk-week wknd-weekend ⊜ No credit cards ⊗ No dogs
See page 7 for details of the AA Camping Card Scheme

LANCASTER — Map 18 SD46

►► 86% New Parkside Farm Caravan Park (SD507633)

Denny Beck, Caton Rd LA2 9HH
☎ 01524 770723
dir: *M6 junct 34, take A683 towards Caton/Kirkby Lonsdale. Site 1m on right*

🚐 £15–£17 🚐 £15–£17 Å £12–£14

Open Mar-Oct

Last arrival 20.00hrs Last departure 16.00hrs

Peaceful, friendly grassy park on a working farm convenient for exploring the historic city of Lancaster and the delights of the Lune Valley. 4 acre site. 40 touring pitches. 40 hardstandings. Caravan pitches. Motorhome pitches. Tent pitches. 16 statics.

AA Pubs & Restaurants nearby: Sun Hotel & Bar, Lancaster 01524 66006

The Waterwitch, Lancaster 01524 63828

Facilities: 🚿⊙🅟♿♻ 🅸
Services: 🚐🔒
Within 3 miles: ↯🎄✎💷
Notes: 🐾 No football. Dogs must be kept on leads.

LYTHAM ST ANNES — Map 18 SD32

See also Kirkham

Places to visit

Blackpool Zoo, BLACKPOOL 01253 830830
www.blackpoolzoo.org.uk

►►► 76% *Eastham Hall Caravan Park* (SD379291)

Saltcotes Rd FY8 4LS
☎ 01253 737907 📠 01253 732559
e-mail: info@easthamhall.co.uk
web: www.easthamhall.co.uk
dir: *M55 junct 3. Straight over 3 rdbts onto B5259. Through Wrea Green & Moss Side, site 1m after level crossing*

🚐 🚐

Open Mar-Oct (rs Oct only super pitches available)

Last arrival 21.00hrs Last departure noon

Secluded park with trees and hedgerows in a rural setting. The helpful owners ensure that facilities are maintained to a high standard and there are 12 fully serviced super pitches available. 15 acre site. 160 touring pitches. 14 hardstandings. Caravan pitches. Motorhome pitches. 150 statics.

Eastham Hall Caravan Park

AA Pubs & Restaurants nearby: Greens Bistro, St Annes-on-Sea 01253 789990

Leisure: Ⓐ
Facilities: 🚿⊙🅟✳♿Ⓢ♻🚿📶
Services: 🚐🔒🔒♻🅣
Within 3 miles: ↯🎄✎💷🅢Ⓤ
Notes: No tents, breathable groundsheets only in awnings. Football field.

MORECAMBE — Map 18 SD46

Places to visit

Leighton Hall, LEIGHTON HALL 01524 734474
www.leightonhall.co.uk

►►► 78% Venture Caravan Park (SD436633)

Langridge Way, Westgate LA4 4TQ
☎ 01524 412986 📠 01524 422029
e-mail: mark@venturecaravanpark.co.uk
dir: *From M6 junct 34 follow Morecambe signs. At rdbt follow signs for Westgate then site signs. 1st right after fire station*

* 🚐 fr £20 🚐 fr £20 Å fr £17

Open all year (rs Winter one toilet block open)

Last arrival 22.00hrs Last departure noon

A large family park with good modern facilities, including a small indoor heated pool, a licensed clubhouse and a family room with children's entertainment. The site has many statics, some of which are for holiday hire, and is close to the town centre. 17.5 acre site. 56 touring pitches. 40 hardstandings. Caravan pitches. Motorhome pitches. Tent pitches. 304 statics.

AA Pubs & Restaurants nearby: Hest Bank Hotel, Hest Bank 01524 824339

Leisure: 🏊Ⓐ☺🔍
Facilities: 🛁🚿⊙🅟✳♿Ⓢ♻
Services: 🚐🔒🍴🅣🎪♨🛒
Within 3 miles: ↯🎄✎🅢🅢
Notes: Dogs must be kept on leads. Amusement arcade, off licence.

ORMSKIRK — Map 15 SD40

Places to visit

Astley Hall Museum & Art Gallery, CHORLEY
01257 515555 www.astleyhall.co.uk

British Commercial Vehicle Museum, LEYLAND
01772 451011 www.bcvm.co.uk

Great for kids: Camelot Theme Park, CHARNOCK RICHARD 01257 452100
www.camelotthemepark.co.uk

AA CAMPING CARD SITE

►►►► 79% Abbey Farm Caravan Park (SD434098)

Dark Ln L40 5TX
☎ 01695 572686 📠 01695 572686
e-mail: abbeyfarm@yahoo.com
dir: *M6 junct 27 onto A5209 to Burscough. 4m left onto B5240. Immediate right into Hobcross Lane. Site 1.5m on right*

* 🚐 £14.80–£20.40 🚐 £14.80–£20.40
Å £8.75–£22.20

Open all year

Last arrival 21.00hrs Last departure noon

Delightful hanging baskets and flower beds brighten this garden-like rural park which is sheltered by hedging and mature trees. Modern, very clean facilities include a family bathroom, and there are suitable pitches, close to the toilet facilities, for disabled visitors. A superb recreation field caters for children of all ages, and there is an indoor games room, large library, fishing lake and dog walk. Tents have their own area with BBQ and picnic tables. 6 acre site. 56 touring pitches. Caravan pitches. Motorhome pitches. Tent pitches. 44 statics.

AA Pubs & Restaurants nearby: Eagle & Child, Parbold 01257 462297

Leisure: ⚙ ◎ ❋

Facilities: ⛟ 🐾 ◎ 🅿 ❋ ⚲ ⊕ 🚰 🚿 ♻ ❶

Services: 🔌 🅖 🍴 🚿 🗍 ⛽

Within 3 miles: 🚴 🎣 🛒 🚆 U

Notes: No camp fires. Off-licence, farm walk.

SILVERDALE

Places to visit

Leighton Hall, LEIGHTON HALL 01524 734474
www.leightonhall.co.uk

Great for kids: RSPB Leighton Moss Nature Reserve, SILVERDALE 01524 701601
www.rspb.org.uk/leightonmoss

SILVERDALE   Map 18 SD47

AA CAMPING CARD SITE

PREMIER PARK

►►►►► 95% Silverdale Caravan Park (SD455762)

Middlebarrow Plain, Cove Rd LA5 0SH
☎ 01524 701508 📄 01524 701580
e-mail: caravan@holgates.co.uk
dir: M6 junct 35. 5m NW of Carnforth. From Carnforth centre take unclass Silverdale road & follow tourist signs after Warton

* 🚐 fr £31 🚛 fr £31 ⛺ fr £31

Open 22 Dec-7 Nov

Last arrival 20.00hrs Last departure noon

A superb family holiday park set in wooded countryside next to the sea, which demonstrates high quality in all areas, and offers a wide range of leisure amenities. Its relaxing position overlooking Morecambe Bay combined with excellent touring facilities mark this park out as special. 100 acre site. 80 touring pitches. 80 hardstandings. 2 seasonal pitches. Caravan

---

pitches. Motorhome pitches. Tent pitches. 339 statics.

AA Pubs & Restaurants nearby: Longland Inn & Restaurant, Carnforth 01524 781256

The Wheatsheaf, Beetham 015395 62123

Leisure: ☂ ⛴ ⚙ ◎ ❋

Facilities: 🐾 ◎ 🅿 ❋ ⚲ ⊕ 🚰 🚿 📶 ♻ ❶

Services: 🔌 🅖 🍴 🛒 🚿 🗍 🍴 🚮 ⚡

Within 3 miles: 🚴 🎣 ◎ 🛒 U

Notes: No unaccompanied children. Dogs must be kept on leads. Sauna, spa pool, steam room, mini-golf.

see advert below

THORNTON   Map 18 SD34

Places to visit

Blackpool Zoo, BLACKPOOL 01253 830830
www.blackpoolzoo.org.uk

►►►► 85% Kneps Farm Holiday Park (SD353429)

River Rd, Stanah FY5 5LR
☎ 01253 823632 📄 01253 863967
e-mail: enquiries@knepsfarm.co.uk
web: www.knepsfarm.co.uk
dir: Exit A585 at rdbt onto B5412 to Little Thornton. Right at mini-rdbt after school onto Stanah Rd, over 2nd mini-rdbt, leading to River Rd

* 🚐 £19-£20.50 🚛 £19-£20.50

Open Mar-mid Nov (rs Mar & mid Nov shop closed)

continued

SERVICES: 🔌 Electric hook up 🅖 Launderette 🍴 Licensed bar 🅖 Calor Gas 🅖 Camping Gaz 🗍 Toilet fluid 🍴 Café/Restaurant 🚮 Fast Food/Takeaway ⚡ Battery charging 🚼 Baby care ⚡ Motorvan service point

ABBREVIATIONS: BH/bank hols-bank holidays Etr-Easter Whit-Whitsun dep-departure fr-from hrs-hours m-mile mdnt-midnight rdbt-roundabout rs-restricted service wk-week wknd-weekend ⊘ No credit cards ⊗ No dogs   See page 7 for details of the AA Camping Card Scheme

THORNTON *continued*

Last arrival 20.00hrs Last departure noon

A quality park adjacent to the River Wyre and the Wyre Estuary Country Park, handily placed for the attractions of Blackpool and the Fylde coast. This family-run park offers an excellent toilet block with immaculate facilities, and a mixture of hard and grass pitches (no tents), plus there are four new camping pods for hire. The park is quietly located, but there is some noise from a nearby plastics plant. 10 acre site. 60 touring pitches. 40 hardstandings. Caravan pitches. Motorhome pitches. 50 statics. 4 wooden pods.

Kneps Farm Holiday Park

AA Pubs & Restaurants nearby: Twelve Restaurant & Lounge Bar, Thornton 01253 821212

Leisure: ⚠

Facilities: ↝ 🅁 ⊙ 🅟 ⚡ ❄ ♿ 🅂 📶 🖥 ♻ ❶

Services: 🕊 🔋 🅐 ✎ 🅣 🛒 ⛟

Within 3 miles: 🕊 🍽 🏌 ⊚ 🚵 🅂 🅑

Notes: No commercial vehicles. Max 2 dogs per group, dogs are chargeable. Dogs must be kept on leads.

LEICESTERSHIRE

See also Wolvey, Warwickshire

CASTLE DONINGTON

Places to visit

Twycross Zoo, TWYCROSS 01827 880250 www.twycrosszoo.org

National Space Centre, LEICESTER 0845 605 2001 www.spacecentre.co.uk

Great for kids: Snibston Discovery Museum, COALVILLE 01530 278444 www.snibston.com

---

CASTLE DONINGTON   Map 11 SK42

▶▶▶ **71% Donington Park Farmhouse** *(SK414254)*

Melbourne Rd, Isley Walton DE74 2RN
☎ 01332 862409   📄 01332 862364
e-mail: info@parkfarmhouse.co.uk
dir: *M1 junct 24, pass airport to Isley Walton, right towards Melbourne. Site 0.5m on right*

🚐 � 🅰

Open Jan-23 Dec (rs Winter hardstanding only)

Last arrival 21.00hrs Last departure noon

A secluded touring site at the rear of a hotel beside Donington Park motor racing circuit, which is very popular on race days when booking is essential. Both daytime and night flights from nearby East Midlands Airport may cause disturbance. 7 acre site. 60 touring pitches. 10 hardstandings. Caravan pitches. Motorhome pitches. Tent pitches.

AA Pubs & Restaurants nearby: Priest House on the River, Castle Donington 0845 072 7502

Leisure: ⚠

Facilities: 🅁 ⊙ ❄ ♿ ✈ 📶 🖥 ♻ ❶

Services: 🕊 🔋 🅐 🅣 🛒 ⛟

Within 3 miles: 🕊 🍽 🚵 🅂 🅑 ∪

Notes: Dogs must be kept on leads. Bread & milk sold, hotel on site for bar/dining.

LINCOLNSHIRE

ANCASTER   Map 11 SK94

Places to visit

Belton House Park & Gardens, BELTON 01476 566116 www.nationaltrust.org.uk

Belvoir Castle, BELVOIR 01476 871002 www.belvoircastle.com

▶▶▶ **82% Woodland Waters** *(SK979435)*

Willoughby Rd NG32 3RT
☎ 01400 230888   📄 01400 230888
e-mail: info@woodlandwaters.co.uk
web: www.woodlandwaters.co.uk
dir: *On A153 W of junct with B6403*

* 🚐 £13.50-£16 � £13.50-£16 🅰 £13.50-£16

Open all year

Last arrival 21.00hrs Last departure noon

Peacefully set around five impressive fishing

---

lakes, with a few log cabins in a separate area, this is a pleasant open park. The access road is through mature woodland, and there is an excellent heated toilet block, and a pub/club house with restaurant. 72 acre site. 62 touring pitches. 2 hardstandings. Caravan pitches. Motorhome pitches. Tent pitches.

AA Pubs & Restaurants nearby: Bustard Inn & Restaurant, South Rauceby 01529 488250

Brownlow Arms, Hough-on-the-Hill 01400 250234

Leisure: ⚠ 🔍

Facilities: 🅁 ⊙ 🅟 ♿ 🅂 🗄 🍴

Services: 🕊 🔋 🅐 🅣 🛒 🏪

Within 3 miles: 🕊 🍽 🅂 🅑 ∪

Notes: Dogs must be kept on leads.

BOSTON   Map 12 TF34

Places to visit

Battle of Britain Memorial Flight Visitor Centre, CONINGSBY 01522 782040 www.lincolnshire.gov.uk/bbmf

Tattershall Castle, TATTERSHALL 01526 342543 www.nationaltrust.org.uk

▶▶▶▶ **81% Long Acre Caravan Park** *(TF385535)*

Station Rd, Old Leake PE22 9RF
☎ 01205 871555   📄 01205 871555
e-mail: lacp@btconnect.com
dir: *From A16 take B1184 at Sibsey (by church); approx 1m at T-junct turn left. 1.5m, after level crossing take next right into Station Rd. Park entrance approx 0.5m on left*

🚐 � 🅰

Open Mar-Oct

Last arrival 20.00hrs Last departure 11.00hrs

A small rural adults-only park in an attractive setting within easy reach of Boston, Spalding and Skegness. The park has a smart toilet block, which is very clean and has an appealing interior, with modern, upmarket fittings. Excellent shelter is provided by the high, mature boundary hedging. A holiday cottage is available to let. 40 touring pitches. 40 hardstandings. Caravan pitches. Motorhome pitches. Tent pitches.

Facilities: 🅁 ⊙ 🅟 ❄ ♿ 📶 ♻ ❶

Services: 🕊 ⛟

Within 3 miles: 🍽 🅂

Notes: Adults only. Washing lines not permitted. Dogs must be kept on leads.

LEISURE: 🏊 Indoor swimming pool 🏊 Outdoor swimming pool ⚠ Children's playground 🛝 Kid's club 🎾 Tennis court 🔍 Games room 📺 Separate TV room 🏌 9/18 hole golf course 🚣 Boats for hire 🎬 Cinema 🎵 Entertainment 🎣 Fishing ⊚ Mini golf 🏄 Watersports 🏋 Gym 🏟 Sports field Spa ∪ Stables
FACILITIES: 🛁 Bath 🚿 Shower ⊙ Electric shaver 🗯 Hairdryer ❄ Ice Pack Facility ♿ Disabled facilities 🕓 Public telephone 🏪 Shop on site or within 200yds 🚚 Mobile shop (calls at least 5 days a week) 🍴 BBQ area 🪑 Picnic area 📶 Wi-fi 🖥 Internet access ♻ Recycling ❶ Tourist info ✈ Dog exercise area

►►►► 80% Orchard Park

(TF274432)

Frampton Ln, Hubbert's Bridge
PE20 3QU
☎ 01205 290328 📠 01205 290247
e-mail: info@orchardpark.co.uk
dir: *On B1192, between A52 (Boston-Grantham) & A1121 (Boston-Sleaford)*

* 🚐 £16 🚐 £16 ▲ £8-£16

Open all year (rs Dec-Feb bar, shop & café closed)

Last arrival 22.30hrs Last departure 16.00hrs

Ideally located for exploring the unique fenlands, this rapidly-improving park has two lakes - one for fishing and the other set aside for conservation. The very attractive restaurant and bar prove popular with visitors. 51 acre site. 87 touring pitches. 15 hardstandings. Caravan pitches. Motorhome pitches. Tent pitches. 164 statics.

Leisure: ⚽ 🎣
Facilities: 🛁 🛖 🛒 ⊙ 🍴 ⚡ ❄ ⚲ 🌀 🚻 🚿 🛗 🚮 wifi ♻ ❶
Services: 🔌 🔋 🍴 🛢 🚿 T 🍴 🛒 ♨
Within 3 miles: 🎣 🌳 ◎ 🏠 🛍 ∪

Notes: Adults only. 🚫 Washing lines not permitted. Dogs must be kept on leads.

►►►► 78% Pilgrims Way Caravan & Camping Park *(TF358434)*

Church Green Rd, Fishtoft PE21 0QY
☎ 01205 366646 & 07973 941955
📠 01205 366646
e-mail:
pilgrimsway@caravanandcampingpark.com
dir: *E from Boston on A52. In 1m, after junct with A16, at Ball House pub turn right. Follow tourist signs to site*

* 🚐 £15-£22 🚐 £15-£22 ▲ £10-£22

Open all year

Last arrival 22.00hrs (21.00hrs in summer) Last departure noon

---

A peaceful and relaxing park situated in the heart of the south Lincolnshire countryside, yet only a mile from the centre of Boston. Enthusiastic, hands-on owners have done a superb job in upgrading the facilities and the park offers quality toilet facilities, 22 electric hook-ups and hardstandings, and tents are welcome in a separate grassy area. 2.5 acre site. 22 touring pitches. 15 hardstandings. Caravan pitches. Motorhome pitches. Tent pitches.

Leisure: 🎱 🎵
Facilities: 🛖 ⊙ 🍴 ❄ ⚲ 🌀 🚮 wifi ♻ ❶
Services: 🔌 🔋 🛢 🚿
Within 3 miles: 🎣 ⛳ 🎯 🌳 ◎ 🏊 🛍 🏠 🛍 ∪

Notes: 🚫 Dogs must be kept on leads. Tea house & sun terrace, day dog kennels.

CLEETHORPES Map 17 TA30

Places to visit

Fishing Heritage Centre, GRIMSBY 01472 323345 www.nelincs.gov.uk/leisure/museums

Great for kids: Pleasure Island Family Theme Park, CLEETHORPES 01472 211511 www.pleasure-island.co.uk

---

81% Thorpe Park Holiday Centre *(TA321035)*

DN35 0PW
☎ 0871 231 0885 📠 01472 812146
e-mail: thorpepark@haven.com
dir: *Take unclassified road from A180 at Cleethorpes, signed Humberstone & Holiday Park*

🚐 🚐 ▲

Open mid Mar-end Oct (rs mid Mar-May & Sep-Oct some facilities may be reduced)

Last arrival anytime Last departure 10.00hrs

A large static site with touring facilities, including fully-serviced pitches, adjacent to

---

the beach. This holiday centre offers excellent recreational and leisure activities, including an indoor pool with bar, bowling greens, crazy golf, tennis courts, and a games area. Parts of the site overlook the sea. 300 acre site. 134 touring pitches. 81 hardstandings. Caravan pitches. Motorhome pitches. Tent pitches. 1357 statics.

AA Pubs & Restaurants nearby: Ship Inn, Barnoldby le Beck 01472 822308

Leisure: 🏊 🏊 🎱 🎿
Facilities: 🛖 🛒 ⊙ 🍴 ⚲ 🌀 🛗 🚿 🚮 wifi 🖥 ♻ ❶
Services: 🔌 🔋 🍴 🛢 🚿 🍴 ♨
Within 3 miles: 🎣 ⛳ 🌳 ◎ 🏊 🏠 🛍 ∪

Notes: Max 2 dogs per booking, certain dog breeds banned, no commercial vehicles, no bookings by persons under 21yrs unless a family booking. Pitch & putt, roller ring, fishing lakes.

see advert on page 236

GREAT CARLTON Map 17 TF48

AA CAMPING CARD SITE

►►► 82% West End Farm *(TF418842)*

Salters Way LN11 8BF
☎ 01507 450949 & 07766 278740
e-mail: westendfarm@talktalkbusiness.net
dir: *From A157 follow Great Carlton signs at Gayton Top. Follow brown sign for West End Farm in 0.5m, right into site*

* 🚐 £12 🚐 £12 ▲ £12

Open 28 Mar-2 Oct

Last arrival 20.30hrs Last departure 14.00hrs

A neat and well-maintained four-acre touring park situated on the edge of the Lincolnshire Wolds. Surrounded by mature trees and bushes and well away from the busy main roads, yet connected by footpaths ideal for walking and cycling, it offers enjoyable peace and quiet close to the popular holiday resort of Mablethorpe. Good clean facilities throughout. 4 acre site. 35 touring pitches. 4 seasonal pitches. Caravan pitches. Motorhome pitches. Tent pitches.

Leisure: 🎱
Facilities: 🛖 🛒 ❄ 🚮 ❶
Services: 🔌 🔋 🚿
Within 3 miles: 🎣 🌳 ◎ 🏠 ∪

Notes: Dogs must be kept on leads.

SERVICES: 🔌 Electric hook up 🔋 Launderette 🍴 Licensed bar 🛢 Calor Gas 🅿 Camping Gaz T Toilet fluid 🍴 Café/Restaurant ♨ Fast Food/Takeaway 🔋 Battery charging 🍼 Baby care 🔧 Motorvan service point
ABBREVIATIONS: BH/bank hols-bank holidays Etr-Easter Whit-Whitsun dep-departure fr-from hrs-hours m-mile mdnt-midnight rdbt-roundabout rs-restricted service wk-week wknd-weekend 🚫 No credit cards 🚫 No dogs
See page 7 for details of the AA Camping Card Scheme

HOLBEACH — Map 12 TF32

Places to visit

Butterfly & Wildlife Park,
SPALDING 01406 363833
www.butterflyandwildlifepark.co.uk

AA CAMPING CARD SITE

▶▶▶ **76% Herons Cottage Touring Park** *(TF364204)*

Frostley Gate PE12 8SR
☎ 01406 540435
e-mail: simon@satleisure.co.uk
dir: *4m S of Holbeach on B1165 between Sutton St James & Whaplode St Catherine*

🚐 £15-£20 🚎 £15-£20 ▲ £15-£20

Open all year

Last arrival 20.00hrs Last departure 11.00hrs

Under the same ownership as Heron's Mead Touring Park in Orby (see entry), this continually improving park is situated in the heart of the Fens beside the Little South Holland Drain, with its extremely good coarse fishing. There's excellent

supervision and 18 fully-serviced pitches. 4.5 acre site. 52 touring pitches. 48 hardstandings. 40 seasonal pitches. Caravan pitches. Motorhome pitches. Tent pitches. 9 statics.

AA Pubs & Restaurants nearby: Ship Inn, Surfleet Seas End 01775 680547

Facilities: 🍴 ⛟ 🎣 🚿

Services: 🚐 🔌 🔒 🧹 🚽 🧺 ↻

Within 3 miles: 🚶 🏠 🎣

Notes: 😊 Strictly no children under 12yrs. Dogs must be kept on leads. Phone available for warden's cottage.

LANGWORTH

Places to visit

Lincoln Castle, LINCOLN 01522 511068
www.lincolnshire.gov.uk/lincolncastle

Usher Gallery, LINCOLN 01522 550990
www.thecollection.lincoln.museum/

Great for kids: Museum of Lincolnshire Life, LINCOLN 01522 528448 www.lincolnshire.gov.uk/museumoflincolnshirelife

LANGWORTH — Map 17 TF07

AA CAMPING CARD SITE

▶▶▶ **79% Lakeside Caravan Park**
(TF065762)

Barlings Ln LN3 5DF
☎ 01522 753200 📠 01522 750444
e-mail: lakesidecaravanpark@btconnect.com
dir: *Take A158 from Lincoln bypass. 4m to Langworth, right at x-rds into Barlings Lane. Site approx 0.25m on left, well signed*

* 🚐 fr £17.50 🚎 fr £17.50 ▲ fr £14

Open all year (rs Winter - access in bad winter conditions may not be possible)

Last arrival 21.00hrs Last departure noon

A well-maintained touring park set in 23 acres of woodlands lawns and lakes, just four miles from the Lincoln bypass, and offering an ideal base for exploring Lincoln and the surrounding countryside. It is a popular venue for campers who like fishing or just the peace and quiet of this parkland-style site. There are large open spaces and a wealth of the wildlife and, with its security gates, CCTV and on-site wardens, offers a safe, secure place to

LEISURE: 🏊 Indoor swimming pool 🏊 Outdoor swimming pool 🛝 Children's playground 🎣 Kid's club 🎾 Tennis court 🎱 Games room 📺 Separate TV room 🏌 9/18 hole golf course ⛵ Boats for hire 🎬 Cinema 🎵 Entertainment 🎣 Fishing ⛳ Mini golf 🏄 Watersports 🏋 Gym ⚽ Sports field Spa ♨ Stables
FACILITIES: 🛁 Bath 🚿 Shower ⚡ Electric shaver 💈 Hairdryer ❄ Ice Pack Facility ♿ Disabled facilities 📞 Public telephone 🏪 Shop on site or within 200yds 🚐 Mobile shop (calls at least 5 days a week) 🍖 BBQ area 🪑 Picnic area 📶 Wi-fi 🌐 Internet access ♻ Recycling ℹ Tourist info 🐕 Dog exercise area

stay the night. 22 acre site. 25 touring pitches. 20 hardstandings. 20 seasonal pitches. Caravan pitches. Motorhome pitches. Tent pitches. 1 static.

AA Pubs & Restaurants nearby: Wig & Mitre, Lincoln 01522 535190

Pyewipe Inn, Lincoln 01522 528708

The Victoria, Lincoln 01522 541000

The Old Bakery, Lincoln 01522 576057

Facilities: ⌐※⚅☆♈〰️⚟♿️🅘

Services: ☗⊡🛢️🔥⚡↯

Within 3 miles: ⤳🏧🔒

Notes: Dogs must be kept on leads.

MABLETHORPE   Map 17 TF58

Places to visit

The Village-Church Farm, SKEGNESS 01754 766658 www.churchfarmvillage.org.uk

Great for kids: Skegness Natureland Seal Sanctuary, SKEGNESS 01754 764345 www.skegnessnatureland.co.uk

 80% Golden Sands Holiday Park *(TF501861)*

Quebec Rd LN12 1QJ
☎ **0871 231 0884** 🖷 **01507 472066**
e-mail: goldensands@haven.com
dir: *From centre of Mablethorpe turn left on seafront road towards north end. Site on left*

🚐 🚌 ▲

Open mid Mar-Oct

Last arrival anytime Last departure 10.00hrs

A large, well-equipped seaside holiday park with separate touring facilities on two sites, including a refurbished toilet block, additional portaloo facilities, and a good shop at reception. The first-floor entertainment rooms are only accessible via stairs (no lifts). 23 acre site. 214 touring pitches. 20 hardstandings. Caravan pitches. Motorhome pitches. Tent pitches. 1500 statics.

Leisure: 🏊‍♂️⛱️♨️🔍

Facilities: 🛁⌐☉🅿️※☆⚅🅘🛒📶

Services: ☗⊡🔥🛢️🚿🔥⚡↯

Within 3 miles: ⤳🏇⤳◉🏧🔒

Notes: Max 2 dogs per booking, certain dog breeds banned, no commercial vehicles, no bookings by persons under 21yrs unless a family booking. Mini bowling alley, snooker/ pool, indoor fun palace.

▶▶▶ 77% Kirkstead Holiday Park

(TF509835)

North Rd, Trusthorpe LN12 2QD
☎ **01507 441483**
e-mail: mark@kirkstead.co.uk
dir: *From Mablethorpe town centre take A52 S towards Sutton-on-Sea. 1m, sharp right by phone box into North Rd. Site signed in 300yds*

* 🚐 £14-£24 🚌 £14-£24 ▲ £10-£20

Open Mar-Nov

Last arrival 22.00hrs Last departure 15.00hrs

A well-established family-run park catering for all age groups, just a few minutes' walk from Trusthorpe and the sandy beaches of Mablethorpe. The main touring area, which is serviced by good quality toilet facilities, has been extended with the addition of 37 fully-serviced pitches on what used to be the football pitch, and here portacabin toilets have been installed. The site is particularly well maintained. 12 acre site. 60 touring pitches. 3 hardstandings. 30 seasonal pitches. Caravan pitches. Motorhome pitches. Tent pitches. 70 statics.

Leisure: 🎱⚽🔍▭🎵

Facilities: ⌐☉🅿️※⚅🕙🅘♈〰️📶♿️🅘

Services: ☗⊡🔥🍽️🛢️🔥↯

Within 3 miles: ↕🏇⤳◉🏧🔒⛳

Notes: No dogs in tents. Dogs must be kept on leads.

OLD LEAKE   Map 17 TF45

Places to visit

Lincolnshire Aviation Heritage Centre, EAST KIRKBY 01790 763207 www.lincsaviation.co.uk

Battle of Britain Memorial Flight Visitor Centre, CONINGSBY 01522 782040 www.lincolnshire.gov.uk/bbmf

▶▶▶ 75% *Old Leake Leisure Park*

(TF415498)

Shaw Ln PE22 9LQ
☎ **01205 870121** 🖷 **01205 870121**
dir: *Just off A52, 7m NE of Boston, opposite B1184*

🚐 🚌 ▲

A pleasant, well-maintained small touring park set down a rural lane just off the A52, surrounded by the tranquillity of the Fenlands. It makes a peaceful base for exploring Boston and the Lincolnshire coast, and there are two holiday statics for hire. 2.5 acre site. 30 touring pitches. Caravan pitches. Motorhome pitches. Tent pitches.

ORBY   Map 17 TF46

Places to visit

The Village-Church Farm, SKEGNESS 01754 766658 www.churchfarmvillage.org.uk

Great for kids: Skegness Natureland Seal Sanctuary, SKEGNESS 01754 764345 www.skegnessnatureland.co.uk

---

AA CAMPING CARD SITE

 ▶▶▶▶ **80% Heron's Mead Fishing Lake & Touring Park**

(TF508673)

Marsh Ln PE24 5JA
☎ **01754 811340**
e-mail: mail@heronsmeadtouringpark.co.uk
dir: *From A158 (Lincoln to Skegness road) turn left at rdbt, through Orby for 0.5m*

* 🚐 £20 🚌 £20 ▲ £15-£20

Open Mar-1 Nov

Last arrival 21.00hrs Last departure noon

A pleasant fishing and touring park with coarse fishing and an eight-acre woodland walk. The owners continue to improve the facilities, which prove particularly appealing to quiet couples and more elderly visitors. 16 acre site. 21 touring pitches. 21 hardstandings. 10 seasonal pitches. Caravan pitches. Motorhome pitches. Tent pitches. 35 statics.

Facilities: ⌐☉🅿️※⚅🕙♈〰️♿️🅘

Services: ☗⊡🛢️↯

Within 3 miles: ↕⤳🚣🏧🔒⛳

Notes: No cars by caravans or tents. No ball games, no motorbikes. Carp lake.

SALTFLEET — Map 17 TF49

 80% Sunnydale
(TF455941)

Sea Ln LN11 7RP
☎ **0871 664 9776**
e-mail: sunnydale@park-resorts.com
dir: *From A16 towards Louth take B1200 through Manby & Saltfleetby. Left into Saltfleet. Sea Lane on right. Site in approx 400mtrs*

Open Mar-Oct (rs BH & peak wks)

Last arrival noon Last departure 10.00hrs

Set in a peaceful and tranquil location in the village of Saltfleet between the seaside resorts of Cleethorpes and Mablethorpe. This park offers modern leisure facilities including an indoor pool, the tavern bar with entertainment, amusements and a coarse fishing pond. There is also direct access to the huge expanse of Saltfleet beach. The touring facilities are incorporated into the leisure complex, and are modern and well cared for. 38 touring pitches. Caravan pitches. Motorhome pitches. 260 statics.

Leisure: 🏊 ⚙ 🎠 🎵
Facilities: 🚿 ♿ ⊙ 🗄 🛒 📶 🖥
Services: 🚐 🔋 🔧 🍴 🍺
Within 3 miles: 🏌 ◎ 🎣 🛒 ⛴

SALTFLEETBY ST PETER — Map 17 TF48

▶▶▶ **83% Saltfleetby Fisheries**
(TF425892)

Main Rd LN11 7SS
☎ **01507 338272**
e-mail: saltfleetbyfish@btinternet.com
dir: *On B1200, 6m E of junct with A16. 3m W of A103*

🚐 🚐 ⛺

Open Mar-Nov

Last arrival 21.00hrs Last departure 10.00hrs

An excellent small site with just 12 touring pitches, each with gravel hardstanding and electric hook-up, set in a sheltered area close to two large and very popular fishing lakes. A spacious, upmarket Swedish chalet doubles as a reception and a well-furnished café with open-plan kitchen. The purpose-built toilet block is light, airy and well maintained. 14 acre site. 12 touring pitches. 12 hardstandings. Caravan pitches. Motorhome pitches. Tent pitches. 3 statics.

AA Pubs & Restaurants nearby: Bistro Bar at Brackenborough Hotel, Louth 01507 609169

Facilities: 🚿 ❄ ♿ ⊙ 🗄 🛒 🐴 🚻
Services: 🚐 T 🍴 🍺
Within 3 miles: 🚴 🏌 🛒 ⛴
Notes: Adults only. 🐕

SKEGNESS — Map 17 TF56

Places to visit

Skegness Natureland Seal Sanctuary, SKEGNESS
01754 764345 www.skegnessnatureland.co.uk

The Village-Church Farm, SKEGNESS
01754 766658 www.churchfarmvillage.org.uk

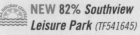 **NEW 82% *Southview Leisure Park*** *(TF541645)*

Burgh Rd PE25 2LA
☎ **01754 896001**
e-mail: southview@park-resorts.com

🚐 🚐

Open Apr-Oct

Last arrival noon Last departure 10.00hrs

A well presented holiday and leisure park close to the resort of Skegness. The leisure and entertainment facilities are modern and well maintained, and are just a short walk from the touring area with its neat pitches and clean and tidy amenity block. The staff are friendly and efficient. 98 touring pitches. Caravan pitches. Motorhome pitches.

LEISURE: 🏊 Indoor swimming pool 🏊 Outdoor swimming pool 🎠 Children's playground 🪁 Kid's club 🎾 Tennis court 🎱 Games room 📺 Separate TV room 🏌 9/18 hole golf course 🚣 Boats for hire 🎬 Cinema 🎵 Entertainment 🎣 Fishing ◎ Mini golf 🏄 Watersports 🏋 Gym ⚽ Sports field Spa ⛴ Stables

FACILITIES: 🛁 Bath 🚿 Shower ⊙ Electric shaver 🪮 Hairdryer ❄ Ice Pack Facility ♿ Disabled facilities 🕿 Public telephone 🏪 Shop on site or within 200yds 🏪 Mobile shop (calls at least 5 days a week) 🍖 BBQ area 🌳 Picnic area 📶 Wi-Fi 💻 Internet access ♻ Recycling ❓ Tourist info 🐕 Dog exercise area

TATTERSHALL   Map 17 TF25

AA CAMPING CARD SITE

▶▶▶▶ 83% Tattershall Lakes Country Park *(TF234587)*

Sleaford Rd LN4 4RL
☎ 01526 348800
e-mail: tattershall.holidays@away-resorts.com
dir: *A153 to Tattershall*

* ⚐ £4-£30 ⚑ £12-£42 ▲ £2-£26

Open end Mar-end Oct

Last arrival 21.00hrs Last departure 10.00hrs

Set amongst woodlands, lakes and parkland on the edge of Tattershall in the heart of the Lincolnshire Fens, this mature country park has been created from old gravel pits and the flat, well-drained and maintained touring area offers plenty of space for campers. There's lots to entertain the youngsters as well as the grown-ups, with good fishing on excellent lakes, and an 18-hole golf course. There is a separate adults-only touring field. The owner has positive future plans for the country park and touring site. 400 acre site. 186 touring pitches. 20 hardstandings. 25 seasonal pitches. Caravan pitches. Motorhome pitches. Tent pitches. 500 statics. 3 bell tents/ yurts.

Leisure: 🏊 🏑 🎣 ⛳ 🎮 🎱 🎯 Spa
Facilities: 🌳 ☉ ☂ 🚿 🛁 🚻 ♿ Wi-Fi 🖥 ♻ ℹ
Services: 🔌 💧 🍽 🍴 🛒 🍼
Within 3 miles: 🚶 🏇 🚲 🏌 🛒 🍴

Notes: No excessive noise after mdnt. Dogs must be kept on leads. Water & jet skiing, family activities.

see advert on opposite page

WADDINGHAM   Map 17 SK99

Places to visit
Gainsborough Old Hall, GAINSBOROUGH
01427 612669 www.english-heritage.org.uk

▶▶▶ 76% Brandy Wharf Leisure Park *(TF014968)*

Brandy Wharf DN21 4RT
☎ 01673 818010   📄 01673 818010
e-mail: brandywharflp@freenetname.co.uk
dir: *From A15 onto B1205 through Waddingham. Site 3m from Waddingham*

⚐ £15 ⚑ £15 ▲ £12

Open all year (rs Nov-Etr no tents)

Last arrival dusk Last departure 17.00hrs

A delightful site in a very rural area on the banks of the River Ancholme, where fishing is available. The toilet block has unisex rooms with combined facilities as well as a more conventional ladies and gents with wash hand basins and toilet. All of the grassy pitches have electricity, and there's a playing and picnic area. The site attracts a lively clientele at weekends, and music around open fires is allowed until 1am. Advance booking is necessary for weekend pitches. 5 acre site. 50 touring pitches. Caravan pitches. Motorhome pitches. Tent pitches.

AA Pubs & Restaurants nearby: The George, Kirton in Lindsey
01652 640600

Leisure: 🎣
Facilities: 🌳 ☉ 🚿 🛁 🚻 ♿ ♻ ℹ
Services: 🔌 💧 🛢 🚮 🍴 🚐 🛒
Within 3 miles: 🚶 🏇 🚲 🛒 🍴 ⛳

Notes: ⊗ No disposable BBQs on grass, no music after 01.00hrs. Fishing, boat mooring, boat launching slipway, canoe hire, pedalos, pets' corner.

WOODHALL SPA   Map 17 TF16

Places to visit
Tattershall Castle, TATTERSHALL 01526 342543
www.nationaltrust.org.uk

Battle of Britain Memorial Flight Visitor Centre,
CONINGSBY 01522 782040
www.lincolnshire.gov.uk/bbmf

PREMIER PARK

NEW ▶▶▶▶▶ 82% Woodhall Country Park *(TF189643)*

Stixwold Rd LN10 6UJ
☎ 01526 353710
e-mail: info@woodhallcountrypark.co.uk
dir: *From rdbt in Woodhall Spa High St into Stixwold Rd, 1m. Site on right, just before Village Limits pub*

* ⚐ £18-£22 ⚑ £18-£22 ▲ £14-£16

Open Mar-Nov

Last arrival 20.00hrs Last departure noon

A peaceful and attractive, newly opened touring park situated just a short walk from Woodhall Spa. The owners have spared no expense in transforming part of the woodland area into a countryside retreat for campers who wish to escape from a hectic lifestyle. Well organised and well laid out, the park offers fishing lakes, three log cabin amenity blocks, fully serviced pitches and high levels of customer care. 80 acre site. 80 touring pitches. 80 hardstandings. Caravan pitches. Motorhome pitches. Tent pitches.

AA Pubs & Restaurants nearby: Village Limits Country Pub & Restaurant, Woodall Spa 01526 353312

Facilities: 🌳 ☉ ☂ 🚿 🛁 🚻 🧺 🚮 ♻ ℹ
Services: 🔌 💧
Within 3 miles: 🚶 🏇 🚲 🛒 🍴 ⛳

Notes: No cars by tents. No fires, chinese lanterns or fireworks, no noise between 23.00hrs- 07.00hrs, BBQs must be off ground. Dogs must be kept on leads.

LONDON

E4 CHINGFORD — Map 6 TQ39

▶▶▶▶ **80%** *Lee Valley Campsite*

(TQ381970)

Sewardstone Rd, Chingford E4 7RA
☎ **020 8529 5689** 📄 **020 8559 4070**
e-mail: scs@leevalleypark.org.uk
dir: *M25 junct 26, A112. Site signed*

🚐 🚙 ⛺

Open Apr-Oct

Last arrival 21.00hrs Last departure noon

Overlooking King George's Reservoir and close to Epping Forest, the touring area of this popular park has been totally revamped and redesigned, and improvements continue apace. It features excellent modern facilities and excellent hardstanding pitches including nine that are able to accommodate the larger motorhomes, and has a very peaceful atmosphere. This impressive park is maintained to a high standard and there are nine camping pods in a separate shady glade for hire, and nine new timber cabins. A bus calls at the site hourly to take passengers to the nearest tube station, and Enfield is easily accessible. 12 acre site. 100 touring pitches. 20 hardstandings. Caravan pitches. Motorhome pitches. Tent pitches. 43 statics.

Leisure: ⚠
Facilities: 🌡🔲⚙🛁🚿⚅♿🕓🏪🛫
Services: 🚰🔌🛢🧽🚽🧺⬇
Within 3 miles: ⚓🎇🏌◎🏪🛒♾

Notes: Under 18s must be accompanied by an adult.

N9 EDMONTON — Map 6 TQ39

▶▶▶ **84%** *Lee Valley Camping & Caravan Park* (TQ360945)

Meridian Way N9 0AR
☎ **020 8803 6900** 📄 **020 8884 4975**
e-mail: leisurecomplex@leevalleypark.org.uk
dir: *M25 junct 25, A10 S, 1st left onto A1055, approx 5m to Leisure Complex. From A406 (North Circular), N on A1010, left after 0.25m, right (Pickets Lock Ln)*

🚐 🚙 ⛺

Open all year (rs Xmas & New Year)

Last arrival 22.00hrs Last departure noon

LEISURE: 🏊 Indoor swimming pool 🏊 Outdoor swimming pool ⚠ Children's playground 🧒 Kid's club 🎾 Tennis court 🎱 Games room 📺 Separate TV room ⛳ 9/18 hole golf course 🚣 Boats for hire 🎬 Cinema 🎵 Entertainment 🎣 Fishing ◎ Mini golf 🏄 Watersports 🏋 Gym ⚽ Sports field Spa ♾ Stables
FACILITIES: 🛁 Bath 🚿 Shower 🪒 Electric shaver 💈 Hairdryer ❄ Ice Pack Facility ♿ Disabled facilities 🕓 Public telephone 🏪 Shop on site or within 200yds 🛒 Mobile shop (calls at least 5 days a week) 🍖 BBQ area 🌲 Picnic area 📶 Wi-fi 💻 Internet access ♻ Recycling ⓘ Tourist info 🐕 Dog exercise area

A pleasant, open site within easy reach of London yet peacefully located close to two large reservoirs. The very good toilet facilities are beautifully kept by dedicated wardens, and the site has the advantage of being adjacent to a restaurant and bar, and a multi-screen cinema. There are also six camping pods and six timber cabins for hire. 4.5 acre site. 160 touring pitches. 41 hardstandings. Caravan pitches. Motorhome pitches. Tent pitches.

Leisure:

Facilities: ⚒ ⊙ 🛠 ⚡ 🔥 🛁 🚿 🛒 ᵂⁱ🔤

Services: 🔌 🗄 🍺 🛢 🖊 Ⓣ 🍴 ⚓

Within 3 miles: ↨ 🏇 🔎 🏌 🛒

Notes: No commercial vehicles.

MERSEYSIDE

SOUTHPORT   Map 15 SD31

Places to visit

The British Lawnmower Museum, SOUTHPORT 01704 501336 www.lawnmowerworld.com

 84% Riverside Holiday Park *(SD405192)*

Southport New Rd PR9 8DF
☎ 01704 228886   📠 01704 505886
e-mail: reception@harrisonleisureuk.com
dir: *M6 junct 27, A5209 towards Parbold/ Burscough, right onto A59. Left onto A565 at lights in Tarleton. Continue to dual carriageway. At rdbt straight across, site 1m on left*

* 🚐 £15-£25 🚍 £15-£25 ⛺ £15-£23

Open 14 Feb-Jan

Last arrival 17.00hrs Last departure 11.00hrs

A large, spacious park with a lively family entertainment complex for cabaret, dancing and theme nights. Children have their own club and entertainer plus games and food. A superb health and leisure centre next door is available at an extra charge. 80 acre site. 260 touring pitches. 130 hardstandings. Caravan pitches. Motorhome pitches. Tent pitches. 355 statics.

AA Pubs & Restaurants nearby: V-Café & Sushi Bar, Southport 01704 883800

Leisure: ⚐ 🏊 ⚓ ♪

Facilities: ⚒ 🛠 ⚡ 🔥 🛁 🐴 🖥 ❶

Services: 🔌 🗄 🍺 🛢 🖊 Ⓣ 🍴 ♨ 👶

Within 3 miles: ↨ 🔎 🏌 🛒 U

Notes: One car per pitch. Dogs must be kept on leads.

AA CAMPING CARD SITE

▶▶▶ **86% Willowbank Holiday Home & Touring Park** *(SD305110)*

Coastal Rd, Ainsdale PR8 3ST
☎ 01704 571566   📠 01704 571576
e-mail: info@willowbankcp.co.uk
web: www.willowbankcp.co.uk
dir: *From A565 between Formby & Ainsdale exit at Woodvale lights onto coast road, site 150mtrs on left. From N: M6 junct 31, A59 towards Preston, A565, through Southport & Ainsdale, right at Woodvale lights*

* 🚐 £15.20-£18.30 🚍 £15.20-£18.30

Open Mar-Jan

Last arrival 21.00hrs Last departure noon

Set in a wooded clearing on a nature reserve next to the beautiful sand dunes, this attractive park is just off the coastal road to Southport. The immaculate toilet facilities are well equipped. 8 acre site. 87 touring pitches. 61 hardstandings. Caravan pitches. Motorhome pitches. 228 statics.

AA Pubs & Restaurants nearby: V-Café & Sushi Bar, Southport 01704 883800

Leisure: ⚐

Facilities: ⚒ ⊙ 🛠 ⚡ 🔥 🛁 🐴 🚮 ♻ ❶

Services: 🔌 🗄 🍺 ⊘ ⚓

Within 3 miles: ↨ ⚓ 🏇 🔎 ◎ 🛒 🛒 U

Notes: No dangerous dog breeds, cannot site continental door entry units, no commercial vehicles. Dogs must be kept on leads. Baby changing facility.

▶▶▶ 80% *Hurlston Hall Country Caravan Park (SD398107)*

Southport Rd L40 8HB
☎ 01704 841064   📠 01704 841404
e-mail: enquiries@hurlstonhallcaravanpark.co.uk
dir: *On A570, 3m from Ormskirk towards Southport*

🚐 🚍

Open Etr-Oct

Last arrival 20.30hrs (18.30hrs at weekends) Last departure 17.00hrs

A peaceful tree-lined touring park next to a static site in attractive countryside about ten minutes' drive from Southport. The park is maturing well, with growing trees and a coarse fishing lake, and the excellent on-site facilities include golf, a bistro, a well-equipped health centre, and a new bowling green and model boat lake. Please note that neither tents nor dogs are accepted at this site. 5 acre site. 60 touring pitches. Caravan pitches. Motorhome pitches. 68 statics.

AA Pubs & Restaurants nearby: V-Café & Sushi Bar, Southport 01704 883800

Leisure: 🎣 ⚐

Facilities: ⚒ ⊙ 🛠 ⚡ 🔥

Services: 🔌 🗄 🍺 🛢 🍴

Within 3 miles: ↨ 🔎 🛒 🛒

Notes: ⊗

SERVICES: 🔌 Electric hook up 🗄 Launderette 🍺 Licensed bar 🛢 Calor Gas ⊘ Camping Gaz Ⓣ Toilet fluid 🍴 Café/Restaurant ♨ Fast Food/Takeaway ⚓ Battery charging 👶 Baby care ⚓ Motorvan service point

ABBREVIATIONS: BH/bank hols-bank holidays Etr-Easter Whit-Whitsun dep-departure fr-from hrs-hours m-mile mdnt-midnight rdbt-roundabout rs-restricted service wk-week wknd-weekend ⊗ No credit cards ⊗ No dogs   See page 7 for details of the AA Camping Card Scheme

Norfolk

Even today, with faster cars and improved road and rail systems, Norfolk still seems a separate entity, as if strangely detached from the rest of the country. There are those who would like it to stay that way. The renowned composer, actor and playwright, Noel Coward, famously described Norfolk as 'very flat' and he was right.

Top of the list of attractions is the North Norfolk Coast, designated an Area of Outstanding Natural Beauty, which has been described as a long way from anywhere, a place of traditions and ancient secrets. The coastline here represents a world of lonely beaches, vast salt marshes and extensive sand dunes stretching as far as the eye can see. It is the same today as it has always been, and is a stark reminder of how this area has been vulnerable to attack and enemy invasion.

Delightful villages

With its old harbour and quaint High Street, Wells-next-the-Sea is a popular favourite with regular visitors to Norfolk, as is Blakeney, famous for its mudflats and medieval parish church, dedicated to the patron saint of seafarers, standing guard over the village and the estuary of the River Glaven.

Cromer is a classic example of a good old fashioned seaside resort where rather grand Victorian hotels look out to sea; the writer and actor Stephen Fry once worked as a waiter at Cromer's Hotel de Paris. A pier, such a key feature of coastal towns, completes the scene.

Farther down the coast, among a string of sleepy villages, is Happisburgh, pronounced Hazeburgh. The Hill House pub here is where Sir Arthur Conan Doyle stayed at the beginning of the 20th century; the Sherlock Holmes' story *The Adventure of the Dancing Men* (1903) is set in a ▶

● The beach at Cromer

Norfolk where 'on every hand enormous square-towered churches bristled up from the flat, green landscape.' Explore this corner of the county today and the scene is remarkably unchanged.

The Broads and nearby area

No visit to Norfolk is complete without a tour of the popular Broads, a network of mostly navigable rivers and lakes. Located a little inland to the south of Happisburgh, the various linked rivers, streams and man-made waterways, offer about 200 miles of highly enjoyable sailing and cruising. Away from the Broads rural Norfolk stretches for miles. If you've the time, you could spend days exploring a network of quiet back roads and winding lanes, visiting en route a generous assortment of picturesque villages and quiet market towns, including Fakenham and Swaffham. Also well worth a look is Thetford, with its delightful Dad's Army Museum. The location filming for the much-loved BBC comedy series was completed in and around Thetford Forest, and fictional Walmington-on-Sea was in fact the town of Thetford.

Ideally, this itinerary should also include the village of Castle Acre, with its impressive

Norfolk Broads

Bure Valley Railway

Hunstanton. There are also good walks around the Burnham villages, Castle Acre and the National Trust's Blickling Hall.

Cycling in Norfolk offers variety and flexibility and the chance to tie it in with a bit of train travel. You can cycle beside the Bure Valley Railway on a 9-mile (14.5km) trail running from Aylsham to Wroxham and return to the start by train. Alternatively, combine an undemanding 5 miles (8km) of mostly traffic-free cycling with a trip on the North Norfolk Railway from Sheringham to Holt, starting and finishing at Kelling Heath. There is also the North Norfolk Coast Cycleway between King's Lynn and Cromer and a series of cycle trails around the Norfolk Broads.

monastic ruins, and, of course, Norwich, with its magnificent cathedral, one of the country's greatest examples of Norman cathedral architecture.

Walking and Cycling
The 93-mile (150km) Peddars Way and North Norfolk Coast Path is one of Britain's most popular national trails. Consisting of two paths joined together to form one continuous route, the trail begins near Thetford on the Suffolk/Norfolk border and follows ancient tracks and stretches of Roman road before reaching the coast near

Festivals and Events
- The Norfolk & Norwich Festival, held in May, is a celebration of creativity, innovation, jazz, comedy, dance and classical music.
- The Sandringham Game & Country Fair in September has falconry, fishing, wildfowling and archery among many other country sports and pursuits.
- The Little Vintage Lovers Fair takes place on different dates and at different venues around the county throughout the year and includes 30 stalls with the emphasis on quality vintage fashion, textiles and accessories.

NORFOLK

See Cycle Ride 4 in Walks & Cycle Rides section at the end of the guide

BARNEY — Map 13 TF93

Places to visit

Baconsthorpe Castle, BACONSTHORPE 01799 322399 www.english-heritage.org.uk

Holkham Hall & Bygones Museum, HOLKHAM 01328 710227 www.holkham.co.uk

Great for kids: Dinosaur Adventure Park, LENWADE 01603 876310 www.dinosaurpark.co.uk

PREMIER PARK

 86% The Old Brick Kilns (TG007328)

Best of British — GOLD

Little Barney Ln NR21 0NL
☎ 01328 878305 📄 01328 878948
e-mail: enquiries@old-brick-kilns.co.uk
dir: From A148 (Fakenham-Cromer) follow brown tourist signs to Barney, left into Little Barney Lane. Site at end of lane

Open mid Mar-6 Jan (rs Low season bar food & takeaway on selected nights only)

Last arrival 21.00hrs Last departure 11.00hrs

A secluded and peaceful park approached via a quiet leafy country lane. The park is on two levels with its own boating and fishing pool and many mature trees. Excellent, well-planned toilet facilities can be found in two blocks, and there is a short dog walk. Due to a narrow access road, no arrivals are accepted until after 1pm. AA-rated B&B accommodation is available and there are four self-catering holiday cottages. 12.73 acre site. 65 touring pitches. 65 hardstandings. Caravan pitches. Motorhome pitches. Tent pitches.

AA Pubs & Restaurants nearby: Chequers Inn, Binham 01328 830297

Old Forge Seafood Restaurant, Thursford 01328 878345

Leisure: ⚑ 🔍 ▢

Facilities: 🅟 ☺ ℗ ✳ & ◷ 🅱 🛒 🖈 Wi-Fi 📶

Services: 🔌 🛢 🔧 🍴 ▢ 🍽 🛒 ⬇

Within 3 miles: 🖊 🅟🛢

Notes: No gazebos. Outdoor draughts, chess, family games.

BELTON — Map 13 TG40

Places to visit

Burgh Castle, BURGH CASTLE www.english-heritage.org.uk

Great for kids: Thrigby Hall Wildlife Gardens, FILBY 01493 369477 www.thrigbyhall.co.uk

BELTON — Map 13 TG40

 **70% Wild Duck Holiday Park** (TG475028)

GOLD

Howards Common NR31 9NE
☎ 0871 231 0876 📄 01493 782308
e-mail: wildduck@haven.com
dir: Phone for detailed directions

🚐 🚲 Å

Open 16 Mar-5 Nov (rs mid Mar-May & Sep-Oct some facilities may be reduced)

Last arrival 21.00hrs Last departure 10.00hrs

This a large holiday complex with plenty to do for all ages both indoors and out. This level grassy site has well laid-out facilities and is set in a forest with small, cleared areas for tourers. Clubs for children and teenagers, sporting activities and evening shows all add to the fun of a stay here. 97 acre site. 117 touring pitches. Caravan pitches. Motorhome pitches. Tent pitches. 560 statics.

LEISURE: 🏊 Indoor swimming pool 🏊 Outdoor swimming pool 🎠 Children's playground 🧒 Kid's club 🎾 Tennis court 🎱 Games room 📺 Separate TV room ⛳ 9/18 hole golf course ⛵ Boats for hire 🎬 Cinema 🎵 Entertainment 🎣 Fishing 🅜 Mini golf 🏄 Watersports 🏋 Gym 🏟 Sports field **Spa** ⛺ Stables
FACILITIES: 🛁 Bath 🚿 Shower 🔌 Electric shaver 💈 Hairdryer ❄ Ice Pack Facility 👨‍🦽 Disabled facilities ☎ Public telephone 🏪 Shop on site or within 200yds 🚐 Mobile shop (calls at least 5 days a week) 🍖 BBQ area 🪑 Picnic area 📶 Wi-fi 💻 Internet access ♻ Recycling ℹ Tourist info 🐕 Dog exercise area

AA Pubs & Restaurants nearby: Fritton House, Fritton 01493 484008

Andover House, Great Yarmouth 01493 843490

Leisure: 🏊 ⛱ 🎱 🎣

Facilities: 🚿 ☉ 🔥 🕐 🍴 🚽 📶 ♻ ❶

Services: 🔌 🔋 🍺 🔧 🍴 🛒 ⛽

Within 3 miles: 🚶 ⛳ 🚴 🛒 🔴 🔋 🍴

Notes: Max 2 dogs per booking, certain dog breeds banned, no commercial vehicles, no bookings by persons under 21yrs unless a family booking.

see advert on opposite page

▶▶▶▶ 87% Rose Farm Touring & Camping Park (TG488033)

Stepshort NR31 9JS
☎ 01493 780896   📠 01493 780896
dir: *Follow signs to Belton off A143, right at lane signed Stepshort, site 1st on right*

🚐 🚙 Å

Open all year

A former railway line is the setting for this very peaceful site which enjoys rural views and is beautifully presented throughout. The ever-improving toilet facilities are spotlessly clean and inviting to use, and the park is brightened with many flower and herb beds. The customer care here is truly exceptional. 10 acre site. 145 touring pitches. 20 hardstandings. Caravan pitches. Motorhome pitches. Tent pitches.

AA Pubs & Restaurants nearby: Fritton House, Fritton 01493 484008

Andover House, Great Yarmouth 01493 843490

Leisure: 🎱 🎣 ⛱ 🏊

Facilities: 🚿 ☉ ✻ 🕐 🍴 🚽 🐴 📶

Services: 🔌 🔋 🍺 🍴

Within 3 miles: 🚶 ⛳ 🚴 🔴 🔋 🔋 ⛳

Notes: No dog fouling.

BURGH CASTLE   Map 13 TG40

Places to visit

Burgh Castle, BURGH CASTLE
www.english-heritage.org.uk

Thrigby Hall Wildlife Gardens, FILBY
01493 369477 www.thrigbyhall.co.uk

Great for kids: Pettitts Animal Adventure Park, REEDHAM 01493 700094
www.pettittsadventurepark.co.uk

77% Breydon Water (TG479042)

Butt Ln NR31 9QB
☎ 0871 664 9710
e-mail: breydon.water@park-resorts.com
dir: *From Gt Yarmouth on A12 towards Lowestoft over 2 rdbts. Follow Burgh Castle sign. Right at lights signed Diss & Beccles. 1.5m, right signed Burgh Castle & Belton. At mini rdbt right onto Stepshort. Site on right*

🚐 🚙 Å

Open Apr-Oct

Last arrival anytime Last departure 10.00hrs

This large park has two village areas just a short walk apart. Yare Village offers touring facilities, family fun and superb entertainment, while Bure Village, which is a quieter base, is now static caravans only. Although the villages are separated, guests are more than welcome to use facilities at both. Yare Village has modern, well maintained toilets, and tents are welcome. The park is are just a short drive from the bright lights of Great Yarmouth and the unique Norfolk Broads. 189 touring pitches. Caravan pitches. Motorhome pitches. Tent pitches. 327 statics.

Breydon Water

AA Pubs & Restaurants nearby: Andover House, Great Yarmouth 01493 843490

Leisure: 🏊 ⛱ 🎱 🎣 🚶 ☉ 🎱 🎵

Facilities: 🚿 🐴 🕐 🍴 📶 🖥

Services: 🔌 🔋 🍺 🍴

Within 3 miles: 🚶 ⛳ 🎣 🔴 ☉ 🔋 🔋

see advert below

CAISTER-ON-SEA Map 13 TG51

80% Caister Holiday Park (TG519132)

Ormesby Rd NR30 5NQ
☎ 0871 231 0873 📱 01493 722016
e-mail: caister@haven.com
dir: *A1064 signed Caister-on-Sea. At rdbt take 2nd exit onto A149, at next rdbt take 1st exit onto Caister by-pass, at 3rd rdbt take 3rd exit to Caister-on-Sea. Park on left*

🚐 🚲

Open mid Mar-end Oct

Last arrival 18.00hrs Last departure 10.00hrs

An all-action holiday park located beside the beach north of the resort of Great Yarmouth, yet close to the attractions of the Norfolk Broads. The touring area offers 46 fully serviced pitches and a modern purpose-built toilet block. Customer care is of an extremely high standard with a full time, experienced and caring warden. Please note that the park does

not accept tents. 138 acre site. 46 touring pitches. Caravan pitches. Motorhome pitches. 900 statics.

Leisure: 🏊 🅰️ 👶 ⊙ 🔍 🎵
Facilities: 🌳 👩‍🦽 🚿 🔥 wifi ♻️ 🌀 ℹ️
Services: 🔌 📞 🛒 🏪 🍴 ⛽ 🚮 ♻️ ↓
Within 3 miles: ↓ 🎣 🏕️ 🎯 ⊙ 🏪

Notes: Max 2 dogs per booking, certain dog breeds banned, no commercial vehicles, no bookings by persons under 21yrs unless a family booking, no sleeping in awnings, no tents.

see advert below

CLIPPESBY

Places to visit

Fairhaven Woodland & Water Garden, SOUTH WALSHAM 01603 270449 www.fairhavengarden.co.uk

Great for kids: Caister Roman Site, CAISTER-ON-SEA www.english-heritage.org.uk

CLIPPESBY Map 13 TG41

PREMIER PARK

▶▶▶▶▶ **90% Clippesby Hall** (TG423147)

Hall Ln NR29 3BL
☎ 01493 367800 📱 01493 367809
e-mail: holidays@clippesby.com
web: www.clippesby.com
dir: *From A47 follow tourist signs for The Broads. At Acle rdbt take A1064, in 2m left onto B1152, 0.5m left opposite village sign, site 400yds on right*

* 🚐 £11.50-£30.50 🚲 £11.50-£30.50 ⛺ £11.50-£30.50

Open all year

Last arrival 17.30hrs Last departure 11.00hrs

A lovely country house estate with secluded pitches hidden among the trees or in sheltered sunny glades. The toilet facilities are appointed to a very good standard, providing a wide choice of cubicles. Amenities include a coffee shop with

LEISURE: 🏊 Indoor swimming pool 🏊 Outdoor swimming pool 🅰️ Children's playground 👶 Kid's club 🎾 Tennis court 🎱 Games room 📺 Separate TV room ⛳ 9/18 hole golf course ⛵ Boats for hire 🎬 Cinema 🎵 Entertainment 🎣 Fishing ⊙ Mini golf 🌊 Watersports 🏋️ Gym ⚽ Sports field **Spa** ♘ Stables
FACILITIES: 🛁 Bath 🚿 Shower ⊙ Electric shaver 💇 Hairdryer ❄️ Ice Pack Facility ♿ Disabled facilities 📞 Public telephone 🏪 Shop on site or within 200yds 🚐 Mobile shop (calls at least 5 days a week) 🍴 BBQ area 🌲 Picnic area wifi Wi-fi 💻 Internet access ♻️ Recycling ℹ️ Tourist info 🐕 Dog exercise area

Wi-fi and wired internet access, family bar and restaurant and family golf. There are pine lodges and holiday cottages available for holiday lets. 30 acre site. 120 touring pitches. 9 hardstandings. Caravan pitches. Motorhome pitches. Tent pitches.

AA Pubs & Restaurants nearby: Fishermans Return, Winterton-on-Sea 01493 393305

Fur & Feather Inn, Woodbastwick 01603 720003

Leisure: ⚓ 🅰 🎱 ⊙ 🔍

Facilities: 🚿 🏮 ⊙ 🅿 ❄ ⚕ 🕐 🎲 🎏 🚻 [Wi-fi] 🖥 ♻ ⓘ

Services: 🔌 🏧 🍺 🛢 ⊘ [T] 🍴 🔋 🐾 ↯

Within 3 miles: ↕ ⚷ ✎ ◎ ⛵ 🎣 🐕 ∪

Notes: Dogs must be kept on leads. Bicycle hire, family golf, volley ball.

CROMER Map 13 TG24

Places to visit

RNLI Henry Blogg Museum, CROMER 01263 511294 www.rnli.org.uk/henryblogg

Felbrigg Hall, FELBRIGG 01263 837444 www.nationaltrust.org.uk/main/w-felbrigghallgardenandpark

▶▶▶▶ 74% *Manor Farm Caravan & Camping Site* (TG198416)

East Runton NR27 9PR
☎ 01263 512858
e-mail: manor-farm@ukf.net
dir: *1m W of Cromer, exit A148 or A149 at Manor Farm sign*

🚐 🚍 Å

Open Etr-Sep

Last arrival 20.30hrs Last departure noon

A well-established family-run site on a working farm enjoying panoramic sea views. There are good modern facilities across the site, including three smart toilet blocks that include two quality family rooms and privacy cubicles, two good play areas and a large expanse of grass for games - the park is very popular with families. 17 acre site. 250 touring pitches. Caravan pitches. Motorhome pitches. Tent pitches.

AA Pubs & Restaurants nearby: The Wheatsheaf, West Beckham 01263 822110

Marmalade's Bistro, Sheringham 01263 822830

White Horse, Overstrand 01263 579237

Frazers, Sea Marge Hotel, Overstrand 01263 579579

Leisure: 🅰

Facilities: 🏮 ⊙ ❄ ⚕ 🐕 🎏

Services: 🔌 🏧 🍺 ⊘ 🔋

Within 3 miles: ↕ 🎢 ✎ ◎ ⛵ 🔋 🎣

Notes: 🐕 2 dog-free fields.

▶▶▶ 85% *Forest Park* (TG233405)

Northrepps Rd NR27 0JR
☎ 01263 513290 📠 01263 511992
e-mail: info@forest-park.co.uk
dir: *A140 from Norwich, left at T-junct signed Cromer, right signed Northrepps, right then immediate left, left at T-junct, site on right*

🚐 🚍 Å

Open 15 Mar-15 Jan

Last arrival 21.00hrs Last departure 11.00hrs

Surrounded by forest, this gently sloping park offers a wide choice of pitches. Visitors have the use of a heated indoor swimming pool, and a large clubhouse with entertainment. 100 acre site. 262 touring pitches. Caravan pitches. Motorhome pitches. Tent pitches. 420 statics.

AA Pubs & Restaurants nearby: The Wheatsheaf, West Beckham 01263 822110

Marmalade's Bistro, Sheringham 01263 822830

White Horse, Overstrand 01263 579237

Frazers, Sea Marge Hotel, Overstrand 01263 579579

Leisure: 🏊 🅰 🔍

Facilities: 🏮 ⊙ 🅿 ❄ ⚕ 🕐 🎲 🚻 [Wi-fi]

Services: 🔌 🏧 🍺 🛢 ⊘ [T] 🍴 🔋 🐾

Within 3 miles: ↕ 🎢 ✎ 🚩 ◎ ⛵ 🔋 🎣 ∪

DOWNHAM MARKET Map 12 TF60

▶▶▶ 82% Lakeside Caravan Park & Fisheries (TF608013)

Sluice Rd, Denver PE38 0DZ
☎ 01366 387074 & 07790 272978
📠 01366 387074
e-mail: richesflorido@aol.com
web: www.westhallfarmholidays.co.uk
dir: *Exit A10 towards Denver, follow signs to Denver Windmill*

🚐 🚍 Å

Open Mar-Oct

Last arrival 21.00hrs Last departure noon

A peaceful, rapidly improving park set around four pretty fishing lakes. Several grassy touring areas are sheltered by mature hedging and trees. There is a function room, shop and laundry. 30 acre site. 100 touring pitches. Caravan pitches. Motorhome pitches. Tent pitches. 1 static.

AA Pubs & Restaurants nearby: Hare Arms, Stow Bardolph 01366 382229

Leisure: 🅰

Facilities: 🏮 ⊙ 🅿 ❄ ⚕ 🎲 🎏 [Wi-fi]

Services: 🔌 🏧 🍺 ⊘ [T] 🔋

Within 3 miles: ↕ 🎢 🚩 ⛵ 🔋 🎣

Notes: Dogs must be kept on leads. Pool table, fishing tackle/bait, caravan accessories.

SERVICES: 🔌 Electric hook up 🏧 Launderette 🍺 Licensed bar 🛢 Calor Gas ⊘ Camping Gaz [T] Toilet fluid 🍴 Café/Restaurant 🔋 Fast Food/Takeaway 🔋 Battery charging 🐾 Baby care ↯ Motorvan service point

ABBREVIATIONS: BH/bank hols-bank holidays Etr-Easter Whit-Whitsun dep-departure fr-from hrs-hours m-mile mdnt-midnight rdbt-roundabout rs-restricted service wk-week wknd-weekend 🚫 No credit cards 🚫 No dogs

See page 7 for details of the AA Camping Card Scheme

FAKENHAM — Map 13 TF92

Places to visit

Houghton Hall, HOUGHTON 01485 528569
www.houghtonhall.com

Great for kids: Penthorpe Nature Reserve & Gardens, FAKENHAM 01328 851465
www.penthorpe.co.uk

►►► 79% Caravan Club M.V.C. Site

(TF926288)

Fakenham Racecourse NR21 7NY
☎ 01328 862388 📠 01328 855908
e-mail: caravan@fakenhamracecourse.co.uk
dir: *From B1146, S of Fakenham follow brown Racecourse signs (with tent & caravan symbols) leads to site entrance*

Open all year

Last arrival 21.00hrs Last departure noon

A very well laid-out site set around the racecourse, with a grandstand offering smart modern toilet facilities. Tourers move to the centre of the course on race days, and enjoy free racing, and there's a wide range of sporting activities in the club house. 11.4 acre site. 120 touring pitches. 25 hardstandings. Caravan pitches. Motorhome pitches. Tent pitches.

AA Pubs & Restaurants nearby: Blue Boar Inn, Great Ryburgh 01328 829212

Brisley Bell Inn & Restaurant, Brisley 01362 668686

Facilities: ⬛◎🅿✳⛄🕐🛉♻

Services: 🔌🔲🔧🛢🚰Ⓣ🍽♨

Within 3 miles: ⚓🎣🏌◎🛒🐴🛖Ù

Notes: Max 2 dogs per unit. TV aerial hook-ups.

►►► 79% Fakenham Campsite

(TF907310)

Burnham Market Rd, Sculthorpe NR21 9SA
☎ 01328 856614
e-mail: fakenham.campsite@gmail.com
dir: *From Fakenham take A148 towards King's Lynn then B1355 Burnham Market road. Site on right in 400yds*

* 🚐 £13-£17 🚗 £13-£17 ⛺ £13-£17

Open all year

Last arrival 22.00hrs Last departure noon

Enthusiastic owners are running this peaceful site

that is surrounded by tranquil countryside and which is part of a par 3, 9-hole golf complex and driving range. The toilet facilities are of good quality, and there is a golf shop and licensed bar. Please note there is no laundry. 4 acre site. 50 touring pitches. 11 hardstandings. Caravan pitches. Motorhome pitches. Tent pitches. 2 statics.

AA Pubs & Restaurants nearby: Blue Boar Inn, Great Ryburgh 01328 829212

Brisley Bell Inn & Restaurant, Brisley 01362 668686

Leisure: ⚠

Facilities: ⬛✳⛄🐴♻ℹ

Services: 🔌🔲🛢

Within 3 miles: ⚓🎣🏌🛖

Notes: No noise after 22.30hrs. Dogs must be kept on leads.

AA CAMPING CARD SITE

►► 72% Crossways Caravan & Camping Park (TF961321)

Crossways, Holt Rd, Little Snoring NR21 0AX
☎ 01328 878335
e-mail: joyholland@live.co.uk
dir: *From Fakenham take A148 towards Cromer. After 3m pass exit for Little Snoring. Site on A148 on left behind Post Office*

Open all year

Last arrival 22.00hrs Last departure noon

Set on the edge of the peaceful hamlet of Little Snoring, this level site enjoys views across the fields towards the North Norfolk coast some seven miles away. Visitors can use the health suite for a small charge, and there is a shop on site, and a good village pub. 2 acre site. 26 touring pitches. 10 hardstandings. Caravan pitches. Motorhome pitches. Tent pitches. 1 static.

AA Pubs & Restaurants nearby: Blue Boar Inn, Great Ryburgh 01328 829212

Brisley Bell Inn & Restaurant, Brisley 01362 668686

Leisure: 🕐

Facilities: ⬛◎✳🕐🛉🏕♻ℹ

Services: 🔌🔲🛢Ⓣ

Within 3 miles: ⚓🎣🏌◎🛒🐴Ù

Notes: Dogs must be kept on leads.

GREAT YARMOUTH — Map 13 TG50

Places to visit

Elizabethan House Museum, GREAT YARMOUTH 01493 855746 www.museums.norfolk.gov.uk

Great Yarmouth Row 111 Houses & Greyfriars' Cloister, GREAT YARMOUTH 01493 857900
www.english-heritage.org.uk

Great for kids: Merrivale Model Village, GREAT YARMOUTH 01493 842097
www.merrivalemodelvillage.co.uk

87% Vauxhall Holiday Park (TG520083)

4 Acle New Rd NR30 1TB
☎ 01493 857231 📠 01493 331122
e-mail: info@vauxhallholidays.co.uk
web: www.vauxhall-holiday-park.co.uk
dir: *On A47 approaching Great Yarmouth*

Open Etr, mid May-Sep & Oct half term

Last arrival 21.00hrs Last departure 10.00hrs

A very large holiday complex with plenty of entertainment and access to beach, river, estuary, lake and the A47. The touring pitches are laid out in four separate areas, each with its own amenity block, and all arranged around the main entertainment. 40 acre site. 220 touring pitches. Caravan pitches. Motorhome pitches. Tent pitches. 421 statics.

AA Pubs & Restaurants nearby: Andover House, Great Yarmouth 01493 843490

Leisure: 🏊🏊⚠🎱🎣🖵

Facilities: ⬛◎✳⛄🕐🛒📶

Services: 🔌🔲🔧🛢🚰Ⓣ🍽🚰🏭

Within 3 miles: ⚓🎣🏌◎🛒🛖Ù

Notes: No pets. Children's pool, sauna, solarium, fitness centre.

see advert on opposite page

AA CAMPING CARD SITE

▶▶▶▶ 77% The Grange Touring Park (TG510142)

Yarmouth Rd, Ormesby St Margaret NR29 3QG
☎ 01493 730306 & 730023 📄 01493 730188
e-mail: info@grangetouring.co.uk
dir: From A419, 3m N of Great Yarmouth. Site at junct of A419 & B1159. Signed

* 🚐 £11.50-£18 🚎 £11.50-£18 ▲ £11.50-£18

Open Etr-Oct

Last arrival 21.00hrs Last departure 11.00hrs

A mature, ever improving park with plenty of trees, located just one mile from the sea, within easy reach of both coastal attractions and the Norfolk Broads. The level pitches have electric hook-ups and include 13 hardstanding pitches, and there are clean, modern toilets including three spacious family rooms. All pitches have Wi-Fi access. 3.5 acre site. 70 touring pitches. 7 hardstandings. Caravan pitches. Motorhome pitches. Tent pitches.

AA Pubs & Restaurants nearby: Andover House, Great Yarmouth 01493 843490

Leisure: ⚠

Facilities: 🟤⊙🅿✳♿🕒 Wi-Fi 🖥 ❶

Services: 🚐🖻🍴🛒🚿🛒↯

Within 3 miles: ↯🟤◎🍴🛒♻

Notes: No football, no gazebos, no open fires. Dogs must be kept on leads.

HUNSTANTON   Map 12 TF64

Places to visit

Lynn Museum, KING'S LYNN 01553 775001
www.museums.norfolk.gov.uk

Norfolk Lavender, HEACHAM 01485 570384
www.norfolk-lavender.co.uk

Great for kids: Hunstanton Sea Life Sanctuary, HUNSTANTON 01485 533576
www.sealsanctuary.co.uk

87% Searles Leisure Resort (TF671400)

South Beach Rd PE36 5BB
☎ 01485 534211 📄 01485 533815
e-mail: bookings@searles.co.uk
web: www.searles.co.uk
dir: A149 from King's Lynn to Hunstanton. At rdbt follow signs for South Beach. Straight on at 2nd rdbt. Site on left

🚐🚎▲

Open all year (rs 25 Dec & Feb-May limited entertainment & restaurant)

Last arrival 20.45hrs Last departure 11.00hrs

A large seaside holiday complex with well-managed facilities, adjacent to sea and beach. The tourers have their own areas, including two excellent toilet blocks, and pitches are individually marked by small maturing shrubs for privacy. The bars and entertainment, restaurant, bistro and takeaway, heated indoor and outdoor pools, golf, fishing and bowling

---

green make this park popular throughout the year. 50 acre site. 332 touring pitches. 100 hardstandings. Caravan pitches. Motorhome pitches. Tent pitches. 460 statics.

AA Pubs & Restaurants nearby: King William IV, Hunstanton 01485 571765

Neptune Restaurant with Rooms, Hunstanton 01485 532122

Gin Trap Inn, Ringstead 01485 525264 Lifeboat Inn, Thornham 01485 512236

Leisure: 🏊⚓⚠🎱🎣

Facilities: 🛏🟤⊙🅿✳♿🕒🖻🚿🎣 Wi-Fi

Services: 🚐🖻🍴🥡🚿T🍴🛒🍺

Within 3 miles: ↯🍴🟤🍴🛒♻♥

Notes: No dangerous dog breeds. Hire shop, beauty salon.

SERVICES: 🚐 Electric hook up 🖻 Launderette 🍴 Licensed bar 🛢 Calor Gas ⊘ Camping Gaz T Toilet fluid 🍴 Café/Restaurant 🛒 Fast Food/Takeaway 🔋 Battery charging 🚼 Baby care ↯ Motorvan service point

ABBREVIATIONS: BH/bank hols-bank holidays Etr-Easter Whit-Whitsun dep-departure fr-from hrs-hours m-mile mdnt-midnight rdbt-roundabout rs-restricted service wk-week wknd-weekend ⊛ No credit cards ⊗ No dogs   See page 7 for details of the AA Camping Card Scheme

HUNSTANTON *continued*

NEW 80% *Manor Park Holiday Village* (TF671399)

BRONZE

Manor Rd PE36 5AZ
☎ 01485 532300
e-mail: manor.park@park-resorts.com

Open Apr-Oct

Last arrival noon Last departure 10.00hrs

Situated just a few yards from the beach on the outskirts of the lively resort of Hunstanton, Manor Farm offers a range of leisure activities, including two heated outdoor swimming pools, children's playground, children's club, amusement arcade, restaurant, bar and cabaret. There are 64 electric, all-grass pitches set out in the heart of the park and adjacent to the leisure complex. Expect high standards of customer care. 64 touring pitches. Caravan pitches. Motorhome pitches.

AA Pubs & Restaurants nearby: King William IV Country Inn & Restaurant, Hunstanton 01485 571765

Neptune Restaurant with Rooms, Hunstanton 01485 532122

KING'S LYNN

See also Stanhoe

Places to visit

Lynn Museum, KING'S LYNN 01553 775001
www.museums.norfolk.gov.uk

African Violet Centre,
KING'S LYNN 01553 828374
www.africanvioletandgardencentre.com

Great for kids: Castle Rising Castle,
CASTLE RISING 01553 631330
www.english-heritage.org.uk

KING'S LYNN   Map 12 TF62

AA CAMPING CARD SITE

NEW ▶▶▶▶ 79% King's Lynn Caravan and Camping Park (TF645160)

New Rd, North Runcton PE33 0RA
☎ 01553 840004
e-mail: klcc@btconnect.com
web: www.kl-cc.co.uk
dir: *From King's Lynn take A47 signed Swaffham & Norwich, right in 1.5m to North Runcton. Site 100yds on left*

* ⊕ £15-£16 ⊕ £15-£16 ▲ £15-£16

Open all year

Last arrival flexible Last departure flexible

Set in approximately 10 acres of parkland, this developing camping park is situated on the edge of North Runcton, just a few miles south of the historic town of King's Lynn. There is a new, eco-friendly toilet block which is powered by solar panels and an air-sourced heat pump, plus it also recycles rainwater; in itself this proves a source of great interest. The three very extensive touring fields are equipped with 150 electric hook-ups and one field is reserved for rallies. 9 acre site. 150 touring pitches. 2 hardstandings. Caravan pitches. Motorhome pitches. Tent pitches.

AA Pubs & Restaurants nearby: Bank House Hotel, King's Lynn 01553 660492

Facilities: ⛶☏⊙℗✳⚲⛉▥⊡ Wi-Fi ♺ ❶
Services: ☏⊡▐⌀⊤☡⛒
Within 3 miles: ↨日ℐ⚲☖☖♨

Notes: No skateboards or fires. Dogs must be kept on leads.

NORTH WALSHAM   Map 13 TG23

Places to visit

Blickling Hall, BLICKLING 01263 738030
www.nationaltrust.org.uk/blickling

Horsey Windpump, HORSEY 01263 740241
www.nationaltrust.co.uk

Regional Winner – AA Heart of England Campsite of the Year 2012

PREMIER PARK

▶▶▶▶▶ 85% Two Mills Touring Park (TG291286)

Best of British
GOLD

Yarmouth Rd NR28 9NA
☎ 01692 405829 ▤ 01692 405829
e-mail: enquiries@twomills.co.uk
dir: *1m S of North Walsham on Old Yarmouth road past police station & hospital on left*

⛶⊡▲

Open Mar-3 Jan

Last arrival 20.30hrs Last departure noon

An intimate, beautifully presented park set in superb countryside in a peaceful, rural spot, which is also convenient for touring. The 'Top Acre' section is starting to mature and features an additional 26 fully serviced pitches, offering panoramic views over the site, an immaculate toilet block and good planting, plus the layout of pitches and facilities is excellent. The very friendly and helpful owners keep the park in immaculate condition. Please note this park does not accept children. 7 acre site. 81 touring pitches. 81 hardstandings. Caravan pitches. Motorhome pitches. Tent pitches.

AA Pubs & Restaurants nearby: Butchers Arms, East Ruston 01692 650237

Beechwood Hotel, North Walsham 01692 403231

Leisure: ▭
Facilities: ☏⊙℗✳⚲☖▥⛉▥ Wi-Fi ❶
Services: ☏⊡▐⌀⊤☡
Within 3 miles: ℐ☖☖

Notes: Adults only. Max 2 dogs per pitch. Dogs must be kept on leads. Library.

ST JOHN'S FEN END — Map 12 TF51

Places to visit

African Violet Centre,
KING'S LYNN 01553 828374
www.africanvioletandgardencentre.com

Oxburgh Hall, OXBOROUGH 01366 328258
www.nationaltrust.org.uk/main/w-oxburghhall

►►►► 73% Virginia Lake Caravan Park (TF538113)

Smeeth Rd PE14 8JF
☎ 01945 430585 & 430167
e-mail: louise@virginialake.co.uk
dir: *From A47 E of Wisbech follow tourist signs to Terrington St John. Site on left*

Open all year

Last arrival 21.00hrs Last departure 15.00hrs

A well-established park beside a two-acre fishing lake with good facilities for both anglers and tourers. The toilet facilities are very good, and security is carefully observed throughout the park. A clubhouse serves a selection of meals. 7 acre site. 97 touring pitches. 20 hardstandings. Caravan pitches. Motorhome pitches. Tent pitches.

AA Pubs & Restaurants nearby: Stuart House Hotel, Bar & Restaurant, King's Lynn 01553 772169

Facilities: 🅿️⊙🅿️✳️🅱️🕒🖐️🎣🛒ℹ️

Services: 🔌🖨️🍴🗂️Ⓣ🍽️♨️♨️⛽

Within 3 miles: 🛴🏇🐾◎🗂️🗂️U

Notes: No camp fires. Dogs must be kept on leads. Pool tables, large-screen TV, fishing lake, fruit machines.

SCRATBY — Map 13 TG51

Places to visit

St Olave's Priory, ST OLAVES
www.english-heritage.org.uk

Time and Tide Museum of Great Yarmouth Life, GREAT YARMOUTH 01493 743930
www.museums.norfolk.gov.uk

Great for kids: Caister Roman Site, CAISTER-ON-SEA www.english-heritage.org.uk

►►► 85% Scratby Hall Caravan Park (TG501155)

NR29 3SR
☎ 01493 730283
e-mail: scratbyhall@aol.com
dir: *5m N of Great Yarmouth. Exit A149 onto B1159, site signed*

Open Spring BH-mid Sep

Last arrival 22.00hrs Last departure noon

A neatly-maintained site with a popular children's play area, well-equipped shop and outdoor swimming pool with sun terrace. The toilets are kept very clean. The beach and the Norfolk Broads are close by. 5 acre site. 85 touring pitches. Caravan pitches. Motorhome pitches. Tent pitches.

AA Pubs & Restaurants nearby: Fishermans Return, Winterton-on-Sea 01493 393305

Nelson Head, Horsey 01493 393378

Leisure: 🅰️

Facilities: 🅿️⊙🅿️✳️🖐️🕒🗂️♻️ℹ️

Services: 🔌🖨️🅱️🖊️Ⓣ♨️

Within 3 miles: 🛴🔱🐾🗂️🗂️U

Notes: No commercial vehicles. Food preparation room.

STANHOE — Map 13 TF83

Places to visit

Norfolk Lavender, HEACHAM 01485 570384
www.norfolk-lavender.co.uk

Walsingham Abbey Grounds & Shirehall Museum, LITTLE WALSINGHAM 01328 820510
www.walsinghamabbey.com

►►► 78% The Rickels Caravan & Camping Park (TF794355)

Bircham Rd PE31 8PU
☎ 01485 518671
dir: *A148 from King's Lynn to Hillington. B1153 to Great Bircham. B1155 to x-rds, straight over, site on left*

Open Mar-Oct

Last arrival 21.00hrs Last departure 11.00hrs

Set in three acres of grassland, with sweeping country views and a pleasant, relaxing atmosphere fostered by being for adults only. The meticulously maintained grounds and facilities are part of the attraction, and the slightly sloping land has some level areas and sheltering for tents. 3 acre site. 30 touring pitches. Caravan pitches. Motorhome pitches. Tent pitches. 1 static.

AA Pubs & Restaurants nearby: Lord Nelson, Burnham Thorpe 01328 738241

The Hoste Arms, Burnham Market 01328 738777

Leisure: 🖵

Facilities: 🅿️⊙✳️🎣♻️ℹ️

Services: 🔌🖨️🅱️🖊️♨️

Within 3 miles: 🐾🗂️

Notes: Adults only. ⊛ No ground sheets. Dogs must be kept on leads. Field available to hire for rallies.

SERVICES: 🔌 Electric hook up 🖨️ Launderette 🍴 Licensed bar 🅱️ Calor Gas 🖊️ Camping Gaz Ⓣ Toilet fluid 🍽️ Café/Restaurant ♨️ Fast Food/Takeaway 🔋 Battery charging 🍼 Baby care ⛽ Motorvan service point
ABBREVIATIONS: BH/bank hols-bank holidays Etr-Easter Whit-Whitsun dep-departure fr-from hrs-hours m-mile mdnt-midnight rdbt-roundabout rs-restricted service wk-week wknd-weekend ⊛ No credit cards ⊗ No dogs
See page 7 for details of the AA Camping Card Scheme

SWAFFHAM — Map 13 TF80

Places to visit

Gressenhall Farm and Workhouse, GRESSENHALL 01362 860563 www.museums.norfolk.gov.uk

AA CAMPING CARD SITE

▶▶▶ **80% Breckland Meadows Touring Park** *(TF809094)*

Lynn Rd PE37 7PT
☎ **01760 721246**
e-mail: info@brecklandmeadows.co.uk
dir: *1m W of Swaffham on old A47*

* ⚕ £11.95-£13.95 ⚕ £11.95-£13.95
Å £8-£11.50

Open all year

Last arrival 21.00hrs Last departure noon

An immaculate, well-landscaped little park on the edge of Swaffham. The impressive toilet block is well equipped, and there are hardstandings, full electricity and laundry equipment. Plentiful planting is resulting in attractive screening. 3 acre site. 45 touring pitches. 35 hardstandings. 5 seasonal pitches. Caravan pitches. Motorhome pitches. Tent pitches.

AA Pubs & Restaurants nearby: Canary & Linnet, Little Fransham 01362 687027

Facilities: ⚕☉⚬⚕⚕⚕⚕⚕⚕⚕⚕⚕⚕⚕
Services: ⚕⚕⚕⚕⚕⚕
Within 3 miles: ⚕⚕⚕⚕⚕⚕

Notes: Adults only. Dogs must be kept on leads. Newspaper deliveries.

SYDERSTONE — Map 13 TF83

Places to visit

Creake Abbey, NORTH CREAKE
www.english-heritage.org.uk

Great for kids: Castle Rising Castle, CASTLE RISING 01553 631330
www.english-heritage.org.uk

▶▶▶ **76% The Garden Caravan Site** *(TF812337)*

Barmer Hall Farm PE31 8SR
☎ **01485 578220 & 578178**
e-mail: nigel@gardencaravansite.co.uk
dir: *Signed from B1454 at Barmer between A148 & Docking, 1m W of Syderstone*

* ⚕ £16.20-£20 ⚕ £16.20-£20 Å

Open Mar-Nov

Last arrival 21.00hrs Last departure noon

In the tranquil setting of a former walled garden beside a large farmhouse, with mature trees and shrubs, a secluded site surrounded by woodland. The site is run mainly on trust, with a daily notice indicating which pitches are available, and an honesty box for basic foods. An ideal site for the discerning camper, and well placed for touring north Norfolk. 3.5 acre site. 30 touring pitches. Caravan pitches. Motorhome pitches. Tent pitches.

AA Pubs & Restaurants nearby: Lord Nelson, Burnham Thorpe 01328 738241

The Hoste Arms, Burnham Market 01328 738777

Facilities: ⚕☉⚕⚕⚕⚕⚕⚕
Services: ⚕⚕⚕
Within 3 miles: ⚕

Notes: ⚕ Max 2 dogs per pitch. Dogs must be kept on leads. Cold drinks, ice creams & eggs available.

THREE HOLES — Map 12 TF50

Places to visit

African Violet Centre, KING'S LYNN
01553 828374
www.africanvioletandgardencentre.com

Norfolk Lavender, HEACHAM 01485 570384
www.norfolk-lavender.co.uk

AA CAMPING CARD SITE

▶▶▶ **77% Lode Hall Holiday Park** *(TF529989)*

Lode Hall, Silt Rd PE14 9JW
☎ **01354 638133** 📄 **01354 638133**
e-mail: dick@lode-hall.co.uk
dir: *From Wisbech take A1101 towards Downham Market. At Outwell continue on A1101 signed Littleport. Site signed from Three Holes. Right onto B1094 to site*

⚕ £15 ⚕ £15 Å £10-£15

Open Apr-Oct

Peace and tranquilly is assured at this deeply rural park in the grounds of Lode Hall. The toilet facilities are located in an imaginative restoration of a former cricket pavilion and include combined toilet/wash basin cubicles and unisex showers. Please note that this is an adults-only site. 5 acre site. 20 touring pitches. 8 hardstandings. Caravan pitches. Motorhome pitches. Tent pitches.

AA Pubs & Restaurants nearby: Hare Arms, Stow Bardolph 01366 382229

Facilities: ⚕☉⚕⚕⚕⚕⚕⚕
Services: ⚕⚕⚕
Within 3 miles: ⚕⚕⚕

Notes: Adults only. ⚕

TRIMINGHAM

Places to visit

RNLI Henry Blogg Museum, CROMER
01263 511294 www.rnli.org.uk/henryblogg

Cromer Museum, CROMER 01263 513543
www.norfolk.gov.uk/tourism/museums

LEISURE: 🏊 Indoor swimming pool 🏊 Outdoor swimming pool 🎠 Children's playground 🧒 Kid's club 🎾 Tennis court 🎱 Games room 📺 Separate TV room
⛳ 9/18 hole golf course 🚤 Boats for hire 🎬 Cinema 🎵 Entertainment 🎣 Fishing ⛳ Mini golf 🏄 Watersports 🏋 Gym 🏟 Sports field Spa ♨ Stables
FACILITIES: 🛁 Bath 🚿 Shower ⚡ Electric shaver 💇 Hairdryer ✳ Ice Pack Facility ♿ Disabled facilities ☎ Public telephone 🏪 Shop on site or within 200yds
🛒 Mobile shop (calls at least 5 days a week) 🍖 BBQ area 🎍 Picnic area 📶 Wi-fi 💻 Internet access ♻ Recycling ℹ Tourist info 🐕 Dog exercise area

TRIMINGHAM — Map 13 TG23

AA CAMPING CARD SITE

►►► 70% Woodland Holiday Park
(TG274388)

NR11 8AL
☎ 01263 579208 📄 01263 576477
e-mail: info@woodland-park.co.uk
web: www.woodlandholidaypark.co.uk
dir: 4m SE on B1159 (coast road)

* 🚐 £19-£29 🚐 £19-£29 ▲ £12-£16

Open Mar-Dec

Last arrival 23.00hrs Last departure noon

A secluded woodland site in an open enclosure, close to the sea but well sheltered from the winds by tall trees. Facilities include two bars, a restaurant, an indoor swimming pool, bowling green and sauna, and entertainment is provided in the clubhouse. There are holiday statics for hire and a large field is available for tents. 55 acre site. 20 touring pitches. Caravan pitches. Motorhome pitches. Tent pitches. 230 statics.

AA Pubs & Restaurants nearby: White Horse, Overstrand 01263 579237

Leisure: 🏊🎭♟🎣🎵
Facilities: 📶⊙🅿✳♿🛍🏪🚿 ♻ ❶
Services: 🔌🛁🍺🛢🍽🔋♨
Within 3 miles: 🛁🎠🅿◎⛵🛍🛒⛳

Notes: Dogs must be kept on leads.

WORTWELL — Map 13 TM28

Places to visit

Bressingham Steam Museum & Gardens, BRESSINGHAM 01379 686900 www.bressingham.co.uk

Great for kids: Banham Zoo, BANHAM 01953 887771 www.banhamzoo.co.uk

►►►► 81% Little Lakeland Caravan Park (TM279849)

IP20 0EL
☎ 01986 788646 📄 01986 788646
e-mail: information@littlelakeland.co.uk
dir: From W: exit A143 at sign for Wortwell. In village turn right 300yds past garage. From E: on A143, left onto B1062, then right. After 800yds turn left

🚐 £15-£20.50 🚐 £15-£20.50 ▲ £15-£20.50

Open 15 Mar-Oct

Last arrival 22.00hrs Last departure noon

A well-kept and pretty site built round a fishing lake, and accessed by a lake-lined drive. The individual pitches are sited in hedged enclosures for complete privacy, and the purpose-built toilet facilities are excellent. 4.5 acre site. 38 touring pitches. 6 hardstandings. 17 seasonal pitches. Caravan pitches. Motorhome pitches. Tent pitches. 21 statics.

AA Pubs & Restaurants nearby: Dove Restaurant with Rooms, Alburgh 01986 788315

Fox & Goose Inn, Fressingfield 01379 586247

Leisure: 🎭
Facilities: 📶⊙🅿✳♿🛍🏪 ♻ ❶
Services: 🔌🛁🍽🛢🍽
Within 3 miles: 🛁🎠🅿🛍

Notes: ❸ No noise after 23.00hrs. Dogs must be kept on leads. Library.

NORTHUMBERLAND

BAMBURGH — Map 21 NU13

Places to visit

Chillingham Wild Cattle Park, CHILLINGHAM 01668 215250 www.chillinghamwildcattle.com

Great for kids: Bamburgh Castle, BAMBURGH 01668 214515 www.bamburghcastle.com

►►►► 79% Waren Caravan Park (NU155343)
GOLD

Waren Mill NE70 7EE
☎ 01668 214366 📄 01668 214224
e-mail: waren@meadowhead.co.uk
dir: 2m E of town. From A1 onto B1342 signed Bamburgh. Take unclassified road past Waren Mill, signed Budle

* 🚐 £14-£24 🚐 £14-£24 ▲ £14-£30

Open Apr-Oct

Last arrival 20.00hrs Last departure noon

Attractive seaside site with footpath access to the beach, surrounded by a slightly sloping grassy embankment giving shelter to caravans. The park offers excellent facilities, including several family bathrooms, and the on-site restaurant serves a good breakfast. There are also wooden wigwams to rent. 4 acre site. 150 touring pitches. 24 hardstandings. Caravan pitches. Motorhome pitches. Tent pitches. 300 statics. 4 tipis.

AA Pubs & Restaurants nearby: Olde Ship Inn, Seahouses 01665 720200

Blue Bell Hotel, Belford 01668 213543

Grays Restaurant, Waren House Hotel, Bamburgh 01668 214581

Leisure: 🏊🎭🎣
Facilities: 🚽📶⊙🅿✳♿🛍🏪🚿🏪 📶 🖥♻❶
Services: 🔌🛁🍺🛢🍽🔋♨⛽
Within 3 miles: 🛁🅿◎🛍⛳

Notes: Dogs must be kept on leads. 100 acres of private heathland.

►►► 71% Glororum Caravan Park
(NU166334)

Glororum Farm NE69 7AW
☎ 01668 214457 📄 01688 214484
dir: Exit A1 at junct with B1341 (Purdy's Lodge). In 3.5m left onto unclass road. Site 300yds on left

* 🚐 £18-£19 🚐 £18-£19

Open Mar-end Oct

Last arrival 18.00hrs Last departure noon

A pleasantly situated site where tourers have their own well-established facilities. A new touring field and toilet block are planned for the 2012 season. The open countryside setting affords good views of Bamburgh Castle and surrounding farmland. 6 acre site. 100 touring pitches. Caravan pitches. Motorhome pitches. 150 statics.

AA Pubs & Restaurants nearby: Olde Ship Inn, Seahouses 01665 720200

Blue Bell Hotel, Belford 01668 213543

Grays Restaurant, Waren House Hotel, Bamburgh 01668 214581

Leisure: 🎭⚽
Facilities: 📶⊙🅿✳🛍🏪🚿
Services: 🔌🛁🛢🍽⛽
Within 3 miles: 🛁🎠🅿🛍⛳

Notes: Dogs must be kept on leads.

BELLINGHAM

Places to visit

Wallington House Walled Garden & Grounds, CAMBO 01670 773600 www.nationaltrust.org.uk/wallington

BELLINGHAM

Map 21 NY88

PREMIER PARK

►►►►► 80% Bellingham Camping & Caravanning Club Site *(NY835826)*

Brown Rigg NE48 2JY

☎ 01434 220175 & 0845 130 7633

📄 01434 220175

dir: *From A69 take A6079 N to Chollerford & B6320 to Bellingham. Pass Forestry Commission land, site 0.5m S of Bellingham*

* 🚐 £14.37-£21.93 � £14.37-£21.93
🏕 £14.37-£21.93

Open 11 Mar-Oct

Last arrival 20.00hrs Last departure noon

A beautiful and peaceful site set in the glorious Northumberland National Park. Exceptionally well-managed, it continues to improve and offers high levels of customer care, maintenance and cleanliness - the excellent toilet facilities are spotlessly clean. There are four camping pods for hire. This is a perfect base for exploring this undiscovered part of England, and it is handily placed for visiting the beautiful Northumberland coast. 5 acre site. 64 touring pitches. 42 hardstandings. Caravan pitches. Motorhome pitches. Tent pitches. 4 wooden pods.

AA Pubs & Restaurants nearby: Pheasant Inn, Falstone 01434 240382

Leisure: 🅰

Facilities: 🏕⊙📻⚡✳🔧🕐🛁🍴📶 🖥 ♻ 🄸

Services: 🔌🔋🍴🛢⊘🅃🖿⛟

Within 3 miles: ⚓🎣🛒🛍🔵⛎

Notes: Site gates closed & quiet time 23.00hrs-07.00hrs. Dogs must be kept on leads.

BERWICK-UPON-TWEED

Places to visit

Berwick-upon-Tweed Barracks, BERWICK-UPON-TWEED 01289 304493 www.english-heritage.org.uk

Paxton House, Gallery & Country Park, BERWICK-UPON-TWEED 01289 386291 www.paxtonhouse.com

Great for kids: Norham Castle, NORHAM 01289 382329 www.english-heritage.org.uk

BERWICK-UPON-TWEED

Map 21 NT95

 80% Haggerston Castle *(NU041435)*

GOLD

Beal TD15 2PA

☎ 0871 231 0865   📄 01289 381433

e-mail: haggerstoncastle@haven.com

dir: *On A1, 7m S of Berwick-upon-Tweed, site signed*

🚐 �

Open mid Mar-end Oct (rs mid Mar-May & Sep-Oct some facilities may be reduced)

Last arrival anytime Last departure 10.00hrs

A large holiday centre with a very well equipped touring park, offering comprehensive holiday activities. The entertainment complex contains amusements for the whole family, and there are several bars, an adventure playground, boating on the lake, a children's club, a 9-hole golf course, tennis courts, and various eating outlets. Please note that this site does not accept tents. 100 acre site. 132 touring pitches. 132 hardstandings. Caravan pitches. Motorhome pitches. 1200 statics.

AA Pubs & Restaurants nearby: Blue Bell Hotel, Belford 01668 213543

Leisure: ⚓🏊🅰🛶🎾🎵

Facilities: 🏕⊙✳🔧🛁🍴📶 🖥 ♻ 🄸

Services: 🔌🔋🍴🛢🍴⛟

Within 3 miles: ⚓🎣🔵🛍🛒⛎

Notes: Max 2 dogs per booking, certain dog breeds banned, no commercial vehicles, no bookings by persons under 21yrs unless a family booking.

PREMIER PARK

►►►►► 80% Ord House Country Park *(NT982515)*

Best of British   GOLD

East Ord TD15 2NS

☎ 01289 305288   📄 01289 330832

e-mail: enquiries@ordhouse.co.uk

dir: *On A1, Berwick bypass, exit at 2nd rdbt at East Ord, follow 'Caravan' signs*

🚐 � 🏕

Open all year

Last arrival 23.00hrs Last departure noon

A very well run park set in the pleasant grounds of an 18th-century country house. Touring pitches

are marked and well spaced, some of them fully-serviced. The very modern toilet facilities include family bath and shower suites, and first class disabled rooms. There is an exceptional outdoor leisure shop with a good range of camping and caravanning spares, as well as clothing and equipment, and an attractive licensed club selling bar meals. 42 acre site. 79 touring pitches. 46 hardstandings. Caravan pitches. Motorhome pitches. Tent pitches. 255 statics.

AA Pubs & Restaurants nearby: Wheatsheaf at Swinton 01890 860257

Leisure: 🅰😊

Facilities: 🛁🏕⊙📻✳🔧🕐🛁🍴📶🍴📶 🖥 ♻ 🄸

Services: 🔌🔋🍴🛢⊘🅃🖿⛟⛟

Within 3 miles: ⚓🎣🔵🎣🔵⊙🛍🛒

Notes: Dogs must be kept on leads. Crazy golf, table tennis, giant draughts.

►► 78% Old Mill Caravan Site *(NU055401)*

West Kyloe Farm, Fenwick TD15 2PG

☎ 01289 381279 & 07971 411625

e-mail: teresamalley@westkyloe.demon.co.uk

dir: *A1 onto B6353, 9m S of Berwick-upon-Tweed. Road signed to Lowick/Fenwick. Site 1.5m signed on left*

* 🚐 £15-£20 � £15-£20 🏕 £15-£20

Open Etr-Oct

Last arrival 19.00hrs Last departure 11.00hrs

Small, secluded site accessed through a farm complex, and overlooking a mill pond complete with resident ducks. Some pitches are in a walled garden, and the amenity block is simple but well kept. Delightful walks can be enjoyed on the 600-acre farm. A holiday cottage is also available. 2.5 acre site. 12 touring pitches. Caravan pitches. Motorhome pitches. Tent pitches.

AA Pubs & Restaurants nearby: Black Bull, Etal 01890 820200

Blue Bell Hotel, Belford 01668 213543

Facilities: 🏕⊙🛁🔧♻ 🄸

Services: 🔌⛟

Within 3 miles: 🛍

Notes: 🐕 Dogs must be kept on leads.

LEISURE: 🏊 Indoor swimming pool ⚓ Outdoor swimming pool 🅰 Children's playground 🛶 Kid's club 🎾 Tennis court 🎱 Games room 🖵 Separate TV room ⛳ 9/18 hole golf course ⛵ Boats for hire 🎬 Cinema 🎵 Entertainment 🎣 Fishing 🔵 Mini golf 🏄 Watersports 🏋 Gym ⊙ Sports field Spa ⛎ Stables
FACILITIES: 🛁 Bath 🚿 Shower ⊙ Electric shaver 🔧 Hairdryer ✳ Ice Pack Facility 🕐 Disabled facilities 🕐 Public telephone 🛍 Shop on site or within 200yds 🚐 Mobile shop (calls at least 5 days a week) 🍴 BBQ area 🎍 Picnic area 📶 Wi-fi 🖥 Internet access ♻ Recycling 🄸 Tourist info 🐕 Dog exercise area

HEXHAM — Map 21 NY96

Places to visit

Vindolanda (Chesterholm), BARDON MILL
01434 344277 www.vindolanda.com

Temple of Mithras (Hadrian's Wall),
CARRAWBROUGH www.english-heritage.org.uk

Great for kids: Housesteads Roman Fort,
HOUSESTEADS 01434 344363
www.english-heritage.org.uk

►►► 65% Hexham Racecourse Caravan Site (NY919623)

Hexham Racecourse NE46 2JP
☎ 01434 606847 & 606881 📠 01434 605814
e-mail: hexrace.caravan@btconnect.com
dir: *From Hexham take B6305 signed Allendale/
Alston. Left in 3m signed to racecourse. Site 1.5m
on right*

* 🚐 £14-£17 🚃 £14-£17 ▲ fr £10

Open May-Sep

Last arrival 20.00hrs Last departure noon

A part-level and part-sloping grassy site situated
on a racecourse overlooking Hexhamshire Moors.
The facilities are functional. 4 acre site. 50
touring pitches. Caravan pitches. Motorhome
pitches. Tent pitches.

AA Pubs & Restaurants nearby: Battlesteads
Hotel & Restaurant, Hexham 01434 230209

Dipton Mill, Hexham 01434 606577 Rat Inn,
Hexham 01434 602814

Leisure: ⚙ 🔍
Facilities: 📶 ⊙ 🄿 ✳ ⊙ 🚿 ⚲ ❶
Services: 🔌 🔟 🛢 ⊘ 🔋
Within 3 miles: 🚴 ⛷ 🎗 🄟 ⌕ ◎ 🛒 🔟
Notes: Dogs must be kept on leads.

NORTH SEATON — Map 21 NZ28

Places to visit

Woodhorn, ASHINGTON 01670 528080
www.experiencewoodhorn.com

Morpeth Chantry Bagpipe Museum, MORPETH
01670 535163 www.experiencewoodhorn.com/
morpeth-bagpipe-museum

72% Sandy Bay (NZ302858)

NE63 9YD
☎ 0871 664 9764
e-mail: sandy.bay@park-resorts.com
dir: *From A1 at Seaton Burn take A19 signed
Tyne Tunnel. Then A189 signed Ashington,
approx 8m, at rdbt right onto B1334 towards
Newbiggin-by-the-Sea. Site on right*

🚐 🚃

Open Apr-Oct

Last arrival anytime Last departure noon

A beach-side holiday park on the outskirts of
the small village of North Seaton, within easy
reach of Newcastle. The site is handily placed
for exploring the magnificent coastline and
countryside of Northumberland, but for those
who do not wish to travel it offers the full range
of holiday centre attractions, both for parents
and their children. New extensive dog walk
for 2011 season. 48 touring pitches. Caravan
pitches. Motorhome pitches. 396 statics.

Leisure: 🏊 ⚙ 🎣 🎵
Facilities: 📶 🄿 ⊙ 🛢 🌐 🖥
Services: 🔌 🔟 🛢 🍽 🔋
Within 3 miles: ✏ 🛒 🔟 **Notes:** Koi carp lake.

NOTTINGHAMSHIRE

CHURCH LANEHAM

Places to visit

Newark Air Museum, NEWARK-ON-TRENT
01636 707170 www.newarkairmuseum.org

Vina Cooke Museum of Dolls & Bygone
Childhood, NEWARK-ON-TRENT 01636 821364
www.vinasdolls.co.uk

Great for kids: Sherwood Forest Country Park &
Visitor Centre, EDWINSTOWE 01623 823202
www.nottinghamshire.gov.uk/sherwoodforestcp

CHURCH LANEHAM — Map 17 SK87

►►► 81% *Trentfield Farm* (SK815774)

DN22 0NJ
☎ 01777 228651 📠 01777 228178
e-mail: post@trentfield.co.uk
dir: *A1 onto A57 towards Lincoln for 6m. Left
signed Laneham, 1.5m, through Laneham &
Church Laneham (pass Ferryboat pub on left).
Site 300yds on right*

🚐 🚃 ▲

Open Etr-Nov

Last arrival 20.00hrs Last departure noon

A delightfully rural and level grass park tucked
away on the banks of the River Trent. The park has
its own river frontage with free coarse fishing
available to park residents. The toilets, showers
and laundry room have now been refurbished. The
cosy local pub, which serves food, is under the
same ownership. 34 acre site. 25 touring pitches.
Caravan pitches. Motorhome pitches. Tent pitches.

Facilities: 📶 ⊙ 🄿 ✳ 🌫 🛢 🄿 ⚲ 🌐
Services: 🔌 🔟 🛢 🔋
Within 3 miles: 🚴 🛒 🔟 ◡
Notes: 24-hour mini shop.

MANSFIELD — Map 16 SK56

Places to visit

Sherwood Forest Country Park & Visitor Centre,
EDWINSTOWE 01623 823202
www.nottinghamshire.gov.uk/sherwoodforestcp

Great for kids: Vina Cooke Museum of Dolls &
Bygone Childhood, NEWARK-ON-TRENT
01636 821364 www.vinasdolls.co.uk

►►► 70% Tall Trees Touring Park (SK551626)

Old Mill Ln, Forest Town NG19 0JP
☎ 01623 626503 & 07770 661957
e-mail: info@talltreestouringpark.co.uk
dir: *A60 from Mansfield towards Worksop. After
1m turn right at lights into Old Mill Lane. Site
approx 0.5m on left*

🚐 fr £12.50 🚃 fr £12.50 ▲ fr £12.50

Open all year

Last arrival anytime

A very pleasant park situated just on the outskirts
of Mansfield and within easy walking distance of
shops and restaurants. It is surrounded on three

continued

SERVICES: 🔌 Electric hook up 🔟 Launderette 🍺 Licensed bar 🛢 Calor Gas ⊘ Camping Gaz 🔲 Toilet fluid 🍽 Café/Restaurant 🍟 Fast Food/Takeaway 🔋 Battery charging 🍼 Baby care ↯ Motorvan service point

ABBREVIATIONS: BH/bank hols-bank holidays Etr-Easter Whit-Whitsun dep-departure fr-from hrs-hours m-mile mdnt-midnight rdbt-roundabout rs-restricted service wk-week wknd-weekend 🚫 No credit cards ⊗ No dogs
See page 7 for details of the AA Camping Card Scheme

MANSFIELD *continued*

sides by trees and shrubbery, and securely set at the back of the residential park. There has been significant development on the site, and the new facilities should be complete for the 2012 season. 3 acre site. 15 touring pitches. 15 hardstandings. Caravan pitches. Motorhome pitches. Tent pitches.

Tall Trees Touring Park

AA Pubs & Restaurants nearby: Forest Lodge, Edwinstowe 01623 824443

Fox & Hounds, Blidworth Bottoms 01623 792383

Leisure: ✪ **Facilities:** ↖⊙☓♿☶♺✪ ❻

Services: ☷⛽ **Within 3 miles:** ⛽

Notes: Dogs must be kept on leads.

NEWARK

See Southwell

See Southwell

RADCLIFFE ON TRENT   Map 11 SK63

Places to visit

Nottingham Castle Museum & Art Gallery, NOTTINGHAM 0115 876 3356 www.mynottingham.gov.uk/nottinghamcastle

Wollaton Hall, Gardens & Park, NOTTINGHAM 0115 915 3900 www.nottingham.gov.uk/wollatonhall

▶▶▶ 77% Thornton's Holt Camping Park *(SK638377)*

Stragglethorpe Rd, Stragglethorpe NG12 2JZ
☎ 0115 933 2125 & 933 4204
📠 0115 933 3318
e-mail: camping@thorntons-holt.co.uk
web: www.thorntons-holt.co.uk
dir: *Take A52, 3m E of Nottingham. Turn S at lights towards Cropwell Bishop. Site 0.5m on left. Or A46 SE of Nottingham. N at lights. Site 2.5m on right*

✳ ⛺ £12.50-£20 ⛟ £12.50-£20 ▲ £12.50-£20

Open Apr-6 Nov (rs Nov-Mar pool & shop closed)

Last arrival 20.00hrs Last departure noon

A well-run family site in former meadowland, with pitches located among young trees and bushes for a rural atmosphere and outlook. The toilets are housed in converted farm buildings, and an indoor swimming pool is a popular attraction. 13 acre site. 155 touring pitches. 35 hardstandings. 20 seasonal pitches. Caravan pitches. Motorhome pitches. Tent pitches.

AA Pubs & Restaurants nearby: Ye Olde Trip to Jerusalem, Nottingham 0115 947 3171

Fellows Morton & Clayton, Nottingham 0115 950 6795

Leisure: ⛱ ⅍ **Facilities:** ↖⊙☓♿☶♺✪ ❻
Services: ☷⛽⌀☕⚑⛟
Within 3 miles: ⚓↜☶⌁♨☰☷⛽∪
Notes: Noise curfew at 22.00hrs.

SOUTHWELL   Map 17 SK65

Places to visit

Galleries of Justice Museum, NOTTINGHAM 0115 952 0555 www.galleriesofjustice.org.uk

The Workhouse, SOUTHWELL 01636 817250 www.nationaltrust.org.uk/main/w-theworkhouse

▶▶▶ 76% New Hall Farm Touring Park *(SK660550)*

New Hall Farm, New Hall Ln NG22 8BS
☎ 01623 883041 📠 01623 883041
e-mail: enquiries@newhallfarm.co.uk
dir: *From A614 at White Post Modern Farm Centre, turn E signed Southwell. Immediately after Edingley turn S into New Hall Ln to site (0.5m)*

⛟ ⛺ ▲

Open Mar-Oct

Last arrival 21.00hrs Last departure 13.00hrs

A park on a working stock farm with the elevated pitching area enjoying outstanding panoramic views. It is within a short drive of medieval Newark and Sherwood Forest. A log cabin viewing gantry offers a place to relax and take in the spectacular views. 2.5 acre site. 25 touring pitches. 10 hardstandings. Caravan pitches. Motorhome pitches. Tent pitches.

AA Pubs & Restaurants nearby: Tom Browns Brasserie, Gunthorpe 0115 966 3642

Facilities: ↖⊙☓☶♺
Services: ☷⛽⚑ **Within 3 miles:** ⚓↜☷⛽∪
Notes: Adults only. 🐾 Dogs must be kept on leads.

TEVERSAL   Map 16 SK46

Places to visit

Sherwood Forest Country Park & Visitor Centre, EDWINSTOWE 01623 823202 www.nottinghamshire.gov.uk/sherwoodforestcp

Hardwick Hall, HARDWICK HALL 01246 850430 www.nationaltrust.org.uk/main/w-hardwickhall

PREMIER PARK

▶▶▶▶▶ 87% Teversal Camping & Caravanning Club Site *(SK472615)*

Silverhill Ln NG17 3JJ
☎ 01623 551838
dir: *M1 junct 28, A38 towards Mansfield. Left at lights onto B6027. At top of hill straight over at lights & left at Tesco Express. Right onto B6014, left at Craven Arms, site on left*

✳ ⛟ £10-£30 ⛟ £10-£30 ▲ £10-£30

Open all year

Last arrival 20.00hrs Last departure noon

A top notch park with excellent purpose-built facilities and innovative, hands-on owners. Each pitch is spacious, the excellent toilet facilities are state-of-the-art, and there are views of and access to the countryside and nearby Silverhill Community Woods. The attention to detail and all-round quality are truly exceptional - guests can even hire a car for a day. New of 2011 are ready-erected safari tents for hire, new tent pitches and a bike/dog washing area. 6 acre site. 126 touring pitches. 92 hardstandings. Caravan pitches. Motorhome pitches. Tent pitches. 1 static. 2 bell tents/yurts.

Leisure: ⅍
Facilities: ↖⊙☓☀♿☶♺✪ ❻
Services: ☷⛽⚑⌀☕⛟
Within 3 miles: ⚓↜☷∪
Notes: Site gates closed 23.00hrs-07.00hrs. Dogs must be kept on leads.

LEISURE: ⛱ Indoor swimming pool ⛲ Outdoor swimming pool ⅍ Children's playground ⚓ Kid's club ⚒ Tennis court ⚔ Games room ⬚ Separate TV room ⛳ 9/18 hole golf course ⛵ Boats for hire ⊞ Cinema ♫ Entertainment ⚲ Fishing ◎ Mini golf ⚑ Watersports ⚐ Gym ✿ Sports field Spa ∪ Stables
FACILITIES: ⚱ Bath ⚲ Shower ⊙ Electric shaver ☓ Hairdryer ☀ Ice Pack Facility ♿ Disabled facilities ☎ Public telephone ⚑ Shop on site or within 200yds ⚑ Mobile shop (calls at least 5 days a week) ☶ BBQ area ⚑ Picnic area ⚑ Wi-fi ⚑ Internet access ♺ Recycling ❻ Tourist info ⚑ Dog exercise area

TUXFORD   Map 17 SK77

Places to visit

Museum of Lincolnshire Life, LINCOLN
01522 528448 www.lincolnshire.gov.uk/
museumoflincolnshirelife

Great for kids: Lincoln Castle,
LINCOLN 01522 511068
www.lincolnshire.gov.uk/lincolncastle

AA CAMPING CARD SITE

**►►► 82% Orchard Park
Touring Caravan &
Camping Park** *(SK754708)*

Marnham Rd NG22 0PY
☎ 01777 870228 📠 01777 870320
e-mail: info@orchardcaravanpark.co.uk
dir: *Exit A1 at Tuxford onto A6075 towards Lincoln.
0.5m, right into Marnham Rd. Site 0.75m on right*

🚐 £18-£25 🚍 £18-£25 ▲ £18-£25

Open mid Mar-Oct

Last arrival mdnt Last departure 18.00hrs

A rural site set in an old fruit orchard with
spacious pitches arranged in small groups
separated by shrubs; many of the pitches are
served with water and electricity. A network of
grass pathways and picnic clearings have been
created in a woodland area, and there's a superb
adventure playground. 7 acre site. 60 touring
pitches. 30 hardstandings. Caravan pitches.
Motorhome pitches. Tent pitches.

AA Pubs & Restaurants nearby: Mussel & Crab,
Tuxford 01777 870491

Robin Hood Inn, Elkesley 01777 838259

Leisure: ⚑

Facilities: 🅿️☉🐾✳&©📵🖨️💈戸🚿 wi-fi
🖥️♻️ ❼

Services: 🔌🛢🧴⌀🔲🔋

Within 3 miles: ⌀💈∪

Notes: Dogs must be kept on leads.

WORKSOP   Map 16 SK57

Places to visit

Clumber Park, WORKSOP 01909 476592
www.nationaltrust.org.uk

►►► 78% Riverside Caravan Park

(SK582790)

Central Av S80 1ER
☎ 01909 474118
dir: *From A57 E of town, take B6040 signed Town
Centre at rdbt. Follow international camping sign
to site*

* 🚐 £18-£20 🚍 £18-£20 ▲ £18-£20

Open all year

Last arrival 18.00hrs Last departure noon

A very well maintained park within the attractive
market town of Worksop and next door to the
cricket and bowls club where Riverside customers
are made welcome. This is an ideal park for those
wishing to be within walking distance of all
amenities yet also within a 10-minute car journey
of the extensive Clumber Park and numerous good
garden centres. The towpath of the adjacent
Chesterfield Canal provides excellent walking
opportunities. 4 acre site. 60 touring pitches. 59
hardstandings. Caravan pitches. Motorhome
pitches. Tent pitches.

Facilities: 🅿️☉✳❼
Services: 🔌🛢⌀🔋
Within 3 miles: ⌀🏴⌀💈

Notes: No bikes around reception or in toilet
block. Dogs must be kept on leads.

OXFORDSHIRE

BANBURY   Map 11 SP44

Places to visit

Banbury Museum, BANBURY 01295 753752
www.cherwell.gov.uk/banburymuseum

Great for kids: Deddington Castle, DEDDINGTON
www.english-heritage.org.uk

**►►►► 84% Bo Peep Farm Caravan
Park** *(SP481348)*

Bo Peep Farm, Aynho Rd, Adderbury OX17 3NP
☎ 01295 810605 📠 01295 810605
e-mail: warden@bo-peep.co.uk
dir: *1m E of Adderbury & A4260, on B4100 (Aynho
road)*

🚐 £17-£20 🚍 £17-£20 ▲ £14-£16

Open Mar-Oct

Last arrival 20.00hrs Last departure noon

A delightful park with good views and a spacious
feel. Four well laid out camping areas including
two with hardstandings and a separate tent field
are all planted with maturing shrubs and trees.
The two facility blocks are built in attractive
Cotswold stone. Unusually there is a bay in which
you can clean your caravan or motorhome. There
are four miles of on-site walks including through
woods and on the river bank. 13 acre site. 104
touring pitches. Caravan pitches. Motorhome
pitches. Tent pitches.

AA Pubs & Restaurants nearby: Ye Olde Reindeer
Inn, Banbury 01295 264031

Wykham Arms, Banbury 01295 788808

Saye and Sele Arms, Broughton 01295 263348

Facilities: 🅿️☉🐾✳&©📵💈戸🚿 wi-fi
🖥️♻️ ❼

Services: 🔌🛢⌀🔲🔋⌀

Within 3 miles: ⌀⌀💈

AA CAMPING CARD SITE

**►►►► 83% *Barnstones Caravan &
Camping Site* *(SP455454)***

Great Bourton OX17 1QU
☎ 01295 750289
dir: *Take A423 from Banbury signed Southam. In
3m turn right signed Gt Bourton/Cropredy, site
100yds on right*

* 🚐 £11-£14 🚍 £11-£14 ▲ £10-£12

Open all year

A popular, neatly laid-out site with plenty of
hardstandings, some fully serviced pitches, a
smart up-to-date toilet block, and excellent rally
facilities. Well run by a very personable owner,
this is an excellent value park. 3 acre site. 49
touring pitches. 44 hardstandings. Caravan
pitches. Motorhome pitches. Tent pitches.

AA Pubs & Restaurants nearby: Ye Olde Reindeer
Inn, Banbury 01295 264031

Wykham Arms, Banbury 01295 788808

Saye and Sele Arms, Broughton 01295 263348

Leisure: ⚑✪

Facilities: 🅿️☉✳&©戸🚿♻️ ❼

Services: 🔌🛢🧴⌀🔲🛒🔋

Within 3 miles: ⌀⌀🏴⌀◎≚💈💈∪

Notes: ◎ Dogs must be kept on leads.

SERVICES: 🔌 Electric hook up 🛢 Launderette 🍺 Licensed bar 🛢 Calor Gas ⌀ Camping Gaz 🔲 Toilet fluid 🍴 Café/Restaurant 🛒 Fast Food/Takeaway 🔋 Battery charging
🍼 Baby care ⌀ Motorvan service point
ABBREVIATIONS: BH/bank hols-bank holidays Etr-Easter Whit-Whitsun dep-departure fr-from hrs-hours m-mile mdnt-midnight rdbt-roundabout rs-restricted service wk-week
wknd-weekend ◎ No credit cards ⊗ No dogs   See page 7 for details of the AA Camping Card Scheme

BLETCHINGDON — Map 11 SP51

Places to visit

Rousham House, ROUSHAM 01869 347110
www.rousham.org

Museum of the History of Science, OXFORD
01865 277280 www.mhs.ox.ac.uk

Great for kids: Oxford University Museum of
Natural History, OXFORD 01865 272950
www.oum.ox.ac.uk

►►►► 83% Greenhill Leisure Park
(SP488178)

Greenhill Farm, Station Rd OX5 3BQ
☎ 01869 351600 📠 01869 350918
e-mail: info@greenhill-leisure-park.co.uk
web: www.greenhill-leisure-park.co.uk
dir: M40 junct 9, A34 S for 3m. Take B4027 to
Bletchingdon. Site 0.5m after village on left

🚐 £13-£15 🚎 £13-£15 ▲ £13-£15

Open all year (rs Oct-Mar no dogs, shop & games
room closed)

Last arrival 21.00hrs (20.00hrs in winter) Last
departure noon

An all-year round park set in open countryside
near the village of Bletchingdon. Fishing is
available in the nearby river or in the parks two
well stocked lakes. Pitches are very spacious and
the park is very family orientated and in keeping
with the owner's theme of 'Where fun meets the
countryside'. The facilities are also very good. 7
acre site. 92 touring pitches. 30 hardstandings.
20 seasonal pitches. Caravan pitches. Motorhome
pitches. Tent pitches.

AA Pubs & Restaurants nearby: King's Head,
Woodstock 01993 812164

Feathers Hotel, Woodstock 01993 812291

Leisure: ⚠ 🔍
Facilities: 🚿⊙📠✳️🧴♿️ṣ⌨🖫🚻 �ℹ️
Services: 🔌🗑️ 🪣🚮🛢️T🚽
Within 3 miles: ↨🎣ṣ
Notes: No camp fires. Pets' corner.

►►►► 81% Diamond Farm Caravan & Camping Park (SP513170)

Islip Rd OX5 3DR
☎ 01869 350909
e-mail: warden@diamondpark.co.uk
dir: M40 junct 9, A34 S for 3m, B4027 to
Bletchingdon. Site 1m on left

* 🚐 £17-£19 🚎 £17-£19 ▲ £12-£17

Open all year

Last arrival dusk Last departure 11.00hrs

A well-run, quiet rural site in good level
surroundings, and ideal for touring the Cotswolds,
situated seven miles north of Oxford in the heart
of the Thames Valley. This popular park has
excellent facilities, and offers a heated outdoor
swimming pool and a games room for children. 3
acre site. 37 touring pitches. 20 hardstandings.
Caravan pitches. Motorhome pitches. Tent pitches.

AA Pubs & Restaurants nearby: King's Head,
Woodstock 01993 812164

Feathers Hotel, Woodstock 01993 812291

Leisure: ≋ ⚠ 🔍
Facilities: 🛁🚿⊙📠✳️ṣ🖫🚻 ♻️ℹ️
Services: 🔌🗑️🪣🛢️🚮T🍽️🛒🚽
Within 3 miles: ↨🎣ṣ
Notes: Dogs must be kept on leads.

CHARLBURY

Places to visit

Blenheim Palace, WOODSTOCK 0800 849 6500
www.blenheimpalace.com

Minster Lovell Hall & Dovecote, MINSTER LOVELL
www.english-heritage.org.uk

Great for kids: Cogges Witney, WITNEY
01993 772602 www.cogges.org.uk

CHARLBURY — Map 11 SP31

►►►► 84% *Cotswold View Touring Park* (SP365210)

Enstone Rd OX7 3JH
☎ 01608 810314 📠 01608 811891
e-mail: bookings@gfwiddows.co.uk
dir: From A44 in Enstone take B4022 towards
Charlbury. Follow site signs. Site 1m from
Charlbury.

🚐 🚎 ▲

Open Etr or Apr-Oct

Last arrival 21.00hrs Last departure noon

A good Cotswold site, well screened and with
attractive views across the countryside. The toilet
facilities include fully-equipped family rooms and
bathrooms, and there are spacious, sheltered
pitches, some with hardstandings. Breakfasts and
takeaway food are available from the shop. The
site has camping pods for hire. Perfect location for
exploring the Cotswolds and anyone heading for
the Charlbury Music Festival. 10 acre site. 125
touring pitches. Caravan pitches. Motorhome
pitches. Tent pitches.

AA Pubs & Restaurants nearby: Bull Inn,
Charlbury 01608 810689

Crown Inn, Church Enstone 01608 677262

Leisure: ⚠ ♨ 🔍
Facilities: 🛁🚿⊙📠✳️♿️🔔ṣ🚻🐕
Services: 🔌🗑️🛢️🚮T🛒🚽
Within 3 miles: 🎣ṣ🗑️
Notes: Off licence, skittle alley, chess, boules.

HENLEY-ON-THAMES

Places to visit

Greys Court, HENLEY-ON-THAMES 01491 628529
www.nationaltrust.org.uk

River & Rowing Museum, HENLEY-ON-THAMES
01491 415600 www.rrm.co.uk

Great for kids: LEGOLAND Windsor, WINDSOR
www.legoland.co.uk

HENLEY-ON-THAMES
Map 5 SU78

PREMIER PARK

▶▶▶▶▶ **82% Swiss Farm Touring & Camping** (SU759837)

Marlow Rd RG9 2HY
☎ **01491 573419**
e-mail: enquiries@swissfarmcamping.co.uk
web: www.swissfarmcamping.co.uk
dir: On A4155, N of Henley, next left after rugby club, towards Marlow

* 🚐 £15-£24 🚗 £15-£24 Å £12-£18.50

Open Mar-Oct

Last arrival 21.00hrs Last departure noon

A conveniently-located site within a few minutes' walk of Henley, and ideal for those visiting Henley during Regatta Week. Pitches are spacious and there are fully serviced pitches available. Facilities are modern, well refurbished and are very clean. There is a well-stocked fishing lake plus a very nice and popular outdoor pool. For those who like walking there are some lovely walks along the nearby River Thames. 6 acre site. 140 touring pitches. 20 hardstandings. Caravan pitches. Motorhome pitches. Tent pitches. 6 statics.

AA Pubs & Restaurants nearby: Little Angel, Henley-on-Thames 01491 411008

Cherry Tree Inn, Stoke Row, 01491 680430

Five Horseshoes, Maidensgrove, 01491 641282

Leisure: 🏊 🅰
Facilities: 🌂⊙🅿❄⚡🕒 Wi-fi 🛈
Services: 🔌🅖🍽🛢⌀🅣
Within 3 miles: 🎣🐾🎯🛒🏪
Notes: No groups, no dogs during high season.

STANDLAKE

Places to visit
Buscot Park, BUSCOT 01367 240786
www.buscotpark.com

Harcourt Arboretum, OXFORD 01865 343501
www.botanic-garden.ox.ac.uk

Great for kids: Cotswold Wildlife Park and Gardens, BURFORD 01993 823006
www.cotswoldwildlifepark.co.uk

STANDLAKE
Map 5 SP30

AA CAMPING CARD SITE

PREMIER PARK

▶▶▶▶▶ **96% Lincoln Farm Park Oxfordshire** (SP395028)

Best of British

High St OX29 7RH
☎ **01865 300239** 📠 **01865 300127**
e-mail: info@lincolnfarmpark.co.uk
web: www.lincolnfarmpark.co.uk
dir: In village of Standlake exit A415 between Abingdon & Witney, 5m SE of Witney

🚐 £17.95-£29.95 🚗 £17.95-£29.95
Å £17.95-£26.95

Open Feb-Nov

Last arrival 20.00hrs Last departure noon

An attractively landscaped park in a quiet village setting, with superb facilities and a high standard of maintenance. Family rooms, fully serviced pitches, two indoor swimming pools and a fully-equipped gym are part of the comprehensive amenities. Overall, an excellent top quality park and the perfect base for visiting the Oxfordshire area and the Cotswolds. A warm welcome is assured from the friendly staff. 9 acre site. 90 touring pitches. 75 hardstandings. Caravan pitches. Motorhome pitches. Tent pitches.

AA Pubs & Restaurants nearby: Bear & Ragged Staff, Cumnor 01865 862329

The Vine Inn, Cumnor 01865 862567

Leisure: 🏊 🅰 🎣
Facilities: 🛏🌂⊙🅿❄⚡🕒🅖🍴🐕 Wi-fi
Services: 🔌🅖⌀🅣🛒⌄
Within 3 miles: 🎣🐾🏊🛒🎯⛳
Notes: No gazebos, no noise after 23.00hrs. Dogs must be kept on leads. Putting green, outdoor chess.

UPPER HEYFORD
Map 11 SP42

▶▶▶ **79% Heyford Leys Camping Park** (SP518256)

Camp Rd OX25 5LX
☎ **01869 232048**
e-mail: heyfordleys@aol.com
dir: M40 junct 10 take B430 towards Middleton Stoney. Right after 1.5m marked The Heyford, follow brown signs to site

* 🚐 £14.29-£17.83 🚗 £14.29-£17.83
Å £10.21-£15

Open all year

Last arrival 22.00hrs Last departure 11.00hrs

This small peaceful park near the Cherwell Valley and the village of Upper Heyford is well positioned for visiting nearby Bicester, Oxford and Banbury, as well as being about a 15-minute drive from Silverstone. The facilities are very clean and guests will be assured of a warm welcome. A small fishing lake is also available to customers. 5 acre site. 25 touring pitches. 5 hardstandings. Caravan pitches. Motorhome pitches. Tent pitches.

Facilities: 🌂⊙🅿❄🅖🐕 Wi-fi ♻ 🛈
Services: 🔌🛒
Within 3 miles: 🎣🐾🏪🛒🎯
Notes: No groups, no noise after 20.00hrs.

SERVICES: 🔌 Electric hook up 🅖 Launderette 🍽 Licensed bar 🛢 Calor Gas ⌀ Camping Gaz 🅣 Toilet fluid 🍴 Café/Restaurant 🛒 Fast Food/Takeaway 🔋 Battery charging 🍼 Baby care ⌄ Motorvan service point
ABBREVIATIONS: BH/bank hols-bank holidays Etr-Easter Whit-Whitsun dep-departure fr-from hrs-hours m-mile mdnt-midnight rdbt-roundabout rs-restricted service wk-week wknd-weekend ⊗ No credit cards ⊗ No dogs
See page 7 for details of the AA Camping Card Scheme

RUTLAND

GREETHAM

Places to visit

Rutland County Museum & Visitor Centre, OAKHAM 01572 758440 www.rutland.gov.uk/museum

Great for kids: Oakham Castle, OAKHAM 01572 758440 www.rutland.gov.uk/castle

GREETHAM   Map 11 SK91

▶▶▶▶ **80% Rutland Caravan & Camping** (SK925148)

Park Ln LE15 7FN
☎ **01572 813520**
e-mail: info@rutlandcaravanandcamping.co.uk
dir: *From A1 onto B668 towards Greetham. Before Greetham turn right at x-rds, 2nd left to site*

Open all year

Last arrival 20.00hrs

This pretty caravan park, built to a high specification and surrounded by well-planted banks, continues to improve due to the enthusiasm and vision of its owner. From the spacious reception and the innovative play area to the upgraded toilet block, everything is of a very high standard. The spacious grassy site is close to the Viking Way and other footpath networks, and well sited for visiting Rutland Water and the many picturesque villages in the area. 5 acre site. 130 touring pitches. 65 hardstandings. Caravan pitches. Motorhome pitches. Tent pitches.

AA Pubs & Restaurants nearby: Ram Jam Inn, Stretton 01780 410776

Jackson Stops Inn, Stretton 01780 410237

Olive Branch, Clipsham 01780 410355

Leisure: 🅰

Facilities: 🌂⊙🅿✳🅸🏢🛱🚻 ♻ 🅸

Services: 🔌🔲💧📋🕎

Within 3 miles: 🚵🔄🅿◎🛶🏢🇺

Notes: Dogs must be kept on leads.

WING

Places to visit

Lyddington Bede House, LYDDINGTON 01572 822438 www.english-heritage.org.uk

Great for kids: Oakham Castle, OAKHAM 01572 758440 www.rutland.gov.uk/castle

WING   Map 11 SK80

▶▶▶ **71%** *Wing Lakes Caravan & Camping* (SK892031)

Wing Hall LE15 8RY
☎ **01572 737283 & 737090**
e-mail: winghall1891@aol.com
dir: *From A1 take A47 towards Leicester, 14m, follow Morcott signs. In Morcott follow Wing signs. 2.5m, follow site signs*

Open all year

Last arrival 21.00hrs Last departure noon

A deeply tranquil and rural park set in the grounds of an old manor house. The four grassy fields with attractive borders of mixed, mature deciduous trees have exceptional views across the Rutland countryside and are within one mile of Rutland Water. There's a good shop, which specialises in locally sourced produce, a licensed café, and there are high quality showers and a fully-equipped laundry. Children and tents are very welcome in a safe environment where there is space to roam. 11 acre site. 250 touring pitches. 4 hardstandings. Caravan pitches. Motorhome pitches. Tent pitches.

AA Pubs & Restaurants nearby: Kings Arms, Wing 01572 737634

Facilities: 🌂🅿✳🅸🛱🚻

Services: 🔌💧

Within 3 miles: 🚵🔄🅿🛶🏢🇺

Notes: 🐟 Farm shop, coarse fishing.

SHROPSHIRE

See Walk 8 in the Walks & Cycle Rides section at the end of the guide

BRIDGNORTH   Map 10 SO79

Places to visit

Benthall Hall, BENTHALL 01952 882159 www.nationaltrust.org.uk/main/w-benthallhall

Great for kids: Dudmaston Estate, QUATT 01746 780866 www.nationaltrust.org.uk/main/w-dudmaston

PREMIER PARK

▶▶▶▶▶ **87% Stanmore Hall Touring Park** (SO742923)

Stourbridge Rd WV15 6DT
☎ **01746 761761** 📠 **01746 768069**
e-mail: stanmore@morris-leisure
dir: *2m E of Bridgnorth on A458*

Open all year

Last arrival 20.00hrs Last departure noon

An excellent park in peaceful surroundings offering outstanding facilities. The pitches, many fully serviced (with Freeview TV), are arranged around the lake close to Stanmore Hall. Handy for touring Ironbridge and the Severn Valley Railway, while Bridgnorth itself is an attractive old market town. 12.5 acre site. 131 touring pitches. 53 hardstandings. Caravan pitches. Motorhome pitches. Tent pitches.

AA Pubs & Restaurants nearby: Halfway House Inn, Eardington 01746 762670

Pheasant Inn, Bridgnorth 01746 762260

Leisure: 🅰⚽

Facilities: 🌂⊙🅿✳🅸🕓🏢🛱🚻 🅸

Services: 🔌💧📋🕎

Within 3 miles: 🚵🔄🅇🅿🏢🇺

Notes: Max of 2 dogs. Dogs must be kept on leads.

LEISURE: 🏊 Indoor swimming pool 🏊 Outdoor swimming pool 🅰 Children's playground 🧒 Kid's club 🎾 Tennis court 🎱 Games room 📺 Separate TV room 🏌 9/18 hole golf course ⛵ Boats for hire 🎬 Cinema 🎵 Entertainment 🎣 Fishing ◎ Mini golf 🏄 Watersports 🏋 Gym ⚽ Sports field Spa 🇺 Stables
FACILITIES: 🛁 Bath 🚿 Shower ⚡ Electric shaver 🅿 Hairdryer ✳ Ice Pack Facility ♿ Disabled facilities ☎ Public telephone 🛒 Shop on site or within 200yds 🛒 Mobile shop (calls at least 5 days a week) 🍖 BBQ area 🪑 Picnic area 📶 Wi-fi 🌐 Internet access ♻ Recycling 🅸 Tourist info 🐕 Dog exercise area

CRAVEN ARMS — Map 9 SO48

Places to visit

Stokesay Castle, STOKESAY 01588 672544
www.english-heritage.org.uk

Great for kids: Ludlow Castle, LUDLOW
01584 873355 www.ludlowcastle.com

▶▶▶ 78% Wayside Camping and Caravan Park (SO399816)

Aston on Clun SY7 8EF
☎ 01588 660218
e-mail: waysidecamping@hotmail.com
dir: From Craven Arms on A49, W onto B4368
(Clun road) towards Clun Valley. Site approx 2m
on right just before Aston-on-Clun

* ☎ £13-£15 ☎ £13-£15 ▲ £8-£13

Open Apr-Oct

A peaceful park with lovely views, close to
excellent local walks and many places of interest.
The modern toilet facilities provide a good level of
comfort, and there are several electric hook-ups.
You are assured of a warm welcome by the helpful
owner. 2.5 acre site. 20 touring pitches. 4
hardstandings. Caravan pitches. Motorhome
pitches. Tent pitches. 1 static.

AA Pubs & Restaurants nearby: Sun Inn, Corfton
01584 861239

Crown Country Inn, Munslow 01584 841205

Facilities: ⓝ⊙ℙ☀�⚙ *ⓘ*
Services: ☎ⓣ☎☕
Within 3 miles: ⅃ℐ🐟🏊

Notes: ⊛ Adults only on BHs, only 1 dog per unit.
Dogs must be kept on leads. Seasonal organic
vegetables on sale.

ELLESMERE

See Lyneal

HUGHLEY — Map 10 SO59

Places to visit

Old Oswestry Hill Fort, OSWESTRY
www.english-heritage.org.uk

Great for kids: Hoo Farm Animal Kingdom,
TELFORD 01952 677917 www.hoofarm.com

▶▶▶ 79% Mill Farm Holiday Park (SO564979)

GOLD

SY5 6NT
☎ 01746 785208
e-mail: mail@millfarmcaravanpark.co.uk
dir: On unclass road off B4371 through Hughley,
3m SW of Much Wenlock, 11m SW of Church
Stretton

☎ fr £16 ☎ fr £16 ▲ fr £16

Open all year

Last arrival 18.00hrs Last departure noon

A well-established farm site set in meadowland
adjacent to river, with mature trees and bushes
providing screening, and situated below Wenlock
Edge. Horse riding can be arranged at the riding
stables on the farm. 20 acre site. 60 touring
pitches. 6 hardstandings. 10 seasonal pitches.
Caravan pitches. Motorhome pitches. Tent
pitches. 90 statics.

AA Pubs & Restaurants nearby: Wenlock Edge
Inn, Much Wenlock 01746 785678

George & Dragon, Much Wenlock 01952 727312

Talbot Inn, Much Wenlock 01952 727077

Longville Arms, Longville in the Dale
01694 771206

Leisure: ⊛
Facilities: ⓝ⊙ℙ☀☰🐕📶 ⚙ *ⓘ*
Services: ☎🖹⊘☎☕
Within 0 miles: ⌂🖥∪

Notes: Site more suitable for adults. Dogs must
be kept on leads. Fishing, horse riding.

LYNEAL (NEAR ELLESMERE) — Map 15 SJ43

Places to visit

Old Oswestry Hill Fort, OSWESTRY
www.english-heritage.org.uk

Great for kids: Hawkstone Historic Park &
Follies, WESTON-UNDER-REDCASTLE
01948 841700 www.principal-hayley.co.uk

▶▶▶▶ 81% Fernwood Caravan Park (SJ445346)

GOLD

SY12 0QF
☎ 01948 710221 🖹 01948 710324
e-mail: enquiries@fernwoodpark.co.uk
dir: From A495 in Welshampton take B5063, over
canal bridge, turn right as signed

* ☎ £22-£29.50 ☎ £22-£29.50

Open Mar-Nov (rs Mar & Nov shop closed)

Last arrival 21.00hrs Last departure 17.00hrs

A peaceful park set in wooded countryside, with a
screened, tree-lined touring area and coarse
fishing lake. The approach is past colourful
flowerbeds, and the static area which is tastefully
arranged around an attractive children's playing
area. There is a small child-free touring area for
those wanting complete relaxation, and the park
has 20 acres of woodland walks. 26 acre site. 60
touring pitches. 8 hardstandings. Caravan
pitches. Motorhome pitches. 165 statics.

Leisure: ⚏
Facilities: ⓝ⊙ℙ☀�ⓢ🖹🐕⚙ *ⓘ*
Services: ☎🖹📶ⓣ☕
Within 3 miles: ⅃ℐ🐟🏊

Notes: Dogs must be kept on leads.

SERVICES: ☎ Electric hook up 🖹 Launderette 🖵 Licensed bar 🖴 Calor Gas ⊘ Camping Gaz ⓣ Toilet fluid 🍽 Café/Restaurant 🍔 Fast Food/Takeaway 🔋 Battery charging
🍼 Baby care ☕ Motorvan service point
ABBREVIATIONS: BH/bank hols-bank holidays Etr-Easter Whit-Whitsun dep-departure fr-from hrs-hours m-mile mdnt-midnight rdbt-roundabout rs-restricted service wk-week
wknd-weekend ⊛ No credit cards ⊗ No dogs See page 7 for details of the AA Camping Card Scheme

MINSTERLEY
Map 15 SJ30

Places to visit

Powis Castle & Garden, WELSHPOOL
01938 551920 www.nationaltrust.org.uk

Great for kids: Shrewsbury Castle and
Shropshire Regimental Museum, SHREWSBURY
01743 358516 www.shrewsburymuseums.com

AA CAMPING CARD SITE

►► 92% The Old School Caravan Park
(SO322977)

Shelve SY5 0JQ
☎ 01588 650410 ▤ 01588 650410
e-mail: t.ward425@btinternet.com
dir: *6.5m SW of Minsterley on A488, site on left 2m
after village sign for Hope*

* ⌑ £17-£20.50 ⌑ £17-£20.50 ▲ £17-£20.50

Open Mar-Jan

Last arrival 21.00hrs Last departure 11.00hrs

Situated in the Shropshire hills with many
excellent walks direct from the site, as well as
being close to many cycle trails. There's also a
shooting range and leisure centre within six miles.
Near Snailbreach Mine, one of the most complete
disused mineral mines in the country, and just a
45-minute drive from Ironbridge. This is a really
beautiful small park with excellent facilities. 1.5
acre site. 22 touring pitches. 10 hardstandings. 6
seasonal pitches. Caravan pitches. Motorhome
pitches. Tent pitches.

AA Pubs & Restaurants nearby: Sun Inn, Marton
01938 561211

Lowfield Inn, Marton 01743 891313

Facilities: ↾ ⊙ ✳ ☉ ✶ ♲ ❻

Services: ♨ ╘

Within 3 miles: ⌿ ☖ ∪

Notes: ⊘ No ball games or cycle riding. Dogs
must be kept on leads. TV aerial connection.

SHREWSBURY

Places to visit

Attingham Park, ATCHAM 01743 708123
www.nationaltrust.org.uk/attinghampark

Great for kids: Wroxeter Roman City, WROXETER
01743 761330 www.english-heritage.org.uk

SHREWSBURY
Map 15 SJ41

AA CAMPING CARD SITE

PREMIER PARK

►►►►► 89% Beaconsfield
Farm Caravan Park *(SJ522189)*

Best of British

Battlefield SY4 4AA
☎ 01939 210370 & 210399 ▤ 01939 210349
e-mail: mail@beaconsfield-farm.co.uk
web: www.beaconsfield-farm.co.uk
dir: *At Hadnall, 1.5m NE of Shrewsbury. Follow
sign for Astley from A49*

⌑ £18-£27 ⌑ £18-£27

Open all year

Last arrival 19.00hrs Last departure noon

A purpose-built family-run park on farmland in
open countryside. This pleasant park offers quality
in every area, including superior toilets, heated
indoor swimming pool, luxury lodges for hire, and
attractive landscaping. Fly and coarse fishing are
available from the park's own fishing lake and The
Bothy restaurant is excellent. Car hire is now
available direct from the site, and there's a steam
room, plus free Wi-fi. 12 luxury lodges are
available for hire or sale. Only adults over 21 years
are accepted. 16 acre site. 60 touring pitches. 50
hardstandings. Caravan pitches. Motorhome
pitches. 35 statics.

AA Pubs & Restaurants nearby: The Armoury,
Shrewsbury 01743 340525

Plume of Feathers, Shrewsbury 01952 727360

Mytton & Mermaid, Shrewsbury 01743 761220

Leisure: ⌂

Facilities: ↾ ⊙ ℘ ✳ ☉ ☉ ♱ ⌶ ⟨Wi-fi⟩ ▢ ♲ ❻

Services: ♨ ◪ ▯ ℉ ⌶ ⌄

Within 3 miles: ↥ ☖ ⌿ ◎ ☖ ☖

Notes: Adults only. Dogs must be kept on leads.

PREMIER PARK

►►►►► 88% Oxon Hall
Touring Park *(SJ455138)*

Best of British

Welshpool Rd SY3 5FB
☎ 01743 340868 ▤ 01743 340869
e-mail: oxon@morris-leisure.co.uk
dir: *Exit A5 (ring road) at junct with A458. Site
shares entrance with 'Oxon Park & Ride'*

⌑ ⌑ ▲

Open all year

Last arrival 21.00hrs

A delightful park with quality facilities, and a
choice of grass and fully-serviced pitches. A warm
welcome is assured from the friendly staff. An
adults-only section proves very popular, and there
is an inviting patio area next to reception and the
shop, overlooking a small lake. This site is ideally
located for visiting Shrewsbury and the
surrounding countryside, and the site also benefits
from the Oxon Park & Ride, a short walk through
the park. 15 acre site. 105 touring pitches. 72
hardstandings. Caravan pitches. Motorhome
pitches. Tent pitches. 60 statics.

AA Pubs & Restaurants nearby: The Armoury,
Shrewsbury 01743 340525

Plume of Feathers, Shrewsbury 01952 727360

Mytton & Mermaid, Shrewsbury 01743 761220

Leisure: ⋀

Facilities: ↾ ⊙ ℘ ✳ ☉ ☉ ⑤ ♱ ⟨Wi-fi⟩ ▢ ♲ ❻

Services: ♨ ◪ ▯ ⌀ ⊤ ⌄

Within 3 miles: ↥ ☖ ⌿ ☖ ☖ ∪

Notes: Max 2 dogs per pitch. Dogs must be kept
on leads.

LEISURE: 🏊 Indoor swimming pool 🏊 Outdoor swimming pool ⋀ Children's playground 🧒 Kid's club 🎾 Tennis court 🎱 Games room ⬜ Separate TV room
⛳ 9/18 hole golf course ⛵ Boats for hire 🎬 Cinema ♫ Entertainment ⌿ Fishing ◎ Mini golf 🏄 Watersports 🏋 Gym ⚽ Sports field **Spa** ∪ Stables
FACILITIES: 🛁 Bath 🚿 Shower ⊙ Electric shaver ℘ Hairdryer ✳ Ice Pack Facility ♿ Disabled facilities ☎ Public telephone 🏪 Shop on site or within 200yds
🛒 Mobile shop (calls at least 5 days a week) 🍖 BBQ area 🏕 Picnic area 〈Wi-fi〉 Wi-fi ▢ Internet access ♲ Recycling ❻ Tourist info ✶ Dog exercise area

TELFORD
Map 10 SJ60

Places to visit

Lilleshall Abbey, LILLESHALL 0121 625 6820
www.english-heritage.org.uk

Ironbridge Gorge Museums, IRONBRIDGE
01952 884391 www.ironbridge.org.uk

Great for kids: The Royal Air Force Museum,
COSFORD 01902 376200 www.rafmuseum.org

PREMIER PARK

▶▶▶▶▶ **79% Severn Gorge Park**

(SJ705051)

Bridgnorth Rd, Tweedale TF7 4JB
☎ 01952 684789 📠 01952 587299
e-mail: info@severngorgepark.co.uk
dir: *Signed off A442, 1m S of Telford*

🚐 🚲

Open all year

Last arrival 22.00hrs Last departure 18.00hrs

A very pleasant wooded site in the heart of Telford, well-screened and well-maintained. The sanitary facilities are fresh and immaculate, and landscaping of the grounds is carefully managed. Although the touring section is small, this is a really delightful park to stay on, and it is also well positioned for visiting nearby Ironbridge and its museums. 6 acre site. 10 touring pitches. 10 hardstandings. Caravan pitches. Motorhome pitches. 120 statics.

AA Pubs & Restaurants nearby: All Nations Inn, Madeley 01952 585747

New Inn, Madeley 01952 601018

Facilities: 🐾 ⊙ 🎱 ⚒ 👤 🛬
Services: 🔌 🗑 ⊘ 🍴 👶 ⚡
Within 3 miles: 🎣 🎠 🎯 ◉ 🏧 🗑 ∪
Notes: Adults only. Well behaved dogs only.

WEM
Map 15 SJ52

Places to visit

Hawkstone Historic Park & Follies,
WESTON-UNDER-REDCASTLE 01948 841700
www.principal-hayley.co.uk

Attingham Park, ATCHAM 01743 708123 www.
nationaltrust.org.uk/attinghampark

Great for kids: Shrewsbury Castle and
Shropshire Regimental Museum, SHREWSBURY
01743 358516 www.shrewsburymuseums.com

AA CAMPING CARD SITE

▶▶▶ **79% Lower Lacon Caravan Park**

(SJ534304)

SY4 5RP
☎ 01939 232376 📠 01939 233606
e-mail: info@llcp.co.uk
web: www.llcp.co.uk
dir: *A49 onto B5065. Site 3m on right*

* 🚐 £10.50-£29.50 🚲 £10.50-£29.50
🅰 £10.50-£29.50

Open all year

Last arrival anytime Last departure 16.00hrs

A large, spacious park with lively club facilities and an entertainments' barn, set safely away from the main road. The park is particularly suited to families, with an outdoor swimming pool and farm animals. 52 acre site. 270 touring pitches. 70 hardstandings. Caravan pitches. Motorhome pitches. Tent pitches. 50 statics.

AA Pubs & Restaurants nearby: Burlton Inn, Burlton 01939 270284

Leisure: 🏊 🅿 🎱 🎱
Facilities: 🚿 🐾 ⊙ 🎱 ⚒ 👤 ⊘ 👤 🛬 📶 ♻ ℹ
Services: 🔌 🗑 🍴 🛢 ⊘ 🚽 🍴 👶 ⚡
Within 3 miles: 🎣 🎠 ◉ 🏧 🗑
Notes: No skateboards, no commercial vehicles, no sign written vehicles. Dogs must be kept on leads. Crazy golf.

WENTNOR
Map 15 SO39

Places to visit

Montgomery Castle, MONTGOMERY
01443 336000 www.cadw.wales.gov.uk

Glansevern Hall Gardens, BERRIEW
01686 640644 www.glansevern.co.uk

▶▶▶ **81% The Green Caravan Park** *(SO380932)*

SY9 5EF
☎ 01588 650605
e-mail: karen@greencaravanpark.co.uk
dir: *1m NE of Bishop's Castle on A489. Right at brown tourist sign*

🚐 🚲 🅰

Open Etr-Oct

Last arrival 21.00hrs Last departure 13.00hrs

A pleasant site in a peaceful setting convenient for visiting Ludlow or Shrewsbury. Very family orientated, with good facilities. The grassy pitches are mainly level, and some hardstandings are available. 15 acre site. 140 touring pitches. 5 hardstandings. Caravan pitches. Motorhome pitches. Tent pitches. 20 statics.

AA Pubs & Restaurants nearby: Crown Inn, Wentnor 01588 650613

Leisure: 🅿
Facilities: 🐾 ⊙ 🎱 ⚒ 👤 🛬 ♻ ℹ
Services: 🔌 🗑 🍴 🛢 ⊘ 🚽 🍴 ⚡
Within 3 miles: 🎠 🏧 ∪
Notes: Dogs must be kept on leads.

SERVICES: 🔌 Electric hook up 🗑 Launderette 🍴 Licensed bar 🛢 Calor Gas ⊘ Camping Gaz 🚽 Toilet fluid 🍴 Café/Restaurant 👶 Fast Food/Takeaway ⚡ Battery charging 👶 Baby care ⚡ Motorvan service point
ABBREVIATIONS: BH/bank hols-bank holidays Etr-Easter Whit-Whitsun dep-departure fr-from hrs-hours m-mile mdnt-midnight rdbt-roundabout rs-restricted service wk-week wknd-weekend ⊗ No credit cards ⊗ No dogs
See page 7 for details of the AA Camping Card Scheme

Somerset

South of Bristol and north-east of the West Country lies Somerset, that most English of counties. You tend to think of classic traditions and renowned honey traps when you think of Somerset – cricket and cider, the ancient and mysterious Glastonbury Tor and the deep gash that is Cheddar Gorge.

Somerset means 'summer pastures' – appropriate given that so much of this old county is rural and unspoiled. At its heart are the Mendip Hills, 25 miles (40km) long by 5 miles (8km) wide. Mainly of limestone over old red sandstone, and rising to just over 1,000 ft (303m) above sea level, they have a striking character and identity and are not really like any of the other Somerset hills.

Landscape of contrasts

By contrast, to the south and south-west are the Somerset Levels, a flat fenland landscape that was the setting for the Battle of Sedgemoor in

● Cheddar Gorge

1685, while close to the rolling acres of Exmoor National Park lie the Quantock Hills, famous for gentle slopes, heather-covered moorland stretches and red deer. From the summit, the Bristol Channel is visible where it meets the Severn Estuary; look to the east and you can see the Mendips.

The Quantocks were the haunt of several distinguished British poets. Coleridge wrote *The Ancient Mariner* and *Kubla Khan* while living in the area. Wordsworth and his sister visited on occasions and often accompanied Coleridge on his country walks.

Along the coast

Somerset's fine coastline takes a lot of beating. Various old-established seaside resorts overlook Bridgwater Bay – among them Minehead, on the edge of Exmoor National Park, and classic Weston-Super-Mare, with its striking new pier (the previous one was destroyed by fire in 2008). Fans of the classic Merchant-Ivory film production of The Remains of the Day, starring Anthony Hopkins and Emma Thompson, will recognise the Royal Pier Hotel in Birnbeck Road as one of the locations. Weston has just about everything for the holidaymaker – including Marine Parade, which runs for 2 miles (3.2km). ▶

Historic Wells

Inland – and not to be missed – is historic Wells, one of the smallest cities in the country, and with its period houses and superb cathedral, it is certainly one of the finest. Adorned with sculptures, Wells Cathedral's West Front is a masterpiece of medieval craftsmanship. Nearby are Vicar's Close, a delightful street of 14th-century houses, and the Bishop's Palace, which is 13th century and moated.

Walking and Cycling

The choice of walks in Somerset is plentiful, as is the range of cycle routes. One of the most attractive of long-distance trails is the 50-mile (80km) West Mendip Way, which runs from Weston to Frome. En route the trail visits Cheddar Gorge and Wells. The local tourist information centres throughout the county offer a varied mix of described walks and longer trails to suit all.

One of Somerset's most popular cycling trails is the delightfully named Strawberry Line which links Yatton railway station with Cheddar and runs for 9 miles (14.5km) along the course of a disused track bed. The trail is relatively easy and along the way are various picnic spots and various public artworks.

Festivals and Events

- The Cheddar Ales Beer Festival in June is a celebration of real ale with a range of beers from micro-breweries across the country.
- The Priddy Sheep Fair in mid-August is a great occasion for country lovers and farming traditions.
- Between July and September there are amazing sand sculptures down on the beach at Weston-Super-Mare.
- The Autumn Steam Gala at the West Somerset Railway in Minehead during late September/early October is a must for steam train enthusiasts.
- The Royal Smithfield Christmas Fair at the Royal Bath and West Showground at Shepton Mallet is popular, with festive food, gift halls, cooking demonstrations and sheep shearing.

Wells Cathedral

SOMERSET

See Walk 9 in the Walks & Cycle Rides section at the end of the guide

BATH

Places to visit

Roman Baths & Pump Room, BATH 01225 477785 www.romanbaths.co.uk

Bath Abbey, BATH 01225 422462 www.bathabbey.org

Great for kids: The Herschel Museum of Astronomy, BATH 01225 446865 www.bath-preservation-trust.org.uk

BATH   Map 4 ST76

AA CAMPING CARD SITE

▶▶▶▶ 82% Newton Mill Holiday Park

(ST715649)

Newton Rd BA2 9JF
☎ 08442 729503
e-mail: enquiries@newtonmillpark.co.uk
dir: *From Bath W on A4 to rdbt by Globe Inn, immediately left, site 1m on left*

* ⊞ £15-£25 ⊞ £15-£25 ▲ £13-£25

Open all year (rs Wknds low season restaurant open)

Last arrival 21.30hrs Last departure 11.30hrs

An attractive, high quality park set in a sheltered valley and surrounded by woodland, with a stream running through. It offers excellent toilet facilities with private cubicles and family rooms, and there is an appealing restaurant and bar offering a wide choice of menus throughout the year. Additional hardstandings have been put in on the top area of the park. The city of Bath is easily accessible by bus or via the Bristol to Bath cycle path. 42 acre site. 106 touring pitches. 67 hardstandings. Caravan pitches. Motorhome pitches. Tent pitches.

Newton Mill Holiday Park

AA Pubs & Restaurants nearby: Marlborough Tavern, Bath 01225 423731

King William, Bath 01225 428096

Hop Pole, Bath 01225 446327

Jamie's Italian, Bath 01225 432430

Leisure:

Facilities: ⬚⬚⬚⬚⬚⬚⬚⬚⬚⬚⬚⬚⬚

Services: ⬚⬚⬚⬚⬚⬚⬚⬚⬚

Within 3 miles: ⬚⬚⬚⬚⬚⬚

Notes: No noise after 22.00hrs. Dogs must be kept on leads. Satellite TV hook up on selected pitches.

see advert below

BREAN   Map 4 ST25

Places to visit

King John's Hunting Lodge, AXBRIDGE 01934 732012 www.nationaltrust.org.uk

North Somerset Museum, WESTON-SUPER-MARE 01934 621028 www.n-somerset.gov.uk/museum

Great for kids: The Helicopter Museum, WESTON-SUPER-MARE 01934 635227 www.helicoptermuseum.co.uk

AA CAMPING CARD SITE

 NEW 90% Holiday Resort Unity (ST294539)

Coast Rd, Brean Sands TA8 2RB
☎ 01278 751235   ▤ 01278 752006
e-mail: admin@hru.co.uk
dir: *M5 junct 22, B3140 through Burnham-on-Sea, then through Berrow to Brean. Site on left just before Brean Leisure Park*

* ⊞ £8-£34 ⊞ £8-£34 ▲ £8-£32

Open Feb-Nov

Last arrival 21.00hrs Last departure 11.00hrs

This is an excellent, family-run holiday park offering very good touring facilities plus a wide range of family oriented activities, including bowling, RJ's entertainment club plus good eating outlets etc. Brean Leisure Park and a new swimming pool complex are availabe directly from the touring park at a discounted

LEISURE: ⬚ Indoor swimming pool ⬚ Outdoor swimming pool ⬚ Children's playground ⬚ Kid's club ⬚ Tennis court ⬚ Games room ⬚ Separate TV room ⬚ 9/18 hole golf course ⬚ Boats for hire ⬚ Cinema ⬚ Entertainment ⬚ Fishing ⬚ Mini golf ⬚ Watersports ⬚ Gym ⬚ Sports field Spa ⬚ Stables
FACILITIES: ⬚ Bath ⬚ Shower ⬚ Electric shaver ⬚ Hairdryer ⬚ Ice Pack Facility ⬚ Disabled facilities ⬚ Public telephone ⬚ Shop on site or within 200yds ⬚ Mobile shop (calls at least 5 days a week) ⬚ BBQ area ⬚ Picnic area ⬚ Wi-fi ⬚ Internet access ⬚ Recycling ⬚ Tourist info ⬚ Dog exercise area

entry price. Ready erected, fully-equipped tents are also available for hire. 200 acre site. 453 touring pitches. 158 hardstandings. 168 seasonal pitches. Caravan pitches. Motorhome pitches. Tent pitches. 650 statics. 8 bell tents/yurts.

Leisure: 🌊🚣🏹🎠🎣❓🎱🎵

Facilities: 🐾📶⊙👪✖♿🕙🖥️🚻🐾📶 🖥️ ♻️ ❓

Services: 🗄️🍴🔒🧼🍽️🛒🐾

Within 3 miles: ↓🏇🍴◎💰🗄️∪

Notes: Family parties of 3 or more, must be over 21 (young persons policy applies). Dogs must be kept on leads.

89% Warren Farm Holiday Centre (ST297564)

Brean Sands TA8 2RP
☎ 01278 751227
e-mail: enquiries@warren-farm.co.uk
dir: M5 junct 22 , B3140 through Burnham-on-Sea to Berrow & Brean. Site 1.5m past Brean Leisure Park

* 🚐 £8–£17.50 🚙 £8–£17.50 ▲ £8–£17.50

Open Apr-Oct

Last arrival 20.00hrs Last departure noon

A large family-run holiday park close to the beach, divided into several fields each with its own designated facilities. Pitches are spacious and level, and enjoy panoramic views of the Mendip Hills and Brean Down. A bar and restaurant are part of the complex, which provide entertainment for all the family, and there is also separate entertainment for children. The park has excellent modern facilities. 100 acre site. 575 touring pitches. Caravan pitches. Motorhome pitches. Tent pitches. 400 statics.

AA Pubs & Restaurants nearby: Crossways Inn, West Huntspill 01278 783756

Leisure: 🎠❓🔍🎱🎵

Facilities: 🐾📶⊙👪✖♿🕙🖥️🚻🐾📶 🖥️ ❓

Services: 🗄️🍴🔒🧼🍽️🛒🐾↓

Within 3 miles: ↓🍴◎💰🗄️∪

Notes: No commercial vehicles. Fishing lake & ponds, indoor play area.

see advert on page 272

►►►► 86% Northam Farm Caravan & Touring Park (ST299556)

TA8 2SE
☎ 01278 751244 📠 01278 751150
e-mail: enquiries@northamfarm.co.uk
dir: M5 junct 22, B3140 to Burnham-on-Sea & Brean. Park on right 0.5m past Brean Leisure Park

* 🚐 £9.75–£25.25 🚙 £9.75–£25.25 ▲ £9.75–£21.25

Open Mar-Oct (rs Mar & Oct shop/café/takeaway open limited hours)

Last arrival 20.00hrs Last departure 10.30hrs

An attractive site a short walk from the sea and a long sandy beach. This quality park also has lots of children's play areas, and also owns the Seagull Inn about 600 yards away, which includes a restaurant and entertainment. There is a fishing lake on the site, which proves very popular. Facilities on this park are excellent. A DVD of the site is available free of charge. 30 acre site. 350 touring pitches. 252 hardstandings. Caravan pitches. Motorhome pitches. Tent pitches.

AA Pubs & Restaurants nearby: Crossways Inn, West Huntspill 01278 783756

Leisure: 🎠❓

Facilities: 🐾📶⊙👪✖♿🕙🖥️🚻🐾♻️ ❓

Services: 🗄️🍴🔒🧼🍽️🛒🐾↓

Within 3 miles: ↓🍴◎💰🗄️∪

Notes: Families & couples only, no motorcycles or commercial vehicles. Dogs must be kept on leads.

see advert on inside back cover

BRIDGETOWN Map 3 SS93

Places to visit
Dunster Castle, DUNSTER 01643 821314
www.nationaltrust.org.uk
Cleeve Abbey, WASHFORD 01984 640377
www.english-heritage.org.uk

►►►► 81% Exe Valley Caravan Site (SS923333)

Mill House TA22 9JR
☎ 01643 851432
e-mail: paul@paulmatt.fsnet.co.uk
dir: Take A396 (Tiverton to Minehead road). Turn W in centre of Bridgetown, site 40yds on right

🚐 £10.50–£16.50 🚙 £10.50–£16.50
▲ £10.50–£19.50

Open 16 Mar-15 Oct

Last arrival 22.00hrs

Set in the Exmoor National Park, this adults-only park occupies an enchanting, peaceful spot in a wooded valley alongside the River Exe. There is free fly-fishing, and an abundance of wildlife, with excellent walks directly from the park. The inn opposite serves lunchtime and evening meals. 4 acre site. 50 touring pitches. 10 hardstandings. Caravan pitches. Motorhome pitches. Tent pitches.

AA Pubs & Restaurants nearby: Rest & Be Thankful Inn, Wheddon Cross 01643 841222

Facilities: 📶⊙👪✖♿🕙🖥️🚻🐾📶 ♻️ ❓

Services: 🗄️🍴🔒🧼🍽️🛒↓

Within 3 miles: ↓🍴💰🗄️∪

Notes: Adults only. ⊗ 17th-century mill, cycle hire.

SERVICES: 🗄️ Electric hook up 🍴 Launderette 🔒 Licensed bar 🧼 Calor Gas 🍽️ Camping Gaz 🛒 Toilet fluid 🐾 Café/Restaurant ↓ Fast Food/Takeaway 🚐 Battery charging
🐾 Baby care ↓ Motorvan service point
ABBREVIATIONS: BH/bank hols-bank holidays Etr-Easter Whit-Whitsun dep-departure fr-from hrs-hours m-mile mdnt-midnight rdbt-roundabout rs-restricted service wk-week
wknd-weekend ⊗ No credit cards ⊗ No dogs See page 7 for details of the AA Camping Card Scheme

BRIDGWATER — Map 4 ST23

Places to visit

Hestercombe Gardens, TAUNTON 01823 413923
www.hestercombe.com

Coleridge Cottage, NETHER STOWEY
01278 732662 www.nationaltrust.org.uk

Great for kids: Tropiquaria Animal and
Adventure Park, WASHFORD 01984 640688
www.tropiquaria.co.uk

81% Mill Farm Caravan & Camping Park (ST219410)

Fiddington TA5 1JQ
☎ 01278 732286
web: www.millfarm.biz
dir: *From Bridgwater take A39 W, left at Cannington rdbt, 2m, right just beyond Apple Inn towards Fiddington. Follow camping signs*

* 🚐 £12-£22 🚎 £12-£22 ⛺ £12-£22

Open all year

Last arrival 23.00hrs Last departure 10.00hrs

A large holiday park with plenty to interest all the family, including indoor and outdoor pools, a boating lake, a gym and horse riding. There is also a clubhouse with bar, and a full entertainment programme in the main season. Although lively and busy in the main season, the park also offers a much quieter environment at other times; out of season some activities and entertainment may not be available. 6 acre site. 125 touring pitches. Caravan pitches. Motorhome pitches. Tent pitches.

AA Pubs & Restaurants nearby: Lemon Tree Restaurant (Walnut Tree Hotel), North Petherton 01278 662255

Leisure: ⌇⌇🏹🎠🎡♜□🎵
Facilities: 🛉🏫☉🄿⚒👤🄺©📷🎡🐕📶 ♨ ❶
Services: 🔌🅂🍴🛢🅰🅃🍴🔋
Within 3 miles: ↓🎣🎡©👤🅂∪

Notes: Dogs must be kept on leads. Canoeing, pool table, trampolines, pony rides.

see advert on opposite page

BURNHAM-ON-SEA — Map 4 ST34

Places to visit

Glastonbury Abbey, GLASTONBURY
01458 832267 www.glastonburyabbey.com

King John's Hunting Lodge, AXBRIDGE
01934 732012 www.nationaltrust.org.uk

Great for kids: Wookey Hole Caves & Papermill, WOOKEY HOLE 01749 672243 www.wookey.co.uk

85% Burnham-on-Sea Holiday Village (ST305485)
GOLD

Marine Dr TA8 1LA
☎ 0871 231 0868 🖨 01278 793776
e-mail: burnham@haven.com
dir: *M5 junct 22, A38 towards Highbridge. Over mini rdbt, right onto B3139 to Burnham. After Total Garage left into Marine Drive. Park 400yds on left*

🚐🚎⛺

Open mid Mar-Oct (rs mid Mar-May & Sep-Oct facilities may be reduced)

Last arrival anytime Last departure 10.00hrs

A large, family-orientated holiday village complex with a separate touring park containing 43 super pitches, newly refurbished toilets and showers and a new touring reception. There is a wide range of activities, including excellent indoor and outdoor pools, plus bars, restaurants and entertainment for all the family. The coarse fishing lake is very popular, and the seafront at Burnham is only half a mile away. 94 acre site. 72 touring pitches. 44 hardstandings. Caravan pitches. Motorhome pitches. Tent pitches. 700 statics.

AA Pubs & Restaurants nearby: Crossways Inn, West Huntspill 01278 783756

Leisure: ⌇⌇🏊🚣☉🎵
Facilities: 🛉🄿⚒👤©📶 ❶
Services: 🔌🅂🍴🅰🍴🔋🛒🚿
Within 3 miles: ↓🎣🎡©👤🅂∪

Notes: Max 2 dogs per booking, certain dog breeds banned, no commercial vehicles, no bookings by persons under 21yrs unless a family booking.

see advert on page 274

BURTLE — Map 4 ST34

Places to visit

Glastonbury Abbey, GLASTONBURY
01458 832267 www.glastonburyabbey.com

The Bishop's Palace, WELLS 01749 988111
www.bishopspalace.org.uk

Great for kids: East Somerset Railway, CRANMORE 01749 880417
www.eastsomersetrailway.com

► 76% Orchard Camping (ST397434)

Ye Olde Burtle Inn, Catcott Rd TA7 8NG
☎ 01278 722269 & 722123 🖨 01278 722269
e-mail: food@theinn.eu
dir: *M5 junct 23, A39, in approx 4m left onto unclass road to Burtle, site by pub in village centre* ⛺

Open all year

Last arrival anytime

A simple campsite set in an orchard at the rear of a lovely 17th-century family inn in the heart of the Somerset Levels. The restaurant offers a wide range of meals, and breakfast can be pre-ordered by campers. The site has a shower and disabled toilet which are available to campers outside pub opening hours. Free internet access and Wi-fi are available. 0.75 acre site. 30 touring pitches. Tent pitches.

AA Pubs & Restaurants nearby: The Burcott Inn, Wookey 01749 673874

Leisure: 🎠 🔍
Facilities: 🛉☉🄿⚒👤🎡📶 ❶
Services: 🍴🍴🔋🛒 **Within 3 miles:** 🎡🅂∪

Notes: No cars by caravans or tents. Cycle & tent hire, sleeping bags & equipment.

CHARD
Map 4 ST30

Places to visit

Forde Abbey, CHARD 01460 221290
www.fordeabbey.co.uk

Barrington Court, BARRINGTON 01460 241938
www.nationaltrust.org.uk

AA CAMPING CARD SITE

▶▶▶▶ 80% **Alpine Grove Touring Park** *(ST342071)*

Forton TA20 4HD
☎ 01460 63479 📠 01460 63479
e-mail: stay@alpinegrovetouringpark.com
dir: *Exit A30 between Chard & Crewkerne towards Cricket St Thomas, follow signs. Site 2m on right*

* 🚐 £11-£20 🚙 £11-£20 ▲ £11-£20

Open 1 wk before Etr-Sep

Last arrival 21.00hrs Last departure 10.30hrs

A warm welcome awaits at this attractive, quiet wooded park that has both hardstandings and grass pitches. The facilities are kept spotlessly clean. Families particularly enjoy the small swimming pool and terrace in summer. Log cabins are also available for hire. This very dog-friendly site offers a dog sitting service. 8.5 acre site. 40 touring pitches. 16 hardstandings. Caravan pitches. Motorhome pitches. Tent pitches. 2 wooden pods.

AA Pubs & Restaurants nearby: George Inn, Crewkerne 01460 73650

New Inn, Ilminster 01460 52413

Leisure: 🏊 /Ⓐ
Facilities: 🖐🔘🅿✳♿🕐🖥🎋🚼 ⬛ ♻ 🏧
Services: 🔌🅱🚿🧺⊤🛒↻
Within 3 miles: ↓✎🅱�#↻

Notes: No open fires. Dogs must be kept on leads. Fire pits to hire.

CHEDDAR
Map 4 ST45

Places to visit

Glastonbury Abbey, GLASTONBURY 01458 832267
www.glastonburyabbey.com

The Helicopter Museum, WESTON-SUPER-MARE
01934 635227 www.helicoptermuseum.co.uk

Great for kids: Wookey Hole Caves & Papermill, WOOKEY HOLE 01749 672243 www.wookey.co.uk

AA CAMPING CARD SITE

 84% **Broadway House Holiday Park** *(ST448547)*

Axbridge Rd BS27 3DB
☎ 08442 729501 📠 01934 744950
e-mail: enquiries@broadwayhousepark.co.uk
dir: *From M5 junct 22 follow signs to Cheddar Gorge & Caves (8m). Site midway between Cheddar & Axbridge on A371*

* 🚐 £15-£30 🚙 £15-£30 ▲ £10-£30

Open Mar-Oct (rs Mar-end May & Oct bar & pool closed, limited shop hours)

Last arrival 22.00hrs Last departure 11.00hrs

A well-equipped holiday park on the slopes of the Mendips with an exceptional range of activities for all ages. This is a busy and lively park in the main holiday periods, but can be quiet and peaceful off-peak. Broadway has its own competition standard BMX track, which is used for National and European Championships, plus a skateboard park and many other activities. The slightly-terraced pitches face south, and are backed by the hills. Lodges are available to let. 30 acre site. 342 touring pitches. 70 hardstandings. Caravan pitches. Motorhome pitches. Tent pitches. 35 statics.

AA Pubs & Restaurants nearby: Wookey Hole Inn, Wookey Hole 01749 676677

Leisure: 🏊 /Ⓐ 🎣 ♫
Facilities: 🛁🖐🔘🅿✳♿🕐🖥🎋🚼 ♻ 🏧
Services: 🔌🅱🍴🧺🔘⊤🍴🛒🛍🐕↻
Within 3 miles: ✎◎🅱🚲

Notes: Children to be supervised at all times. Dogs must be kept on leads. Table tennis, skate park, BMX track.

see advert on page 276

LEISURE: 🏊 Indoor swimming pool 🏊 Outdoor swimming pool /Ⓐ Children's playground 🧒 Kid's club 🎾 Tennis court 🎱 Games room 📺 Separate TV room ⛳ 9/18 hole golf course 🚣 Boats for hire 🎬 Cinema ♫ Entertainment 🎣 Fishing ◎ Mini golf 🏄 Watersports 💪 Gym 🏅 Sports field **Spa** ↻ Stables
FACILITIES: 🛁 Bath 🖐 Shower ⊝ Electric shaver 🅿 Hairdryer ✳ Ice Pack Facility ♿ Disabled facilities 🕐 Public telephone 🖥 Shop on site or within 200yds 🏪 Mobile shop (calls at least 5 days a week) 🎋 BBQ area 🚼 Picnic area ⬛ Wi-fi 🖳 Internet access ♻ Recycling 🏧 Tourist info 🐕 Dog exercise area

►►►► 84% Cheddar Bridge Touring Park *(ST459529)*

Draycott Rd BS27 3RJ
☎ 01934 743048 📄 01934 743048
e-mail: enquiries@cheddarbridge.co.uk
dir: *M5 junct 22 (Burnham-on-Sea), A38 towards Cheddar & Bristol, approx 5m. Right onto A371 at Cross, follow Cheddar signs. Through Cheddar village towards Wells, site on right just before Caravan Club site*

🏕 🚐 ⛺

Open Mar-Oct

Last arrival 22.00hrs Last departure 11.00hrs

A peaceful adults-only park on the edge of the village of Cheddar, with the River Yeo passing attractively through its grounds. It is handy for exploring Cheddar Gorge and Wookey Hole, Wells and Bath. The toilet and shower facilities are very good. 4 acre site. 45 touring pitches. 10 hardstandings. Caravan pitches. Motorhome pitches. Tent pitches. 4 statics.

AA Pubs & Restaurants nearby: Wookey Hole Inn, Wookey Hole 01749 676677

Facilities: 🚿 ⊙ 🅿 ⚒ ❄ & 🛒 🛁 🎏

Services: 🔌 🗑 ♿

Within 3 miles: ↕ 🏌 ◎ ⛴ 🛒 🛁 ↻

Notes: Adults only. Quiet 23.00hrs-08.00hrs.
see advert on page 276

COWSLIP GREEN

Places to visit

Clevedon Court, CLEVEDON 01275 872257
www.nationaltrust.org.uk

Bristol Museum & Art Gallery, BRISTOL
0117 922 3571 www.bristol.gov.uk/museums

Great for kids: HorseWorld, BRISTOL
01275 540173 www.horseworld.org.uk

COWSLIP GREEN Map 4 ST46

►►► 83% *Brook Lodge Farm Camping & Caravan Park (Bristol)* *(ST486620)*

BS40 5RB
☎ 01934 862311 📄 01934 862311
e-mail: info@brooklodgefarm.com
dir: *M5 junct 18 follow signs for Bristol Airport. Site 3m on left of A38 at bottom of hill. M5 junct 22 follow A38 to Churchill. Site 4m on right opposite Holiday Inn*

🏕 🚐 ⛺

Open Mar-Oct

Last arrival 21.30hrs Last departure noon

A naturally sheltered country touring park nestling in a valley of the Mendip Hills, surrounded by trees and a historic walled garden. A friendly welcome is always assured by the family owners who are particularly keen on preserving the site's environment and have now won a green tourism award. This park is particularly well placed for visiting the Bristol Balloon Festival, held in August, plus the many country walks in the area. 3.5 acre site. 29 touring pitches. 3 hardstandings. Caravan pitches. Motorhome pitches. Tent pitches.

AA Pubs & Restaurants nearby: Ship & Castle, Congresbury 01934 833535

Leisure: ⛰ **Facilities:** 🚿 ⊙ 🅿 ⚒ ❄ 🛁 🐕

Services: 🔌 🗑 🛢 🗑 ♿

Within 3 miles: ↕ 🏌 🛁 ↻

Notes: Dogs by prior arrangement. Cycle hire, walking maps available.

CREWKERNE

See Drimpton, Dorset

CROWCOMBE Map 3 ST13

Places to visit

Cleeve Abbey, WASHFORD 01984 640377
www.english-heritage.org.uk

Great for kids: Dunster Castle, DUNSTER
01643 821314 www.nationaltrust.org.uk

AA CAMPING CARD SITE

►►►► 86% Quantock Orchard Caravan Park *(ST138357)*

Flaxpool TA4 4AW
☎ 01984 618618
e-mail: member@flaxpool.freeserve.co.uk
web: www.quantock-orchard.co.uk
dir: *Take A358 from Taunton, signed Minehead & Wiliton. In 8m turn left just past Flaxpool Garage. Park immediately on left*

* 🏕 £14-£26.50 🚐 £14-£26.50 ⛺ £14-£26.50

Open all year (rs 10 Sep-20 May swimming pool closed)

Last arrival 22.00hrs Last departure noon

This small family run park is set at the foot of the beautiful Quantock Hills and makes an ideal base for touring Somerset, Exmoor and north Devon. It is also close to the West Somerset Railway. It has excellent facilities and there is a lovely heated outdoor swimming pool, plus gym and fitness centre; bike hire is also available. There are static homes for hire. 3.5 acre site. 69 touring pitches. 30 hardstandings. Caravan pitches. Motorhome pitches. Tent pitches. 8 statics.

AA Pubs & Restaurants nearby: White Horse, Stogumber 01984 656277

Blue Ball, Triscombe 01984 618242

Leisure: 🏊 🎯 ⛰ 🎣 🎱 Spa

Facilities: 🛁 🚿 ⊙ 🅿 ⚒ ❄ & 🛒 🛁 🎏 📶 💻 ♻ ❓

Services: 🔌 🗑 🛢 🗑 🚰 ♿

Within 3 miles: ↕ 🏌 🛒 🛁 ↻

Notes: Dogs must be kept on leads. Off-licence.

CROWCOMBE *continued*

DULVERTON

See also East Anstey (Devon)

Places to visit

Knightshayes Court,
KNIGHTSHAYES COURT 01884 254665
www.nationaltrust.org.uk/knightshayes

Killerton House & Garden, KILLERTON HOUSE &
GARDEN 01392 881345
www.nationaltrust.org.uk

Great for kids: Tiverton Castle, TIVERTON
01884 253200 www.tivertoncastle.com

DULVERTON
Map 3 SS92

►►► 80% Wimbleball Lake *(SS960300)*

Brompton Regis TA22 9NU
☎ 01398 371257 & 371460
e-mail: wimbleball@swlakestrust.org.uk
dir: *From A396 (Tiverton-Minehead road) take
B3222 signed Dulverton Services, follow signs
to Wimbleball Lake. Ignore 1st entry (fishing) &
take 2nd entry for tea-room & camping. (NB care
needed - narrow roads)*

Open Mar-Oct

Last departure 11.30hrs

A grassy site overlooking Wimbleball Lake, set
high up on Exmoor National Park. The camping
area is adjacent to the Visitor Centre and café,
which also includes the refurbished camping
toilets and showers. The camping field, which
includes 11 electric hook-ups, is in a quiet and
peaceful setting with good views of the lake,
which is nationally renowned for its trout fishing,
and boats can be hired with advance notice. 1.25
acre site. 30 touring pitches. 4 hardstandings.
Caravan, motorhome and tent pitches.

AA Pubs & Restaurants nearby: Masons Arms,
Knowstone 01398 341231

Leisure: ⚑

Facilities: ⚐⊙℘⚹⚒⚘⚕⚐⚐⚘⚕

Services: ⚑⚐⊙

Within 3 miles: ⚹℘⚒⚐⚐U

Notes: Dogs must be kept on leads. Watersports
& activity centre, cycling, lakeside walks.

LEISURE: 🏊 Indoor swimming pool 🏊 Outdoor swimming pool ⚑ Children's playground 🏐 Kid's club ⚑ Tennis court 🎱 Games room 📺 Separate TV room ⚑ 9/18 hole golf course ⛵ Boats for hire 🎬 Cinema ♫ Entertainment 🎣 Fishing ◎ Mini golf 🏄 Watersports 🏋 Gym 🏟 Sports field Spa ∪ Stables
FACILITIES: 🛁 Bath 🚿 Shower ⊙ Electric shaver 🗲 Hairdryer ❄ Ice Pack Facility 🚽 Disabled facilities ☏ Public telephone 🛒 Shop on site or within 200yds 🚐 Mobile shop (calls at least 5 days a week) 🍖 BBQ area 🎍 Picnic area 📶 Wi-fi 🖥 Internet access ♻ Recycling ⓘ Tourist info 🐕 Dog exercise area

EMBOROUGH
Map 4 ST65

Places to visit

Glastonbury Abbey, GLASTONBURY 01458 832267 www.glastonburyabbey.com

King John's Hunting Lodge, AXBRIDGE 01934 732012 www.nationaltrust.org.uk

Great for kids: East Somerset Railway, CRANMORE 01749 880417 www.eastsomersetrailway.com

AA CAMPING CARD SITE

►►► 83% Old Down Touring Park
(ST628513)

Old Down House BA3 4SA
☎ 01761 232355   📄 01761 232355
e-mail: jsmallparkhomes@aol.com
dir: A37 from Farrington Gurney through Ston Easton. In 2m left onto B3139 to Radstock. Site opposite Old Down Inn

* 🚐 £15-£20 🚐 £15-£20 ▲ £15-£20

Open all year

Last arrival 20.00hrs Last departure noon

A small family-run site set in open parkland, surrounded by well-established trees. The excellent toilet facilities are well maintained as is every other aspect of the park. Children are welcome. 4 acre site. 30 touring pitches. 15 hardstandings. 6 seasonal pitches. Caravan pitches. Motorhome pitches. Tent pitches.

AA Pubs & Restaurants nearby: Moody Goose, Old Priory, Midsomer Norton 01761 416784

Facilities: 🅁 ⊙ 🅟 ✳ 🔊 🖙 ♻ 🅘

Services: 🔌 🔒 ⊘ 🅣 🖘

Within 3 miles: 🖈 🗏 🖊 🔊 🔊 U

Notes: Dogs must be kept on leads.

EXFORD
Map 3 SS83

Places to visit

Dunster Castle, DUNSTER 01643 821314 www.nationaltrust.org.uk

West Somerset Railway, MINEHEAD 01643 704996 www.west-somerset-railway.co.uk

Great for kids: Exmoor Zoological Park, BLACKMOOR GATE 01598 763352 www.exmoorzoo.co.uk

►► 84% Westermill Farm (SS825398)

TA24 7NJ
☎ 01643 831238   📄 01643 831216
e-mail: aa@westermill.com
dir: From Exford on Porlock road. Left in 0.25m left, to Westermill sign on tree. Fork left (NB recommended route)

* 🚐 £15.50 ▲

Open all year (rs Nov-May larger toilet block & shop closed)

An idyllic site for peace and quiet, in a sheltered valley in the heart of Exmoor, which has won awards for conservation. There are four waymarked walks over the 500-acre working farm and self-catering accommodation is also available. Please note that the site should only be approached from Exford (other approaches are difficult). 6 acre site. 60 touring pitches. Motorhome pitches. Tent pitches.

AA Pubs & Restaurants nearby: Crown Hotel, Exford 01643 831554

Facilities: 🅁 ⊙ 🅟 ✳ 🕒 🔊 🖙 ♻ 🅘

Services: 🔊 🔒 ⊘

Within 3 miles: 🖊 🔊 🔊

Notes: 🐕 Shallow river for fishing & bathing, waymarked walks.

FROME
Map 4 ST74

Places to visit

Stourhead, STOURHEAD 01747 841152 www.nationaltrust.org.uk/main/w-stourhead

Dyrham Park, DYRHAM 0117 937 2501 www.nationaltrust.org.uk

Great for kids: Longleat, LONGLEAT 01985 844400 www.longleat.co.uk

►►► 83% Seven Acres Caravan & Camping Site (ST777444)

Seven Acres, West Woodlands BA11 5EQ
☎ 01373 464222
dir: A361 (Frome bypass) onto B3092 at rdbt, 0.75m to site

* 🚐 £15-£20 🚐 £15-£20 ▲ £10-£15

Open Mar-Oct

A level meadowland site beside the shallow River Frome, with a bridge across to an adjacent field, and plenty of scope for families. The facilities are spotless. Set on the edge of the Longleat Estate with its stately home, wildlife safari park, and many other attractions. 3 acre site. 16 touring pitches. 16 hardstandings. Caravan pitches. Motorhome pitches. Tent pitches.

AA Pubs & Restaurants nearby: Horse & Groom, Frome 01373 462802

The George at Nunney, Nunney 01373 836458

Vobster Inn, Lower Vobster 01373 812920

Leisure: 🄰

Facilities: 🅁 ⊙ 🅟 ✳ 🖙 🖙

Services: 🔌

Within 3 miles: 🖈 🗏 🖊 🔊 🔊 U

Notes: 🐕 Dogs must be kept on leads.

SERVICES: 🔌 Electric hook up   🔊 Launderette   🍺 Licensed bar   🔋 Calor Gas   ⊘ Camping Gaz   🅣 Toilet fluid   🍽 Café/Restaurant   🍟 Fast Food/Takeaway   🔋 Battery charging   🍼 Baby care   ⚡ Motorvan service point
ABBREVIATIONS: BH/bank hols-bank holidays   Etr-Easter   Whit-Whitsun   dep-departure   fr-from   hrs-hours   m-mile   mdnt-midnight   rdbt-roundabout   rs-restricted service   wk-week   wknd-weekend   ⊗ No credit cards   ⊗ No dogs
See page 7 for details of the AA Camping Card Scheme

GLASTONBURY   Map 4 ST53

Places to visit

Lytes Cary Manor, KINGSDON 01458 224471
www.nationaltrust.org.uk/
main/w-lytescarymanor

Fleet Air Arm Museum, YEOVILTON
01935 840565 www.fleetairarm.com

Great for kids: Haynes International Motor
Museum, SPARKFORD 01963 440804
www.haynesmotormuseum.co.uk

PREMIER PARK

▶▶▶▶▶ **94% The Old**
Oaks Touring Park

(ST521394)

Wick Farm, Wick BA6 8JS
☎ 01458 831437
e-mail: info@theoldoaks.co.uk
dir: On A361 from Glastonbury towards Shepton
Mallet. In 1.75m left at Wick sign, site on left in
1m

🚐 £16-£30.50 🚗 £16-£30.50 ▲ £15-£22.50

Open 10 Feb-12 Nov (rs Low season reduced shop
& reception hours)

Last arrival 20.00hrs (18.00hrs in low season)
Last departure noon

An idyllic park on a working farm with panoramic
views towards the Mendip Hills. Old Oaks offers
sophisticated services whilst retaining a farming
atmosphere, and there are some 'super' pitches as
well as en suite toilet facilities. Glastonbury's two
famous 1,000-year-old oak trees, Gog and Magog,
are on site. This is an adult-only park, and
three camping cabins are available for hire. 10 acre
site. 100 touring pitches. 90 hardstandings.
Caravan pitches. Motorhome pitches. Tent pitches.

AA Pubs & Restaurants nearby: Ring O'Bells,
Ashcott 01458 210232

Ashcott Inn, Ashcott 01458 210282

Facilities: 🚿🏠⊙ℱ✳🚿🕒🏧🚽🛁 📶
🖥 ♻ ❶

Services: 🚐🚽🔒🚮 🔁🛒🚽⟴

Within 3 miles: 🖊🏧🛍∪

Notes: Adults only. Group or block bookings
accepted only at owners' discretion. Dogs must be
kept on leads. Fishing, cycle hire, off licence, dog
shower, dog sitting.

▶▶▶▶ **79%** *Isle of Avalon Touring*
Caravan Park (ST494397)

Godney Rd BA6 9AF
☎ 01458 833618   📄 01458 833618
dir: M5 junct 23, A39 to outskirts of Glastonbury,
2nd exit signed Wells at B&Q rdbt, straight over
next rdbt, 1st exit at 3rd rdbt (B3151), site 200yds
on right

🚐 🚗 ▲

Open all year

Last arrival 21.00hrs Last departure 11.00hrs

A popular site on the south side of this historic
town and within easy walking distance of the town
centre. This level park offers a quiet environment
in which to stay and explore the many local
attractions including the Tor, Wells, Wookey Hole
and Clarks Village. 8 acre site. 120 touring
pitches. 70 hardstandings. Caravan pitches.
Motorhome pitches. Tent pitches.

AA Pubs & Restaurants nearby: Ring O'Bells,
Ashcott 01458 210232

Ashcott Inn, Ashcott 01458 210282

Leisure: 🅰

Facilities: 🏠⊙ℱ✳🕒🏧🛁🚽

Services: 🚐🔒🚮🚽🛒🛁🚽

Within 3 miles: 🖊🏧🛍∪

Notes: Cycle hire.

LANGPORT   Map 4 ST42

Places to visit

Montacute House, MONTACUTE 01935 823289
www.nationaltrust.org.uk

Lytes Cary Manor, KINGSDON 01458 224471
www.nationaltrust.org.uk/
main/w-lytescarymanor

Great for kids: Fleet Air Arm Museum,
YEOVILTON 01935 840565 www.fleetairarm.com

▶▶▶ **77% Thorney Lakes**
Caravan Park (ST430237)

Thorney Lakes, Muchelney TA10 0DW
☎ 01458 250811
e-mail: enquiries@thorneylakes.co.uk
dir: From A303 at Podimore rdbt take A372 to
Langport. At Huish Episcopi Church turn left for
Muchelney. In 100yds left (signed Muchelney
& Crewkerne). Site 300yds after John Leach Pottery

✳ 🚐 £10-£16 🚗 £10-£16 ▲ £10-£16

Open Etr-Oct

A small, basic but very attractive park set in a
cider apple orchard, with coarse fishing in the
three well-stocked, on-site lakes. The famous John
Leach pottery shop is close at hand, and The
Lowland Games are held nearby in July. 6 acre
site. 36 touring pitches. Caravan pitches.
Motorhome pitches. Tent pitches.

AA Pubs & Restaurants nearby: Rose & Crown,
Huish Episcopi 01458 250494

Old Pound Inn, Langport 01458 250469

Devonshire Arms, Long Sutton 01458 241271

Halfway House, Pitney 01458 252513

Facilities: 🏠⊙✳📶 ♻ ❶

Services: 🚐

Within 3 miles: ⌯🖊🏧

Notes: 🐾

MARTOCK

Places to visit

Montacute House, MONTACUTE 01935 823289
www.nationaltrust.org.uk

Montacute House, MONTACUTE 01935 823289
www.nationaltrust.org.uk

Great for kids: Fleet Air Arm Museum,
YEOVILTON 01935 840565 www.fleetairarm.com

MARTOCK
Map 4 ST41

AA CAMPING CARD SITE

▶▶▶▶ **82% Southfork Caravan Park** *(ST448188)*

Parrett Works TA12 6AE
☎ **01935 825661** 📄 **01935 825122**
e-mail: southforkcaravans@btconnect.com
dir: *8m NW of Yeovil, 2m off A303. From E, take exit after Cartgate rdbt. From W, 1st exit off rdbt signed South Petherton, follow camping signs*

* 🚐 £11-£22 🚃 £11-£22 ▲ £11-£19

Open all year

Last arrival 22.30hrs Last departure noon

A neat, level mainly grass park in a quiet rural area, just outside the pretty village of Martock. Some excellent spacious hardstandings are available. The facilities are always spotless and the whole site well cared for by the friendly owners, who will ensure your stay is a happy one, a fact borne out by the many repeat customers. The park is unique in that it also has a fully-approved caravan repair and servicing centre with accessory shop. There are also static caravans available for hire. 2 acre site. 27 touring pitches. 2 hardstandings. Caravan pitches. Motorhome pitches. Tent pitches. 3 statics.

AA Pubs & Restaurants nearby: Nag's Head Inn, Martock 01935 823432

Ilchester Arms, Ilchester 01935 840220

Leisure: 🅰
Facilities: 🏷⊙📍✳🕐📷🔊⌨ ♻ 🅸
Services: 🔌🅖 🛢⌀🅣🔋
Within 3 miles: 🚶🎣🅟
Notes: Dogs must be kept on leads.

MINEHEAD
Map 3 SS94

Places to visit

West Somerset Railway, MINEHEAD 01643 704996 www.west-somerset-railway.co.uk

Dunster Castle, DUNSTER 01643 821314 www.nationaltrust.org.uk

Great for kids: Tropiquaria Animal and Adventure Park, WASHFORD 01984 640688 www.tropiquaria.co.uk

▶▶▶ **75% Minehead & Exmoor Caravan & Camping Park** *(SS950457)*

Porlock Rd TA24 8SW
☎ **01643 703074**
dir: *1m W of Minehead town centre, take A39 towards Porlock. Site on right*

* 🚐 £12-£18 🚃 £12-£18 ▲ £12-£18

Open Mar-Oct (rs Nov-Feb open certain weeks only (phone to check))

Last arrival 22.00hrs Last departure noon

A small terraced park on the edge of Exmoor, spread over five small paddocks and screened by the mature trees that surround it. The level pitches provide a comfortable space for each unit on this family-run park. There is a laundrette in nearby Minehead. 3 acre site. 50 touring pitches. 10 hardstandings. 9 seasonal pitches. Caravan pitches. Motorhome pitches. Tent pitches.

AA Pubs & Restaurants nearby: Luttrell Arms, Dunster 01643 821555

The Smugglers, Blue Anchor 01984 640385

Leisure: 🅰
Facilities: 🏷⊙📍✳🕐📷🔊♻ 🅸
Services: 🔌🔒⌀🔋
Within 3 miles: 🚶🎣🅟◎🔊🅟🅖🔊U
Notes: 🐾 No open fires.

OARE
Map 3 SS74

Places to visit

Watermouth Castle & Family Theme Park, ILFRACOMBE 01271 863879 www.watermouthcastle.com

Marwood Hill Gardens, BARNSTAPLE 01271 342528 www.marwoodhillgarden.co.uk

Great for kids: Exmoor Zoological Park, BLACKMOOR GATE 01598 763352 www.exmoorzoo.co.uk

▶▶▶ **76% Cloud Farm** *(SS794467)*

EX35 6NU
☎ **01598 741278**
e-mail: stay@cloudfarmcamping.co.uk
web: www.cloudfarmcamping.com
dir: *M5 junct 24, A39 towards Minehead & Porlock then Lynton. Left in 6.5m, follow signs to Oare, right, site signed*

🚐 🚃 ▲

Open all year

Set in the heart of Exmoor's Doone Valley, this quiet, sheltered park is arranged over four riverside fields, with modern toilet facilities. It offers a good shop and café serving all day food, including breakfasts, with a large garden for outdoor eating, and there are self-catering holiday cottages. 110 acre site. 70 touring pitches. Caravan pitches. Motorhome pitches. Tent pitches.

AA Pubs & Restaurants nearby: Rockford Inn, Brendon 01598 741214

Facilities: 🏷⊙📍✳🔊🕐🅖🛏🚻 📶
Services: 🔌🅖 ⌀🍽🍴🔋
Within 3 miles: 🚶🎣🅟🚶🅖🅖U

PORLOCK

Places to visit

West Somerset Railway, MINEHEAD 01643 704996 www.west-somerset-railway.co.uk

Dunster Castle, DUNSTER 01643 821314 www.nationaltrust.org.uk

Great for kids: Tropiquaria Animal and Adventure Park, WASHFORD 01984 640688 www.tropiquaria.co.uk

---

SERVICES: 🔌 Electric hook up 🅖 Launderette 🍸 Licensed bar 🛢 Calor Gas ⌀ Camping Gaz 🅣 Toilet fluid 🍽 Café/Restaurant 🍴 Fast Food/Takeaway 🔋 Battery charging 🍼 Baby care ⚒ Motorvan service point
ABBREVIATIONS: BH/bank hols-bank holidays Etr-Easter Whit-Whitsun dep-departure fr-from hrs-hours m-mile mdnt-midnight rdbt-roundabout rs-restricted service wk-week wknd-weekend 🚫 No credit cards ⊗ No dogs   See page 7 for details of the AA Camping Card Scheme

PORLOCK
Map 3 SS84

AA CAMPING CARD SITE

PREMIER PARK

►►►►► 83% Porlock Caravan Park (SS882469)

TA24 8ND
☎ 01643 862269   📠 01643 862269
e-mail: info@porlockcaravanpark.co.uk
dir: *Through village fork right signed Porlock Weir, site on right*

* 🚐 £12-£19.50 🚍 £12-£19.50 ▲ £13-£20

Open 15 Mar-Oct

Last arrival 20.00hrs Last departure 11.00hrs

A sheltered touring park, attractively laid-out in the centre of lovely countryside, on the edge of the village of Porlock. The famous Porlock Hill which starts a few hundred yards from the site, takes you to some spectacular parts of Exmoor with stunning views. The toilet facilities are superb, and there's a popular kitchen area with microwave and freezer. Holiday statics for hire. 3 acre site. 40 touring pitches. 14 hardstandings. Caravan pitches. Motorhome pitches. Tent pitches. 55 statics.

AA Pubs & Restaurants nearby: Ship Inn, Porlock 01643 862507

The Bottom Ship, Porlock 01643 863288

Facilities: 🖍 ⊙ 🗗 ✳ 🕭 🕒 🚻 🖭 ♻ 🛈

Services: 🔌 🗑 🖉 🚽 ↓

Within 3 miles: ⅃ 🖋 🖺 🗊 🖰 ∪

Notes: No fires. Dogs must be kept on leads.

►►►► 84% Burrowhayes Farm Caravan & Camping Site & Riding Stables (SS897460)

West Luccombe TA24 8HT
☎ 01643 862463
e-mail: info@burrowhayes.co.uk
dir: *A39 from Minehead towards Porlock for 5m. Left at Red Post to Horner & West Luccombe, site 0.25m on right, immediately before humpback bridge*

🚐 🚍 ▲

Open 15 Mar-Oct

Last arrival 22.00hrs Last departure noon

A delightful site on the edge of Exmoor, sloping gently down to Horner Water. The farm buildings have been converted into riding stables, from where escorted rides onto the moors can be taken, and the excellent toilet facilities are housed in timber-clad buildings. There are many walks into the countryside that can be directly accessed from the site. 8 acre site. 120 touring pitches. 10 hardstandings. Caravan pitches. Motorhome pitches. Tent pitches. 20 statics.

Burrowhayes Farm Caravan & Camping Site

AA Pubs & Restaurants nearby: Ship Inn, Porlock 01643 862507

The Bottom Ship, Porlock 01643 863288

Facilities: 🖍 ⊙ 🗗 ✳ 🕭 🕒 🖺 🚻 🖭 🖳

Services: 🔌 🗑 🖉 🚽 ↓

Within 3 miles: ⅃ 🖋 ◎ 🖺 🗊 ∪

PRIDDY
Map 4 ST55

Places to visit

Glastonbury Abbey, GLASTONBURY 01458 832267 www.glastonburyabbey.com

The Helicopter Museum, WESTON-SUPER-MARE 01934 635227 www.helicoptermuseum.co.uk

Great for kids: Wookey Hole Caves & Papermill, WOOKEY HOLE 01749 672243 www.wookey.co.uk

►►►► 85% Cheddar Camping & Caravanning Club Site (ST522519)

Townsend BA5 3BP
☎ 01749 870241   & 0845 130 7633
dir: *From A39 take B3135 to Cheddar. Left in 4.5m. Site 200yds on right*

🚐 🚍 ▲

Open 15 Mar-5 Nov

Last arrival 20.00hrs Last departure noon

A gently sloping site set high on the Mendip Hills and surrounded by trees. This excellent site offers really good facilities, including top notch family rooms and private cubicles which are spotlessly maintained. Fresh bread is baked daily and available from the well-stocked shop. The site is well positioned for visiting local attractions such as Cheddar, Wookey Hole, Wells and Glastonbury, and is popular with walkers. 4.5 acre site. 90 touring pitches. 37 hardstandings. Caravan pitches. Motorhome pitches. Tent pitches. 2 statics.

AA Pubs & Restaurants nearby: Wookey Hole Inn, Wookey Hole 01749 676677

The Burcott Inn, Wookey 01749 673874

Leisure: 🎢

Facilities: 🖍 ⊙ 🗗 ✳ 🕭 🕒 🖺 🚻 🖭 ♻ 🛈

Services: 🔌 🗑 🖉 🗑 T 🚽 ↓

Within 3 miles: 🖺 ∪

Notes: Site gates closed 23.00hrs-07.00hrs. Dogs must be kept on leads.

SHEPTON MALLET
Map 4 ST64

Places to visit

Stourhead, STOURHEAD 01747 841152 www.nationaltrust.org.uk/main/w-stourhead

Westwood Manor, WESTWOOD 01225 863374 www.nationaltrust.org.uk

Great for kids: Longleat, LONGLEAT 01985 844400 www.longleat.co.uk

AA CAMPING CARD SITE

►► 95% Greenacres Camping (ST553416)

Barrow Ln, North Wootton BA4 4HL
☎ 01749 890497
e-mail: stay@greenacres-camping.co.uk
dir: *Approx halfway between Glastonbury & Shepton Mallet on A361 turn at Steanbow Farm signed North Wootton. Or from A39 between Upper Coxley & Wells turn at Brownes Garden Centre into Woodford Ln. Follow North Wootton & site signs*

* 🚍 £16-£20 ▲ £16-£20

Open Apr-Sep

Last arrival 21.00hrs Last departure 11.00hrs

An immaculately maintained site peacefully set within sight of Glastonbury Tor. Mainly family orientated with many thoughtful extra facilities provided, and there is plenty of space for children to play games in a very safe environment. There is even a 'glow worm safari' at certain times of the year. Facilities are exceptionally clean. 4.5 acre site. 40 touring pitches. Motorhome pitches. Tent pitches.

LEISURE: 🏊 Indoor swimming pool 🏊 Outdoor swimming pool 🎢 Children's playground 🪁 Kid's club 🎾 Tennis court 🎱 Games room 📺 Separate TV room
🏌 9/18 hole golf course ⛵ Boats for hire 🎬 Cinema 🎭 Entertainment 🎣 Fishing ◎ Mini golf 🚣 Watersports 💪 Gym ⊕ Sports field **Spa** ∪ Stables
FACILITIES: 🛁 Bath 🚿 Shower ⊙ Electric shaver 🗗 Hairdryer ✳ Ice Pack Facility 🕭 Disabled facilities 🕒 Public telephone 🖺 Shop on site or within 200yds
🛒 Mobile shop (calls at least 5 days a week) 🍖 BBQ area 🌲 Picnic area 🖭 Wi-fi 🖳 Internet access ♻ Recycling 🛈 Tourist info 🖰 Dog exercise area

AA Pubs & Restaurants nearby: Bull Terrier, Croscombe 01749 343658

Leisure: ⚲ ✥

Facilities: ⬉ ⊙ ☞ ✳ 🛁 🕯 🎠 ₩ℹ ♻ ❶

Services: 🔌 🛢 ⌀ 🍴 🛒

Within 3 miles: ⚓ 🗗 ✎ 🖳 📮 ↺

Notes: ⊗ No cars by caravans. No caravans or large motorhomes. Free use of fridges & freezers, book library.

SPARKFORD   Map 4 ST62

Places to visit

Lytes Cary Manor, KINGSDON 01458 224471
www.nationaltrust.org.uk/
main/w-lytescarymanor

Montacute House, MONTACUTE 01935 823289
www.nationaltrust.org.uk

▶▶▶ 83% Long Hazel Park *(ST602262)*

High St BA22 7JH
☎ **01963 440002**
e-mail: longhazelpark@hotmail.com
dir: *Exit A303 at Hazlegrove rdbt, follow signs for Sparkford. Site 400yds on left*

* 🚐 £16-£20 🚍 £16-£20 ▲ £16-£20

Open all year

Last arrival 22.00hrs Last departure 11.00hrs

A very neat, adults-only park next to the village inn in the high street. This attractive park is run by friendly owners to a very good standard. Many of the spacious pitches have hardstandings. There are also luxury lodges on site for hire or purchase. 3.5 acre site. 50 touring pitches. 30 hardstandings. 21 seasonal pitches. Caravan pitches. Motorhome pitches. Tent pitches. 1 static.

AA Pubs & Restaurants nearby: Walnut Tree, West Camel 01935 851292

Queens Arms, Corton Denham 01963 220317

Facilities: ⬉ ⊙ ☞ ✳ ♿ 🕙 ₥ ₩ℹ ♻ ❶

Services: 🔌 🗄 🛢 ⌀ 🚽 🛒 ⚡

Within 3 miles: ⚓ ✎ 📮

Notes: Adults only. ⊛ Dogs must be kept on leads and exercised off site. Picnic tables available, camping spares.

TAUNTON   Map 4 ST22

Places to visit

Hestercombe Gardens, TAUNTON 01823 413923
www.hestercombe.com

Barrington Court, BARRINGTON 01460 241938
www.nationaltrust.org.uk

Great for kids: Sunnycroft, WELLINGTON 01952 242884 www.nationaltrust.org.uk/sunnycroft

---

▶▶▶▶ 84% Cornish Farm Touring Park *(ST235217)*

Shoreditch TA3 7BS
☎ **01823 327746** 🖷 **01823 354946**
e-mail: info@cornishfarm.com
web: www.cornishfarm.com
dir: *M5 junct 25 towards Taunton. Left at lights. 3rd left into Ilminster Rd (follow Corfe signs). Right at rdbt, left at next rdbt. Right at T-junct, left into Killams Dr, 2nd left into Killams Ave. Over motorway bridge. Site on left, take 2nd entrance*

🚐 £14-£18 🚍 £14-£18 ▲ £14-£18

Open all year

Last arrival anytime Last departure 11.30hrs

This smart park provides really top quality facilities throughout. Although only two miles from Taunton, it is set in open countryside and is a very convenient base for visiting the many attractions of the area such as Clarks Village, Glastonbury and Cheddar Gorge. 3.5 acre site. 50 touring pitches. 25 hardstandings. Caravan pitches. Motorhome pitches. Tent pitches.

AA Pubs & Restaurants nearby: Queens Arms, Pitminster 01823 421529

Hatch Inn, Hatch Beauchamp 01823 480245

Willow Tree Restaurant, Taunton 01823 352835

Facilities: ⬉ ⊙ ☞ ♿ ₥ ₩ℹ 🖥 ❶

Services: 🔌 🗄 🛢 🚽 ⚡

Within 3 miles: ⚓ 🗗 ◎ 📮 🖳 ↺

Notes: Dogs must be kept on leads.

▶▶▶ 81% Ashe Farm Camping & Caravan Site *(ST279229)*

Thornfalcon TA3 5NW
☎ **01823 443764 & 07891 989482**
e-mail: info@ashefarm.co.uk
dir: *M5 junct 25, A358 E for 2.5m. Right at Nags Head pub. Site 0.25m on right*

🚐 🚍 ▲

Open Apr-Oct

Last arrival 22.00hrs Last departure noon

A well-screened site surrounded by mature trees and shrubs, with two large touring fields. A modern facilities block includes toilets and showers plus a separate laundry room. Not far from the bustling market town of Taunton, and handy for both south and north coasts. 7 acre site. 30 touring pitches. 11 hardstandings. Caravan pitches. Motorhome pitches. Tent pitches. 3 statics.

AA Pubs & Restaurants nearby: Queens Arms, Pitminster 01823 421529

Hatch Inn, Hatch Beauchamp 01823 480245

Willow Tree Restaurant, Taunton 01823 352835

Leisure: ⚲ ♨

Facilities: ⬉ ⊙ ☞ ✳ ♿ 🎠 ♻ ❶

Services: 🔌 🗄

Within 3 miles: ⚓ 🗗 ✎ 📮 🖳 ↺

Notes: ⊛ Baby changing facilities.

WATCHET
Map 3 ST04

Places to visit

West Somerset Railway,
MINEHEAD 01643 704996
www.west-somerset-railway.co.uk

Dunster Castle, DUNSTER 01643 821314
www.nationaltrust.org.uk

Great for kids: Tropiquaria Animal and
Adventure Park, WASHFORD 01984 640688
www.tropiquaria.co.uk

▶▶▶ 85% Home Farm Holiday Centre (ST106432)

St Audries Bay TA4 4DP
☎ 01984 632487 ▤ 01984 634687
e-mail: dib@homefarmholidaycentre.co.uk
dir: A39 towards Minehead, right onto B3191 at
West Quantoxhead after St Audries garage, right
in 0.25m

* ⬛ £12-£27.50 ⬛ £12-£27.50 ▲ £12-£27.50

Open all year (rs mid Nov-Etr shop & bar closed)

Last arrival dusk Last departure noon

In a hidden valley beneath the Quantock Hills, this
park overlooks its own private beach. The
atmosphere is friendly and quiet, and there are
lovely sea views from the level pitches.
Flowerbeds, woodland walks, and a Koi carp pond
all enhance this very attractive site, along with a
lovely indoor swimming pool and a beer garden.
45 acre site. 40 touring pitches. 35
hardstandings. Caravan pitches. Motorhome
pitches. Tent pitches. 230 statics.

AA Pubs & Restaurants nearby: The Smugglers,
Blue Anchor 01984 640385

Leisure: 🐟 /△

Facilities: 🛁☉🗜☀&🕐🗑🐕♻❶

Services: 🔌🔄🍴⟋▣

Within 3 miles: ⟋🏧🔄

Notes: No cars by caravans or tents. No noise
after mdnt. Dogs must be kept on leads.

WELLINGTON
Map 3 ST12

Places to visit

Sunnycroft, WELLINGTON 01952 242884
www.nationaltrust.org.uk/sunnycroft

Hestercombe Gardens, TAUNTON 01823 413923
www.hestercombe.com

Great for kids: Diggerland, CULLOMPTON
0871 227 7007 www.diggerland.com

▶▶▶▶ 82% Greenacres Touring Park (ST156001)

Haywards Ln, Chelston TA21 9PH
☎ 01823 652844
e-mail: enquiries@wellington.co.uk
dir: M5 junct 26, right at rdbt signed Wellington,
approx 1.5m. At Chelston rdbt, 1st left, signed A38
West Buckland Rd. 500mtrs follow sign

* ⬛ £14-£17 ⬛ £14-£17

Open Apr-end Sep

Last arrival 20.00hrs Last departure 11.00hrs

This attractively landscaped adults-only park is
situated close to the Somerset/Devon border in a
peaceful setting with great views of the
Blackdown and Quantock Hills. It is in a very
convenient location for overnight stays, being just
one and half miles from the M5. It is also close to
a local bus route. It has excellent facilities, which
are spotlessly clean and well maintained. 2.5 acre
site. 40 touring pitches. 30 hardstandings.
Caravan pitches. Motorhome pitches.

AA Pubs & Restaurants nearby: White Horse Inn,
Bradford-on-Tone 01823 461239

Facilities: 🛁☉🗜&🏧🐕♻❶

Services: 🔌 Within 3 miles: ⟋🏧⟋▣🔄U

Notes: Adults only. ⊘ No RVs. Dogs must be kept
on leads.

▶▶▶ 79% Gamlins Farm Caravan Park (ST083195)

Gamlins Farm House, Greenham TA21 0LZ
☎ 01823 672859 ✆ 07967 683738
e-mail: nataliehowe@hotmail.com
dir: M5 junct 26, A38 towards Tiverton & Exeter.
5m, right for Greenham, site 1m on right

⬛ £8-£12 ⬛ £8-£12 ▲ £6-£12

Open Mar-Oct

A well-planned site in a secluded position with
panoramic views. The friendly owners keep the
toilet facilities to a good standard of cleanliness.
4 acre site. 35 touring pitches. 6 hardstandings.
Caravan, motorhome and tent pitches. 3 statics.

AA Pubs & Restaurants nearby: White Horse Inn,
Bradford-on-Tone 01823 461239

Leisure: 🎣 **Facilities:** 🛁☉🗜☀🏧🐕♻❶

Services: 🔌🔄🔒 Within 3 miles: ⟋⟋▣🔄U

Notes: ⊘ No loud noise after 22.00hrs. Dogs
must be kept on leads. Free coarse fishing on site.

WELLS
Map 4 ST54

Places to visit

Glastonbury Abbey, GLASTONBURY
01458 832267 www.glastonburyabbey.com

Great for kids: Haynes International Motor
Museum, SPARKFORD 01963 440804
www.haynesmotormuseum.co.uk

▶▶▶▶ 85% Wells Holiday Park (ST531459)

Haybridge BA5 1AJ
☎ 01749 676869
e-mail: jason@wellsholidaypark.co.uk
dir: From A38 follow Axbridge, Cheddar & Wells
signs

* ⬛ £10-£25 ⬛ £10-£25 ▲ £10-£19

Open all year

Last arrival 20.00hrs Last departure noon

This well established, completely upgraded
holiday park has first-class toilet facilities and
many hardstandings, all with electricity. A restful
park set in countryside on the outskirts of Wells, it
is within easy walking distance of the city, with its
spectacular cathedral and Bishop's Palace.
Cheddar Gorge and Caves, Bath, Bristol, Weston-
Super-Mare, Wookey Hole and Glastonbury are all
within easy driving distance. Holiday cottages are
available for hire. 7.5 acre site. 72 touring
pitches. 54 hardstandings. Caravan pitches.
Motorhome pitches. Tent pitches.

AA Pubs & Restaurants nearby: City Arms, Wells
01749 673916

Fountains Inn & Boxer's Restaurant, Wells
01749 672317

Goodfellows, Wells 01749 673866

The Old Spot, Wells 01749 689099

Facilities: 🛁☉🗜☀&🏧🕐🏧♻❶

Services: 🔌🔄🔒⟋▣🔄🔔⬆⬇

Within 3 miles: ⟋🏧⟋◎▣🔄U

Notes: No cars by tents. Dogs must be on leads.

LEISURE: 🏊 Indoor swimming pool 🏊 Outdoor swimming pool /△ Children's playground 🪁 Kid's club ⚲ Tennis court 🎯 Games room 📺 Separate TV room
⛳ 9/18 hole golf course 🚤 Boats for hire 🎦 Cinema ♫ Entertainment 🎣 Fishing ◎ Mini golf 🏄 Watersports 🏋 Gym 🏟 Sports field Spa U Stables
FACILITIES: 🛁 Bath 🚿 Shower ☉ Electric shaver 🗜 Hairdryer ☀ Ice Pack Facility & Disabled facilities 🕐 Public telephone 🏪 Shop on site or within 200yds
🏧 Mobile shop (calls at least 5 days a week) 🍴 BBQ area 🌲 Picnic area 📶 Wi-fi 💻 Internet access ♻ Recycling ❶ Tourist info 🐕 Dog exercise area

►► 84% Homestead Park (ST532474)

Wookey Hole BA5 1BW
☎ 01749 673022 📄 01749 673022
e-mail: homesteadpark@onetel.com
dir: *0.5m NW off A371 (Wells to Cheddar road). (NB weight limit on bridge into touring area now 1 tonne)*

* 🏕 £15.80

Open Etr-Sep

Last arrival 20.00hrs Last departure noon

This attractive, small site for tents only is set on a wooded hillside and meadowland with access to the river and Wookey Hole. This park is for adults only and the statics are residential caravans. 2 acre site. 30 touring pitches. Tent pitches. 28 statics.

AA Pubs & Restaurants nearby: City Arms, Wells 01749 673916

Fountains Inn & Boxer's Restaurant, Wells 01749 672317

Goodfellows, Wells 01749 673866

The Old Spot, Wells 01749 689099

Facilities: 🄺☉🅿✳🄾
Services: 🄰🄰🄰
Within 3 miles: 🄷🄿🄸🄹🄾🅄
Notes: Adults only. 🚫 Dogs must be kept on leads.

WESTON-SUPER-MARE

Places to visit
North Somerset Museum, WESTON-SUPER-MARE 01934 621028 www.n-somerset.gov.uk/museum

Great for kids: The Helicopter Museum, WESTON-SUPER-MARE 01934 635227 www.helicoptermuseum.co.uk

WESTON-SUPER-MARE   Map 4 ST36

►►► 82% Country View Holiday Park (ST335647)

Sand Rd, Sand Bay BS22 9UJ
☎ 01934 627595
e-mail: info@cvhp.co.uk
dir: *M5 junct 21, A370 towards Weston-Super-Mare. Immediately into left lane, follow Kewstoke/ Sand Bay signs. Straight over 3 rdbts onto Lower Norton Ln. At Sand Bay right into Sand Rd, site on right*

* 🚐 £10-£25 🚃 £10-£25 🏕 £10-£25

Open Mar-Jan

Last arrival 20.00hrs Last departure noon

A pleasant open site in a rural area a few hundred yards from Sandy Bay and the beach. The park is also well placed for energetic walks along the coast at either end of the beach and is only a short drive away from Weston-Super-Mare. The facilities are excellent and well maintained. 8 acre site. 120 touring pitches. 90 hardstandings. 90 seasonal pitches. Caravan pitches. Motorhome pitches. Tent pitches. 65 statics.

AA Pubs & Restaurants nearby: The Cove, Weston-Super-Mare 01934 418217

Leisure: 🏊🎿🎱
Facilities: 🄺☉🅿✳🄰🄾🅆🄸💻🄾🄾
Services: 🄰🄰🄰🄰
Within 3 miles: 🄹🄷🄿🄾🄾🄹🄾🅄
Notes: Dogs must be kept on leads.

►►► 82% West End Farm Caravan & Camping Park (ST354600)

Locking BS24 8RH
☎ 01934 822529
e-mail: robin@westendfarm.org
dir: *M5 junct 21 onto A370. Follow International Helicopter Museum signs. Right at rdbt, follow signs to site*

🚐 £14.50-£19.50 🚃 £14.50-£19.50
🏕 £14.50-£19.50

Open all year

Last arrival 21.00hrs Last departure noon

A spacious and well laid out park bordered by hedges, with good landscaping, and well kept facilities. Fully serviced pitches are available. It is handily located next to a helicopter museum, and offers good access to Weston-Super-Mare and the Mendips. 10 acre site. 75 touring pitches. 10

hardstandings. 30 seasonal pitches. Caravan pitches. Motorhome pitches. Tent pitches. 11 statics.

AA Pubs & Restaurants nearby: The Cove, Weston-Super-Mare 01934 418217

Leisure: 🏊
Facilities: 🄺☉🄰🄰🄰🄰🄾
Services: 🄰🄰🄰🄰🄰
Within 3 miles: 🄹🄷🄿🄾🄾🄹🄾🅄
Notes: 🚫 No noise after 22.00hrs. Dogs must be kept on leads.

WINSFORD   Map 3 SS93

Places to visit
Dunster Castle, DUNSTER 01643 821314 www.nationaltrust.org.uk

Cleeve Abbey, WASHFORD 01984 640377 www.english-heritage.org.uk

Great for kids: Tropiquaria Animal and Adventure Park, WASHFORD 01984 640688 www.tropiquaria.co.uk

►►► 79% Halse Farm Caravan & Camping Park (SS894344)

TA24 7JL
☎ 01643 851259
e-mail: info@halsefarm.co.uk
web: www.halsefarm.co.uk
dir: *Signed from A396 at Bridgetown. In Winsford turn left, bear left past pub. 1m up hill, entrance on left immediately after cattle grid*

🚐🚃🏕

Open 16 Mar-Oct

Last arrival 22.00hrs Last departure noon

A peaceful little site on Exmoor overlooking a wooded valley with glorious views. This moorland site is quite remote, but it provides good modern toilet facilities which are kept immaculately clean. This is a good base for exploring the Exmoor

continued

WINSFORD continued

National Park. 3 acre site. 44 touring pitches. Caravan pitches. Motorhome pitches. Tent pitches.

AA Pubs & Restaurants nearby: Crown Hotel, Exford 01643 831554

Leisure: ⏢

Facilities: ⬡⊙☂✳⬅⊙🐾♻ ❶

Services: ⬛⬚🔋⬕

Within 3 miles: ✎🛒∪

Notes: Dogs must be kept on leads.

WIVELISCOMBE   Map 3 ST02

Places to visit

Sunnycroft, WELLINGTON 01952 242884 www.nationaltrust.org.uk/sunnycroft

Hestercombe Gardens, TAUNTON 01823 413923 www.hestercombe.com

---

PREMIER PARK

►►►►► 86% Waterrow Touring Park (ST053251)

Best of British

TA4 2AZ
☎ 01984 623464
e-mail: waterrowpark@yahoo.co.uk
dir: M5 junct 25, A358 (signed Minehead) bypassing Taunton, B3227 through Wiveliscombe. Site in 3m at Waterrow, 0.25m past Rock Inn

* 🚐 £15-£25 ⬕ £15-£25 ⛺ £15-£25

Open all year

Last arrival 19.00hrs Last departure 11.30hrs

This really delightful park for adults only has spotless facilities and plenty of spacious hardstandings. The River Tone runs along a valley beneath the park, accessed by steps to a nature area created by the owners, where fly-fishing is permitted. Watercolour painting workshops and other activities are available, and the local pub is a short walk away. 6 acre site. 45 touring pitches. 38 hardstandings. Caravan pitches. Motorhome pitches. Tent pitches. 1 static.

AA Pubs & Restaurants nearby: White Hart, Wiveliscombe 01984 623344

Rock Inn, Waterrow 01984 623293

Facilities: ⬡⊙☂✳⬅⊙🐾♻🔲🖥♻ ❶

Services: ⬛⬚🔋⬕🚻⬆

Within 3 miles: ✎🛒

Notes: Adults only. No gazebos, max 2 dogs per unit. Dogs must be kept on leads. Frozen meals.

YEOVIL   Map 4 ST51

Places to visit

Montacute House, MONTACUTE 01935 823289 www.nationaltrust.org.uk

Lytes Cary Manor, KINGSDON 01458 224471 www.nationaltrust.org.uk/main/w-lytescarymanor

Great for kids: Fleet Air Arm Museum, YEOVILTON 01935 840565 www.fleetairarm.com

---

►► 81% Halfway Caravan & Camping Park (ST530195)

Trees Cottage, Halfway, Ilchester Rd BA22 8RE
☎ 01935 840342
e-mail: halfwaycaravanpark@earthlink.net
web: www.halfwaycaravanpark.com
dir: On A37 between Ilchester & Yeovil

🚐 £10-£12.50 ⬕ £10-£12.50 ⛺ £7-£10

Open Mar-Oct

Last arrival 19.00hrs Last departure noon

An attractive little park near the Somerset and Dorset border, and next to the Halfway House pub and restaurant, which also has excellent AA-graded accommodation. It overlooks a fishing lake and is surrounded by attractive countryside, with free fishing for people staying at the park. Dogs are welcome here. 2 acre site. 20 touring pitches. 10 hardstandings. Caravan pitches. Motorhome pitches. Tent pitches.

AA Pubs & Restaurants nearby: Masons Arms, Yeovil 01935 862591

Helyar Arms, East Coker 01935 862332

Facilities: ⬅⬡☂ ❶

Services: ⬛⬚🖥

Within 3 miles: ♨🎏✎🛒⬚

Notes: ♿

CHEADLE   Map 10 SK04

Places to visit

Wedgwood Visitor Centre, STOKE-ON-TRENT 01782 282986 www.wedgwoodvisitorcentre.com

The Potteries Museum & Art Gallery, STOKE-ON-TRENT 01782 232323 www.stoke.gov.uk/museums

Great for kids: Alton Towers Resort, ALTON 0871 222 3330 www.altontowers.com

Etruria Industrial Museum, STOKE-ON-TRENT 01782 233144 www.stoke.gov.uk/museums

---

►►►► 73% Quarry Walk Park (SK045405)

Coppice Ln, Croxden Common, Freehay ST10 1RQ
☎ 01538 723412
e-mail: quarry@quarrywalkpark.co.uk
dir: From A522 (Uttoxeter-Cheadle road) turn at Crown Inn at Mabberley signed Freehay. In 1m at rdbt by Queen pub turn to Great Gate. Site signed on right in 1.25m

* 🚐 £20-£23 ⬕ £20-£23 ⛺ £12-£21

Open all year

Last arrival 18.00hrs Last departure 11.00hrs

A pleasant park, close to Alton Towers, developed in an old quarry with well-screened pitches, all with water and electricity, and mature trees and shrubs, which enhance the peaceful ambience of the park. There are seven glades of varying sizes used exclusively for tents, one with ten electric hook-ups. There are timber lodges for hire, each with its own hot tub. 46 acre site. 16 touring pitches. 16 hardstandings. 13 seasonal pitches. Caravan pitches. Motorhome pitches. Tent pitches. 1 wooden pod.

AA Pubs & Restaurants nearby: The Queens at Freehay, Cheadle 01538 722383

Leisure: ⏢

Facilities: ⬡⊙☂✳⬅🎏⬅🔲🖥♻ ❶

Services: ⬛⬚🔋⬕

Within 3 miles: 🎏✎◎⬚⬚∪

Notes: Dogs must be kept on leads.

LEISURE: 🏊 Indoor swimming pool 🏊 Outdoor swimming pool ⏢ Children's playground 🏌 Kid's club 🎾 Tennis court 🎱 Games room 📺 Separate TV room ⛳ 9/18 hole golf course ⛵ Boats for hire 🎬 Cinema 🎵 Entertainment 🎣 Fishing ⛳ Mini golf 🏄 Watersports 🏋 Gym ⚽ Sports field **Spa** ∪ Stables
FACILITIES: 🛁 Bath 🚿 Shower ⊙ Electric shaver ☂ Hairdryer ✳ Ice Pack Facility ♿ Disabled facilities ☎ Public telephone 🏪 Shop on site or within 200yds 🚐 Mobile shop (calls at least 5 days a week) 🍖 BBQ area 🎏 Picnic area 📶 Wi-fi 🖥 Internet access ♻ Recycling ❶ Tourist info 🐾 Dog exercise area

Suffolk

Suffolk's superb Heritage Coast is the jewel in the county's crown. The beaches, often windswept and completely deserted, run for miles, with the waves of the North Sea breaking beside them in timeless fashion. But it is an ecologically fragile coastline with much of it claimed by the sea over the years. The poet, George Crabbe, perfectly summed up the fate of this area when he wrote:

'The ocean roar whose greedy waves devour the lessening shore.'

With its huge skies and sense of space and solitude, Suffolk's crumbling, time-ravaged coastline is highly evocative and wonderfully atmospheric. This is where rivers wind lazily to the sea and 18th-century smugglers hid from the excise men.

Suffolk's coast

Between Felixstowe and Lowestoft the coast offers something for everyone. For example, Orford Ness is a unique visitor attraction where ecology meets military history. This internationally important nature reserve – home to many breeding birds, including the avocet – was once the setting for a highly secret military testing site. These days, Orford Ness is managed by the National Trust.

Aldeburgh is all about the arts and in particular the Aldeburgh Music Festival. Benjamin Britten lived at nearby Snape and wrote *Peter Grimes*

here. The Suffolk coast is where both the sea and the natural landscape have influenced generations of writers, artists and musicians. The charm of Southwold, further north, is undimmed and reminiscent of a fashionable, genteel seaside resort from a bygone era.

Inland towns and villages

But there is much more to Suffolk than its scenic coastline. Far away to the west lies Newmarket and the world of horseracing. Apart from its equine associations, the town boasts some handsome buildings and memorable views. Palace House in Palace Street was the home of Charles II while the High Street is the setting for ▶

the National Horseracing Museum, illustrating how this great sporting tradition has evolved over the last 400 years.

Bury St Edmunds, Sudbury and Ipswich also feature prominently on the tourist trail and the county's smaller towns offer a wealth of attractions, too. With their picturesque, timber-framed houses, Lavenham, Kersey and Debenham are a reminder of Suffolk's key role in the wool industry and the vast wealth it yielded for the merchants.

Constable's legacy

It was the artist John Constable who really put Suffolk's delightful countryside on the map. Son of a wealthy miller, Constable spent much of his early life sketching in the vicinity of Dedham Vale. Situated on the River Stour at Flatford, Constable's mill is now a major tourist attraction in the area but a close look at the surroundings confirms rural Suffolk is little changed since the family lived here. Constable himself maintained that the Suffolk countryside *made me a painter and I am grateful.'*

Walking and Cycling

With 3,300 miles of rights of way, walkers in the county have plenty of choice. There are many publicised trails and waymarked routes, including the Angles Way which runs along Norfolk and Suffolk's boundary in the glorious Waveney Valley. Hard to beat is the county's famous Suffolk Coast Path which runs for 50 miles (80km) between Felixstowe and Lowestoft and is the best way to explore Suffolk's dramatic eastern extremity.

The county offers plenty of potential for cycling, too. There is the Heart of Suffolk Cycle Route, which extends for 78 miles (125km), while the National Byway, a 4,000-mile (6,436km) cycle route around Britain takes in part of Suffolk and is a highly enjoyable way to tour the county.

Festivals and Events

- The popular Aldeburgh Literary Festival takes place in March.
- The Alde Valley Spring Festival is staged in April and May with a 4-week celebration of food, farming, landscape and the arts. The venue is Great Glemham near Saxmundham.
- There is the Lattitude Music Festival at Southwold in July and the two-day Lowestoft Seafront Airshow in August, with over four hours of breathtaking precision flying displays.
- The 3-day Christmas Fayre at Bury St Edmunds showcases the ancient town and in recent years has attracted 70,000 visitors.

Little Hall, Lavenham

Tidemill, Woodbridge

Flatford Mill, East Bergholt

SUFFOLK

See Walk 10 in the Walks & Cycle Rides section at the end of the guide

BUCKLESHAM   Map 13 TM24

Places to visit

Ipswich Museum, IPSWICH 01473 433550
www.ipswich.gov.uk

Christchurch Mansion, IPSWICH 01473 433554
www.ipswich.gov.uk

AA CAMPING CARD SITE

►►►► 84% Westwood Caravan Park

(TM253411)

Old Felixstowe Rd IP10 0BN
☎ 01473 659637 & 07814 570973
e-mail: caroline.pleace@westwoodcaravanpark.co.uk
dir: *A14 towards Felixstowe, after junct 58 take 1st exit signed to Kirton. Follow road to Bucklesham for 1.5m. Site on right*

* 🚐 £15-£20 🚐 £15-£20 ▲ £15-£20

Open Mar-15 Jan

Last arrival 22.00hrs Last departure 15.00hrs

This site is in the heart of rural Suffolk in an idyllic, peaceful setting. All buildings are of traditional Suffolk style, and the toilet facilities are of outstanding quality. There is also a spacious room for disabled visitors, and plenty of space for children to play. 4.5 acre site. 100 touring pitches. 35 hardstandings. Caravan pitches. Motorhome pitches. Tent pitches.

AA Pubs & Restaurants nearby: Ship Inn, Levington 01473 659573

Mariners, Ipswich 01473 289748

The Eaterie at Salthouse Harbour Hotel, Ipswich 01473 226789

Leisure: 🅰 🔍
Facilities: 🐾 ☉ ✻ & 🚿 🚻 🚮 WiFi ♻ 🛈
Services: 🚐 🚽 💧 🍴 T 🛒 ⛴
Within 3 miles: 🎣 🐾 🛶 ⛴ 🏪
Notes: Dogs must be kept on leads.

BUNGAY   Map 13 TM38

►►► 68% Outney Meadow Caravan Park *(TM333905)*

Outney Meadow NR35 1HG
☎ 01986 892338 📠 01986 896627
e-mail: c.r.hancy@ukgateway.net
dir: *At Bungay, site signed from rdbt junction of A143 & A144*

* 🚐 £14-£20 🚐 £14-£20 ▲ £14-£20

Open Mar-Oct

Last arrival 21.00hrs Last departure 16.00hrs

Three pleasant grassy areas beside the River Waveney, with screened pitches. The central toilet block offers good modern facilities, especially in the ladies, and is open at all times. The views from the site across the wide flood plain could be straight out of a Constable painting. Canoeing and boating, coarse fishing and cycling are all available here. 6 acre site. 45 touring pitches. 5 hardstandings. Caravan pitches. Motorhome pitches. Tent pitches. 30 statics.

AA Pubs & Restaurants nearby: Earsham Street Café, Bungay 01986 893103

Wicked at St Peter's Hall, St Peter South Elmham 01986 782288

Facilities: 🐾 ☉ ℘ ✻ 🚿 🚮 ♻ 🛈
Services: 🚐 🚽 💧 🍴 T 🛒
Within 3 miles: 🎣 ≒ 🐾 🛶 ⛴ 🏪
Notes: Dogs must be kept on leads. Boat, canoe & cycle hire.

BURY ST EDMUNDS   Map 13 TL86

Places to visit

Moyse's Hall Museum, BURY ST EDMUNDS 01284 706183 www.moyseshall.org

Ickworth House, Park & Gardens, HORRINGER 01284 735270 www.nationaltrust.org.uk/ickworth

Great for kids: National Horseracing Museum and Tours, NEWMARKET 01638 667333 www.nhrm.co.uk

AA CAMPING CARD SITE

►►►► 85% Dell Touring Park

(TL928640)

Beyton Rd, Thurston IP31 3RB
☎ 01359 270121
e-mail: thedellcaravanpark@btinternet.com
dir: *Signed from A14 at Beyton/Thurston (4m E of Bury St Edmunds) & from A143 at Barton/Thurston*

🚐 £15-£19 🚐 £15-£19 ▲ £12-£35

Open all year

Last arrival 20.00hrs Last departure noon

A small site with enthusiastic owners that has been developed to a high specification with more improvements planned. Set in a quiet spot with lots of mature trees, the quality purpose-built toilet facilities include family rooms, dishwashing and laundry. This is an ideal base for exploring this picturesque area. 6 acre site. 60 touring pitches. 12 hardstandings. Caravan pitches. Motorhome pitches. Tent pitches.

AA Pubs & Restaurants nearby: Old Cannon Brewery, Bury St Edmunds 01284 768769

Linden Tree, Bury St Edmunds 01284 754600

Maison Bleue, Bury St Edmunds 01284 760623

Leaping Hare Restaurant & Country Store, Bury St Edmunds 01359 250287

LEISURE: 🅰 Indoor swimming pool 🅰 Outdoor swimming pool 🅰 Children's playground 🅰 Kid's club 🅰 Tennis court 🔍 Games room ⬜ Separate TV room 🅰 9/18 hole golf course 🅰 Boats for hire 🅷 Cinema 🎵 Entertainment 🎣 Fishing ◉ Mini golf 🅰 Watersports 🅰 Gym ⚫ Sports field **Spa** ∪ Stables
FACILITIES: 🅰 Bath 🅰 Shower ☉ Electric shaver ℘ Hairdryer ✻ Ice Pack Facility & Disabled facilities 🅾 Public telephone 🏠 Shop on site or within 200yds 🅰 Mobile shop (calls at least 5 days a week) 🚻 BBQ area 🚮 Picnic area WiFi Wi-fi ⬛ Internet access ♻ Recycling 🛈 Tourist info 🅰 Dog exercise area

Facilities: 🚼 📶 ⊙ 🅿 ⚒ ✳ 🔥 🐕 ♻ ✥ 🛈

Services: 🔌 🗑 🚿 ⊘ 🎦 ⚡

Within 3 miles: ✎ 🏠

Notes: No footballs, no noise after 23.00hrs. Dogs must be kept on leads.

DUNWICH — Map 13 TM47

►► 71% Haw Wood Farm Caravan Park *(TM421717)*

Hinton IP17 3QT
☎ **01986 784248**
e-mail: bookings@hawwoodfarm.co.uk
dir: *Exit A12, 1.5m N of Darsham level crossing at Little Chef. Site 0.5m on right*

* 🚐 £15-£19 🚎 £15-£19 ▲ £15-£19

Open Mar-14 Jan

Last arrival 21.00hrs Last departure noon

An unpretentious family-orientated park set in two large fields surrounded by low hedges. The toilets are clean and functional, and there is plenty of space for children to play. 15 acre site. 60 touring pitches. Caravan pitches. Motorhome pitches. Tent pitches. 55 statics.

AA Pubs & Restaurants nearby: Westleton Crown, Westleton 01728 648777

Ship Inn, Dunwich 01728 648219

Queen's Head, Halesworth 01986 784214

Leisure: 🏞

Facilities: 📶 ⊙ ✳ 🔥 🐕 🛈

Services: 🔌 🚿 ⊘ Ⓣ

Within 3 miles: ⌁ ✎ 🏠 ↻

Notes: ⊗ Dogs must be kept on leads.

FELIXSTOWE — Map 13 TM33

Places to visit

Ipswich Museum, IPSWICH 01473 433550 www.ipswich.gov.uk

Christchurch Mansion, IPSWICH 01473 433554 www.ipswich.gov.uk

►►► 75% Peewit Caravan Park *(TM290338)*

Walton Av IP11 2HB
☎ **01394 284511**
e-mail: peewitpark@aol.com
dir: *Signed from A14 in Felixstowe, 100mtrs past Dock Gate 1, 1st on left*

🚐 £16.50-£30 🚎 £16.50-£30 ▲ £13.50-£33

Open Apr (or Etr if earlier)-Oct

Last arrival 21.00hrs Last departure 11.00hrs

A grass touring area fringed by trees, with well-maintained grounds and a colourful floral display. This handy urban site is not overlooked by houses, and the toilet and shower facilities are clean and well cared for. A function room contains a TV and library. The beach is a few minutes away by car. 13 acre site. 45 touring pitches. 4 hardstandings. Caravan pitches. Motorhome pitches. Tent pitches. 200 statics.

AA Pubs & Restaurants nearby: Ship Inn, Levington 01473 659573

Leisure: 🏞

Facilities: 📶 ⊙ 🅿 ✳ 🔥 ⚓ 🐕 ♻ 🛈

Services: 🔌 🗑 🎦 ⚡

Within 3 miles: ⌁ ⚡ ⼻ ✎ ◎ ⼻ 🏠 🗑

Notes: Only foam footballs are permitted. Dogs must be kept on leads. Boules area, bowling green, adventure trail.

HOLLESLEY — Map 13 TM34

Places to visit

Woodbridge Tide Mill, WOODBRIDGE 01728 746959 www.woodbridgetidemill.org.uk

Sutton Hoo, WOODBRIDGE 01394 389700 www.nationaltrust.org.uk/suttonhoo

Great for kids: Orford Castle, ORFORD 01394 450472 www.english-heritage.org.uk

►►► 85% Run Cottage Touring Park *(TM350440)*

Alderton Rd IP12 3RQ
☎ **01394 411309**
e-mail: info@run-cottage.co.uk
dir: *From A12 (Ipswich-Saxmundham) onto A1152 at Melton. 1.5m, right at rdbt onto B1083. 0.75m, left to Hollesley. In Hollesley right into The Street, through village, down hill, over bridge, site 100yds on left*

* 🚐 £16 🚎 £16 ▲ £14

Open all year

Last arrival 20.00hrs Last departure 11.00hrs

Located in the peaceful village of Hollesley on the Suffolk coast, this landscaped park is set behind the owners' house. The generously-sized pitches are serviced by a well-appointed and immaculately maintained toilet block. This site is handy for the National Trust's Sutton Hoo, and also by travelling a little further north, the coastal centre and beach at Dunwich Heath, and the RSPB bird reserve at Minsmere. 2.5 acre site. 20 touring pitches. 6 hardstandings. Caravan pitches. Motorhome pitches. Tent pitches.

AA Pubs & Restaurants nearby: The Crown, Woodbridge 01394 384242

Seckford Hall Hotel, Woodbridge 01394 385678

Facilities: 📶 ⊙ 🅿 ✳ 🔥 🐕 ♻ 🛈

Services: 🔌 ⚡

Within 3 miles: ⌁ ✎ ⼻ 🏠 ↻

Notes: No groundsheets, ball games or cycles.

SERVICES: 🔌 Electric hook up 🗑 Launderette 🍴 Licensed bar 🛢 Calor Gas ⊘ Camping Gaz Ⓣ Toilet fluid 🍽 Café/Restaurant 🍟 Fast Food/Takeaway ⚡ Battery charging 🍼 Baby care ⚓ Motorvan service point
ABBREVIATIONS: BH/bank hols-bank holidays Etr-Easter Whit-Whitsun dep-departure fr-from hrs-hours m-mile mdnt-midnight rdbt-roundabout rs-restricted service wk-week wknd-weekend ⊗ No credit cards ⊗ No dogs
See page 7 for details of the AA Camping Card Scheme

IPSWICH

See Bucklesham

KESSINGLAND
Map 13 TM58

Places to visit

East Anglia Transport Museum, LOWESTOFT 01502 518459 www.eatm.org.uk

Maritime Museum, LOWESTOFT 01502 561963 www.lowestoftmaritimemuseum.org.uk

Great for kids: Pleasurewood Hills, LOWESTOFT 01502 586000 (admin) www.pleasurewoodhills.com

 74% Kessingland Beach Holiday Park *(TM535852)*

Beach Rd NR33 7RN
☎ 01502 740636 📄 01502 740907
e-mail: holidaysales.kessinglandbeach@park-resorts.com
dir: *From Lowestoft take A12 S. At Kessingland take 3rd exit at rdbt towards beach. Through village. At beach follow road to right. In 400yds fork left for park*

🚐 🚐 Å

Open Apr-Oct

Last departure 10.00hrs

A large holiday centre with direct access onto the beach, and a variety of leisure facilities. The touring area is tucked away from the statics, and served by a clean and functional toilet block. A fish and chip shop and the Boat House Restaurant are popular features. 69 acre site. 90 touring pitches. Caravan pitches. Motorhome pitches. Tent pitches. 95 statics.

Leisure: 🏊 ⛱ 🎮 🎾 🏐 🎱 🎯 📺 🎵
Facilities: 🚿 👁 ⚡ ✂ ❄ ♿ 🕐 🏪 🔥 📶 💻 ♻ ℹ
Services: 🚐 🔋 🍴 🛒 🛝
Within 3 miles: 🎣 ⛳ 🚣 🎿 🏪 🎱 ⛺

Notes: Archery.

AA CAMPING CARD SITE

▶▶▶▶ **86% Heathland Beach Caravan Park** *(TM533877)*

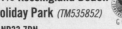

London Rd NR33 7PJ
☎ 01502 740337 📄 01502 742355
e-mail: heathlandbeach@btinternet.com
web: www.heathlandbeach.co.uk
dir: *1m N of Kessingland exit A12 onto B1437*

🚐 🚐 Å

Open Apr-Oct

Last arrival 21.00hrs Last departure 11.00hrs

A well-run and maintained park offering superb toilet facilities. The park is set in meadowland, with level grass pitches, and mature trees and bushes. There is direct access to the sea and beach, and good provisions for families on site with a heated swimming pool and three play areas. 5 acre site. 63 touring pitches. Caravan pitches. Motorhome pitches. Tent pitches. 200 statics.

Leisure: ⛱ 🎮 🎱
Facilities: 🚿 👁 ⚡ ✂ ❄ ♿ 🕐 🏪 🔥 📶
Services: 🚐 🔋 🍴 🛒 📞
Within 3 miles: 🎣 ⛳ 🎬 ⛳ 🎿 🏪 🎱 ⛺

Notes: One dog only per unit. Freshwater & sea fishing.

LEISTON

Places to visit

Long Shop Museum, LEISTON 01728 832189 www.longshopmuseum.co.uk

Leiston Abbey, LEISTON 01728 831354 www.leistonabbey.co.uk

Great for kids: Easton Farm Park, EASTON 01728 746475 www.eastonfarmpark.co.uk

---

LEISTON
Map 13 TM46

▶▶▶ **86% Cakes & Ale** *(TM432637)*

Abbey Ln, Theberton IP16 4TE
☎ 01728 831655
e-mail: cakesandalepark@gmail.com
web: www.cakesandale.net
dir: *From Saxmundham E on B1119. 3m follow minor road over level crossing, turn right, in 0.5m straight on at x-rds, entrance 0.5m on left*

* 🚐 £20-£28 🚐 £20-£28 Å £20-£28

Open Apr-Oct (rs Low season club, shop & reception limited hours)

Last arrival 20.00hrs Last departure 13.00hrs

A large, well spread out and beautifully maintained site with many trees and bushes on a former Second World War airfield. The spacious touring area includes plenty of hardstandings and super pitches, and there is a good bar and a well-maintained toilet block, a fully-serviced family/disabled room and a washing-up room. 45 acre site. 50 touring pitches. 50 hardstandings. Caravan pitches. Motorhome pitches. Tent pitches. 200 statics.

AA Pubs & Restaurants nearby: 152 Aldeburgh, Aldeburgh 01728 454594

Mill Inn, Aldeburgh 01728 452563

Regatta Restaurant, Aldeburgh 01728 452011

Leisure: 🎮 🎱 🏐
Facilities: 🛁 🚿 👁 ⚡ ✂ ❄ 🕐 🏪 🔥 📶 💻 ♻ ℹ
Services: 🚐 🔋 🍴 🛒 🛝
Within 3 miles: 🎣 ⛳ 🎬 ⛳ 🏪 🎱 ⛺

Notes: No group bookings, no noise between 21.00hrs-08.00hrs. Dogs must be kept on leads. Practice range/net, volleyball court, boules, football nets.

see advert on opposite page

LOWESTOFT

See Kessingland

SAXMUNDHAM
Map 13 TM36

Places to visit

Long Shop Museum, LEISTON 01728 832189
www.longshopmuseum.co.uk

Leiston Abbey, LEISTON 01728 831354
www.leistonabbey.co.uk

Great for kids: Museum of East Anglian Life,
STOWMARKET 01449 612229
www.eastanglianlife.org.uk

▶▶▶▶ 85% *Carlton Meres Country Park* (TM372637)

Rendham Rd, Carlton IP17 2QP
☎ 01728 603344 📠 01728 652015
e-mail: enquiries@carlton-meres.co.uk
dir: *From A12 , W of Saxmundham, take B1119 towards Framlingham. Site signed from A12*

Open Etr-Oct

Last arrival 17.00hrs Last departure 10.00hrs

With two large fishing lakes, a modern fitness suite, a beauty salon, sauna and steam rooms, tennis court, a bar, and a heated outdoor swimming pool, Carlton Meres offers a wealth of leisure facilities, and all for the exclusive use for those staying on the site (holiday statics and lodges for hire). There is a modern heated toilet block and excellent security. This site is well-placed for all the Suffolk coast attractions.

Please note that this site does not accept tents. 52 acre site. 96 touring pitches. 56 hardstandings. Caravan pitches. Motorhome pitches.

AA Pubs & Restaurants nearby: 152 Aldeburgh, Aldeburgh 01728 454594

Crown Inn, Great Glemham 01728 663693

Leisure:

Facilities:

Services:

Within 3 miles:

▶▶▶ 80% Whitearch Touring Caravan Park (TM379610)

Main Rd, Benhall IP17 1NA
☎ 01728 604646 & 603773
dir: *At junct of A12 & B1121*

* 🚐 fr £15.50 🚍 fr £15.50 ▲ fr £13

Open Apr-Oct

Last arrival 20.00hrs

A small, maturing park set around an attractive coarse-fishing lake, with good quality, imaginatively appointed toilet facilities and secluded pitches tucked away among trees and shrubs. The park is popular with anglers; there is some traffic noise from the adjacent A12. 14.5 acre site. 50 touring pitches. 50 hardstandings. Caravan pitches. Motorhome pitches. Tent pitches.

AA Pubs & Restaurants nearby: Mill Inn, Aldeburgh 01728 452563

Regatta Restaurant, Aldeburgh 01728 452011

Leisure:

Facilities:

Services:

Within 3 miles:

Notes: No cars by caravans. No bicycles. Dogs must be kept on leads.

▶▶ 82% *Marsh Farm Caravan Site* (TM385608)

Sternfield IP17 1HW
☎ 01728 602168
dir: *A12 onto A1094 (Aldeburgh road), at Snape x-roads left signed Sternfield, follow signs to site*

Open all year

Last arrival 21.00hrs Last departure 17.00hrs

A very pretty site overlooking reed-fringed lakes which offer excellent coarse fishing. The facilities are very well maintained, and the park is a truly peaceful haven. 30 acre site. 45 touring pitches. Caravan pitches. Motorhome pitches. Tent pitches.

AA Pubs & Restaurants nearby: 152 Aldeburgh, Aldeburgh 01728 454594

Crown Inn, Great Glemham 01728 663693

Facilities: **Services:**

Within 3 miles:

Notes: Dogs must be kept on leads.

SERVICES: 🔌 Electric hook up 🌀 Launderette 🍺 Licensed bar 🛢 Calor Gas ⛽ Camping Gaz 🅃 Toilet fluid 🍴 Café/Restaurant 🍔 Fast Food/Takeaway 🔋 Battery charging 👶 Baby care ♿ Motorvan service point
ABBREVIATIONS: BH/bank hols-bank holidays Etr-Easter Whit-Whitsun dep-departure fr-from hrs-hours m-mile mdnt-midnight rdbt-roundabout rs-restricted service wk-week wknd-weekend 🚫 No credit cards ⊗ No dogs
See page 7 for details of the AA Camping Card Scheme

LEISURE: 🏊 Indoor swimming pool 🏊 Outdoor swimming pool 🎠 Children's playground 🏌 Kid's club 🎾 Tennis court 🎱 Games room 📺 Separate TV room ⛳ 9/18 hole golf course ⛵ Boats for hire 🎬 Cinema 🎵 Entertainment 🎣 Fishing ⛳ Mini golf 🏄 Watersports 🏋 Gym ⚽ Sports field **Spa** ♘ Stables
FACILITIES: 🛁 Bath 🚿 Shower 🔌 Electric shaver ✂ Hairdryer ❄ Ice Pack Facility ♿ Disabled facilities 📞 Public telephone 🏪 Shop on site or within 200yds 🚐 Mobile shop (calls at least 5 days a week) 🍴 BBQ area 🍴 Picnic area 📶 Wi-fi 💻 Internet access ♻ Recycling ℹ Tourist info 🐕 Dog exercise area

SUDBURY — Map 13 TL84

Places to visit

Melford Hall, LONG MELFORD 01787 379228
www.nationaltrust.org.uk/melfordhall

Kentwell Hall, LONG MELFORD 01787 310207
www.kentwell.co.uk

Great for kids: Colne Valley Railway &
Museum, CASTLE HEDINGHAM 01787 461174
www.colnevalleyrailway.co.uk

►►► 75% Willowmere Caravan Park
(TL886388)

Bures Rd, Little Cornard CO10 0NN
☎ 01787 375559 & 310422 🖹 01787 375559
e-mail: awillowmere@aol.com
dir: 1.5m S of Sudbury on B1508 (Bures road)

🔌 £12-£13 🚐 £12-£13 ▲ £9-£13

Open Etr-Oct

Last arrival anytime Last departure noon

A pleasant little site in a quiet location tucked
away beyond a tiny residential static area,
offering spotless facilities. 3 acre site. 40 touring
pitches. Caravan pitches. Motorhome pitches.
Tent pitches. 9 statics.

AA Pubs & Restaurants nearby: Scutchers
Restaurant, Long Melford 01787 310200

White Hart, Great Yeldham 01787 237250

Bell Inn, Great Hadingham 01787 460350

Facilities: 🔦 ⊙ ※ 🔥 🕓
Services: 🔌 🖥
Within 3 miles: ↓ ♪ ◎ 🔥 🖥 U
Notes: ⊛ Fishing.

WOODBRIDGE — Map 13 TM24

Places to visit

Sutton Hoo, WOODBRIDGE 01394 389700
www.nationaltrust.org.uk/suttonhoo

Orford Castle, ORFORD 01394 450472
www.english-heritage.org.uk

Great for kids: Easton Farm Park, EASTON
01728 746475 www.eastonfarmpark.co.uk

AA CAMPING CARD SITE

PREMIER PARK

►►►►► 92% Moon & Sixpence
(TM263454)

Newbourn Rd, Waldringfield IP12 4PP
☎ 01473 736650 🖹 01473 736270
e-mail: info@moonandsixpence.eu
web: www.moonandsixpence.eu
dir: Follow caravan & Moon & Sixpence signs from
A12 Ipswich (east bypass). 1.5m, left at x-roads

* 🔌 £20-£32 🚐 £20-£32 ▲ £20-£32

Open Apr-Oct (rs Low season club, shop, reception
open limited hours)

Last arrival 20.00hrs Last departure noon

A well-planned site, with tourers occupying a
sheltered valley position around an attractive
boating lake with a sandy beach. Toilet facilities
are housed in a smart Norwegian-style cabin, and
there is a laundry and dishwashing area. Leisure
facilities include two tennis courts, a bowling
green, fishing, boating and a games room. There
is an adult-only area, and a strict 'no groups and
no noise after 9pm' policy. 5 acre site. 65 touring
pitches. Caravan pitches. Motorhome pitches.
Tent pitches. 225 statics.

AA Pubs & Restaurants nearby: The Crown,
Woodbridge 01394 384242

Seckford Hall Hotel, Woodbridge 01394 385678

Leisure: 🎿 🏊 😎 🎣
Facilities: 🛁 🔦 ⊙ 🌳 ※ 🖥 🚿 WiFi ♻ ❶
Services: 🔌 🖥 🍺 🌡 🏺 🚰 ◎ 🛒 ↯
Within 3 miles: ↓ 🗄 ♪ ⛷ 🔥 🖥
Notes: No group bookings or commercial vehicles,
quiet 21.00hrs-08.00hrs. Lake, cycle trail, 10-acre
sports area, 9-hole golf, tennis courts.

see advert on opposite page

►►► 85% Moat Barn Touring
Caravan Park *(TM269530)*

Dallinghoo Rd, Bredfield IP13 6BD
☎ 01473 737520
dir: Exit A12 at Bredfield, 1st right at village
pump. Through village, 1m site on left

* 🔌 fr £16 🚐 fr £16 ▲ fr £16

Open Mar-15 Jan

Last arrival 22.00hrs Last departure noon

An attractive small park set in idyllic Suffolk
countryside, perfectly located for touring the
heritage coastline and for visiting the National
Trust's Sutton Hoo. The modern toilet block is well
equipped and maintained. There are ten tent
pitches and the park is located on the popular
Hull to Harwich cycle route. Cycle hire is available,
but there are no facilities for children. 2 acre site.
34 touring pitches. Caravan pitches. Motorhome
pitches. Tent pitches.

AA Pubs & Restaurants nearby: The Crown,
Woodbridge 01394 384242

Seckford Hall Hotel, Woodbridge 01394 385678

Facilities: 🔦 ⊙ 🌳 ※ 🖥 WiFi ♻
Services: 🔌
Within 3 miles: ↓ 🗄 ♪ 🔥 🖥 U

Notes: Adults only. ⊛ No ball games, breathable
groundsheets only. Dogs must be kept on leads.

SERVICES: 🔌 Electric hook up 🖥 Launderette 🍺 Licensed bar 🌡 Calor Gas ⊘ Camping Gaz 🅃 Toilet fluid ◎ Café/Restaurant 🛒 Fast Food/Takeaway 🔋 Battery charging
🚼 Baby care ↯ Motorvan service point
ABBREVIATIONS: BH/bank hols-bank holidays Etr-Easter Whit-Whitsun dep-departure fr-from hrs-hours m-mile mdnt-midnight rdbt-roundabout rs-restricted service wk-week
wknd-weekend ⊛ No credit cards ⊗ No dogs See page 7 for details of the AA Camping Card Scheme

Beachy Head

Sussex

Sussex, deriving its name from 'South Saxons' is divided into two - East and West - but the name is so quintessentially English that we tend to think of it as one entity. Mention its name anywhere in the world and for those who are familiar with 'Sussex by the sea', images of rolling hills, historic towns and villages and miles of spectacular chalky cliffs immediately spring to mind. Perhaps it is the bare South Downs with which Sussex is most closely associated.

This swathe of breezy downland represents some of the finest walking in southern England. Now a National Park, the South Downs provide country-loving locals and scores of visitors with a perfect natural playground. As well as walkers and cyclists, you'll find kite flyers, model aircraft enthusiasts and hang gliders.

Beaches and cliffs

The coast is one of the county's gems. At its western end lies sprawling Chichester harbour, with its meandering channels, creeks and sleepy inlets, and on the horizon is the imposing outline of the cathedral, small but beautiful. To the east are the seaside towns of Worthing, Brighton, Eastbourne, Bexhill and Hastings. Here, the South Downs sweep down towards the sea with two famous landmarks, Birling Gap and Beachy Head, demonstrating how nature and the elements have shaped the land over time.

The heart of the county

Inland is Arundel, with its rows of elegant Georgian and Victorian buildings standing in the shadow of the great castle, ancestral home of the Dukes of Norfolk, and the magnificent French Gothic-style Roman Catholic cathedral. Mid Sussex is the setting for a chain of attractive, typically English towns, including Midhurst, Petworth, Pulborough, Billingshurst, Uckfield and Haywards Heath.

There are grand country houses, too. Parham, built during the reign of Henry VIII, was one of the first stately homes to open its doors to the public, while the National Trust's Petworth House, in 2,000 acres of parkland, retains the 13th-century chapel of an earlier mansion and has a fine art ▶

collection including works by Rembrandt and
Van Dyck.

Walking and Cycling

In terms of walking, this county is spoilt for
choice. Glancing at the map reveals innumerable
paths and bridleways, while there are many more
demanding and adventurous long-distance paths
– a perfect way to get to the heart of rural East
and West Sussex. The Sussex Border Path
meanders along the boundary between the two
counties; the Monarch's Way broadly follows
Charles II's escape route in 1651; the most
famous of all of them, the South Downs Way,

follows hill paths and clifftop tracks all the way
from Winchester to Eastbourne; the West Sussex
Literary Trail links Horsham with Chichester and
recalls many literary figures associated with this
area – Shelley, Tennyson and Wilde among them.

East and West Sussex offer exciting cycle rides
through the High Weald, along the South Downs
Way and via coastal routes between Worthing and
Rye. Brighton to Hastings via Polegate is part of
the Downs and Weald Cycle Route. There is also
the Forest Way through East Grinstead to
Groombridge and the Cuckoo Trail from Heathfield
to Eastbourne. For glorious coastal views and stiff
sea breezes, the very easy ride between

● Net sheds, Hastings

● South Downs Way

Chichester and West Wittering is recommended. You can vary the return by taking the Itchenor Ferry to Bosham.

Festivals and Events

- March is the month for the Pioneer Motorcycle Run from Epsom Downs to Brighton. All the participating motorcycles are pre 1915 and the event offers a fascinating insight into the early history of these machines – 300 of which are on display.
- During April there is A Taste of Sussex Fine Food Fair at the Weald and Downland Open Air Museum near Chichester.

- The 15th-century moated Herstmonceux Castle hosts England's Medieval Festival on August Bank Holiday weekend, complete with minstrels, magicians, lords, ladies and serfs.
- Goodwood is the venue for the Motor Circuit Revival Meeting in September. This is when fast cars and track legends celebrate the golden age of British motor sport from the 1940s and '50s.
- The same month – September – sees Uckfield Bonfire and Carnival Society's Annual Carnival with fancy dress and a torchlight procession.

SUSSEX, EAST

BATTLE Map 7 TQ71

Places to visit

1066 Story in Hastings Castle, HASTINGS & ST LEONARDS 01424 781111 www.discoverhastings.co.uk/hastings-castle-1066/

Blue Reef Aquarium, HASTINGS & ST LEONARDS 01424 718776 www.bluereefaquarium.co.uk

Great for kids: Smugglers Adventure, HASTINGS & ST LEONARDS 01424 422964 www.discoverhastings.co.uk

▶▶▶ 80% Brakes Coppice Park

(TQ765134)

Forewood Ln TN33 9AB
☎ 01424 830322
e-mail: brakesco@btinternet.com
web: www.brakescoppicepark.co.uk
dir: From Battle on A2100 towards Hastings. After 2m turn right for Crowhurst. Site 1m on left

* ⊞ £16-£20 ⊞ £16-£20 ▲ £14-£18

Open Mar-Oct

Last arrival 21.00hrs Last departure noon

A secluded farm site in a sunny meadow deep in woodland with a small stream and a coarse fishing lake. The toilet block has quality fittings and there's a good fully-serviced family/disabled room. Hardstanding pitches are neatly laid out on a terrace, and tents are pitched on grass edged by woodland. The hands-on owners offer high levels of customer care and this tucked away gem proves a peaceful base for exploring Battle and the south coast. 3 acre site. 30 touring pitches. 10 hardstandings. Caravan pitches. Motorhome pitches. Tent pitches.

AA Pubs & Restaurants nearby: Ash Tree Inn, Ashburnham Place 01424 892104 Wild Mushroom Restaurant, Westfield 01424 751137

Leisure: ⚑
Facilities: ⋔⊙⌿⋇☐⊙圄⊼⊼🐕ℹ
Services: ⊡⊡🔒⊘⊤🍴
Within 3 miles: ⌿⊙圄∪

Notes: No fires, footballs or kite flying. Dogs must be kept on leads.

▶▶▶ 71% Senlac Wood Holiday Park

(TQ722153)

Catsfield Rd, Catsfield TN33 9LN
☎ 01424 773969
e-mail: senlacwood@xlninternet.co.uk
dir: A271 from Battle onto B2204 signed Bexhill. Site on left

* ⊞ £15-£17 ⊞ £15-£17 ▲ £15-£17

Open Mar-Oct

Last arrival 22.00hrs Last departure noon

An woodland site with many secluded bays with hardstanding pitches, and two peaceful grassy glades for tents. The functional toilet facilities are clean, and at the time of our inspection, due for refurbishment. The site is ideal for anyone looking for seclusion and shade. Well placed for visiting nearby Battle and the south coast beaches. 20 acre site. 35 touring pitches. 16 hardstandings. Caravan pitches. Motorhome pitches. Tent pitches.

AA Pubs & Restaurants nearby: Ash Tree Inn, Ashburnham Place 01424 892104 Wild Mushroom Restaurant, Westfield 01424 751137

Leisure: ⚑🔍
Facilities: ⋔⊙⌿⋇☐圄⊼
Services: ⊡⊤🍴
Within 3 miles: ⌿⊙圄⊙∪
Notes: No camp fires.

BEXHILL Map 6 TQ70

Places to visit

Pevensey Castle, PEVENSEY 01323 762604 www.english-heritage.org.uk

1066 Story in Hastings Castle, HASTINGS & ST LEONARDS 01424 781111 www.discoverhastings.co.uk/hastings-castle-1066/

Great for kids: The Observatory Science Centre, HERSTMONCEUX 01323 832731 www.the-observatory.org

PREMIER PARK

▶▶▶▶▶ 87% Kloofs Caravan Park

(TQ709091)

Sandhurst Ln TN39 4RG
☎ 01424 842839
e-mail: camping@kloofs.com
dir: NE of Bexhill exit A259 at Little Common rdbt, N into Peartree Lane, left at x-rds, site 300mtrs on left

⊞ ⊞ ▲

Open all year

Last arrival anytime Last departure 11.00hrs

Hidden away down a quiet lane, just inland from Bexhill and the coast, Kloofs is a friendly, family-run park surrounded by farmland and oak woodlands, with views extending to the South Downs from hilltop pitches. Lovingly developed by the owners over the past 16 years, the site is well landscaped and thoughtfully laid out, with excellent hardstandings (some large enough for RVs), colourful flower beds, and spacious pitches, each with mini patio, bench and barbeque stand. Spotless, upmarket toilet facilities include a family shower room and a unisex block with privacy cubicles, a dog shower, a drying room, and a dishwasher. 22 acre site. 50 touring pitches. 50 hardstandings. Caravan pitches. Motorhome pitches. Tent pitches. 75 statics.

Leisure: ⚑
Facilities: ⋔⊙⌿⋇☐⊙圄⊼⊼♻ℹ
Services: ⊡⊡🔒⊘⊤🍴♿
Within 3 miles: ⌿日⌿◎≋圄⊙∪

Notes: No noise between 22.30hrs-07.00hrs. Dogs must be kept on leads. Hanging/drying room, kitchens.

LEISURE: 🏊 Indoor swimming pool 🏊 Outdoor swimming pool ⚑ Children's playground 🪁 Kid's club ⊙ Tennis court 🔍 Games room ▭ Separate TV room ⌿ 9/18 hole golf course ⛵ Boats for hire 🎬 Cinema 🎵 Entertainment ⌿ Fishing ◎ Mini golf ≋ Watersports 💪 Gym ⊙ Sports field Spa ∪ Stables
FACILITIES: 🛁 Bath 🚿 Shower ⊙ Electric shaver ⌿ Hairdryer ⋇ Ice Pack Facility ⓹ Disabled facilities ⊙ Public telephone 圄 Shop on site or within 200yds 📱 Mobile shop (calls at least 5 days a week) 🍴 BBQ area ⊼ Picnic area 📶 Wi-fi 💻 Internet access ♻ Recycling ℹ Tourist info 🐕 Dog exercise area

NEW ▶▶▶ 79% Cobbs Hill Farm Caravan & Camping Park *(TQ736102)*

Watermill Ln TN39 5JA
☎ **01424 213460 & 07708 958910**
e-mail: cobbshillfarmuk@hotmail.com
dir: *Exit A269 into Watermill Lane, park 1m on left*

* 🚐 £12-£14 🚐 £12-£14 ▲ £10-£15

Open Apr-Oct

Last arrival 20.00hrs Last departure noon

A well established farm site tucked away in pleasant rolling countryside close to Bexhill and a short drive from Battle, the South Downs and good beaches. Neat, well maintained camping paddocks, one with eight new hardstanding pitches, are sheltered by mature trees and hedging; the toilet block is clean and freshly painted. Children will love the menagerie of farm animals. 17 acre site. 55 touring pitches. 8 hardstandings. 20 seasonal pitches. Caravan pitches. Motorhome pitches. Tent pitches. 15 statics.

AA Pubs & Restaurants nearby: Ash Tree Inn, Ashburton Place 01424 892104

Leisure: ⚙ ✣
Facilities: 🏵⊙🅟✳⚒⚙🅗🚽🛁 Wi-Fi 🅘
Services: 🔌🅢🍺⚙🆃🛒
Within 3 miles: ↕🅟🛥🅢🅢
Notes: Dogs must be kept on leads.

CAMBER Map 7 TQ91

Places to visit
Rye Castle Museum, RYE 01797 226728 www.ryemuseum.co.uk

Lamb House, RYE 01580 762334 www.nationaltrust.org.uk/main/w-lambhouse

Great for kids: 1066 Story in Hastings Castle, HASTINGS & ST LEONARDS 01424 781111 www.discoverhastings.co.uk/hastings-castle-1066/

66% Camber Sands *(TQ972184)*

New Lydd Rd TN31 7RT
☎ **0871 664 9719**
e-mail: camber.sands@park-resorts.com
dir: *M20 junct 10 (Ashford International Station), A2070 signed Brenzett. Follow Hastings & Rye signs on A259. 1m before Rye, left signed Camber. Site in 3m*

🚐🚐▲

Open Apr-Oct

Last arrival anytime Last departure 10.00hrs

Located opposite Camber's vast sandy beach, this large holiday centre offers a good range of leisure and entertainment facilities. The touring area is positioned close to the reception and entrance, and is served by a clean and functional toilet block. 110 acre site. 40 touring pitches. 6 hardstandings. Caravan pitches. Motorhome pitches. Tent pitches. 921 statics.

AA Pubs & Restaurants nearby: Mermaid Inn, Rye 01797 223065

Globe Inn, Rye 01797 227918 Ypres Castle, Rye 01797 223248

George in Rye, Rye 01797 222114

Leisure: 🏊⚙🛝🏃🎣🎵 Spa
Facilities: 🏵⊙⚙⚙🅗🚽 Wi-Fi 💻 ♻ 🅘
Services: 🔌🅢🍺🍽🛒💻
Within 3 miles: ↕🅟◎🛥🅢🅢
Notes: Quiet between 23.00hrs-7.00hrs. Dogs must be kept on leads.

FURNER'S GREEN Map 6 TQ42

Places to visit
Sheffield Park Garden, SHEFFIELD PARK 01825 790231 www.nationaltrust.org.uk/main/w-sheffieldparkgarden

Nymans, HANDCROSS 01444 405250 www.nationaltrust.org.uk/main/w-nymansgarden2

▶▶ 81% Heaven Farm *(TQ403264)*

TN22 3RG
☎ **01825 790226** 📠 **01825 790881**
e-mail: heavenfarmleisure@btinternet.com
dir: *On A275 between Lewes & East Grinstead, 1m N of Sheffield Park Gardens*

🚐🚐▲

Open Apr-Oct

Last arrival 21.00hrs Last departure noon

A delightful, small, rural site on a popular farm complex incorporating a farm museum, craft shop, organic farm shop, tea room and nature trail. Good clean toilet facilities are housed in well-converted outbuildings. Ashdown Forest, the Bluebell Railway and Sheffield Park Garden are nearby. 1.5 acre site. 25 touring pitches. 2 hardstandings. Caravan pitches. Motorhome pitches. Tent pitches.

AA Pubs & Restaurants nearby: Coach & Horses, Danehill 01825 740369

Griffin Inn, Fletchling 01825 722890

Facilities: 🏵⊙✳⚙🅗🚽🛝
Services: 🔌🆃🍽🛒⚙
Within 3 miles: ↕🅟🅢∪
Notes: ⊛ No children between 6-18yrs preferred. Dogs must be kept on leads. Fishing.

HEATHFIELD — Map 6 TQ52

Places to visit

Pashley Manor Gardens, TICEHURST 01580 200888 www.pashleymanorgardens.com

The Truggery, HERSTMONCEUX 01323 832314 www.truggery.co.uk

Great for kids: Bentley Wildfowl & Motor Museum, HALLAND 01825 840573 www.bentley.org.uk

►► 77% *Greenviews Caravan Park*

(TQ605223)

Burwash Rd, Broad Oak TN21 8RT
☎ 01435 863531 ▤ 01435 863531
dir: *Through Heathfield on A265 for 1m. Site on left after Broad Oak sign*

🚐 🚑 Å

Open Apr-Oct (rs Apr & Oct bookings only, subject to weather)

Last arrival 22.00hrs Last departure 10.30hrs

A small touring area adjoining a residential park, with a smart clubhouse. The facility block includes a room for disabled visitors. The owners always offer a friendly welcome, and they take pride in the lovely flower beds which adorn the park. 3 acre site. 10 touring pitches. Caravan pitches. Motorhome pitches. Tent pitches. 51 statics.

AA Pubs & Restaurants nearby: The Middle House, Mayfield 01435 872146

Best Beech Inn, Wadhurst 01892 782046

Facilities: 🔦 ⊙ ♿ ◐
Services: 🚽 🗑 🍴 🛒 ⊘
Within 3 miles: 🖫
Notes: 🐾 ⊗

PEVENSEY BAY — Map 6 TQ60

Places to visit

"How We Lived Then" Museum of Shops & Social History, EASTBOURNE 01323 737143 www.how-we-lived-then.co.uk

Alfriston Clergy House, ALFRISTON 01323 870001 www.nationaltrust.org.uk/main/w-alfristonclergyhouse

Great for kids: The Observatory Science Centre, HERSTMONCEUX 01323 832731 www.the-observatory.org

AA CAMPING CARD SITE

►►► 83% Bay View Park

(TQ648028)

Old Martello Rd BN24 6DX
☎ 01323 768688 ▤ 01323 769637
e-mail: holidays@bay-view.co.uk
web: www.bay-view.co.uk
dir: *Signed from A259 W of Pevensey Bay. On seaward side of A259 take private road towards beach*

* 🚐 £16-£23 🚑 £16-£23 Å £16-£23

Open Mar-Oct

Last arrival 20.00hrs Last departure noon

A pleasant well-run site just yards from the beach, in an area east of Eastbourne town centre known as 'The Crumbles'. The level grassy site is very well maintained and the toilet facilities feature fully-serviced cubicles. 6 acre site. 94 touring pitches. 10 hardstandings. Caravan pitches. Motorhome pitches. Tent pitches. 8 statics.

AA Pubs & Restaurants nearby: Lamb Inn, Wartling 01323 832116

Leisure: ⚠
Facilities: 🔦 ⊙ 🌡 ✳ ♿ ◐ 🖫 📶 ♻ ❶
Services: 🚽 🗑 🛒 ⊘ T 🍴 ⚡
Within 3 miles: 🖔 🎏 ◉ 🛶 🖫 🖫
Notes: Families & couples only, no commercial vehicles. Dogs must be kept on leads. 9-hole golf course.

SUSSEX, WEST

ARUNDEL — Map 6 TQ00

Places to visit

Arundel Castle, ARUNDEL 01903 882173 www.arundelcastle.org

Harbour Park, LITTLEHAMPTON 01903 721200 www.harbourpark.com

Great for kids: Look & Sea! Visitor Centre, LITTLEHAMPTON 01903 718984 www.lookandsea.co.uk

►► 78% Ship & Anchor Marina

(TQ002040)

Station Rd, Ford BN18 0BJ
☎ 01243 551262 ▤ 01243 555256
e-mail: enquiries@shipandanchormarina.co.uk
dir: *From A27 at Arundel take road S signed Ford. Site 2m on left after level crossing*

* 🚐 £14-£19 🚑 £14-£19 Å £14-£19

Open Mar-Oct

Last arrival 21.00hrs Last departure noon

A neat and tidy site with dated but spotlessly clean toilet facilities enjoying a pleasant position beside the Ship & Anchor pub and the tidal River Arun. There are good walks from the site to Arundel and the coast. 12 acre site. 120 touring pitches. 11 hardstandings. Caravan pitches. Motorhome pitches. Tent pitches.

AA Pubs & Restaurants nearby: The Townhouse, Arundel 01903 883847

George & Dragon, Burpham 01903 883131

Leisure: ⚠
Facilities: 🛁 🔦 ⊙ 🌡 ✳ ♿ ◐ 🖫 🐾 ❶
Services: 🚽 🍴 🛒 ⊘ T 🍴 🎒
Within 3 miles: 🖔 🎏 🖈 ◉ 🛶 🖫 🖫 ↻
Notes: 🐾 No music audible to others. Dogs must be kept on leads. River fishing from site, pub on site.

LEISURE: 🏊 Indoor swimming pool 🏊 Outdoor swimming pool ⚠ Children's playground 🧒 Kid's club 🎾 Tennis court 🎱 Games room 📺 Separate TV room 🏌 9/18 hole golf course 🚣 Boats for hire 🎬 Cinema 🎵 Entertainment 🎣 Fishing ◉ Mini golf 🏄 Watersports 🏋 Gym 🏟 Sports field Spa ↻ Stables
FACILITIES: 🛁 Bath 🔦 Shower ⊙ Electric shaver 🌡 Hairdryer ✳ Ice Pack Facility ♿ Disabled facilities ◐ Public telephone 🖫 Shop on site or within 200yds 🛒 Mobile shop (calls at least 5 days a week) 🍴 BBQ area 🎏 Picnic area 📶 Wi-fi 🖥 Internet access ♻ Recycling ❶ Tourist info 🐾 Dog exercise area

BARNS GREEN Map 6 TQ12

Places to visit

Parham House & Gardens, PULBOROUGH 01903 744888 www.parhaminsussex.co.uk

Great for kids: Bignor Roman Villa & Museum, BIGNOR 01798 869259 www.bignorromanvilla.co.uk

►►►► 84% Sumners Ponds Fishery & Campsite *(TQ125268)*

GOLD

Chapel Rd RH13 0PR
☎ 01403 732539
e-mail: sumnersponds@dsl.co.uk
dir: *From A272 at Coolham x-rds, N towards Barns Green. In 1.5m take 1st left at small x-rds. 1m, over level crossing. Site on left just after right bend*

* 🚐 £18.50-£24.50 🚌 £18.50-£24.50 ⛺ £18.50-£24.50

Open all year

Last arrival 20.00hrs Last departure noon

Diversification towards high quality camping continues at this working farm set in attractive surroundings on the edge of the quiet village of Barns Green. There are three touring areas; one is under development and includes camping pods, and another, which will have a new toilet block for 2012, has excellent pitches (and pods) on the banks of one of the well-stocked fishing lakes. A woodland walk has direct access to miles of footpaths. Horsham and Brighton are within easy reach. 40 acre site. 85 touring pitches. 45 hardstandings. Caravan pitches. Motorhome pitches. Tent pitches.

AA Pubs & Restaurants nearby: Cricketers Arms, Wisborough Green 01403 700369

Black Horse Inn, Nuthurst 01403 891272

White Horse, Maplehurst 01403 891208

Leisure: 🛝

Facilities: 🚿 🪒 💨 ❄ ♿ [S] 🪑 🐕 [Wi-fi]

Services: 🔌 🧺 ⛽ [T] 🍴 🍔 ⚓

Within 3 miles: ⛳ 🎣 🏊 [S] 🧺 🐴

Notes: Only one car per pitch. Cycling paths, cycle racks.

BILLINGSHURST Map 6 TQ02

Places to visit

Borde Hill Garden, HAYWARDS HEATH 01444 450326 www.bordehill.co.uk

Petworth Cottage Museum, PETWORTH 01798 342100 www.petworthcottagemuseum.co.uk

►► 72% Limeburners Arms Camp Site *(TQ072255)*

Lordings Rd, Newbridge RH14 9JA
☎ 01403 782311
e-mail: chippy.sawyer@virgin.net
dir: *From A29 take A272 towards Petworth for 1m, left onto B2133. Site 300yds on left*

* 🚐 fr £14 🚌 fr £14 ⛺ fr £14

Open Apr-Oct

Last arrival 22.00hrs Last departure 14.00hrs

A secluded site in rural West Sussex, at the rear of the Limeburners Arms public house, and surrounded by fields. It makes a pleasant base for touring the South Downs and the Arun Valley. The toilets are basic but very clean. 2.75 acre site. 40 touring pitches. Caravan pitches. Motorhome pitches. Tent pitches.

AA Pubs & Restaurants nearby: Cricketers Arms, Wisborough Green 01403 700369

Black Horse Inn, Nuthurst 01403 891272

White Horse, Maplehurst 01403 891208

Leisure: 🛝

Facilities: 🚿 🪒 ❄ 📞

Services: 🔌 🍺 🍴 🔋 ⚓

Within 3 miles: ⛳ [S] 🐴

Notes: Dogs must be kept on leads.

BIRDHAM Map 5 SU80

Places to visit

Chichester Cathedral, CHICHESTER 01243 782595 www.chichestercathedral.org.uk

Pallant House Gallery, CHICHESTER 01243 774557 www.pallant.org.uk

► 72% Tawny Touring Park *(SZ818991)*

Tawny Nurseries, Bell Ln PO20 7HY
☎ 01243 512168
e-mail: tawny@pobox.co.uk
dir: *From A27 at Stockbridge rdbt take A286 towards The Witterings. 5m to mini rdbt in Birdham. 1st exit onto B2198. Site 300mtrs on left*

* 🚐 £14-£16 🚌 £14-£16

Open all year

Last arrival 21.00hrs Last departure 19.00hrs

A small site for the self-contained tourer only, on a landscaped field adjacent to the owners' nurseries. There are six hardstanding pitches for American RVs but no toilet facilities. The beach is just one mile away. 4.5 acre site. 30 touring pitches. 7 hardstandings. Caravan pitches. Motorhome pitches.

AA Pubs & Restaurants nearby: Crab & Lobster, Sidlesham 01243 641233

Facilities: [S] 🐕 ♻ ℹ

Services: 🔌 🔥 [T] ⚓

Within 3 miles: ⛳ ⛵ 🎬 🎣 🎯 🏊 [S] 🧺 🐴

Notes: Dogs must be kept on leads. RV charge £20-£22.

SERVICES: 🔌 Electric hook up 🧺 Launderette 🍺 Licensed bar 🔥 Calor Gas ⛽ Camping Gaz [T] Toilet fluid 🍴 Café/Restaurant 🍔 Fast Food/Takeaway 🔋 Battery charging 👶 Baby care ⚓ Motorvan service point

ABBREVIATIONS: BH/bank hols-bank holidays Etr-Easter Whit-Whitsun dep-departure fr-from hrs-hours m-mile mdnt-midnight rdbt-roundabout rs-restricted service wk-week wknd-weekend 💳 No credit cards 🚫 No dogs

See page 7 for details of the AA Camping Card Scheme

CHICHESTER
Map 5 SU80

Places to visit

Chichester Cathedral, CHICHESTER
01243 782595 www.chichestercathedral.org.uk

Pallant House Gallery, CHICHESTER
01243 774557 www.pallant.org.uk

►►► 81% Ellscott Park *(SU829995)*

Sidlesham Ln, Birdham PO20 7QL
☎ 01243 512003 📄 01243 512003
e-mail: camping@ellscottpark.co.uk
dir: *From Chichester take A286 towards The Witterings for approx 4m, left at Butterfly Farm sign, site 500yds right*

🚐 �90 Å   Open Apr-3rd wk in Oct

Last arrival daylight Last departure variable

A well-kept park set in meadowland behind the owners' nursery and van storage area. The park attracts a peace-loving clientele, and is handy for the beach, Chichester, Goodwood House, the racing at Goodwood and walking on the South Downs. Home-grown produce is for sale. 2.5 acre site. 50 touring pitches. 25 seasonal pitches. Caravan pitches. Motorhome pitches. Tent pitches.

AA Pubs & Restaurants nearby: Crab & Lobster, Sidlesham 01243 641233

Leisure: 🅰 ⚽

Facilities: 🅽 ⊙ ✳ 🕭 🅰 🛒 ♻ ℹ

Services: 🔧 🖾 ⌀ T 🖃 ☕

Within 3 miles: ↧ 🎣 ♂ ☕ 🖾 🖥 ∪

Notes: 🐕 Dogs must be kept on leads.

DIAL POST
Map 6 TQ11

Places to visit

Bignor Roman Villa & Museum, BIGNOR
01798 869259 www.bignorromanvilla.co.uk

Great for kids: Amberley Working Museum, AMBERLEY 01798 831370
www.amberleymuseum.co.uk

AA CAMPING CARD SITE

►►►► 85% Honeybridge Park

(TQ152183)

Honeybridge Ln RH13 8NX
☎ 01403 710923 📄 01403 712815
e-mail: enquiries@honeybridgepark.co.uk
dir: *10m S of Horsham, just off A24 at Dial Post. Behind Old Barn Nursery*

* 🚐 £18-£24.50 �90 £18-£24.50 Å £15-£24.50

Open all year

Last arrival 19.00hrs Last departure noon

An attractive and very popular park on gently-sloping ground surrounded by hedgerows and mature trees. A comprehensive amenities building houses upmarket toilet facilities including luxury family and disabled rooms, as well as a laundry, shop and off-licence. There are plenty of hardstandings and electric hook-ups, and an excellent children's play area. 15 acre site. 130 touring pitches. 70 hardstandings. 20 seasonal pitches. Caravan pitches. Motorhome pitches. Tent pitches. 50 statics.

AA Pubs & Restaurants nearby: Countryman Inn, Shipley 01403 741383

George & Dragon, Shipley 01403 741320

Queens Head, West Chiltington 01798 812244

Leisure: 🅰 🎣 🖵

Facilities: 🚿 🅽 ⊙ 🅿 ✳ 🕭 🖹 🛒 ℹ

Services: 🔧 🖾 🖾 ⌀ T 🍴 ☕

Within 3 miles: ♂ ☕ 🖾 🖥 ∪

Notes: No open fires. Dogs must be kept on leads. Fridges available.

HENFIELD
Map 6 TQ21

►► 70% *Blacklands Campsite*

(TQ231180)

Blacklands Farm, Wheatsheaf Rd BN5 9AT
☎ 01273 493528
e-mail: info@blacklandsfarm.co.uk
dir: *A23, B2118, B2116 towards Henfield. Site approx 4m on right*

🚐 �90 Å

Open Mar-Jan

Last arrival 20.00hrs Last departure noon

Tucked away off the B2116, east of Henfield, and well placed for visiting Brighton and exploring the South Downs National Park, this simple, grassy site has great potential, and the owners plan positive improvements that will not spoil the traditional feel of the campsite. The clean and tidy portaloos have been smartly clad in wood, but future plans include building a new toilet block, developing the central children's play area, and

LEISURE: 🏊 Indoor swimming pool   🏊 Outdoor swimming pool   🅰 Children's playground   🛝 Kid's club   🎾 Tennis court   🎱 Games room   🖵 Separate TV room   ↧ 9/18 hole golf course   🚣 Boats for hire   🎬 Cinema   🎵 Entertainment   🎣 Fishing   ⊙ Mini golf   🏄 Watersports   🏋 Gym   ⚽ Sports field   **Spa**   ∪ Stables
FACILITIES: 🚿 Bath   🅽 Shower   ⊙ Electric shaver   🅿 Hairdryer   ✳ Ice Pack Facility   🕭 Disabled facilities   ☎ Public telephone   🖹 Shop on site or within 200yds   🏪 Mobile shop (calls at least 5 days a week)   🍴 BBQ area   🛒 Picnic area   📶 Wi-fi   🖥 Internet access   ♻ Recycling   ℹ Tourist info   🐕 Dog exercise area

adding a few hardstanding pitches. 5 acre site. 75 touring pitches. Caravan pitches. Motorhome pitches. Tent pitches.

AA Pubs & Restaurants nearby: The Fountains Inn, Ashurst 01403 710219

The Royal Oak, Poynings 01273 857389

Leisure:

Facilities: ⌂ ✳ 🖎 ♯ 🖎

Services: 🖴

Within 3 miles: ↕ ⌐ 🖎🖎 U

Notes: 🚫 No camp fires, no commercial vehicles.

HORSHAM

See Barns Green & Dial Post

SELSEY   Map 5 SZ89

Places to visit

Chichester Cathedral, CHICHESTER 01243 782595 www.chichestercathedral.org.uk

Pallant House Gallery, CHICHESTER 01243 774557 www.pallant.org.uk

▶▶ 79% Warner Farm Touring Park (SZ845939)

Warner Ln, Selsey PO20 9EL
☎ **01243 604499**
e-mail: touring@bunnleisure.co.uk
web: www.warnerfarm.co.uk
dir: From B2145 in Selsey turn right into School Lane & follow signs

* 🚐 £21-£47.50 🚛 £21-£47.50 ▲ £19-£37

Open Mar-Oct

Last arrival 17.30hrs Last departure 10.00hrs

A well-screened touring site with refurbished toilet facilities that adjoins the three static parks under the same ownership. A courtesy bus runs around the complex to entertainment areas and supermarkets. The park backs onto open grassland, and the leisure facilities

with bar, amusements and bowling alley, and swimming pool/sauna complex are also accessible to tourers. 10 acre site. 250 touring pitches. 60 hardstandings. Caravan pitches. Motorhome pitches. Tent pitches. 1500 statics.

AA Pubs & Restaurants nearby: Crab & Lobster, Sidlesham 01243 641233

Leisure: 🏊 🌊 ⚓ 🎱 🕊 👋 🎯 🎮 🍷 🎵

Facilities: ⌂ ⊙ 🅿 ✳ ♿ 🖎 📷 ♯ 🖎 WiFi 🔁 🛈

Services: 🖴 🖶 🍴 🛢 ⌀ 🅣 🍽 🚮 ⚡

Within 3 miles: ↕ 🚲 ⌐ ◎ 🖎 🖎 U

Notes: Dogs must be kept on leads.

see advert on opposite page

TYNE & WEAR

SOUTH SHIELDS   Map 21 NZ36

Places to visit

Arbeia Roman Fort & Museum, SOUTH SHIELDS 0191 456 1369 www.twmuseums.org.uk/arbeia

Tynemouth Priory and Castle, TYNEMOUTH 0191 257 1090 www.english-heritage.org.uk

Great for kids: Blue Reef Aquarium, TYNEMOUTH 0191 258 1031 www.bluereefaquarium.co.uk

▶▶▶ 80% Lizard Lane Caravan & Camping Site (NZ399648)

Lizard Ln NE34 7AB
☎ **0191 454 4982** 📠 **0191 455 4466**
e-mail: info@littlehavenhotel.com
dir: 2m S of town centre on A183
* 🚐 £13.55-£26.50 🚛 £13.55-£26.50

Open Feb-28 Jan

Last arrival anytime Last departure 11.00hrs

Completely renovated in recent years, this site is located in an evelated position with good sea views. All touring pitches are fully serviced and the modern smart amenities block is equipped with superb fixtures and fittings. A shop is also provided. Please note that tents are not accepted. 2 acre site. 47 touring pitches. Caravan pitches. Motorhome pitches. 70 statics.

Facilities: ⌂ ⊙ 🅿 ✳ ♿ 🖎 ♯ 🔁 🛈

Services: 🖴 ⌀ ⚡

Within 3 miles: ↕ 🕊 🎌 ⌐ 🖎 🖎 🖎 U

Notes: Dogs must be kept on leads. 9-hole putting green.

WARWICKSHIRE

ASTON CANTLOW   Map 10 SP16

Places to visit

Mary Arden's Farm, WILMCOTE 01789 201844 www.shakespeare.org.uk

Charlecote Park, CHARLECOTE 01789 470277 www.nationaltrust.org.uk/main/w-charlecotepark

Great for kids: Warwick Castle, WARWICK 0871 265 2000 www.warwick-castle.com

AA CAMPING CARD SITE

▶▶▶ 78% Island Meadow Caravan Park (SP137596)

The Mill House B95 6JP
☎ **01789 488273** 📠 **01789 488273**
e-mail: holiday@islandmeadowcaravanpark.co.uk
dir: From A46 or A3400 follow signs for Aston Cantlow. Site signed 0.25m W off Mill Lane

* 🚐 £20 🚛 £20 ▲ £15-£20

Open Mar-Oct

Last arrival 21.00hrs Last departure noon

A small well-kept site bordered by the River Alne on one side and its mill stream on the other. Mature willows line the banks, and this is a very pleasant place to relax and unwind. There are six holiday statics for hire. 7 acre site. 24 touring pitches. 14 hardstandings. Caravan pitches. Motorhome pitches. Tent pitches. 56 statics.

AA Pubs & Restaurants nearby: The Stag, Red Hill 01789 764634

Blue Boar Inn, Temple Grafton 01789 750010

Facilities: ⌂ ⊙ 🅿 ✳ ♿ 🖎 🖎 🔁 🛈

Services: 🖴 🖶 🛢 ⌀ 🅣 ⚡

Within 3 miles: ↕ ⌐ ◎ 🖎

Notes: Dogs must be kept on leads. Free fishing for visitors.

SERVICES: 🖴 Electric hook up 🖶 Launderette 🍴 Licensed bar 🛢 Calor Gas ⌀ Camping Gaz 🅣 Toilet fluid 🍽 Café/Restaurant 🚮 Fast Food/Takeaway ⚡ Battery charging 👶 Baby care ⚙ Motorvan service point
ABBREVIATIONS: BH/bank hols-bank holidays Etr-Easter Whit-Whitsun dep-departure fr-from hrs-hours m-mile mdnt-midnight rdbt-roundabout rs-restricted service wk-week wknd-weekend 🚫 No credit cards 🚫 No dogs
See page 7 for details of the AA Camping Card Scheme

HARBURY — Map 11 SP35

Places to visit

Warwick Castle, WARWICK 0871 265 2000
www.warwick-castle.com

Farnborough Hall, FARNBOROUGH 01295 690002
www.nationaltrust.org.uk

Great for kids: Stratford Butterfly Farm,
STRATFORD-UPON-AVON 01789 299288
www.butterflyfarm.co.uk

►►►► 87% *Harbury Fields* (SP352604)

Harbury Fields Farm CV33 9JN
☎ 01926 612457
e-mail: rdavis@harburyfields.co.uk
dir: *M40 junct 12, B4451 (signed Kenton/Gaydon).
0.75m, right signed Lightborne. 4m, right at rdbt
onto B4455 (signed Harbury). 3rd right by petrol
station, site in 700yds (by two cottages)*

🚐 🚃

Open 2 Jan-19 Dec

Last arrival 21.30hrs Last departure noon

This developing park is in a peaceful farm setting
with lovely countryside views. All pitches have
hardstandings with electric and the facilities are
spotless. It is well positioned for visiting Warwick
and Leamington Spa as well as the exhibition
centres at NEC Birmingham, and the National
Agricultural Centre at Stoneleigh Park. 3 acre site.
32 touring pitches. 31 hardstandings. Caravan
pitches. Motorhome pitches.

AA Pubs & Restaurants nearby: Duck on the Pond,
Long Itchington 01926 815876

Facilities: 🏠 ☉ ⚲ ⊙ 🛱
Services: 🔌 🗑 ⏚
Within 3 miles: ⬆ 🏤
Notes: ♻

KINGSBURY — Map 10 SP29

Places to visit

Sarehole Mill, BIRMINGHAM 0121 777 6612
www.bmag.org.uk

Museum of the Jewellery Quarter, BIRMINGHAM
0121 554 3598 www.bmag.org.uk

► 70% Tame View Caravan Site

(SP209979)

Cliff B78 2DR
☎ 01827 873853
dir: *400yds off A51 (Tamworth-Kingsbury road),
1m N of Kingsbury opposite pub. Signed Cliff Hall
Lane*

🚐 🚃 ⛺

Open all year

Last arrival 23.00hrs Last departure 23.00hrs

A secluded spot overlooking the Tame Valley and
river, sheltered by high hedges. Sanitary facilities
are minimal but clean on this small park. The site
is popular with many return visitors who like a
peaceful basic site. 5 acre site. 5 touring pitches.
Caravan pitches. Motorhome pitches. Tent pitches.

AA Pubs & Restaurants nearby: Chapel House
Restaurant with Rooms, Atherstone 01827 718949

Facilities: ✳ 🗑 🛱 🐕 ♻
Services: ⚞
Within 3 miles: ⬆ ⚲ 🗓 🎣 ◎ ⛵ 🏤 🗑 U
Notes: ♻ Dogs must be kept on leads. Fishing.

RUGBY — Map 11 SP57

Places to visit

The Webb Ellis Rugby Football Museum, RUGBY
01788 567777 www.webb-ellis.co.uk

Coventry Transport Museum, COVENTRY
024 7623 4270 www.transport-museum.com

Great for kids: Lunt Roman Fort, COVENTRY
024 7629 4734 www.theherbert.org

►► 69% Lodge Farm Campsite

(SP476748)

Bilton Ln, Long Lawford CV23 9DU
☎ 01788 560193
e-mail: jane@lodgefarm.com
web: www.lodgefarm.com
dir: *From Rugby take A428 (Lawford road),
towards Coventry, 1.5m. At Sheaf & Sickle pub left
into Bilton Ln, site 500yds*

* 🚐 fr £15 🚃 fr £15 ⛺ fr £10

Open all year (rs Winter - extreme weather
conditions limit access)

Last arrival 22.00hrs

A small, simple farm site set behind the friendly
owner's home and self-catering cottages, with
converted stables housing the toilet facilities.
Rugby is only a short drive away, and the site is
tucked well away from the main road. 2.5 acre
site. 35 touring pitches. 3 hardstandings. 10
seasonal pitches. Caravan pitches. Motorhome
pitches. Tent pitches.

AA Pubs & Restaurants nearby: Bell Inn, Monks
Kirby 01788 832352

Golden Lion, Easenhall 01788 832265 Old Smithy,
Church Lawford 02476 542333

Facilities: 🏠 ☉ ✳ ⚲ 🛱 📶 ♻ ❶
Services: 🔌 🔋 ⚞
Within 3 miles: ⬆ ⚲ 🗓 🎣 ◎ ⛵ 🏤 🗑 U
Notes: Dogs must be kept on leads.

LEISURE: 🏊 Indoor swimming pool 🏊 Outdoor swimming pool 🎠 Children's playground 🧒 Kid's club 🎾 Tennis court 🎯 Games room 📺 Separate TV room
⛳ 9/18 hole golf course 🚣 Boats for hire 🎬 Cinema 🎵 Entertainment 🎣 Fishing ◎ Mini golf 🏄 Watersports 🏋 Gym ⚽ Sports field Spa U Stables
FACILITIES: 🛁 Bath 🚿 Shower ⊙ Electric shaver 🗓 Hairdryer ✳ Ice Pack Facility ⚲ Disabled facilities ⏚ Public telephone 🏪 Shop on site or within 200yds
🚚 Mobile shop (calls at least 5 days a week) 🍖 BBQ area 🛱 Picnic area 📶 Wi-fi 💻 Internet access ♻ Recycling ❶ Tourist info 🛱 Dog exercise area

WOLVEY
Map 11 SP48

Places to visit

Arbury Hall, NUNEATON 024 7638 2804
www.arburyestate.co.uk

Jaguar Daimler Heritage Centre, COVENTRY
024 7640 1291 www.jdht.com

Great for kids: Lunt Roman Fort, COVENTRY
024 7629 4734 www.theherbert.org

▶▶▶ 77% Wolvey Villa Farm Caravan & Camping Site (SP428869)

LE10 3HF
☎ 01455 220493 & 220630
dir: M6 junct 2, B4065 follow Wolvey signs. Or
M69 junct 1 & follow Wolvey signs

⚐ £13-£16 ⚐ £13-£16 ⚐ £13-£16

Open all year

Last arrival 22.00hrs Last departure noon

A level grass site surrounded by trees and shrubs,
on the borders of Warwickshire and Leicestershire.
This quiet country site has its own popular fishing
lake, and is convenient for visiting the cities of
Coventry and Leicester. 7 acre site. 110 touring
pitches. 24 hardstandings. Caravan pitches.
Motorhome pitches. Tent pitches.

AA Pubs & Restaurants nearby: Bell Inn, Monks
Kirby 01788 832352

The Pheasant, Withybrook 01455 220480

Leisure: ⊕ ⚲ ☐
Facilities: �📷 ⊙ ⟟ ⚹ ⚫ ☺ 🈵 ⚒ ❶
Services: ⚡ ⑤ 🛢 ⊘ Ⓣ ⚞
Within 3 miles: ⚓ 🛢 ⚟ 🛢 ⑤ ↺

Notes: ⊗ No twin axles. Dogs must be kept on
leads. Putting green, off licence.

WEST MIDLANDS

MERIDEN
Map 10 SP28

Places to visit

Blakesley Hall, BIRMINGHAM 0121 464 2193
www.bmag.org.uk

Aston Hall, BIRMINGHAM 0121 464 2193
www.bmag.org.uk/aston -hall

AA CAMPING CARD SITE

▶▶▶▶ 89% Somers Wood Caravan Park (SP225824)

Bestof British

Somers Rd CV7 7PL
☎ 01676 522978 ▤ 01676 522978
e-mail: enquiries@somerswood.co.uk
dir: M42 junct 6, A45 signed Coventry. Keep left
(do not take flyover). Then right onto A452 signed
Meriden & Leamington. At next rdbt left onto
B4102 (Hampton Lane). Site in 0.5m on left

⚐ £18-£24 ⚐ £18-£24

Open all year

Last arrival variable Last departure variable

A peaceful adults-only park set in the heart of
England with spotless facilities. The park is well
positioned for visiting the National Exhibition
Centre (NEC), the NEC Arena and National Indoor
Arena (NIA), and Birmingham is only 12 miles
away. The park also makes an ideal touring base
for Warwick, Coventry and Stratford-upon-Avon
just 22 miles away. Please note that tents are not
accepted. 4 acre site. 48 touring pitches. 48
hardstandings. Caravan pitches. Motorhome
pitches.

AA Pubs & Restaurants nearby: White Lion,
Hampton-in-Arden 01675 442833

Facilities: 📷 ⊙ ⟟ ⚹ ⚫ ☺ 🛜 ♲ ❶
Services: ⚡ 🛢 ⊘ Ⓣ ⚞
Within 3 miles: ⚓ ⚟ ⑤ ↺

Notes: Adults only. Dogs must be kept on leads.
Laundry service available.

SERVICES: ⚡ Electric hook up ⑤ Launderette ⚑ Licensed bar 🛢 Calor Gas ⊘ Camping Gaz Ⓣ Toilet fluid 🍴 Café/Restaurant 🍟 Fast Food/Takeaway ⚞ Battery charging
⚒ Baby care ↯ Motorvan service point
ABBREVIATIONS: BH-bank hols-bank holidays Etr-Easter Whit-Whitsun dep-departure fr-from hrs-hours m-mile mdnt-midnight rdbt-roundabout rs-restricted service wk-week
wknd-weekend ⊗ No credit cards ⊗ No dogs   See page 7 for details of the AA Camping Card Scheme

Isle of Wight

Generations of visitors to the Isle of Wight consistently say the same thing, that to go there is akin to stepping back to the 1950s and '60s. The pace of life is still gentle and unhurried and the place continues to exude that familiar salty tang of the sea we all remember from childhood, when bucket and spade holidays were an integral part of growing up. Small and intimate – just 23 miles by 13 miles – the Isle of Wight is just the place to get away-from-it-all.

Being an island, it has a unique and distinctive identity. With its mild climate, long hours of sunshine and exuberant architecture, the Isle of Wight has something of a continental flavour. In the summer the place understandably gets very busy, especially during Cowes week in August – a key date in the country's sporting calendar. Elsewhere, seaside towns such as Ventnor, Shanklin and Sandown are popular during the season for their many and varied attractions.

● Ventnor

Variety is the key on this delightful and much-loved holiday island. Queen Victoria made the place fashionable and popular when she and Prince Albert chose it as the setting for their summer home, Osborne House, and the island has never looked back. In recent years the steady increase in tourism has ushered in many new visitor attractions to meet the demands of the ▶

Coastal path, Bembridge

● Racing off Cowes

late 20th and early 21st centuries, but there are still the perennial old favourites. The Needles, the iconic series of chalk stacks, is a classic example, and just about everyone who has visited over the years can recall buying tubes of sand from nearby Alum Bay – a multi-coloured mix of white quartz, red iron oxide and yellow limonite.

Walking and Cycling

Despite the large numbers of summer visitors, there are still plenty of places on the island where you can be alone and savour its tranquillity. The 65-mile Isle of Wight Coast Path allows walkers to appreciate the natural beauty and diversity of its coastal scenery. Much of the path in the southern half of the island is a relatively undemanding walk over sweeping chalk downs, and beyond Freshwater Bay the coast is often remote and essentially uninhabited. Completing the whole trail or just part of it is the ideal way to discover the island's coastline without the aggravation. Mostly, the route is over cliff-top paths, tracks, sea walls and esplanades. Nearly 40 miles of it is beside the coast, though the inland stretches are never far from the sea. However, beware of erosion and expect to find the path diverted in places. The Isle of Wight's hinterland may lack the sea views but the scenery is no less appealing.

Here walkers can explore a vast and well publicised network of paths that reach the very heart of the island. In all, the Isle of Wight has more than 500 miles of public rights of way and more than half the island is recognised as an Area of Outstanding Natural Beauty.

For cyclists there is also a good deal of choice. The Round the Island Cycle Route runs for 49 miles and takes advantage of quiet roads and lanes. There are starting points at Yarmouth, Cowes and Ryde and the route is waymarked with official Cycle Route blue signs.

Festivals and Events

Among a host of festivals and events held on the Isle of Wight throughout the year are:-

- The Real Ale Festival in May
- The Isle of Wight Walking Festival in May and the Isle of Wight Weekend Walking Festival held in October
- The Cycling Festival in September
- The Garlic Festival in August

For more information visit
www.islandbreaks.co.uk

WIGHT, ISLE OF

See Walk 11 in the Walks & Cycle Rides section at the end of the guide

BEMBRIDGE

See Whitecliff Bay

COWES
Map 5 SZ49

Places to visit

Osborne House, OSBORNE HOUSE 01983 200022 www.english-heritage.org.uk

Bembridge Windmill, BEMBRIDGE 01983 873945 www.nationaltrust.org.uk/isleofwight

Great for kids: Robin Hill Country Park, ARRETON 01983 527352 www.robin-hill.com

 85% Thorness Bay Holiday Park (SZ448928)

Thorness PO31 8NJ
☎ 01983 523109 📠 01983 822213
e-mail: holidaysales.thornessbay@park-resorts.com
dir: On A3054 towards Yarmouth, 1st right after BMW garage, signed Thorness Bay

🚐 🚏 Å

Open Apr–1 Nov

Last arrival anytime Last departure 10.00hrs

Splendid views of The Solent can be enjoyed from this rural park located just outside Cowes. A footpath leads directly to the coast, while on site there is an all-weather sports court, entertainment clubs for children, and cabaret shows, and a bar for all the family. There are 23 serviced pitches, in the separate touring area, with TV boosters. 148 acre site. 124 touring pitches. 21 hardstandings. 8 seasonal pitches. Caravan pitches. Motorhome pitches. Tent pitches. 560 statics.

AA Pubs & Restaurants nearby: The Folly, Cowes 01983 297171

Leisure: 🏊 ⛰ 🛝 🎱 🎵

Facilities: 🛁 🚿 ⚡ ✂ 🦽 🕿 🛍 🔥 📶 📺 ♻ ℹ

Services: 🚐 🔧 🛢 🧺 🚾 🍽 🛒 ↻

Within 3 miles: 🎣 🛥 🏪 🛍

Notes: Dogs must be kept on leads. Water slide.

FRESHWATER
Map 5 SZ38

Places to visit

Dimbola Lodge Museum, FRESHWATER 01983 756814 www.dimbola.co.uk

Great for kids: Blackgang Chine Fantasy Park, BLACKGANG 01983 730330 www.blackgangchine.com

▶▶▶▶ **84% Heathfield Farm Camping** (SZ335879)

Heathfield Rd PO40 9SH
☎ 01983 407822
e-mail: web@heathfieldcamping.co.uk
dir: 2m W from Yarmouth ferry port on A3054, left to Heathfield Rd, entrance 200yds on right

✱ 🚐 £10.50–£18.50 🚏 £10.50–£18.50
Å £10.50–£18.50

Open May–Sep

Last arrival 20.00hrs Last departure 11.00hrs

A very good quality park with friendly and welcoming staff. There are lovely views across the Solent to Hurst Castle. The toilet facilities, the amenities, which include an excellent new backpackers' area, and the very well maintained grounds, make this park now amongst the best on the island. 10 acre site. 60 touring pitches. Caravan pitches. Motorhome pitches. Tent pitches.

AA Pubs & Restaurants nearby: Red Lion, Freshwater 01983 754925

Leisure: ⚽

Facilities: 🚿 ⚡ 🦽 🔥 📶 ♻ ℹ

Services: 🚐 🛢 ↻

Within 3 miles: 🎣 🛥 🏪 🛍 ↻

Notes: Family camping only.

NEWBRIDGE

Places to visit

Brighstone Shop and Museum, BRIGHSTONE 01983 740689 www.nationaltrust.org.uk/isleofwight

Great for kids: Yarmouth Castle, YARMOUTH 01983 760678 www.english-heritage.org.uk

LEISURE: 🏊 Indoor swimming pool 🏊 Outdoor swimming pool ⛰ Children's playground 🛝 Kid's club 🎾 Tennis court 🎱 Games room 📺 Separate TV room ⛳ 9/18 hole golf course 🛥 Boats for hire 🎬 Cinema 🎵 Entertainment 🎣 Fishing ⛳ Mini golf 🏄 Watersports 🏋 Gym ⚽ Sports field Spa ↻ Stables
FACILITIES: 🛁 Bath 🚿 Shower ⚡ Electric shaver 🧴 Hairdryer ✱ Ice Pack Facility 🦽 Disabled facilities 🕿 Public telephone 🛍 Shop on site or within 200yds 🏪 Mobile shop (calls at least 5 days a week) 🔥 BBQ area 🌲 Picnic area 📶 Wi-fi 💻 Internet access ♻ Recycling ℹ Tourist info 🐕 Dog exercise area

NEWBRIDGE Map 5 SZ48

PREMIER PARK

►►►►► 92% The Orchards Holiday Caravan Park *(SZ411881)*

Main Rd PO41 0TS

☎ 01983 531331 & 531350 01983 531666

e-mail: info@orchards-holiday-park.co.uk

web: www.orchards-holiday-park.co.uk

dir: *4m E of Yarmouth; 6m W of Newport on B3401. Take A3054 from Yarmouth, after 3m turn right at Horse & Groom Inn. Follow signs to Newbridge. Entrance opposite Post Office*

Open 11 Feb-2 Jan (rs Nov-Feb takeaway, shop, outdoor pool closed)

Last arrival 23.00hrs Last departure 11.00hrs

A really excellent, well-managed park set in a peaceful village location amid downs and meadowland, with glorious downland views. Pitches are terraced and offer a good provision of hardstandings, including water serviced pitches. There is a high quality facility centre offering excellent spacious showers and family rooms, plus there is access for disabled visitors to all site facilities and disabled toilets. The park has indoor and outdoor swimming pools, a shop, takeaway and licensed coffee shop. 15 acre site. 171 touring pitches. 74 hardstandings. Caravan pitches. Motorhome pitches. Tent pitches. 65 statics.

AA Pubs & Restaurants nearby: New Inn, Shalfleet 01983 531314

Leisure:

Facilities:

Services:

Within 3 miles:

Notes: No cycling. Dogs must be kept on leads. Petanque, table tennis room, poolside coffee shop/café.

NEWPORT Map 5 SZ58

Places to visit

Carisbrooke Castle, CARISBROOKE 01983 522107 www.english-heritage.org.uk

Osborne House, OSBORNE HOUSE 01983 200022 www.english-heritage.org.uk

►►► 74% Riverside Paddock Camp Site *(SZ503911)*

Dodnor Ln PO30 5TE

☎ 01983 821367 & 07962 400533

e-mail: enquiries@riversidepaddock.co.uk

dir: *From Newport take dual carriageway towards Cowes. At 1st rdbt take 3rd exit, immediately left at next rdbt. Follow until road meets National Cycle Route. Site on left*

* £11-£16 £11-£16 £11-£16

Open all year

Last arrival 20.00hrs Last departure 11.00hrs

Although fairly close to Newport this quiet campsite offers a really peaceful environment and has direct access to the national cycle route from Newport to Cowes.The Medina River with its riverside walks is also nearby. The park has improved toilet facilities (two fully serviced unisex cubicles), good hardstandings many with electric plus spotless facilities. The location of the park makes it perfect for people who like to walk or to ride their bikes. 8 acre site. 28 touring pitches. 18 hardstandings. Caravan pitches. Motorhome pitches. Tent pitches. 5 tipis.

AA Pubs & Restaurants nearby: White Lion, Arreton 01983 528479

Facilities: Wi-fi

Services:

Within 3 miles:

Notes: Adults only. No loud music, no generators. Dogs must be kept on leads.

RYDE Map 5 SZ59

Places to visit

Nunwell House & Gardens, BRADING 01983 407240

Bembridge Windmill, BEMBRIDGE 01983 873945 www.nationaltrust.org.uk/isleofwight

Great for kids: Robin Hill Country Park, ARRETON 01983 527352 www.robin-hill.com

PREMIER PARK

►►►►► 91% Whitefield Forest Touring Park *(SZ604893)*

Brading Rd PO33 1QL

☎ 01983 617069

e-mail: pat&louise@whitefieldforest.co.uk

web: www.whitefieldforest.co.uk

dir: *From Ryde follow A3055 towards Brading, after Tesco rdbt site 0.5m on left*

* £15-£20.80

Open Etr-Oct

Last arrival 21.00hrs Last departure 11.00hrs

This park is beautifully laid out in Whitefield Forest, and offers a wide variety of pitches, all of which have electricity. It offers excellent modern facilities, which are spotlessly clean. The park takes great care in retaining the natural beauty of the forest, and is a haven for wildlife, including the red squirrel, which may be seen on the park's nature walk. 23 acre site. 80 touring pitches. 20 hardstandings. Caravan pitches. Motorhome pitches. Tent pitches.

AA Pubs & Restaurants nearby: Ryde Castle, Ryde 01983 563755

Boathouse, Seaview 01983 810616

Leisure:

Facilities: Wi-fi

Services:

Within 3 miles:

RYDE *continued*

►►► 84% *Roebeck Camping and Caravan Park* (SZ581903)

Gatehouse Rd, Upton Cross PO33 4BP
☎ **01983 611475 & 07930 992080**
e-mail: info@roebeck-farm.co.uk
dir: *Right from Fishbourne ferry terminal (west of Ryde). At lights left onto A3054 towards Ryde. In outskirts straight on at 'All Through Traffic' sign. At end of Pellhurst Rd right into Upton Rd. Site 50yds beyond mini-rdbt*

Open Apr-Nov

A quiet park in a country setting on the outskirts of Ryde offering very nice facilities, especially for campers, including an excellent dishwashing/ kitchen cabin. The unique, ready-erected tipis, which are available for hire, add to the ambience of the site. There is also an excellent fishing lake. 4 acre site. 37 touring pitches. Caravan pitches. Tent pitches.

AA Pubs & Restaurants nearby: Ryde Castle, Ryde 01983 563755

Boathouse, Seaview 01983 810616

Facilities: ⬆🅿✳🎋🐕 📶
Services: 🗲🔔
Within 3 miles: ⬇🛶🎣◎♨🏦🛒U

ST HELENS   Map 5 SZ68

Places to visit

Brading The Experience, BRADING 01983 407286
www.bradingtheexperience.co.uk

Bembridge Windmill, BEMBRIDGE 01983 873945
www.nationaltrust.org.uk/isleofwight

Great for kids: Lilliput Antique Doll & Toy Museum, BRADING 01983 407231
www.lilliputmuseum.org.uk

86% *Nodes Point Holiday Park* (SZ636897)

Nodes Rd PO33 1YA
☎ **01983 872401 🖨 01983 874696**
e-mail: gm.nodespoint@park-resorts.com
dir: *From Ryde take B3330 signed Seaview/ Puckpool. At junct for Puckpool bear right. 1m past Road Side Inn in Nettlestone, site on left*

Open Apr-Oct

Last arrival 21.00hrs Last departure 10.00hrs

A well-equipped holiday centre on an elevated position overlooking Bembridge Bay with direct access to the beach. The touring area is mostly sloping with some terraces. Activities are organised for youngsters, and there is entertainment for the whole family. Buses pass the main entrance road. The touring area has very well appointed, ready-erected tents

---

for hire. 16 acre site. 150 touring pitches. 4 hardstandings. 4 seasonal pitches. Caravan pitches. Motorhome pitches. Tent pitches. 195 statics.

Nodes Point Holiday Park

AA Pubs & Restaurants nearby: Windmill Inn, Bembridge 01983 872875

Leisure: 🏊♨🎮🛝🎵
Facilities: ⬆🐈◎🅿✳🐾🕐🔔🛁🎋🐕📶🖥
Services: 🗲🔔🚐⊘🍽🛒
Within 3 miles: ⬇🛶🎣◎♨🏦🛒U

see advert below

SANDOWN

Places to visit

Nunwell House & Gardens, BRADING 01983 407240

Bembridge Windmill, BEMBRIDGE 01983 873945
www.nationaltrust.org.uk/isleofwight

Great for kids: Dinosaur Isle, SANDOWN 01983 404344 www.dinosaurisle.com

---

LEISURE: 🏊 Indoor swimming pool 🏊 Outdoor swimming pool 🛝 Children's playground 🛝 Kid's club 🎾 Tennis court 🎮 Games room 📺 Separate TV room ⬇ 9/18 hole golf course 🛶 Boats for hire 🎬 Cinema 🎵 Entertainment 🎣 Fishing ◎ Mini golf ♨ Watersports 🏋 Gym ⚽ Sports field **Spa** U Stables
FACILITIES: 🛁 Bath 🚿 Shower ⊖ Electric shaver 🅿 Hairdryer ✳ Ice Pack Facility 🕐 Disabled facilities 🔔 Public telephone 🛒 Shop on site or within 200yds 🏪 Mobile shop (calls at least 5 days a week) 🍖 BBQ area 🎋 Picnic area 📶 Wi-fi 🖥 Internet access ♻ Recycling ⊙ Tourist info 🐕 Dog exercise area

SANDOWN — Map 5 SZ58

▶▶▶▶ 78% Old Barn Touring Park (SZ573833)

GOLD

Cheverton Farm, Newport Rd, Apse Heath PO36 9PJ
☎ 01983 866414 📠 01983 865988
e-mail: oldbarn@weltinet.com
dir: On A3056 from Newport, site on left after Apse Heath rdbt

* 🚐 £15-£19.50 🚃 £15-£19.50 ▲ £15-£19.50

Open May-Sep

Last arrival 21.00hrs Last departure noon

A terraced site with good quality facilities, bordering onto open farmland. The spacious pitches are secluded and fully serviced, and there is a decent, modern toilet block. 5 acre site. 60 touring pitches. 9 hardstandings. 6 seasonal pitches. Caravan pitches. Motorhome pitches. Tent pitches.

AA Pubs & Restaurants nearby: Windmill Inn, Bembridge 01983 872875

Leisure: 🄰 🔍 ⬜

Facilities: 🌂 ⊙ 🅿 ✳ 🕭 & ⚓ ♲ ❼

Services: 🔌 🅱 🛢 ⊘ 🚽 ⛟ ⚡

Within 3 miles: ⌚ ⛟ 🖉 ◎ ≽ 🅱 🅱 U

Notes: Dogs must be kept on leads.

▶ 78% Queenbower Dairy Caravan Park (SZ567846)

Alverstone Rd, Queenbower PO36 0NZ
☎ 01983 403840 📠 01983 409671
e-mail: queenbowerdairy@aol.com
dir: 3m N of Sandown from A3056 right into Alverstone Rd, site 1m on left

* 🚐 £6.50-£10 🚃 £6.50-£10 ▲ £6.50-£10

Open May-Oct

A small site with basic amenities that will appeal to campers keen to escape the crowds and the busy larger sites. The enthusiastic owners keep the facilities very clean. 2.5 acre site. 20 touring pitches. Caravan pitches. Motorhome pitches. Tent pitches.

AA Pubs & Restaurants nearby: Windmill Inn, Bembridge 01983 872875

Facilities: ✳ 🅱

Services: 🔌 ⚡

Within 3 miles: ⌚ ⛟ 🖉 ◎ ≽ 🅱 🅱

Notes: 🚫 Dogs must be exercised off site.

SHANKLIN — Map 5 SZ58

Places to visit

Shanklin Chine, SHANKLIN 01983 866432
www.shanklinchine.co.uk

Ventnor Botanic Garden, VENTNOR 01983 855397 www.botanic.co.uk

Great for kids: Dinosaur Isle, SANDOWN 01983 404344 www.dinosaurisle.com

84% Lower Hyde Holiday Park (SZ575819)

SILVER

Landguard Rd PO37 7LL
☎ 01983 866131 📠 01983 862532
e-mail: holidaysales.lowerhyde@park-resorts.com
dir: From Fishbourne ferry terminal follow A3055 to Shanklin. Site signed just past lake

🚐 🚃 ▲

Open Apr-Oct

Last arrival anytime Last departure 10.00hrs

A popular holiday park on the outskirts of Shanklin, close to the sandy beaches. There is an outdoor swimming pool and plenty of organised activities for youngsters of all ages. In the evening there is a choice of family entertainment. The touring facilities are located in a quiet area away from the main complex, with good views over the downs. 65 acre site. 148 touring pitches. 25 hardstandings. Caravan pitches. Motorhome pitches. Tent pitches. 313 statics.

AA Pubs & Restaurants nearby: Bonchurch Inn, Bonchurch 01983 852611

The Taverners, Godshill 01983 840707

Leisure: ≋ ≈ 🄰 ⬇ ⚽ ⊙ ⬜ ♫

Facilities: 🌂 ⊙ 🅿 ✳ 🕭 & ⊙ 🅱 WiFi 🖥

Services: 🔌 🅱 🛢 ⊘ 🍴 ⛟

Within 3 miles: ⌚ ⛟ H 🖉 ◎ ≽ 🅱 🅱 U

Notes: No cars by caravans. Water flume.

▶▶▶ 84% Ninham Country Holidays (SZ573825)

Ninham PO37 7PL
☎ 01983 864243
e-mail: office@ninham-holidays.co.uk
dir: Signed from A3056 (Newport to Sandown road)

🚐 £15.50-£24 🚃 £13-£24 ▲ £12-£22

Open May Day BH-5 Sep (rs Etr-1 Oct reception open)

Enjoying a lofty rural position with fine country views, this delightful, spacious park occupies two separate, well-maintained areas in a country park setting near the sea and beach. There's a good outdoor swimming pool. 12 acre site. 98 touring pitches. 4 hardstandings. Caravan pitches. Motorhome pitches. Tent pitches.

AA Pubs & Restaurants nearby: Bonchurch Inn, Bonchurch 01983 852611

The Taverners, Godshill 01983 840707

Leisure: ≋ 🄰 ⊙ 🔍

Facilities: 🌂 ⊙ ✳ 🕭 🅱 🚻 WiFi ♲ ❼

Services: 🔌 🅱 🛢 ⊘ ⚡

Within 3 miles: ⌚ ⛟ 🖉 ◎ ≽ 🅱 🅱 U

Notes: Swimming pool & coarse fishing rules apply. Dogs must be kept on leads. Fully serviced pitches. Late night/arrival area available.

NEW ▶▶▶ 81% Landguard Camping (SZ580825)

SILVER

Manor Rd PO37 7PJ
☎ 01983 863100
e-mail: landguard@park-resorts.com
dir: A3056 towards Sandown. After Morrisons on left, turn right into Whitecross Ln. Follow brown signs to site

🚐 🚃 ▲

Open Apr-Oct

Last arrival noon Last departure 10.00hrs

Now owned by Park Resorts, this peaceful and secluded park offers good touring facilities, including a refurbished toilet block. Customers here also have the benefit of using the swimming pool and entertainment facilities at Lower Hyde Holiday Park nearby. 141 touring pitches. Caravan pitches. Motorhome pitches. Tent pitches.

SERVICES: 🔌 Electric hook up 🅱 Launderette 🍺 Licensed bar 🛢 Calor Gas ⊘ Camping Gaz 🚽 Toilet fluid 🍴 Café/Restaurant 🍟 Fast Food/Takeaway 🔋 Battery charging 🍼 Baby care ⛟ Motorvan service point
ABBREVIATIONS: BH-bank hols-bank holidays Etr-Easter Whit-Whitsun dep-departure fr-from hrs-hours m-mile mdnt-midnight rdbt-roundabout rs-restricted service wk-week wknd-weekend 🚫 No credit cards ⊗ No dogs
See page 7 for details of the AA Camping Card Scheme

TOTLAND BAY — Map 5 SZ38

Places to visit

Dimbola Lodge Museum, FRESHWATER 01983 756814 www.dimbola.co.uk

Mottistone Manor Garden, MOTTISTONE 01983 741302 www.nationaltrust.org.uk/isleofwight

Great for kids: Yarmouth Castle, YARMOUTH 01983 760678 www.english-heritage.org.uk

▶▶▶ **76% Stoats Farm Caravan & Camping** *(SZ324865)*

PO39 0HE
☎ 01983 755258 & 753416
e-mail: david@stoats-farm.co.uk
dir: *On Alum Bay road, 1.5m from Freshwater & 0.75m from Totland*

* 🚐 £11-£16 🚐 £11-£16 ▲ £10-£12

Open Apr-Oct

A friendly, personally run site in a quiet country setting close to Alum Bay, Tennyson Down and The Needles. It has good laundry and shower facilities, and the shop, although small, is well stocked. Popular with families, walkers and cyclists, it makes the perfect base for campers wishing to explore this part of the island. 10 acre site. 100 touring pitches. Caravan pitches. Motorhome pitches. Tent pitches.

AA Pubs & Restaurants nearby: Red Lion, Freshwater 01983 754925

Facilities: 🔦⊙☂☀🅹⦵🔥🐕🔤ℹ️
Services: 🔌🔷🛒🚮
Within 3 miles: 🎣🚣⚓◎⛵🎱♨️U

Notes: No loud noise after 23.00hrs, no camp fires. Dogs must be kept on leads. Campers' fridge available.

WHITECLIFF BAY — Map 5 SZ68

AA CAMPING CARD SITE

84% Whitecliff Bay Holiday Park *(SZ637862)*

GOLD

Hillway Rd, Bembridge PO35 5PL
☎ 01983 872671   🖨 01983 872941
e-mail: holiday@whitecliff-bay.com
dir: *1m S of Bembridge, signed from B3395 in village*

* 🚐 £6-£31 🚐 £17-£52 ▲ fr £4

Open Mar-Oct

Last arrival 21.00hrs Last departure 10.30hrs

A large seaside complex on two sites, with camping on one and self-catering chalets and statics on the other. There is an indoor pool with flume and spa pool, and an outdoor pool with a kiddies' pool, a family entertainment club, and plenty of traditional on-site activities including crazy golf, a soft play area and table tennis, plus a restaurant and a choice of bars. Activities include a new 'My Active' programme for all the family in partnership with 'Fit4Life'. The Canvas Village now has 12 ready-erected tents for hire. There is easy access to Whitecliff Beach. Dogs are welcome. 49 acre site. 400 touring pitches. 50 hardstandings. Caravan pitches. Motorhome pitches. Tent pitches. 227 statics. 12 bell tents/yurts.

AA Pubs & Restaurants nearby: Windmill Inn, Bembridge 01983 872875

Leisure: 🏊♨️🎢🎱🔲
Facilities: 🔦⊙☂☀🅹⦵🔥🐕📶💻♻️ℹ️
Services: 🔌🔷🍽🧺🧹🚰🍴🚚🛒🚮
Within 3 miles: 🎣🚣⚓◎⛵🏪🎱U

Notes: Adults & families only. Dogs must be kept on leads. Secluded beach, sauna, sunbed, sports TV lounge, kids' indoor soft play area.

See advert below

LEISURE: 🏊 Indoor swimming pool 🏊 Outdoor swimming pool 🎢 Children's playground 🛝 Kid's club 🎾 Tennis court 🎱 Games room 🔲 Separate TV room 🏌️ 9/18 hole golf course 🚣 Boats for hire 🎬 Cinema 🎵 Entertainment 🎣 Fishing ◎ Mini golf 🏄 Watersports 🏋️ Gym 🏟️ Sports field **Spa** U Stables
FACILITIES: 🛁 Bath 🚿 Shower ⊙ Electric shaver ☂ Hairdryer ☀ Ice Pack Facility 🅹 Disabled facilities ⦵ Public telephone 🏪 Shop on site or within 200yds 🚐 Mobile shop (calls at least 5 days a week) 🔥 BBQ area 🪑 Picnic area 📶 Wi-Fi 💻 Internet access ♻️ Recycling ℹ️ Tourist info 🐕 Dog exercise area

WOOTTON BRIDGE — Map 5 SZ59

Places to visit

Osborne House, OSBORNE HOUSE 01983 200022
www.english-heritage.org.uk

Bembridge Windmill, BEMBRIDGE 01983 873945
www.nationaltrust.org.uk/isleofwight

Great for kids: Robin Hill Country Park,
ARRETON 01983 527352 www.robin-hill.com

►►► 85% Kite Hill Farm Caravan & Camping Park (SZ549906)

Firestone Copse Rd PO33 4LE
☎ 01983 882543 & 883261 📄 01983 883883
e-mail: welcome@kitehillfarm.co.uk
dir: Signed off A3054 at Wootton Bridge, between
Ryde & Newport

🚐 £12-£15 🚗 £12-£15 ▲ £12-£15

Open all year

Last arrival anytime Last departure anytime

The park, on a gently sloping field, is tucked away behind the owners' farm, just a short walk from the village and attractive river estuary. The facilities are excellent and very clean. This park provides a nice relaxing atmosphere to stay on the island. 12.5 acre site. 50 touring pitches. 10 hardstandings. Caravan pitches. Motorhome pitches. Tent pitches.

AA Pubs & Restaurants nearby: The Folly, Cowes
01983 297171

Ryde Castle, Ryde 01983 563755

Leisure: ⚙

Facilities: 🏾☉✳🔥🕙🐕𝑖

Services: 🔌🗑🔋🖼

Within 3 miles: ↕日🖉🛒🗑∪

Notes: Owners must clean up after pets. Dogs must be kept on leads.

WROXALL — Map 5 SZ57

Places to visit

Appuldurcombe House, WROXALL 01983 852484
www.english-heritage.org.uk

Great for kids: Blackgang Chine Fantasy Park,
BLACKGANG 01983 730330
www.blackgangchine.com

►►►► 87% Appuldurcombe Gardens Holiday Park (SZ546804)

Appuldurcombe Rd PO38 3EP
☎ 01983 852597 📄 01983 856225
e-mail: info@appuldurcombegardens.co.uk
dir: From Newport take A3020 towards Shanklin & Ventnor. Through Rookley & Godshill. Right at Whiteley Bank rdbt towards Wroxall village, then follow brown signs

* 🚐 £14.50-£25 🚗 £14.50-£25 ▲ £14.50-£25

Open Mar-Nov

Last arrival 21.00hrs Last departure 11.00hrs

This well-appointed park is set in a unique setting fairly close to the town of Ventnor. It has modern and spotless facilities plus a very tasteful lounge bar and function room. There is an excellent, screened outdoor pool and paddling pool plus café and shop. The site is close to cycle routes and is only 150 yards from the bus stop making it perfect for those with a motorhome or those not wanting to take the car out. Static caravans and apartments are also available for hire. 14 acre site. 100 touring pitches. 2 hardstandings. Caravan pitches. Motorhome pitches. Tent pitches.

AA Pubs & Restaurants nearby: Pond Café,
Ventnor 01983 855666

Leisure: 🏊 ⚙ 🎱

Facilities: 🐄🏾☉✳✂🔥🕙🛝🗑🖼🚻♻𝑖

Services: 🔌🗑🔋🖼T🍽🍔♨⚡

Within 3 miles: ↕🎣日🖉◎↕🗑∪

Notes: No skateboards. Entertainment in high season.

YARMOUTH

See Newbridge

WILTSHIRE

AMESBURY — Map 5 SU14

Places to visit

Stonehenge, STONEHENGE 0870 333 1181
www.english-heritage.org.uk

Heale Gardens, MIDDLE WOODFORD
01722 782504

Great for kids: Wilton House, WILTON [NEAR SALISBURY] 01722 746720
www.wiltonhouse.com

►►► 80% Stonehenge Touring Park (SU061456)

SP3 4SH
☎ 01980 620304
e-mail: stay@stonehengetouringpark.com
dir: From A360 towards Devizes turn right, follow lane, site at bottom of village on right

🚐 £9.50-£15.50 🚗 £9.50-£15.50
▲ £9.50-£26.50

Open all year

Last arrival 21.00hrs Last departure 11.00hrs

A quiet site adjacent to the small village of Orcheston near the centre of Salisbury Plain and four miles from Stonehenge. There's an excellent on-site shop. 2 acre site. 30 touring pitches. 12 hardstandings. Caravan pitches. Motorhome pitches. Tent pitches.

Leisure: ⚙

Facilities: 🏾☉🖉✳🕙🛝🗑🖼♻𝑖

Services: 🔌🗑🔋🖉T⚡

Within 3 miles: 🗑🗑

Notes: No noise after 23.00hrs. Dogs must be kept on leads.

CALNE   Map 4 ST97

Places to visit

Avebury Manor & Garden, AVEBURY
01672 539250 www.nationaltrust.org.uk

Bowood House & Gardens, CALNE 01249 812102
www.bowood.org

Great for kids: Alexander Keiller Museum,
AVEBURY 01672 539250
www.nationaltrust.org.uk

AA CAMPING CARD SITE

►►► 70% Blackland Lakes Holiday & Leisure Centre (ST973687)

Stockley Ln SN11 0NQ
☎ 01249 810943 📠 01249 811346
e-mail: blacklandlakes.bookings@btconnect.com
web: www.blacklandlakes.co.uk
dir: From Calne take A4 E for 1.5m, right at camp
sign. Site 1m on left

🚐 🚍 ▲

Open all year (rs 30 Oct-1 Mar pre-paid bookings
only)

Last arrival 22.00hrs Last departure noon

A rural site surrounded by the North and West
Downs. The park is divided into several paddocks
separated by hedges, trees and fences, and there
are two well-stocked carp fisheries for the angling
enthusiast. There are some excellent walks close
by, and the interesting market town of Devizes is
just a few miles away. 15 acre site. 180 touring
pitches. 25 hardstandings. Caravan pitches.
Motorhome pitches. Tent pitches.

AA Pubs & Restaurants nearby: Red Lion Inn,
Lacock 01249 730456

George Inn, Lacock 01249 730263 Rising Sun,
Lacock 01249 730363

Leisure: ⚙
Facilities: 🏕 ⊙ 🅿 ✳ ♿ 🛢 🏪 🌂
Services: 🔌 🗑 🔋 🗜 🚽 ♨ ⬇
Within 3 miles: ♨ ✏ 🏪 🛢 ∪
Notes: Wildfowl sanctuary, cycle trail.

LACOCK   Map 4 ST96

Places to visit

Lacock Abbey, Fox Talbot Museum & Village,
LACOCK 01249 730459
www.nationaltrust.org.uk/lacock

Corsham Court, CORSHAM 01249 701610
www.corsham-court.co.uk

►►► 87% Piccadilly Caravan Park

(ST913683)

Folly Lane West SN15 2LP
☎ 01249 730260 📠 01249 730260
e-mail: piccadillylacock@aol.com
dir: 4m S of Chippenham just past Lacock. Exit
A350 signed Gastard. Site 300yds on left

🚐 £17-£19 🚍 £17-£19 ▲ £17-£22.50

Open Etr/Apr-Oct

Last arrival 21.00hrs Last departure noon

A peaceful, pleasant site, well established and
beautifully laid-out, close to the village of Lacock.
Facilities and grounds are immaculately kept, and
there is very good screening. A section of the park
has been developed to provide spacious pitches,
especially for tents, although the toilet block has
yet to be completed. 2.5 acre site. 41 touring
pitches. 12 hardstandings. Caravan pitches.
Motorhome pitches. Tent pitches.

AA Pubs & Restaurants nearby: Red Lion Inn,
Lacock 01249 730456

George Inn, Lacock 01249 730263 Rising Sun,
Lacock 01249 730363

Leisure: ⚙ ♟
Facilities: 🏕 ⊙ 🅿 ✳ 🕐 🌂 ♻ ℹ
Services: 🔌 🗑 🔋 🗜 ♨
Within 3 miles: ♨ 🎬 ✏ 🛢 🛢 ∪
Notes: ⊗ Dogs must be kept on leads.

LANDFORD   Map 5 SU21

Places to visit

Furzey Gardens, MINSTEAD 023 8081 2464
www.furzey-gardens.org

Mottisfont Abbey & Garden,
MOTTISFONT 01794 340757
www.nationaltrust.org.uk/mottisfontabbey

Great for kids: Paultons Park, OWER
023 8081 4442 www.paultonspark.co.uk

►►► 78% Greenhill Farm Caravan & Camping Park (SU266183)

Greenhill Farm, New Rd SP5 2AZ
☎ 01794 324117
e-mail: info@greenhillholidays.co.uk
dir: M27 junct 2, A36 towards Salisbury, approx
3m after Hants/Wilts border, (Shoe Inn pub on
right, BP garage on left) take next left into New
Rd, signed Nomansland, 0.75m on left

* 🚐 £17-£24 🚍 £17-£24 ▲ £13.50-£24

Open all year

Last arrival 21.30hrs Last departure 11.00hrs

A tranquil, well-landscaped park hidden away in
unspoilt countryside on the edge of the New
Forest. Pitches overlooking the fishing lake include
hardstandings and are for adults only. The other
section of the park is for families and includes a
play area and games room. Well placed for visiting
Paulton's Park. 13 acre site. 160 touring pitches.
45 hardstandings. Caravan pitches. Motorhome
pitches. Tent pitches.

AA Pubs & Restaurants nearby: Royal Oak,
Fritham 023 8081 2606

Leisure: ⚙ ♦
Facilities: 🏕 🅿 ✳ 🕐 🛢 🌂
Services: 🔌 🗑 🗜 🚽 ♨ ⬇
Within 3 miles: ♨ ✏ 🏪 🛢 🛢 ∪
Notes: Dogs must be kept on leads. Disposable
BBQs.

MARSTON MEYSEY — Map 5 SU19

Places to visit

Lydiard Park, LYDIARD PARK 01793 770401
www.lydiardpark.org.uk

Buscot Park, BUSCOT 01367 240786
www.buscotpark.com

Great for kids: STEAM - Museum of the Great
Western Railway, SWINDON 01793 466646
www.swindon.gov.uk/steam

AA CAMPING CARD SITE

►► 78% Second Chance Touring Park
(SU140960)

SN6 6SZ
☎ 01285 810675 & 810939
e-mail: secondchancepark@hotmail.co.uk
dir: *A419 from Cirencester towards Swindon, exit
at Latton junct. Through Latton, left at next mini-
rdbt, towards Fairford. Follow signs to site. From
M4 junct 15, A419 towards Fairford, right after
Marston Meysey*

* ⚌ £12-£14 ⚌ £12-£14 ▲ £10-£14

Open Mar-Nov

Last arrival 21.00hrs Last departure noon

An attractive and much improved quiet site
located near the source of the Thames, and well
positioned for those wishing to visit the nearby
Cotswold Water Park. 1.75 acre site. 22 touring
pitches. 10 hardstandings. Caravan pitches.
Motorhome pitches. Tent pitches. 3 statics.

AA Pubs & Restaurants nearby: Masons Arms,
Meysey Hampton 01285 850164

Jolly Tarr, Hannington 01793 762245

Facilities: ↖ ☉ ✳ ⊟ ♻ ✪

Services: ⚌ 🔒

Within 3 miles: 🚴 ⚐

Notes: 🚫 No loud music or parties. Dogs must be
kept on leads. Fishing, river access for canoes.

SALISBURY — Map 5 SU12

Places to visit

Salisbury & South Wiltshire Museum, SALISBURY
01722 332151 www.salisburymuseum.org.com

Salisbury Cathedral, SALISBURY 01722 555120
www.salisburycathedral.org.uk

Great for kids: The Medieval Hall, SALISBURY
01722 412472 www.medieval-hall.co.uk

►►►► 85% Coombe Touring Park
(SU099282)

Race Plain, Netherhampton SP2 8PN
☎ 01722 328451 📠 01722 328451
e-mail: enquiries@coombecaravanpark.co.uk
dir: *A36 onto A3094, 2m SW, site adjacent to
Salisbury racecourse*

⚌ ⚌ ▲

Open 3 Jan-20 Dec (rs Oct-May shop closed)

Last arrival 21.00hrs Last departure noon

A very neat and attractive site adjacent to the
racecourse with views over the downs. The park is
well landscaped with shrubs and maturing trees,
and the very colourful beds are stocked from the
owner's greenhouse. A comfortable park with a
superb luxury toilet block, and four static holiday
homes for hire. 3 acre site. 50 touring pitches.
Caravan pitches. Motorhome pitches. Tent
pitches. 4 statics.

AA Pubs & Restaurants nearby: Haunch of
Venison, Salisbury 01722 411313

Wig & Quill, Salisbury 01722 335665

Facilities: ↖ ☉ ☏ ✳ ⚙ ⏱ 🛢 ✪

Services: ⚌ ▣ ⊘ T ⚓ ⚌

Within 3 miles: 🚴 🛢 ▣ ∪

Notes: 🚫 No disposable BBQs or fires, no mini
motorbikes, no noise between 23.00hrs-07.00hrs.
Dogs must be kept on leads. Children's bathroom.

►►► 78% Alderbury Caravan & Camping Park *(SU197259)*

Southampton Rd, Whaddon SP5 3HB
☎ 01722 710125
e-mail: alderbury@aol.com
dir: *Just off A36, 3m from Salisbury, opposite The
Three Crowns*

* ⚌ £16-£19 ⚌ £16-£19 ▲ £16-£19

Open all year

Last arrival 21.00hrs Last departure 12.30hrs

A pleasant, attractive park set in the village of
Whaddon not far from Salisbury. The small site is
well maintained by friendly owners, and is ideally
positioned near the A36 for overnight stops to and
from the Southampton ferry terminals. 2 acre site.
39 touring pitches. 12 hardstandings. Caravan
pitches. Motorhome pitches. Tent pitches. 1 static.

AA Pubs & Restaurants nearby: Salisbury Seafood
& Steakhouse, Salisbury 01722 417411

The Haunch of Venison, Salisbury 01722 411313

Facilities: ↖ ☉ ✳ ⚙ ✪

Services: ⚌ ▣ 🛢 ⊘ ⚌

Within 3 miles: 🚴 ⚐ ⊟ ⚲ 🛢 ▣ ∪

Notes: No open fires. Dogs must be kept on leads.
Microwave & electric kettle available.

SERVICES: ⚌ Electric hook up ▣ Launderette ⚌ Licensed bar 🛢 Calor Gas ⊘ Camping Gaz T Toilet fluid ⚌ Café/Restaurant ⚌ Fast Food/Takeaway ⚌ Battery charging
⚌ Baby care ⚲ Motorvan service point
ABBREVIATIONS: BH/bank hols-bank holidays Etr-Easter Whit-Whitsun dep-departure fr-from hrs-hours m-mile mdnt-midnight rdbt-roundabout rs-restricted service wk-week
wknd-weekend 🚫 No credit cards 🚫 No dogs
See page 7 for details of the AA Camping Card Scheme

TROWBRIDGE — Map 4 ST85

Places to visit

Great Chalfield Manor and Garden, BRADFORD-ON-AVON 01225 782239 www.nationaltrust.org.uk

The Courts Garden, HOLT 01225 782875 www.nationaltrust.org.uk

Great for kids: Longleat, LONGLEAT 01985 844400 www.longleat.co.uk

►► 74% Stowford Manor Farm

(ST810577)

Stowford, Wingfield BA14 9LH
☎ **01225 752253**
e-mail: stowford1@supanet.com
dir: *From Trowbridge take A366 W towards Radstock. Site on left in 3m*

* ⊞ £12-£14 ⊞ £12-£14 ▲ £12-£14

Open Etr-Oct

A very simple farm site set on the banks of the River Frome behind the farm courtyard. The owners are friendly and relaxed, and the park enjoys a similarly comfortable ambience. 1.5 acre site. 15 touring pitches. Caravan pitches. Motorhome pitches. Tent pitches.

AA Pubs & Restaurants nearby: Red or White, Trowbridge 01225 781666

George Inn, Norton St Philip 01373 834224

Facilities: ♠⊙❄⊀⊀♻

Services: ♨⊠⊞

Within 3 miles: ⌘⊀⌘⊀🛇🛈U

Notes: No open fires. Dogs must be kept on leads. Fishing, boating, swimming in river.

WESTBURY — Map 4 ST85

Places to visit

Great Chalfield Manor and Garden, BRADFORD-ON-AVON 01225 782239 www.nationaltrust.org.uk

The Courts Garden, HOLT 01225 782875 www.nationaltrust.org.uk

AA CAMPING CARD SITE

►►►► 83% Brokerswood Country Park *(ST836523)*

GOLD

Brokerswood BA13 4EH
☎ **01373 822238** ⊟ **01373 858474**
e-mail: info@brokerswoodcountrypark.co.uk
web: www.brokerswoodcountrypark.co.uk
dir: *M4 junct 17, S on A350. Right at Yarnbrook to Rising Sun pub at North Bradley, left at rdbt. Left on bend approaching Southwick, 2.5m, site on right*

⊞ £12-£32 ⊞ £12-£32 ▲ £12-£32

Open all year

Last arrival 21.30hrs Last departure 11.00hrs

A popular park on the edge of an 80-acre woodland park with nature trails and fishing lakes. An adventure playground offers plenty of fun for all ages, and there is a miniature railway, an indoor play centre, and a café. There are high quality toilet facilities and fully-equipped, ready-erected tents are available for hire. 5 acre site. 69 touring pitches. 21 hardstandings. Caravan pitches. Motorhome pitches. Tent pitches.

AA Pubs & Restaurants nearby: Full Moon, Rudge 01373 830936

Bell Inn, Great Cheverell 01380 813277

Leisure: ⚠

Facilities: ⊁♠⊙🅟❄⊱🔟🎄⊀♻🛈

Services: ♨⊠⊞🔟⊞⊘🔟⊞♻⊍

Within 3 miles: ⌘🛈

Notes: Families only.

WORCESTERSHIRE

HONEYBOURNE — Map 10 SP14

Places to visit

Kiftsgate Court Garden, MICKLETON 01386 438777 www.kiftsgate.co.uk

Hidcote Manor Garden, MICKLETON 01386 438333 www.nationaltrust.org.uk/hidcote

Great for kids: Anne Hathaway's Cottage, SHOTTERY 01789 201844 www.shakespeare.org.uk

PREMIER PARK

►►►►► 80% Ranch Caravan Park *(SP113444)*

GOLD

Station Rd WR11 7PR
☎ **01386 830744** ⊟ **01386 833503**
e-mail: enquiries@ranch.co.uk
dir: *Through village x-rds towards Bidford, site 400mtrs on left*

* ⊞ £22-£26 ⊞ £22-£26

Open Mar-Nov (rs Mar-May & Sep-Nov swimming pool closed, shorter club hours)

Last arrival 20.00hrs Last departure noon

An attractive and well-run park set amidst farmland in the Vale of Evesham and landscaped with trees and bushes. Tourers have their own excellent facilities in two locations, and the use of an outdoor heated swimming pool in peak season. There is also a licensed club serving meals. Please note that this site does not accept tents. 12 acre site. 120 touring pitches. 43 hardstandings. Caravan pitches. Motorhome pitches. 218 statics

AA Pubs & Restaurants nearby: Fleece Inn, Bretforton 01386 831173

Ebrington Arms, Ebrington 01386 593223

LEISURE: 🏊 Indoor swimming pool 🏊 Outdoor swimming pool ⚠ Children's playground 🛶 Kid's club 🎾 Tennis court 🎱 Games room 📺 Separate TV room ⛳ 9/18 hole golf course ⛵ Boats for hire 🎬 Cinema 🎭 Entertainment 🎣 Fishing 🔵 Mini golf 🌊 Watersports 🏋 Gym 🏟 Sports field **Spa** U Stables
FACILITIES: 🛁 Bath 🚿 Shower ⊙ Electric shaver 🅟 Hairdryer ❄ Ice Pack Facility ⬥ Disabled facilities 🕿 Public telephone 🛒 Shop on site or within 200yds 🚐 Mobile shop (calls at least 5 days a week) 🍖 BBQ area 🌲 Picnic area 🛜 Wi-fi 💻 Internet access ♻ Recycling 🛈 Tourist info 🐕 Dog exercise area

Leisure: ⚓ ⛳ ⚠ ◎ ✎ ▭ ♫ Spa
Facilities: ⚘ ☉ ⚿ ✳ ᴥ ◔ ⓢ ♨ ♻ ❶
Services: ⊞ ⬙ ⬛ ▥ ∅ ⊤ ⑩ ⛟ 🖁 ⬱ ↯
Within 3 miles: ↓ ✐ ⬙ ⬚ U

Notes: No unaccompanied minors. Dogs must be kept on leads.

WORCESTER   Map 10 SO85

Places to visit

City Museum & Art Gallery, WORCESTER 01905 25371 www.museumsworcestershire.org.uk

The Greyfriars, WORCESTER 01905 23571 www.nationaltrust.org.uk

Great for kids: West Midland Safari & Leisure Park, BEWDLEY 01299 402114 www.wmsp.co.uk

---

▶▶▶ 85% *Peachley Leisure Touring Park (SO807576)*

Peachley Ln, Lower Broadheath WR2 6QX
☎ **01905 641309** 🖷 **01905 641854**
e-mail: info@peachleyleisure.com
dir: *M5 junct 7, A44 (Worcester ring road) towards Leominster. Exit at sign for Elgar's Birthplace Museum. Pass museum, at x-roads turn right. In 0.75m at T-junct turn left. Park signed on right*

🚐 🚙 ⅄

Open all year

Last arrival 21.30hrs Last departure noon

The park is set in its own area in the grounds of Peachley Farm. It has all hardstanding and fully-serviced pitches. There are two fishing lakes, and a really excellent quad bike course. The park provides a peaceful haven, and is an excellent base from which to explore the area, which includes the Elgar Museum. 8 acre site. 82 touring pitches. 82 hardstandings. Caravan pitches. Motorhome pitches. Tent pitches.

AA Pubs & Restaurants nearby: The Talbot, Knightwick 01886 821235

Bear & Ragged Staff, Bransford 01886 833399

Facilities: ⚘ ☉ ✳ ᴥ ♨

Services: ⊞ ⬙ ⑩

Within 3 miles: ⅄ 🎱 ✐ ⬱ ⬙ ⬚ U

Notes: No skateboards, no riding of motorbikes or scooters.

Yorkshire

There is nowhere in the British Isles quite like Yorkshire. By far the largest county, and with such scenic and cultural diversity, it is almost a country within a country. For sheer scale, size and grandeur, there is nowhere to beat it.

Much of it in the spectacular Pennines, Yorkshire is a land of castles, grand houses, splendid rivers, tumbling becks and historic market towns.

But it is the natural, unrivalled beauty of the Yorkshire Dales and the North York Moors that captures the heart and leaves a lasting impression. Surely no-one could fail to be charmed by the majestic landscapes of these two much-loved National Parks.

● Flamborough Head

The Dales

Wherever you venture in the Yorkshire Dales, stunning scenery awaits you; remote emerald green valleys, limestone scars and timeless villages of charming stone cottages. The Dales, beautifully represented in the books of James Herriot, are characterised and complemented by their rivers – the Wharfe, Ribble, Ure, Nidd and Swale among them.

Touring this glorious region reveals the broad sweep of Wensleydale, the delights of Arkengarthdale and the charming little villages of ▶

● Hutton-le-Hole   ● Digging at Filey Beach

Swaledale. There is also the spectacular limestone country of the western Dales – the land of the Three Peaks. Perhaps here, more than anywhere else in the area, there is a true sense of space and freedom. This is adventure country – a place of endless views and wild summits.

The Moors

To the east lies another sprawling landscape – the North York Moors. This is where the purple of the heather gives way to the grey expanse of the North Sea. Covering 554 square miles (1,436km) and acknowledged as an internationally important site for upland breeding birds, the North York Moors National Park is a vast, intricately-woven tapestry of heather moorland, narrow valleys, rolling dales, broad-leaved woodland and extensive conifer forests. Few places in Britain offer such variety and breadth of terrain.

Extending for 36 miles (58km), the North Yorkshire and Cleveland Heritage Coast forms the Park's eastern boundary. The popular holiday resorts of Whitby and Scarborough are the two largest settlements on this stretch of coastline, which is rich in fossils and minerals and protected for its outstanding natural beauty and historic interest.

Further south

To the south of the North York Moors is the beautiful city of York, its history stretching back 2,000 years. At its heart stands the minster, constructed between 1220 and 1470 and the largest medieval church in northern Europe. There is so much to see and do in this ancient, vibrant city that you can easily lose track of time.

Farther south, despite the relics of the county's industrial heritage, is Yorkshire's magical *Last of the Summer Wine* country. The BBC's long-running and much-loved comedy series, *Last of the Summer Wine*, ran for 37 years and was filmed in and around the town of Holmfirth, near Huddersfield.

● Ribblehead Viaduct

Walking and Cycling

Not surprisingly, Yorkshire offers a myriad of circular walks and long-distance trails throughout the county. For the more ambitious walker there is the Pennine Way, which runs through Yorkshire from top to bottom, from the Scottish Borders as far south as Derbyshire. The 81-mile (130km) Dales Way, another popular route, is a perfect way to explore the magnificent scenery of Wharfedale, Ribblesdale and Dentdale, while the 50-mile (80km) Calderdale Way offers a fascinating insight into the Pennine heartland of industrial West Yorkshire.

Yorkshire also boasts a great choice of cycle routes. You can cycle to York on the track bed of the former King's Cross to Edinburgh railway line, or ride along a 20-mile (32.2km) stretch of the former Whitby to Scarborough line, looping around Robin Hood's Bay. There are also cycle routes through the Yorkshire Wolds, Dalby Forest in the North York Moors National Park and around Castle Howard, the magnificent estate near Malton where Evelyn Waugh's *Brideshead Revisited* was filmed.

Festivals and Events

- The long established Jorvik Festival is held in York in February and lasts eight days. The festival celebrates Viking heritage with various lectures, arts and crafts and river events.
- Easter Monday is the date for Ossett's Coal Carrying Championships where competitors carry a sack of coal through the streets.
- November sees the three-day Northern Antiques Fair at Harrogate. This event includes various indoor stalls, as well as displays of glass and ceramics.
- The Yorkshire Dales has numerous events and festivals throughout the year, including the Masham Arts Festival in October, the Lunesdale Agricultural Show in August and the Grassington Festival of Music & Arts in June.

YORKSHIRE, EAST RIDING OF

BRANDESBURTON Map 17 TA14

Places to visit

The Guildhall, BEVERLEY 01482 392783
www.eastriding.gov.uk/museums

Burton Constable Hall, SPROATLEY
01964 562400 www.burtonconstable.com

Great for kids: `Streetlife' - Hull Museum of
Transport, KINGSTON UPON HULL 01482 613902
www.hullcc.gov.uk

NEW ►►► 85% *Blue Rose Caravan Country Park* (TA110464)

Star Carr Ln YO25 8RU
☎ 01964 543366 📠 01964 543366
e-mail: info@bluerosepark.com
dir: *From A165 at rdbt into New Rd signed Brandesburton (becomes Star Carr Ln). Approx 1m, site on left*

Open all year

Last arrival 20.00hrs Last departure noon

A neat and well maintained adult-only site well placed for visiting Hornsea and the Yorkshire coastline. The park is walking distance of Brandesburton and offers an idyllic stopover for caravanners wanting a peaceful break in the countryside. At the time of our inspection finishing touches were being made to the smart toilet block. Future plans include the addition of a small clubhouse. 12 acre site. 58 touring pitches. Caravan pitches. Motorhome pitches.

Notes: Adults only.

►►► 80% *Dacre Lakeside Park* (TA118468)

YO25 8RT
☎ 0800 1804556 📠 01964 544040
e-mail: dacrepark@btconnect.com
dir: *Off A165 bypass, midway between Beverley & Hornsea*

Open Mar-Oct

Last arrival 21.00hrs Last departure noon

A large lake popular with watersports enthusiasts is the focal point of this grassy site. The clubhouse offers indoor activities; there's a fish and chip shop, a pub and a Chinese takeaway in the village, which is within walking distance. The six-acre lake is used for windsurfing, sailing, kayaking, canoeing and fishing. Three camping

pods are available for hire. 8 acre site. 120 touring pitches. Caravan pitches. Motorhome pitches. Tent pitches.

Leisure: 🏊 🎣
Facilities: 🚿🔌📷✂️♿🕙🏪🐕
Services: 🔌🛒🍳🍴🚽🗑️
Within 3 miles: ⛳🚤🎣⛵🐴🐴

Notes: Wind surfing, fishing, canoeing, sailing & bowling.

BRIDLINGTON Map 17 TA16

See also Rudston

Places to visit

Sewerby Hall & Gardens, BRIDLINGTON
01262 673769 www.sewerby-hall.co.uk

Hornsea Museum, HORNSEA 01964 533443
www.hornseamuseum.com

Great for kids: Flamingo Land Theme Park & Zoo, KIRBY MISPERTON 01653 668287
www.flamingoland.co.uk

►►► 80% Fir Tree Caravan Park (TA195702)

Jewison Ln, Sewerby YO16 6YG
☎ 01262 676442
e-mail: info@flowerofmay.com
dir: *1.5m from centre of Bridlington. Left onto B1255 at Marton Corner. Site 600yds on left*

Open Mar-Oct (rs Early & late season bar & entertainment restrictions)

Last arrival dusk Last departure noon

Fir Tree Park has a well laid out touring area with its own facilities within a large, mainly static park. It has an excellent swimming pool complex, and the adjacent bar-cum-conservatory serves meals. There is also a family bar, games room and outdoor children's play area. 22 acre site. 45 touring pitches. 45 hardstandings. 45 seasonal pitches. Caravan pitches. 400 statics.

AA Pubs & Restaurants nearby: Seabirds Inn, Flamborough 01262 850242

Old Star Inn, Kilham 01262 420619

Leisure: 🏊🎠🎣🎵
Facilities: 🚿⊙✂️♿🕙🏪🐕📶♻️ℹ️
Services: 🔌🛒🍳🍴🗑️
Within 3 miles: ⛳🚤🎪🎣◎⛵🐴🐴🐴

Notes: Dogs accepted by prior arrangement only, no noise after mdnt.

KINGSTON UPON HULL

See Sproatley

RUDSTON Map 17 TA06

Places to visit

Sewerby Hall & Gardens, BRIDLINGTON
01262 673769 www.sewerby-hall.co.uk

►►► 86% Thorpe Hall Caravan & Camping Site (TA108677)

☎ 01262 420393 & 420574
Thorpe Hall YO25 4JE
e-mail: caravansite@thorpehall.co.uk
dir: *5m from Bridlington on B1253 (West)*

✱ 🚐 £15.50-£30.50 🚐 £15.50-£30.50 ⛺ £11-£26

Open Mar-Oct (rs Limited opening hours reception & shop)

Last arrival 22.00hrs Last departure noon

A delightful, peaceful small park within the walled gardens of Thorpe Hall yet within a few miles of the bustling seaside resort of Bridlington. The site offers a games field, its own coarse fishery, pitch and putt, and a games and TV lounge, and there are numerous walks locally. 4.5 acre site. 90 touring pitches. Caravan pitches. Motorhome pitches. Tent pitches.

AA Pubs & Restaurants nearby: Old Star Inn, Kilham 01262 420619

Leisure: 🎠🎣🖵
Facilities: 🚿⊙✂️♿🕙🏪🐕📶♻️ℹ️
Services: 🔌🛒🍴🚽🗑️
Within 3 miles: 🎣◎⛵🐴

Notes: Dogs must be well behaved and kept on leads, no ball games (field provided). Golf practice area (4.5 acres).

see advert on opposite page

SKIPSEA — Map 17 TA15

Places to visit

Hornsea Museum, HORNSEA 01964 533443
www.hornseamuseum.com

Sewerby Hall & Gardens, BRIDLINGTON
01262 673769 www.sewerby-hall.co.uk

AA CAMPING CARD SITE

 84% Low Skirlington Leisure Park (TA188528)

YO25 8SY
☎ 01262 468213 & 468466 ▤ 01262 468105
e-mail: info@skirlington.com
dir: From M62 towards Beverley then Hornsea. Between Skipsea & Hornsea on B1242

⌂ ⌂

Open Mar-Oct

A large well-run seaside park set close to the beach in partly-sloping meadowland with young trees and shrubs. The site has five toilet blocks, a supermarket and an amusement arcade, with occasional entertainment in the clubhouse. The wide range of family amenities includes an indoor heated swimming pool complex with sauna, jacuzzi and sunbeds. A 10-pin bowling alley and indoor play area for children are added attractions. 24 acre site. 285 touring pitches. 15 hardstandings. Caravan pitches. Motorhome pitches. 450 statics.

Leisure: ⌂ ⌂ ⌂ ⌂
Facilities: ⌂ ⌂ ⌂ ⌂ ⌂ ⌂ ⌂ ⌂ ⌂ ⌂ ⌂ ⌂ ⌂
Services: ⌂ ⌂ ⌂ ⌂ ⌂ ⌂ ⌂
Within 3 miles: ⌂ ⌂ ⌂ ⌂ ⌂ ⌂ ⌂ ⌂ ⌂
Notes: Dogs must be kept on leads. Putting green.

 NEW 80% Skipsea Sands (TA176563)

Mill Ln YO25 8TZ
☎ 01262 468210
e-mail: skipsea.sands@park-resorts.com
dir: From A165 (Bridlington to Kingston upon Hull road) 8m S of Bridlington take B1242 to Skipsea. Follow Skipsea Sands signed to left just after sharp left bend

⌂ ⌂ Å

Open Apr-Oct

Last arrival noon Last departure 10.00hrs

A busy and popular holiday park just a stone's throw from the beach, and offering an excellent range of leisure and entertainment facilities for families and couples. There's a good, well maintained touring area with clean toilets and neat grass pitches. A dedicated team ensure that standards are high across the park. 91 touring pitches. Caravan pitches. Motorhome pitches. Tent pitches.

SPROATLEY — Map 17 TA13

Places to visit

Burton Constable Hall, SPROATLEY
01964 562400 www.burtonconstable.com

Maritime Museum, LOWESTOFT 01502 561963
www.lowestoftmaritimemuseum.org.uk

Great for kids: The Deep, KINGSTON UPON HULL
01482 381000 www.thedeep.co.uk

►►►► **80% Burton Constable Holiday Park & Arboretum** (TA186357)

Old Lodges HU11 4LN
☎ 01964 562508 ▤ 01964 563420
e-mail: info@burtonconstable.co.uk
dir: A165 onto B1238 to Sproatley. Follow signs to site

* ⌂ £16-£28 ⌂ £16-£28 Å £16-£29

Open Mar-Jan (rs Mar-Oct tourers/tents)

Last arrival 22.00hrs Last departure 14.00hrs

A very attractive parkland site overlooking the fishing lakes, in the grounds of Burton Constable Hall. The toilet facilities are kept very clean, and the Lakeside Club provides a focus for relaxing in the evening. Children will enjoy the extensive adventure playground. 90 acre site. 140 touring pitches. 14 hardstandings. 14 seasonal pitches. Caravan pitches. Motorhome pitches. Tent pitches. 350 statics.

continued

SERVICES: ⌂ Electric hook up ⌂ Launderette ⌂ Licensed bar ⌂ Calor Gas ⌂ Camping Gaz ⌂ Toilet fluid ⌂ Café/Restaurant ⌂ Fast Food/Takeaway ⌂ Battery charging ⌂ Baby care ⌂ Motorvan service point
ABBREVIATIONS: BH/bank hols-bank holidays Etr-Easter Whit-Whitsun dep-departure fr-from hrs-hours m-mile mdnt-midnight rdbt-roundabout rs-restricted service wk-week wknd-weekend ⌂ No credit cards ⌂ No dogs
See page 7 for details of the AA Camping Card Scheme

SPROATLEY *continued*

Burton Constable Holiday Park & Arboretum

\Leisure: ⚓ 🎪 ♣ 🎵

Facilities: 🚿 ⊙ 🅿 🔥 ♿ 🕒 🛒 🍴 🛒 ♻ ❶

Services: 🔌 🔋 🍴 💧 🗑 T 🛒 ♻

Within 3 miles: 🏊 🗲 🛒 🚶 U

Notes: No skateboards or rollerblades. Dogs must be kept on leads. Two 10-acre fishing lakes, snooker table.

WITHERNSEA   Map 17 TA32

Places to visit

Wilberforce House, KINGSTON UPON HULL
01482 613902 www.hullcc.gov.uk

Maister House, KINGSTON UPON HULL
01723 879900 www.nationaltrust.org.uk

Great for kids: The Deep, KINGSTON UPON HULL
01482 381000 www.thedeep.co.uk

 76% Withernsea Sands
(TA335289)

Waxholme Rd HU19 2BS
☎ 0871 664 9803
e-mail: withernsea.sands@park-resorts.com
dir: M62 junct 38, A63 through Hull. At end of dual carriageway, right onto A1033, follow Withernsea signs. Through village, left at mini-rdbt onto B1242. 1st right at lighthouse. Site 0.5m on left

🚐 🚍 Å

Open Apr-Oct (rs BH & peak wknds sports available)

Last arrival 22.00hrs Last departure noon

Touring is very much at the heart of this holiday park's operation, with 100 all-electric pitches and additional space for tents. The owners, Park Resorts, continue to upgrade the facilities and attractions, and the leisure complex with its futuristic design is especially impressive. 115 touring pitches. Caravan pitches. Motorhome pitches. Tent pitches. 400 statics.

Leisure: ⚓ 🎪 ♣ ⚽ ♣ 🎵
Facilities: 🚿 🔥 ⊙ 🅿 🔥 ♿ 🕒 🛒 🍴 🛒 🚶 WI-FI 💻 ♻

Services: 🔌 🔋 🍴 💧 🗑 T 🍴 🛒 🚐

Within 3 miles: 🏊 🗲 🛒 U

Notes: No noise between 23.00hrs & 07.00hrs. Dogs must be kept on leads. Extension leads & utilities from reception.

YORKSHIRE, NORTH

See Walk 12 & Cycle Ride 5 in the Walks & Cycle Rides section at the end of the guide

ACASTER MALBIS   Map 16 SE54

Places to visit

Yorkshire Museum, YORK 01904 551800
www.yorkshiremuseum.org.uk

York Art Gallery, YORK 01904 687687
www.york.trust.museum

Great for kids: Jorvik Viking Centre, YORK
01904 615505 www.jorvik-viking-centre.com

►►► **78% Moor End Farm** *(SE589457)*

YO23 2UQ
☎ 01904 706727 & 07860 405872
e-mail: moorendfarm@acaster99.fsnet.co.uk
dir: Follow signs to Acaster Malbis from junct of A64 & A1237 at Copmanthorpe

* 🚐 £14-£18 🚍 £12-£18 Å £12-£20

Open Etr or Apr-Oct
Last arrival 22.00hrs Last departure 12.00hrs

A very pleasant farm site with modernised facilities including a heated family/disabled shower room. A riverboat pickup to York is 150 yards from the site entrance, and the village inn and restaurant are a short stroll away. A good place to hire a boat or simply watch the boats go by. 1 acre site. 10 touring pitches. Caravan pitches. Motorhome pitches. Tent pitches. 6 statics.

AA Pubs & Restaurants nearby: Ye Old Sun Inn, Colton 01904 744261

Leisure: 🎪

Facilities: 🚿 ⊙ 🅿 🔥 ♿ 🛒 ♻

Services: 🔌 🔋 🛒

Within 3 miles: 🏊 ♣ 🗲 🛒 🛒

Notes: ⊗ Dogs must be kept on leads. Use of fridge, freezer & microwave.

ALLERSTON   Map 19 SE88

Places to visit

Scarborough Castle, SCARBOROUGH
01723 372451 www.english-heritage.org.uk

Pickering Castle, PICKERING 01751 474989
www.english-heritage.org.uk

Great for kids: Sea Life & Marine Sanctuary, SCARBOROUGH 01723 376125 www.sealife.co.uk

---

PREMIER PARK

►►►►► **80% Vale of Pickering Caravan Park**
(SE879808)

GOLD

Carr House Farm YO18 7PQ
☎ 01723 859280 ▤ 01723 850060
e-mail: tony@valeofpickering.co.uk
dir: On B1415, 1.75m from A170 (Pickering-Scarborough road)

* 🚐 £15.50-£26 🚍 £15.50-£26 Å £12.50-£23

Open 5 Mar-3 Jan (rs Mar)
Last arrival 21.00hrs Last departure 11.30hrs

A well-maintained, spacious family park with excellent facilities including a well-stocked shop and immaculate toilet facilities, and an interesting woodland walk. Younger children will enjoy the attractive play area, while the large ball sports area will attract older ones. The park is set in open countryside bounded by hedges, has manicured grassland and stunning seasonal floral displays, and is handy for the North Yorkshire Moors and the attractions of Scarborough. 13 acre

---

LEISURE: ⚓ Indoor swimming pool ⚓ Outdoor swimming pool 🎪 Children's playground ♣ Kid's club ♣ Tennis court ♣ Games room ⊡ Separate TV room 🏌 9/18 hole golf course ⛵ Boats for hire 🎬 Cinema 🎵 Entertainment 🎣 Fishing ⊙ Mini golf 🌊 Watersports 🏋 Gym ⊕ Sports field **Spa** U Stables
FACILITIES: 🛁 Bath 🚿 Shower ⊙ Electric shaver 🅿 Hairdryer ✳ Ice Pack Facility ♿ Disabled facilities 🕒 Public telephone 🛒 Shop on site or within 200yds 🏪 Mobile shop (calls at least 5 days a week) 🍴 BBQ area 🛒 Picnic area WI-FI Wi-fi 💻 Internet access ♻ Recycling ❶ Tourist info 🚶 Dog exercise area

site. 120 touring pitches. 100 hardstandings. Caravan pitches. Motorhome pitches. Tent pitches.

AA Pubs & Restaurants nearby: New Inn, Thornton le Dale 01751 474226

Coachman Inn, Snainton 01723 859231 Cayley Arms, Brompton-by-Sawdon 01723 859372

Leisure: ⚙ ✦

Facilities: ⟿ ♠ ☺ ℗ ✳ ⅙ ☺ ⓢ ⌸ ☀

Services: ⚡ ⓢ ⓐ ⊘ ⊤ ⇶

Within 3 miles: ⫰ ⋆ ◎ ⓢ ⓢ ∪

Notes: Microwave available.

ALNE — Map 19 SE46

Places to visit

Castle Howard, MALTON 01653 648333 www.castlehoward.co.uk

Sutton Park, SUTTON-ON-THE-FOREST 01347 810249 www.statelyhome.co.uk

Great for kids: National Railway Museum, YORK 01904 621261 www.nrm.org.uk

►►►► 80% Alders Caravan Park

(SE497654)

Home Farm YO61 1RY
☎ 01347 838722 ⓘ 01347 838722
e-mail: enquiries@homefarmalne.co.uk
dir: From A19 exit at Alne sign, in 1.5m left at T-junct, 0.5m site on left in village centre

* ⇘ £17-£19 ⇚ £17-£19 ▲ £17-£19

Open Mar-Oct

Last arrival 21.00hrs Last departure 14.00hrs

A tastefully developed park on a working farm with screened pitches laid out in horseshoe-shaped areas. This well designed park offers excellent toilet facilities including a bathroom and fully-serviced washing and toilet cubicles. A woodland area and a water meadow are pleasant places to walk. 12 acre site. 87 touring pitches. 6 hardstandings. 71 seasonal pitches. Caravan pitches. Motorhome pitches. Tent pitches. 2 wooden pods.

AA Pubs & Restaurants nearby: Black Bull Inn, Boroughbridge 01423 322413

The Dining Room Restaurant, Boroughbridge 01423 326426

Facilities: ⟿ ♠ ☺ ℗ ✳ ⅙ ☺ ⓢ ⌸ ☀

Services: ⚡ ⓢ ⓐ ⇶

Within 3 miles: ⫰ ⋆ ⓢ ⓢ

Notes: Max 2 dogs per pitch. Dogs must be kept on leads. Summer house, bread, eggs, milk & other farm produce for sale.

BISHOP MONKTON — Map 19 SE36

Places to visit

Newby Hall & Gardens, RIPON 01423 322583 www.newbyhall.com

Fountains Abbey & Studley Royal, RIPON 01765 643197 www.fountainsabbey.org.uk

Great for kids: Stump Cross Caverns, PATELEY BRIDGE 01756 752780 www.stumpcrosscaverns.co.uk

►►► 75% Church Farm Caravan Park (SE328660)

Knaresborough Rd HG3 3QQ
☎ 01765 676578 & 07861 770164
ⓘ 01765 676578
e-mail: churchfarmcaravan@btinternet.com
dir: From A61 at x-rds follow Bishop Monkton signs. 1.25m to village. At x-rds right into Knaresborough Rd, site approx 500mtrs on right

* ⇘ £12-£17 ⇚ ▲ £10-£17

Open Mar-Oct

Last arrival 22.30hrs Last departure 15.30hrs

A very pleasant rural site on a working farm, on the edge of the attractive village of Bishop Monkton with its well-stocked shop and pubs. Whilst very much a place to relax, there are many attractions close by, including Fountains Abbey, Newby Hall, Ripon and Harrogate. 4 acre site. 45 touring pitches. 3 hardstandings. Caravan pitches. Motorhome pitches. Tent pitches. 3 statics.

AA Pubs & Restaurants nearby: Black Bull Inn, Boroughbridge 01423 322413

The Dining Room Restaurant, Boroughbridge 01423 326426

Facilities: ♠ ☺ ℗ ✳ ⅙ ⓢ ☀ ⓸

Services: ⚡ ⇶ ⇙

Within 3 miles: ⫰ ⋆ ⓢ ⓢ ∪

Notes: ⊛ No ball games. Dogs must be kept on leads.

BOLTON ABBEY — Map 19 SE05

Places to visit

RHS Garden Harlow Carr, HARROGATE 01423 565418 www.rhs.org.uk/harlowcarr

Parcevall Hall Gardens, PARCEVALL HALL GARDENS 01756 720311 www.parcevallhallgardens.co.uk

Great for kids: Stump Cross Caverns, PATELEY BRIDGE 01756 752780 www.stumpcrosscaverns.co.uk

►►► 83% Howgill Lodge

(SE064592)

Barden BD23 6DJ
☎ 01756 720655
e-mail: info@howgill-lodge.co.uk
dir: From Bolton Abbey take B6160 signed Burnsall. In 3m at Barden Tower right signed Appletreewick. 1.5m at phone box right into lane to site

* ⇘ £18-£26.50 ⇚ £18-£26.50 ▲ £18-£30.50

Open mid Mar-Oct

Last arrival 20.00hrs Last departure noon

A beautifully-maintained and secluded site offering panoramic views of Wharfedale. The spacious hardstanding pitches are mainly terraced, and there is a separate tenting area with numerous picnic tables. There are three toilet facilities spread throughout the site, with the main block (including private, cubicled wash facilities) refurbished to a high standard. There is also a well stocked shop. 4 acre site. 40 touring pitches. 20 hardstandings. Caravan pitches. Motorhome pitches. Tent pitches.

AA Pubs & Restaurants nearby: The Fleece, Addingham 01943 830491

Craven Arms, Appletreewick 01756 720270

Leisure: ✦

Facilities: ♠ ☺ ℗ ✳ ☺ ⓢ ☀ ⅏ ⓸ ⓿

Services: ⚡ ⓢ ⓐ ⊘ ⊤ ⇶

Within 3 miles: ⋆ ⓢ ⓢ

Notes: Dogs must be kept on leads.

CONSTABLE BURTON   Map 19 SE19

Places to visit

Middleham Castle, MIDDLEHAM 01969 623899
www.english-heritage.org.uk

Great for kids: Bedale Museum, BEDALE
01677 427516

▶▶▶▶ **80% Constable Burton Hall Caravan Park** *(SE158907)*

DL8 5LJ
☎ **01677 450428**
e-mail: caravanpark@constableburton.com
dir: *Off A684*

🚐 £18-£23 🚐 £18-£23

Open Apr-Oct

Last arrival 20.00hrs Last departure noon

A pretty site in the former deer park of the adjoining Constable Burton Hall, screened from the road by the deer park walls and surrounded by mature trees in a quiet rural location. The laundry is housed in a converted 18th-century deer barn, there is a pub and restaurant opposite, and seasonal pitches are available. Please note that this site does not accept tents. 10 acre site. 120 touring pitches. Caravan pitches. Motorhome pitches.

AA Pubs & Restaurants nearby: Old Horn Inn, Spennithorne 01969 622370

Sandpiper Inn, Leyburn 01969 622206

White Swan, Middleham 01969 622093

Black Swan, Middleham 01969 622221

Wensleydale Heifer, West Witton 01969 622322

Facilities: 🐾☉🅿✳♿🚽🖥♻

Services: 🔌🅖🔒🏕

Within 3 miles: ♨🅢

Notes: No commercial vehicles, no games. Dogs must be kept on leads.

FILEY

Places to visit

Scarborough Castle, SCARBOROUGH
01723 372451 www.english-heritage.org.uk

Sea Life & Marine Sanctuary, SCARBOROUGH
01723 376125 www.sealife.co.uk

FILEY   Map 17 TA18

 90% Flower of May Holiday Park *(TA085835)*

Lebberston Cliff YO11 3NU
☎ **01723 584311** 📄 **01723 585716**
e-mail: info@flowerofmay.com
dir: *Signed from A165 on Scarborough side of Filey*

* 🚐 £15-£21 🚐 £15-£21 ⛺ £13-£21

Open Etr-Oct (rs Early & late season restricted opening in café, shop & bars)

Last arrival dusk Last departure noon

A well-run, high quality family holiday park with top class facilities. This large landscaped park offers a full range of recreational activities, with plenty to occupy everyone. Grass and hard pitches are available, all on level ground, and arranged in avenues screened by shrubs. Enjoy the 'Scarborough Fair' museum, with its collection of restored fairground attractions, including rides, organs and vintage cars. 13 acre site. 300 touring pitches. 250 hardstandings. 100 seasonal pitches. Caravan pitches. Motorhome pitches. Tent pitches. 193 statics.

AA Pubs & Restaurants nearby: Cayley Arms, Brompton-by-Sawdon 01723 859372

Leisure: 🏊⛰🎣⚽□🎵

Facilities: 🐾☉✳♿🅒🚽🏕♻🎈♻ ❶

Services: 🔌🅖🍴🔒🅣🍴🏕⚡

Within 3 miles: ♨♣🕌🎣◎⛷🅢🅢♻

Notes: 1 dog per pitch by arrangement only, no noise after mdnt. Dogs must be kept on leads. Squash, bowling, 9-hole golf, basketball court, skate park.

see advert on opposite page

81% Primrose Valley Holiday Park *(TA123778)*

YO14 9RF
☎ **0871 231 0892** 📄 **01723 513777**
e-mail: primrosevalley@haven.com
dir: *Signed from A165 (Scarborough-Bridlington road), 3m S of Filey*

🚐 🚐

Open mid Mar-end Oct

Last arrival anytime Last departure 10.00hrs

A large all-action holiday centre with a wide range of sports and leisure activities to suit everyone from morning until late in the evening. The touring area is completely separate from the main park with its own high quality amenity block. All touring pitches are fully-serviced hardstandings with grassed awning strips. 2012 - a new 9-hole golf course. 160 acre site. 50 touring pitches. 50 hardstandings. Caravan pitches. Motorhome pitches. 1514 statics.

AA Pubs & Restaurants nearby: Cayley Arms, Brompton-by-Sawdon 01723 859372

Leisure: 🏊⛰🎣⚽♻🎵

Facilities: 🐾🅟♿🅒🚽🏕♻🚾🖥♻❶

Services: 🔌🅖🍴🔒🍴🏕⚡

Within 3 miles: ♨♣🎣◎🅢🅢

Notes: Max 2 dogs per booking, certain dog breeds banned, no commercial vehicles, no bookings by persons under 21yrs unless a family booking.

FILEY *continued*

77% Blue Dolphin Holiday Park (TA095829)

Gristhorpe Bay YO14 9PU
☎ 0871 231 0893 📠 01723 512059
e-mail: bluedolphin@haven.com
dir: On A165, 2m N of Filey

🚐 🚃 ▲

Open mid Mar-end Oct (rs mid Mar-May & Sep-Oct some facilities may be reduced & outdoor pool closed)

Last arrival mdnt Last departure 10.00hrs

There are great cliff-top views to be enjoyed from this fun-filled holiday centre with an extensive and separate touring area. The emphasis is on non-stop entertainment, with organised sports and clubs, all-weather leisure facilities, heated swimming pools (extended with new multi-slide in 2011), and plenty of well-planned amusements. Pitches are mainly on level or gently-sloping grass plus some fully-serviced hardstandings, the toilet facilities have now been upgraded; the beach is just two miles away. 85 acre site. 329 touring pitches. 43 hardstandings. 20 seasonal pitches. Caravan pitches. Motorhome pitches. Tent pitches. 850 statics.

AA Pubs & Restaurants nearby: Cayley Arms, Brompton-by-Sawdon 01723 859372

Leisure: 🏊 🏖 🛝 ♨ 🎱 🎵

Facilities: 🔥 ☺ ☀ 🛁 🕙 🚿 ♿ 🏧 WiFi ♻ ℹ

Services: 🚐 🗃 🍴 🍳 📷 T 🍽 🛒 ⛽ ♨

Within 3 miles: 🛴 🚲 ◎ 🛍 🔒

Notes: Max 2 dogs per booking, certain dog breeds banned, no commercial vehicles, no bookings by persons under 21yrs unless a family booking. Dogs must be kept on leads.

see advert below

77% Reighton Sands Holiday Park (TA142769)

Reighton Gap YO14 9SH
☎ 0871 231 0894 📠 01723 891043
e-mail: reightonsands@haven.com
dir: On A165, 5m S of Filey at Reighton Gap, signed

🚐 🚃 ▲

Open mid Mar-end Oct (rs mid Mar-May & Sep-Oct some facilities may be reduced)

Last arrival 22.00hrs Last departure 10.00hrs

A large, lively holiday centre with a wide range of entertainment and all-weather leisure facilities, located just a 10-minute walk from a

LEISURE: 🏊 Indoor swimming pool 🏖 Outdoor swimming pool 👶 Children's playground 🪁 Kid's club 🎾 Tennis court 🎱 Games room 📺 Separate TV room ⛳ 9/18 hole golf course 🚤 Boats for hire 🎬 Cinema 🎵 Entertainment 🎣 Fishing ◎ Mini golf 🤿 Watersports 💪 Gym 🏑 Sports field Spa ♨ Stables

FACILITIES: 🛁 Bath 🚿 Shower 🪒 Electric shaver 💇 Hairdryer ❄ Ice Pack Facility ♿ Disabled facilities 📞 Public telephone 🛍 Shop on site or within 200yds 🚚 Mobile shop (calls at least 5 days a week) 🍖 BBQ area 🪑 Picnic area WiFi Wi-fi 📶 Internet access ♻ Recycling ℹ Tourist info 🐕 Dog exercise area

long sandy beach. There are good all-weather pitches and a large tenting field. The site is particularly geared towards families with young children. There is a new 9-hole golf course with 18 tees for the 2011 season. 229 acre site. 83 touring pitches. 83 hardstandings. 5 seasonal pitches. Caravan pitches. Motorhome pitches. Tent pitches. 800 statics.

AA Pubs & Restaurants nearby: Cayley Arms, Brompton-by-Sawdon 01723 859372

Leisure: 🏊 ⚲ 🔍

Facilities: 🚿 ♿ ⊙ 🌣 ♿ 🕓 🛒 🚿 📶 🖥 ♻ 🕖

Services: 🔌 🗑 🍴 T 🍽 🎂 🚮 ♨

Within 3 miles: 🚵 ♨ 🅿 ◎ 🗑 🗑 ⛱

Notes: Max 2 dogs per booking, certain dog breeds banned, no commercial vehicles, no bookings by persons under 21yrs unless a family booking. Indoor play area.

see advert below

►►►► **86% Lebberston Touring Park** *(TA077824)*

Filey Rd YO11 3PE
☎ 01723 585723
e-mail: info@lebberstontouring.co.uk
dir: *Off A165. Site signed*

🚐 🚗

Open Mar-Oct

Last arrival 20.00hrs Last departure 11.00hrs

A peaceful family park in a gently-sloping rural area, where the quality facilities are maintained to a high standard of cleanliness. The keen owners are friendly and helpful, and create a relaxing atmosphere. A natural area offers views of the surrounding countryside through the shrubbery. Please note that this park does not accept tents. 7.5 acre site. 125 touring pitches. 25 hardstandings. Caravan pitches. Motorhome pitches.

Facilities: 🚿 ♿ ⊙ 🌣 🌣 ♿ 🕓 🗑 🚿 📶

Services: 🔌 🗑 🍴 ⊘ T

Within 3 miles: 🚵 ♨ 🅿 ◎ 🗑 🗑 ⛱

Notes: Dogs must be kept on leads.

►►► **79% Centenary Way Camping & Caravan Park** *(TA115798)*

Muston Grange YO14 0HU
☎ 01723 516415 & 512313
dir: *Just off A1039 near A165 junct towards Bridlington*

* 🚐 £10.50-£17 🚗 £10.50-£17 ▲ £7.50-£17

Open Mar-Oct

Last arrival 21.00hrs Last departure noon

A well set-out family-owned park, with footpath access to nearby beach. Close to the seaside resort of Filey, and caravan pitches enjoy views over open countryside. 3 acre site. 75 touring pitches. 25 hardstandings. Caravan pitches. Motorhome pitches. Tent pitches.

AA Pubs & Restaurants nearby: Cayley Arms, Brompton-by-Sawdon 01723 859372

Leisure: ⚲

Facilities: ♿ ⊙ 🌣 ♿ 🗑 🚿 ♻ 🕖

Services: 🔌 🗑 🛒 🍴

Within 3 miles: 🚵 ♨ 🅿 ◎ 🗑 🗑

Notes: ⊘ No group bookings in peak period, no 9-12 berth tents, no gazebos. Dogs must be kept on leads.

SERVICES: 🔌 Electric hook up 🗑 Launderette 🍴 Licensed bar 🛒 Calor Gas ⊘ Camping Gaz T Toilet fluid 🍽 Café/Restaurant 🚮 Fast Food/Takeaway 🔋 Battery charging 🚿 Baby care ♨ Motorvan service point

ABBREVIATIONS: BH/bank hols-bank holidays Etr-Easter Whit-Whitsun dep-departure fr-from hrs-hours m-mile mdnt-midnight rdbt-roundabout rs-restricted service wk-week wknd-weekend ⊘ No credit cards ⊗ No dogs

See page 7 for details of the AA Camping Card Scheme

FILEY continued

▶▶▶ 76% Crows Nest Caravan Park

(TA094826)

Gristhorpe YO14 9PS
☎ 01723 582206 📠 01723 582206
e-mail: enquires@crowsnestcaravanpark.com
dir: 5m S of Scarborough & 2m N of Filey. On seaward side of A165, signed from rdbt, near petrol station

* 🚐 £15-£25 🚍 £15-£25 ▲ £15-£25

Open Mar-Oct

Last departure noon

A beautifully situated park on the coast between Scarborough and Filey, with excellent panoramic views. This large and mainly static park offers lively entertainment, and two bars. The touring caravan area is near the entertainment complex, whilst the tenting pitches are at the top of the site. 20 acre site. 49 touring pitches. 49 hardstandings. Caravan pitches. Motorhome pitches. Tent pitches. 217 statics.

AA Pubs & Restaurants nearby: Cayley Arms, Brompton-by-Sawdon 01723 859372

Leisure: 🏊♨♿🔍🎵
Facilities: 🍴☉✳🕐🚿🛅🚮📶🖥♻ℹ
Services: 🚐🛢🔧🛗🛢🚽🛒🧺🚙
Within 3 miles: ↧🔗◎♨🛶🎣🎰🎱U

see advert below

▶▶▶ 76% Filey Brigg Touring Caravan & Country Park (TA115812)

North Cliff YO14 9ET
☎ 01723 513852
e-mail: fileybrigg@scarborough.gov.uk
dir: 0.5m from Filey town centre on coast road from Scarborough, A165

* 🚐 £14.50-£22.50 🚍 £14.50-£22.50 ▲ £11.50-£17

Open Etr-2 Jan

Last arrival 18.00hrs Last departure noon

A municipal park overlooking Filey Brigg with splendid views along the coast, and set in a country park. The beach is just a short walk away, as is the resort of Filey. There is a good quality amenity block, and 50 all-weather pitches are available. The electric hook-ups and the amenity blocks have been upgraded and an excellent children's adventure playground was built adjacent to the park for the 2011 season. 9 acre site. 158 touring pitches. 82 hardstandings. Caravan pitches. Motorhome pitches. Tent pitches.

AA Pubs & Restaurants nearby: Cayley Arms, Brompton-by-Sawdon 01723 859372

Leisure: ♨♿
Facilities: 🍴☉✳♿🕐🚿🛅🚮♻ℹ
Services: 🚐🛢🛗🍽🛒
Within 3 miles: ↧🛶🔗◎🎰🎱U

LEISURE: 🏊 Indoor swimming pool 🏊 Outdoor swimming pool 🅰 Children's playground 🪁 Kid's club 🎾 Tennis court 🎱 Games room 📺 Separate TV room ⛳ 9/18 hole golf course 🛶 Boats for hire 🎬 Cinema 🎵 Entertainment 🎣 Fishing ◎ Mini golf 🏄 Watersports 🏋 Gym 🅾 Sports field Spa U Stables
FACILITIES: 🛁 Bath 🚿 Shower ☉ Electric shaver 🎀 Hairdryer ✳ Ice Pack Facility ♿ Disabled facilities 🕐 Public telephone 🛅 Shop on site or within 200yds 🏪 Mobile shop (calls at least 5 days a week) 🍖 BBQ area 🏕 Picnic area 📶 Wi-fi 🖥 Internet access ♻ Recycling ℹ Tourist info 🐕 Dog exercise area

HARROGATE   Map 19 SE35

PREMIER PARK

►►►►► 80% Rudding Holiday Park *(SE333531)*

Follifoot HG3 1JH
☎ 01423 871350   🖹 01423 870859
e-mail: holiday-park@ruddingpark.com
web: www.ruddingpark.co.uk/caravans-camping
dir: *From A1 take A59 to A658 signed Bradford. 4.5m then right, follow signs*

* ⚐ £19-£37 ⚐ £19-£37 ▲ £19-£37

Open Mar-Jan (rs Nov-Jan shop & Deer House Pub - limited opening, summer open times only for outdoor swimming pool)

Last arrival 23.00hrs Last departure 11.00hrs

A spacious park set in the stunning 200 acres of mature parkland and walled gardens of Rudding Park. The setting has been tastefully enhanced with terraced pitches and dry-stone walls. A separate area houses super pitches where all services are supplied including a picnic table and TV connection, and there are excellent toilets. An 18-hole golf course, a 6-hole short course, driving range, golf academy, heated outdoor swimming pool, the Deer House Pub, and a children's play area complete the amenities. 55 acre site. 109 touring pitches. 20 hardstandings. Caravan pitches. Motorhome pitches. Tent pitches. 57 statics.

AA Pubs & Restaurants nearby: van Zeller, Harrogate 01423 508762

Boars Head Hotel, Ripley Castle Estate, 01423 771888

General Tarleton, Knaresborough 01423 340284

Leisure: ⚓ Ⓜ ⊕ ✎ ♫ Spa
Facilities: ⊷ 🅵 ☉ 🅿 ✶ ⅋ Ⓢ ⑧ 🅷 📶 🖥 ❶
Services: 🔌 🅾 🍴 🛢 ⌀ 🚾 🍽 🔋 🚿 ⚲ ↧
Within 3 miles: ↧ 🎣 🅟 ⑧ 🅾 ∪

Notes: Under 18s must be accompanied by an adult.

PREMIER PARK

►►►►► 73% Ripley Caravan Park *(SE289610)*

GOLD

Knaresborough Rd, Ripley HG3 3AU
☎ 01423 770050   🖹 01423 770050
e-mail: ripleycaravanpark@talk21.com
web: www.ripleycaravanpark.com
dir: *3m N of Harrogate on A61. Right at rdbt onto B6165 signed Knaresborough. Site 300yds left*

* ⚐ £15.50-£18.50 ⚐ £15.50-£18.50
▲ £15.50-£20.50

Open Etr-Oct

Last arrival 21.00hrs Last departure noon

A well-run rural site in attractive meadowland which has been landscaped with mature tree plantings. The resident owners lovingly maintain the facilities, and there is a heated swimming pool and sauna, a TV and games room, and a covered nursery playroom for small children. 18 acre site. 100 touring pitches. 35 hardstandings. 35 seasonal pitches. Caravan pitches. Motorhome pitches. Tent pitches. 50 statics.

AA Pubs & Restaurants nearby: van Zeller, Harrogate 01423 508762

Boars Head Hotel, Ripley Castle Estate, 01423 771888

Malt Shovel Inn, Brearton 01423 862929

General Tarleton, Knaresborough 01423 340284

Leisure: ⚓ Ⓜ ✎
Facilities: 🅵 ☉ 🅿 ✶ ⅋ Ⓢ ⑧ 🚾 ⚲ ❶
Services: 🔌 🅾 🛢 ⌀ 🚾 ⚲ ↧
Within 3 miles: ↧ ☇ 🎣 🅟 ⊚ ⑧ 🅾 ∪

Notes: Family camping only, BBQs must be off ground, no skateboards. Dogs must be kept on leads. Football, sauna.

►►►► 77% High Moor Farm Park *(SE242560)*

Skipton Rd HG3 2LT
☎ 01423 563637 & 564955   🖹 01423 529449
e-mail: highmoorfarmpark@btconnect.com
dir: *4m W of Harrogate on A59 towards Skipton*

⚐ fr £22 ⚐ fr £22

Open Etr or Apr-Oct

Last arrival 23.30hrs Last departure 15.00hrs

An excellent site with very good facilities, set beside a small wood and surrounded by thorn hedges. The numerous touring pitches are located in meadowland fields, each area with its own toilet block. A large heated indoor swimming pool, games room, 9-hole golf course, full-sized crown bowling green, and a bar serving meals and snacks are all popular. Please note that this park does not accept tents. 15 acre site. 320 touring pitches. 51 hardstandings. 57 seasonal pitches. Caravan pitches. Motorhome pitches. 158 statics.

AA Pubs & Restaurants nearby: van Zeller, Harrogate 01423 508762

Boars Head Hotel, Ripley Castle Estate, 01423 771888

General Tarleton, Knaresborough 01423 340284

Leisure: ⚓ Ⓜ ✎
Facilities: ⊷ 🅵 ☉ 🅿 ✶ ⅋ Ⓢ ⑧ 🅷 ⚲ ❶
Services: 🔌 🅾 🍴 🛢 ⌀ 🚾 🍽 🔋 🍴
Within 3 miles: ↧ 🅟 ⑧ 🅾 ∪

Notes: Dogs must be kept on leads. Coarse fishing.

SERVICES: 🔌 Electric hook up   🅾 Launderette   🍴 Licensed bar   🛢 Calor Gas   ⌀ Camping Gaz   🚾 Toilet fluid   🍽 Café/Restaurant   🔋 Fast Food/Takeaway   🍴 Battery charging   🚿 Baby care   ⚲ Motorvan service point
ABBREVIATIONS: BH/bank hols-bank holidays   Etr-Easter   Whit-Whitsun   dep-departure   fr-from   hrs-hours   m-mile   mdnt-midnight   rdbt-roundabout   rs-restricted service   wk-week
wknd-weekend   ⊗ No credit cards   ⊗ No dogs   See page 7 for details of the AA Camping Card Scheme

HARROGATE *continued*

►►► 76% *Bilton Park* (SE317577)

Village Farm, Bilton Ln HG1 4DH
☎ **01423 863121**
e-mail: welcome@biltonpark.co.uk
dir: *In Harrogate, exit A59 (Skipton Rd) at Skipton Inn into Bilton Lane. Site approx 1m*

Open Apr-Oct

An established family-owned park in open countryside yet only two miles from the shops and tearooms of Harrogate. The spacious grass pitches are complemented by a well-appointed toilet block with private facilities. The Nidd Gorge is right on the doorstep. 4 acre site. 50 touring pitches. Caravan pitches. Motorhome pitches. Tent pitches.

AA Pubs & Restaurants nearby: van Zeller, Harrogate 01423 508762

Boars Head Hotel, Ripley Castle Estate, 01423 771888

Malt Shovel Inn, Brearton 01423 862929

General Tarleton, Knaresborough 01423 340284

Leisure: ⚙
Facilities: ↖ ☞ ✳ ⑤ ↯
Services: ⊡ ⑤ 🔒 🖉 ⛟
Within 3 miles: ♨ ⚘ ⒣ 🖉 ⑤ ⑤
Notes: ⊗

►►► 64% Shaws Trailer Park

(SE325557)

Knaresborough Rd HG2 7NE
☎ **01423 884432** 🖷 **01423 883622**
dir: *On A59 1m from town centre. 0.5m SW of Starbeck railway crossing, by Johnsons (dry cleaners)*

* ⛺ £13-£16 ⛟ £13-£16 ▲ £12-£16

Open all year

Last arrival 20.00hrs Last departure 14.00hrs

A long-established site just a mile from the centre of Harrogate. The all-weather pitches are arranged around a carefully kept grass area, and the toilets are basic but functional and clean. The entrance is on the bus route to Harrogate. 11 acre site. 60 touring pitches. 24 hardstandings. Caravan pitches. Motorhome pitches. Tent pitches. 146 statics.

AA Pubs & Restaurants nearby: van Zeller, Harrogate 01423 508762

Boars Head Hotel, Ripley Castle Estate, 01423 771888

Malt Shovel Inn, Brearton 01423 862929

General Tarleton, Knaresborough 01423 340284

Facilities: ↤ ↖ ☉ ⑤ ⚙ ⑤
Services: ⊡ ⑤ 🔒
Within 3 miles: ♨ ⚘ ⒣ 🖉 ⑤ ⑤ ∪
Notes: Adults only. ⊗

Places to visit

Dales Countryside Museum & National Park Centre, HAWES 01969 666210
www.yorkshiredales.org.uk/dcm

►►► 76% Bainbridge Ings Caravan & Camping Site (SD879895)

DL8 3NU
☎ **01969 667354**
e-mail: janet@bainbridge-ings.co.uk
dir: *Approaching Hawes from Bainbridge on A684, left at Gayle sign, site 300yds on left*

* ⛺ fr £16.50 ⛟ fr £13.50 ▲ fr £13.50

Open Apr-Oct

Last arrival 22.00hrs Last departure noon

A quiet, well-organised site in open countryside close to Hawes in the heart of Upper Wensleydale, popular with ramblers. Pitches are sited around the perimeter of several fields, each bounded by traditional stone walls. 5 acre site. 70 touring pitches. 8 hardstandings. Caravan pitches. Motorhome pitches. Tent pitches. 15 statics.

AA Pubs & Restaurants nearby: Moorcock Inn, Hawes 01969 667488

Facilities: ↖ ☉ ☞ ✳ ♻ ⓘ
Services: ⊡ ⑤ 🔒 🖉 ⛟
Within 3 miles: 🖉 ⑤ ⑤

Notes: ⊗ No noise after 23.00hrs. Dogs must be kept on leads.

Places to visit

Duncombe Park, HELMSLEY 01439 778625
www.duncombepark.com

Helmsley Castle, HELMSLEY 01439 770442
www.english-heritage.org.uk

Great for kids: Flamingo Land Theme Park & Zoo, KIRBY MISPERTON 01653 668287
www.flamingoland.co.uk

LEISURE: 🏊 Indoor swimming pool 🏊 Outdoor swimming pool ⚙ Children's playground ⚓ Kid's club ⚘ Tennis court ⚙ Games room ▭ Separate TV room ♨ 9/18 hole golf course ⚓ Boats for hire ⒣ Cinema ♫ Entertainment 🖉 Fishing ◎ Mini golf ⚓ Watersports ⚙ Gym ⚙ Sports field Spa ∪ Stables
FACILITIES: ↤ Bath ↖ Shower ☉ Electric shaver ☞ Hairdryer ✳ Ice Pack Facility ⚙ Disabled facilities ☎ Public telephone ⑤ Shop on site or within 200yds ⚙ Mobile shop (calls at least 5 days a week) 🍖 BBQ area ⚙ Picnic area ▬ Wi-fi 🖥 Internet access ♻ Recycling ⓘ Tourist info ↯ Dog exercise area

HELMSLEY — Map 19 SE68

PREMIER PARK

▶▶▶▶▶ **78% Golden Square Touring Caravan Park** *(SE604797)*

Oswaldkirk YO62 5YQ
☎ 01439 788269 📄 01439 788236
e-mail: reception@goldensquarecaravanpark.com
dir: *From York take B1363 to Oswaldkirk. Left onto B1257, 2nd left onto unclassified road signed Ampleforth, site 0.5m on right. Or A19 from Thirsk towards York. Left, follow 'Caravan Route avoiding Sutton Bank' signs, through Ampleforth to site in 1m*

* 🚐 fr £16 🚙 fr £16 ⛺ fr £16

Open Mar-Oct

Last arrival 21.00hrs Last departure noon

An excellent, popular and spacious site with very good facilities. This friendly, immaculately maintained park is set in a quiet rural situation with lovely views over the North York Moors. Terraced on three levels and surrounded by mature trees, it caters particularly for families, with excellent play areas and space for ball games. Country walks and mountain bike trails start here and an attractive holiday home development is underway. 12 acre site. 129 touring pitches. 10 hardstandings. Caravan pitches. Motorhome pitches. Tent pitches. 10 statics.

AA Pubs & Restaurants nearby: The Star Inn, Harome 01439 770397

Leisure: ⚠ ❄ 🔍
Facilities: 🛁 🚿 ⊙ ℱ ✳ ⚖ ⊙ 🔥 🛒 🐾 ♻ 🛈
Services: 🔌 🕎 🔋 ⊘ 🚽 🛒 ⚡
Within 3 miles: ↥ 🏇 ℱ ◎ 🚲 🛒 ∪
Notes: ⊘ No skateboards or fires. Dogs must be kept on leads. Microwave available.

▶▶▶ **75% Foxholme Caravan Park**
(SE658828)

Harome YO62 5JG
☎ 01439 771904
dir: *A170 from Helmsley towards Scarborough, right signed Harome, left at church, through village, follow signs*

🚐 £20 🚙 £20 ⛺ £20

Open Etr-Oct

Last arrival 23.00hrs Last departure noon

A quiet park set in secluded wooded countryside, with well-shaded pitches in individual clearings divided by mature trees. The facilities are well maintained, and the site is ideal as a touring base or a place to relax. Please note that caravans are prohibited on the A170 at Sutton Bank between Thirsk and Helmsley. 6 acre site. 60 touring pitches. Caravan pitches. Motorhome pitches. Tent pitches.

AA Pubs & Restaurants nearby: The Star Inn, Harome 01439 770397

Facilities: 🛁 🚿 ⊙ ℱ ✳ ⚖ ⊙ 🔥 🛈
Services: 🔌 🕎 🔋 ⊘ 🚽 🛒 ⚡
Within 3 miles: ↥ 🚲 🛒 ∪
Notes: Adults only. ⊘

HIGH BENTHAM

Places to visit

Lancaster Maritime Museum, LANCASTER 01524 382264 www.lancashire.gov.uk/museums

Lancaster City Museum, LANCASTER 01524 64637 www.lancashire.gov.uk/museums

Great for kids: Lancaster Castle, LANCASTER 01524 64998 www.lancastercastle.com

---

HIGH BENTHAM — Map 18 SD66

Regional Winner –
AA North West of England
Campsite of the Year 2012

PREMIER PARK

▶▶▶▶▶ **80%** Riverside Caravan Park *(SD665688)*

LA2 7FJ
☎ 015242 61272 📄 015242 62835
e-mail: info@riversidecaravanpark.co.uk
dir: *Exit B6480, signed from High Bentham town centre*

* 🚐 £19.25-£25 🚙 £19.25-£25

Open Mar-16 Dec (rs 28 Dec-2 Jan)

Last arrival 20.00hrs Last departure noon

A well-managed riverside park developed to a high standard, with level grass pitches set in avenues separated by trees, and there are excellent facilities for children, who are made to feel as important as the adults! It has an excellent, modern amenity block, including a family bathroom, and an excellent shop, laundry and information room. The superb games room and adventure playground are hugely popular, and the market town of High Bentham is close by. Please note that this site does not accept tents. Bentham Golf Club (within one mile) is also under same ownership with facilities available for Riverside customers. 12 acre site. 61 touring pitches. 27 hardstandings. Caravan pitches. Motorhome pitches. 206 statics.

AA Pubs & Restaurants nearby: The Traddock, Austwick 015242 51224

Game Cock Inn, Austwick 015242 51226

New Inn, Clapham 015242 51203

Leisure: ⚠ 🔍
Facilities: 🚿 ⊙ ℱ ⚖ ⊙ 🔥 🐾 📶 🖥 ♻ 🛈
Services: 🔌 🕎 🔋 ⊘ 🚽 🛒 ⚡
Within 3 miles: ↥ ℱ 🚲 🛒 ∪
Notes: Permits for private fishing (chargeable), discounted golf green fees.

SERVICES: 🔌 Electric hook up 🕎 Launderette 🍷 Licensed bar 🔋 Calor Gas ⊘ Camping Gaz 🚽 Toilet fluid 🍴 Café/Restaurant 🍔 Fast Food/Takeaway 🔋 Battery charging 🚼 Baby care ⚡ Motorvan service point
ABBREVIATIONS: BH/bank hols-bank holidays Etr-Easter Whit-Whitsun dep-departure fr-from hrs-hours m-mile mdnt-midnight rdbt-roundabout rs-restricted service wk-week wknd-weekend ⊘ No credit cards ⊗ No dogs
See page 7 for details of the AA Camping Card Scheme

HIGH BENTHAM *continued*

▶ 81% Lowther Hill Caravan Park

(SD696695)

LA2 7AN
☎ 015242 61657 & 07985 478750
web: www.caravancampingsites.co.uk/
northyorkshire/lowtherhill.htm
dir: *From A65 at Clapham onto B6480 signed Bentham. 3m to site on right*

* ☎ £16.50-£17.50 ☎ £16.50-£17.50 ▲

Open Mar-Nov

Last arrival 21.00hrs Last departure 14.00hrs

A simple site with stunning panoramic views from every pitch. Peace reigns on this little park, though the tourist villages of Ingleton, Clapham and Settle are not far away. All pitches have electricity, and there is a heated toilet/washroom and dishwashing facilities. 1 acre site. 9 touring pitches. 4 hardstandings. Caravan pitches. Motorhome pitches. Tent pitches.

AA Pubs & Restaurants nearby: The Traddock, Austwick 015242 51224

Game Cock Inn, Austwick 015242 51226

New Inn, Clapham 015242 51203

Facilities: ⋒ & ♻

Services: ☎

Within 3 miles: ↋ ⌀ 🖭 🖸

Notes: ⊕ Payment on arrival. Dogs must be kept on leads.

| HINDERWELL | Map 19 NZ71 |

Places to visit

Whitby Abbey, WHITBY 01947 603568
www.english-heritage.org.uk

RNLI Zetland Museum, REDCAR 01642 494311

▶▶▶ 78% Serenity Touring and Camping Park *(NZ792167)*

26A High St TS13 5JH
☎ 01947 841122
e-mail: patandni@aol.com
web: www.serenitycaravanpark.co.uk
dir: *Off A174 in Hinderwell*

* ☎ £18-£22 ☎ £18-£22 ▲ £8

Open Mar-Oct

Last arrival 21.00hrs Last departure noon

A charming park mainly for adults, being developed by enthusiastic owners. It lies behind the village of Hinderwell with its two pubs and store, and is handy for backpackers on the Cleveland Way. The sandy Runswick Bay and old fishing port of Staithes are close by, whilst Whitby is a short drive away. 5.5 acre site. 20 touring pitches. 3 hardstandings. 10 seasonal pitches. Caravan pitches. Motorhome pitches. Tent pitches.

AA Pubs & Restaurants nearby: Magpie Café, Whitby 01947 602058

Facilities: ⋒ ⊙ ℱ ✳ ⊼ ♻ ❶

Services: ☎ 🖸 ⬥ ⌀ Ⓣ ⬥ ↥

Within 3 miles: ⌀ 🖭 ∪

Notes: ⊕ No ball games, kites or frisbees. Dogs must be kept on leads.

| HUNMANBY | Map 17 TA07 |

Places to visit

Sewerby Hall & Gardens, BRIDLINGTON
01262 673769 www.sewerby-hall.co.uk

Scarborough Castle, SCARBOROUGH
01723 372451 www.english-heritage.org.uk

Great for kids: Sea Life & Marine Sanctuary, SCARBOROUGH 01723 376125 www.sealife.co.uk

▶▶▶▶ 79% Orchard Farm Holiday Village *(TA105779)*

Stonegate YO14 0PU
☎ 01723 891582 ▤ 01723 891582
e-mail: info@orchardfarmholidayvillage.co.uk
dir: *A165 from Scarborough towards Bridlington. Turn right signed Hunmanby, site on right just after rail bridge*

☎ £14-£22 ☎ £14-£22 ▲ £14-£22

Open Mar-Oct (rs Off peak some facilities restricted)

Last arrival 23.00hrs Last departure 11.00hrs

Pitches are arranged around a large coarse fishing lake at this grassy park. The young owners are keen and friendly, and offer a wide range of amenities including an indoor heated swimming pool and a licensed bar. 14 acre site. 91 touring pitches. 34 hardstandings. Caravan pitches. Motorhome pitches. Tent pitches. 46 statics.

Leisure: ⛱ ⚠ 🎣 ⏹

Facilities: ⋒ ⊙ ℱ ✳ & Ⓢ 🖫 ⊼ ↢

Services: ☎ 🖸 ⬥ Ⓣ ⬥

Within 3 miles: ↋ ⌀ ⓞ ≋ 🖭 🖸

Notes: ⊕ Dogs must be kept on leads. Minature railway.

LEISURE: ⛱ Indoor swimming pool ⛱ Outdoor swimming pool ⚠ Children's playground ↆ Kid's club ⚲ Tennis court 🎣 Games room ⏹ Separate TV room ↋ 9/18 hole golf course ⬦ Boats for hire ⊟ Cinema ♫ Entertainment ⌀ Fishing ⓞ Mini golf ≋ Watersports ↤ Gym ⊗ Sports field Spa ∪ Stables
FACILITIES: ⬥ Bath ⋒ Shower ⊙ Electric shaver ℱ Hairdryer ✳ Ice Pack Facility & Disabled facilities Ⓢ Public telephone 🖫 Shop on site or within 200yds ⌂ Mobile shop (calls at least 5 days a week) 🖳 BBQ area ⊼ Picnic area ᴡɪғɪ Wi-fi ⬛ Internet access ♻ Recycling ❶ Tourist info ↢ Dog exercise area

HUTTON-LE-HOLE　　　Map 19 SE79

Places to visit

Nunnington Hall, NUNNINGTON 01439 748283
www.nationaltrust.org.uk

Rievaulx Abbey, RIEVAULX 01439 798228
www.english-heritage.org.uk

Great for kids: Pickering Castle, PICKERING
01751 474989 www.english-heritage.org.uk

►►►► 80% Hutton-le-Hole Caravan Park *(SE705895)*

Westfield Lodge YO62 6UG
☎ **01751 417261** 🗎 **01751 417876**
e-mail: rwstrickland@farmersweekly.net
dir: From A170 at Keldholme follow Hutton-le-Hole signs. Approx 2m, over cattle grid, left in 500yds into Park Drive, site signed

* 🚐 fr £15 🚎 fr £15 ▲ fr £12.50

Open Etr-Oct

Last arrival 21.00hrs Last departure noon

A small high quality park on a working farm in the North York Moors National Park. The purpose-built toilet block offers en suite family rooms, and there is a choice of hard-standing or grass pitches within a well-tended area surrounded by hedges and shrubs. The village facilities are a 10-minute walk away. Please note that caravans are prohibited from the A170 at Sutton Bank between Thirsk and Helmsley. 5 acre site. 42 touring pitches. 36 hardstandings. Caravan pitches. Motorhome pitches. Tent pitches.

AA Pubs & Restaurants nearby: Blacksmiths Arms, Lastingham 01751 417247

The Moors Inn, Appleton-le-Moors 01751 417435

Facilities: 🅵⊙🄿✳🕭◐🖵🛖♻ 🅸
Services: 🔌🛢🅃🛒
Within 3 miles: 🍴⊙🚲📮

Notes: Farm walks.

KNARESBOROUGH　　　Map 19 SE35

Places to visit

RHS Garden Harlow Carr, HARROGATE
01423 565418 www.rhs.org.uk/harlowcarr

The Royal Pump Room Museum,
HARROGATE 01423 556188
www.harrogate.gov.uk/museums

Great for kids: Knaresborough Castle & Museum, KNARESBOROUGH 01423 556188
www.harrogate.gov.uk/museums

►►► 74% Kingfisher Caravan Park *(SE343603)*

Low Moor Ln, Farnham HG5 9JB
☎ **01423 869411** 🗎 **01423 869411**
dir: From Knaresborough take A6055. Left in 1m towards Farnham, left in village signed Scotton. Site 1m on left

* 🚐 £14-£18 🚎 £14-£18 ▲ £14-£18

Open Mar-Oct

Last arrival 21.00hrs Last departure 16.00hrs

A large grassy site with open spaces set in a wooded area in rural countryside. Whilst Harrogate, Fountains Abbey and York are within easy reach, anglers will want to take advantage of on-site coarse and fly fishing lakes. The park has a separate flat tenting field with electric hook-ups available. 14 acre site. 35 touring pitches. Caravan pitches. Motorhome pitches. Tent pitches. 80 statics.

AA Pubs & Restaurants nearby: General Tarleton, Knaresborough 01423 340284

Leisure: 🄰
Facilities: 🅵⊙🄿✳🕭◐🖲🖵🛖 🅸
Services: 🔌🛢🛒🧺
Within 3 miles: 🚶🚣🏕📮🖲🖺🚲

Notes. 🐕 Pets must be kept under strict adult control, no football.

MARKINGTON　　　Map 19 SE26

Places to visit

Fountains Abbey & Studley Royal, RIPON
01765 643197 www.fountainsabbey.org.uk

Norton Conyers, RIPON 01765 640333

Great for kids: Stump Cross Caverns, PATELEY BRIDGE 01756 752780
www.stumpcrosscaverns.co.uk

►►► 77% Yorkshire Hussar Inn Holiday Caravan Park *(SE288650)*

High St HG3 3NR
☎ **01765 677327 & 677715**
e-mail: yorkshirehussar@yahoo.co.uk
dir: From A61 between Harrogate & Ripon at Wormald Green follow Markington signs, 1m, left past Post Office into High Street. Site signed on left

🚐 £16.50-£20 🚎 £16.50-£20 ▲ £14-£20

Open Etr-Oct

Last arrival 19.00hrs Last departure noon

A terraced site behind the village inn with well-kept grass. This pleasant site offers spacious pitches with some hardstandings and electricity, and there are a few holiday statics for hire. Although the pub does not provide food, an alternative food pub is available within walking distance. 5 acre site. 20 touring pitches. 2 hardstandings. 12 seasonal pitches. Caravan pitches. Motorhome pitches. Tent pitches. 73 statics.

AA Pubs & Restaurants nearby: Sawley Arms, Sawley 01765 620642

Leisure: 🄰
Facilities: 🅵⊙🄿✳🕭♻ 🅸
Services: 🔌🛢🍴🛒🧺
Within 3 miles: 🚲📮🖲🖺🎣

Notes: 🚫 Dogs must be kept on leads. Paddling pool.

MASHAM Map 19 SE28

Places to visit

Theakston Brewery & Visitor Centre, MASHAM 01765 680000 www.theakstons.co.uk

Norton Conyers, RIPON 01765 640333

Great for kids: Lightwater Valley Theme Park, NORTH STAINLEY 0871 720 0011 www.lightwatervalley.co.uk

►►► 78% Old Station Holiday Park (SE232812)

Old Station Yard, Low Burton HG4 4DF
☎ 01765 689569 📠 01765 689569
e-mail: oldstation@tiscali.co.uk
dir: *A1 onto B6267 signed Masham & Thirsk. In 8m left onto A6108. In 100yds left into site*

* 🚐 £16-£19.50 🚌 £16-£19.50 ⛺ fr £15

Open Mar-Nov

Last arrival 20.00hrs Last departure noon

An interesting site on a former station. The enthusiastic and caring family owners have maintained the railway theme in creating a park with high quality facilities. The small town of Masham with its Theakston and Black Sheep breweries are within easy walking distance of the park. The reception/café in a carefully restored wagon shed provides a range of meals using local produce. 3.75 acre site. 50 touring pitches. Caravan pitches. Motorhome pitches. Tent pitches. 12 statics.

AA Pubs & Restaurants nearby: Kings Head Hotel, Masham 01765 689295

Black Sheep Brewery, Masham 01765 680101

Vennell's, Masham 01765 689000

Facilities: 🚿 ⊙ 💨 ❄ ♿ 📞 🛒 ⛱ Wi-fi 💻 ♻ ℹ

Services: 🔌 🧺 🔥 [T] 🍴 🧊 🛍 ⚓

Within 3 miles: ⛳ 🎣 🛒 🧺 🐎

Notes: No fast cycling around site, no campfires. Dogs must be kept on leads.

NABURN Map 16 SE54

Places to visit

Clifford's Tower, YORK 01904 646940 www.english-heritage.org.uk

Fairfax House, YORK 01904 655543 www.fairfaxhouse.co.uk

Great for kids: Jorvik Viking Centre, YORK 01904 615505 www.jorvik-viking-centre.com

►►►► 78% *Naburn Lock Caravan Park* (SE596446)

GOLD

YO19 4RU
☎ 01904 728697 📠 01904 728697
e-mail: wilks@naburnlock.co.uk
dir: *From A64 (McArthur Glen designer outlet) take A19 N, turn left signed Naburn on B1222, site on right 0.5m past village*

🚐 🚌 ⛺

Open Mar-6 Nov

Last arrival 20.00hrs Last departure 13.00hrs

A family park where the enthusiastic owners are steadily improving its quality. The mainly grass pitches are arranged in small groups separated by mature hedges. The park is close to the River Ouse, and the river towpath provides excellent walking and cycling opportunities. The river bus to nearby York leaves from a jetty beside the park. 7 acre site. 100 touring pitches. 12 hardstandings. Caravan pitches. Motorhome pitches. Tent pitches.

AA Pubs & Restaurants nearby: Blue Bell, York 01904 654904

Lysander Arms, York 01904 640845

Facilities: 🚿 ⊙ 💨 ❄ ♿ 🛒 ⛱ 🐕

Services: 🔌 🧺 🔥 🌿 [T] 🧊 ⚓

Within 3 miles: 🎣 🛒 🧺 🐎

Notes: Adults-only section. River fishing.

NETHERBY Map 16 SE34

Places to visit

Abbey House Museum, LEEDS 0113 230 5492 www.leeds.gov.uk

Royal Armouries Museum, LEEDS 0113 220 1866 www.royalarmouries.org

Great for kids: Tropical World, LEEDS 0113 214 5721 www.leeds.gov.uk

►►►► 80% *Maustin Caravan Park* (SE332470)

GOLD

Kearby with Netherby LS22 4DA
☎ 0113 288 6234
e-mail: info@maustin.co.uk
dir: *From A61 (Leeds-Harrogate road) follow signs for Kirkby Overblow. Right towards Kearby, pass farm buildings to x-rds. Right to site*

🚐 🚌 ⛺

Open Mar-28 Jan

A secluded park for adults only, with pitches set around a well-tended grassed area. Adjacent to the pitching area, the amenity block offers a high standard of facilities. The charming Stables Restaurant, with its cosy bar and patio, is open at weekends and bank holidays, and the park has its own flat bowling green where competitions are held throughout the season. 8 acre site. 25 touring pitches. Caravan pitches. Motorhome pitches. Tent pitches. 70 statics.

AA Pubs & Restaurants nearby: Windmill Inn, Linton 01937 582209

Facilities: 🚿 ⊙ 💨 ❄ Wi-fi

Services: 🔌 🧺 🍷 🍴

Within 3 miles: ⛳ 🎣 🛒 🐎

Notes: Adults only.

LEISURE: 🏊 Indoor swimming pool 🏖 Outdoor swimming pool 🛝 Children's playground 👋 Kid's club 🎾 Tennis court 🎱 Games room 📺 Separate TV room ⛳ 9/18 hole golf course 🚣 Boats for hire 🎬 Cinema 🎵 Entertainment 🎣 Fishing ⚪ Mini golf 🌊 Watersports 🏋 Gym ⚽ Sports field **Spa** 🐎 Stables
FACILITIES: 🛁 Bath 🚿 Shower ⊙ Electric shaver 💨 Hairdryer ❄ Ice Pack Facility ♿ Disabled facilities 📞 Public telephone 🛒 Shop on site or within 200yds 🚚 Mobile shop (calls at least 5 days a week) 🍖 BBQ area ⛱ Picnic area Wi-fi Wi-fi 💻 Internet access ♻ Recycling ℹ Tourist info 🐕 Dog exercise area

NORTHALLERTON — Map 19 SE39

Places to visit

Mount Grace Priory, OSMOTHERLEY
01609 883494 www.english-heritage.org.uk

Theakston Brewery & Visitor Centre, MASHAM
01765 680000 www.theakstons.co.uk

Great for kids: Falconry UK - Birds of Prey
Centre, THIRSK 01845 587522
www.falconrycentre.co.uk

►►►► 79% Otterington Park

(SE378882)

Station Farm, South Otterington DL7 9JB
☎ **01609 780656**
e-mail: info@otteringtonpark.com
dir: *From A168 midway between Northallerton
& Thirsk onto unclassified road signed South
Otterington. Site on right just before South
Otterington*

* 🚐 £18-£22 🚐

Open Mar-Oct

Last arrival 21.00hrs Last departure 13.00hrs

A high quality park on a working farm with open
outlooks across the Vale of York. Now extended to
include another paddock with 22 hardstanding
pitches and three camping pods, it enjoys a
peaceful location with a lovely nature walk and
on-site fishing, which is very popular. Young
children will enjoy the play area. Toilet facilities
are very good. The attractions of Northallerton and
Thirsk are a few minutes' drive away. 6 acre site.
62 touring pitches. 62 hardstandings. Caravan
pitches. Motorhome pitches. 3 wooden pods.

Leisure: 🅰 ⚙

Facilities: 🛁 🐾 ☉ ⌂ ✳ ⚅ 🕙 🖥 🎋 🛒 WiFi ♻ ⓘ

Services: 🔌 🖥 🛢 🔋

Within 3 miles: ⬇ 🏇 🎣 ◎ 🛒 🖥

Notes: Hot tub, fitness equipment.

NORTH STANLEY — Map 19 SE27

Places to visit

Norton Conyers, RIPON 01765 640333

Falconry UK - Birds of Prey Centre, THIRSK
01845 587522 www.falconrycentre.co.uk

Great for kids: Lightwater Valley Theme Park,
NORTH STANLEY 0871 720 0011
www.lightwatervalley.co.uk

►►►► 76% Sleningford Watermill Caravan Camping Park *(SE280783)*

HG4 3HQ
☎ **01765 635201**
web: www.sleningfordwatermill.co.uk
dir: *Adjacent to A6108. 5m N of Ripon & 1m N of
North Stanley*

🚐 🚐 ⛺

Open Etr & Apr-Oct

Last arrival 21.00hrs Last departure 12.30hrs

The old watermill and the River Ure make an
attractive setting for this touring park which is
laid out in two areas. Pitches are placed in
meadowland and close to mature woodland, and
the park has two enthusiastic managers. This is a
popular place with canoeists. 14 acre site. 140
touring pitches. 8 hardstandings. 40 seasonal
pitches. Caravan pitches. Motorhome pitches.
Tent pitches.

AA Pubs & Restaurants nearby: Bruce Arms, West
Tanfield 01677 470325

Black Sheep Brewery, Masham 01765 680101

Leisure: ⚙

Facilities: 🐾 ☉ ✳ ⚅ 🎋 🛒 ♻ ⓘ

Services: 🔌 🖥 🛢 🔋 🔋

Within 3 miles: ⬇ 🏊 🎣 ⚓ 🛒 🖥

Notes: Groups by prior arrangement only, booked
through organisations or associations. Dogs must
be kept on leads. Fly fishing, outdoor activities,
canoe sales, hire & tuition.

OSMOTHERLEY — Map 19 SE49

Places to visit

Mount Grace Priory, OSMOTHERLEY
01609 883494 www.english-heritage.org.uk

Gisborough Priory, GUISBOROUGH 01287 633801
www.english-heritage.org.uk

Great for kids: Falconry UK - Birds of Prey
Centre, THIRSK 01845 587522
www.falconrycentre.co.uk

PREMIER PARK

►►►►► 79% *Cote Ghyll Caravan & Camping Park* *(SE459979)*

DL6 3AH
☎ **01609 883425**
e-mail: hills@coteghyll.com
dir: *Exit A19 dual carriageway at A684
(Northallerton junct). Follow signs to Osmotherley.
Left in village centre. Site entrance 0.5m on right*

🚐 🚐 ⛺

Open Mar-Oct

Last arrival 22.00hrs Last departure noon

A quiet, peaceful site in a pleasant valley on the
edge of moors, close to the village. The park is
divided into terraces bordered by woodland, and
the extra well-appointed amenity block is a
welcome addition to this attractive park. Mature
trees, shrubs and an abundance of fresh seasonal
floral displays create a relaxing and peaceful
atmosphere and the whole park is immaculately
maintained. Major investment has delivered high
standards in landscaping and facilities. There are
pubs and shops nearby and holiday statics for
hire. 7 acre site. 77 touring pitches. 22
hardstandings. Caravan pitches. Motorhome
pitches. Tent pitches. 18 statics.

AA Pubs & Restaurants nearby: Golden Lion,
Osmotherley 01609 883526

Leisure: 🅰

Facilities: 🛁 🐾 ☉ ⌂ ✳ ⚅ 🕙 🖥 🎋 WiFi ⓘ

Services: 🔌 🖥 🛢 ⚗ 🔋 🔋 🔋

Within 3 miles: 🎣 🖥 🖥 ⛳

Notes: Family park. Dogs must be kept on leads.

SERVICES: 🔌 Electric hook up 🖥 Launderette 🍺 Licensed bar 🛢 Calor Gas ⚗ Camping Gaz 🕙 Toilet fluid 🍽 Café/Restaurant 🍟 Fast Food/Takeaway 🔋 Battery charging 🍼 Baby care ⚓ Motorvan service point

ABBREVIATIONS: BH/bank hols-bank holidays Etr-Easter Whit-Whitsun dep-departure fr-from hrs-hours m-mile mdnt-midnight rdbt-roundabout rs-restricted service wk-week wknd-weekend ⊛ No credit cards ⊗ No dogs   See page 7 for details of the AA Camping Card Scheme

PICKERING
Map 19 SE78

Places to visit

Pickering Castle, PICKERING 01751 474989
www.english-heritage.org.uk

North Yorkshire Moors Railway, PICKERING
01751 472508 www.nymr.co.uk

Great for kids: Flamingo Land Theme Park &
Zoo, KIRBY MISPERTON 01653 668287
www.flamingoland.co.uk

▶▶▶▶ **78% Wayside Holiday Park**

(SE764859)

Wrelton YO18 8PG
☎ **01751 472608** 🖨 **01751 472608**
e-mail: wrelton@waysideholidaypark.co.uk
web: www.waysideparks.co.uk
dir: *2.5m W of Pickering off A170, follow signs at
Wrelton*

🚐 🚐

Open Etr-end Oct

Last arrival 22.00hrs Last departure noon

Located in the village of Wrelton, this well-
maintained mainly seasonal touring and holiday
home park is divided into small paddocks by
mature hedging. Major investment has resulted in
the complete refurbishment of the amenity block,
which now has smart, modern facilities. The
village pub and restaurant are within a few
minutes' walk of the park. Please note that
caravans are prohibited from the A170 at Sutton
Bank between Thirsk and Helmsley. 10 acre site.
40 touring pitches. 5 hardstandings. Caravan
pitches. Motorhome pitches. 122 statics.

AA Pubs & Restaurants nearby: Fox & Hounds
Country Inn, Sinnington, 01751 431577

White Swan Inn, Pickering 01751 472288

Fox & Rabbit Inn, Lockton 01751 460213

Leisure: ⚬

Facilities: ⚬⚬⚬⚬⚬⚬

Services: ⚬⚬⚬⚬⚬

Within 3 miles: ⚬⚬⚬⚬⚬⚬

Notes: Dogs must be kept on leads.

RICHMOND
Map 19 NZ10

Places to visit

Green Howards Museum, RICHMOND
01748 826561 www.greenhowards.org.uk

Bolton Castle, CASTLE BOLTON 01969 623981
www.boltoncastle.co.uk

Great for kids: Richmond Castle, RICHMOND
01748 822493 www.english-heritage.org.uk

▶▶▶▶ **77% Brompton Caravan Park**

(NZ199002)

Brompton-on-Swale DL10 7EZ
☎ **01748 824629** 🖨 **01748 826383**
e-mail: brompton.caravanpark@btinternet.com
dir: *Exit A1 signed Catterick. Take B6271 to
Brompton-on-Swale, site 1m on left*

🚐 🚐 🛖

Open mid Mar-Oct

Last arrival 21.00hrs Last departure noon

An attractive and well-managed family park where
pitches have an open outlook across the River
Swale. There is a good children's playground, an
excellent family recreation room, a takeaway food
service, and fishing is available on the river.
Electric hook ups and camping pods are to be
installed in tent field for 2012 season. Holiday
apartments are also available. 14 acre site. 177
touring pitches. 2 hardstandings. Caravan
pitches. Motorhome pitches. Tent pitches. 22
statics.

AA Pubs & Restaurants nearby: Charles Bathurst
Inn, Arkengarthdale 01748 884567

Leisure: ⚬ ⚬

Facilities: ⚬⚬⚬⚬⚬⚬⚬⚬⚬⚬

Services: ⚬⚬⚬⚬⚬⚬

Within 3 miles: ⚬⚬⚬⚬⚬⚬

Notes: No gazebos, no motor, electric cars or
scooters, no open fires or wood burners. Quiet at
mdnt.

AA CAMPING CARD SITE

▶▶▶ **76% Swale View Caravan Park**

(NZ134013)

Reeth Rd DL10 4SF
☎ **01748 823106** & **07736 820283**
🖨 **01748 823123**
e-mail: swaleview@teesdaleonline.co.uk
dir: *3m W of Richmond on A6108 (Reeth to
Leyburn road)*

* 🚐 £18-£28 🚐 £18-£28 🛖 £18-£28

Open Mar-15 Jan

Last arrival 21.00hrs Last departure noon

Shaded by trees and overlooking the River Swale is
this attractive, mainly grassy site, which has a
number of attractive holiday homes and seasonal
tourers. The facilities continue to be improved by
enthusiastic owners and the park offers facilities
for 30 tourers, all with electric and hardstandings.
It is a short distance from Richmond, and well
situated for exploring Swaledale and Wensleydale.
13 acre site. 30 touring pitches. 30
hardstandings. 15 seasonal pitches. Caravan
pitches. Motorhome pitches. Tent pitches. 100
statics.

AA Pubs & Restaurants nearby: Charles Bathurst
Inn, Arkengarthdale 01748 884567

Leisure: ⚬

Facilities: ⚬⚬⚬⚬⚬⚬⚬⚬⚬⚬

Services: ⚬⚬⚬⚬⚬⚬⚬

Within 3 miles: ⚬⚬⚬⚬⚬

Notes: 1 dog per pitch. Dogs must be kept on
leads. Vending machine.

RIPON

See also North Stainley

Places to visit

Fountains Abbey & Studley Royal, RIPON
01765 643197 www.fountainsabbey.org.uk

Norton Conyers, RIPON 01765 640333

Great for kids: Falconry UK - Birds of Prey
Centre, THIRSK 01845 587522
www.falconrycentre.co.uk

LEISURE: 🏊 Indoor swimming pool 🏊 Outdoor swimming pool ⚬ Children's playground 🪁 Kid's club 🎾 Tennis court 🎱 Games room 📺 Separate TV room
⚬ 9/18 hole golf course ⚓ Boats for hire 🎬 Cinema 🎵 Entertainment 🎣 Fishing ⚬ Mini golf 🏄 Watersports 💪 Gym ⚬ Sports field **Spa** ⚬ Stables
FACILITIES: 🛁 Bath 🚿 Shower ⚬ Electric shaver ⚬ Hairdryer ❄ Ice Pack Facility ♿ Disabled facilities ⚬ Public telephone 🏪 Shop on site or within 200yds
🚐 Mobile shop (calls at least 5 days a week) 🍖 BBQ area ⚬ Picnic area ⚬ Wi-fi 🌐 Internet access ♻ Recycling ⚬ Tourist info ⚬ Dog exercise area

RIPON
Map 19 SE37

▶▶▶▶ 78% Riverside Meadows Country Caravan Park (SE317726)

Ure Bank Top HG4 1JD
☎ 01765 602964 📠 01765 604045
e-mail: info@flowerofmay.com
dir: *On A61 at N end of bridge out of Ripon, W along river (do not cross river). Site 400yds, signed*

* 🚐 £15-£21 � £15-£21 ▲ £13-£21

Open Etr-Oct (rs Low-mid season bar open wknds only)

Last arrival dusk Last departure noon

This pleasant, well-maintained site stands on high ground overlooking the River Ure, one mile from the town centre. The site has an excellent club with family room and quiet lounge. There is no access to the river from the site. 28 acre site. 80 touring pitches. 40 hardstandings. 40 seasonal pitches. Caravan pitches. Motorhome pitches. Tent pitches. 269 statics.

AA Pubs & Restaurants nearby: Sawley Arms, Sawley 01765 620642

Leisure: ⚙ 🎣 ⊡ 🎵
Facilities: 🅿 ⊙ ✳ ♿ 🕙 🛆 🎪 📬 WiFi ♻ 🅸
Services: 🔌 🚾 🍴 🔋 ⊘ Ⓣ 🚼 ⚓
Within 3 miles: ♨ ⛳ 🗓 🔗 🚴 🛒 🎢 ⛵ ∪

Notes: No noise after mdnt. Dogs by arrangement only. Dogs must be kept on leads.

ROBIN HOOD'S BAY
Map 19 NZ90

See also Whitby

▶▶▶▶ 80% Grouse Hill Caravan Park (NZ928002)

Flask Bungalow Farm, Fylingdales YO22 4QH
☎ 01947 880543 & 880560 📠 01947 880543
e-mail: info@grousehill.co.uk
dir: *Off A171 (Whitby-Scarborough road), entered via loop road at Flask Inn*

🚐 � ▲

Open Mar-Oct (rs Etr-May shop & reception restricted)

Last arrival 20.30hrs Last departure noon

A spacious family park on a south-facing slope, with many terraced pitches overlooking the North Yorkshire Moors National Park. Major investment in recent years has greatly improved the touring areas and amenities, in particular one of the toilet blocks, which has a superb fully-serviced shower room and a private bathroom, and 4 camping pods were added in 2011. An ideal base for walking and touring. 14 acre site. 175 touring pitches. 30 hardstandings. Caravan pitches. Motorhome pitches. Tent pitches. 1 static. 4 wooden pods.

Grouse Hill Caravan Park

AA Pubs & Restaurants nearby: Laurel Inn, Robin Hood's Bay 01947 880400

Magpie Café, Whitby 01947 602058

Leisure: ⚙ 🎣
Facilities: 🛏 🅿 ⊙ 🅿 ✳ ♿ 🕙 🛆 🎪 ♻ 🅸
Services: 🔌 🚾 🔋 ⊘ Ⓣ 🚼 ⚓
Within 3 miles: ♨ 🛒 🎢 ∪

Notes: Dogs must be kept on leads. Fish & chip van on Saturdays from 20.15hrs.

see advert below

SERVICES: 🔌 Electric hook up 🚾 Launderette 🍴 Licensed bar 🔋 Calor Gas ⊘ Camping Gaz Ⓣ Toilet fluid 🍴 Café/Restaurant ⚓ Fast Food/Takeaway 🔋 Battery charging 🚼 Baby care ⚓ Motorvan service point
ABBREVIATIONS: BH/bank hols-bank holidays Etr-Easter Whit-Whitsun dep-departure fr-from hrs-hours m-mile mdnt-midnight rdbt-roundabout rs-restricted service wk-week wknd-weekend ⊛ No credit cards ⊗ No dogs
See page 7 for details of the AA Camping Card Scheme

ROBIN HOOD'S BAY *continued*

▶▶▶▶ 80% Middlewood Farm
Holiday Park *(NZ945045)*

Middlewood Ln, Fylingthorpe YO22 4UF
☎ 01947 880414 📠 01947 880871
e-mail: info@middlewoodfarm.com
dir: *From A171 towards Robin Hood's Bay & into Fylingthorpe. Site signed from A171*

⁕ ⊞ £15-£25 ⚌ £15-£25 ▲ £12-£22

Open Mar-Oct

Last arrival 20.00hrs Last departure 11.00hrs

A peaceful, friendly family park enjoying panoramic views of Robin Hood's Bay in a picturesque fishing village. The park has two toilet blocks with private facilities. The village pub is a five-minute walk away, and the beach can be reached via a new path leading directly from the site, which is also accessible by wheelchair users. 7 acre site. 100 touring pitches. 19 hardstandings. Caravan pitches. Motorhome pitches. Tent pitches. 30 statics.

AA Pubs & Restaurants nearby: Laurel Inn, Robin Hood's Bay 01947 880400

Magpie Café, Whitby 01947 602058

Leisure: ⚏

Facilities: ⌇🏠⊙🏋🌂⚴🛁📮 WiFi ♻ 🄋

Services: 🖭🗄🚽🍽🛒🚚🖦

Within 3 miles: 🚴🏇🎣🛍🎯∪

Notes: Dangerous dog breeds are not accepted, no radios or noise after 22.00hrs. Dogs must be kept on leads.

see advert below

ROSEDALE ABBEY

Places to visit

Pickering Castle, PICKERING 01751 474989 www.english-heritage.org.uk

North Yorkshire Moors Railway, PICKERING 01751 472508 www.nymr.co.uk

Great for kids: Flamingo Land Theme Park & Zoo, KIRBY MISPERTON 01653 668287 www.flamingoland.co.uk

---

ROSEDALE ABBEY   Map 19 SE79

▶▶▶▶ 78% Rosedale Caravan & Camping Park *(SE725958)*

YO18 8SA
☎ 01751 417272
e-mail: info@flowerofmay.com
dir: *From Pickering take A170 towards Sinnington for 2.25m. At Wrelton turn right onto unclassified road signed Cropton & Rosedale, 7m. Site on left in village*

⁕ ⊞ £15-£21 ⚌ £15-£21 ▲ £15-£21

Open Mar-Oct

Last arrival dusk Last departure noon

Set in a sheltered valley in the centre of the North Yorkshire Moors National Park, and divided into separate areas for tents, tourers and statics. A very popular park, with well-tended grounds, and close to the pretty village of Rosedale Abbey. Two toilet blocks offer private, combined facilities. 10 acre site. 100 touring pitches. 20 seasonal pitches. Caravan pitches. Motorhome pitches. Tent pitches. 35 statics.

AA Pubs & Restaurants nearby: Blacksmiths Arms, Lastingham 01751 417247

New Inn, Cropton 01751 417330

Leisure: ⚏

Facilities: 🏠⊙🌂⚴🛁🖭🛍📮🎣🄋

Services: 🖭🗄🚽🍽T🛒

Within 3 miles: 🚴🎣🛍🎯∪

Notes: Dogs by arrangement only, no noise after mdnt. Dogs must be kept on leads.

LEISURE: 🏊 Indoor swimming pool 🏊 Outdoor swimming pool 🎠 Children's playground 🎪 Kid's club 🎾 Tennis court 🎱 Games room 📺 Separate TV room ⛳ 9/18 hole golf course 🚣 Boats for hire 🎬 Cinema 🎵 Entertainment 🎣 Fishing ⛳ Mini golf 🏄 Watersports 🏋 Gym 🏟 Sports field Spa ∪ Stables
FACILITIES: 🛁 Bath 🚿 Shower ⊙ Electric shaver 🖊 Hairdryer ❄ Ice Pack Facility ♿ Disabled facilities 📞 Public telephone 🛍 Shop on site or within 200yds 🚐 Mobile shop (calls at least 5 days a week) 🍖 BBQ area 🌳 Picnic area WiFi Wi-fi 🖥 Internet access ♻ Recycling 🄋 Tourist info 🐕 Dog exercise area

SCARBOROUGH
Map 17 TA08

See also Filey & Wykeham

Places to visit

Scarborough Castle, SCARBOROUGH
01723 372451 www.english-heritage.org.uk

Pickering Castle, PICKERING 01751 474989
www.english-heritage.org.uk

Great for kids: Sea Life & Marine Sanctuary,
SCARBOROUGH 01723 376125 www.sealife.co.uk

PREMIER PARK

►►►►► 75% **Jacobs Mount
Caravan Park** *(TA021868)*

Jacobs Mount, Stepney Rd YO12 5NL
☎ 01723 361178 📄 01723 361178
e-mail: jacobsmount@yahoo.co.uk
dir: *Direct access from A170*

* 🚐 £11-£21 🚎 £11-£21 ▲ £11-£21

Open Mar-Nov (rs Mar-May & Oct limited hours
at shop/bar)

Last arrival 22.00hrs Last departure noon

An elevated family-run park surrounded by
woodland and open countryside, yet only two miles
from the beach. Touring pitches are terraced gravel
stands with individual services. The Jacobs Tavern
serves a wide range of appetising meals and
snacks, and there is a separate well-equipped
games room for teenagers. 18 acre site. 156 touring
pitches. 131 hardstandings. Caravan pitches.
Motorhome pitches. Tent pitches. 60 statics.

AA Pubs & Restaurants nearby: Cayley Arms,
Brompton-by-Sawdon 01723 859372

Anvil Inn, Sawdon 01723 859896

Leisure: 🏛 🔍 🖵 🎵
Facilities: 🖛 🌪 ☺ 🌳 🐾 ✳ ♿ 🕐 🖻 ✈ ❶
Services: 🔌 🗄 🍴 🛢 ⊘ T 🍴 🛒 🏧 ⚙
Within 3 miles: ↧ ⅞ 目 🏌 ◎ 🌥 🖻 🗄 U

Notes: Dogs must be kept on leads. Food
preparation area.

AA CAMPING CARD SITE

►►►► 78% **Scalby Close Park**

(TA020925)

Burniston Rd YO13 0DA
☎ 01723 365908
e-mail: info@scalbyclosepark.co.uk
web: www.scalbyclosepark.co.uk
dir: *2m N of Scarborough on A615 (coast road),
1m from junct with A171*

* 🚐 £19-£27 🚎 £19-£27

Open Mar-Oct

Last arrival 22.00hrs Last departure noon

An attractive park with enthusiastic owners who
have carried out many improvements. The site has
a shower block, a laundry and fully-serviced
pitches, and the landscaping is also very good.
This is an ideal base from which to explore the
nearby coast and countryside. 3 acre site. 42
touring pitches. 42 hardstandings. Caravan
pitches. Motorhome pitches. 5 statics.

AA Pubs & Restaurants nearby: Cayley Arms,
Brompton-by-Sawdon 01723 859372

Anvil Inn, Sawdon 01723 859896

Facilities: 🌪 ☺ 🌳 ✳ ♿ 🕐 🖻
Services: 🔌 🗄 ⊘ T 🛒 ⚙
Within 3 miles: ↧ ⅞ 目 🏌 🖻 🗄 U
Notes: 🐾

►►► 80% **Killerby Old Hall** *(TA063829)*

Killerby YO11 3TW
☎ 01723 583799 📄 01723 581608
e-mail: killerbyhall@btconnect.com
dir: *Direct access via B1261 at Killerby, near
Cayton*

🚐 🚎

Open 14 Feb-4 Jan

Last arrival 20.00hrs Last departure noon

A small secluded park, well sheltered by mature
trees and shrubs, located at the rear of the old
hall. Use of the small indoor swimming pool is
shared by visitors to the hall's holiday
accommodation. There is a children's play area. 2
acre site. 20 touring pitches. 20 hardstandings.
Caravan pitches. Motorhome pitches.

Killerby Old Hall

AA Pubs & Restaurants nearby: Cayley Arms,
Brompton-by-Sawdon 01723 859372

Anvil Inn, Sawdon 01723 859896

Leisure: 🏊 🏛 ☺ 🔍
Facilities: 🌪 ☺ 🌳 🐾 ✳ ♻ ❶
Services: 🔌 🗄
Within 3 miles: ↧ 🏌 ◎ 🌥 🖻 🗄 U

NEW ►►► 77% **Arosa Caravan &
Camping Park** *(TA014830)*

Ratten Row, Seamer YO12 4QB
☎ 01723 862166 & 07858 694077
e-mail: info@arosacamping.co.uk
dir: *Off A64 towards Scarborough, take B1261.
At rdbt signed Seamer 1st turn left on entering
village. From Pickering on A171 turn right at
Seamer rdbt. Last turn right in village*

🚐 £13-£28 🚎 £13-£28 ▲ £13-£28

Open Mar-4 Jan

Last arrival 21.00hrs Last departure by
arrangement

A mature park in a secluded location, but with
easy access to costal attractions. Touring areas
are hedge-screened to provide privacy, and a well
stocked bar, serving food is also available.
Barbecues and hog roasts are a feature during the
warmer months. 9 acre site. 118 touring pitches.
25 hardstandings. 40 seasonal pitches. Caravan
pitches. Motorhome pitches. Tent pitches. 8
statics.

AA Pubs & Restaurants nearby: Cayley Arms,
Brompton-by-Sawdon 01723 859372 $Coachman
Inn, Snainton 01723 859231

Leisure: 🏛 🔍 🎵
Facilities: 🌪 🌳 ✳ ♿ 🕐 wifi 🖥 ❶
Services: 🔌 🗄 🍴 🛢 ⊘ T 🍴 🏧
Within 3 miles: ↧ 🏌 🖻 🗄 U

Notes: No noise after 23.00hrs, no generators, no
powered bikes or scooters. Dogs must be kept on
leads.

SERVICES: 🔌 Electric hook up 🗄 Launderette 🍴 Licensed bar 🛢 Calor Gas ⊘ Camping Gaz T Toilet fluid 🍴 Café/Restaurant 🏧 Fast Food/Takeaway 🔋 Battery charging
🚼 Baby care ⚙ Motorvan service point
ABBREVIATIONS: BH/bank hols-bank holidays Etr-Easter Whit-Whitsun dep-departure fr-from hrs-hours m-mile mdnt-midnight rdbt-roundabout rs-restricted service wk-week
wknd-weekend 🐾 No credit cards 🚫 No dogs   See page 7 for details of the AA Camping Card Scheme

SCOTCH CORNER — Map 19 NZ20

Places to visit

Green Howards Museum, RICHMOND
01748 826561 www.greenhowards.org.uk

Bolton Castle, CASTLE BOLTON 01969 623981
www.boltoncastle.co.uk

Great for kids: Raby Castle, STAINDROP
01833 660202 www.rabycastle.com

►►► 75% Scotch Corner Caravan Park (NZ210054)

DL10 6NS
☎ 01748 822530   🖨 01748 822530
e-mail: marshallleisure@aol.com
dir: From Scotch Corner junct of A1 & A66 take A6108 towards Richmond. 250mtrs, cross central reservation, return 200mtrs to site entrance

🚐 🚎 ⛺

Open Etr-Oct

Last arrival 22.30hrs Last departure noon

A well-maintained site with good facilities, ideally situated as a stopover, and an equally good location for touring. The Vintage Hotel, which serves food, can be accessed from the rear of the site. 7 acre site. 96 touring pitches. 4 hardstandings. Caravan pitches. Motorhome pitches. Tent pitches.

AA Pubs & Restaurants nearby: Black Bull Inn, Moulton 01325 377289

Hack & Spade, Whashton 01748 823721

Facilities: 🖍⊙☂❋⛅🚿🏕🐕♻❶
Services: 🚐🗑🍴🛢⊘🅣🍽🛒⛟
Within 3 miles: ⬇🏇🏩🛍🛒∪

Notes: 🐕 Dogs must be kept on leads. Recreation area for children, soft ball.

SELBY

Places to visit

York Castle Museum, YORK 01904 687687
www.yorkcastlemuseum.org.uk

Micklegate Bar Museum, YORK 01904 615505
www.micklegatebar.com

Great for kids: DIG, YORK 01904 615505
www.digyork.co.uk

SELBY — Map 16 SE63

►►► 79% The Ranch Caravan Park
(SE664337)

Cliffe Common YO8 6EF
☎ 01757 638984   🖨 01757 630089
e-mail: contact@theranchcaravanpark.co.uk
dir: Exit A63 at Cliffe signed Skipwith. Site 1m N on left

✱ 🚐 £16.50-£18.50 🚎 £16.50-£18.50
⛺ £16.50-£18.50

Open 5 Feb-5 Jan

Last arrival 20.00hrs Last departure noon

A compact, sheltered park in open countryside offering excellent amenities. The enthusiastic and welcoming family owners have created a country club feel, with a tasteful bar serving food at weekends. There are timber lodge holiday homes for sale. 7 acre site. 50 touring pitches. 50 hardstandings. Caravan pitches. Motorhome pitches. Tent pitches.

Leisure: 🅐
Facilities: 🖍⊙☂❋⛅🚿🏠🏕📶♻❶
Services: 🚐🗑🍴🛢⊘🅣🍽⛟
Within 3 miles: 🏇🏩🛍

Notes: No ball games, no campfires, no hanging of washing from trees. Dogs must be kept on leads.

SLINGSBY — Map 19 SE67

Places to visit

Nunnington Hall, NUNNINGTON 01439 748283
www.nationaltrust.org.uk

Castle Howard, MALTON 01653 648333
www.castlehoward.co.uk

►►►► 77% Robin Hood Caravan & Camping Park (SE701748)

Green Dyke Ln YO62 4AP
☎ 01653 628391   🖨 01653 628392
e-mail: info@robinhoodcaravanpark.co.uk
dir: Access from B1257 (Malton to Helmsley road)

✱ 🚐 £17-£27 🚎 £17-£27 ⛺ £15-£25

Open Mar-Oct

Last arrival 18.00hrs Last departure noon

A pleasant, well-maintained grassy park, in a good position for touring North Yorkshire. Situated on the edge of the village of Slingsby, the park has hardstandings and electricity for every pitch. 2 acre site. 32 touring pitches. 22 hardstandings. Caravan pitches. Motorhome pitches. Tent pitches. 35 statics.

Robin Hood Caravan & Camping Park

AA Pubs & Restaurants nearby: Worsley Arms Hotel, Hovingham 01653 628234

Malt Shovel, Hovingham 01653 628264

Royal Oak Inn, Nunnington 01439 748271

Leisure: 🅐
Facilities: 🖍⊙☂❋⛅🚿🏠🏕📶🖥♻❶
Services: 🚐🗑🍴🛢⊘🅣🛒
Within 3 miles: 🏇🛍∪

Notes: No noise after 23.00hrs. Dogs must be kept on leads. Caravan hire, off-licence, fish & chip shop once a week.

see advert on opposite page

SNAINTON — Map 17 SE98

Places to visit

Scarborough Castle, SCARBOROUGH
01723 372451 www.english-heritage.org.uk

Pickering Castle, PICKERING 01751 474989
www.english-heritage.org.uk

Great for kids: Sea Life & Marine Sanctuary, SCARBOROUGH 01723 376125 www.sealife.co.uk

►►►► 85% Jasmine Caravan Park
(SE928813)

Cross Ln YO13 9BE
☎ 01723 859240
e-mail: enquiries@jasminepark.co.uk
dir: Turn S off A170 in Snainton, then follow signs

✱ 🚐 £18-£30 🚎 £18-£30 ⛺ £18-£30

Open Mar-Oct

Last arrival 20.00hrs Last departure noon

A peaceful and beautifully-presented park on the edge of a pretty village, and sheltered by high hedges. The toilet block with individual wash cubicles is maintained to a very high standard, and there is a licensed shop. This picturesque park lies midway between Pickering and Scarborough on the southern edge of the North Yorkshire Moors. Please note there is no motorhome service point but two additional super pitches for motorhomes were added for the 2011

LEISURE: 🏊 Indoor swimming pool 🏊 Outdoor swimming pool 🅐 Children's playground 🅚 Kid's club 🎾 Tennis court 🎱 Games room 📺 Separate TV room
⛳ 9/18 hole golf course ⛵ Boats for hire 🎬 Cinema 🎵 Entertainment 🎣 Fishing ⛳ Mini golf 🏄 Watersports 🏋 Gym ⚽ Sports field Spa ∪ Stables
FACILITIES: 🛁 Bath 🚿 Shower ⊙ Electric shaver 🖐 Hairdryer ❋ Ice Pack Facility ⛅ Disabled facilities 🕾 Public telephone 🏠 Shop on site or within 200yds
🚐 Mobile shop (calls at least 5 days a week) 🍴 BBQ area 🏕 Picnic area 📶 Wi-fi 🖥 Internet access ♻ Recycling ❶ Tourist info 🐕 Dog exercise area

season. 5 acre site. 94 touring pitches. 42 hardstandings. 42 seasonal pitches. Caravan pitches. Motorhome pitches. Tent pitches. 16 statics.

Jasmine Caravan Park

AA Pubs & Restaurants nearby: Coachman Inn, Snainton 01723 859231

New Inn, Thornton le Dale 01751 474226

Cayley Arms, Brompton-by-Sawdon 01723 859372

Leisure: 🛝 ⚽

Facilities: 🛁 🚿 ⊙ 🚿 ✲ ♿ ✆ $ ⛩ [Wi-fi] 💻 ♻ ℹ

Services: 🔌 🧺 🔥 ⛺ [T] 🚼

Within 3 miles: ⛳ 🎣 ◎ $ 🧺 Ʊ

Notes: Dogs must be kept on leads. Baby changing unit.

STAINFORTH — Map 18 SD86

Places to visit

Brodsworth Hall & Gardens, DONCASTER 01302 722598 www.english-heritage.org.uk

Doncaster Museum & Art Gallery, DONCASTER 01302 734293 www.doncaster.gov.uk/museums

Great for kids: The Yorkshire Waterways Museum, GOOLE 01405 768730 www.waterwaysmuseum.org.uk

►►►► 78% Knight Stainforth Hall Caravan & Campsite *(SD816672)*

BD24 0DP

☎ 01729 822200 📠 01729 823387

e-mail: info@knightstainforth.co.uk

dir: *From W, on A65 take B6480 for Settle, left before swimming pool signed Little Stainforth. From E, through Settle on B6480, over bridge to swimming pool, turn right*

* 🚐 £16-£22 🚌 £16-£22 ⛺ £16-£22

Open Mar-Oct

Last arrival 22.00hrs Last departure noon

Located near Settle and the River Ribble in the Yorkshire Dales National Park, this well-maintained family site is sheltered by mature woodland. It is an ideal base for walking or touring in the beautiful surrounding areas. The toilet block is appointed to a very high standard. 6 acre site. 100 touring pitches. 30 hardstandings. Caravan pitches. Motorhome pitches. Tent pitches. 60 statics.

AA Pubs & Restaurants nearby: Black Horse Hotel, Giggleswick 01729 822506

Game Cock Inn, Austwick 015242 51226

The Traddock, Austwick 015242 51224

New Inn, Clapham 015242 51203

Leisure: 🛝 ⚽ 🏓 📺

Facilities: 🚿 ⊙ 🚿 ✲ ♿ ✆ $ ⛩ 🐕 [Wi-fi] 💻 ♻ ℹ

Services: 🔌 🧺 🔥 ⛺ [T] 🔋 🚰

Within 3 miles: ⛳ 🎣 $ 🧺 Ʊ

Notes: No groups of unaccompanied minors. Dogs must be kept on leads. Fishing.

STILLINGFLEET

Places to visit

Merchant Adventurers' Hall, YORK 01904 654818 www.theyorkcompany.co.uk

Mansion House, YORK 01904 613161 www.mansionhouseyork.co.uk

Great for kids: National Railway Museum, YORK 01904 621261 www.nrm.org.uk

See page 7 for details of the AA Camping Card Scheme

STILLINGFLEET
Map 16 SE54

▶▶▶ 70% Home Farm Caravan & Camping (SE595427)

Moreby YO19 6HN
☎ 01904 728263   📄 01904 720059
e-mail: home_farm@hotmail.co.uk
dir: *6m from York on B1222, 1.5m N of Stillingfleet*

🚐 🚃 Å

Open Feb-Dec

Last arrival 22.00hrs

A traditional meadowland site on a working farm bordered by parkland on one side and the River Ouse on another. Facilities are in converted farm buildings, and the family owners extend a friendly welcome to tourers. An excellent site for relaxing and unwinding in, yet only a short distance from the attractions of York. There are four log cabins for holiday hire. 5 acre site. 25 touring pitches. Caravan pitches. Motorhome pitches. Tent pitches.

Facilities: 🏕️☉♿✳☉🚱🛁♻🅹
Services: 🔌🚽🧺💧🅣🚌
Within 3 miles: ♿♻
Notes: 🐕 Dogs must be kept on leads.

SUTTON-ON-THE-FOREST
Map 19 SE56

Places to visit

Sutton Park, SUTTON-ON-THE-FOREST 01347 810249 www.statelyhome.co.uk

Treasurer's House, YORK 01904 624247 www.nationaltrust.org.uk

Great for kids: Jorvik Viking Centre, YORK 01904 615505 www.jorvik-viking-centre.com

PREMIER PARK

▶▶▶▶▶ 80% Goosewood Caravan Park (SE595636)

YO61 1ET
☎ 01347 810829   📄 01347 811498
e-mail: enquiries@goosewood.co.uk
dir: *From A1237 take B1363. After 5m turn right. Turn right after 0.5m, site on right*

* 🚐 £15-£21 🚃 £15-£21

Open Mar-2 Jan

Last arrival dusk Last departure noon

A relaxing and immaculately maintained park with its own lake and seasonal fishing, set in attractive woodland just six miles north of York. Mature shrubs and stunning seasonal floral displays at the entrance create an excellent first impression and the well located toilet facilities are kept spotlessly clean. The generous patio pitches are randomly spaced throughout the site, providing optimum privacy, and there's a good adventure play area for younger children, with a recreation barn for teenagers, plus a health spa. 20 acre site. 100 touring pitches. 75 hardstandings. Caravan pitches. Motorhome pitches. 35 statics.

AA Pubs & Restaurants nearby: Blackwell Ox Inn, Sutton-on-the-Forest 01347 810328

Rose & Crown, Sutton-on-the-Forest 01347 811333

Leisure: 🅰🔍
Facilities: 🏕️☉♿✳♿☉🛁🚱🛁♻🅹
Services: 🔌🚽🧺🅣🚌♻
Within 3 miles: ♿🎣♻🅟
Notes: Dogs by arrangement only, no noise after mdnt. Dogs must be kept on leads.

THIRSK
Map 19 SE48

Places to visit

Monk Park Farm Visitor Centre, THIRSK 01845 597730 www.monkparkfarm.co.uk

Norton Conyers, RIPON 01765 640333

Great for kids: Falconry UK - Birds of Prey Centre, THIRSK 01845 587522 www.falconrycentre.co.uk .

▶▶▶▶ 81% Hillside Claravan Park (SE447889)

Canvas Farm, Moor Rd, Knayton YO7 4BR
☎ 01845 537349   & 07711 643652
e-mail: info@hillsidecaravanpark.co.uk
dir: *From Thirsk take A19 north. Left at Knayton sign. In 0.25m right (crossing bridge over A19), through village. Site on left in approx 1.5m*

* 🚐 £18-£28 🚃 £18-£28

Open 4 Feb-4 Jan

Last arrival 21.00hrs Last departure noon

A high quality, spacious park with first-class facilities, set in open countryside. It is an excellent base for walkers and for those wishing to explore the Thirsk area. Please note that the park does not accept tents. 5 acre site. 35 touring pitches. 35 hardstandings. Caravan pitches. Motorhome pitches.

AA Pubs & Restaurants nearby: Black Swan, Oldstead 01347 868387

Bagby Inn, Bagby 01845 597315

Leisure: 🅰🎣
Facilities: 🏕️☉♿✳♿🚱🛁🚱♻🅹
Services: 🔌🚽🧺🅣
Within 3 miles: ♿🎣♻🅟
Notes: 🐕 Dogs must be kept on leads.

▶▶▶ 76% Thirkleby Hall Caravan Park (SE472794)

Thirkleby YO7 3AR
☎ 01845 501360   & 07799 641815
e-mail: greenwood.parks@virgin.net
web: www.greenwoodparks.com
dir: *3m S of Thirsk on A19. Turn E through arched gatehouse into site*

🚐 £21-£23 🚃 £21-£23 Å £13-£19

Open Mar-Oct

Last arrival 20.00hrs Last departure 14.30hrs

A long-established site in the grounds of the old hall, with statics in wooded areas around a fishing lake and tourers based on slightly sloping grassy pitches. There is a quality amenities block and laundry. This well-screened park has superb views of the Hambledon Hills. 53 acre site. 50 touring pitches. 3 hardstandings. 20 seasonal pitches. Caravan pitches. Motorhome pitches. Tent pitches. 185 statics.

AA Pubs & Restaurants nearby: Black Swan, Oldstead 01347 868387

Bagby Inn, Bagby 01845 597315

Leisure: 🅰♻
Facilities: 🏕️☉♿✳♿🚱♻
Services: 🔌🚽🍴🧺🚌
Within 3 miles: ♿🎣♻🅟
Notes: 🐕 No noise after 23.00hrs. Dogs must be kept on leads. 12-acre woods.

LEISURE: 🏊 Indoor swimming pool 🏊 Outdoor swimming pool 🅰 Children's playground 🧒 Kid's club 🎾 Tennis court 🎱 Games room 📺 Separate TV room
🏌 9/18 hole golf course ⛵ Boats for hire 🎬 Cinema 🎵 Entertainment 🎣 Fishing ⛳ Mini golf 🏄 Watersports 🏋 Gym 🏐 Sports field Spa Ů Stables
FACILITIES: 🛁 Bath 🚿 Shower ☉ Electric shaver ♿ Hairdryer ✳ Ice Pack Facility ♿ Disabled facilities ☎ Public telephone 🏪 Shop on site or within 200yds
🏪 Mobile shop (calls at least 5 days a week) 🍖 BBQ area 🛋 Picnic area 📶 Wi-fi 💻 Internet access ♻ Recycling 🅹 Tourist info 🐕 Dog exercise area

AA CAMPING CARD SITE

▶▶▶ 63% Sowerby Caravan Park

(SE437801)

Sowerby YO7 3AG
☎ 01845 522753 📠 01845 574520
e-mail: sowerbycaravans@btconnect.com
dir: *From A19 approx 3m S of Thirsk, turn W for Sowerby. Turn right at junct. Site 1m on left*

* 🚐 £11.25-£12.75 🚍 £11.25-£12.75

Open Mar-Oct

Last arrival 22.00hrs

A grassy site beside a tree-lined river bank, with basic but functional toilet facilities. Tourers enjoy a separate grassed area with an open outlook, away from the statics. 1 acre site. 25 touring pitches. 5 hardstandings. Caravan pitches. Motorhome pitches. 85 statics.

AA Pubs & Restaurants nearby: Black Swan, Oldstead 01347 868387

Bagby Inn, Bagby 01845 597315

Leisure: 🅰 🔍
Facilities: 🐾⊙☀♿⏰🚰♻
Services: 🔌🗑🍺🧺🛁🔋
Within 3 miles: ⛳🏇🗑⛳
Notes: 🚫

TOLLERTON

Places to visit

The York Brewery Co Ltd, YORK 01904 621162
www.yorkbrew.co.uk

Yorkshire Museum, YORK 01904 551800
www.yorkshiremuseum.org.uk

Great for kids: Jorvik Viking Centre, YORK 01904 615505 www.jorvik-viking-centre.com

TOLLERTON
Map 19 SE56

AA CAMPING CARD SITE

▶▶▶▶ 76% Tollerton Holiday Park

(SE513643)

Station Rd YO61 1RD
☎ 01347 838313 📠 01347 838313
e-mail: greenwood.parks@virgin.net
dir: *From York take A19 towards Thirsk. At Cross Lanes left towards Tollerton. 1m to Chinese restaurant just before rail bridge. Site entrance through restaurant car park*

🚐 £20-£22 🚍 £20-£22 ⛺ £13-£19

Open Mar-Oct

Last arrival 20.00hrs Last departure 15.00hrs

Set in open countryside within a few minutes' walk of Tollerton and just a short drive from the Park & Ride for York, this small park has seen recent major improvements. There's a new amenities block of real quality, which includes a family bathroom and laundry, and additional hardstandings have been installed. There is little disturbance from the East Coast mainline which passes near to the park. 5 acre site. 50 touring pitches. 6 hardstandings. 18 seasonal pitches. Caravan pitches. Motorhome pitches. Tent pitches. 75 statics.

AA Pubs & Restaurants nearby: Blackwell Ox Inn, Sutton-on-the-Forest 01347 810328

Rose & Crown, Sutton-on-the-Forest 01347 811333

Leisure: 🅰
Facilities: 🐾⊙🏥☀♿⏰🚰🐕♻ ⓘ
Services: 🔌🗑🍺🍴🛁🏪
Within 3 miles: ⛳🏇🗑⛳
Notes: 🚫 No groups. Dogs must be kept on leads. Small fishing lake, large recreation field.

TOWTHORPE
Map 19 SE65

Places to visit

Malton Museum, MALTON 01653 695136
www.maltonmuseum.co.uk

Wolds Way Lavender, MALTON 01944 758641
www.woldswaylavender.co.uk

Great for kids: Eden Camp Modern History Theme Museum, MALTON 01653 697777
www.edencamp.co.uk

AA CAMPING CARD SITE

▶▶▶▶ 77% York Touring Caravan Site *(SE648584)*

Greystones Farm, Towthorpe Moor Ln YO32 9ST
☎ 01904 499275 📠 01904 499271
e-mail: info@yorkcaravansite.co.uk
web: www.yorkcaravansite.co.uk
dir: *From A64 follow Strensall & Haxby signs, site 1.5m on left*

* 🚐 £16-£22 🚍 £16-£22 ⛺ £16-£19

Open all year

Last arrival 21.00hrs Last departure noon

This purpose-built golf complex and caravan park is situated just over five miles from York. There is a 9-hole golf course, driving range and golf shop with a coffee bar/café. The generous sized, level pitches are set within well-manicured grassland with a backdrop of trees and shrubs. 6 acre site. 44 touring pitches. 12 hardstandings. Caravan pitches. Motorhome pitches. Tent pitches.

AA Pubs & Restaurants nearby: Blackwell Ox Inn, Sutton-on-the-Forest 01347 810328

Rose & Crown, Sutton-on-the-Forest 01347 811333

Leisure: ⚽
Facilities: 🐾⊙🏥☀♿⏰🚰📶♻ ⓘ
Services: 🔌🗑🍺🍴🛁↯
Within 3 miles: 🏇🗑◎⛳
Notes: Dogs must be kept on leads.

WEST KNAPTON

Places to visit

Pickering Castle, PICKERING 01751 474989
www.english-heritage.org.uk

North Yorkshire Moors Railway, PICKERING 01751 472508 www.nymr.co.uk

Great for kids: Eden Camp Modern History Theme Museum, MALTON 01653 697777
www.edencamp.co.uk

SERVICES: 🔌 Electric hook up 🗑 Launderette 🍺 Licensed bar 🍴 Calor Gas 🚿 Camping Gaz ⏹ Toilet fluid 🍴 Café/Restaurant 🏪 Fast Food/Takeaway 🔋 Battery charging 🍼 Baby care ↯ Motorvan service point
ABBREVIATIONS: BH/bank hols-bank holidays Etr-Easter Whit-Whitsun dep-departure fr-from hrs-hours m-mile mdnt-midnight rdbt-roundabout rs-restricted service wk-week wknd-weekend 🚫 No credit cards 🚫 No dogs
See page 7 for details of the AA Camping Card Scheme

WEST KNAPTON   Map 19 SE87

▶▶▶▶ 78% *Wolds Way Caravan and Camping* (SE896743)

West Farm YO17 8JE
☎ 01944 728463 & 728180
e-mail: knapton.wold.farms@farming.co.uk
dir: *Signed between Rillington & West Heslerton on A64 (Malton to Scarborough road). Site 1.5m*

Open Mar-Oct

Last arrival 22.30hrs Last departure 19.00hrs

A park on a working farm in a peaceful, high position on the Yorkshire Wolds, with magnificent views over the Vale of Pickering. This is an excellent walking area, with the Wolds Way passing the entrance to the park. A pleasant one and a half mile path leads to a lavender farm, with its first-class coffee shop. 7.5 acre site. 70 touring pitches. 5 hardstandings. Caravan pitches. Motorhome pitches. Tent pitches.

AA Pubs & Restaurants nearby: Coachman Inn, Snainton 01723 859231

New Inn, Thornton le Dale 01751 474226

Cayley Arms, Brompton-by-Sawdon 01723 859372

Leisure: ⚂

Facilities: ⛟ ⛾ ☉ ✳ ⛾ ⛐ ⛾ ⛾

Services: ⛽ ⛾ ⛾ ⛾ ⛾ ⛾

Within 3 miles: ⛾ ⛾

Notes: Free use of microwave, toaster & TV. Drinks machine.

WHITBY

See also Robin Hood's Bay

Places to visit

Whitby Abbey, WHITBY 01947 603568
www.english-heritage.org.uk

Scarborough Castle, SCARBOROUGH
01723 372451 www.english-heritage.org.uk

Great for kids: Sea Life & Marine Sanctuary,
SCARBOROUGH 01723 376125 www.sealife.co.uk

WHITBY   Map 19 NZ81

▶▶▶▶ 80% Ladycross Plantation Caravan Park (NZ821080)

(GOLD badge)

Egton YO21 1UA
☎ 01947 895502
e-mail: enquiries@ladycrossplantation.co.uk
dir: *From A171 (Whitby-Teesside road) onto unclassified road (site signed).*

* ⛺ £16.80-£19.80 ⛺ £16.80-£19.80
🛆 £15-£19.80

Open Mar-Oct

Last arrival 20.30hrs Last departure noon

A unique forest setting creates an away-from-it-all feeling at this peaceful touring park, which is under enthusiastic ownership. Pitches are sited in small groups in clearings around two smartly refurbished amenity blocks, which offer excellent facilities. The site is well placed for visiting Whitby and exploring the Moors. Children will enjoy exploring the woodland around the site, which also has a new dog walk. 30 acre site. 130 touring pitches. 18 hardstandings. 60 seasonal pitches. Caravan pitches. Motorhome pitches. Tent pitches.

AA Pubs & Restaurants nearby: Wheatsheaf Inn, Egton 01947 895271

Horseshoe Hotel, Egton Bridge 01947 895245

Magpie Café, Whitby 01947 602058

Facilities: ⛾ ☉ ⛾ ✳ ⛾ ⛾ ⛾ ♻ ⛾

Services: ⛽ ⛾ ⛾ ⛾ ⛾ ⛾ ⛾

Within 3 miles: ⛾ ⛾ ⛾ ◎ ⛾ ⛾

WYKEHAM

Places to visit

Scarborough Castle, SCARBOROUGH
01723 372451 www.english-heritage.org.uk

Pickering Castle, PICKERING 01751 474989
www.english-heritage.org.uk

Great for kids: Sea Life & Marine Sanctuary,
SCARBOROUGH 01723 376125 www.sealife.co.uk

WYKEHAM   Map 17 SE98

Regional Winner –
AA North East of England
Campsite of the Year 2012

PREMIER PARK

▶▶▶▶▶ 83% St Helens Caravan Park (SE967836)

YO13 9QD
☎ 01723 862771   🖷 01723 866613
e-mail: caravans@wykeham.co.uk
dir: *On A170 in village, 150yds on left beyond Downe Arms Hotel towards Scarborough*

* ⛺ £15.50-£25 ⛺ £15.50-£25 🛆 £11-£21

Open 15 Feb-15 Jan (rs Nov-Jan shop/laundry closed)

Last arrival 22.00hrs Last departure 17.00hrs

Set on the edge of the North York Moors National Park this delightfully landscaped park is immaculately maintained and thoughtfully laid out with top quality facilities and a high level of customer care. The site is divided into terraces with tree-screening creating smaller areas, including an adults' zone, and the stunning floral displays around the park are impressive. 12 super pitches and 2 camping pods were added for the 2011 season. A cycle route leads through the surrounding Wykeham Estate, and there is a short pathway to the adjoining Downe Arms country pub. 25 acre site. 250 touring pitches. 40 hardstandings. Caravan pitches. Motorhome pitches. Tent pitches. 2 wooden pods.

AA Pubs & Restaurants nearby: Coachman Inn, Snainton 01723 859231

New Inn, Thornton le Dale 01751 474226

Cayley Arms, Brompton-by-Sawdon
01723 859372

Leisure: ⚂

Facilities: ⛟ ⛾ ☉ ⛾ ✳ ⛾ ⛾ ⛾ ⛾ ⛾ wifi ♻ ⛾

Services: ⛽ ⛾ ⛾ ⛾ ⛾ ⛾ ⛾ ⛾ ⛾

Within 3 miles: ⛾ ⛾ ⛾ ◎ ⛾ ⛾ ⛾ ⛾

Notes: No noise after 22.00hrs. Dogs must be kept on leads. Caravan storage, adult-only super pitches with water & drainage.

LEISURE: 🏊 Indoor swimming pool   🏊 Outdoor swimming pool   ⚂ Children's playground   🧒 Kid's club   ⚞ Tennis court   🎱 Games room   📺 Separate TV room
⛳ 9/18 hole golf course   🚣 Boats for hire   🎬 Cinema   🎵 Entertainment   🎣 Fishing   ◎ Mini golf   🌊 Watersports   🏋 Gym   ⚽ Sports field   Spa   ♉ Stables
FACILITIES: ⛟ Bath   ⛾ Shower   ☉ Electric shaver   ⛾ Hairdryer   ✳ Ice Pack Facility   ⛾ Disabled facilities   ⏰ Public telephone   ⛾ Shop on site or within 200yds
⛾ Mobile shop (calls at least 5 days a week)   🍖 BBQ area   ⛾ Picnic area   wifi Wi-fi   🌐 Internet access   ♻ Recycling   ⛾ Tourist info   ⛾ Dog exercise area

YORKSHIRE, SOUTH

WORSBROUGH Map 16 SE30

Places to visit

Monk Bretton Priory, BARNSLEY
www.english-heritage.org.uk

Millennium Gallery, SHEFFIELD 0114 278 2600
www.museums-sheffield.org.uk

Great for kids: Magna Science Adventure
Centre, ROTHERHAM 01709 720002
www.visitmagna.co.uk

►► 74% Greensprings Touring Park

(SE330020)

Rockley Abbey Farm, Rockley Ln S75 3DS
☎ 01226 288298 ▤ 01226 288298
dir: *M1 junct 36, A61 to Barnsley. Left after 0.25m
signed Pilley. Site 1m at bottom of hill*

* ▥ fr £15 ▱ fr £15 Å fr £10

Open Apr-Oct

Last arrival 21.00hrs Last departure noon

A secluded and attractive farm site set amidst
woods and farmland, with access to the river and
several good local walks. There are two touring
areas, one gently sloping. Although not far from
the M1, there is almost no traffic noise, and this
site is convenient for exploring the area's
industrial heritage, as well as the Peak District. 4
acre site. 65 touring pitches. 5 hardstandings. 22
seasonal pitches. Caravan pitches. Motorhome
pitches. Tent pitches.

Leisure: ◔

Facilities: ♠ ⊙ ✳ ♔ ❼

Services: ▱ ▪

Within 3 miles: ↕ ⊞ ♪ ◎ ▣ ▧ ∪

Notes: ⊜ Dogs must be kept on leads.

YORKSHIRE, WEST

BARDSEY Map 16 SE34

Places to visit

Bramham Park, BRAMHAM 01937 846000
www.bramhampark.co.uk

Thackray Museum, LEEDS 0113 244 4343
www.thackraymuseum.org

Great for kids: Leeds Industrial Museum at
Armley Mills, LEEDS 0113 263 7861
www.leeds.gov.uk/armleymills

►►► 85% Moor Lodge Park *(SE352423)*

Blackmoor Ln LS17 9DZ
☎ 01937 572424 ▤ 01937 572424
e-mail: rodatmlcp@aol.com
dir: *From A1(M) take A659 (S of Wetherby) signed
Otley. Left onto A58 towards Leeds for 5m. Right
after New Inn pub (Ling Lane), right at x-rds, 1m.
Site on right*

* ▥ £15 ▱ £15 Å £15

Open all year

Last arrival 20.00hrs Last departure noon

A well-kept site in a peaceful and beautiful
setting, close to Harewood House and only 25
minutes' drive from York and the Dales; the centre
of Leeds is just 15 minutes away. The touring area
is for adults only. 7 acre site. 12 touring pitches.
Caravan pitches. Motorhome pitches. Tent
pitches. 60 statics.

AA Pubs & Restaurants nearby: Windmill Inn,
Linton 01937 582209

Facilities: ♠ ⊙ ☞ ✳ ⊙ ♬ ▥

Services: ▱ ▧ ▪ ∅ ▰

Within 3 miles: ↕ ♪ ◎ ▣ ∪

Notes: Adults only.

►►► 83% Glenfield Caravan Park

(SE351421)

120 Blackmoor Ln LS17 9DZ
☎ 01937 574657 ▤ 01937 579529
e-mail: glenfieldcp@aol.com
web: www.ukparks.co.uk/glenfield/
dir: *From A58 at Bardsey into Church Ln, past
church, up hill. 0.5m, site on left*

▥ fr £15 ▱ fr £15 Å £10-£20

Open all year

Last arrival 21.00hrs Last departure noon

A quiet family-owned rural site in a well-screened,
tree-lined meadow. The site has an excellent toilet
block complete with family room. A convenient
touring base for Leeds and the surrounding area.
Discounted golf and food are both available at the
local golf club. 4 acre site. 30 touring pitches. 30
hardstandings. Caravan pitches. Motorhome
pitches. Tent pitches. 1 static.

AA Pubs & Restaurants nearby: Windmill Inn,
Linton 01937 582209

Facilities: ♠ ⊙ ☞ ✳ ☕ ⊙ ♬

Services: ▱ ▧ ▰ ▪

Within 3 miles: ↕ ⊞ ♪ ▣ ▧ ∪

Notes: ⊜ Children must be supervised. Dogs
must be kept on leads.

SERVICES: ▱ Electric hook up ▧ Launderette ▯ Licensed bar ▪ Calor Gas ∅ Camping Gaz ⊡ Toilet fluid ☕ Café/Restaurant ▰ Fast Food/Takeaway ▰ Battery charging
▱ Baby care ↯ Motorvan service point
ABBREVIATIONS: BH/bank hols-bank holidays Etr-Easter Whit-Whitsun dep-departure fr-from hrs-hours m-mile mdnt-midnight rdbt-roundabout rs-restricted service wk-week
wknd-weekend ⊜ No credit cards ⊗ No dogs See page 7 for details of the AA Camping Card Scheme

HORSFORTH
Map 19 SE23

Places to visit

Cartwright Hall Art Gallery, BRADFORD
01274 431212 www.bradfordmuseums.org

National Media Museum,
BRADFORD 01274 202030
www.nationalmediamuseum.org.uk

►►► 78% *St Helena's Caravan Park*

(SE240421)

Otley Old Rd LS18 5HZ
☎ **0113 284 1142**
dir: *From A658 follow signs for Leeds/Bradford
Airport. Then follow site signs*

Open Apr-Oct

Last arrival 19.30hrs Last departure 14.00hrs

A well-maintained parkland setting surrounded by
woodland yet within easy reach of Leeds with its
excellent shopping and cultural opportunities,
Ilkley, and the attractive Wharfedale town of Otley.
Some visitors may just want to relax in this
adults-only park's spacious and pleasant
surroundings. 25 acre site. 60 touring pitches.
Caravan pitches. Motorhome pitches. Tent pitches.
40 statics.

Facilities: ⛟ ☏ ⊙ ℗ ✳ ⛐ ☉ 🐕

Services: ⛽ ◻ Ⓣ Within 3 miles: ⌕ ⌀ 🏪 🛒

Notes: Adults only.

CHANNEL ISLANDS

GUERNSEY

On Guernsey only islanders may own and
use towed caravans, but a limited number
of motor caravans are now permitted on the
island. The motor caravan, used for overnight
accommodation, must be not more than 6.9mtrs
long, must be booked into an authorised site
(Fauxquets Valley Campsite or Le Vaugrat
Camp Site) and must obtain a permit from the
site operator before embarking on a ferry for
Guernsey - Condor Ferries will not accept motor
caravans without this permit. A window sticker
must be displayed, motor caravans must return
to the site each night, and the visits are limited
to a maximum of one month. Permission is not
required to bring a trailer tent to the island. For
further details see:
www.visitguernsey.com/faqs.aspx

CASTEL
Map 24

Places to visit

Sausmarez Manor, ST MARTIN 01481 235571
www.sausmarezmanor.co.uk

Fort Grey Shipwreck Museum, ROCQUAINE BAY
01481 265036 www.museum.gov.gg

►►►► 84% *Fauxquets Valley Campsite*

GY5 7QL
☎ **01481 236951 & 07781 413333**
e-mail: info@fauxquets.co.uk
dir: *From pier, take 2nd exit off rdbt. At top of hill
left into Queens Rd. 2m. Right into Candie Rd. Site
opposite sign for German Occupation Museum*

Open mid Jun-Aug

A beautiful, quiet farm site in a hidden valley
close to the sea. The friendly and helpful owners,
who understand campers' needs, offer good
quality facilities and amenities, including
spacious pitches, an outdoor swimming pool, bar/
restaurant, a nature trail and sports areas. Fully
equipped tents and two lodges are available for
hire. Motorhomes up to 6.9 metres are now
allowed on Guernsey - contact the site for details
and a permit. 3 acre site. 120 touring pitches.
Tent pitches.

AA Pubs & Restaurants nearby: Fleur du Jardin,
Castel 01481 257996

Hotel Hogue du Pommier, Castel 01481 256531

Cobo Bay Restaurant, Castel 01481 257102

Leisure: ⚊ ⅍ ⚲ ▭

Facilities: ☏ ⊙ ℗ ✳ ⛐ ☉ 🏪 🐕

Services: ⛽ ◻ 🍽 ⌀ Ⓣ 🍴 ⛟ 🛒

Within 3 miles: ⌕ ⚓ 日 ⌀ ◎ �‑ 🏪 🛒 ∪

Notes: Birdwatching.

ST SAMPSON
Map 24

Places to visit

Sausmarez Manor, ST MARTIN 01481 235571
www.sausmarezmanor.co.uk

Castle Cornet, ST PETER PORT 01481 721657
www.museums.gov.gg

►►► 84% *Le Vaugrat Camp Site*

Route de Vaugrat GY2 4TA
☎ **01481 257468** 🖹 **01481 251841**
e-mail: enquiries@vaugratcampsite.com
web: www.vaugratcampsite.com
dir: *From main coast road on NW of island, site
signed at Port Grat Bay into Route de Vaugrat,
near Peninsula Hotel*

Open May-mid Sep

Overlooking the sea and set within the grounds of
a lovely 17th-century house, this level grassy park
is backed by woodland, and is close to the lovely
sandy beaches of Port Grat and Grand Havre. It is
run by a welcoming family who pride themselves
on creating magnificent floral displays. The
facilities here are excellent. Motorhomes up to 6.9
metres are now allowed on Guernsey - contact the
site for details and permit. 6 acre site. 150 touring
pitches. Tent pitches.

AA Pubs & Restaurants nearby: The Admiral de
Saumarez, St Peter Port 01481 721431

Governor's, St Peter Port 01481 738623

The Absolute End, St Peter Port 01481 723822

Mora Restaurant & Grill, St Peter Port
01481 715053

Leisure: ⅍ ▭

Facilities: ☏ ⊙ ℗ ✳ ⛐ ☉ 🏪

Services: ⛽ ◻ 🔋 ⌀ ⛟

Within 3 miles: ⌕ 日 ⌀ ◎ �‑ 🏪 🛒 ∪

Notes: No animals.

LEISURE: ⚊ Indoor swimming pool ⚊ Outdoor swimming pool ⅍ Children's playground ⚐ Kid's club ⚲ Tennis court ⚲ Games room ▭ Separate TV room ⌕ 9/18 hole golf course ⚓ Boats for hire 日 Cinema ♫ Entertainment ⌀ Fishing ◎ Mini golf �‑ Watersports ⚑ Gym ⚐ Sports field Spa ∪ Stables
FACILITIES: ⛟ Bath ☏ Shower ⊙ Electric shaver ℗ Hairdryer ✳ Ice Pack Facility ⛐ Disabled facilities ☉ Public telephone 🏪 Shop on site or within 200yds 🚗 Mobile shop (calls at least 5 days a week) 🍽 BBQ area 🪑 Picnic area wïfï Wi-fi 🖥 Internet access ♺ Recycling ⓘ Tourist info 🐕 Dog exercise area

JERSEY

Visiting caravans are now allowed onto Jersey, provided they are to be used as holiday accommodation only. Caravans will require a permit for travelling to and from the port and campsite on their arrival and departure days only. Motorists may travel around the island on a daily basis, but must return to the campsite each night. Bookings should be made through the chosen campsite, who will arrange for a permit. Early booking is strongly recommended during July and August.

ST MARTIN — Map 24

Places to visit

Mont Orgueil Castle, GOREY 01534 853292 www.jerseyheritage.org

Maritime Museum & Occupation Tapestry Gallery, ST HELIER 01534 811043 www.jerseyheritage.org

Great for kids: Elizabeth Castle, ST HELIER 01534 723971 www.jerseyheritage.org

PREMIER PARK

►►►►► 83% *Beuvelande Camp Site*

Beuvelande JE3 6EZ
☎ 01534 853575 📠 01534 857788
e-mail: info@campingjersey.com
web: www.campingjersey.com
dir: *Take A6 from St Helier to St Martin & follow signs to site before St Martins Church*

⛺

Open Apr-Sep (rs Apr-May & Sep pool & restaurant closed, shop hours limited)

A well-established site with excellent toilet facilities, accessed via narrow lanes in peaceful countryside close to St Martin. An attractive bar/restaurant is the focal point of the park, especially in the evenings, and there is a small swimming pool and playground. Motorhomes and towed caravans will be met at the ferry and escorted to the site if requested when booking. The new owners have made positive changes, including upgrading the shop and restaurant, and adding two yurts. 6 acre site. 150 touring pitches. Tent pitches. 75 statics.

AA Pubs & Restaurants nearby: Royal Hotel, St Martin 01534 856289

Leisure: 🏊 🛝 🎱 📺

Facilities: 🚿 ⊙ ❄ ♿ 📞 [$] 🐕

Services: 🔌 🧺 🍺 🛢 ⛽ [T] 🍴 🔋 🚰

Within 3 miles: ⛳ ⛵ 🎣 🏄 [$] 🐎

►►►► 86% *Rozel Camping Park*

Summerville Farm JE3 6AX
☎ 01534 855200 📠 01534 856127
e-mail: rozelcampingpark@jerseymail.co.uk
web: www.rozelcamping.co.uk
dir: *Take A6 from St Helier through Five Oaks to St Martins Church, turn right onto A38 towards Rozel, site on right*

🚐 🚙 ⛺

Open May-mid Sep

Last departure noon

Customers can be sure of a warm welcome at this delightful family run park. Set in the north east of the island, it offers large spacious pitches, many with electric, for tents, caravans and motorhomes. The lovely Rozel Bay is just a short distance away and spectacular views of the French coast can be seen from one of the four fields on the park. The site also offers excellent facilities including a swimming pool. Motorhomes and caravans will be met at the ferry and escorted to the park by arrangement when booking. 4 acre site. 100 touring pitches. Caravan pitches. Motorhome pitches. Tent pitches. 20 statics.

AA Pubs & Restaurants nearby: Royal Hotel, St Martin 01534 856289

Leisure: 🏊 🛝 🎱 📺

Facilities: 🚿 ⊙ 💨 ❄ ♿ 📞 [$] [Wi-fi]

Services: 🔌 🧺 🛢 ⛽ [T] 🔋 🍔 🚰

Within 3 miles: ⛳ ⛵ 🎣 🏄 [$] 🧺 🐎

Notes: Mini golf.

ISLE OF MAN

Motor caravans may enter with prior permission. Trailer caravans are generally only allowed in connection with trade shows and exhibitions, or for demonstration purposes, not for living accommodation. Written application for permission should be made to the Secretary, Planning Committee, Isle of Man Local Government Board, Murray House, Mount Havelock, Douglas. The shipping line cannot accept caravans without this written permission.

KIRK MICHAEL — Map 24 SC39

Places to visit

Peel Castle, PEEL 01624 648000 www.storyofmann.com

House of Manannan, PEEL 01624 648000 www.storyofmann.com

Great for kids: Curraghs Wild Life Park, BALLAUGH 01624 897323 www.gov.im/wildlife

►►► 76% *Glen Wyllin Campsite*

(SC302901)

IM6 1AL
☎ 01624 878231 & 878836 📠 01624 878836
e-mail: michaelcommissioners@manx.net
dir: *From Douglas take A1 to Ballacraine, right at lights onto A3 to Kirk Michael. Left onto A4 signed Peel. Site 100yds on right*

🚙 ⛺

Open mid Apr-mid Sep

Last departure noon

Set in a beautiful wooded glen with bridges over a pretty stream dividing the camping areas. A gently-sloping tarmac road gives direct access to a good beach. Hire tents are available. 9 acre site. 90 touring pitches. Motorhome pitches. Tent pitches. 18 statics.

AA Pubs & Restaurants nearby: The Creek Inn, Peel 01624 842216

Leisure: 🛝 📺

Facilities: 🚿 ⊙ 💨 ❄ ♿ 📞 [$] 🪑 🐕 [Wi-fi]

Services: 🔌 🧺 🛢 ⛽ 🍴 🔋 🍔

Within 3 miles: 🎣 [$] 🧺 🐎

Notes: No excess noise after midnight, dogs must be kept on leads and under control.

SERVICES: 🔌 Electric hook up 🧺 Launderette 🍺 Licensed bar 🛢 Calor Gas ⛽ Camping Gaz [T] Toilet fluid 🍴 Café/Restaurant 🍔 Fast Food/Takeaway 🔋 Battery charging 🍼 Baby care 🚰 Motorvan service point
ABBREVIATIONS: BH/bank hols-bank holidays Etr-Easter Whit-Whitsun dep-departure fr-from hrs-hours m-mile mdnt-midnight rdbt-roundabout rs-restricted service wk-week wknd-weekend 💳 No credit cards 🚫🐕 No dogs
See page 7 for details of the AA Camping Card Scheme

Scotland

Glen Coe and Loch Atriochan, Highlands

Scotland

It is virtually impossible to distil the spirit and essence of Scotland in a few short sentences. It is a country with a particular kind of beauty and something very special to offer. Around half the size of England but with barely one fifth of its population, the statistics alone are enough to make you want to rush there and savour its solitude and sense of space.

The Borders, maybe the most-obvious place to begin a tour of Scotland, was for so long one of Britain's most bitterly contested frontiers. The border has survived the years of lawlessness, battle and bloodshed, though few crossing it today would probably give its long and turbulent history a second thought. Making up 1,800 square miles of dense forest, rolling hills and broad sweeps of open heather, this region includes some of the most spectacular scenery anywhere in the country. Next door is Dumfries & Galloway, where just across the English/Scottish border is Gretna Green, famous for the 'anvil marriages' of eloping couples.

Travelling north and miles of open moorland and swathes of forest stretch to the Ayrshire coast where there are views towards the islands of Bute and Arran.

The country's two great cities, Glasgow and Edinburgh, include innumerable historic sites,

Eilean Donan Castle, Loch Duich

popular landmarks and innovative visitor attractions. To the north lies a landscape of tranquil lochs, fishing rivers, wooded glens and the cities of Perth and Dundee. There's also the superb scenery of the Trossachs, Loch Lomond and Stirling, which, with its wonderful castle perched on a rocky crag, is Scotland's heritage capital.

Further north

The country's prominent north-east shoulder is the setting for the mountain landscape of the Cairngorms and the Grampians, while Aberdeenshire and the Moray coast enjoy a pleasantly mild, dry climate with plenty of sunshine. Here, the River Spey, one of Scotland's great rivers and a mecca for salmon anglers, winds between lush pastures to the North Sea. Various famous distilleries can be found along its banks, some offering visitors the chance to sample a wee dram!

The remote far north is further from many parts of England than a good many European destinations. Names such as Pentland Firth, Sutherland, Caithness and Ross and Cromarty spring to mind, as does Cape Wrath, Britain's most northerly ▶

● Iona

● Glen Muick

outpost. The stunning coast is known for its spectacular sea cliffs and deserted beaches – the haunt of some of the rarest mammals.

Highlands and Islands

The beauty of the Western Highlands and the islands has to be seen to be believed. It is, without question, one of Europe's wildest and most spectacular regions, evoking a truly breathtaking sense of adventure. There are a great many islands, as a glance at the map will reveal – Skye, Mull, Iona, Coll, Jura and Islay to name but a few; all have their own individual character and identity. The two most northerly island groups are Orkney and the Shetlands, which, incredibly, are closer to the Arctic Circle than London.

Walking and Cycling

There are numerous excellent walks in Scotland. Among the best is the 95-mile (152km) West Highland Way, Scotland's first long-distance path. The trail runs from Glasgow to Fort William. The Southern Upland Way and St Cuthbert's Way explore the best of the Scottish Borders, which is also the northerly terminus for the 250-mile (402km) Pennine Way.

Scotland's majestic landscapes are perfect for exploring by bike. There are scores of popular routes and trails – among them a ride through Dumfries & Galloway to Drumlanrig Castle and the museum where blacksmith, Kirkpatrick MacMillan, invented the bicycle. Alternatively, there's the chance to get away from the city and head for the coast along disused railway lines; perhaps the route from Edinburgh to Cramond, with good views of the Firth of Forth.

● The Quirang, Isle of Skye

Festivals and Events

- The Viking Festival is staged at Largs on the Ayrshire coast during the August Bank Holiday week. This is where the last Viking invasion of Britain took place in 1263. There are birds of prey displays, battle re-enactments, fireworks and the ritual burning of a longship.
- Also in August is the internationally famous Edinburgh Military Tattoo, which draws numerous visitors and participants from many parts of the world.
- The Highland Games, another classic fixture in the Scottish calendar, run from May onwards; the most famous being the Braemar gathering in September.

ABERDEENSHIRE

ABOYNE — Map 23 NO59

Places to visit

Alford Valley Railway, ALFORD 019755 64236 www.alfordvalleyrailway.org.uk

Crathes Castle Garden & Estate, CRATHES 0844 4932166 www.nts.org.uk

Great for kids: Craigievar Castle, ALFORD 0844 493 2174 www.nts.org.uk

►►► 71% Aboyne Loch Caravan Park *(NO538998)*

AB34 5BR

☎ 013398 86244 & 82589 📠 013398 86244

e-mail: heatherreid24@yahoo.co.uk

dir: *On A93, 1m E of Aboyne*

* 🚐 fr £18 🚌 fr £18 ⛺ fr £12

Open 31 Mar-Oct

Last arrival 20.00hrs Last departure 11.00hrs

An attractively sited caravan park set amidst woodland on the shores of the lovely Aboyne Loch in scenic Deeside. The facilities are modern and immaculately maintained, and amenities include boat-launching, boating and fishing. An ideally situated park for touring Royal Deeside and the Aberdeenshire uplands. 6 acre site. 20 touring pitches. 25 hardstandings. Caravan pitches. Motorhome pitches. Tent pitches. 120 statics.

AA Pubs & Restaurants nearby: Milton Restaurant, Crathes 01330 844566

Leisure: 🛝 ♠

Facilities: 🚿 ⊙ 💨 ✲ ♿ 📞 🏪 🐕 ♻ ℹ

Services: 🚐 🧺 🔒 🌿 [T] ⚓

Within 3 miles: ⛳ ⚽ ★ 🍷 🎣 ◎ 🏄 🏪 🧺 U

Notes: 🚭 Coarse & pike fishing, boats for hire.

FORDOUN — Map 23 NO77

Places to visit

Edzell Castle and Garden, EDZELL 01356 648631 www.historic-scotland.gov.uk

House of Dun, MONTROSE 0844 493 2144 www.nts.org.uk

►►► 74% Brownmuir Caravan Park *(NO740772)*

AB30 1SJ

☎ 01561 320786 📠 01561 320786

e-mail: brownmuircaravanpark@talk21.com

web: www.brownmuircaravanpark.co.uk

dir: *From N: A90 take B966 signed Fettercairn, site 1.5m on left. From S: A90, exit 4m N of Laurencekirk signed Fordoun, site 1m on right*

* 🚐 £14-£15.50 🚌 £14-£15.50 ⛺ £8-£13

Open Apr-Oct

Last arrival 23.00hrs Last departure noon

A mainly static site set in a rural location with level pitches and good touring facilities. The area is ideal for cyclists, walkers and golfers, as well as those wanting to visit Aberdeen, Banchory, Ballater, Balmoral, Glamis and Dundee. 7 acre site. 11 touring pitches. 7 hardstandings. 7 seasonal pitches. Caravan pitches. Motorhome pitches. Tent pitches. 49 statics.

AA Pubs & Restaurants nearby: Tolbooth Restaurant, Stonehaven 01569 762287

Carron Art Deco Restaurant, Stonehaven 01569 760460

Leisure: 🛝

Facilities: 🚿 ⊙ 💨 ✲ ♿ 📞 🧺 🐕 📶 ♻ ℹ

Services: 🚐 🧺

Within 3 miles: ⛳ 🎣 🏪

Notes: 🚭 Dogs must be kept on leads.

HUNTLY — Map 23 NJ53

Places to visit

Leith Hall, Garden & Estate, RHYNIE 0844 493 2175 www.nts.org.uk

Glenfiddich Distillery, DUFFTOWN 01340 820373 www.glenfiddich.com

Great for kids: Archaeolink Prehistory Park, OYNE 01464 851500 www.archaeolink.co.uk

AA CAMPING CARD SITE

PREMIER PARK

►►►►► 83% Huntly Castle Caravan Park *(NJ525405)*

The Meadow AB54 4UJ

☎ 01466 794999

e-mail: enquiries@huntlycastle.co.uk

web: www.huntlycastle.co.uk

dir: *From Aberdeen on A96 to Huntly. 0.75m after rdbt (on outskirts of Huntly) right towards town centre, left into Riverside Drive*

* 🚐 £17.50-£22.75 🚌 £17.50-£22.75 ⛺ £15.25-£18.50

Open Apr-Oct (rs Wknds & school hols indoor activity centre open)

Last arrival 20.00hrs Last departure noon

A quality parkland site within striking distance of the Speyside Malt Whisky Trail, the beautiful Moray coast, and the Cairngorm Mountains. The park provides exceptional toilet facilities, and there are some fully serviced pitches. The indoor activity centre provides a wide range of games; the attractive town of Huntly is only a five-minute walk away, with its ruined castle plus a wide variety of restaurants and shops. 15 acre site. 90 touring pitches. 51 hardstandings. Caravan pitches. Motorhome pitches. Tent pitches. 40 statics.

Leisure: 🛝

Facilities: 🚿 ⊙ 💨 ✲ ♿ 🐕 📶 ♻ ℹ

Services: 🚐 🧺 🔒 [T] 🍴 ⚓

Within 3 miles: ⛳ 🎣 🏪 🧺

Notes: Indoor activity centre, indoor children's play area, snooker table.

KINTORE — Map 23 NJ71

Places to visit

Pitmedden Garden, PITMEDDEN 0844 493 2177
www.nts.org.uk

Tolquhon Castle, PITMEDDEN 01651 851286
www.historic-scotland.gov.uk

Great for kids: Castle Fraser, KEMNAY
0844 493 2164 www.nts.org.uk

►►►► 77% Hillhead Caravan Park

(NJ777163)

AB51 0YX
☎ 01467 632809 & 0870 413 0870
🖷 01467 633173
e-mail: enquiries@hillheadcaravan.co.uk
dir: From A96 follow signs to site on B994, then
unclassified road

🚐 🚙 Å

Open all year

Last arrival 21.00hrs Last departure 13.00hrs

An attractive, nicely landscaped site, located on
the outskirts of Kintore in the valley of the River
Dee with excellent access to forest walks and
within easy reach of the many attractions in rural
Aberdeenshire. Since the new owners have taken
over the management of the site, significant
improvements have been made to upgrade the
toilet facilities to a high standard, and additional
hardstanding pitches have also been created.
There are good play facilities for smaller children
and a modern lodge-style games room, with TV
and internet access, for older teenagers will be
installed for autumn 2011. 1.5 acre site. 29
touring pitches. 14 hardstandings. Caravan
pitches. Motorhome pitches. Tent pitches.

AA Pubs & Restaurants nearby: Old Blackfriars,
Aberdeen 01224 581922

Leisure: ⚑
Facilities: ♠☉🅟✳🕭⚲🔥🚿
Services: 🔌🅢🖉🆃🔋
Within 3 miles: ⚓🖉🖻🅢
Notes: Caravan storage, accessories shop.

MACDUFF

Places to visit

Duff House, BANFF 01261 818181
www.historic-scotland.gov.uk

Banff Museum, BANFF 01771 622807
www.aberdeenshire.gov.uk/museums

MACDUFF — Map 23 NJ76

►► 65% Wester Bonnyton Farm Site

(NJ741638)

Gamrie AB45 3EP
☎ 01261 832470 🖷 01261 831853
e-mail: westerbonnyton@fsmail.net
dir: From A98 (1m S of Macduff) take B9031
signed Rosehearty. Site 1.25m on right

🚐 🚙 Å

Open Mar-Oct

A spacious farm site in a screened meadow, with
level touring pitches enjoying views across the
Moray Firth. The site is continually improving, and
offers some electric hook-ups and a laundry. 8
acre site. 10 touring pitches. 5 hardstandings.
Caravan pitches. Motorhome pitches. Tent
pitches. 50 statics.

Leisure: ⚑ ✎
Facilities: ♠☉🅟🕭🔥🚿 📶 ♻ 🛈
Services: 🔌🅢 🔋🔌
Within 3 miles: ⚓✦🖉🖻🅢
Notes: 🐾 Dogs must be kept on leads. Children's
playbarn.

NORTH WATER BRIDGE — Map 23 NO66

►►► 77% Dovecot Caravan Park (NO648663)

GOLD

AB30 1QL
☎ 01674 840630 🖷 01674 840630
e-mail: adele@dovecotcaravanpark.co.uk
dir: Take A90, 5m S of Laurencekirk. At Edzell
Woods sign turn left. Site 500yds on left

* 🚐 £13-£14 🚙 £13-£14 Å £10-£11

Open Apr-Oct

Last arrival 20.00hrs Last departure noon

A level grassy site in a country area close to the
A90, with mature trees screening one side and the
River North Esk on the other. The immaculate
toilet facilities make this a handy overnight stop
in a good touring area. 6 acre site. 25 touring
pitches. 8 hardstandings. 8 seasonal pitches.
Caravan pitches. Motorhome pitches. Tent
pitches. 44 statics.

Leisure: ⚑ ✎
Facilities: ♠☉🅟✳🕭⚲🔥 📶 ♻ 🛈
Services: 🔌🅢🔋🆃↯

ST CYRUS — Map 23 NO76

Places to visit

House of Dun, MONTROSE 0844 493 2144
www.nts.org.uk

Pictavia Visitor Centre, BRECHIN 01356 626241
www.pictavia.org.uk

Great for kids: Brechin Town House Museum,
BRECHIN 01356 625536
www.angus.gov.uk/history/museum

►►►► 79% East Bowstrips Caravan Park (NO745654)

DD10 0DE
☎ 01674 850328 🖷 01674 850328
e-mail: tully@bowstrips.freeserve.co.uk
web: www.caravancampingsites.co.uk/
aberdeenshire/eastbowstrips.htm
dir: From S on A92 (coast road) into St Cyrus. Pass
hotel on left. 1st left then 2nd right signed

* 🚐 £15-£18 🚙 £15-£18 Å fr £9

Open Etr or Apr-Oct

Last arrival 20.00hrs Last departure noon

A quiet, rural site close to a seaside village, with
modernised facilities and a particular welcome for
disabled visitors. The park is surrounded by
farmland on the edge of a village, with extensive
views. Touring pitches are sited on rising ground
amongst attractive landscaping. 4 acre site. 32
touring pitches. 22 hardstandings. Caravan
pitches. Motorhome pitches. Tent pitches. 17
statics.

Leisure: ⚑
Facilities: ♠☉🅟✳🕭⚲⚲🔥🛈
Services: 🔌🅢 🔋🖉
Within 3 miles: 🖉🅢
Notes: 🐾 If camping no dogs allowed, if touring
dogs must be kept on leads at all times. Separate
garden with boule pitch.

SERVICES: 🔌 Electric hook up 🅢 Launderette 🍺 Licensed bar 🔋 Calor Gas 🖉 Camping Gaz 🆃 Toilet fluid 🍽 Café/Restaurant 🍟 Fast Food/Takeaway 🔋 Battery charging
🚼 Baby care ↯ Motorvan service point
ABBREVIATIONS: BH/bank hols-bank holidays Etr-Easter Whit-Whitsun dep-departure fr-from hrs-hours m-mile mdnt-midnight rdbt-roundabout rs-restricted service wk-week
wknd-weekend 🐾 No credit cards 🐾 No dogs See page 7 for details of the AA Camping Card Scheme

ANGUS

MONIFIETH   Map 21 N043

Places to visit

Barry Mill, BARRY 0844 493 2140
www.nts.org.uk

HM Frigate Unicorn, DUNDEE 01382 200900
www.frigateunicorn.org

Great for kids: Discovery Point & RRS
Discovery, DUNDEE 01382 309060
www.rrsdiscovery.com

▶▶▶▶ **79% Riverview**
Caravan Park (NO502322)

Marine Dr DD5 4NN
☎ 01382 535471 & 817979 📠 01382 811525
e-mail: info@riverview.co.uk
web: www.riverview.co.uk
dir: From Dundee on A930 follow signs to
Monifieth, past supermarket, right signed golf
course, left under rail bridge. Site signed on left

🚗 🚐

Open Mar-Jan

Last arrival 22.00hrs Last departure 12.30hrs

A well-landscaped seaside site with individual
hedged pitches, and direct access to the beach.
The modernised toilet block has excellent facilities
which are immaculately maintained. Amenities
include a multi-gym, sauna and steam rooms. 5.5
acre site. 49 touring pitches. 45 hardstandings.
Caravan pitches. Motorhome pitches. 46 statics.

AA Pubs & Restaurants nearby: Royal Arch Bar,
Broughty Ferry, 01382 779741

Dalhousie Restaurant at Carnoustie Golf Hotel,
Carnoustie 01241 411999

Leisure: ⚑ 瓜 ⊙ ⚲
Facilities: 🅝 ⊙ ℙ ✳ 👶 ⓒ ⌂ ⊓ 🚻 wwa 🖳 ♻ 🛈
Services: 🔌 🖪 🛢 🇹 ⛽ 🚐 ⚒
Within 3 miles: ⬇ 🏢 ℘ ◎ ⛵ 🛍 🖪 ∪
Notes: Dogs must be kept on leads.

ARGYLL & BUTE

CARRADALE   Map 20 NR83

▶▶▶ **85% Carradale Bay Caravan
Park** (NR815385)

PA28 6QG
☎ 01583 431665
e-mail: info@carradalebay.com
dir: A83 from Tarbert towards Campbeltown, left
onto B842 (Carradale road), right onto B879. Site
0.5m

✳ £16.10-£22.40 🚐 £16.10-£22.40
⛺ £14.05-£18.05

Open Apr-Sep

Last arrival 22.00hrs Last departure noon

A beautiful, natural site on the sea's edge with
superb views over Kilbrannan Sound to the Isle of
Arran. Pitches are landscaped into small bays
broken up by shrubs and bushes, and backed by
dunes close to the long sandy beach. The toilet
facilities are appointed to a very high standard.
An environmentally-aware site that requires the
use of green toilet chemicals - available on the
site. Lodges and static caravans for holiday hire. 8
acre site. 74 touring pitches. Caravan pitches.
Motorhome pitches. Tent pitches. 15 statics.

AA Pubs & Restaurants nearby: Dunvalanree,
Carradale 01583 431226

Facilities: 🅝 ⊙ ℙ ✳ 👶 ⓒ 🖪 ⌂ ⊓ 🚻 wwa ♻ 🛈
Services: 🔌 🖪 🚐
Within 3 miles: ⬇ 🛥 ℘ ⛵ 🛍 🖪 ∪

GLENDARUEL   Map 20 NR98

Places to visit

Benmore Botanic Garden, BENMORE
01369 706261 www.rbge.org.uk

AA CAMPING CARD SITE

▶▶▶ **77% Glendaruel Caravan Park**
(NR005865)

PA22 3AB
☎ 01369 820267
e-mail: mail@glendaruelcaravanpark.com
web: www.glendaruelcaravanpark.com
dir: A83 onto A815 to Strachur, 13m to site on
A886. By ferry from Gourock to Dunoon then B836,
then A886 for approx 4m N. (NB this route not
recommended for towing vehicles - 1:5 uphill
gradient on B836)

🚐 £18-£20.50 🚐 £18-£20.50 ⛺ £14-£18

Open Apr-Oct

Last arrival 22.00hrs Last departure noon

A very pleasant, well-established site in the
beautiful Victorian gardens of Glendaruel House.
The level grass and hardstanding pitches are set
in 23 acres of wooded parkland in a valley
surrounded by mountains, with many rare
specimen trees. Static caravans are available for
hire. 6 acre site. 27 touring pitches. 15
hardstandings. 12 seasonal pitches. Caravan
pitches. Motorhome pitches. Tent pitches. 32
statics. 1 wooden pod.

AA Pubs & Restaurants nearby: Kilfinan Hotel
Bar, Kilfinan 01700 821201

Leisure: 瓜 ⊙
Facilities: 🅝 ⊙ ℙ ✳ 🖪 ⊓ 🚻 wwa ♻ 🛈
Services: 🔌 🖪 🛢 🖉 🇹 ⛽
Within 3 miles: ℘ 🛍 🖪
Notes: Dogs must be kept on leads. Sea trout &
salmon fishing, woodland walks, 24-hour
emergency phone available.

LEISURE: 🏊 Indoor swimming pool 🏊 Outdoor swimming pool 瓜 Children's playground 🏐 Kid's club 🎾 Tennis court 🎱 Games room 📺 Separate TV room
⛳ 9/18 hole golf course 🚤 Boats for hire 🎭 Cinema 🎵 Entertainment 🎣 Fishing ◎ Mini golf 🏄 Watersports ⚑ Gym 🥅 Sports field Spa ∪ Stables
FACILITIES: 🛁 Bath 🚿 Shower ⊙ Electric shaver ℙ Hairdryer ✳ Ice Pack Facility 👶 Disabled facilities ⓒ Public telephone 🛍 Shop on site or within 200yds
🚐 Mobile shop (calls at least 5 days a week) 🔥 BBQ area ⊓ Picnic area wwa Wi-fi 🖳 Internet access ♻ Recycling 🛈 Tourist info ⊓ Dog exercise area

MACHRIHANISH · Map 20 NR62

▶▶▶▶ 80% Machrihanish Caravan Park (NR647208)

East Trodigal PA28 6PT
☎ 01586 810366
e-mail: mail@campkintyre.co.uk
dir: A82 from Glasgow to Tarbet, A83 to Inveraray, then to Campbeltown. Take B843 to Machrihanish. Site 300yds before village on right

⌂ ⌂ Å

Open Mar-Oct & Dec

Last arrival 22.00hrs Last departure 11.30hrs

Machrihanish is an open and breezy coastal site close to the Mull of Kintyre and a glorious three mile sandy beach. There is a campers' room, static caravans and four wooden wigwams for hire and great sea views to the isles of Jura and Islay. The park is adjacent to a fine links golf course, and Campbeltown, with its shops and restaurants, is five miles away. 8 acre site. 90 touring pitches. 12 hardstandings. 7 seasonal pitches. Caravan pitches. Motorhome pitches. Tent pitches. 5 statics.

Leisure: ⊡
Facilities: ♠⊙☐☀⚙⚒⚿⚑⚐
Services: ⚡⚑☐
Within 3 miles: ⚐⚑⚒⚙⚒⚑
Notes: ⚙ No campfires, 10mph speed limit. Crazy golf & fishing on site.

OBAN · Map 20 NM82

Places to visit

Dunstaffnage Castle and Chapel, OBAN
01631 562465 www.historic-scotland.gov.uk

Bonawe Historic Iron Furnace, TAYNUILT
01866 822432 www.historic-scotland.gov.uk

▶▶▶ 75% Oban Caravan & Camping Park (NM831277)

Gallanachmore Farm, Gallanach Rd PA34 4QH
☎ 01631 562425
e-mail: info@obancaravanpark.com
dir: From Oban follow Mull Ferry signs then Gallanach sign, 2m

⌂ ⌂ Å

Open Etr/Apr-Oct

Last arrival 23.00hrs Last departure noon

A tourist park in an attractive location close to the sea and ferries. This family park is a popular base for walking, sea-based activities and for those who just want to enjoy the peace and tranquillity. There are self-catering holiday lodges for hire. 15 acre site. 120 touring pitches. 35 hardstandings. Caravan pitches. Motorhome pitches. Tent pitches. 17 statics.

AA Pubs & Restaurants nearby: Coast, Oban 01631 569900

Leisure: ⚑⚒ **Facilities:** ♠⊙☐☀⚙⚑⚐
Services: ⚡⚑⚒⚙☐⚒⚑
Within 3 miles: ⚐⚒⚑⚙⚒⚙⚑⚙
Notes: No commercial vehicles. Indoor kitchen for tent campers.

DUMFRIES & GALLOWAY

ANNAN

Places to visit

Ruthwell Cross, RUTHWELL 0131 550 7612
www.historic-scotland.gov.uk

Great for kids: Caerlaverock Castle, CAERLAVEROCK 01387 770244
www.historic-scotland.gov.uk

ANNAN · Map 21 NY16

▶▶ 73% Galabank Caravan & Camping Group (NY192676)

North St DG12 5DQ
☎ 01461 203539 & 204108
dir: Enter site via North Street

⌂ ⌂ Å

Open Apr-early Sep Last departure noon

A tidy, well-maintained grassy little park with spotless facilities close to the centre of town but with pleasant rural views, and skirted by River Annan. 1 acre site. 30 touring pitches. Caravan pitches. Motorhome pitches. Tent pitches.

AA Pubs & Restaurants nearby: Smiths of Gretna Green, Gretna 01461 337007

Facilities: ♠⚙☐⚑ **Services:** ⚡
Within 3 miles: ⚐⚒⚙⚒⚙
Notes: ⚙ Dogs must be kept on leads. Social club adjacent.

BARGRENNAN · Map 20 NX37

▶▶▶ 78% Glentrool Holiday Park (NX350769)

DG8 6RN
☎ 01671 840280 ⚐ 01671 840342
e-mail: enquiries@glentroolholidaypark.co.uk
dir: Exit Newton Stewart on A714 towards Girvan, right at Bargrennan towards Glentrool. Site on left before village

⌂ ⌂ Å

Open Mar-Oct

Last arrival 21.00hrs Last departure noon

A small park close to the village of Glentrool, and bordered by the Galloway Forest Park. Both the touring and static area with vans for hire are immaculately presented and the amenity block is clean and freshly painted. The on-site shop is well stocked. 6 acre site. 16 touring pitches. 13 hardstandings. 3 seasonal pitches. Caravan pitches. Motorhome pitches. Tent pitches. 26 statics.

AA Pubs & Restaurants nearby: Creebridge House Hotel, Newton Stewart 01671 402121

Leisure: ⚑
Facilities: ♠⊙☐☀⚙⚒⚙⚑⚙ ⚙
Services: ⚡⚒ ⚑⚙⚒ **Within 3 miles:** ⚙
Notes: ⚙ No cars by tents. No ball games, no groups. Dogs must be kept on leads.

BRIGHOUSE BAY — Map 20 NX64

PREMIER PARK

▶▶▶▶▶ 74% Brighouse Bay *Best of British*
Holiday Park *(NX628453)*

DG6 4TS

☎ 01557 870267 📠 01557 870319
e-mail: info@brighouse-bay.co.uk
dir: *From Gatehouse-of-Fleet take A75 towards Castle Douglas, onto B727 (signed Kirkcudbright & Borgue). Or from Kirkcudbright take A755 onto B727. Site signed*

* 🚐 £15.30-£21.60 🚐 £15.30-£21.60
⛺ £15.30-£21.60

Open all year (rs Nov-Mar leisure club closed 3 days each week)

Last arrival 21.30hrs Last departure 11.30hrs

This top class park has a country club feel and enjoys a marvellous coastal setting adjacent to the beach and with superb sea views. Pitches have been imaginatively sculpted into the meadowland, with stone walls and hedges blending in with the site's mature trees. These features, together with the large range of leisure activities, make this an excellent park for families who enjoy an active holiday. Many of the facilities are at an extra charge. A range of self-catering units is available for hire. 120 acre site. 190 touring pitches. 100 hardstandings. 60 seasonal pitches. Caravan pitches. Motorhome pitches. Tent pitches. 285 statics.

Leisure: 🏊 ⛳ 🎠 🎣 🎵
Facilities: 🛁 🚿 ⊙ 🧴 ✳ ⚕ Ⓩ 🏪 🛒 WiFi ℹ
Services: 🔌 🚽 🍽 🔋 🧺 🚰 ⓣ 🍴 🛒 🐕 ⚡
Within 3 miles: ⚓ ⛳ 🎣 ◎ ⛵ 🏪 Ⓢ ♻

Notes: No motorised scooters, jet skis or own quad bikes. Dogs must be kept on leads. Mini golf, 18-hole golf, quad bikes for hire, riding, fishing.

CREETOWN — Map 20 NX46

Places to visit
Cardoness Castle, CARDONESS CASTLE
01557 814427 www.historic-scotland.gov.uk

Great for kids: Creetown Gem Rock Museum, CREETOWN 01671 820357 www.gemrock.net

AA CAMPING CARD SITE

PREMIER PARK

▶▶▶▶▶ 81% Castle Cary Holiday Park *(NX475576)*

DG8 7DQ

☎ 01671 820264 📠 01671 820670
e-mail: enquiries@castlecarypark.f9.co.uk
web: www.castlecary-caravans.com
dir: *Signed with direct access off A75, 0.5m S of village*

* 🚐 £14.65-£18.30 🚐 £14.65-£18.30
⛺ £14.65-£18.30

Open all year (rs Oct-Mar reception/shop, no heated outdoor pool)

Last arrival anytime Last departure noon

This attractive site in the grounds of Cassencarie House is sheltered by woodlands, and faces south towards Wigtown Bay. The park is in a secluded location with beautiful landscaping and excellent facilities. The bar/restaurant is housed in part of an old castle, and enjoys extensive views over the River Cree estuary. 12 acre site. 50 touring pitches. 50 hardstandings. Caravan pitches. Motorhome pitches. Tent pitches. 26 statics. 2 bell tents/yurts.

AA Pubs & Restaurants nearby: Creebridge House Hotel, Newton Stewart 01671 402121

Galloway Arms Hotel, Newton Stewart 01671 402653

Kirroughtree House, Minnigaff, Newton Stewart 01671 402141

Cally Palace Hotel, Gatehouse-of-Fleet 01557 814341

Leisure: 🏊 🏊 🎠 ⚽ 🎣 🖵
Facilities: 🛁 🚿 ⊙ 🧴 ✳ ⚕ Ⓩ 🏪 🐕 WiFi ℹ
Services: 🔌 🚽 🍽 🔋 🧺 ⓣ 🍴 🛒 🐕
Within 3 miles: ⚓ 🎣 ◎ 🏪 Ⓢ

Notes: Dogs must be kept on leads. Bike hire, crazy golf, coarse fishing, full size football pitch.

CROCKETFORD — Map 21 NX87

Places to visit
Drumcoltran Tower, DRUMCOLTRAN TOWER
www.historic-scotland.gov.uk

Sweetheart Abbey, NEW ABBEY 01387 850397
www.historic-scotland.gov.uk

Great for kids: Threave Castle, CASTLE DOUGLAS
07711 223101 www.historic-scotland.gov.uk

▶▶▶▶ 74% *The Park of Brandedleys (NX830725)*

DG2 8RG

☎ 01387 266700 📠 01556 690681
e-mail: brandedleys@holgates.com
web: www.holgates.com
dir: *In village on A75, from Dumfries towards Stranraer site on left on unclassified road (signed), entrance 200yds on right*

🚐 🚐 ⛺

Open all year (rs Nov-Mar bar/restaurant open Fri-Sun afternoon)

Last arrival 22.00hrs Last departure noon

A well-maintained site in an elevated position off the A75, with fine views of Auchenreoch Loch and beyond. This comfortable park offers a wide range of amenities, including a fine games room and a tastefully-designed bar with adjoining bistro. There are attractive holiday homes for sale and hire on this park, which is well placed for enjoying walking, fishing, sailing and golf. 24 acre site. 49 touring pitches. 29 hardstandings. Caravan pitches. Motorhome pitches. Tent pitches. 60 statics.

Leisure: 🏊 🎠 🎾 🎣
Facilities: 🛁 🚿 ⊙ 🧴 ✳ ⚕ Ⓩ 🏪 🐕
Services: 🔌 🚽 🍽 🔋 🧺 ⓣ 🍴 🛒
Within 3 miles: 🎣 🎣 🏪 Ⓢ ♻

Notes: Guidelines issued on arrival. Badminton court.

LEISURE: 🏊 Indoor swimming pool 🏊 Outdoor swimming pool 🎠 Children's playground 🧒 Kid's club 🎾 Tennis court 🎣 Games room 🖵 Separate TV room ⛳ 9/18 hole golf course ⛵ Boats for hire 🎬 Cinema 🎵 Entertainment 🎣 Fishing ◎ Mini golf 🏄 Watersports ⛳ Gym ⚽ Sports field **Spa** ♨ Stables
FACILITIES: 🛁 Bath 🚿 Shower ⊙ Electric shaver 🧴 Hairdryer ✳ Ice Pack Facility ⚕ Disabled facilities Ⓟ Public telephone 🏪 Shop on site or within 200yds 🚐 Mobile shop (calls at least 5 days a week) 🍖 BBQ area 🪵 Picnic area WiFi Wi-fi 🖥 Internet access ♻ Recycling ℹ Tourist info 🐕 Dog exercise area

DALBEATTIE   Map 21 NX86

Places to visit

Threave Garden & Estate, CASTLE DOUGLAS
08449 4932245 www.nts.org.uk

Orchardton Tower, PALNACKIE
www.historic-scotland.gov.uk

▶▶▶▶ 81% Glenearly Caravan Park

(NX838628)

DG5 4NE
☎ 01556 611393   📠 01556 612058
e-mail: glenearlycaravan@btconnect.com
dir: From Dumfries take A711 towards Dalbeattie.
Site entrance after Edingham Farm on right
(200yds before boundary sign)

🚐 🚌 Å

Open all year

Last arrival 19.00hrs Last departure noon

An excellent small park set in open countryside
with panoramic views of Long Fell, Maidenpap
and Dalbeattie Forest. The park is located in 84
beautiful acres of farmland which visitors are
invited to enjoy. The attention to detail here is of
the highest standard and this is most notable in
the presentation of the amenity block. Static
holiday caravans for hire. 10 acre site. 39 touring
pitches. 33 hardstandings. Caravan pitches.
Motorhome pitches. Tent pitches. 74 statics.

Leisure: 🎱 🔍
Facilities: 🍴 ☺ 🏴 ✳ & ◎ 🐕 ✆
Services: 🔌 🔋 🛢 🔌
Within 3 miles: ↓ ✈ 🏌 ◎ 🛒 🎱 ∪

Notes: No commercial vehicles. Dogs must be
kept on leads.

ECCLEFECHAN   Map 21 NY17

Places to visit

Robert Burns House, DUMFRIES 01387 255297
www.dumgal.gov.uk/museums

Old Bridge House Museum, DUMFRIES
01387 256904 www.dumgal.gov.uk/museums

Great for kids: Dumfries Museum & Camera
Obscura, DUMFRIES 01387 253374
www.dumgal.gov.uk/museums

PREMIER PARK

▶▶▶▶▶ 75% Hoddom Castle
Caravan Park (NY154729)

Hoddom DG11 1AS
☎ 01576 300251   📠 01576 300757
e-mail: hoddomcastle@aol.com
dir: M74 junct 19, follow signs to site. From A75,
W of Annan, take B723 for 5m, follow signs to site

🚐 🚌 Å

Open Etr or Apr-Oct (rs Early season cafeteria
closed)

Last arrival 21.00hrs Last departure 14.00hrs

The peaceful, well-equipped park can be found on
the banks of the River Annan, and offers a good
mix of grassy and hard pitches, beautifully
landscaped and blending into the surroundings.
There are signed nature trails, maintained by the
park's countryside ranger, a 9-hole golf course,
trout and salmon fishing, and plenty of activity
ideas for children. 28 acre site. 200 touring
pitches. 150 hardstandings. Caravan pitches.
Motorhome pitches. Tent pitches. 54 statics.

Leisure: 🎱 🏊 🔍 🎵
Facilities: 🚻 🍴 ☺ 🏴 ✳ & ◎ 🛒 🐕
Services: 🔌 🔋 🛢 🚿 ⊘ 🚰 🍴 🛒 🔧 ↓
Within 3 miles: ↓ 🏌 ◎ 🛒 🎱

Notes: No electric scooters, no gazebos, no fires.
Visitor centre.

GATEHOUSE OF FLEET   Map 20 NX55

Places to visit

MacLellan's Castle, KIRKCUDBRIGHT
01557 331856 www.historic-scotland.gov.uk

Great for kids: Galloway Wildlife Conservation
Park, KIRKCUDBRIGHT 01557 331645
www.gallowaywildlife.co.uk

 ### 87% Auchenlarie Holiday Park

(NX536522)

DG7 2EX
☎ 01556 506200 & 206201   📠 01556 206220
e-mail: enquiries@auchenlarie.co.uk
web: www.auchenlarie.co.uk
dir: Direct access from A75, 5m W of Gatehouse
of Fleet

🚐 £16-£22 🚌 £16-£22 Å £16-£22

Open Mar-Oct

Last arrival 20.00hrs Last departure noon

A well-organised family park set on cliffs
overlooking Wigtown Bay, with its own sandy
beach. The tenting area, in sloping grass
surrounded by mature trees, has its own
sanitary facilities, while the marked caravan
pitches are in paddocks, with open views
and the provision of high quality toilets. The
leisure centre includes a swimming pool, gym,
solarium and sports hall. There are six self-
catering holiday apartments for let. 32 acre
site. 49 touring pitches. 52 hardstandings.
Caravan pitches. Motorhome pitches. Tent
pitches. 400 statics.

AA Pubs & Restaurants nearby: Cally Palace
Hotel, Gatehouse-of-Fleet 01557 814341

Leisure: 🏊 🎱 🏊 🔍
Facilities: 🚻 🍴 ☺ 🏴 ✳ & ◎ 🛒 🐕 🐾 📶 🖥
Services: 🔌 🔋 🛢 🚿 ⊘ 🚰 🍴 🔧 🔧
Within 3 miles: ↓ 🏌 ◎ 🛒 🎱 ∪

Notes: Dogs must be kept on leads. Baby
changing facilities, internet café, crazy golf.

GATEHOUSE OF FLEET *continued*

AA CAMPING CARD SITE

▶▶▶▶ 80% Anwoth Caravan Site

(NX595563)

DG7 2JU
☎ 01557 814333 & 01556 506200
📄 01557 814333
e-mail: enquiries@auchenlarie.co.uk
dir: *From A75 into Gatehouse of Fleet, site on right towards Stranraer. Signed from town centre*

🚐 🚏 ⛺

Open Mar-Oct

Last arrival 20.00hrs Last departure noon

A very high quality park in a peaceful sheltered setting within easy walking distance of the village, ideally placed for exploring the scenic hills, valleys and coastline. Grass, hardstanding and fully serviced pitches are available and guests may use the leisure facilities at the sister site, Auchenlarie Holiday Park (see entry). 2 acre site. 28 touring pitches. 13 hardstandings. Caravan pitches. Motorhome pitches. Tent pitches. 44 statics.

AA Pubs & Restaurants nearby: Cally Palace Hotel, Gatehouse-of-Fleet 01557 814341

Facilities: 🛁 🚿 ⊙ ℗ ✳ & ◐ 🎱 🚻 Wi-Fi

Services: 🔌 🗑 ⊘

Within 3 miles: ↕ ℘ 🏪 🗑

GRETNA

Places to visit

Carlisle Cathedral, CARLISLE 01228 535169 www.carlislecathedral.org.uk

Tullie House Museum & Art Gallery, CARLISLE 01228 618718 www.tulliehouse.co.uk

Great for kids: Carlisle Castle, CARLISLE 01228 591992 www.english-heritage.org.uk

---

GRETNA Map 21 NY36

▶▶▶▶ 77% Braids Caravan Park

(NY313674)

Annan Rd DG16 5DQ
☎ 01461 337409
e-mail: enquiries@thebraidscaravanpark.co.uk
dir: *On B721, 0.5m from village on right, towards Annan*

✱ 🚐 £15.50-£19 🚏 £15.50-£19

Open all year

Last arrival 21.00hrs (20.00hrs in winter) Last departure noon

A very well-maintained park conveniently located on the outskirts of Gretna village. Within walking distance is Gretna Gateway Outlet Village, and Gretna Green with the World Famous Old Blacksmith's Shop is nearby. It proves a convenient stop-over for anyone travelling to and from both the north of Scotland, and Northern Ireland (via the ferry at Stranraer). The park has first-class toilet facilities and generous-sized all-weather pitches. Please note that tents are not accepted. A rally field and a meeting room are available. 6 acre site. 93 touring pitches. 46 hardstandings. Caravan pitches. Motorhome pitches.

Facilities: 🚿 ⊙ ℗ ✳ & ◐ ♻

Services: 🔌 🗑 🧴 T ↓

Within 3 miles: 🗑

Notes: Dogs must be kept on leads.

▶▶▶▶ 73% King Robert the Bruce's Cave Caravan & Camping Park

(NY266705)

Cove Estate, Kirkpatrick Fleming DG11 3AT
☎ 01461 800285 & 07779 138694
📄 01461 800269
e-mail: enquiries@brucescave.co.uk
web: www.brucescave.co.uk
dir: *Exit A74(M) junct 21 for Kirkpatrick Fleming, follow N through village, pass Station Inn, left at Bruce's Court. Over rail crossing to site*

✱ 🚐 fr £14 🚏 fr £14 ⛺ £10-£22

Open Apr-Nov (rs Nov shop closed, water restriction)

Last arrival 22.00hrs Last departure 16.00hrs

The lovely wooded grounds of an old castle and mansion are the setting for this pleasant park. The mature woodland is a haven for wildlife, and there is a riverside walk to Robert the Bruce's Cave. A toilet block with en suite facilities is of special appeal to families. 80 acre site. 75 touring pitches. 60 hardstandings. Caravan pitches. Motorhome pitches. Tent pitches. 35 statics.

King Robert the Bruce's Cave Caravan & Camping Park

AA Pubs & Restaurants nearby: Smiths of Gretna Green, Gretna 01461 337007

Leisure: 🅰 ☺ 🔍 ⊡ ⎕

Facilities: 🛁 🚿 ⊙ ℗ ✳ & ◐ 🎱 🚻 🛒 ♻ ❶

Services: 🔌 🗑 🧴 ⊘ T 🍴 ♨ ↓

Within 3 miles: ↕ ☐ ℘ ≈ 🏪 🗑 ∪

Notes: Dogs must be kept on leads. BMX bike hire, coarse fishing, first aid available.

KIPPFORD Map 21 NX85

Places to visit

Orchardton Tower, PALNACKIE www.historic-scotland.gov.uk

AA CAMPING CARD SITE

▶▶▶ 75% Kippford Holiday Park *(NX844564)*

DG5 4LF
☎ 01556 620636 📄 01556 620607
e-mail: info@kippfordholidaypark.co.uk
dir: *From Dumfries take A711 to Dalbeattie, left onto A710 (Solway coast road) for 3.5m. Park 200yds beyond Kippford turn on right*

🚐 £21-£27 🚏 £21-£27 ⛺ £19-£25

Open all year

Last arrival 21.30hrs Last departure noon

An attractively landscaped park set in hilly countryside close to the Urr Water estuary and a sand/shingle beach, and with spectacular views. The level touring pitches are on grassed hardstands with private garden areas, and many are fully serviced, and there are attractive lodges for hire. The Doon Hill and woodland walks separate the park from the lovely village of

---

LEISURE: 🏊 Indoor swimming pool 🏊 Outdoor swimming pool 🅰 Children's playground 🧒 Kid's club 🎾 Tennis court 🎱 Games room 📺 Separate TV room ⛳ 9/18 hole golf course ⛵ Boats for hire 🎬 Cinema 🎵 Entertainment ℘ Fishing ⛳ Mini golf 🏄 Watersports 🏋 Gym ⚽ Sports field **Spa** ∪ Stables
FACILITIES: 🛁 Bath 🚿 Shower ⊙ Electric shaver ℘ Hairdryer ✳ Ice Pack Facility & Disabled facilities ◐ Public telephone 🛒 Shop on site or within 200yds 🛒 Mobile shop (calls at least 5 days a week) 🍴 BBQ area 🌲 Picnic area Wi-Fi Wi-fi 💻 Internet access ♻ Recycling ❶ Tourist info 🐕 Dog exercise area

Kippford. 18 acre site. 45 touring pitches. 35 hardstandings. Caravan pitches. Motorhome pitches. Tent pitches. 119 statics.

Kippford Holiday Park

AA Pubs & Restaurants nearby: Balcary Bay Hotel, Auchencairn 01556 640217

Leisure: ⚙ ☉

Facilities: 🔭 ☉ ☏ ✳ ⚷ ⊙ 🖻 🛒 🐕 📶 💻 ♻ ✿

Services: 🔌 🖻 🛢 ⊘ 🍴 🛒 ⚒

Within 3 miles: ↨ ╱ ⊙ ≋ 🖻 🖻 ∪

Notes: No camp fires. Dogs must be kept on leads. Golf, fly fishing, nature walk, cycle hire.

see advert below

▶▶▶▶ **80% Seaward Caravan Park**

(NX662494)

Dhoon Bay DG6 4TJ

☎ 01557 870267 & 331079 📠 01557 870319

e-mail: info@gillespie-leisure.co.uk

dir: *2m SW off B727 (Borgue road)*

* 🔌 £13.15-£18.90 🚐 £13.15-£18.90
⛺ £13.15-£18.90

Open Mar-Oct (rs Mar-mid May & mid Sep-Oct swimming pool closed)

Last arrival 21.30hrs Last departure 11.30hrs

A very attractive elevated park with outstanding views over Kirkcudbright Bay which forms part of the Dee Estuary. Access to a sandy cove with rock pools is just across the road. Facilities are well organised and neatly kept, and the park offers a very peaceful atmosphere. The leisure facilities at the other Gillespie parks are available to visitors to Seaward Caravan Park. 23 acre site. 26 touring pitches. 20 hardstandings. Caravan pitches. Motorhome pitches. Tent pitches. 54 statics.

AA Pubs & Restaurants nearby: Selkirk Arms Hotel, Kirkcudbright 01557 330402

Leisure: ⚓ ⚙ 🔍

Facilities: 🛏 🔭 ☉ ☏ ✳ ⚷ ⊙ 🖻 🛒 ✿

Services: 🔌 🖻 🛢 ⊘ ⊤

Within 3 miles: ↨ ╱ ⊙ 🖻 🖻 ∪

Notes: No motorised scooters or bikes (except disabled vehicles), no jet skis or own quad bikes. Dogs must be kept on leads. Pitch & putt, volley ball, badminton, table tennis.

SERVICES: 🔌 Electric hook up 🖻 Launderette 🍷 Licensed bar 🛢 Calor Gas ⊘ Camping Gaz ⊤ Toilet fluid 🍴 Café/Restaurant 🍟 Fast Food/Takeaway 🔋 Battery charging 🍼 Baby care ⚒ Motorvan service point

ABBREVIATIONS: BH/bank hols-bank holidays Etr-Easter Whit-Whitsun dep-departure fr-from hrs-hours m-mile mdnt-midnight rdbt-roundabout rs-restricted service wk-week wknd-weekend ⊛ No credit cards ⊗ No dogs   See page 7 for details of the AA Camping Card Scheme

KIRKGUNZEON — Map 21 NX86

AA CAMPING CARD SITE

►►► 71% Mossband Caravan Park

(NX872665)

Mossband DG2 8JP
☎ 01387 760505 & 07818 518119
e-mail: mossbandcp@btconnect.com
dir: *Adjacent to A711 to Dalbeattie, 1.5m E of Kirkgunzeon*

➤ £12-£18 ➤ £12-£18 ▲ £9-£18

Open Mar-Oct

Last arrival 21.00hrs Last departure 11.00hrs

A level park on the site of an old railway station, set in a peaceful rural location with good views. The experienced owners have certainly made a difference by refreshing some of the dated facilities. 3 acre site. 25 touring pitches. 3 hardstandings. Caravan pitches. Motorhome pitches. Tent pitches. 12 statics.

Facilities: 🚿 ☺ ✻ ♻ ❶
Services: 🚻 🗑 🛒 📧
Within 3 miles: ⚓ 🎣
Notes: 🐕 Dogs must be kept on leads.

LANGHOLM — Map 21 NY38

Places to visit

Hermitage Castle, HERMITAGE 01387 376222
www.historic-scotland.gov.uk

►► 65% *Ewes Water Caravan & Camping Park* *(NY365855)*

Milntown DG13 0BG
☎ 013873 80386 📠 013873 81670
e-mail: aeneasmn@aol.com
dir: *Directly off A7 approx 0.5m N of Langholm. Site in Langholm Rugby Club*

➤ ➤ ▲

Open Apr-Sep

Last departure noon

On the banks of the River Esk, this attractive park lies in a sheltered wooded valley close to an unspoilt Borders' town. 2 acre site. 24 touring pitches. Caravan pitches. Motorhome pitches. Tent pitches.

Facilities: 🚿 ☺ ✻ ♿ ☏ 🏕 🐕
Services: 🚻 🛒 ♻ 📧
Within 3 miles: ⚓ 🎣 🏧
Notes: 🐕 Large playing area.

LOCKERBIE

See Ecclefechan

NEWTON STEWART — Map 20 NX46

►►► 67% Creebridge Caravan Park

(NX415656)

Minnigaff DG8 6AJ
☎ 01671 402324 & 402432 📠 01671 402324
e-mail: john_sharples@btconnect.com
dir: *0.25m E of Newton Stewart at Minnigaff on bypass, signed off A75*

* ➤ £14-£18 ➤ £14-£18 ▲ £12-£18

Open all year (rs Mar only one toilet block open)

Last arrival 20.00hrs Last departure 10.30hrs

A small family-owned site a short walk from the town's amenities. The site is surrounded by mature trees, and the toilet facilities are clean and functional. 5.5 acre site. 26 touring pitches. 9 hardstandings. Caravan pitches. Motorhome pitches. Tent pitches. 60 statics.

AA Pubs & Restaurants nearby: Creebridge House Hotel, Newton Stewart 01671 402121

Galloway Arms Hotel, Newton Stewart 01671 402653

Kirroughtree House, Minnigaff, Newton Stewart 01671 402141

Leisure: 🎪
Facilities: 🚿 ☺ 📺 ✻ ♿ ☏ 🏧 🏕 ♻ ❶
Services: 🚻 🗑 ♻ 📧
Within 3 miles: ⚓ 🍴 🎣 ⛵ 🏧 🗑 ⛺
Notes: Dogs must be kept on leads. Security street lighting.

PALNACKIE — Map 21 NX85

Places to visit

Orchardton Tower, PALNACKIE
www.historic-scotland.gov.uk

►►► 79% Barlochan Caravan Park

(NX819572)

DG7 1PF
☎ 01556 600256 & 01557 870267
📠 01557 870319
e-mail: aa@barlochan.co.uk
dir: *On A711, N of Palnackie, signed*

* ➤ £12.55-£18.05 ➤ £12.55-£18.05
▲ £12.55-£18.05

Open Apr-Oct (rs Apr-May & Sep-Oct swimming pool closed)

Last arrival 21.30hrs Last departure 11.30hrs

A small terraced park with quiet landscaped pitches in a level area backed by rhododendron bushes. There are spectacular views over the River Urr estuary, and the park has its own coarse fishing loch nearby. The amenity block includes combined wash facilities. The leisure facilities at Brighouse Bay are available to visitors. 9 acre site. 20 touring pitches. 3 hardstandings. Caravan pitches. Motorhome pitches. Tent pitches. 65 statics.

AA Pubs & Restaurants nearby: Balcary Bay Hotel, Auchencairn 01556 640217

Leisure: 🏊 🎪 🎣 🖥
Facilities: 🚿 📺 ✻ ♿ ☏ 🏧 🏕 ♻ ❶
Services: 🚻 🗑 🛒 ♻ 📧 📶
Within 3 miles: ⚓ 🎣 ⚓ 🏧 🗑
Notes: Dogs must be kept on leads. Pitch & putt.

LEISURE: 🏊 Indoor swimming pool 🏊 Outdoor swimming pool 🎪 Children's playground 🧒 Kid's club 🎾 Tennis court 🎱 Games room 📺 Separate TV room ⚓ 9/18 hole golf course ⛵ Boats for hire 🎬 Cinema 🎵 Entertainment 🎣 Fishing ◎ Mini golf 🏄 Watersports 🏋 Gym 🏆 Sports field **Spa** Spa ⛎ Stables
FACILITIES: 🛁 Bath 🚿 Shower ☺ Electric shaver 📺 Hairdryer ✻ Ice Pack Facility ♿ Disabled facilities ☏ Public telephone 🏧 Shop on site or within 200yds 🚐 Mobile shop (calls at least 5 days a week) 🍖 BBQ area 🏕 Picnic area 📶 Wi-fi 🖥 Internet access ♻ Recycling ❶ Tourist info 🏕 Dog exercise area

PARTON · Map 20 NX67

Places to visit

The Rum Story, WHITEHAVEN 01946 592933
www.rumstory.co.uk

The Beacon, WHITEHAVEN 01946 592302
www.thebeacon-whitehaven.co.uk

►►► 83% Loch Ken Holiday Park (NX687702)

DG7 3NE
☎ 01644 470282
e-mail: office@lochkenholidaypark.co.uk
web: www.lochkenholidaypark.co.uk
dir: On A713, N of Parton. (NB do not follow Sat Nav directions. Site on main road)

* 🚐 £17-£22 ⛺ £17-£22 ▲ £10-£20

Open Mar-mid Nov (rs Mar (ex Etr) & Nov restricted shop hours)

Last departure noon

Much improved, with completely refurbished toilets to an excellent standard, following a huge injection of energy, enthusiasm and commitment from the hands-on Bryson family, this busy and popular park, with a natural emphasis on water activities, is set on the eastern shores of Loch Ken, with superb views. It is in a peaceful and beautiful spot opposite the RSPB reserve, with direct access to the loch for fishing and boat launching. The park offers a variety of watersports, as well as farm visits and nature trails. Static caravans are available for hire. 15 acre site. 40 touring pitches. 12 hardstandings. 12 seasonal pitches. Caravan pitches. Motorhome pitches. Tent pitches. 35 statics.

Leisure: 🎠 ⚽ ☺
Facilities: 🖮 ⊙ 🅿 ⚒ ⚙ 🖫 🏕 🛒 WiFi ♻ 🛈
Services: 🔌 🗄 🛢 ⊘ 🗆 🍴 🛒
Within 3 miles: ⚓ 🎣 🚣 🛒 🗄

Notes: No noise after 22.00hrs. Dogs must be kept on leads. Bike, boat & canoe hire, water skiing, sailing.

PORT WILLIAM · Map 20 NX34

Places to visit

Glenluce Abbey, GLENLUCE 01581 300541
www.historic-scotland.gov.uk

►►► 78% *Kings Green Caravan Site* (NX340430)

South St DG8 9SG
☎ 01988 700489
dir: Direct access from A747 at junct with B7085, towards Whithorn

🚐 ⛺ ▲

Open Etr, May & Jul-Aug

Last arrival 20.00hrs Last departure noon

Set beside the unspoilt village with all its amenities and the attractive harbour, this level grassy park is community owned and run. Approached via the coast road, the park has views reaching as far as the Isle of Man. 3 acre site. 30 touring pitches. Caravan pitches. Motorhome pitches. Tent pitches.

AA Pubs & Restaurants nearby: Steam Packet Inn, Isle of Whithorn 01988 500334

Facilities: 🖮 ⊙ 🅿 ⚙ ⊙ 🖫 🏕
Services: 🔌 🗄 **Within 3 miles:** ⚓ 🎣 🚣 🗄
Notes: ⊗ No golf or fireworks permitted on site. Free book lending.

SANDHEAD · Map 20 NX04

Places to visit

Glenwhan Gardens, STRANRAER 01581 400222
www.glenwhangardens.co.uk

Great for kids: Castle Kennedy & Gardens, STRANRAER 01776 702024
www.castlekennedygardens.co.uk

►►►► 78% Sands of Luce Holiday Park (NX103510)

Sands of Luce DG9 9JN
☎ 01776 830456 　 📠 01776 830477
e-mail: info@sandsofluceholidaypark.co.uk
web: www.sandsofluceholidaypark.co.uk
dir: From S & E: left from A75 onto B7084 signed Drummore. Site signed at junct with A716. From N: A77 through Stranraer towards Portpatrick, 2m, follow A716 signed Drummore, site signed in 5m

* 🚐 £20-£25 ⛺ £20-£25 ▲ £15-£22

Open Mar-Jan

Last arrival 20.00hrs Last departure noon

This is a large, well managed park with a balance of static and touring caravans and enjoys a stunning position with direct access to a sandy beach and with views across Luce Bay. It has its own boat storage area and boasts an excellent static hire fleet and a tastefully decorated well-managed club. 30 acre site. 120 touring pitches. Caravan pitches. Motorhome pitches. Tent pitches. 250 statics.

Leisure: 🎠 ☺ ⚓ 🎵
Facilities: 🖮 ⊙ 🅿 ⚒ ⚙ 🖫 🏕 🛒 WiFi 🖥 ♻ 🛈
Services: 🔌 🗄 🍴 ⊕ 🛒 🛒
Within 3 miles: ⚓ 🎣 🚣 🗄 🗄 ⛳

Notes: Dog fouling must be cleared up by owners. No quad bikes. Dogs must be kept on leads. Boat launching.

SANDYHILLS · Map 21 NX85

Places to visit

Threave Garden & Estate, CASTLE DOUGLAS 08449 4932245 www.nts.org.uk

Great for kids: Threave Castle, CASTLE DOUGLAS 07711 223101 www.historic-scotland.gov.uk

►►►► 75% Sandyhills Bay Leisure Park (NX892552)

DG5 4NY
☎ 01557 870267 　& 01387 780257
📠 01557 870319
e-mail: info@gillespie-leisure.co.uk
dir: On A710, 7m from Dalbeattie, 6.5m from Kirkbean

* 🚐 £12.55-£18.05 ⛺ £12.55-£18.05
▲ £12.55-£18.05

Open Apr-Oct

Last arrival 21.30hrs Last departure 11.30hrs

A well-maintained park in a superb location beside a beach, and close to many attractive villages. The level, grassy site is sheltered by woodland, and the south-facing Sandyhills Bay and beach are a treasure trove for all the family, with their caves and rock pools. The leisure facilities at Brighouse Bay are available to visitors here. Two camping pods with TV, fridge, kettle and microwave are available for hire. 15 acre site. 24 touring pitches. Caravan pitches. Motorhome pitches. Tent pitches. 32 statics. 2 tipis.

continued

SANDYHILLS *continued*

AA Pubs & Restaurants nearby: Cavens, Kirkbean 01387 880234

Leisure: 🅐

Facilities: 🏠⊙🅿✳⊙🖥🚿🕭🐕❶

Services: 🔌🖲🍴🛢🚰🚽📮🛒⚡

Within 3 miles: ⬆🏌🎣🛍🛒⛲

Notes: No motorised scooters, jet skis or own quad bikes. Dogs must be kept on leads.

SOUTHERNESS Map 21 NX95

 82% Southerness Holiday Village
GOLD

(NX976545)

Off Sandy Ln DG2 8AZ
☎ 0844 335 3756 📠 01387 880429
e-mail: touringandcamping@parkdeanholidays.com
web: www.parkdeantouring.com
dir: *From S: A75 from Gretna to Dumfries. From N: A74, exit at A701 to Dumfries. Take A710 (coast road), approx 16m, site easily visible*

* 🚐 £15-£34.50 🚏 £15-£34.50 ▲ £13-£30.50

Open Mar-Oct

Last arrival 21.00hrs Last departure 10.00hrs

There are stunning views across the Solway Firth from this holiday park at the foot of the Galloway Hills. A sandy beach on the Solway Firth is accessible directly from the park. The emphasis is on family entertainment, and facilities include an indoor pool, show bar, coast bar and kitchen. A very well organised park with excellent all-weather, fully-serviced pitches available. 50 acre site. 110 touring pitches. Caravan pitches. Motorhome pitches. Tent pitches. 611 statics.

AA Pubs & Restaurants nearby: Cavens, Kirkbean 01387 880234

Leisure: 🅐🏊🚣🎣🎵

Facilities: 🏠⊙🅿✳♿⊙🖥🚿🕭

Services: 🔌🖲🍴🛢🚽📮🍴🛒

Within 3 miles: 🏌🎣◎🛍🛒

Notes: Amusements centre, live entertainment.

see advert in preliminary section

STRANRAER Map 20 NX06

Places to visit
Ardwell House Gardens, ARDWELL 01776 860227

AA CAMPING CARD SITE

▶▶▶▶ **79% Aird Donald Caravan Park** *(NX075605)*

London Rd DG9 8RN
☎ 01776 702025
e-mail: enquiries@aird-donald.co.uk
dir: *From A75 left on entering Stranraer (signed). Opposite school, site 300yds*

* 🚐 £17-£18 🚏 £17-£18 ▲ £13-£15

Open all year

Last departure 16.00hrs

A spacious touring site, mainly grass but with tarmac hardstanding areas, with pitches large enough to accommodate a car and caravan overnight without unhitching. On the fringe of town screened by mature shrubs and trees. A 25 pitch rally field is also available. This is the ideal stopover en route for the Stranraer to Belfast ferry. Please note that this site only accepts tents from April to September. 12 acre site. 100 touring pitches. 50 hardstandings. Caravan pitches. Motorhome pitches. Tent pitches.

AA Pubs & Restaurants nearby: Knockinaam Lodge, Portpatrick 01776 810471

Leisure: 🅐

Facilities: 🏠⊙🅿♿🕭

Services: 🔌🖲🛢🛢🚰

Within 3 miles: ⬆🎾🎣🛍🛒⛲

Notes: ⊘ Dogs must be kept on leads.

WIGTOWN Map 20 NX45

▶▶▶ **85% Drumroamin Farm Camping & Touring Site** *(NX444512)*

1 South Balfern DG8 9DB
☎ 01988 840613 & 07752 471456
e-mail: enquiry@drumroamin.co.uk
dir: *A75 towards Newton Stewart, onto A714 for Wigtown. Left on B7005 through Bladnock, A746 through Kirkinner. Take B7004 signed Garlieston, 2nd left opposite Kilsture Forest, site 0.75m at end of lane*

🚐 £17 🚏 £17 ▲ £14-£17

Open all year

Last arrival 21.00hrs Last departure noon

An open, spacious park in a quiet spot a mile from the main road, and close to Wigtown Bay. A superb toilet block offers spacious showers, and there's a lounge/games room and plenty of room for children to play. Also provides a store and pitch facility . 5 acre site. 48 touring pitches. Caravan pitches. Motorhome pitches. Tent pitches. 3 statics.

AA Pubs & Restaurants nearby: Creebridge House Hotel, Newton Stewart 01671 402121

Galloway Arms Hotel, Newton Stewart 01671 402653

Kirroughtree House, Minnigaff, Newton Stewart 01671 402141

Leisure: 🅐🔍

Facilities: 🏠⊙🅿✳♿🕭🐕♻❶

Services: 🔌🖲🚰⚡

Within 3 miles: ⬆🎣🛍

Notes: ⊘ No fires. Dogs must be kept on leads. Ball games area.

EAST LOTHIAN

ABERLADY

Places to visit
Dirleton Castle and Gardens, DIRLETON 01620 850330 www.historic-scotland.gov.uk

Hailes Castle, EAST LINTON www.historic-scotland.gov.uk

Great for kids: Myreton Motor Museum, ABERLADY 01875 870288

ABERLADY
Map 21 NT47

►► 75% Aberlady Caravan Park
(NT482797)

Haddington Rd EH32 0PZ
☎ 01875 870666 🖺 01875 870666
dir: *From Aberlady take A6137 towards Haddington. Right in 0.25m, site on right*

🚐 fr £17.50 🚐 fr £17.50 ▲ fr £10

Open Mar-Oct

Last arrival 22.00hrs Last departure noon

A small, simple campsite in pleasantly wooded surroundings, with a delightful outlook towards the Lammermuir Hills. It offers level pitches in a well-maintained meadow with electric hook-ups, and is within easy reach of Edinburgh and the East Lothian coast. 4.5 acre site. 15 touring pitches. 8 hardstandings. Caravan pitches. Motorhome pitches. Tent pitches. 3 wooden pods.

AA Pubs & Restaurants nearby: La Potinière, Gullane 01620 843214

Macdonald Marine Hotel & Spa, North Berwick 0870 400 8129

Leisure: Ⓐ
Facilities: ⋔☉ℙ⚘𝄞ⅇ🖃⛱🐾ᴡɪғɪ ♻ ❶
Services: 🔌🖨🎍🖉Ⓣ🍴🔋
Within 3 miles: ↨🌮◎⛴🖟🖥Ⓤ
Notes: ⊘ No ball games, no loud music. Dogs must be kept on leads.

DUNBAR

Places to visit

Preston Mill & Phantassie Doocot, EAST LINTON 0844 493 2128 www.nts.org.uk

Great for kids: Tantallon Castle, NORTH BERWICK 01620 892727 www.historic-scotland.gov.uk

DUNBAR
Map 21 NT67

PREMIER PARK

►►►►► 83% Thurston Manor Leisure Park *(NT712745)*

Innerwick EH42 1SA
☎ 01368 840643 🖺 01368 840261
e-mail: holidays@thurstonmanor.co.uk
dir: *4m S of Dunbar, signed off A1*

🚐 £19-£29.75 🚐 £19-£29.75 ▲ £9-£25.50

Open Mar-7 Jan (rs 1-22 Dec site open wknds only)

Last arrival 23.00hrs Last departure noon

A pleasant park set in 250 acres of unspoilt countryside. The touring and static areas of this large park are in separate areas. The main touring area occupies an open, level position, and the toilet facilities are modern and exceptionally well maintained. The park boasts a well-stocked fishing loch, a heated indoor swimming pool, steam room, sauna, jacuzzi, mini-gym and fitness room and seasonal entertainment. There is a superb family toilet block. 250 acre site. 120 touring pitches. 53 hardstandings. Caravan pitches. Motorhome pitches. Tent pitches. 490 statics.

AA Pubs & Restaurants nearby: Macdonald Marine Hotel & Spa, North Berwick 0870 400 8129

Leisure: ⍨🏑Ⓐ🎣▭🎵
Facilities: ⋔☉ℙ⚘𝄞ⅇ🖃⛱🐾ᴡɪғɪ 🖥♻ ❶
Services: 🔌🖨🎍🖉🚰Ⓣ🍴🎍🔋🖉
Within 3 miles: 🌮🖟🖥Ⓤ
Notes: Dogs must be kept on leads.

►►► 75% Belhaven Bay Caravan & Camping Park

(NT661781)

Belhaven Bay EH42 1TS
☎ 01368 865956 🖺 01368 865022
e-mail: belhaven@meadowhead.co.uk
dir: *A1 onto A1087 towards Dunbar. Site (1m) in John Muir Park*

🚐 ▲

Open Mar-13 Oct

Last arrival 20.00hrs Last departure noon

Small, well-maintained park in a sheltered location and within walking distance of the beach. This is an excellent spot for seabird watching, and there is a good rail connection with Edinburgh

from Dunbar. A children's play area and additional electric hook-ups have now been added. 40 acre site. 52 touring pitches. 11 hardstandings. Caravan pitches. Tent pitches. 64 statics.

AA Pubs & Restaurants nearby: Macdonald Marine Hotel & Spa, North Berwick 0870 400 8129

Leisure: Ⓐ
Facilities: ⋔☉ℙ⚘𝄞ⅇ🖃⛱🐾ᴡɪғɪ 🖥
Services: 🔌🖨Ⓣ🖉
Within 3 miles: ↨🌮◎⛴🖟🖥Ⓤ
Notes: Dogs must be kept on leads.

LONGNIDDRY
Map 21 NT47

Places to visit

Crichton Castle, CRICHTON 01875 320017 www.historic-scotland.gov.uk

65% Seton Sands Holiday Village

(NT420759)

EH32 0QF
☎ 0871 231 0867 🖺 01875 813531
e-mail: setonsands@haven.com
dir: *A1 to A198 exit, then B6371 to Cockenzie. Right onto B1348. Site 1m on right*

🚐 🚐 ▲

Open mid Mar-end Oct (rs mid Mar-May & Sep-Oct some facilities may be reduced)

Last arrival 22.00hrs Last departure 10.00hrs

A well-equipped holiday centre with plenty of organised entertainment, clubs and bars, restaurants, and sports and leisure facilities. A multi-sports court, heated swimming pool, and various play areas ensure that there is plenty to do, and there is lots to see and do in and around Edinburgh which is nearby. The touring facilities are separate from the large static areas. 1.75 acre site. 38 touring pitches. Caravan pitches. Motorhome pitches. Tent pitches. 635 statics.

AA Pubs & Restaurants nearby: La Potinière, Gullane 01620 843214

Leisure: ⍨Ⓐ🛝⚽🎵
Facilities: ⋔☉ℙ⚘ⅇ🖃ᴡɪғɪ ♻ ❶
Services: 🔌🖨🎍🍴🎍🖉
Within 3 miles: 🌮🖟Ⓤ
Notes: Max 2 dogs per booking, certain dog breeds banned, no commercial vehicles, no bookings by persons under 21yrs unless a family booking. Dogs must be kept on leads.

SERVICES: 🔌 Electric hook up 🖨 Launderette 🎍 Licensed bar ▪ Calor Gas ⊘ Camping Gaz Ⓣ Toilet fluid 🍴 Café/Restaurant 🎍 Fast Food/Takeaway 🔋 Battery charging 🖉 Baby care 🖉 Motorvan service point
ABBREVIATIONS: BH/bank hols-bank holidays Etr-Easter Whit-Whitsun dep-departure fr-from hrs-hours m-mile mdnt-midnight rdbt-roundabout rs-restricted service wk-week wknd-weekend ⊘ No credit cards ⊗ No dogs
See page 7 for details of the AA Camping Card Scheme

MUSSELBURGH — Map 21 NT37

Places to visit

Dalmeny House, SOUTH QUEENSFERRY
0131 331 1888 www.dalmeny.co.uk

Lauriston Castle, EDINBURGH 0131 336 2060
www.edinburghmuseums.org.uk

AA CAMPING CARD SITE

►►►► 80% Drum Mohr Caravan Park (NT373734)

Levenhall EH21 8JS
☎ 0131 665 6867 📠 0131 653 6859
e-mail: admin@drummohr.org
web: www.drummohr.org
dir: Exit A1 at A199 junct through Wallyford, at rdbt onto B1361 signed Prestonpans. 1st left, site 400yds

* 🚐 £18-£28 🚌 £18-£28 ▲ £18-£25

Open all year (rs Winter arrivals by arrangement)

Last arrival 17.00hrs Last departure noon

This attractive park is sheltered by mature trees on all sides, and carefully landscaped within. The park is divided into separate areas by mature hedging and planting of trees and ornamental shrubs. the pitches are generous in size, and there are a number of fully serviced pitches plus first-class amenities. There are bothys for hire. 9 acre site. 120 touring pitches. 50 hardstandings. Caravan pitches. Motorhome pitches. Tent pitches. 12 statics. 10 wooden pods.

AA Pubs & Restaurants nearby: The Kitchen, Leith, Edinburgh 0131 555 1755

Plumed Horse, Leith 0131 554 5556

The Vintners Rooms, Leith 0131 554 6767

Leisure: 🎠

Facilities: 🏪⊙📷✳&🔥🚻📶♻️ℹ️

Services: 🔌🔋🧺Ⓣ🛒🚰♿

Within 3 miles: ↓🏌️🛒🔌

Notes: Max of 2 dogs per pitch. Dogs must be kept on leads. Freshly baked bread & croissants, tea & coffee in high season.

FIFE

LUNDIN LINKS — Map 21 NO40

Places to visit

Kellie Castle & Gardens, KELLIE CASTLE & GARDENS 0844 493 2184 www.nts.org.uk

►►► 82% Woodland Gardens Caravan & Camping Site (NO418031)

Blindwell Rd KY8 5QG
☎ 01333 360319
e-mail: enquiries@woodland-gardens.co.uk
dir: Exit A915 (coast road) at Largo at E end of Lundin Links, 0.5m, site signed

🚐 £15-£20 🚌 £18-£20 ▲ £12-£18

Open Apr-Oct

Last arrival 21.00hrs Last departure noon

A secluded and sheltered little jewel of a site in a small orchard under the hill called Largo Law. This very attractive site is family owned and run to an immaculate standard, and pitches are grouped in twos and threes by low hedging and gorse. Please note that larger units cannot be accommodated. 1 acre site. 20 touring pitches. 12 hardstandings. 6 seasonal pitches. Caravan pitches. Motorhome pitches. Tent pitches. 5 statics.

AA Pubs & Restaurants nearby: Inn at Lathones, Largoward 01334 840494

The Orangery at Balbirnie House, Markinch 01592 610066

Leisure: 🎣🖵

Facilities: 🏪⊙📷✳🔥♻️ℹ️

Services: 🔌🔋🧺🚰

Within 3 miles: ↓🏌️🛒♿

Notes: Adults only. Dogs must be kept on leads.

ST ANDREWS — Map 21 NO51

Places to visit

Castle & Visitor Centre, ST ANDREWS
01334 477196

British Golf Museum, ST ANDREWS
01334 460046 www.britishgolfmuseum.co.uk

Great for kids: St Andrews Aquarium,
ST ANDREWS 01334 474786
www.standrewsaquarium.co.uk

PREMIER PARK

►►►►► 91% Craigtoun Meadows Holiday Park (NO482150)

Mount Melville KY16 8PQ
☎ 01334 475959 📠 01334 476424
e-mail: craigtoun@aol.com
web: www.craigtounmeadows.co.uk
dir: M90 junct 8, A91 to St Andrews. Just after Guardbridge right for Strathkinness. At 2nd x-rds left for Craigtoun

* 🚐 £22-£28.50 🚌 £22-£28.50 ▲ £19

Open 15 Mar-Oct (rs Mar-Etr & Sep-Oct no shop & restaurant open shorter hours)

Last arrival 21.00hrs Last departure 11.00hrs

An attractive site set unobtrusively in mature woodlands, with large pitches in spacious hedged paddocks. All pitches are fully serviced, and there are also some patio pitches and a summerhouse containing picnic tables and chairs. The modern toilet block provides cubicled en suite facilities as well as spacious showers, baths, disabled facilities and baby changing areas. The licensed restaurant and coffee shop are popular, and there is a takeaway, a launderette, and indoor and outdoor games areas. Located near the sea and sandy beaches. 32 acre site. 57 touring pitches. 57 hardstandings. 3 seasonal pitches. Caravan pitches. Motorhome pitches. Tent pitches. 199 statics.

AA Pubs & Restaurants nearby: Jigger Inn, St Andrews 01334 474371

Inn at Lathones, Largoward 01334 840494

Leisure: 🎠⚽🎣

Facilities: 🛁🏪⊙📷&🕘🔥🖥️♻️ℹ️

Services: 🔌🔋🍽️🛒🏪♿

Within 3 miles: ↓🎪🏌️◎⛵🔌U

Notes: No groups of unaccompanied minors, no pets. Putting green.

LEISURE: 🏊 Indoor swimming pool 🏊 Outdoor swimming pool 🎠 Children's playground 🚸 Kid's club 🎾 Tennis court 🎱 Games room 🖵 Separate TV room ↓ 9/18 hole golf course ⛵ Boats for hire 🎬 Cinema 🎭 Entertainment 🎣 Fishing ◎ Mini golf 🏄 Watersports 🏋️ Gym ⚽ Sports field Spa U Stables
FACILITIES: 🛁 Bath 🏪 Shower ⊙ Electric shaver 📷 Hairdryer ✳ Ice Pack Facility & Disabled facilities 🕘 Public telephone 🛒 Shop on site or within 200yds 🚚 Mobile shop (calls at least 5 days a week) 🔥 BBQ area 🎪 Picnic area 📶 Wi-fi 🖥️ Internet access ♻️ Recycling ℹ️ Tourist info 🐕 Dog exercise area

AA CAMPING CARD SITE

PREMIER PARK

NEW ►►►►► 88% Cairnsmill Holiday Park *(NO502142)*

Largo Rd KY16 8NN
☎ 01334 473604 ▯ 01334 474410
e-mail: cairnsmill@aol.com
dir: *A915 from St Andrews towards Lathones. Approx 2m, site on right*

* ⚎ £23-£24.50 ⚍ £23-£24.50 ▲ £16-£18

Open Mar-Oct

Last arrival flexible Last departure 11.00hrs

Hidden behind mature trees and hedging in open countryside on the outskirts of St Andrews, this top quality park is ideally placed for visiting St Andrews and exploring the Fife area. It is a family owned and run site providing high levels of customer care and excellent facilities, including a swimming pool, licensed bar and café, numerous play areas for children and a small fishing lochan, stocked annually with rainbow trout. Toilet facilities are first class, and the tent area has its own amenity block and outdoor kitchen area. Bunk house accommodation is also available. 27 acre site. 62 touring pitches. 33 hardstandings. 24 seasonal pitches. Caravan pitches. Motorhome pitches. Tent pitches. 194 statics.

AA Pubs & Restaurants nearby: The Inn at Lathones, Largoward 01334 840494

Leisure: ⚎ ⚏ ⚐ ⚑ ⚒

Facilities: ⚓ ⚔ ⚕ ⚖ ⚗ ⚘ ⚙ ⚚ ⚛ ⚜ ⚝ ⚞ ⚟ ⚠

Services: ⚡ ⚢ ⚣ ⚤ ⚥ ⚦ ⚧ ⚨ ⚩

Within 3 miles: ⚪ ⚫ ⚬ ⚭ ⚮ ⚯ ⚰ ⚱ ⚲ ⚳

Notes: Dogs must be kept on leads.

HIGHLAND

BALMACARA   Map 22 NG82

Places to visit

Balmacara Estate & Lochalsh Woodland Garden, BALMACARA 0844 493 2233
www.nts.org.uk

►►► 78% Reraig Caravan Site
(NG815272)

IV40 8DH
☎ 01599 566215
e-mail: warden@reraig.com
dir: *On A87 3.5m E of Kyle, 2m W of junct with A890*

* ⚎ £14.90 ⚍ £14.90 ▲ £12.90

Open May-Sep

Last arrival 22.00hrs Last departure noon

Set on level, grassy ground surrounded by trees, the site is located on the saltwater Sound of Sleet, and looks south towards Loch Alsh and Skye. Very nicely organised with a high standard of maintenance, and handy for the bridge crossing to the Isle of Skye. 2 acre site. 40 touring pitches. 36 hardstandings. Caravan pitches. Motorhome pitches. Tent pitches.

AA Pubs & Restaurants nearby: Waterside Seafood Restaurant, Kyle of Lochalsh 01599 534813

Plockton Inn & Seafood Restaurant, Plockton 01599 544222

Plockton Hotel, Plockton 01599 544274

Facilities: ⚓ ⚔ ⚕ ⚖ ⚗ ⚘ ⚙

Services: ⚡ ⚩

Within 3 miles: ⚵

Notes: No awnings Jul & Aug. Only small tents permitted. Dogs must be kept on leads. Ramp access to block.

CORPACH

Places to visit

West Highland Museum, FORT WILLIAM 01397 702169
www.westhighlandmuseum.org.uk

Great for kids: Inverlochy Castle, FORT WILLIAM www.historic-scotland.gov.uk

---

CORPACH   Map 22 NN07

PREMIER PARK

►►►►► 85% Linnhe Lochside Holidays *(NN074771)*

PH33 7NL
☎ 01397 772376 ▯ 01397 772007
e-mail: relax@linnhe-lochside-holidays.co.uk
dir: *On A830, 1m W of Corpach, 5m from Fort William*

⚎ £18-£20 ⚍ £18-£20 ▲ £12.75-£19.50

Open Dec-Oct (rs Dec-Etr shop closed out of season, unisex showers during peak season only)

Last arrival 21.00hrs Last departure 11.00hrs

An excellently maintained site in a beautiful setting on the shores of Loch Eil, with Ben Nevis to the east and the mountains and Sunart to the west. The owners have worked in harmony with nature to produce an idyllic environment, where the highest standards of design and maintenance are evident. 5.5 acre site. 85 touring pitches. 63 hardstandings. 20 seasonal pitches. Caravan pitches. Motorhome pitches. Tent pitches. 20 statics.

AA Pubs & Restaurants nearby: Inverlochy Castle Hotel, Fort William 01397 702177

Moorings Hotel, Fort William 01397 772797

Lime Tree Hotel & Restaurant, Fort William 01397 701806

Leisure: ⚏

Facilities: ⚊ ⚓ ⚔ ⚕ ⚖ ⚗ ⚘ ⚙ ⚚ ⚛ ⚜ ⚝ ⚞ ⚟ ⚠

Services: ⚡ ⚢ ⚣ ⚤ ⚥ ⚨ ⚩

Within 3 miles: ⚪ ⚫ ⚮ ⚰ ⚱ ⚲ ⚳

Notes: No cars by tents. No large groups. Launching slipway, free fishing.

see advert page 374

SERVICES: ⚡ Electric hook up ⚢ Launderette ⚣ Licensed bar ⚤ Calor Gas ⚥ Camping Gaz ⚦ Toilet fluid ⚧ Café/Restaurant ⚨ Fast Food/Takeaway ⚩ Battery charging
⚬ Baby care ⚩ Motorvan service point
ABBREVIATIONS: BH/bank hols-bank holidays Etr-Easter Whit-Whitsun dep-departure fr-from hrs-hours m-mile mdnt-midnight rdbt-roundabout rs-restricted service wk-week
wknd-weekend ⊛ No credit cards ⊗ No dogs   See page 7 for details of the AA Camping Card Scheme

DORNOCH   Map 23 NH78

Places to visit

Dunrobin Castle, GOLSPIE 01408 633177
www.dunrobincastle.co.uk

77% Grannie's Heilan Hame Holiday Park

(NH818924)

GOLD

Embo IV25 3QD
☎ 0844 335 3756   📠 01862 810368
e-mail:
touringandcamping@parkdeanholidays.com
web: www.parkdeantouring.com
dir: *A949 to Dornoch, left in square. Follow Embo signs*

* ⊞ £14-£31.50 ⊞ £14-£31.50 ▲ £11.50-£27

Open Mar-Oct

Last arrival 21.00hrs Last departure 10.00hrs

A holiday park on the Highland coast, with a wide range of leisure facilities, including indoor swimming pool with sauna and solarium, spa

bath, separate play areas, crazy golf, tennis courts and very much more. The sanitary facilities are clean and well maintained, and there is a family pub and entertainment. 60 acre site. 125 touring pitches. Caravan pitches. Motorhome pitches. Tent pitches. 273 statics.

AA Pubs & Restaurants nearby: Dornoch Castle Hotel, Dornoch 01862 810216

Leisure: 🏊🎠🚸🎾🎱🎵

Facilities: 🔦⊙🏪✳🚿🕐🏬🚮Wi-fi

Services: 🔌🗑🔥🚽🚮🚰🛒🏧

Within 3 miles: 🚣🎣◎🏬🏧

Notes: Mini ten-pin bowling, sauna & solarium.

see advert in preliminary section

DUROR   Map 22 NM95

►►► 80% Achindarroch Touring Park

(NM997554)

PA38 4BS
☎ 01631 740329   & 07739 554813
e-mail: stay@achindarrochtp.co.uk
dir: *A82 onto A828 at Ballachulish Bridge then towards Oban for 5.2m. In Duror site on left, signed*

* ⊞ fr £17 ⊞ fr £17 ▲ fr £17

Open 24 Jan-16 Jan

Last departure 11.00hrs

A long established, well-laid out park which continues to be upgraded to a high standard by an enthusiastic and friendly family team. There is a

well-appointed heated toilet block and spacious all-weather pitches and there are also 2- and 4-person camping pods for hire. The park is well placed for visits to Oban, Fort William and Glencoe. A wide variety of outdoor sports is available in the area. 5 acre site. 40 touring pitches. 21 hardstandings. 10 seasonal pitches. Caravan pitches. Motorhome pitches. Tent pitches. 2 wooden pods.

Facilities: 🔦⊙🏪✳🚿🕐🚮Wi-fi♻🛈

Services: 🔌🗑🔥🚽🚰🏧

Within 3 miles: 🎣🚽⛳

Notes: Groups by prior arrangement only. Dogs must be kept on leads. Campers' kitchen (freezer, toaster, kettle, microwave, boot dryer).

FORT WILLIAM

See also Corpach

Places to visit

West Highland Museum,
FORT WILLIAM 01397 702169
www.westhighlandmuseum.org.uk

Great for kids: Inverlochy Castle, FORT WILLIAM
www.historic-scotland.gov.uk

LEISURE: 🏊 Indoor swimming pool   🏊 Outdoor swimming pool   🎠 Children's playground   🚸 Kid's club   🎾 Tennis court   🎱 Games room   📺 Separate TV room   ⛳ 9/18 hole golf course   🚣 Boats for hire   🎬 Cinema   🎵 Entertainment   🎣 Fishing   ◎ Mini golf   🏄 Watersports   🏋 Gym   🏟 Sports field   Spa   ⛎ Stables
FACILITIES: 🛁 Bath   🚿 Shower   ⊙ Electric shaver   🔌 Hairdryer   ✳ Ice Pack Facility   ♿ Disabled facilities   🕐 Public telephone   🏪 Shop on site or within 200yds   🚚 Mobile shop (calls at least 5 days a week)   🍖 BBQ area   🌲 Picnic area   Wi-fi Wi-fi   💻 Internet access   ♻ Recycling   🛈 Tourist info   🐾 Dog exercise area

FORT WILLIAM
Map 22 NN17

▶▶▶▶ 88% *Glen Nevis Caravan & Camping Park*

(NN124722)

Glen Nevis PH33 6SX
☎ 01397 702191 📄 01397 703904
e-mail: holidays@glen-nevis.co.uk
web: www.glen-nevis.co.uk
dir: *On northern outskirts of Fort William follow A82 to mini-rdbt. Exit for Glen Nevis. Site 2.5m on right*

🚐 🚙 ⛺

Open 13 Mar-9 Nov (rs Mar & mid Oct-Nov limited shop & restaurant facilities)

Last arrival 22.00hrs Last departure noon

A tasteful site with well-screened enclosures, at the foot of Ben Nevis in the midst of some of the most spectacular Highland scenery; an ideal area for walking and touring. The park boasts a restaurant which offers a high standard of cooking and provides good value for money. 30 acre site. 380 touring pitches. 150 hardstandings. Caravan pitches. Motorhome pitches. Tent pitches. 30 statics.

AA Pubs & Restaurants nearby: Inverlochy Castle Hotel, Fort William 01397 702177

Moorings Hotel, Fort William 01397 772797

Lime Tree Hotel & Restaurant, Fort William 01397 701806

Leisure: ⚘
Facilities: 🖕⊙🅟✳&Ⓢⓖ🚻♒
Services: 🔌ⓖ🍴🛢⌀Ⓣ🍽🍴⛽🔋
Within 3 miles: ⬇🎣🏌ⓖ🏬
Notes: Quiet 23.00hrs-08.00hrs.

see advert below

GAIRLOCH

Places to visit

Gairloch Heritage Museum, GAIRLOCH 01445 712287 www.gairlochheritagemuseum.org

Inverewe Garden, POOLEWE 0844 493 2225 www.nts.org.uk

GAIRLOCH
Map 22 NG87

AA CAMPING CARD SITE

▶▶▶ 78% **Gairloch Caravan Park**

(NG798773)

Strath IV21 2BX
☎ 01445 712373
e-mail: info@gairlochcaravanpark.com
dir: *From A832 take B8021 signed Melvaig towards Strath. In 0.5m turn right, just after Millcroft Hotel. Immediately right again*

* 🚐 £7-£30 🚙 £7-£30 ⛺ £7-£30

Open Etr-Oct

Last arrival 21.00hrs Last departure noon

A clean, well-maintained site on flat coastal grassland close to Loch Gairloch. The owners and managers are hard working and well organised and continued investment in recent years has seen significant improvements around the park, including the hardstandings, good shrub and flower planting, and the building of a bunkhouse that provides accommodation for families. 6 acre site. 70 touring pitches. 13 hardstandings. 8 seasonal pitches. Caravan pitches. Motorhome pitches. Tent pitches.

AA Pubs & Restaurants nearby: Old Inn, Gairloch 01445 712006

Badachro Inn, Badachro 01445 741255

Facilities: 🖕⊙🅟✳Ⓢⓖ📶 ♻ ❶
Services: 🔌ⓖ Ⓣ🏬
Within 3 miles: ⬇🏌◎🏬ⓖⓖ⛳
Notes: Dogs must be kept on leads.

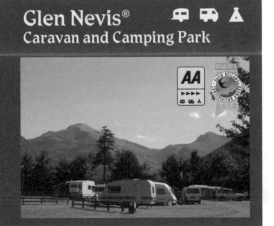

SERVICES: 🔌 Electric hook up ⓖ Launderette 🍴 Licensed bar 🛢 Calor Gas ⌀ Camping Gaz Ⓣ Toilet fluid 🍽 Café/Restaurant ⛽ Fast Food/Takeaway 🔋 Battery charging 🍼 Baby care ⛟ Motorvan service point

ABBREVIATIONS: BH/bank hols-bank holidays Etr-Easter Whit-Whitsun dep-departure fr-from hrs-hours m-mile mdnt-midnight rdbt-roundabout rs-restricted service wk-week wknd-weekend ⊛ No credit cards ⊗ No dogs

See page 7 for details of the AA Camping Card Scheme

GLENCOE
Map 22 NN15

Places to visit

Glencoe & Dalness, GLENCOE 0844 493 2222
www.nts.org.uk

Great for kids: Glencoe & North Lorn Folk
Museum, GLENCOE 01855 811664
www.glencoefolkmuseum.com

▶▶▶▶ 79% Invercoe Caravan & Camping Park (NN098594)

PH49 4HP
☎ 01855 811210 📠 01855 811210
e-mail: holidays@invercoe.co.uk
web: www.invercoe.co.uk
dir: Exit A82 at Glencoe Hotel onto B863 for 0.25m

🚐 🚍 ⛺

Open all year

Last departure noon

A level grass site set on the shore of Loch Leven,
with excellent mountain views. The area is ideal
for both walking and climbing, and also offers a
choice of several freshwater and saltwater lochs.
Convenient for the good shopping in Fort William.
5 acre site. 60 touring pitches. Caravan pitches.
Motorhome pitches. Tent pitches. 4 statics. 2
wooden pods.

AA Pubs & Restaurants nearby: Loch Leven Hotel,
North Ballachulish 01855 821236

The Restaurant at Onich Hotel, Onich
01855 821214

Leisure: ⚠
Facilities: 🥾 ☺ 🄿 ✳ & ◔ 🔯 🐎
Services: 🔌 🔲 ⊘ 🅣 🛒 ↯
Within 3 miles: ⚓ ✛ 🖉 🔯 🔲
Notes: No large group bookings.

JOHN O'GROATS
Map 23 ND37

Places to visit

The Castle & Gardens of Mey, THURSO
01847 851473 www.castleofmey.org.uk

▶▶▶ 78% John O'Groats Caravan Site (ND382733)

KW1 4YR
☎ 01955 611329 📱 07762 336359
e-mail: info@johnogroatscampsite.co.uk
dir: At end of A99

✱ 🚐 £15-£17.50 🚍 £15-£17.50 ⛺ £11-£15

Open Apr-Sep

Last arrival 22.00hrs Last departure 11.00hrs

An attractive site in an open position above the
seashore and looking out towards the Orkney
Islands. Nearby is the passenger ferry that makes
day trips to the Orkneys, and there are grey seals
to watch, and sea angling can be organised by the
site owners. 4 acre site. 90 touring pitches. 30
hardstandings. Caravan pitches. Motorhome
pitches. Tent pitches.

Facilities: 🥾 ☺ 🄿 ✳ & ◔ 🔯 🐎 ♻ 🛈
Services: 🔌 🔲 ⊘ 🛒 ↯
Within 3 miles: 🖉 🔯 🔲
Notes: 🚫

LAIRG
Map 23 NC50

▶▶▶ 73% *Dunroamin Caravan and Camping Park* (NC585062)

Main St IV27 4AR
☎ 01549 402447 📠 01549 402784
e-mail: enquiries@lairgcaravanpark.co.uk
dir: 300mtrs from centre of Lairg on S side of
A839

🚐 🚍 ⛺

Open Apr-Oct

Last arrival 21.00hrs Last departure noon

An attractive little park with clean and functional
facilities, adjacent to a licensed restaurant. The
park is close to the lower end of Loch Shin. 4 acre
site. 40 touring pitches. 8 hardstandings. Caravan
pitches. Motorhome pitches. Tent pitches. 9
statics.

Facilities: 🥾 ☺ 🄿 ✳ ◔ 🔯
Services: 🔌 🔲 🛢 ⊘ 🅣 🍽 🛒 ⛲
Within 3 miles: ✛ 🖉 ⛷ 🔯 🔲
Notes: No vehicles to be driven on site between
21.00hrs-07.00hrs.

▶▶▶ 67% Woodend Caravan & Camping Site (NC551127)

Achnairn IV27 4DN
☎ 01549 402248 📠 01549 402248
dir: 4m N of Lairg off A836 onto A838, signed at
Achnairn

🚐 🚍 ⛺

Open Apr-Sep

Last arrival 23.00hrs

A clean, simple site set in hilly moors and
woodland with access to Loch Shin. The area is
popular with fishing and boating enthusiasts, and
there is a choice of golf courses within a 30 mile
radius. A spacious campers' kitchen is a useful
amenity. There's also a holiday cottage to hire. 4
acre site. 55 touring pitches. 5 hardstandings.
Caravan pitches. Motorhome pitches. Tent pitches.

Leisure: ⚠
Facilities: 🥾 ☺ 🄿 ✳
Services: 🔌 🔲
Within 3 miles: ✛ 🖉 🔯
Notes: 🚫

NAIRN

Places to visit

Sueno's Stone, FORRES 01667 460232
www.historic-scotland.gov.uk

Dallas Dhu Distillery, FORRES 01309 676548
www.historic-scotland.gov.uk

Great for kids: Brodie Castle, BRODIE CASTLE
0844 493 2156 www.nts.org.uk

LEISURE: 🏊 Indoor swimming pool 🏊 Outdoor swimming pool ⚠ Children's playground 🪅 Kid's club ⚲ Tennis court 🎱 Games room ▭ Separate TV room
🏌 9/18 hole golf course 🚣 Boats for hire 🎬 Cinema 🎵 Entertainment 🎣 Fishing ◉ Mini golf 🏄 Watersports 🏋 Gym 🔅 Sports field **Spa** ♘ Stables
FACILITIES: 🛁 Bath 🚿 Shower ⊙ Electric shaver 🄿 Hairdryer ✳ Ice Pack Facility & Disabled facilities ◔ Public telephone 🏪 Shop on site or within 200yds
🏪 Mobile shop (calls at least 5 days a week) 🔥 BBQ area 🌲 Picnic area 🆆🅸🅵🅸 Wi-Fi 🌐 Internet access ♻ Recycling 🛈 Tourist info 🐎 Dog exercise area

NAIRN
Map 23 NH85

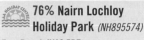

76% Nairn Lochloy Holiday Park *(NH895574)*

East Beach IV12 5DE

☎ 0844 335 3756 📠 01667 454721

e-mail:
touringandcamping@parkdeanholidays.com
web: www.parkdeantouring.com
dir: *From A96 (Bridge St) in Nairn follow site signs onto unclassified raod at Bridgemill Direct shop*

* 🚐 £13-£36 🚈 £13-£36 ▲ £10.50-£32

Open Mar-Oct

Last arrival 21.00hrs Last departure 10.00hrs

A small touring site situated within a popular holiday park with a wide range of leisure facilities including heated pool, sauna, spa bath, children's play-area and clubs, crazy golf, amusements, bars, restaurant and mini supermarket. A small, well-maintained toilet block exclusively serves the touring area where all pitches have electricity. Handily placed in the centre of Nairn, only minutes from the beach and within striking distance of Inverness and the Highlands. 15 acre site. 13 touring pitches. Caravan pitches. Motorhome pitches. Tent pitches. 263 statics.

AA Pubs & Restaurants nearby: Cawdor Tavern, Cawdor 01667 404777

Boath House, Nairn (AA Hotel of the Year for Scotland 2010-11) 01667 454896

Newton Hotel, Nairn 01667 453144

Golf View Hotel & Leisure Club, Nairn 01667 452301

Leisure: 🏊 🅰 🚣 🎣 🎵
Facilities: 🛁 🛏 ⊙ 🅿 🦽 🕐 🔥 wifi
Services: 🔌 🔲 🍴 🔋 🧺 🍽 🏪
Within 3 miles: 🦮 🏌 ⊚ 🎿 🏧 🔲 🔵 ∪

see advert in preliminary section

ULLAPOOL
Map 22 NH19

►►► 72% Broomfield Holiday Park
(NH123939)

West Shore St IV26 2UT

☎ 01854 612020 & 612664 📠 01854 613151
e-mail: sross@broomfieldhp.com
web: www.broomfieldhp.com
dir: *Take 2nd right past harbour*

* 🚐 fr £17 🚈 fr £16 ▲ £15-£17

Open Etr/Apr-Sep

Last departure noon

Set right on the water's edge of Loch Broom and the open sea, with lovely views of the Summer Isles. The clean, well maintained and managed park is close to the harbour and town centre with their restaurants, bars and shops. 12 acre site. 140 touring pitches. Caravan pitches. Motorhome pitches. Tent pitches.

Leisure: 🅰
Facilities: 🛏 ⊙ ✳ 🦽 🅱 🅰
Services: 🔌 🔲 🍴 🔋
Within 3 miles: 🦮 🏌 🔲 🔵

Notes: No noise at night. Dogs must be kept on leads.

MORAY

ABERLOUR
Map 23 NJ24

Places to visit

Balvenie Castle, DUFFTOWN 01340 820121
www.historic-scotland.gov.uk

►►► 80% Aberlour Gardens Caravan Park
(NJ282434)

AB38 9LD

☎ 01340 871586 📠 01340 871586
e-mail: info@aberlourgardens.co.uk
dir: *Midway between Aberlour & Craigellachie on A95 turn onto unclassified road. Site signed. (NB vehicles over 10' 6" use A941 (Dufftown to Craigellachie road) where park is signed)*

* 🚐 £17-£21.25 🚈 £17-£21.25 ▲ £13.45-£21.25

Open Mar-27 Dec (rs Winter park opening dates weather dependant)

Last arrival 19.00hrs Last departure noon

This attractive parkland site is set in the five-acre walled garden of the Victorian Aberlour House, surrounded by the full range of spectacular scenery from the Cairngorm National Park, through pine clad glens, to the famous Moray coastline; the park is also well placed for the world renowned Speyside Malt Whisky Trail. It offers a small, well-appointed toilet block, laundry and small licensed shop. 5 acre site. 34 touring pitches. 10 hardstandings. 10 seasonal pitches. Caravan pitches. Motorhome pitches. Tent pitches. 32 statics.

AA Pubs & Restaurants nearby: Craigellachie Hotel, Craigellachie 01340 881204

Archiestown Hotel, Archiestown 01340 810218

Leisure: 🅰
Facilities: 🛏 ⊙ 🅿 ✳ 🦽 🕐 🅱 wifi ♻ 🛈
Services: 🔌 🔲 🔋 🧺 🔲 🍴
Within 3 miles: 🦮 🏌 🔲 🔵

Notes: No ball games, max 5mph speed limit, no noise after 23.00hrs. Dogs must be kept on leads.

ALVES
Map 23 NJ16

Places to visit

Pluscarden Abbey, ELGIN 01343 890257
www.pluscardenabbey.org

Elgin Museum, ELGIN 01343 543675
www.elginmuseum.org.uk

Great for kids: Duffus Castle, DUFFUS
01667 460232 www.historic-scotland.gov.uk

►►► 67% North Alves Caravan Park
(NJ122633)

IV30 8XD
☎ 01343 850223
dir: From Elgin towards Forres on A96, follow signs
for site (sign in Alves), turn right onto unclassified
road. Approx 1m site on right

* ➡ £16-£20 ➡ £16-£20 ▲ £12-£18

Open Apr-Oct

Last arrival 23.00hrs Last departure noon

A quiet rural site in attractive rolling countryside
within three miles of a good beach. The site is on
a former farm, and the stone buildings are quite
unspoilt. 10 acre site. 45 touring pitches. Caravan
pitches. Motorhome pitches. Tent pitches. 45
statics.

Leisure: 🅰 ⊕ ⚲ ▭

Facilities: 🅵 ⊙ 🅿 ✳ 🛫

Services: 🔌 🛢 ⌀ T 🧺

Within 3 miles: ↕ ⁂ 🎱 🎣 🍴 🛥 ∪

Notes: 🐾 Dogs must be kept on leads.

FOCHABERS
Map 23 NJ35

Places to visit

Strathisla Distillery, KEITH 01542 783044
www.chivas.com

Glen Grant Distillery, ROTHES 01340 832118
www.glengrant.com

►►► 76% Burnside Caravan Park
(NJ350580)

IV32 7ET
☎ 01343 820511   📄 01343 820511
e-mail: burnside7et@googlemail.com
dir: 0.5m E of town off A96

* ➡ £17-£22 ➡ £17-£22 ▲ £10-£25

Open all year

Last departure noon

An attractive site in a tree-lined, sheltered valley
with a footpath to the village and owned by the
garden centre on the opposite side of the A96. The
site has fully serviced pitches and there is a
camping area for 20 tents, all with water and
electricity. 5 acre site. 56 touring pitches. 31
hardstandings. Caravan pitches. Motorhome
pitches. Tent pitches. 104 statics.

AA Pubs & Restaurants nearby: Gordon Arms
Hotel, Fochabers 01343 820508

Leisure: 🏊 🅰 ⚲ ▭

Facilities: 🅵 ⊙ 🅿 ⚙ 🕒 🧴 🛫 WI-FI ♻ ❶

Services: 🔌 🛢 🛢 ⌀ T ↧

Within 3 miles: ↕ 🎣 ◎ 🧴 ∪

Notes: Dogs must be kept on leads. Jacuzzi &
sauna.

LOSSIEMOUTH
Map 23 NJ27

Places to visit

Elgin Cathedral, ELGIN 01343 547171
www.historic-scotland.gov.uk

►►►► 80% Silver Sands Leisure Park
(NJ205710)

Covesea, West Beach IV31 6SP
☎ 01343 813262   📄 01343 815205
e-mail: enquiries@silver-sands.co.uk
dir: From Lossiemouth follow B9040, 2m W to site

➡ ➡ ▲

Open 15 Feb-15 Jan (rs 15 Feb-Jun & Oct-15 Jan
shops & entertainment restricted)

Last arrival 22.00hrs Last departure noon

A large holiday park with entertainment during the
peak season, set on the links beside the shore of
the Moray Firth. Touring campers and caravans
are catered for in three areas: one offers de-luxe,
fully-serviced facilities, while the others are either
unserviced or include electric hook-ups and water.
There's a well-stocked shop, a clubroom and bar,
and takeaway food outlet. 60 acre site. 140
touring pitches. 30 hardstandings. Caravan
pitches. Motorhome pitches. Tent pitches. 200
statics.

Leisure: 🅰 🏊 ⚲ ▭ 🎵

Facilities: 🛁 🅵 ⊙ 🅿 ✳ ⚙ 🕒 🧴 🛫 🖥 ♻ ❶

Services: 🔌 🛢 🛢 ⌀ T 🍴 🧺 🛒

Within 3 miles: ↕ ⁂ 🎣 🛥 🧴 ◎ ∪

Notes: Over 16yrs only in bar. Dogs must be kept
on leads.

LEISURE: 🏊 Indoor swimming pool ⊕ Outdoor swimming pool 🅰 Children's playground ⚐ Kid's club ⚲ Tennis court ⚲ Games room ▭ Separate TV room ↕ 9/18 hole golf course ⚓ Boats for hire 🎬 Cinema 🎵 Entertainment 🎣 Fishing ◎ Mini golf 🛥 Watersports 🏋 Gym ⚽ Sports field **Spa** ∪ Stables
FACILITIES: 🛁 Bath 🚿 Shower ⊙ Electric shaver 🅿 Hairdryer ✳ Ice Pack Facility ⚙ Disabled facilities 🕒 Public telephone 🧴 Shop on site or within 200yds 🛒 Mobile shop (calls at least 5 days a week) 🍴 BBQ area 🛫 Picnic area WI-FI Wi-fi 🖥 Internet access ♻ Recycling ❶ Tourist info 🛫 Dog exercise area

NORTH AYRSHIRE

SALTCOATS   Map 20 NS24

Places to visit

North Ayrshire Museum,
SALTCOATS 01294 464174
www.north-ayrshire.gov.uk/museums

Kelburn Castle and Country Centre, LARGS
01475 568685 www.kelburnestate.com

Great for kids: Scottish Maritime Museum,
IRVINE 01294 278283
www.scottishmaritimemuseum.org

75% Sandylands
(NS258412)

**James Miller Crescent, Auchenharvie
Park KA21 5JN**
☎ 0871 664 9767
e-mail: sandylands@park-resorts.com
dir: *From Glasgow take M77 & A77 to
Kilmarnock, A71 towards Irvine. Follow signs for
Ardrossan. Take A78 follow Stevenston signs.
Through Stevenston, past Auchenharvie Leisure
Centre, 1st left follow signs to site on left*

🚐 🚃 Å

Open Apr-Oct

Last arrival mdnt Last departure 10.00hrs

A holiday centre with on-site recreational and
entertainment facilities for all ages, including
an indoor swimming pool. There is a links golf
course nearby. With good transport links and
easy access to the ferry terminal in Ardrossan,
day trips to the Isle of Arran are possible. A new
amenity block will open for the 2012 season
to provide touring customers with modern
facilities. 55 acre site. 20 touring pitches. 20
hardstandings. Caravan pitches. Motorhome
pitches. Tent pitches. 438 statics.

Leisure: 📶 🎣 ⬇ 🔍 ♫
Facilities: 🔂 ☉ 🅿 ♿ 🕒 🐕 🏇 Wi-fi 🖥
Services: 🔌 🔲 🔇 ♨
Within 3 miles: 🚲 🎯 🟎 🏪 🔲

PERTH & KINROSS

See Walk 13 in the Walks & Cycle Rides section
at the end of the guide

BLAIR ATHOLL   Map 23 NN86

Places to visit

Blair Castle, BLAIR ATHOLL 01796 481207
www.blair-castle.co.uk

Killiecrankie Visitor Centre, KILLIECRANKIE
0844 493 2194 www.nts.org.uk

PREMIER PARK

►►►►► 84% Blair Castle Caravan Park *(NN874656)*

PH18 5SR
☎ 01796 481263   📄 01796 481587
e-mail: mail@blaircastlecaravanpark.co.uk
dir: *From A9 junct with B8079 at Aldclune, then
NE to Blair Atholl. Site on right after crossing
bridge in village*

* 🚐 £16.50-£19.50 🚃 £16.50-£19.50
Å £16.50-£28

Open Mar-Nov

Last arrival 21.30hrs Last departure noon

An attractive site set in impressive seclusion
within the Atholl estate, surrounded by mature
woodland and the River Tilt. Although a large
park, the various groups of pitches are located
throughout the extensive parkland, and each has
its own sanitary block with all-cubicled facilities
of a very high standard. There is a choice of grass
pitches, hardstandings, or fully-serviced pitches.
This park is particularly suitable for the larger
type of motorhome. 32 acre site. 241 touring
pitches. Caravan pitches. Motorhome pitches.
Tent pitches. 107 statics.

AA Pubs & Restaurants nearby: Killiecrankie
House Hotel, Killiecrankie 01796 473220

Moulin Hotel, Pitlochry 01796 472196

Leisure: 🎱 ⚽ 🔍
Facilities: 🚿 🔂 ☉ 🅿 ✳ ♿ 🕒 🛁 🏇 🏕 Wi-fi 🖥 ♻
Services: 🔌 🔲 🔇 🛒 🍴 🔲 🧺 ⬆
Within 3 miles: 🚲 🎯 🟎 🏪 🔲 ↺
Notes: Family park, no noise after 23.00hrs. Dogs
must be kept on leads.

PREMIER PARK

►►►►► 81% *River Tilt Caravan Park (NN875653)*

PH18 5TE
☎ 01796 481467   📄 01796 481511
e-mail: stuart@rivertilt.co.uk
dir: *7m N of Pitlochry on A9, take B8079 to Blair
Atholl & site at rear of Tilt Hotel*

🚐 🚃 Å

Open 16 Mar-12 Nov

Last arrival 21.00hrs Last departure noon

An attractive park with magnificent views of the
surrounding mountains, idyllically set in hilly
woodland country on the banks of the River Tilt,
adjacent to the golf course. There is also a leisure
complex with heated indoor swimming pool, sun
lounge area, spa pool and multi-gym, all available
for an extra charge; outdoors there is a short
tennis court. The toilet facilities are very good. 2
acre site. 30 touring pitches. Caravan pitches.
Motorhome pitches. Tent pitches. 69 statics.

AA Pubs & Restaurants nearby: Killiecrankie
House Hotel, Killiecrankie 01796 473220

Moulin Hotel, Pitlochry 01796 472196

Leisure: 🎱 🏊
Facilities: 🔂 ☉ 🅿 ✳ 🕒 🛁 🏇
Services: 🔌 🔲 🛒 🔇 ♨ 🍴
Within 3 miles: 🚲 🎯 🟎 🏪 🔲 ↺
Notes: Sauna, solarium, steam room.

DUNKELD   Map 21 NO04

Places to visit

The Ell Shop & Little Houses, DUNKELD
0844 4932192 www.nts.org.uk

Castle Menzies, WEEM 01887 820982
www.menzies.org

AA CAMPING CARD SITE

►►► **78% Inver Mill Farm Caravan Park** *(NO015422)*

Inver PH8 0JR
☎ 01350 727477   📠 01350 727477
e-mail: invermill@talk21.com
dir: *A9 onto A822 then immediately right to Inver*

🚐 £17-£18 🚎 £17-£18 ▲ £15-£21

Open end Mar-Oct

Last arrival 22.00hrs Last departure noon

A peaceful park on level former farmland, located on the banks of the River Braan and surrounded by mature trees and hills. The active resident owners keep the park in very good condition. 5 acre site. 65 touring pitches. Caravan pitches. Motorhome pitches. Tent pitches.

Facilities: 🍴☉🌳⚲🔥👦⚲

Services: 🔌🚿🗑️🍴

Within 3 miles: ⚓🎣🛒🗑️

Notes: 🐕

KINLOCH RANNOCH   Map 23 NN65

► **67% Kilvrecht Campsite** *(NN623567)*

PH16 5QA
☎ 01350 727284   📠 01350 727811
e-mail: tay.fd@forestry.gsi.gov.uk
dir: *3m along S shore of Loch Rannoch. Approach via unclass road along Loch, with Forestry Commission signs*

🚐 fr £8 🚎 fr £8 ▲ £5-£8

Open Apr-Oct

Last arrival 22.00hrs Last departure 10.00hrs

Set in a remote and beautiful spot in a large forest clearing, about three-quarters of a mile from Loch Rannoch shore. This small and basic campsite has no hot water, but the few facilities are very well maintained. 17 acre site. 60 touring pitches. Caravan pitches. Motorhome pitches. Tent pitches.

AA Pubs & Restaurants nearby: Dunalistair Hotel, Kinloch Rannoch 01882 632323

Facilities: ⚲🚿🔥ℹ️

Within 3 miles: 🎣🎣🛒

Notes: 🐕 No fires. Dogs must be kept on leads.

PITLOCHRY   Map 23 NN95

Places to visit

Edradour Distillery, PITLOCHRY 01796 472095
www.edradour.co.uk

Great for kids: Scottish Hydro Electric Visitor Centre, Dam & Fish Pass, PITLOCHRY 01796 473152

►►►► **84% Milton of Fonab Caravan Site** *(NN945573)*

Bridge Rd PH16 5NA
☎ 01796 472882   📠 01796 474363
e-mail: info@fonab.co.uk
dir: *0.5m S of town off A924*

* 🚐 £17.50-£20.50 🚎 £17.50-£20.50 ▲ £17.50-£20.50

Open Apr-Oct

Last arrival 21.00hrs Last departure 13.00hrs

Set on the banks of the River Tummel, with extensive views down the river valley to the mountains, this park is close to the centre of Pitlochry, adjacent to the Pitlochry Festival Theatre. The sanitary facilities are exceptionally good, with most contained in combined shower/wash basin and toilet cubicles. 15 acre site. 154 touring pitches. Caravan pitches. Motorhome pitches. Tent pitches. 34 statics.

continued

LEISURE: 🏊 Indoor swimming pool 🏊 Outdoor swimming pool 🛝 Children's playground 👦 Kid's club 🎾 Tennis court 🎱 Games room 📺 Separate TV room ⛳ 9/18 hole golf course ⛵ Boats for hire 🎬 Cinema 🎵 Entertainment 🎣 Fishing ⛳ Mini golf 🏄 Watersports 🏋️ Gym ⚽ Sports field Spa ♨ Stables
FACILITIES: 🛁 Bath 🚿 Shower ⊙ Electric shaver ✂ Hairdryer ❄ Ice Pack Facility ♿ Disabled facilities ☏ Public telephone 🏪 Shop on site or within 200yds 🛒 Mobile shop (calls at least 5 days a week) 🍖 BBQ area 🏕 Picnic area 📶 Wi-fi 💻 Internet access ♻ Recycling ℹ Tourist info 🐕 Dog exercise area

AA Pubs & Restaurants nearby: Moulin Hotel, Pitlochry 01796 472196

Killiecrankie House Hotel, Killiecrankie 01796 473220

Facilities: ⊷ ⋔ ⊙ ⚑ ✻ ⅙ ⊙ 🛇 ⊞ 🚐 [wi-fi] ♻ ❶

Services: 🔌 🖥 🧺 ⌿

Within 3 miles: ⌕ ⋔ 🖊 ◎ 🖥 🖥

Notes: ⊛ Couples & families only, no motor cycles. Free trout fishing.

►►►► 72% *Faskally Caravan Park*

(NN916603)
PH16 5LA
☎ 01796 472007   📠 01796 473896
e-mail: info@faskally.co.uk
dir: 1.5m N of Pitlochry on B8019

🚐 🚑 ▲

Open 15 Mar-Oct

Last arrival 23.00hrs

A large park attractively divided into sections by mature trees, set in gently-sloping meadowland beside the tree-lined River Garry. The excellent amenities include a leisure complex with heated indoor swimming pool, spa, sauna and steam room, bar, restaurant and indoor amusements. The park is close to, but unaffected by, the A9. 27 acre site. 300 touring pitches. Caravan pitches. Motorhome pitches. Tent pitches. 130 statics.

AA Pubs & Restaurants nearby: Moulin Hotel, Pitlochry 01796 472196

Killiecrankie House Hotel, Killiecrankie 01796 473220

Leisure: 🏊 ⅍ 🔍 Spa
Facilities: ⋔ ⊙ ⚑ ✻ ⅙ ⊙ 🛇
Services: 🔌 🖥 🍴 🛢 ⌿ 🇹 🍽
Within 3 miles: ⌕ ⋔ 🖊 🖥 🖥 ⛳

Notes: Dogs must be kept on leads.

see advert on opposite page

 ### 72% Tummel Valley Holiday Park *(NN764592)*

PH16 5SA
☎ 0844 335 3756   📠 01882 634302
e-mail: touringandcamping@ parkdeanholidays.com
web: www.parkdeantouring.com
dir: From Perth take A9 N to bypass Pitlochry. 3m after Pitlochry take B8019 signed Tummel Bridge. Site 11m on left

* 🚐 £13.50-£33 🚑 £13.50-£33

Open Mar-Oct

Last arrival 21.00hrs Last departure 10.00hrs

A well-developed site amongst mature forest in an attractive valley, beside the famous bridge on the banks of the River Tummel. Play areas and the bar are sited alongside the river, and there is an indoor pool, children's clubs and live family entertainment. This is an ideal base in which to relax. Please note that this park does not accept tents or trailer tents. 55 acre site. 28 touring pitches. 28 hardstandings. Caravan pitches. Motorhome pitches. 169 statics.

AA Pubs & Restaurants nearby: Dunalastair Hotel, Kinloch Rannoch 01882 632323

Moulin Hotel, Pitlochry 01796 472196

Killiecrankie House Hotel, Killiecrankie 01796 473220

Leisure: 🏊 ⅍ 🔍 🔍 🎵
Facilities: ⊷ ⋔ ⊙ ⚑ ✻ ⅙ ⊙ 🛇 🚐 [wi-fi]
Services: 🔌 🖥 🍴 🛢 🍽 🍟
Within 3 miles: 🖊 ◎ 🖥 🖥

Notes: Sports courts, sauna, solarium, toddlers' pool, amusements, rod hire.

see advert in preliminary section

Places to visit

Manderston, DUNS 01361 883450 www.manderston.co.uk

Great for kids: Eyemouth Museum, EYEMOUTH 018907 50678

 ### 73% Eyemouth *(NT941646)*

Fort Rd TD14 5BE
☎ 0871 664 9740
e-mail: eyemouth@park-resorts.com
dir: From A1, approx 6m N of Berwick-upon-Tweed take A1107 to Eyemouth. On entering town, site signed. Right after petrol station, left at bottom of hill into Fort Rd

🚐 🚑

Open Apr-Oct

Last arrival mdnt Last departure 10.00hrs

A cliff-top holiday park on the outskirts of the small fishing village of Eyemouth, within easy reach of Edinburgh and Newcastle. The site is handily placed for exploring the beautiful Scottish Borders, and the magnificent coastline and countryside of north Northumberland. 22 acre site. 17 touring pitches. 7 hardstandings. 17 seasonal pitches. Caravan pitches. Motorhome pitches. 276 statics.

Leisure: ⅍ ⬇ ⊙ 🔍 🎵
Facilities: ⋔ 🖊 ⅙ ⊙ 🛇 🚐 [wi-fi] 🖥 ♻ ❶
Services: 🔌 🖥 🍴 🍽 🍟
Within 3 miles: ⌕ 🖊 🖥 🖥 🖥

Notes: Dogs must be kept on leads.

SERVICES: 🔌 Electric hook up 🖥 Launderette 🍴 Licensed bar 🛢 Calor Gas ⌿ Camping Gaz 🇹 Toilet fluid 🍽 Café/Restaurant 🍟 Fast Food/Takeaway 🔋 Battery charging 🍼 Baby care ⚡ Motorvan service point
ABBREVIATIONS: BH/bank hols-bank holidays Etr-Easter Whit-Whitsun dep-departure fr-from hrs-hours m-mile mdnt-midnight rdbt-roundabout rs-restricted service wk-week wknd-weekend ⊛ No credit cards ⊗ No dogs
See page 7 for details of the AA Camping Card Scheme

KELSO Map 21 NT73

Places to visit

Kelso Abbey, KELSO 0131 668 8800
www.historic-scotland.gov.uk

Smailholm Tower, SMAILHOLM 01573 460365
www.historic-scotland.gov.uk

Great for kids: Floors Castle, KELSO
01573 223333 www.floorscastle.com

►►►► 80% Springwood Caravan Park *(NT720334)*

TD5 8LS
☎ 01573 224596 ▤ 01573 224033
e-mail: admin@springwood.biz
dir: *1m E of Kelso on A699, signed Newtown St Boswells*

* ⊕ fr £20 ⊕ fr £20

Open 25 Mar-17 Oct

Last arrival 23.00hrs Last departure noon

Set in a secluded position on the banks of the tree-lined River Teviot, this well-maintained site enjoys a pleasant and spacious spot in which to relax. It offers a high standard of modern toilet facilities, which are mainly contained in cubicled units. Floors Castle and the historic town of Kelso are close by. 2 acre site. 20 touring pitches. 20 hardstandings. Caravan pitches. Motorhome pitches. 180 statics.

AA Pubs & Restaurants nearby: Roxburghe Hotel & Golf Course, Kelso 01573 450331

Leisure: ⋀ ⚞

Facilities: ⋔ ⊙ ⚟ ⚹ ⅘ ⊙ ⊶ ♻ ⓘ

Services: ⊕ ⓕ ⅏

Within 3 miles: ⅃ ⚟ ⓑⓕⓤ

Notes: Dogs must be kept on leads.

LAUDER

Places to visit

Abbotsford, MELROSE 01896 752043
www.scottsabbotsford.co.uk

Harmony Garden, MELROSE 0844 493 2251
www.nts.org.uk

Great for kids: Thirlestane Castle, LAUDER
01578 722430 www.thirlestanecastle.co.uk

LAUDER Map 21 NT54

►►► 74% Thirlestane Castle Caravan & Camping Site *(NT536473)*

Thirlestane Castle TD2 6RU
☎ 01578 718884 & 07976 231032
e-mail: thirlestanepark@btconnect.com
dir: *Signed off A68 & A697, just S of Lauder*

* ⊕ £14-£17 ⊕ £16-£17 ⋀ £14-£17

Open Apr-1 Oct

Last arrival 20.30hrs Last departure noon

Set in the grounds of the impressive Thirlestane Castle, with mainly level grassy pitches. The park and facilities are kept in sparkling condition. 5 acre site. 60 touring pitches. 17 hardstandings. Caravan pitches. Motorhome pitches. Tent pitches. 24 statics.

AA Pubs & Restaurants nearby: Black Bull, Lauder 01578 722208

Facilities: ⋔ ⊙ ⚹ ⊙ ⊟ ♻ ⓘ

Services: ⊕ ⓕ ⅏

Within 3 miles: ⅃ ⚟ ⓑⓕ

Notes: ⊛ Dogs must be kept on leads.

PEEBLES Map 21 NT24

Places to visit

Kailzie Gardens, PEEBLES 01721 720007
www.kailziegardens.com

Robert Smail's Printing Works, INNERLEITHEN
0844 493 2259 www.nts.org.uk

Great for kids: Culzean Castle & Country Park,
CULZEAN CASTLE 0844 493 2149 www.nts.org.uk

►►►► 78% Crossburn Caravan Park *(NT248417)*

Edinburgh Rd EH45 8ED
☎ 01721 720501 ▤ 01721 720501
e-mail: enquiries@crossburncaravans.co.uk
web: www.crossburncaravans.co.uk
dir: *0.5m N of Peebles on A703*

* ⊕ £22-£24 ⊕ £22-£24 ⋀ £9-£19

Open Apr-Oct

Last arrival 21.00hrs Last departure 14.00hrs

A peaceful site in a relatively quiet location, despite the proximity of the main road which partly borders the site, as does the Eddleston Water. There are lovely views, and the park is well stocked with trees, flowers and shrubs. Facilities are maintained to a high standard, and fully-serviced pitches are available. A large caravan dealership is on the same site. 6 acre site. 45 touring pitches. 15 hardstandings. Caravan pitches. Motorhome pitches. Tent pitches. 85 statics.

Crossburn Caravan Park

AA Pubs & Restaurants nearby: Cringletie House, Peebles 01721 725750

Renwicks at Macdonald Cardrona Hotel, Peebles 0844 879 9024

Leisure: ⋀ ⚞

Facilities: ⇃ ⋔ ⊙ ⚟ ⅘ ♻ ⓘ

Services: ⊕ ⓕ ⬛ ⌀ Ⓣ ⛟ ⅏

Within 3 miles: ⅃ ⚟ ⓑⓤ

Notes: Dogs must be kept on leads.

SOUTH AYRSHIRE

AYR Map 20 NS32

78% Craig Tara Holiday Park *(NS300184)*

KA7 4LB
☎ 0871 231 0866 ▤ 01292 445206
e-mail: craigtara@haven.com
dir: *Take A77 towards Stranraer, 2nd right after Bankfield rdbt. Follow signs for A719 & to park*

Open mid Mar-end Oct (rs mid Mar-May & Sep-Oct some facilities may be limited)

Last arrival 20.00hrs Last departure 10.00hrs

A large, well-maintained holiday centre with on-site entertainment and sporting facilities to suit all ages. The touring area is set apart from the main complex at the entrance to the park, and campers can use all the facilities, including a water world, soft play areas, sports zone, show bars, and supermarket with in-house bakery. There is a bus service to Ayr. 213 acre site. 38 touring pitches. 38 hardstandings. Caravan pitches. Motorhome pitches. 1100 statics.

LEISURE: 🏊 Indoor swimming pool 🏊 Outdoor swimming pool ⋀ Children's playground Kid's club Tennis court Games room Separate TV room
9/18 hole golf course Boats for hire Cinema Entertainment Fishing Mini golf Watersports Gym Sports field **Spa** Stables
FACILITIES: Bath Shower Electric shaver Hairdryer Ice Pack Facility Disabled facilities Public telephone Shop on site or within 200yds
Mobile shop (calls at least 5 days a week) BBQ area Picnic area Wi-fi Internet access Recycling Tourist info Dog exercise area

AA Pubs & Restaurants nearby: Fairfield House Hotel, Ayr 01292 267461

Western House Hotel, Ayr 0870 055 5510

Leisure: ⌇ ⌂

Facilities: ⌂ ⊙ ⌂ ⌂ ⌂ ⌂ ⌂ ♻ ⊘

Services: ⌂ ⌂ ⌂ ⌂ ⌂ ⌂ ⌂

Within 3 miles: ⌂ ⌂ ⌂ ⊚ ⌂ ⌂ ∪

Notes: Max 2 dogs per booking, certain dog breeds banned, no commercial vehicles, no bookings by persons under 21yrs unless a family booking. Access to beach from park.

BARRHILL   Map 20 NX28

AA CAMPING CARD SITE

▶▶▶▶ 77% **Barrhill Holiday Park**

(NX216835)

KA26 0PZ
☎ 01465 821355 ▤ 01465 821355
e-mail: barrhill@surfree.co.uk
dir: On A714 (Newton Stewart to Girvan road). 1m N of Barrhill

* ⌂ fr £15 ⌂ ▲ £7-£13

Open Mar-Jan

Last arrival 22.00hrs Last departure 10.00hrs

A small, friendly park in a tranquil rural location, screened from the A714 by trees. The park is terraced and well landscaped, and a high quality amenity block includes disabled facilities. 6 acre site. 30 touring pitches. 30 hardstandings. Caravan pitches. Motorhome pitches. Tent pitches. 42 statics.

Leisure: ⌂

Facilities: ⌂ ⊙ ⌂ ✳ ⌂ ⌂ ⌂ ⌂ ♻

Services: ⌂ ⌂ ⌂ ⌂ ⌂ ⌂

Within 3 miles: ⌂ ⌂

Notes: ⊚ No noise after 23.00hrs.

COYLTON   Map 20 NS41

 81% **Sundrum Castle Holiday Park** (NS405208)

KA6 5JH
☎ 0844 335 3756 ▤ 01292 570065
e-mail: touringandcamping@parkdeanholidays.com
web: www.parkdeantouring.com
dir: Just off A70, 4m E of Ayr near Coylton

* ⌂ £16-£35.50 ⌂ £16-£35.50 ▲ £14-£31.50

Open Mar-Oct

Last arrival 21.00hrs Last departure 10.00hrs

A large family holiday park, in rolling countryside and just a 10-minute drive from the centre of Ayr, with plenty of on-site entertainment. Leisure facilities include an indoor swimming pool complex with flume, crazy golf, clubs for young children and teenagers. The touring pitch areas and amenity block have been appointed to a high standard. 30 acre site. 30 touring pitches. Caravan pitches. Motorhome pitches. Tent pitches. 247 statics.

AA Pubs & Restaurants nearby: Browne's at Enterkine, Annbank 01292 520580

Leisure: ⌇ ⌂ ⌂ ⌂ ⌂ ⌂

Facilities: ⌂ ⊙ ⌂ ⌂ ⌂ ⌂ ⌂

Services: ⌂ ⌂ ⌂ ⌂ ⌂ ⌂ ⌂ ⌂

Within 3 miles: ⌂ ⌂ ⌂ ⊚ ⌂ ⌂ ∪

Notes: No cars by tents. Adventure play area, nature trail.

see advert in preliminary section

SOUTH LANARKSHIRE

ABINGTON   Map 21 NS92

Places to visit

Moat Park Heritage Centre, BIGGAR 01899 221050 www.biggarmuseumtrust.co.uk

Gladstone Court Museum, BIGGAR 01899 221050 www.biggarmuseumtrust.co.uk

Great for kids: National Museum of Rural Life, EAST KILBRIDE 0300 123 6789 www.nms.ac.uk/rural

▶▶▶ 74% **Mount View Caravan Park**

(NS935235)

ML12 6RW
☎ 01864 502808
e-mail: info@mountviewcaravanpark.co.uk
dir: M74 junct 13, A702 S into Abington. Left into Station Rd, over river & railway. Site on right

⌂ £15-£18 ⌂ £15-£18 ▲ £8-£24

Open Mar-Oct

Last arrival 20.45hrs Last departure 11.30hrs

A delightfully maturing family park, surrounded by the Southern Uplands and handily located between Carlisle and Glasgow. It is an excellent stopover site for those travelling between Scotland and the south, and the West Coast Railway passes beside the park. 5.5 acre site. 51 touring pitches. 51 hardstandings. Caravan pitches. Motorhome pitches. Tent pitches. 20 statics.

Leisure: ⌂

Facilities: ⌂ ⊙ ⌂ ⌂ ⌂

Services: ⌂ ⌂ ⌂

Within 3 miles: ⌂ ⌂ ⌂

Notes: No cars by tents. Dogs must be kept on leads and exercised off site. 5mph speed limit. Emergency phone.

SERVICES: ⌂ Electric hook up ⌂ Launderette ⌂ Licensed bar ⌂ Calor Gas ⌂ Camping Gaz ⌂ Toilet fluid ⌂ Café/Restaurant ⌂ Fast Food/Takeaway ⌂ Battery charging ⌂ Baby care ⌂ Motorvan service point
ABBREVIATIONS: BH/bank hols-bank holidays Etr-Easter Whit-Whitsun dep-departure fr-from hrs-hours m-mile mdnt-midnight rdbt-roundabout rs-restricted service wk-week wknd-weekend ⊚ No credit cards ⊗ No dogs
See page 7 for details of the AA Camping Card Scheme

STIRLING

ABERFOYLE
Map 20 NN50

Places to visit

Inchmahome Priory, PORT OF MENTEITH
01877 385294 www.historic-scotland.gov.uk

▶▶▶▶ **80%** *Trossachs HolidayPark* (NS544976)

Best of British
GOLD

FK8 3SA

☎ **01877 382614** 📠 **01877 382732**

e-mail: info@trossachsholidays.co.uk
web: www.trossachsholidays.co.uk
dir: *Access on E side of A81, 1m S of junct A821 & 3m S of Aberfoyle*

🚐 🚐 ▲

Open Mar-Oct

Last arrival 21.00hrs Last departure noon

An imaginatively designed terraced site offering a high degree of quality all round, with fine views across Flanders Moss. All touring pitches are fully serviced with water, waste, electricity and TV aerial, and customer care is a main priority. Set in grounds within the Queen Elizabeth Forest Park, with plenty of opportunities for cycling off-road on mountain bikes, which can be hired or purchased on site. There are self-catering units including lodges for rental. 40 acre site. 66 touring pitches. 46 hardstandings. Caravan pitches. Motorhome pitches. Tent pitches. 84 statics.

Leisure: ⚠ 🔍 ▭

Facilities: ▮⊙♥✳⊙🖻🎢🚿 wifi

Services: 🖪🖥 🛒Ⓣ🍴🍽

Within 3 miles: ↨≄♪🛍🛒∪

Notes: Groups by prior arrangement only.

see advert below

AUCHENBOWIE

Places to visit

Stirling Old Town Jail, STIRLING 01786 450050
www.oldtownjail.com

Stirling Smith Art Gallery & Museum, STIRLING 01786 471917
www.smithartgallery.demon.co.uk

Great for kids: Stirling Castle, STIRLING 01786 450000 www.stirlingcastle.gov.uk

AUCHENBOWIE
Map 21 NS78

▶▶▶ **66% Auchenbowie Caravan & Camping Site** (NS795880)

FK7 8HE

☎ **01324 823999** 📠 **01324 822950**

dir: *From junct 9 on M9 or M80 follow A872/Denny signs. 0.5m, site signed*

✱ 🚐 £12-£15 🚐 £12-£15 ▲ £9-£12

Open Apr-Oct

Last departure noon

A pleasant little site in a rural location, with mainly level grassy pitches. The friendly warden creates a relaxed atmosphere, and given its position close to the junction of the M9 and M80, this is a handy stopover spot for tourers. 3.5 acre site. 60 touring pitches. Caravan pitches. Motorhome pitches. Tent pitches. 12 statics.

Leisure: ⚠

Facilities: ▮⊙♥⊙🎢ℹ

Services: 🖪🛒⌀

Within 3 miles: ↨Ⴙ♪🛍🛒∪

Notes: Dogs must be kept on leads.

see advert on opposite page

LEISURE: 🏊 Indoor swimming pool 🏊 Outdoor swimming pool ⚠ Children's playground 🧒 Kid's club 🎾 Tennis court 🎱 Games room ▭ Separate TV room ⛳ 9/18 hole golf course ⛵ Boats for hire 🎬 Cinema 🎵 Entertainment 🎣 Fishing ⊙ Mini golf 🏄 Watersports 🏋 Gym ⚽ Sports field Spa ∪ Stables
FACILITIES: 🛁 Bath 🚿 Shower ⊙ Electric shaver ♥ Hairdryer ✳ Ice Pack Facility ♿ Disabled facilities Ⓒ Public telephone 🏪 Shop on site or within 200yds 🏪 Mobile shop (calls at least 5 days a week) 🍖 BBQ area 🎢 Picnic area wifi Wi-fi 💻 Internet access ♻ Recycling ℹ Tourist info 🐕 Dog exercise area

BLAIRLOGIE — Map 21 NS89

Places to visit

Alloa Tower, ALLOA 0844 493 2129
www.nts.org.uk

The Regimental Museum of the Argyll &
Sutherland Highlanders, STIRLING
01786 475165 www.argylls.co.uk

►►►► 85% Witches Craig Caravan & Camping Park

(NS821968)

FK9 5PX
☎ 01786 474947
e-mail: info@witchescraig.co.uk
dir: *3m NE of Stirling on A91 (Hillfoots to St Andrews road)*

* 🚐 £17-£21.50 🚘 £17-£21.50 ▲ £16-£20.50

Open Apr-Oct

Last arrival 20.00hrs Last departure noon

In an attractive setting with direct access to the lower slopes of the dramatic Ochil Hills, this is a well-maintained family-run park. It is in the centre of 'Braveheart' country, with easy access to historical sites and many popular attractions. 5 acre site. 60 touring pitches. 53 hardstandings. 6 seasonal pitches. Caravan pitches. Motorhome pitches. Tent pitches.

Leisure: 🅰

Facilities: 🦌⊙ℙ✳🔥🔥🅾🚰🚻📶♻🅾

Services: 🔌🖥🔋🖊🅃🔋🖊

Within 3 miles: 🖊🏇🖊🅖🖊🅾🔋🔋∪

Notes: Dogs must be kept on leads. Food preparation area, baby bath & changing area.

CALLANDER — Map 20 NN60

Places to visit

Doune Castle, DOUNE 01786 841742
www.historic-scotland.gov.uk

►►►► 81% Gart Caravan Park

(NN643070)

The Gart FK17 8LE
☎ 01877 330002 📠 01877 330002
e-mail: enquiries@theholidaypark.co.uk
dir: *1m E of Callander on A84*

* 🚐 £22 🚘 £22

Open Etr or Apr-15 Oct

Last arrival 22.00hrs Last departure 11.30hrs

A very well maintained spacious parkland site within easy walking distance of Callander. The on-site play area for children is excellent, whilst free fishing is available on a private stretch of the River Teith. A wide range of leisure activities is available within the locality. 26 acre site. 128 touring pitches. Caravan pitches. Motorhome pitches. 66 statics.

AA Pubs & Restaurants nearby: Roman Camp Country House Hotel, Callander 01877 330003

Callander Meadows, Callander 01877 330181

Leisure: 🅰🎡

Facilities: 🦌⊙✳🔥🅾🚰♻🅾

Services: 🔌🖥🔋🖊

Within 3 miles: 🖊🏇🖊🅖🖊🔋🔋∪

Notes: No commercial vehicles. Dogs must be kept on leads.

LUIB — Map 20 NN42

Places to visit

Balmacara Estate & Lochalsh Woodland Garden, BALMACARA 0844 493 2233
www.nts.org.uk

►►►► 75% Glendochart Holiday Park *(NN477278)*

FK20 8QT
☎ 01567 820637 📠 01567 820024
e-mail: info@glendochart-caravanpark.co.uk
dir: *On A85 (Oban to Stirling road), midway between Killin & Crianlarich*

* 🚐 £17-£18.50 🚘 £17-£18.50 ▲ £6-£13.50

Open Mar-Nov

Last arrival 21.00hrs Last departure noon

A small, well maintained park on a hillside in Glendochart, with imaginative landscaping and glorious mountain and hill views. The site is well located for trout and salmon fishing, and ideal for walking. 15 acre site. 35 touring pitches. 28 hardstandings. Caravan pitches. Motorhome pitches. Tent pitches. 60 statics.

Facilities: 🦌⊙ℙ✳🔥🅾🚰🅾

Services: 🔌🖥🔋🖊📶

Within 3 miles: 🖊

Notes: Dogs must be kept on leads.

SERVICES: 🔌 Electric hook up 🖥 Launderette 🍺 Licensed bar 🔋 Calor Gas ⊘ Camping Gaz 🅃 Toilet fluid 🍽 Café/Restaurant 🍟 Fast Food/Takeaway 📶 Battery charging 🍼 Baby care 🖊 Motorvan service point

ABBREVIATIONS: BH/bank hols-bank holidays Etr-Easter Whit-Whitsun dep-departure fr-from hrs-hours m-mile mdnt-midnight rdbt-roundabout rs-restricted service wk-week wknd-weekend ⊛ No credit cards ⊗ No dogs

See page 7 for details of the AA Camping Card Scheme

STIRLING

See Auchenbowie & Blairlogie

STRATHYRE
Map 20 NN51

►►► 72% Immervoulin Caravan and Camping Park (NN560164)

FK18 8NJ

☎ 01877 384285 📄 01877 384390

dir: *Off A84, approx 1m S of Strathyre*

Open Mar-Oct

Last arrival 22.00hrs

A family run park on open meadowland next to the River Balvaig, where fishing, canoeing and other water sports can be enjoyed. A riverside walk leads to Loch Lubnaig, and the village of Strathyre offers restaurants. The park has a modern, well-appointed amenity block. 5 acre site. 50 touring pitches. Caravan pitches. Motorhome pitches. Tent pitches.

AA Pubs & Restaurants nearby: Creagan House, Strathyre 01877 384638

Roman Camp Country House Hotel, Callander 01877 330003

Callander Meadows, Callander 01877 330181

Facilities: ⌐◉ℱ☀⚴⊘⌂⚒♲ 𝒊

Services: 🔌🗑🛢⊘🅣🏧↯

Within 3 miles: ✎⚲

Notes: No noise after 23.00hrs.

WEST DUNBARTONSHIRE

BALLOCH
Map 20 NS38

Places to visit

Finlaystone Country Estate, LANGBANK 01475 540505 www.finlaystone.co.uk

The Tall Ship at Glasgow Harbour, GLASGOW 0141 222 2513 www.thetallship.com

►►►► 79% *Lomond Woods Holiday Park* (NS383816)

Old Luss Rd G83 8QP

☎ 01389 755000 📄 01389 755563

e-mail: lomondwoods@holiday-parks.co.uk

web: www.holiday-parks.co.uk

dir: *From A82, 17m N of Glasgow, take A811 (Stirling to Balloch road). Left at 1st rdbt, follow holiday park signs, 150yds on left*

🔌🚐

Open all year

Last arrival 20.00hrs Last departure noon

A mature park with well-laid out pitches and self-catering lodges screened by trees and shrubs, surrounded by woodland and hills. The park is within walking distance of Loch Lomond Shores, a leisure and retail complex, which is the main gateway to Scotland's first National Park. Amenities include the Loch Lomond Aquarium, an Interactive Exhibition, and loch cruises. Please note that this park does not accept tents. 13 acre site. 100 touring pitches. 100 hardstandings. Caravan pitches. Motorhome pitches. 35 statics.

AA Pubs & Restaurants nearby: Cameron Grill 01389 755565 & Martin Wishart Loch Lomond 01389 722504 - both at Cameron House Hotel, Balloch

Leisure: 🅐🎱▯

Facilities: 🛏⌐◉ℱ☀⚴🗑🎡🐕📶

Services: 🔌🗑🛢⊘🅣🏧↯

Within 3 miles: ⚓🚣✎⚲🛥⌂🗑∪

Notes: No jet skis.

WEST LOTHIAN

EAST CALDER
Map 21 NT06

Places to visit

Suntrap Garden, GOGAR 0131 339 7283 www.suntrap-garden.org.uk

Malleny Garden, BALERNO 0844 493 2123 www.nts.org.uk

►►► 85% Linwater Caravan Park (NT104696)

West Clifton EH53 0HT

☎ 0131 333 3326 📄 0131 333 1952

e-mail: linwater@supanet.com

dir: *M9 junct 1, signed to B7030 or from Wilkieston on A71*

🔌 £15-£21 🚐 £15-£21 🅐 £13-£19

Open late Mar-late Oct

Last arrival 21.00hrs Last departure noon

A farmland park in a peaceful rural area within easy reach of Edinburgh. The very good facilities are housed in a Scandinavian-style building, and are well maintained by resident owners, who are genuinely caring hosts and nothing is too much trouble to ensure campers are enjoying themselves. There are 'timber tents' for hire and nearby are plenty of pleasant woodland walks. 5 acre site. 60 touring pitches. 18 hardstandings. Caravan pitches. Motorhome pitches. Tent pitches. 4 wooden pods.

AA Pubs & Restaurants nearby: Bridge Inn, Ratho 0131 333 1320

Leisure: 🅐

Facilities: ⌐◉ℱ☀⚴⊘🎡📶♲ 𝒊

Services: 🔌🗑🛢⊘🅣🏧

Within 3 miles: ⚓✎⌂🗑

Notes: No noise after 23.00hrs. Dogs must be kept on leads.

LINLITHGOW — Map 21 NS97

Places to visit

Linlithgow Palace, LINLITHGOW 01506 842896 www.historic-scotland.gov.uk

House of The Binns, LINLITHGOW 0844 493 2127 www.nts.org.uk

Great for kids: Blackness Castle, LINLITHGOW 01506 834807 www.historic-scotland.gov.uk

►►►► 81% Beecraigs Caravan & Camping Site *(NT006746)*

Beecraigs Country Park, The Park Centre EH49 6PL
☎ 01506 844516 📠 01506 846256
e-mail: mail@beecraigs.com
web: www.beecraigs.com
dir: *From Linlithgow on A803 or from Bathgate on B792, follow signs to country park. Reception either at restaurant or visitor centre*

* 🚐 £15.30-£17.80 🚌 £15.30-£17.80 ⛺ £13-£21.30

Open all year (rs 25-26 Dec, 1-2 Jan no new arrivals Xmas, New Year or BH)

Last arrival 21.00hrs Last departure noon

A wildlife enthusiast's paradise where even the timber facility buildings are in keeping with the environment. Beecraigs is situated peacefully in the open countryside of the Bathgate Hills. Small bays with natural shading offer intimate pitches, and there's a restaurant serving lunch and evening meals. The smart toilet block on the main park includes en suite facilities, and there is a luxury toilet block for tenters. 6 acre site. 36 touring pitches. 36 hardstandings. Caravan pitches. Motorhome pitches. Tent pitches.

AA Pubs & Restaurants nearby: The Chop & Ale House, Champany Inn, Linlithgow 01506 834532

Leisure: /⚠\

Facilities: 🛁 🚿 ⊙ 💨 ✻ ♿ ☎ 🍴 🐕 ♻ ⓘ

Services: 🔌 🧺 🔥 [T] 🍽

Within 3 miles: ⛳ 🎣 🏊 [S] 🧺 U

Notes: No cars by tents. No ball games near caravans, no noise after 22.00hrs. Dogs must be kept on leads. Children's bath, country park facilities.

SERVICES: 🔌 Electric hook up 🧺 Launderette 🍺 Licensed bar 🔥 Calor Gas 🔥 Camping Gaz [T] Toilet fluid 🍽 Café/Restaurant 🍔 Fast Food/Takeaway 🔋 Battery charging 👶 Baby care ⛽ Motorvan service point
ABBREVIATIONS: BH/bank hols-bank holidays Etr-Easter Whit-Whitsun dep-departure fr-from hrs-hours m-mile mdnt-midnight rdbt-roundabout rs-restricted service wk-week wknd-weekend 🚫 No credit cards 🚫 No dogs

See page 7 for details of the AA Camping Card Scheme

ISLE OFARRAN

LOCHRANZA   Map 20 NR25

►►► 79% Lochranza Caravan & Camping Site *(NR942500)*

KA27 8HL
☎ **01770 830273 & 07733 611083**
e-mail: info@arran-campsite.com
dir: *On A841 at N of island, beside Kintyre ferry & 14m N of Brodick for ferry to Ardrossan*

* ⊞ £15-£16 ⊟ £15-£16 ▲ £14-£16

Open Mar-30 Oct

Last arrival 22.00hrs Last departure 16.00hrs

A lovely site located on the outskirts of Lochranza with spectacular views which easily justifies the 'Scotland in Miniature' tag given to the Isle of Arran. Red deer frequent the newly re-developed 9-hole pay & play golf course, there is a restaurant and shop at the site entrance; Arran Distillery is only a short walk away. There is a good local bus service and the ferry from Lochranza only takes 30 minutes to reach the Mull of Kintyre making day trips a possibility. 2.2 acre site. 60 touring pitches. 10 hardstandings. Caravan pitches. Motorhome pitches. Tent pitches.

AA Pubs & Restaurants nearby: Kilmichael Country House Hotel, Brodick 01770 302219

Leisure: ⚽

Facilities: ⋔ ☉ ℉ ✳ ᴦ 🛒 ♻ ❶

Services: 🔌 🚽 🛢 ⊘ T 🍽 🚮 ⏚ ⏟

Within 3 miles: ♪ ✎ ⇟ 🛍 🛒

Notes: No fires. Putting green.

ISLE OF MULL

CRAIGNURE — Map 20 NM73

Places to visit

Mull & West Highland Narrow Gauge Railway, CRAIGNURE 01680 812494 (in season) www.mullrail.co.uk

AA CAMPING CARD SITE

▶▶▶▶ 78% Shieling Holidays

(NM724369)

PA65 6AY
☎ 01680 812496 & 0131 556 0068
e-mail: sales@shielingholidays.co.uk
web: www.shielingholidays.co.uk
dir: *From ferry left onto A849 to Iona. 400mtrs left at church, follow site signs towards sea*

* 🚐 £16-£18.50 🚐 £16-£18.50 ▲ £15-£17

Open 9 Mar-5 Nov

Last arrival 22.00hrs Last departure noon

A lovely site on the water's edge with spectacular views, and less than one mile from the ferry landing. Hardstandings and service points are provided for motorhomes, and there are astro-turf pitches for tents. The park also offers unique, en suite cottage tents for hire and bunkhouse accommodation for families. There is also a wildlife trail on site. 7 acre site. 90 touring pitches. 30 hardstandings. Caravan pitches. Motorhome pitches. Tent pitches. 15 statics.

Leisure: ⚑ ⚓ ▢
Facilities: 🚽 🍴 ⊙ ☂ ✳ ⅃ ⊙ 🗪 🚲 WiFi ♻ ❼
Services: 🔌 🔋 🔒 ⌀ 🅃 ⬇
Within 3 miles: ⚓ ⌔ 🖫 🔋
Notes: Bikes available.

ISLE OF SKYE

EDINBANE — Map 22 NG35

AA Campsite of the Year for Scotland 2012

▶▶▶▶ 83% Skye Camping & Caravanning Club Site *(NG345527)*

Loch Greshornish, Borve, Arnisort IV51 9PS
☎ 01470 582230 📠 01470 582230
e-mail: skye.site@thefriendlyclub.co.uk
dir: *Approx 12m from Portree on A850 (Dunvegan road). Site by loch shore*

🚐 🚐 ▲

Open Apr-Oct

Last arrival 22.00hrs Last departure noon

The Club site on Skye stands out for its stunning waterside location and glorious views, the generous pitch density, the overall range of facilities, and the impressive ongoing improvements under enthusiastic franchisee owners. The layout maximises the beauty of the scenery and genuine customer care is very evident with an excellent tourist information room and campers' shelter being just two examples. The amenities block has that definite 'wow' factor with smart, modern fittings, including excellent showers, a generously proportioned disabled room and a family bathroom. This is a green site that uses only green toilet fluids, which are available on site. There are 2 camping pods to let, plus car hire is available on the site. 7.5 acre site. 105 touring pitches. 36 hardstandings. Caravan pitches. Motorhome pitches. Tent pitches. 2 wooden pods.

AA Pubs & Restaurants nearby: Stein Inn, Stein 01470 592362

Loch Bay Seafood Restaurant, Stein 01470 592235

Three Chimneys Restaurant, Colbost 01470 511258

Facilities: 🍴 ⊙ ☂ ✳ ⅃ ⊙ 🖫 🚲 WiFi ♻ ❼
Services: 🔌 🔋 🔒 ⌀ 🅃 🔋 ⬇
Within 3 miles: ⌔ 🖫 🔋
Notes: Dogs must be kept on leads.

STAFFIN — Map 22 NG46

AA CAMPING CARD SITE

▶▶▶ 75% Staffin Camping & Caravanning *(NG492670)*

IV51 9JX
☎ 01470 562213 📠 01470 562213
e-mail: staffincampsite@btinternet.com
dir: *On A855, 16m N of Portree. Turn right before 40mph signs*

* 🚐 fr £13 🚐 fr £13 ▲ fr £12

Open Apr-Oct

Last arrival 22.00hrs Last departure 11.00hrs

A large sloping grassy site with level hardstandings for motor homes and caravans, close to the village of Staffin. The toilet block is appointed to a very good standard and the park has a laundry. Mountain bikes are available for hire. 2.5 acre site. 50 touring pitches. 18 hardstandings. Caravan pitches. Motorhome pitches. Tent pitches.

AA Pubs & Restaurants nearby: The Glenview, Staffin 01470 562248

Flodigarry Country House Hotel, Staffin 01470 552203

Facilities: 🍴 ⊙ ☂ ✳ ⅃ 🗪 🚲 WiFi ♻ ❼
Services: 🔌 🔋 🔒 ⌀ 🔋
Within 3 miles: ⚓ ⌔ 🖫 🔋
Notes: No music after 22.00hrs. Dogs must be kept on leads. Picnic tables, kitchen area, campers' bothy.

Wales

Tryfan, Ogwen Valley, Snowdonia National Park

Wales

Wales may be small but it certainly packs a punch. Its scenery is a matchless mix of magnificent mountains, rolling green hills and craggy coastlines. But it is not just the landscape that makes such a strong impression - Wales is renowned for its prominent position in the world of culture and the arts.

This is a land of ancient myths and traditions, of male voice choirs, exceptionally gifted singers and leading actors of stage and screen. Richard Burton hailed from the valleys in south Wales, Anthony Hopkins originates from Port Talbot and Tom Jones, born Thomas Jones Woodward, comes from Pontypridd. One man who is inextricably linked to Wales is the poet Dylan Thomas. Born in Swansea in 1914, he lived at the Boat House in Laugharne,

● Nant Gwynant Valley & Snowdon

on the Taf and Tywi estuaries, overlooking Carmarthen Bay. He is buried in the local churchyard.

The valleys

East of here are the old industrial valleys of the Rhondda, once a byword for hardship and poverty and the grime of the local coal and iron workings, it has been transformed into now a very different place. Also vastly altered and improved by the passage of time are the great cities of Swansea and Cardiff, the latter symbolising New Labour's 'Cool Britannia' philosophy with its café culture and Docklands-style apartments. ▶

Going west and north

Tenby in west Wales still retains the charm of a
typical seaside resort while the Pembrokeshire
coast, overlooking Cardigan Bay, is one of the
country's scenic treasures. Lower Fishguard has a
connection with Dylan Thomas. In 1971, less than
20 years after his death, some of the theatre's
greatest names – Richard Burton and Peter
O'Toole among them – descended on this
picturesque village to film *Under Milk Wood*,
which Thomas originally wrote as a radio play.

Farther north is Harlech Castle, built by Edward I
around 1283, with the peaks of Snowdonia in the
distance. The formidable Caernarfon Castle, the
setting for the investiture of the Prince of Wales in
1969, stands in the north-west corner of the
country. Both castles are part of a string of massive
strongholds built by Edward to establish a united
Britain.

The mountains

With its many attractions and miles of natural
beauty, the coast of Wales is an obvious draw for
its many visitors but ultimately it is the country's
spectacular hinterland that people make for.
Snowdonia, with its towering summits and craggy
peaks, is probably top of the list of adventure
destinations. Heading back south reveals still

Harlech Castle

Marloes, Pembrokeshire

be prepared for some tough ascents and dramatic terrain. Try the Taff Trail, which runs north from Cardiff to Caerphilly and includes three castles en route; it's a fairly easy trail, quite flat and largely free of traffic.

For something completely different, cycle from Swansea to Mumbles, enjoying memorable views of the Gower Peninsula.

Festivals and Events

- May is the month for the Royal Welsh Smallholder & Garden Festival, held on the Royal Welsh Showground at Llanelwedd. The event features all manner of farming and horticultural activities.
- The August Bank Holiday weekend sees the Summer Harp Festival at the National Botanic Garden of Wales at Llanarthne in Carmarthenshire. There are concerts, talks and workshops.
- The Abergavenny Food Festival takes place in September with more than 80 events, including masterclasses, tutored tastings, talks and debates.

more scenic landscapes – the remote country of the Welsh Borders and the stunning scenery of the dramatic Brecon Beacons among them.

Walking and Cycling

With mile upon mile of natural beauty, it's hardly surprising that Wales offers so much potential for walking. There's the Cistercian Way, which circles the country by incorporating its Cistercian abbeys; the Glyndwr's Way, named after the 15th-century warrior statesman; and the Pembrokeshire Coast Path, which is a great way to explore the Pembrokeshire National Park.

Cycling is understandably very popular here but

ANGLESEY, ISLE OF

DULAS
Map 14 SH48

PREMIER PARK

▶▶▶▶▶ 85% Tyddyn Isaf
Caravan Park (SH486873)
GOLD

Lligwy Bay LL70 9PQ
☎ 01248 410203 & 410667 ▤ 01248 410667
e-mail: mail@tyddynisaf.co.uk
dir: Take A5025 through Benllech to Moelfre rdbt,
left towards Amlwch to Brynrefail. Turn right
opposite craft shop. Site 0.5m down lane on right
* ➡ £20-£32.50 ➡ £20-£32.50 ▲ £20-£27.50

Open Mar-Oct (rs Mar-Jul & Sep-Oct bar & shop
opening limited)

Last arrival 21.30hrs Last departure 11.00hrs

A beautifully situated, very spacious family park
on rising ground adjacent to a sandy beach, with
magnificent views overlooking Lligwy Bay. A
private footpath leads direct to the beach and
there is an excellent nature trail around the park.
There are very good toilet facilities, including a
block with under-floor heating and excellent
unisex privacy cubicles, a well-stocked shop, and
café/bar serving meals, which are best enjoyed on
the terrace with its magnificent coast and sea
views. 16 acre site. 30 touring pitches. 50
hardstandings. Caravan pitches. Motorhome
pitches. Tent pitches. 56 statics.

AA Pubs & Restaurants nearby: The Ship Inn,
Red Wharf Bay 01248 852568

Ye Olde Bulls Head Inn, Beaumaris 01248 810329

Leisure: ⚠ ▢
Facilities: ↖ ☉ ☞ ✳ ⚅ ⊙ 🄴 🪑 ☂ WiFi
Services: ⚡ 🔋 🛢 ⊘ 🅣 🍽 ⛴ ⛟ ↓
Within 3 miles: ↓ ≭ ◢ 🄶 ◡

Notes: ☻ No groups, maximum 3 units together.
Dogs must be kept on leads. Baby changing unit.

MARIAN-GLAS
Map 14 SH58

Places to visit
Bryn Celli Ddu Burial Chamber, BRYNCELLI DDU
01443 336000 www.cadw.wales.gov.uk

PREMIER PARK

▶▶▶▶▶ 93% Home
Farm Caravan Park
(SH498850)
Best of British / GOLD

LL73 8PH
☎ 01248 410614 ▤ 01248 410900
e-mail: enq@homefarm-anglesey.co.uk
web: www.homefarm-anglesey.co.uk
dir: On A5025, 2m N of Benllech. Site 300mtrs
beyond church

➡ ➡ ▲

Open Apr-Oct

Last arrival 21.00hrs Last departure noon

A first-class park, run with passion and
enthusiasm, set in an elevated and secluded
position sheltered by trees, with good planting and
landscaping. The peaceful rural setting affords
views of farmland, the sea, and the mountains of
Snowdonia. The modern toilet blocks are spotlessly
clean and well maintained, and there are excellent
play facilities for children both indoors and out.
Improvements include a super visitors' parking
area, a stunning water feature, a children's play
area with top-notch equipment, and a smart new
reception and shop for 2011. The area is blessed
with sandy beaches, and local pubs and shops
cater for everyday needs. 6 acre site. 98 touring
pitches. 21 hardstandings. Caravan pitches.
Motorhome pitches. Tent pitches. 84 statics.

AA Pubs & Restaurants nearby: The Ship Inn,
Red Wharf Bay 01248 852568

Ye Olde Bulls Head Inn, Beaumaris 01248 810329

Bishopsgate House Hotel, Beaumaris
01248 810302

Leisure: ⚠ ⚞ ☉ ◖ ▢
Facilities: ↝ ↖ ☉ ☞ ✳ ⚅ ⊙ 🄴 ☂ WiFi
Services: ⚡ 🔋 ⊘ 🅣 ⛴ ↓
Within 3 miles: ↓ ◢ ≭ 🄶 🄶 ◡

Notes: No roller blades, skateboards or scooters.
Indoor adventure playground.

PENTRAETH
Map 14 SH57

Places to visit
Bryn Celli Ddu Burial Chamber, BRYNCELLI DDU
01443 336000 www.cadw.wales.gov.uk

Plas Newydd, PLAS NEWYDD 01248 714795
www.nationaltrust.org.uk/main/plasnewydd

▶▶▶ 78% Rhos Caravan Park
(SH517794)

Rhos Farm LL75 8DZ
☎ 01248 450214 ▤ 01248 450214
e-mail: rhosfarm@googlemail.com
web: www.rhoscaravanpark.co.uk
dir: Site on A5025, 1m N of Pentraeth

➡ ➡ ▲

Open Etr-Oct

Last arrival 22.00hrs Last departure 16.00hrs

A warm welcome awaits families at this spacious
park on level, grassy ground with easy access to
the main road to Amlwch. A 200-acre working
farm that has two play areas and farm animals to
keep children amused, with good beaches, pubs,
restaurants and shops nearby. The two toilet
blocks are kept to a good standard by enthusiastic
owners, who are constantly improving the
facilities. The administration and bookings are via
the sister park, Bryn Awel, which is located
opposite - Tel 01248 450801. 15 acre site. 98
touring pitches. Caravan pitches. Motorhome
pitches. Tent pitches. 66 statics.

AA Pubs & Restaurants nearby: The Ship Inn,
Red Wharf Bay 01248 852568

Ye Olde Bulls Head Inn, Beaumaris 01248 810329

Bishopsgate House Hotel, Beaumaris
01248 810302

Leisure: ⚠
Facilities: ↝ ☉ ✳ ☂
Services: ⚡ 🔋 🔋 ⊘ ⛴
Within 3 miles: ↓ ≭ ◢ 🄶 🄶 🄶 ◡

Notes: ☻

LEISURE: ☝ Indoor swimming pool ⚞ Outdoor swimming pool ⚠ Children's playground ↓ Kid's club ☉ Tennis court ◖ Games room ▢ Separate TV room
↓ 9/18 hole golf course ⚓ Boats for hire ☲ Cinema ♫ Entertainment ◢ Fishing ◉ Mini golf ☲ Watersports 🏋 Gym ☉ Sports field Spa ◡ Stables
FACILITIES: ↝ Bath ↖ Shower ☉ Electric shaver ☞ Hairdryer ✳ Ice Pack Facility ⚅ Disabled facilities ⊙ Public telephone 🄴 Shop on site or within 200yds
☻ Mobile shop (calls at least 5 days a week) ▤ BBQ area ⛴ Picnic area WiFi Wi-fi ◗ Internet access ☼ Recycling ◷ Tourist info ☂ Dog exercise area

RHOS LLIGWY   Map 14 SH48

►►► 68% Ty'n Rhos Caravan Park
(SH495867)

Lligwy Bay, Moelfre LL72 8NL
☎ 01248 852417 📠 01248 853417
e-mail: robert@bodafonpark.co.uk
dir: *Take A5025 from Benllech to Moelfre rdbt, right to T-junct in Moelfre. Left, then approx 2m to site, pass x-roads leading to beach, site 50mtrs on right*

* 🚐 £17-£25 🚏 £17-£25 ▲ £14-£20

Open Mar-Oct

Last arrival 21.00hrs Last departure noon

A family park close to the beautiful beach at Lligwy Bay, and cliff walks along the Heritage Coast. Historic Din Lligwy, and the shops at picturesque Moelfre are nearby. Please note that guests should register at Bodafon Caravan Park in Benllech where detailed directions will be given and pitches allocated. 10 acre site. 30 touring pitches. 4 hardstandings. 48 seasonal pitches. Caravan pitches. Motorhome pitches. Tent pitches. 80 statics.

AA Pubs & Restaurants nearby: The Ship Inn, Red Wharf Bay 01248 852568

Ye Olde Bulls Head Inn, Beaumaris 01248 810329

Bishopsgate House Hotel, Beaumaris 01248 810302

Facilities: 🌣⊙❄♿🕐🐾❼
Services: 🔌🗑🔒
Within 3 miles: ⏲🎣🛒🏪♨
Notes: No campfires. Dogs must be kept on leads.

RHOSNEIGR   Map 14 SH37

►►► 77% Ty Hen (SH327738)
GOLD

Station Rd LL64 5QZ
☎ 01407 810331 📠 01407 810331
e-mail: info@tyhen.com
web: www.tyhen.com
dir: *From A55 junct 5 follow signs to Rhosneigr, at clock turn right. Entrance 50mtrs before Rhosneigr railway station*

🚐 🚏 ▲

Open mid Mar-Oct

Last arrival 21.00hrs Last departure noon

Attractive seaside position near a large fishing lake and riding stables, in lovely countryside. A smart toilet block offers a welcome amenity at this popular family park, where friendly owners are always on hand. The park is close to RAF Valley, which is great for plane spotters, but expect some aircraft noise during the day. 7.5 acre site. 38 touring pitches. 5 hardstandings. Caravan pitches. Motorhome pitches. Tent pitches. 42 statics.

AA Pubs & Restaurants nearby: Ye Olde Bulls Head Inn, Beaumaris 01248 810329

Bishopsgate House Hotel, Beaumaris 01248 810302

Leisure: 🏊⚽🎯
Facilities: 🌣⊙❄♿🕐🐾 Wi-fi
Services: 🔌🗑🍺⚓
Within 3 miles: ⏲🎣🛒🏪🗑
Notes: 1 motor vehicle per pitch, children must not be out after 22.00hrs. Dogs must be kept on leads. Fishing, family room, walks.

BRIDGEND

PORTHCAWL

Places to visit

Newcastle, BRIDGEND 01443 336000
www.cadw.wales.gov.uk

Coity Castle, COITY 01443 336000
www.cadw.wales.gov.uk

PORTHCAWL   Map 9 SS87

►► 72% Brodawel Camping & Caravan Park (SS816789)

Moor Ln, Nottage CF36 3EJ
☎ 01656 783231
dir: *M4 junct 37, A4229 towards Porthcawl. Site on right off A4229*

🚐 🚏 ▲

Open Apr-Sep

Last arrival 19.00hrs Last departure 11.00hrs

A family run park catering mainly for families, on the edge of the village of Nottage. It is very convenient for Porthcawl and the Glamorgan Heritage Coast, each is within a five-minute drive. 4 acre site. 100 touring pitches. Caravan pitches. Motorhome pitches. Tent pitches.

AA Pubs & Restaurants nearby: Prince of Wales Inn, Kenfig 01656 740356

Leisure: 🎯🎱
Facilities: 🌣⊙❄♿🕐🗑🎯
Services: 🔌🗑🔒⚓🚰
Within 3 miles: ⏲🎯🎣🛒🏪🗑🗑♨
Notes: ⊗

CARMARTHENSHIRE

HARFORD   Map 8 SN64

AA CAMPING CARD SITE

►►► 86% Springwater Lakes
(SN637430)

SA19 8DT
☎ 01558 650788
dir: *4m E of Lampeter on A482, entrance well signed on right*

* 🚐 £20 🚏 £20 ▲ £16

Open Mar-Oct

Last arrival 20.00hrs Last departure 11.00hrs

In a rural setting overlooked by the Cambrian Mountains, this park is adjoined on each side by four spring-fed and well-stocked fishing lakes. All pitches have hardstandings, electricity and TV hook-ups, and there is a small and very clean toilet block and a shop. New fully serviced hardstanding pitches have been created beside one of the lakes. 20 acre site. 30 touring pitches. 30 hardstandings. Caravan pitches. Motorhome pitches. Tent pitches.

continued

HARFORD *continued*

Facilities: ⊓⊙✳⛬☉🛏🐾❔

Services: 🖳💧🗑🚮🛒

Within 3 miles: ✐⛱🛍⛷

Notes: ☺ Children must be supervised around lakes, no cycling on site, no ball games. Dogs must be kept on leads. Bait & tackle shop.

LLANDOVERY   Map 9 SN73

Places to visit

Dolaucothi Gold Mines, PUMSAINT 01558 650177 www.nationaltrust.org.uk/main/w-dolaucothigoldmines

► ► ► ► **89% Erwlon Caravan & Camping Park**

Best of British GOLD

(SN776343)

Brecon Rd SA20 0RD

☎ 01550 721021 & 720332

e-mail: peter@erwlon.co.uk

dir: *0.5m E of Llandovery on A40*

✱ 🚐 £12-£19 🚙 £12-£19 ⛺ £5-£19

Open all year

Last arrival anytime Last departure noon

A long-established, family-run site set beside a brook in the Brecon Beacons foothills. The town of Llandovery and the hills overlooking the Towy Valley are a short walk away. The superb, Scandinavian-style facilities block has cubicled washrooms, family and disabled rooms and is an impressive feature; ongoing improvements include a campers' kitchen. 8 acre site. 75 touring pitches. 15 hardstandings. Caravan pitches. Motorhome pitches. Tent pitches.

Leisure: ⚑

Facilities: ⊓⊙⚓✳⛬☉🛏🐾 Wi-Fi ♻ ❔

Services: 🖳🔌💧🛒🚮

Within 3 miles: ⚓✐🛍⛷

Notes: ☺ Quiet after 22.30hrs. Dogs must be kept on leads. Fishing, cycle storage & hire.

► ► **73% Llandovery Caravan Park**

(SN762342)

Church Bank SA20 0DT

☎ 01550 721993 & 07970 650 606

e-mail: drovers.rfc@btinternet.com

dir: *A40 from Carmarthen, over rail crossing, past junct with A483 (Builth Wells). Turn right for Llangadog, past church, 1st right signed Rugby Club & Camping*

🚐 🚙 ⛺

Open all year

Last arrival 20.00hrs Last departure 20.00hrs

A level, spacious and developing small site adjacent to the rugby club on the outskirts of Llandovery. Toilets facilities are adequate but there are plans to upgrade and improve the facilities. 8 acre site. 100 touring pitches. 32 hardstandings. Caravan pitches. Motorhome pitches. Tent pitches.

Leisure: ⚑⚽🏕

Facilities: ⊓⊙⛬🐾♻ ❔

Services: 🖳🛒🛍

Within 3 miles: ⚓✐🛍⛷

Notes: ☺ Dogs must be kept on leads.

LLANGADOG   Map 9 SN72

Places to visit

Dinefwr Park and Castle, LLANDEILO 01558 823902 www.nationaltrust.org.uk/main/w-dinefwrpark

Carreg Cennen Castle, CARREG CENNEN CASTLE 01558 822291 www.cadw.wales.gov.uk

► ► ► **76% Abermarlais Caravan Park**

(SN695298)

SA19 9NG

☎ 01550 777868 & 777797

dir: *On A40 midway between Llandovery & Llandeilo, 1.5m NW of Llangadog*

✱ 🚐 £11-£13 🚙 £11-£13 ⛺ £11-£13

Open 15 Mar-15 Nov (rs Mar & Nov 1 toilet block, water point no hot water)

Last arrival 23.00hrs Last departure noon

An attractive, well-run site with a welcoming atmosphere. This part-level, part-sloping park is in a wooded valley on the edge of the Brecon Beacons National Park, beside the River Marlais. 17 acre site. 88 touring pitches. 2 hardstandings. Caravan pitches. Motorhome pitches. Tent pitches.

Leisure: ⚑

Facilities: ⊓⊙✳⛬☉🛏🐾❔

Services: 🖳🔌💧T🛒

Within 3 miles: ✐🛍⛷

Notes: No open fires, silence from 23.00hrs-08.00hrs. Dogs must be kept on leads. Volleyball, badminton court, softball tennis net.

LLANWRDA

See Harford

NEWCASTLE EMLYN   Map 8 SN34

Places to visit

Cilgerran Castle, CILGERRAN 01239 621339 www.cadw.wales.gov.uk

Castell Henllys Iron Age Fort, CRYMYCH 01239 891319 www.castellhenllys.com

Great for kids: Felinwynt Rainforest Centre, FELINWYNT 01239 810882 www.butterflycentre.co.uk

AA CAMPING CARD SITE

PREMIER PARK

► ► ► ► ► **85% Cenarth Falls Holiday Park** *(SN265421)*

Best of British

Cenarth SA38 9JS

☎ 01239 710345 📠 01239 710344

e-mail: enquiries@cenarth-holipark.co.uk

dir: *Off A484 on outskirts of Cenarth village towards Cardigan*

🚐 £16-£27 🚙 £16-£27 ⛺ £16-£27

Open Mar-Nov

Last arrival 20.00hrs Last departure 11.00hrs

A high quality park with excellent facilities, close to the village of Cenarth where the River Teifi (famous for its salmon and sea trout) cascades through the Cenarth Falls Gorge. A well-landscaped park with an indoor heated swimming

LEISURE: 🏊 Indoor swimming pool 🏊 Outdoor swimming pool ⚑ Children's playground 🧒 Kid's club 🎾 Tennis court 🎱 Games room 📺 Separate TV room ⛳ 9/18 hole golf course ⛵ Boats for hire 🎬 Cinema 🎵 Entertainment 🎣 Fishing ⛳ Mini golf 🏄 Watersports 🏋 Gym ⚽ Sports field **Spa** ⛷ Stables
FACILITIES: 🛁 Bath 🚿 Shower ⊙ Electric shaver ⚓ Hairdryer ✳ Ice Pack Facility ⛬ Disabled facilities ☉ Public telephone 🛍 Shop on site or within 200yds 🛒 Mobile shop (calls at least 5 days a week) 🍖 BBQ area 🛏 Picnic area Wi-Fi Wi-fi 🖥 Internet access ♻ Recycling ❔ Tourist info 🐾 Dog exercise area

pool and fitness suite, and a restaurant and bar. 2 acre site. 30 touring pitches. 30 hardstandings. Caravan pitches. Motorhome pitches. Tent pitches. 89 statics.

AA Pubs & Restaurants nearby: Nags Head Inn, Abercych 01239 841200

Webley Waterfront Inn & Hotel, St Dogmaels 01239 612085

Leisure: ♨ ♨ ♈ ⚔ ❋ ♫

Facilities: ⌾ ⊙ ℗ ✳ ⚓ ⚘ ⚙ ❶

Services: ⚡ ⏚ ⛁ ∅ ⚱ ⱶ ❤ ⚟

Within 3 miles: ✠ ✦ ≿ ⚏ ⚎

Notes: No skateboards. Dogs must be kept on leads. Pool table, health & leisure complex.

AA CAMPING CARD SITE

▶▶▶ 85% Argoed Meadow Caravan and Camping Site *(SN268415)*

Argoed Farm SA38 9JL
☎ 01239 710690
dir: *From Newcastle Emlyn on A484 towards Cenarth, take B4332. Site 300yds on right*

⚑ ⚑ ▲

Open all year

Last arrival anytime Last departure noon

Pleasant open meadowland on the banks of the River Teifi, very close to Cenarth Falls gorge, this site has a modern toilet block which adds to the general appeal of this mainly adults-only park. 3 acre site. 30 touring pitches. 5 hardstandings. Caravan pitches. Motorhome pitches. Tent pitches. 5 statics.

AA Pubs & Restaurants nearby: Nags Head Inn, Abercych 01239 841200

Webley Waterfront Inn & Hotel, St Dogmaels 01239 612085

Facilities: ⌾ ⊙ ℗ ✳ ⚓ ⚘ ⛁ ⚟ ⚘ ❶

Services: ⚡ ⏚ ⚱ ∅ ❤ ⚟

Within 3 miles: ⚏ ✦ ⚎ ⚏ ⚎

Notes: ⊗ No bikes or skateboards. Dogs must be kept on leads.

▶▶▶ 82% Moelfryn Caravan & Camping Park *(SN321370)*

Ty-Cefn, Pant-y-Bwlch SA38 9JE
☎ 01559 371231
e-mail: moelfryn@moelfryncaravanpark.co.uk
dir: *A484 from Carmarthen towards Cynwyl Elfed. Pass Blue Bell Inn on right, 200yds take left fork onto B4333 towards Hermon. In 7m brown sign on left. Turn left, site on right*

* ⚑ £12-£15 ⚑ £12-£15 ▲ £10-£15

Open Mar-10 Jan

Last arrival 22.00hrs Last departure noon

A small, beautifully maintained, family-run park in a glorious elevated location overlooking the valley of the River Teifi. Pitches are level and spacious, and well screened by hedging and mature trees. Facilities are spotlessly clean and tidy, and the playing field is well away from the touring area. Home-cooked meals can be ordered and Sunday breakfast delivered to the tent/caravan door. 3 acre site. 25 touring pitches. 16 hardstandings. 12 seasonal pitches. Caravan pitches. Motorhome pitches. Tent pitches.

AA Pubs & Restaurants nearby: Nags Head Inn, Abercych 01239 841200

Webley Waterfront Inn & Hotel, St Dogmaels 01239 612085

Leisure: ⚔

Facilities: ⌾ ⊙ ℗ ✳ ⛁ ⱳⱳ ⚘ ❶

Services: ⚡ ⏚ ⚱ ❤

Within 3 miles: ✠ ✦ ⚏ ✦ ≿ ⚏ ⚎ ⚎

Notes: Games to be played in designated area only. Dogs must be kept on leads. Caravan storage.

▶▶▶ 77% Afon Teifi Caravan & Camping Park *(SN338405)*

Pentrecagal SA38 9HT
☎ 01559 370532
e-mail: afonteifi@btinternet.com
dir: *Signed from A484, 2m E of Newcastle Emlyn*

⚑ £18-£20 ⚑ £18-£20 ▲ £10-£20

Open Apr-Oct

Last arrival 23.00hrs

Set on the banks of the River Teifi, a famous salmon and sea trout river, this park is secluded with good views. Family owned and run, and only two miles from the market town of Newcastle Emlyn. 6 acre site. 110 touring pitches. 22 hardstandings. Caravan pitches. Motorhome pitches. Tent pitches. 10 statics.

AA Pubs & Restaurants nearby: Nags Head Inn, Abercych 01239 841200

Webley Waterfront Inn & Hotel, St Dogmaels 01239 612085

Leisure: ⚔ ⚘ ⚓

Facilities: ❤ ⌾ ⊙ ℗ ✳ ⚓ ⛁ ⚟ ⚏ ✠ ⚘ ❶

Services: ⚡ ⏚ ⚱ ∅ ⊤ ❤

Within 3 miles: ✠ ✦ ≿ ⚏ ⚎ ⚎

Notes: ⊛ 15 acres of woodland, fields & walks.

CEREDIGION

ABERAERON
Map 8 SN46

Places to visit

Llanerchaeron, ABERAERON 01545 570200
www.nationaltrust.org.uk

►►► 86% Aeron Coast Caravan Park

(SN460631)

North Rd SA46 0JF
☎ 01545 570349 📠 01545 571289
e-mail: enquiries@aeroncoast.co.uk
web: www.aeroncoast.co.uk
dir: *On A487 (coast road) on N edge of Aberaeron, signed. Filling station at entrance*

🚐 £16-£26 �Ⓜ £16-£26 ⚕ £16-£26

Open Mar-Oct

Last arrival 23.00hrs Last departure 11.00hrs

A well-managed family holiday park on the edge of the attractive resort of Aberaeron, with direct access to the beach. The spacious pitches are all level. On-site facilities include an extensive outdoor pool complex, a multi-activity outdoor sports area, an indoor children's play area, a small lounge bar which serves food, a games room and an entertainment suite. 22 acre site. 100 touring pitches. 23 hardstandings. Caravan pitches. Motorhome pitches. Tent pitches. 200 statics.

AA Pubs & Restaurants nearby: Harbourmaster, Aberaeron 01545 570755

Ty Mawr Mansion, Aberaeron 01570 470033

Leisure: ⚓ 🎠 ♨ ♦ ▢ ♪
Facilities: ☕ ⊙ ✳ ₺ ☺ 🗑 ❶
Services: 🔌 ⌷ 🛢 🔋 🗋 🖵 🍴 🧺 🛒 🛗
Within 3 miles: ♦ ♨ ☺ ∪

Notes: Families only, no motorcycles. Dogs must be kept on leads.

ABERYSTWYTH
Map 8 SN58

Places to visit

The National Library of Wales, ABERYSTWYTH
01970 632800 www.llgc.org.uk

AA CAMPING CARD SITE

►►► 80% Ocean View Caravan Park

(SN592842)

North Beach, Clarach Bay SY23 3DT
☎ 01970 828425 & 623361
e-mail: enquiries@oceanviewholidays.com
dir: *Exit A487 in Bow Street. Straight on at next x-roads. Site 2nd on right*

* 🚐 £16.50-£21 🚐 £16.50-£21 ⚕

Open Mar-Oct

Last arrival 20.00hrs Last departure noon

This site is in a sheltered valley on gently sloping ground, with wonderful views of both the sea and the countryside. The beach of Clarach Bay is just 200 yards away, and this welcoming park is ideal for all the family. Campers may use the Clarach Bay pub & restaurant. 9 acre site. 24 touring pitches. 15 hardstandings. Caravan pitches. Motorhome pitches. Tent pitches. 56 statics.

Facilities: ☕ ⊙ 🗑 ✳ ☺ 🗑 🔧 ❀ ❶
Services: 🔌 🛢 🔋 🧺
Within 3 miles: ♦ 🎣 ♦ ⊙ ♨ ☺ 🗑 ∪

Notes: Dogs must be kept on leads.

BETTWS EVAN
Map 8 SN34

Places to visit

Pentre Ifan Burial Chamber, NEWPORT
01443 336000 www.cadw.wales.gov.uk

Tredegar House & Park, NEWPORT 01633 815880
www.newport.gov.uk

AA CAMPING CARD SITE

►►► 80% Pilbach Holiday Park

(SN306476)

SA44 5RT
☎ 0845 050 8176
e-mail: info@barkersleisure.com
web: www.barkersleisure.com
dir: *S on A487, turn left onto B4333*

🚐 🚐 ⚕

Open Mar-Oct (rs Mar-Spring BH & Oct swimming pool closed)

Last arrival 22.00hrs Last departure noon

This park is set in secluded countryside, with two separate paddocks and pitches clearly marked in the grass, close to nearby seaside resorts. It has a heated outdoor swimming pool, and entertainment in the club two or three times a week in high season. 15 acre site. 65 touring pitches. 10 hardstandings. Caravan pitches. Motorhome pitches. Tent pitches. 70 statics.

AA Pubs & Restaurants nearby: Nags Head Inn, Abercych 01239 841200

Leisure: ⚓ 🎠 ♦
Facilities: ☕ ⊙ 🗑 ⊙ ☺ 🗑 🔧 ❀
Services: 🔌 🛢 🔋 🍴 🛒
Within 3 miles: ♦ 🎣 ♦ ♨ ☺ 🗑 ∪

Notes: Bike/skateboard parks.

LEISURE: ⚓ Indoor swimming pool ⚓ Outdoor swimming pool 🎠 Children's playground ♦ Kid's club ♨ Tennis court ♦ Games room ▢ Separate TV room ♦ 9/18 hole golf course ♦ Boats for hire 🎬 Cinema ♪ Entertainment 🎣 Fishing ⊙ Mini golf ♨ Watersports 🏌 Gym ♨ Sports field **Spa** ∪ Stables
FACILITIES: ♦ Bath ☕ Shower ⊙ Electric shaver 🗑 Hairdryer ✳ Ice Pack Facility ₺ Disabled facilities ☺ Public telephone 🗑 Shop on site or within 200yds 🗑 Mobile shop (calls at least 5 days a week) 🍖 BBQ area 🌲 Picnic area 📶 Wi-fi 🖳 Internet access ♻ Recycling ❶ Tourist info ♦ Dog exercise area

BORTH

Places to visit

The National Library of Wales, ABERYSTWYTH
01970 632800 www.llgc.org.uk

 74% Brynowen Holiday Park (SN608893)
GOLD

SY24 5LS
☎ 01970 871366 🖷 01970 871125
e-mail: brynowen@park-resorts.com
dir: Signed from B4353, S of Borth

🚐 🚏

Open Apr-Oct

Last arrival mdnt Last departure 10.00hrs

Enjoying spectacular views across Cardigan Bay and the Cambrian Mountains, a small touring park in a large and well-equipped holiday centre. The well-run park offers a wide range of organised activities and entertainment for all the family from morning until late in the evening. A long sandy beach is a few minutes' drive away. 52 acre site. 16 touring pitches. 16 hardstandings. 4 seasonal pitches. Caravan pitches. Motorhome pitches. 480 statics.

Leisure: 🏊 🎇 👋 🚣 🎯 🎣 🎵
Facilities: 🍴 ⊙ 🚿 🕙 🚽 🚻 W-fi 🖥 ♻
Services: 🔌 🔄 🍴 🍴 🛒
Within 3 miles: ⚓ 🏌 🏧 🛒

Notes: No cars by caravans. Dogs must be kept on leads. Mini ten-pin bowling.

LLANON
Map 8 SN56

Places to visit

The National Library of Wales, ABERYSTWYTH
01970 632800 www.llgc.org.uk

►►► 75% Woodlands Caravan Park
(SN509668)

SY23 5LX
☎ 01974 202342 & 202454 🖷 01974 202342
dir: Through Llanon, exit A487 at international sign, site 280yds right

🚐 £20 🚏 £20 ⚠ £15

Open Mar-Oct

Last arrival 21.30hrs Last departure noon

A well maintained, mainly grass site surrounded by mature trees and shrubs near woods and meadowland, adjacent to the sea and a stony beach. The park is half a mile from the village. 4 acre site. 40 touring pitches. 10 hardstandings. Caravan pitches. Motorhome pitches. Tent pitches. 59 statics.

AA Pubs & Restaurants nearby: Harbourmaster, Aberaeron 01545 570755

Ty Mawr Mansion, Aberaeron 01570 470033

Facilities: 🍴 ⊙ 🚿 🕙 W-fi 🖥 ♻ ❓
Services: 🔌 🔄 🔋 🌊 🇹 🛒
Within 3 miles: ⚓ 🏌 🏧 🛒

Notes: Dogs must be kept on leads.

YSTRAD AERON
Map 8 SN55

Places to visit

Llanerchaeron, ABERAERON 01545 570200
www.nationaltrust.org.uk

►►► 72% *Hafod Brynog* (SN525563)

SA48 8AE
☎ 01570 470084
e-mail: hafod@brynog.wanadoo.co.uk
dir: On A482 (Lampeter to Aberaeron road) in Ystrad Aeron. Entrance adjacent to Brynog Arms pub, opposite church

🚐 🚏 ⚠

Open Apr-Oct

Last arrival 21.00hrs Last departure noon

This peaceful, mainly adult park with fine views over the countryside is a perfect place to unwind, yet is within easy reach of the coastal resort of Aberaeron. The village pubs serve meals and are only a short walk from the park. 7 acre site. 30 touring pitches. 2 hardstandings. Caravan pitches. Motorhome pitches. Tent pitches. 40 statics.

AA Pubs & Restaurants nearby: The Harbourmaster, Aberaeron 01545 570755

Falcondale Hotel & Restaurant, Lampeter 01570 422910

Facilities: 🍴 ⊙ 🚿 🕙 🛒
Services: 🔌 🔄 🔋
Within 3 miles: 🏌 🛒
Notes: 🐾

CONWY

BETWS-YN-RHOS
Map 14 SH97

Places to visit

Denbigh Castle, DENBIGH 01745 813385
www.cadw.wales.gov.uk

►►►► 79% Hunters Hamlet Caravan Park (SH928736)

Sirior Goch Farm LL22 8PL
☎ 01745 832237 & 07721 552106
e-mail: huntershamlet@aol.com
web: www.huntershamlet.co.uk
dir: From A55 W'bound, A547 into Abergele. At 2nd lights turn left by George & Dragon pub, onto A548. 2.75m right at x-rds onto B5381. Site 0.5m on left

🚐 £17-£27 🚏

Open 21 Mar-Oct

Last arrival 22.00hrs Last departure noon

A quiet working farm park next to the owners' Georgian farmhouse. Pitches are in two grassy paddocks with pleasant views, and the beach is three miles away. The very good toilets, including unisex bathrooms, are kept in spotless condition. Please note that this site does not accept tents. 2 acre site. 23 touring pitches. 23 hardstandings. Caravan pitches. Motorhome pitches.

AA Pubs & Restaurants nearby: Wheatsheaf Inn, Betws-Yn-Rhos 01492 680218

Leisure: 🎇
Facilities: 🛁 🍴 ⊙ 🚿 🕙 ♿ W-fi ♻ ❓
Services: 🔌 🔄 🔋 🛒
Within 3 miles: 🏌 🛒

Notes: No football, dogs must be kept on leads and not left unattended. Baby bath & changing facilities.

BETWS-YN-RHOS *continued*

►►►► 79% *Plas Farm Caravan Park* (SH897744)

GOLD

LL22 8AU
☎ **01492 680254** & **07831 482176**
e-mail: info@plasfarmcaravanpark.co.uk
dir: *A547 Abergele, right Rhyd y Foel Rd, 3m then left signed B5381, 1st farm on right*

⊞ ⊞ Å

Open Mar-Oct

Last departure 11.00hrs

A small, quiet caravan park on a working farm, surrounded by rolling countryside and farmland. The park continues to improve, with an additional field with 20 excellent pitches and a separate amenities block for the 2011 season, plus 4,000 trees and shrubs have been planted. It is an ideal holiday location for both families and couples, with its modern facilities, fully-serviced pitches, and well-equipped children's play area, as well as spacious fields to roam through. The park is close to Bodnant Gardens and glorious beaches. 10 acre site. 40 touring pitches. 40 hardstandings. Caravan pitches. Motorhome pitches. Tent pitches.

AA Pubs & Restaurants nearby: Wheatsheaf Inn, Betws-Yn-Rhos 01492 680218

Leisure: ⚠

Facilities: ⚫⊙☂✳⚭⚪⚙☐☍✈ⓦ

Services: ⚫⚙⚭☐⚒⚘⚙

Within 3 miles: ⚭☐⚮⚙⚭

Notes: Cycle hire, dog kennels available.

NEW ►►► 78% Peniarth Bach Farm
(SH926737)

Roadside LL22 8PL
☎ **07545 572744**
e-mail: geoff-wilson@btinternet.com
dir: *A55 junct 25, left into Abergele. Left at lights onto B5381 towards Llanfairth. Right after 3m signed Betws-yn-Rhos. Site signed on right*

⊞ ⊞ Å

Open Mar-Oct

Last arrival flexible Last departure 11.00hrs

New for the 2011 season and part of a working farm which also offers quality stone holiday cottages for hire. Most pitches are hardstanding, with electric hook-up and water supply, and the smart purpose-built amenities block provides modern and efficient facilities. 40 acre site. 38 touring pitches. 15 hardstandings. Caravan pitches. Motorhome pitches. Tent pitches.

AA Pubs & Restaurants nearby: Wheatsheaf Inn, Betws-Yn-Rhos 01492 680218

Hawk & Buckle Inn, Llannefydd 01745 540249

Kinmel Arms, Abergele 01745 832207

Facilities: ⚫⊙☂✳⚭⚪☐✈ⓦⓡ♺⚙

Services: ⚫⚙☐⚒⚘

Within 3 miles: ⚭✣☐⚮⊚⚭⚙⚭⚙∪

Notes: ⊘ No noise after mdnt. Dogs must be kept on leads. Family room.

LLANDDULAS

Places to visit

Great Orme Bronze Age Copper Mines, LLANDUDNO 01492 870447 www.greatormemines.info

Bodelwyddan Castle, BODELWYDDAN 01745 584060 www.bodelwyddan-castle.co.uk

---

LLANDDULAS   Map 14 SH97

PREMIER PARK

►►►►► 83% Bron-Y-Wendon Caravan Park *(SH903785)*

Wern Rd LL22 8HG
☎ **01492 512903** ▤ 01492 512903
e-mail: stay@northwales-holidays.co.uk
dir: *Take A55 W. Turn right at sign for Llanddulas A547 junct 23, then sharp right. 200yds, under A55 bridge. Park on left*

* ⊞ £20-£23 ⊞ £20-£23

Open all year

Last arrival anytime Last departure 11.00hrs

A top quality site in a stunning location, with panoramic sea views from every pitch and excellent purpose-built toilet facilities including heated shower blocks. Pitch density is excellent, offering a high degree of privacy, and the grounds are beautifully landscaped and immaculately maintained. Staff are helpful and friendly, and everything from landscaping to maintenance has a stamp of excellence. An ideal seaside base for touring Snowdonia and visiting Colwyn Bay, Llandudno and Conwy. 8 acre site. 130 touring pitches. 85 hardstandings. Caravan pitches. Motorhome pitches.

AA Pubs & Restaurants nearby: Pen-y-Bryn, Colwyn Bay 01492 533360

Leisure: ⚲

Facilities: ⚫⊙☂✳⚭⚙⚘⚙ⓦ⚑♺⚙

Services: ⚫⚙⚭⚘⚙

Within 3 miles: ⚭✣⚮⚭⚙⚭∪

Notes: Dogs must be kept on leads.

LLANRWST

Places to visit

Gwydyr Uchaf Chapel, LLANRWST 01492 640578 www.cadw.wales.gov.uk

Dolwyddelan Castle, DOLWYDDELAN 01690 750366 www.cadw.wales.gov.uk

Great for kids: Conwy Valley Railway Museum, BETWS-Y-COED 01690 710568 www.conwyrailwaymuseum.co.uk

---

LEISURE: 🏊 Indoor swimming pool   🏊 Outdoor swimming pool   ⚠ Children's playground   🚩 Kid's club   🎾 Tennis court   ⚲ Games room   📺 Separate TV room
⚮ 9/18 hole golf course   ⚓ Boats for hire   🎬 Cinema   🎵 Entertainment   🎣 Fishing   ⚬ Mini golf   🌊 Watersports   🏌 Gym   ⚙ Sports field   **Spa**   ∪ Stables
FACILITIES: 🛁 Bath   🚿 Shower   ⊙ Electric shaver   ☂ Hairdryer   ✳ Ice Pack Facility   ⚭ Disabled facilities   ⚙ Public telephone   ☐ Shop on site or within 200yds
🏪 Mobile shop (calls at least 5 days a week)   🍖 BBQ area   🏕 Picnic area   ⓦ Wi-fi   💻 Internet access   ♺ Recycling   ⓘ Tourist info   ✈ Dog exercise area

LLANRWST
Map 14 SH86

PREMIER PARK

▶▶▶▶▶ 85% Bron Derw Touring Caravan Park *(SH798628)*

LL26 0YT
☎ 01492 640494 📠 01492 640494
e-mail: bronderw@aol.com
web: www.bronderw-wales.co.uk
dir: *A55 onto A470 for Betwys-y-Coed & Llanwrst. In Llanwrst left into Parry Rd signed Llanddoged. Left at T-junct, site signed at 1st farm entrance on right*

🚐 £18-£20 🚃 £18-£20

Open Mar-Oct

Last arrival 22.00hrs Last departure 11.00hrs

Surrounded by hills and beautifully landscaped from what was once a dairy farm, Bron Derw has been built to a very high standard and is fully matured, with stunning flora and fauna displays. All pitches are fully serviced, and there is a heated, stone-built toilet block with excellent and immaculately maintained facilities. The new Parc Derwen adults-only field opened in 2011, complete with 23 fully serviced pitches and its own designated amenities block. CCTV security cameras cover the whole park. 4.5 acre site. 43 touring pitches. 43 hardstandings. 15 seasonal pitches. Caravan pitches. Motorhome pitches.

AA Pubs & Restaurants nearby: Ty Gwyn Inn, Betws-Y-Coed 01690 710383

Facilities: 🏪⊙🅿🔥🅾🚿🐴♻ 🄯

Services: 🔌🗄 �🔧

Within 3 miles: ✎🏠🗄

Notes: Children must be supervised, no bikes, scooters or skateboards. Dogs must be kept on leads.

▶▶▶▶ 81% *Bodnant Caravan Park*

(SH805609)

Nebo Rd LL26 0SD
☎ 01492 640248
e-mail: ermin@bodnant-caravan-park.co.uk
dir: *S in Llanrwst, exit A470 opposite Birmingham garage onto B5427 signed Nebo. Site 300yds on right, opposite leisure centre*

🚐 🚃 Å

Open Mar-end Oct

Last arrival 21.00hrs Last departure 11.00hrs

This well maintained and stunningly attractive park is filled with flower beds, and the landscape includes shrubberies and trees. The statics are unobtrusively sited and the quality toilet blocks are spotlessly clean, with the fully serviced private cubicles refurbished for 2011. All caravan pitches are multi-service, and the tent pitches serviced. There is a separate playing field and rally field, and there are lots of farm animals on the park to keep children entertained, and Victorian farming implements are on display around the touring fields. 5 acre site. 54 touring pitches. 20 hardstandings. Caravan pitches. Motorhome pitches. Tent pitches. 2 statics.

AA Pubs & Restaurants nearby: Ty Gwyn Inn, Betws-Y-Coed 01690 710383

Facilities: 🏪⊙🅿🔥🅾🐴

Services: 🔌🗄🚿

Within 3 miles: ↨✎🏠🗄

Notes: No bikes or skateboards. Main gates locked 23.00hrs-08.00hrs, no noise after 23.00hrs.

TAL-Y-BONT (NEAR CONWY)
Map 14 SH76

Places to visit

Bodnant Garden, TAL-Y-CAFN 01492 650460 www.bodnant-garden.co.uk

Great for kids: Smallest House, CONWY 01492 593484

▶ 89% Tynterfyn Touring Caravan Park *(SH768695)*

LL32 8YX
☎ 01492 660525
dir: *5m S of Conwy on B5106, signed Tal-y-Bont, 1st on left*

* 🚐 fr £12 🚃 fr £12 Å fr £5

Open Mar-Oct (rs 28 days in year tent pitches only)

Last arrival 22.00hrs Last departure noon

A quiet, secluded little park set in the beautiful Conwy Valley, and run by family owners. The grounds are tended with care, and the older-style toilet facilities sparkle. There is lots of room for children and dogs to run around. 2 acre site. 15 touring pitches. 4 hardstandings. Caravan pitches. Motorhome pitches. Tent pitches.

Leisure: ⚙☺

Facilities: 🏪⊙🅿🔥🐴♻ 🄯

Services: 🔌🛒🗄🚿🚂

Within 3 miles: ↨✎🏠

Notes: ☺ Dogs must be kept on leads.

TOWYN (NEAR ABERGELE)

Places to visit

Rhuddlan Castle, RHUDDLAN 01745 590777 www.cadw.wales.gov.uk

Great for kids: Welsh Mountain Zoo, COLWYN BAY 01492 532938 www.welshmountainzoo.org

---

SERVICES: 🔌 Electric hook up 🗄 Launderette 🍺 Licensed bar ▪ Calor Gas ⊘ Camping Gaz 🚽 Toilet fluid 🍽 Café/Restaurant 🍟 Fast Food/Takeaway 🔋 Battery charging 🍼 Baby care 🚐 Motorvan service point
ABBREVIATIONS: BH/bank hols-bank holidays Etr-Easter Whit-Whitsun dep-departure fr-from hrs-hours m-mile mdnt-midnight rdbt-roundabout rs-restricted service wk-week wknd-weekend ⊛ No credit cards ⊗ No dogs
See page 7 for details of the AA Camping Card Scheme

TOWYN (NEAR ABERGELE) Map 14 SH97

  73% Ty Mawr Holiday Park (SH965792)

Towyn Rd LL22 9HG
☎ 01745 832079 📠 01745 827454
e-mail: admin.tymawr@parkresorts.com
dir: On A548, 0.25m W of Towyn

Open Apr-Oct (rs Apr (excluding Etr))

Last arrival mdnt Last departure 10.00hrs

A very large coastal holiday park with extensive leisure facilities including sports and recreational amenities (the indoor swimming pool was refurbished in 2011), and club and eating outlets. The toilet facilities in The Warren have also been refurbished to a high standard. Ideally located for both Rhyl's attractions and the nearby historical site of Rhuddlan Castle. 18 acre site. 406 touring pitches. Caravan pitches. Motorhome pitches. Tent pitches. 464 statics.

AA Pubs & Restaurants nearby: Kinmel Arms, Abergele 01745 832207

Barratt's at Ty'n Rhyl, Rhyl 01745 344138

Leisure: 🏊 🎠 👶 🎾 🏹 🎵
Facilities: 📡 ⊙ 🔥 🍴 ⏰ 🏠 🚿 🔌 wifi 💻
Services: 🔌 🛒 🍴 🍽 ♿
Within 3 miles: ⛳ 🎬 🎡 🛒 🍴 🐴

see advert below

DENBIGHSHIRE

CORWEN Map 15 SJ04

See also Llandrillo

Places to visit

Rug Chapel, CORWEN 01490 412025
www.cadw.wales.gov.uk

Ewe-Phoria Sheepdog Centre, CORWEN
01490 460369 www.ewe-phoria.co.uk

▶▶ **70% Llawr-Betws Farm Caravan Park** (SJ016424)

LL21 0HD
☎ 01490 460224 & 460296
dir: 3m W of Corwen off A494 (Bala road)

🚐 🚙 🏕

Open Mar-Oct

Last arrival 23.00hrs Last departure noon

A quiet grassy park with mature trees and gently sloping pitches. The friendly owners keep the

facilities in good condition. 12.5 acre site. 35 touring pitches. Caravan pitches. Motorhome pitches. Tent pitches. 68 statics.

Leisure: 🎠 🎾
Facilities: 📡 ⊙ 🔥 🏠 🚿 🐴
Services: 🔌 🛒 🔥 💧 🚽 ♿
Within 3 miles: ⛳ 🛒 🍴
Notes: 🎣 Fishing.

LLANDRILLO Map 15 SJ03

Places to visit

Chirk Castle, CHIRK 01691 777701
www.nationaltrust.org.uk/main/w-chirkcastle

Rug Chapel, CORWEN 01490 412025
www.cadw.wales.gov.uk

▶▶▶ **77% Hendwr Country Park** (SJ042386)

LL21 0SN
☎ 01490 440210
dir: From Corwen (A5) take B4401 for 4m. Right at Hendwr sign. Site 0.5m on right down wooded driveway. Or follow brown signs from A5 at Corwen

* 🚐 £18-£20 🚙 £18-£20 🏕 £18-£20

Open Apr-Oct

Last arrival 22.00hrs Last departure 16.00hrs

Set in parkland at the end of a tree-lined lane, Hendwr (it means 'old tower') has a stream meandering through its grounds, and all around is the stunning Snowdonia mountain range. The toilet facilities are good. Self-catering holiday

LEISURE: 🏊 Indoor swimming pool 🏊 Outdoor swimming pool 🎠 Children's playground 👶 Kid's club 🎾 Tennis court 🎱 Games room 📺 Separate TV room ⛳ 9/18 hole golf course 🚤 Boats for hire 🎬 Cinema 🎵 Entertainment 🎣 Fishing 🏌 Mini golf 🏄 Watersports 🏋 Gym 🏉 Sports field **Spa** 🐴 Stables
FACILITIES: 🛁 Bath 🚿 Shower ⊙ Electric shaver 🔥 Hairdryer ❄ Ice Pack Facility ♿ Disabled facilities 📞 Public telephone 🛒 Shop on site or within 200yds 🚐 Mobile shop (calls at least 5 days a week) 🍴 BBQ area 🏠 Picnic area wifi Wi-fi 💻 Internet access ♻ Recycling ℹ Tourist info 🐕 Dog exercise area

lodges are available. 11 acre site. 40 touring pitches. 3 hardstandings. 26 seasonal pitches. Caravan pitches. Motorhome pitches. Tent pitches. 80 statics.

Facilities: 📶⊙❄🖳🎣🐾♻ ❼

Services: 🔌🗑🔥⌀🚽💺⛽

Within 3 miles: ✎🖳

Notes: Dogs must be kept on leads. Wet weather camping facilities.

LLANGOLLEN   Map 15 SJ24

Places to visit

Plas Newydd, LLANGOLLEN 01978 861314 www.denbighshire.gov.uk

Valle Crucis Abbey, LLANGOLLEN 01978 860326 www.cadw.wales.gov.uk

Great for kids: Llangollen Railway, LLANGOLLEN 01978 860979 www.llangollen-railway.co.uk

---

▶▶ 76% Ty-Ucha Caravan Park

(SJ232415)

Maesmawr Rd LL20 7PP

☎ 01978 860677

dir: *1m E of Llangollen. Signed 250yds off A5*

* 🔌 fr £11 🚐 fr £10

Open Etr-Oct

Last arrival 22.00hrs Last departure 13.00hrs

A very spacious site in beautiful unspoilt surroundings, with a small stream on site, and superb views. Ideal for country and mountain walking, and handily placed near the A5. Pitch density is excellent, facilities are clean and well maintained, and there is a games room with table tennis. Please note that this site does not accept tents. 4 acre site. 40 touring pitches. Caravan pitches. Motorhome pitches.

Leisure: ⊙🔍

Facilities: 📶⊙❼

Services: 🔌

Within 3 miles: ↓≉🎃✎≥🔒🗑∪

Notes: ⊗ Dogs must be kept on leads.

PRESTATYN   Map 15 SJ08

Places to visit

Basingwerk Abbey, HOLYWELL 01443 336000 www.cadw.wales.gov.uk

Great for kids: Rhuddlan Castle, RHUDDLAN 01745 590777 www.cadw.wales.gov.uk

---

78% Presthaven Sands

(SJ091842)

Gronant LL19 9TT

☎ 0871 231 0888   ▤ 01745 886646

e-mail: presthavensands@haven.com

dir: *A548 from Prestatyn towards Gronant. Site signed. (NB For Sat Nav use LL19 9ST)*

🔌🚐

Open mid Mar-end Oct (rs mid Mar-May & Sep-Oct facilities may be reduced)

Last arrival 20.00hrs Last departure 10.00hrs

Set beside two miles of superb sandy beaches and dunes, this large holiday centre offers extensive leisure and sports facilities and lively entertainment for all the family. The leisure complex houses clubs, swimming pools (with a new 'Lazy River' attraction for 2011), restaurants, shops, launderette and pub, and the touring area is separate from the much larger static section. 21 acre site. 34 touring pitches. Caravan pitches. Motorhome pitches. 1052 statics.

AA Pubs & Restaurants nearby: Nant Hall Restaurant & Bar, Prestatyn 01745 886766

Leisure: 🏊⚽♨👣

Facilities: 📶⊙♿🕐🗑🚻

Services: 🔌🗑🔥🍴💺⛽

Within 3 miles: ↓🎃✎◎🔒🗑∪

Notes: Max 2 dogs per booking, certain dog breeds banned, no commercial vehicles, no bookings by persons under 21yrs unless a family booking. Dogs must be kept on leads.

RHUALLT   Map 15 SJ07

Places to visit

Rhuddlan Castle, RHUDDLAN 01745 590777 www.cadw.wales.gov.uk

Bodelwyddan Castle, BODELWYDDAN 01745 584060 www.bodelwyddan-castle.co.uk

Great for kids: Denbigh Castle, DENBIGH 01745 813385 www.cadw.wales.gov.uk

---

AA CAMPING CARD SITE

▶▶▶▶ 89% Penisar Mynydd Caravan Park (SJ093770)

Caerwys Rd LL17 0TY

☎ 01745 582227   & 07831 408017

▤ 01745 582227

e-mail: contact@penisarmynydd.co.uk

web: www.penisarmynydd.co.uk

dir: *From A55 junct 29 follow Dyserth & brown caravan signs. Site 500yds on right*

🔌 £15-£17 🚐 £15 ⛺ £12

Open Mar-15 Jan

Last arrival 21.00hrs Last departure 21.00hrs

A very tranquil, attractively laid-out park set in three grassy paddocks with superb facilities block including a disabled room and dishwashing area. The majority of pitches are super pitches. Everything is immaculately maintained, and the amenities of the seaside resort of Rhyl are close by. 6.6 acre site. 75 touring pitches. 75 hardstandings. Caravan pitches. Motorhome pitches. Tent pitches.

AA Pubs & Restaurants nearby: Plough Inn, St Asaph 01745 585080

Leisure: ⊙

Facilities: 📶⊙❄♿🕐🕯🎣🐾🚻 ♻ ❼

Services: 🔌🗑 🔥💺⛽

Within 3 miles: ↓🎃✎◎≥🔒🗑∪

Notes: ⊗ No cycling. Dogs must be kept on leads. Rally area.

SERVICES: 🔌 Electric hook up 🗑 Launderette 🔥 Licensed bar 🛢 Calor Gas ⌀ Camping Gaz ⊤ Toilet fluid 🍴 Café/Restaurant 🍟 Fast Food/Takeaway 💺 Battery charging 🍼 Baby care ⛽ Motorvan service point

ABBREVIATIONS: BH/bank hols-bank holidays Etr-Easter Whit-Whitsun dep-departure fr-from hrs-hours m-mile mdnt-midnight rdbt-roundabout rs-restricted service wk-week wknd-weekend ⊗ No credit cards ⊗ No dogs

See page 7 for details of the AA Camping Card Scheme

RUABON
Map 15 SJ34

Places to visit

Plas Newydd, LLANGOLLEN 01978 861314 www.denbighshire.gov.uk

Valle Crucis Abbey, LLANGOLLEN 01978 860326 www.cadw.wales.gov.uk

Great for kids: Horse Drawn Boats Centre, LLANGOLLEN 01978 860702 www.horsedrawnboats.co.uk

►►► 73% James' Caravan Park
(SJ300434)

LL14 6DW
☎ 01978 820148   📄 01978 820148
e-mail: ray@carastay.demon.co.uk
dir: *Approach on A483 South, at rdbt with A539, turn right (signed Llangollen) over dual carriageway bridge, site 500yds on left*

* 🚐 fr £15 🚐 fr £15

Open all year

Last arrival 21.00hrs Last departure 11.00hrs

A well-landscaped park on a former farm, with modern heated toilet facilities. Old farm buildings house a collection of restored original farm machinery, and the village shop, four pubs, takeaway and launderette are a 10-minute walk away. 6 acre site. 40 touring pitches. 4 hardstandings. Caravan pitches. Motorhome pitches.

Facilities: 🍴⊙ 🅿 🌣 & 🕓 🐾
Services: 🔌🔒 ⊘ 🖾
Within 3 miles: ⅃ 🏤 🖾

Notes: 🐕 Dogs must be kept on leads. Chest freezer available.

GWYNEDD

See Walk 14 in the Walks & Cycle Rides section at the end of the guide

ABERSOCH
Map 14 SH32

Places to visit

Plas-yn-Rhiw, PLAS YN RHIW 01758 780219 www.nationaltrust.org.uk

Penarth Fawr, PENARTH FAWR 01443 336000 www.cadw.wales.gov.uk

Great for kids: Criccieth Castle, CRICCIETH 01766 522227 www.cadw.wales.gov.uk

►►►► 81% Beach View Caravan Park *(SH316262)*

Bwlchtocyn LL53 7BT
☎ 01758 712956
dir: *Through Abersoch & Sarn Bach. Over x-rds, next left signed Porthtocyn Hotel. Pass chapel to another Porthtocyn Hotel sign. Turn left, site on left*

🚐 🚐 ▲

Open mid Mar-mid Oct

Last arrival 19.00hrs Last departure 11.00hrs

A compact family park run by a very enthusiastic owner who makes continual improvements. Just a six-minute walk from the beach, the site's immaculately maintained grounds, good hardstanding pitches (mostly seasonal) and excellent facilities are matched by great sea and country views. 4 acre site. 47 touring pitches. Caravan pitches. Motorhome pitches. Tent pitches.

AA Pubs & Restaurants nearby: Porth Tocyn Hotel, Abersoch 01758 713303

Neigwl Hotel, Abersoch 01758 712363

Facilities: 🍴⊙ 🅿 🖙
Services: 🔌🔒 ⊘
Within 3 miles: ⅃ 🏤 🖋 🖾 🏤 🕓
Notes: 🐕 Dogs must be kept on leads.

AA CAMPING CARD SITE

►►►► 79% *Deucoch Touring & Camping Park* *(SH301269)*

Sarn Bach LL53 7LD
☎ 01758 713293 & 07740 281770
📄 01758 713293
e-mail: info@deucoch.com
dir: *From Abersoch take Sarn Bach road, at x-rds turn right, site on right in 800yds*

🚐 🚐 ▲

Open Mar-Oct

Last arrival 22.00hrs Last departure 11.00hrs

A sheltered site with sweeping views of Cardigan Bay and the mountains, just a mile from Abersoch and a long sandy beach. The facilities block is well maintained and has new outdoor hot showers for washing wet suits. This site is of special interest to watersports enthusiasts and those touring the Llyn Peninsula. 5 acre site. 70 touring pitches. 10 hardstandings. Caravan pitches. Motorhome pitches. Tent pitches.

AA Pubs & Restaurants nearby: Porth Tocyn Hotel, Abersoch 01758 713303

Neigwl Hotel, Abersoch 01758 712363

Leisure: ⏲ 🔍
Facilities: 🍴⊙ 🅿 🌣 & 🕓 ⊘
Services: 🔌🔒 ⊘
Within 3 miles: ⅃ 🏤 🖋 🖾 🏤 🕓
Notes: 🐕 Families only.

►►► 82% Tyn-y-Mur Touring & Camping *(SH304290)*

Lon Garmon LL53 7UL
☎ 01758 712328
e-mail: info@tyn-y-mur.co.uk
dir: *From Pwllheli into Abersoch on A499, sharp right at Land & Sea Garage. Site approx 0.5m on left*

* 🚐 £25 🚐 £25 ▲ £18-£25

Open Apr-Oct

Last arrival 22.00hrs Last departure 11.00hrs

A family-only park in a glorious hill-top location overlooking a lush valley and with views extending across Abersoch to the mountains beyond Cardigan Bay. Good, clean modernised toilet facilities and spacious tent pitches in a level grassy field. The beach at Abersoch is just a short walk away and the park offers boat storage facilities. 22 acre site. 50 touring pitches. 37 hardstandings. Caravan pitches. Motorhome pitches. Tent pitches.

AA Pubs & Restaurants nearby: Porth Tocyn Hotel, Abersoch 01758 713303

Neigwl Hotel, Abersoch 01758 712363

Leisure: ⏲ ⚙
Facilities: 🍴⊙ 🌣 & 🕓 🖙 ⊘ ⓘ
Services: 🔌🔒 ⊘ 🖵 🖾 🧺
Within 3 miles: ⅃ 🏤 🖋 🖾 🏤 🕓
Notes: 🐕 No open fires, no motorcycles, no noisy activity after 23.00hrs, 1 dog per unit. Dogs must be kept on leads.

LEISURE: 🏊 Indoor swimming pool 🏊 Outdoor swimming pool ⏲ Children's playground 🪁 Kid's club 🎾 Tennis court 🎱 Games room 📺 Separate TV room ⅃ 9/18 hole golf course 🚣 Boats for hire 🎬 Cinema 🎵 Entertainment 🎣 Fishing ⛳ Mini golf 🤿 Watersports 🏋 Gym ⚽ Sports field Spa 🕓 Stables
FACILITIES: 🛁 Bath 🍴 Shower ⊙ Electric shaver 🅿 Hairdryer 🌣 Ice Pack Facility & Disabled facilities 🕓 Public telephone 🏬 Shop on site or within 200yds 🏪 Mobile shop (calls at least 5 days a week) 🍖 BBQ area 🏕 Picnic area 📶 Wi-Fi 💻 Internet access ♻ Recycling ⓘ Tourist info 🖙 Dog exercise area

►►► 79% Bryn Bach Caravan & Camping Site *(SH315258)*

Tyddyn Talgoch Uchaf, Bwlchtocyn LL53 7BT
☎ 01758 712285 & 07789 390808
e-mail: brynbach@abersochcamping.co.uk
dir: From Abersoch take Sarn Bach road for approx 1m, left at sign for Bwlchtocyn. Site approx 1m on left

⚑ ⛺ Å

Open Mar-Oct

Last arrival 20.00hrs Last departure 11.00hrs

This well-run, elevated park overlooks Abersoch Bay, with lovely sea views towards the Snowdonia mountain range. Pitches are well laid out in sheltered paddocks, with well-placed modern facilities. Fishing, watersports, golf and beach access are all nearby. 4 acre site. 8 touring pitches. 1 hardstanding. 30 seasonal pitches. Caravan pitches. Motorhome pitches. Tent pitches. 2 statics.

AA Pubs & Restaurants nearby: Porth Tocyn Hotel, Abersoch 01758 713303

Neigwl Hotel, Abersoch 01758 712363

Leisure: ⚑

Facilities: ⛏ ⌂ ⊙ ⚡ ✳ ⚷ ⎍ WiFi ♻ ❶

Services: ⚡ ⓢ 🔋 ⌀ ⊡ ⚓

Within 3 miles: ⌿ ⚷ ⌿ ⚓ ⓢ ⓢ ∪

Notes: Families & couples only. Dogs must be kept on leads. Private shortcut to beach, boat storage.

►►► 70% Tanrallt Farm *(SH296288)*

Tanrallt, Llangian LL53 7LN
☎ 01758 713527
e-mail: www.abersoch-holiday.co.uk
dir: A499 to Abersoch, right up hill, follow signs for Llangian. Site in village on left

⚑ ⛺ Å

Open Etr-end Oct

Last arrival 21.30hrs Last departure 10.30hrs

Tanrallt Farm site is in a secluded valley on a working farm. Friendly owners make their guests feel welcome, providing a BBQ area, very clean and serviceable toilets, a laundry room with washer, dryer, spin dryer, iron and ironing board plus a drying area for wet clothing. There are also

three bunk rooms and a kitchen. 1.5 acre site. 12 touring pitches. 12 hardstandings. Caravan pitches. Motorhome pitches. Tent pitches.

Tanrallt Farm

AA Pubs & Restaurants nearby: Porth Tocyn Hotel, Abersoch 01758 713303

Neigwl Hotel, Abersoch 01758 712363

Facilities: ⌂ ✳ ⚷ ⓢ ⎍

Services: ⚡ ⓢ ⚓ ⚓

Within 3 miles: ⌿ ⚷ ⌿ ◎ ⚓ ⓢ ⓢ ∪

Notes: ⊗ Families & couples only. No noise after 23.00hrs.

►►► 69% Rhydolion *(SH283276)*

Rhydolion, Llangian LL53 7LR
☎ 01758 712342
e-mail: enquiries@rhydolion.co.uk
dir: From A499 take unclassified road to Llangian for 1m, turn left, through Llangian. Site 1.5m after road fork towards Hell's Mouth/Porth Neigwl

* ⚑ £15-£25 Å £12-£16

Open Mar-Oct

Last arrival 22.00hrs Last departure noon

A peaceful small site with good views, on a working farm close to the long sandy surfers beach at Hell's Mouth. The simple, revamped toilet facilities are kept to a high standard by the friendly owners, and nearby Abersoch is a mecca for boat owners and water sports enthusiasts. 1.5 acre site. 20 touring pitches. Caravan pitches. Tent pitches.

AA Pubs & Restaurants nearby: Porth Tocyn Hotel, Abersoch 01758 713303

Neigwl Hotel, Abersoch 01758 712363

Leisure: ⚑ ⊗

Facilities: ⌂ ⊙ ✳ ⌁ ♻ ❶

Services: ⚡ ⓢ ⚓

Within 3 miles: ⌿ ⚷ ⌿ ◎ ⚓ ⓢ ⓢ ∪

Notes: ⊜ Families & couples only, dogs by arrangement only. Dogs must be kept on leads. 3 fridge freezers.

Places to visit

Bala Lake Railway, LLANUWCHLLYN
01678 540666 www.bala-lake-railway.co.uk

Rug Chapel, CORWEN 01490 412025
www.cadw.wales.gov.uk

Great for kids: Ewe-Phoria Sheepdog Centre, CORWEN 01490 460369 www.ewe-phoria.co.uk

---

►►►► 81% Pen-y-Bont Touring Park *(SH932350)*

Llangynog Rd LL23 7PH
☎ 01678 520549 📠 01678 520006
e-mail: penybont-bala@btconnect.com
dir: From A494 take B4391. Site 0.75m on right

⚑ ⛺ Å

Open Mar-Oct

Last arrival 21.00hrs Last departure noon

A family run attractively landscaped park in a woodland country setting. Set close to Bala Lake and the River Dee, with plenty of opportunities for water sports including kayaking and white water rafting. The park offers good facilities including a motorhome service point, and many pitches have water and electricity. Around the park are superb large wood carvings of birds and mythical creatures depicting local legends. New for 2011 are ready-erected tents for hire. 7 acre site. 95 touring pitches. 59 hardstandings. Caravan pitches. Motorhome pitches. Tent pitches. 1 bell tents/yurts.

Facilities: ⌂ ⊙ ⚡ ✳ ⚷ ⊗ ⓢ ⌂ ⎍ ⥺ WiFi ♻ ❶

Services: ⚡ ⓢ 🔋 ⌀ ⊡ ⚓ ⚓

Within 3 miles: ⌿ ⚷ ⽥ ⌿ ⚓ ⓢ ⓢ

Notes: No camp fires. BBQs must be kept off ground, quiet after 22.30hrs. Dogs must be kept on leads.

BALA *continued*

AA CAMPING CARD SITE

▶▶▶▶ **79% Tyn Cornel Camping & Caravan Park** *(SH895400)*

Frongoch LL23 7NU
☎ **01678 520759**
e-mail: tyncornel@mail.com
dir: *From Bala take A4212 (Porthmadog road) for 4m. Site on left before National White Water Centre*

* ⊕ £14-£18 ⊕ £16-£18 ▲ £14-£20

Open Etr-Oct

Last arrival 20.00hrs Last departure 11.00hrs

A delightful riverside park with mountain views, popular with those seeking a base for river kayaks and canoes, with access to the nearby White Water Centre and riverside walk with tearoom. The helpful, resident owners keep the modern facilities, including a laundry and dishwashing room, very clean. 10 acre site. 67 touring pitches. 10 hardstandings. Caravan pitches. Motorhome pitches. Tent pitches.

Leisure: ☺

Facilities: ♠⊙☏✱๕☉🗄♨≻✻📶♻❶

Services: ⊕🖵💧⏃⛟

Within 3 miles: ↨⚞⯀⌨⟋🍽🎱🎰

Notes: Quiet after 23.00hrs, no cycling, no camp fires or wood burning. Dogs must be kept on leads. Fridge, freezer & tumble dryer available.

▶▶▶ **68% Treborth Hall Farm Caravan Park** *(SH554707)*

The Old Barn, Treborth Hall Farm LL57 2RX
☎ **01248 364399** 📠 **01248 364333**
e-mail: enquiries@treborthleisure.co.uk
dir: *A55 junct 9, 1st left at rdbt, straight over 2nd rdbt, site approx 800yds on left*

⊕ ⊕ ▲

Open Etr-end Oct

Last arrival 22.30hrs Last departure 10.30hrs

Set in eight acres of beautiful parkland with its own trout fishing lake and golf course, this park offers serviced pitches in a sheltered, walled orchard. Tents have a separate grass area, and there is a good clean toilet block. This is a useful base for families, with easy access for the Menai Straits, Anglesey beaches, Snowdon and the Lleyn peninsula. 8 acre site. 34 touring pitches. 34 hardstandings. Caravan pitches. Motorhome pitches. Tent pitches. 4 statics.

Leisure: ⚠

Facilities: ♠☉≻

Services: ⊕

Within 3 miles: ↨⟋◎🍽🎱🎰

Notes: Dogs must be kept on leads.

PREMIER PARK

▶▶▶▶▶ **91% Trawsdir Touring Caravans & Camping Park** *(SH596198)*   Best of British

Llanaber LL42 1RR
☎ **01341 280611 & 280999** 📠 **01341 280740**
e-mail: enquiries@barmouthholidays.co.uk
web: www.barmouthholidays.co.uk
dir: *3m N of Barmouth on A496, just past Wayside pub on right*

* ⊕ £15-£30 ⊕ £15-£30 ▲ £10-£25

Open Mar-Jan

Last arrival 20.00hrs Last departure noon

Well run by enthusiastic wardens, this quality park enjoys spectacular views to the sea and hills, and is very accessible to motor traffic. The facilities are appointed to a very high standard, and include spacious cubicles containing showers and washbasins, individual showers, smart toilets with sensor-operated flush, and under-floor heating. Tents and caravans have their own designated areas divided by dry-stone walls (both have spacious fully serviced pitches) and the site is very convenient for large recreational vehicles. There is an excellent children's play area, plus glorious seasonal floral displays and an illuminated dog walk that leads directly to the nearby pub! There are also luxury holiday lodges for hire. 15 acre site. 70 touring pitches. 70 hardstandings. Caravan pitches. Motorhome pitches. Tent pitches.

Leisure: ⚠

Facilities: ♠⊙☏✱๕🗄♨≻✻📶♻❶

Services: ⊕🖵💧⏃🛆Ⓣ🎪≻⛟

Within 3 miles: ⟋🍽🎱🎰

Notes: Families & couples only. Dogs must be kept on leads. Milk/bread etc available from reception, takeaway food can be delivered from sister site.

PREMIER PARK

►►►►► 82% **Hendre Mynach Touring Caravan & Camping Park**

(SH605170)

Llanaber Rd LL42 1YR
☎ 01341 280262 ▤ 01341 280586
e-mail: mynach@lineone.net
web: www.hendremynach.co.uk
dir: *0.75m N of Barmouth on A496*

⊞ ⊞ Å

Open Mar-9 Jan (rs Nov-Jan shop closed)

Last arrival 22.00hrs Last departure noon

A lovely site with enthusiastic owners and immaculate facilities, just off the A496 and near the railway, with almost direct access to the promenade and beach. Caravanners should not be put off by the steep descent, as park staff are always on hand if needed. Spacious pitches have TV and satellite hook-up as well as water and electricity. A small café serves light meals and takeaways. 10 acre site. 240 touring pitches. 75

hardstandings. Caravan pitches. Motorhome pitches. Tent pitches. 1 static.

Leisure: ⚠

Facilities: ⋒ ⊙ ⎙ ✳ ⅋ ⊙ ⑤ ⌀ WiFi 💻 ♻ ❼

Services: ⊞ ⑤ ⬤ ⊘ ⊺ ⎁ ⛟ ⬇

Within 3 miles: ⊞ ⅋ ⑤ ⑤ ∪

BETWS GARMON   Map 14 SH55

Places to visit

Snowdon Mountain Railway, LLANBERIS
01286 870223 www.snowdonrailway.co.uk

Great for kids: Dolbadarn Castle, LLANBERIS
01443 336000 www.cadw.wales.gov.uk

AA CAMPING CARD SITE

►►►► 79% **Bryn Gloch Caravan & Camping Park** *(SH534574)*

LL54 7YY
☎ 01286 650216
e-mail: eurig@bryngloch.co.uk
web: www.campwales.co.uk
dir: *On A4085, 5m SE of Caernarfon*

* ⊞ £15-£30 ⊞ £15-£30 Å £15-£30

Open all year

Last arrival 23.00hrs Last departure 17.00hrs

An excellent family-run site with immaculate modern facilities, and all level pitches in beautiful surroundings. The park offers the best of two worlds, with its bustling holiday atmosphere and the peaceful natural surroundings. The 28 acres of level fields are separated by mature hedges and

trees, guaranteeing sufficient space for families wishing to spread themselves out. There are static holiday caravans for hire and plenty of walks in the area. 28 acre site. 160 touring pitches. 60 hardstandings. 50 seasonal pitches. Caravan pitches. Motorhome pitches. Tent pitches. 17 statics.

Bryn Gloch Caravan & Camping Park

AA Pubs & Restaurants nearby: Snowdonia Parc Brewpub, Waunfawr 01286 650409

Leisure: ⚠ ⚲ ⛝

Facilities: ⬅ ⋒ ⊙ ⎙ ✳ ⅋ ⊙ ⑤ ⊓ ⋔ WiFi 💻 ♻ ❼

Services: ⊞ ⑤ ⬤ ⊘ ⊺ ⛟ ⬇

Within 3 miles: ↓ ⅋ ⅋ ◎ ⑤ ⑤ ∪

Notes: Dogs must be kept on leads. Family bathroom, mother & baby room.

see advert below

SERVICES: ⊞ Electric hook up ⑤ Launderette ⎁ Licensed bar ⬤ Calor Gas ⊘ Camping Gaz ⊺ Toilet fluid ⎁ Café/Restaurant ⛟ Fast Food/Takeaway ⬆ Battery charging ⬌ Baby care ⬇ Motorvan service point

ABBREVIATIONS: BH/bank hols-bank holidays Etr-Easter Whit-Whitsun dep-departure fr-from hrs-hours m-mile mdnt-midnight rdbt-roundabout rs-restricted service wk-week wknd-weekend ⊗ No credit cards ⊗ No dogs   See page 7 for details of the AA Camping Card Scheme

CAERNARFON Map 14 SH46

See also Dinas Dinlle & Llandwrog

Places to visit

Segontium Roman Museum, CAERNARFON 01286 675625 www.segontium.org.uk

Welsh Highland Railway, CAERNARFON 01286 677018 www.festrail.co.uk

Great for kids: Caernarfon Castle, CAERNARFON 01286 677617 www.cadw.wales.gov.uk

AA CAMPING CARD SITE

►►►► 82% Riverside Camping

(SH505630)

Seiont Nurseries, Pont Rug LL55 2BB
01286 678781 & 673276 01286 677223
e-mail: brenda@riversidecamping.co.uk
web: www.riversidecamping.co.uk
dir: *2m from Caernarfon on right of A4086 towards Llanberis, also signed Seiont Nurseries*

* £12-£19 £12-£19 £12-£19

Open Etr-end Oct

Last arrival anytime Last departure noon

Set in the grounds of a large garden centre beside the small River Seiont, this park is approached by an impressive tree-lined drive. Immaculately maintained by the owners, there are good grassy riverside tent pitches, clean and tidy toilet facilities and an excellent café/restaurant. A haven of peace close to Caernarfon, Snowdonia and some great walking opportunities. 4.5 acre site. 60 touring pitches. 8 hardstandings. 4 seasonal pitches. Caravan pitches. Motorhome pitches. Tent pitches.

AA Pubs & Restaurants nearby: Seiont Manor Hotel, Llanrug 01286 673366

Rhiwafallen Restaurant with Rooms, Llandwrog 01286 830172

Leisure:

Facilities:

Services:

Within 3 miles:

Notes: No fires, no loud music. Dogs must be kept on leads. Family shower room & baby changing facilities.

AA CAMPING CARD SITE

►►► 80% Plas Gwyn Caravan & Camping Park

(SH520633)

Llanrug LL55 2AQ
01286 672619
e-mail: info@plasgwyn.co.uk
web: www.plasgwyn.co.uk
dir: *A4086, 3m E of Caernarfon, site on right. Between River Seiont & Llanrug*

* £16-£19.50 £16-£19.50 £14-£17

Open Mar-Oct

Last arrival 22.00hrs Last departure 11.30hrs

A secluded park in an ideal location for visiting the glorious nearby beaches, historic Caernarfon, the Snowdonia attractions, and for walking. The site is set within the grounds of Plas Gwyn House, a Georgian property with colonial additions, and the friendly owners are gradually upgrading the park. There are four fully serviced pitches, two wooden camping tents with beds, kettle and fridge, and five static caravans for hire. 3 acre site. 42 touring pitches. 8 hardstandings. 8 seasonal pitches. Caravan pitches. Motorhome pitches. Tent pitches. 18 statics. 2 wooden pods.

AA Pubs & Restaurants nearby: Seiont Manor Hotel, Llanrug 01286 673366

Rhiwafallen Restaurant with Rooms, Llandwrog 01286 830172

Facilities:

Services:

Within 3 miles:

Notes: Minimal noise between 22.00hrs-mdnt, complete quiet between mdnt-08.00hrs.

►►► 79% Cwm Cadnant Valley

(SH487628)

Cwm Cadnant Valley, Llanberis Rd LL55 2DF
01286 673196 01286 675941
e-mail: aa@cwmcadnant.co.uk
web: www.cwmcadnant.co.uk
dir: *On outskirts of Caernarfon on A4086 towards Llanberis, next to fire station*

* £12.50-£19.50 £12.50-£19.50 £9-£16

Open 14 Mar-3 Nov

Last arrival 22.00hrs Last departure 11.00hrs

Set in an attractive wooded valley with a stream is this terraced site with secluded pitches, a good camping area for backpackers and clean, modernised toilet facilities. It is located on the outskirts of Caernarfon in a rural location, close to the main Caernarfon-Llanberis road and just a 10-minute walk from the castle and town centre. 4.5 acre site. 60 touring pitches. 9 hardstandings. 5 seasonal pitches. Caravan pitches. Motorhome pitches. Tent pitches.

Cwm Cadnant Valley

AA Pubs & Restaurants nearby: Seiont Manor Hotel, Llanrug 01286 673366

Rhiwafallen Restaurant with Rooms, Llandwrog 01286 830172

Leisure:

Facilities:

Services:

Within 3 miles:

Notes: No noise after 23.00hrs, no wood fires. Dogs must be kept on leads. Family room with baby changing facilities.

►►► 75% Ty'n yr Onnen Caravan Park *(SH533588)*

Waunfawr LL55 4AX
01286 650281 & 07503 702886
01286 650043
e-mail: tynronnen.farm@btconnect.com
dir: *At Waunfawr on A4085, onto unclass road opposite church. Site signed*

£14-£20 £14-£20 £14-£18

Open Apr-Oct

Last arrival 22.00hrs Last departure noon

A gently sloping site on a 200-acre sheep farm set in magnificent surroundings close to Snowdon and enjoying stunning mountain views. This secluded park is well equipped and has quality toilet facilities. Access is via a very narrow, unclassified road, which would be a challenge for the larger unit or the faint hearted. 3.5 acre site. 20 touring pitches. Caravan pitches. Motorhome pitches. Tent pitches.

LEISURE: Indoor swimming pool Outdoor swimming pool Children's playground Kid's club Tennis court Games room Separate TV room 9/18 hole golf course Boats for hire Cinema Entertainment Fishing Mini golf Watersports Gym Sports field **Spa** Stables
FACILITIES: Bath Shower Electric shaver Hairdryer Ice Pack Facility Disabled facilities Public telephone Shop on site or within 200yds Mobile shop (calls at least 5 days a week) BBQ area Picnic area Wi-fi Internet access Recycling Tourist info Dog exercise area

Leisure: 🎢 🐾 🖵

Facilities: 🌂⊙✕♿🏕🛗 WiFi ♻

Services: 🔌🔋🛢🚿🅣🔌

Within 3 miles: 🚶🚴🎣◎🛒🅿🏪⛳

Notes: ⊗ No music after 23.00hrs. Dogs must be kept on leads. Fishing & nature park.

CRICCIETH
Map 14 SH43

Places to visit

Criccieth Castle, CRICCIETH 01766 522227
www.cadw.wales.gov.uk

Portmeirion, PORTMEIRION 01766 770000
www.portmeirion-village.com

Great for kids: Ffestiniog Railway, PORTHMADOG 01766 516000 www.festrail.co.uk

▶▶▶▶ **82% Eisteddfa** (SH518394)

Eisteddfa Lodge, Pentrefelin LL52 0PT
☎ **01766 522696**
e-mail: eisteddfa@criccieth.co.uk
dir: From Porthmadog take A497 towards Criccieth. After approx 3.5m, through Pentrefelin, site signed 1st right after Plas Gwyn Nursing Home

* 🚐 £14.50-£21.50 🚃 £14.50-£21.50
▲ £13-£21.50

Open Mar-Oct

Last arrival 22.30hrs Last departure 11.00hrs

A quiet, secluded park on elevated ground, sheltered by the Snowdonia Mountains and with lovely views of Cardigan Bay; Criccieth is nearby. The owners are carefully improving the park whilst preserving its unspoilt beauty, and are keen to welcome families, who will appreciate the cubicled facilities. There's a field and play area, woodland walks, a new cocoon, two tipis, six superb slate-based hardstandings, three static holiday caravans for hire, and a three-acre coarse fishing lake adjacent to the park. £4 acre site. 100 touring pitches. 17 hardstandings. Caravan pitches. Motorhome pitches. Tent pitches. 3 statics. 2 tipis. 1 wooden pod.

AA Pubs & Restaurants nearby: Bron Eifion Country House Hotel, Criccieth 01766 522385

Plas Bodegroes, Pwllheli 01758 612363

Leisure: 🎢 ♻ 🐾

Facilities: 🌂⊙🛎✕♿🏕🛗♻ ❶

Services: 🔌🔋🛢🚿🔌

Within 3 miles: 🚶🚴🎽🎣◎🛒🅿🏪⛳

Notes: No noise after 22.30hrs. Dogs must be kept on leads. Baby bath available.

AA CAMPING CARD SITE

▶▶ **82% Llwyn-Bugeilydd Caravan & Camping Site** (SH498398)

LL52 0PN
☎ **01766 522235**
dir: From Porthmadog on A497, 1m N of Criccieth on B4411. Site 1st on right. From A55 take A487 through Caernarfon. After Bryncir right onto B4411, site on left in 3.5m

🚐🚃▲

Open Mar-Oct

Last arrival anytime Last departure 11.00hrs

A quiet rural site with sea and Snowdon mountain views, and well tended grass pitches. The toilets are kept very clean, and the resident owner is always on hand. 6 acre site. 45 touring pitches. 2 hardstandings. Caravan pitches. Motorhome pitches. Tent pitches.

AA Pubs & Restaurants nearby: Bron Eifion Country House Hotel, Criccieth 01766 522385

Plas Bodegroes, Pwllheli 01758 612363

Leisure: 🎢

Facilities: 🌂⊙🛎✕♿🛗♻ ❶

Services: 🔌🔌

Within 3 miles: 🚶🚴🎽🎣◎🛒🅿🏪⛳

Notes: ⊗ No skateboards. Dogs must be kept on leads.

AA CAMPING CARD SITE

▶ **64% Tyddyn Morthwyl Camping & Caravan Site** (SH491399)

LL52 0NF
☎ **01766 522115** & 07983 716292
e-mail: trumper@henstabl147freeserve.co.uk
dir: 1.5m N of Criccieth on B4411. Sign at entrance

* 🚐 £10-£15 🚃 £10-£15 ▲ £10-£15

Open Etr-Oct (rs Mar & Oct unsuitable for heavy motorhomes due to wet ground)

Last departure 14.00hrs

A simple and very quiet sheltered site on a farm with level grass pitches in three fields, which offer plenty of space. The simple facilities include some electric hook-ups, basic yet clean toilets, lovely surrounding walks, bunkhouse accommodation, and Criccieth and the sea are close by. At the remarkable age of 100, owner Mrs Trumper must be our oldest campsite operator. 10 acre site. 40 touring pitches. Caravan pitches. Motorhome pitches. Tent pitches. 22 statics.

AA Pubs & Restaurants nearby: Bron Eifion Country House Hotel, Criccieth 01766 522385

Plas Bodegroes, Pwllheli 01758 612363

Facilities: 🌂⊙♻ ❶

Services: 🔌🔌

Within 3 miles: 🚶🚴🎣🏪🅿⛳

Notes: ⊗ Dogs must be kept on leads.

SERVICES: 🔌 Electric hook up 🔋 Launderette 🍺 Licensed bar 🛢 Calor Gas 🚿 Camping Gaz 🅣 Toilet fluid 🍽 Café/Restaurant 🍟 Fast Food/Takeaway 🔌 Battery charging 🍼 Baby care ⛟ Motorvan service point
ABBREVIATIONS: BH/bank hols-bank holidays Etr-Easter Whit-Whitsun dep-departure fr-from hrs-hours m-mile mdnt-midnight rdbt-roundabout rs-restricted service wk-week wknd-weekend ⊗ No credit cards ⊗ No dogs
See page 7 for details of the AA Camping Card Scheme

DINAS DINLLE
Map 14 SH45

Places to visit

Snowdon Mountain Railway, LLANBERIS
01286 870223 www.snowdonrailway.co.uk

St Cybi's Well, LLANGYBI 01443 336000
www.cadw.wales.gov.uk

Great for kids: Dolbadarn Castle, LLANBERIS
01443 336000 www.cadw.wales.gov.uk

AA CAMPING CARD SITE

▶▶▶▶ 86% Dinlle Caravan Park

(SH438568)

LL54 5TW
☎ 01286 830324 📠 01286 831526
e-mail: enq@thornleyleisure.co.uk
dir: *S on A499 turn right at sign for Caernarfon Airport. 2m W of Dinas Dinlle coast*

* ⊕ £10-£21 ⊕ £10-£21 ▲ £10-£21

Open Mar-Oct

Last arrival 23.00hrs Last departure noon

A very accessible, well-kept grassy site, adjacent to sandy beach, with good views to Snowdonia.

The park is situated in acres of flat grassland, with plenty of room for even the largest groups. A lounge bar and family room are comfortable places in which to relax, and children are well provided for with an exciting adventure playground. The beach road gives access to the golf club, a nature reserve, and to Air World at Caernarfon Airport. The man-made dunes offers campers additional protection from sea breezes. 20 acre site. 175 touring pitches. 20 hardstandings. Caravan pitches. Motorhome pitches. Tent pitches. 167 statics.

AA Pubs & Restaurants nearby: Rhiwafallen Restaurant with Rooms, Llandwrog 01286 830172

Leisure: 🏊 🄰 🎱 🎵
Facilities: 🅿 ⊙ 🄿 ✳ 🄳 ⏲ wifi ❶
Services: 🄌 🄌 🄌 🄌 🄌 🄌
Within 3 miles: 🄿 🄌 ∪
Notes: No skateboards.

see advert below

DYFFRYN ARDUDWY

Places to visit

Cymer Abbey, CYMER ABBEY 01443 336000
www.cadw.wales.gov.uk

Great for kids: Harlech Castle, HARLECH
01766 780552 www.cadw.wales.gov.uk

DYFFRYN ARDUDWY
Map 14 SH52

▶▶▶ 79% Murmur-yr-Afon Touring Park *(SH586236)*

LL44 2BE
☎ 01341 247353 📠 01341 247353
e-mail: murmuryrafon1@btinternet.com
dir: *On A496 N of village*

⊕ ⊕ ▲

Open Mar-Oct

Last arrival 22.00hrs Last departure 11.00hrs

A pleasant family-run park alongside a wooded stream on the edge of the village, and handy for large sandy beaches. Expect good, clean facilities, and lovely views of rolling hills and mountains. 6 acre site. 77 touring pitches. 37 hardstandings. Caravan pitches. Motorhome pitches. Tent pitches.

AA Pubs & Restaurants nearby: Victoria Inn, Llanbedr 01341 241213

Leisure: 🄰
Facilities: 🅿 ⊙ 🄿 ✳ 🄳 ⏲ 🄌 🄌 ❶
Services: 🄌 🄌 🄌
Within 3 miles: 🄿 🄌 🄌
Notes: 🐕 Dogs must be kept on leads.

LEISURE: 🏊 Indoor swimming pool 🏊 Outdoor swimming pool 🄰 Children's playground 🄌 Kid's club 🄌 Tennis court 🎱 Games room 🄌 Separate TV room 🄌 9/18 hole golf course 🄌 Boats for hire 🄌 Cinema 🎵 Entertainment 🄿 Fishing 🄌 Mini golf 🄌 Watersports 🄌 Gym 🄌 Sports field Spa ∪ Stables
FACILITIES: 🄌 Bath 🅿 Shower ⊙ Electric shaver 🄿 Hairdryer ✳ Ice Pack Facility 🄳 Disabled facilities ⏲ Public telephone 🄌 Shop on site or within 200yds 🄌 Mobile shop (calls at least 5 days a week) 🄌 BBQ area 🄌 Picnic area wifi Wi-fi 🄌 Internet access 🄌 Recycling ❶ Tourist info 🄌 Dog exercise area

LLANDWROG — Map 14 SH45

Places to visit

Sygun Copper Mine, BEDDGELERT 01766 890595
www.syguncoppermine.co.uk

Great for kids: Caernarfon Castle, CAERNARFON
01286 677617 www.cadw.wales.gov.uk

AA CAMPING CARD SITE

►►►► 77% White Tower Caravan Park (SH453582)

LL54 5UH
☎ 01286 830649 & 07802 562785
📄 01286 830649
e-mail: whitetower@supanet.com
web: www.whitetowerpark.co.uk
dir: 1.5m from village on Tai'r Eglwys road. From Caernarfon take A487 (Porthmadog road). Cross rdbt, 1st right. Site 3m on right

* 🚐 £18-£25 🚃 £18-£25 ▲ £18-£25

Open Mar-10 Jan (rs Mar-mid May & Sep-Oct bar open wknds only)

Last arrival 23.00hrs Last departure noon

There are lovely views of Snowdonia from this park located just two miles from the nearest beach at Dinas Dinlle. A well-maintained toilet block has key access, and the hardstanding pitches have water and electricity. Popular amenities include an outdoor heated swimming pool, a lounge bar with family room, and a games and TV room. 6 acre site. 68 touring pitches. 68 hardstandings. 58 seasonal pitches. Caravan pitches. Motorhome pitches. Tent pitches. 68 statics.

AA Pubs & Restaurants nearby: Rhiwafallen Restaurant with Rooms, Llandwrog 01286 830172

Leisure: 🏊 🎱 🎣 🎵
Facilities: 🛁 ☉ 🅿 ✳ 👶 🕐 📶 🖥 ❶
Services: 🔌 📺 🚽 🚿 ▓ 🔋 🚐
Within 3 miles: 🚣 🎣 🐾 ⛳ 🏧 🎯
Notes: Dogs must be kept on leads.

LLANRUG — Map 14 SH56

Places to visit

Segontium Roman Museum, CAERNARFON
01286 675625 www.segontium.org.uk

Dolbadarn Castle, LLANBERIS 01443 336000
www.cadw.wales.gov.uk

Great for kids: Greenwood Forest Park, Y FELINHELI 01248 670076
www.greenwoodforestpark.co.uk

►►►► 83% Llys Derwen Caravan & Camping Site (SH539629)

Ffordd Bryngwyn LL55 4RD
☎ 01286 673322
e-mail: llysderwen@aol.com
dir: A55 junct 13 (Caernarfon) onto A4086 to Llanberis, through Llanrug, turn right at pub, site 60yds on right

🚐 🚃 ▲

Open Mar-Oct

Last arrival 22.00hrs Last departure noon

A pleasant, beautifully maintained small site set in woodland within easy reach of Caernarfon, Snowdon, Anglesey and the Lleyn Peninsula. Visitors can expect a warm welcome from enthusiastic, hands-on owners, who keep the toilet facilities spotlessly clean. 5 acre site. 20 touring pitches. Caravan pitches. Motorhome pitches. Tent pitches. 2 statics.

AA Pubs & Restaurants nearby: Seiont Manor Hotel, Llanrug 01286 673366

Facilities: 🛁 ☉ ✳ 👶 🍴
Services: 🔌 📺 🔋
Within 3 miles: 🚣 🎣 🐾 ⛳ 🏧 🎯
Notes: No open fires, no noise after 22.00hrs, no ball games.

PONT-RUG

See Caernarfon

PORTHMADOG

Places to visit

Inigo Jones Slateworks, GROESLON
01286 830242 www.inigojones.co.uk

Great for kids: Ffestiniog Railway, PORTHMADOG
01766 516000 www.festrail.co.uk

PORTHMADOG — Map 14 SH53

76% Greenacres (SH539374)

Black Rock Sands,Morfa Bychan LL49 9YF
☎ 0871 231 0886 📄 01766 512781
e-mail: greenacres@haven.com
dir: From Porthmadog High Street follow Black Rock Sands signs between The Factory Shop & Post Office. Park 2m on left at end of Morfa Bychan

🚐 🚃

Open mid Mar-Oct (rs mid Mar-May & Sep-Oct some facilities may be reduced)

Last arrival anytime Last departure 10.00hrs

A quality holiday park on level ground just a short walk from Black Rock Sands, and set against a backdrop of Snowdonia National Park. All touring pitches are on hardstandings surrounded by closely-mown grass, and near the entertainment complex. A full programme of entertainment, organised clubs, indoor and outdoor sports and leisure, pubs, shows and cabarets all add to a holiday here. A bowling alley and a large shop/bakery are useful amenities. 121 acre site. 52 touring pitches. 52 hardstandings. Caravan pitches. Motorhome pitches. 900 statics.

AA Pubs & Restaurants nearby: Royal Sportsman Hotel, Porthmadog 01766 512015

Hotel Portmeirion, Portmeirion Village, Penrhyndeudraeth 01766 770000

Castell Deudraeth, Portmeirion Village 01766 772400

Leisure: 🏊 🎱 🎮 ☉ 🎣 🎵
Facilities: 🛁 ☉ 🅿 👶 🕐 🖥 🍴 📶 ♻ ❶
Services: 🔌 📺 🔌 🚿 🍴 🍟 ▓
Within 3 miles: 🚣 ◎ 🏧 🎯 🎯
Notes: Max 2 dogs per booking, certain dog breeds banned, no commercial vehicles, no bookings by persons under 21yrs unless a family booking.

SERVICES: 🔌 Electric hook up 📺 Launderette 🍷 Licensed bar 🛢 Calor Gas ⛽ Camping Gaz 🚽 Toilet fluid 🍴 Café/Restaurant 🍟 Fast Food/Takeaway 🔋 Battery charging 👶 Baby care 🚐 Motorvan service point

ABBREVIATIONS: BH/bank hols-bank holidays Etr-Easter Whit-Whitsun dep-departure fr-from hrs-hours m-mile mdnt-midnight rdbt-roundabout rs-restricted service wk-week wknd-weekend 🚫 No credit cards 🚫 No dogs

See page 7 for details of the AA Camping Card Scheme

PWLLHELI — Map 14 SH33

Places to visit

Penarth Fawr, PENARTH FAWR 01443 336000
www.cadw.wales.gov.uk

Plas-yn-Rhiw, PLAS YN RHIW 01758 780219
www.nationaltrust.org.uk

Great for kids: Criccieth Castle, CRICCIETH
01766 522227 www.cadw.wales.gov.uk

76% Hafan Y Mor Holiday Park (SH431368)

LL53 6HJ

☎ 0871 231 0887 📠 01766 810379
e-mail: hafanymor@haven.com
dir: From Caernarfon take A499 to Pwllheli.
A497 to Porthmadog. Park on right, approx
3m from Pwllheli. Or from Telford, A5, A494
to Bala. Right for Porthmadog. Left at rdbt in
Porthmadog signed Criccieth & Pwllheli. Park
on left 3m from Criccieth

🚐 🚙

Open 20 Mar-2 Nov (rs Mar-May & Sep-Oct
reduced facilities)

Last arrival 21.00hrs Last departure 10.00hrs

Set between the seaside towns of Pwllheli and
Criccieth on the sheltered Llyn Peninsula, this
is an all action caravan park with direct beach
access. Facilities include an indoor splash pool
with flumes and bubble pools, wave rider, aqua
jet racer and boating lake. 500 acre site. 73
touring pitches. Caravan pitches. Motorhome
pitches. 800 statics.

AA Pubs & Restaurants nearby: Plas
Bodegroes, Pwllheli 01758 612363

Leisure: 🏊 🎠 ✋

Facilities: 🍴 📮 ♿ ⏰ 🛎️ 📶

Services: 🚰 🔥 🔧 🔒 🍴 ⛲

Within 3 miles: ⚓ 🎣 ◎ 🚴 🛒 🎡 ♻ ♨

Notes: Max 2 dogs per booking, certain dog
breeds banned, no commercial vehicles, no
bookings by persons under 21yrs unless a
family booking.

►►► 68% Abererch Sands Holiday Centre (SH403359)

LL53 6PJ

☎ 01758 612327 📠 01758 701556
e-mail: enquiries@abererch-sands.co.uk
dir: On A497 (Porthmadog to Pwllheli road), 1m
from Pwllheli

🚐 🚙 ▲

Open Mar-Oct

Last arrival 21.00hrs Last departure 21.00hrs

Glorious views of Snowdonia and Cardigan Bay
can be enjoyed from this very secure, family-run
site adjacent to a railway station and a four-mile
stretch of sandy beach. A large heated indoor
swimming pool, snooker room, pool room, fitness
centre and children's play area make this an ideal
holiday venue. 85 acre site. 70 touring pitches. 70
hardstandings. Caravan pitches. Motorhome
pitches. Tent pitches. 90 statics.

AA Pubs & Restaurants nearby: Plas Bodegroes,
Pwllheli 01758 612363

Leisure: 🏊 🎠 🔍

Facilities: 🍴 ⊙ ✳ ♿ ⏰ 🛎️ 🏀 📶

Services: 🚰 🔥 🔒 🔧 🍴 ⛲ ⚙

Within 3 miles: ⚓ 🎣 🎣 🚴 🛒 🎡 ♻ ♨

TALSARNAU — Map 14 SH63

Places to visit

Portmeirion, PORTMEIRION 01766 770000
www.portmeirion-village.com

Harlech Castle, HARLECH 01766 780552
www.cadw.wales.gov.uk

Great for kids: Ffestiniog Railway, PORTHMADOG
01766 516000 www.festrail.co.uk

►►►► 82% Barcdy Touring Caravan & Camping Park (SH620375)

LL47 6YG

☎ 01766 770736
e-mail: anwen@barcdy.co.uk
dir: From Maentwrog take A496 for Harlech. Site
4m on left

* 🚐 £22-£26 🚙 £20-£26 ▲ £16-£20

Open Apr-Sep (rs Selected dates 2nd facility
building closed)

Last arrival 21.00hrs Last departure noon

A quiet picturesque park on the edge of the Vale of
Ffestiniog near the Dwryd estuary. Two touring
areas serve the park, one near the park entrance,
and the other with improved and more secluded
terraced pitches beside a narrow valley. The tent
area is secluded and peaceful, and the toilet
facilities are clean and tidy. Footpaths through
adjacent woodland lead to small lakes and an
established nature trail. 12 acre site. 80 touring
pitches. 40 hardstandings. 15 seasonal pitches.
Caravan pitches. Motorhome pitches. Tent pitches.
30 statics.

AA Pubs & Restaurants nearby: Hotel Portmeirion,
Portmeirion Village, Penrhyndeudraeth
01766 770000

Castell Deudraeth, Portmeirion Village
01766 772400

Facilities: 🍴 ⊙ 📮 ✳ 🏀 📶 ♻ ❶

Services: 🚰 🔥 🔒 ⚙

Within 3 miles: ⚓ 🎣 🛒 ♨

Notes: ⊗ No noisy parties, quiet families &
couples only, no groups except Duke of Edinburgh
award students.

TAL-Y-BONT

Places to visit

Cymer Abbey, CYMER ABBEY 01443 336000
www.cadw.wales.gov.uk

Great for kids: Fairbourne Railway, FAIRBOURNE
01341 250362 www.fairbournerailway.com

ISLAWRFFORDD CARAVAN PARK

A family owned park Est. 1957

TALYBONT, NR BARMOUTH, GWYNEDD, LL43 2AQ, NORTH WALES

01341 247269

Email: info@islawrffordd.co.uk   www.islawrffordd.co.uk

AA

Family owned and run since being established in 1957, Islawrffordd Caravan Park offers the very best in quality which you are immediately aware of when entering the award winning reception building now to be complimented in 2011 with similar architectural design to the laundry, bar and amusement/take-away facilities.

Situated at the southern end of the magnificent Snowdonia National Park coastline in the village of Talybont, Islawrffordd offers 201 holiday home bases, 75 touring caravan/motorhome plots and 30 camping pitches all benefitting from the very best facilities, including a heated indoor swimming pool/sauna/ jacuzzi and tanning suite.

Nigel Mansell, O.B.E. & 1992 Formula 1 World Champion & Indy Car World Champion 1993 has a Holiday Home association with Islawrffordd that stretches back from the present day to his childhood and his opinion of the Snowdonia Coastline area and our park is still the same
"It's absolutely fantastic".

Choice of a Champion

TAL-Y-BONT — Map 14 SH52

AA Campsite of the Year for Wales 2012

AA CAMPING CARD SITE

PREMIER PARK

►►►►► 88% Islawrffordd Caravan Park (SH584215)

LL43 2AQ

☎ 01341 247269 📠 01341 242639
e-mail: jane@islawrffordd.co.uk
dir: On sea side of main A496 (coast road), 4m N of Barmouth, 6m S of Harlech

🚐 £27.50-£32.50 🚌 £27.50-£32.50
⛺ £20-£32.50

Open Mar-1 Nov

Last arrival 20.00hrs Last departure noon

Situated on the coast between Barmouth and Harlech, and within the Snowdonia National Park, with clear views of Cardigan Bay and the mountains, this excellent, family-run and family-friendly park has seen considerable investment in recent years. Now matured, the touring area boasts fully serviced pitches, a superb toilet block with under-floor heating and top-quality fittings, and the park has private access to miles of sandy beach. The restaurant, bar and games room were smartly refurbished in 2011. 25 acre site. 105 touring pitches. 75 hardstandings. Caravan pitches. Motorhome pitches. Tent pitches. 201 statics.

Leisure: 🏊 ⅍ 🎱 ⬜
Facilities: 🌂 ⊙ ℱ ✳ ⅙ 🕒 ⓢ 📶 ♻ ❶
Services: 🔌 🗄 🍴 🛢 ⌀ Ⓣ 🍽 🛒 ⅄
Within 3 miles: ⚓ ℐ ◎ ⅙ 🏦 🏪 ♨
Notes: Strictly families & couples only, no groups. Dogs must be kept on leads.

see advert on page 415

TYWYN — Map 14 SH50

Places to visit

Talyllyn Railway, TYWYN 01654 710472 www.talyllyn.co.uk

Castell-y-Bere, LLANFIHANGEL-Y-PENNANT 01443 336000 www.cadw.wales.gov.uk

Great for kids: King Arthur's Labyrinth, MACHYNLLETH 01654 761584 www.kingarthurslabyrinth.com

►►►► 81% *Ynysymaengwyn Caravan Park* (SH602021)

LL36 9RY

☎ 01654 710684 📠 01654 710684
e-mail: rita@ynysy.co.uk
dir: On A493, 1m N of Tywyn, towards Dolgellau

🚐 🚌 ⛺

Open Etr or Apr-Oct

Last arrival 23.00hrs Last departure noon

A lovely park set in the wooded grounds of a former manor house, with designated nature trails through 13 acres of wildlife-rich woodland, scenic river walks, fishing and a sandy beach nearby. The attractive stone amenity block is clean and well kept, and this smart municipal park is ideal for families. 4 acre site. 80 touring pitches. Caravan pitches. Motorhome pitches. Tent pitches. 115 statics.

Leisure: ⅍
Facilities: 🌂 ⊙ ℱ ✳ ⅙ 🕒 🔩 🚻 🐕
Services: 🔌 🗄 🛢 ⌀ 🛒
Within 3 miles: ⚓ 🎯 ℐ ◎ ⅙ 🏦 🏪 ♨
Notes: 🐕 Dogs must be kept on leads.

MONMOUTHSHIRE

ABERGAVENNY — Map 9 SO21

Places to visit

White Castle, WHITE CASTLE 01600 780380 www.cadw.wales.gov.uk

Hen Gwrt, LLANTILIO CROSSENNY 01443 336000 www.cadw.wales.gov.uk

Great for kids: Raglan Castle, RAGLAN 01291 690228 www.cadw.wales.gov.uk

AA CAMPING CARD SITE

►►► 79% Pyscodlyn Farm Caravan & Camping Site (SO266155)

Llanwenarth Citra NP7 7ER

☎ 01873 853271 & 07816 447942
e-mail: pyscodlyn.farm@virgin.net
dir: From Abergavenny take A40 (Brecon road), site 1.5m from entrance of Nevill Hall Hospital, on left 50yds past phone box

* 🚐 £14-£15 🚌 £14-£15 ⛺ £13-£15

Open Apr-Oct

With its outstanding views of the mountains, this quiet park in the Brecon Beacons National Park makes a pleasant venue for country lovers. The Sugarloaf Mountain and the River Usk are within easy walking distance and, despite being a working farm, dogs are welcome. Please note that credit cards are not taken on this site. 4.5 acre site. 60 touring pitches. Caravan pitches. Motorhome pitches. Tent pitches. 6 statics.

AA Pubs & Restaurants nearby: Angel Hotel, Abergavenny 01873 857121

Llansantffraed Court Hotel, Llanvihangel Gobion, Abergavenny 01873 840678

Facilities: 🌂 ⊙ ✳ ⅙ 🐕 ♻ ❶
Services: 🔌 🗄 🛢 ⌀
Within 3 miles: ⚓ 🎯 ℐ ◎ 🏪 ♨
Notes: 🐕 Dogs must be kept on leads.

LEISURE: 🏊 Indoor swimming pool 🏊 Outdoor swimming pool ⅍ Children's playground 🎣 Kid's club 🎾 Tennis court 🎱 Games room ⬜ Separate TV room
⛳ 9/18 hole golf course 🚣 Boats for hire 🎬 Cinema 🎭 Entertainment 🎣 Fishing ◎ Mini golf 🏄 Watersports 🏋 Gym ⚽ Sports field Spa ♨ Stables
FACILITIES: 🛁 Bath 🚿 Shower ⊙ Electric shaver ℱ Hairdryer ✳ Ice Pack Facility ⅙ Disabled facilities 🕒 Public telephone 🏪 Shop on site or within 200yds
🚚 Mobile shop (calls at least 5 days a week) 🍴 BBQ area 🏕 Picnic area 📶 Wi-fi 🖥 Internet access ♻ Recycling ❶ Tourist info 🐕 Dog exercise area

DINGESTOW
Map 9 SO41

Places to visit

Raglan Castle, RAGLAN 01291 690228
www.cadw.wales.gov.uk

Tintern Abbey, TINTERN PARVA 01291 689251
www.cadw.wales.gov.uk

Great for kids: The Nelson Museum & Local
History Centre, MONMOUTH 01600 710630

AA CAMPING CARD SITE

►►► **80% Bridge Caravan Park &
Camping Site** (SO459104)

Bridge Farm NP25 4DY
☎ 01600 740241   📄 01600 740241
e-mail: info@bridgecaravanpark.co.uk
dir: Signed from Raglan. Off A449 (S Wales-
Midlands road)

* 🚐 £15-£18 ⛟ £15-£18 ⛺ £15-£18

Open Etr-Oct

Last arrival 22.00hrs Last departure 16.00hrs

The River Trothy runs along the edge of this quiet
village park, which has been owned by the same
family for many years. Touring pitches are both
grass and hardstanding, and there is a backdrop
of woodland. The quality facilities are enhanced
by good laundry equipment. 4 acre site. 94 touring
pitches. 15 hardstandings. Caravan pitches.
Motorhome pitches. Tent pitches.

AA Pubs & Restaurants nearby: Beaufort Arms
Coaching Inn & Brasserie, Raglan 01291 690412

Facilities: 🅿 ⊙ 🖰 ⚘ ⅋ ⊛ 🅱 ⊞ 🚿 ♻ 🅸

Services: 🔌 🖥 🛢 ⊘ ⊤ 🔋 ⚙

Within 3 miles: ⅃ ⅄ ⊞ ℘ ℗ 🛒 ⌗ ∪

Notes: 🐕 Dogs must be kept on leads. Fishing.

USK
Places to visit

Caerleon Roman Baths, CAERLEON
01663 422518 www.cadw.wales.gov.uk

Big Pit National Coal Museum, BLAENAVON
01495 790311 www.museumwales.ac.uk

Great for kids: Greenmeadow Community
Farm, CWMBRAN 01633 647662
www.greenmeadowcommunityfarm.org.uk

USK
Map 9 SO30

PREMIER PARK

►►►►► **84% Pont Kemys Caravan
& Camping Park** (SO348058)

Chainbridge NP7 9DS
☎ 01873 880688   📄 01873 880270
e-mail: info@pontkemys.com
web: www.pontkemys.com
dir: On B4598 (Usk to Abergavenny road), 300yds
N of Chainbridge, 4m from Usk

* 🚐 £15-£19 ⛟ £15-£19 ⛺ £15-£17

Open Mar-Oct

Last arrival 21.00hrs Last departure noon

A peaceful park next to the River Usk, offering an
excellent standard of toilet facilities with family
rooms. A section of the park has fully serviced
pitches. The park is in a rural area with mature
trees and country views, and attracts quiet
visitors who enjoy the many attractions of this
area. The local golf club is open during the day
and serves breakfast and lunches. 8 acre site. 65
touring pitches. 29 hardstandings. 25 seasonal
pitches. Caravan pitches. Motorhome pitches.
Tent pitches.

AA Pubs & Restaurants nearby: Raglan Arms,
Llandenny 01291 690800

Nags Head Inn, Usk 01291 672820

Three Salmons Hotel, Usk 01291 672133

Leisure: ⊛ ▢

Facilities: 🅿 ⊙ 🖰 ⚘ ⅋ ⊛ 🅱 🚿 🚿 📶 ♻ 🅸

Services: 🔌 🖥 🛢 ⊘ ⊤ 🔋 ⚙

Within 3 miles: ⅃ ⅄ ℘ 🛒

Notes: Dogs must be kept on leads. Mother &
baby room, kitchen facilities for groups.

PEMBROKESHIRE

BROAD HAVEN
Map 8 SM81

Places to visit

Pembroke Castle, PEMBROKE 01646 681510
www.pembrokecastle.co.uk

Llawhaden Castle, LLAWHADEN 01443 336000
www.cadw.wales.gov.uk

Great for kids: Scolton Manor Museum &
Country Park, SCOLTON 01437 731328
(Museum)

►►► **85% Creampots Touring
Caravan & Camping Park** (SM882131)

Broadway SA62 3TU
☎ 01437 781776
e-mail: creampots@btconnect.com
dir: From Haverfordwest take B4341 to Broadway.
Turn left, follow brown tourist signs to site

🚐 ⛟ ⛺

Open Mar-Jan

Last arrival 21.00hrs Last departure noon

Set just outside the Pembrokeshire National Park,
this quiet site is just one and a half miles from a
safe sandy beach at Broad Haven, and the coastal
footpath. The park is well laid out and carefully
maintained, and the toilet block offers a good
standard of facilities. The owners welcome
families. 8 acre site. 71 touring pitches. 20
hardstandings. Caravan pitches. Motorhome
pitches. Tent pitches. 1 static.

AA Pubs & Restaurants nearby: Swan Inn, Little
Haven 01437 781880

Facilities: 🅿 ⊙ 🖰 ⚘ ⅋ ⊛ 🚿 ♻ 🅸

Services: 🔌 🖥 🛢 ⊘ 🔋

Within 3 miles: ⅄ ⊞ ℘ 🛒 ⌗ ∪

Notes: Dogs must be kept on leads.

SERVICES: 🔌 Electric hook up 🖥 Launderette 🍷 Licensed bar 🛢 Calor Gas ⊘ Camping Gaz ⊤ Toilet fluid 🍽 Café/Restaurant 🍟 Fast Food/Takeaway 🔋 Battery charging 🚼 Baby care ⚙ Motorvan service point
ABBREVIATIONS: BH/bank hols-bank holidays Etr-Easter Whit-Whitsun dep-departure fr-from hrs-hours m-mile mdnt-midnight rdbt-roundabout rs-restricted service wk-week wknd-weekend 🚫 No credit cards 🚫 No dogs
See page 7 for details of the AA Camping Card Scheme

BROAD HAVEN *continued*

►►► 77% South Cockett Caravan & Camping Park *(SM878136)*

South Cockett SA62 3TU
☎ 01437 781296 & 781760 📠 01437 781296
e-mail: esmejames@hotmail.co.uk
dir: *From Haverfordwest take B4341 to Broad Haven, at Broadway turn left, site 300yds*

* 🚐 £13.75-£16.20 🚙 £13.75-£16.20
⛺ £12.85-£14.95

Open Etr-Oct

Last arrival 22.30hrs

A small park on a working farm, with touring areas divided into neat paddocks by high, well-trimmed hedges. Good toilet facilities, and in a convenient location for the lovely beach at nearby Broad Haven. 6 acre site. 73 touring pitches. Caravan pitches. Motorhome pitches. Tent pitches.

AA Pubs & Restaurants nearby: Swan Inn, Little Haven 01437 781880

Facilities: 🌾⊙✳🕒🛒♨

Services: 🔌🗑🧺♻

Within 3 miles: ⛷🏌🛶📦🎞️⛹

Notes: 🐕 Dogs must be kept on leads.

FISHGUARD

Places to visit

Pentre Ifan Burial Chamber, NEWPORT
01443 336000 www.cadw.wales.gov.uk

Tredegar House & Park, NEWPORT
01633 815880 www.newport.gov.uk

Great for kids: OceanLab, FISHGUARD
01348 874737 www.ocean-lab.co.uk

FISHGUARD   Map 8 SM93

►►► 89% Fishguard Bay Caravan & Camping Park *(SM984383)*

Garn Gelli SA65 9ET
☎ 01348 811415 📠 01348 811425
e-mail: enquiries@fishguardbay.com
web: www.fishguardbay.com
dir: *If approaching Fishguard from Cardigan on A487 ignore Sat Nav to turn right. Turn at campsite sign onto single track road*

* 🚐 £17-£21 🚙 £17-£21 ⛺ £16-£30

Open Mar-9 Jan

Last arrival anytime Last departure noon

Set high up on cliffs with outstanding views of Fishguard Bay, and the Pembrokeshire Coastal Path running right through the centre. The park is extremely well kept, with three good toilet blocks, a common room with TV, a lounge/library, decent laundry, and well-stocked shop. 5 acre site. 50 touring pitches. 4 hardstandings. Caravan pitches. Motorhome pitches. Tent pitches. 50 statics.

AA Pubs & Restaurants nearby: Sloop Inn, Porthgain 01348 831449

The Shed, Porthgain 01348 831518

Salutation Inn, Felindre Farchog 01239 820564

Leisure: 🅰🎱💬

Facilities: 🌾⊙✳🕒🛒♨🛜♻ℹ️

Services: 🔌🗑🛒🧺📞🏺

Within 3 miles: ⛷📅🏌📦🎞️⛹

Notes: Dogs must be kept on leads.

►►► 75% Gwaun Vale Touring Park *(SM977356)*

Llanychaer SA65 9TA
☎ 01348 874698
e-mail: margaret.harries@talk21.com
dir: *B4313 from Fishguard. Site 1.5m on right*

🚐🚙⛺

Open Apr-Oct

Last arrival anytime Last departure 11.00hrs

Located at the opening of the beautiful Gwaun Valley, this well-kept park is set on the hillside with pitches tiered on two levels. There are lovely views of the surrounding countryside, and good facilities. 1.6 acre site. 29 touring pitches. 5 hardstandings. Caravan pitches. Motorhome pitches. Tent pitches. 1 static.

AA Pubs & Restaurants nearby: Sloop Inn, Porthgain 01348 831449

The Shed, Porthgain 01348 831518

Salutation Inn, Felindre Farchog 01239 820564

Leisure: 🅰

Facilities: 🌾⊙✳🕒🛒♨🏺🪁

Services: 🔌🗑🧺

Within 3 miles: ⛷📅🏌📦🎞️⛹

Notes: 🐕 No skateboards. Dogs must be kept on leads. Guidebooks available.

HASGUARD CROSS   Map 8 SM80

Places to visit

Pembroke Castle, PEMBROKE 01646 681510
www.pembrokecastle.co.uk

►►► 82% Hasguard Cross Caravan Park *(SM850108)*

SA62 3SL
☎ 01437 781443 📠 01437 781443
e-mail: hasguard@aol.com
dir: *From Haverfordwest take B4327 towards Dale. In 7m right at x-rds. Site 1st right*

🚐🚙⛺

Open all year (rs Aug tent field for 28 days)

Last arrival 21.00hrs Last departure 10.00hrs

A very clean, efficient and well-run site in the Pembrokeshire National Park, just one and a half miles from the sea and beach at Little Haven, and with views of the surrounding hills. The toilet and shower facilities are immaculately clean, and there is a licensed bar (evenings only) serving a

---

LEISURE: 🏊 Indoor swimming pool 🏊 Outdoor swimming pool 🅰 Children's playground ⚓ Kid's club 🎾 Tennis court 🎱 Games room 💬 Separate TV room ⛳ 9/18 hole golf course 🛶 Boats for hire 🎬 Cinema 🎵 Entertainment 🎣 Fishing ⛳ Mini golf 🏄 Watersports 🏋 Gym ⚽ Sports field Spa 🧖 Stables
FACILITIES: 🛁 Bath 🚿 Shower ⊙ Electric shaver 💇 Hairdryer ✳ Ice Pack Facility ♿ Disabled facilities 🕒 Public telephone 🛒 Shop on site or within 200yds 🚐 Mobile shop (calls at least 5 days a week) 🔥 BBQ area 🪑 Picnic area 🛜 Wi-fi 💻 Internet access ♻ Recycling ℹ️ Tourist info 🪁 Dog exercise area

good choice of food. 4.5 acre site. 12 touring pitches. Caravan pitches. Motorhome pitches. Tent pitches. 42 statics.

AA Pubs & Restaurants nearby: Swan Inn, Little Haven 01437 781880

Leisure: ⚽

Facilities: 🅿⊙ℱ✳🔥⊙🚿🚮♻ ❶

Services: 🔌🗑🔚📶🍽🛄⛟

Within 3 miles: ⤋🎣ℐ🚴🎣🅱∪

AA CAMPING CARD SITE

►►► 82% Redlands Touring Caravan & Camping Park *(SM853109)*

SA62 3SJ
☎ 01437 781300
e-mail: info@redlandscamping.co.uk
dir: *From Haverfordwest take B4327 towards Dale. Site 7m on right*

* 🚐 fr £13.75 🚐 fr £13.75 ▲ fr £13.25

Open Mar-Dec

Last arrival 21.00hrs Last departure 11.30hrs

Set in the Pembrokeshire National Park, close to sandy beaches and the famous coastal path, this family owned and run park is set in five acres of immaculately kept grassland and offers spacious, level pitches with glorious sea views for caravans, motorhomes and tents. Facilities are clean and well maintained, the park is well laid out with good hardstanding pitches, and the camping area offers two sizes of pitches, all with electric hook-up. Ideally situated for exploring the whole of Pembrokeshire. 6 acre site. 60 touring pitches. 32 hardstandings. Caravan pitches. Motorhome pitches. Tent pitches.

AA Pubs & Restaurants nearby: Swan Inn, Little Haven 01437 781880

Facilities: 🅿⊙ℱ✳⊙🚿♻ ❶

Services: 🔌🗑🔚⊘🅣🛄⛟

Within 3 miles: 🎣ℐ🚴🅱

Notes: ⊗ No commercial vans or minibuses, max 2 dogs in high season. Dogs must be kept on leads. Use of freezers.

HAVERFORDWEST   Map 8 SM91

Places to visit

Llawhaden Castle, LLAWHADEN 01443 336000 www.cadw.wales.gov.uk

Carew Castle & Tidal Mill, CAREW 01646 651782 www.carewcastle.com

Great for kids: Oakwood Theme Park, NARBERTH 01834 861889 www.oakwoodthemepark.co.uk

AA CAMPING CARD SITE

►► 81% Nolton Cross Caravan Park *(SM879177)*

Nolton SA62 3NP
☎ 01437 710701 📠 01437 710329
e-mail: info@noltoncross-holidays.co.uk
web: www.noltoncross-holidays.co.uk
dir: *1m off A487 (Haverfordwest to St David's road) at Simpson Cross, towards Nolton & Broadhaven*

* 🚐 £7.75-£14.25 🚐 £7.75-£14.25 ▲ £7.75-£14.25

Open Mar-Dec

Last arrival 22.00hrs Last departure noon

High grassy banks surround the touring area of this park next to the owners' working farm. It is located on open ground above the sea and St Bride's Bay (within one and a half miles), and there is a coarse fishing lake close by - equipment for hire and reduced permit rates for campers are available. 4 acre site. 15 touring pitches. Caravan pitches. Motorhome pitches. Tent pitches. 30 statics.

AA Pubs & Restaurants nearby: Swan Inn, Little Haven 01437 781880

Leisure: ⚑

Facilities: 🅿⊙✳⊙🚿♻ ❶

Services: 🔌🗑⊘🅣🔚

Within 3 miles: ℐ🚴🅱∪

Notes: No youth groups. Dogs must be kept on leads.

AA CAMPING CARD SITE

NEW ►► 78% The Rising Sun Inn *(SM930171)*

St Davids Rd SA62 6EA
☎ 01437 765171 & 07876 236692
e-mail: therisingsuninn@hotmail.co.uk
dir: *On A487 from Haverfordwest towards St David's for 1.5m, site on left*

🚐 £11-£14.50 🚐 £11-£14.50 ▲ £11-£14.50

Open 31 Mar-7 Oct

Last arrival flexible Last departure 10.30hrs

The new owners are gradually sprucing up this great little site which is tucked behind a pub close to St David's and the Pembrokeshire beaches and coastal path. The amenity block had been refurbished and the pitches improved, and plans for 2012 include new hardstandings and a disabled room. 2.5 acre site. 8 touring pitches. Caravan pitches. Motorhome pitches. Tent pitches. 1 static.

Leisure: 🔍

Facilities: 🅿⊙ℱ✳⊙🔥🚿♻ ❶

Services: 🔌🗑🔚📶🅣🍽🛄⛟

Within 3 miles: ⤋🅷ℐ🚴🅱∪

LITTLE HAVEN

See Hasguard Cross

SERVICES: 🔌 Electric hook up 🗑 Launderette 🔚 Licensed bar 🅰 Calor Gas ⊘ Camping Gaz 🅣 Toilet fluid 🍽 Café/Restaurant 🛄 Fast Food/Takeaway ⛟ Battery charging 📶 Baby care ⛟ Motorvan service point

ABBREVIATIONS: BH/bank hols-bank holidays Etr-Easter Whit-Whitsun dep-departure fr-from hrs-hours m-mile mdnt-midnight rdbt-roundabout rs-restricted service wk-week wknd-weekend ⊗ No credit cards ⊗ No dogs

See page 7 for details of the AA Camping Card Scheme

ROSEBUSH — Map 8 SN02

Places to visit

Cilgerran Castle, CILGERRAN 01239 621339
www.cadw.wales.gov.uk

OceanLab, FISHGUARD 01348 874737
www.ocean-lab.co.uk

►► 72% Rosebush Caravan Park (SN073293)

GOLD

Rhoslwyn SA66 7QT
☎ 01437 532206 & 07831 223166
📠 01437 532206
dir: From A40, near Narberth, take B4313, between Haverfordwest & Cardigan take B4329, site 1m

🚐 �+🏕

Open 14 Mar-Oct

Last arrival 23.00hrs Last departure noon

A most attractive park with a large ornamental lake at its centre and good landscaping. Set off the main tourist track, it offers lovely views of the Presely Hills which can be reached by a scenic walk. Rosebush is a quiet village with a handy pub, and the park owner also runs the village shop. Please note that due to the deep lake on site, children are not accepted. 12 acre site. 65 touring pitches. Caravan pitches. Motorhome pitches. Tent pitches. 15 statics.

AA Pubs & Restaurants nearby: Tafarn Sinc, Rosebush 01437 532214

Facilities: 🅟 ⊙ 🦷 ☀ 🔌 🛒 ♻
Services: 🚰 🛒
Within 3 miles: 🎣 ◎
Notes: Adults only. 🐾

ST DAVID'S

Places to visit

St David's Bishop's Palace, ST DAVID'S 01437 720517 www.cadw.wales.gov.uk

St David's Cathedral, ST DAVID'S 01437 720202 www.stdavidscathedral.org.uk

Great for kids: Oakwood Theme Park, NARBETH 01834 861889 www.oakwoodthemepark.co.uk

ST DAVID'S — Map 8 SM72

PREMIER PARK

►►►►► 83% Caerfai Bay Caravan & Tent Park (SM759244)

Caerfai Bay SA62 6QT
☎ 01437 720274 📠 01437 720577
e-mail: info@caerfaibay.co.uk
web: www.caerfaibay.co.uk
dir: At St David's exit A487 at Visitor Centre/Grove Hotel. Follow signs for Caerfai Bay. Right at end of road

🚐 £13.50-£18 🚖 £11.50-£18 🏕 £11.50-£16

Open Mar-mid Nov

Last arrival 21.00hrs Last departure 11.00hrs

Magnificent coastal scenery and an outlook over St Bride's Bay can be enjoyed from this delightful site, located just 300 yards from a bathing beach. The excellent toilet facilities include four family rooms, which are a huge asset to the park, and ongoing improvements include a second, solar-heated wet suit shower room, upgraded roadways, and modernised water points. There is an excellent farm shop just across the road. 10 acre site. 106 touring pitches. 24 hardstandings. Caravan pitches. Motorhome pitches. Tent pitches. 33 statics.

AA Pubs & Restaurants nearby: Cwtch, St David's 01437 720491

Sloop Inn, Porthgain 01348 831449

The Shed, Porthgain 01348 831518

Cambrian Inn, Solva 01437 721210

Facilities: 🅟 ⊙ 🦷 ☀ ♿ 🔌 🛒 🐕 📶 🖥 ♻ 🔁 ℹ
Services: 🚰 🗑 🔒 ⚡ 🛒 ➡ ⛽
Within 3 miles: 🎣 ◎ 🏊 🐴 🐕
Notes: No dogs in tent field mid Jul-Aug, no skateboards or rollerblades. Dogs must be kept on leads. Family washrooms.

AA CAMPING CARD SITE

►►► 80% Hendre Eynon Camping & Caravan Site (SM771284)

SA62 6DB
☎ 01437 720474 📠 01437 720474
dir: Take A487 (Fishguard road) from St David's, left at rugby club signed Llanrhian. Site 2m on right (NB do no take turn to Whitesands)

* 🚐 £14-£22 🚖 £14-£22 🏕 £14-£22

Open Apr-Sep

Last arrival 21.00hrs Last departure noon

A peaceful country site on a working farm, with a modern toilet block including family rooms. Within easy reach of many lovely sandy beaches, and two miles from the cathedral city of St David's. 7 acre site. 50 touring pitches. 20 seasonal pitches. Caravan pitches. Motorhome pitches. Tent pitches.

AA Pubs & Restaurants nearby: Cwtch, St David's 01437 720491

Sloop Inn, Porthgain 01348 831449

The Shed, Porthgain 01348 831518

Cambrian Inn, Solva 01437 721210

Facilities: 🅟 ⊙ ☀ ♿ 🔌 🐕 ℹ
Services: 🚰 🗑 🔒 ⚡ 🛒
Within 3 miles: 🎣 ➕ 🎣 🏊 🐴 🔁 U
Notes: 🐾 Maximum 2 dogs per unit. Dogs must be kept on leads.

►►► 78% Tretio Caravan & Camping Park (SM787292)

SA62 6DE
☎ 01437 781600 📠 01437 781594
e-mail: info@tretio.com
dir: From St David's take A487 towards Fishguard, left at Rugby Football Club, straight on for 3m. Site signed, left to site

🚐 🚖 🏕

Open Mar-Oct

Last arrival 20.00hrs Last departure 10.00hrs

An attractive site in a very rural spot with distant country views, and beautiful local beaches. A mobile shop calls daily at peak periods, and the tiny cathedral city of St David's is only three miles away. 6.5 acre site. 40 touring pitches. 8 seasonal pitches. Caravan pitches. Motorhome pitches. Tent pitches. 30 statics.

LEISURE: 🏊 Indoor swimming pool 🏊 Outdoor swimming pool 🅜 Children's playground 🛝 Kid's club 🎾 Tennis court 🎱 Games room 📺 Separate TV room ⛳ 9/18 hole golf course 🚣 Boats for hire 🎬 Cinema 🎵 Entertainment 🎣 Fishing ◎ Mini golf 🏄 Watersports 🏋 Gym 🏟 Sports field Spa U Stables
FACILITIES: 🛁 Bath 🚿 Shower ⊙ Electric shaver 🦷 Hairdryer ☀ Ice Pack Facility ♿ Disabled facilities 📞 Public telephone 🛒 Shop on site or within 200yds 🚚 Mobile shop (calls at least 5 days a week) 🔥 BBQ area 🎡 Picnic area 📶 Wi-fi 🖥 Internet access ♻ Recycling ℹ Tourist info 🐕 Dog exercise area

AA Pubs & Restaurants nearby: Cwtch, St David's 01437 720491

Sloop Inn, Porthgain 01348 831449

The Shed, Porthgain 01348 831518

Cambrian Inn, Solva 01437 721210

Leisure: ⚑ ✪

Facilities: ℝ ☉ ℙ ✳ ⚒ ♿ ⛟ ♻ 🛈

Services: 🔌 🔋 🧺 T 🔋

Within 3 miles: ↓ ✈ 🎣 ◎ ♨ 🛒 🔋

Notes: Dogs must be kept on leads. Pitch & putt.

TENBY

Places to visit

Tudor Merchant's House, TENBY 01834 842279
www.nationaltrust.org.ukmain-w-
tudormerchantshouse

Tenby Museum & Art Gallery, TENBY
01834 842809 www.tenbymuseum.org.uk

Great for kids: Colby Woodland Garden,
AMROTH 01834 811885
www.nationaltrust.org.uk/main

TENBY
Map 8 SN10

85% Kiln Park Holiday Centre (SN119002)

GOLD

Marsh Rd SA70 7RB
☎ **0871 231 0889** 📠 **01834 845159**
e-mail: kilnpark@haven.com
dir: Follow A477, A478 to Tenby for 6m, then
follow signs to Penally, site 0.5m on left

🚐 🚓 Å

Open mid Mar-Oct (rs mid Mar-May & Sep-Oct
some facilities may be reduced)

Last arrival dusk Last departure 10.00hrs

A large holiday complex complete with leisure
and sports facilities, and lots of entertainment
for all the family. There are bars and cafés, and
plenty of security. This touring, camping and
static site is on the outskirts of town, with a
short walk through dunes to the sandy beach.
The well-equipped toilet block is very clean. 103
acre site. 193 touring pitches. Caravan pitches.
Motorhome pitches. Tent pitches. 703 statics.

AA Pubs & Restaurants nearby: Stackpole Inn,
Stackpole 01646 672324

New Inn, Amroth 01834 812368

Leisure: ≋ ≈ ⚑ 🖐 ⚽ ♫

Facilities: ℝ ℙ ✳ ♿ ◎ 🛖 ⛟ WiFi ♻

Services: 🔌 🔋 🧺 🍴 ◎ 🍽 🚿 🔋

Within 3 miles: ↓ ✈ H 🎣 ◎ ♨ 🛒 🔋 U

Notes: Max 2 dogs per booking, certain dog
breeds banned, no commercial vehicles, no
bookings by persons under 21yrs unless a
family booking. Entertainment complex, bowling
& putting green.

see advert below

▶▶▶▶ **85% Trefalun Park** (SN093027)

Devonshire Dr, St Florence SA70 8RD
☎ **01646 651514** 📠 **01646 651746**
e-mail: trefalun@aol.com
dir: 1.5m NW of St Florence & 0.5m N of B4318

🚐 🚓 Å

Open Etr-Oct

Last arrival 19.00hrs Last departure noon

Set within 12 acres of sheltered, well-kept
grounds, this quiet country park offers well-
maintained level grass pitches separated by
bushes and trees, with plenty of space to relax in.
Children can feed the park's friendly pets. Plenty
of activities are available at the nearby
Heatherton Country Sports Park, including go-
karting, indoor bowls, golf and bumper boating

continued

SERVICES: 🔌 Electric hook up 🔋 Launderette 🍸 Licensed bar 🛢 Calor Gas ⊘ Camping Gaz T Toilet fluid 🍴 Café/Restaurant 🍽 Fast Food/Takeaway 🔋 Battery charging 🚼 Baby care ⛟ Motorvan service point

ABBREVIATIONS: BH/bank hols-bank holidays Etr-Easter Whit-Whitsun dep-departure fr-from hrs-hours m-mile mdnt-midnight rdbt-roundabout rs-restricted service wk-week wknd-weekend 🚫 No credit cards ⊗ No dogs

See page 7 for details of the AA Camping Card Scheme

TENBY *continued*

12 acre site. 90 touring pitches. 54 hardstandings. Caravan pitches. Motorhome pitches. Tent pitches. 10 statics.

Trefalun Park

AA Pubs & Restaurants nearby: Stackpole Inn, Stackpole 01646 672324

New Inn, Amroth 01834 812368

Leisure: ⚠

Facilities: ⚘⊙🜂✳♿🕐🐾🛒

Services: ⊡🗑🔌🧺T🚽

Within 3 miles: ⚓🎣🏇🎣◎⛷🏧🔒

Notes: No motorised scooters.

see advert below

▶▶▶▶ **81% Well Park Caravan & Camping Site** *(SN128028)*

SA70 8TL
☎ **01834 842179** 🖷 **01834 842179**
e-mail: enquiries@wellparkcaravans.co.uk
dir: *A478 towards Tenby. At rdbt at Kilgetty follow Tenby/A478 signs. 3m to next rdbt, take 2nd exit, site 2nd right*

⊡ 🚐 ⚠

Open Mar-Oct (rs Mar-mid Jun & mid Sep-Oct bar, launderette, baby room may be closed)

Last arrival 22.00hrs Last departure 11.00hrs

An attractive, well-maintained park with good landscaping from trees, ornamental shrubs, and attractive flower borders. The amenities include a launderette and indoor dishwashing, games room with table tennis, and an enclosed play area. Tenby is just a 15-minute walk away or can be reached via a traffic-free cycle track. 10 acre site. 100 touring pitches. 16 hardstandings. Caravan pitches. Motorhome pitches. Tent pitches. 42 statics.

AA Pubs & Restaurants nearby: Stackpole Inn, Stackpole 01646 672324

New Inn, Amroth 01834 812368

Leisure: ⚠🔍🖵

Facilities: ⚘⊙🜂✳♿🕐🛒♻🅸

Services: ⊡🗑🔌🍴🧺🚽

Within 3 miles: ⚓🎣🏇🎣◎⛷🏧🔒U

Notes: ❸ Family parties only. Dogs must be kept on leads. TV hookups.

AA CAMPING CARD SITE

▶▶▶ **76% Wood Park Caravans**

(SN128025)

New Hedges SA70 8TL
☎ **0845 129 8314 & 129 8344 (winter)**
e-mail: info@woodpark.co.uk
dir: *At rdbt 2m N of Tenby follow A478 towards Tenby, then take 2nd right & right again*

* ⊡ £15-£25 🚐 £15-£25 ⚠ £13-£23

Open Spring BH-Sep (rs May & mid-end Sep bar, laundrette & games room may not be open)

Last arrival 22.00hrs Last departure 10.00hrs

LEISURE: 🏊 Indoor swimming pool 🏊 Outdoor swimming pool ⚠ Children's playground 🪁 Kid's club ⛳ Tennis court 🎱 Games room 🖵 Separate TV room ⚓ 9/18 hole golf course ⛵ Boats for hire ⊞ Cinema 🎵 Entertainment 🎣 Fishing ◎ Mini golf ⛷ Watersports 💪 Gym ⚙ Sports field **Spa** U Stables
FACILITIES: 🛁 Bath 🚿 Shower ⊙ Electric shaver 🜂 Hairdryer ✳ Ice Pack Facility ♿ Disabled facilities 🕐 Public telephone 🏧 Shop on site or within 200yds 🏪 Mobile shop (calls at least 5 days a week) 🍖 BBQ area 🍴 Picnic area 📶 Wi-fi 💻 Internet access ♻ Recycling 🅸 Tourist info 🐾 Dog exercise area

Situated in beautiful countryside between the popular seaside resorts of Tenby and Saundersfoot, and with Waterwynch Bay just a 15-minute walk away, this peaceful site provides a spacious and relaxing atmosphere for holidays. The slightly sloping touring area is partly divided by shrubs into three paddocks. 10 acre site. 60 touring pitches. 40 hardstandings. 10 seasonal pitches. Caravan pitches. Motorhome pitches. Tent pitches. 90 statics.

AA Pubs & Restaurants nearby: Stackpole Inn, Stackpole 01646 672324

New Inn, Amroth 01834 812368

Leisure: ⚠ 🔍

Facilities: 🛉⊙🅿☀♨ 🟢 ❶

Services: 🔌🍴🔋🧺∅🛒

Within 3 miles: ⬇🚶☰🅿◎⬇🛒🛒∪

Notes: ⬤ No groups. 1 car per unit, only small dogs accepted, no dogs Jul-Aug & BHs. Dogs must be kept on leads.

POWYS

See Walk 15 in the Walks & Cycle Rides section at the end of the guide

BRECON
Map 9 SO02

Places to visit

Brecknock Museum & Art Gallery, BRECON 01874 624121 www.powys.gov.uk/breconmuseum

Regimental Museum of The Royal Welsh, BRECON 01874 613310 www.rrw.org.uk

PREMIER PARK

▶▶▶▶▶ **88% Pencelli Castle Caravan & Camping Park**

GOLD

(SO096248)

Pencelli LD3 7LX
☎ **01874 665451**
e-mail: pencelli@tiscali.co.uk
dir: *Exit A40 2m E of Brecon onto B4558, follow signs to Pencelli*

* �GBP 17.50-£22.60 🚐 £17.50-£22.60
▲ £17.50-£22.60

Open Feb-27 Nov (rs 30 Oct-Etr shop closed)

Last arrival 22.00hrs Last departure noon

Lying in the heart of the Brecon Beacons National Park, this charming park offers peace, beautiful scenery and high quality facilities. The park is bordered by the Brecon and Monmouth Canal. The attention to detail is superb, and the well-equipped heated toilets with en suite cubicles are matched by a drying room for clothes and boots, full laundry, and a shop. Regular buses stop just outside the gate go to Brecon, Abergavenny and Swansea. 10 acre site. 80 touring pitches. 40 hardstandings. Caravan pitches. Motorhome pitches. Tent pitches.

AA Pubs & Restaurants nearby: Felin Fach Griffin, Felin Fach 01874 620111

White Swan Inn, Llanfrynach 01874 665276

Old Ford Inn, Llanhamlach 01874 665391

Leisure: ⚠

Facilities: 🛉⊙🅿☀♿🕐🧺🍴 📶 🟢 ❶

Services: 🔌🍴🔋∅🚽🔋⬇

Within 3 miles: 🚶☰🅿🛒∪

Notes: ⊗ Assistance dogs only. No radios, music or campfires. Cycle hire.

BRONLLYS
Map 9 SO13

Places to visit

Brecknock Museum & Art Gallery, BRECON 01874 624121 www.powys.gov.uk/breconmuseum

Regimental Museum of The Royal Welsh, BRECON 01874 613310 www.rrw.org.uk

AA CAMPING CARD SITE

▶▶▶▶ **80% Anchorage Caravan Park** *(SO142351)*

LD3 0LD
☎ **01874 711246 & 711230** 📠 **01874 711711**
dir: *8m NE of Brecon in village centre*

🚐 fr £12 🚐 fr £12 ▲ fr £12

Open all year (rs Nov-Mar TV room closed)

Last arrival 23.00hrs Last departure 18.00hrs

A well-maintained site with a choice of south-facing, sloping grass pitches and superb views of the Black Mountains, or a more sheltered lower area with a number of excellent super pitches. The site is a short distance from the water sports centre at Llangorse Lake. 8 acre site. 110 touring pitches. 8 hardstandings. 60 seasonal pitches. Caravan pitches. Motorhome pitches. Tent pitches. 101 statics.

Anchorage Caravan Park

AA Pubs & Restaurants nearby: Castle Inn, Talgarth 01874 711353

Old Black Lion, Hay-on-Wye 01497 820841

Kilverts Inn, Hay-on-Wye 01497 821042

Leisure: ⚠ 🖵

Facilities: 🛉⊙🅿☀♿🕐🧺🍴🏕♨ ❶

Services: 🔌🍴🔋∅🚽⬇

Within 3 miles: 🅿🛒∪

Notes: ⬤ Dogs must be kept on leads. Post office, hairdresser.

BUILTH WELLS
Map 9 SO05

▶▶▶ **83% *Fforest Fields Caravan & Camping Park***

GOLD

(SO100535)

Hundred House LD1 5RT
☎ **01982 570406**
e-mail: office@fforestfields.co.uk
web: www.fforestfields.co.uk
dir: *From town follow New Radnor signs on A481. 4m to signed entrance on right, 0.5m before Hundred House village*

🚐🚐▲

Open Etr & Apr-Oct

Last arrival 21.00hrs Last departure 18.00hrs

A sheltered park in a hidden valley with wonderful views and plenty of wildlife. Set in unspoilt countryside, this is a peaceful park with delightful hill walks beginning on site. The historic town of

continued

SERVICES: 🔌 Electric hook up 🔋 Launderette 🍴 Licensed bar 🔋 Calor Gas ∅ Camping Gaz 🚽 Toilet fluid 🍴 Café/Restaurant 🔋 Fast Food/Takeaway 🔋 Battery charging 🔋 Baby care ⬇ Motorvan service point
ABBREVIATIONS: BH/bank hols-bank holidays Etr-Easter Whit-Whitsun dep-departure fr-from hrs-hours m-mile mdnt-midnight rdbt-roundabout rs-restricted service wk-week wknd-weekend ⬤ No credit cards ⊗ No dogs
See page 7 for details of the AA Camping Card Scheme

BUILTH WELLS *continued*

Builth Wells and the Royal Welsh Showground are only four miles away, and there are plenty of outdoor activities in the vicinity. 12 acre site. 60 touring pitches. 17 hardstandings. Caravan pitches. Motorhome pitches. Tent pitches.

AA Pubs & Restaurants nearby: Laughing Dog, Howey 01597 822406

Facilities: ↟☉🝖❋🕓🚾📶

Services: 🔌🔋🔒💧🚮

Within 3 miles: ⚓🎠🐾🛒

Notes: 🐾 No loud music or revelry. Bread, dairy produce & cured bacon available.

CRICKHOWELL — Map 9 SO21

Places to visit

Tretower Court & Castle, TRETOWER 01874 730279 www.cadw.wales.gov.uk

Big Pit National Coal Museum, BLAENAVON 01495 790311 www.museumwales.ac.uk

►►► 78% Riverside Caravan & Camping Park *(SO215184)*

New Rd NP8 1AY
☎ 01873 810397
dir: *On A4077, well signed from A40*

* 🚐 fr £15 🚐 fr £15 ▲ fr £12

Open Mar-Oct

Last arrival 21.00hrs

A very well tended adults-only park in delightful countryside on the edge of the small country town of Crickhowell. The adjacent riverside park is an excellent facility for all, including dog-walkers. Crickhowell has numerous specialist shops including a first-class delicatessen. Within a few minutes' walk of the park are several friendly pubs with good restaurants. 3.5 acre site. 35 touring pitches. Caravan pitches. Motorhome pitches. Tent pitches. 20 statics.

AA Pubs & Restaurants nearby: Nantyffin Cider Mill Inn, Crickhowell 01873 810775

Facilities: ↟☉🝖❋🛒

Services: 🔌🔒🚮

Within 3 miles: ⚓🎠🛒U

Notes: Adults only. 🐾 No hangliders or paragliders. Dogs must be kept on leads. Large canopied area for drying clothes, cooking & socialising.

LLANDRINDOD WELLS — Map 9 SO06

Places to visit

The Judge's Lodging, PRESTEIGNE 01544 260650 www.judgeslodging.org.uk

AA CAMPING CARD SITE

►►► 81% Disserth Caravan & Camping Park *(SO035583)*

Disserth, Howey LD1 6NL
☎ 01597 860277
e-mail: disserthcaravan@btconnect.com
dir: *1m from A483, between Newbridge-on-Wye & Howey, by church. Follow brown signs from A483 or A470*

🚐🚐▲

Open Mar-Oct

Last arrival 22.00hrs Last departure noon

A delightfully secluded and predominantly adult park nestling in a beautiful valley on the banks of the River Ithon, a tributary of the River Wye. This little park is next to a 13th-century church, and has a small bar open at weekends and busy periods. The chalet toilet block offers spacious, combined cubicles. 4 acre site. 30 touring pitches. 6 hardstandings. Caravan pitches. Motorhome pitches. Tent pitches. 25 statics.

AA Pubs & Restaurants nearby: Laughing Dog, Howey 01597 822406

Bell Country Inn, Llanyre 01597 823959

Facilities: ↟☉🝖❋🕓📶♻🛈

Services: 🔌🔋🔌🔒💧🚮

Within 3 miles: ⚓🎠🐾🛒🛒

Notes: 🐾 Dogs must be kept on leads. Private trout fishing.

AA CAMPING CARD SITE

►► 82% Dalmore Camping & Caravanning Park *(SO045568)*

Howey LD1 5RG
☎ 01597 822483 📄 01597 822483
dir: *3m S of Llandrindod Wells off A483. 4m N of Builth Wells, at top of hill*

🚐 £9-£12 🚐 £9-£12 ▲ £9-£12

Open Mar-Oct

Last arrival 22.00hrs Last departure noon

An intimate and well laid out adults-only park. Pitches are attractively terraced to ensure that all enjoy the wonderful views from this splendidly landscaped little park. Please note, dogs are not allowed. 3 acre site. 20 touring pitches. 12 hardstandings. 6 seasonal pitches. Caravan pitches. Motorhome pitches. Tent pitches. 20 statics.

AA Pubs & Restaurants nearby: Laughing Dog, Howey 01597 822406

Bell Country Inn, Llanyre 01597 823959

Facilities: ↟☉🝖❋🕓🚜🛈

Services: 🔌🔒💧🚮🔽

Within 3 miles: ⚓🎠🎠🐾◎🛒🛒

Notes: Adults only. 🐾🐕 Gates closed 23.00hrs-07.00hrs, no ball games.

LEISURE: 🏊 Indoor swimming pool 🏊 Outdoor swimming pool 🎠 Children's playground 👶 Kid's club 🎾 Tennis court 🎱 Games room 📺 Separate TV room ⛳ 9/18 hole golf course ⛵ Boats for hire 🎬 Cinema 🎵 Entertainment 🎣 Fishing ◎ Mini golf 🏄 Watersports 🏋 Gym ⚽ Sports field **Spa** U Stables
FACILITIES: 🛁 Bath 🚿 Shower ⊙ Electric shaver 🝖 Hairdryer ❋ Ice Pack Facility ♿ Disabled facilities 🕓 Public telephone 🛒 Shop on site or within 200yds 🚙 Mobile shop (calls at least 5 days a week) 🍖 BBQ area 🪑 Picnic area 🚾 Wi-fi 💻 Internet access ♻ Recycling 🛈 Tourist info 🐾 Dog exercise area

LLANGORS
Map 9 SO12

Places to visit

Llanthony Priory, LLANTHONY 01443 336000
www.cadw.wales.gov.uk

Great for kids: Tretower Court & Castle,
TRETOWER 01874 730279
www.cadw.wales.gov.uk

▶▶▶ 76% **Lakeside Caravan Park** (SO128272)

LD3 7TR
☎ **01874 658226**
e-mail: holidays@llangorselake.co.uk
dir: Exit A40 at Bwlch onto B4560 towards
Talgarth. Site signed towards lake in Llangors
centre

* ⊞ £12.50-£14.50 ⚏ £12.50-£14.50
Å £12.50-£14.50

Open Etr or Apr-Oct (rs Mar-May & Oct clubhouse,
restaurant, shop limited)

Last arrival 21.30hrs Last departure 10.00hrs

Next to Llangors common and lake this attractive
park has launching and mooring facilities and is
an ideal centre for water sports enthusiasts.
Popular with families, and offering a clubhouse/
bar, with a well-stocked shop and café/takeaway
next door. Boats, bikes and windsurfing
equipment can be hired on site. 2 acre site. 40
touring pitches. 8 hardstandings. Caravan
pitches. Motorhome pitches. Tent pitches. 72
statics.

AA Pubs & Restaurants nearby: Usk Inn,
Talybont-on-Usk 01874 676251

Star Inn, Talybont-on-Usk 01874 676635

Leisure: ⚏ ✎

Facilities: ⛿ ☉ ℗ ☀ ⓢ ⌂ ⌶ ⚞ ♻ ❂

Services: ⛿ ⓢ ⊞ ⛿ ⌖ ⊤ ⓧ ⛻

Within 3 miles: ⇟ ℘ ⇟ ⓢ ⓢ ∪

Notes: No open fires. Dogs must be kept on leads.
Boat hire during summer season.

MIDDLETOWN
Map 15 SJ31

Places to visit

Powis Castle & Garden, WELSHPOOL
01938 551920 www.nationaltrust.org.uk

Great for kids: Old Oswestry Hill Fort, OSWESTRY
www.english-heritage.org.uk

AA CAMPING CARD SITE

▶▶▶ 79% **Bank Farm Caravan Park**
(SJ293123)

SY21 8EJ
☎ **01938 570526**
e-mail: bankfarmcaravans@yahoo.co.uk
dir: 13m W of Shrewsbury, 5m E of Welshpool on
A458

⊞ ⚏ Å

Open Mar-Oct

Last arrival 20.00hrs

An attractive park on a small farm, maintained to
a high standard. There are two touring areas, one
on either side of the A458, and each with its own
amenity block, and immediate access to hills,
mountains and woodland. A pub serving good
food, and a large play area are nearby. 2 acre site.
40 touring pitches. Caravan pitches. Motorhome
pitches. Tent pitches. 33 statics.

AA Pubs & Restaurants nearby: Old Hand &
Diamond Inn, Coedway 01743 884379

Leisure: ⚏ ✎

Facilities: ⛿ ☉ ☀ ⓢ ⌂ ⌶

Services: ⛿ ⓢ ⇶

Within 3 miles: ⇟ ℘ ⓢ

Notes: ⊗ Coarse fishing, jacuzzi, snooker room.

RHAYADER
Map 9 SN96

Places to visit

Blaenavon Ironworks, BLAENAVON 01495 792615
www.cadw.wales.gov.uk

White Castle, WHITE CASTLE 01600 780380
www.cadw.wales.gov.uk

Great for kids: Raglan Castle, RAGLAN
01291 690228 www.cadw.wales.gov.uk

▶▶▶ 75% *Wyeside Caravan &
Camping Park* (SO967690)

Llangurig Rd LD6 5LB
☎ **01597 810183**
e-mail: info@wyesidecamping.co.uk
dir: 400mtrs N of Rhayader town centre on A470

⊞ ⚏ Å

Open Feb-Nov

Last arrival 22.30hrs Last departure noon

With direct access from the A470, the park sits on
the banks of the River Wye. Situated just 400
metres from the centre of the market town of
Rhayader, and next to a recreation park with
tennis courts, bowling green and children's
playground. There are good riverside walks from
here, though the river is fast flowing and
unfenced, and care is especially needed when
walking with children. 6 acre site. 140 touring
pitches. 22 hardstandings. Caravan pitches.
Motorhome pitches. Tent pitches. 39 statics.

AA Pubs & Restaurants nearby: Bell Country Inn,
Llanyre 01597 823959

Facilities: ⛿ ☉ ℗ ☀ ⓢ ☉ wifi

Services: ⛿ ⓢ ⌖ ⊘ ⊤ ⇶

Within 3 miles: ℘ ◎ ⇟ ⓢ ⓢ ∪

SERVICES: ⛿ Electric hook up ⓢ Launderette ⛿ Licensed bar ⌖ Calor Gas ⊘ Camping Gaz ⊤ Toilet fluid ⓧ Café/Restaurant ⛻ Fast Food/Takeaway ⇶ Battery charging
⛿ Baby care ⚓ Motorvan service point
ABBREVIATIONS: BH/bank hols-bank holidays Etr-Easter Whit-Whitsun dep-departure fr-from hrs-hours m-mile mdnt-midnight rdbt-roundabout rs-restricted service wk-week
wknd-weekend ⊗ No credit cards ⊗ No dogs See page 7 for details of the AA Camping Card Scheme

SWANSEA

PONTARDDULAIS

Places to visit

The National Botanic Garden of Wales, LLANARTHNE 01558 668768 www.gardenofwales.org.uk

Glynn Vivain Art Gallery, SWANSEA 01792 516900 www.glynnviviangallery.org

Great for kids: Plantasia, SWANSEA 01792 474555 www.plantasia.org

PONTARDDULAIS Map 8 SN50

►►►► 87% River View Touring Park *(SN578086)*

The Dingle, Llanedi SA4 0FH
☎ 01269 844876
e-mail: info@riverviewtouringpark.com
web: www.riverviewtouringpark.com
dir: *M4 junct 49, A483 signed Llandeilo. 0.5m, 1st left after lay-by, follow lane to site*

🚐 🚙 ⛺

Open Mar-late Nov

Last arrival 20.00hrs Last departure noon

This peaceful park is set on one lower and two upper levels in a sheltered valley with an abundance of wild flowers and wildlife. The River Gwli flows around the bottom of the park in which fishing for brown trout is possible. The excellent toilet facilities are an added bonus. This park is ideally situated for visiting the beaches of South Wales, The Black Mountains and the Brecon Beacons. 6 acre site. 60 touring pitches. 39 hardstandings. Caravan pitches. Motorhome pitches. Tent pitches.

Leisure: ⚽

Facilities: 🚿 ⊙ 💨 ❄ ♿ 🏪 🐕 ♻ ℹ

Services: 🔌 🌀 🔒 🍃 [T]

Within 3 miles: ⛳ 🎬 🎣 🏪 🌀 🐴

Notes: Dogs must be kept on leads.

PORT EINON Map 8 SS48

Places to visit

Weobley Castle, LLANRHIDIAN 01792 390012 www.cadw.wales.gov.uk

Gower Heritage Centre, PARKMILL 01792 371206 www.gowerheritagecentre.co.uk

Great for kids: Oxwich Castle, OXWICH 01792 390359 www.cadw.wales.gov.uk

►►► 81% Carreglwyd Camping & Caravan Park *(SS465863)*

SA3 1NL
☎ 01792 390795 📠 01792 390796
dir: *A4118 to Port Einon, site adjacent to beach*

🚐 🚙 ⛺

Open Mar-Dec

Last arrival 18.00hrs Last departure 15.00hrs

Set in an unrivalled location alongside the safe sandy beach of Port Einon on the Gower Peninsula, this popular park is an ideal family holiday spot. Close to an attractive village with pubs and shops, most pitches offer sea views. The sloping ground has been partly terraced, and facilities are excellent. 12 acre site. 150 touring pitches. Caravan pitches. Motorhome pitches. Tent pitches.

AA Pubs & Restaurants nearby: Fairyhill, Reynoldston 01792 390139

King Arthur Hotel, Reynoldston 01792 390775

Facilities: 🚿 ⊙ ♿ 🏪 🐕 ♻

Services: 🔌 🌀 🔒 🍃 [T] ⚓

Within 3 miles: 🎣 🏄 🏪 🐴

Notes: Dogs must be kept on leads.

RHOSSILI Map 8 SS48

Places to visit

Weobley Castle, LLANRHIDIAN 01792 390012 www.cadw.wales.gov.uk

Gower Heritage Centre, PARKMILL 01792 371206 www.gowerheritagecentre.co.uk

Great for kids: Oxwich Castle, OXWICH 01792 390359 www.cadw.wales.gov.uk

►►► 84% Pitton Cross Caravan & Camping Park *(SS434877)*

SA3 1PH
☎ 01792 390593 📠 01792 391010
e-mail: admin@pittoncross.co.uk
web: www.pittoncross.co.uk
dir: *2m W of Scurlage on B4247*

* 🚐 £16.50-£24.95 🚙 £16.50-£24.95 ⛺ £9-£31.50

Open all year (rs Nov-Mar no bread, milk or papers)

Last arrival 20.00hrs Last departure 11.00hrs

Surrounded by farmland close to sandy Menslade Bay, which is within walking distance across the fields, this grassy park is divided by hedging into paddocks. Nearby Rhossili Beach is popular with surfers. Performance kites are sold, and instruction in flying is given. 6 acre site. 100 touring pitches. 25 hardstandings. Caravan pitches. Motorhome pitches. Tent pitches.

AA Pubs & Restaurants nearby: Fairyhill, Reynoldston 01792 390139

King Arthur Hotel, Reynoldston 01792 390775

Kings Head, Llangennith 01792 386212

Leisure: 🛝

Facilities: 🚿 ⊙ 💨 ❄ ♿ ☎ 🏪 🧺 ♻ ℹ

Services: 🔌 🌀 🔒 🍃 [T]

Within 3 miles: 🎣 🏄 🏪 🌀

Notes: Quiet at all times, charcoal BBQs must be off ground. Dogs must be kept on leads. Baby bath available.

LEISURE: 🏊 Indoor swimming pool 🏊 Outdoor swimming pool 🛝 Children's playground 🤸 Kid's club 🎾 Tennis court 🎱 Games room 📺 Separate TV room ⛳ 9/18 hole golf course ⛵ Boats for hire 🎬 Cinema 🎵 Entertainment 🎣 Fishing ◎ Mini golf 🏄 Watersports 🏋 Gym ⚽ Sports field Spa 🐴 Stables
FACILITIES: 🛁 Bath 🚿 Shower ⊙ Electric shaver 💨 Hairdryer ❄ Ice Pack Facility ♿ Disabled facilities ☎ Public telephone 🏪 Shop on site or within 200yds 🚚 Mobile shop (calls at least 5 days a week) 🍖 BBQ area 🧺 Picnic area [Wi-fi] Wi-fi 💻 Internet access ♻ Recycling ℹ Tourist info 🐕 Dog exercise area

SWANSEA
Map 9 SS69

Places to visit

Swansea Museum, SWANSEA 01792 653763
www.swanseaheritage.net

Glynn Vivain Art Gallery, SWANSEA
01792 516900 www.glynnviviangallery.org

 78% Riverside Caravan Park
(SS679991)

Ynys Forgan Farm, Morriston SA6 6QL
☎ 01792 775587   📄 01792 795751
e-mail: reception@riversideswansea.com
dir: Exit M4 junct 45 towards Swansea. Left into
private road signed to site

🚗 🚐 Å

Open all year (rs Winter months pool & club
closed)

Last arrival mdnt Last departure noon

A large and busy park close to the M4 but
in a quiet location beside the River Taw.
This friendly, family orientated park has a
licensed club and bar with a full high-season
entertainment programme. There is a choice of
eating outlets with the clubhouse restaurant,
takeaway or chip shop. The park has a good
indoor pool. 5 acre site. 90 touring pitches.
Caravan pitches. Motorhome pitches. Tent
pitches. 256 statics.

AA Pubs & Restaurants nearby: Hanson at the
Chelsea Restaurant, Swansea 01792 464068

Leisure: 🏊 🎱 🎣 🖵
Facilities: 🅿 ⊙ ℗ ⚒ 🔧 🕐 ⓢ 🛁 🐾 WI-FI
Services: 🔌 🛢 🍴 🔥 🧴 Ⓣ 🛒 ♨
Within 3 miles: ♨ ⅔ ⽮ ℐ ⓢ 🔄 ∪

Notes: Dogs by arrangement only (no
aggressive dog breeds permitted). Fishing on
site by arrangement.

VALE OF GLAMORGAN

LLANTWIT MAJOR
Map 9 SS96

Places to visit

Old Beaupre Castle, ST HILARY 01443 336000
www.cadw.wales.gov.uk

Great for kids: Ogmore Castle, OGMORE
01443 336000 www.cadw.wales.gov.uk

►►► **83% Acorn Camping & Caravan
Site** (SS973678)

Ham Lane South CF61 1RP
☎ 01446 794024
e-mail: info@acorncamping.co.uk
dir: B4265 to Llantwit Major, follow camping
signs. Approach site through Ham Manor
residential park

* 🚗 £15.15-£16.50 🚐 £15.15-£16.50
Å £11.15-£12.50

Open Feb-8 Dec

Last arrival 21.00hrs Last departure 11.00hrs

A peaceful country site in level meadowland, with
some individual pitches divided by hedges and
shrubs. It is about one mile from the beach, which
can be reached via a cliff top walk, and the same
distance from the historic town of Llantwit Major.
An internet station and a full-size snooker table
are useful amenities. 5.5 acre site. 90 touring
pitches. 10 hardstandings. Caravan pitches.
Motorhome pitches. Tent pitches. 25 statics.

AA Pubs & Restaurants nearby: Illtud's 216,
Llantwit Major 01446 793800

Plough & Harrow, Monknash 01656 890209

Blue Anchor Inn, East Aberthaw 01446 750329

Leisure: 🎱 🎣
Facilities: 🅿 ⊙ ℗ ⚒ 🔧 🕐 ⓢ WI-FI 🖵 ♻ ❶
Services: 🔌 🛢 🍴 🔥 Ⓣ 🍴 🛒 ♨ ⅃
Within 3 miles: ℐ ⓢ ∪

Notes: No noise 23.00hrs-07.00hrs. Dogs must be
kept on leads.

SERVICES: 🔌 Electric hook up ⓢ Launderette 🍴 Licensed bar 🛢 Calor Gas ⊘ Camping Gaz Ⓣ Toilet fluid 🍴 Café/Restaurant 🛒 Fast Food/Takeaway ♨ Battery charging
🍼 Baby care ⅃ Motorvan service point
ABBREVIATIONS: BH/bank hols-bank holidays Etr-Easter Whit-Whitsun dep-departure fr-from hrs-hours m-mile mdnt-midnight rdbt-roundabout rs-restricted service wk-week
wknd-weekend 🚫 No credit cards 🚫 No dogs
See page 7 for details of the AA Camping Card Scheme

WREXHAM

EYTON	Map 15 SJ34

Places to visit

Erddig, WREXHAM 01978 355314
www.nationaltrust.org.uk

Chirk Castle, CHIRK 01691 777701
www.nationaltrust.org.uk/main/w-chirkcastle

AA CAMPING CARD SITE

PREMIER PARK

►►►►► 92% The
Plassey Leisure Park

(SJ353452)

The Plassey LL13 0SP
☎ 01978 780277 📠 01978 780019
e-mail: enquiries@plassey.com
web: www.plassey.com
dir: *From A483 at Bangor-on-Dee exit onto B5426
for 2.5m. Site entrance signed on left*

🚐 £14.50-£25 🚙 £14.50-£25 ▲ £14.50-£25

Open Feb-Nov

Last arrival 20.30hrs Last departure noon

A lovely park set in several hundred acres of quiet farm and meadowland in the Dee Valley. The superb toilet facilities include individual cubicles for total privacy and security, while the Edwardian farm buildings have been converted into a restaurant, coffee shop, beauty studio, and various craft outlets. There is plenty here to entertain the whole family, from scenic walks and swimming pool to free fishing, and use of the 9-hole golf course. 10 acre site. 90 touring pitches. 45 hardstandings. 60 seasonal pitches. Caravan pitches. Motorhome pitches. Tent pitches. 15 statics.

The Plassey Leisure Park

AA Pubs & Restaurants nearby: Hanmer Arms, Hanmer 01948 830532

Leisure: 🏊 ⛳ 🎱 🎣

Facilities: 🛁 ☉ 🚿 ⚡ ✂ 👤 🛎 🚻 🛒 📶 ♻ ℹ

Services: 🚱 🔄 🚽 🧺 🔌 📞 🍴 🛒 ⛽ 🚮

Within 3 miles: ↓🏇🚵 ⛳ ◎ 🛒 🎣 ⛹

Notes: No footballs, bikes or skateboards. Dogs must be kept on leads. Sauna, badminton & table tennis.

see advert below

LEISURE: 🏊 Indoor swimming pool 🏊 Outdoor swimming pool 🎠 Children's playground 🪁 Kid's club 🎾 Tennis court 🎱 Games room 📺 Separate TV room ⛳ 9/18 hole golf course ⛵ Boats for hire 🎬 Cinema 🎵 Entertainment 🎣 Fishing ◎ Mini golf 🏄 Watersports 🏋 Gym 🏟 Sports field **Spa** ⛹ Stables

FACILITIES: 🛁 Bath 🚿 Shower ☉ Electric shaver ✂ Hairdryer ❄ Ice Pack Facility ♿ Disabled facilities 📞 Public telephone 🛒 Shop on site or within 200yds 🚐 Mobile shop (calls at least 5 days a week) 🍖 BBQ area 🍴 Picnic area 📶 Wi-fi 💻 Internet access ♻ Recycling ℹ Tourist info 🐕 Dog exercise area

SERVICES: 🔌 Electric hook up 🌀 Launderette 🍸 Licensed bar 🛢 Calor Gas 🔥 Camping Gaz 🚽 Toilet fluid 🍽 Café/Restaurant 🍔 Fast Food/Takeaway 🔋 Battery charging
🐾 Baby care ⚓ Motorvan service point
ABBREVIATIONS: BH/bank hols-bank holidays Etr-Easter Whit-Whitsun dep-departure fr-from hrs-hours m-mile mdnt-midnight rdbt-roundabout rs-restricted service wk-week
wknd-weekend 💳 No credit cards 🚫 No dogs   See page 7 for details of the AA Camping Card Scheme

Ireland

Wicklow Mountains, Co Wicklow

NORTHERN IRELAND

CO ANTRIM

ANTRIM
Map 1 D5

Places to visit

Antrim Round Tower, ANTRIM 028 9023 5000 www.ehsni.gov.uk

Bonamargy Friary, BALLYCASTLE 028 9023 5000 www.ehsni.gov.uk

Great for kids: Belfast Zoological Gardens, BELFAST 028 9077 6277 www.belfastzoo.co.uk

▶▶▶ **83% Six Mile Water Caravan Park** (J137870)

Lough Rd BT41 4DG
☎ 028 9446 4963 & 9446 3113
e-mail: sixmilewater@antrim.gov.uk
web: www.antrim.gov.uk/caravanpark
dir: *1m from town centre, follow Antrim Forum/ Loughshore Park signs. On Dublin road take Lough road (pass Antrim Forum on right). Site at end of road on right*

* ⊕ £20-£22 ⊕ £20-£22 ▲ fr £15

Open Mar-Oct

Last arrival 21.45hrs Last departure noon

A pretty tree-lined site in a large municipal park, within walking distance of Antrim and the Antrim Forum leisure complex yet very much in the countryside. The modern toilet block is well equipped, and other facilities include a laundry and electric hook-ups. All the pitches are precisely set on generous plots. 9.61 acre site. 67 touring pitches. 37 hardstandings. Caravan pitches. Motorhome pitches. Tent pitches.

AA Pubs & Restaurants nearby: Galgorm Resort & Spa, Ballymena 028 2588 1001

Leisure: ◆ ⊡
Facilities: ⋔ ⊙ ℗ ⅄ ⅃ ⊙ ⓢ ⍭
Services: ⊕ ⓢ ⅇ ⣿ ⅊
Within 3 miles: ⅃ ⊟ ℘ ⅃ ⓢ ⅃

Notes: Max stay 14 nights, no noise between 22.00hrs-08.00hrs. Dogs must be kept on leads. Watersports, angling stands.

BALLYCASTLE
Map 1 D6

Places to visit

Bonamargy Friary, BALLYCASTLE 028 9023 5000 www.ehsni.gov.uk

Great for kids: Dunluce Castle, PORTBALLINTRAE 028 2073 1938 www.ehsni.gov.uk

▶▶▶ **74% Watertop Farm** (D115407)

188 Cushendall Rd BT54 6RN
☎ 028 2076 2576
e-mail: watertopfarm@aol.com
dir: *Take A2 from Ballycastle towards Cushendall. Site opposite Ballypatrick forest*

⊕ fr £18 ⊕ fr £18 ▲ fr £10

Open Etr-Oct (rs Etr-Jun & Sep-Oct farm activities not available)

Located on a family hill sheep farm set in the glens of Antrim, the farm offers a range of activities and attractions including pony trekking, boating, pedal go-karts, farm tours, tea room and lots more. The touring facilities consist of three individual sections, two reserved for caravans and the other for tents. The toilets are housed in a converted traditional Irish cottage, and the attached small rural museum serves as a night time social area. 0.5 acre site. 14 touring pitches. 9 hardstandings. Caravan pitches. Motorhome pitches. Tent pitches.

AA Pubs & Restaurants nearby: Frances Anne Restaurant, Londonderry Arms Hotel, Carnlough 028 2888 5255

Leisure: ⚑ ◆
Facilities: ⋔ ⊙ ✳ ⅄ ⍭ ⊙
Services: ⊕ ⓢ ⅆ ⣿ ⅇ ⅊ ⅃
Within 3 miles: ⅃ ⅄ ℘ ⅃ ⓢ ⅃ ⎈

Notes: No camp fires, no BBQ trays on grass. Dogs must be kept on leads.

BALLYMONEY
Map 1 C6

Places to visit

Leslie Hill Open Farm, BALLYMONEY 028 2766 6803 www.lesliehillopenfarm.co.uk

Bonamargy Friary, BALLYCASTLE 028 9023 5000 www.ehsni.gov.uk

Great for kids: Dunluce Castle, PORTBALLINTRAE 028 2073 1938 www.ehsni.gov.uk

PREMIER PARK

▶▶▶▶▶ **78% Drumaheglis Marina & Caravan Park** (C901254)

36 Glenstall Rd BT53 7QN
☎ 028 2766 0280 & 2766 0227
⊟ 028 2766 0222
e-mail: drumaheglis@ballymoney.gov.uk
dir: *Signed off A26, approx 1.5m from Ballymoney towards Coleraine. Also accessed from B66, S of Ballymoney*

⊕ £23-£24 ⊕ £23-£24 ▲ £16.50

Open 17 Mar-Oct

Last arrival 20.00hrs Last departure 13.00hrs

Exceptionally well-designed and laid out park beside the Lower Bann River, with very spacious pitches (all fully serviced) and two quality toilet blocks. Ideal base for touring Antrim and for watersports enthusiasts. 16 acre site. 55 touring pitches. 55 hardstandings. 20 seasonal pitches. Caravan pitches. Motorhome pitches. Tent pitches.

Leisure: ⚑
Facilities: ⋔ ⊙ ℗ ✳ ⅃ ⊙ ⅄ ⍭ ⅲ ⊙ ⓘ
Services: ⊕ ⓢ ⅆ ⅊
Within 3 miles: ⅃ ℘ ⅃ ⓢ ⅃

Notes: Dogs must be kept on leads. Marina berths. Table tennis & volleyball.

BUSHMILLS

Places to visit

Old Bushmills Distillery, BUSHMILLS 028 2073 3218 www.bushmills.com

Great for kids: Belfast Zoological Gardens, BELFAST 028 9077 6277 www.belfastzoo.co.uk

---

LEISURE: ≋ Indoor swimming pool ≋ Outdoor swimming pool ⚑ Children's playground ✦ Kid's club ⚑ Tennis court ◆ Games room ⊡ Separate TV room
⅃ 9/18 hole golf course ⚓ Boats for hire ⊟ Cinema ♫ Entertainment ℘ Fishing ◎ Mini golf ⚑ Watersports ⅄ Gym ⊛ Sports field Spa ⎈ Stables
FACILITIES: ⚑ Bath ⋔ Shower ⊙ Electric shaver ℗ Hairdryer ✳ Ice Pack Facility ⅃ Disabled facilities ⊙ Public telephone ⓢ Shop on site or within 200yds
⍭ Mobile shop (calls at least 5 days a week) ⍭ BBQ area ⍭ Picnic area ⅲ Wi-fi ⍭ Internet access ⍭ Recycling ⓘ Tourist info ⅄ Dog exercise area

BUSHMILLS Map 1 C6

AA CAMPING CARD SITE

PREMIER PARK

▶▶▶▶▶ **87% Ballyness Caravan Park** *(C944393)*

GOLD

40 Castlecatt Rd BT57 8TN
☎ 028 2073 2393 📠 028 2073 2713
e-mail: info@ballynesscaravanpark.com
web: www.ballynesscaravanpark.com
dir: 0.5m S of Bushmills on B66, follow signs

🚐 £22 🚛 £22

Open 17 Mar-Oct

Last arrival 21.00hrs Last departure noon

A quality park with superb toilet and other facilities, on farmland beside St Columb's Rill, the stream that supplies the famous nearby Bushmills Distillery. The friendly owners built this park with the discerning camper in mind, and they continue to improve it to ever higher standards. There is a pleasant walk around several ponds, and the park is peacefully located close to the beautiful north Antrim coast. There is a holiday cottage to let. 16 acre site. 48 touring pitches. 48 hardstandings. Caravan pitches. Motorhome pitches. 65 statics.

AA Pubs & Restaurants nearby: Bushmills Inn Hotel, Bushmills 028 2073 3000

Leisure: 🅰

Facilities: 🔛 🌂 ⊙ 🅿 ✳ 🔥 🕒 ⑤ 🐕 🚾 🖥 ♻ ❶

Services: 🔌 ⑤ 🔋 ⊘ 🇹 ⛽ ↯

Within 3 miles: ↨ 🎣 ⑤

Notes: No skateboards or roller blades. Dogs must be kept on leads. Library.

CUSHENDUN Map 1 D6

Places to visit
Bonamargy Friary, BALLYCASTLE 028 9023 5000 www.ehsni.gov.uk

Antrim Round Tower, ANTRIM 028 9023 5000 www.ehsni.gov.uk

Great for kids: Giant's Causeway Centre, GIANT'S CAUSEWAY 028 2073 1855 www.northantrim.com

▶▶▶ **77% *Cushendun Caravan Park*** *(D256332)*

14 Glendun Rd BT44 0PX
☎ 028 2176 1254 📠 028 2076 2515
e-mail: cushenduncp@moyle-council.org
dir: From A2 take B92 for 1m towards Glenarm, park clearly signed

🚐 🚛 ⛺

Open Apr-Sep

Last arrival 22.00hrs Last departure 12.30hrs

A pretty little grassy park surrounded by trees, with separate secluded areas offering some privacy, and static vans discreetly interspersed with tourers. The beautiful north Antrim coast is a short drive away through scenic countryside. 3 acre site. 12 touring pitches. Caravan pitches. Motorhome pitches. Tent pitches. 64 statics.

AA Pubs & Restaurants nearby: Frances Anne Restaurant, Londonderry Arms Hotel, Carnlough 028 2888 5255

Leisure: 🎣 ⬚

Facilities: 🌂 ⊙ 🕒 ⑤ 🈂

Services: 🔌 ⑤ ↯

Within 3 miles: ↨ 🎣 🎣 ◎ ⑤ ∪

Notes: Dogs must be kept on leads.

BELFAST

DUNDONALD Map 1 D5

Places to visit
Mount Stewart House & Gardens, NEWTOWNARDS 028 4278 8387 www.nationaltrust.org.uk

Giant's Ring, BELFAST 028 9023 5000 www.ehsni.gov.uk

Great for kids: Belfast Zoological Gardens, BELFAST 028 9077 6277 www.belfastzoo.co.uk

▶▶▶ **75% Dundonald Touring Caravan Park** *(J410731)*

111 Old Dundonald Rd BT16 1XT
☎ 028 9080 9123 & 9080 9129
📠 028 9048 9604
e-mail: sales@castlereagh.gov.uk
dir: From Belfast city centre follow M3 & A20 to City Airport. Then A20 to Newtownards, follow signs to Dundonald & Ulster Hospital. At hospital right at sign for Dundonald Ice Bowl. Follow to end, turn right (Ice Bowl on left)

✳ 🚐 fr £23 🚛 fr £8 ⛺ fr £15

Open 16 Mar-Oct (rs Nov-Mar Aire de Service restricted to motorhomes)

Last arrival 23.00hrs Last departure noon

A purpose-built park in a quiet corner of Dundonald Leisure Park on the outskirts of Belfast. This peaceful park is ideally located for touring County Down and exploring the capital. In the winter it offers an 'Aire de Service' for motorhomes. 1.5 acre site. 22 touring pitches. 22 hardstandings. Caravan pitches. Motorhome pitches. Tent pitches.

AA Pubs & Restaurants nearby: Clandeboye Lodge Hotel, Clandeboye 028 9185 2500

Facilities: 🌂 ⊙ 🅿 ✳ 🔥 🕒 🅰 🚾 🖥 ❶

Services: 🔌 ⑤ 🍴 🍔 ↯

Within 3 miles: ↨ 🎳 🎣 ◎ ⑤ ⑤ ∪

Notes: No commercial vehicles. Dogs must be kept on leads. Bowling, indoor play area, Olympic ice rink (additional charges apply).

see advert on page 434

SERVICES: 🔌 Electric hook up ⑤ Launderette 🍸 Licensed bar 🛢 Calor Gas ⊘ Camping Gaz 🇹 Toilet fluid 🍴 Café/Restaurant 🍔 Fast Food/Takeaway 🔋 Battery charging 🍼 Baby care ↯ Motorvan service point

ABBREVIATIONS: BH/bank hols-bank holidays Etr-Easter Whit-Whitsun dep-departure fr-from hrs-hours m-mile mdnt-midnight rdbt-roundabout rs-restricted service wk-week wknd-weekend ⊜ No credit cards ⊗ No dogs See page 7 for details of the AA Camping Card Scheme

CO FERMANAGH

BELCOO
Map 1 C5

PREMIER PARK

►►►►► 82% Rushin House Caravan Park (H835047)

Holywell BT93 5DY
☎ 028 6638 6519
e-mail: enquiries@rushinhousecaravanpark.com
dir: *From Enniskillen take A4 W for 13m to Belcoo. Right onto B52 towards Garrison for 1m. Site signed*

🚐 fr £24 ⛺ fr £24 ⛺ £15-£22

Open mid Mar-Oct (rs Nov-Mar (Aire de Service facilities available))

Last arrival 21.00hrs Last departure 13.00hrs

This park occupies a scenic location overlooking Lough MacNean, close to the picturesque village of Belcoo, and is the product of meticulous planning and execution. There are 24 very generous, fully-serviced pitches standing on a terrace overlooking the lough, with additional tenting pitches below; all are accessed by excellent wide tarmac roads. Play facilities include a lovely well-equipped play area and a hard surface and fenced five-a-side football pitch. There is a slipway providing boat access to the lough and, of course, fishing. Excellent toilet facilities are housed in a purpose-built structure and include family rooms. 5 acre site. 38 touring pitches. 38 hardstandings. Caravan pitches. Motorhome pitches. Tent pitches.

Leisure: 🅰 🏊 ⚽ 📺
Facilities: 🍴 ⊙ 🧴 ✳ ⛄ 🔍 🚿 ♿ 🌳 WI-FI ♻ ❶
Services: 🚐 🔋 🍺 📶 🛒 ⬇
Within 3 miles: ⚓ 🚲 ⛵ 🏪 🔋

Notes: No cars by tents. Dogs must be kept on leads. Fishing, lakeside walk.

IRVINESTOWN
Map 1 C5

Places to visit

Castle Coole, ENNISKILLEN 028 6632 2690
www.nationaltrust.org.uk

Great for kids: Castle Balfour, LISNASKEA 028 9023 5000 www.ehsni.gov.uk

►►►► 82% Castle Archdale Caravan Park & Camping Site (H176588)

Lisnarick BT94 1PP
☎ 028 6862 1333 📠 028 6862 1176
e-mail: info@castlearchdale.com
dir: *From Irvinestown take B534 signed Lisnarick. Left onto B82 signed Enniskillen. Approx 1m right by church (site signed)*

🚐 £25-£30 ⛺ £25-£30 ⛺ £20-£40

Open Apr-Oct (rs Apr-Jun & Sep-Oct shop, restaurant & bar open wknds only)

Last departure noon

This park is located within the grounds of Castle Archdale Country Park on the shores of Lough Erne which boasts stunning scenery, forest walks and also war and wildlife museums. The site is ideal for watersport enthusiasts with its marina and launching facilities. Also on site are a shop, licenced restaurant, takeaway and play park. There are 56 fully serviced, hardstanding pitches. 11 acre site. 158 touring pitches. 120 hardstandings. Caravan pitches. Motorhome pitches. Tent pitches. 139 statics.

AA Pubs & Restaurants nearby: Catalina Restaurant, Lough Erne Resort, Enniskillen 028 6632 3230

Leisure: 🅰 Facilities: 🍴 ⊙ ✳ ⛄ 🔍 🚿 🚐 🌳 WI-FI
Services: 🚐 🔋 🍴 📶 🚾 🍽 🛒 ⬇
Within 3 miles: ⚓ 🚲 ⛵ 🏪 🔋

Notes: No open fires. Dogs must be kept on leads.

LISNASKEA

Places to visit

Castle Balfour, LISNASKEA 028 9023 5000
www.ehsni.gov.uk

Florence Court, ENNISKILLEN 028 6634 8249
www.nationaltrust.org.uk

Great for kids: Castle Coole, ENNISKILLEN 028 6632 2690 www.nationaltrust.org.uk

LEISURE: 🏊 Indoor swimming pool 🏊 Outdoor swimming pool 🅰 Children's playground 🧒 Kid's club 🎾 Tennis court 🎱 Games room 📺 Separate TV room ⛳ 9/18 hole golf course ⛵ Boats for hire 🎬 Cinema 🎭 Entertainment 🎣 Fishing ⛳ Mini golf 🏄 Watersports 🏋 Gym 🏐 Sports field **Spa** ⛎ Stables
FACILITIES: 🛁 Bath 🚿 Shower ⊙ Electric shaver 🔌 Hairdryer ✳ Ice Pack Facility ♿ Disabled facilities 🕐 Public telephone 🛒 Shop on site or within 200yds 🚗 Mobile shop (calls at least 5 days a week) 🍖 BBQ area 🌳 Picnic area 🚾 Wi-fi 💻 Internet access ♻ Recycling ❶ Tourist info 🐕 Dog exercise area

LISNASKEA — Map 1 C5

▶▶▶ 81% *Lisnaskea Caravan Park*

(H297373)

BT92 0NZ
☎ 028 6772 1040
dir: *From Lisnaskea take B514 signed Carry Bridge, site signed*

⊞ ⊟ 🅰 Open Mar-Sep

Last arrival 21.00hrs Last departure 14.00hrs

A pretty riverside site set in peaceful countryside, with well-kept facilities and friendly owners. Fishing is available on the river, and this quiet area is an ideal location for touring the lakes of Fermanagh. 6 acre site. 43 touring pitches. 43 hardstandings. Caravan pitches. Motorhome pitches. Tent pitches. 8 statics.

Leisure: 🄰 **Facilities:** 🌣⊙❋♿🛍 🔥
Services: 🔌🔲🔒
Within 3 miles: ♨⚓🅿🍴🛍🔲U **Notes:** 🚭

CO TYRONE

DUNGANNON — Map 1 C5

Places to visit

The Argory, MOY 028 8778 4753
www.nationaltrust.org.uk

Greencastle, KILKEEL 028 9181 1491
www.ehsni.gov.uk

Great for kids: Mountjoy Castle, MOUNTJOY
028 9023 5000 www.ehsni.gov.uk

▶▶▶ 81% Dungannon Park *(H805612)*

Moy Rd BT71 6DY
☎ 028 8772 8690 📠 028 8772 9169
e-mail: dpreception@dungannon.gov.uk
dir: *M1 junct 15, A29, left at 2nd lights*

⊞ ⊟ 🅰 Open Mar-Oct

Last arrival 20.30hrs Last departure 14.00hrs

Modern caravan park in a quiet area of a public park with fishing lake and excellent facilities, especially for disabled visitors. 2 acre site. 20 touring pitches. 12 hardstandings. Caravan pitches. Motorhome pitches. Tent pitches.

Leisure: 🄰🛝🔲
Facilities: 🌣⊙❋♿🛍🔥🄰
Services: 🔌🔲🔋
Within 3 miles: ♨⚓🅿🛍🔲U

Notes: Hot & cold drinks, snacks available.

REPUBLIC OF IRELAND

CO CORK

BALLINSPITTLE — Map 1 B2

Places to visit

Cork City Gaol, CORK 021 4305022
www.corkcitygaol.com

Blarney Castle & Rock Close, BLARNEY
021 4385252 www.blarneycastle.ie

Great for kids: Muckross House, Gardens & Traditional Farms, KILLARNEY 064 6670144
www.muckross-house.ie

▶▶▶▶ 80% Garrettstown House Holiday Park *(W588445)*

☎ 021 4778156 & 4775286 📠 021 4778156
e-mail: reception@garrettstownhouse.com
dir: *6m from Kinsale, through Ballinspittle, past school & football pitch on main road to beach. Beside stone estate entrance*

✱ ⊞ €16-€23 ⊟ €16-€23 🅰 €16-€20

Open 4 May-9 Sep (rs Early season-1 Jun shop closed)

Last arrival 22.00hrs Last departure noon

Elevated holiday park with tiered camping areas and superb panoramic views. Plenty of on-site amenities, and close to beach and forest park. 7 acre site. 60 touring pitches. 20 hardstandings. Caravan pitches. Motorhome pitches. Tent pitches. 80 statics.

Leisure: 🎾🄰🛝🛟🔲🎵
Facilities: 🌣⊙🅿❋♿🛍🔥🄰 🔄🄰
Services: 🔌🔲🔒🅿🔧🍴🔋🚼↯
Within 3 miles: ♨⚓🅿◎🛍🔲U

Notes: 🐕 Dogs must be kept on leads. Crazy golf, video shows, snooker, adult reading lounge, tots' playroom.

see advert on page 436

BALLYLICKEY — Map 1 B2

Places to visit

Muckross House, Gardens & Traditional Farms, KILLARNEY 064 6670144
www.muckross-house.ie

Great for kids: Fota Wildlife Park, CARRIGTWOHILL 021 4812678
www.fotawildlife.ie

▶▶▶▶ 85% Eagle Point Caravan and Camping Park *(V995535)*

☎ 027 50630
e-mail: eaglepointcamping@eircom.net
dir: *N71 to Bandon, then R586 to Bantry, then N71, 4m to Glengarriff, opposite petrol station*

⊞ €26-€29 ⊟ €26-€29 🅰 €26-€29

Open 20 Apr-24 Sep

Last arrival 21.00hrs Last departure noon

An immaculate park set in an idyllic position on a headland overlooking the rugged Bantry Bay and the mountains of West Cork. There are boat launching facilities, small and safe pebble beaches, a football field, tennis court, a small playground, and TV rooms for children and adults on the park. There is an internet café at reception and a shop and petrol station across from the park entrance. Nearby are two golf courses, riding stables, a sailing centre and cycle hire facilities. 20 acre site. 125 touring pitches. 20 hardstandings. 60 seasonal pitches. Caravan pitches. Motorhome pitches. Tent pitches.

AA Pubs & Restaurants nearby: Sea View House Hotel, Ballylickey 027 50073

Leisure: 🄰🛟⊙🔲
Facilities: 🌣⊙❋🕐🛍🔥🖥🔄🄰🄰
Services: 🔌🔲🔋↯
Within 3 miles: ♨🅿🛍🔲

Notes: ⊗ No commercial vehicles, bikes, skates, scooters or jet skis.

SERVICES: 🔌 Electric hook up 🔲 Launderette 🍻 Licensed bar 🛍 Calor Gas 🔥 Camping Gaz 🔲 Toilet fluid 🍴 Café/Restaurant 🔋 Fast Food/Takeaway 🔋 Battery charging 🚼 Baby care ↯ Motorvan service point
ABBREVIATIONS: BH/bank hols-bank holidays Etr-Easter Whit-Whitsun dep-departure fr-from hrs-hours m-mile mdnt-midnight rdbt-roundabout rs-restricted service wk-week wknd-weekend 🚭 No credit cards ⊗ No dogs
See page 7 for details of the AA Camping Card Scheme

CO DONEGAL

PORTNOO
Map 1 B5

Places to visit

Glebe House & Gallery, LETTERKENNY 074 9137071 www.glebegallery@opw.ie

Tower Museum, LONDONDERRY 028 7137 2411 www.derrycity.gov.uk/museums

►► 70% Boyle's Caravan Park
(G702990)

☎ 074 9545131 & 086 8523131
🖹 074 9545130
e-mail: pboylecaravans@gmail.com
dir: *Exit N56 at Ardra onto R261 for 6m. Follow signs for Santa Anna Drive*

🚐 � 🏕 Open 18 Mar-Oct

Last arrival 23.00hrs Last departure 11.00hrs

This open park nestles among the sand dunes overlooking Narin Beach and close to a huge selection of water activities, including windsurfing, fishing, scuba diving and kayaking on a magnificent stretch of the Atlantic on the Donegal coast. There is an 18-hole golf links, and a café and shop at the entrance to the site. The park is very well maintained by the Boyle family. 1.5 acre site. 20 touring pitches. Caravan pitches. Motorhome pitches. Tent pitches. 80 statics.

Facilities: 🌧⊙❄🌭🔌🛒🎯

Services: 🔋🍽🧺🍲🚮

Within 3 miles: ↨🎣🏊🌰🎱🎮⛳

Notes: ⊜ No skateboards. 1.5m Blue Flag beach.

CO DUBLIN

CLONDALKIN
Map 1 D4

Places to visit

Castletown, CELBRIDGE 01 6288252 www.heritageireland.ie

Irish Museum of Modern Art, DUBLIN 01 6129900 www.imma.ie

Great for kids: Dublin Zoo, DUBLIN 01 4748900 www.dublinzoo.ie

►►►► 81% *Camac Valley Tourist Caravan & Camping Park* *(0056300)*

Naas Rd, Clondalkin
☎ 01 4640644 🖹 01 4640643
e-mail: info@camacvalley.com
dir: *M50 junct 9, W on N7, site on right of dual carriageway after 2km. Site signed from N7*

🚐 🚐 🏕 Open all year

Last arrival anytime Last departure noon

A pleasant, lightly wooded park with good facilities, security and layout, situated within an hour's drive, or a bus ride, from city centre. 15 acre site. 163 touring pitches. 113 hardstandings. Caravan pitches. Motorhome pitches. Tent pitches.

AA Pubs & Restaurants nearby: Finnstown Country House Hotel, Lucan 01 6010700

Leisure: 🎪 **Facilities:** 🌧⊙🅿❄🌭🔌🛒🎯🪑

Services: 🔋🚽🧺🍽🛒⛟

Within 3 miles: ↨🎭🌰◎🎱🎮⛳

CO MAYO

CASTLEBAR
Map 1 B4

Places to visit

King House - Georgian Mansion & Military Barracks, BOYLE 071 9663242 www.kinghouse.ie

►►►► 80% *Lough Lannagh Caravan Park* *(M140890)*

Old Westport Rd
☎ 094 9027111 🖹 094 9027295
e-mail: info@loughlannagh.ie
web: www.loughlannagh.ie
dir: *N5, N60, N84 to Castlebar. At ring road follow signs for Westport. Signs for Lough Lannagh Village on all approach roads to Westport rdbt*

🚐 🚐 🏕

Open 22 Apr-Sep

Last arrival 18.00hrs Last departure 10.00hrs

This park is part of the Lough Lannagh Village which is situated in a wooded area a short walk from Castlebar. Leisure facilities include a

LEISURE: 🏊 Indoor swimming pool 🏊 Outdoor swimming pool 🎪 Children's playground 🪁 Kid's club 🎾 Tennis court 🎱 Games room 📺 Separate TV room ⛳ 9/18 hole golf course ⛵ Boats for hire 🎬 Cinema 🎵 Entertainment 🎣 Fishing ◎ Mini golf 🏄 Watersports 💪 Gym 🏟 Sports field **Spa** ⛲ Stables

FACILITIES: 🛁 Bath 🚿 Shower ⊙ Electric shaver 💈 Hairdryer ❄ Ice Pack Facility 🔌 Disabled facilities 🕐 Public telephone 🛒 Shop on site or within 200yds 🚚 Mobile shop (calls at least 5 days a week) 🍖 BBQ area 🪑 Picnic area 📶 Wi-fi 🌐 Internet access ♻ Recycling ❶ Tourist info 🐕 Dog exercise area

purpose-built fitness and relaxation centre, tennis courts, children's play area and café. 2.5 acre site. 20 touring pitches. 20 hardstandings. Caravan pitches. Motorhome pitches. Tent pitches.

AA Pubs & Restaurants nearby: Knockranny House Hotel, Westport 098 28600

Bluewave Restaurant, Carlton Atlantic Coast Hotel, Westport 098 29000

Leisure: 🏊

Facilities: 🛁🍴⊙📷✳&🔥 Wi-fi

Services: 🔌🧺🍴

Within 3 miles: 🎣🏇🎱🏊◎🏌🍴U

Notes: No pets Jul & Aug. Fitness club, table tennis, boules.

KNOCK — Map 1 B4

Places to visit
King House - Georgian Mansion & Military Barracks, BOYLE 071 9663242 www.kinghouse.ie

►►►► 76% Knock Caravan and Camping Park (M408828)

Claremorris Rd
☎ 094 9388100 📠 094 9388295
e-mail: caravanpark@knock-shrine.ie
dir: From rdbt in Knock, through town. Site entrance on left 1km, opposite petrol station

🚐🚚🏕

Open Mar-Nov

Last arrival 22.00hrs Last departure noon

A pleasant, very well maintained caravan park within the grounds of Knock Shrine, offering spacious terraced pitches and excellent facilities. 10 acre site. 88 touring pitches. 88 hardstandings. Caravan pitches. Motorhome pitches. Tent pitches. 12 statics.

Leisure: 🎮🎣🏓

Facilities: 🍴⊙📷✳&🔥🐕 Wi-fi

Services: 🔌🧺🚿T🍴🍔U

Within 3 miles: 🎣🏌🍴U

Notes: Dogs must be kept on leads.

CO ROSCOMMON

BOYLE — Map 1 B4

Places to visit
King House - Georgian Mansion & Military Barracks, BOYLE 071 9663242 www.kinghouse.ie

Florence Court, ENNISKILLEN 028 6634 8249 www.nationaltrust.org.uk

►►► 74% Lough Key Caravan & Camping Park (G846039)

Lough Key Forest Park
☎ 071 9662212 📠 071 9673140
e-mail: info@loughkey.ie
web: www.loughkey.ie
dir: Site 3km E of Boyle on N4. Follow Lough Key Forest Park signs, site within grounds. Approx 0.5km from entrance

🚐🚚🏕

Open Apr-20 Sep

Last arrival 18.00hrs Last departure noon

Peaceful and very secluded site within the extensive grounds of a beautiful forest park. Lough Key offers boat trips and waterside walks, and there is a viewing tower. 15 acre site. 72 touring pitches. 52 hardstandings. Caravan pitches. Motorhome pitches. Tent pitches.

Leisure: 🎮

Facilities: 🛁🍴⊙&◎🔥🐕

Services: 🔌🧺

Within 3 miles: 🎣🏇🏌🚣🏌🍴

Notes: No cars by tents.

CO WATERFORD

CLONEA — Map 1 C2

Places to visit
Waterford Crystal Visitor Centre, WATERFORD 051 332500 www.waterfordvisitorcentre.com

Brú Ború Heritage Centre, CASHEL 062 61122 www.comhaltas.com

Great for kids: Johnstown Castle Gardens, WEXFORD 053 9184671 www.irishagrimuseum.ie

►►►► 83% Casey's Caravan & Camping Park (X320937)

☎ 058 41919 📠 058 41919
dir: From R675 (Dungarvan road), follow signs to Clonea Bay. Site at end of road

🚐🚚🏕

Open 5 Apr-9 Sep

Last arrival 21.30hrs Last departure noon

A spacious, well-kept park with excellent toilet facilities, situated next to the beach. 4.5 acre site. 111 touring pitches. 34 hardstandings. Caravan pitches. Motorhome pitches. Tent pitches. 170 statics.

Leisure: 🎮🎣🏓

Facilities: 🍴⊙📷✳&🧺

Services: 🔌🧺🚿U

Within 3 miles: 🎣🏇🏌🍴🧺

Notes: Dogs must be kept on leads. Crazy golf, games room & tiny tots' play area.

Killiecrankie

WALKS & CYCLE RIDES
Contents

WALKS & CYCLE RIDES
Walking and cycling in safety

WALKING

All the walks are suitable for families, but less experienced family groups, especially those with younger children, should try the shorter or easier walks first. Route finding is usually straightforward, but the maps are for guidance only and we recommend that you always take the suggested Ordnance Survey map with you.

Risks

Although each walk has been researched with a view to minimising any risks, no walk in the countryside can be considered to be completely free from risk. Walking in the outdoors will always require a degree of common sense and judgement to ensure safety, especially for young children.

- Be particularly careful on cliff paths and in upland terrain, where the consequences of a slip can be serious.
- Remember to check tidal conditions before walking on the seashore.
- Some sections of routes are by, or cross, busy roads. Remember traffic is a danger even on minor country lanes.
- Be careful around farmyard machinery and livestock.
- Be aware of the consequences of changes in the weather and check the forecast before you set out. Ensure the whole family is properly equipped, wearing appropriate clothing and a good pair of boots or sturdy walking shoes. Take waterproof clothing with you and carry spare clothing and a torch if you are walking in the winter months. Remember the weather can change quickly at any time of the year, and in moorland and heathland areas, mist and fog can make route finding much harder. In summer, take account of the heat and sun by wearing a hat and carrying enough water.
- On walks away from centres of population you should carry a whistle and survival bag. If you do have an accident requiring emergency services, make a note of your position as accurately as possible and dial 999.

CYCLING

Cycling is a fun activity which children love, and teaching your child to ride a bike, and going on family cycling trips, are rewarding experiences. Not only is cycling a great way to travel, but as a regular form of exercise it can make an invaluable contribution to a child's health and fitness, and increase their confidence and independence.

The growth of motor traffic has made Britain's roads increasingly dangerous and unattractive to cyclists. Cycling with children is an added responsibility and, as with everything, there is a risk when taking them out cycling. However, in recent years measures have been taken to address this, including the on-going development of the National Cycle Network (more than 12,600 miles utilising quiet lanes and traffic-free paths) and local designated off-road routes for families, such as converted railway lines, canal tow paths and forest tracks.

In devising the cycle rides included in this guide, every effort has been made to use these designated cycle paths, or to link them with quiet country lanes and waymarked byways and bridleways. Unavoidably, in a few cases, some relatively busy B-roads link the quieter, more attractive routes.

Taking care on the road

- Ride in single file on narrow and busy roads.
- Be alert, look and listen for traffic, especially on narrow lanes and blind bends and be extra careful when descending steep hills, as loose gravel can lead to an accident.
- In wet weather make sure you keep a good distance between you and other riders.
- Make sure you indicate your intentions clearly.
- Brush up on The Highway Code before venturing out on to the road.

Off-road safety code of conduct

- Only ride where it is legal to do so. It is forbidden to cycle on public footpaths. The only 'rights of way' open to cyclists are bridleways and unsurfaced tracks, known as byways, which are open to all traffic.
- Canal tow paths: you need a permit to cycle on some stretches of tow path (**www.waterscape.com**). Remember that access paths can be steep and slippery and always get off and push your bike under low bridges and by locks.
- Always yield to walkers and horses, giving adequate warning of your approach.
- Don't expect to cycle at high speeds.
- Keep to the main trail to avoid any unnecessary erosion to

the area beside the trail and to prevent skidding, especially if it is wet.

- Remember the Countryside Code. (**www.naturalengland.org.uk**)

Cycling with children

Children can use a child seat from the age of eight months, or from the time they can hold themselves upright. A number of child seats fit on the front or rear of a bike, and it's worth investigating towable two-seat trailers. 'Trailer bicycles', suitable for five- to ten-year-olds, can be attached to the rear of an adult's bike, so that the adult has control, allowing the child to pedal if he/she wishes. Family cycling can be made easier by using a tandem, as it can carry a child seat and tow trailers. 'Kiddy-cranks' for shorter legs can be fitted to the rear seat tube, enabling either parent to take their child out cycling. For older children it is better to purchase the right size bike: an oversized bike will be difficult to control, and potentially dangerous.

Preparing your bicycle

Basic routine includes checking the wheels for broken spokes or excess play in the bearings, and checking for punctures, undue tyre wear and the correct tyre pressures. Ensure that the brake blocks are firmly in place and not worn, and that cables are not frayed or too slack. Lubricate hubs, pedals, gear mechanisms and cables. Make sure you have a pump, a bell, a rear rack to carry panniers and, if cycling at night, a set of working lights.

Preparing yourself

Equipping the family with cycling clothing need not be expensive; comfort is the key. Essential items for cycling are padded cycling shorts, warm stretch leggings (avoid tight-fitting and seamed trousers like jeans or baggy tracksuit trousers that may become caught in the chain), stiff-soled training shoes, and a wind/waterproof jacket. Fingerless gloves are comfortable.

A cycling helmet provides essential protection and are essential for young children learning to cycle.

Wrap your child up with several layers in colder weather. Make sure you and those with you are easily visible by all road users, by wearing light-coloured or luminous clothing in daylight and reflective strips or sashes in failing light and when it is dark.

What to take with you

Invest in a pair of medium-sized panniers (rucksacks can affect balance) to carry the necessary gear for the day. Take extra clothes with you, the amount depending on the season, and always pack a light wind/waterproof jacket. Carry a basic tool kit (tyre levers, adjustable spanner, a small screwdriver, puncture repair kit, a set of Allen keys) and practical spares, such as an inner tube, a universal brake/gear cable, and a selection of nuts and bolts. Also, always take a pump and a strong lock.

Cycling, especially in hilly terrain and off-road, saps energy, so take enough food and drink. Always carry plenty of water, especially in hot and humid weather. Consume high-energy snacks like cereal bars, cake or fruits, eating little and often to combat feeling weak and tired. Remember that children get thirsty (and hungry) much more quickly than adults so always have food and diluted juices available for them.

And finally, the most important advice of all – enjoy yourselves!

Useful cycling websites

- National Cycle Network: **www.sustrans.org.uk**
- British Waterways (tow path cycling): **www.waterscape.com**
- Forestry Commission (for cycling on Forestry Commission woodland): **www.forestry.gov.uk**
- Cyclists Touring Club: **www.ctc.org.uk**

▷

WALKS & CYCLE RIDES

continued

Each walk and cycle ride starts with a panel giving essential information, including the distance, terrain, nature of the paths, and where to park your car.

WALKS AND CYCLE ROUTES

Minimum time: The time stated for each route is the estimated minimum time that a reasonably fit family group would take to complete the circuit. This does not include rest or refreshment stops.

Maps: Each main route is shown on a detailed map. However, some detail is lost because of the scale. For this reason, we always recommend that you use the maps alongside the suggested Ordnance Survey (OS) map.

Start/Finish: Indicates the start and finish point and parking. The six-figure grid reference prefixed by two letters refers to a 100km square of the National Grid. You'll find more information on grid references on most OS maps.

Level of difficulty: The walks and cycle rides have been graded from 1 to 3. Easier routes, such as those with little total ascent, on easy footpaths or level trails, or those covering shorter distances are graded 1. The hardest routes, either because they include a lot of ascent, greater distances, or are in hilly, more demanding terrains, are graded 3.

Parking: Local parking information for the walks.

Tourist information: A contact number for the nearest tourist information office is provided to help find local information.

Cycle hire: For the cycle rides, this lists, within reason, the nearest cycle hire shop/centre.

❗ This highlights at a glance any potential difficulties or hazards along the route. If a particular route is suitable for older, fitter children it says so here.

All the walks and cycle rides featured in this guide appear in the *AA 365 Pub Walks and Cycle Rides*. This is a comprehensive ring-binder format directory offering a vast collection of routes for the whole family. See the AA website for more details
http://shop.theaa.com/store/anywhere-and-everywhere

A loop walk on the most accessible section of a prominent sandstone ridge.

Minimum time:	2hrs
Walk length:	5.5 miles (8.8km)
Ascent/gradient:	919ft (280mtrs) ▲▲▲
Difficulty level:	✚✚✚
Paths:	Field and woodland paths, plus some lane walking; 6 stiles
Landscape:	Richly varied woodland and farmland, some rocky outcrops and views over lush plains
Map:	OS Explorer 257 Crewe & Nantwich
Start/finish:	Grid reference: SJ 521551
Dog friendliness:	On lead in Peckforton Estate and near grazing stock. Beware of electric fences
Parking:	Verges at end of tarmac on Coppermines Lane, off A534 car park and picnic area
Public toilets:	None en route

● Burwardsley

Beeston Castle, which is visible from afar, was built in the 13th century, its strategic hilltop site looking towards the turbulent Welsh border. It saw no real battles until the English Civil War around 400 years later. After changing hands several times, it was largely demolished in 1646 on the orders of Parliament. Nearby Peckforton Castle is a 19th-century imitation of a medieval fortress.

Layers of History

Distant views of these grand castle-crowned ridges might lead you to anticipate airy ridge walking. In fact there is little of that to be found here, though Raw Head hill does provide its own brand of unique moments of drama. Generally, however, this walk delivers something different and equally pleasurable for walkers.

The castles proclaim the long history of the area, but there are other layers of history to be found. The name of Coppermines Lane, where the walk starts, is a reminder of an industrial element. Where the walk first leaves the tarmac, a chimney glimpsed below marks the site of the old copper works. Just above, the map still marks the site of a mine, though there's little to be seen of it now.

Sandstone Trail

From here your route climbs to Raw Head hill, then continues along a steep slope which breaks into startling crags at Musket's Hole. The summit, at 745ft (227mtrs), is the highest point on the Sandstone Trail, a 34-mile (55km) route from Frodsham to Whitchurch. However, a screen of trees means it is far from the best viewpoint. The walk does serve up some great views, but never an all-round panorama: more a series of tasty morsels than a grand main course. But there is plenty of charm in their sudden and often fleeting appearance.

High Point

After Raw Head hill the walk winds down through woods, fields and along a quiet lane to Burwardsley village then up an even quieter one to Higher Burwardsley. Then it climbs again to the National Trust-owned Bulkeley Hill Wood. The high point, literally and metaphorically, is a wonderful grove of sweet chestnut trees on a broad shelf rimmed by low sandstone crags. With virtually no undergrowth, you can fully appreciate the gnarled, multi-stemmed trees, which seem hunched with age. From here it is an enjoyable and easy stroll down through a plantation and then across a field back to reach Coppermines Lane.

Walk Directions

1 Walk down Coppermines Lane to a sharp left-hand bend. Cross a stile beside an arched sandstone overhang. Cross a field then ascend the edge of a wooded area. Cross fields to the edge of another wood. Go up right, signposted 'Raw Head, Beeston', joining a track towards Chiflik Farm.

2 Go through a kissing gate by the farm and up a fenced path. The path generally runs just below the top of a steep slope, climbing to the trig point on Raw Head hill.

3 The path goes right and into a slight dip. Go left down steps then back right, slanting through a steep plantation. Go left down a narrow lane for 300yds (274mtrs). Opposite a track and footpath sign, descend through newly planted woodland. At the bottom cross a stile and go up towards Bodnook Cottage. Just below this bear left and into a wood. Follow a firm path, roughly level then slightly left and downhill among spindly beech trees.

4 Cross a stile at the edge of the wood, then another immediately to its right. There's a faint path, aim directly for a stile below a large tree, 50yds (46mtrs) left of a

house. Continue through the next field. At the far end cross a stile and follow the road ahead.

5 On the edge of Burwardsley village turn right up the first lane. Go right again up Sarra Lane, then

fork left at an 'Unsuitable for Motor Vehicles' sign. Follow the lane up past Cheshire Workshops. Just beyond this the road forks.

6 Go right and over the junction up Rock Lane. Keep right at the next fork. The lane meets the Crewe and Nantwich boundary.

7 Just before the boundary sign go right through a gate and follow the field-edge path. Keep ahead to meet a narrow lane and go up left. On the crest, opposite a gatehouse,

go right on a track into Bulkeley Hill Wood.

8 Go left up steps into the wood and continue less steeply. Where the path splits, the left branch follows the brink of a steep slope. Keep fairly close to this edge as the path levels. Go through a gap in a fence then descend through a plantation, to a kissing gate beside a big iron gate. Go diagonally right on a clear track across a field to Coppermines Lane.

what to look out for...

Sweet chestnuts, like those in Bulkeley Hill Wood, are not a native species; they probably arrived with the Romans. Nor are they related to the horse chestnut, which gets its name from the chance resemblance of its fruit. In fact the sweet chestnut is related to the oaks.

WALK 2
Rollercoaster Path to Port Quin

An exhilarating hike between the North Cornish villages of Port Isaac and Port Quin.

Minimum time:	4hrs
Walk length:	6 miles/9.7km
Ascent/Gradient:	984ft (300mtrs) ▲▲▲
Difficulty level:	+++
Paths:	Good coastal and field paths. Several sections of coast path run very close to unguarded cliff edges. May not be suitable for children and dogs. 14 stiles.
Landscape:	Coastal scenery and inland fields, one wooded valley
Map:	Map OS Explorer 106 Newquay and Padstow
Start/finish:	Grid reference: SW 999809
Dog friendliness:	Dogs on lead in grazed areas
Parking:	Port Isaac. Large car park on outskirts of village, can be busy. Allowed on stony beach, but this is tidal so you need to know tides. Small car park at Port Quin.
Public toilets:	Port Isaac car park and at start of Roscarrock Hill

● Port Isaac

The North Cornish coast between the sea inlets of Port Isaac and Port Quin is a marvellous chaos of tumbled cliffs and convoluted hills. The price of all this, for the keen walker, is a strenuous passage along the coastal footpath between the two. You rise and fall like a dipping gull, but without the same ease and effortlessness. The inland return, across fields, to Port Isaac, is undramatic but is not strenuous. On the coastal section, be prepared for airy clifftop paths that in places are pinned narrowly between thin air on the unprotected seaward edge and a lengthy stretch of wooden fencing inland, said by some ironic locals to be as visible from space as the Great Wall of China.

Port Isaac

The North Cornish village of Port Isaac is one of the West Country's most popular visitor destinations. The appeal of Port Isaac, however, lies partly in its relative freedom from too many visitors' vehicles. The village is enclosed between the steep slopes of a narrow valley that reaches the sea at a protected

inlet, a natural haven for vessels. It is this orientation to the sea that has produced the densely compact nature of the village. The sea was the common highway here, long before the modern road became so; until the early 20th century trading ships brought coal, limestone, timber and other commodities to Port Isaac and carried away, fish, farm produce, mineral ore and building stone.

It's worth taking a little time to explore the village of Port Isaac before setting off uphill on the coastal footpath. The path leads round the smooth-browed Lobber Point, then traces a remarkable rollercoaster route along the folded coastline to Kellan Head and then to Port Quin. There is a slightly haunted air about Port Quin today. It is a remote, silent place, yet in 1841 nearly 100 people lived here in a village of over 20 households. Now only a few cottages remain, not all of them occupied permanently. Like most inlets on the North Cornish coast Port Quin survived until the 19th century on pilchard fishing and on coastal trade that involved the import of coal and lime in exchange for slate, and lead from small mining concerns. Legend claims that most of the men of Port Quin were lost at sea in some kind of fishing or smuggling disaster and that the womenfolk and children moved away. There was certainly rapid depopulation, but it may simply have been through emigration when mining failed and pilchard fishing declined in the late 19th century. The route you follow through the fields back to bustling Port Isaac must once have been a local highway between two thriving communities.

Walk Directions

1 Leave the Port Isaac main car park by the lower terrace and turn left along a track, keeping right where it branches, signposted 'Coast Path'. At the road, keep ahead and down Fore Street to reach the open space known as the Platt at the entry to the harbour. Just past Port Isaac Fishermen Ltd, turn right up Roscarrock Hill, signposted 'Coast Path'.

2 At the top of the lane, pass a public footpath sign on the left, then, in 30yds (27mtrs), keep to the right of the gateway to a terrace of houses and bear right, signposted 'Coastal Footpath'. Follow the path round Lobber Point.

3 Descend to Pine Haven Cove and then cross over a wooden stile. (A wooden fence marches alongside the inside edge of the path from here on.) Climb steeply uphill and round the edge of an enormous gulf. Go over a stile at the end of the fenced section and cross Varley Head. The path ahead again runs close to the cliff edge and is fenced on the inside.

4 Just beyond a bench descend steep steps (there is a hand rail) into Downgate Cove and Reedy Cliff. Follow the coast path up some very steep sections to reach the seaward edge of Kellan Head. Continue along the coast path until you reach Port Quin.

5 Turn left at Port Quin and go up the road past the car park

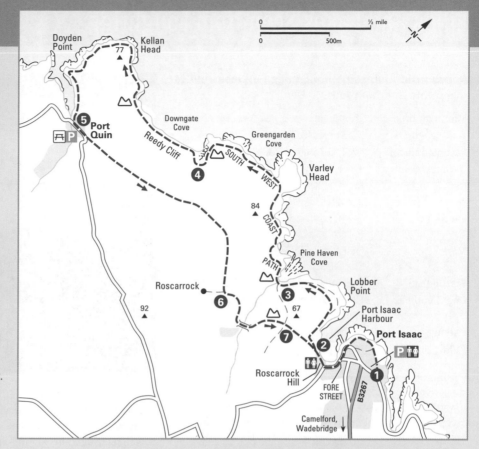

entrance. At a bend in the road bear off left, signposted 'Public Footpath to Port Isaac'. Go past cottages and keep up the slope to a gate with a stone stile. Dogs should be kept under strict control from here on. Follow the path alongside a hedge, then climb to a stile between two gates. Keep alongside the right-hand edge of the next fields.

6 Go over a stile beside an open gateway near Roscarrock (right), then turn left and follow the left field-edge to a wooden stile. Go left over the stile and descend into the wooded valley bottom. Cross a wooden footbridge over a

stream, then go over a stone stile. Keep ahead and climb very steeply through gorse to reach an open field slope. Keep ahead across the field (no apparent path), aiming to the left of a tall wooden pole that soon comes into view.

7 Cross a stone stile and follow the left field-edge downhill to a junction with the lane at Point **2**. Turn right and retrace your steps to Port Isaac and the car park.

what to look out for...

The tangled vegetation of the Reedy Cliff area makes an ideal habitat for small birds such as the stonechat. This is a typical passerine, or percher. The male bird is easily distinguished by its russet breast, white collar and dark head while the female is a duller brown overall. The 'stonechat' name derives from the bird's distinctive chattering note that resembles a rapid tapping of stone on stone.

Above little Ambleside, Loughrigg Fell looks out to lake, dale and high fell.

Minimum time:	1hr 45min
Walk length:	3.25 miles (5.2km)
Ascent/gradient:	575ft (175mtrs) ▲▲▲
Difficulty level:	✚✚✚
Paths:	Road, paths and tracks, can be muddy in places, 3 stiles
Landscape:	Town, park and open hillside with views to high fells
Map:	OS Explorer OL7 The English Lakes (SE)
Start/finish:	Grid reference: NY 375047
Dog friendliness:	Under control; busy roads, park, sheep grazing
Parking:	Ambleside central car park
Public toilets:	At car park

● Loughrigg Fell

The favourite of many, Loughrigg is a delightful low fell, which runs from Ambleside and the head of Windermere lake towards both Langdale and Grasmere. This circuit walk crosses the River Rothay by Miller Bridge and rises to a craggy viewpoint before traversing the small Lily Tarn to return via the stone lane of Miller Brow.

With the exception of possibly thick mist or cloud, this is a walk for all seasons and most weather conditions. The views, south over Waterhead and down Windermere and north over the wooded vale of Rydal into the high mountain drama of the Fairfield Horseshoe, are some of the most evocative in the region. The delightful detail of tree, rocky knoll, heather, bracken and the white and green cup and saucers of the lilies on Lily Tarn, contrast with the grand open views of mountain, dale and lake.

Ambleside

Even before the heights of lovely Loughrigg are reached, the varied slate stone buildings of Ambleside provide an intriguing start to the walk. Indeed, despite recent developments, there is a lot more to this little town than just being the outdoor equipment capital of Britain. Sited in the old county of Westmorland, Ambleside has long been a site of occupation. Bronze Age remains, c2000 bc can be seen on the nearby

fells and the Galava Roman fort, near Waterhead, was one of the most important in north-west England.

How Head, just up the Kirkstone road, one of the oldest surviving buildings in old Ambleside, is located in the area known as Above Stock. Sections of this fine stone house date back to the 16th century and it was once the lodge of the Master Forester of the Barony of Kendal. It has massive circular chimneys, a typical Westmorland feature, stone mullioned windows and incorporates stone from the old Roman fort at Waterhead and cobbles from the bed of Stock Ghyll Beck.

Stock Ghyll once served as the heartbeat of the town when, some 150 years ago, it provided water power for 12 watermills. On this walk we pass a restored waterwheel, immediately followed by the famous Bridge House, one of the most photographed buildings in the Lake District. Spanning the beck, this tiny 17th-century building is said to have been built thus to avoid paying land tax. Locally it is said to have once housed a family with six children. It is now a shop and information centre for the National Trust. Ambleside has become a major tourist resort with shops, hotels and restaurants, and is a convenient base for exploring the rest of the Lake District.

Walk Directions

1 Take the wooden footbridge from the car park and go right, along the Rydal road to pass the waterwheel and Bridge House. At the junction bear right along Compston Road. Continue to the next junction, with the cinema on the corner, then bear right to cross the side road and enter Vicarage Road alongside the chip shop. Pass the school and enter Rothay Park. Follow the main path through the park to emerge by a flat bridge over Stock Ghyll Beck. Cross this then go left to cross over the stone arched Miller Bridge spanning the River Rothay.

2 Bear right along the road over the cattle grid until, in a few paces, a steep surfaced road rises to the left. Climb the road, which becomes unsurfaced, by the buildings of Brow Head Farm. At the S-bend beyond the buildings, a stone stile leads up and off left. Pass through the trees to find, in a few dozen paces, a stone squeeze stile. Pass through this, cross a little bridge and climb the open hillside above. The paths are well worn and a variety of routes

are possible. For the best views over Windermere keep diagonally left. Rising steeply at first, the path levels before rising again to ascend the first rocky knoll. Cross a stile and a higher, larger knoll offering definitive views of the

Fairfield Horseshoe to the north and over Windermere to the south.

3 Beyond this, the way descends to the right, dropping to a well-defined path. Follow the path to pass a little pond before cresting a rise and falling to lovely little Lily Tarn (flowers bloom late June to September). The path skirts the right edge of the tarn, roughly following the crest of Loughrigg Fell before joining a wall on the left. Follow this down through a kissing gate and the base of a further knoll. This is ascended to another worthy viewpoint.

4 Take the path descending right to a prominent track below. Bear right to a gate which leads through the stone wall boundary of the open fell and into a field. Continue to descend the track passing an interesting building on the left, the old golf clubhouse. Intercept the original route just above the buildings of Brow Head.

5 Continue to cross Miller Bridge then, before the flat bridge, bear left to follow the track by the side of Stock Ghyll Beck. Beyond the meadows a lane through the houses leads to the main Rydal road. Bear right on the road to the car park beyond the fire station.

while you're there...

The Lakes Discovery Museum @ the Armitt, opposite the car park, provides a fascinating look at Ambleside and its environs in times past. An area is devoted to Beatrix Potter, where her desk and some of her natural history watercolours are on display. Borrans Park at Waterhead, with Galava Roman Fort next to it, and Rothay Park both provide pleasant recreational areas for those with a little time to spare, the latter having an excellent children's play area.

A fine linear walk from Ravenglass to Eskdale Green, returning on La'al Ratty.

Minimum time:	2hrs 30min
Walk length:	6 miles (9.7km)
Ascent/gradient:	730ft (220mtrs) ▲▲▲
Difficulty level:	✚✚✚
Paths:	Clear tracks and paths, muddy after rain, 1 stile
Landscape:	Woodlands, moderately rugged fell and gentle valley
Map:	OS Explorer OL6 The English Lakes (SW)
Start:	Grid reference: SD 085964
Finish:	Grid reference: SD 145998
Dog friendliness:	Under close control where sheep are grazing
Parking:	Village car park at Ravenglass, close to station
Public toilets:	Ravenglass village and Ravenglass and Eskdale Station

Muncaster Fell is a long and knobbly fell of no great height. The summit rises to 758ft (231mtrs), but is a little off the route described. A winding path negotiates the fell from end to end and this can be linked with other paths and tracks to offer a fine walk from Ravenglass to Eskdale Green. It's a linear walk, but when the Ravenglass and Eskdale Railway is in full steam, a ride back on the train is simply a joy.

Affectionately known as La'al Ratty, the Ravenglass and Eskdale Railway has a history of fits and starts. It was originally opened as a standard gauge track in 1875 to serve a granite quarry and was converted to narrow gauge between 1915 and 1917. After a period of closure it was bought by

while you're there...

Don't forget to explore the little village of Ravenglass. It's essentially a fishing village at the confluence of the rivers Irt, Mite and Esk. Apart from being a Roman port, by 1280 it had charters for a weekly market and annual fair, though its trade was eclipsed as the port of Whitehaven developed and it became a rum-smuggling centre.

enthusiasts in 1960, overhauled and re-opened, and is now a firm favourite. The line runs from Ravenglass to Dalegarth Station, near Boot at the head of Eskdale, and is open almost all year, but there are times in the winter when there are no services. Obtain a timetable and study it carefully. When the trains are running, there are few Lakeland journeys to compare with a trip both ways.

The Romans operated an important port facility at Ravenglass. Fortifications were built all the way around the Cumbrian coast to link with Hadrian's Wall and a Roman road cut through Eskdale, over the passes to Ambleside, then along the crest of High Street to link with the road network near Penrith. Some people think the Romans planned to invade Ireland from Ravenglass, though this is a subject of debate. The mainline railway sliced through the old Roman fort in 1850, leaving only the bathouse intact, though even this ruin is among the tallest Roman remains in Britain. The Romans also operated a tileworks on the lower slopes of Muncaster Fell.

Surrounded by luxuriant rhododendrons, Muncaster Castle is almost completely hidden from view. It has been the home of the Pennington family since about 1240, though they occupied a nearby site even earlier than that. The estate around the castle includes a church that was founded in 1170, as well as a network of paths and tracks to explore. Owls are bred and reared at Muncaster, then released into the wild.

● Ravenglass station

Walk Directions

1 Leave the car park by crossing the mainline and miniature railway line, using the footbridges, then follow a narrow path to a road junction. Turn right on a footpath by the side of a narrow road, signposted 'Walls Castle'. The bathouse is soon on the left.

2 Continue along the access road and turn left along a track signposted 'Newtown'. Turn left again before the cottage and follow another track up a little wooded valley. Go through four gates, following the track from the wood, across fields and into another wood. Turn left to reach Home Farm and a busy main road.

3 Cross the road and turn right, passing Muncaster Castle car park and the Muncaster Country Guest House. The road leads up to a bend, where Fell Lane is signposted uphill. Ascend the clear track, cross a little wooded dip, then fork right and left, noticing Muncaster Tarn on the left. Go through a gate at the top of the lane to reach Muncaster Fell.

4 A path forges through boggy patches along the edge of a coniferous plantation, then the path runs free across the slopes of Muncaster Fell. A path rising to the left leads to the summit, otherwise keep right to continue.

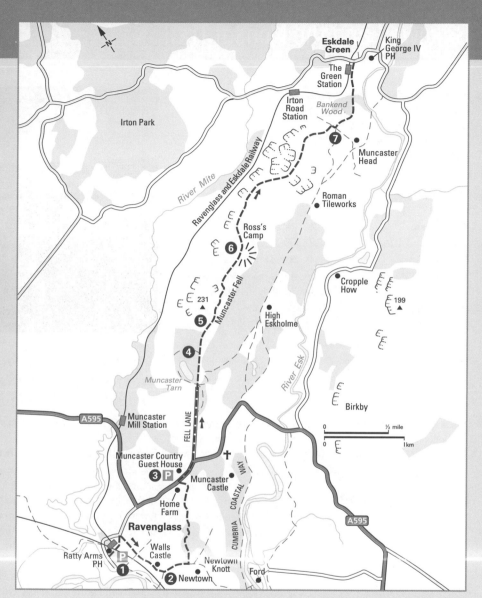

5 Views develop as the path winds about on the slope overlooking Eskdale. A panorama of fells opens up as a curious structure is reached at Ross's Camp. Here, a large stone slab was turned into a picnic table for a shooting party in 1883.

6 Continue along the footpath, looping round a broad and boggy area to reach a corner of a dry-stone wall. Go down through a gateway and bear in mind that the path can be muddy. There is a short ascent on a well-buttressed stretch, then the descent continues on a sparsely wooded slope, through a gate, ending on a track near another gate.

7 Go through the gate and then turn left, crossing a field to reach a stone wall seen at the edge of Bankend Wood. Walk on, keeping to the right side of the wall to reach a stile and a stream. A narrow track continues, becoming better as it draws close to a road. Turn left at the end of the road to reach The Green Station.

Minimum time:	3hrs
Ride length:	8 miles/12.9km
Difficulty level:	✚✚✚
Short Alternative Route	
Minimum time:	1hr 15min
Ride length:	5.25 miles/8.4km
Difficulty level:	✚✚✚
Map:	OS Explorer OL24 White Peak
Start/finish:	Bakewell Old Station, grid ref SK223690
Trails/tracks:	old railway trackbed and back lanes
Landscape:	woods and pastures below limestone edges, river valley, hay meadows
Public toilets:	central Bakewell
Tourist information:	Bakewell, tel 01629 813227
Cycle hire:	none nearby
❶	One short climb, one long downhill stretch

● Bakewell

Getting to the start

The old railway station in Bakewell is on Station Road – the road that forks off to the right at the memorial as you take the A619 for Baslow out of the town centre and cross the bridge over the River Wye. There's ample parking at the old station.

Why do this cycle ride?

This is an easy, largely level ride from Bakewell into the folded, wooded countryside that characterises the eastern fringes of the national park. A couple of shorter add-ons include one of the Peak's charming little villages and a pleasant ride above the Wye Valley.

did you know?

According to tradition the recipe for Bakewell Pudding was the result of a mistake by the cook in Bakewell's Rutland Arms Hotel in 1860. The cook put the jam in first and topped it off with the egg mixture intended for the pastry – the dish was a triumph. The famous Bakewell Pudding Shop is a popular venue for those who want to taste the real thing.

An easy ride from the town of Bakewell, with its railway heritage, which loops through a picturesque limestone village and riverside hay meadows.

Bakewell and the Monsal Trail

The Monsal Trail is largely the trackbed of the former main line railway linking Manchester Central to Derby and London St Pancras. Opened in 1849 and built by the Midland Railway, it was latterly renowned for its comfortable Pullman carriages before closing in 1969. There are ambitious plans to restore services through the Peak District, and a start has been made at nearby Rowsley, from where Peak Rail runs seasonal services through to Matlock and the surviving branch line to Derby. During the summer months the railway's banks (and the roadside verges) are bright with the vivid blue flower of the meadow cranesbill, that can often be seen in great drifts along with the ox-eye daisies and willowherb.

Bakewell is famed for its puddings, but there's much more to look out for here, including the Old House Museum and the lively market (Wednesdays are particularly busy and vibrant). Great Longstone was once a renowned centre for stocking manufacture, established by immigrant Flemish weavers who often traded their goods at the village market cross.

The Ride

1 Access to the trackbed remains via the gap at the left side of the imposing structure. Turn left along the level track, a compacted and well-surfaced route that, beyond the industrial units that occupy the former goods yard, runs initially through thin woods. Passing beneath the main road, the buildings of Bakewell are left behind and soon *Hassop Old Station* comes into view.

2 The station buildings are largely gone, although an old warehouse has been converted to other uses. Beyond here, the trees become less constricting, and views to the hill slopes climbing towards *Longstone Edge* draw the eye. There's an abundance of summer wild flowers along this section. The old trackbed passes under and over several roads and lanes before reaching the impressive buildings at Great Longstone's *old station*. The station partially retains its canopy, while next door is one of the buildings of the Thornbridge Estate.

3 A sign here warns that there is no exit for cycles beyond this point, but it is worth cycling the extra 0.25 mile (400mtrs) to the end of the useable track for some great views across towards the hidden *River Wye* in its deep valley. You can choose here to simply retrace your route back to Bakewell, a total distance of 5.25 miles (8.4km). Another option, though, is to return to *Great Longstone Station* and take the steep flight of steps, left,

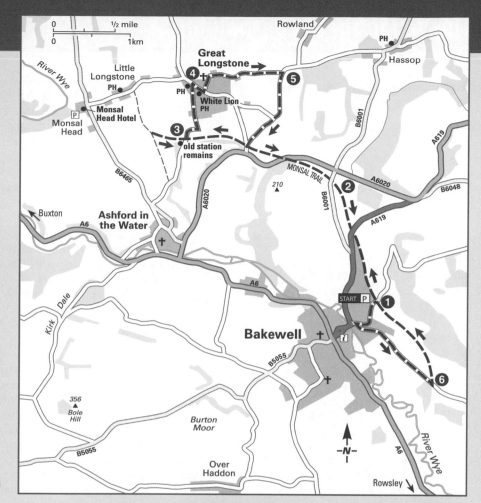

to a minor road. Turn left along this, an easy, level ride to the village centre at *Great Longstone*.

4 At the market cross and village green, fork right along either of the lanes. Both wind down to the main street, lined with fine limestone cottages and houses, to reach the White Lion. Just beyond this, take *Church Lane*, left, to rise up a gentle hill to the parish *church*. The road bends right here, commencing an undulating, easy ride along this narrow road, *Beggarway Lane*, offering excellent views up

to *Longstone Edge* and occasional glimpses back towards Bakewell.

5 In about 0.75 miles (1.2km), turn right along the lane that starts at a left bend. *Longreave Lane*, is an easy downhill coast for nearly a mile (1.6km), eventually reaching a junction at a railway overbridge. Fork left here just before the bridge, up a gravelly ramp to regain the old railway. Turn left to return to *Bakewell*. To extend the route you can now cycle across the car park and take *Station Road* downhill (take care by the parked cars). At

the junction at the bottom turn sharp left along *Coombs Road*, passing the car park entrance. This peaceful, level lane runs for about a mile (1.6km), amid pastures and hay meadows to reach a high-arched viaduct crossing.

6 Immediately before the viaduct, look for the *Monsal Trail* board on the left, indicating a short, sharp incline up which you wheel your bicycle to gain the old railway. Turn left to return to *Bakewell*; there are some good views across the town from this elevated route.

WALK 5
The Vision that is Dartington

A gentle walk around the Dartington Hall Estate, with a pretty pub loop.

Minimum time:	2hrs 30min
Walk length:	6.5 miles (10.4km)
Ascent/gradient:	164ft (50mtrs) ▲ ▲ ▲
Difficulty level:	✦✦✦
Paths:	Fields, woodland tracks and country lanes, 4 stiles
Landscape:	River meadows, parkland and mixed woodland
Map:	OS Explorer 110 Torquay & Dawlish
Start/finish:	Grid reference: SX 799628
Dog friendliness:	Keep on lead; dogs (except assist dogs) not allowed within Dartington Hall grounds
Parking:	Opposite entrance to Dartington Hall
Public toilets:	Outside entrance to Dartington Hall and Staverton village
Note:	Larger organised groups require permission from the Property Administrator (01803 847000) in advance

You could be forgiven for thinking that Dartington is really nothing more than what you see as you cross the roundabout on the A382 leading south from the A38 to Totnes – just somewhere you pass en route to the South Hams. But there's so much more to Dartington than that, and the story behind 'the vision' of Leonard and Dorothy Elmhirst, who bought the estate in 1925, is a fascinating one. This walk circles the estate and you should allow time at the end to visit its central buildings.

The Most Spectacular Medieval Mansion
Dartington Hall was described by Nikolaus Pevsner in his classic book on the buildings of Devon as 'the most spectacular medieval mansion' in Devon. The great hall and main courtyard were built for John Holand, Duke of Exeter, at the end of the 14th century, and although all the buildings have since been carefully restored, to walk through the gateway into the courtyard today, with the superb Great Hall with its hammerbeam roof opposite, is to step back in time.

Arthur Champernowne came to own the manor in 1554, and made various alterations, and the estate stayed in the hands of the Champernowne family until 1925. Further restoration work was carried out in Georgian times, but by the time the Elmhirsts came on the scene the Hall was derelict. Visitors can explore the Great Hall, courtyard and gardens, if they are not in use, in return for a moderate fee.

St Mary's Church can be found on the northern edge of the estate just off the Totnes road. You'll pass the site of the original estate church just to the north of the Hall. It was demolished in 1873, leaving only the tower, which can be seen today. The new church, which is wonderfully light and spacious, was built in 1880, following the exact dimensions of the original building, and re-using various items from it, such as the south porch with its lovely star vault, the chancel screen, font, pulpit and roof. A tablet in the outer east wall records the rebuilding and subsequent consecration of the church by Frederick, Bishop of Exeter. The Dartington Hall Trust, a registered charity, was set up in 1935, and evolved from the vision of Leonard Elmhirst and his American wife Dorothy Whitney Straight, who bought the derelict hall and 1,000 acres (405ha) of the estate and set about making their dream reality. He was interested in farming and forestry, and in increasing rural employment opportunities. She believed passionately in the arts as a way of promoting personal and social improvement. Their joint aim was to provide a foundation where both dreams could be realised, and Dartington Hall, home to Dartington College of Arts (today faced with closure) and other educational facilities, provides the perfect setting.

Staverton bridge

Walk Directions

1 From the car park turn left downhill. Follow the pavement until you reach the River Dart.

2 Turn left through a gate (no footpath sign) and follow the river northwards. This part of the walk is likely to be very muddy after rainfall. The Dart here is broad, tree-lined and slow-moving. Pass through one gate, then another, through woodland and a gate. Continue through riverside meadows, and eventually pass through an open gateway on to a wooded track.

3 Walk along the river edge of the next field (Park Copse left). At the end of that field a gate leads into Staverton Ford Plantation. Where the track bears left go through the gate in the wall ahead, then right to follow a narrow path back towards the river, bearing left over a footbridge. This path runs parallel with the Dart, becoming a broad woodland track through North Wood. When you see buildings nearby through the trees on the right, leave the track and walk downhill to a metal gate and a lane.

4 Turn right to cross Staverton Bridge. At the level crossing turn right to pass through Staverton Station yard into a park-like area between the railway and river. Follow the path across the single-track railway and walk on to meet a lane by Sweet William Cottage.

5 Turn right and follow the lane to its end. Go straight ahead on a small gritty path to pass the Church of St Paul de Leon, who was a 9th-century travelling preacher. Turn left at the lane to pass the public toilets, and left at the junction to the Sea Trout Inn. After your break retrace your steps to the metal gate past Staverton Bridge.

6 Turn immediately right to rejoin the track. Follow this until it runs downhill and bends left. Walk towards the gate on the right, then turn left on the narrow concrete path. The houses of Huxham's Cross can be seen, right. Keep on the concrete path, which leaves the woodland to run between wire fences to meet a concrete drive at the Dartington Crafts Education Centre. Follow the drive to meet the road.

7 Turn left to pass Old Parsonage Farm. Keep on the road back to Dartington Hall, passing the gardens and ruins of the original church (right), until you see the car park on the left.

what to look out for...

The South Devon Railway, which runs from Buckfastleigh to Totnes. Staverton Station has featured in many television programmes and films, such as *The Railway Children*. The station at Buckfastleigh has old locomotives and rolling stock on display, a museum and café, riverside walks and a picnic area. Nearby is Dartmoor Otters & Buckfast Butterflies.

CYCLE 2
The Plym Valley Trail

Minimum time:	3hrs
Ride length:	13.5 miles/21.7km
Difficulty level:	+++
Short Alternative Route	
Minimum time:	2hrs 15min
Ride length:	10.5 miles/16.9km
Difficulty level:	+++
Map:	OS Explorer OL20 South Devon
Start/finish:	Clearbrook parking area above village, grid ref SX 518650
Trails/tracks:	mix of bumpy and well-surfaced track
Landscape:	wooded valley, townscape, estuary and parkland on extension
Public toilets:	Coypool (Point 5)
Tourist information:	Plymouth, tel 01752 304849
Cycle hire:	Tavistock Cycles, Tavistock, tel 01822 617630
❗	First 0.75 mile (1.2km) rough and bumpy (alternative lane access given), steep hills at Bickleigh and busy roads on extension

Getting to the start

Clearbrook lies on Dartmoor's western edge, clearly signposted off the A386 Tavistock to Plymouth road, 2.5 miles (4km) south of Yelverton. Follow the lane across the down and park at the furthest parking area on the right where the road forks.

Why do this cycle ride?

This ride – particularly if the extension to Saltram House is included – covers an impressive range of landscapes: moorland, woodland, river estuary and parkland. The views at both the northern (Dartmoor) and southern (Plym Estuary) ends are impressive, and the outskirts of Plymouth, for Saltram House, are passed quickly.

Plym Bridge Woods and Blaxton Meadow

This railway line opened in 1859 under the South Devon and Tavistock Railway, and ran for 16 miles (25.7km) from Plymouth to Tavistock. The cycle route through Plym Bridge Woods is one of the best bits. The woods became popular with daytrippers who alighted at Plym Bridge Halt, built in

1906 (on the site of the car park mentioned in Point 5). You'll also see evidence of industrial activity: there were several quarries here, workers' cottages, a small lead/silver mine, a canal and three railway lines. The remains of 18th-century Rumple Quarry – from which slate was extracted – and engine house are passed on the right, soon after entering the woods. Plym Bridge Woods are particularly lovely in spring, thick with wood anemones, primroses, bluebells and ransoms.

Once in the Saltram estate you soon pass Blaxton Meadow on your right, an area of managed saltmarsh on the Plym Estuary. It was enclosed in 1886 and developed as agricultural land, and around the time of World War Two supported a cricket ground! Plans to regenerate the saltmarsh started in 1995, and today it provides suitable habitats for a wide range of flora and fauna, with large numbers of migrant waders; look out for flocks of curlews in winter, and deep red samphire beds in autumn.

A pleasant ride along the line of the old Plym Valley railway, with an optional extension to the National Trust's magnificent house and parkland at Saltram.

The Ride

❶ Return to the lane, turn right and descend into Clearbrook and continue past *The Skylark Inn* for about 500yds (457mtrs). Turn right opposite the village hall on a track. After 100yds (91mtrs) turn right up a steep, narrow path; at the top by the *pylon* bear left downhill (cyclists should dismount). Turn sharp left, then right through a gate onto the rough, gritty, old railway line. Follow for about 0.5 mile (0.8km) to Goodameavy: tarmac takes over. (NB to avoid this initial rough section turn left at the fork by the parking area, signed '*Goodameavy*', and cycle steeply downhill to join the railway.)

❷ Soon after Goodameavy the track passes through *Shaugh Tunnel* (note: there are lights, but these are turned off between dusk and dawn – there's a colony of roosting bats in the tunnel), and then under an aqueduct. Pass Shaugh Bridge Halt and cross *Ham Green viaduct*; look back left and you'll catch sight of the Dewerstone Rock above the wooded Plym Valley just above its junction with the River Meavy.

❸ At *Ham Bridge* the route meets a lane; turn right uphill towards *Bickleigh*. At the T-junction turn left and proceed very steeply downhill (young children should dismount). Turn right on a narrow wooded path back onto the railway line and continue through deciduous woodland. Pass over Bickleigh viaduct and into the National Trust's *Plym Bridge Woods*. Continue over Cann viaduct – look over the left side to see the remains of Rumple wheelpit by the river below, and the face of *Cann Quarry* beyond.

4 At Plym Bridge follow signs sharp left to leave the track. For a picnic by the river, turn left under the railway towards the 18th-century bridge; the meadow is on the right (leave your bikes on the lane). For *Saltram House* – created in the 18th century with 500 acres (202ha) of parkland – cross the car park entrance and turn right on a level woodland track. Cycle towards Plymouth (note that Plymouth is one end of the Devon Coast to Coast route, which runs for 102 miles (163km) to Ilfracombe – watch out for serious and speedy cyclists!) to emerge by *Coypool Park-and-Ride* on the right.

5 Cross the road at the T junction and follow the narrow path ahead (barrier); cross the next road and take the rough track opposite. Just past the *playing field gates* (right) bear right on a narrow path to emerge under the A38. Bear diagonally right to find a railed tarmac path uphill left. Follow that up and down, then along the edge of the Plym Estuary to reach the National Trust's *Saltram Estate*.

6 At the edge of parkland keep right, and follow the estuary to *Point Cottage*. Turn left inland on an estate lane to cross the parking area, with the house and shop left.

At the signpost bear left, signed '*Riverside walk and bird hide*' and cycle carefully downhill, avoiding pedestrians, keeping straight on where the tarmac way bears

left towards offices. Re-enter the *parkland* and keep ahead to rejoin the outward route.

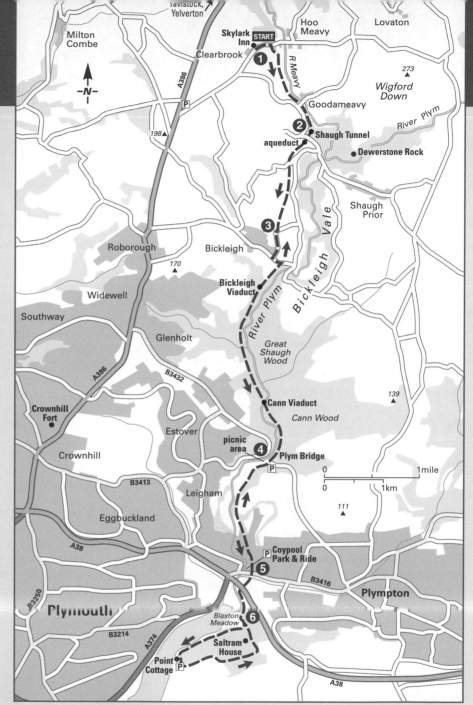

WALK 6
Kimmeridge and Ghostly Tyneham

A coastal walk by army ranges to a not-quite-deserted village.

Minimum time:	3hrs 30min
Walk length:	7.5 miles (12.1km)
Ascent/gradient:	1,165ft (355mtrs) ▲ ▲ ▲
Difficulty level:	✚✚✚
Paths:	Grassy tracks and bridlepaths, some road walking, 12 stiles
Landscape:	Folded hills and valleys around Kimmeridge Bay
Map:	OS Explorer OL15 Purbeck & South Dorset
Start/finish:	Grid reference: SY 918800
Dog friendliness:	Notices request dogs on leads in some sections; some road walking
Parking:	Car park (free) in old quarry north of Kimmeridge village
Public toilets:	Near Marine Centre at Kimmeridge Bay and Tyneham
Note:	Range walks open most weekends throughout year and during main holiday periods; call 01929 462 721, ext 4819 for further information. Keep strictly to paths, between yellow-marked posts

There's a bleakness about Kimmeridge Bay which the high energy of the surfers and the cheerful picture of families on the beach, eyes down as they potter in the rock pools, can't quite dispel. Giant slabs of black rock shelving out to sea, with crumbling cliffs topped by clumps of wild cabbage, create something of this mood. The slow, steady nodding donkey-head of the oil well above a little terrace of unmistakably industrial cottages reinforces it.

Kimmeridge Coal and Oil

The story of the bay is intriguing. Iron Age tribes spotted the potential of the band of bituminous shale that runs through Kimmeridge, polishing it up into blackstone arm rings and ornaments, and later into chair and table legs. People have have been trying to exploit it ever since. The shale, permeated with crude oil, is also known as Kimmeridge coal, but

successive attempts to work it on an industrial scale seemed doomed to failure. These included alum extraction (for dyeing) in the 16th century; use of the coal to fuel a glassworks in the 17th century (it was smelly and inefficient); and use for a variety of chemical distillations, including paraffin wax and varnish, in the 19th century. And for one brief period the street lights of Paris were lit by gas extracted from the shale oil. However, nothing lasted very long. Since 1959 BP has drilled down 1,716ft (520m) below the sea, and its beam engine sucks out some 80 barrels (2,800 gallons/12,720 litres) of crude oil a day. Transported to the Wytch Farm collection point (near Corfe Castle), the oil is then pumped to Hamble, to be shipped around the world.

In contrast to Kimmeridge, just over the hill lies Tyneham, a cosy farming village clustered around its church in a glorious valley. As you get up close, however, you realise that it's uncannily neat, like a film set from the 1940s – Greer Garson's 'Mrs Miniver' could appear at any moment. There's a spreading oak tree by the church gate; a quaint old phone box; even a village pump. The gravestones all look freshly scrubbed – no lichen here. The farmyard is swept clean and empty. The stone cottages are newly repointed, but roofless. And the church, as you enter on a chill mid-winter day, is warm! Inside is an exhibition to explain all. The villagers were asked to give up their homes in December 1943 for the 'war effort', and Tyneham became absorbed into the vast Lulworth Ranges, as part of the live firing range. It's a touching memorial, though perhaps nothing can make up for the fact that the villagers were never allowed back to their homes. Emerging again, you half expect to see soldiers popping out of the windows, but relax, you can only visit when the ranges are closed.

● Kimmeridge Bay

Walk Directions

1 Turn right up the road and soon left over a stile, signposted 'Kimmeridge' – enjoy the sweeping views as you descend. Go through a gate by the church, then another at the bottom. Turn right past some houses, go through a gateway and bear left. Go over a stile below a coppice and bear immediately left along the hedge, following it round to a pair of stiles. Go straight ahead to the next stile and turn right to follow the path along the hedge towards the sea. Turn left on to the road and turn right, across a car park after approximately 0.5 mile (800mtrs).

2 Bear left to visit the marine centre (closed in winter), otherwise turn right on the coastal path to continue. Descend some steps, cross a bridge and bear right, signposted 'Range Walks'. Pass some cottages, on the right, and the oil well. Go through the gate on to the range walk and continue around the coast on a track between yellow posts, crossing several cattle grids. The cliffs of Brandy Bay stagger away to the west.

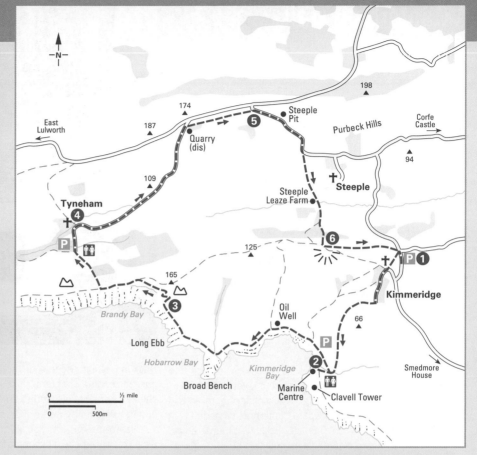

3 After a mile (1.6km) cross a stile and follow the path as it zig-zags sharply uphill. Continue around the top of Brandy Bay on the cliff path. When you reach a stile and marker stone turn down to the right, signposted 'Tyneham'. Soon cross a stile to the left and follow the track down into Tyneham village.

4 After exploring, take the exit road up the hill. At the top, by a gate, turn right over a stile and go along a path parallel with the road.

5 Emerge at a gate and turn right down the road, to go past Steeple Pit. Where the road turns sharp left, go straight ahead down the gravel drive through Steeple Leaze Farm and take the gravel track ahead, leading straight up the hill. Go through a gate and keep left up a muddy path that winds through gorse and scrub, up the hill. Cross a stile at the top and continue straight ahead, with superb views over Kimmeridge.

6 Turn left across a stile and go straight along the edge of the field, following the ridge of the hill, for 0.5 mile (800mtrs), with views to Smedmore House and Corfe Castle. Go through the gate and turn right to return to the start.

while you're there...

The Clavell family have been at Smedmore since the 13th century. In 1575 John Clavell was attempting to exploit the Kimmeridge shale for alum (an essential ingredient for the dyeing industry), and the current Smedmore House, a handsome twin-bayed affair dating from 1761, still keeps a firm eye on activities in the bay. The house is open in high summer when you can enjoy its attractive gardens, the rococo details, period furniture and a museum collection of dolls.

WALK 7
A Canterbury Trail

Canterbury Cathedral

Canterbury's streets have attracted pilgrims for centuries.

Minimum time:	1hr 45min
Walk length:	3.75 miles (6km)
Ascent/gradient:	115ft (35mtrs) ▲▲▲
Difficulty level:	+++
Paths:	City streets and firm footpaths
Landscape:	Ancient cathedral city and tracks once followed by pilgrims
Map:	OS Explorer 150 Canterbury & the Isle of Thanet
Start/finish:	Grid reference: TR 146574
Dog friendliness:	Keep on lead in city but can mostly run free on footpaths
Parking:	Castle Street or one of several car parks in Canterbury
Public toilets:	Castle Row, off Burgate and off High Street

As you walk through the streets of Canterbury, you can't help but be aware that you are following in the footsteps of millions of pilgrims. They have been drawn to Canterbury cathedral every year since 1170, when Thomas Becket was murdered at the cathedral, and have included some notable historic figures. Yet, out of all these people, the most famous pilgrims of all are fictional – they are the characters created by Geoffrey Chaucer (*c*1345–1400) in his epic poem *The Canterbury Tales* (1387): 'And specially from every shires ende, Of Engelond to Caunterbury they wende'.

Roving Ambassador

Chaucer is acknowledged as the father of English literature, but writing wasn't his main occupation, it was just a hobby. Chaucer was born while the Hundred Years War was raging between England and France, and after several years working in the Royal household, he joined the army. He was taken prisoner in France but was released after the English paid a ransom for him. Chaucer then became a sort of roving ambassador travelling throughout Europe on various high level diplomatic missions. He could read French, Latin and Italian and when he travelled he took the opportunity to study foreign literature, which he put to good use in his own works.

Back in England, he took on various official posts including customs controller of furs, skins and hides, and knight of the shire for Kent. He also found time to write several long poems and translate many works of prose.

He wrote *The Canterbury Tales* around 1387 and created a cast of lively, believable characters that tell us a great deal about life in the 14th century. There's the earthy Wife of Bath, who's already had five husbands and seems to have set out on this pilgrimage to catch her sixth; the too worldly Prioress, who puts on affected table manners and speaks French – unfortunately more like Del Boy Trotter than anything else; and then there's the corrupt Friar, who's not at all bothered about those in need, but who sells absolution to anyone who can afford it. The poem, written in Middle English, became the first printed work of English literature and is known all over the world. Chaucer is buried in Westminster Abbey.

where to eat and drink...

West Gate, Canterbury

what to look out for...

Canterbury Cathedral was the first cathedral built in England. It was founded in AD 597 by St Augustine. The present structure dates back to 1071 and is a spectacular example of ecclesiastical architecture. However, it was a murder that first attracted pilgrims to the cathedral. In 1170 Thomas Becket, the Archbishop of Canterbury, was killed by men loyal to the King, Henry II. The Primate had only just returned from exile, after a disagreement with Henry over constitutional reform. The King was overcome with guilt, following the murder, and made a pilgrimage to the cathedral, walking barefoot to show his humility. Becket was buried at Canterbury and was credited with so many miracles that he was soon canonised. The city was established as a site of pilgrimage.

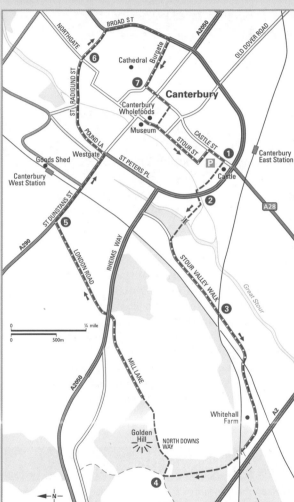

Walk Directions

1 Go right from Castle Street car park then right again down Gas Street to pass the castle. At the end turn left on Centenary Walk. Where this finishes go right and walk beside the road. Cross a bridge, turn left, go under another bridge and along the river to the other side of the road.

2 Cross some grassland, go over a bridge and through a children's play area. Walk across the car park and turn left up the road to join the Stour Valley Walk.

3 Go under a bridge and continue to a level crossing. Cross the railway, then stroll up past Whitehall Farm. Walk under the bridge, through a gate and over a stream. The path bends round and the main road is on your left. At a junction turn right along the North Downs Way.

4 Go over a bridge and up a lane. To your left is Golden Hill – from which pilgrims traditionally had their first view of the city. When you come to a track, turn left and follow it round. Go right along Mill Lane to the main road. Take the underpass to cross Rheims Way, walk down London Road, then turn right into St Dunstans Street.

5 Walk into Canterbury to the Westgate, turn left along Pound Lane and into St Radigund Street.

6 Continue into Northgate, go left then right down Broad Street. You're now walking around the outside of the city walls. Turn right along Burgate, past a tiny 16th-century building called the Pilgrim's Shop. Soon come to a pedestrianised area that brings you out at the Butter Market and war memorial. On your right is the entrance to the cathedral.

7 Turn left, cross The Parade into St Margaret's Street and turn right down Beer Cart Lane. Turn left into Stour Street and on the right is the city museum, and almost opposite, down Jewry Lane, is Canterbury Wholefoods where you can finish your walk. To return to Castle Street, retrace your steps along Stour Street, turn left along Rosemary Lane and then right.

CYCLE 3
Glasson Dock to Lancaster

Minimum time:	2hrs 30min
Ride length:	14 miles/22km
Difficulty level:	✚✚✚
Map:	OS Explorer 296 Lancaster, Morecambe and Fleetwood
Start/finish:	Quayside, Glasson Dock; grid ref: SD 446561
Trails/tracks:	good route, though cyclists will need to dismount at a few points on the canal while passing waterfront pubs
Landscape:	mainly old railway trackbed or canal towpaths
Public toilets:	at the start
Tourist information:	Lancaster, tel 01524 32878
Cycle hire:	none locally
❶	Cycles will need to be carried up and down steps to reach the canal tow path

● Lancaster Canal

Getting to the start

Glasson Dock is on the Lune Estuary, 4 miles (6.4km) south west of Lancaster. It is best reached from Lancaster, or Cockerham to the south, along the A588, but may also be reached from Junction 33 on the M6 via Galgate – turn left at the traffic lights in the village centre and follow signs.

Why do this cycle ride?

A superb introduction to coastal Lancashire. The old trackbed and the return along the Lancaster Canal makes for easy riding, while the traffic-free cycle route through riverside Lancaster is ingenious. You can opt out at the Millennium Bridge and explore Lancashire's ancient capital.

while you're there...

Glasson itself is worth a little more time: there's usually something going on in the outer harbour or the inner yacht basin. There's also a gallery/craft shop and, round the corner, the Smokehouse offers a wide range of delicacies.

Follow the River Lune to explore Lancaster, and share the delights of its canal towpath on the way back.

Wildlife along the way

Aldcliffe Marsh is a Site of Special Scientific Interest because of its importance for waders such as redshank and lapwing.

At one time the lapwing was a common sight on ploughed fields, but the use of insecticides and farming machinery has driven it to meadows and marshes in summer. Keep an eye open for the bright yellow ragwort, a plant that attracts the cinnabar moth, which lays its eggs on the stems and produces gaudy black-and-yellow caterpillars. In Freeman's Wood is a black poplar (*Populus nigra*), a native tree of lowland marshes and of this area, but not all that common. There are thought to be fewer than 3,000 black poplars in Britain today. The tree in Freeman's Wood is one of only two in Lancashire.

The Ride

❶ Begin from the large car park near the dock by crossing the road onto a cycleway along the edge of the *Lune Estuary*. A gravel track leads on to cross the River Conder before turning north through the *Conder Green car park*. (Follow the road right for The Stork pub.) Beyond the car park, ride onto a tree-lined track, and keep following this until it reaches a surfaced lane end, not far from the village of Aldcliffe.

❷ Turn left into a *gravel area*, and then immediately, just before a footpath stile, onto a broad vehicle track. At a cross-track, keep forward along a bridleway for *New Quay Road*, and going into *Freeman's Wood*. The track, now surfaced,

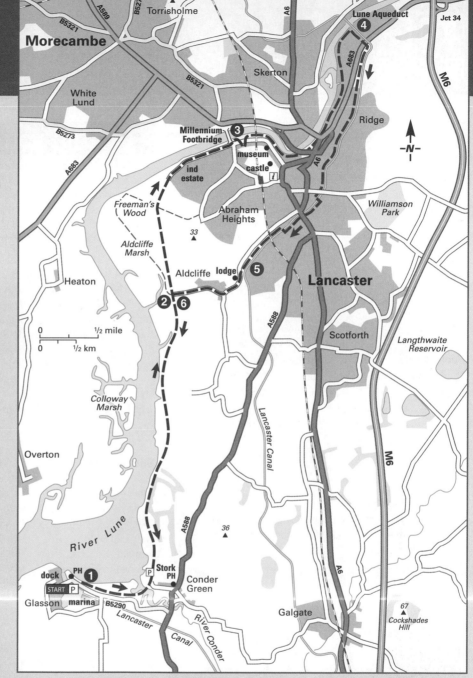

crosses a section of *Aldcliffe Marsh*, and eventually comes out to meet a much wider road near a small light industrial complex. Keep forward until you reach an old arched bridge with the modern, *Millennium* (foot) *Bridge* nearby.

3 Turn onto the footbridge, and then immediately right to leave it, without crossing the river. Go left on a surfaced *cycle lane* (signed for Halton and Caton). Follow the lane until it rises, to run briefly alongside the main road. Almost immediately turn right to perform a loop to the left into an *underpass* – you may need to dismount here. On the other side, go forward on a *signed cycle route*, which passes beneath a bridge and goes forward on a surfaced track down an avenue of trees. When it forks, keep left, and carry on to reach the stone *Lune Aqueduct*. Just before it, turn right onto a narrow path that leads to the foot of a flight of steps. Here you will need to dismount and carry your cycle up the steps to reach the tow path – a breathless few minutes, but well worth the effort.

4 Turn right along the tow path. At *Whitecross*, dismount again to change to the other side of the canal. At a couple of places now you may need to dismount again as you pass canalside pubs, but eventually a *bridge* leads back over the canal. Over the bridge, turn immediately right down steps (dismount again) to rejoin the *tow path*.

5 Continue until you pass *Bridge 95*, following which the canal has a road on the right, and bends to the

left. A short way on, leave the tow path and go onto the road (near a *lodge* on the right, dated 1827). Go forward, climbing steadily into the village of *Aldcliffe*. At the top of the climb, on a bend, take care, and turn right into the first lane on the

right, descending quite steeply, and continuing down past *houses*, to ride along a narrow country lane to rejoin the outward near the gravel area.

6 Turn left onto the *trackbed*, and follow this back to Conder Green, turning left into the village for *The Stork*, or continue round the coast to *Glasson Dock*.

CYCLE 4
Blickling Hall and The Marriott Way

Minimum time:	3hrs
Ride length:	19 miles/30.6km
Difficulty level:	✚✚✚
Short Alternative Route	
Minimum time:	2hrs
Ride length:	13.5 miles/12.8km
Difficulty level:	✚✚✚
Map:	OS Explorer 252 Norfolk Coast East
Start/finish:	National Trust car park at Blickling Hall; grid ref: TG176285
Trails/tracks:	parkland tracks, narrow country lanes, old railway track
Landscape:	open and gently rolling agricultural countryside and parkland
Public toilets:	Blickling Hall and Aylsham
Tourist information:	Aylsham, tel 01263 733903
Cycle hire:	Blickling Hall (mid-March to October), tel 01263 738015 www.nationaltrust.org.uk/blickling
❗	Puddles after rain along the Marriott Way, care to be taken crossing B1354 and through Aylsham

Getting to the start
Blickling Hall is located on the B1354 Aylsham to Holt road, 1.5 miles (2.4km) north-west of Aylsham and 15 miles (24.1km) north of Norwich.

Blickling Hall

Why do this cycle ride?
A level and easy-going ride, this enjoyable route begins at the Blickling splendid National Trust property of Blickling Hall, and incorporates a variety of parkland tracks, peaceful country lanes and a 6-mile (9.7km) section of disused railway track, the Marriott Way. Diversions along the way include a fascinating church and the little market town of Aylsham.

Cycle peaceful country lanes and a former railway track from Blickling Hall

Blickling Hall
Flanked by 17ft (5mtrs) dark yew hedges planted in the 17th century, Blickling Hall (NT) is a magnificent Jacobean brick-fronted hall and one of the great houses of East Anglia. Dutch gabling, mullioned windows and domed turrets characterise the exterior. Inside there are fine collections of furniture, pictures and tapestries, and a spectacular Jacobean plaster ceiling in the 123ft (37.5mtrs) Long Gallery (moulded in the 1620s) is very impressive. The gardens are also well worth exploring.

Salle
The tiny village of Salle is the unlikely setting for a 15th-century cathedral-like church full of rich treasures, apparently totally out of proportion to the tiny parish it serves. It was built by three wealthy families – the Briggs, the Fontaynes and the Boleyns – who made their fortunes from the weaving industry. Of particular note is the unusual seven-sacrament font, of which only 39 are said to exist. Well worth looking at are the 26 carved oak stalls. Some have good carvings of human heads, others boast birds and animals; note the swan, squirrel, dragon and ape.

The Ride

1 From the car park follow the path to the information board and sign stating 'Park Only'. Turn left along the estate road, bearing right at a fork to enter *Blickling Park*. In a few yards, at a fork, take the bridleway left across the park (Weavers Way). Proceed for 1 mile (1.6km), passing a track to the Mausoleum, and keeping to the left of *Great Wood* to reach a parking area and lane.

2 Turn left, then turn left at the junction in *Itteringham Common*, following the lane uphill to a T-junction. Turn right, then left for Oulton and shortly reach the B1354. Turn right and then left in 100mtrs, signposted Oulton. Pass *Oulton Hall*, turn left at a crossroads and pass Oulton church. Keep to the lane for a mile (1.6km) to a T-junction and turn right into Oulton Street.

3 The road crosses a *disused airfield* to reach the busy B1149. Cross straight over and follow the lane for 0.75 mile (1.2km) to a crossroads by cottages (Southgate). (For the short ride, continue towards Cawston and at an old railway crossing turn left to join *Marriott's Way*, signed 'Aylsham 4', Point 6). Turn right at the crossroads, signposted Heydon, and continue to a T-junction (unsigned).

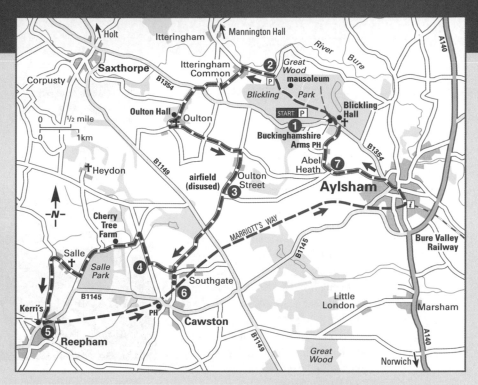

4 Turn right, then in 0.5 mile (800mtrs) turn left for Salle. Pass *Cherry Tree Farm* and keep left at the next junction. Take the next right turning and soon pass the impressive church at *Salle*. Pass through the hamlet to a junction and follow the road left, signposted to Reepham. Continue to *Reepham* and a T-junction on the outskirts of the village.

5 For refreshments at the old Reepham Station turn right, then right again (Kerri's). Turn left, then cross the road and pass through a gate to join the Marriott Way, a good, surfaced cycling trail along the former railway track. In 2 miles (3km) pass under a bridge and immediately fork left to climb an *embankment* (former platform of Cawston Station). Continue to a level crossing and cross a by-road.

6 Proceed for a further 4 miles (6.4km) through open country to the end of the trail in *Aylsham*, almost opposite the Bure Valley Railway (toilets). Turn left towards the town centre. Pass Budgens and follow the road left, signed to *Blickling Hall*. Pass the square and remain on the road for 0.5 mile (800mtrs) before forking left on to a lane, signposted Abel Heath.

7 In 1 mile (1.6km) at *Abel Heath*, fork right and pass through the hamlet of Silvergate to reach the B1354, opposite Blickling Church. Turn left to return to the National Trust car park and *The Buckinghamshire Arms*.

while you're there...

Deep in the lovely valley of the River Bure, which winds its way through fertile agricultural land on its way to the Broads, lie two stately homes. These are Mannington Hall and Wolterton Hall, both owned by Lord and Lady Walpole. The grounds are run with a view to conservation and ecologically safe management, so they are a haven for many species of birds, small mammals and plants.

WALK 8
Close to the Edge at Diddlebury

Former drovers' roads link the crest of Wenlock Edge to the meadows of beautiful Corve Dale.

Minimum time:	3hrs
Walk length:	6.25 miles (10.1km)
Ascent/gradient:	689ft (210mtrs) ▲▲▲
Difficulty level:	✦✦✦
Paths:	Mostly good but ford on Dunstan's Lane can be deep after rain, 10 stiles
Landscape:	Wooded ridge of Wenlock Edge, patchwork of Corve Dale
Map:	OS Explorer 217 The Long Mynd & Wenlock Edge
Start/finish:	Grid reference: SO 479875
Dog friendliness:	On lead near livestock; notices warn sheep chasers will be shot
Parking:	Car park/picnic site on east side of unclassified road between Middlehope and Westhope
Public toilets:	None en route

● Tortoiseshell butterfly

Wenlock Edge needs a book to itself, so all you will get here is the merest glimpse, but it should whet your appetite for more. This great tree-clad escarpment is one of Shropshire's most famous landscape features, partly because it plays a role in A E Housman's collection of poems entitled *A Shropshire Lad*, some of which were set to music by the composer Vaughan Williams. It is best seen from the west, appearing as an unbroken escarpment running from the Severn Gorge to Craven Arms. From the east it is more elusive, rising almost imperceptibly. Within a basic ridge structure, it seems to form a series of waves or steps, and consists for part of its length of two parallel edges, divided by Hope Dale.

Ancient Woodland
Wenlock Edge is composed of Silurian limestone formed about 420 million years ago. Developing as a barrier reef in a tropical sea on the edge of a continental shelf, it was built up from the accumulation of sediments and the skeletons of marine creatures such as corals, brachiopods and crinoids. Earth movements and erosion then sculpted it into the escarpment.

Most of it is wooded, and much of this is ancient woodland, growing on steep slopes where there has been continuous tree cover since the end of the last ice age. The dominant species is ash, which has a special affinity with limestone, but many other types are present. Beneath the trees are lime-loving shrubs such as spurge laurel, spindle and dogwood. The ground flora is rich and varied, especially along the rides and in newly coppiced areas, where flowers respond to the increased light by growing more profusely and attracting many butterflies.

Exploitation
In the past, the Edge was always seen as a valuable resource to be exploited. Timber provided building materials, tools and charcoal for iron smelting. Limestone was used for building, for making lime, for iron smelting and, more recently, as an aggregate. This latter use still continues and there are unsightly quarries between Presthope and Much Wenlock, where you can walk the ridge and look down on the unedifying spectacle of monstrous machines digging up Shropshire so that heavy lorries can carry it away. There's nothing like that on this walk, where the quarries you pass are small ones, long since abandoned and now transformed by nature into mossy, fern-filled caverns of green.

Walk Directions

1 Turn left out of the car park along the lane. When you come to a junction, turn left again, signposted 'Middlehope'. Keep straight on at the next, signposted 'Upper Westhope', where the road becomes a track and soon bends left towards a house. Enter a gate on the right instead and join a grassy bridleway that soon enters woodland. Keep straight on at two cross paths.

2 The bridleway emerges into pasture; keep straight on along to the corner. Go through a gate and turn right on a field-edge path, which soon becomes a wide track.

3 After passing a cottage, and with a group of barns ahead, look for blue arrows that direct you sharp right through a gate. Turn immediately left and walk above Corfton Bache, a deep valley, until more blue arrows direct you zig-zagging down into the valley. Follow it to the road at Corfton and cross to a lane opposite.

4 As the lane degenerates into a track, look on the left for an iron kissing gate. Cross cattle pasture to a prominent stile at the far side. Cross a farm track and walk to the far right corner of an arable field.

5 Go through a gate, then a little way along the left-hand edge of another field until a gate gives access to parkland. Head in the direction indicated by the waymarker. St Peter's Church at Diddlebury soon comes into view, providing an infallible guide.

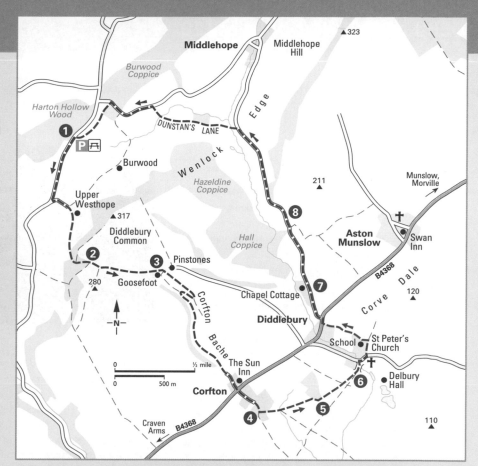

6 Cross two stiles at the far side of the park and go straight on down. Cross a track to find a footbridge and a path into Diddlebury. Turn right, then left by the church. Join a footpath which passes to the right of the village hall, then goes diagonally right through the school, to stiles immediately right of the buildings. Cross fields to the road. Cross to the lane opposite, forking right after a few paces.

7 A footpath leaves the lane on the right, almost opposite Chapel Cottage. Continue up the lane.

8 At a junction at the top of the hill, keep left, still on the lane. As the lane reaches the valley bottom, turn left on a stony track, Dunstan's Lane, soon reaching a ford. Follow it, with waymarks appearing, to the Middlehope road and turn left. Keep straight on at a Y-junction. Turn left on a footpath with Shropshire Way sign. The sometimes muddy path leads through the woods back to the picnic site.

what to look out for...

St Peter's Church at Diddlebury has a Saxon nave, its north wall constructed of herringbone masonry, which was the style favoured by the Saxons. The north doorway is typically Saxon, and there is a Saxon window. The tower also seems to be partly Saxon, though even the experts are unsure. Do go inside – very few churches of this kind survive in England.

WALK 9
Deep Romantic Ebbor Gorge

The small but sublime limestone gorge that inspired Coleridge to write one of his best-known poems, '*Kubla Khan*'.

Minimum time:	2hrs 30min
Walk length:	4.75 miles (7.7km)
Ascent/gradient:	1000ft (305mtrs) ▲ ▲ ▲
Difficulty level:	+++
Paths:	Small paths and field-edges, with a rugged descent, 10 stiles
Landscape:	Vast view across the Levels, then tight little gorge
Map:	OS Explorer 141 Cheddar Gorge
Start/finish:	Grid reference: ST 521484
Dog friendliness:	English Nature asks that dogs to be on leads in reserve
Parking:	Lane above Wookey Hole or Wookey Hole's car park below Point ②
Public toilets:	At Wookey Hole's visitor car park

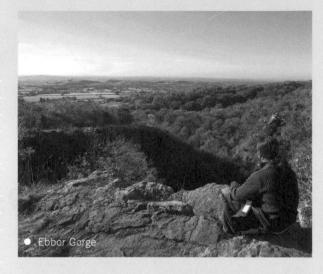

● Ebbor Gorge

When Samual Taylor Coleridge (1772–1834) wanted to paint in words the ultimate in sublime landscape, he based his poem not on Snowdonia (which he had visited) but on Somerset. The setting of *Kubla Khan* (1816) is based partly on Culbone Combe, on the Exmoor Coast, and partly on memories of a visit to Wookey Hole and Ebbor. So we have: 'the deep romantic chasm that slanted, down a green hill, athwart a cedern covert; a savage place!' While down at Wookey Hole: 'Alph, the sacred river ran, through caverns measureless to man…'

To the writers and painters of the Romantic period, a landscape could be merely beautiful – or it could be sublime. A scene that's 'sublime' goes far beyond the merely pretty: it induces awe and even terror. It stills the noisy chattering mind, to the point of breaking through into the 'divine Reality' that lies behind the world. Today most of us don't believe in the divine Reality, and aren't driven to sort our views into categories and seek out the sublime. And yet it is possible to experience it on Glastonbury Tor at sunset and at midnight on the Quantocks even while staring down on some very 21st-century streetlights.

Ornamental Vision

It's interesting to compare *Kubla Khan* with Stourhead Garden: the walls and towers are there; the incense-bearing trees; even the domed shapes of the buildings. Stourhead's designer, Henry Hoare, wasn't copying the poem, it's just that he and Coleridge sought the same thing.

The third category of scenery was picturesque. This is one that's arranged correctly, with foreground, middleground, and a hill wall shutting off the end. The foreground should have some ornamental peasants or brigands, from whom a carefully placed river or lane leads the eye into the scene.

Coleridge did pronounce 'Kubla Khan' to rhyme with 'Measureless to man'. We know this from a letter of Dorothy Wordsworth's where she puns on 'Kubla Khan' and 'watering Khan'. Wordsworth himself mocked those who go walking for the sake of the view – the 'craving for a prospect', as he called it. But Ebbor Gorge is impressive whatever its landscape category.

what to look out for...

Keep your eyes open for wailing women and demon lovers, obviously. But also note how the cramped narrow passage of the Ebbor Gorge has clearly been a waterfall. The stream now runs underground and there are some cave entrances below the gorge.

Walk Directions

1 From the noticeboard at the top end of the car park descend a stepped path. After a clearing, turn left, signposted 'The Gorge'. The wide path crosses the stream to another junction.

2 Turn right, away from the gorge down the valley to a road. Turn left, to pass through Wookey Hole village. At its end the road bends right; take a kissing gate on the left with a 'West Mendip Way' post. After two more kissing gates turn left up a spur to a stile and the top of Arthur's Point.

3 Bear right for 60yds (55mtrs) into woods again. The path now bears right to a stile. Go down left to a kissing gate back into the wood. At once, and before the lime kiln just ahead, turn up left between boulders to pass between high quarry crags. Bear right along the wood foot to join a short track ahead. It leads to a four-track junction with a waymarker post standing in a stone plinth.

4 Turn sharp left, on to tarred track that bends right then left through Model Farm, to Tynings Lane. Turn left for 85yds (78mtrs) to a signposted stile on the right. Go up with a fence on your right, then bear left to a gate with a stile. Go straight up the next field, aiming for a gateway below the top left corner with tractor ruts running into it. A track leads up through a wood and a field. From the gate at its top slant upwards in the same direction to another gate next to a stile 100yds (91mtrs) below the field's top left corner.

5 A small path runs along the tops of three fields with a long view across the Levels away to your left. With a stile on the right and a gate and horse trough in front, turn downhill keeping the fence on your right; follow it to a stile leading into the Ebbor Gorge Nature Reserve.

6 A second stile leads into a wood. At a junction with a red arrow and sign marked 'Car Park' pointing forward, turn right into the valley and go down it – this narrows to an exciting, rocky gully. At the foot of the gorge turn right, signposted 'Car Park'. You are now back at Point **2** of the outward walk. After crossing a stream turn left at a T-junction to the wood edge, and back right to the car park.

while you're there...

Wookey Hole Caves – the 'absolutely top hole' – was first recorded as a tourist attraction in 1480, when visitors had to bring their own rushlight tapers. The underground River Axe and the vast chambers are now dramatically illuminated by electric lighting.

A walk in the footsteps of Britain's best-known 20th-century composer.

Minimum time:	2hrs 30min
Walk length:	5.75 miles (9.2km)
Ascent/gradient:	Negligible ▲ ▲ ▲
Difficulty level:	✚ ✚ ✚
Paths:	River and sea wall, meadows, old railway track
Landscape:	Town, river, marshes and beach
Map:	OS Explorer 212 Woodbridge & Saxmundham
Start/finish:	Grid reference: TM 463555
Dog friendliness:	Off lead on river wall, on lead on permissive path – not allowed on beach between May and September
Parking:	Slaughden Quay free car park
Public toilets:	Slaughden Quay, Fort Green, Moot Hall

Aldeburgh is one of those places that has been put on the map by one man. In medieval times this was a busy port with fishing and shipbuilding industries, but in a story which has been repeated up and down the Suffolk coast, its harbour silted up and it went into decline as the River Alde was diverted southwards by the shingle bank of Orford Ness. Today, Aldeburgh is buzzing once again and the cafés on the seafront are full of excited chatter as visitors come in their thousands to pay homage to the town's most famous resident, Benjamin Britten.

Britain's Leading Composer

Britten (1913–76) was the leading British composer of the 20th century and the man who introduced many people to classical music through works like *The Young Person's Guide to the Orchestra* and his opera for children, *Noye's Fludde*. Born in Lowestoft, the son of a local dentist, he grew up with the sound of the sea and began composing at the age of five. During World War Two he moved to the United States as a conscientious objector, and it was here that he first read the work of George Crabbe (1754–1832), an Aldeburgh poet. Crabbe's father was a salt-master and two of his brothers had been lost at sea.

It was through Crabbe that Britten rediscovered his Suffolk roots. He returned to Snape to write *Peter Grimes*, an opera

based on Crabbe's poems about the gritty lives of Aldeburgh fishermen. If ever a piece of music had a sense of place, this is it. You hear the waves breaking on the shingle beach, the seagulls swooping over the coast, the wind coming in on the tide. The leading role was created for Britten's lifelong partner and collaborator, the operatic tenor Peter Pears.

Aldeburgh Festival

Benjamin Britten's most lasting contribution to Aldeburgh was the foundation of the Aldeburgh Festival, which he achieved together with Pears and the librettist Eric Crozier in 1948. A number of Britten's best-known works were first performed at the festival, including *Noye's Fludde, Curlew River* and *A Midsummer Night's Dream*. At first the concerts took place in local churches and the Jubilee Hall, but eventually a larger venue was needed. In 1967, the festival was moved to a new concert hall at Snape Maltings, a 19th-century granary outside Aldeburgh that now hosts musical events throughout the year and not just during the main festival in June. Britten and Pears continued to live in Aldeburgh, initially in a seafront house on Crabbe Street and later in a large farmhouse on the edge of town. They are buried side by side in the churchyard of the parish church of St Peter and St Paul.

● Aldeburgh

Walk Directions

1 Start at Slaughden Quay, once a thriving port, now a yacht club. Walk back briefly in the direction of Aldeburgh and turn left along the river wall on the north bank of the River Alde. There are good views to your left of the Martello tower that marks the northern end of Orford Ness. Stay on the river wall for 2 miles (3.2km) as the river swings to the right towards Aldeburgh.

2 When the river bends left, go down the wooden staircase to your right and keep straight ahead across a meadow with a water tower visible ahead. Go through a gate and bear half-left across the next meadow to cross over a footbridge. Next, follow the waymarks, bearing half right, then keep straight ahead across the next field to come to another footbridge. After crossing a fifth footbridge, the path runs alongside allotments and goes through a gate to reach a lane.

3 Turn left by a brick wall and cross the recreation ground. Continue past the fire station to reach a road. Turn right for

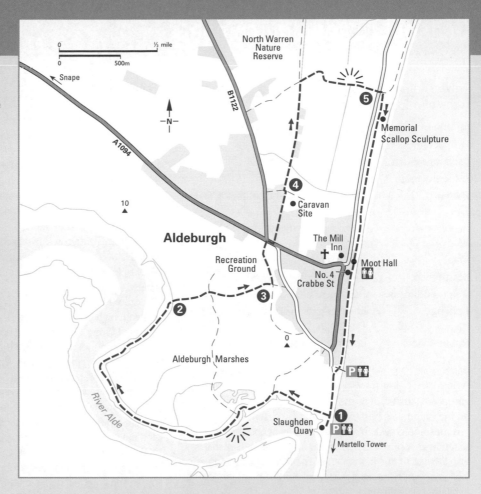

75yds (69mtrs) then go left on a signposted footpath almost opposite the hospital entrance. Follow this path between houses, cross a road and keep straight ahead with a caravan site on the right.

4 When you see a footpath on the right, leading to a track across the caravan park, turn left and immediately right on a permissive path that follows the trackbed of an old railway. Stay on this path for 0.5 mile (800mtrs) as it climbs steadily between farmland to the left and woodland and marshes to the right. Turn right at a junction of paths to reach the open meadows. Stay on this path, crossing the North Warren nature reserve with views of Sizewell power station to your left.

5 Cross the road and turn right along a tarmac path that runs parallel to the beach. As you approach Aldeburgh, you pass a striking scallop sculpture on the shingle (erected in 2003 to celebrate Benjamin Britten's life in Aldeburgh), fishermen's huts and fishing boats that have been pulled up on to the shingle. Pass the timber-framed Moot Hall and continue along Crag Path, past a lifeboat station and a pair of 19th-century look-out towers. At the end of Crag Path, bear right across a car park and walk around the old mill to return to Slaughden Quay.

while you're there...

The Moot Hall, in a 16th-century building on the seafront, doubles as the council chamber and a small local museum, open on summer afternoons with exhibitions on history, fishing and the Anglo-Saxon ship burial at Snape. You should also pay a visit to Snape Maltings, 5 miles (8km) from Aldeburgh, with its concert hall, craft shops, tea rooms, pub and boat trips on the River Alde in summer.

Traverse unspoilt downland from Godshill to the ruins of a Palladian mansion.

Minimum time:	2hrs
Walk length:	4.5 miles (7.2km)
Ascent/gradient:	639ft (195mtrs) ▲▲▲
Difficulty level:	+++
Paths:	Downland, woodland paths, tracks, metalled drive, 2 stiles
Landscape:	Farmland, woodland, and open downland
Map:	OS Explorer OL 29 Isle of Wight
Start/finish:	Grid reference: SZ 530817
Dog friendliness:	Dogs must be kept on lead in places
Parking:	Free car park in Godshill, opposite The Griffin
Public toilets:	Godshill, opposite The Griffin

With its village street lined with pretty thatched cottages, flower-filled gardens, wishing wells, souvenir shops, and tea gardens, Godshill, at its most visible, is the tourist 'honey-pot' on the island. It is best explored out of season, when the coaches and crowds have gone, and its period buildings and magnificent church can be better appreciated. Godshill is also located in the heart of an unspoilt landscape and perfect walking country, making it a useful starting point for several exhilarating downland rambles.

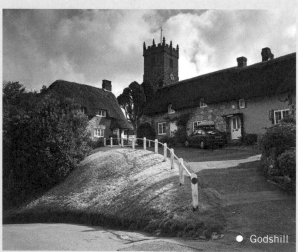

● Godshill

Family Tie

The history of Godshill is closely tied to the Worsley family, builders of the Palladian-style mansion of Appuldurcombe in the neighbouring village of Wroxall and the focus of this walk. Several of the buildings in the village were built by various owners of Appuldurcombe and their fine memorials can be seen in the church. Your walk quickly escapes Godshill and the throng of summer visitors, steadily climbing through woods and farmland to the top of Stenbury Down, where you can catch your breath and take in the far-reaching island views, from Tennyson Down in the west to Culver Cliff in the east. From these lofty heights, you quickly descend towards Wroxall to reach the magnificent ruins of Appuldurcombe House.

Cradled in a sheltered and secluded natural amphitheatre beneath high downland slopes, Appuldurcombe, the great house of Wroxall, began as a priory in 1100. It later became a convent and then the home of the Leigh family in 1498. The connection with the illustrious Worsleys began when the Leighs' daughter Anne married Sir James Worsley, the richest man in Wight, who obtained a new lease. Following the Dissolution of the Monasteries, the Worsley's gained outright possession of the property, pulled down the old Tudor house and built a fine mansion with a pillared front towards the end of the 18th century. They also employed 'Capability' Brown to landscape the immediate surroundings of the house. It was, by far, the grandest house on the island until Queen Victoria built Osborne House. After 300 years as the home of the Worsley family, it was sold in 1854 and in succeeding years became a school, the home of Benedictine monks, and a temporary base for troops during World War One. Already damaged and decaying, it was finally reduced to a ruined shell in 1943, courtesy of a stray German land mine.

What you see today has been achieved by English Heritage and its predecessors, who since 1952 have repaired and restored the dramatic shell of the building, finally re-roofing and replacing windows in the Great Hall, Drawing Room and Dining Parlour in 1986. Visitors can wander through the eerily empty rooms, admire the splendid east front and stroll through the ornamental gardens and 11 acres (4.5ha) of grounds.

Walk Directions

1 From the car park in Godshill, cross the road and walk down Hollow Lane beside the Griffin Inn. Just before Godshill Cherry Orchard, take the footpath left, signed to Beech Copse. Keep to the right of the pub garden and continue gently uphill through the valley to a kissing gate on the edge of Beech Copse.

2 Just beyond, at a fork, bear right uphill through trees to a junction of paths by a gate. Turn right through the gate and walk towards Sainham Farm. Keep left of the farm to a gate and turn left uphill (Worsley Trail), signed to Stenbury Down. Steadily climb this fenced track, passing two large metal gates to enter a copse.

3 At a junction of paths below Gat Cliff, take bridleway GL49 right through a gate beside a fingerpost, signed 'Stenbury Down'. Shortly, disregard footpath right and keep to the bridleway as it veers left and climbs to a gate. Skirting around the base of Gat Cliff and then Appuldurcombe Down, the path follows field-edges before climbing steeply beside a stone wall to a gate and open grassland on the top of Stenbury Down.

4 Keep left beside the hedge to a gate and, in a few paces, bear right along the track towards a radio station. Pass to the left of the building; then, just before reaching a stile and footpath on the right, turn left through a waymarked gate along the

field-edge. Head downhill, then at the field boundary, bear left to descend steps to a metalled track.

5 Turn left and steeply descend to a T-junction. Turn left then, where the lane curves right, keep ahead to pass Span Lodge and a large barn to a gate. Keep ahead between fields to a stile. Keep to the left-hand field-edge in front of Appuldurcombe House, ignoring the waymarked path right, to a stile by the entrance to the house.

6 Take the footpath to the left of the car park, signed 'Godshill'. Walk along the drive to Appuldurcombe Farm then, where it curves left, keep straight ahead through two gateways (with stiles to the left) and soon pass through Freemantle Gate on the edge of Godshill Park.

7 Proceed downhill towards Godshill Park Farm. Ignore paths right and left, pass in front of Godshill Park House and join the metalled drive that leads to the A3020. Cross over and turn left along the pavement back to the car park.

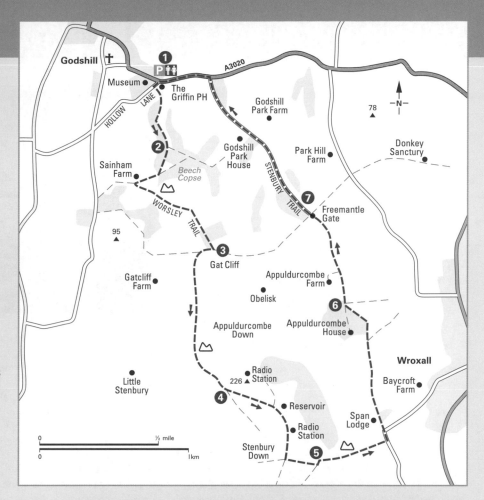

From the ancient site of St Cedd's monastery to the attractive village of Hutton-le-Hole.

Minimum time:	2hrs
Walk length:	4.5 miles (7.2km)
Ascent/gradient:	463ft (141mtrs) ▲▲▲
Difficulty level:	✚✚✚
Paths:	Farm tracks and field paths, 2 stiles
Landscape:	Moorland and woodland, with views
Map:	OS Explorer OL 26 North York Moors – Western
Start/finish:	Grid reference: SE 729905
Dog friendliness:	Dogs should be on lead
Parking:	Village street in Lastingham. Alternative parking in car park at north end of Hutton-le-Hole
Public toilets:	Hutton-le-Hole

● Hutton-le-Hole

In high and isolated hills, more fitted as a place of robbers and the haunt of wild animals than somewhere fit for men to live.'

So wrote the 8th-century historian Bede about Lastingham, which he had visited. This was where St Cedd, Bishop of the East Saxons and once a monk from Lindisfarne, founded his monastery in ad 654, and where he died in ad 664. Although nothing survives of his church, Lastingham remains a holy place, not least in the ancient and impressive crypt beneath the Norman church. This was built in 1078, when the monastery was refounded after destruction in Danish raids in the 9th century.

Court in Spaunton

Leaving Lastingham, the walk quickly reaches the single village street of Spaunton. Lined with cottages and farmhouses from the 17th century onwards, it seems typical of many villages on the North York Moors. But Spaunton has hidden secrets; the fields surrounding it are set out on a Roman pattern, and at the beginning of the 19th century, a Roman burial was found near the village. Excavations, some

60 years later, also unearthed the foundations of a very large medieval hall, which indicated that Spaunton was once a large and important village, owned by St Mary's Abbey in York. When the estate was sold in the 16th century, the new landowners constituted a special court for the manor, grandly called the Court Leet and Court Baron with View of Frankpledge, which still meets to deal with the rights of those who can graze animals on the commons.

Hutton-le-Hole and the Quakers

Reckoned by many people to be one of the prettiest of North Yorkshire's villages, Hutton-le-Hole clusters around an irregular green and along the banks of the Hutton Beck. The village has an old Meeting House and a long association with the Society of Friends. One Quaker inhabitant, John Richard, was a friend of William Penn, founder of Pennsylvania. He spent much time preaching in America; it is said he rode more than 3,726 miles (5,995km) and acted as a mediator between the white settlers and the Native Americans. He finally retired to the village, where he died in 1753.

The Millennium Stone

Near the end of the walk you'll come across a new local landmark. Marking the year 2000, the people of Lastingham have placed a boulder carved with a cross on the hillside above the village. On it are two dates – ad 2000 and ad 654, the year in which St Cedd founded the original Lastingham monastery.

Walk Directions

1 Begin by The Green and follow signs to Cropton, Pickering and Rosedale, past the red telephone box. Where the road swings left, go right to wind over a small bridge and beside a stream. Ascend to a footpath sign, and go right, uphill, through a gate and through woodland to a handgate on to a road. Turn right, signed 'Spaunton'.

2 Follow the road through Spaunton, and bend right at the end of the village, then turn left by the public footpath sign over the cattle grid into the farmyard. The waymarked track curves through the farm to reach another footpath signpost, where the track bends left. After 100yds (91mtrs), at a barn, the track bends left again.

3 After about 200yds (183mtrs), follow a public footpath sign right and walk on to follow another sign as the track bends left. After 100yds (91mtrs), take a footpath to the right, down the hill into woodland. Follow the track as it bends left, then go right, following the waymarks, down a steep grassy path into the valley. Descend to a gate beside a stream, and on to the road through Hutton-le-Hole.

4 Turn right up the main street and then right again at a footpath signpost opposite the Village Hall. Follow the waymarked route along the field-edges and through five waymarked gates to a kissing gate before a footbridge. Follow the path through woodland to a gate and follow the grassy track to the road.

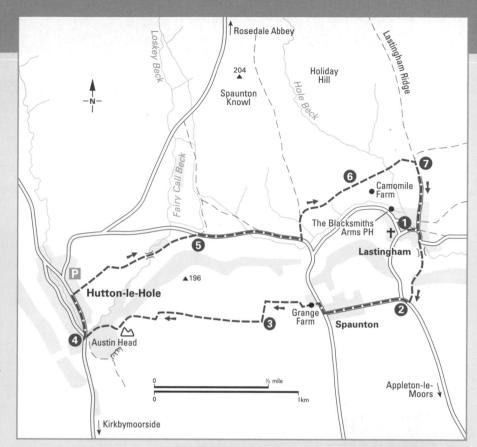

5 Turn right and follow the road for 0.5 mile (800mtrs). Turn left at a footpath sign just before the road descends to a stone bridge. Continue on the grassy path, going over a stile, and follow the track towards a farm.

6 Follow the waymarked posts, bending left alongside the wall beside a clump of trees and descending into a valley. Cross over the stream and follow the wall on your right-hand side uphill. You will reach a bench and then a carved stone with a cross and a three-pointed sign nearby.

7 Take none of the directions indicated by the sign, but turn right, downhill through a gate and on to the metalled road. Follow the road downhill back into the village of Lastingham.

what to look out for...

There is a full range of activities at the Ryedale Folk Museum in Hutton-le-Hole, where old structures from around the North York Moors have been reconstructed as a hamlet. As well as an authentic Elizabethan manor house with a massive oak cruck frame, farm buildings, cottages and traditional long houses, you can see an early photographer's studio, a medieval glass kiln and a variety of agricultural tools and transport. There's also a fire engine and a hearse. Maypole dancing, rare breeds days and quilting are just some of the activities that take place during the year and you may catch the historic farm machinery working, or have the chance to try your hand at some of the almost-forgotten crafts.

CYCLE 5
Terrington and Castle Howard

Minimum time:	2hrs
Ride length:	9.3 miles/15km
Difficulty level:	✚✚✚
Map:	OS Explorer 300 Howardian Hills and Malton
Start/finish:	roadside parking in the main street, Terrington; grid ref: SE 670706
Trails/tracks:	country lanes with some hills
Landscape:	rolling pastoral hills and parkland
Public toilets:	at Castle Howard
Tourist information:	Malton, tel: 01653 600048
Cycle hire:	none locally
❗	The hilly terrain might be a little tiring for younger children. Take care on the Stray (Point 3) – some of the traffic here is faster than it should be

● Mausoleum, Castle Howard

while you're there...

Visit Yorkshire Lavender at Terrington where you can see row upon row of different varieties of lavender in a fantastic array of colours ranging from white through to blues, lilacs and a magnificent deep purple.

Getting to the start
From the A64 northeast of York, follow the signs for Castle Howard and take the first left after the castle entrance. Alternatively, from Helmsley follow the B1257 signed 'Malton' to Slingsby and turn right for Castle Howard. Turn right by the castle's Great Lake.

Why do this cycle ride?
This pleasant ride combines the sophistication of the Castle Howard Estate and the simple beauty and rural charm of the Howardian Hills.

A ride through Yorkshire's most magnificent estate.

Castle Howard
Six years after Henderskelfe Castle burned down in 1693, Charles Howard, the 3rd Earl of Carlisle, asked his friend, Sir John Vanbrugh, to design its replacement, Castle Howard. Vanbrugh at this time was a complete novice, though he would later design Blenheim Palace. However, he formed a successful team with Christopher Wren's clerk, Nicholas Hawksmoor. The building programme would last 100 years, the lifetime of three earls, but the legacy left Yorkshire with one of Britain's most elegant palaces, set among magnificent and colourful gardens, complete with lakes, fountains, classical statues and temples.

In the house itself, the marble entrance hall is lit subtly by a dome. Explore further and you'll see treasures built up over centuries, including antique sculptures, fine porcelain, and paintings by Rubens, Reynolds and Gainsborough. In 1940 fire came to haunt the Howards once more.

A devastating blaze destroyed the dome and twenty of the rooms, leaving the palace open to the elements and in need of extremely costly renovation. That it was done so successfully is all down to George Howard, who inherited the estate after the death of his two brothers in World War Two.

The Ride

1 Terrington is a peaceful little village with fine sloping greens either side of the main street, giving the place a spacious feel. The cottages, which are largely Victorian, are built with local limestone. Above them, just off the main street, stands the church, a square-towered building that dates back to Saxon times – there's an Anglo-Saxon window in the south aisle. Much of the structure is 13th-century but was modernised around 1860. Heading east past the ivy-clad *Bay Horse Inn* towards Castle Howard is slightly downhill, a nice start – the tea rooms tempt you straight away. If it's hot, a splendid avenue of trees on the way out of the village will offer some welcome shade.

2 Take the right fork, signed 'to Ganthorpe, York', 0.5 mile (800mtrs) out of the village. Now you pay for your downhill as the road climbs to the top of *Cross Hill*, where there's a good view back to Terrington. The lane levels out as it passes through the stone cottages and farms of *Ganthorpe*. This hamlet was the birthplace of the historian, Arthur Toynbee (1886–1975) and the botanist, Richard Spruce (1817–93), who travelled to places like the Andes and the Amazon in search of specimens for scientific research. There's another short downhill section as the lane bends right by *Sata Wood*, then it's uphill again.

3 Turn left at the T-junction, where you get glimpses of a couple of the *Castle Howard domes*, then left at the crossroads following the directions to Slingsby and Castle Howard. The road, known as *The Stray*, is straight and madly undulating like a Roman road, with wide verges and avenues of trees lining the way. Some of the traffic is speedy so take care! Soon you pass beneath the extremely narrow stone arch of the Castle Howard estate's *Carrmire Gate*, which is flanked by castellated walls, then you come upon the gate house with its pyramidal roof. There's a roundabout next to a 100ft (91mtrs) *obelisk* of 1714 dedicated to Lady Cecilia Howard. Here you need to decide whether or not to visit the palace (highly recommended).

4 Continuing down *The Stray* you'll pass the *Obelisk Ponds*, which are enshrouded by woodland, then the *Great Lake*, across which you get a great view of the palace and its many domes.

5 Turn left for 'Terrington' at the crossroads just beyond the lake. The lane soon swings right and climbs through the trees of *Shaw Wood*. If you have mountain bikes and are experienced riders you could take the bridleway at the next bend (*South Bell Bottom*) then double back on the track over Husket and Ling Hills to meet the lane further west. If not, continue with the lane, which winds downhill across *Ganthorpe Moor* to meet the outward route by the first T-junction east of Terrington. Though you've still got the trees for shade, the downhill is now an uphill so you'll probably deserve that refreshment at the *Bay Horse Inn*.

Map: The Ride route through Terrington, Ganthorpe and Castle Howard area, showing START at Terrington, The Park, Huskit Hill, Terrington Moor, South Bell Bottom, Ganthorpe Moor, Shaw Wood, Coneysthorpe Banks Wood, Slingsby, Coneysthorpe, Great Lake, Cross Hill, Ganthorpe, Obelisk Ponds, Castle Howard, obelisk, Sata Wood, gate house, THE STRAY, Mowthorpe Dale, Mowthorpe Hill, Stittenham Wood, Bulmer, Carrmire Gate, Welburn, Malton, York, Sheriff Hutton, Scackleton, Hovingham, Nunnington. Spot heights 122, 91, 101, 95. Scale 0–1 mile / 0–1km.

A deeply wooded riverside leads from the famous battlefield to Loch Faskally.

Minimum time:	4hrs
Walk length:	8.75 miles (14.1km)
Ascent/gradient:	492ft (150mtrs) ▲▲▲
Difficulty level:	✚✚✚
Paths:	Wide riverside paths, minor road, no stiles
Landscape:	Oakwoods on banks of two rivers
Map:	OS Explorer 386 Pitlochry & Loch Tummel
Start/finish:	Grid reference: NN 917626
Dog friendliness:	Off lead on riverside paths
Parking:	Killiecrankie visitor centre
Public toilets:	At start

The song commemorating the victory of the Battle of Killiecrankie in July 1689 is still sung wherever anyone with an accordion sits down in a pub full of patriotic tourists. In fact, both sides in the battle were Scots. When James II was ousted from England in a bloodless coup in 1688, the Scots Parliament (the Estates) voted to replace him with William of Orange. The Stuarts had neglected and mismanaged Scotland, and had mounted a bloody persecution of the fundamentalist Protestants (Covenanters) of the Southern Uplands.

● Killiecrankie

'Bluidy Clavers'

John Claverhouse, 'Bonnie Dundee', had earned the rather different nickname 'Bluidy Clavers' in those persecutions. He now raised a small army of Highlanders in support of King James. The Estates sent a larger army north under another Highlander, General Hugh Mackay, to sort things out. Dundee, outnumbered two to one, was urged to ambush Mackay in the Pass of Killiecrankie. He refused, on the grounds of chivalry. The path above the river was steep, muddy and wide enough for only two soldiers; a surprise attack on such difficult ground would give his broadsword-wielding Highlanders too great an advantage against Mackay's inexperienced troops. Just one of the Lowlanders was picked off by an Atholl sharpshooter at the Trouper's Den (below today's visitor centre), and the battle actually took place on open ground, to the north of the pass.

*Ye wouldna been sae swanky o
If ye'd hae seen where I hae seen
On the braes o Killiecrankie o'*

Claymore Victorious

Killiecrankie was the last time the claymore conquered the musket in open battle, due to a deficiency in the musket. Some 900 of the 2,500 Highlanders were shot down as they charged, but then the troopers had to stop to fix their bayonets, which plugged into the muzzle of the musket. By this time the Highlanders were upon them, and they broke and fled. The battle had lasted just three minutes. Half of Mackay's army was killed, wounded, captured or drowned in the Garry. One escaped by leaping 18ft (5.5mtrs) across the river: the 'Soldier's Leap'. Dundee died in battle. A month later his army was defeated at Dunkeld, and 25 years later, when the Highlanders next brought their claymores south for the Stuarts, the troopers had learnt to fix a bayonet to the side of a musket where it didn't block the barrel.

where to eat and drink....

There are cafés at the start and at Lochside, Pitlochry. Pitlochry itself is the town of the tea room. One of them is Macdonald's, on the main street, which serves traditional Scottish high teas to the very hungry.

Walk Directions

1 From the back corner of the visitor centre steps, signed 'Soldier's Leap', lead down into the wooded gorge. A footbridge crosses the waterfall of Trouper's Den. At the next junction, turn left ('Soldier's Leap'). Ten steps down, a spur path on the right leads to the viewpoint above the Soldier's Leap.

2 Return to the main path, signed 'Linn of Tummel', which runs down to the River Garry below the railway viaduct. After 1 mile (1.6km) the path reaches a footbridge.

3 Don't cross this footbridge, but continue ahead, signed 'Pitlochry', along the riverside under the tall South Garry road bridge. The path bears left to a footbridge. Cross and turn right, signed 'Pitlochry', back to the main river. The path runs around a huge river pool to a tarred lane; turn right here. The lane leaves the lochside, then passes a track on the right, blocked by a vehicle barrier. Ignore this track; shortly afterwards turn right at a signpost, 'Pitlochry'.

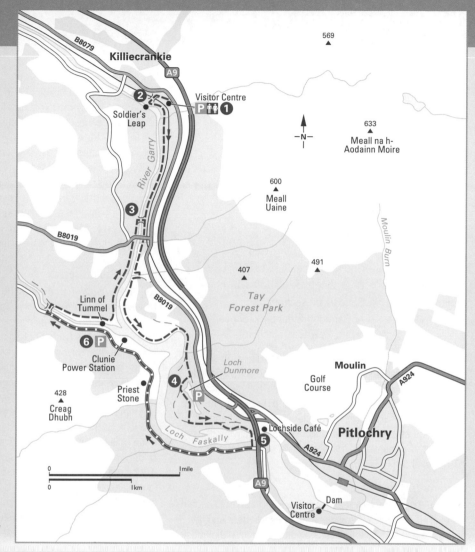

4 Immediately bear left to pass along the right side of Loch Dunmore, following red-top posts. A footbridge crosses the loch, but turn away from it, half right, on to a small path that becomes a dirt track. After 270yds (250mtrs) it reaches a wider track. Turn left, with a white/yellow waymarker. After 220yds (201mtrs) the track starts to climb; here the white/yellow markers indicate a smaller

path on the right, which follows the lochside to a point below the A9 road bridge.

5 Cross Loch Faskally on the Clunie footbridge below the road's bridge and turn right, on a quiet road around the loch. In 1 mile (1.6km), at the top of the grass bank on the left, is the Priest Stone. After you pass the Clunie power station, you reach a

car park on the left. Here a sign indicates a steep little path down to the Linn of Tummel.

6 Return to the road above for 0.5 mile (800mtrs), to cross a grey suspension bridge on the right. Turn right, downstream, to pass above the Linn. A spur path back right returns to the falls at a lower level, but the main path continues along the riverside

(signed 'Killiecrankie'). It bends left and goes down wooden steps to the Garry, then continues upstream and under the high road bridge. Take the side-path up on to the bridge for the view of the river, then return to follow the descending path signed 'Pitlochry via Faskally'. This runs down to the bridge, Point **3**. Return upstream to the start.

Walk in the footsteps of Wordsworth, Darwin and Ruskin who visited here to work and to explore.

Minimum time:	4hrs
Walk length:	6 miles (9.7km)
Ascent/gradient:	656ft (200mtrs) ▲ ▲ ▲
Difficulty level:	✚✚✚
Paths:	A bridge, good tracks and woodland paths, 6 stiles
Landscape:	Estuary and wooded hills
Map:	OS Explorer OL23 Cadair Idris & Llyn Tegid
Start/finish:	Grid reference: SH 613155
Dog friendliness:	Dogs should be on lead at all times
Parking:	Car park on seafront
Public toilets:	At Barmouth's car park, or near Morfa Mawddach Station

Barmouth (once better known in Welsh as Y Bermo), used to be a seaport, trading the coarse woollen goods of Merionydd with the Americas. In those days the village cottages were strung out across terraces in the cliffs and there was one pub, the Corsygedol Arms, for the traveller. There wasn't enough room to squeeze the main road from Harlech between those rocks and the sea, so it bypassed the village and instead went inland, over the Rhinog mountain passes.

Barmouth: the New Era

In the mid-19th century it all changed. Barmouth built a main street on the beach. Visitors became more frequent and the resort's sea and sand attracted the gentry from the Midlands. Barmouth also came to the notice of the famous: the poet,

Wordsworth said of the Mawddach Estuary that it was sublime and equal to any in Scotland. Artists like J M W Turner and Richard Wilson came to capture the changing light and renowned beauty of estuary and mountainside.

In 1867 the railway came, and a new bridge was engineered across the estuary sands. It was half a mile (800mtrs) long and had a swing section across the Mawddach's main channel to allow shipping to pass. Today you can see that Barmouth is not as smart as it was in its heyday. It's still in the most wonderful situation though and, as you step on to the wooden boards of that half-mile foot and railway bridge, you can feel exactly what Wordsworth felt.

Mighty Cadair Idris

The view is best when the sun's shining and the tide's half out. That way the waters of the Mawddach will be meandering like a pale blue serpent amid pristine golden sandbars. Across the estuary your eyes cannot help but be drawn to mighty Cadair Idris. This is not one mountain, but a long ridge with several peaks, each displaying fierce cliffs that soar above the wooded foothills. The biggest is Penygadair at 2,927ft (893mtrs), but the most prominent is Tyrrau Mawr, a shapely peak with a seemingly overhanging crag. As you get to the other side you can look back to Barmouth, and you will see how this town has been built into the rocks of the lower Rhinogs. Across the bridge you're ready to explore those wooded foothills. Through Arthog the path climbs between oak trees and you find yourself looking across to some waterfalls, thundering into a wooded chasm. At the top you are presented with an elevated view of all that you have seen so far, the estuary, the sandbars, the mountains and the yawning bridge. By the time you return to Barmouth you will have experienced that 'sublime' Mawddach.

● Barmouth estuary

Walk Directions

1 Follow the promenade round the harbour, then go over the footbridge across the estuary (toll). On reaching the path along the south shore of the estuary, turn left to follow the grassy embankment that leads to a track rounding the wooded knoll of Fegla Fawr on its seaward side.

2 Reaching the terraced houses of Mawddach Crescent, follow the track that passes to their rear. Rejoin the track along the shoreline until you reach a gate on the right marking the start of a bridleway heading inland across the marshes of Arthog.

3 Turn left along the old railway track, then leave it just before the crossing of the little Arthog Estuary and turn right along a tarmac lane by a small car park. Bear left over a ladder stile and follow a raised embankment to a wall which now leads the path to the main Dolgellau road next to St Catherine's Church.

4 Opposite the church gate is a footpath beginning with some steps into woodland. A good waymarked path now climbs by the Arthog.

5 Beyond a stile at the top of the woods, turn right to come to a lane. Turn right along the descending lane, then left along a stony track passing the cottage of Merddyn. The track gets narrower and steeper as it descends into more woodland, beneath the boulders of an old quarry and down to the

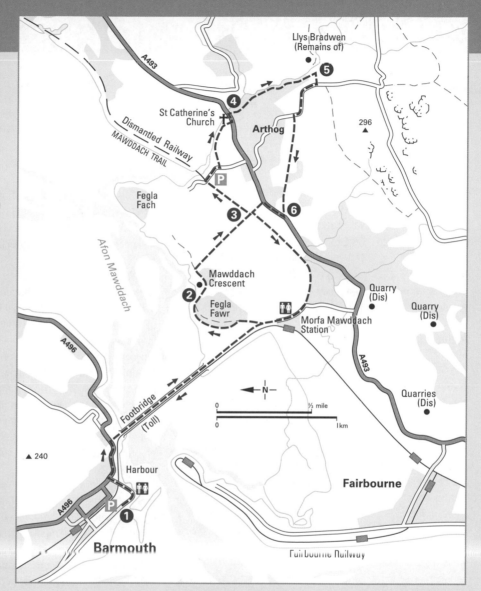

Dolgellau road by Arthog Village Hall.

6 Turn right along the road, then left along a path back to the railway track and the Mawddach Trail. Turn left along the trail and follow it past Morfa Mawddach Station and back across Barmouth's bridge.

what to look out for...

Near the place you cross the Arthog River, at the top of the woods, is Llys Bradwen. These days it's no more than banks covered by grass, but here are the remains of large wooden hall from a Dark Ages house. In those times it would have been occupied by the local chieftain, Ednowain ap Bradwen.

WALK 15
Sweet Walking on Sugar Loaf

Escape the crowds and see another side of the most distinctive of the Abergavenny peaks.

Minimum time:	2hrs 30min
Walk length:	4.5 miles (7.2km)
Ascent/gradient:	1,150ft (350mtrs) ▲▲▲
Difficulty level:	✛✛✛
Paths:	Grassy tracks, no stiles
Landscape:	Bracken-covered hillsides, secluded valley and rugged mountain top
Map:	OS Explorer OL13 Brecon Beacons National Park Eastern area
Start/finish:	Grid reference: SO 268167
Dog friendliness:	Care needed near sheep
Parking:	Top of small lane running north from A40, to west of Abergavenny
Public toilets:	None en route

The Sugar Loaf, or Mynydd Pen-y-fal to give it its Welsh name, is without a doubt one of the most popular mountains in the National Park. The distinctive, cone-shaped outline of the rock-strewn summit is visible from miles around and the convenient placing of a car park on the southern flanks of the mountain makes it easy for those who just want to 'climb a mountain'. To follow the well-trodden trade route is to miss the best of the hill, which, despite its popularity, remains a formidable and dignified peak.

This walk takes a more subtle approach, leaving the masses on Mynydd Llanwenarth and dipping into a lonely combe, before making an enjoyable push, up the less-walked west ridge. The steep walls of the valley give a much better sense of scale to the gentle giant you're about to climb. The descent follows the more ordinary route back to the car park.

The National Trust
The Sugar Loaf, and some of the land that surrounds it, belongs to the National Trust, who own around 4 per cent of the land within the National Park. The Trust was founded in 1895 with the objective of protecting places of beauty and value from the onslaught of industrial development – particularly pertinent in South Wales. It is not, as is sometimes believed, a government-run agency, but a registered charity that relies on membership and donations to carry out its work. The Trust currently acts as a guardian for over 300 historic houses and gardens, 49 industrial monuments, 612,808 acres (248,187ha) of countryside, including the Brecon Beacons' highest peaks of Pen y Fan and Corn Du, and over 600 miles (965km) of coast. It has the statutory power to declare land inalienable, meaning that it can't be sold or purchased against the National Trust's wishes without special parliamentary procedures. Wherever possible, the Trust offers open access to its common land enabling walkers to explore this beautiful landscape at will.

So Many Sheep
Wales has one of the highest densities of sheep in the world. In the Brecon Beacons National Park they outnumber people by 30 to 1. Most of the farms in the National Park are sheep farms, but many also maintain a small herd of beef cattle on the lower ground. The sheep you'll see while walking across the upland commons are mainly the hardy Welsh mountain sheep, the smallest of the commercially bred sheep with a small head, small ears and a white or tanned face with dark eyes. They thrive in the harsh mountain environment – the ewes spend as many as 36 weeks every year on the high ground – and can eke a living out of the very poor grazing available.

Typically, the ewes celebrate the New Year by being returned to the hill – around 80 per cent of them will be carrying lambs. They're scanned for twins in February and those carrying two lambs will be retained on the low ground with supplementary food until they've given birth. Around April, the rest of the flock is brought down for lambing, then returned to the high ground, with their lambs, by mid-May. In July the ewes are sheared, in August and September the lambs are weaned and the male lambs and surplus ewe lambs sold or retained on lower ground for finishing. By November, the older ewes are 'drafted' on to lower ground and usually sold for cross-breeding with lower level breeds. The young, replacement ewes are also brought down on to lowland pastures for the winter. Late in the month, the mature ewes are mated and the cycle begins again.

Walk Directions

1 Standing in the car park and looking up the slope you'll see three obvious tracks leading away. The lowest, down to the left, is a tarmac drive; above this, but still heading out left, is a broad grassy track. Take this and follow it for 500yds (457mtrs) to the corner of a dry-stone wall.

2 This marks a crossroads where you keep straight ahead, to follow the wall on your left. Continue along this line for another 0.5 mile (800mtrs), ignoring any right forks, and keeping the wall down to your left. Eventually, you'll start to drop down into a valley, where you leave the wall and head diagonally towards a wood. At the end of the wood, keep left to descend a grassy path to the stream.

3 Climb out of the valley, keeping to the main, steepest, right-hand path. This leads around a shoulder and meets another dry-stone wall. Follow this, still climbing a little, until it levels by a corner and gate in the wall. Turn right here, cross some lumpy ground and follow the grassy path up.

4 As the track levels, you'll be joined by another track from the left. Continue ahead and climb on to the rocks at the western end of the summit ridge. Follow the ridge to the white-painted trig point.

5 Looking back towards the car park, you'll see that the hillside is criss-crossed with tracks. Most will lead you back eventually, but the easiest route follows a path that traverses right, from directly below the trig point. This veers left and drops steeply down a blunt spur.

6 Follow this down until it levels and pass a right fork and another right turn. As the track veers left, continue past another right fork and then take the next, to follow an almost sunken track along a broken wall, which leads to a junction by a wall. This is the track that you followed on the outward leg. Bear left and retrace your steps back to the car park.

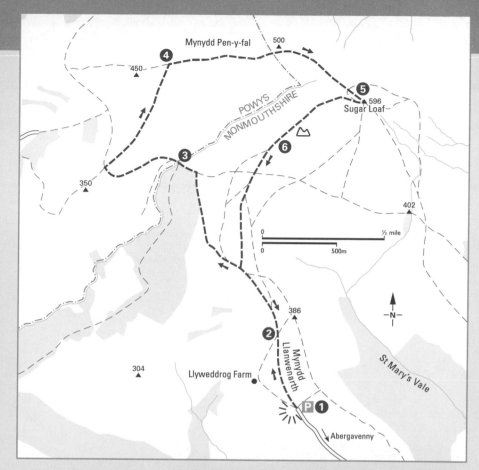

County Maps

The county map shown here will help you identify the counties within each country. You can look up each county in the guide using the county names at the top of each page. To find towns featured in the guide use the atlas and the index.

England

1 Bedfordshire
2 Berkshire
3 Bristol
4 Buckinghamshire
5 Cambridgeshire
6 Greater Manchester
7 Herefordshire
8 Hertfordshire
9 Leicestershire
10 Northamptonshire
11 Nottinghamshire
12 Rutland
13 Staffordshire
14 Warwickshire
15 West Midlands
16 Worcestershire

Scotland

17 City of Glasgow
18 Clackmannanshire
19 East Ayrshire
20 East Dunbartonshire
21 East Renfrewshire
22 Perth & Kinross
23 Renfrewshire
24 South Lanarkshire
25 West Dunbartonshire

Wales

26 Blaenau Gwent
27 Bridgend
28 Caerphilly
29 Denbighshire
30 Flintshire
31 Merthyr Tydfil
32 Monmouthshire
33 Neath Port Talbot
34 Newport
35 Rhondda Cynon Taff
36 Torfaen
37 Vale of Glamorgan
38 Wrexham

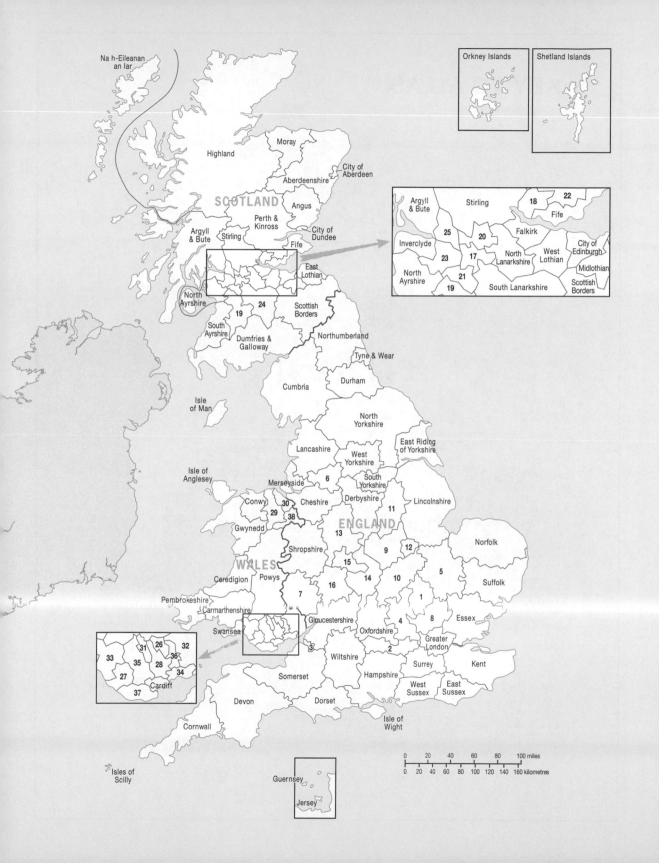

KEY TO ATLAS

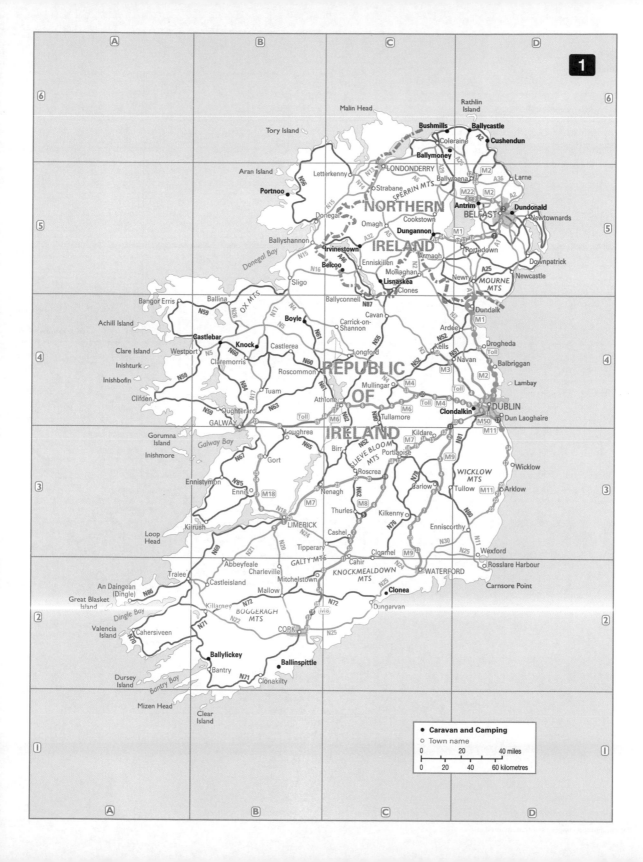

Legend:

M6	Motorway/toll motorway
	Motorway junction full/restricted. Service area
A33	Primary route single/dual carriageway
A34	Other A road single/dual carriageway
B3400	B road
	Unclassified road
V	Vehicle ferry
C	Fast vehicle ferry or catamaran
● Edale	Caravan and Camping
● Wykeham	AA Campsite Award Winner
○ Oundle	Town/Village name
	National boundary
ESSEX	English county name & boundary
CONWY	Welsh county name & boundary
MORAY	Scottish county name & boundary
	National Park

ISLES OF SCILLY

Bryher
New Grimsby
Tresco
St Martin's
Higher Town
Hugh Town
St Mary's
Old Town
ISLES OF SCILLY (ST MARY'S)
Middle Town
St Agnes

SV

SW

Lundy

Hartland Point
Hartland
Morwenstow
Kilkhampton
Bude
Stratton
Bude Bay
Widemouth Bay
Bridgerule
Week St Mary
Crackington Haven
Jacobstow
Boscastle
Otterham
Tintagel
Delabole
Camelford
Laun
Port Isaac
Pendoggett
BODMIN MOOR
Bolventor
Polzeath
St Minver
St Tudy
Blisland
Rock
Harlyn
St Merryn
Padstow
Wadebridge
Porthcothan
Rumford
Ruthernbridge
Bodmin
CORNWALL
St Cleer
Mawgan Porth
St Mawgan
St Columb Major
Lanivet
Dobwalls
Liskeard
Watergate Bay
NEWQUAY
Roche
St Keyne
Newquay
A3059
Bugle
Luxulyan
Lostwithiel
West Pentire
Indian Queens
Pelynt
Holywell Bay
Cubert
Rejerrah
Summercourt
St Blazey Gate
St Blazey
Wide
Perranporth
Goonhavern
St Austell
Carlyon Bay
Fowey
Looe
St Agnes
Ladock
St Allen
St Stephen
Polruan
Polperro
Porthtowan
Marazanvose
Pentewan
Portreath
Blackwater
Grampound
Mevagissey
St Day
Carnon Downs
Truro
Gorran
Gorran Haven
St Ives Bay
St Ives
Gwithian
Redruth
Tregony
Portloe
Zennor
Camborne
A393
St Just-in-Roseland
Lelant
Hayle
Carnhell Green
Penryn
Portscatho
St Just
Leedstown
Edgcumbe
Falmouth
St Mawes
Land's End
Penzance
Marazion
St Hilary
Ashton
Constantine
Mawnan Smith
Newlyn
Rosudgeon
Praa Sands
Helston
Gweek
St Buryan
Mousehole
Porthleven
Manaccan
Sennen
Treen
Porthcurno
St Keverne
Mullion
Coverack
Kennack Sands
Cadgwith
Lizard
Lizard Point

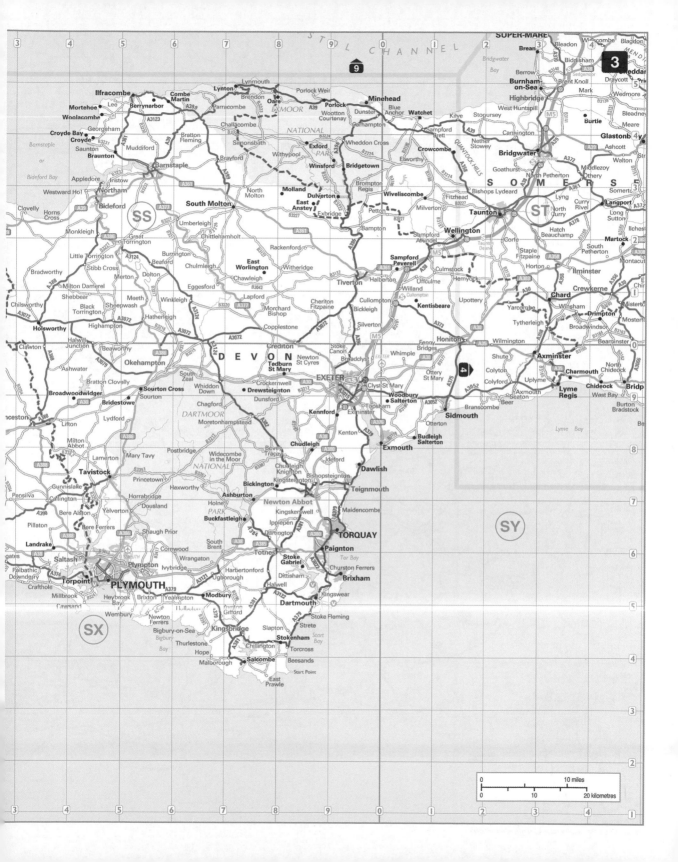

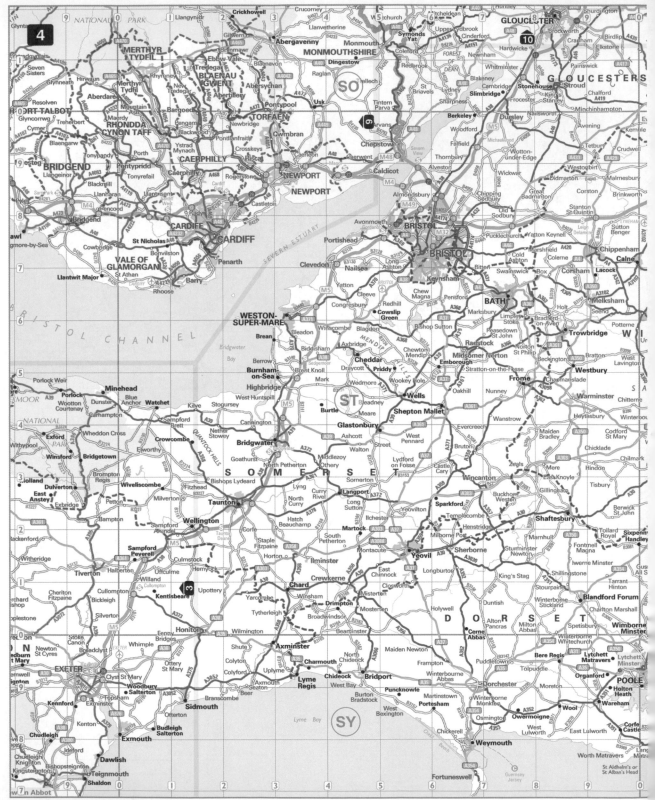

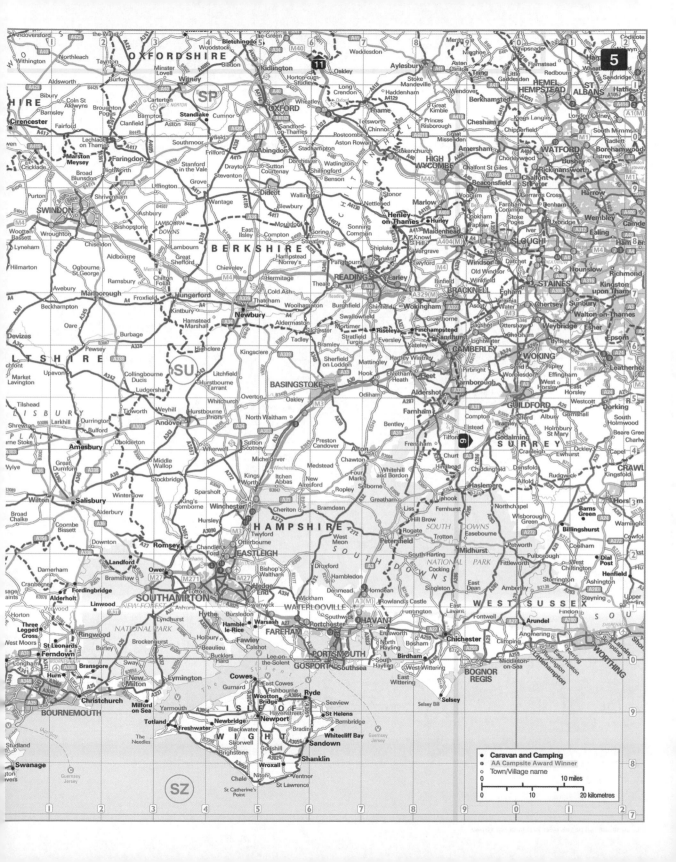

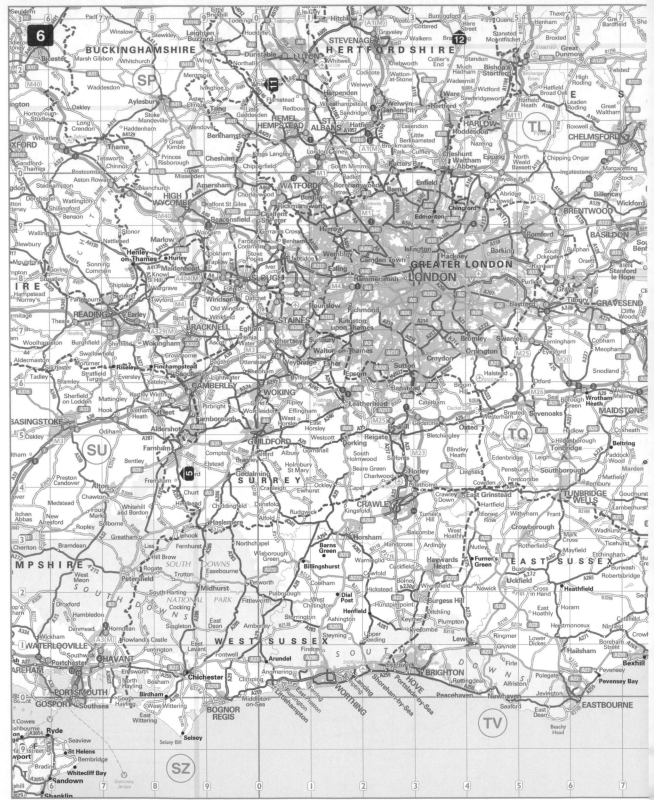

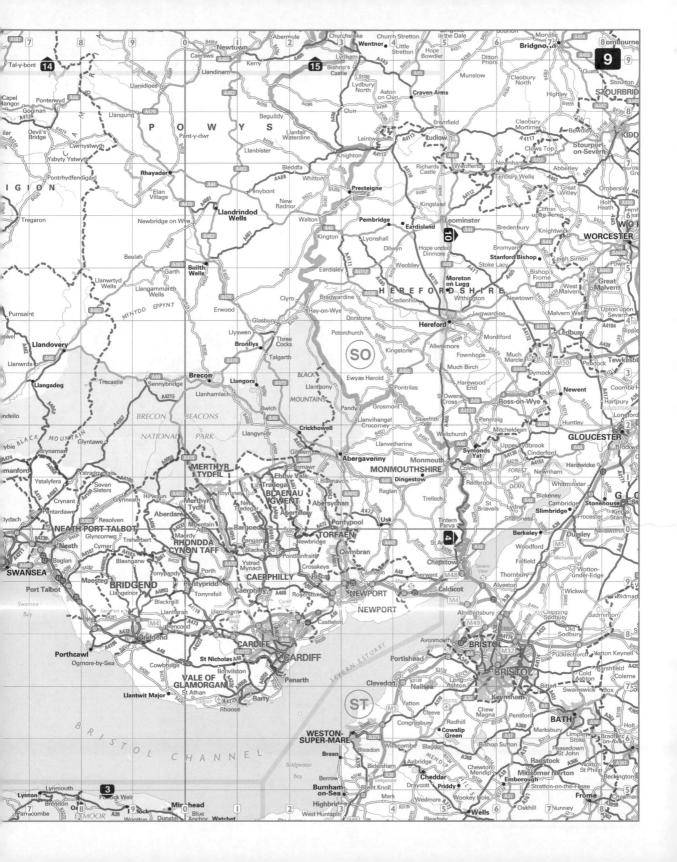

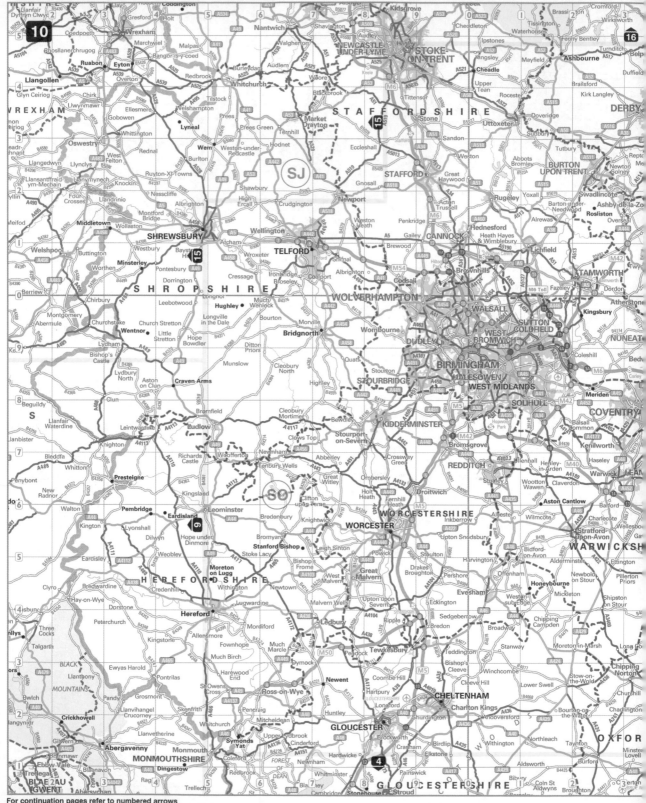

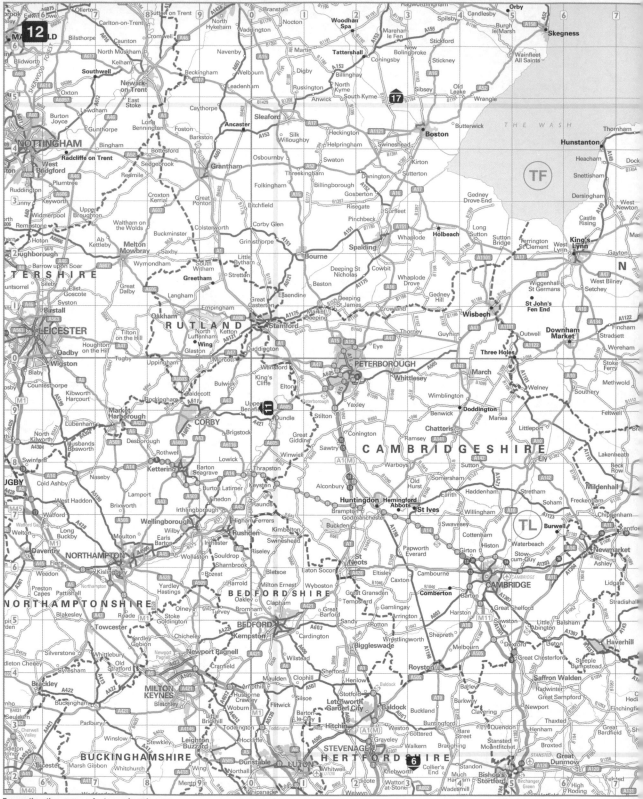

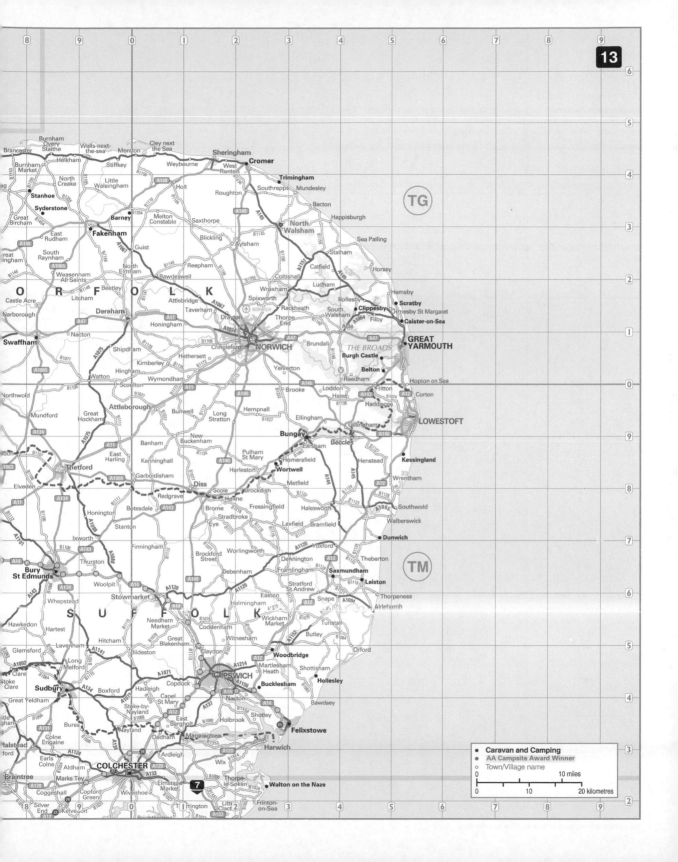

14

ISLE OF
ANGLESEY

Cemaes
Amlwch
Dulas
Rhôs Lligwy
Marian-Glas
Llanerchymedd
Llanfachraeth
Red Wharf Bay
Benllech
Holyhead
Pentraeth
Llangoed
Trearddur Bay
Llangefni
Penmaenmawr
Beaumaris
Menai
Holy Island
Bridge
Llanfair P.G.
Llanfairfechan
Rhosneigr
Bangor
Llanllechid
Aberffraw
Y Felinheli
Bethesda
Tal-y-Bont
Newborough
Caernarfon
Llanrug
Bontnewydd
Llanberis
Dinas Dinlle
Llanwnda
Betws Garmon
Capel Curig
Betws-y-Coed
Llandwrog
Penygroes
Rhyd-Ddu
Dolwyddelan
Clynnog-fawr
Penmachno
Beddgelert
Blaenau Ffestiniog
Llanaelhaearn
PENINSULA
Prenteg
Ffestiniog
Morfa Nefyn
Nefyn
Tremadog
Maentwrog
Bodfuan
Llanystumdwy
Porthmadog
Penrhyndeudraeth
LLEYN
Criccieth
Borth-y-Gest
Talsarnau
Sarn
Pwllheli
Trawsfynydd
Llanbedrog
Harlech
Aberdaron
Y Rhiw
Abersoch
Llanbedr
Ganllwyd
Bardsey Island
Dyffryn Ardudwy
Tal-y-bont
Barmouth
Dolgellau
Dinas-Mawddwy
Fairbourne
Mallwyd
Llwyngwril
Corris
Cemmaes Road
Bryncrug
Tywyn
Pennal
Machynlleth
Carno
Aberdyfi
Borth
Tal-y-bont
Llandre
Capel Bangor
Aberystwyth
Ponterwyd

Llandudno
Deganwy
Rhôs-on-Sea
Rhyl
Colwyn Bay
Towyn
Conwy
Llanddulas
Abergele
Llansanffraid Glan Conwy
Betws-yn-Rhos
Llannefydd
Tal-y-Cafn
Henll
Llangernyw
Llanfair Talhaiarn
Llansannan
Trefriw
Llanrwst
Bylchau
CONWY
Pentrefoelas
Cerrigydrudion
Y Maerd

SNOWDONIA
NATIONAL
PARK
GWYNEDD
Llanuwchllyn
Bala
Llandderfel

SH

SN

9

CARDIGAN BAY

Llanidloes
Llanbrynmair
Llangadfan

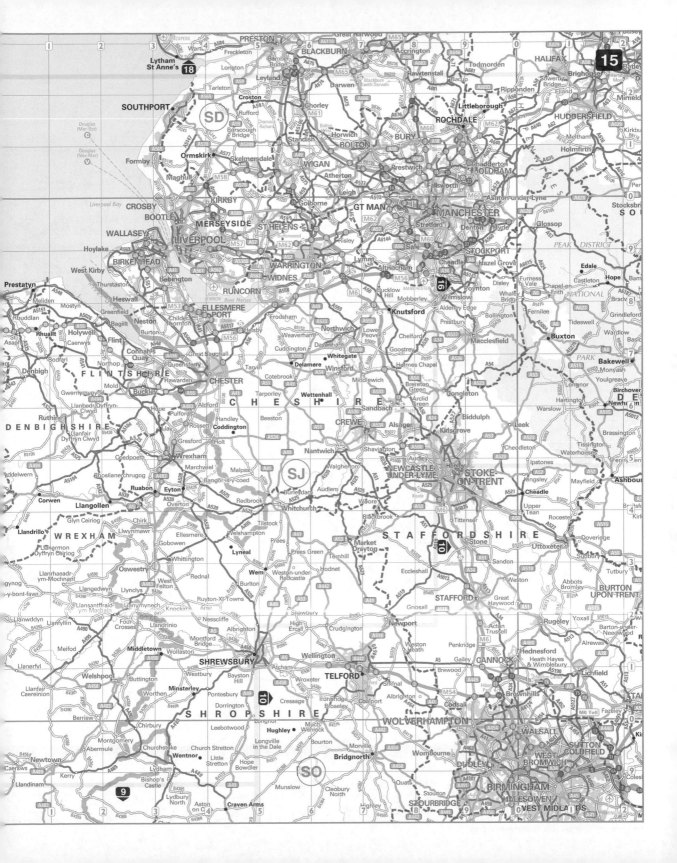

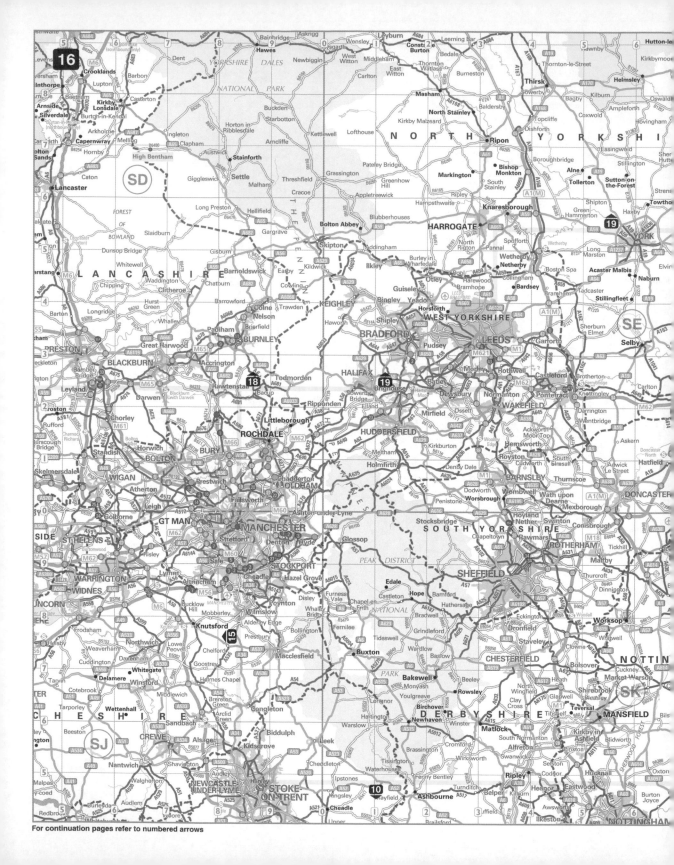

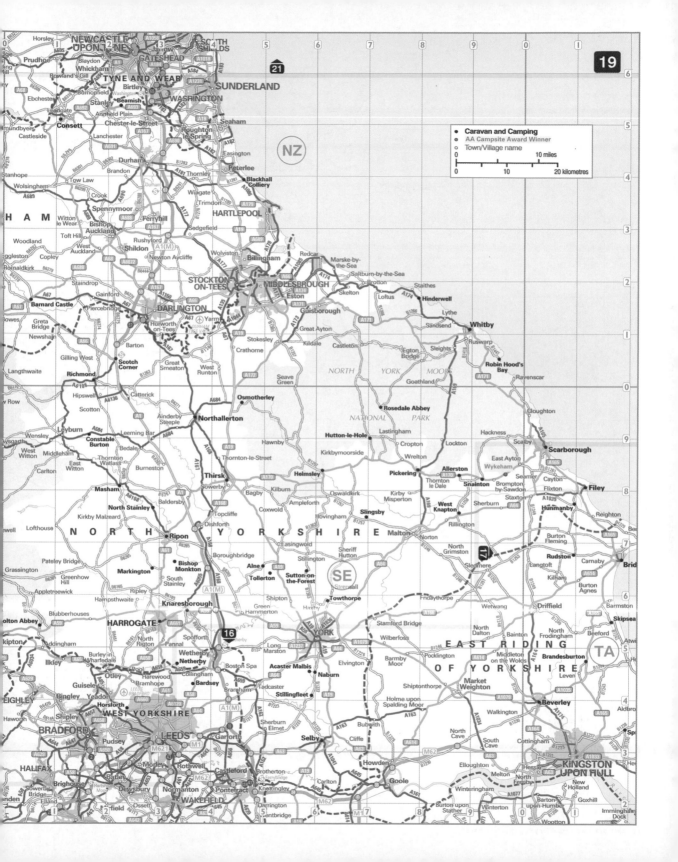

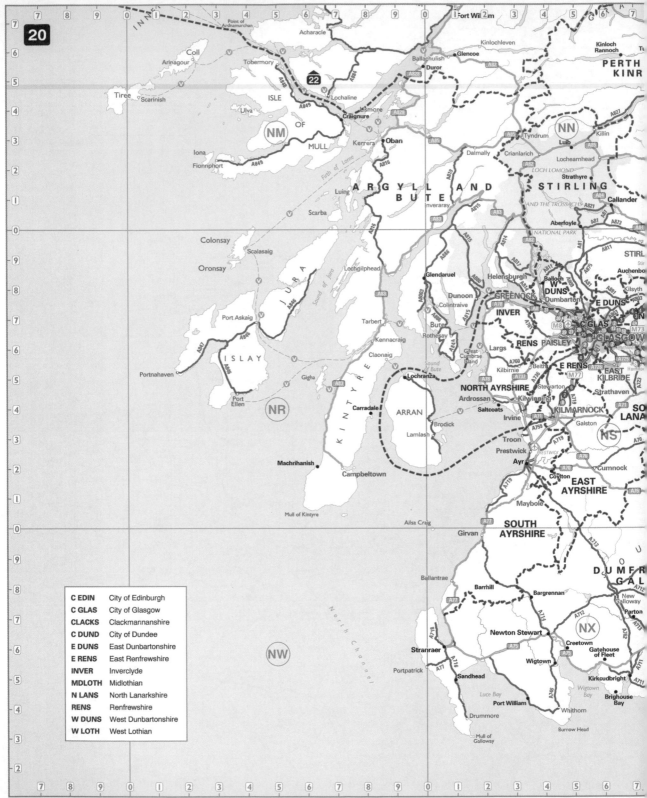

Point of Ardnamurchan
Acharacle
Kinlochleven
Kinloch Rannoch
Fort Wil 2 m
PERTH
KINR
Tu

Coll
Arinagour
Tobermory
Glencoe
Ballachulish
Duror
A82

Tiree
Scarinish
ISLE
22
Lochaline
OF
Craignure
Lismore
Kerrera
Oban

Ulva
MULL
A849
A816

Iona
Fionnphort
A849
Firth of Lorne
Luing
Scarba
Inveraray
A85
Dalmally
Crianlarich
Lochearnhead
Tyndrum
Luib
Killin
NN
Locheathead
Strathyre
A82
LOCH LOMOND

ARGYLL AND
BUTE
A83
A815
STIRLING
AND THE TROSSACHS
Callander

Colonsay
Scalasaig
NATIONAL PARK
Aberfoyle
A81 A873

Oronsay
Lochgilphead
Glendaruel
Helensburgh
Balloch
W DUNS
Auchenbo
STIR
Stir

Port Askaig
A846
A83
Dunoon
Colintraive
GREENOCK
Dumbarton
E DUNS
Kilsyth
A803

ISLAY
Tarbert
Bute
INVER
M8
C GLAS
M73

Portnahaven
A846
Kennacraig
Rothesay
A78
PAISLEY
GLASGOW
A725

NR
Gigha
Claonaig
Great Cumbrae Island
Largs
RENS
E RENS
EAST KILBRIDE
Hamilton
SO LANA

Port Ellen
Carradale
ARRAN
Lochranza
Sound of Bute
NORTH AYRSHIRE
Kilbirnie
M77
Strathaven

Machrihanish
Brodick
Lamlash
Saltcoats
Ardrossan
Kilwinning
Stewarton
Irvine
A71
KILMARNOCK
Galston
A70
NS
A76

Campbeltown
Troon
Prestwick
A719
Coylton
Cumnock
EAST AYRSHIRE
A70

Mull of Kintyre
Ayr
PRESTWICK
Maybole
A76

Ailsa Craig
Girvan
SOUTH AYRSHIRE
A77
A713
DUMFR GAL
U

North Channel
Ballantrae
Barrhill
Bargrennan
New Galloway
Parton
A712

NW
A77
Stranraer
A718
Newton Stewart
A75
NX
Creetown
Gatehouse of Fleet
A711

Portpatrick
A716
Wigtown
Kirkcudbright
A711

Sandhead
Luce Bay
Port William
Wigtown Bay
Brighouse Bay

Drummore
Whithorn
Burrow Head

Mull of Galloway

C EDIN	City of Edinburgh
C GLAS	City of Glasgow
CLACKS	Clackmannanshire
C DUND	City of Dundee
E DUNS	East Dunbartonshire
E RENS	East Renfrewshire
INVER	Inverclyde
MDLOTH	Midlothian
N LANS	North Lanarkshire
RENS	Renfrewshire
W DUNS	West Dunbartonshire
W LOTH	West Lothian

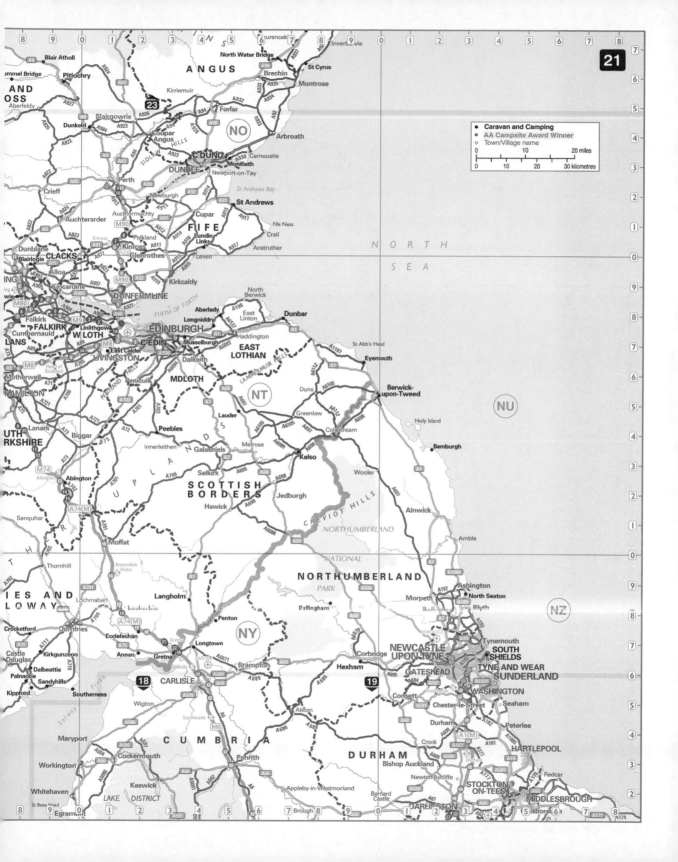

3 4 5 6 7 8 9 0 1 2 3 4 5 6 7 8 9 0 1 2 3

Cape Wrath

Rudha Rhobhanais
(Butt of Lewis)
Port Nis
(Port of Ness)

Handa Island
Scourie

NA

LEWIS

NB

A857

Cellar
Head

A859

Great
Bernera

Carlabhagh
(Carloway)

A858

A857

Tiumpan
Head

Lochinver

Achnadamph

A837

Scarp

ISLE
OF
Steornabhagh
(Stornoway)

STORNOWAY

A859

A859

A866

NA H–EILEANAN
AN IAR

A859

A855

A859

A858

A894

A835

A837

Taransay

Tairbeart
(Tarbert)

Scalpay

THE MINCH

Ullapool

A832

HIGHLANDS

Pabbay

HARRIS

A859

Gruinard
Bay

A835

Boreray

Berneray

THE LITTLE MINCH

Gairloch

A832

Kinlochewe

A832

Loch nam Madadh
(Lochmaddy)

Uig

A865

NORTH UIST

A865

A867

A865

Ronay

Edinbane

NG

A87

Achnasheen

A890

A832

WEST

NF

Benbecula

A865

Wiay

Dunvegan

ISLE

Portree

Inner Sound

A896

A890

A96

A890

SOUTH
UIST

A865

Drynoch

OF

Raasay

A87

Scalpay

Kyle of
Lochalsh

Balmacara

Cannich

NORTH

A87

Loch Baghasdail
(Lochboisdale)

SKYE

A87

A87

Invergarry

Eriskay

Canna

Ardvasar

Sound of Sleat

A861

BARRA

A888

Rùm

Mallaig

Cuillin Sound

A82

Bagh a Chaisteil
(Castlebay)

Sandray

Eigg

Arisaig

A830

Corpach

A82

Spean
Bridge

NL

Mingulay

INNER HEBRIDES

Muck

A830

A861

Fort William

Kinlochleven

Point of
Ardnamurchan

NM

Acharacle

A861

Coll

Tobermory

Ballachulish

Glencoe

Arinagour

A884

A828

Duror

A82

Tiree

Scarinish

20

ISLE

A848

Lochaline

Lismore

A828

A85

Ulva

OF

A849

Craignure

Iona

Fionnphort

A849

MULL

Kerrera

Oban

A85

Dalmally

A816

Lorne

Craiglaric

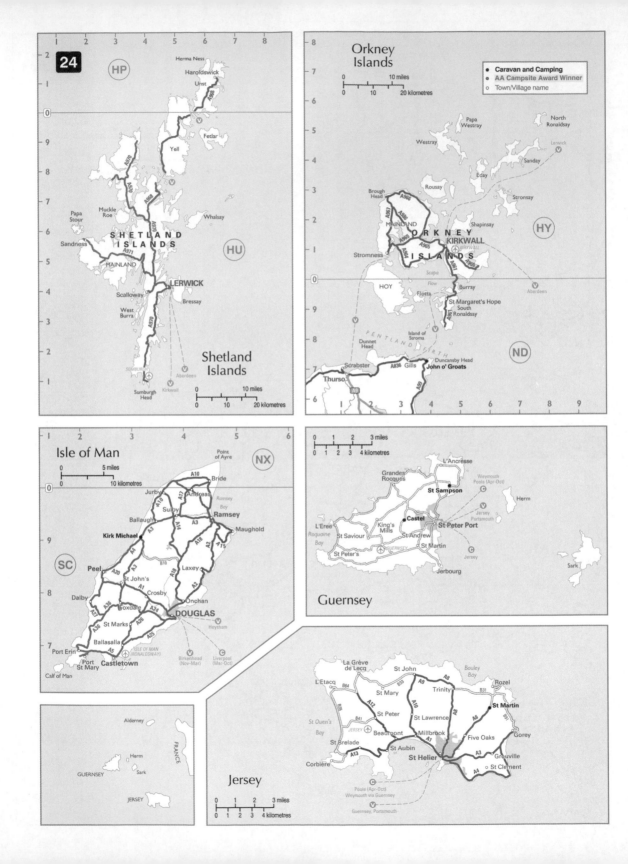

24

Shetland Islands

HP

Herma Ness
Haroldswick
Unst

Fetlar

Yell

Papa Stour
Muckle Roe
Whalsay

Sandness
SHETLAND ISLANDS
MAINLAND
HU
A971

Scalloway
LERWICK
Bressay

West Burra

Sumburgh
Head
Sumburgh
Aberdeen
Kirkwall

0 — 10 miles
0 — 10 — 20 kilometres

Orkney Islands

Caravan and Camping
AA Campsite Award Winner
Town/Village name

0 — 10 miles
0 — 10 — 20 kilometres

Papa Westray
North Ronaldsay
Westray
Sanday
Eday
Rousay
Shapinsay
Stronsay
HY
Brough Head
MAINLAND
ORKNEY
KIRKWALL
Stromness
ISLANDS
Burray
HOY
Scapa Flow
Flotta
St Margaret's Hope
South Ronaldsay
Aberdeen
Lerwick

PENTLAND FIRTH
Dunnet Head
Island of Stroma
ND
Scrabster
Gills
Duncansby Head
John o' Groats
Thurso
A9

Isle of Man

NX
Point of Ayre

0 — 5 miles
0 — 10 kilometres

A10
Bride
Jurby
Andreas
Ramsey Bay
Sulby
Ramsey
Ballaugh
Maughold
SC
Kirk Michael
Laxey
Peel
St John's
Crosby
Dalby
Onchan
Foxdale
DOUGLAS
St Marks
Heysham
Ballasalla
Port Erin
Port St Mary
Castletown
ISLE OF MAN (RONALDSWAY)
Birkenhead (Nov-Mar)
Liverpool (Mar-Oct)
Calf of Man

Guernsey

0 — 1 — 2 — 3 miles
0 — 1 — 2 — 3 — 4 kilometres

L'Ancresse
Grandes Rocques
Weymouth Poole (Apr-Oct)
St Sampson
Herm
L'Eree
King's Mills
Castel
St Peter Port
Jersey Portsmouth
Roquaine Bay
St Saviour
St Andrew
St Peter's
St Martin
Jersey
Jerbourg
Sark

Jersey

Alderney
Herm
FRANCE
Sark
GUERNSEY
JERSEY

La Grève de Lecq
St John
Bouley Bay
L'Etacq
St Mary
Trinity
Rozel
St Peter
St Lawrence
St Martin
St Ouen's Bay
Beaumont
Millbrook
Five Oaks
Gorey
St Brelade
St Aubin
St Helier
Grouville
Corbière
St Clement

0 — 1 — 2 — 3 miles
0 — 1 — 2 — 3 — 4 kilometres

Poole (Apr-Oct)
Weymouth via Guernsey
Guernsey, Portsmouth

AA Camping Card Sites

The following list shows AA rated campsites that accept the AA Camping Card which is valid until 31st January 2013. See page 7 for further details of the card.

ENGLAND

BERKSHIRE
FINCHAMPSTEAD
California Chalet & Touring Park
0118 973 3928
RISELEY
Wellington Country Park
0118 932 6444

CAMBRIDGESHIRE
ST IVES
Stroud Hill Park
01487 741333

CHESHIRE
CODDINGTON
Manor Wood Country Caravan Park
01829 782990
DELAMERE
Fishpool Farm Caravan Park
01606 883970
WETTENHALL
New Farm Caravan Park
01270 528213

CORNWALL & ISLES OF SCILLY
BLACKWATER
Chiverton Park
01872 560667
BODMIN
Mena Caravan & Camping Park
01208 831845
BOLVENTOR
Colliford Tavern Campsite
01208 821335

BRYHER (ISLES OF SCILLY)
Bryher Camp Site
01720 422559
BUDE
Sandymouth Holiday Park
08442 729530
Widemouth Fields Caravan & Camping Park
01288 361351
Wooda Farm Holiday Park
01288 352069
CARNHELL GREEN
Lavender Fields Touring Park
01209 832188
COVERACK
Little Trevothan Caravan & Camping Park
01326 280260
CRANTOCK
Quarryfield Holiday Park
01637 872792
GOONHAVERN
Penrose Holiday Park
01872 573185
GORRAN
Treveague Farm Caravan & Camping Site
01726 842295
HELSTON
Poldown Caravan Park
01326 574560
Skyburriowe Farm
01326 221646
KENNACK SANDS
Silver Sands Holiday Park
01326 290631
LOOE
Tencreek Holiday Park
01503 262447
LOSTWITHIEL
Eden Valley Holiday Park
01208 872277
MARAZION
Wheal Rodney Holiday Park
01736 710605
MEVAGISSEY
Seaview International Holiday Park
01726 843425

NEWQUAY
Hendra Holiday Park
01637 875778
Treloy Touring Park
01637 872063
PERRANPORTH
Higher Golla Touring & Caravan Park
01872 573963
Tollgate Farm Caravan & Camping Park
01872 572130
POLRUAN
Polruan Holidays-Camping & Caravanning
01726 870263
REDRUTH
Lanyon Holiday Park
01209 313474
Stithians Lake Country Park
01209 860301
RUMFORD
Music Water Touring Park
01841 540257
RUTHERNBRIDGE
Ruthern Valley Holidays
01208 831395
SCORRIER
Wheal Rose Caravan & Camping Park
01209 891496
ST AGNES
Beacon Cottage Farm Touring Park
01872 552347
ST IVES
Trevalgan Touring Park
01736 792048
ST JUST
[NEAR LAND'S END]
Secret Garden Caravan & Camping Park
01736 788301
ST MERRYN
Atlantic Bays Holiday Park
01841 520855
SUMMERCOURT
Carvynick Country Club
01872 510716

TRURO
Carnon Downs Caravan & Camping Park
01872 862283
Cosawes Park
01872 863724
WADEBRIDGE
The Laurels Holiday Park
01209 313474
Little Bodieve Holiday Park
01208 812323
St Mabyn Holiday Park
01208 841677
WATERGATE BAY
Watergate Bay Touring Park
01637 860387

CUMBRIA
APPLEBY-IN-WESTMORLAND
Wild Rose Park
017683 51077
KESWICK
Burns Farm Caravan Park
017687 79225
PENTON
Twin Willows
01228 577313
POOLEY BRIDGE
Park Foot Caravan & Camping Park
017684 86309
WATERMILLOCK
Cove Caravan & Camping Park
017684 86549
The Quiet Site
07768 727016

DERBYSHIRE
BAKEWELL
Greenhills Holiday Park
01629 813052
BIRCHOVER
Barn Farm Campsite
01629 650245
BUXTON
Lime Tree Park
01298 22988

continued

AA Camping Card Sites *continued*

SHARDLOW
Shardlow Marina Caravan Park
01332 792832

DEVON

AXMINSTER
Hawkchurch Country Park
08442 729502

BRIDESTOWE
Bridestowe Caravan Park
01837 861261

BUDLEIGH SALTERTON
Pooh Cottage Holiday Park
01395 442354

CHAPMANS WELL
Chapmanswell Caravan Park
01409 211382

COMBE MARTIN
Newberry Valley Park
01271 882334

DARTMOUTH
Woodlands Grove Caravan
& Camping Park
01803 712598

DAWLISH
Cofton Country Holidays
01626 890111
Leadstone Camping
01626 864411

EAST ALLINGTON
Mounts Farm Touring Park
01548 521591

EAST ANSTEY
Zeacombe House
Caravan Park
01398 341279

HOLSWORTHY
Headon Farm Caravan Site
01409 254477
Tamarstone Farm
01288 381734

ILFRACOMBE
Hele Valley Holiday Park
01271 862460

LYNTON
Channel View Caravan and
Camping Park
01598 753349

MORTEHOE
Warcombe Farm Caravan
& Camping Park
01271 870690

NEWTON ABBOT
Dornafield
01803 812732
Ross Park
01803 812983

PAIGNTON
Beverley Parks Caravan &
Camping Park
01803 661979
Whitehill Country Park
01803 782338

SALCOMBE
Alston Camping and
Caravan Site
01548 561260

SIDMOUTH
Oakdown Country
Holiday Park
01297 680387
Salcombe Regis Caravan
& Camping Park
01395 514303

SOURTON CROSS
Bundu Camping &
Caravan Park
01837 861611

SOUTH MOLTON
Riverside Caravan &
Camping Park
01769 579269

STOKE GABRIEL
Broadleigh Farm Park
01803 782422

STOKENHAM
Old Cotmore Farm
01548 580240

TAVISTOCK
Harford Bridge Holiday Park
01822 810349
Langstone Manor Camping
& Caravan Park
01822 613371
Woodovis Park
01822 832968

TEDBURN ST MARY
Springfield Holiday Park
01647 24242

WOOLACOMBE
Woolacombe Sands
Holiday Park
01271 870569

DORSET

ALDERHOLT
Hill Cottage Farm Camping
and Caravan Park
01425 650513

BRIDPORT
Highlands End Holiday Park
01308 422139

CERNE ABBAS
Giants Head Caravan &
Camping Park
01300 341242

CHIDEOCK
Golden Cap Holiday Park
01308 422139

LYME REGIS
Hook Farm Caravan &
Camping Park
01297 442801

LYTCHETT MATRAVERS
Huntick Farm Caravan Park
01202 622222

LYTCHETT MINSTER
South Lytchett Manor
Caravan & Camping Park
01202 622577

ORGANFORD
Pear Tree Holiday Park
0844 272 9504

OWERMOIGNE
Sandyholme Holiday Park
01308 422139

PUNCKNOWLE
Home Farm Caravan and
Campsite
01308 897258

SWANAGE
Herston Caravan &
Camping Park
01929 422932

WAREHAM
Wareham Forest Tourist Park
01929 551393

WEYMOUTH
Sea Barn Farm
01305 782218
West Fleet Holiday Farm
01305 782218

WIMBORNE MINSTER
Charris Camping &
Caravan Park
01202 885970

ESSEX

CANEWDON
Riverside Village Holiday Park
01702 258297

GLOUCESTERSHIRE

BERKELEY
Hogsdown Farm Caravan
& Camping Park
01453 810224

CHELTENHAM
Briarfields Motel &
Touring Park
01242 235324

CIRENCESTER
Mayfield Touring Park
01285 831301

LANCASHIRE

BOLTON LE SANDS
Bay View Holiday Park
01524 732854

CROSTON
Royal Umpire Caravan Park
01772 600257

FAR ARNSIDE
Hollins Farm Camping &
Caravanning
01524 701508

GARSTANG
Claylands Caravan Park
01524 791242

ORMSKIRK
Abbey Farm Caravan Park
01695 572686

SILVERDALE
Silverdale Caravan Park
01524 701508

LINCOLNSHIRE
GREAT CARLTON
West End Farm
01507 450949

HOLBEACH
Herons Cottage Touring Park
01406 540435

LANGWORTH
Lakeside Caravan Park
01522 753200

ORBY
Heron's Mead Fishing Lake
& Touring Park
01754 811340

TATTERSHALL
Tattershall Lakes
Country Park
01526 348800

MERSEYSIDE
SOUTHPORT
Willowbank Holiday Home
& Touring Park
01704 571566

NORFOLK
FAKENHAM
Crossways Caravan &
Camping Park
01328 878335

GREAT YARMOUTH
The Grange Touring Park
01493 730306

KING'S LYNN
King's Lynn Caravan and
Camping Park
01553 840004

SWAFFHAM
Breckland Meadows
Touring Park
01760 721246

THREE HOLES
Lode Hall Holiday Park
01354 638133

TRIMINGHAM
Woodland Holiday Park
01263 579208

NOTTINGHAMSHIRE
TUXFORD
Orchard Park Touring
Caravan & Camping Park
01777 870228

OXFORDSHIRE
BANBURY
Barnstones Caravan &
Camping Site
01295 750289

STANDLAKE
Lincoln Farm Park
Oxfordshire
01865 300239

SHROPSHIRE
MINSTERLEY
The Old School Caravan Park
01588 650410

SHREWSBURY
Beaconsfield Farm Caravan
Park
01939 210370

WEM
Lower Lacon Caravan Park
01939 232376

SOMERSET
BATH
Newton Mill Holiday Park
08442 729503

BREAN
Holiday Resort Unity
01278 751235

CHARD
Alpine Grove Touring Park
01460 63479

CHEDDAR
Broadway House
Holiday Park
08442 729501

CROWCOMBE
Quantock Orchard
Caravan Park
01984 618618

EMBOROUGH
Old Down Touring Park
01761 232355

MARTOCK
Southfork Caravan Park
01935 825661

PORLOCK
Porlock Caravan Park
01643 862269

SHEPTON MALLET
Greenacres Camping
01749 890497

SUFFOLK
BUCKLESHAM
Westwood Caravan Park
01473 659637

BURY ST EDMUNDS
Dell Touring Park
01359 270121

KESSINGLAND
Heathland Beach
Caravan Park
01502 740337

WOODBRIDGE
Moon & Sixpence
01473 736650

SUSSEX, EAST
PEVENSEY BAY
Bay View Park
01323 768688

SUSSEX, WEST
DIAL POST
Honeybridge Park
01403 710923

WARWICKSHIRE
ASTON CANTLOW
Island Meadow Caravan Park
01789 488273

WEST MIDLANDS
MERIDEN
Somers Wood Caravan Park
01676 522978

WIGHT, ISLE OF
WHITECLIFF BAY
Whitecliff Bay Holiday Park
01983 872671

WILTSHIRE
CALNE
Blackland Lakes Holiday
& Leisure Centre
01249 810943

MARSTON MEYSEY
Second Chance Touring Park
01285 810675

WESTBURY
Brokerswood Country Park
01373 822238

YORKSHIRE,
EAST RIDING OF
SKIPSEA
Low Skirlington Leisure Park
01262 468213

YORKSHIRE, NORTH
HARROGATE
Shaws Trailer Park
01423 884432

RICHMOND
Swale View Caravan Park
01748 823106

SCARBOROUGH
Scalby Close Park
01723 365908

THIRSK
Sowerby Caravan Park
01845 522753

TOLLERTON
Tollerton Holiday Park
01347 838313

TOWTHORPE
York Touring Caravan Site
01904 499275

continued

AA Camping Card Sites *continued*

SCOTLAND

ABERDEENSHIRE
HUNTLY
Huntly Castle Caravan Park
01466 794999

ARGYLL & BUTE
CRAIGNURE
Shieling Holidays
01680 812496
GLENDARUEL
Glendaruel Caravan Park
01369 820267

DUMFRIES & GALLOWAY
CREETOWN
Castle Cary Holiday Park
01671 820264
GATEHOUSE OF FLEET
Anwoth Caravan Site
01557 814333
KIPPFORD
Kippford Holiday Park
01556 620636
KIRKGUNZEON
Mossband Caravan Park
01387 760505
STRANRAER
Aird Donald Caravan Park
01776 702025

EAST LOTHIAN
MUSSELBURGH
Drum Mohr Caravan Park
0131 665 6867

FIFE
ST ANDREWS
Cairnsmill Holiday Park
01334 473604

HIGHLAND
GAIRLOCH
Gairloch Caravan Park
01445 712373

STAFFIN
Staffin Camping &
Caravanning
01470 562213

PERTH & KINROSS
DUNKELD
Inver Mill Farm Caravan Park
01350 727477

SOUTH AYRSHIRE
BARRHILL
Barrhill Holiday Park
01465 821355

WALES

CARMARTHENSHIRE
HARFORD
Springwater Lakes
01558 650788
NEWCASTLE EMLYN
Argoed Meadow Caravan and
Camping Site
01239 710690
Cenarth Falls Holiday Park
01239 710345

CEREDIGION
ABERYSTWYTH
Ocean View Caravan Park
01970 828425
BETTWS EVAN
Pilbach Holiday Park
0845 050 8176

DENBIGHSHIRE
RHUALLT
Penisar Mynydd Caravan Park
01745 582227

GWYNEDD
ABERSOCH
Deucoch Touring &
Camping Park
01758 713293
Tanrallt Farm
01758 713527

BALA
Pen-y-Bont Touring Park
01678 520549
Tyn Cornel Camping &
Caravan Park
01678 520759
BETWS GARMON
Bryn Gloch Caravan &
Camping Park
01286 650216
CAERNARFON
Plas Gwyn Caravan &
Camping Park
01286 672619
Riverside Camping
01286 678781
CRICCIETH
Llwyn-Bugeilydd Caravan &
Camping Site
01766 522235
CRICCIETH
Tyddyn Morthwyl Camping &
Caravan Site
01766 522115
DINAS DINLLE
Dinlle Caravan Park
01286 830324
LLANDWROG
White Tower Caravan Park
01286 830649
TAL-Y-BONT
Islawrffordd Caravan Park
01341 247269

MONMOUTHSHIRE
ABERGAVENNY
Pyscodlyn Farm Caravan &
Camping Site
01873 853271
DINGESTOW
Bridge Caravan Park &
Camping Site
01600 740241

PEMBROKESHIRE
HASGUARD CROSS
Redlands Touring Caravan &
Camping Park
01437 781300

HAVERFORDWEST
Nolton Cross Caravan Park
01437 710701
The Rising Sun Inn
01437 765171
ST DAVID'S
Hendre Eynon Camping &
Caravan Site
01437 720474
TENBY
Wood Park Caravans
0845 129 8314

POWYS
BRONLLYS
Anchorage Caravan Park
01874 711246
LLANDRINDOD WELLS
Dalmore Camping &
Caravanning Park
01597 822483
Disserth Caravan &
Camping Park
01597 860277
MIDDLETOWN
Bank Farm Caravan Park
01938 570526

WREXHAM
EYTON
The Plassey Leisure Park
01978 780277

NORTHERN IRELAND

CO ANTRIM
BUSHMILLS
Ballyness Caravan Park
028 2073 2393

Index

Entries are listed alphabetically by town name, then campsite name. The following abbreviations have been used
C&C - Caravan & Camping; HP - Holiday Park; CP - Caravan Park; C&C Club - Camping & Caravanning Club Site